LAW OF THE EUROPEAN UNION

LAW OF THE EUROPEAN UNION

TREVOR REDMOND
LL.B., M.Phil., LL.M., Ph.D., B.L.

CLARUS
PRESS

Published by
Clarus Press Ltd,
Griffith Campus,
South Circular Road,
Dublin 8.
www.claruspress.ie

Typeset by
Gough Typesetting Services, Dublin

Printed by
CPI Antony Rowe,
United Kingdom.

ISBN
978-1-911611-17-2

Cover designed using resources from www.slon.pics/freepik

Do Patricia, ar ndóigh.

PREFACE

> *European Union, the redeeming parathesis of Europe's higher unity, is not a federation or a confederation, actual or potential, but a state of mind. It is not merely a union of states or governments, but a unity of consciousness. It is a new process of social self-constituting in the dimensions of ideas, of power, and of law.*
>
> Philip Allott, 'The Concept of European Union' (1999) 2 *Cambridge Yearbook of European Legal Studies* 31, 59.

The law of the European Union is not simply a subject of law governing human behaviour within a particular field, such as commercial law or employment law. Whereas international law is a system of rules for governing relations between states, it is often accused of lacking any deep sense of purpose. EU law, in contrast, is a new type of law, brought into being in order to constitute a European realm in which conflict born of division was replaced by solidarity developed through cooperation. To borrow a phrase: 'Stronger Together'. It is difficult to make any ontological assumptions as to the realm in which the study of EU law takes place. We made this, and therefore we preserve it. And so, to be able to make a small contribution to this collective endeavour, however modest, is a very real privilege. The cosmopolitan spirit that imbues the study of EU law – a feature that pings from almost every footnote – makes writing a book such as this a joy. However easy it may be, the European Union, its body of laws and consequent continental community of lawyers, ought not to be taken for granted.

How, then, is the law of the European Union, as both a system of law and of governance and distinct fields of legal rules, to be approached in an introductory textbook such as this? Given its breadth, difficult choices had to be made. Topics such as competition law, the area of freedom, security and justice, human rights protection and external relations law are not given any detailed treatment in this book. Such is their depth and complexity that these areas are deserving of a more substantive discussion than space here would allow.

Instead, the seven parts of this book aim to provide a comprehensive overview of, first, the development of the Treaties and their current incarnation in the form of the TEU, the TFEU and the Charter of Fundamental Rights. In ease of the reader, current Treaty numbering has been used throughout, indicated by square brackets where updated. Robert Schütze has made the point that many authors on EU law from a common law background tend towards a court-centric view that can lead to downplaying the significance of the Treaties themselves, such that it can seem as if a Treaty provision only comes into existence when the Court of Justice (CJEU) first refers to it. Part One goes into some detail, therefore, to explain the development of the Treaties and their current structure and content. The role and function of the EU institutions is dealt with in Part Two, including the CJEU and the important role played by the preliminary reference procedure. It should be noted that content in parentheses (usually a list of relevant cases) has been omitted from quotations from judgments of the CJEU and so the original judgment should be consulted for the complete version.

With a view to developing a deep understanding of the unique nature of EU law, Part Three takes a close look at its sources and the critically important principles of competence, supremacy, direct effect, effectiveness and national procedural autonomy. The EU legal remedies available against both Member States and the EU itself are the subject of Part Four, while Part Five is concerned with the Internal Market, Customs Union and free movement of goods, establishment and services. The individual forms the focus of Part Six, which deals with the free movement of persons both under the Citizens Directive and as workers, and the complex and evolving area of Union citizenship. Finally, financial matters frame Part Seven's consideration of the free movement of capital and Economic and Monetary Union.

Reflecting a principal motivation behind its publication, the book seeks to highlight Irish experiences, engagement and interaction with EU law and its development. This has included momentous occasions and contributions: from the Dooge Report to the McCreevy Draft; from delaying the entry into force of the Single European Act, to causing nail-baiting waits for ratification of the Treaties of Nice and Lisbon; from hosting the first ever formal European Council in Dublin Castle in 1975 to celebrating the accession of ten new Member States in the Phoenix Park in 2004; from initiating the first inter-state proceedings to making a preliminary reference questioning the first use of the simplified revision procedure to amend the Treaties; from the unattractively named P(ortugal), I(reland), G(reece) and S(pain) to the altogether grander titled New Hanseatic League; from the Irish Protocol to the Irish Backstop. The recent rapid growth in the number of preliminary rulings requested by the Irish courts is indicative of the ever-deepening engagement between the Irish and EU legal systems.

For those studying EU law, the Eur-Lex website (www.eur-lex.europa.eu) is an invaluable resource that is worth exploring. A useful way in which to see how the law-making process operates in practice is to frequently visit the Official Journal via the Eur-Lex site. Consulting the L (Legislative) series will show the legal acts that have been published on any given day. Each Monday, the C (Information) series includes the diary of the Court of Justice of the European Union, providing a summary of recently delivered judgments. Useful Twitter accounts include @EUCourtPress and @EURLex, while two excellent blogs are europeanlawblog.eu and eulawanalysis.blogspot.com. The European Commission Representation in Ireland also operates a hugely informative weekly email service – "EU News You Can Use" – that can be subscribed to on its website www.ec.europa.eu/ireland.

Law is very much a collaborative activity. Sincere thanks are due to the many wonderful people who, directly or indirectly, actually or potentially, assisted me in exploring matters of EU law reflected in the book, including esteemed colleagues in the Department of Foreign Affairs and Trade, the Office of the Attorney General and students in the Institute of Public Administration. A heartfelt thank you to Annette Redmond, Terry Redmond, Kenneth Redmond, Enya Murray, the Quirkes and the Hanson-Brazils, Anne-Marie O'Sullivan, Barra Lysaght, Brídín O'Donoghue, Carl Grainger, Colm O'Dwyer, Darren Lehane, David Brophy, David Kelly, Declan Smyth, Garrett Cunnane, Glen Gibbons,

Kyra Hild, Mark Callanan, Michael Dillon, James Kingston, Patrick McEvoy, Peter White and Stephen Ryan. Thank you, David McCartney of Clarus Press, for having faith in the original idea and very patiently seeing it through to the end with constant good humour, as well as to the fantastic Shane Gough, Marsha Swan, Anne-Marie Giblin and Wendy Simpson. All errors or omissions are, however, my own. Views expressed are solely those of the author and are not to be taken as representative or indicative of the views of any other person or office.

By some considerable ocean, however, the greatest thanks are due to Patricia Brazil. While it may sound a little trite, it is no less true. Without Patricia, this book would never have been even remotely possible. Go raibh maith agat, mo ghrá, don dara huair. Ar deireadh, agus an ceann deireanach!

Trevor Redmond
1 September 2019

TABLE OF CONTENTS

PART TWO

PART FIVE

PART SIX

TABLE OF CASES

Court of Justice

General Court

European Court of Human Rights

Other Jurisdictions

TABLE OF TREATIES AND LEGAL ACTS

Declarations to the TEU and TFEU

Other EU Treaties

Declarations, Conclusions, Interinstitutional Agreements, Rules of Procedure

International Agreements

Regulations

Delegated Regulations

Implementing Regulations

Directives

Decisions

Primary Legislation

Secondary Legislation

PART ONE

CHAPTER 1

ORIGINS OF THE EUROPEAN UNION 1944–1973

A. THE EMERGENCE OF SUPRANATIONALISM

[1–01] It is striking to recall that the modern world was forged while the Second World War was still being fought. In July 1944, as bombs fell on London and Paris remained occupied, over 700 delegates assembled in Bretton Woods, New Hampshire, for the United Nations Monetary and Financial Conference. Its work would lead to the establishment of the International Monetary Fund and the World Bank. The opening address by US Treasury Secretary Henry Morgenthau was a call to arms of a very different kind:

> [T]he world is a community. On battlefronts the world over, the young men of all our united countries have been dying together – dying for a common purpose. It is not beyond our powers to enable the young men of all our countries to live together – to pour their energies, their skills, their aspirations into mutual enrichment and peaceful progress. Our final responsibility is to them. As they prosper or perish, the work which we do here will be judged. The opportunity before us has been bought with blood. Let us meet it with faith in one another, with faith in our common future, which these men fought to make free.[1]

[1–02] The unprecedented extent of the devastation and outrages wrought by the War led to a genuine willingness to explore novel and progressive approaches to international governance, as exemplified in a speech by former Prime Minister Winston Churchill to the University of Zurich in 1946:

> If Europe were once united in the sharing of its common inheritance, there would be no limit to the happiness, to the prosperity and glory which its three or four hundred

---

1 Proceedings and Documents of the United Nations Monetary and Financial Conference, Bretton Woods, New Hampshire, 1–22 July 1944, Volume I, cited in Ed Conway, *The Summit* (Abacus, 2014) 213–214.

> million people would enjoy. Yet it is from Europe that have sprung that series of frightful nationalistic quarrels … which we have seen even in this twentieth century and in our own lifetime, wreck the peace and mar the prospects of all mankind. …
>
> Yet all the while there is a remedy which, if it were generally and spontaneously adopted, would as if by a miracle transform the whole scene, and would in a few years make all Europe, or the greater part of it, as free and as happy as Switzerland is today. What is this sovereign remedy? It is to re-create the European Family, or as much of it as we can, and provide it with a structure under which it can dwell in peace, in safety and in freedom. We must build a kind of United States of Europe. …
>
> There is no reason why a regional organisation of Europe should in any way conflict with the world organisation of the United Nations. On the contrary, I believe that the larger synthesis will only survive if it is founded upon coherent natural groupings. There is already a natural grouping in the Western Hemisphere. We British have our own Commonwealth of Nations. These do not weaken, on the contrary they strengthen, the world organisation. They are in fact its main support. …
>
> I am now going to say something that will astonish you. The first step in the re-creation of the European family must be a partnership between France and Germany. … The structure of the United States of Europe, if well and truly built, will be such as to make the material strength of a single state less important. Small nations will count as much as large ones and gain their honour by their contribution to the common cause. The ancient states and principalities of Germany, freely joined together for mutual convenience in a federal system, might each take their individual place among the United States of Europe. …
>
> Our constant aim must be to build and fortify the strength of the United Nations Organisation. Under and within that world concept, we must re-create the European family in a regional structure called, it may be, the United States of Europe. The first step is to form a Council of Europe. If at first all the States of Europe are not willing or able to join the Union, we must nevertheless proceed to assemble and combine those who will and those who can. … Great Britain, the British Commonwealth of Nations, mighty America, and I trust Soviet Russia – for then indeed all would be well – must be the friends and sponsors of the new Europe and must champion its right to live and shine.

[1–03] Debate continues as to whether Churchill envisaged the UK forming part of such a "United Europe" or remaining outside it, and he maintains a somewhat uneasy role as a possible founding father of the European Union.[2] The speech is, nevertheless, an important signpost on the road towards the creation of what we would now term a regional economic integration organisation. It is interesting, too, for the manner in which it foresees a "synthesis" between the newly formed United Nations, and regional groupings of states acting in support of it. Also of note is the reference to the possibility that the "ancient states and principalities" of Germany might take their own place within a United States of Europe. Whilst this did not transpire, the EU did provide a framework

[2] Two years later, the enthusiastic reception he received in delivering a similar speech to the Congress of Europe moved Churchill to tears. See Felix Klos, *Churchill on Europe: The Untold Story of Churchill's European Project* (IB Tauris, 2016).

in which traditional bilateral relations could be transformed – the relationship between Ireland and the UK being a good example[3] – and in which regionalism could develop.[4]

[1–04] The story of the European Union is one of gradual evolution. When cooperation within limited fields was deemed a success, confidence in the effectiveness of European integration and its institutions was strengthened. As a result, successive treaties have conferred additional areas of competence on the EU, including areas that were once deemed too sensitive to be dealt with on a supranational basis. The geographic scope of integration has also widened. Beginning with just six Member States in 1957, three more joined in 1973, including Ireland, followed by one in 1981, two in 1986, three in 1995, ten in 2004, two in 2007 and one in 2013, bringing the total to 28.[5] Whilst, from an Irish perspective, the decision of the United Kingdom to leave undoubtedly casts a shadow over its sense of cohesion, it is worth remembering the extent to which the EU has transformed European life over the past sixty years. Meeting in the Brussels suburb of Laeken in December 2001 to contemplate the Union's further enlargement, the European Council began the Laeken Declaration on the Future of the European Union by setting out the EU's historic achievement:

> The debilitating effects of two bloody wars and the weakening of Europe's position in the world brought a growing realisation that only peace and concerted action could make the dream of a strong, unified Europe come true. In order to banish once and for all the demons of the past, a start was made with a coal and steel community. Other economic activities, such as agriculture, were subsequently added in. A genuine single market was eventually established for goods, persons, services and capital, and a single currency was added in 1999. On 1 January 2002, the euro is to become a day-to-day reality for 300 million European citizens.
>
> The European Union has thus gradually come into being. In the beginning, it was more of an economic and technical collaboration. Twenty years ago, with the first direct elections to the European Parliament, the Community's democratic legitimacy, which until then had lain with the Council alone, was considerably strengthened. Over the last ten years, construction of a political union has begun and cooperation has been established on social policy, employment, asylum, immigration, police, justice, foreign policy and a common security and defence policy.

---

3 See Elizabeth Meehan, "'Britain's Irish Question: Britain's European Question?' British–Irish Relations in the Context of European Union and the Belfast Agreement" (2000) 26 *Review of International Studies* 83; Brigid Laffan, "Ireland, Britain, Northern Ireland and the European Dimension", IBIS Working Paper 27, Institute for British–Irish Studies, 2003; Katy Hayward, "Mediating the European Ideal: Cross-border Programmes and Conflict Resolution on the Island of Ireland" (2007) 45 *Journal of Common Market Studies* 675; Katy Hayward, "Reiterating National Identities: The European Union conception of conflict resolution in Northern Ireland" (2006) 41 *Cooperation and Conflict* 261.

4 See Karolina Borońska-Hryniewiecka, "Regional Parliamentary Empowerment in EU Affairs: Building an Analytical Framework" (2017) 23 *Journal of Legislative Studies* 144; Tony Cole, "The Committee of the Regions and Subnational Representation to the European Union" (2005) 12 *Maastricht Journal of European and Comparative Law* 49; Stephen Weatherill and Ulf Bernitz (eds), *The Role of Regions and Sub-National Actors in Europe* (Hart Publishing, 2005); Jan Kottmann, "Europe and the Regions: Subnational Entity Representation at Community Level" (2001) 26 *European Law Review* 159.

5 Together with Ireland, the UK and Denmark joined in 1973, followed by Greece (1981), Spain and Portugal (1986), Austria, Finland and Sweden (1995), Cyprus, Czech Republic, Estonia, Hungary, Latvia, Lithuania, Malta, Poland, Slovakia and Slovenia (2004), Bulgaria and Romania (2007) and Croatia (2013). On further expansion see John O'Brennan, "EU Enlargement to the Western Balkans: Towards 2025 and Beyond" (Institute of International and European Affairs, 2018).

> The European Union is a success story. For over half a century now, Europe has been at peace. Along with North America and Japan, the Union forms one of the three most prosperous parts of the world. As a result of mutual solidarity and fair distribution of the benefits of economic development, moreover, the standard of living in the Union's weaker regions has increased enormously and they have made good much of the disadvantage they were at.[6]

(i) The Council of Europe

[1–05] One element within Churchill's Zurich speech that did come to early fruition was the establishment, in 1949, of the Council of Europe, with Ireland amongst the 10 founding states.[7] The Council of Europe adopted an innovative institutional structure that included a "Committee of Ministers", comprised of the foreign ministers of the states parties or their representatives, and a "Parliamentary Assembly", made up of national parliamentarian delegations reflecting the political spectrum within each national parliament. Compared with a body consisting solely of meetings of foreign ministers, the fact that the Assembly included representatives from *opposition* parliamentary parties within each state tempered the "intergovernmental" nature of the Council of Europe, as their inclusion meant that the Assembly did more than merely reflect the views of the governments of the states belonging to the organisation.

[1–06] At this time, international organisations were mainly *intergovernmental* in nature. Such an organisation provides a framework for states to cooperate on an equal basis, whilst maintaining their overall control through operating by consensus, allowing each state to veto any new proposal or amendment that it does not like. The states that are party to the organisation tend to retain ultimate control, with no organ of the organisation having a superior authority to override the interests of one or more states in favour of the interests of the organisation as a whole. In contrast to intergovernmentalism, the term "supranationalism" is used to indicate an entity that, by departing from the traditional elements of an intergovernmental organisation, becomes greater than the sum of its component member states and thereby takes on an independent authority of its own.

[1–07] A *supranational* organisation moves beyond providing a framework in which a number of states can cooperate consensually in order to further their individual national interests.[8] By joining a supranational organisation, a state cedes some of its authority to the organisation and accepts that it may operate in certain ways that are contrary to its own national preferences. This is typically achieved through the use of majority voting, rendering a state unable to veto proposals or amendments not to its liking, or by a creating an organ that is mandated to pursue the interests of the organisation as a whole, with the authority to take decisions independent from the states parties, or through a combination of the two. The creation of a Parliamentary Assembly of the Council

---

6 Annex I to the Presidency Conclusions of the Laeken European Council, 14 and 15 December 2001, 19–23.

7 See Michael Kennedy and Eunan O'Halpin, *Ireland and the Council of Europe: From Isolation towards Integration* (Council of Europe Publishing, 2000). More generally, see Stefanie Schmahl and Marten Breur (eds), *The Council of Europe* (Oxford University Press, 2017).

8 See Bernd Meyring, "Intergovernmentalism and Supranationality: Two Stereotypes for a Complex Reality" (1997) 22 *European Law Review* 221; Antje Wiener, Tanja A Börzel, and Thomas Risse (ed) *European Integration Theory* (3rd ed, Oxford University Press, 2018); Liesbet Hooghe and Gary Marks, "Grand Theories of European Integration in the Twenty-first Century" (2019) 26 *Journal of European Public Policy* 113.

of Europe that included national delegates other than those representing governments marked the beginning of a departure away from strict intergovernmentalism.

[1–08] While there are certain overlaps and similarities between the EU and the Council of Europe, such as common anthems and flags, and all EU Member States being members of the Council of Europe, the two organisations are entirely separate and distinct, with the Council having a total 47 members, including Russia, Turkey and Switzerland. The Council of Europe acts in large part through the adoption of international agreements aimed at addressing certain issues, the best known of which is the 1950 European Convention for the Protection of Human Rights and Fundamental Freedoms, on foot of which the European Court of Human Rights was established in 1959. Media references often fail to distinguish between the European Court of Human Rights in Strasbourg, an organ of the Council of Europe, and the Court of Justice of the European Union, based in Luxembourg, referring in an imprecise way to "the European Court".

[1–09] As set out in the first article of its Statute, the aim of the Council of Europe was to "achieve a greater unity between its members for the purpose of safeguarding and realising the ideals and principles which are their common heritage and facilitating their economic and social progress".[9] This broad aim was to be pursued through the organs of the Council by discussion of more specific questions of common concern and by "agreements and common action in economic, social, cultural, scientific, legal and administrative matters and in the maintenance and further realisation of human rights and fundamental freedoms".[10] Over 200 treaties have been adopted within the Council of Europe framework, dealing with issues such as extradition, prevention of terrorism, mutual assistance in criminal matters, transfer of sentenced persons, human trafficking, cybercrime, animal welfare, television broadcasts, patents, access to official documents, as well as 16 protocols to the Convention on Human Rights.

B. European Coal and Steel Community

[1–10] The Council of Europe did not have a particularly economic focus, and while it aimed at fostering greater European unity, it was not concerned with adopting practical measures to enhance integration. In this way, the Council much reflected the preferences of the UK, which was one of its leading founding members. In contrast, in 1950 the French Foreign Minister, Robert Schuman, set out a proposal for a highly functional approach to integration, as contained in what is known as the "Schuman Declaration". The Declaration's significance is reflected in the fact that the date of its delivery, 9 May, continues to be marked throughout the EU as "Europe Day". Schuman set out his idea of incremental and progressive integration based on functionalism as follows:

> Europe will not be made all at once, or according to a single plan. It will be built through concrete achievements which first create a de facto solidarity. The coming together of the nations of Europe requires the elimination of the age-old opposition of France and Germany. Any action taken must in the first place concern these two countries. With this aim in view, the French Government proposes that action be taken immediately on one limited but decisive point.

---

9 Art 1, Statute of the Council of Europe (European Treaty Series No 1).
10 *ibid.*

It proposes that Franco-German production of coal and steel as a whole be placed under a common High Authority, within the framework of an organization open to the participation of the other countries of Europe. The pooling of coal and steel production should immediately provide for the setting up of common foundations for economic development as a first step in the federation of Europe, and will change the destinies of those regions which have long been devoted to the manufacture of munitions of war, of which they have been the most constant victims.

The solidarity in production thus established will make it plain that any war between France and Germany becomes not merely unthinkable, but materially impossible. The setting up of this powerful productive unit, open to all countries willing to take part and bound ultimately to provide all the member countries with the basic elements of industrial production on the same terms, will lay a true foundation for their economic unification. …

By pooling basic production and by instituting a new High Authority, whose decisions will bind France, Germany and other member countries, this proposal will lead to the realization of the first concrete foundation of a European federation indispensable to the preservation of peace. …

To achieve these objectives, starting from the very different conditions in which the production of member countries is at present situated, it is proposed that certain transitional measures should be instituted, such as the application of a production and investment plan, the establishment of compensating machinery for equating prices, and the creation of a restructuring fund to facilitate the rationalization of production. The movement of coal and steel between member countries will immediately be freed from all customs duty, and will not be affected by differential transport rates. Conditions will gradually be created which will spontaneously provide for the more rational distribution of production at the highest level of productivity. In contrast to international cartels, which tend to impose restrictive practices on distribution and the exploitation of national markets, and to maintain high profits, the organization will ensure the fusion of markets and the expansion of production.

The essential principles and undertakings defined above will be the subject of a treaty signed between the States and submitted for the ratification of their parliaments. …

The common High Authority entrusted with the management of the scheme will be composed of independent persons appointed by the governments, giving equal representation. A chairman will be chosen by common agreement between the governments. The Authority's decisions will be enforceable in France, Germany and other member countries. Appropriate measures will be provided for means of appeal against the decisions of the Authority.[11]

[1–11] The initiative set out in the Schuman Declaration led to the signing on 18 April 1951 of the European Coal and Steel Community (ECSC) Treaty by the six states of France, Germany, Italy, Belgium, the Netherlands and Luxembourg. The Treaty entered into force on 23 July 1952. As the ECSC was established for a period of 50 years, it expired on 23 July 2002, with its subject matter thereafter falling under the Treaty establishing the European Community.[12]

---

[11] The Schuman Declaration, 9 May 1950, available at https://europa.eu/european-union/about-eu/symbols/europe-day/schuman-declaration_en.

[12] Decision 2002/595 of the Representatives of the Governments of the Member States, meeting within the Council, of 19 July 2002, on the consequences of the expiry of the European Coal and Steel Community on international agreements concluded by the ECSC provided that, from 24 July 2002, the rights and obligations arising under international agreements concluded by the ECSC were to be taken over by the European Community [2002] OJ L194/35.

[1–12] Although having a limited sectoral focus, the more wide-ranging political ambition underlying the ECSC was plain to see in the broad sweep of its preambular language, which recalled the fact that "Europe can be built only by concrete actions which create a real solidarity and by the establishment of common bases for economic development", and expressed the resolve of the Member States to "substitute for historic rivalries a fusion of their essential interests; to establish, by creating an economic community, the foundation of a broad and independent community among peoples long divided by bloody conflicts; and to lay the bases of institutions capable of giving direction to their future common destiny".

[1–13] At this time, intergovernmental organisations typically operated on the basis of the unanimous agreement of its Member States, thereby affording each member a veto. The ECSC Treaty introduced a novel degree of supranationalism by establishing a High Authority (subsequently renamed the Commission), comprised of nine independent appointees of the six states who were granted the power to adopt binding decisions by majority.[13] As set out in the Treaty, the members of the High Authority were to exercise their functions "in complete independence, in the general interest of the Community", while in the fulfilment of their duties they were to "neither solicit nor accept instructions from any government or from any organization".[14] As a corollary, each Member State agreed to "respect this supranational character and to make no effort to influence the members of the High Authority in the execution of their duties".

[1–14] In addition to the High Authority, an Assembly of national parliamentarians had certain supervisory and advisory powers, a Council comprising representatives of the Member States had the task of harmonising the activities of the Community and the states, and a Court of Justice was charged with ensuring the rule of law in the interpretation and application of the Treaty and its implementing regulations.

[1–15] From a contemporary EU law perspective, the principal significance of the ECSC is the legacy it established, with many elements of the ECSC Treaty still finding echoes in the two core Treaties of the European Union – the Treaty on European Union (TEU) and the Treaty on the Functioning of the European Union (TFEU). Indeed, certain rules and instruments first introduced by the ECSC Treaty will reappear in an EU law guise later in this book. For example, the mission of the ECSC was defined as being to contribute to economic expansion, employment and improved standards of living through the creation of a "common market" for coal and steel. To this end, the Treaty expressly prohibited:

(a) import and export duties, or charges with an equivalent effect, and quantitative restrictions on the movement of coal and steel;
(b) measures or practices discriminating among producers, among buyers or among consumers, specifically as concerns prices, delivery terms and transportation rates, as well as measures or practices which hamper the buyer in the free choice of his supplier;
(c) subsidies or state assistance, or special charges imposed by the state, in any form whatsoever;

[13] For a contemporary analysis see Gerhard Bebr's "The European Coal and Steel Community: A Political and Legal Innovation" (1953–1954) 63 *Yale Law Journal* 1 and "The Relation of the European Coal and Steel Community to the Law of the Member States: A Peculiar Legal Symbiosis" (1958) 58 *Columbia Law Review* 767.

[14] Art 9, ECSC Treaty.

(d) restrictive practices tending towards the division of markets or the exploitation of the consumer.[15]

[1–16] These elements – a ban on import or export duties or charges having an equivalent effect, non-discrimination, freedom to access the market and rules governing state aids and unfair competition – continue to form a central part of the creation and maintenance of the Single Market. The High Authority was conferred with the power to issue "decisions" that were to be binding in all their details, "recommendations" that were binding with respect to the specified objectives but left to those to whom they were directed the choice of appropriate means for attaining those objectives and non-binding "opinions" – a distinction that has clear echoes in the modern EU legal acts of binding regulations, directives and decisions and non-binding recommendations and opinions.

[1–17] A key figure in the creation of the ECSC was Jean Monnet, a French diplomat who influenced Robert Schuman and served both as chairman of the intergovernmental conference that negotiated the ECSC Treaty and as the first president of the High Authority. His speech delivered at the inauguration of the High Authority provides a contemporary insight into the novel project being embarked upon:

> For the first time, the traditional relations between States are now transformed. Under the methods of the past, even when European States are convinced of the need for common action, even when they set up an international organisation, they retain their complete sovereignty. Thus the international organisation can neither make decisions nor carry them out, but can only make recommendations to the States. These methods cannot eliminate our national antagonisms; as long as national sovereignty is not surmounted, such antagonisms can only be aggravated.
>
> But today, six Parliaments have decided after careful deliberation, by substantial majorities, to create the first European Community which merges a portion of their respective national sovereignties and submits it to the common interest.
>
> Within the limits of the powers conferred upon it by the Treaty, the *High Authority* has received from the six States a mandate to take decisions with complete independence, decisions which immediately become effective throughout their territory. The Authority obtains its financial resources, not from contributions by the States, but from direct levies on the industries under its control.
>
> It is responsible, not to the States, but to a European *Assembly*. The Assembly was elected by the national parliaments, but it has already been provided that it may be elected directly by the people. From the beginning, the members of the Assembly are not bound by any national mandate; they vote freely and individually, not by national blocs. Each of them represents not his own country but the whole Community. The Assembly controls our activities. It has the power to refuse us its confidence. It is the first European Assembly endowed with sovereign powers.
>
> The acts of the High Authority are subject to review. But such review will be not by national courts, but by a European court, the *Court of Justice*.
>
> Any of these institutions may be changed and improved in the light of experience. What cannot be challenged is the principle that they are supra-national — in other words federal — institutions. They are institutions which are sovereign within the limits of

[15] Art 4, ECSC Treaty.

> their competence — that is to say, which are endowed with the right to make decisions and carry them out.
>
> However, coal and steel represent only a part of economic life. For this reason there must be continual liaison between the High Authority and the Governments which are still responsible for the overall economic policy of their States. The *Council of Ministers* was set up, not to exercise control and guardianship, but to provide this liaison and to assure the coordination of the policies of the High Authority and those of the member States.[16]

[1–18] This institutional architecture, made up of a High Authority/Commission, Council of Ministers, Assembly/Parliament and Court, was replicated in the European Economic Community and continues to form the core framework for the European Union to this day. Whereas most states share a similar separation of powers as between the legislative, executive and judicial branches, the novel nature of the ECSC meant that its institutions did not follow this traditional model. It is sometimes said that, rather than a separation of powers, EU institutions can be seen to entail a separation of *interests* in which the Commission represents the supranational interests of the institution as a whole; the Council represents the interests of the Member States; the Parliament represents the collective interests of the citizens of the Member States and is intended to confer democratic legitimacy on an institution otherwise lacking directly elected officials, while the Court ensures adherence to the legal framework and legal principles. Although this involves a generalisation, it is a useful way in which to position the institutions when first becoming familiar with them.

[1–19] The ECSC Treaty was, therefore, an international agreement under public international law through which the six Member States "instituted amongst themselves" a community with a legal personality of its own with defined objectives and the authority or competence to take certain actions to achieve those objectives. Interestingly, however, while the High Authority was empowered to make binding decisions and recommendations, neither it nor the Council of Ministers had a general law-making power. While policies could be further developed, the rules governing the ECSC were set out in the founding treaty itself. As will be seen, this contrasts sharply with the approach taken in the European Economic Community (EEC) Treaty, which established an institutional framework and core principles which were to be expanded upon by detailed laws to be adopted by the EEC institutions in the form of regulations, directives and decisions, rather than being set out in every detail in the EEC Treaty itself.

(i) Western European Union

[1–20] Before considering measures towards further *economic* integration, it is worth noting that an attempt had been made amongst the six European Coal and Steel Community states to develop a parallel European Defence Community, with a Treaty signed by those states in 1952, which was supplemented by a proposal for a European Political Community. This would have seen the integration of the defence forces of the Member States through the creation of a European army under the command of a supranational political institution. As a result of a vote by the French National Assembly in August 1954 not to ratify the European Defence Community Treaty, the project

[16] Speech delivered by Jean Monnet on the occasion of the inauguration of the High Authority, Luxembourg, 10 August 1952, available at https://www.cvce.eu/en.

could not proceed to conclusion and both proposals were subsequently abandoned, for the time being.[17]

[1–21] Defence cooperation continued, albeit on a strictly intergovernmental basis, through the establishment two months later of a separate international organisation entitled the Western European Union (WEU). At its peak, it had 10 member countries, all of whom were EU Member States, as well as six "associate member" countries, seven "associate partner" countries and five "observer countries", including Ireland. Since the Lisbon Treaty's entry into force on 1 December 2009, Art 42.7 of the Treaty on European Union now provides that, without prejudice to the specific character of the security and defence policy of certain Member States, if a Member State is the victim of armed aggression on its territory, the other Member States shall have towards it an obligation of aid and assistance by all the means in their power, in accordance with Art 51 of the United Nations Charter.[18] This emptied the WEU of much of its purpose and it was eventually wound up on 30 June 2011. Aspects of the WEU's activities continue to be carried out by the EU's three Common Security and Defence Policy agencies, namely the European Defence Agency, the EU Institute for Security Studies and the EU Satellite Centre. Article 42.7 TEU was invoked for the first time by France following terrorist attacks in Paris on 13 November 2015.[19]

C. European Economic Community and Euratom

[1–22] The failure of proposals for a European Defence Community and a European Political Community prompted the realisation that political integration had to be preceded by greater cooperation at the economic level. Following a meeting of the foreign ministers of the ECSC states in Messina, Sicily, in 1955, it was agreed to adopt the objectives of establishing a European common market and to develop atomic energy for peaceful purposes. The Belgian Foreign Minister, Paul-Henri Spaak, chaired an intergovernmental committee tasked with formulating proposals, which produced the Spaak Report in 1956. Spaak spoke openly of the motivations driving the Report's approach:

> After the [European Defence Community] venture it was not reasonable to repeat exactly the same experiment a few months later. A means must be found of reaching the same goal – the distant goal of an integrated Europe – by other methods and through other channels. We then considered that, having failed on the *political* plane, we should take up the question on the *economic* plane and use the so-called *functional method*, availing

[17] For a contemporary account see AH Robertson, "The European Political Community" (1952) 29 *British Yearbook of International Law* 383 and Gerhard Bebr, "The European Defence Community and the Western European Union: An Agonizing Dilemma" (1954–1945) 7 *Stanford Law Review* 169.

[18] Art 3 of the Protocol on the Concerns of the Irish People on the Treaty of Lisbon provides, *inter alia*, that the EU's common security and defence policy "does not prejudice the security and defence policy of each Member State, including Ireland, or the obligations of any Member State. The Treaty of Lisbon does not affect or prejudice Ireland's traditional policy of military neutrality. It will be for Member States – including Ireland, acting in a spirit of solidarity and without prejudice to its traditional policy of military neutrality – to determine the nature of aid or assistance to be provided to a Member State which is the object of a terrorist attack or the victim of armed aggression on its territory."

[19] See Niklas IM Nováky, "The Invocation of the European Union's Mutual Assistance Clause: A Call for Enforced Solidarity" (2017) 22 *European Foreign Affairs Review* 357.

ourselves to some extent … of the admittedly successful experiment already made with the European Coal and Steel Community.[20]

[1–23] The recommendations of the Spaak Report were taken up in negotiations which led to the six ECSC states signing in Rome, on 25 March 1957, the European Economic Community Treaty (also known as the Treaty of Rome) and the European Atomic Energy Community Treaty (also known as the Euratom Treaty), both of which entered into force on 1 January 1958.

[1–24] The reason why two separate treaties were employed was in order to maximise the chances for the entry into force of the Euratom Treaty, should the French National Assembly reject the EEC Treaty.[21] The Euratom Treaty essentially applied the model of the ECSC Treaty to the field of civil nuclear energy, which was believed at the time to be a vital energy source of the future, and foresaw the development of nuclear energy and its distribution throughout the Community, with any surplus being sold to third countries. Unlike the ECSC Treaty, however, the Euratom Treaty did provide for law-making at the EU level. Euratom has not developed to the extent originally envisaged, as a result of which the Euratom Treaty has never been substantively amended, and its focus is primarily on research and the promotion of nuclear safety.[22]

[1–25] A third treaty, the Convention on Certain Institutions Common to the European Communities, was signed on the same day, providing for the EEC and Euratom to share a common Assembly and Court with the ECSC. Each of the two new Communities had their own separate Commission and Council, until finally, in July 1967, the Treaty establishing the Single Council and a Single Commission for the European Communities (the "Merger Treaty") entered into force, merging the three Councils and three Commissions into one Council and one Commission, which were to serve all three communities.

[1–26] The EEC Treaty, in particular, marks the birth of what is now the European Union. Indeed, the two principal Treaties governing the EU today are the Treaty on European Union (TEU), which was originally adopted in Maastricht in 1992, and the EEC Treaty as significantly amended over a number of occasions and renamed, since the Lisbon Treaty, the Treaty on the Functioning of the European Union (TFEU). As originally adopted, the EEC Treaty had 248 articles, divided into six Parts as follows:

PART ONE:	**PRINCIPLES**
PART TWO:	**BASES OF THE COMMUNITY**
Title I	**Free Movement of Goods**
	Chapter 1 – The Customs Union
	Section 1 – The Elimination of Customs Duties as between Member States
	Section 2 – Establishment of the Common Customs Tariff
	Chapter 2 – The Elimination of Quantitative Restriction as between Member States
Title II	**Agriculture**

[20] Address to Parliament, 21 October 1955, cited in Robert Schütze, *European Union Law* (Cambridge University Press, 2015) 12. Emphasis added.

[21] Trevor C Hartley, *The Foundations of European Community Law* (5th ed, Oxford University Press, 2003) 3.

[22] See Anna Södersten, *Euratom at the Crossroads* (Edward Elgar Publishing, 2018).

Title III	**Free Movement of Persons, Services and Capital**
	Chapter 1 – Workers
	Chapter 2 – The Right of Establishment
	Chapter 3 – Services
	Chapter 4 – Capital
Title IV	**Transport**
PART THREE:	**POLICY OF THE COMMUNITY**
Title I	**Common Rules**
	Chapter 1 – Common Rules
	Section 1 – Rules Governing Competition
	Section 2 – Rules Applying to Enterprises
	Section 3 – Dumping Practices
	Chapter 2 – Fiscal Provisions
	Chapter 3 – Approximation of Laws
Title II	**Economic Policy**
	Chapter 1 – Policy Relating to Economic Trends
	Chapter 2 – Balance of Payments
	Chapter 3 – Commercial Policy
Title III	**Social Policy**
	Chapter 1 – Social Provisions
	Chapter 2 – The European Social Fund
Title IV	**European Investment Bank**
PART FOUR:	**THE ASSOCIATION OF OVERSEAS COUNTRIES AND TERRITORIES**
PART FIVE:	**INSTITUTIONS OF THE COMMUNITY**
Title I	**Provisions Governing Institutions**
	Chapter 1 – Institutions
	Section 1 – The Assembly [later Parliament]
	Section 2 – The Council
	Section 3 – The Commission
	Section 4 – The Court of Justice
	Chapter 2 – Provisions Common to Several Institutions
	Chapter 3 – The Economic and Social Committee
Title II	**Final Provisions**
PART SIX:	**GENERAL AND FINAL PROVISIONS**

[1–27] The European Economic Community was assigned, in Art 2, with no less a task than to promote throughout the Community "a harmonious development of economic activities, a continuous and balanced expansion, an increase in stability, an accelerated raising of the standard of living and closer relations between the States belonging to it". These aims were to be achieved, first, through the creation of a customs union with no internal tariffs and a common external tariff. Secondly, by establishing a "common market" over a 12-year transitional period and by "progressively approximating the economic policies of Member States", including competition policy and rules regarding state aid. Thirdly, integration would be deepened in specific areas in which the six Member States were comfortable cooperating within the EEC framework, namely agriculture, transport and aspects of social policy.

(i) The Customs Union

[1–28] In terms of the progressive stages of economic integration, a customs union advances upon a free trade area, while a common market further advances on a customs union. In a free trade area, the states that form part of the area agree not to impose duties or quantitative restrictions on each other's goods moving from one participating state to another. Each state, however, remains free to decide on the duties it will impose on imports coming from a third country and so can conclude their own trade deals with such countries. What are known as "rules of origin" checks must be applied in order to determine whether a good crossing a border within the free trade area is one that originates from within one of the participating states and is therefore free from any duties, or has been imported into a participating state from a third country. In a customs union, a free trade area is combined with a common external tariff on goods coming from outside of the union, with the result that states within the customs union must adhere to a common commercial policy towards the rest of the world and are no longer free to conclude their own trade deals with third countries. This then avoids the need for any rules of origin checks to be conducted at the internal borders within the customs union. Finally, a common market builds further on a customs union through the "creation of a single market achieving conditions similar to those of a domestic market".[23]

[1–29] When it came to establishing a customs union, in addition to the sectoral areas covered by the ECSC, a precedent had already been established amongst the three Benelux countries (Belgium, the Netherlands and Luxembourg). From 1 January 1948, these countries had formed a customs union within which goods could move freely, and into which imports were subject to a uniform customs tariff, followed by a removal of restrictions on capital and, later, of workers, resulting in a 50 per cent increase in trade by 1956. Wishing to emulate this success, included amongst the eleven activities assigned to the EEC by the Art 3 of the Treaty of Rome were: (i) the elimination, as between Member States, of customs duties and of quantitative restrictions on the import and export of goods, and of all other measures having equivalent effect and (ii) the establishment of a common customs tariff and of a common commercial policy towards third countries. From this it can be seen that the creation of the Customs Union entailed both internal and external elements, with the external elements involving the application of a Common External Tariff on goods entering the EEC and the implementation of a Common Commercial Policy aimed at ensuring the "harmonious development of world trade, the progressive abolition of restrictions on international exchanges and the lowering of customs barriers", through entering into agreements with third states.

(ii) The Common Market

[1–30] A core objective of the EEC was the creation of a common market amongst its Member States, within which not only would goods move freely, but so too would the factors of production – labour and capital – and services. Accordingly, Art 3 included as among the activities of the EEC: (i) the abolition, as between Member States, of obstacles to freedom of movement for persons, services and capital; (ii) the institution of a system for ensuring that competition in the Common Market is not distorted, and (iii) the approximation of the laws of Member States to the extent required for the proper functioning of the Common Market. The Court of Justice has described the establishment of a Common Market as involving the

> elimination of all obstacles to intra-Community trade in order to merge the national markets into a single market bringing about conditions as close as possible to those of a genuine internal market. It is important that not only commerce as such but also private persons

[23] Case 26/76 *Metro v Commission* [1977] ECR 1875, 1904.

who happen to be conducting an economic transaction across national frontiers should be able to enjoy the benefits of that market.[24]

[1–31] Part Two of the EEC Treaty established what are known as the "Four Freedoms", which continue to form the cornerstone of today's Single Market, and of EU law generally: the free movement within the Union of goods, persons, services and capital.

[1–32] The creation of the Common Market involved both *negative* elements, requiring the removal of direct and indirect barriers to trade between Member States, and *positive* elements through the adoption of certain common policies and Community measures that would harmonise the laws of its Member States. In order to achieve this positive harmonisation it was important that, in contrast to the ECSC, the EEC be endowed with a law-making power. This meant that, unlike most previous international agreements, the content of the rules governing the Community were not to be found exhaustively within the EEC Treaty itself, but rather the Treaty provided the overall framework within which such rules were to be adopted and adjudicated. The Community's institutions were given the power to enact laws for the "approximation of such legislative and administrative provisions of the Member States as have a direct incidence on the establishment or functioning of the Common Market" or to address a "disparity existing between the legislative or administrative provisions of the Member States [that] distorts the conditions of competition in the Common Market".[25] In order to ensure that these rules were not undermined by the practices of private economic operators, it was also considered necessary to enable the EEC to enforce a competition policy. Accordingly, the Treaty prohibited any "agreements between enterprises, any decisions by associations of enterprises and any concerted practices which are likely to affect trade between the Member States and which have as their object or result the prevention, restriction or distortion of competition". For similar reasons, there were also rules governing state aid and dumping practices.

(iii) Other Policy Areas

[1–33] As an international organisation established by treaty, the EEC had what is known as "conferred competence". This means that the EEC only had the authority to carry out those functions that had been conferred upon it by the Member States (the principle of conferral). Given the extent to which the competence of the EU has been expanded in successive treaty amendments, it is useful to recall the degree to which the remit of the EEC beyond the Customs Union and the Common Market was initially quite limited. So, in addition to the five activities related to the establishment of the Customs Union and the Common Market mentioned above, Art 3 of the EEC Treaty also mandated:

- the adoption of a common policy in the spheres of agriculture and of transport;
- the application of procedures by which the economic policies of Member States could be co-ordinated and disequilibria in their balances of payments remedied;
- the creation of a European Social Fund in order to improve employment opportunities for workers and to contribute to the raising of their standard of living;

[24] Case 15/81 *Schul* [1982] ECR 1409, 1431–1432.

[25] Arts 100 and 101, EEC Treaty.

- the establishment of a European Investment Bank to facilitate the economic expansion of the Community by opening up fresh resources, and
- the association of the overseas countries and territories in order to increase trade and to promote jointly economic and social development.

[1–34] On foot of this, the EEC developed a Common Transport Policy, a Common Agricultural Policy and a Common Fisheries Policy, and began to coordinate the economic policies of the Member States. In addition to creating both a European Social Fund and a European Investment Bank, a limited social policy enshrined within the Treaty the principle of equal pay for men and women for equal work, and provided that the Commission would promote close collaboration amongst the Member States particularly in the areas of employment law, working conditions and safety, social security, collective bargaining and occupational and continual training. Finally, the intention of the Association Policy was to promote the economic and social development of certain countries and territories identified as having a special relationship with the six Member States and to establish close economic relations between them and the Community as a whole.

D. European Free Trade Association

[1–35] As it is often overlooked, it is worth noting here that on 4 January 1960 the seven countries of Austria, Denmark, Norway, Sweden, Switzerland, Portugal and the UK signed the Stockholm Convention establishing the European Free Trade Association (EFTA). The Convention entered into force on 3 May 1960. The need to maintain preferential access for Irish agricultural products to the UK was a primary reason for Ireland not seeking to join EFTA, which did not cover trade in agricultural goods.[26] As mentioned above, a free trade area is a less intense form of integration than a customs union in that it does not impose a common external tariff but merely entails the absence of tariffs between the states that make up the free trade area. EFTA was established by these "Outer Seven" states as an economic-focused and less political counterpoint to the EEC. Article 2 of the Stockholm Convention set out the four objectives of the Association as follows:

(a) to promote in the Area of the Association and in each Member State a sustained expansion of economic activity, full employment, increased productivity and the rational use of resources, financial stability and continuous improvement in living standards,
(b) to secure that trade between Member States takes place in conditions of fair competition,
(c) to avoid significant disparity between Member States in the conditions of supply of raw materials produced within the Area of the Association, and
(d) to contribute to the harmonious development and expansion of world trade and to the progressive removal of barriers to it.

[1–36] The history of EFTA is complex given the changing make-up of its composition, as some members joined only to eventually leave so as to accede to the

---

[26] Michael Breen and James Dorgan, "The Death of Irish Trade Protectionism: A Political Economy Analysis" (2013) 24 *Irish Studies in International Affairs* 1, 8; Denis Maher, *The Tortuous Path: The Course of Ireland's Entry into the EEC, 1948–1973* (Institute of Public Administration, 1986) 106-111.

EEC. Finland joined in 1961, Iceland in 1970 and Liechtenstein in 1991. Of these 10, all but the current EFTA members of Norway, Switzerland, Iceland and Liechtenstein left to join the EU. In addition, on 2 May 1992 the EU and EFTA states signed the European Economic Area (EEA) Agreement, which entered into force on 1 January 1994.[27] A referendum in Switzerland rejected ratification of the Agreement and so of the four EFTA states, Norway, Iceland and Liechtenstein are also in the EEA, whereas Switzerland's relationship with the EU is governed by a series of bilateral agreements.[28] The EEA Agreement extends the four freedoms of the Single Market to the three non-EU states. In return, the non-EU states are required to accept EU legislation in these fields (subject to certain modifications) and to make financial contributions to the EU.

E. Accession by Ireland

[1–37] In the same year as the Treaty of Rome entered into force, a committed intergovernmentalist, Charles de Gaulle, assumed the French presidency and quickly moved towards establishing France's Fifth Republic. His victory would have a major impact on both the EEC – leading to the Luxembourg Compromise that would significantly slow down progress towards integration until the reforms of the Single European Act of 1986 – and on Ireland.[29] Ireland first applied for membership of the EEC on 31 July 1961. As Ireland's application was, in reality, made in parallel with that of the UK, France's veto of UK membership in January 1963 meant that Ireland's application was similarly stalled, even though it was not formally vetoed.[30] When the UK renewed its application on 10 May 1967, Ireland did likewise on the following day, expressing the hope that "discussions for the admission of Ireland to the Community would be brought to completion at the same time as those for the United Kingdom". The UK's application was once again vetoed by France in November 1967.

[1–38] Between the time of Ireland's original application in 1961 and eventual

---

27 See Sven Norberg, "The Agreement on a European Economic Area" (1992) 29 *Common Market Law Review* 1171; Christophe Reymond, "Institutions, Decision-Making Procedure and Settlement of Disputes in the European Economic Area" (1993) 30 *Common Market Law Review* 449; Noel Travers, "The European Economic Area and the European Communities: A Constitutional Dilemma Partially Resolved" (1994) 3 *Irish Journal of European Law* 74; Halvard Haukeland Fredriksen and Christian NK Franklin, "Of Pragmatism and Principles: The EEA Agreement 20 Years On" (2015) 52 *Common Market Law Review* 629; Carl Baudenbacher (ed), *The Handbook of EEA Law* (Springer, 2016); Christophe Hillion, "Brexit means Br(EEA)xit: The UK Withdrawal from the EU and its Implications for the EEA" (2018) 55 *Common Market Law Review* 135.

28 See Matthias Oesch, *Switzerland and the European Union* (Nomos, 2018); Christine Kaddous, "The Relations between the EU and Switzerland" in Alan Dashwood and Marc Maresceau (eds), *Law and Practice of EU External Relations* (Cambridge University Press, 2008) 227.

29 See ch 5, paras [5–25] to [5–31].

30 See Michael Geary, *An Inconvenient Wait: Ireland's Quest for Membership of the EEC 1957–1973* (Institute of Public Administration, 2010); Michael Geary, *Enlarging the European Union: The Commission Seeking Influence, 1961–1973* (Palgrave Macmillan, 2013); Denis Maher, *The Tortuous Path: The Course of Ireland's Entry into the EEC, 1948–1973* (Institute of Public Administration, 1986); Dermot Keogh and Aoife Keogh, "Ireland and European Integration: From the Treaty of Rome to Membership" in Mark Callanan (ed), *Foundations of an Ever Closer Union: An Irish Perspective on the Fifty Years since the Treaty of Rome* (Institute of Public Administration, 2007) 6; Maurice FitzGerald, *Protectionism to Liberalisation: Ireland and the EEC, 1957 to 1966* (Ashgate, 2000); Gary Murphy, *Economic Realignment and the Politics of EEC Entry: Ireland, 1948–1972* (Academica Press, 2003).

membership in 1973, important developments continued to shape the legal nature and institutional architecture of the EEC. In 1962, the Assembly adopted a resolution changing its name to Parliament (purportedly to align different language versions), a change that was not formally recognised until the Single European Act of 1986. The Merger Treaty, combining the separate Councils and Commissions of the three Communities, was signed in 1965 and entered into force in 1967. Nineteen sixty-five also saw the outbreak of the "empty chair" crisis, which would see a disagreement over voting rules cause France to absent itself from the Council until a resolution was reached the following year in the form of the Luxembourg Compromise.[31] On 1 July 1968, the establishment of the Customs Union and the application of a Common External Tariff were completed, slightly ahead of schedule. In 1970, the Council adopted its first decision providing for a system of "own resources" financing of the EEC, whereby it would be funded through the Common External Tariff and a percentage of VAT rather than being entirely reliant on contributions from Member States. A Budgetary Treaty of the same year amended the EEC Treaty in order to confer further powers on the Parliament in respect of the budget (a second Budgetary Treaty of 1975 amended the EEC Treaty once again so as to further enhance the power of the Parliament and create the European Court of Auditors). Nineteen seventy was also the year in which "European Political Cooperation" began, which involved regular meetings of the foreign ministers of the six Member States with a view to harmonising their foreign policies. Such meetings occurred in parallel to the institutions of the EEC and were not formally part of the Community's activity. On the same day as Ireland's accession negotiations began in June 1970, the Council adopted measures providing for the establishment of a Common Fisheries Policy.

[1–39] Alongside these institutional developments, the Court of Justice was delivering a number of landmark judgments that radically altered the understanding of EEC law. First, in its 1963 judgment in *Van Gend en Loos*, the Court established that certain provisions of the EEC Treaty not only had *direct application* in the national law of the Member States, but also had *direct effect*, in the sense that a national of a Member State may rely on an article of the EEC Treaty in order to claim rights which the national court must protect.[32] This was the case even if a Member State was dualist when it came to the incorporation of international law into its domestic legal system, and the decision was reached notwithstanding that three of the six Member States made clear to the Court that this was not their intention when they adopted the EEC Treaty six years earlier. According to the Court, the EEC constituted:

> a new legal order of international law for the benefit of which the States have limited their sovereign rights, albeit within limited fields, and the subjects of which comprise not only member states but also their nationals. Independently of the legislation of Member States, Community law therefore not only imposes obligations on individuals but is also intended to confer upon them rights which become part of their legal heritage.[33]

[1–40] The following year, in *Costa v ENEL*, the Court established the equally important doctrine of the *supremacy* of EEC law over conflicting national laws.[34] In contrast with ordinary international treaties, the EEC Treaty was said to have created its

---

[31] See ch 5, paras [5–25] to [5–31].

[32] Case 26/62 *Van Gend en Loos* [1963] ECR 1.

[33] *ibid*, 12.

[34] Case 6/64 *Costa v ENEL* [1964] ECR 585.

own legal system which, upon its entry into force on 1 January 1958, became an integral part of the legal systems of the Member States and which their courts were bound to apply. In a passage that would become one of its best known, the Court reasoned that:

> By creating a Community of unlimited duration, having its own institutions, its own personality, its own legal capacity and capacity of representation on the international plane and, more particularly, real powers stemming from a limitation of sovereignty or a transfer of powers from the States to the Community, the Member States have limited their sovereign rights, albeit within limited fields, and have thus created a body of law which binds their nationals and themselves.
>
> The integration into the laws of each Member State of provisions which derive from the Community, and more generally the terms and spirit of the Treaty, make it impossible for the states, as a corollary, to accord precedence to a unilateral and subsequent measure over a legal system accepted by them on the basis of reciprocity. Such a measure cannot therefore be inconsistent with that legal system. The executive force of Community law cannot vary from one State to another in deference to subsequent domestic laws, without jeopardising the attainment of the objectives of the Treaty ... and giving rise to discrimination ...
>
> The obligations undertaken under the Treaty establishing the Community would not be unconditional, but merely contingent, if they could be called into question by subsequent legislative acts of the signatories ...[35]

[1–41] The doctrine of supremacy requires that, in the event of a conflict between EU law and national law, national law must be set aside in order to enable EU law to be applied. In the 1970 case of *Internationale Handelsgesellschaft* the Court of Justice confirmed that the doctrine of supremacy applied to all forms of national law, even constitutional law.[36]

[1–42] While each of these cases will be considered in detail in subsequent chapters, they are worth noting here as part of the historical context in which Ireland voted to join the EEC. Although neither the direct effect nor the supremacy of EEC law was set out in express terms in the Treaty of Rome, the Court's case law formed part of the *acquis communautaire* or body of law that Ireland would be required to accommodate within its legal system from the moment of joining this "new legal order of international law". Theoretical debates flourished, and still do, as to the precise nature of this new form of international organisation with its own parliament, court and executive bodies and the power to make laws that override even the constitutional norms of its Member States. What was clear was that the EEC was quite unlike anything that had come before, and that its unique nature defied any neat description. As Laurent Pech has described, because European integration

> has always evolved by a successive set of compromises between "federalism" and "sovereignists", the EU is, and will remain, an ongoing "experiment in transnational politics". Therefore, even though the qualification may certainly appear frustrating, the original political and legal nature of the EU makes it a *sui generis* entity: an entity not bestowed with statehood but whose legal system is reminiscent of a federal state.[37]

[1–43] Negotiations on Ireland's accession to the EEC and Euratom eventually

35 *ibid*, 593–594.

36 Case 11/70 *Internationale Handelsgesellschaft* [1970] ECR 1125.

37 Laurent Pech, *The European Union and its Constitution* (Clarus Press, 2008) 15.

took place from June 1970 to January 1972.[38] Just as the negotiations began on 30 June 1970, within the same building the Council was adopting measures to establish the first ever Common Fisheries Policy, prompting each of the candidate countries to make sure to mention this fresh cause of concern in their introductory speeches.[39] Having no deep-sea fishing fleet of its own, Ireland was at that time reliant on inshore fishing that remained within shallower waters. After 18 months of negotiations, a compromise was reached as part of which Ireland obtained a 10-year fisheries reserve of 12 nautical miles from Lough Foyle to Cork Harbour, and from Carlingford Lough to Carnsore Point in respect of shellfish. The Accession Treaty would also permit Ireland to apply transitional arrangements until 1977 allowing for the gradual dismantling of its existing trade protection system, the maintaining of certain aids and incentives to industrial development, as well as special arrangements for the Irish steel industry so as to allow it to reorganise and quota restrictions on certain textile imports from low cost countries. Special arrangements were permitted until 1985 in order to allow the Irish motor assembly industry to adapt to competing within the Customs Union. A Treaty of Accession in respect of Ireland, the UK, Denmark and Norway was signed on 22 January 1972, with a separate Decision of the Council of the same day allowing for accession to the ECSC.

[1–44] In Ireland, the Third Amendment to the Constitution Bill was subject to a referendum in 1972, in which there was a vote of 1,041,890 (83 per cent) in favour and just 211,891 (17 per cent) against. As a referendum in Norway voted against ratification, the Treaty entered into force for Ireland, the UK and Denmark on 1 January 1973, marking the first enlargement of the EEC since its founding 15 years earlier. The Constitution was amended by the insertion of a new sub-paragraph, Art 29.4.3°, as follows:

> The State may become a member of the European Coal and Steel Community (established by Treaty signed at Paris on the 18 April 1951), the European Economic Community (established by Treaty signed at Rome on the 25 March 1957) and the European Atomic Energy Community (established by Treaty signed at Rome on the 25 March 1957). No provision of this Constitution invalidates laws enacted, acts done or measures adopted by the State necessitated by the obligations of membership of the Communities or prevents laws enacted, acts done or measures adopted by the Communities, or institutions thereof, from having the force of law in the State.

(i) European Communities Act 1972

[1–45] In addition to a constitutional amendment, legislation was required in order to give the EEC Treaty, and related treaties, the force of law in Ireland.[40] This followed

---

[38] See "Negotiations with Denmark, Ireland and Norway" (1971) 8 *Common Market Law Review* 67; KR Simmonds, "The Dublin Conference, October 1970" (1971) 8 *Common Market Law Review* 266; "Ireland's Negotiations with the European Communities, September 1970–July 1971" (1971) 8 *Common Market Law Review* 517; "Negotiations with Ireland, July–November 1971" (1972) 9 *Common Market Law Review* 80; "Negotiations with Ireland, November 1971–January 1972" (1972) 9 *Common Market Law Review* 185; LJ Brinkhorst and MJ Kuiper, "The Integration of New Member States in the Community Legal Order" (1972) 9 *Common Market Law Review* 364.

[39] Giancarlo Olmi, "Agriculture and Fisheries in the Treaty of Brussels of January 22, 1972" (1972) 9 *Common Market Law Review* 293, 314.

[40] See Jane Cochrane, "Implications for Ireland of Membership of the European Communities" (1970) 7 *Common Market Law Review* 336; John Temple Lang, "Legal and Constitutional Implications for Ireland of Adhesion to the EEC Treaty" (1972) 9 *Common Market Law Review* 167; Bryan

from the dualist nature of Ireland as regards the incorporation of international law, with Art 29.6 of the Constitution providing that no international agreement shall be part of the domestic law of the State save as may be determined by the Oireachtas. To this end, the European Communities Act 1972 was enacted, s 2 of which provided that:

> From the 1st day of January, 1973, the treaties governing the European Communities and the existing and future acts adopted by the institutions of those Communities shall be binding on the State and shall be part of the domestic law thereof under the conditions laid down in those treaties.

[1–46] Although amended 19 times, the 1972 Act continues to provide the legislative basis for Ireland's EU membership. In particular, on each occasion on which the primary treaties of the EU are amended, the Act's definition of the term "the treaties governing the European Communities" requires updating. As defined in 1972 these were the ECSC Treaty, EEC Treaty, Euratom Treaty, the Convention on Institutions Common to the Communities, the Merger Treaty, the (first) Budgetary Treaty, the Treaty of Accession to the EEC and Euratom, and the Decision of the Council on the Accession of Ireland to the ECSC.[41] The Act also provided for the making of ministerial regulations for the purpose of giving effect to EU law, a power that will be considered in Chapter 12. The Act came into operation on 6 December 1972 and between then and the end of the year was used to make 11 regulations on matters such as customs, immigration, the recognition of EEC judgments,[42] and allowing for judicial notice to be taken of the Official Journal,[43] while the European Communities (State Financial Transactions) Regulations authorised (and continues to authorise) the making of any payments from the Central Fund necessitated by membership of the Communities.[44]

[1–47] Writing a few years after its enactment, Henchy J described the "sweeping" effect of the 1972 Act as being as if,

> the people of Ireland had adopted Community law as a second but transcendent Constitution, with the difference that Community law is not to be found in any single document – it is a living growing organism and the right to interpret it and give it conclusive judicial interpretation is reserved to the institutions of the Community and to its Court.[45]

McMahon, "Constitutional Adjustments necessitated by Community Membership" (1976) 1 *European Law Review* 86; Bryan McMahon, "The Oireachtas and Community Legislation" (1977) 2 *European Law Review* 150.

41 Mary Robinson, "The Irish European Communities Act 1972" (1973) 10 *Common Market Law Review* 352; Mary Robinson, "Recent Legal Developments in Ireland in Relation to the European Communities" (1973) 10 *Common Market Law Review* 465. Separate from the European Communities Acts, a definition of "Member State" is provided for in s 21(2) of the Interpretation Act 2005 as meaning, where the context so admits, a Member State of the European Communities or of the European Union.

42 See now the European Communities (Enforcement of Community Judgments, Orders and Decisions) Regulations 2007 (SI No 121 of 2007).

43 European Communities (Judicial Notice and Documentary Evidence) Regulations 1972 (SI No 341 of 1972).

44 SI No 329 of 1972, as amended by the European Communities (State Financial Transactions) (Amendment) Regulations 1999 (SI No 30 of 1999).

45 Séamus Henchy, "The Irish Constitution and the EEC" (1977) 1 *Dublin University Law Journal* 20, 23.

[1–48] In *Tate v Minister for Social Welfare*, Carroll J memorably described s 2 of the Act as:

> the conduit pipe through which community law became part of domestic law. The Constitution was amended to enable accession to the community, the European Communities Act 1972 was passed and the Treaty of Accession was agreed, and thereby the whole body of community law, past, present and future was incorporated into domestic law. But community law did not thereby become constitutional law or statute law. It is still community law governed by community law but with domestic effect. And it is in that form that it is part of domestic law.[46]

[1–49] The manner in which Member States choose to give effect to EU law within their domestic legal order, and how this is perceived by their highest courts, is closely linked to the doctrine of the supremacy of EU law and is considered further in Chapter 13.

Timeline – From Origins to Accession

19 September 1946	Churchill's Zurich speech
5 May 1949	Signing of the Statute of the Council of Europe
9 May 1950	Schuman Declaration
4 November 1950	Adoption of the European Convention on Human Rights by the Council of Europe
18 April 1951	Signing of the European Coal and Steel Community Treaty (Treaty of Paris)
27 May 1952	Signing of the European Defence Community Treaty
23 July 1952	Entry into force of the European Coal and Steel Community Treaty (expired 23 July 2002)
30 August 1954	French National Assembly votes against ratification of the European Defence Community Treaty
23 October 1954	Establishment of the Western European Union (expired 30 June 2011)
25 March 1957	Signing of the European Economic Community Treaty (Treaty of Rome), the Euratom Treaty and the Convention on Certain Institutions Common to the European Communities (relating to the Parliamentary Assembly and Court)
1 January 1958	Entry into force of the European Economic Community Treaty (Treaty of Rome), the Euratom Treaty and the Convention on Certain Institutions Common to the European Communities (relating to the Parliamentary Assembly and Court)
21 January 1959	Establishment of the European Court of Human Rights with the election of its first judges
4 January 1960	Signing of the Treaty of Stockholm, establishing the European Free Trade Association (EFTA)
3 May 1960	Treaty of Stockholm enters into force, establishing the European Free Trade Association (EFTA)

[46] [1995] 1 IR 418, 437; [1995] 1 ILRM 507, 521.

31 July 1961	Ireland applies for membership of the EEC
March 1962	Assembly of the EEC, ECSC and Euratom adopts resolution changing its name to European Parliament (although not formally changed until the Single European Act 1986)
January 1963	France vetoes the UK's application to join the EEC, ending the accession process for Ireland
5 February 1963	*Van Gend en Loos* judgment establishes the principle of direct effect of EU law
15 July 1964	*Costa v ENEL* judgment establishes the principle of supremacy of EU law
8 April 1965	Signing of the Treaty Establishing a Single Council and a Single Commission of the European Communities (Merger Treaty) (concerning the Council and Commission)
June 1965	Beginning of the "Empty Chair" crisis and France's absence from the Council
28 January 1966	"Luxembourg Compromise" agreed upon as a resolution to the "Empty Chair" crisis
1 July 1967	Entry into force of the Treaty Establishing a Single Council and a Single Commission of the European Communities (Merger Treaty) (concerning the Council and Commission)
November 1967	France vetoes the UK's second application to join the EEC, ending the process for Ireland
1 July 1968	Completion of establishment of the Customs Union and application of a Common External Tariff
1970	Beginning of "European Political Cooperation"
21 April 1970	Own Resources Decision, establishing method of financing EEC budget
22 April 1970	Signing of the Treaty amending Certain Budgetary Provisions of the Treaties establishing the European Communities (Budgetary Treaty)
30 June 1970	Opening of accession negotiations and adoption by the Council of measure establishing a Common Fisheries Policy
17 December 1970	*Internationale Handelsgesellschaft* judgment confirms that the doctrine of supremacy of EEC law applies to the constitutional law of the Member States
1 January 1971	Entry into force of the Treaty amending Certain Budgetary Provisions of the Treaties establishing the European Communities (Budgetary Treaty)
22 January 1972	Signing of Instrument of Accession to the EEC and Euratom of Ireland, Denmark, the UK and Norway, and the adoption of a Decision of the Council on Accession to the ECSC
10 May 1972	Irish people vote in favour of joining the EEC, ECSC and Euratom by 83 per cent to 17 per cent
6 December 1972	Enactment of European Communities Act 1972
1 January 1973	Ireland, Denmark and the UK become members of the EEC, ECSC and Euratom

CHAPTER 2

DEVELOPMENT OF THE EU TREATIES 1974–2003

A. INTRODUCTION

[2–01] Slightly earlier than provided for in the EEC Treaty, the Customs Union was established by July 1968. In comparison, progress in creating the Common Market was considerably slower than had been anticipated. This was despite the best efforts of an activist and integrationist Court of Justice. Having already developed the principles of direct effect and supremacy, in the 1974 case of *Dassonville* the Court gave a very broad definition to the concept of a "measure having the equivalent effect to a quantitative restriction" on imports or exports. The EEC Treaty required such measures to be prohibited as an unlawful restriction on the free movement of goods. According to the *Dassonville* formula, the concept included "all trading rules enacted by a Member State which are capable of hindering, directly or indirectly, actually or potentially, intra-community trade".[1] The wide-sweep of such an expansive definition gave a hefty boost to the establishment of the Common Market through the means of negative integration. The Court delivered yet another landmark judgment in 1979, known as *Cassis de Dijon*, in which it established the fundamental principles of mutual recognition (or equivalence) and the "rule of reason".[2] Unless a Member State could point to a particular public policy reason why a good made in another Member State according to that state's laws should not be imported for sale, goods made in accordance with the law of one Member State were to be capable of being sold in any Member State. In other words, unless there was a good reason not to, standards within each Member State were to be recognised as being equivalent.

[2–02] Yet, whereas *negative* integration was being driven by Court of Justice findings that particular national rules were invalid in light of Treaty provisions, the pace of

---

1 Case 8/74 *Procureur du Roi v Dassonville* [1974] ECR 837, 852, discussed further in ch 19, paras [19–31] to [19–37].

2 Case 120/78 *Cassis de Dijon* [1979] ECR 649, discussed further in ch 19, paras [19–44] to [19–53].

positive integration through the adoption of harmonisation measures was considered to be very disappointing. This was due in part to the fact that the "Damoclean sword of the Luxembourg Compromise led to consensual decision-making within the Council even for legal bases that allowed for (qualified) majority voting".[3] The example is often given of a directive on the minimum training requirements for architects that took 17 years to negotiate. As a result, this period came to be known as one of "Euro-sclerosis": "The twenty-fifth anniversary of the Treaty of Rome, observed in March 1982, was a dismal affair. Remarking on a report that the Council had cancelled the official celebration, the president of the European Parliament compared the Community to 'a feeble cardiac patient whose condition is so poor that he cannot even be disturbed by a birthday party'."[4]

[2–03] During this period, institutional developments within the EEC included the entry into force of the Second Budgetary Treaty in 1977, creating the Court of Auditors and granting the Parliament the power to reject the Community budget as a whole, and the holding of the first direct elections to the European Parliament in 1979. Greece acceded to the EEC in 1981 while Portugal and Spain would do so on 1 January 1986.

[2–04] More significant developments, however, were taking place on the margins of the EEC, on an intergovernmental basis. These changes evolved organically and were not provided for in the EEC Treaty itself. First established in 1970, European Political Cooperation continued in the form of regular meetings of foreign ministers. In 1974, the leaders of the Member States decided to formalise their high-level summits in the guise of the European Council, the first proper meeting of which took place in Dublin in March 1975. In December 1975, following discussions within European Political Cooperation, the European Council established the "TREVI" mechanism in order to discuss issues related to terrorism, radicalism, extremism and international violence. In 1978, by a combination of a resolution of the European Council and an agreement between national central banks, the European Monetary System was established, made up of the Exchange Rate Mechanism and the European Currency Unit (ECU). Each participating currency was set against the ECU, with fluctuation to be limited to no more than 2.25 per cent. A final development worth mentioning started out as very much independent from the EEC, but would eventually come to be subsumed within it. In 1985, Belgium, the Netherlands, Luxembourg, France and Germany signed the Schengen Agreement on the Gradual Abolition of Checks at Common Borders, which had the aim of establishing an area comprising the five states within which there would be the free movement of persons without any border controls.

[2–05] Whilst these important developments were taking place outside of the EEC framework, at the Stuttgart European Council in June 1983 the leaders subscribed to a "Solemn Declaration on the Future of Europe" in which they committed to a "renewed impetus" in the completion of the Common Market in which the four freedoms were guaranteed, reaffirmed the Luxembourg Compromise and the voting rules as provided for in the EEC Treaty, as well as agreeing that:

> [i]n order to achieve ever increasing solidarity and joint action, the construction of Europe must be more clearly oriented towards its general political objectives, more efficient decision-making procedures, greater coherence and close coordination between the

---

[3] Robert Schütze, *European Union Law* (Cambridge University Press, 2015) 16.

[4] Desmond Dinan, *Ever Closer Union* (2nd ed, Palgrave, 1999) 81.

> different branches of activity, and the search for common policies in all areas of common interest, both within the Community and in relation to third countries.

[2–06] The Community's institutions were mandated to work on initiatives that would bring an end to a period of prolonged stagnation. Amongst the various reports commissioned, two in particular are worth highlighting. In March 1985, the report of the *Ad Hoc Committee on Institutional Affairs* (the "Dooge Report") was presented to the European Council by its chair, former Irish Foreign Minister James Dooge. Reflecting its significance, the Report is also known as the Spaak II Report as a successor to the first Spaak Report which led to the EEC Treaty itself. The Report acknowledged that the EEC was in a state of crisis and suffered from serious deficiencies, and responded by setting out the "objectives, policies and institutional reforms which are necessary to restore to Europe the vigour and ambition of its inception". These included the creation of a genuine internal market, the strengthening of the European Monetary System, the expansion of the EEC's social policies, the incorporation of European Political Cooperation within the Community framework and a series of institutional reforms that would see a strengthened Parliament and Commission and the default use of qualified majority voting within the Council. As an expression of Ireland's traditional policy of military neutrality, Dooge recorded his own disagreement with the report's recommendation that the EEC also develop coordination on security and defence matters.

[2–07] Three months later, in June 1985, the Commission published its seminal *White Paper on the Completion of the Internal Market*, setting out a legislative roadmap of 282 measures necessary to complete the Internal Market by removing physical, technical and fiscal barriers to trade by the end of 1992.[5] The two reports were considered at the Milan European Council, during which Italy proposed the opening of an intergovernmental conference (IGC) to negotiate a treaty on foreign policy and security cooperation, as well as a revision of the EEC Treaty to improve decision-making and extend the Community's competence. The proposal proved contentious, and of the four Member States to have acceded since 1957, only Ireland supported the holding of a conference:

> Jealous of their national sovereignty, Britain and Denmark objected to the holding of an IGC, and obstructionist Greece followed suit. Italy again forced the issue by calling for a vote under [the EEC Treaty], which permit[ted] an IGC to be convened if a majority of member states approve. It was unprecedented for the heads of state and government to vote on anything at a European Council. In the ensuing ballot seven voted in favour of an IGC and three – the British, Danish and Greek prime ministers – voted against.[6]

B. The Single European Act

[2–08] Confusingly, the resultant Single European Act is so called because it addressed two quite separate reforms in one single international agreement.[7] Late in the negotiations it was decided to combine into one text what, until that point, had been seen as two separate treaties dealing with amending the EEC Treaty and providing

---

5 European Commission, COM(85) 310, 14 June 1985.

6 Desmond Dinan, *Ever Closer Union* (2nd ed, Palgrave, 1999) 115.

7 For a contemporary analysis see Finbarr Murphy, "The Single European Act" (1985) 20 *Irish Jurist* 17 and 239; Dermot McAleese and Alan Matthews, "The Single European Act and Ireland: Implications for a Small Member State" (1987) 21 *Journal of Common Market Studies* 38.

for a nascent foreign and security policy. Of its four Titles, Titles I and IV dealt with common provisions and general and final provisions. The main substance, therefore, was dealt with in Title II, which amended the EEC Treaty's institutional provisions as well as adding a number of new competences, and also amended aspects of the ECSC and Euratom Treaties. Title III dealt exclusively with European Political Cooperation in the sphere of foreign policy.

Title I	**Common Provisions**
Title II	**Provisions Amending the Treaties Establishing the European Communities**
	Chapter I – Provisions Amending the European Coal and Steel Community Treaty
	Chapter II – Provisions Amending the European Economic Community Treaty
	Section I – Institutional Provisions
	Section II – Provisions Relating to the Foundations and the Policy of the Community
	I – Internal Market
	II – Monetary Capacity
	III – Social Policy
	IV – Economic and Social Cohesion
	V – Research and Technological Development
	VI – Environment
	Chapter III – Provisions Amending the European Atomic Energy Community Treaty
	Chapter IV – General Provisions
Title III	**Treaty Provisions on European Co-operation in the Sphere of Foreign Policy**
Title IV	**General and Final Provisions**

[2–09] The Single European Act was signed by nine Member States (including Ireland) on 17 February 1986, and by the remaining three 11 days later, with the intention of it entering into force the following January. As will be seen, a decision by the Irish Supreme Court that a referendum was required in order for Ireland to ratify the Act caused a delay, such that it did not enter into force until 1 July 1987.

[2–10] In amending the EEC Treaty, the principal aim of the Single European Act was to facilitate the completion of the Common Market. As a form of reboot and a break with the slow progress of the past decade, the new term "Internal Market" was introduced and given the definition of an area without internal frontiers in which the free movement of goods, persons, services and capital is ensured. The deadline of 31 December 1992 was set by which to progressively establish the Internal Market. The main change introduced in order to assist in achieving this goal was a significant extension of the use of qualified majority voting (QMV) within the Council,[8] including a new legal basis that allowed for the use of QMV in the adoption of measures to approximate the laws of the Member States (now Art 114 TFEU). In light of the particular sensitivities of the insurance industry in Ireland, Ireland made a declaration to the Act indicating that, in the event of QMV being used in respect of a measure to harmonise the insurance sector, Ireland "would expect to be able to rely on a sympathetic attitude from the

[8] See ch 5, paras [5–19] to [5–24].

Commission and from the other Member States".[9] A further amendment gave effect to a recommendation that the Council make greater use of the ability to delegate to the Commission the power to implement the rules laid down in EU legal acts.

[2–11] In addition to these Internal Market focused reforms, the Single European Act also provided the EEC with new competences in the areas of research and technological development, environmental policy, economic and social cohesion (which would lead to the Regional Development Fund) and social policy. Although not fully incorporating it within the EEC, the Act recognised the need to converge economic and monetary policies for the further development of the Community and imposed on Member States a duty to "take account of the experience acquired in cooperation within the framework of the European Monetary System and in developing the ECU".[10] For the time being, however, both the European Monetary System and the ECU would remain a form of intergovernmental cooperation outside of the Community framework. The same was true of the tentative first steps in cooperating in the areas security and criminal law that was beginning to take place within the TREVI mechanism.

[2–12] The Single European Act also introduced significant institutional changes. As well as formally recognising the change of name from Assembly to Parliament, the Parliament's role in the legislative process was strengthened by the introduction of a "co-operation procedure", which required the Council to engage in a dialogue in respect of legislative proposals to which the procedure applied. If certain proposals were rejected by the Parliament, a unanimous vote of the Council was to be required to override its objections. In addition, the assent of the Parliament was henceforward to be required for any new accession to the EEC, or for the entry into association agreements with third countries. In response to a growing backlog of cases before the Court of Justice, the Act provided for the establishment of a Court of First Instance (now named the General Court). Summit meetings of heads of state or government having been formalised since 1975, the Act brought the European Council within the EEC framework by formally recognising it, albeit that it would not be until the Lisbon Treaty's entry into force in 2009 that the European Council would be included as one of the Union's seven institutions.

[2–13] Finally, Title III of the Act gave a formal legal basis to European Political Cooperation. Although this cooperation in the sphere of foreign policy would continue on an intergovernmental basis, and in parallel to the EEC Treaty, it was now codified within an international agreement. Given its importance to the Supreme Court decision in *Crotty v An Taoiseach*, it is worth setting out the full detail of Title III, which provided as follows:

---

[9] "Ireland, in confirming its agreement to qualified majority voting under Article 57(2), wishes to recall that the insurance industry in Ireland is a particularly sensitive one and that special arrangements have had to be made by the Government of Ireland for the protection of insurance policy holders and third parties. In relation to harmonization of legislation on insurance, the Government of Ireland would expect to be able to rely on a sympathetic attitude from the Commission and from the other Member States of the Community should Ireland later find itself in a situation where the Government of Ireland considers it necessary to have special provision made for the position of the industry in Ireland." Declaration by the Government of Ireland on Art 57(2) of the EEC Treaty [1987] OJ L169/27.

[10] New Art 102a of the EEC Treaty, as inserted by Art 20 of the Single European Act.

1. The High Contracting Parties, being members of the European Communities, shall endeavour jointly to formulate and implement a European foreign policy.

2. (a) The High Contracting Parties undertake to inform and consult each other on any foreign policy matters of general interest so as to ensure that their combined influence is exercised as effectively as possible through co-ordination, the convergence of their positions and the implementation of joint action.
   (b) Consultations shall take place before the High Contracting Parties decide on their final position.
   (c) In adopting its positions and in its national measures each High Contracting Party shall take full account of the positions of the other partners and shall give due consideration to the desirability of adopting and implementing common European positions. In order to increase their capacity for joint action in the foreign policy field, the High Contracting Parties shall ensure that common principles and objectives are gradually developed and defined. The determination of common positions shall constitute a point of reference for the policies of the High Contracting Parties.
   (d) The High Contracting Parties shall endeavour to avoid any action or position which impairs their effectiveness as a cohesive force in international relations or within international organizations.

3. (a) The Ministers for Foreign Affairs and a member of the Commission shall meet at least four times a year within the framework of European Political Co-operation. They may also discuss foreign policy matters within the framework of Political Co-operation on the occasion of meetings of the Council of the European Communities.
   (b) The Commission shall be fully associated with the proceedings of Political Co-operation.
   (c) In order to ensure the swift adoption of common positions and the implementation of joint action, the High Contracting Parties shall, as far as possible, refrain from impeding the formation of a consensus and the joint action which this could produce.

4. The High Contracting Parties shall ensure that the European Parliament is closely associated with European Political Co-operation. To that end the Presidency shall regularly inform the European Parliament of the foreign policy issues which are being examined within the framework of Political Co-operation and shall ensure that the views of the European Parliament are duly taken into consideration.

5. The external policies of the European Community and the policies agreed in European Political Co-operation must be consistent. The Presidency and the Commission, each within its own sphere of competence, shall have special responsibility for ensuring that such consistency is sought and maintained.

6. (a) The High Contracting Parties consider that closer co-operation on questions of European security would contribute in an essential way to the development of a European identity in external policy matters. They are ready to co-ordinate their positions more closely on the political and economic aspects of security.
   (b) The High Contracting Parties are determined to maintain the technological and industrial conditions necessary for their security. They shall work to that end both at national level and, where appropriate, within the framework of the competent institutions and bodies.
   (c) Nothing in this Title shall impede closer co-operation in the field of security between certain of the High Contracting Parties within the framework of the Western European Union or the Atlantic Alliance.

7. (a) In international institutions and at international conferences which they attend, the High Contracting Parties shall endeavour to adopt common positions on the subjects covered by this Title.
   (b) In international institutions and at international conferences in which not all the High Contracting Parties participate, those who do participate shall take full account of positions agreed in European Political Co-operation.

8. The High Contracting Parties shall organize a political dialogue with third countries and regional groupings whenever they deem it necessary.

9. The High Contracting Parties and the Commission, through mutual assistance and information, shall intensify co-operation between their representations accredited to third countries and to international organizations.

10. (a) The Presidency of European Political Co-operation shall be held by the High Contracting Party which holds the Presidency of the Council of the European Communities.
    (b) The Presidency shall be responsible for initiating action and co-ordinating and representing the positions of the Member States in relations with third countries in respect of European Political Cooperation activities. It shall also be responsible for the management of Political Co-operation and in particular for drawing up the timetable of meetings and for convening and organizing meetings.
    (c) The Political Directors shall meet regularly in the Political Committee in order to give the necessary impetus, maintain the continuity of European Political Co-operation and prepare Ministers' discussions.

    …

    (g) A Secretariat based in Brussels shall assist the Presidency in preparing and implementing the activities of European Political Co-operation and in administrative matters. It shall carry out its duties under the authority of the Presidency.

(i) *Crotty v An Taoiseach*

[2–14] As seen in the previous chapter, in order to allow Ireland to join the EEC, Art 29.4.3° was inserted into the Constitution providing that: (i) the State may become a member of the EEC, established by the EEC Treaty of 1957; (ii) no provision of the Constitution invalidates laws enacted, acts done or measures adopted by the State necessitated by the obligations of such membership and (iii) no provision of the Constitution prevents Community laws, acts or measures from having the force of law in the State. The European Communities Act 1972 was passed in order to give the EEC Treaty (as well as the ECSC and Euratom Treaties) force as part of Irish law.

[2–15] When it came to ratifying the Single European Act before the scheduled date of 1 January 1987, the Oireachtas enacted the European Communities (Amendment) Act 1986 which was signed into law on 23 December. That Act amended the definition of the "treaties governing the European Communities" in s 1 of the 1972 Act by inserting a reference to certain provisions of the Single European Act that were to have the force of law in the State. Given the intergovernmental nature of European Political Cooperation, no provision of Title III was included within the Act's revised definition of the treaties. This process was stopped, however, on 24 December, when the High Court granted an injunction to a private citizen, Mr Crotty, who sought to restrain the Government from proceeding with ratification. On appeal, the Supreme Court delivered two separate judgments.[11] The first related to the constitutionality of the 1986 Act and was delivered by Finlay CJ on behalf of the Court. The second related to whether Ireland could proceed to ratify the Single European Act given the inclusion of Title III on European Political Cooperation and resulted in a 3 to 2 majority judgment (Walsh, Henchy and Hederman JJ for the majority and Finlay CJ and Griffin J for the minority).[12]

[2–16] Regarding those aspects of the Single European Act that amended the EEC Treaty, the Supreme Court held that neither the Single European Act, nor the 1986 Act giving it the force of law, could be regarded as being "necessitated" by Ireland's membership of the EEC such that Art 29.4.3° would afford them a form of constitutional immunity. This did not mean, however, that every single amendment to the EEC Treaty would require a referendum as this would be "too narrow a construction".[13] Rather, Art 29.4.3° "must be construed as an authorisation given to the State not only to join the Communities as they stood in 1973, but also to join in amendments of the Treaties so long as such amendments do not alter the essential scope or objectives of the Community".[14] This is often described by saying that in acceding to the EEC, Ireland boarded a moving train not a static legal entity.[15]

[2–17] The question that was to be addressed in this judgment, therefore, became whether or not the changes to the EEC Treaty were within its original scope or objectives. Mr Crotty argued that the following changes brought about by the Single European Act were outside the constitutional authorisation granted in 1972: (i) the instances in which the voting procedure within the Council was switched from unanimity to QMV; (ii) the new legal base that allowed for measures to be adopted, by QMV, to approximate national laws that were necessitated to complete the Single Market; (iii) the addition of new objectives dealing with the environment, economic and social cohesion, research and technological development, social policy and cooperation in economic and monetary policy and (iv) the provision allowing for the establishment of a Court of First Instance.

---

11 See Gerard Hogan, "The Supreme Court and the Single European Act" (1987) 22 *Irish Jurist* 55; John Temple Lang, "The Irish Court Case which Delayed the Single European Act: *Crotty v An Taoiseach and Others*" (1987) 24 *Common Market Law Review* 709; Kieran Bradley, "The Referendum on the Single European Act" (1987) *European Law Review* 301; Bryan McMahon and Finbarr Murphy, *European Community Law in Ireland* (Butterworths, 1989) 267–271; James Casey, "*Crotty v An Taoiseach*: A Comparative Perspective" in James O'Reilly (ed), *Essays in Honour of Brian Walsh* (Butterworths, 1992) 189; Gerard Hogan and Anthony Whelan, *Ireland and the European Union* (Sweet and Maxwell, 1995) 25–49; Diarmuid Rossa Phelan, *Revolt or Revolution* (Round Hall, 1997) 334–337; Gavin Barrett, "The Evolving Door to Europe: Reflections on an Eventful 40 Years for Article 29.4 of the Constitution" (2012) 48 *Irish Jurist* 132; Gavin Barrett, *A Road Less Travelled: Reflections on the Supreme Court Rulings in Crotty, Coughlan and McKenna (No.2)* (Institute of International and European Affairs, 2011); Gavin Barrett, "Building a Swiss Chalet in an Irish Legal Landscape? Referendums on European Union Treaties in Ireland and the Impact of Supreme Court Jurisprudence" (2009) 5 *European Constitutional Law Review* 32; David Fennelly, "*Crotty*'s Long Shadow: the European Union, the United Nations and the Changing Framework of Ireland's International Relations" in Eoin Carolan (ed), *The Constitution of Ireland: Perspectives and Prospects* (Bloomsbury, 2012); Maria Cahill, "*Crotty* after *Pringle*: The Revival of the Doctrine of Implied Amendment" (2014) 17 *Irish Journal of European Law* 1; Ruadhán Mac Cormaic, *The Supreme Court* (Penguin, 2016) 251–268.

12 *Crotty v An Taoiseach* [1987] IR 713; [1987] ILRM 400.

13 *ibid*, 767; 444.

14 *ibid*.

15 Gavin Barrett, *A Road Less Travelled: Reflections on the Supreme Court Rulings in Crotty, Coughlan and McKenna (No.2)* (Institute of International and European Affairs, 2011) 8.

[2–18] In addressing these changes, the Supreme Court noted that the EEC Treaty had provided for a transitional period, at the end of which certain instances where unanimity was required within the Council would change to QMV (as had been at issue when the "Empty Chair" crisis arose in 1965). This led the Court to conclude that the EEC was:

> a developing organism with diverse and changing methods for making decisions and an inbuilt and clearly expressed objective of expansion and progress, both in terms of the number of its Member States and in terms of the mechanics to be used in the achievement of its agreed objectives.[16]

[2–19] Accordingly, the change from unanimity to QMV was deemed to be within the original aims and objectives of the EEC Treaty. The addition of new areas of competence did not confer any new powers on the Council that would "alter the essential character of the Communities".[17] Finally, the creation of a Court of First Instance would not "affect in any material way the extent to which the judicial power had already been ceded to the European Court".[18] As a result, the Supreme Court concluded that those parts of the Single European Act other than Title III were not such as to require a referendum.

[2–20] In contrast, in its second judgment dealing with the formalisation of European Political Cooperation within the Single European Act, a majority of the Supreme Court considered that to enter into a binding commitment as regards a coordinated approach to foreign policy would infringe upon the requirement in Art 1 of the Constitution that Ireland, as an independent, sovereign state, "determine its relations with other nations … in accordance with its *own* genius and traditions".[19] For the majority, while it may have been the case that Ireland had already been participating in a coordination of foreign policy on an informal basis, it was something else to enter into "a solemnly covenanted commitment to the conduct of foreign policy in a way that will lead to European political union, at least in the sphere of foreign policy".[20] The difference in the approaches of the majority and minority judgments is explained by Ann Sherlock as follows:

> For the minority judges the fact that cooperation on the political level had already been taking place was clearly of some relevance. Griffin J. observed that there had been European Political Cooperation since 1970 with the states undertaking to co-operate in the field of foreign policy by consulting regularly, harmonising views and opinions and taking joint action. Article 1 made clear that Title III was designed to confirm and supplement the procedures previously agreed and practices gradually established. However, in Henchy J.'s view [forming part of the majority], to regard Title III as merely formalising existing practise was to underestimate the nature of a treaty in international law as distinct from a mere practice or procedure. In his view, as a Treaty, Title III required changes which would erode national independence in the conduct of external relations.[21]

[2–21] It is fair to say that reaction to the judgment has not been favourable, with a prediction being made at the time that the Supreme Court's "remarkable display of judicial activism" would "probably rank as one of the most extraordinary [judgments]

---

16 [1987] IR 713, 770; [1987] ILRM 400, 446.

17 *ibid.*

18 *ibid.*

19 Emphasis added.

20 Henchy J, [1987] IR 713, 786; [1987] ILRM 400, 444.

21 Ann Sherlock, "Constitutional Law – Sovereignty, the Constitution and the Single European Act" (1986) 9 *Dublin University Law Journal* 101, 108.

ever delivered by that Court".[22] Its legacy has variously been described as a ghost that continues to haunt us,[23] and a "legal and political noose on the nation as regards EU Treaty ratification",[24] while it has been said that it is "difficult to find any objective commentator who is convinced by the approach of the Supreme Court majority to sovereignty in the latter part of the *Crotty* ruling".[25] Former Chief Justice Ronan Keane has observed that, given that the case concerned

> the capacity of the executive arm to enter into an international treaty designed to promote cooperation in foreign policy, but which preserved Ireland's right as a sovereign State to refuse to accept the positions adopted by the other contracting States, it is difficult to understand how … the question as to whether it was appropriate for the State to enter into contractual commitments to endeavour to reach such common positions was other than a political, and hence non-justiciable, question.[26]

[2–22] In remarks delivered in 2013, Peter Sutherland (who was Ireland's European Commissioner at the time of the judgment) spoke of his disagreement with the conclusions of the majority with respect to Title III:

> I do not know of any analysis by a political scientist that would consider that its provisions abrogate national sovereignty. Indeed developments in this area ever since have proven the minority was correct in its conclusions. No country can be forced to take any position in foreign policy decisions of which is disapproves. Indeed EU countries took entirely divergent positions regarding the invasion of Iraq in 2003. Title III poses no threat whatsoever to our sovereignty but this judgment has still created an understandable uncertainty in the minds of Attorneys General and governments ever since that has influenced the subsequent referenda that have taken place.[27]

[2–23] Reflecting on the fact that every amending constitutive EU Treaty since *Crotty* has been the subject of a referendum in Ireland, Gavin Barrett similarly observes that on each occasion the government has "found itself under immense pressure to hold a referendum even when there is merely a reasonable probability of Treaties going beyond the essential scope/objectives of existing constitutive Treaties".[28] Given the inherent vagueness of the test of remaining within the "scope or objectives" of a constitutionally authorised treaty, he concedes that it is difficult to be too critical of a government for feeling that recourse to a referendum "is effectively *de rigeur* under Irish constitutional law as so as to avoid later difficulties associated with an unsuccessful parliamentary ratification".[29] While Sutherland feared that this may have led to a minimalist approach

---

[22] Gerard Hogan, "The Supreme Court and the Single European Act" (1987) 22 *Irish Jurist* 55, 55.

[23] Ronan Keane, "Reconciling Ireland's Sovereignty with Membership of the European Union – The Lessons of *Crotty* and *Pringle*" in Kieran Bradley, Noel Travers and Anthony Whelan (eds), *Of Courts and Constitutions: Liber Amicorum in Honour of Nial Fennelly* (Hart, 2014) 195, 211.

[24] Elaine Fahey, *EU Law in Ireland* (Clarus Press, 2010) 9.

[25] Gavin Barrett, *A Road Less Travelled: Reflections on the Supreme Court Rulings in Crotty, Coughlan and McKenna (No.2)* (Institute of International and European Affairs, 2011) 7.

[26] Ronan Keane, "Reconciling Ireland's Sovereignty with Membership of the European Union – The Lessons of *Crotty* and *Pringle*" in Kieran Bradley, Noel Travers and Anthony Whelan (eds), *Of Courts and Constitutions: Liber Amicorum in Honour of Nial Fennelly* (Hart, 2014) 195, 203.

[27] Peter Sutherland, "The Constitution, the Courts and the Legislature", Second Brian Lenihan Memorial Lecture, 16 February 2013, published by the Institute of International and European Affairs and in (2014) 103 *Studies: An Irish Quarterly Review* 20.

[28] Gavin Barrett, *A Road Less Travelled: Reflections on the Supreme Court Rulings in Crotty, Coughlan and McKenna (No.2)* (Institute of International and European Affairs, 2011) 7.

[29] *ibid*, 9.

by Irish negotiators whenever Treaty reform is being discussed, it is possible that a consistent practice of consulting the people on EU treaty change results in a deeper engagement on EU issues, even if only from time to time, as well as helping to ensure that the EU itself remains responsive to the wishes of its citizens.

[2–24] A referendum held on 25 May 1987 approved Ireland's ratification of the Single European Act by 70 per cent to 30 per cent (755,423 to 324,977), paving the way for its entry into force on 1 July 1987, six months later than scheduled. It would not be until 2012 that the Supreme Court would have cause to revisit the issues in *Crotty* in the case of *Pringle v The Government of Ireland*, when a constitutional challenge was brought to Ireland's impending ratification of the Treaty Establishing the European Stability Mechanism (ESM).[30]

[2–25] The objective of the ESM Treaty was to establish a mechanism among Euro Area states to facilitate the mobilising of funding in support of a member in financial difficulty whenever such support is indispensable to safeguard the financial stability of the Euro Area as a whole and of its members. The Treaty created the ESM as a financial institution, the Board of Governors of which is comprised of the Ministers of Finance of each participating state. The ESM has an authorised capital of €700 billion, divided amongst each of its members. Ireland's portion of the authorised capital is just over €11 billion, only a portion of which was required to be paid in at the outset. Subject to two exceptions, the Board of Governors operates by unanimity. First, a qualified majority of 85 per cent is to be used to decide on granting financial assistance where the Commission and the ECB both conclude that a failure to do so would threaten the economic and financial stability of the Euro Area. Secondly, a member that has failed to pay their contribution loses their entitlement to vote. In either of those circumstances, therefore, a decision could be made without Ireland's approval. The majority of the Supreme Court accepted, however, that under the terms of the ESM Treaty, Ireland's financial exposure could not be increased beyond the €11 billion figure without the prior approval of the Dáil.

[2–26] According to the plaintiff, participation in the ESM Treaty impinged upon Ireland's budgetary, economic and fiscal sovereignty. It was claimed that the Treaty entailed an open-ended and irreversible transfer of powers to an autonomous institution that exposed Ireland to a permanent commitment to provide funding and assume liability, without limit, for the debts of other members, on the basis of decisions that could be made in opposition to Ireland's views. This argument was rejected by a majority of the Supreme Court (Denham CJ, Murray, Clarke, O'Donnell, Fennelly and McKechnie JJ), with only Hardiman J dissenting.[31] In applying the constitutional principles set out in *Crotty* to the facts of this case, the majority concluded that Ireland's ratification of the ESM Treaty would not involve an impermissible transfer of sovereignty by abdicating, alienating or subordinating constitutional power conferred on the Government to another.[32] According to Clarke J:

> The limit on the discretion which the Government holds arises where the relevant treaty involves Ireland in committing itself to undefined policies not specified in the treaty and

[30] [2013] 3 IR 1. On the ESM Treaty see ch 27, paras [27–42] to [27–58].

[31] For a favourable analysis of Hardiman J's dissent see Maria Cahill, "*Crotty* after *Pringle*: The Revival of the Doctrine of Implied Amendment" (2014) 17 *Irish Journal of European Law* 1.

[32] [2013] 3 IR 1, 173.

> in circumstances where those policies, which Ireland will be required to support, are to be determined not by the Government but by institutions or bodies specified in the treaty. It is an abdication, alienation or subordination of policy formation and adoption which is not permitted. A transference of the means of implementing a policy agreed by the Government, and specified in the treaty concerned, to an appropriate implementation institution or body may be permitted provided that it does not go so far as to amount, in substance, to an abdication, alienation or subordination of the role of government under the Constitution.[33]

[2–27] In his judgment, O'Donnell J specifically addressed the plaintiff's assertion that the essence of the decision in *Crotty* was to be found in the statement by Walsh J to the effect that "the essential nature of sovereignty is the right to say yes or to say no".[34] Pointing to the dangers of "substituting the invocation of a vivid and memorable phrase for the analysis of the substance of a judgment", O'Donnell J concluded that there was "nothing in *Crotty* or indeed in logic" to suggest that the Constitution required that Ireland, when entering into international agreements, "insist that it retain the capacity to change its mind".[35] In his view, the decision to participate in the ESM Treaty was:

> an exercise in sovereignty rather than an alienation of it, and was taken by the organ of government to which such decisions are consigned by the Constitution. In one sense it is a one off decision by Ireland to invest up to a defined maximum pursuant to a scheme which prescribes the countries to whom funds can be lent, the procedure under which any decision to lend will be made, and the criteria for such a decision. It is no more a breach of Irish sovereignty asserted under the Constitution and defended in *Crotty v. An Taoiseach* [1987] IR 713, than a person who decides to invest a large portion of his or her wealth in a limited company with a defined investment objective could be said to lose his or her status as a citizen.
>
> There is no doubt that the figures involved here are very substantial and the decision to ratify the ESM is one which may have significant consequences for the Irish economy, but the quantum of a decision does not alter the identity of the actor required by the Constitution to make the decision.[36]

[2–28] There is consensus that the more recent judgment in *Pringle* has tempered the more expansive understandings of the earlier majority decision in *Crotty*. As Oran Doyle has observed, the majority in *Pringle* "took at least a minimalist interpretation of *Crotty*" and so "may signal a less exacting approach than that evident in *Crotty*".[37] On the other hand, the precise extent to which *Pringle* is viewed as having altered the continuing significance of *Crotty* varies. For former judge of the Supreme Court, Hugh Geoghegan, writing in an article entitled "*Crotty* put to sleep by *Pringle*", the "influence and effect of *Crotty* will now be considerably diminished".[38] In contrast, former Chief Justice Ronan Keane feared that the Supreme Court's decision "left unresolved the uncertainties as to the limitations on the conduct of foreign policy by Irish Governments which have persisted since *Crotty*".[39] The authors of *Kelly: The Irish*

---

33 *ibid*, 152.
34 [1987] IR 713, 781; [1987] ILRM 400, 457.
35 [2013] 3 IR 1, 112–113.
36 *ibid*, 112.
37 Oran Doyle, *The Constitution of Ireland* (Hart, 2018), 35.
38 Hugh Geoghegan, "*Crotty* Put to Sleep by *Pringle*" in Kieran Bradley, Noel Travers and Anthony Whelan (eds), *Of Courts and Constitutions: Liber Amicorum in Honour of Nial Fennelly* (Hart, 2014) 213.
39 Ronan Keane, "Reconciling Ireland's Sovereignty with Membership of the European Union – The

Constitution have described the judgment in *Pringle* as a "more nuanced view" that has "presaged a significant change in direction", at least in some respects.[40] Indeed, they suggest that it is "hard to disagree with the conclusion of many observers that the effect of *Pringle* has been to neutralise at least that part of *Crotty* which dealt with restrictions on the executive power of the State".[41] Nevertheless, they caution against reading too much into the judgment, noting that had it been delivered at the time, it would probably still have led to the holding of a referendum in respect of the Lisbon Treaty and the Treaty on Stability, Coordination and Governance in the Economic and Monetary Union (the "Fiscal Treaty").[42]

C. The Treaty on European Union

[2–29] Whereas the Single European Act was concerned with enhancing the drive towards the completion of an Internal Market, the Treaty on European Union (TEU) was a response to the political ambition to supplement the Internal Market with an Economic and Monetary Union (EMU). Within months of the Single European Act coming into force, work began on examining ways in which to advance EMU through three progressive stages, the last of which would require treaty change. At the same time, there were those that had been disappointed by the scale of ambition of the Single European Act and wanted to deepen European integration through the creation of a European *political union*. At the Dublin European Council in June 1990, the Irish Presidency "prepared a deliberately non-provocative paper that included almost all the suggestions so far made by others on treaty reform".[43] The discussion proved less contentious than had been expected and agreement was reached to convene an intergovernmental conference (IGC) having as its objective the "transformation of the Community from an entity mainly based on economic integration and political cooperation into a union of a political nature, including a common foreign and security policy".[44]

[2–30] In fact, two parallel IGCs were held dealing respectively with EMU and European political union, eventually leading to the signing in Maastricht on 7 February 1992 of the Treaty on European Union. It was intended that the Treaty would enter into force on 1 January 1993, coinciding with the deadline set for the completion of the Internal Market. A "no" vote in a Danish referendum prevented this, and the Treaty eventually entered into force on 1 November 1993.

[2–31] A referendum held in Ireland on 18 June 1992 resulted in a 69 per cent to 31 per cent vote in favour of ratification.[45] Abortion featured as a prominent issue in the

---

Lessons of *Crotty* and *Pringle*" in Kieran Bradley, Noel Travers and Anthony Whelan (eds), *Of Courts and Constitutions: Liber Amicorum in Honour of Nial Fennelly* (Hart, 2014) 195, 210.

40 Gerard Hogan, Gerry Whyte, David Kenny and Rachel Walsh, *Kelly: The Irish Constitution* (5th ed, Bloomsbury Professional, 2018) 597–598.

41 *ibid*, 599.

42 *ibid*, 600.

43 Desmond Dinan, *Ever Closer Union* (2nd ed, Palgrave, 1994) 134.

44 Paragraph 2 of Annex 1 to Presidency Conclusions, Dublin European Council, 25–26 June 1990 (SN 60/1/90).

45 See Anthony Collins, "The Eleventh Amendment – Problems and Perspectives" (1992) 10 *Irish Law Times* 209; Patrick Keatinge, *Maastricht and Ireland: What the Treaty Means* (Institute for International and European Affairs, 1992); Gerard Hogan and Anthony Whelan, *Ireland and the European Union* (Sweet and Maxwell, 1995) 89–120.

campaign due, in part, to a 1991 judgment of the Court of Justice in *Society for the Protection of the Unborn Child v Grogan*.[46] In reply to a preliminary reference from the Irish High Court, the Court held that medical termination of pregnancy, performed in accordance with the law of the state in which it is carried out, constitutes a service within the meaning of the EEC Treaty. Alert to the sensitivities surrounding the issue, Ireland succeeded in having a protocol annexed to both the EC Treaty and the TEU stating that nothing in either Treaty, or in the Treaties or Acts modifying or supplementing those Treaties, affected the application in Ireland of Art 40.3.3° of the Constitution on the right to life of the unborn (now Protocol No 35 annexed to the TEU and TFEU). Article 40.3.3° was amended by referendum in 2018 so that it now provides that provision may be made by law for the regulation of termination of pregnancy.

(i) The Pillar Structure

[2–32] The Treaty on European Union radically altered the overarching framework within which the EEC operated. Up until then, the three distinct communities established by the ECSC Treaty, the EEC Treaty and the Euratom Treaty shared institutions but were otherwise quite separate. Outside of these three communities, but in close association with them, intergovernmental cooperation took place with regard to European Political Cooperation, Economic and Monetary Union and certain aspects of international terrorism and serious crime. Whereas some Member States were keen to apply the supranational method of cooperation found in the EEC Treaty to these additional areas, others felt that their sensitive nature was more suited to intergovernmental cooperation.

[2–33] The political compromise that emerged was to create a new overarching structure – the European Union – within which EMU would be pursued in the EEC Treaty framework or "Community Pillar", and cooperation in the field of Common Foreign and Security Policy (CFSP) and Justice and Home Affairs (JHA) would be pursued through separate pillars that did not involve the same degree of supranationalism. Unlike the ECSC, EEC and Euratom, the European Union was not conferred with a legal personality of its own. Indeed, it was only in 2009, when the Lisbon Treaty replaced the pillar structure with a unified approach, that the EU became a legal entity in its own right. Under this arrangement, the CFSP and JHA pillars would remain predominantly intergovernmental in nature and the institutional arrangements that had become known as the "Community method" would not apply to them. The Community method was characterised by the Commission having the power to initiate proposals, the Council making decisions by majority voting, the Parliament having certain rights to be consulted and the Court of Justice having jurisdiction to interpret EU measures.

[2–34] The term "pillar structure" comes from the idea that the architecture established by the TEU represents a Greek temple. The roof of the temple is found in Title I of the TEU, setting out common provisions that established the European Union and its relationship to the three existing Communities. Famously, Art A of the TEU declared that the Treaty marked "a new stage in the process of creating an ever closer union among the peoples of Europe, in which decisions are taken as closely as possible to the citizen". It went on to describe the Union as being "founded on the European

---

[46] Case C-159/90 *Society for the Protection of the Unborn Child (Ireland) Ltd v Grogan* [1991] ECR I-4685. See ch 13, paras [13–51] to [13–55].

Communities, supplemented by the policies and forms of cooperation established by this Treaty". Article B then set out the objectives of the Union as being:

- to promote economic and social progress which is balanced and sustainable, in particular through the creation of an area without internal frontiers, through the strengthening of economic and social cohesion and through the establishment of economic and monetary union, ultimately including a single currency in accordance with the provisions of this Treaty;
- to assert its identity on the international scene, in particular through the implementation of a common foreign and security policy including the eventual framing of a common defence policy, which might in time lead to a common defence;
- to strengthen the protection of the rights and interests of the nationals of its Member States through the introduction of a citizenship of the Union;
- to develop close cooperation on justice and home affairs;
- to maintain in full the *acquis communautaire* and build on it with a view to considering … to what extent the policies and forms of cooperation introduced by this Treaty may need to be revised with the aim of ensuring the effectiveness of the mechanisms and the institutions of the Community.

[2–35] To achieve these objectives, the Council, Commission, Parliament and Court were to exercise the powers conferred on them by both the Treaties establishing the Communities and the TEU. So, for example, whereas until now foreign ministers meeting as part of European Political Cooperation did not meet as the Council of Ministers as such, under the TEU they were free to do so. The European Council was given a particular role in overseeing the development of the new European Union and its relationship with the European Communities, being assigned the task of providing the Union with general political guidelines and the necessary impetus for its development. In this overarching role, the European Council formed a key part of the temple's "roof".

[2–36] If the common provisions in Title I of the TEU formed the roof, the temple's foundation comprised the final provisions set out in Title VII which provided for a uniform procedure to amend the Community Treaties or the TEU. Finally, the substance of the Treaties formed the three pillars, representing the Community Treaties (the First Pillar), CFSP (Second Pillar) and JHA (Third Pillar).

[2–37] The CFSP Pillar brought European Political Cooperation in under the EU umbrella and established the objectives of the common policy as being to: (i) safeguard the common values, fundamental interests and independence of the Union; (ii) strengthen the security of the Union and its Member States in all ways; (iii) preserve peace and strengthen international security in accordance with the principles of the UN Charter; (iv) promote international cooperation, and (v) develop and consolidate democracy and the rule of law, and respect for human rights and fundamental freedoms.

[2–38] A delicate balance was reached regarding the security policy aspect of CFSP, which was said to include "all questions related to the security of the Union, including the *eventual* framing of a common defence policy, which *might* in time lead to a common defence".[47] On the one hand, the TEU requested the Western European Union – a separate organisation of which Ireland was not a member – to elaborate and implement decisions and actions of the EU which had defence implications. On the other hand, it was stated that the security policy of the EU "shall not prejudice the specific character

[47] Art J 4(1).

of the security and defence policy of certain Member States".[48] A declaration to the TEU was made by the Member States who were also members of the WEU, which was all bar Ireland, Denmark and Greece, agreeing "on the need to develop a genuine European security and defence identity and a greater European responsibility for defence matters" and setting out the means by which the WEU would contribute to this.[49]

[2–39] Just as the CFSP Pillar brought European Political Cooperation within the EU umbrella, the JHA Pillar did the same for the TREVI Mechanism, providing that for the purposes of pursuing the objectives of the Union, in particular the free movement of persons, nine areas were to be regarded as matters of common concern in relation to which the Member States agreed to inform and consult one another within the Council with a view to coordinating their action. These nine areas were:

(i) Asylum policy;
(ii) Rules governing the crossing by persons of external borders of the Member States and the exercise of controls thereon;
(iii) Immigration policy and policy regarding nationals of third countries including conditions of entry, movement, residence, family reunion, access to employment and combatting unauthorised immigration;
(iv) Combatting drug addiction;
(v) Combatting fraud on an international scale;
(vi) Judicial cooperation in civil matters;
(vii) Judicial cooperation in criminal matters;
(viii) Customs cooperation, and
(ix) Police cooperation for the purposes of preventing and combatting terrorism, drug trafficking and serious international crime, including if necessary certain aspects of customs cooperation, in connection with a Union-wide system for exchanging information within a European Police Office (Europol).

[2–40] Although the Lisbon Treaty eventually did away with the pillar structure, it was a defining feature of the EU from 1 November 1993 to 1 December 2009. An awareness of the structure is necessary, therefore, in order to understand how the EU developed during this period. For example, different legal acts were to be used when operating in the CFSP and JHA Pillars than the trio of regulations, directives and decisions used in the First Pillar, such as common positions, joint actions and conventions. Secondly, issues arose as to the inclusion of CFSP and JHA content in international agreements entered into by the European Community such as would require the direct participation of the Member States themselves, known as "cross-pillar mixity". Finally, given that it meant the difference between applying the Community Method or an alternative method likely to entail a more limited role for the Court, Parliament or Commission, or to require unanimity rather than a qualified majority vote, disputes often arose as to whether the correct Treaty article had been cited as the legal base for a particular measure, or whether a legal base from a different pillar ought to have been used instead. An understanding of the pillar structure is also necessary to appreciate important aspects of contemporary EU law. The structure of the very Treaties themselves – the TFEU and the TEU – derives from the EEC Treaty and the TEU. The area of CFSP, in particular, continues to retain many vestiges of the intergovernmental nature with which it was

[48] Art J 4(4).
[49] Declaration on Western European Union, Declaration No 30 to the Final Act of the Treaty on European Union.

endowed back in 1993, with no power to adopt legislative acts and the jurisdiction of the Court of Justice still generally precluded.

Single European Act architecture

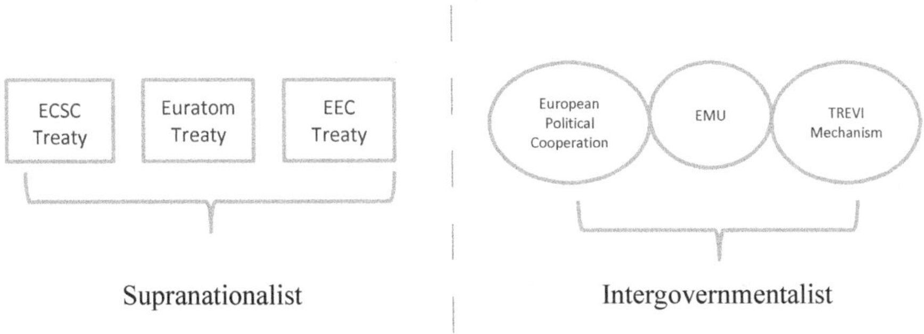

Treaty on European Union architecture

EUROPEAN UNION
(Title I TEU – Common Provisions)

Pillar One European Communities	Pillar Two	Pillar Three
EC Treaty (Title II TEU) ECSC (Title III TEU) Euratom Treaty (Title IV TEU)	Common Foreign and Security Policy (Title V TEU)	Justice and Home Affairs (Title VI TEU)

Supranationalist/Community Method — Predominantly Intergovernmentalist

Title VII – Final Provisions

(ii) Amendments to the EEC Treaty

[2–41] Although the most striking change brought about by the Maastricht Treaty was the creation of the European Union and its pillar structure, the majority of its provisions, comprising 80 of its 140 pages, is made up of Title II amending the EEC Treaty, beginning with a change to its name. Reflecting its widening focus and increased areas of competence, the EEC was now simply to be known as the European Community, with that term replacing the "European Economic Community" throughout the Treaty.

Economic and Monetary Union

[2–42] The most significant new Community competence was in relation to economic and monetary union, which included, effectively, an agreement within an agreement in the form of detailed protocols containing the statutes of the European Monetary Institute, the European System of Central Banks and the European Central Bank as well as a protocol on the Excessive Deficit Procedure.[50] The Member States agreed to regard their economic policies as a matter of common concern and to conduct them with a view to contributing to achieving the objectives of the Community. To this end, they agreed to coordinate their economic policies in light of guidelines to be adopted by the European Council aimed at ensuring closer coordination of economic policies and sustained convergence of the economic performance of the Member States. This would also entail a surveillance and assessment of the extent to which Member States' economic policies remained consistent with the guidelines, with the possibility for recommendations to be adopted in the event that they risked jeopardising the proper functions of the economic and monetary union. The Member States also committed to avoiding excessive government deficits, with the Commission tasked with monitoring each Member State's government deficit to gross domestic product ratio. If a Member State failed to follow Council recommendations to remedy an excessive deficit the Council could adopt a number of measures, including imposing a fine.

[2–43] The second stage of monetary union began two months after the entry into force of the TEU, on 1 January 1994. During this stage, Member States agreed to regard their exchange rate policy as a matter of common interest. Monetary union was to be advanced through the establishment of a European Central Bank (ECB), which would eventually have the sole power to issue bank notes, and a European System of Central Banks comprising the ECB and national central banks. A protocol set out the convergence criteria to be used in order to determine whether Member States were ready to be locked in to a single currency unit, which would launch the start of stage three, which in turn would lead to the adoption of the euro as a single currency.

Citizenship

[2–44] The TEU established Union citizenship for the first time, inserting into the EC Treaty a provision to the effect that every person holding the nationality of a Member State shall be a citizen of the Union as well as providing for certain rights of citizenship such as the right to move and reside freely within the territory of the Member States, the right to vote in municipal (ie local) elections and elections to the European Parliament in the Member State in which he or she resides, and the right to petition the European Parliament and apply to the Ombudsman.[51] The nature of Union citizenship has undergone significant evolution and is considered further in Chapter 25.

Social Policy

[2–45] In 1989, 11 of the Member States had participated in the making of a solemn declaration entitled the Community Charter of the Fundamental Social Rights of Workers, also known as the Social Charter. The UK declined to participate. The purpose of the Charter was to consolidate the progress made in the social field and to "declare solemnly that the implementation of the Single European Act must take full account of the social dimension of the Community and that it is necessary in this context to

---

[50] Each of these are discussed further in ch 27, paras [27–12] to [27–32].

[51] See Síofra O'Leary, *The Evolving Concept of Community Citizenship: From the Free Movement of Persons to Union Citizenship* (Kluwer, 1996); Jo Shaw, "The Interpretation of European Union Citizenship" (1998) 61 *Modern Law Review* 293.

ensure at appropriate levels the development of the social rights of workers of the European Community".

[2–46] Because the UK remained unwilling to participate, a protocol to the TEU authorised the 11 Member States to have recourse to the institutions, procedures and mechanisms of the EC Treaty for the purpose of taking among themselves acts required for giving effect to an Agreement on Social Policy among the 11 Member States, which was also annexed to the TEU. The Agreement provided that the Community and the 11 Member States should have as their objective the promotion of employment, improving living and working conditions, proper social protection, dialogue between management and labour, the development of human resources with a view to lasting high employment and the combating of exclusion.

Other Additional Competences

[2–47] In addition to EMU, citizenship and social policy, the TEU also conferred additional competences on the EC in the areas of public health, consumer protection, education, culture, trans-European networks in transport, energy and telecommunications, industrial policy and development cooperation.

Conferral and Subsidiarity

[2–48] The TEU expressly introduced the important concepts of conferral and subsidiarity into the EC Treaty by inserting a provision to the effect that the Community shall act within the limits of the powers conferred upon it, and objectives assigned to it, by the Treaty. Secondly, in areas which did not fall within its exclusive competence, any action by the Community was to be taken in accordance with the principle of subsidiarity. According to this principle, Community action was only to be taken if, and in so far as, the objectives of the proposed action could not be sufficiently achieved by the Member States and could therefore, by reason of the scale or effects of the proposed action, be better achieved by the Community. Thirdly, it was reaffirmed that any action by the Community should not go beyond what was necessary to achieve the objectives set out in the EC Treaty. The twin principles of conferral and subsidiarity are examined in Chapter 9.

Institutional Reforms

[2–49] Conscious of criticisms that the Community suffered from a "democratic deficit", the TEU built upon the SEA's enhancement of the powers of the Parliament by introducing a new legislative procedure known as the Co-Decision Procedure (now referred to as the Ordinary Legislative Procedure). Where applicable, this procedure gave the Parliament a role in the legislative process that was effectively co-equal to that of the Council, allowing for a conciliation procedure in order to reconcile any conflicting views. Ultimately, however, the Parliament was now empowered to block legislation not to its liking. The Parliament was also granted the power to request the Commission to bring forward a legislative proposal, as well as the power to block the appointment of a new Commission. In addition, a declaration to the Treaty encouraged greater involvement of national parliaments in the activities of the EU, including through greater contacts between national parliaments and the European Parliament.

To this end, the Member States agreed to ensure that their national parliaments received Commission legislative proposals in good time for information or possible examination.

[2–50] In addition to providing for the establishment of a European System of Central Banks and a European Central Bank, the TEU also created the Committee of the Regions and the Parliamentary Ombudsman. Finally, the TEU extended the number of areas in which QMV was to be used by the Council.

Variable Geometry

[2–51] A final feature of the TEU worth highlighting is the manner in which it introduced a degree of flexibility or "variable geometry" to the EU Treaties. A clear example of this can be seen in the Agreement on Social Policy annexed to the TEU that was concluded between all of the Member States except the UK. In a related Protocol, the 12 Member States authorised the 11 to have recourse to the institutions and mechanisms of the EC Treaty in order to give effect to the Agreement amongst themselves, spelling out that the UK would not take part in the adoption by the Council of Commission proposals made on the basis of the Agreement. Another example was the Declaration on Western European Union, made by all Member States except Ireland, Denmark and Greece. With an eye towards the 1985 Schengen Agreement on the Gradual Abolition of Checks at Common Borders, entered into by some but not all Member States, the JHA Pillar was said not to prevent the establishment or development of closer cooperation between two or more Member States so long as it did not conflict with, or impede, what was provided for in the JHA Pillar. The most significant piece of variable geometry, however, was an opt-out obtained by the UK and Denmark allowing them not to participate in the third stage of EMU and the adoption of a single currency. In the case of Denmark, this followed a referendum in which ratification of the TEU was rejected and paved the way for a second referendum that resulted in a vote in favour of ratification – a precedent that would be taken up again following Ireland's original vote against ratification of the Lisbon Treaty.[52]

[2–52] Debates as to the merits of a "two-speed Europe" continue today. For many, the possibility of enhanced cooperation amongst willing Member States is an essential means of ensuring that the pace towards deeper integration is not set by the most reluctant member. The counter-argument, however, is that enhanced cooperation risks creating a fragmented and two-tier Europe. One of the best-known commentaries on the Maastricht Treaty sums up this view by describing the constitutional structure established by the Treaty as a Europe "of bits and pieces". For Deirdre Curtin, if a *process* of integration was to have any meaning at all, it must imply "that you can't take one step forward and two steps backwards at the same time. Built into the principle of an 'ever closer union among the peoples of Europe' is the notion that integration should be one way."[53]

---

52 See Deirdre Curtin and Ronald van Ooik, "Denmark and the Edinburgh Summit: Maastricht without Tears" in David O'Keeffe and Patrick Twomey (eds), *Legal Issues of the Maastricht Treaty* (Chancery Law Publishing, 1994) 349. The Protocol obtained by Ireland following the first referendum on the Lisbon Treaty is discussed further in ch 3, paras [3–10] to [3–17].

53 Deirdre Curtin, "The Constitutional Structure of the Union: A Europe of Bits and Pieces" (1993) 30 *Common Market Law Review* 17, 67. For a contrasting view, see Jean-Claude Piris, *The Future of Europe: Towards a Two-Speed Europe?* (Cambridge University Press, 2012). See ch 3, para [3–26].

D. The Treaty of Amsterdam

[2–53] The TEU provided that an intergovernmental conference (IGC) was to take place in 1996 in order to consider any institutional reforms that were required to accommodate the accession of new Member States, as well to review the operation of the three pillar structure. The IGC led to the signing of the Treaty of Amsterdam on 2 October 1997.[54] A referendum held on 22 May 1998 (the same day as the referendum on the Good Friday Agreement) resulted in a 62 per cent to 38 per cent vote in favour of Ireland's ratification of the Treaty, and the Treaty entered into force on 1 May 1999.

[2–54] As the IGC failed to reach agreement on institutional reforms, these were taken up in the Treaty of Nice a few years later. The key elements of the Amsterdam Treaty, therefore, concerned changes to the JHA Pillar, elements of which were transferred to the Community Pillar and the remainder renamed "Police and Judicial Cooperation in Criminal Matters". Significantly, for Ireland in particular, the Schengen Agreement of 1985 and the related *acquis*, or body of decisions that had built up around it, were brought not only within the EU framework, but into the Community Pillar as part of a new title within the EC Treaty. This supra-nationalisation of the Schengen *acquis* came at the price of differential integration, as the UK opted-out of the new title and would remain outside of the Schengen Area.[55] Because of the Common Travel Area between Ireland and the UK, Ireland also opted out of the new title and did not join the Schengen Area. Denmark obtained a separate opt-out of its own whereby it would continue to be bound by the Schengen Agreement as a matter of international law, but not by virtue of its membership of the EU. The Amsterdam Treaty also addressed debates concerning the democratic legitimacy of the EU by introducing new provisions on human rights, non-discrimination and transparency as well as enhancing the role of the European Parliament and national parliaments.

(i) Splitting the Third Pillar

[2–55] Over time, the view increasingly developed that as a corollary to the free movement of persons, the EU ought also to address the related justice and security issues that inevitably arose as a result. For example, the greater the extent to which EU citizens moved to another Member State, the more likely it was that Member States would wish to exchange information on criminal records or that a person under investigation for a crime in one Member State might end up living in another. Similarly, having exercised the right of free movement, an individual may need to rely on a civil court judgment in a Member State other than that in which the judgment was granted. This wish to further develop cooperation in the field described as an "Area of Freedom, Security and Justice" was strengthened by the decision to incorporate within the Community Pillar, via a protocol to the Amsterdam Treaty, the Schengen Agreement of 1985 and its Implementing Convention of 1990. In addition, it is often said that, having become familiar with the manner in which intergovernmental cooperation had been carried out since the TEU first introduced the JHA Pillar, Member States were willing to forego

[54] As Ireland held the Presidency of the Council from July to December 1996, preceding the Dutch Presidency, it had an active role in the IGC and was responsible for producing an outline of the draft treaty. For a detailed insight by one of the Irish negotiators, see Bobby McDonagh, *Original Sin in a Brave New World, An Account of the Negotiation of the Treaty of Amsterdam* (Institute of European Affairs, 1998).

[55] Robert Schütze, *European Union Law* (Cambridge University Press, 2015) 29.

some of their concerns as to applying supranational cooperation to this sensitive area. A further argument in favour of doing so was that, as this field touched upon the civil liberties of individuals, it was particularly appropriate that it should be carried out according to the Community method, which afforded a greater role to the Parliament and the Court of Justice.

[2–56] As Member States were not yet ready to go so far as to incorporate all of the JHA Pillar within the Community Pillar, a compromise was reached whereby visas, asylum, immigration and judicial cooperation in civil matters were transferred to the Community Pillar as a new Title IIIa of Part Three of the EC Treaty. Reflecting its narrower remit, the remaining Third Pillar was renamed "Police and Judicial Cooperation in Criminal Matters". The EU objective of maintaining an Area of Freedom, Security and Justice was to be achieved through a combination of Community method acts adopted under Title IIIa of the EC Treaty and the particular acts, such as framework decisions and joint actions, available under the Third Pillar with respect to police and judicial cooperation in criminal matters.

[2–57] As neither the UK nor Ireland were a party to the Schengen Convention, the Protocol integrating the Schengen *acquis* into the framework of the European Union did not apply to them. The Protocol did, however, permit either state to request at any time to participate in some or all of the Schengen *acquis*, which would be subject to a unanimous decision of the other Member States (now provided for in Protocol No 19 to the TEU and TFEU).

[2–58] Given that the UK and Ireland were remaining outside of the Schengen Area, a separate protocol expressly allowed for them to continue to exercise border controls for the purpose of verifying the right of EEA nationals, or their dependants, to enter their territory or for determining whether or not to grant other persons permission to enter their territory.[56] Having regard to the "existence for many years of special travel arrangements between the United Kingdom and Ireland", this protocol also confirmed that the UK and Ireland "may continue to make arrangements between themselves relating to the movement of persons between their territories ('the Common Travel Area')", while fully respecting the rights of EEA nationals and their dependants (now Protocol No 20 to the TEU and TFEU) – a provision that has taken on a particular significance in the context of the UK's withdrawal from the EU.[57] As one of Irish negotiators of the Amsterdam Treaty has explained:

---

[56] Protocol on the application of certain aspects of Article 7a of the Treaty establishing the European Community to the United Kingdom and to Ireland.

[57] See Graham Butler and Gavin Barrett, "Europe's 'Other' Open Border Zone: the Common Travel Area under the Shadow of Brexit" (2018) 20 *Cambridge Yearbook of European Legal Studies* 252; Imelda Maher, "Crossing the Irish Land Borders after Brexit: The Common Travel Area and the Challenge of Trade" (2016–2017) 11–12 *Irish Yearbook of International Law* 51; Elizabeth Meehan, "The Origins of the Common Travel Area between Ireland and the United Kingdom and its Fate in the Era of Governmental Concern about Undocumented Migration and International Terrorism", ESRI Working Paper No 48, 2011; Elaine Fahey, "Swimming in a Sea of Law: Reflections on Water Borders, Irish (-British)-Euro Relations and Opting-In and Opting-Out after the Treaty of Lisbon" (2010) 47 *Common Market Law Review* 673; Bernard Ryan, "The Common Travel Area between Britain and Ireland" (2001) 64 *Modern Law Review* 855; Elizabeth Meehan, *Free Movement Between Ireland and the UK: From the 'common travel area' to the Common Travel Area* (Policy Institute, 2000); Gerard Hogan, "The Common Travel Area and Community Law"

> Ireland was in a distinctive position. In line with our strong commitment to the process of European integration, we did not object to the transfer to the first pillar of free movement, asylum and immigration as such. Nor indeed did our non-participation in Schengen essentially reflect problems of principle in that regard. However, we had to have regard to our Common Travel Area with the United Kingdom which we greatly value and to which we must give priority.
>
> That long-standing Common Travel Area constitutes an area of free movement – without the requirement of travel documents – between Ireland and the United Kingdom. It is indeed an area of free movement older and more complete than that between the Schengen countries. Much the greater part of travel out of Ireland (leaving Northern Ireland out of the equation) is to or through Britain. If Ireland were to participate in Schengen, and this were to lead to the establishment of controls (and travel documents) within the Common Travel Area, this would ironically reduce rather than increase free movement to and from Ireland. Thus – as far as we would be concerned – the very purpose of Schengen would be negated. Moreover, the level of mutual cooperation and trust regarding entry to the CTA, facilitated by the absence of land borders to be controlled, makes it possible for Ireland and the UK to forgo the more intrusive internal personal identity cards and controls which are standard in continental Member States.[58]

[2–59] Finally, the only basis on which the UK would agree to certain elements of the JHA Pillar being transferred to the Community Pillar was if it was given a right to choose to opt-in to such measures, rather than being bound by them automatically. As a result, a second protocol provided that the UK and Ireland would not be bound by the new Title IIIa of the EC Treaty dealing with visas, asylum, immigration and judicial cooperation in civil matters, but could choose to opt-in to measures adopted under that Title on case-by-case basis (now Protocol No 21 to the TEU and TFEU). Ireland made a declaration on this protocol expressing its intention to exercise its right to opt-in to the adoption of such measures "to the maximum extent compatible with the maintenance of its Common Travel Area with the United Kingdom".[59] The declaration also recalled that Ireland's participation in the protocol on the maintenance of external borders "reflects its wish to maintain its Common Travel Area with the United Kingdom in order to maximise freedom of movement into and out of Ireland".[60]

[2–60] Given that the Amsterdam Treaty created certain opt-ins for Ireland, the amendment to Art 29.5 of the Constitution not only authorised the State to ratify the Treaty but also permitted the State to exercise the options and discretions provided for in relation to the Area of Freedom, Security and Justice (under both Title IV of the EC Treaty and the Third Pillar) and enhanced cooperation, subject to the prior approval of both Houses of the Oireachtas.

---

in Niamh Hyland (ed), *The Free Movement of Workers within the European Union* (Irish Centre for European Law, 1999) 9.

58 Bobby McDonagh, *Original Sin in a Brave New World, An Account of the Negotiation of the Treaty of Amsterdam* (Institute of European Affairs, 1998) 169–170. See Anthony M Collins, "Freedom through Security? The Third Pillar" (1998) 7 *Irish Journal of European Law* 36.

59 Declaration by Ireland on Article 3 of the Protocol on the position of the United Kingdom and Ireland, Declaration No 3 of the Declarations of which the Conference Took Note. See now Declaration No 56 to the TEU and TFEU.

60 *ibid.*

(ii) Addressing Legitimacy Concerns

[2–61] A number of the reforms introduced by the Treaty of Amsterdam can be categorised as addressing ongoing concerns as to the legitimacy of the EU from the point of view of democratic principles and the rule of law:

- within the preamble to the TEU a new commitment was inserted to take decisions "as openly as possible and as closely as possible to the citizen";
- a protocol set out how, in exercising the powers conferred on it, each institution would ensure that the principles of subsidiarity and proportionality were complied with;
- a protocol on the role of national parliaments provided that, in addition to legislative proposals, all Commission communications and green and white papers would be promptly sent to national parliaments. So as to allow national parliaments time to consider Commission proposals, a six-week period was to be maintained between a Commission legislative proposal being made available in all languages to the Council and European Parliament and the date when it was placed on a Council agenda for decision;
- a new statement was added to the TEU declaring that the Union is founded on the principles of liberty, democracy, respect for human rights and fundamental freedoms, and the rule of law, and making respect for these principles a condition for EU membership. Provision was made to allow for the suspension of certain of a Member State's rights under the Treaties, including voting rights, in the event of a serious and persistent breach of these principles.

[2–62] The concerns of the citizen were also at the forefront of the additional competences conferred on the EC, most notably in the areas of addressing unemployment and various forms of discrimination, as well as expanding on existing competences in relation to consumer protection and public health. As a result of the UK's acceptance, the Agreement on Social Policy was now finally incorporated within the Community Pillar.

[2–63] Institutional changes continued the trend introduced by the SEA and TEU, furthering the use of QMV within the Council and expanding the use of the Co-Decision Procedure to the extent that the Co-Operation Procedure was now mostly confined to use in connection with EMU. Adding to the Parliament's power of assent over the appointment of a new Commission, it was now given the power to assent to the appointment of the Commission President. Whereas, through various opt-outs, the TEU had introduced a degree of flexibility to the Treaties, the Amsterdam Treaty built upon this by inserting a new general provision on enhanced cooperation, allowing for an authorisation to be granted for the use of the institutions, mechanisms and procedures of the EC Treaty by those Member States wishing to establish closer cooperation between themselves.

E. The Treaty of Nice

[2–64] The failure of the Treaty of Amsterdam to fully address the institutional reforms needed to allow for the EU's enlargement rendered a further IGC inevitable. Before this was to take place, however, a novel development occurred in the form of a "Convention", rather than an IGC, made up of 15 representatives of national governments, 30 representatives of national parliaments, 16 representatives of the European Parliament and a single representative of the Commission. Tasked with drafting a Charter of Fundamental Rights, the Convention met in open session and operated by consensus. In October 2000 it adopted the Charter of Fundamental Rights of the European Union, which was solemnly proclaimed by the European Council held in Nice in December 2000. The Charter was eventually given binding force by the Lisbon Treaty and now has the same legal value as the TEU and TFEU themselves.[61]

[2–65] Somewhat harshly, the Treaty of Nice is often characterised as dealing with the leftovers of the Amsterdam Treaty and is remembered for a difficult IGC during which an exasperated Prime Minister Tony Blair is said to have exclaimed that "we cannot go on working like this".[62] Rather than carry out a comprehensive review of the Union's institutional structure, the Nice Treaty reduced the number of Commissioners to one per Member State, adjusted the weighting of Member States for the purposes of QMV and redistributed an increased number of members of the European Parliament. Like the Amsterdam Treaty, it further extended the use of QMV and the Co-Decision Procedure and relaxed the criteria under which some Member States could participate in enhanced cooperation. Changes to the statute of the Court of Justice widened the jurisdiction of the Court of First Instance and allowed for the greater use of chambers. As a further streamlining measure, it was agreed that once EU membership reached 18 Member States, European Council meetings were to be held in Brussels rather than in the Member State holding the rotating Presidency.

[2–66] In the area of CFSP, the Nice Treaty amended Art 17 of the TEU by removing the provisions defining the relations between the Union and the WEU, such that it now reads as follows:

> 1. The common foreign and security policy shall include all questions relating to the security of the Union, including the progressive framing of a common defence policy, which might lead to a common defence, should the European Council so decide. It shall in that case recommend to the Member States the adoption of such a decision in accordance with their respective constitutional requirements. The policy of the Union in accordance with this Article shall not prejudice the specific character of the security and defence policy of certain Member States and shall respect the obligations of certain Member States, which see their common defence realised in the North Atlantic Treaty Organisation (NATO), under the North Atlantic Treaty and be compatible with the common security and defence policy established within that framework. The progressive framing of a common defence policy will be supported, as Member States consider appropriate, by cooperation between them in the field of armaments.
>
> 2. Questions referred to in this Article shall include humanitarian and rescue tasks, peacekeeping tasks and tasks of combat forces in crisis management, including peacemaking.
>
> 3. Decisions having defence implications dealt with under this Article shall be taken without prejudice to the policies and obligations referred to in paragraph 1, second subparagraph.
>
> 4. The provisions of this Article shall not prevent the development of closer cooperation between two or more Member States on a bilateral level, in the framework of the Western European Union (WEU) and NATO, provided such cooperation does not run counter to or impede that provided for in this Title.

[61] The Charter is discussed further in ch 3, paras [3–48] to [3–64] and ch 11, paras [11–39] to [11–49].

[62] Philippe de Schoutheete, "The European Council" in John Peterson and Michael Shackleton (eds), *The Institutions of the European Union* (3rd ed, Oxford University Press, 2012) 43, 64.

[2–67] The Nice Treaty also renamed the Political Committee the Political and Security Committee which, in order to manage a crisis, could be authorised by the Council to take appropriate decisions under the CFSP Pillar in order to ensure the political control and strategic leadership of a crisis management operation. In addition, the Nice European Council approved a report by the Presidency on European Security and Defence Policy that provided for the development of the Union's military capacity, the creation of permanent political and military structures and the incorporation into the Union of the crisis management functions of the WEU. In its Conclusions, the European Council called for the work set out in the report to be taken forward with the objective of quickly making the Union operational in this area, with a decision to be taken as soon as possible and no later than the European Council to be held in Laeken, Belgium in December 2001.

[2–68] In a referendum in June 2001, a vote of 54 per cent to 46 per cent disapproved of Ireland's ratification of the Treaty of Nice. The result came as a surprise and, despite being held on the same day as votes on the abolition of the death penalty and ratification of the Statute of the International Criminal Court, was based on a low turn-out of just 35 per cent. The high level of abstention was attributed to a lack of knowledge, with polling finding that more than two-thirds of people had an inadequate understanding of the Treaty. In response, the Government established the National Forum on Europe with a mandate to "provide the basis for an inclusive and broadly-based debate on Ireland's participation in the European Union, and on the overall functioning and future development of the Union".[63] The Forum continued to operate until 2009, when the Government decided to bring it to an end.

[2–69] As the following contemporary assessment suggests, a variety of factors contributed to the outcome, although prominent among them were concerns as to the development of the Union's defence policy and the possibility that this might undermine Ireland's traditional policy of military neutrality:

> The defeat of the referendum ought not to be regarded as a vote against enlargement (since even the 'No' campaigners expressed their support for the enlargement process), but rather the expression of concern about the political direction which the European Union is taking. For example, the traditional Catholic right were anxious not only about the perennial issue of abortion, but also the drift towards a secular super-state in which the role of religion is marginalised while, on the other hand, peace groups were anxious about the steady erosion of Irish neutrality and Irish participation in the rapid reaction force. Other factors were also at play: the formal reprimand of Irish economic policy by the Council of Ministers earlier this year alienated some voters as did the persistent demands for tax harmonization by M. Jospin, the French Prime Minister.[64]

---

63 See Tony Brown, "Ireland's National Forum on Europe: Helping to Make Up for the Democratic Deficit?" in Gavin Barrett (ed), *National Parliaments and the European Union* (Clarus Press, 2008) 323; Maurice Hayes, "The National Forum on Europe: A Model of Democratic Engagement" (2005) 12 *Irish Journal of European Law* 272.

64 Gerard Hogan, "The Nice Treaty and the Irish Constitution" (2001) 7 *European Public Law* 565, 571–572. See also Cathryn Costello, "Peoples' Vengeances: Ireland's Nice Referenda" (2005) 1 *European Constitutional Law* Review 357; James O'Reilly and Anthony Collins, "Reflections on the Nice Referendum" (2001) 10 *Irish Journal of European Law* 1; Ben Tonra, "Ireland: A Tale of Two Referenda" in Finn Laursen (ed), *The Treaty of Nice* (Martinus Nijhoff, 2006) 179.

[2–70] In order to address concerns regarding neutrality, at the Seville European Council in June 2002 Ireland made the following Declaration on the Treaty of Nice:

> 1. Ireland reaffirms its attachment to the aims and principles of the Charter of the United Nations, which confers primary responsibility for the maintenance of international peace and security upon the United Nations Security Council.
>
> 2. Ireland recalls its commitment to the common foreign and security policy of the European Union as set out in the Treaty on European Union, adopted at Maastricht, amended at Amsterdam and approved on each occasion by the Irish people through referendum.
>
> 3. Ireland confirms that its participation in the European Union's common foreign and security policy does not prejudice its traditional policy of military neutrality. The Treaty on European Union makes clear that the Union's security and defence policy shall not prejudice the specific character of the security and defence policy of certain Member States.
>
> 4. In line with its traditional policy of military neutrality, Ireland is not bound by any mutual defence commitment. Nor is Ireland party to any plans to develop a European army. Indeed, the Nice European Council recognised that the development of the Union's capacity to conduct humanitarian and crisis management tasks does not involve the establishment of a European army.
>
> 5. The Treaty on European Union specifies that any decision by the Union to move to a common defence would have to be taken by unanimous decision of the Member States and adopted in accordance with their respective constitutional requirements. The Government of Ireland have made a firm commitment to the people of Ireland, solemnised in this Declaration, that a referendum will be held in Ireland on the adoption of any such decision and on any future Treaty which would involve Ireland departing from its traditional policy of military neutrality.
>
> 6. Ireland reiterates that the participation of contingents of the Irish Defence Forces in overseas operations, including those carried out under the European security and defence policy, requires (a) the authorisation of the operation by the Security Council or the General Assembly of the United Nations, (b) the agreement of the Irish Government and (c) the approval of Dáil Éireann, in accordance with Irish law.

[2–71] In response, the European Council issued a Declaration of its own in which it took cognisance of the National Declaration and Ireland's intention to associate it with its act of ratification should the second referendum result in a "yes" vote. The Declaration also noted that the TEU provided for the following three elements, none of which would be changed by the entry into force of the Nice Treaty: (i) any decision to move to a common defence was to be adopted in accordance with the respective constitutional requirements of the Member States; (ii) the policy of the Union was not to prejudice the specific character of the security and defence policy of certain Member States, in which regard Ireland had drawn attention to its traditional policy of military neutrality, and (iii) no binding mutual defence commitments were imposed, nor did the development of the Union's capacity to conduct humanitarian and crisis management tasks involve the establishment of a European army. Finally, the Declaration recognised that, like all Member States, after the entry into force of the Nice Treaty, Ireland would retain the right to take its own sovereign decision, in accordance with its Constitution and its laws, whether to commit military personnel to participate in any operation carried out under the European Security and Defence Policy.

[2–72] Believing that, for some, the "firm commitment" in paragraph 5 of the

National Declaration to hold a referendum was insufficient, the Government in fact went beyond this commitment by including within the second proposed constitutional amendment on the Nice Treaty an additional clause to the effect that "the State shall not adopt a decision taken by the European Council to establish a common defence ... where that common defence would include the State".[65] A referendum in October 2002 approved ratification by 63 per cent to 37 per cent and this preclusion of participation in a European common defence now forms Art 29.4.9° of the Constitution. The Treaty of Nice entered into force on 1 February 2003.

New Competences

Single European Act	Treaty on European Union	Amsterdam Treaty	Nice Treaty
– Research & Technological Development – Environmental Policy – Economic and Social Cohesion – Social Policy	– EMU – Citizenship – CFSP – Public Health – Consumer Protection – Development Cooperation – Culture – Trans-European Networks – Agreement on Social Policy *JHA Cooperation re:* – Asylum – Immigration – Rules regarding the crossing of external borders – Drugs – International fraud – Judicial cooperation in civil matters – Judicial cooperation in criminal matters – Cooperation between customs services – Police cooperation	– Employment – Council given power to conclude international agreements in CFSP field – Combatting racism, xenophobia and other forms of discrimination – Agreement on Social Policy replaced by bringing it within the EC Treaty – Incorporated Schengen Acquis *Moved from JHA Pillar to Community Pillar:* – Visas – Asylum – Immigration – Rules relating to free movement of persons – Judicial cooperation in civil matters	– Amended aspects of CFSP Pillar – Nice European Council adopted report on European Security and Defence Policy

[65] Art 42(2) TEU states: "The common security and defence policy shall include the progressive framing of a common Union defence policy. This will lead to a common defence, when the European Council, acting unanimously, so decides. It shall in that case recommend to the Member States the adoption of such a decision in accordance with their respective constitutional requirements."

Institutional Reforms

Single European Act	Treaty on European Union	Amsterdam Treaty	Nice Treaty
– Co-Operation Procedure – Parliament's Assent required for new accessions to the EEC and for association agreements – Court of First Instance – Recognition of European Council	– Establishment of ESCB and ECB – Co-Decision Procedure – Parliament permitted to request Commission to propose legislation – Parliament empowered to block appointment of new Commission – Extension of use of QMV – Parliamentary Ombudsman – Committee of the Regions – Principles of Subsidiarity and Conferral – Declaration on National Parliaments	– Extension of use of QMV – Extension of use of Co-Decision Procedure – High Representative for CFSP – Parliament's assent required for appointment of Commission President – Power to suspend a Member State's voting rights for persistent breach of fundamental principles – Court of Justice permitted to sit in chambers – Protocol on role of National Parliaments – General provision allowing for enhanced cooperation	– Extension of use of QMV – Extension of use of Co-Decision Procedure – Re-weighting of QMV voting – Increase in the number of MEPs and changes to their distribution – Broadening of jurisdiction of Court of First Instance – Relaxing of conditions for the use of enhanced cooperation and allowing for some forms of CFSP enhanced cooperation – Once there were 18 Member States, all European Councils to be held in Brussels

Timeline – From Single European Act to Nice Treaty

11 July 1974	*Dassonville* judgment gives a broad definition to a measure equivalent to a quantitative restriction
September 1974	Decision taken to formalise meetings of the European Council
10–11 March 1975	First formal meeting of the European Council takes place in Dublin
22 July 1975	Signing of the Second Budgetary Treaty
1 December 1975	Establishment of the TREVI Mechanism (Terrorism, Radicalism, Extremism and International Violence)
1 June 1977	Entry into force of the Second Budgetary Treaty
December 1978	Establishment of the European Monetary System and Exchange Rate Mechanism
20 February 1979	*Cassis de Dijon* judgment establishes the principles of mutual recognition and the "rule of reason"

June 1979	First direct elections to the European Parliament
1 January 1981	Greece becomes the EEC's tenth Member State
19 June 1983	Solemn Declaration on European Union adopted at the Stuttgart European Council
14 June 1985	Signing of the Schengen Agreement on the Gradual Abolition of Checks at Common Borders by Belgium, Netherlands, Luxembourg, France and Germany
14 June 1985	Commission publishes its White Paper on the Completion of the Internal Market
1 January 1986	Portugal and Spain accede to the EEC, bringing membership to 12
17, 28 February 1986	Signing of the Single European Act
24 December 1986	High Court grants an injunction in *Crotty v An Taoiseach* preventing ratification of the Single European Act
9 April 1987	Supreme Court judgment in *Crotty v An Taoiseach*
25 May 1987	Referendum approves ratification of the Single European Act by 70 per cent to 30 per cent
1 July 1987	Entry into force of the Single European Act
9 December 1989	Adoption of the Community Charter of the Fundamental Social Rights of Workers ("the Social Charter")
11 October 1991	Court of Justice judgment in *SPUC v Grogan*
7 February 1992	Signing of the Treaty on European Union (the Maastricht Treaty)
2 May 1992	Signing of the European Economic Area (EEA) Agreement
18 June 1992	Referendum approves ratification of the Treaty on European Union by 69 per cent to 31 per cent
1 November 1993	Entry into force of the Treaty on European Union (the Maastricht Treaty)
1 January 1994	European Economic Area (EEA) Agreement enters into force for Norway, Iceland and Liechtenstein and EU Member States
1 January 1995	Austria, Finland and Sweden accede to the EU, bringing membership to 15
2 October 1997	Signing of the Treaty of Amsterdam
22 May 1998	Referendum approves ratification of the Treaty of Amsterdam by 62 per cent to 38 per cent
1 May 1999	Entry into force of the Treaty of Amsterdam
7 December 2000	Charter of Fundamental Rights of the European Union solemnly proclaimed by the European Council
26 February 2001	Signing of the Treaty of Nice
7 June 2001	Referendum rejects ratification of the Treaty of Nice by 54 per cent to 46 per cent
1 January 2002	Introduction of Euro notes

21 June 2002	Ireland makes a National Declaration on the Treaty of Nice at the Seville European Council
19 October 2002	Second referendum approves ratification of the Treaty of Nice by 63 per cent to 37 per cent
1 February 2003	Entry into force of the Treaty of Nice

Chapter 3

TREATY ON EUROPEAN UNION AND TREATY ON THE FUNCTIONING OF THE EUROPEAN UNION

A. The Constitutional Treaty

[3–01] So far, Chapter 1 has set out the historical origins of the European Union and the establishment of the EEC, while Chapter 2 looked at the various amendments to the EEC Treaty carried out by the Single European Act of 1986, the (Maastricht) Treaty on European Union of 1992, the Amsterdam Treaty of 1997 and the Nice Treaty of 2001. This chapter deals with the current versions of the EU Treaties – the Treaty on European Union (TEU) and the Treaty on the Functioning of the European Union (TFEU), including the Charter of Fundamental Rights of the European Union.

[3–02] The origin of the current Treaty on European Union is found in the initial version of that Treaty adopted in Maastricht in 1992, while the Treaty on the Functioning of the European Union is the new name for the EEC Treaty of 1957, as amended and expanded upon in successive treaty changes. Their more direct history, however, begins with the Nice Treaty of 2001. Whereas the Amsterdam Treaty is commonly accused of having failed to provide the institutional reforms necessary for EU enlargement, the Nice Treaty took up this unfinished work but did so in a rather perfunctory manner. Conscious of their own shortcomings, the Member States annexed to the Nice Treaty a Declaration on the Future of the Union. This called for a "deeper and wider debate about the future of the European Union" involving "wide-ranging discussions with all interested parties: representatives of national parliaments and all those reflecting public opinion, namely political, economic and university circles, representatives of civil society etc". It was agreed that the European Council to be held in the Brussels suburb of Laeken in December 2001 would issue a declaration setting out initiatives for the continuation of a process to consider:

(i) how to establish and monitor a more precise delimitation of powers between the EU and the Member States, reflecting the principle of subsidiarity;

(ii) the status of the Charter of Fundamental Rights of the EU that had been proclaimed at the Nice European Council;
(iii) a simplification of the Treaties with a view to making them clearer and better understood without changing their meaning; and
(iv) the role of national parliaments in the European architecture.

[3–03] The resultant Laeken Declaration on the Future of the European Union called for the establishment of a European Convention to identify reforms for the future development of the EU, including means of achieving greater transparency, democratic legitimacy and bringing the Union closer to its citizens. Following the precedent set by the Convention on the Charter of Fundamental Rights, the Convention on the Future of Europe was made up of one government representative and two national parliament representatives from each of the 15 Member States, 16 representatives from the European Parliament and two from the Commission. The Irish Government was represented by former Commissioner Ray McSharry, while the Oireachtas was represented by former Taoiseach John Bruton (who also served on the Convention's 10-person Praesidium) and Proinsias De Rossa. Accession countries were also represented, albeit that they were unable to prevent any consensus emerging among the Member States.

[3–04] The Convention worked through 11 working groups dealing with: subsidiarity; the Charter of Fundamental Rights and European Convention on Human Rights; legal personality; national parliaments; complementary competences; economic governance; external action; defence; simplification; freedom, security and justice, and social Europe. From the very outset, however, the Chair of the Convention, former French President Giscard d'Estaing, made clear an intention not to pursue a number of possible options for reform, but rather to work on drafting a single proposal that would provide the basis for a constitutional text. What emerged was a draft Treaty establishing a Constitution for the European Union, or "Constitutional Treaty", that was intended to replace the existing Treaties with one single, foundational document. Following a relatively short intergovernmental conference (IGC), agreement on the Constitutional Treaty was reached in June 2004 at the end of Ireland's six-month rotation of the Presidency of the Council (a highpoint to an eventful Presidency that had also seen a welcoming ceremony held in Dublin on 1 May to mark the accession of 10 new Member States).[1] Reflecting its significance as the successor to the Treaty of Rome, the Constitutional Treaty was signed in Rome in October 2004.

[3–05] In May and June 2005, voters in the Netherlands and France rejected ratification of the Constitutional Treaty, eventually prompting a "period of reflection" during which the remaining Member States suspended their progress towards ratification. As a result, a referendum was never held in Ireland. By June 2007, it was decided to convene a new IGC with the task of preparing a "reform treaty" that would amend the EC Treaty and TEU in order to implement the majority of the non-contentious reforms that had been contained in the Constitutional Treaty.

[3–06] Under this new amending treaty, the pillar structure was still to be replaced by a single European Union framework, with the Union being given a legal personality of its own in order to take the place of the European Community. The EC Treaty was to be renamed the Treaty on the Functioning of the European Union (TFEU) and all references

[1] See Brian Cowen, "The European Constitution" (2005) 12 *Irish Journal of European Law* 169.

to the Community were to be replaced. The more symbolically constitutional aspects of the draft treaty, however, were to be dropped, such as provisions establishing an EU flag, anthem and motto.[2] The position of Minister for Foreign Affairs was replaced by the less eye-catching title of High Representative of the Union for Foreign Affairs and Security Policy. A new provision declaring the primacy of EU law over national law was demoted to become a declaration annexed to the TEU and TFEU, while a provision that would have introduced the terminology of EU "laws" was jettisoned altogether.

[3–07] It is this complicated political history that explains why, although there is now only one legal entity – the European Union – it has two foundational Treaties. Not wishing to be accused of merely repackaging the Constitutional Treaty under a new title, the Reform Treaty followed the technique of earlier amending treaties and consists of a series of amendments to the EC Treaty (including its renaming) and the TEU. In contrast to the Constitutional Treaty, the Charter of Fundamental Rights is not incorporated within the existing Treaties but remains formally separate, while being conferred with the same legal status as the Treaties. To convey the unity of the Union, the TEU and TFEU cross-reference each other and are themselves said to be of the same legal value, while the various protocols are annexed to both Treaties. Some disparities do remain, however. Whereas the TEU (the much shorter of the two) deals with common provisions, democratic principles, institutions and enhanced cooperation, it also contains the chapter on Common Foreign and Security Policy (CFSP). All other policies are provided for in the TFEU. This is because the Member States wished to emphasise the special status of CFSP, which continues to retain elements of the separate pillar structure such as, for example, a general exclusion of the jurisdiction of the Court of Justice and an inability to adopt legislative acts. Secondly, rather than placing all institutional provisions within the TEU, there continues to be a large degree of overlap, with such provisions being spread out over the two Treaties.

[3–08] The Reform Treaty was signed in Lisbon on 13 December 2007 and thereafter became known as the Lisbon Treaty.

B. The Lisbon Treaty

[3–09] The changes introduced by the Lisbon Treaty are wide-ranging and include both institutional and substantive changes. As many of these will be highlighted throughout this book, it is proposed here to identify 12 of the most significant reforms, most of which will be returned to in later chapters. The Lisbon Treaty:

(i) Dismantled the pillar structure, replacing the EU/European Community duality with a unified European Union which was conferred with legal personality for the first time.

(ii) Simplified the area of EU competences by expressly setting out the categories of

[2] Ireland is not among the 16 Member States that entered a declaration to the TEU and TFEU (Declaration No 52) confirming that the flag, anthem, motto, euro currency and Europe Day of 9 May "will for them continue as symbols to express the sense of community of the people in the European Union and their allegiance to it". See Laurent Pech, "The Fabulous Destiny of the EC Treaty: From Treaty to Constitution to Treaty Again?" (2008) 15 *Irish Journal of European Law* 49; Maria Cahill, "The Constitutional Success of Ratification Failure" (2006) 7 *German Law Journal* 947.

(i) exclusive competence; (ii) shared competence and (iii) supporting, coordinating or complementary competences.

(iii) Added new express competences in the areas of energy, space, sport, intellectual property, climate change, humanitarian aid and civil protection.

(iv) Extended the exclusive external competence of the Union under the Common Commercial Policy to include foreign direct investment and all aspects of trade in services.

(v) Created the full-time position of President of the European Council and made the European Council an EU institution for the first time. The European Central Bank is also made an EU institution, bringing the total number of institutions to seven.

(vi) Renamed the Co-Decision Procedure as the Ordinary Legislative Procedure, which was applied to around forty new areas and deemed the default legislative procedure to be used in all cases other than those to which the Special Legislative Procedure applied.[3] The Co-Operation Procedure is done away with.

(vii) Made Qualified Majority Voting (QMV) the default voting method except where the Treaties provide otherwise and extended the use of QMV to almost 50 new instances by switching 18 existing legal bases to QMV and adding 31 new bases to which QMV applies. Unanimity or common agreement continues to apply in around 80 areas (61 in the Council and around 20 in the European Council), including most CFSP measures, taxation, the conclusion of trade agreements in sensitive fields, social security and social policy, certain police co-operation matters, Own Resources of the EU and the Multiannual Financial Framework.[4]

(viii) Introduced a provision providing for the withdrawal of a Member State from the Union (Art 50 TEU).

(ix) Gave legally binding force, and the same legal value as the Treaties, to the Charter of Fundamental Rights and mandated the EU to accede to the European Convention on Human Rights.

(x) Created the Citizens' Initiative, whereby a petition supported by one million citizens requires the Commission to consider a matter.

(xi) Introduced a "Yellow Card" procedure whereby national parliaments have eight weeks to consider a legislative proposal and, if one-third of them object (or a lower-threshold of one-quarter in the Area of Freedom, Security and Justice) that the proposal is not in accordance with the principle of subsidiarity, it must be reviewed.

(xii) Incorporated the provisions of the old Third Pillar on Police and Judicial Cooperation on Criminal Matters into what became Title V of Part Three of the TFEU, extending the jurisdiction of the Court of Justice over these provisions. In response, Ireland's right to opt-in was extended to the entirety of the Area of Freedom, Security and Justice with the sole exception of Art 75 TFEU permitting asset-freezing measures to be adopted to prevent terrorism (a provision that has yet

[3] The Ordinary Legislative Procedure and Special Legislative Procedure are discussed further in ch 7, paras [7–26] to [7–41].

[4] Jean-Claude Piris, *The Lisbon Treaty* (Cambridge University Press, 2010) 212–213.

to be used). Whereas the original right to opt-in had been explained by reference to the maintenance of the Common Travel Area, the Government explained its extension to all of AFSJ as follows:

> One of the most substantive areas of change between the Constitutional Treaty, agreed in 2004, and the Reform Treaty was the amendment of the Protocol, which has existed since 1997. It extends our existing arrangement with regard to visas, asylum, immigration and judicial co-operation in civil matters to judicial co-operation in criminal matters and to police co-operation. This decision was taken because of the sensitive nature of co-operation in this area and particularly the fact that Ireland, like the UK, has a distinctive common law system of criminal justice which is different from the legal systems in place in the majority of our EU partners. For this reason, Ireland decided to avail of an extension of these flexible arrangements first agreed in 1997.
>
> These arrangements mean that we will be able to choose, on a case-by-case basis, which criminal justice or police co-operation measures we will participate in. We have clearly indicated in a declaration made during the intergovernmental conference that we will study how EU policy evolves in this area and review these arrangements within a period of three years.
>
> We have consistently and strongly supported practical EU anti-terrorism measures and concerted action against organised crime, and we will continue along those lines. In that regard, Ireland has made a declaration, which is annexed to the final act adopting the Reform Treaty, stating our clear intention to participate to the maximum extent possible in relevant JHA proposals and particularly in police co-operation proposals.[5]

(i) Protocol on the Concerns of the Irish People and other "Irish Guarantees"

[3–10] Ireland was the only Member State to hold a referendum on the Lisbon Treaty and, on 12 June 2008, by 53 per cent to 47 per cent, the Irish people once again rejected an EU treaty. Given the prolonged attempts to ensure treaty reform, beginning with the Laeken Declaration in December 2001, the vote caused a crisis of confidence not just in Ireland, but in the EU as a whole. Extensive polling was carried out in order to understand the reasons that led to a "no" vote. Following a combination of the precedents set by Denmark after its rejection of the Maastricht Treaty and Ireland after the rejection of the Nice Treaty, a package of measures, known as the "Irish Guarantees" was agreed upon.[6] These comprised three separate elements, the first of which was agreed at the December 2008 European Council. Under the Lisbon Treaty,

---

5 Minister for Foreign Affairs, Dermot Ahern, 2 April 2008, Dáil Debates, Vol 650, No 3. See Elaine Fahey, "Swimming in a Sea of Law: Reflections on Water Borders, Irish (British)-Euro Relations and Opting-Out and Opting-In after the Treaty of Lisbon" (2010) 47 *Common Market Law Review* 645; Clara Hurley, "Legislating Criminal Matters at EU-Level and the Minimisation of the Opt-Out Protocols" (2015) 33 *Irish Law Times* 298; Eugene Regan (ed), *European Criminal Justice Post Lisbon: An Irish Perspective*, Institute of International and European Affairs, 2012.

6 See Hans Jürgen Papier, "The Lisbon Treaty: The Irish 'No': Europe's New Realism" (2008) 4 *European Constitutional Law Review* 421; Maria Cahill, "Ireland's Constitutional Amendability and Europe's Constitutional Ambition: The Lisbon Referendum in Context" (2008) 9 *German Law Journal* 1191; Desmond Dinan, "Institutions and Governance: Saving the Lisbon Treaty – An Irish Solution to a European Problem" (2009) 47 *Journal of Common Market Studies Annual Review* 113; Laurent Pech and Patrick B Griffin, "Fixing a Hole Where the Rain Gets In: The Lisbon Treaty and the Irish 'Legal Guarantees'" (2009) 16 *Irish Journal of European Law* 5; Ece Özlem Atikcan, "The Puzzle of Double Referendums in the European Union" (2015) 53 *Journal of Common Market Studies* 937.

in 2014 the number of Commissioners was to be reduced to correspond to two-thirds of the Member States unless the European Council decided otherwise. As a result, each Member State would no longer be guaranteed one Commissioner. The potential loss of an "Irish" Commissioner was seen as a contributing factor towards a "no" vote and so, in the event of the Lisbon Treaty's entry into force, the European Council undertook to adopt a decision to maintain a Commission comprising one national from each Member State.[7] Such a decision was adopted in 2013.[8]

[3–11] The second, central element of the Irish Guarantees was a "Decision of the Heads of State or Government of the 27 Member States of the EU, meeting within the European Council, on the Concerns of the Irish People on the Treaty of Lisbon". This Decision was considered to be a binding international agreement entered into by the EU Member States (effectively, while they happened to be meeting as the European Council), a fact copper-fastened by Ireland registering it as such with the Secretariat of the United Nations pursuant to Art 102 of the UN Charter.[9] As agreed by the European Council, the Decision was eventually converted into a Protocol to the TEU and TFEU around the time of Croatia's accession to the EU (with a view to Member States completing ratification procedures for the Protocol while also doing so for the Accession Treaty). The Protocol entered into force on 1 December 2014 and is now Protocol No 38 to the Treaties.[10] Its three substantive articles confirm that the Lisbon Treaty is not to have any effect on certain aspects of Irish policy of a sensitive nature, namely: (i) the right to life, protection of the family and right to education as enshrined in the Constitution; (ii) national competence over tax affairs and (iii) Ireland's traditional policy of military neutrality. They read as follows:

> TITLE I RIGHT TO LIFE, FAMILY AND EDUCATION
> Article 1
> Nothing in the Treaty of Lisbon attributing legal status to the Charter of Fundamental Rights of the European Union, or in the provisions of that Treaty in the area of Freedom, Security and Justice affects in any way the scope and applicability of the protection of the right to life in Article 40.3.1, 40.3.2 and 40.3.3, the protection of the family in Article 41 and the protection of the rights in respect of education in Articles 42 and 44.2.4 and 44.2.5 provided by the Constitution of Ireland.
>
> TITLE II TAXATION
> Article 2
> Nothing in the Treaty of Lisbon makes any change of any kind, for any Member State, to the extent or operation of the competence of the European Union in relation to taxation.
>
> TITLE III SECURITY AND DEFENCE
> Article 3
> The Union's action on the international scene is guided by the principles of democracy, the rule of law, the universality and indivisibility of human rights and fundamental freedoms, respect for human dignity, the principles of equality and solidarity, and respect for the principles of the United Nations Charter and international law.

---

7 European Council 11/12 December 2008, Presidency Conclusions, para 2.

8 European Council Decision 2013/272/EU of 22 May 2013 concerning the number of members of the European Commission [2013] OJ L165/98.

9 Irish Treaty Series No 20 of 2010.

10 [2013] OJ L60/129; [2016] OJ L293/1; Irish Treaty Series No 25 of 2014. See Corrigendum to the consolidated versions of the Treaty on European Union and the Treaty on the Functioning of the European Union [2016] OJ C400/1.

> The Union's common security and defence policy is an integral part of the common foreign and security policy and provides the Union with an operational capacity to undertake missions outside the Union for peace-keeping, conflict prevention and strengthening international security in accordance with the principles of the United Nations Charter.
>
> It does not prejudice the security and defence policy of each Member State, including Ireland, or the obligations of any Member State.
>
> The Treaty of Lisbon does not affect or prejudice Ireland's traditional policy of military neutrality.
>
> It will be for Member States – including Ireland, acting in a spirit of solidarity and without prejudice to its traditional policy of military neutrality – to determine the nature of aid or assistance to be provided to a Member State which is the object of a terrorist attack or the victim of armed aggression on its territory.
>
> Any decision to move to a common defence will require a unanimous decision of the European Council. It would be a matter for the Member States, including Ireland, to decide, in accordance with the provisions of the Treaty of Lisbon and with their respective constitutional requirements, whether or not to adopt a common defence.
>
> Nothing in this Title affects or prejudices the position or policy of any other Member State on security and defence.
>
> It is also a matter for each Member State to decide, in accordance with the provisions of the Treaty of Lisbon and any domestic legal requirements, whether to participate in permanent structured cooperation or the European Defence Agency.
>
> The Treaty of Lisbon does not provide for the creation of a European army or for conscription to any military formation. It does not affect the right of Ireland or any other Member State to determine the nature and volume of its defence and security expenditure and the nature of its defence capabilities.
>
> It will be a matter for Ireland or any other Member State, to decide, in accordance with any domestic legal requirements, whether or not to participate in any military operation.

[3–12] The third and final element of the Irish guarantees took the form of: (i) a National Declaration by Ireland concerning neutrality that was to be associated with its ratification of the Lisbon Treaty and of which the European Council "took cognisance" and (ii) a Solemn Declaration by the European Council on Workers' Rights, Social Policy and Other Issues.

[3–13] The declaration by Ireland repeated, in the first three paragraphs, the terms of the first three paragraphs of its National Declaration on the Treaty of Nice, while paragraph 6 repeated the same paragraph of the earlier declaration recalling that a triple-lock decision of the UN Security Council or General Assembly, the Government and the Dáil is required for a contingent of the Irish Defence Forces to participate in an overseas operation.[11] The remaining paragraphs of the National Declaration expanded further on the Nice Treaty Declaration by setting out that:

> In line with its traditional policy of military neutrality, Ireland is not bound by any mutual defence commitment. The Treaty on European Union specifies that any decision by the Union to move to a common defence would have to be taken by unanimous decision of the

[11] See ch 2, para [2–70].

Member States and adopted in accordance with their respective constitutional requirements. The Constitution of Ireland requires that a referendum be held on the adoption of any such decision applicable to Ireland and this requirement will not be affected should Ireland ratify the Treaty of Lisbon.

Ireland reiterates its commitment to the ideal of peace and friendly cooperation amongst nations and to the principle of the peaceful resolution of international disputes. It reaffirms its strong commitment to conflict prevention, resolution and peace-keeping, and recalls the record of achievement of its personnel, military and civilian, in this regard.

[*Repeated paragraph 6 of Ireland's Declaration on the Treaty of Nice*]

Ireland notes that nothing obliges it to participate in permanent structured cooperation as provided for in the Treaty on European Union. Any decision enabling Ireland to participate will require the approval of Dáil Éireann in accordance with Irish law.

Ireland notes also that nothing obliges it to participate in the European Defence Agency, or in specific projects or programmes initiated under its auspices. Any decision to participate in such projects or programmes will be subject to national decision-making and the approval of Dáil Éireann in accordance with Irish law. Ireland declares that it will participate only in those projects and programmes that contribute to enhancing the capabilities required for participation in UN-mandated missions for peace-keeping, conflict prevention and strengthening international security, in accordance with the principles of the United Nations Charter.

[3–14] In order to give effect to the elements of the National Declaration concerning a decision to participate in Permanent Structured Cooperation[12] or the European Defence Agency (EDA), the Defence (Miscellaneous Provisions) Bill was introduced in September 2009 and enacted a month after the second referendum, in November 2009. Mirroring the triple-lock for the participation of a contingent of the Defence Forces on an overseas operation, the Act provides that Ireland shall not participate in an EDA project or programme, or in Permanent Structured Cooperation, without the prior approval of the Government and the Dáil, where the approval of the Government is conditional on it first satisfying itself that participation would contribute to the enhancement of capabilities for UN mandated missions engaged in peace-keeping, conflict prevention or the strengthening of international security in accordance with the principles of the UN Charter.

[3–15] In November 2017, 23 Member States jointly notified the Council and the High Representative of the Union for Foreign Affairs and Security Policy of their intention to participate in Permanent Structured Cooperation, or PESCO, as provided for in Art 46 TEU and Protocol 10 to the Treaties. Following the passing of the required Dáil motion on 7 December 2017, Ireland (together with Portugal) joined in the notification, bringing the total number of participating states to 25. In introducing the motion, the Minister for Foreign Affairs and Trade confirmed that "the Government is fully satisfied that

[12] Art 42(6) TEU states: "Those Member States whose military capabilities fulfil higher criteria and which have made more binding commitments to one another in [the area of common security and defence] with a view to the most demanding missions shall establish permanent structured cooperation with the Union framework." Art 46(1) TEU provides that: "Those Member States which wish to participate in the permanent structured cooperation referred to in Article 42(6), which fulfil the criteria and have the commitments on military capabilities set out in the Protocol on permanent structured cooperation, shall notify their intention to the Council and to the High Representative of the Union for Foreign Affairs and Security Policy."

Ireland's participation in PESCO will enhance the capability of UN-mandated missions engaged in peacekeeping, conflict prevention or the strengthening of international security. This is in accordance with the principles specified in the charter of the United Nations, as required by section (3)(2) of the 2009 Act."[13] PESCO was then formally established by a Council Decision.[14] A list of 17 initial PESCO projects was established, later expanded to 34, with Ireland committing to participate in two – the EU Training Mission Competence Centre and the Maritime Surveillance project.[15]

[3–16] The Solemn Declaration by the European Council on Workers' Rights, Social Policy and Other Issues was of a much broader nature and not specific to Ireland. In it, the European Council confirmed the high importance attached by the EU to social progress and the protection of workers' rights, public services, the responsibility of Member States for the delivery of education and health services and the essential role and wide discretion of national, regional and local authorities in providing, commissioning and organising services of general economic interest. To underline this further, the Declaration recalled a number of features of the Treaties, as modified by the Lisbon Treaty, including that they:

- establish an Internal Market and aim at working for the sustainable development of Europe based on balanced economic growth and price stability, a highly competitive social market economy, aiming at full employment and social progress, and a high level of protection and improvement of the quality of the environment;
- aim to combat social exclusion and discrimination, and to promote social justice and protection, equality between women and men, solidarity between generations and protection of the rights of the child;
- oblige the Union, when defining and implementing its policies and activities, to take into account requirements linked to the promotion of a high level of employment, the guarantee of adequate social protection, the fight against social exclusion, and a high level of education, training and protection of human health;
- include, as a shared value of the Union, the essential role and the wide discretion of national, regional and local authorities in providing, commissioning and organising services of general economic interest as closely as possible to the needs of the users;
- do not affect in any way the competence of Member States to provide, commission and organise non-economic services of general interest;
- provide that the Council, when acting in the area of Common Commercial Policy, must act unanimously when negotiating and concluding international agreements in the field of trade in social, education and health services, where those agreements risk seriously disturbing the national organisation of such services and prejudicing the responsibility of Member States to deliver them; and
- provide that the Union recognises and promotes the role of the social partners at the

---

13 Minister for Foreign Affairs and Trade, Simon Coveney, Dáil Debates, 7 December 2017, Vol 962, No 8.

14 Council Decision (CFSP) 2017/2315 of 11 December 2017 establishing permanent structured cooperation (PESCO) and determining the list of participating Member States [2017] OJ L331/57; Council Decision (CFSP) 2018/909 establishing a common set of rules for PESCO projects [2018] OJ L161/37. See Steven Blockmans, "The EU's Modular Approach to Defence Integration: An Inclusive, Ambitious and Legally Binding PESCO?" (2018) 55 *Common Market Law Review* 1785; Niklas Nováky, "The EU's Permanent Structured Cooperation in defence: Keeping Sleeping Beauty from snoozing" (2018) 17 *European View* 97.

15 Council Decision (CFSP) 2018/340 of 6 March 2018 establishing the list of projects to be developed under PESCO [2018] OJ L65/24; Council Decision (CFSP) 2018/1797 of 19 November 2018 amending Council Decision (CFSP) 2018/340 [2018] OJ L294/18.

level of the EU, and facilitates dialogue between them, taking account of the diversity of national systems and respecting the autonomy of social partners.

[3–17] Many of the issues touched upon in the Solemn Declaration have been taken up in the European Pillar of Social Rights that was proclaimed by the European Parliament, Council and Commission in November 2017.[16] The Social Pillar sets out 20 principles relating to equal opportunities and access to the labour market, fair working conditions and social protection and inclusion. In its preamble, the Social Pillar is described as reaffirming "some of the rights already present in the Union acquis. It adds new principles which address the challenges arising from societal, technological and economic developments. For them to be legally enforceable, the principles and rights first require dedicated measures or legislation to be adopted at the appropriate level."[17] As part of deliberations on the Future of Europe, the Commission in the same year published a Reflection Paper on the Social Dimension of Europe.[18] Furthermore, a European Labour Authority has been established as a new EU agency, which is due to become operational in 2019.

[3–18] A second referendum on 2 October 2009 approved ratification by 67 per cent to 33 per cent and the Lisbon Treaty finally entered into force on 1 December 2009. In addition to Art 29.4.7°, providing for Ireland's availing of the right to participate in enhanced cooperation under Art 20 TEU or to opt-in under Protocol No 19 (Schengen) or Protocol No 21 (Area of Freedom, Security and Justice), a new Art 29.4.8° was inserted into the Constitution so as to manage how Ireland might agree to the use of certain new optional decisions contained within the Treaties. It provides that, subject to the approval of both Houses of the Oireachtas, the State may agree to regulations, decisions or other acts:

(i) under the TEU and TFEU authorising the Council of the EU to act other than by unanimity;
(ii) under the TEU and TFEU authorising the adoption of the ordinary legislative procedure; and

---

16 Interinstitutional Proclamation on the European Pillar of Social Rights (2017/C 428/09) [2017] OJ C428/10. See ch 10, para [10–02]; Sacha Garben, "The European Pillar of Social Rights: Effectively Addressing Displacement?" (2018) 14 *European Constitutional Law Review* 210; Sacha Garben, "The European Pillar of Social Rights: An Assessment of its Meaning and Significance" (2019) Cambridge Yearbook of European Legal Studies (forthcoming); Commission Communication, "Establishing a European Pillar of Social Rights", COM/2017/0250 final, 26 April 2017.

17 Recital 14.

18 "Reflection Paper on the Social Dimension of Europe", European Commission, COM(2017) 206, 26 April 2017.

(iii) relating to the Area of Freedom, Security and Justice under Art 82(2)(d) TFEU,[19] the third subparagraph of Art 83.1 TFEU[20] and Art 86(1) and (4) TFEU.[21]

[3–19] Paragraphs (i) and (ii) of Art 29.4.8° are mainly concerned with a new general "passerelle clause" ("little bridge") introduced by the Lisbon Treaty as Art 48(7) TEU. This clause allows for a simplified means of changing Treaty provisions governing the applicable voting rules and legislative procedure without having to go through the formal methods of amending the Treaties. Essentially, Art 48(7) TEU allows for a decision to be adopted by the European Council to switch the use of unanimity to QMV, or to switch the special legislative procedure to the ordinary legislative procedure, in certain areas. Under Art 48(7), such a decision shall not be adopted if any national parliament makes known its opposition within six months of being notified. This was given effect to in Art 29.4.8° by requiring the *prior* approval of both Houses of the Oireachtas before Ireland may agree to the adoption of any such decision. As the Minister for Foreign Affairs explained when introducing the referendum Bill:

> The [TEU] provides that national parliaments must have at least six months' notice of any intention on the part of the European Council to use the provisions of the Treaty relating

---

19 Art 82(2) TFEU: "To the extent necessary to facilitate mutual recognition of judgments and judicial decisions and police and judicial cooperation in criminal matters having a cross-border dimension, the European Parliament and the Council may, by means of directives adopted in accordance with the ordinary legislative procedure, establish minimum rules. Such rules shall take into account the differences between the legal traditions and systems of the Member States. They shall concern … (d) any other specific aspects of criminal procedure which the Council has identified in advance by a decision; for the adoption of such a decision, the Council shall act unanimously after obtaining the consent of the European Parliament."

20 Art 83(1) TFEU: "The European Parliament and the Council may, by means of directives adopted in accordance with the ordinary legislative procedure, establish minimum rules concerning the definition of criminal offences and sanctions in the areas of particularly serious crime with a cross-border dimension resulting from the nature or impact of such offences or from a special need to combat them on a common basis.

These areas of crime are the following: terrorism, trafficking in human beings and sexual exploitation of women and children, illicit drug trafficking, illicit arms trafficking, money laundering, corruption, counterfeiting of means of payment, computer crime and organised crime.

On the basis of developments in crime, the Council may adopt a decision identifying other areas of crime that meet the criteria specified in this paragraph. It shall act unanimously after obtaining the consent of the European Parliament."

21 Art 86(1) and (4) TFEU: "1. In order to combat crimes affecting the financial interests of the Union, the Council, by means of regulations adopted in accordance with a special legislative procedure, may establish a European Public Prosecutor's Office from Eurojust. The Council shall act unanimously after obtaining the consent of the European Parliament.

In the absence of unanimity in the Council, a group of at least nine Member States may request that the draft regulation be referred to the European Council. In that case, the procedure in the Council shall be suspended. After discussion, and in case of a consensus, the European Council shall, within four months of this suspension, refer the draft back to the Council for adoption.

Within the same timeframe, in case of disagreement, and if at least nine Member States wish to establish enhanced cooperation on the basis of the draft regulation concerned, they shall notify the European Parliament, the Council and the Commission accordingly …

…

4. The European Council may, at the same time or subsequently, adopt a decision amending paragraph 1 in order to extend the powers of the European Public Prosecutor's Office to include serious crime having a cross-border dimension and amending accordingly paragraph 2 as regards the perpetrators of, and accomplices in, serious crimes affecting more than one Member State. The European Council shall act unanimously after obtaining the consent of the European Parliament and after consulting the Commission."

to voting in the Council of Ministers and extension of the co-decision procedure between the Council and the European Parliament. Unanimity is also required in the European Council for any such move. This means that, under the treaty, Ireland has a double veto, exercisable by either the Government or the Houses of the Oireachtas. Furthermore, under the terms of the proposed new subsection 8°, the prior approval of both Houses of the Oireachtas will be required before the Government can proceed with any such proposal. This means Irish parliamentarians have more than the negative veto provided by the Treaty; the Government will be required to seek affirmatively their permission before the Taoiseach can commit himself to any change at the European Council. [22]

[3–20] In addition to inserting this new clause, the opportunity was taken to overhaul Art 29.4 generally, given the significant changes to the EU's primary treaties. As explained to the Dáil by the Minister for Foreign Affairs:

> After 35 years of membership, the Government considers it both timely and appropriate to set out an updated version of our constitutional arrangements relating to the EU. Accordingly, the relevant provisions of Article 29.4, which have been amended four times since joining the EU, becoming increasingly complex each time, are being replaced in their entirety. The new provisions set out in a streamlined and more user-friendly form how our engagement with the EU is to be governed. It is proposed that part of subsection 3° dealing with the European Coal and Steel Community, the European Economic Community and the Single European Act be deleted as well, since the references are redundant. The other subsections dealing with our membership of the EU — subsections 4° to 11°— will be replaced with new subsections, 4° to 9° …
>
> A proposed new subsection 4° would contain a short statement of our commitment to the Union "within which the Member States … work together to promote peace, shared values and the well-being of their peoples". This reflects our highly positive experience of membership going back to 1973. It is in keeping with the values set out in Article 29.1, which affirms Ireland's devotion to peace and friendly co-operation among nations founded on international justice and morality.
>
> The proposed new subsection 5° of Article 29.4 provides that the State may ratify the Lisbon Treaty and be a member of the Union established by that Treaty. Since the Treaty establishes a new Union with legal personality, it is proposed that the current subsections 4°, 5° and 7° providing for the ratification of the treaties of Maastricht, Amsterdam and Nice be deleted as they will be made redundant by Lisbon.[23]

C. Treaty on European Union

[3–21] The Treaty on European Union (TEU) is the much shorter of the two foundational treaties, containing just 55 articles that are divided into six Titles. Twenty-five of these articles are found in Title V dealing with the EU's external action and the Common Foreign and Security Policy (CFSP), comprising a major part of the TEU as a whole. In addition, whereas the rest of the TEU is concerned with general principles and institutional matters, Chapter 2 of Title V, on the CFSP, is unique within the Treaty in that it sets out substantive provisions governing a particular area of EU activity. All other policy areas are provided for in the TFEU.

---

22 Minister for Foreign Affairs, Micheál Martin, Dáil Debates, 8 July 2009, Vol 687, No 4.
23 *ibid.*

Title I	**Common Provisions**	*Art 1–8*
Title II	**Provisions on Democratic Principles**	*Art 9–12*
Title III	**Provisions on the Institutions**	*Art 13–19*
Title IV	**Provisions on Enhanced Cooperation**	*Art 20*
Title V	**General Provisions on Union's External Action and Specific Provisions on Common Foreign and Security Policy**	
	Chapter 1 – General Provisions on the Union's External Action	*Art 21–22*
	Chapter 2 – Specific Provisions on the CFSP	*Art 23–46*
Title VI	**Final Provisions**	*Art 47–55*

[3–22] Title I effectively defines the EU, its fundamental values and its objectives. It also establishes some of the fundamental principles in accordance with which the EU is to exercise its competence, such as conferral, subsidiarity and proportionality, as well as the equality of Member States and the duty of sincere cooperation. Article 6 confers legally binding status on the Charter of Fundamental Rights, obliges the Union to accede to the European Convention on Human Rights and recognises that fundamental rights form part of the general principles of EU law.[24] Article 7 provides a mechanism through which the EU may monitor the extent to which its Member States adhere to the fundamental values set out in Art 2, such as respect for human dignity, freedom, democracy, equality, the rule of law and respect for human rights.

[3–23] In 2014, the Commission introduced a Framework for strengthening the Rule of Law, which establishes a three-stage process that is intended to precede and implement the Art 7 mechanism: Commission assessment; Commission recommendation and follow-up to the Commission recommendation.[25] The Framework was invoked for the first time against Poland in 2016 following changes to the composition of the Polish constitutional tribunal and proposed reforms to the governance of state broadcasters. This resulted in a series of Commission Recommendations,[26] culminating in a reasoned proposal from the Commission in accordance with Art 7 TEU for a Council Decision

---

[24] See ch 8, para [8–01].

[25] Commission Communication, "A New EU Framework to Strengthen the Rule of Law", COM(2014) 158 final/2, 19 March 2014; Commission Communication, "Further Strengthening the Rule of Law within the Union: State of play and possible next steps", COM(2019) 163 final, 3 April 2019; Commission Communication, "Further Strengthening the Rule of Law within the Union: A blueprint for action", COM(2019) 3433 final, 17 July 2019.

[26] Commission Recommendation (EU) 2016/1374 of 27 July 2016 regarding the Rule of Law in Poland, [2016] OJ L217/53; Commission Recommendation (EU) 2018/103 of 20 December 2017 regarding the Rule of Law in Poland complementary to Recommendations (EU) 2016/1374, (EU) 2017/146 and (EU) 2017/1520 [2018] OJ L17/50. See also Case C-619/18 R *Commission v Poland* EU:C:2018:852, 19 October 2018, EU:C:2018:1021, 17 December 2018, EU:C:2019:325, 11 April 2019 and EU:C:2019:531, 24 June 2019, where the Court of Justice took the unusual step of provisionally granting interim orders against Poland requiring it not to apply certain national laws relating to the lowering of the retirement age of Supreme Court judges. See Patrick Lavelle, "Europe's Rule of Law Crisis: An Assessment of the EU's Capacity to Address Systemic Breaches of its Foundational Values in Member States" (2019) 22 *Trinity College Law Review* 35; Anthony M Collins, "The Rule of Law in Europe – Threats and Challenges" (2018) 21 *Irish Journal of European Law* 1; Matthias Schmidt and Piotr Bogdanowicz, "The Infringement Procedure in the Rule of Law Crisis: How to Make Effective Use of Article 258 TFEU" 55 (2018) *Common Market Law Review* 1061; Laurent Pech and Kim Lane Scheppele, "Illiberalism Within: Rule of Law Backsliding in the EU" (2017) 19 *Cambridge Yearbook of European Legal Studies* 3; Armin von Bogandy and Michael Ioannidis, "Systemic Deficiency in the Rule of Law: What It Is, What Has Been Done, What Can Be Done" (2014) 51 *Common Market Law Review* 59. The rule of law

determining a clear risk of a serious breach by Poland of the rule of law.[27] In turn, these Recommendations were drawn upon by the Irish High Court in requesting a preliminary reference from the Court of Justice as to whether rule of law issues in Poland presented an obstacle to the surrender of a person for trial under a European Arrest Warrant.[28] The Court of Justice clarified the test to be applied and the High Court ultimately ordered the surrender, finding that the systemic and generalised deficiencies in the independence of the judiciary in Poland of themselves did not reach the threshold of amounting to a real risk that there would be a flagrant denial of a right to a fair trial.[29] In 2018, the European Parliament passed a resolution that, for the first time, called upon the Council to determine, pursuant to Art 7 TEU, the existence of a clear risk of a serious breach of the rule of law in Hungary.[30] The rule of law is also featuring in proposals for the next EU budget, to run from 2021–2027, with initial Commission proposals including the suggestion that, in the future, cohesion funding should be made conditional on Member States' adherence to rule of law principles.[31]

[3–24] Title II of the TEU sets out the core democratic principles of the Union, including that every national of a Member State shall, in addition, be a citizen of the Union, which is founded on representative democracy through the European Parliament and, indirectly, by the participation of elected governments in the European Council and Council. Article 11 provides for a Citizens' Initiative – introduced by the Lisbon Treaty – whereby a petition of one million citizens may invite the Commission to submit proposals on a matter. Article 12 sets out the ways in which national parliaments contribute actively to the good functioning of the Union, including through the mechanisms established in the Protocol No 1 on the role of national parliaments and the Protocol No 2 on the application of the principles of subsidiarity and proportionality.

[3–25] Title III deals with the Union's seven institutions: the European Parliament, European Council, Council, European Commission, Court of Justice of the European Union, European Central Bank and Court of Auditors. The fundamental principles and characteristics of the Parliament (Art 14), European Council (Art 15), Council (Art 16), Commission (Art 17) and Court of Justice (Art 19) are set out here, with more detailed provisions contained in Part Six of the TFEU. The European Central Bank and the Court of Auditors are dealt with entirely in the TFEU. In addition, Art 13 provides that the Parliament and Commission shall be assisted by an Economic and Social Committee and a Committee of the Regions acting in an advisory capacity, both of which are dealt with in Part Six of the TFEU.

---

was also at issue in Case C-64/16 *Associação Sindical dos Juízes Portugueses* EU:C:2018:117, 27 February 2018, discussed in ch 14, para [14–02].

[27] European Commission, Reasoned Proposal in accordance with Art 7(1) of the Treaty on European Union regarding the Rule of Law in Poland, COM(2017) 835 final, 20 December 2017.

[28] *Minister for Justice and Equality v Celmer (No 1)* [2018] IEHC 119, 12 March 2018, Donnelly J; *Minister for Justice and Equality v Celmer (No 2)* [2018] IEHC 153, 23 March 2018, Donnelly J.

[29] Case C-216/18 PPU *Minister for Justice and Equality v LM* EU:C:2018:586, 25 July 2018. *Minister for Justice and Equality v Celmer (No 5)* [2018] IEHC 639, 19 November 2018, Donnelly J.

[30] European Parliament resolution of 12 September 2018 on a proposal calling on the Council to determine, pursuant to Art 7(1) of the Treaty on European Union, the existence of a clear risk of a serious breach by Hungary of the values on which the Union is founded, 2017/2131(INL). Hungary has brought proceedings seeking the annulment of the resolution, Case C-650/18 *Hungary v European Parliament* [2018] OJ C436/33 (ongoing).

[31] See Viorica Viță, "Revisiting the Dominant Discourse on Conditionality in the EU: The Case of EU Spending Conditionality" (2017) 19 *Cambridge Yearbook of European Legal Studies* 116.

[3–26] Title IV comprises just Art 20 and provides that where at least nine Member States wish to establish enhanced cooperation between themselves within the framework of the Union's non-exclusive competences, they may make use of its institutions and exercise those competences by applying the relevant provisions of the Treaties. The cooperation must be open at any time to all Member States. More detailed rules are set out in Arts 326 to 334 TFEU. The introduction of a system of unitary patent protection is one area where enhanced cooperation has been used, with all Member States bar Spain and Croatia participating.[32]

[3–27] Title V is made up of a short chapter setting out the general principles and institutional arrangements for the Union's external action generally, followed by a much longer chapter dealing substantively with the EU's Common Foreign and Security Policy (CFSP). The location of this substantive CFSP chapter within the TEU dates back to the introduction of the pillar structure by the original version of the TEU adopted in Maastricht, and the fact that Pillar Two on CFSP was never incorporated into the Community Pillar. As has been explained, this separation from the rest of Union policies in the TFEU is "intended to emphasise and indeed reinforce the highly differentiated nature of the CFSP within the Union legal order".[33] As well as excluding both the role of the CJEU and the possibility of adopting legislative acts, it is also:

> widely assumed that decisions adopted specifically pursuant to the CFSP will remain distinct, as regards their potential effects within the national legal systems, from decisions adopted in any other field of Union activity, to the extent that CFSP acts should not generally be capable of having independent effects (such as direct effect and/or supremacy) within the domestic legal orders.[34]

[3–28] A CFSP area where the Court of Justice does, exceptionally, have jurisdiction is in relation to restrictive measures, or sanctions, adopted by the Union. These are typically imposed by way of a CFSP decision together with a parallel regulation adopted pursuant to the TFEU which provides for, say, the freezing of assets or the prohibition of certain imports or exports. In this context, the Court has emphasised that, pursuant to Art 29 TEU, Member States must ensure that their national policies conform to the Union position adopted under a CFSP decision and that, were a sanctions regulation to be declared invalid, that would, as a matter of principle, have no effect on the obligation of

---

[32] Regulation (EU) No 1257/2012 of the European Parliament and of the Council implementing enhanced cooperation in the area of the creation of unitary patent protection [2012] OJ L361/1. See Cases C-274/11 and C-275/11 *Spain and Italy v Council* EU:C:2013:240, 16 April 2013; Federico Fabbrini, "Enhanced Cooperation under Scrutiny: Revisiting the Law and Practice of Multi-Speed Integration in Light of the First Involvement of the EU Judiciary" (2013) 40 *Legal Issues of Economic Integration* 197; Matthias Lamping, "Enhanced Cooperation in the Area of Unitary Patent Protection – Testing the Boundaries of the Rule of Law" (2013) 20 *Maastricht Journal of European and Comparative Law* 589; Tuomas Mylly, "Hovering between Intergovernmentalism and Unionization: The Shape of Unitary Patents" (2017) 54 *Common Market Law Review* 1381; Bruno de Witte, "An Undivided Union? Differentiated Integration in Post-Brexit Times" (2018) 55 *Common Market Law Review* 227; Noel Travers, "From *Merck v Stephar* to the Unitary Patent Regulations and Court: Reflections on the Incremental Development of an EU Patent Law and Legal System" in Kieran Bradley, Noel Travers and Anthony Whelan (eds), *Of Courts and Constitutions: Liber Amicorum in Honour of Nial Fennelly* (Hart, 2014), 155. More generally, see Bruno De Witte, "The Law as Tool and Constraint of Differentiated Integration", EUI Working Paper, RSCAS 2019/47, 2019.

[33] Alan Dashwood, Michael Dougan, Barry Rodger, Eleanor Spaventa and Derrick Wyatt, *Wyatt and Dashwood's European Union Law* (6th ed, Hart, 2011) 28.

[34] *ibid.*

Member States to ensure that their national policies conform to the sanctions established pursuant to the separate CFSP decision.[35]

[3–29] While CFSP is dealt with in the TEU, Part Five of the TFEU further deals with the other aspects of the Union's external action such as the Common Commercial Policy, cooperation with third countries, humanitarian aid, the procedure for entering into international agreements and, as referred to above, the adoption of the necessary measures to impose sanctions in line with a CFSP decision.

[3–30] Lastly, Title VI deals with final provisions such as the Treaty's language versions, its duration and territorial scope, the Union's legal personality (Art 47) and how the Treaties may be amended (Art 48), acceded to (Art 49) or withdrawn from (Art 50).[36] Following a referendum held on 23 June 2016, the UK submitted notification of its intention to withdraw from the EU pursuant to Art 50 TEU on 29 March 2017.[37]

---

35 Case C-72/15 *Rosneft* EU:C:2017:236, 28 March 2017, para 56.

36 On Art 50 TEU see Case C-621/18 *Wightman v Secretary of State for Exiting the EU* EU:C:2018:999, 10 December 2018; Case C-340/17 P *Alcohol Countermeasure Systems (International) Inc v European Union Intellectual Property Office* EU:C:2018:965, 29 November 2018, paras 115–120; Case C-327/18 *Minister for Justice and Equality v RO* EU:C:2018:733, 19 September 2018 ; Case C-661/17 *MA v International Protection Appeals Tribunal* EU:C:2019:53, 23 January 2019; Case T-458/17 *Shindler v Council* EU:T:2018:838, 26 November 2018; Daniel Benrath, "Bona Fide and Revocation of Withdrawal: How Art 50 Handles the Potential Abuse of a Unilateral Revocation of Withdrawal" (2018) 43 *European Law Review* 234; Christophe Hillion, "Withdrawal under Article 50 TEU: An Integration-Friendly Process" (2018) 55 *Common Market Law Review* 29; Aurel Sari, "Reversing a Withdrawal Notification under Article 50 TEU: Can a Member State Change Its Mind?" (2014) 42 *European Law Review* 451; Patrick Ostendorf, "The Withdrawal Cannot be Withdrawn: The Irrevocability of a Withdrawal Notification under Art 50(2) TEU" (2017) 42 *European Law Review* 767; Jens Dammann, "Revoking Brexit: Can Member States Rescind Their Declaration of Withdrawal from the European Union?" (2017) 23 *Columbia Journal of European Law* 265; Phedon Nicolaides, "Withdrawal from the European Union: A Typology of Effects" (2013) 20 *Maastricht Journal of European and Comparative Law* 209; Hannes Hofmeister, "Should I Stay or Should I Go? – A Critical Analysis of the Right to Withdraw from the EU" (2010) 16 *European Law Journal* 589; Adam Lazowski, "Withdrawal from the European Union and Alternatives to Membership" (2012) 37 *European Law Review* 523; Allan Tatham, "'Don't Mention Divorce at the Wedding, Darling!' EU Accession and Withdrawal after Lisbon" in Andrea Biondi, Piet Eeckhout and Stefanie Ripley (eds), *EU Law After Lisbon* (Oxford University Press, 2012) 128; Raymond Friel, "Providing a Constitutional Framework for a Withdrawal from the EU: Art 59 of the Draft European Constitution" (2004) 53 *International and Comparative Law Quarterly* 407; Jochen Herbst, "Observations on the Right to Withdraw from the European Union: Who Are the 'Masters of the Treaties'?" (2005) 6 *German Law Journal* 1755.

37 See Kevin O'Rourke, *A Short History of Brexit: From Brentry to Backstop* (Pelican, 2019); Ivan Rogers, *9 Lessons in Brexit* (Short Books, 2019); Steve Peers, *Brexit: What Happens Next* (Hart, 2019); Francis B Jacobs, *The EU After Brexit* (Palgrave, 2018); Oonagh Fitzgerald and Eva Lein (eds), *Complexity's Embrace: The International Law Implications of Brexit* (CIGI Press, 2018); Benjamin Martill and Uta Staiger (eds), *Brexit and Beyond* (UCL Press, 2018); Andrea Biondi, Patrick J Birkinshaw and Maria Kendrick (eds), *Brexit: The Legal Implications* (Wolters Kluwer, 2018); John Armour and Horst Eidenmüller (eds), *Negotiating Brexit* (Hart, 2017); Kenneth Armstrong, *Brexit Time* (Cambridge University Press, 2017); Michael Dougan (ed), *The UK after Brexit* (Intersentia, 2017); Tony Connelly, *Brexit and Ireland* (Penguin, 2017); Federico Fabbrini (ed), *The Law and Politics of Brexit* (Oxford University Press, 2017); Nazaré da Costa Cabral, José Renato Gonçalves and Nuno Cunha Rodrigues (eds), *After Brexit: Consequences for the European Union* (Palgrave Macmillan, 2017); Jennifer Hillman and Gary Horlick (eds), *Legal Aspects of Brexit* (Institute of International Economics Law, Washington, 2017); Anthony M Collins, "EU Law in Ireland Post-Brexit" (2018) 21 *Trinity College Law Review* 9; Gerard Hogan, "Laws in Common? What is the future of the common law within the European Union after Brexit?" (2019)

Negotiations on a withdrawal agreement began on 19 June 2017.[38]

[3–31] The first phase of negotiations focused on three principal issues, namely: (i) the "financial settlement" of the UK's outstanding liabilities to the Union, less certain assets or monies owed to it, and the means by which this is to be paid; (ii) the rights of EU citizens who have exercised the right of free movement by moving to the UK, and the rights of UK nationals who have moved to another EU Member State (often referred to as "acquired rights") and (iii) issues relating to the island of Ireland including the maintenance of the Common Travel Area, the protection of the Good Friday Agreement and the avoidance of the creation of a hard border between Ireland and Northern Ireland.[39] Indeed, in establishing its first set of guidelines for the negotiations, the European Council agreed to a declaration within its minutes to confirm the understanding that, in the event of a united Ireland being brought about in accordance with the Good Friday Agreement, the entire territory of such a united Ireland would be part of the Union.[40]

[3–32] A fully negotiated Withdrawal Agreement was finally published in November 2018, together with a political declaration setting out the framework for the future relationship between the EU and the UK.[41] The European Council endorsed the draft

---

24 *Bar Review* 22; Michael Dougan, "An Airbag for Crash Test Dummies? EU–UK Negotiations for a Post-Withdrawal 'Status Quo' Transitional Arrangement under Article 50 TEU" (2018) 55 *Common Market Law Review* 57; Ramses Wessel, "Consequences of Brexit for International Agreements concluded by the EU and its Member States" (2018) 55 *Common Market Law Review* 101; Giesela Rühl, "Judicial Cooperation in Civil and Commercial Matters after Brexit: Which Way Forward?" (2018) 67 *International and Comparative Law Quarterly* 99; Piet Eeckhout and Eleni Frantziou, "Brexit and Article 50 TEU: A Constitutional Reading" (2017) 54 *Common Market Law Review* 695; Nanette Neuwahl, "CETA as a Potential Model for (Post-Brexit) UK–EU Relations" (2017) 22 *European Foreign Affairs Review* 279; Vincent Power, "The Implications of Brexit for Competition Law – An Irish Perspective" (2017) 20 *Irish Journal of European Law* 1; Elaine Fahey, "The Global Reach of EU Law and Brexit: Between Theory and Praxis" (2017) 20 *Irish Journal of European Law* 16; Jed Odermatt, "Brexit and International Law: Disentangling Legal Orders" (2017) 31 *Emory International Law Review* 1051; *Brexit Supplement* (2016) 17 *German Law Journal*; *Brexit Special Issue* (2016) 27(3) *King's Law Journal*; Paul Craig, "Brexit: A Drama in Six Acts" (2016) 41 *European Law Review* 447; Adam Łazowski and Ramses Wessel, "The External Dimension of Withdrawal from the European Union" (2016) *Revue des Affaires européennes* 623; Dora Kostakopoulou, "Brexit, Voice and Loyalty: Reflections on Article 50 TEU" (2016) 41 *European Law Review* 488; Takis Tridimas, "Article 50: An Endgame without an End?" (2016) 27 *King's Law Journal* 297; Christa Tobler, "One of Many Challenges after 'Brexit': The Institutional Framework of an Alternative Agreement — Lessons from Switzerland and Elsewhere?" (2016) 23 *Maastricht Journal of European and Comparative Law* 275.

38 See European Council Guidelines following the United Kingdom's Notification under Art 50 TEU, 29 April 2017, EUCO XT 20004/17; Council Decision of 22 May 2017 authorising the opening of negotiations with the United Kingdom of Great Britain and Northern Ireland for an agreement setting out the arrangements for its withdrawal from the European Union; European Council Guidelines, 15 December 2017, EUCO XT 20011/17.

39 See Mary C Murphy, *Europe and Northern Ireland's Future: Negotiating Brexit's Unique Case* (Columbia University Press, 2018); Sylvia de Mars, Colin Murray, Aoife O'Donoghue and Ben Warwick, *Bordering Two Unions: Northern Ireland and Brexit* (Policy Press, 2018).

40 See Tony Connelly, *Brexit and Ireland* (Penguin, 2017) 297–302; Dáil Debates, Leader's Questions, Taoiseach Enda Kenny, 2 May 2017, Vol 948, No 1.

41 [2019] OJ C66I/1. For the text of these, together with background negotiating documents, see <https://ec.europa.eu/ commission/brexit-negotiations_en>.

Withdrawal Agreement and approved the political declaration at a specially convened summit on 25 November.[42]

[3–33] In order to address the significant consequences of the UK's withdrawal for Northern Ireland, the Withdrawal Agreement has a dedicated Protocol on Ireland/Northern Ireland. The Protocol includes provision for a so-called "backstop", aimed at preventing a hard border on the island of Ireland should this not be achieved through the UK's future relationship with the EU. As eventually agreed upon, the backstop requires that the operation of a single customs territory comprising the EU and the UK. In addition, the Protocol enshrines a commitment to no diminution of rights as set out in the Good Friday Agreement,[43] provides for the continuation of the Common Travel Area arrangements between Ireland and the UK,[44] ensures that the necessary conditions for continued North–South cooperation are maintained,[45] and preserves the Single Electricity Market on the island of Ireland. The provisions of the Protocol are as follows:

Art 1	Objectives and relationship to subsequent agreement
Art 2	Subsequent agreement
Art 3	Extension of transition period
Art 4	Rights of Individuals
Art 5	Common Travel Area
Art 6	Single Customs Territory, movement of goods
Art 7	Protection of the UK internal market
Art 8	Technical regulations, assessments, registrations, certificates, approvals, authorisations
Art 9	VAT and Excise
Art 10	Agriculture and environment
Art 11	Single electricity market
Art 12	State aid
Art 13	Other areas of North–South cooperation
Art 14	Implementation, application, supervision and enforcement
Art 15	Common provisions
Art 16	Specialised Committee
Art 17	Joint Consultative Working Group
Art 18	Safeguards
Art 19	Protection of Financial Interests
Art 20	Review
Art 21	Annexes

[3–34] The Protocol is highly complex in nature, which is perhaps unsurprising given the difficult and multi-faceted problem that it seeks to resolve. A useful summary of

42 Conclusions of the special meeting of the European Council (Art 50), 25 November 2018, EUCO XT 20015/18.

43 See Christopher McCrudden, "The Belfast–Good Friday Agreement, Brexit, and Rights", Royal Irish Academy – British Academy Brexit Briefing Paper Series, October 2017; Christopher McCrudden, "Brexit, Rights and the Ireland-Northern Ireland Protocol to the Withdrawal Agreement", Royal Irish Academy – British Academy Brexit Briefing Paper Series, December 2018.

44 See Imelda Maher, "Crossing the Irish Land Borders after Brexit: The Common Travel Area and the Challenge of Trade" (2016–2017) 11–12 *Irish Yearbook of International Law* 51; Gavin Barrett and Graham Butler, "Europe's 'Other' Open-Border Zone: The Common Travel Area under the Shadow of Brexit" (2018) 20 *Cambridge Yearbook of European Legal Studies* 252.

45 See European Commission, "Mapping of North-South cooperation and Implementation Bodies. Report and key findings of the exercise", 21 June 2019.

how the backstop is intended to operate is provided by a Commission explanatory document as follows:

> If an agreement on the future EU–UK relationship is not applicable by 31 December 2020, the EU and the UK have agreed that a backstop solution will apply until such a time as a subsequent agreement is in place.
>
> Alternatively, the UK may, before 1 July 2020, request an extension of the transition period. Such a request would be dealt with under Art 132 of the Withdrawal Agreement and must therefore be agreed by the Joint Committee.
>
> In the scenario where the "backstop solution" would apply, this would mean the following in practice:
>
> - There will be a single EU–UK customs territory. This will avoid the need for tariffs, quotas or checks on rules of origin between the EU and the UK.
> - The EU and the UK have agreed on a set of measures to ensure that there is a level playing field between the EU and the UK.
> - The Union's Customs Code, which sets out, inter alia, the provisions for releasing products into free circulation within the EU, will continue to apply to Northern Ireland. This will ensure that Northern Irish businesses will not face restrictions when placing products on the EU's Single Market.
> - The UK in respect of Northern Ireland will remain aligned to a limited set of rules that are related to the EU's Single Market and indispensable for avoiding a hard border: legislation on goods, sanitary rules for veterinary controls, rules on agricultural production/marketing, VAT and excise in respect of goods, and state aid rules.
>
> … a single EU–UK customs territory will apply from the end of the transition period until such a time as a subsequent agreement becomes applicable. This single customs territory will comprise of the customs territory of the Union … and the customs territory of the United Kingdom.
>
> This means that:
>
> - the UK will align the tariffs and rules applicable to its customs territory to the Union's external tariffs and rules of origin;
> - there will therefore be no tariffs, quotas and checks on rules of origin between the EU and the UK, with the exception of fishery and aquaculture products;
> - both the EU and the UK have agreed on a series of measures ensuring a level playing field;
> - the UK will harmonise its commercial policy with the EU's common commercial policy to the extent necessary for the functioning of the single customs territory. Under no circumstances can the UK apply a lower customs tariff to its customs territory than the EU Common Customs Tariff for any good imported from any third country or apply different rules of origin.
> - The Union shall apply its trade defence policy and Generalised System of Preferences to both parts of the single customs territory; it shall consult the UK on any measures or actions which it considers taking.[46]

[3–35] For a sizeable element of the governing Conservative Party, the "backstop"

[46] European Commission Fact Sheet, "Protocol on Ireland and Northern Ireland", 14 November 2018, MEMO/18/6423. On the consequences of not agreeing a withdrawal agreement see Eric Pickett and Michael Lux, "The Irish Land Border: Existing and Potential Customs Facilitations in a No-Deal Scenario", Northern Ireland Department for the Economy, 10 June 2019; Sam Lowe, "Northern Ireland and the backstop: Why 'alternative arrangements' aren't an alternative", Centre for European Reform, 29 May 2019.

was perceived as limiting the freedom of the UK to leave a customs arrangement with the EU and to pursue an independent trade policy. When attempts to have the Protocol renegotiated failed, attention turned to seeking binding assurances as to the temporary nature of the backstop, building on the shared intention that the future relationship between the UK and the EU should provide an alternative means of avoiding a hard border on the island of Ireland. In January 2019, letters were exchanged between the British Prime Minister and the Presidents of the European Council and the Commission in which it was confirmed that:

> if the backstop were nevertheless to be triggered, it would only apply temporarily, unless and until it is superseded by a subsequent agreement that ensures that a hard border is avoided, and that the European Union, in such a case, would use its best endeavours to negotiate and conclude expeditiously a subsequent agreement that would replace the backstop, and would expect the same of the United Kingdom, so that the backstop would only be in place for as long as strictly necessary.
>
> … As for the link between the Withdrawal Agreement and the Political Declaration … it can be made clear that these two documents, while being of a different nature, are part of the same negotiated package.

[3–36] In a further attempt to facilitate the House of Commons' approval of the Withdrawal Agreement, in March 2019 an Instrument relating to the Withdrawal Agreement and a Joint Statement supplementing the Political Declaration were agreed between the UK and the Commission and subsequently endorsed by the European Council on 21 March.[47] The European Council also agreed to a UK request to extend the two year negotiation period beyond the scheduled exit date of 29 March to 12 April 2019, if the Withdrawal Agreement had not been approved by the House of Commons, and 22 May 2019 if it had been approved.[48] When it continued to prove impossible to obtain approval of the Agreement in Westminster, on 10 April the European Council agreed to a further extension of the negotiation period until 31 October 2019.[49] A Council Decision was adopted to make the necessary technical changes to the Withdrawal Agreement to reflect this.[50]

[3–37] Assuming it is ratified by the UK, the Withdrawal Agreement will provide for a transition period, to last until 31 December 2020, during which the UK will no longer be an EU Member State but EU law will nevertheless continue to apply. This could be extended once, for a period of either one or two years.[51] In Irish law, such a transition period is provided for in s 98 of the Withdrawal of the United Kingdom from the European Union (Consequential Provisions) Act 2019. The remainder of this Act provides for a series of necessary amendments to the Irish statute book in the scenario that the UK leaves without ratifying the Withdrawal Agreement. A number of EU legal

---

47 Conclusions of the special meeting of the European Council (Art 50), 21 March 2019, EUCO XT 20004/19.

48 European Council Decision (EU) 2019/476 taken in agreement with the United Kingdom of 22 March 2019 extending the period under Article 50(3) TEU [2019] OJ L80I/1.

49 European Council Decision (EU) 2019/584 taken in agreement with the United Kingdom of 11 April 2019 extending the period under Article 50(3) TEU [2019] OJ L101/1; Conclusions of the special meeting of the European Council (Art 50), 10 April 2019, EUCO XT 20015/19.

50 Council Decision (EU) 2019/642 of 13 April 2019 [2019] OJ L110I/1.

51 Art 132 of the Withdrawal Agreement.

acts have also been adopted as a contingency for a "no-deal" scenario, together with the publication of a series of Commission Communications[52] and Stakeholders Notices.[53]

D. Treaty on the Functioning of the European Union

[3–38] The Treaty on the Functioning of the European Union (TFEU) is the new name for what was originally the 1957 EEC Treaty, or Treaty of Rome. Through successive treaty reforms, it has been altered and added to significantly. It is considerably longer than the TEU, containing 358 articles, as compared with the 55 found in the TEU. The articles are divided into seven parts, the longest of which by some measure is Part Three, which contains 170 articles and sets out the Union's polices and internal actions including the Internal Market, the free movement of goods, persons, services and capital, the Area of Freedom, Security and Justice, economic and monetary policy, competition rules and a whole host of sectoral policies such as agriculture, transport, employment, social policy, education, public health, energy and the environment.

PART ONE:	**PRINCIPLES**		*Art 1*
	Title I	**Categories and Areas of Union Competence**	*Art 2–6*
	Title II	**Provisions having General Application**	*Art 7–17*
PART TWO:	**NON-DISCRIMINATION AND CITIZENSHIP OF THE UNION**		*Art 18–25*
PART THREE:	**UNION POLICIES AND INTERNAL ACTIONS**		
	Title I	**The Internal Market**	*Art 26–27*
	Title II	**Free Movement of Goods**	*Art 28–29*
	Chapter 1 – The Customs Union		*Art 30–32*
	Chapter 2 – Customs Cooperation		*Art 33*
	Chapter 3 – Prohibition on Quantitative Restrictions between MS		*Art 34–37*
	Title III	**Agriculture and Fisheries**	*Art 38–44*
	Title IV	**Free Movement of Persons, Services and Capital**	
	Chapter 1 – Workers		*Art 45–48*
	Chapter 2 – Right of Establishment		*Art 49–55*
	Chapter 3 – Services		*Art 56–62*
	Chapter 4 – Capital and Payments		*Art 63–66*
	Title V	**Area of Freedom, Security and Justice**	
	Chapter 1 – General Provisions		*Art 67–76*
	Chapter 2 – Policies on Border Checks, Asylum and Immigration		*Art 77–80*
	Chapter 3 – Judicial Cooperation in Civil Matters		*Art 81*
	Chapter 4 – Judicial Cooperation in Criminal Matters		*Art 82–86*
	Chapter 5 – Police Cooperation		*Art 87–89*
	Title VI	**Transport**	*Art 90–100*
	Title VII	**Common Rules of Competition, Taxation and Approximation of Laws**	
	Chapter 1 – Rules on Competition		
		Section 1 – Rules Applying to Undertakings	*Art 101–106*
		Section 2 – Aids Granted by States	*Art 107–109*

[52] Commission Communication COM(2019) 276 final, 12 June 2019; Commission Communication COM(2019) 195 final, 10 April 2019; Commission Communication COM(2018) 890 final, 19 December 2018; Commission Communication COM(2018) 880 final, 13 November 2018; Commission Communication COM(2018) 556 final/2, 27 August 2018.

[53] See <https://ec.europa.eu/info/brexit/brexit-preparedness/preparedness-notices_en>.

	Chapter 2 – Legal Acts of the Union, Adoption Procedures etc	
	Section 1 – Legal Acts of the Union	*Art 288–292*
	Section 2 – Procedures for the Adoption of Acts	*Art 293–299*
	Chapter 3 – Union's Advisory Bodies	*Art 300*
	Section 1 – Economic and Social Committee	*Art 301–304*
	Section 2 – Committee of the Regions	*Art 305–307*
	Chapter 4 – European Investment Bank	*Art 308–309*
	Title II Financial Provisions	*Art 310*
	Chapter 1 – Union's Own Resources	*Art 311*
	Chapter 2 – Multiannual Financial Framework	*Art 312*
	Chapter 3 – Union's Annual Budget	*Art 313–316*
	Chapter 4 – Implementation of the Budget and Discharge	*Art 317–319*
	Chapter 5 – Common Provisions	*Art 320–324*
	Chapter 6 – Combatting Fraud	*Art 325*
	Title III Enhanced Cooperation	*Art 326–334*
PART SEVEN:	**GENERAL AND FINAL PROVISIONS**	*Art 335–358*

[3–39] Mirroring the opening of the TEU, Part One of the TFEU sets out the constitutional principles governing the Union. Articles 2 to 6 define the concepts of exclusive, shared and supporting competence, a topic that will be taken up in Chapter 9. Article 3(1) defines the five areas of EU exclusive competence, while Art 3(2) details the three ways in which the Union may have exclusive competence to enter into an international agreement.[54] By way of a default rule, Art 4 provides that other than those competences dealt with in Art 3 (exclusive) and Art 6 (supporting), all other competences conferred by the Treaties shall be shared. The article then sets out a non-exhaustive list of the principal areas in which shared competence applies. Similarly, Art 6 provides examples of some areas in which the Union is empowered to play a supplementing, supporting or coordinating role.

Exclusive Competence (Art 3)	**Shared Competence** (Art 4)	**Supporting, Coordinating Competence** (Art 6)
– Customs Union; – the establishing of the competition rules necessary for the functioning of the Internal Market; – monetary policy for the Member States whose currency is the euro; – the conservation of marine biological resources under the Common Fisheries Policy;	– Internal Market; – social policy; – economic, social and territorial cohesion; – agriculture and fisheries, excluding the conservation of marine biological resources; – environment; – consumer protection; – transport; – trans-European networks; – energy;	– protection and improvement of human health; – industry; – culture; – tourism; – education, vocational training, youth and sport; – civil protection; – administrative cooperation.

[54] The Union shall have exclusive competence for the conclusion of an international agreement when its conclusion is: (i) provided for in a legislative act of the Union; (ii) is necessary to enable the Union to exercise its internal competence; or (iii) in so far as its conclusion may affect common rules or alter their scope. On the Union's external competence to conclude agreements more generally see Case C-600/14 *Germany v Commission (OTIF)* EU:C:2017:935, 5 December 2017, paras 43-73.

– Common Commercial Policy; – the conclusion of an international agreement when its conclusion is provided for in a legislative act of the Union; – the conclusion of an international agreement when its conclusion is necessary to enable the Union to exercise its internal competence; – the conclusion of an international agreement in so far as its conclusion may affect common rules or alter their scope.	– area of freedom, security and justice; – common safety concerns in public health matters; – research, technological development and space (albeit that the exercise of Union competence does not prevent Member States from exercising theirs); – development cooperation and humanitarian aid (albeit that the exercise of Union competence does not prevent Member States from exercising theirs).	

[3–40] Other principles set out in Part One include certain directions that are to guide the Union in the conduct of its activities. For example, the Union is obliged to take into account requirements linked to: the promotion of a high level of employment, the guarantee of adequate social protection, the fight against social exclusion, and a high level of education, training and protection of human health (Art 9); the elimination of discrimination (Art 10); environmental protection (Art 11); consumer protection (Art 12) and animal welfare (Art 13). The importance of services of general economic interest is acknowledged in Art 14, while Art 15 outlines the Union's commitment to transparency and access to public documents and Art 16 guarantees the right to the protection of personal data.

[3–41] Part Two supplements Title II of the TEU in providing for a prohibition on discrimination on the grounds of nationality (Art 18), a legal base for Union action to combat discrimination based on sex, racial or ethnic origin, religion or belief, disability, age or sexual orientation (Art 19), and a number of articles detailing the rights that come with EU citizenship (Arts 20–25).

[3–42] Part Three contains the substantive rules governing the Internal Market and its Four Freedoms allowing for the free movement of goods, persons, services and capital. A separate title deals with common rules of competition, taxation and approximation of laws, each of which are considered necessary flanking measures in order to ensure the maintenance of an effective Internal Market. Title V of Part Three relates to the Area of Freedom, Security and Justice, in respect of which Ireland has a right to choose whether or not to opt-in to measures pursuant to Protocol No 21. Part Three also provides for the Union's economic and monetary policy, as well as the wide gamut of 24 other policy areas.

[3–43] Part Four consists of just seven articles and deals with the Union's association with non-European countries and territories which have special relations with Denmark, France, the Netherlands and the UK, as listed in Annex II to the TFEU. The purpose of association is to promote the economic and social development of the countries and territories and to establish close economic relations between them and the Union as a whole.

[3–44] Part Five expands further on Chapter I of Title V of the TEU, which sets out general principles on the EU's external action. It provides for the Common Commercial Policy, development cooperation, economic, financial and technical cooperation with third countries, humanitarian aid and the imposition of restrictive measures (ie sanctions). Article 218 is an important technical provision setting out the procedure to be followed by the Union in entering into international agreements. An innovation of the Lisbon Treaty, Art 222 is a new "solidarity clause" which provides that:

> 1. The Union and its Member States shall act jointly in a spirit of solidarity if a Member State is the object of a terrorist attack or the victim of a natural or man-made disaster. The Union shall mobilise all the instruments at its disposal, including the military resources made available by the Member States, to:
> (a) – prevent the terrorist threat in the territory of the Member States;
> – protect democratic institutions and the civilian population from any terrorist attack;
> – assist a Member State in its territory, at the request of its political authorities, in the event of a terrorist attack;
> (b) assist a Member State in its territory, at the request of its political authorities, in the event of a natural or man-made disaster.[55]

[3–45] Part Six details the rules governing the Union's seven institutions as well as its two advisory bodies – the Economic and Social Committee and the Committee of the Regions – and the procedures for the adoption of EU legal acts. It also regulates the Union's budget and financing through its "own resources" and provides detailed rules on enhanced cooperation.

[3–46] Lastly, Part Seven deals with final provisions, including matters such as the location of the seat of the institutions (Art 341), the languages of the institutions (Art 342) and the Union's privileges and immunities (Art 343). In Art 344, the Member States undertake not to submit a dispute concerning the interpretation or application of the Treaties to any method of settlement other than those provided for in the Treaties – a provision which Ireland has fallen foul of on one occasion.[56] Article 351 provides that the rights and obligations arising from agreements concluded before 1 January 1958 or, for acceding states, before the date of their accession, between one or more Member States on the one hand, and one or more third countries on the other, shall not be affected by the provisions of the Treaties. However, to the extent that such agreements

[55] See Council Decision of 24 June 2014 on the arrangements for the implementation by the Union of the solidarity clause (2014/415/EU) [2014] OJ L192/53; Philip Hilpold, "Filling a Buzzword with Life: The Implementation of the Solidarity Clause in Article 222 TFEU" (2015) 42 *Legal Issues of Economic Integration* 209.

[56] Case C-459/03 *Commission v Ireland* (*Mox Plant*) [2006] ECR I-4635, discussed further in ch 15, para [15–12]. See also the more recent judgment in Case C-284/16 *Slovakia v Achmea* EU:C:2018:158, 6 March 2018 in which it was held that Art 267 TFEU (providing for the preliminary reference procedure) and Art 344 TFEU preclude a provision in an international agreement between Member States under which an investor from one of the Member States, in the event of a dispute concerning investments in the other Member State, may bring proceedings against that Member State before an arbitral tribunal, the jurisdiction of which the Member States have undertaken to accept. See Cristina Contartese and Mads Andenas, "EU Autonomy and Investor State Dispute Settlement between EU Member States: *Achmea*" (2019) 56 *Common Market Law Review* 157.

are not compatible with the Treaties, a Member State shall take all appropriate steps to eliminate the incompatibilities established.

[3–47] Somewhat hidden within Part Seven, Art 352 provides a residual legislative competence to the Union in respect of any EU policy other than CFSP. Known as the "flexibility clause", it states that if action by the Union should prove necessary, within the framework of the policies defined in the Treaties, to attain one of the objectives set out in the Treaties, and the Treaties have not provided the necessary powers, the Council, acting unanimously on a proposal from the Commission and after obtaining the consent of the European Parliament, shall adopt the appropriate measures.[57]

E. Charter of Fundamental Rights

[3–48] The Charter of Fundamental Rights is annexed to the TEU and TFEU and, according to Art 6 TEU, has the same legal value as the Treaties.[58] The Charter consists of 54 articles divided into seven titles. The first three titles (Dignity, Freedoms and Equality) and Title VI (Justice) deal, in the main, with the more traditional civil and political rights, although Title III includes provisions on the rights of children and the elderly, and the integration of persons with disabilities. Title IV, Solidarity, is primarily concerned with workers' rights, but also includes provisions on health care, consumer protection, environmental protection and access to services of a general economic interest. Title V largely replicates provisions of the TEU and TFEU setting out the rights of EU citizens such as the right to vote, to move amongst Member States and to avail of consular protection.

Title I – Dignity

Art 1 – Human dignity
Art 2 – Right to life
Art 3 – Right to the integrity of the person
Art 4 – Prohibition of torture and inhuman or degrading treatment or punishment
Art 5 – Prohibition of slavery and forced labour

Title II – Freedoms

---

57 This is discussed further in ch 9, paras [9–04] to [9–07].

58 For an account of the development of human rights as an element of EU law leading up to the Charter, see James Kingston, "Human Rights and the European Union – An Evolving System" in Mary Catherine Lucey and Cathrina Keville (eds), *Irish Perspectives on EC Law* (Round Hall, 2003) 271; Nial Fennelly, "Pillar Talk: Fundamental Rights Protection in the European Union" (2008) 8 *Judicial Studies Institute Journal* 95; Sionaidh Douglas-Scott, "A Tale of Two Courts: Luxembourg, Strasbourg and the Growing European Human Rights *Acquis*" (2006) 43 *Common Market Law Review* 629. See also Síofra O'Leary, "A Tale of Two Cities: Fundamental Rights Protection in Strasbourg and Luxembourg" (2018) 20 *Cambridge Yearbook of European Legal Studies* 3; Síofra O'Leary, "Courts, charters and conventions: making sense of fundamental rights in the EU" (2016) 56 *Irish Jurist* 4; Sionaidh Douglas-Scott, "The European Union and Human Rights after the Treaty of Lisbon" (2011) 11 *Human Rights Law Review* 645; Sara Iglesias Sánchez, "The Court and the Charter: The Impact of the Entry into Force of the Lisbon Treaty on the ECJ's Approach to Fundamental Rights" (2012) 49 *Common Market Law Review* 1565; Gráinne de Búrca, "After the EU Charter of Fundamental Rights: The Court of Justice as a Human Rights Adjudicator?" (2013) 20 *Maastricht Journal of European and Comparative Law* 168; T John O'Dowd, "Boston or Berlin? EU Charter of Fundamental Rights: Some Irish Perspectives" (2002) 14 *European Review of Public Law* 427.

Art 6 – Right to liberty and security
Art 7 – Respect for private and family life
Art 8 – Protection of personal data
Art 9 – Right to marry and right to found a family
Art 10 – Freedom of thought, conscience and religion
Art 11 – Freedom of expression and information
Art 12 – Freedom of assembly and of association
Art 13 – Freedom of the arts and sciences
Art 14 – Right to education
Art 15 – Freedom to choose an occupation and right to engage in work
Art 16 – Freedom to conduct a business
Art 17 – Right to property
Art 18 – Right to asylum
Art 19 – Protection in the event of removal, expulsion or extradition

Title III – Equality

Art 20 – Equality before the law
Art 21 – Non-discrimination
Art 22 – Cultural, religious and linguistic diversity
Art 23 – Equality between men and women
Art 24 – The rights of the child
Art 25 – The rights of the elderly
Art 26 – Integration of persons with disabilities

Title IV – Solidarity

Art 27 – Workers' right to information and consultation within the undertaking
Art 28 – Right of collective bargaining and action
Art 29 – Right of access to placement services
Art 30 – Protection in the event of unjustified dismissal
Art 31 – Fair and just working conditions
Art 32 – Prohibition of child labour and protection of young people at work
Art 33 – Family and professional life
Art 34 – Social security and social assistance
Art 35 – Health care
Art 36 – Access to services of general economic interest
Art 37 – Environmental protection
Art 38 – Consumer protection

Title V – Citizens' rights

Art 39 – Right to vote and to stand as a candidate at elections to the European Parliament
Art 40 – Right to vote and to stand as a candidate at municipal elections
Art 41 – Right to good administration
Art 42 – Right of access to documents
Art 43 – European Ombudsman
Art 44 – Right to petition
Art 45 – Freedom of movement and of residence
Art 46 – Diplomatic and consular protection

Title VI – Justice

Art 47 – Right to an effective remedy and to a fair trial
Art 48 – Presumption of innocence and right of defence
Art 49 – Principles of legality and proportionality of criminal offences and penalties
Art 50 – Right not to be tried or punished twice in criminal proceedings for the same criminal offence

Title VII – General Provisions governing interpretation and application of the Charter

Art 51 – Field of application
Art 52 – Scope and interpretation of rights and principles

Art 53 – Level of protection
Art 54 – Prohibition of abuse of rights

[3–49] Guidance as to the proper interpretation of the Charter is set out in Title VII. First, Art 51 clarifies that the Charter is addressed to the institutions, bodies, offices and agencies of the Union with due regard for the principle of subsidiarity and to the Member States *only when they are implementing Union law*. Secondly, Art 52 establishes that, in so far as the Charter contains rights which correspond to rights guaranteed by the European Convention of Human Rights, the meaning and scope of those rights shall be the same as those laid down by the Convention. Thirdly, an important distinction is drawn between "rights" and "principles". A right or freedom provided for in the Charter may only be limited: (i) as provided for by law; (ii) while respecting the essence of the right or freedom; and (iii) as is genuinely necessary and proportionate in order to meet objectives of general interest recognised by the Union or the need to protect the rights and freedoms of others. In contrast, *principles* are only judicially cognisable in the interpretation, or ruling on the legality, of legislative and executive acts taken by EU institutions, bodies, offices and agencies in order to implement the principles, and by acts of Member States when implementing Union law.

[3–50] Additional guidance is provided by the "Explanations" prepared under the authority of the Praesidium of the Convention which drafted the Charter.[59] Although they do not have the status of law, they are a valuable tool of interpretation intended to clarify the meaning of the Charter's provisions. Indeed, Art 52(7) mandates that the Explanations shall be given due regard by the courts of the Union and of the Member States. The Explanations seek to clarify the distinction between rights and principles as follows:

> [S]ubjective rights shall be *respected*, whereas principles shall be *observed* (Article 51(1)). Principles may be implemented through legislative or executive acts (adopted by the Union in accordance with its powers, and by the Member States only when they implement Union law); accordingly, they become significant for the Courts only when such acts are interpreted or reviewed. They do not however give rise to direct claims for positive action by the Union's institutions or Member States authorities. This is consistent both with case-law of the Court of Justice … and with the approach of the Member States' constitutional systems to 'principles', particularly in the field of social law. ... In some cases, an Article of the Charter may contain both elements of a right and of a principle.[60]

[3–51] Fourthly, Art 53 provides that nothing in the Charter shall be interpreted as restricting or adversely affecting human rights and fundamental freedoms as recognised, in their respective fields of application, by: (i) EU law and international law; (ii) international agreements to which the EU or all the Member States are party, including the European Convention on Human Rights; and (iii) the Member States' constitutions.

[3–52] An important question in applying the Charter is that of determining its proper scope of application. Here, unhelpfully, the terms of the Charter and the Explanations differ. Whereas Art 51 provides that the Charter is addressed to Member States only when they are *implementing* Union law, the Explanations state that "it follows unambiguously from the case-law of the Court of Justice that the requirement to respect fundamental

---

59 Explanations relating to the Charter of Fundamental Rights [2007] OJ C303/17.

60 *ibid*, Explanation on Art 52.

rights defined in the context of the Union is only binding on the Member States when they *act in the scope of* Union law".[61]

[3–53] On the same day in February 2013, differently constituted Grand Chambers of the Court of Justice delivered two important judgments clarifying the Charter's scope. In *Åkerberg Fransson*, the Court was required to consider whether the Charter applied in circumstances where one Swedish authority imposed a fine on Mr Åkerberg Fransson for submitting false tax returns, including avoiding payments of VAT, and a second authority subsequently initiated criminal proceeding for tax offences.[62] Article 50 of the Charter guarantees the right not to be tried or punished twice in criminal proceedings for the same criminal offence.

[3–54] Ireland was among five Member States to intervene in the case and argue that the imposition of the fine did not entail the implementation of EU law, such that the Charter did not apply. The Grand Chamber rejected this argument by turning to the Explanations as support for a broad interpretation of the phrase "implementing Union law", to include all situations governed by EU law. In its view:

> Since the fundamental rights guaranteed by the Charter must ... be complied with where national legislation falls within the scope of European Union law, situations cannot exist which are covered in that way by European Union law without those fundamental rights being applicable. The applicability of European Union law entails applicability of the fundamental rights guaranteed by the Charter.
>
> Where, on the other hand, a legal situation does not come within the scope of European Union law, the Court does not have jurisdiction to rule on it and any provisions of the Charter relied upon cannot, of themselves, form the basis for such jurisdiction.[63]

[3–55] In applying this test to the facts, the Grand Chamber was satisfied that the conduct of the Swedish authorities fell within the scope of EU law, notwithstanding that the relevant Swedish law under which the fine was imposed did not specifically transpose the VAT Directive. First, the VAT Directive imposed an obligation on Member States to take the necessary measures to collect VAT and prevent evasion. Secondly, Art 325 TFEU obliged Member States to counter fraudulent activities that may affect the financial interests of the Union in the same way as they protect their own interests. Thirdly, VAT formed part of the EU's Own Resources, comprising a direct link between national provisions for the collection of VAT and the EU's financial interests. As a result, "tax penalties and criminal proceedings for tax evasion, such as those to which the defendant ... has been or is subject because the information concerning VAT that was provided was false, constitute implementation of [the VAT] Directive and of Article 325 TFEU and, therefore, of European Union law, for the purposes of Article 51(1) of the Charter".[64]

---

[61] See Michael Dougan, "Judicial Review of Member State Action under the General Principles and the Charter: Defining the 'Scope of Union Law'" (2015) 22 *Common Market Law Review* 1201; Koen Lenaerts, "Exploring the Limits of the EU Charter of Fundamental Rights" (2012) 8 *European Constitutional Law Review* 375.

[62] Case C-617/10 *Åkerberg Fransson* EU:C:2013:105, 26 February 2013.

[63] *ibid*, paras 21–22.

[64] *ibid*, para 27. See Daniel Sarmiento, "Who's Afraid of the Charter? The Court of Justice, National Courts and the new Framework of Fundamental Rights Protection in Europe" (2013) 50 *Common Market Law Review* 1267; Emily Hancox, "The Meaning of 'Implementing' EU Law under Article

[3–56] Delivered on the same day, the judgment in *Melloni* addressed Art 53 of the Charter and the slightly different question of whether that article allowed Member States to apply a higher domestic standard of fundamental rights protection when a matter fell within the scope of EU law. In that case, Mr Melloni had been convicted *in absentia* by an Italian court for a fraud offence and an appeal by his lawyers had been dismissed. Mr Melloni was later arrested in Spain and his surrender to Italy ordered on foot of a European Arrest Warrant. He appealed the surrender order on the basis that the right to a fair trial, as enshrined in the Spanish constitution, had been interpreted by the Spanish courts to mean that a person could only be surrendered on foot of an *in absentia* conviction if there was the possibility of having the conviction reviewed. In contrast, the EAW Framework Decision specifically provided that a surrender on foot of an *in absentia* conviction could not be refused if a person had been duly represented during his trial.

[3–57] The Grand Chamber placed reliance on the supremacy of EU law, as originally set out in the case of *Internationale Handelsgesellschaft*, to conclude that Art 53 could not be interpreted as allowing a Member State to disapply EU legal rules which are fully in compliance with the Charter on the basis that they nonetheless infringe fundamental rights guaranteed by that state's constitution. By virtue of the principle of supremacy of EU law, which was an essential feature of the EU legal order, rules of national law, even of a constitutional order, could not be allowed to undermine the effectiveness of EU law on the territory of that state. As a result, the freedom afforded to Member States under Art 53 to apply their own fundamental rights standards was subject to the critical caveat that the level of protection provided for by the Charter, and the primacy, unity and effectiveness of EU law, were not thereby to be compromised.[65] On the facts of the case, the Grand Chamber concluded that the standard set by the EAW Framework Decision as regards *in absentia* trials could not be departed from, reasoning as follows:

> [The EAW] framework decision effects a harmonisation of the conditions of execution of a European arrest warrant in the event of a conviction rendered *in absentia*, which reflects the consensus reached by all the Member States regarding the scope to be given under EU law to the procedural rights enjoyed by persons convicted in absentia who are the subject of a European arrest warrant.
>
> Consequently, allowing a Member State to avail itself of Article 53 of the Charter to make the surrender of a person convicted in absentia conditional upon the conviction being open to review in the issuing Member State, a possibility not provided for under [the] Framework Decision, in order to avoid an adverse effect on the right to a fair trial and the rights of the defence guaranteed by the constitution of the executing Member State, by casting doubt on the uniformity of the standard of protection of fundamental rights as defined in that framework decision, would undermine the principles of mutual trust and recognition which that decision purports to uphold and would, therefore, compromise the efficacy of that framework decision.[66]

[3–58] The nature of the effect that the Charter enjoys in the domestic legal systems of the Member States is discussed further in Chapter 11. It is worth noting here,

---

51(1) of the Charter: *Åkerberg Fransson*" (2013) 50 *Common Market Law Review* 1411; Stephen Brittain, "The EU Charter of Fundamental Rights and the Member States: An Originalist Analysis" (2013) 36 *Dublin University Law Journal* 277.

[65] Case C-399/11 *Melloni* EU:C:2013:107, 23 February 2013, para 60.

[66] *ibid*, paras 62–63. See Nik de Boer, "Addressing Rights Divergences under the Charter: *Melloni*" (2013) 50 *Common Market Law Review* 1083.

however, that a number of significant judgments interpreting the Charter have resulted from preliminary references from the Irish courts. For example, in *Digital Rights Ireland Ltd*, the High Court made a preliminary reference asking whether the Data Retention Directive, which required electronic communication services providers, such as mobile phone companies, to retain certain data so that it might be available to assist in the investigation of serious crime, was compatible with the rights to privacy, protection of personal data, freedom of expression and good administration enshrined in the Charter.[67] The Directive was found to be invalid on the basis that it exceeded the limits imposed by compliance with the principle of proportionality in light of the Charter rights to privacy and protection of personal data. The Directive was viewed by the Court of Justice as entailing a wide-ranging and particularly serious interference with those rights, without being precisely circumscribed by provisions to ensure that the interference was limited to what was strictly necessary.

[3–59] Data protection was also at issue in a reference by the High Court in *Schrems v Data Protection Commissioner*.[68] There, the Court of Justice was asked for guidance as to whether the Irish Data Protection Commissioner ought to abide by an existing determination by the European Commission that the United States provided an adequate level of protection over personal data transferred from the EU to the United States or whether, in light of the Charter, the Data Protection Commissioner ought to be required to make her own, independent assessment. Mr Schrems argued that in light of leaked material made available by Edward Snowden, the level of protection afforded by the US was not sufficient, such that the Data Protection Commissioner ought not to allow his personal data, kept by Facebook Ireland, to be sent to Facebook Inc in the US. The Court of Justice concluded that the fact that the European Commission had made a prior determination that the protection of data in the US was adequate did not prevent a national supervisory authority, such as the Data Protection Commissioner, from examining a claim such as that made by Mr Schrems. If it were otherwise the case, persons whose personal data could be transferred to the third country concerned would be denied the right, guaranteed by Art 8 of the Charter, to lodge with the national supervisory authorities a claim for the purpose of protecting their fundamental rights.[69] On foot of a further complaint by Mr Schrems to the Data Protection Commissioner, the Commissioner brought proceedings against Facebook Ireland in which she successfully sought the making of another preliminary reference from the High Court, this time concerning the validity of certain Commission decisions regarding the transfer of data

---

[67] Case C-293/12 *Digital Rights Ireland Ltd v Minister for Communications, Marine and Natural Resources* EU:C:2014:238, 8 April 2014. See Andrew Roberts, "Privacy, Data Retention and Domination: *Digital Rights Ireland Ltd v Minister for Communications*" 78 (2015) *Modern Law Review* 535; Maria Helen Murphy, "Data Retention in the Aftermath of *Digital Rights Ireland* and *Seitlinger*" (2014) 24 *Irish Criminal Law Journal* 105; Marie-Pierre Granger and Kristina Irion, "The Court of Justice and the Data Retention Directive in *Digital Rights Ireland*: Telling Off the EU Legislator and Teaching a Lesson in Privacy and Data Protection" (2014) 39 *European Law Review* 835.

[68] Case C-362/14 *Schrems v Data Protection Commissioner* EU:C:2015:650, 6 October 2015. See Loïc Azoulai and Marijn van der Sluis, "Institutionalizing Personal Data Protection in Times of Global Institutional Distrust: *Schrems*" (2016) 53 *Common Market Law Review* 1343; Andrea Mulligan, "Constitutional Aspects of International Data Transfer and Mass Surveillance" (2016) 55 *Irish Jurist* 199, 199–208; Sergio Carrera and Elspeth Guild, "The End of Safe Harbor: What Future for EU–US Data Transfers?" (2015) 22 *Maastricht Journal of European and Comparative Law* 651.

[69] *ibid*, para 58.

to the United States in light of EU law, and the Charter's guarantee of a right to an effective remedy in particular.[70] Finally, although not involving a reference, in *Dwyer v Commissioner of An Garda Síochána*, the High Court granted a declaration that provisions of the Communications (Retention of Data) Act 2011, which allowed for the use in criminal proceedings of mobile phone data kept by service providers, were inconsistent with a data protection directive read in light of the Charter's guarantee of the respect for private and family life and the protection of personal data.[71]

[3–60] In *MM v Minister for Justice* the Court of Justice placed significant reliance on the Charter's guarantee of the right to be heard and to have an effective remedy in answering a preliminary reference from the High Court on the interpretation of the Qualification Directive relating to persons applying for refugee status or who are otherwise in need of international protection.[72] Although a second preliminary reference would be required in order to clarify precisely what the right to be heard entailed, in answer to the first reference the Court of Justice emphasised that when a Member State has chosen to establish two separate procedures, one following upon the other, for examining asylum applications and applications for subsidiary protection, "it is important that the applicant's right to be heard, in view of its fundamental nature, be fully guaranteed in each of those two procedures".[73]

[3–61] A final example of an Irish reference concerning the Charter is *Donnellan v Revenue Commissioners*.[74] Mr Donnellan, who was employed as truck driver, was convicted in Greece of transporting contraband cigarettes in a consignment of olive oil that was destined for Ireland. On appeal, he was acquitted. Seven years later, Greek customs authorities issued a notice concerning their intention to fine him an administrative penalty of over €1 million. Although a letter was sent to him from the Greek Embassy in Dublin informing him of important documents requiring his attention, the High Court accepted that this letter was not received by him. Some months later, the Greek authorities proceeded to issue the fine, notice of which was published in the official journal of Greece. A further three years later, Greek authorities sought to rely on an EU directive to request the assistance of the Revenue Commissioners in enforcing recovery of the claim. That directive included a rule whereby disputes concerning the validity of a claim, or the notification of a claim, could only be contested in the Member State seeking the assistance, and not in the Member State from whom assistance was requested.

[3–62] In making the request for assistance, the Greek authorities indicated that the claim was not contested and could no longer be contested by a court appeal. Upon being notified of the claim by the Revenue Commissioners, Mr Donnellan contested

---

70 *Data Protection Commissioner v Facebook Ireland Ltd* [2017] IEHC 545, 3 October 2017, Costello J.

71 [2019] 1 ILRM 461; [2019] 1 ILRM 523. The judgment is under appeal to the Supreme Court [2019] IESCDET 108, 28 May 2019.

72 Case C-277/11 *MM v Minister for Justice, Equality and Law Reform* EU:C:2012:744, 22 November 2012.

73 *ibid*, paras 91–92. The precise meaning of the Court's ruling, and whether a right to be heard required an oral hearing in particular, was the matter of further litigation upon the case's return to Dublin, leading to a second reference. See *MM v Minister for Justice and Equality* [2013] 1 IR 370 (High Court); Case C-560/14 EU:C:2017:101, 9 February 2017; [2018] 1 ILRM 361 (Supreme Court).

74 Case C-34/17 *Donnellan v Revenue Commissioners* EU:C:2018:282, 26 April 2018.

the recovery procedure in the Irish High Court, claiming that as the letter from the Greek Embassy was never delivered to him he had been denied an effective remedy in Greece. In those circumstances, he claimed that the Revenue Commissioners could not proceed with the recovery process. In contrast, the Revenue Commissioner took the view that, in line with the directive, Mr Donnellan would have to bring a challenge in Greece in order to test the validity of the assistance request made. The High Court sought a preliminary ruling on the question of whether the right to an effective remedy under Art 47 of the Charter precluded it from giving effect to the recovery request.

[3–63] The Court of Justice accepted that, in line with the directive, a challenge to the validity of a claim would have to be taken in the requesting state. Nevertheless, the Court went on to hold that, in exceptional circumstances, a requested state may decline to provide assistance if enforcement would be contrary to its public policy. The Court recalled that, in order to be able to exercise one's right to an effective legal remedy within the meaning of Art 47 of the Charter, a person concerned must know the reasons upon which the decision affecting his or her interests has been taken. Accordingly, respect for the rights laid down in Art 47 required not only that a person receive notice of a decision, but also that he is able to understand completely the meaning of the action brought against him in the requesting state. In the Court's view, therefore,

> in the case where a request for recovery is presented, even though the person concerned has not had the opportunity to raise the matter before the courts of the applicant Member State under conditions compatible with the fundamental right to an effective remedy, the rule laid down [in the directive], as transposed into national law, cannot reasonably be invoked against that person.
>
> That is *a fortiori* so where, as in the present case, the applicant authority itself indicated, in the request for recovery, and therefore at a point in time earlier than that at which the person concerned became aware of the existence of the claim in question, that it was no longer possible to bring administrative or judicial proceedings in the applicant Member State with a view to contesting that claim. …
>
> It follows from the foregoing that an exceptional situation such as that at issue … in the present case, in which an authority of a Member State requests an authority of another Member State to recover a claim relating to a fine of which the person concerned was unaware, may legitimately lead to a refusal of assistance with the recovery by that latter authority. The assistance provided for in [the directive] is, as is indicated by the title and various recitals of that directive, described as 'mutual', which implies, in particular, that it is for the applicant authority to create, before it makes a request for recovery, the conditions under which the requested authority will be able to grant its assistance in a meaningful manner and in conformity with the fundamental principles of EU law.[75]

---

[75] *ibid*, paras 58–61. Compatibility with the Charter was also at issue in Case C-363/12 *Z* EU:C:2014:159, 18 March 2014, where a preliminary reference was made by the Equality Tribunal as to the proper interpretation of the Equal Treatment Directive and the Employment Equality Directive. A teacher who was unable to give birth arranged to have a child born by surrogacy and, following the birth, applied for maternity leave. Finding that Ms Z was not entitled to either maternity leave, as she had not given birth, or adoptive leave, as she had not adopted a child, such leave was refused (with certain other leave arrangements put in place). The Equality Tribunal sought a determination from the Court of Justice as to whether, in light of the Charter's provisions on equal treatment for men and women and the integration of persons with disabilities, there was discrimination within the meaning of either Directive if a woman in Ms Z's position was refused the equivalent of maternity leave. The Court concluded that there was no discrimination between men and women given that Irish fathers of children born by surrogacy were treated in the same

[3–64] In examining recourse to the Charter by Irish courts from the entry into force of the Lisbon Treaty on 1 December 2009 to November 2012, Gráinne de Búrca identified 69 High and Supreme Court cases, one Labour Court and one Equality Tribunal case in which the Charter was referred to.[76] By topic, 28 of these were immigration cases, 19 criminal (mostly concerning the European Arrest Warrant), seven custody and four civil. A more recent review has reached similar findings. Between 2006 and 2014, by far the provisions of the Charter referred to most frequently in judgments of the Superior Courts were the right to an effective remedy and a fair trial (29), the rights of the child (29) and the right to respect for private and family life (20), followed by the right to good administration (13).[77] Drawing on her analysis, de Búrca reached a number of tentative conclusions, albeit acknowledging that the Charter's relatively new legal force, and the question marks over its proper scope of application, may account for some of these:

> [R]ather than examining specific arguments based on particular violations of the Charter, the Irish courts have largely tended to sideline or ignore these arguments and to decide the cases on the grounds of domestic law. … Thus, even where applicant's counsel raised a Charter argument, the court more often than not would only briefly address the provisions allegedly breached. Indeed, the Irish courts have thus far only rarely actually applied the Charter in the cases in which it is raised before them, and even where they did, they did not generally do so in a way which suggested that the Charter was a central aspect of the court's decision. In quite a number of cases, the Charter was invoked by one of the parties but the court simply ignored these arguments altogether. Further, the Irish courts appear to be more comfortable making use of the provisions of the [European Convention on Human Rights] and the case law of the Strasbourg court, in cases in which both the Charter and the ECHR are cited, than they are using the Charter and the case law of the Luxembourg court. This is interesting for a number of reasons, including the fact that the Irish courts in the past were more receptive to EU law than to ECHR law, and that the Charter currently has a somewhat stronger legal force – even if a more limited scope of application – in Irish law than the ECHR.[78]

Timeline

15 December 2001	Laeken Declaration on the Future of the European Union adopted by the European Council
28 February 2002	Opening session of the Convention on the Future of Europe
1 May 2004	Membership of the EU rises to 25 through accession of Czech Republic,

fashion. It also held that Ms Z's inability to give birth was not a disability within the meaning of the Employment Equality Directive. As a result, the Court did not consider it necessary to assess the validity of the Directives in light of the Charter's provisions.

76 Gráinne de Búrca, "The Domestic Impact of the EU Charter of Fundamental Rights" (2013) 49 *Irish Jurist* 49, 61.

77 Suzanne Kingston and Liam Thornton, "A Report on the Application of the European Commission on the Human Rights Act 2003 and the European Charter of Fundamental Rights: Evaluations and Review", Law Society of Ireland, Dublin Solicitors Bar Association, 2015.

78 *ibid*, 62–63. On the relationship between the Charter and the European Convention on Human Rights, see Síofra O'Leary, "A Tale of Two Cities: Fundamental Rights Protection in Strasbourg and Luxembourg" (2018) 20 *Cambridge Yearbook of European Legal Studies* 3; Síofra O'Leary, "Courts, Charters and Conventions: Making Sense of Fundamental Rights in the EU" (2016) 56 *Irish Jurist* 4; Christopher McCrudden, "Using Comparative Reasoning in Human Rights Adjudication: The Court of Justice of the European Union and the European Court of Human Rights Compared" (2013) 15 *Cambridge Yearbook of European Legal Studies* 383.

	Cyprus, Estonia, Hungary, Latvia, Lithuania, Malta, Poland, Slovenia and Slovakia
29 October 2004	Signing of the Constitutional Treaty
29 May 2005	Referendum in the Netherlands rejects ratification of the Constitutional Treaty
1 June 2005	Referendum in France rejects ratification of the Constitutional Treaty
1 January 2007	Bulgaria and Romania accede to the EU, bringing the membership to 27
13 December 2007	Signing of the Lisbon Treaty
12 June 2008	Referendum rejects ratification of the Lisbon Treaty by 53 per cent to 47 per cent
18–19 June 2009	Decision of the Heads of State or Government on the Concerns of the Irish People adopted, together with a Solemn Declaration of the European Council on Workers' Rights, Social Policy and Other Issues and a National Declaration by Ireland (on neutrality)
2 October 2009	Second referendum approves ratification of the Lisbon Treaty by 67 per cent to 33 per cent
1 December 2009	Entry into force of the Lisbon Treaty
26 February 2013	Judgments of the Court of Justice in *Åkerberg Fransson* and *Melloni*
1 December 2014	Entry into force of the Protocol on the Concerns of the Irish People on the Lisbon Treaty
18–19 February 2016	Heads of State and Government, meeting at the European Council, agree a "New Settlement for the United Kingdom", to take effect upon the UK informing that it has decided to remain within the EU
23 June 2016	In a referendum, the UK votes by 52 per cent to 48 per cent to leave the EU
29 March 2017	The UK submits notification of its intention to leave from the EU, triggering the two year withdrawal process provided for under Art 50 TEU
29 April 2017	European Council adopts Guidelines on UK Withdrawal negotiations and includes within its minutes a declaration on the eventuality of a united Ireland
17 November 2017	European Pillar of Social Rights proclaimed by the European Parliament, the Commission and the Council
7 December 2017	Ireland notifies of its intention to participate in Permanent Structured Cooperation (PESCO) in CSDP matters
8 December 2017	Publication of Joint Progress Report on the UK Withdrawal negotiations, which includes a commitment to a "backstop" to prevent a hard border on the island of Ireland
25 November 2018	European Council endorses draft EU–UK Withdrawal Agreement, providing for a transition period to end on 31 December 2020, with the possibility of one extension for either one or two years, and a Protocol on Ireland/Northern Ireland, and approves the Political Declaration on a future relationship with the UK
22 March 2019	European Council and UK agree to extend the UK's membership of the EU until 12 April 2019 and European Council endorses an Instrument relating

	to the Withdrawal Agreement and a Joint Statement supplementing the Political Declaration
10 April 2019	European Council and UK agree to extend the UK's membership of the EU until 31 October 2019.

PART TWO

CHAPTER 4

THE EUROPEAN COUNCIL

A. INTRODUCTION

[4–01] The European Council is the forum in which the leaders of the Member States meet on a regular basis in order to hold high-level discussions on the state and future development of the European Union and its economy, as well as to exchange views on ongoing political events within the Union and globally. Initially, the 1957 Treaty of Rome did not provide for such gatherings, and so they were organised on an ad hoc basis as the need arose, with eight such meetings held throughout the 1960s and early 1970s. In 1974 it was decided that they should be formalised, with the first meeting of the European Council, as such, taking place in Dublin Castle in March 1975.

[4–02] The European Council was eventually given legal recognition by the Single European Act of 1986, although it was chosen not to go so far as to include it among the list of the institutions of the EEC. As a result, its precise legal status remained unclear until 1 December 2009, when the Lisbon Treaty regularised its position by making the European Council one of the EU's seven institutions. This formalisation has been described as merely taking stock of the "pre-Lisbon reality of a Union where the European Council has progressively emerged as the decisive player when strategic or controversial decisions ought to be taken",[1] and as "consecrating its role as the only institution which has overall political leadership on all EU affairs".[2]

[4–03] The European Council is the Union's most senior political body, providing it with overall direction, deciding upon changes to the EU itself and resolving disagreements that cannot be resolved at a lower level. It is important to distinguish it from the similarly named Council of the European Union, which is made up of representatives from each Member State at *ministerial* level (and used to be known as the Council of Ministers). Given that it is tasked with providing high-level political direction to the EU as a whole, including in relation to its future direction and possible changes to the Treaties, the European Council is not limited in its discussions to considering

[1] Laurent Pech, "The Institutional Development of the EU Post-Lisbon: A Case of *plus ça change*...?" in Diamond Ashiagbor, Nicola Countouris and Ionannis Lianos (eds), *The European Union after the Treaty of Lisbon*, (Cambridge University Press, 2012) 24.

[2] Jean-Claude Piris, *The Lisbon Treaty* (Cambridge University Press, 2010) 208.

only matters that fall within the scope of the EU's competence in the same way as is the Council of the European Union.

B. Meetings of the European Council

[4–04] While the position of President of the European Council now gives it a degree of permanence, the European Council is unique among the EU's seven institutions in that it takes the form of short, regularly convened meetings (often referred to as "summits"), rather than an institution operating on a day-to-day basis in the more traditional sense. For example, one might hear expressions such as there "will be a European Council next month", or that "six European Councils were held last year". It is, therefore, an institution that takes the form of convened meetings. It used to meet in a city of the Member State holding the six-month rotating Presidency (always Dublin in Ireland's case), and often came to be known by reference to that city. Since 2003, however, all formal meetings of the European Council take place in Brussels, with a new dedicated premises – the Europa Building – opened in 2017. The European Council is assisted by a relatively small administrative staff within the General Secretariat of the Council.

[4–05] The European Council consists solely of a very select group of individuals: the heads of state or government of each Member State, the President of the European Council and the President of the Commission, although the latter two do not participate in any vote. The High Representative of the Union for Foreign Affairs and Security Policy also takes part in the work of the European Council without having a vote – a remnant of the fact that, when the EU had fewer Member States, foreign ministers also attended the European Council.

[4–06] European Council meetings are usually held over a two-day period and, by a custom dating from 1988, begin with an address by the President of the European Parliament. Other than a very small number of EU officials, no one else attends the meeting and this characteristic has been described as its essence: "a limited number of political figures, including the chief executives of all Member States, meeting in a closed room with no assistants".[3] Although each national delegation may comprise up to twenty persons, only two delegates are issued with red badges which allow them to enter the room to speak with the head of state or government, or to pass a note, but they may not stay. Note takers from the Council Secretariat are within the room and provide regular oral read-outs of the discussion to a separate, dedicated room comprising of the assistants to the Permanent Representatives of the Member States (known as "Antici" attachés, named after the first chair of the group). The Anticis may then leave that room in order to further relay the information to their own national delegations.

[4–07] There are at least two meetings of the European Council every six months. Further meetings can be scheduled should the need arise, as it frequently does, with almost monthly meetings held following the collapse of Lehman Brothers in 2008. In addition to traditionally focusing on economic matters at the spring meeting on foot of the Commission's Annual Growth Survey, the European Council can hold *thematic* meetings, as it has done on a number of occasions in relation to the Area of

---

[3] Philippe de Schoutheete, "The European Council" in John Peterson and Michael Shackleton (eds), *The Institutions of the European Union* (3rd ed, Oxford University Press, 2012) 44.

Freedom, Security and Justice, for example. *Informal* meetings are also occasionally held. Following the UK referendum on leaving on the EU, for instance, the European Council met informally, without the UK, in Bratislava in order to adopt a roadmap on the future of Europe as the Union approached its 60th anniversary. *Extraordinary* meetings can be scheduled at short notice as occurred following the attacks of 11 September 2001, prior to the second Iraq War in February 2003, in order to adopt guidelines on negotiating the withdrawal of the UK in April 2017, and in order to endorse the draft EU–UK withdrawal agreement in November 2018.

[4–08] Preparatory work for each meeting is carried out by the General Affairs Council, which is attended by foreign ministers or by ministers for European affairs, depending on how a Member State assigns ministerial responsibility. This preparatory work includes considering draft "conclusions" to be adopted by the European Council at the end of its meeting. These conclusions can cover a wide range of topics and are an important statement of the agreed position of the Member States on topical events and matters that have been discussed. As such, European Council conclusions can have significant political or legal weight, depending on the matter being addressed. For instance, at a political level, conclusions in June 1995 addressing the conflict in the former Yugoslavia included the following unequivocal message that is considered to have influenced events:

> The European Union strongly advises all the parties in the conflict to refrain from placing obstacles in the way of the freedom of movement and action of UNPROFOR and of the humanitarian organizations bringing aid to the civilian population. It warns them that the peace forces are determined to overcome such obstacles. The siege of Sarajevo must be lifted. The European Union demands freedom of access to Sarajevo, its enclaves and the safe areas.

[4–09] A good example of conclusions having legal weight can be seen in the efforts to address the concerns of the Irish people following their rejection of the Lisbon Treaty in a referendum. Whilst certain matters were dealt with in a decision of the heads of state or government that took the form of an international agreement, Ireland's concern as to the maintaining of one Commissioner for each Member State was addressed in European Council conclusions of December 2008 as follows:

> On the composition of the Commission, the European Council recalls that the Treaties currently in force require that the number of Commissioners be reduced in 2009. The European Council agrees that provided the Treaty of Lisbon enters into force, a decision will be taken, in accordance with the necessary legal procedures, to the effect that the Commission shall continue to include one national of each Member State.[4]

[4–10] Such was the weight attached to this conclusion that the Irish Government were willing to point to it as a firm commitment to maintain one Commissioner per Member State in the second referendum campaign in autumn 2009. The European Council followed through on the commitment by a Decision in May 2013.[5] More recently, the nature of European Council conclusions became a feature of the UK Government's efforts to persuade the House of Commons to approve the Withdrawal Agreement on

4 Presidency Conclusions of 11–12 December 2008, Document 17271/1/08 Rev 1. See ch 3, para [3–10].

5 European Council Decision of 22 May 2013 concerning the number of members of the European Commission (2013/272/EU) [2013] OJ L 165/98.

exiting the EU. This centred on the so-called "backstop" arrangement in the Protocol on Ireland/Northern Ireland intended to avoid a hard border on the island of Ireland.[6] European Council conclusions had set out the intention of the 27 EU Member States to work speedily on a subsequent agreement with the UK that would establish alternative arrangements so that the backstop would not need to be triggered. In an exchange of letters with the UK Prime Minister, the President of the European Council explained the nature of its conclusions as follows:

> European Council conclusions have a legal value in the Union commensurate to the authority of the European Council under the Treaties to define directions and priorities for the European Union at the highest level and, in the specific context of withdrawal, to establish, in the form of guidelines, its framework. They may commit the European Union in the most solemn manner. European Council conclusions therefore constitute part of the context in which an international agreement, such as the Withdrawal Agreement, will be interpreted.[7]

C. President of the European Council

[4–11] A very significant change introduced by the Lisbon Treaty was to create the full-time position of President of the European Council. The President is a permanent chair who may not hold national office, thus ending the practice whereby the European Council was chaired by the Member State holding the rotating, six-month presidency of the Council of the European Union.[8] The President is elected by the European Council by a qualified majority vote for a two-and-a-half year term, renewable once. To date, both holders of the position have been former prime ministers (and so former members of the European Council): Herman Van Rompuy of Belgium (1 January 2010 – 1 December 2014) and Donald Tusk of Poland (1 December 2014 and reappointed in March 2017). Article 15(6) TEU sets out the functions of the President as being to:

- chair the European Council and drive its work forward;
- ensure the preparation and continuity of the work of the European Council in cooperation with the President of the Commission and on the basis of the work of the General Affairs Council;
- facilitate cohesion and consensus within the European Council;
- present a report to the European Parliament after each of the meetings of the European Council; and
- without prejudice to the powers of the High Representative of the Union for Foreign Affairs and Security Policy, ensure the external representation of the EU on issues concerning its common foreign and security policy.

[4–12] Before the first appointment was made, expectations as to the role of the President differed considerably. Whereas for some, the role was seen as a rather technical and narrow one, confined to facilitating the work of the European Council, others preferred to see the appointment of a well-known statesperson, someone, it was said,

---

6 See ch 3, paras [3–30] to [3–36].

7 Letter from the President of the European Council and President of the European Commission to Prime Minister of the United Kingdom, 14 January 2019.

8 See Henri de Waele and Hansko Broeksteeg, "The Semi-Permanent European Council Presidency: Some Reflections on the Law and Early Practice" (2012) 49 *Common Market Law Review* 1039. Six Taoisigh served as President of the European Council during Irish Presidencies of the Council: Liam Cosgrave, Jack Lynch, Garrett FitzGerald, Charles Haughey, John Bruton and Bertie Ahern.

who would stop the traffic when making overseas visits, or would provide an answer to the question posed by foreign leaders: Who should I call if I want to talk to Europe?[9] According to Damian Chalmers, the position has emerged as a "powerful external figurehead for the European Union in a way that no national leader or supranational institution could: the former being too associated with their own state, and the latter mistrusted by national governments".[10] Paul Craig and Gráinne de Búrca also note that, in the post-Lisbon world, executive authority within the EU continues to remain divided, and so the key issue is the relationship between the President of the European Council, the President of the Commission and the Member State holding the Presidency of the Council, with the interplay between them shaping the EU's policies and priorities.[11]

D. Powers and Functions

[4–13] Article 15(1) TEU describes the European Council's role as being to provide the Union with the necessary impetus for its development and to define its general political directions and priorities, explicitly adding that it shall not exercise legislative functions. The TFEU also prescribes a role for the European Council in some specific areas where it has a particular involvement given their political or sensitive nature:

- regarding the Common Foreign and Security Policy, where it plays a central role, the European Council shall "identify the Union's strategic interest, determine the objectives of and define the general guidelines" (Art 26);
- in the Area of Freedom, Security and Justice it shall "define the strategic guidelines for legislative and operational planning" (Art 28); and
- in relation to economic policies it shall, acting on the basis of reports from the Council, "discuss a conclusion on the broad guidelines of the economic policies of the Member States and of the Union" (Art 121).

[4–14] A dedicated role for the European Council can also lend political weight to an issue. For instance, Art 148 TFEU provides that, each year, the European Council shall consider the employment situation in the Union and adopt conclusions thereon, on the basis of a joint annual report by the Council and the Commission. On the basis of the conclusions of the European Council, the Council, on a proposal from the Commission, shall then draw up guidelines which the Member States are to take into account in their employment policies. Here, the European Council is adding overall political direction on the issue of employment while also lending its political authority to the preparatory work of the Council and the Commission, who are then tasked with giving operational effect to the conclusions of the European Council. This role of providing high-level guidance can also be seen in the context of negotiations on the UK's withdrawal from the EU, where the European Council provided broad guidelines which were then translated into a more detailed negotiating mandate by the General Affairs Council. At regular intervals, the European Council considered updates on the negotiations and gave an assessment as to whether sufficient progress had been made to allow moving to the next phase of negotiations.

[4–15] The President of the European Council is tasked with facilitating consensus

---

9 Christian Tomuschat, "Calling Europe by Phone" (2010) 47 *Common Market Law Review* 3.

10 Damian Chalmers, Gareth Davies and Giorgio Monti, *European Union Law* (3rd ed, Cambridge University Press, 2014) 92.

11 Paul Craig and Gráinne de Búrca, *EU Law* (6th ed, Oxford University Press, 2015) 49.

amongst its members and Art 15(4) TEU provides that, unless the Treaties provide otherwise, this is how decisions are to be taken. Formal votes are extremely rare and usually consensus is achieved where a proposal is presented and no objection is raised. The difference between consensus and unanimity has been described as turning on the formality of the procedure used: whereas consensus involves no Member State voicing opposition, a unanimous decision implies a decision put to a vote and no negative vote being recorded.[12] The Treaties specify that decisions are to be taken by unanimity in the following instances, which can be regarded as being of a particularly sensitive or important nature:

– A finding of a persistent breach of EU values by a Member State	Art 7(2) TEU
– Deciding on the composition of the European Parliament	Art 14(2) TEU
– Modifying the number of Commissioners	Art 17(5) TEU
– Identifying strategic interests, objectives and general guidelines for Common Foreign and Security Policy	Art 22(1), 26(1) TEU
– Using *passerelle* clause for Common Foreign and Security Policy	Art 31(3) TEU
– Establishing a Common Defence	Art 42(2) TEU
– Using simplified treaty revision for EU internal competences	Art 48(6) TEU
– Using *passerelle* clause for simplified treaty revision	Art 48(7) TEU
– Extending negotiations on withdrawal of a Member State from the EU	Art 50(3) TEU
– Powers of the European Public Prosecutor's Office	Art 86(4) TFEU
– Rotation of Commissioners	Art 244 TFEU
– Using *passerelle* clause for Multiannual Financial Framework	Art 312(2) TFEU
– Amending the status of Overseas Territories	Art 355(6) TFEU

[4–16] The Treaties also specify that the European Council is to act by qualified majority vote when: electing (or deciding to end the term of) the President of the European Council[13]; proposing a candidate for President of the Commission to the European Parliament[14]; appointing (or deciding to end the term of) the High Representative of the Union for Foreign Affairs and Security Policy[15]; deciding on

---

[12] Philippe de Schoutheete, "The European Council" in John Peterson and Michael Shackleton (eds), *The Institutions of the European Union* (3rd ed, Oxford University Press, 2012) 50.

[13] Art 15(5) TEU.

[14] Art 17(7) TEU.

[15] Art 18(1) TEU.

the list of Council configurations and Presidency of the Council configurations[16] and appointing the board of the European Central Bank.[17]

[4–17] The list above highlights that, in addition to providing overall political guidance and direction, especially in the area of CFSP, the European Council also has roles of a more specific nature, that might be characterised as constitutional, institutional and arbitral.[18] In its *constitutional* role, the European Council shapes the very nature and future of the EU itself in that it establishes the criteria for new Member States to join (Art 49 TEU), provides guidelines for the negotiations on a Member State's withdrawal (Art 50 TEU), determines the existence of a serious and persistent breach of the Union's values by a Member State, which can lead to a suspension of its membership rights (Art 7 TEU) and plays a key role in initiating any amendments to the Treaties themselves (Art 48 TEU) through the ordinary and simplified revision procedures and the use of the *passerelle* clause, discussed below.

[4–18] In its *institutional* role, the European Council also plays a critical part in the most senior appointments, namely the Presidents of the European Council and Commission, the Commissioners, the High Representative of the Union for Foreign Affairs and Security Policy and the Executive Board of the ECB. It also influences the composition of the Commission and the Parliament and the configurations of the Council.

[4–19] Finally, there are instances where the European Council is identified as an *arbitrator* whenever disagreement arises amongst the Member States. This role arises in the context of what are known as "emergency break" provisions within the Treaties, such as Art 48 TFEU, which allows for the adoption of legislative measures in the field of social security by the ordinary legislative procedure (through the use of QMV). Where, within the Council of Ministers, a Member State declares that a proposed legislative act under this article would affect important aspects or the financial balance of its social security system, it may request that the matter be referred to the European Council, in which case the ordinary legislative procedure is suspended. After discussion, and within four months, the European Council is to either refer the proposal back to the Council, which then terminates the suspension of the ordinary legislative procedure, or take no action or request the Commission to submit a new proposal, in which case the original proposal will be deemed not to have been adopted. Articles 82(3) and 83(3) TFEU provide for a similar emergency break mechanism where a legislative proposal is considered to affect a fundamental aspect of a Member State's criminal justice system. A further instance arises in the context of CFSP, where the default rule is that decisions are adopted by unanimity. Exceptionally, Art 31(2) TEU provides for decisions to be adopted by QMV where they define a Union action or position on the basis of a decision of, or a specific request from, the European Council, or where the decision implements an earlier decision defining a Union action or position, or appoints a special representative. Even in these exceptional cases, however, Art 31(2) provides that if a Member State declares that, for vital and stated reasons of national policy, it intends to oppose the use of QMV to adopt a decision, a vote shall not be

16 Art 236 TFEU.

17 Art 283(2) TFEU. The European Council acts by a simple majority when deciding to examine amendments to the TEU or TFEU or when deciding not to convene a Convention (Art 48(3) TFEU) and when adopting its own rules of procedure (Art 253(3) TFEU).

18 Following Robert Schütze, *European Union Law* (Cambridge University Press, 2015) 172.

taken. The High Representative is to search for an acceptable solution but, in the event of not finding one, by QMV the Council may request that the matter be referred to the European Council for a decision by unanimity.

E. Amending the Treaties

[4–20] There are two principal methods by which amendments can be made to the EU Treaties, with an additional third method that allows for specific changes to be made to the voting rules or the legislative procedure that is to apply to a particular area. The European Council has a critical role in all three.

(i) Ordinary Revision Procedure

[4–21] Under the "ordinary revision procedure" for amending the Treaties, as set out in Article 48(2)–(4) TEU, the government of any Member State, the European Parliament or the Commission may submit to the Council of the European Union a proposal for the amendment of the Treaties. Such a proposal can include an amendment that would either increase or reduce the Union's competences. The Council is to then submit the proposal to the European Council and notify the national parliaments.

[4–22] If, after *consulting* the European Parliament and the Commission, the European Council adopts by a simple majority a decision in favour of examining the proposed amendment, the President of the European Council convenes a Convention. The Convention is composed of representatives of the: (i) national parliaments; (ii) heads of state or government of the Member States; (iii) European Parliament; and (iv) Commission. The European Central Bank is also consulted in the case of institutional changes in the monetary area. The Convention will examine the proposals for amendment and adopt by consensus a recommendation to a conference of representatives of the governments of the Member States, known as an "intergovernmental conference" (IGC). Alternatively, after obtaining the *consent* of the European Parliament, by a simple majority the European Council may decide not to convene a Convention should this not be justified by the extent of the proposed amendments. In that case, the European Council will move directly to defining the terms of reference for an intergovernmental conference.

[4–23] Whether either following a recommendation of a Convention, or simply a decision of the European Council, an IGC is then convened by the President of the Council of the European Union for the purpose of determining by common accord the amendments to be made to the Treaties. The amendments will only enter into force after being ratified by all the Member States in accordance with their respective constitutional requirements.

[4–24] The ordinary revision procedure was the method used in order to add to the TEU and TFEU a Protocol on the Concerns of the Irish People on the Treaty of Lisbon, which had been promised as part of a package of guarantees aimed at encouraging support for the Lisbon Treaty in a second referendum on its ratification. The addition of the Protocol followed a proposal being presented to the Council by the Irish Government on 20 July 2011.[19] The proposal was then submitted to the European Council and to national parliaments. The European Parliament adopted a favourable opinion on the proposed amendments and gave its consent not to convene a Convention on account of this not being justified by the extent of the proposed amendments. The Commission also adopted a favourable opinion. The European Council therefore adopted a decision in which it decided not to convene a Convention and to submit the proposed protocol directly to an IGC for examination.[20] Although signed in May 2012, the requirement for the Protocol to be ratified by each Member State meant that it did not enter into force until 1 December 2014.

(ii) Simplified Revision Procedure

[4–25] Article 48(6) and (7) TEU also provides for two forms of "simplified revision procedure". The first concerns amendments to the internal policies of the EU, as set out in Part Three of the TFEU, other than by increasing the Union's competence. Acting by unanimity and after having consulted the European Parliament and the Commission (as well as the European Central Bank with regard to the monetary area), the European Council may adopt a decision amending all or part of the provisions of Part Three of the TFEU. In order to enter into force, the decision must first be approved by the Member States in accordance with their respective constitutional requirements. This version of the simplified revision procedure was used for the first time in 2013 in order to amend Art 136 TFEU so as to expressly provide that the Member States whose currency is the euro may establish a stability mechanism to be activated if indispensable to safeguard the stability of the euro area as a whole.[21] The Court of Justice upheld the use of the simplified revision procedure in a preliminary reference from the Supreme Court in *Pringle v Government of Ireland*.[22]

[4–26] The second form of simplified revision procedure is known as the *passerelle* clause, meaning "little bridge". This allows that, having obtained the consent of the European Parliament, the European Council may decide by unanimity to change a requirement for a unanimous vote to one taken by a qualified majority. Such an amendment can be made anywhere where unanimity is required in the TFEU, or in Title V TEU dealing with CFSP, with the exception of decisions with military implications or those in the area of defence. Likewise, a decision can be made that the use of the Special Legislative Procedure be changed to the Ordinary Legislative Procedure. Before adopting a decision to use the *passerelle* clause, any proposal to do so must first be notified to Member States' national parliaments and, if any parliament opposes the proposal, the decision will not be adopted.

---

[19] See ch 3, paras [3–10] to [3–11].

[20] European Council Decision of 11 May 2012 on the examination by a conference of representatives of the governments of the Member States of the amendment to the Treaties proposed by the Irish Government in the form of a Protocol on the concerns of the Irish people on the Treaty of Lisbon, to be annexed to the Treaty on European Union and to the Treaty on the Functioning of the European Union, and not to convene a Convention (2013/106/EU) [2013] OJ L60/129.

[21] European Council Decision of 25 March 2011 amending Article 136 of the Treaty on the Functioning of the European Union with regard to a stability mechanism for Member States whose currency is the euro (2011/199/EU) [2011] OJ L91/1; Irish Treaty Series No 14 (Treaty Action) of 2014.

[22] Case C-370/12 *Pringle v Government of Ireland* EU:C:2012:756, 27 November 2012. The amendment to Art 136 TFEU and the *Pringle* case are discussed further in ch 27, paras [27–45] to [27–58].

F. Legal Form

[4–27] Whereas the Court of Justice had previously held it to be implicit, post-Lisbon the Treaties explicitly provide that the Court of Justice may review the legality of acts of the European Council intended to produce legal effects *vis-à-vis* third parties (Art 263 TFEU) and that an action may be brought against the European Council on the basis that its failure to act has infringed the Treaties (Art 265 TFEU).

[4–28] Although Art 15(1) TEU states that the European Council shall not exercise legislative functions, since 2009 it does have a number of defined, quasi-constitutional functions, as well as certain powers to adopt binding acts having legal effect, such that it "needs to pay due attention to legal form".[23] With this in mind, it quickly adopted rules of procedure in December 2009, Art 12 of which provides that:

> 1. Decisions adopted by the European Council shall be signed by its President and by the Secretary-General of the Council. Where they do not specify to whom they are addressed, they shall be published in the Official Journal of the European Union. Where they specify to whom they are addressed, they shall be notified to those to whom they are addressed by the Secretary-General of the Council.
>
> 2. The provisions concerning the form of acts set out in Annex VI to the Rules of Procedure of the Council shall apply mutatis mutandis to decisions of the European Council.[24]

[4–29] Particular care must be taken by the Member States whenever they choose to meet at the same time as a meeting of the European Council (often referred to as "in the margins" of such a meeting), *as* Member States, rather than as the institution comprising the European Council. This arose in the context of a political agreement reached at a meeting between the leaders of the EU Member States and Turkey on 18 March 2016, which led to the issuing of a joint statement in the form of a press release. This meeting followed a European Council that had taken place on 17–18 March. In the statement, the EU and Turkey agreed a number of action points to address an ongoing migration crisis, including an agreement that, as and from 20 March, all new irregular migrants crossing from Turkey to Greek islands would be returned to Turkey. A legal challenge to the agreement was subsequently brought, in which it was alleged that the agreement was a legally binding agreement that had been entered into on behalf of the EU Member States by the European Council. The General Court summed up the position of the European Council as follows:

> According to the European Council, the EU–Turkey statement was issued by the participants in an international summit held, in this instance, on 18 March 2016 in the margins of and following the meeting of the European Council. Therefore, that statement is attributable to the Members of the European Council, which are the Member States of the European Union, and their "Turkish counterpart", since they met in the context of a meeting distinct from that of the European Council. … The European Council contends that the EU–Turkey statement cannot therefore be classified as a measure adopted by it.[25]

[4–30] The General Court acknowledged that measures adopted by the representatives of the Member States physically gathered in the grounds of one of the EU institutions

---

[23] Philippe de Schoutheete, "The European Council" in John Peterson and Michael Shackleton (eds), *The Institutions of the European Union* (3rd ed, Oxford University Press, 2012) 44.

[24] [2009] OJ L 315/51.

[25] Case T–192/16 *NF v European Council* EU:T:2017:128, 28 February 2017, para 38.

and acting, not in their capacity as members of the Council or European Council, but in their capacity as heads of state or government of the Member States, are not subject to judicial review by the EU courts. Nevertheless, it was for the Court to review whether, having regard to the content of a measure and the circumstances of its adoption, it was, or was not, a decision of the European Council. The General Court was critical of the language used in the press release of 18 March 2016, which referred to the joint meeting as having involved "Members of the European Council" and an agreement having been reached between the "EU and Turkey". The Court considered that this language could be read as implying that the agreement had been reached with the European Council, and in this regard was "regrettably ambiguous".[26] Nevertheless, having examined in detail the documentation for the preparation of the meeting, the Court concluded that it was, in fact, a meeting of the heads of state and government acting as such. This was the case even though, although not formally invited, the President of the European Council and the President of the Commission had also attended the meeting.

[4–31] On the other hand, there have been occasions when the heads of state or government have taken decisions within the setting of the European Council that they wish to have the force of a binding agreement under public international law. These are not decisions of the European Council, as such, but rather "Decisions of the Heads of State or Government of the Members of the EU *meeting within the European Council*". Such a decision was first used in 1992 to allow Denmark to hold a second referendum on the Maastricht Treaty,[27] a precedent that was followed by Ireland in 2009 to obtain a set of guarantees addressing the concerns of the Irish people that preceded a second referendum on the Lisbon Treaty. Indeed, this decision was annexed to the European Council conclusions from the meeting at which it was agreed.[28] Upon the Lisbon Treaty entering into force, the contents of the decision were to be set out in a Protocol to the TEU and TFEU (as an amendment to the Treaties) at the time of the next accession to the EU. This was arranged in parallel to the accession of Croatia, with the Protocol entering into force on 1 December 2014.[29] This practice was followed once again, in February 2016, with a decision on a "New Settlement for the United Kingdom within the European Union", which had been intended to shore up support for the EU in the pending referendum on membership,[30] and in December 2016, with a decision on the Association Agreement with Ukraine, intended to overcome a Dutch referendum which voted against ratification of the Agreement by the Netherlands.[31]

---

[26] *ibid*, para 66.

[27] See Helle Krunke, "Peoples' Vengeances: from Maastricht to Edinburgh: the Danish Solution" (2005) 1 *European Constitutional Law Review* 339.

[28] Presidency Conclusions, European Council 18–19 June 2009, Document 11225/2/09 Rev 2.

[29] Protocol on the Concerns of the Irish people on the Treaty of Lisbon [2013] OJ L60/131 and [2016] OJ L293/1; Irish Treaty Series No 25 of 2014. See also Corrigendum to the consolidated versions of the Treaty on European Union and the Treaty on the Functioning of the European Union [2016] OJ C400/1.

[30] European Council Conclusions, 18–19 February 2016, EUCO 1/16, [2016] OJ C69I/1.

[31] European Council Conclusions, 15 December 2016, EUCO 34/16; Irish Treaty Series No 12 of 2017. See Ramses Wessel, "The EU Solution to Deal with the Dutch Referendum Result on the EU-Ukraine Association Agreement" (2016) 1 *European Papers* 1305.

Chapter 5

THE COUNCIL OF THE EUROPEAN UNION

A. Introduction

[5–01] Historically, the Council of the European Union (previously known as the Council of Ministers and generally referred to simply as "the Council") was both the prime legislative and executive body of the EEC, and the core intergovernmental element within its institutional architecture. Successive Treaty reforms have seen the Council's preeminent position squeezed from both sides, with the European Council becoming the formal EU institution charged with providing overall political guidance and direction and the European Parliament being given a co-equal role in the legislative process. As defined by Art 16(1) TEU, the role of the Council is to, jointly with the European Parliament, exercise legislative and budgetary functions, and to carry out policy-making and coordinating functions as laid down in the Treaties. It has been observed that there is an interesting dynamic between these two types of powers such that the more that the Council's legislative and budgetary functions came to be shared with the Parliament, the more the second two functions of policy-making and coordination grew in scope and importance.[1]

[5–02] Article 16(2) TEU provides that the Council shall consist of a representative of each Member State at ministerial level, who may commit the government of the Member State in question and cast its vote. The unique feature of the Council is that it meets in ten different "configurations" or formations depending on the subject matter being considered (set out below). While the General Affairs Council (GAC) and Foreign Affairs Council (FAC) are expressly provided for in the TFEU, the remaining configurations are decided upon by the European Council. The remit of each configuration is self-evident from their titles, with the exception of the General Affairs Council, which plays an important role in preparing for European Councils and ensuring the necessary follow-up after each meeting. The GAC is attended by foreign ministers or ministers for European affairs (depending on the internal arrangements

---

1 Sabina Kajnč, "The Council of the EU and the European Council" in Alan Hardacre (ed), *How the EU Institutions Work and ... How to Work with the EU Institutions*" (John Harper, 2011) 47, 53.

within each Member State) and is also charged with coordinating the work of the other configurations and is responsible for institutional, administrative and horizontal matters.

[5–03] Thus, the Council is comprised of ten distinct configurations of governmental politicians who, when taken altogether, meet formally around 80 times a year, with a number of additional informal meetings. Certain configurations such as the GAC, FAC and Economic and Financial Affairs Council (ECOFIN) meet on a monthly basis and others less frequently. Notwithstanding that there are ten configurations, in a legal sense there is only one Council, such that if a particular need arises, one configuration can adopt a decision relating to the subject area of a different configuration.

B. Preparatory Bodies

[5–04] Iceberg-like, the great bulk of the Council's work occurs beneath the level of ministerial Council meetings in what are known as "preparatory bodies", which take the form of over 160 Committees and Working Parties (with some Working Parties in turn having internal sub-groups which number around 90).

[5–05] The level closest to the Council consists of two Committees made up respectively of the permanent representatives and deputy permanent representatives of each Member State known as COREPER (Comité des représentants permanents). Somewhat counter-intuitively, COREPER 2 is attended by the Permanent Representatives and deals with four of the more horizontal and politically sensitive configurations, while COREPER 1 is attended by Deputy Permanent Representatives and deals with the remaining six configurations, which are of a more sectoral nature. Meetings of COREPER are held weekly and are also attended by a delegation from the Commission and the General Secretariat of the Council.

[5–06] In addition to COREPER 1 and 2, there are five Committees established by the Treaties (the Economic and Financial Committee, Employment Committee, Trade Policy Committee, Political and Security Committee, Standing Committee on Operational Cooperation on Internal Security (COSI) and Social Protection Committee), one established by an intergovernmental decision (the Special Committee on Agriculture) and five established by Council act (the EU Military Committee, Committee for Civilian Aspects of Crisis Management (CivCom), Economic Policy Committee, Financial Services Committee and Security Committee).[2] The nature of these Committees vary, with some meeting regularly, attended by national officials who are posted to the Member State's permanent representation in Brussels, and others meeting only a few times a year with national experts travelling to Brussels from capitals. As an example, Art 38 TFEU provides that, without prejudice to Art 240 TFEU which establishes COREPER, the Political and Security Committee shall:

> monitor the international situation in the areas covered by the common foreign and security policy and contribute to the definition of policies by delivering opinions to the Council at the request of the Council or of the High Representative of the Union for Foreign Affairs

[2] For an example of establishment by the Council, see Council Decision 2010/131 of 25 February 2010 on setting up the Standing Committee on operational cooperation in internal security (COSI) [2010] OJ L52/50.

and Security Policy or on its own initiative. It shall also monitor the implementation of agreed policies, without prejudice to the powers of the High Representative.

Within the scope of this Chapter [on Common Foreign and Security Policy], the Political and Security Committee shall exercise, under the responsibility of the Council and of the High Representative, the political control and strategic direction of the crisis management operations referred to in Article 43.

The Council may authorise the Committee, for the purpose and for the duration of a crisis management operation, as determined by the Council, to take the relevant decisions concerning the political control and strategic direction of the operation.

[5–07] The Political and Security Committee (PSC) meets weekly, attended by a senior official from each of the permanent representations, often titled "PSC Ambassadors", and is chaired by a representative of the High Representative of the Union for Foreign Affairs and Security Policy. It has been noted that although the PSC is not a parallel counterpart to COREPER 2, issues considered by the PSC are rarely reopened in COREPER 2.[3] In contrast, uniquely, the Special Committee on Agriculture is a parallel counterpart to COREPER 1 in preparing for the Agriculture and Fisheries Committee.

[5–08] Like the Committees, the frequency with which Working Parties meet varies considerably, some meeting almost daily and attended by Brussels-based national officials, while others might meet only four to six times a year, attended by capital-based experts.[4] By way of illustration, the ten Council configurations, with their distribution as between COREPER 1 and 2, the number of meetings held in 2016 (including informal meetings) and the number of Working Parties reporting to them, were as follows:

[3] Sabina Kajnč, "The Council of the EU and the European Council" in Alan Hardacre ed., *How the EU Institutions Work and ... How to Work with the EU Institutions*" (John Harper, 2011) 47, 68.

[4] For an example of the establishment of a Working Party by the Council, see Council Decision (EU) 2017/900 concerning the establishment of the ad hoc Working Party on Art 50 TEU chaired by the General Secretariat of the Council [2017] OJ L137/138.

COREPER 2		***Meetings in 2016***	***Working Parties***
(Permanent Representatives assisted by Antici Group)			
Foreign Affairs Council	FAC	19	38
General Affairs Council	GAC	12	21
Economic and Financial Affairs Council	ECOFIN	12	14
Justice and Home Affairs Council	JHA	11	28
COREPER 1			
(Deputy Permanent Representatives assisted by Mertens Group)			
Employment, Social Policy, Health & Consumer Affairs	EPSCO	7	5
Agriculture and Fisheries Council	AgFish	11	29
Transport, Telecommunications & Energy	TTE	5	7
Competitiveness	COMP	6	24
Environment	ENV	7	2
Education, Youth and Culture	EYC	3	5

[5–09] The idea behind the hierarchy of Working Parties, Committees, COREPER and finally the Council is to achieve as much agreement as possible at each level, such that the Permanent Representatives need only deal with the more difficult, contentious issues, whilst the Ministers in Council need only debate those issues that COREPER has been unable to resolve. Indeed, it has been estimated that roughly 70 to 80 per cent of all Council decisions are taken as items that have already been agreed and can be adopted without discussion (known as "A" points on the agenda).[5] Even where the applicable rules prescribe the use of qualified majority voting in the Council, COREPER tends to strive for, and operate by, consensus. As Jeffrey Lewis describes:

> As a continuous negotiation chamber in the EU, COREPER is a place where many decisions are effectively made. But the permanent representatives have no *formal* decision-making authority. Juridical decision-making authority is a power exclusively reserved for the ministers, and formal voting is expressly prohibited at any other level of the Council. But in practice, or *de facto*, COREPER has evolved into a veritable decision-making factory. There are ways around the formality of *de jure* voting, such as the 'indicative vote' of how a delegation would vote if the matter were put before the ministers. More common is the tactful packaging of a discussion by the presidency, in which the chair will ask "I assume no one else requests the floor?" or state "A sufficient majority exists". No vote is taken. There is no raising of hands. But many agreements are reached in this manner and many decisions are thus made.[6]

5 Thomas Christiansen, "The Council of Ministers, Facilitating Interaction and Developing Actorness in the EU" in Jeremy Richardson (ed), *European Union: Power and Policy Making* (Routledge, 2006) 147, 162.

6 Jeffrey Lewis, "National Interests: The Committee of Permanent Representatives" in John Peterson

[5–10] The Presidency of the Council rotates amongst the Member States on a six-monthly basis in a pre-determined order set by the European Council. During a Member State's Presidency, it chairs all of the Council configurations (and COREPER and Working Parties) with the exception of the Foreign Affairs Council, which is chaired by the High Representative of the Union for Foreign Affairs and Security Policy.[7] Many of the Working Parties which report to the Foreign Affairs Council are chaired by officials from the European External Action Service. An important part of the Presidency is to be impartial and to act as an honest-broker in the search for compromises and consensus. Nevertheless, by being able to schedule the pace of meetings and set the agenda, it offers a Member State a great deal of influence over the working of the Council, an opportunity that smaller Member States might not otherwise have. Post-Lisbon, trios of Member States coordinate and assist one another on their three consecutive Presidencies over an 18-month period.

[5–11] Given the rotating nature of the Presidency, there is a clear need for a permanent body of officials to assist both the ten Council configurations, Committees, Working Parties and the Member States in their role as President. This is provided by the 3,000 or so staff that make up the General Secretariat of the Council. In addition to providing administrative support, through a number of sectoral directorates it makes important policy contributions, while the opinions of its Legal Service are usually highly influential.

C. High Representative of the Union for Foreign Affairs and Security Policy

[5–12] Further assistance to the rotating Presidency is provided by the fact that, post-Lisbon, the Foreign Affairs Council is chaired by the High Representative of the Union for Foreign Affairs and Security Policy, who is appointed by the European Council with the agreement of the President of the Commission. According to Arts 18 and 27 TEU, the High Representative's role is to:

- preside over the Foreign Affairs Council;
- conduct the Union's Common Foreign and Security Policy (CFSP) and Common Security and Defence Policy (CSDP);
- contribute by her proposals to the development of the CFSP and CSDP;
- represent the Union for matters relating to the CFSP;
- conduct political dialogue with third parties on the Union's behalf;
- express the Union's position in international organisations and at international conferences; and
- ensure the implementation of decisions adopted by the European Council and the Council.

[5–13] As the last task illustrates, while the High Representative presides over the FAC and conducts the CFSP and CSDP on a day-to-day basis, both of these policies are to be carried out by the High Representative "as mandated by the Council", which

and Michael Shackleton (eds), *The Institutions of the European Union* (3rd ed, Oxford University Press, 2012) 315, 325.

7 European Council Decision of 1 December 2009 on the exercise of the Presidency of the Council (2009/881/EU) [2009] OJ L315/50.

remains in charge of providing overall direction and which, in turn, is guided by the European Council and the conclusions adopted by it.

[5–14] The role of High Representative is unusual in that it is "double-hatted", in the sense that she is chair of the FAC and mandated by it to conduct the EU's foreign policy, while simultaneously also being a vice-president of the Commission. In this second role, the High Representative is charged with ensuring the consistency of the Union's external action and is responsible within the Commission for its responsibilities in external relations and for coordinating other aspects of the EU's external action. Paul Craig and Gráinne de Búrca have commented that the position is a "complex and difficult one since, apart from its double- or triple-hatted nature, the holder lacks real political power and cannot realistically seek to define or lead the EU's foreign policy. Instead, the High Representative has sought to build consensus amongst states with very different foreign policy positions on many issues, and to manage conflict".[8]

[5–15] Another significant change introduced by the Lisbon Treaty was the creation of the European External Action Service (EEAS), an EU diplomatic service tasked with assisting the High Representative in the fulfilment of her mandate, working in cooperation with the diplomatic services of the Member States.[9] The EEAS operates 139 delegations worldwide and is made up of officials from the General Secretariat of the Council, the Commission as well as staff seconded from national diplomatic services of the Member States. It has been established as a "functionally autonomous body of the European Union, separate from the General Secretariat of the Council and from the Commission with the legal capacity necessary to perform its tasks and attain its objectives", that is under the authority of the High Representative.[10] While separate from the Council and the Commission, the EEAS is also tasked with assisting the President of the European Council, the President of the Commission, and the Commission in the exercise of their respective functions in the area of external relations.[11] In addition, it is to support and work in cooperation with the diplomatic services of the Member States, the General Secretariat of the Council and the Commission in order to ensure consistency between the different areas of the Union's external action and between those areas and its other policies. The Commission and the EEAS are also to consult each other on all matters relating to the external action of the Union in the exercise of their respective functions, except on matters covered by the CSDP.

D. Powers and Functions

[5–16] The Council has a number of distinct roles which are a mixture of the legislative and executive functions typically found in national systems of government. An old maxim on EU legislation summed up the roles of the institutions as "the Commission proposes and the Council disposes", reflecting that, in the past, the Council was the sole or predominant legislative organ of the EU. Now, under the ordinary legislative procedure, the Council shares a co-legislative role with the European Parliament.

8 Paul Craig and Gráinne de Búrca, *EU Law* (6th ed, Oxford University Press, 2015) 320.

9 See Bart Van Vooren, "A Legal–Institutional Perspective on the European External Action Service" (2011) 48 *Common Market Law Review* 490.

10 Council Decision 2010/427/EU of 26 July 2010 establishing the organisation and functioning of the European External Action Service [2010] OJ L201/30, Art 1(2).

11 *ibid*, Art 2(2).

Council meetings are divided into two parts, dealing respectively with deliberations on legislative acts and non-legislative activities. When it deliberates and votes on a draft legislative act, the Council must meet in public, which is facilitated by live video streaming. In addition, although the Commission retains the prerogative to propose legislative measures, the Council may now request the Commission to undertake any studies that the Council considers desirable for the attainment of common objectives, and to submit to it any appropriate proposals. If the Commission does not submit a proposal, it shall inform the Council of the reasons (Art 241 TFEU). Jointly with the European Parliament, the Council also approves the EU's annual budget.

[5–17] As well as having legislative and budgetary functions, the Council is also responsible for policy-making, general coordination and ensuring the implementation of objectives set by the European Council. The manner in which the Council carries out this function will vary depending on the extent to which the subject area is a matter of EU competence. For example, Art 121 TFEU assigns to the Council a general *coordinating* role with regard to the economic policies of Member States, which are said to be a matter of common concern. On a recommendation from the Commission, the Council formulates draft broad guidelines for the economic policies of the Member States and reports its findings to the European Council. On the basis of the subsequent conclusions adopted by the European Council, the Council then makes a recommendation setting out these broad guidelines. In order to ensure closer coordination of economic policies and convergence of the economic performances of the Member States, the Council monitors economic developments in each Member State, including assessing the consistency of economic policies with the broad guidelines recommended by it. For members of the Euro Zone, the Council may make certain findings – such as an excessive budget deficit or a failure to secure a balanced budget – that may lead to it imposing a fine in order to ensure that corrective measures are taken.

[5–18] As illustrated by the position of the High Representative, the frequency of Foreign Affairs Council meetings and the large number of Working Parties reporting to it, the Council plays a central role in the implementation of the EU's Common Foreign and Security Policy and Common Security and Defence Policy. It is also the Council that must provide a mandate to the Commission to negotiate any international agreement between the EU and non-EU countries and international organisations. At the end of negotiations, it is the Council that must authorise signature of the agreement, based on a proposal from the Commission. For certain types of agreement, as listed in Art 218(6) TFEU, the consent of the European Parliament must first be obtained before the Council can proceed to authorise conclusion by the Union, which is the final step in the process of expressing consent to be bound by an agreement.

E. Qualified Majority Voting

[5–19] Given that they impact upon the influence a Member State has over a given policy area, the rules governing how the Council votes on a legislative proposal are naturally politically sensitive. As we have already seen, throughout the 1970s and early 1980s the requirement for unanimity led to a severe slow-down in the rate of EU legislation adopted by the Council, prompting calls for the wider use of "qualified majority voting" (QMV). Up until the Lisbon Treaty, this involved weighting the votes of Member States in proportion to their size and population, albeit not equating strictly to population. So, for example, when Ireland first joined the EEC, as one of nine Member States, it had a weighted vote of 3 out of a total of 58, or 5.2 per cent of the vote – the highest it would ever be. Within the Union of 28 Member States, Ireland had a weighted vote of 7 out of 352, or 1.99 per cent – the lowest it had been. As will be seen below, the calculation of QMV is now based on a combination of a percentage of Member States and a percentage of the Union population, with Ireland representing 0.93 per cent of the total population. A method has been developed for calculating the probability that a Member State's vote will prove decisive within the Council, known as the "Banzhaf power index".[12] This is considered to give an indication of the relative power of each Member State within the Council. With 28 Member States, Germany has the highest power index of 10.2 per cent, whereas Ireland has 2.2 per cent. The effect of the UK's withdrawal would be to increase the power index of the most populous Member States, with Germany's rising to 11.9 per cent. By a statistical quirk, Ireland is the only Member State whose power index would remain precisely the same.

[5–20] In general terms, the Single European Act of 1986 extended the use of QMV to 12 instances, the Maastricht Treaty of 1992 to 30 more, with a further 40 added by the Amsterdam Treaty in 1997 and 30 by the Nice Treaty of 2001. Finally, the Lisbon Treaty applied the use of QMV an additional 50 times, leaving just over 80 instances where unanimity would continue to apply.[13] Significantly, the Lisbon Treaty also established QMV as the *default* rule to apply unless the Treaties provide otherwise, such as they do in relation to CFSP, CSDP, tax, social security and certain budgetary matters where unanimity is still required.[14] Now, QMV is used in adopting roughly 80 per cent of EU legislation.

[5–21] In order to ease in these changes gradually, the Lisbon Treaty included a series of transitional arrangements that were set out in Protocol No 36 on Transitional Provisions and Declaration No 7, both annexed to the Treaties. These arrangements came to an end on 1 April 2017, from which date the definition of QMV as set out in Art 16(4) TEU applied. In place of the system of weighted votes, a qualified majority is now "at least 55% of the members of the Council, comprising at least 15 of them and representing Member States comprising at least 65% of the population of the Union". In practice, 55 per cent of the Member States means 16 out of the 28. Member States are required to provide annual statistics on their population to facilitate the calculation of QMV.[15] In addition, it is provided that a blocking minority must include at least four Council members, failing which the qualified majority is deemed to have been attained. Jean-Claude Piris suggests that the reasons for this choice of "double majority" system were because: (i) it was considered to be easier for the public to understand; (ii) it was perceived as closer to the essential nature of the EU as both a union of states and a union of citizens; and (iii) it kept the QMV threshold sufficiently low as to facilitate

[12] Werner Kirsch, *Brexit and the Distribution of Power in the Council of the EU* (Centre for European Policy Studies, 2016); Cian McCarthy, *EU Decision-making after Brexit: QMV and the balance of power* (Institute of International and European Affairs, 2019).

[13] Jean-Claude Piris, *The Lisbon Treaty* (Cambridge University Press, 2011) 212–213 and Appendices 5 and 7.

[14] See Commission Communication, "Towards a more efficient and democratic decision making in EU tax policy" COM(2019) 8 final, 15 January 2019; Commission Communication, "A stronger global actor: a more efficient decision-making for EU Common Foreign and Security Policy" COM(2018) 647 final, 12 September 2018.

[15] Regulation (EU) No 1260/2013 of the European Parliament and of the Council of 20 November 2013 on European demographic statistics [2013] OJ L330/39, Arts 4-5.

the adoption of acts in a Council of 28 Member States.[16] The new system also avoids the need to redefine the voting weights upon each new accession or withdrawal. Commenting on the importance of these rules for Member States, Piris observes that:

> Each time a new method of calculating QMV is being negotiated, Member States try their best to keep their maximum power to protect their national interests. All of them try to imagine every possible scenario in which they could be outvoted, and try to calculate their blocking power in such situations. They also study all theoretical possibilities available for constructing qualified majorities or blocking minorities through alliances with "like-minded" Member States. Diplomats try to turn themselves into mathematicians.[17]

[5–22] Given the complexity of the formula, as well as different voting configurations such as the Euro Group or where Ireland, Denmark and the UK do not participate in the adoption of an AFSJ matter, the Council has developed a useful voting calculator that is available online or as an app.[18] More precise details on how QMV operates are found in Art 238 TFEU, such as rules governing abstentions and the situation where not all members of the Council are participating in a vote (such as where Ireland chooses not to participate in a vote on a proposal in the Area of Freedom, Security and Justice pursuant to Protocol No 21, or where Member States that have not adopted the euro do not participate in a vote under Art 136 TFEU). Article 238 also provides for a "strong" form of QMV in the relatively rare circumstances in which the Council is voting on a proposal that does not come from the Commission or the High Representative.[19] For example, Art 50 TEU requires the use of strong QMV by the Council in approving a withdrawal agreement with a Member State leaving the EU.

[5–23] The sensitivities of Member States are further catered for by what is known as the "Ioannina Mechanism", set out in Declaration No 7 to the Treaties and named after an earlier, similar decision adopted in the Greek city in 1994. The Ioannina Mechanism also bears some similarity to the Luxembourg Compromise, discussed below. From 1 April 2017, it provides that if members of the Council, representing either at least 55 per cent of the population, or at least 55 per cent of the number of Member States, necessary to constitute a blocking minority under Art 16(4) or Art 238(2) TFEU, indicate their opposition to the Council adopting an act by a qualified majority, the Council shall discuss the issue. These percentages correlate to roughly 20 per cent of the population (which could be achieved by two large Member States) or 25 per cent of the Member States. In the course of its discussions, and within a reasonable time, the Council shall do all in its power to reach a satisfactory solution to address concerns raised. To this end, with the assistance of the Commission and the Member States, the President of the Council shall undertake any initiative necessary to facilitate a wider basis of agreement.

[5–24] While it is important to understand the nature of QMV, it must also be borne in mind that, in practice, most decisions in the Council are adopted without a vote. A study of contested voting in the Council between 1995 and 2010 found that Ireland was the fifth least likely of 27 Member States to contest a legislative proposal by abstaining or voting against. During that period, Ireland contested 2.1 per cent of proposals, voting

---

16 *ibid*, 214.

17 *ibid*, 220–221.

18 Available at <http://www.consilium.europa.eu/en/council-eu/voting-system/voting-calculator/>.

19 In which case, 72 per cent of the Council members, representing at least 66 per cent of the EU population, is required.

against 1.3 per cent and abstaining in 0.8 per cent of votes. To put this in context, as the most frequent contester, Germany voted against 4.5 per cent and abstained in 3.2 per cent of votes. When voting patterns were clustered, Ireland was included amongst a group of 18 Member States labelled the "silent majority" that contest less and are seldom outvoted.[20] Another study has noted that over the seven years of 2004 to 2010, Ireland abstained, and voted against a proposal, under QMV on seven occasions each, out of a total of just over 1,000 proposals. During this time, 79 per cent of legislative acts subject to QMV were agreed by unanimity.[21]

F. The Luxembourg Compromise

[5–25] Although now largely considered to be an interesting historical episode, when examining the rules on voting in the Council one must remain alert to the possibility that a Member State might choose to invoke what is known as the "Luxembourg Compromise". In the same year as the EEC Treaty entered into force, a committed intergovernmentalist, Charles de Gaulle, assumed the Presidency of one of the Community's largest states, and quickly oversaw the move from the French Fourth to the Fifth Republic. France's reservations as to supranationalism resulted in a significant disagreement in 1965, leading France to absent itself from the Council for seven months, including during its own Presidency, in furtherance of an "empty chair policy", leaving the Council without a chair and France without a Permanent Representative in Brussels.

[5–26] The disagreement occurred at a time when preparations were being made for the extension of the use of qualified majority voting in the Council following the end, on 1 January 1966, of a transitional period provided for in the Treaty of Rome. The Commission had presented three proposals as a package deal, to be accepted or rejected as such, relating to increased powers for the Parliament, a system of "own resources" to independently finance the Communities, and financial regulations for the Common Agricultural Policy (CAP). France, which favoured the CAP regulations but opposed the two other proposals, absented itself until a somewhat awkward resolution was eventually reached in the form of an agreement to disagree. The Luxembourg Compromise took the form of Conclusions to the extraordinary session of the Council held in Luxembourg in January 1966.[22] It was, in essence, a non-legally binding political statement or communiqué that encapsulated the following informal arrangement:

1. Where, in the case of decisions which may be taken by majority vote on a proposal

---

[20] Wim Van Aken, "Voting in the Council of the European Union Contested Decision-Making in the EU Council of Ministers (1995–2010)", Swedish Institute for European Policy Studies (2012) 43, 54. The other members of the silent majority were Belgium, Bulgaria, Cyprus, Estonia, France, Greece, Hungary, Italy, Latvia, Lithuania, Luxembourg, Poland, Portugal, Slovakia, Slovenia, Spain and Romania.

[21] Fiona Hayes-Renshaw, "The Council of Ministers" in John Peterson and Michael Shackleton (eds), *The Institutions of the European Union* (3rd ed, Oxford University Press, 2012) 68, 80, 85.

[22] See W Nicoll, "The Luxembourg Compromise" (1984) 23 *Journal of Common Market Studies* 35; Jean-Marie Palayret, Helen Wallace and Pascaline Winard (eds), *Visions, Votes and Vetoes: The Empty Chair Crisis and the Luxembourg Compromise Forty Years On* (PIE–Peter Lang, Brussels, 2006); Luuk Van Middlelaar, "Spanning the River: The Constitutional Crisis of 1965–1966 as the Genesis of Europe's Political Order" (2008) 4 *European Constitutional Law Review* 98; Jan Herman Reestman and Thomas Beuker, "Not Dead Yet: Revisiting the 'Luxembourg Veto' and its Foundations" (2017) 13 *European Constitutional Law Review* 1.

of the Commission, very important interests of one or more partners are at stake, the Members of the Council will endeavour, within a reasonable time, to reach solutions which can be adopted by all the Members of the Council while respecting their mutual interests and those of the Community, in accordance with Article 2 of the Treaty.

2. With regard to the preceding paragraph, the French delegation considers that where very important interests are at stake the discussion must be continued until unanimous agreement is reached.
3. The six delegations note that there is a divergence of views on what should be done in the event of a failure to reach complete agreement.
4. The six delegations nevertheless consider that this divergence does not prevent the Community's work being resumed in accordance with the normal procedure.

[5–27] Anthony Teasdale has noted how the Compromise led to "pervasive immobilism" within the Council until the early 1980s, during which time it was not necessary to formally invoke the Compromise (which happened around 10 times between 1966 and 1980), in order for a Member State to oppose a proposal it disliked.[23] Nor were the national interests that were required to be at stake as fundamental as one might expect, as often illustrated by Germany's blocking of a 1985 Council decision which would have reduced CAP support prices for cereals and rapeseed oil by less than 2 per cent.[24]

[5–28] A weakening of the Compromise began in 1982, when the UK unsuccessfully sought to invoke it in order to oppose an annual measure on agricultural prices, when the real cause of its concern was the seeking of a reduction in the UK contribution to the Community Budget. All Member States except the UK, Greece and Denmark indicated that the Compromise could only be relied upon with respect to the particular national interest claimed to be at stake, and could not be invoked with regard to any proxy issue. At the June 1983 European Council in Stuttgart, a "Solemn Declaration on European Union" was agreed, in which it was stated that the "application of the decision-making procedures laid down in the Treaties is of vital importance in order to improve the EC's capacity to act". The Member States clarified their position towards the Compromise in national statements. At one end of the spectrum, the UK and Denmark stated that whenever a Member State "considers its very important interests are at stake, the discussion should continue until unanimous agreement is reached". The Netherlands, Belgium, Luxembourg, Germany and Italy, on the other hand, declared that "the Presidency must have recourse to the vote where the Treaties allow for this". Ireland, together with France, was of the view that "the President shall have recourse to the vote where the Treaties allow for this, while accepting that the vote will be postponed if one or several Member States so request, in the name of defending a vital national interest of direct relevance to the subject under discussion, which they will confirm in writing".[25]

---

23 Anthony Teasdale, "The Life and Death of the Luxembourg Compromise" (1993) 31 *Journal of Common Market Studies* 568, 570.

24 See Martin Vasey, "The 1985 Farm Price Negotiations and the Reform of the Common Agriculture Policy" (1985) 22 *Common Market Law Review* 649.

25 A similar position was taken by Ireland's representative on the Ad Hoc Committee for Institutional Affairs (and also the Chair of the Committee) established in 1984. Although in agreement with the principle underlying the Report's text on majority voting within the Council, Senator James Dooge "felt unable to support the text because, though not excluding the pleading in exceptional circumstances of a vital interest it did not include any explicit reference to the protection of vital national interests in exceptional circumstances". Ad Hoc Committee for Institutional Affairs, "Report to the European Council, Brussels, 29–30 March 1985", 27. According to Patrick Keatinge,

[5–29] In 1986, during a UK Presidency (which, given its stated position, was unlikely to have called a vote), Ireland invoked national interests in seeking to block a Council decision on reform of the beef market until it received an additional premium for Irish beef producers, in order to compensate for a reduction in prices. A unanimous agreement was reached, avoiding an impasse. The last attempt to rely on the Compromise is regarded to have been a failed effort by Greece in 1988, on which occasion Ireland joined with the UK, Denmark, France and Portugal in accepting that discussions should continue, whereas all other Member States objected.

[5–30] The precise status of the Compromise is disputed, with one former judge of the Court of Justice dismissing it as a "mere press release", and in more recent times it has fallen into disuse.[26] Whilst not going so far as to declare it entirely extinct, the sixth edition of *Wyatt and Dashwood* confines reference to it to a footnote, deciding that "it no longer deserves such detailed consideration" as contained in past editions.[27] Nevertheless, there remains a perception that it may continue to be invoked by a Member State should it consider that the need arises. Whereas Teasdale notes that, in practice, the Compromise "effectively died" with the entry into force of the Single European Act in July 1987, in discussing the Act in the House of Commons the UK Foreign Secretary argued that "as a last resort, the Luxembourg Compromise remains in place untouched and unaffected ... [It] is not a provision of the Treaty; it is a component of political reality in the Community ... [and] is in no way affected one way or the other by the Single European Act".[28] Even in 1990, the then Foreign Secretary declared the Compromise to be "alive and well" and available to any government.[29] In response to a European Parliament question provided in September 2001, the Council indicated that the status of the Compromise would "remain the same" after the entry into force of the Nice Treaty.[30]

[5–31] Although stated to not necessarily reflect the official position of the Union, an EU publication on European Union law observes that the Compromise "remains a major political factor, at least as far as voting practice is concerned".[31] Trevor Hartley appears to conclude that although the Compromise has "to some extent withered away", "one cannot say that the convention is dead, since many decisions are still taken without a vote and considerable efforts are made to reach a consensus".[32] Indeed, recourse

Ireland's reservation was placed "apparently with some reluctance ... having as recently as March 1984 invoked the veto (on the milk super levy). Dr FitzGerald's government felt unable to ignore altogether the concept of vital national interest. Nevertheless, when the political decision was taken to proceed with the reform proposals, in June 1985 at Milan, Ireland did side with the reformist camp against the United Kingdom, Denmark and Greece." Patrick Keatinge, "Ireland's European Policies: The Single European Act and Beyond" (1989) XIV *Études Irlandaises* 165, 166.

26 Pierre Pescatore, "Some Critical Remarks on the Single European Act" (1987) 24 *Common Market Law Review* 9, 13.

27 Alan Dashwood, Michael Dougan, Barry Rodger, Eleanor Spaventa and Derrick Wyatt, *Wyatt and Dashwood's European Union Law* (6th ed, Hart, 2011) 50, footnote 65.

28 Anthony Teasdale, "The Life and Death of the Luxembourg Compromise" (1993) 31 *Journal of Common Market Studies* 568, 574–575.

29 *ibid.*

30 Reply to Written Question E–1109/01 by Jens-Peter Bonde to the Council, *Official Journal* 364 E, 20 December 2001, 48.

31 Klaus-Dieter Borchardt, *The ABC of European Union Law* (Publications Office of the European Union, 2010) 61.

32 Trevor Hartley, *The Foundations of European Community Law* (5th ed, Oxford University Press, 2003) 25.

to the Compromise was threatened as lately as 2014 when the UK sought to oppose the appointment of Jean-Claude Juncker as President of the European Commission. Accordingly, the conclusion to a recent editorial entitled "Not Dead Yet" would seem to accurately sum up the Compromise's continuing half-life, suggesting that:

> a Union with limited political and executive authority simply cannot afford to outvote a Member State that fundamentally opposes a draft-decision and that is politically unwilling or unable to execute it. From this perspective we are still living in the same world as that of De Gaulle.[33]

[33] Jan Herman Reestman and Thomas Beuker, "Not Dead Yet: Revisiting the 'Luxembourg Veto' and its Foundations" (2017) 13 *European Constitutional Law Review* 1, 12.

Chapter 6

THE EUROPEAN COMMISSION

A. Introduction

[6–01] The European Commission is commonly perceived as the EU's bureaucracy or civil service, and this is largely true. When compared with national administrations, however, it is clear that the Commission has a number of unique features and a combination of functions that reflect the novel nature of the EU itself. Within the Irish system, for example, sectoral departments are headed at a political level by a minister, who is a member of the Government, and managed by a Secretary General, who is a senior civil servant. Each Government will have its own legislative programme which is implemented by relevant departments, which will also provide policy input as to what legislation is needed and how it should be drafted. Departments also play a role in implementing existing legislation and, in certain cases, have enforcement powers to ensure that legislation is being adhered to. In these roles, departments may propose legislation to establish statutory bodies or agencies to assist in technical areas such as in the transport sector, the Road Safety Authority, the Irish Aviation Authority and the Commission for Aviation Regulation, as just three examples.

[6–02] At the top, the Commission comprises a "college" of 28 Commissioners. The college provides leadership and has formal decision-making authority for the Commission as a whole. In its entirety, the Commission is a body of over 30,000 officials (roughly around the same size as the Irish civil service) who are arranged into around 30 sectoral "Directorates-General", each headed by a Director General. The Directorates-General (DGs) broadly align with the 26 portfolios assigned to the Commissioners, although not exactly, and some Commissioners may have responsibility for more than one DG or parts of a DG. There are also a small number of units that provide general services of a horizontal nature such as a Legal Service and an Internal Audit Service. In carrying out its functions, the Commission is assisted by 36 agencies, 24 of which have been established since 2000. Whereas the Council is the forum in which Member States exert their influence, Commissioners act entirely independently from their state of nationality and are nominated on the basis of their "European commitment". Accordingly, the Commission is generally seen as representing the interests of the Union in a supranational sense and "has always been the political force most committed to integration".[1]

[6–03] The key difference between the Commission and, say, the Irish system of Government departments is that the college of Commissioners does not equate to the Cabinet in the same way that departments are headed by Government ministers. As seen in the previous chapter, the Council of the EU, made up of ministers from each Member State, is the co-decision-maker on legislative proposals with the European Parliament. So, while the college of Commissioners is instrumental in influencing the EU's policy in areas in which the Union has competence – and was very much the driver of integration in the period of establishing the Single Market – ultimately political decisions are made by the Council and the European Parliament. This means that there may be differences of opinion, and institutional rivalry, between the Commission and the Council in a manner that would not arise as between departments and the Government in the Irish system. This rivalry is a manifestation of the perpetual tension between intergovernmentalism and supranationalism that the EU's institutional architecture seeks to defuse. As Fiona Hayes-Renshaw describes, "Council-Commission relations have always been typified by a complex mixture of cooperation and competition" and yet the political rhetoric that accompanies their public skirmishes "coexists with very real cooperation, the result of a long and close working relationship across all areas of EU activity".[2]

[6–04] Notwithstanding that it has to defer to the Council and the Parliament as joint decision-makers, the Commission has close to a monopoly in initiating legislative proposals. This means that it is "both an agenda-setter and a veto player. Nothing can happen without the Commission deciding to make a proposal and this proposal, furthermore, will frame the terms of the legislation".[3] As a result, it has been observed that the Commission tends to be more politicised than a traditional civil service. Whereas the purpose of a Government department is to implement policy as decided upon by the Minister, the Commission is independent from the Council and takes its instructions from the Commissioners, each of whom swears an oath to respect the Treaties in the fulfilment of all their duties and to be completely independent in carrying out their responsibilities, in the general interest of the Union.

B. Composition and Appointment

[6–05] The European Commission is led by a college of 28 Commissioners, made up of the President of the Commission, the High Representative of the Union for Foreign Affairs and Security Policy and 26 other Commissioners, each nominated by the governments of the Member States, for a five-year term that roughly coincides with that of the European Parliament. As the number of EU Member States grew, it was agreed as part of the Lisbon Treaty that, from 1 November 2014, the Commission would consist of a number of members corresponding to two-thirds of the number of

1 Paul Craig and Gráinne de Búrca, *EU Law* (6th ed, Oxford University Press, 2015) 39.
2 Fiona Hayes-Renshaw, "The Council of Ministers" in John Peterson and Michael Shackleton (eds), *The Institutions of the European Union* (3rd ed, Oxford University Press, 2012) 68, 89.
3 Damian Chalmers, Gareth Davies and Giorgio Monti, *European Union Law* (3rd ed, Cambridge University Press, 2014) 73.

Member States, unless the European Council, acting unanimously, decided to alter this number.[4] Following the rejection of the Lisbon Treaty in a referendum, Ireland sought a number of guarantees before holding a second referendum, one of which was that Member States would each retain at least one Commissioner. The European Council agreed to this in principle in July 2009 and gave formal effect to it in a Decision of May 2013.[5] Before the appointment of the next Commission in 2019 the decision will be reviewed in light of its effect on the functioning of the Commission.

[6–06] The election of a new college of Commissioners takes places in two distinct stages. First, the European Council, "taking into account the elections to the European Parliament" will propose a nomination for Commission President to the European Parliament. This process is known as "Spitzenkandidaten", from the German for lead candidate.[6] The Parliament then elects the Commission President if he or she succeeds in obtaining a majority vote in their favour. While the requirement for the European Council to "take account" of the make-up of the new Parliament is expressed in vague terms, it is intended to add further democratic legitimacy to a Commission that is made up of government appointees and not directly elected; essentially, it is a compromise between direct election by the European Parliament and unilateral appointment by the Member States. It is noteworthy that in 2019, the European Council nominated as Commission President an individual – the then German Defence Minister, Ursula von der Leyen – who had not been the lead candidate of any political group within the European Parliament in the elections in May of that year. Her nomination formed part of a compromise reached after the European Council failed to reach agreement on a nominee from among the lead candidates of the political groups. Declaration No 11 to the Treaties expands on the provision in Art 17(7) TEU by establishing an understanding that:

> in accordance with the provisions of the Treaties, the European Parliament and the European Council are jointly responsible for the smooth running of the process leading to the election of the President of the European Commission. Prior to the decision of the European Council, representatives of the European Parliament and of the European Council will thus conduct the necessary consultations in the framework deemed the most appropriate. These consultations will focus on the backgrounds of the candidates for President of the Commission, taking account of the elections to the European Parliament, in accordance with the first subparagraph of Article 17(7). The arrangements for such consultations may be determined, in due course, by common accord between the European Parliament and the European Council.

[6–07] The role of the President is to decide on the internal organisation within the Commission, including by allocating portfolios and appointing Vice-Presidents (other than the High Representative), to lay down guidelines within which the Commission is to work, and to represent the Commission. Upon assuming office, a new Commission President will set out his or her priorities in the form of strategic guidelines or objectives

---

4 Art 17(5) TEU.

5 European Council Decision 2013/371/EU of 22 May 2013 concerning the number of members of the European Commission [2013] OJ L165/98. See ch 3, para 3–10.

6 See Marco Goldini, "Politicising EU Lawmaking? The *Spitzenkandidaten* Experiment as a Cautionary Tale" (2016) 22 *European Law Journal* 269; Desmond Dinan, "Governance and Institutions: The Year of the *Spitzenkandidaten*" (2015) 53 *Journal of Common Market Studies* 93; Nereo Peñalver García and Julian Priestley, *The Making of a European President* (Palgrave Macmillan, 2015).

for the next five years, which will then find their way into the Commission's annual work programmes. Every September, the President delivers a "State of the Union" address to the European Parliament, setting out progress made and initiating a dialogue with the Parliament and the Council on the Commission's annual programme for the forthcoming year.

[6–08] In the second stage of the appointment process, nominations for individual commissioners are received from the government of each Member State. According to Art 17 TEU, Commissioners are to be chosen on the ground of their "general competence and European commitment from persons whose independence is beyond doubt". Of the ten Irish Commissioners, eight were former Government ministers while the remaining two had served as Attorney General. In carrying out its responsibilities, Commissioners are to act completely independently, shall neither seek nor take instructions from any government or other institution, body, office or entity and shall refrain from any action incompatible with their duties or the performance of their tasks. By common accord with the President, the Council (specifically, the General Affairs and Council) then adopts a list of persons whom it proposes for appointment as Commissioners. Following individual hearings, the Commission as a whole is subject to a vote of consent by the Parliament, after which it is formally appointed by the European Council.

[6–09] In addition to the President's power to request an individual Commissioner to resign, Art 17(8) TEU provides that the Commission, as a body, shall be responsible to the European Parliament and that, should the Parliament pass a motion of censure, the Commission shall resign. The threat of such a motion following a critical report by the Court of Auditors in 1999 caused the resignation of the entire Jacques Santer Commission, while in 2004 President José Manuel Barroso withdrew his proposed Commission after it became clear that it would not be supported by the Parliament as a result of controversial views expressed by the Italian nominee, Rocco Buttiglione, during the course of his hearing.

[6–10] The portfolios currently allocated amongst the 26 Commissioners (other than President and High Representative) are as follows:

Better Regulation, Inter-Institutional Relations, Rule of Law and Charter of Fundamental Rights	European Neighbourhood Policy and Enlargement Negotiations
Agriculture and Rural Development	Health and Food Safety
Budget and Human Resources	Humanitarian Aid and Crisis Management
Climate Action and Energy	Internal Market, Industry, Entrepreneurship, SMEs
Competition	International Cooperation and Development
Digital Economy and Society	Jobs, Growth, Innovation and Competitiveness
Digital Single Market	Justice, Consumers and Gender Equality
Economic and Financial Affairs, Taxation and Customs	Migration, Home Affairs and Citizenship
Education, Culture, Youth and Sport	Regional Policy
Employment, Social Affairs, Skills and Labour Mobility	Research, Science and Innovation

Energy Union	Security Union
Environment, Maritime Affairs and Fisheries	Trade
Euro, Social Dialogue, Fiscal Stability, Financial Services, Capital Markets Union	Transport

C. Powers and Functions

[6–11] Article 17 TEU sets out the role of the Commission, beginning with the objective of promoting the general interests of the Union and taking appropriate initiatives to this end. The Commission is also tasked in a broad manner with exercising coordinating, executive and management functions. Giving rise to the title of "guardian of the Treaties", under Art 17 the Commission is responsible for ensuring the "application of the Treaties, and of measures adopted by the institutions pursuant to them", as well as for overseeing the application of Union law under the control of the Court of Justice. In the exercise of this role, the Commission monitors the implementation of EU law by the Member States so as to ensure that it is being correctly applied and promptly "transposed" into national law where necessary. Another core function is typically summed up by the phrase "motor of integration", and results from the fact that, traditionally, it was only the Commission that could formally submit a legislative proposal. In the words of Art 17, "Union legislative acts may only be adopted on the basis of a Commission proposal, except where the Treaties provide otherwise". The Commission is also to initiate the Union's annual and multiannual programming with a view to achieving inter-institutional agreements. Supplementing these two core activities, the Commission has a number of executive functions, particularly in the areas of the EU budget and aid programme, representing the EU abroad and conducting its Common Commercial Policy, as well as managing and implementing a range of EU policies more generally.

(i) Motor of Integration

[6–12] Throughout successive Treaty changes, the Commission has succeeded in maintaining its closely guarded prerogative as the institution that must prepare, draft and present every formal legislative proposal. This is known as the Commission's power of initiative and has been described as a "fundamental characteristic of the European constitutional order".[7] Through it, the Commission has the power to influence the overall legislative agenda and frame the terms of the debate on specific proposals by putting forward the initial draft for discussion. As Alan Hardacre has observed, "the ability to draft the initial text in the EU system of compromise and consensus means that a very high portion of what the Commission originally includes in a proposal remains at the end of the process".[8] Indeed, it has been noted that "as one of the potential architects of compromise between conflicting positions in the Council, the Commission delegation can be regarded by beleaguered member governments in the Council as their greatest ally on particular issues under discussion".[9]

7 Robert Schütze, *European Union Law* (Cambridge University Press, 2015) 193.

8 Alan Hardacre (ed), *How the EU Institutions Work and How to Work with the EU Institutions* (John Harper, 2011) 13.

9 Fiona Hayes-Renshaw, "The Council of Ministers" in John Peterson and Michael Shackleton (eds), *The Institutions of the European Union* (3rd ed, Oxford University Press, 2012) 68, 89.

[6–13] There are limited exceptions within the Treaties where a legislative act may be initiated by a group of Member States, or on foot of a recommendation from the Court of Justice or the European Central Bank. The prerogative of the Commission is more significantly impinged upon by the power of the Council (Art 241 TFEU) and the Parliament (Art 225 TFEU) to consider a particular matter and bring forward such proposals as it considers appropriate. In addition, the Citizens' Initiative, introduced by the Lisbon Treaty, allows for a petition of one million citizens to prompt the Commission to consider appropriate proposals on the issue of concern. More generally, while the Commission retains the power to set the legislative programme, it must be acknowledged that both the Council and (increasingly) the European Council also play a prominent role in setting legislative priorities.

(ii) Other Legislative Functions

[6–14] In addition to its power of initiative, the Commission also plays a legislative role through making forms of secondary law known as delegated acts (which only the Commission can make) and implementing acts (which the Commission and, in limited circumstances, the Council may make). Delegated acts are provided for in Art 290 TFEU, which reads as follows:

> 1. A legislative act may delegate to the Commission the power to adopt non-legislative acts of general application to supplement or amend certain non-essential elements of the legislative act.
>
> The objectives, content, scope and duration of the delegation of power shall be explicitly defined in the legislative acts. The essential elements of an area shall be reserved for the legislative act and accordingly shall not be the subject of a delegation of power.
>
> 2. Legislative acts shall explicitly lay down the conditions to which the delegation is subject; these conditions may be as follows:
> (a) the European Parliament or the Council may decide to revoke the delegation;
> (b) the delegated act may enter into force only if no objection has been expressed by the European Parliament or the Council within a period set by the legislative act.

[6–15] Article 290 bears a similarity to the "principles and policies" test that governs the delegation of the power to make statutory instruments under Irish law, in that it requires the essential elements of the relevant area to be defined in the parent legislative act. While the types of EU legal act will be considered further in Chapter 10, here it might be noted that although Art 290 describes delegated acts as "non-legislative acts of general application", they are only non-legislative "in the formal sense that they are not legislative acts, because they have not been made by the ordinary or special legislative procedure. Many such delegated acts will nonetheless be legislative in nature. … The reality is therefore that a delegated act will often be what would be regarded as secondary or delegated legislation."[10]

[6–16] Where a legally binding EU act requires *uniform conditions for its implementation*, but does not require that the legal act itself be supplemented or amended

[10] Paul Craig and Gráinne de Búrca, *EU Law* (6th ed, Oxford University Press, 2015) 115–116. See Paul Craig, "Delegated Acts, Implementing Acts and the New Comitology Regulation" (2011) 36 *European Law Review* 671.

as in the case of delegated acts, Art 291 TFEU provides that such an act may confer implementing powers on the Commission (or, in limited instances, the Council) to make the implementing acts necessary to achieve these uniform conditions. Regulation 182/2011 (known as the "Comitology" Regulation) lays down the rules and general principles concerning a mechanism for control by Member States of the Commission's exercise of its implementing powers.[11]

[6–17] Finally, in addition to setting out annual and multi-annual legislative programmes, the Commission can also drive legislative policy through wide-ranging policy strategies as set out in White and Green Papers. The most oft-cited example of this is, justifiably, the Commission's White Paper on the Completion of the Internal Market. The White Paper not only shaped the Single European Act but also set out in an annex close to 300 measures that would need to be enacted in order to complete the Internal Market.

(iii) Guardian of the Treaties

[6–18] Given the decentralised nature of the EU legal system, a critical function performed by the Commission is that of enforcing proper compliance with EU law. Under Art 258 TFEU, if the Commission considers that a Member State has failed to fulfil an obligation under the Treaties, it shall deliver a reasoned opinion on the matter after giving the Member State an opportunity to submit its observations. If the Member State does not comply with the reasoned opinion within the period laid down by the Commission, the Commission may bring the matter before the Court of Justice. Such "infringement proceedings" may be brought where a Member State is deliberately breaching an EU law, applying it in an incorrect manner or where it has failed to implement or "transpose" a directive into national law within the prescribed deadline. Where an infringement proceeding under Art 258 relates to the failure to transpose a directive in time and ends up before the Court, the Commission may specify what it considers to be an appropriate lump sum or penalty payment to be paid by the Member State.[12]

[6–19] In addition, if the Commission considers that a Member State has failed to comply with a judgment of the Court in which it was found to have infringed the Treaties, the Commission may bring the case before the Court a second time, after first giving the state the opportunity to submit its observations, and may specify the lump sum or penalty payment that it considers appropriate. The Commission publishes an annual report on monitoring the application of EU law, detailing its work in this area and including a short report on each Member State.[13] The following figures indicate the extent of the Commission's activity with respect to Ireland in recent years:

---

[11] Regulation (EU) No 182/2011 of the European Parliament and of the Council of 16 February 2011, laying down the rules and general principles concerning mechanisms for control by Member States of the Commission's exercise of implementing powers [2011] OJ L55/13.

[12] Art 260(3) TFEU. The Commission's role in infringement proceedings is discussed further in ch 15.

[13] Report from the Commission, "Monitoring the Application of European Union Law, 2017 Annual Report", COM (2018) 540 final, 12 July 2018.

	2010	2011	2012	2013	2014	2015	2016	2017
New EU pilot files opened	N/A	44	40	58	32	31	25	6
Infringement cases open	58	42	39	38	42	35	53	56
New late transposition cases	31	28	8	10	9	15	36	21

(iv) Other Supervisory Functions

[6–20] As well as the broad power to bring infringement proceedings against Member States under Art 258 TFEU, the Commission is also conferred with more specific supervisory functions in certain Treaty provisions or EU legal acts. For example, in relation to competition law, Art 105 TFEU provides that:

> 1. … the Commission shall ensure the application of the principles laid down in Articles 101 and 102. On application by a Member State or on its own initiative, and in cooperation with the competent authorities in the Member States, which shall give it their assistance, the Commission shall investigate cases of suspected infringement of these principles. If it finds that there has been an infringement, it shall propose appropriate measures to bring it to an end.
>
> 2. If the infringement is not brought to an end, the Commission shall record such infringement of the principles in a reasoned decision. The Commission may publish its decision and authorise Member States to take the measures, the conditions and details of which it shall determine, needed to remedy the situation.

[6–21] Similarly, in relation to the rules governing state aid, Art 108 TFEU provides that:

> 1. The Commission shall, in cooperation with Member States, keep under constant review all systems of aid existing in those States. It shall propose to the latter any appropriate measures required by the progressive development or by the functioning of the internal market.
>
> 2. If, after giving notice to the parties concerned to submit their comments, the Commission finds that aid granted by a State or through State resources is not compatible with the internal market having regard to Article 107, or that such aid is being misused, it shall decide that the State concerned shall abolish or alter such aid within a period of time to be determined by the Commission.
>
> If the State concerned does not comply with this decision within the prescribed time, the Commission or any other interested State may, in derogation from the provisions of Articles 258 and 259, refer the matter to the Court of Justice of the European Union direct.

[6–22] For example, following an investigation into the tax affairs of Apple in Ireland, in 2016 the Commission issued a decision in which it required Ireland to recover €13 billion in unpaid taxes which it regarded as a form of prohibited state aid.[14] Ireland disagreed with the Commission's assessment and instituted annulment proceedings in the General Court.[15]

---

[14] Commission Decision of 30 August 2016 on State Aid SA.38373 (2014/C) (ex 2014/NN) (ex 2014/CP) implemented by Ireland to Apple, C (2016) 5605 final, [2017] OJ L187/1.

[15] Case T–778/16 *Commission v Ireland* [2016] OJ C38/35 (ongoing).

[6–23] Another supervisory role played by the Commission relates to monitoring the economic policies of Member States. For example, Art 126 TFEU commits the Member States to avoiding excessive government deficits. To this end, the Commission is tasked with monitoring the development of the budgetary situation and of the stock of government debt in the Member States with a view to identifying gross errors, and with examining compliance with budgetary discipline on the basis of set criteria. Ireland experienced intensive Commission supervision of economic policies in the context of loans received from the European Financial Stability Facility in 2011. The Facility was replaced by the European Stability Mechanism Treaty in 2012. This Treaty tasks the Commission, in liaison with the European Central Bank, with negotiating a memorandum of understanding (MoU) with the Member State setting out the conditions for financial assistance and the timescale for meeting those conditions, as well as with monitoring the degree of compliance. As Damian Chalmers has observed, "monitoring compliance will typically involve Commission officials being on the ground in the state concerned, checking that the state is implementing, inter alia, the competitiveness reforms, privatisations, tax increases and public spending cuts that the MoU will require. The Commission will also publish extensive reviews of the state's performance every three months."[16] As he rightly notes, however, these supervisory powers are less about policing compliance with EU law, and more in the nature of monitoring contractual obligations entered into by the Member State in order to avail of a loan facility.

(v) Managing and Implementing EU Policies

[6–24] Across a range of areas, the Commission has a general responsibility to manage, implement and develop EU policies. For instance, the Commission is central to the running of the Common Agricultural Policy, the Common Customs Policy and EU competition policy. As one example, where a proposed merger involves businesses of a combined annual turnover that exceeds specified thresholds in global and European sales, it must be notified to the Commission for examination. This applies even if both companies have their registered offices outside of the EU. The Commission may also examine mergers which are referred to it from the national competition authorities of the Member States. This may take place on the basis of a request by the merging companies or a request by the national competition authority. For instance, the Commission approved the acquisition of Sky by the US media company, Twenty-First Century Fox, and the acquisition of EMI by Universal Music, provided that EMI first divested its Parlophone label and certain other music assets.[17] Having found that certain information provided by Facebook with respect to its acquisition of WhatsApp was misleading, the Commission fined Facebook €110 million.[18] From time to time the Commission will publish white papers and impact assessments on aspects of merger control, as well as reports on the effectiveness of existing EU legislation in the area, and may carry out consultations on possible improvements.

---

[16] Damian Chalmers, Gareth Davies and Giorgio Monti, *European Union Law* (3rd ed, Cambridge University Press, 2014) 76. The role of the Commission in the context of Economic and Monetary Union is discussed further in ch 27.

[17] Case M.8354 Fox/Sky, Commission decision of 7 April 2017 [2017] OJ C238/1; Case M.6458 Universal Music Group/EMI Music, Commission decision of 21 September 2012 [2013] OJ C220/15.

[18] Case M.8228 Facebook/WhatsApp (Art 14(1) procedure) Commission decision of 18 May 2017 [2017] OJ C286/6.

(vi) Managing the EU Budget and Aid Programme

[6–25] The Commission is responsible for presenting an annual budget to the Parliament and Council (Art 314 TFEU), as well as for submitting an annual account of the preceding financial year relating to the implementation of the budget, together with a financial statement of the assets and liabilities of the Union (Art 318 TFEU). The Commission is also responsible for implementing the budget and may, subject to certain limitations, transfer appropriations from one chapter to another.

[6–26] The Commission administers the EU's extensive development aid and humanitarian programmes and may "take any useful initiative" to promote coordination between actions of the Union and those of the Member States in order to enhance the efficiency and complementarity of their actions (Arts 210 and 214 TFEU).

(vii) Representing the EU in External Relations and Trade Negotiations

[6–27] Other than with respect to the Common Foreign and Security Policy, the Commission is responsible for the external representation of the EU. This unusual arrangement is reflected in the "double-hatted" nature of the position of High Representative of the Union for Foreign Affairs and Security Policy, who both chairs the Foreign Affairs Council and is a Vice-President of the Commission. It is reflected, too, in the make-up of the European External Action Service (EEAS), which is comprised of seconded officials from Member States and of staff from both the Council Secretariat and the Commission. Indeed, prior to the establishment of the EEAS in 2009, the EU's delegations across the world were run by the Commission. The Commission acts as the EU's negotiator for all bilateral trade negotiations (Art 207 TFEU) and at the World Trade Organisation, and is typically appointed as the negotiator of EU agreements with third countries under Art 218 TFEU. It also leads on accession negotiations and is the appointed negotiator for the EU in respect of an agreement on the withdrawal of the United Kingdom.

D. EU Agencies

[6–28] The Commission is assisted in its tasks by two forms of EU agency – "executive agencies" and "independent", "decentralised" or "regulatory agencies". Executive agencies are set up for a limited period of time to manage specific tasks related to EU programmes and are under the control and responsibility of the Commission. There are currently six executive agencies.[19]

[6–29] In contrast, decentralised agencies are independent from the Commission, having their own legal personality and, usually, a board of management composed of one representative from each Member State and one from the Commission. Whereas executive agencies are based in Belgium or Luxembourg, decentralised agencies are

[19] The six executive agencies are: (i) Education, Audiovisual and Culture Executive Agency; (ii) Executive Agency for Small and Medium-sized Enterprises; (iii) European Research Council Executive Agency; (iv) Consumers, Health, Agriculture and Food Executive Agency; (v) Research Executive Agency and Innovation and (vi) Networks Executive Agency. See Council Regulation (EC) No 58/2003 of 19 December 2002 laying down the statute for executive agencies to be entrusted with certain tasks in the management of Community programmes [2003] OJ L11/1.

spread throughout the Member States. The European Foundation for the Improvement of Living and Working Conditions (Eurofound) is the only agency located in Ireland (although the Food and Veterinary Office, a part of DG Health and Food Safety, is based in County Meath).[20]

1975	**1990**
– European Centre for the Development of Vocational Training – European Foundation for the Improvement of Living and Working Conditions (Eurofound)	– European Environment Agency – European Union Institute for Security Studies
1992	**1993**
– Europol – European Police Office	– European Monitoring Centre for Drugs and Drug Addiction
1994	**1995**
– Community Plant Variety Office – European Training Foundation – Translation Centre for the Bodies of the EU – European Agency for Safety and Health at Work	– European Medicines Agency
1996	**2001**
– EU Intellectual Property Office (formerly Office for Harmonisation in the Internal Market – Trade Marks and Designs (OHIM))	– EU Satellite Centre *(CSDP)*
2002	**2004**
– European Food Safety Authority – European Aviation Safety Agency – European Maritime Safety Agency – Eurojust – EU's Judicial Cooperation Unit	– Frontex – European Border and Coast Guard Agency – EU Agency for Network and Information Security European Global Navigation Satellite Systems Agency *(CSDP)* – EU Agency for Railways – European Defence Agency *(CSDP)*
2005	**2006**
– European Fisheries Control Agency – EU Agency for Law Enforcement Training – European Centre for Disease Prevention and Control	– European Chemicals Agency
2007	**2009**
– European Institute for Gender Equality – EU Agency for Fundamental Rights	– Office of the Body of European Regulators for Electronic Communications

[20] A Seat Agreement between Ireland and Eurofound was entered into on 10 November 2015 (Irish Treaty Series No 14 of 2016), which was given effect to by the European Foundation for the Improvement of Living and Working Conditions (Privileges and Immunities) Order 2016 (SI No 428 of 2016). As a result of the UK's withdrawal notification, a process was run to select cities for the relocation of the European Medicines Agency (EMA) and the European Banking Authority (EBA). Dublin was a candidate for both and tied with Paris for the relocation of the EBA, losing out in a subsequent drawing of lots.

2010	2011
– Agency for the Cooperation of Energy Regulators – European Asylum Support Office	– European Banking Authority – European Insurance and Occupational Pensions Authority – European Securities and Markets Authority – European Agency for the operational management of large-scale IT systems in the area of freedom, security and justice (EU-LISA)
2015	**2019**
– Single Resolution Board	– European Labour Authority

[6–30] Including the three CSDP agencies, there are 36 decentralised agencies, 24 of which were established since 2000. This expansion followed criticism of the Commission arising out of the BSE food health crisis and the auditing issues that led to the resignation of the Santer Commission in 1999. As part of the response, a Commission White Paper in 2000 recommended the creation of EU agencies in fields marked by specialisation, complexity and where there was a single, predominant public interest.[21] A chronological list of agencies, set out below, illustrates that a particular crisis can continue to prompt the creation of new agencies, with the Banking Authority, Insurance and Occupational Pensions Authority, Securities and Markets Authority and the Single Resolution Board all established following the financial crisis of 2008–2011.

[6–31] There is no single definition of an agency within EU law, and their functions vary considerably. Generally, it may be said that agencies tend to become the source of scientific or technical expertise in a narrow field. As such, agencies can assist the Commission in developing policy and in drafting either legislation for submission to the Council and Parliament, or delegated and implementing acts that the Commission may adopt itself. Agencies are also known for developing networks of stakeholders, including national competent authorities, from across the Member States, providing a forum for sharing information and expertise and discussing implementation issues. Indeed, it has been suggested that the success of the network model has been crucial to the proliferation of agencies:

> By relying on networks of national regulatory authorities, EU agencies render themselves less threatening to those who oppose centralisation of power. Nevertheless, by creating and coordinating networks of national regulatory authorities, the EU agencies can encourage the spread of common regulatory norms and practices across the member states. Ultimately, the agencies manage to harness the capacities of existing national regulatory authorities to serve European ends.[22]

[6–32] The Commission has itself acknowledged this tendency in its 2008 communication on the topic, noting that agencies "have proved particularly relevant in the field of shared competences, when the implementation of new policies at Community level needs to be accompanied by close cooperation between the Member States and

[21] European Commission, *European Governance: A White Paper*, COM(2011) 428, 24.

[22] R Daniel Kelemen and Giandomenico Majone, "Managing Europeanisation: the European Agencies" in John Peterson and Michael Shackleton (eds), *The Institutions of the European Union* (3rd ed, Oxford University Press, 2012) 219, 238.

the EU. The establishment of agencies can make possible a pooling of powers at EU level which would be resisted if centred on the institutions themselves".[23]

[6–33] According to the *Meroni* doctrine, based on a 1958 judgment of the same name, there are limits to the extent to which discretionary powers may be delegated to bodies not established by the EU Treaties themselves, such as powers that would require an agency to arbitrate conflicting public interests, exercise political discretion or carry out complex economic assignments.[24] As a result, some agencies, such as the European Medicines Agency, prepare an assessment of whether an authorisation should be granted and then submit the assessment to the Commission so as to allow it to make a formal decision. There are other agencies, however, such as the Community Plant Office and the EU Intellectual Property Office, which do grant binding decisions. For example, it has been suggested that the regulatory powers granted to the Chemicals Agency and the Aviation Safety Agency would "seem to push them into the realm of discretionary decision-making", such that over time one can observe "a gradual decrease in the constraints imposed by the *Meroni* doctrine and a gradual increase in the authority delegated to EU agencies".[25] A more recent judgment by the Court of Justice refusing a challenge by the UK to a decision of the European Securities and Markets Authority based, in part, on the *Meroni* doctrine, would seem to support this view.[26] A useful categorisation of the functions of decentralised agencies is provided in the Commission's 2008 communication as follows:

Agencies adopting individual decisions which are legally binding on third parties[27]	• Community Plant Office • EU Intellectual Property Office • European Aviation Safety Agency • European Chemicals Agency
Agencies providing direct assistance to the Commission and, where necessary, to the Member States, in the form of technical or scientific advice and/or inspection reports	• European Maritime Safety Agency • European Food Safety Authority • European Railway Agency • European Medicines Agency
Agencies in charge of operational activities	• European Global Navigation Satellite Systems Agency • Community Fisheries Control Agency • FRONTEX • EUROJUST • EUROPOL • European Union Agency for Law Enforcement Training

23 Communication from the Commission to the European Parliament and the Council, "European Agencies – The Way Forward", COM/2008/0135 final, 11 March 2008, 5.

24 Case 9/56 *Meroni v High Authority* [1958] ECR 135. See Stefan Griller and Andreas Orator, "Everything Under Control? The 'Way Forward' for European Agencies in the Footsteps of the Meroni Doctrine" (2010) 35 *European Law Review* 3; Madalina Busuioc, "Accountability, Control and Independence: The Case of European Agencies" (2009) 15 *European Law Journal* 599.

25 R Daniel Kelemen and Giandomenico Majone, "Managing Europeanisation: The European Agencies" in John Peterson and Michael Shackleton, *The Institutions of the European Union* (3rd ed, Oxford University Press, 2012) 219, 228. See Elizabeth Howell, "EU Agencification and the Rise of ESMA: Are its Governance Arrangements Fit for Purpose?" (2019) *Cambridge Law Journal* (forthcoming).

26 Case C-270/12 *United Kingdom v Council* EU:C:2014:18, 22 January 2014.

27 See Edoardo Chiti, "European Agencies' Rulemaking: Powers, Procedures and Assessment" (2013) 19 *European Law Journal* 93.

Agencies responsible for gathering, analysing and forwarding objective, reliable and easy to understand information / networking	• European Centre for Development of Vocational Training • EUROFOUND • European Environment Agency • European Training Foundation • European Monitoring Centre for Drugs and Drugs Addiction • European Agency for Safety and Health at Work • European Network and Information Security Agency • European Centre for Disease Prevention and Control • Fundamental Rights Agency • European Institute for Gender Equality
Services to other agencies and institutions	• Translation Centre for the Bodies of the EU

Chapter 7

THE EUROPEAN PARLIAMENT

A. Introduction

[7–01] As the EU's only directly elected institution, the European Parliament is the principal source of the Union's democratic legitimacy. Indeed, elections to the Parliament are the largest transnational elections in the world. In 1957, the Treaty of Rome provided that the Parliament would initially be comprised of "representatives of the peoples" of the Member States, in the form of delegates selected by national parliaments, but that this would give way to elections by direct universal suffrage in accordance with a uniform procedure in all Member States. The first direct elections to the Parliament eventually took place in 1979.[1]

[7–02] Article 10 TEU expressly acknowledges that the functioning of the Union shall be founded on representative democracy, with EU citizens to be directly represented at Union level in the European Parliament, while governments represented in the European Council and the Council are "themselves democratically accountable either to their national Parliaments, or to their citizens". Article 10 also recognises that "political parties at European level contribute to forming European political awareness and to expressing the will of citizens of the Union". In accordance with Art 22 TFEU, every citizen of the Union residing in a Member State of which he or she is not a national shall have the right to vote and to stand as a candidate in elections to the European Parliament in the Member State in which he or she resides, under the same conditions as nationals of that state.

B. Composition and Election

[7–03] There are 750 members of the European Parliament (MEPs) plus the President. According to Art 14 TEU, no Member State shall have fewer than six or more than

---

[1] This was provided for by the Act concerning the Election of the Members of the European Parliament by direct universal Suffrage, annexed to Decision 76/787/ECSC, EEC, Euratom, [1976] OJ L278/5, as amended by Council Decision 2002/772/EC, Euratom [2002] OJ L283/1 (entered into force 1 April 2004) and Council Decision (EU, Euratom) 2018/994 [2018] OJ L178/1 (not yet in force).

96 MEPs, who are to be allocated on a "degressively proportional" basis, meaning that the size of a state's population is not the sole criterion in allocating the number of MEPs. So, for example, while Germany has one MEP for every 854,000 inhabitants (96 MEPs for a population of 82 million), Malta has one for every 66,000 inhabitants (six MEPs for a population of 400,000). The allocation of MEPs to each Member State is decided upon by the European Council acting by unanimity and with the consent of the Parliament.[2] Ireland has 11 MEPs for a population of 4.7 million, or one for every 427,000 inhabitants, which have been divided amongst three constituencies of Dublin (3), South (4) and Midlands-North-West (4).[3] On account of the UK's withdrawal from the EU and the reallocation of its European Parliament seats, a decision of the European Council decided that, in the event of the UK's withdrawal, Ireland is to have 13 MEPs in a reduced Parliament comprising 705 MEPs.[4] The two additional seats have been allocated to the Dublin (4) and South (5) constituencies, with the counties of Laois and Offaly moved from Midlands-North-West to South. The candidates who came fourth in Dublin, and fifth in the South constituency, in the May 2019 elections are essentially on a reserve list pending the outcome of the withdrawal process. The allocation amongst the 28/27 Member States is as follows:

96	96	Germany	18	19	Austria
74	79	France	17	17	Bulgaria
73	0	United Kingdom	13	14	Denmark, Slovakia, Finland
73	76	Italy	11	13	Ireland
54	59	Spain	11	12	Croatia
51	52	Poland	11	11	Lithuania
32	33	Romania	8	8	Latvia, Slovenia
26	29	The Netherlands	6	7	Estonia
21	21	Belgium, Czech Republic, Greece, Hungary, Portugal	6	6	Cyprus, Luxembourg, Malta
20	21	Sweden	751	705	

[7–04] Although not set out in the Treaties, the 1976 decision establishing direct elections provides that they must be conducted by proportional representation and held in each Member State within the same four-day period between a Thursday and a Sunday. Article 223 TFEU envisages that the Parliament shall draw up a proposal to lay down the provisions necessary for elections by direct universal suffrage in accordance with "a uniform procedure in all Member States or in accordance with principles common to all Member States". Reflecting national sensitivities, after obtaining the consent of the Parliament, such a proposal would be adopted by the Council acting unanimously in accordance with a special legislative procedure. While proposals have been made, thus far it has proved difficult to reach agreement on them. Use has been made, however, of

[2] See 2013/312/EU European Council Decision of 28 June 2013 establishing the Composition of the European Parliament [2013] OJ L181/57.

[3] See the European Parliament Elections Act 1997 as amended by the European Parliament Elections (Amendment) Act 2004, the Electoral, Local Government and Planning and Development Act 2013, the European Parliament Elections (Amendment) Act 2014 and the European Parliament Elections (Amendment) Act 2019.

[4] European Council Decision (EU) 2018/937 of 28 June 2018 establishing the composition of the European Parliament [2018] OJ L165I/1.

Art 224 TFEU, which provides a legal basis for the adoption of regulations governing political parties at European level, and in particular the rules regarding their funding.[5] The Parliament has also adopted a statute laying down regulations governing the performance and duties of MEPs, providing that they shall be free and independent and shall not be bound by instructions, as well as providing for their level of salary.[6]

[7–05] An important feature of the European Parliament is that its members do not sit as national delegations. Rather, MEPs align themselves with one of eight European level political groups or decide to sit as a non-attached member. Two of the seven groups are particularly dominant – the European People's Party or EPP (to which Fine Gael is affiliated) and the Progressive Alliance of Socialists and Democrats or S&D (to which the Labour Party is affiliated), which respectively have 24 and 20 per cent of the seats in the 2019–2024 Parliament. Having being joined by Emmanuel Macron's La République En Marche, the former Alliance of Liberals and Democrats in Europe (ALDE) (to which Fianna Fáil is affiliated) has grown significantly and been renamed Renew Europe. It has 14 per cent of the seats in the current Parliament, while the Greens/European Free Alliance and Identity and Democracy both have 10 per cent. The European Conservatives and Reformists have 8 per cent, while the Confederal Group of the European United Left – Nordic Green Left (GUE/NGL) (to which Sinn Féin is affiliated) and the Europe of Freedom and Direct Democracy Group both have just under 6 per cent of the seats. The remaining 7 members are non-attached.

[7–06] MEPs are elected for a five-year term, which coincides roughly with the appointment of a new Commission. According to the Parliament's rules of procedure, however, the President of the Parliament serves a term of two-and-a-half years. The Presidency is usually held by the nominee of either the EPP or S&D, as the two largest groupings. An exception to this, however, was Irish MEP, Pat Cox, of the ALDE Group, who served as President from 2002 to 2004. The President acts as the speaker of the Parliament and represents the Parliament externally, including in its relations with other institutions. For example, as a matter of practice the President of the Parliament addresses the European Council at the beginning of each of its meetings, even though he or she is not a member of the European Council and does not attend the remainder of its meeting.

[7–07] The Parliament formally acts through its plenary sessions, which usually take place one week per month in Strasbourg (with occasional sittings in Brussels). As a default rule, the Treaties provide that the Parliament shall act by a majority of the votes cast, which is generally done by a show of hands.[7]

[7–08] The detailed work of the Parliament is conducted in the form of 20 standing committees which consider legislative proposals and can hold hearings and prepare

---

[5] Regulation (EU, Euratom) No 1141/2014 of the European Parliament and of the Council of 22 October 2014 on the statute and funding of European political parties and European political foundations [2014] OJ L317/1; Regulation (EU, Euratom) No 1142/2014 of the European Parliament and of the Council of 22 October 2014 amending Regulation (EU, Euratom) No 966/2012 as regards the financing of European political parties [2014] OJ L317/28.

[6] Decision of the European Parliament of 28 September 2005 adopting the Statute for Members of the European Parliament (2005/684/EC, Euratom) [2005] OJ L 262/2.

[7] Art 231 TFEU.

reports on their own initiative.[8] Committees usually meet in Brussels and are made up of between 30 to 60 MEPs reflecting the composition of the Parliament, with the same number of substitute members. Most MEPs, therefore, will serve on one committee as a full member and act as a substitute for another. A legislative proposal is referred by the plenary session directly to a committee, without debate, which then examines the matter before returning it to the plenary for a vote. If a committee decides that it wishes to react to a legislative proposal it will appoint a rapporteur from among its members who will steer the committee's consideration and be responsible for preparing a draft report. In some ways the committees can be seen as mini versions of the Parliament: their membership reflects the Parliament as a whole, their meetings are held in public and they enjoy a high level of autonomy in carrying out their role. The Parliament can also establish temporary, special committees with a particular limited mandate. For example, a committee was established to consider the alleged use of European countries by the CIA for the transport and detention of prisoners. A committee of inquiry can also be established, as was done in 2015 in order to consider the diesel car emissions scandal.

C. Powers and Functions

[7–09] Of the EU's original institutions, the Parliament is the one that has changed the most radically since 1957, with increasing powers granted to it in successive Treaty reforms. At first, the Parliament was essentially a supervisory and consultative body that played no role in the legislative process. Until 1962, the Parliament was known as the Parliamentary Assembly (a change only formally reflected in the Treaties through the Single European Act of 1986), with direct elections not taking place until 1979. An enhancement of its powers did occur, however, with the introduction of "own resources" financing in the Budget Treaties of 1970 and 1975, which granted the Parliament the right to reject the EU's budget, make limited modifications within it, and to approve the annual accounts. A more significant change followed in the Single European Act, which introduced a new "cooperation" procedure for adopting legislation according to which, if the Commission agreed with amendments proposed by the Parliament, unanimity was required within the Council in order to overrule them. An "assent" procedure was also introduced for non-legislative measures, whereby the Parliament's assent was required for the accession of new Member States or for the conclusion of certain international agreements with third countries.

[7–10] It was with the introduction of the Maastricht Treaty of 1992 that the Parliament assumed a genuine co-legislative role through what was then termed the "co-decision procedure". This is now referred to as the "ordinary legislative procedure", since it has become the default rule. The detail of the ordinary legislative procedure is described below. In essence, it elevated the Parliament to a co-equal with the Council in legislative affairs in respect of 15 legal bases, requiring the two institutions to negotiate in order to reach a compromise as between their respective positions. The Maastricht Treaty

---

[8] The 20 standing committees are: (i) Agriculture and Rural Development; (ii) Budgets; (iii) Budgetary Control; (iv) Civil Liberties, Justice and Home Affairs; (v) Constitutional Affairs; (vi) Culture and Education; (vii) Development; (viii) Economic and Monetary Affairs; (ix) Employment and Social Affairs; (x) Environment, Public Health and Food Safety; (xi) Fisheries; (xii) Foreign Affairs; (xiii) Industry, Research and Energy; (xiv) Internal Market and Consumer Protection; (xv) International Trade; (xvi) Legal Affairs; (xvii) Regional Development; (xviii) Transport and Tourism; (xix) Petitions; and (xx) Women's Rights and Gender Equality.

also granted the Parliament the power to: (i) request the Commission to submit a proposal on a matter; (ii) approve the Commission before it took office; (iii) appoint an Ombudsman; and (iv) establish committees of inquiry. In 1997, the Amsterdam Treaty gave the Parliament the power to approve the Commission President and extended the use of the co-decision procedure to 32 legal bases, while the Nice Treaty of 2000 extended this further to 37 legal bases.

[7–11] Following the entry into force of the Lisbon Treaty on 1 December 2009, the ordinary legislative procedure is now applied in 90 legal bases. This was achieved by switching 27 existing legal bases to the procedure (including the common agricultural and fisheries policies, legal immigration, judicial cooperation in criminal matters, police cooperation, the definition of criminal offences and the fight against terrorism) and applying it in the case of 14 new legal bases. Under the Treaty, the requirement for the Council to consult the Parliament before using the residual competence provision under Art 352 TFEU has been changed to a requirement to obtain its consent, and the Parliament has been given a role in the control of delegated Acts under Art 290 TFEU.

[7–12] The Lisbon Treaty also provides that the Parliament is to be kept informed of negotiations on international agreements and that its consent is required for all international agreements covering fields to which the ordinary legislative procedure applies (as well as any withdrawal agreements). In addition, the Treaty elevates the Parliament to a co-equal with the Council in exercising budgetary functions and requires the European Council to take account of the result of European Parliament elections when nominating a candidate for Commission President (in addition to requiring his or her election by the Parliament).

[7–13] As suggested by Michael Shackleton, an interesting way of understanding the Parliament's role is to view it as comprising three broad categories: history-making decisions (such as in relation to new accessions to the Union or the appointment of a new Commission); policy-making decisions and policy-implementing decisions. To this might be added a fourth, supervisory function.[9]

(i) History-Making Decisions

[7–14] The Parliament elects the President of the Commission, on the basis of a nomination by the European Council that must take account of the Parliamentary election results.[10] This process is known as "Spitzenkandidaten", from the German for lead candidate. The Parliament must also approve the Commission as a whole, for the purposes of which it holds hearings with each individual candidate for Commissioner. If the Parliament passes a vote of censure by a two-thirds majority of votes cast (and representing a majority of all MEPs), the Commission is required to resign.[11]

[7–15] The Parliament's consent is required for new accessions to the EU as well as for any agreement providing for the withdrawal of a Member State.[12] Other than

9 Michael Shackleton, "The European Parliament" in John Peterson and Michael Shackleton (eds), *The Institutions of the European Union* (3rd ed, Oxford University Press, 2012) 135.

10 Art 17(7) TEU. See ch 6, paras [6 05] to [6–10].

11 Art 234 TFEU.

12 Arts 49 and 50 TEU.

agreements that relate exclusively to the Common Foreign and Security Policy, the Parliament's consent is required for most international agreements, including association agreements with third countries and trade agreements.[13] Where the agreement is one that does not require the Parliament's consent, the Parliament must be first be consulted.[14]

[7–16] It is likely that the requirement for the European Parliament's consent to international agreements will serve to strengthen its influence and prominence by giving it a high profile in deciding upon politically sensitive issues. For example, the requirement for the Parliament's consent before concluding an agreement with the UK on its withdrawal from the EU resulted in the Parliament securing a role for itself in the negotiations of that agreement, appointing one of its most prominent MEPs – a former prime minister of Belgium – as its "negotiator". Instances of the Parliament exerting its influence include, in 2010, the initial withholding of its consent for the EU's conclusion of the SWIFT Agreement with the United States, concerning the exchange of data on international money transactions. Commentators have noted the seriousness with which the US Government treated the Parliament, with Secretary of State Clinton calling the President of the Parliament before the vote, and Vice-President Biden subsequently addressing the Parliament in order to allay its concerns. The Parliament eventually voted in favour of a modified version of the Agreement. When however, revelations of US espionage emerged, the Parliament passed a resolution asking the Commission to suspend the Agreement (albeit acknowledging that it did not itself have the power to do so).[15]

[7–17] Similarly, in December 2011, the European Parliament rejected a proposed Fisheries Partnership Agreement with Morocco due to certain environmental concerns and a dissatisfaction with the manner in which it applied to the territory of Western Sahara. The negotiations were re-opened to take these concerns into account and a revised Agreement was eventually consented to by the Parliament. Again, in 2012, potential civil liberty implications led the Parliament to reject the EU's ratification of the Anti-Counterfeiting Trade Agreement (ACTA), a multilateral agreement on the enforcement of intellectual property rights, by a margin of 478 to 39.

[7–18] As part of a 2016 Interinstitutional Agreement on Better Law-Making, the Parliament, Council and Commission acknowledged the importance of ensuring that

---

[13] Art 218(6)(a) TFEU: the consent of the European Parliament is required before concluding: (i) association agreements; (ii) agreement on Union accession to the European Convention on Human Rights; (iii) agreements establishing a specific institutional framework by organising cooperation procedures; (iv) agreements with important budgetary implications for the Union; (v) agreements covering fields to which either the ordinary legislative procedure applies, or the special legislative procedure where consent by the European Parliament is required. See Andrea Ott, "The European Parliament's Role in EU Treaty-Making" (2016) 23 *Maastricht Journal of European Law* 1009; Katharina Meissner, "Democratizing EU External Relations: The European Parliament's Informal Role in SWIFT, ACTA, and TTIP" (2016) 21 *European Foreign Affairs Review* 269; Christina Eckes, "How the European Parliament's Participation in International Relations Affects the Deep Tissue of the EU's Power Structures" (2014) 12 *International Journal of Constitutional Law* 904.

[14] Art 218(6)(b) TFEU.

[15] See Jörg Monar, "The Rejection of the EU–US SWIFT Agreement by the European Parliament: A Historic Vote and Its Implications" (2010) 15 *European Foreign Affairs Review* 143; Marieke de Goede, "The SWIFT Affair and the Global Politics of European Security" (2012) 50 *Journal of Common Market Studies* 214; Deirdre Curtin, "Official Secrets and the Negotiation of International Agreements: Is the EU Executive Unbound?" (2013) 50 *Common Market Law Review* 423.

each institution can exercise its rights and fulfil its obligations regarding the negotiation and conclusion of international agreements.[16] To this end, the institutions committed to negotiating improved practical arrangements for carrying out the cooperation and information-sharing that is mandated by the Treaties, as interpreted by the Court of Justice. These negotiations have, however, yet to reach a successful conclusion.

(ii) Policy-Making Powers

[7–19] Through the ordinary legislative procedure, the Parliament and the Council act as the EU's joint legislature. Since the entry into force of the Lisbon Treaty, the ordinary legislative procedure is now the default process used to adopt around 90 per cent of legislative acts. As a result, the position of the Parliament has been significantly further enhanced. The Parliament also has a role under the special legislative procedure. The detail of both of these procedures is set out below.

[7–20] Under Art 225 TFEU, the Parliament may request the Commission to submit a proposal on a matter on which it considers that a Union act is required for the purpose of implementing the Treaties. Such a request from the Parliament usually comes about through an own-initiative report by the relevant standing committee, which would then form the basis for a resolution of the Parliament requesting the Commission to submit a proposal. An individual MEP can also initiate the process by submitting a proposal to the President of the Parliament, who would then request the relevant standing committee to consider the matter. If, having considered the matter, the Commission decides not to submit a proposal, it must inform the Parliament of the reasons why.

[7–21] The Parliament and the Council jointly form the EU's budgetary authority, together negotiating the annual budget and monitoring its execution by the Commission.

(iii) Policy-Implementing Powers

[7–22] The implementation of legislative acts at EU level can take the form of *delegated* acts that supplement or amend certain non-essential elements of the legislative act (Art 290 TFEU) and *implementing* acts, which are used when the parent legislative act requires uniform conditions for its implementation, but does not require that the legal act itself be supplemented or amended (Art 291 TFEU). Under Art 290, the Parliament has a role in respect of the adoption of delegated acts.[17] In contrast, Art 291 does not provide for a role for the Parliament in respect of implementing acts, other than to participate in the adoption of regulations to provide mechanisms for the "control by Member States of the Commission's exercise of implementing powers". To this end, Regulation 182/2011 establishes a series of committees (known as "comitology committees") made up of national experts.[18] As the Parliament does not have a role under Regulation 182/2011, it tends to favour the use of delegated acts over implementing

[16] Paragraph 40 of the Interinstitutional Agreement between the European Parliament, the Council of the European Union and the European Commission of 13 April 2016 on Better Law-Making [2016] OJ L123/1. As between the Parliament and the Commission, paras 23–27 and Annex III of the 2010 Framework Agreement on relations between the European Parliament and the European Commission address cooperation on international agreements [2010] OJ L304/47.

[17] See Michael Kaeding and Alan Hardacre, "The European Parliament and the Future of Comitology after Lisbon" (2013) 19 *European Law Journal* 382.

[18] Regulation (EU) No 182/2011 of the European Parliament and of the Council of 16 February 2011

acts. It has been pointed out that the co-equal nature of the Council and Parliament as the EU's legislature is somewhat undermined by this situation, and that the Parliament "still exercises less-effective influence over policy-implementing decisions than it does over policy-making".[19]

(iv) Supervisory Functions

[7–23] There is a myriad of ways in which the Parliament exercises supervisory powers over the other institutions. For example, the President of the European Council is required to report to the Parliament after each European Council meeting, while the Commission is required to answer questions posed by MEPs. The Parliament can establish committees of inquiry and hold hearings, while the EU Ombudsman is required to submit a report of each of her investigations, as well as an annual report, to the Parliament.[20] In addition, any EU citizen, or any person residing in the EU, may petition the Parliament on any matter which comes within the EU's fields of activity and affects him or her directly.[21]

[7–24] In relation to the Common Foreign and Security Policy (CFSP) and the Common Security and Defence Policy (CSDP), Art 36 TEU obliges the High Representative for Foreign Affairs and Security Policy to regularly consult the Parliament on the main aspects and basic choices of both, inform it of how those policies evolve and ensure that the views of the Parliament are duly taken into consideration. The Parliament may address questions or make recommendations to the Council or the High Representative, and twice a year holds a debate on progress in implementing the CFSP and CSDP.

[7–25] The Parliament also has standing to bring annulment proceedings (Art 263 TFEU) or proceedings alleging a failure to act (Art 265 TFEU) against the other EU institutions.

D. Ordinary Legislative Procedure

[7–26] The Lisbon Treaty greatly streamlined the legislative procedures used to adopt "legislative acts", renaming the co-decision procedure as the ordinary legislative procedure and doing away with the coordination procedure.

[7–27] In a circular definition, Art 289 TFEU provides that "legal acts adopted by legislative procedure shall constitute legislative acts". Article 289 sets out two legislative procedures – the ordinary legislative procedure as the default procedure, applicable around 90 per cent of the time, and the special legislative procedure. Both procedures involve the adoption of a regulation, directive or decision with the participation of both the Council and the Parliament. Accordingly, a legislative act may only take the form of a regulation, directive or decision and has the defining characteristic that both the Council and the Parliament participated in the process leading to its adoption.

---

laying down the rules and general principles concerning mechanisms for control by Member States of the Commission's exercise of implementing powers [2011] OJ L55/13.

[19] Michael Shackleton, "The European Parliament" in John Peterson and Michael Shackleton (eds), *The Institutions of the European Union* (3rd ed, Oxford University Press, 2012) 139.

[20] Arts 226 and 228 TFEU.

[21] Art 227 TFEU.

[7–28] The difference between the two procedures is that, under the ordinary legislative procedure, the act is *jointly adopted* by the Parliament and the Council, with both having an equal role. In contrast, under the special legislative procedure, the act is adopted by either the Council or the Parliament *alone*, with the other institution being either consulted or requested to consent depending on the process prescribed by the relevant Treaty article that forms the legal base for the act's adoption. Each separate legal base within a policy area determines the procedure that is to apply in adopting EU acts, and whether that procedure is a legislative procedure. The legal base may also require that one or both of the EU's advisory bodies be consulted – the Economic and Social Committee and the Committee of the Regions.

[7–29] Although daunting at first, the ordinary legislative procedure comprises, at most, four distinct steps – first reading, second reading, conciliation committee and third reading. As will be seen, in recent years a distinct trend has emerged whereby the Parliament, Council and Commission seek to negotiate an agreement within the framework of the first reading stage, with only a small minority of proposals requiring a second reading, and even fewer needing the establishment of a conciliation committee.

(i) First Reading

[7–30] The ordinary legislative procedure begins with a proposal from the Commission, which is submitted simultaneously to the Council and the Parliament. The plenary of the Parliament will assign it to one of its 20 standing committees, who will appoint a rapporteur from amongst its members. The options open to the Parliament are to reject the proposal (by asking the Commission to withdraw it), to accept it as is, or to suggest amendments. If the committee decides to propose amendments to the text it will seek the views of the Commission and Council on these amendments.

[7–31] In practice, the Council Presidency might make contact with the rapporteur to see whether there is a willingness to enter into negotiations with a view to arriving at a "first-reading agreement" on a compromise text that both the Parliament and the Council could agree to. This would involve the Parliament adopting an amended text as its first reading position, which the Council would then approve. In order to assist in reaching an agreement, informal discussions take place throughout the process in what are known as "trilogues", typically made up of: (i) a senior Commission official from the relevant Directorate-General; (ii) a senior official from the permanent representation of the Member State holding the rotating Council Presidency and the chair of the relevant Council working party; and (iii) two or three MEPs from the relevant standing committee, usually including the rapporteur and the chair of the committee. Indeed, in a Joint Declaration in 2007 the institutions committed to "cooperate in good faith throughout the procedure with a view to reconciling their positions as far as possible and thereby clearing the way, where appropriate, for the adoption of the act concerned at an early stage of the procedure".[22] This is a commitment that has borne fruit, with 85 per cent of proposals agreed to at first reading during the 2009 to 2014 Parliamentary term, compared to a mere 28 per cent between 1999 and 2004.[23] As Damian Chalmers

22 Joint Declaration on Practical Arrangements for the Co-Decision Procedure [2007] OJ C145/2, para 4.

23 European Parliament, Activity Report on Codecision and Conciliation 14 July 2009–30 June 2014 (DV\1031024EN.doc), 8.

observes, "in practice, for three-quarters of law-making under the ordinary legislative procedure, law-making is very simple. Representatives of the Commission, Parliament and Council meet to negotiate a Commission proposal in a closed room. This is then ratified by the Council and the Parliament. The rest of the procedure simply spells out the consequences if there is no agreement."[24]

[7–32] The Parliament adopts its position by a majority of votes cast in the plenary, with the resulting resolution setting out the Parliament's position, which is then sent to the Council. During the period in which the Council is considering the Parliament's position, the Commission retains the freedom to submit a revised proposal. However, if the Parliament considers that the revised proposal substantially alters the version as put forward by it, it may request that the proposal be referred back to the Parliament.

[7–33] If, at its first reading, the Council does not fully agree with the Parliament's position, it may either disagree with some or all of the Parliament's position/proposed amendments, or put forward additional or alternative amendments of its own. The Council will then send a reasoned explanation of its position to the Parliament, which will also receive from the Commission information as to its position.

[7–34] If, on the other hand, the Council and the Parliament reach an agreement on the Commission's proposal, the Council, acting by qualified majority voting (QMV), will adopt the legislative act. The act is then submitted to the Presidents and Secretaries–General of the Parliament and Council for signing and is published in the Official Journal. Where an entry into force date is specified in the act, it will enter into force on that date; otherwise, the act enters into force on the twentieth day following its publication in the Official Journal.

(ii) Second Reading

[7–35] In order to encourage progress, for the stages that follow the first reading, Art 294 TFEU establishes time limits within which the institutions must respond to the latest proposals received by them. So, within the second reading, if the Parliament fails to respond to the Council's position within three months (with a possible extension of a fourth month), the act is deemed to have been adopted in the form submitted by the Council. The Parliament can approve the Council's position by a majority of votes cast, or may reject it by the majority of its component members (thereby making rejection more difficult to achieve than acceptance). If the Parliament rejects the Council's position, the procedure comes to an end without the act being adopted. Alternatively, by a majority of its component members, the Parliament may propose amendments to the Council's position, which are then forwarded to the Council and to the Commission, which delivers an opinion on those amendments. Significantly, the Parliament's Rules of Procedure confine the amendments that it can propose at this stage to those which:

- (i) restore wholly or partly the position adopted by Parliament at its first reading;
- (ii) reach a compromise between the Council and Parliament;
- (iii) amend a part of the text of a Council position which was not included in – or differs in content from – the proposal submitted at first reading; or

---

[24] Damian Chalmers, Gareth Davies and Giorgio Monti, *European Union Law* (3rd ed, Cambridge University Press, 2014) 122.

(iv) take account of a new fact or legal situation which has arisen since the adoption of Parliament's position at first reading.[25]

[7–36] Within three months of receiving the Parliament's amendments, the Council can vote by QMV to approve all of the text as amended, in which case the act will be adopted. However, if the Commission has delivered a negative opinion in respect of any of the Parliament's amendments, the Council must vote unanimously in order to approve them. If the Council does not approve all of the Parliament's amendments, a "Conciliation Committee" – an ad hoc committee that is constituted separately for each legislative proposal requiring conciliation – is to be established within six weeks. During the 2009 to 2014 term, 13 per cent of acts were agreed at second reading (with 8 per cent agreed early within the second reading and 5 per cent agreed through eventual adoption by the Council).[26]

(iii) Conciliation Committee

[7–37] The mandate of the Conciliation Committee is confined to reaching, within six weeks (with the possibility of an extension of two weeks), an agreement on a joint text on the basis of the positions of the Parliament and the Council at second reading, thereby seeking to narrow the range of discussion. Nevertheless, the Court of Justice has taken a pragmatic approach in accepting that, should a consensus solution within the Committee involve straying beyond the positions at second reading, the Committee ought not to be prevented from doing so.[27] This makes sense given that Art 294 TFEU provides that the Commission shall participate in the Conciliation Committee and "take all necessary initiatives with a view to reconciling the positions" of the Parliament and the Council. The Committee has an equal number of MEPs and Council representatives, with the Council members acting by QMV and the MEPs by a majority of their members. If agreement cannot be reached within six weeks, the proposal is not adopted and the procedure ends. If agreement is reached, the Committee must return the joint text to the Parliament and Council, by way of a third reading, as the formal bodies that must approve it. Only nine Conciliation Committees (representing 2 per cent of legislative proposals) were established during the 2009 to 2014 term.[28]

(iv) Third Reading

[7–38] If the Conciliation Committee succeeds in reaching agreement, the Parliament and Council have six weeks in which to approve the act, by a majority of votes cast and by QMV respectively. In the unlikely event that they fail to do so, the act is not adopted and the procedure ends. As a final procedural step, Art 297 TFEU provides that legislative acts adopted under the ordinary legislative procedure must be signed by the Presidents of the Parliament and Council and then published in the Official Journal (where they appear in the "L" series). As mentioned above, the act will enter

[25] Rules of Procedure of the European Parliament, January 2017, Rule 69.

[26] European Parliament, Activity Report on Codecision and Conciliation 14 July 2009–30 June 2014 (DV\1031024EN.doc), 8.

[27] Case C-344/04, *R ex p. International Air Transport Association v Department of Transport* [2006] ECR I-403.

[28] European Parliament, Activity Report on Codecision and Conciliation 14 July 2009–30 June 2014 (DV\1031024EN.doc), 31.

into force on the date specified in the act itself, or otherwise 20 days from the date of publication in the Official Journal.

E. Special Legislative Procedure

[7–39] The second legislative procedure for the adoption of legislative acts in the form of regulations, directives or decisions is known as the "special legislative procedure" and is provided for in Art 289(2) TFEU. There are in fact three variations of this procedure which, moving from the least to the most common, are: (i) the act is formally adopted by the Parliament only, with the *consent* of the Council; (ii) the act is formally adopted by the Council only, with the *consent* of the Parliament; and (iii) the act is formally adopted by the Council only, having *consulted* the Parliament. Where the special legislative procedure applies, the Council is usually required by the relevant Treaty article to act by unanimity. Acts made under this procedure are signed by the President of the institution that adopts the act, and then published in the Official Journal in the "L" series.

[7–40] A special legislative procedure requiring the consent of the Parliament tends to be used in relation to sensitive matters of EU competence such as relating to the EU finances, the creation of the Public Prosecutor's Office,[29] the addition of new citizens' rights or the creation of a uniform method for electing MEPs. It is only in rare instances that it is the Parliament which adopts, with the consent of the Council, and these relate to the rules governing MEPs, the temporary committees of inquiry established by the Parliament and the EU Ombudsman. Most instances of the special legislative procedure, therefore, require that the Council consults with the Parliament, such as in the area of tax policy.[30] In the important case of *Roquette Frères*, the Court of Justice described the consultation procedure as "an essential feature in the institutional balance intended by the Treaty" and as an "essential formality disregard of which means that the measure concerned is void".[31] There, the failure of the Council to wait for an opinion of the Parliament before making a regulation was held to have rendered the act void. To similar effect, if the Council significantly amends a proposal following its consultation with the Parliament, it is required to consult once again on the revised version, unless the amendments give effect to the wishes of the Parliament.[32] Nevertheless, as the obligation is merely to consult, the Council is not required to take account of the Parliament's views in the final text.

[7–41] As noted in Chapter 4, one of the simplified means of amending the Treaties is by use of a *passerelle* clause.[33] One of the two applications of this clause is that the European Council, having obtained the consent of the Parliament, may unanimously decide that a particular use of the special legislative procedure be changed to the ordinary legislative procedure. Before adopting such a decision, any proposal to do so

---

29 Council Regulation (EU) 2017/1939 of 12 October 2017 implementing enhanced cooperation on the establishment of the European Public Prosecutor's Office [2017] OJ L283/1.

30 See Commission Communication, "Towards a more efficient and democratic decision making in EU tax policy" COM(2019) 8 final, 15 January 2019.

31 Case 138/79 *Roquette Frères v Council* [1980] ECR 3333, 3360.

32 Case C-65/93 *Parliament v Council* [1995] ECR I-643.

33 See ch 4, para [4–26].

must be notified to Member States' national parliaments and if any parliament opposes the proposal, the decision will not be adopted.

Chapter 8

THE COURT OF JUSTICE OF THE EUROPEAN UNION

A. Introduction

[8–01] The Court of Justice of the European Union (CJEU) is based in Luxembourg and comprises three separate elements: (i) the Court of Justice (formerly known as the European Court of Justice); (ii) the General Court (formerly known as the Court of First Instance); and (iii) such specialised courts as may be established. The rules in relation to the Court are laid down in Art 19 TEU, Arts 251–281 TFEU, Protocol No 3 on the Statute of the CJEU[1] and the Rules of Procedure of the respective courts.[2] Although media reports will often refer rather loosely to the "European Court", it is important to maintain a distinction between the CJEU in Luxembourg and the entirely separate European Court of Human Rights, which is an institution of the Council of Europe located in Strasbourg.[3] While there is a commitment in Art 6 TEU that the EU shall become a party to the European Convention on Human Rights, this has yet to take place given that, in 2014, a proposed accession agreement was found by the Court of Justice to be incompatible with the EU Treaties.[4]

---

1 See also Regulation (EU, Euratom) 2015/2422 of the European Parliament and of the Council of 16 December 2015 amending Protocol No 3 on the Statute of the Court of Justice of the European Union [2015] OJ L341/14; Regulation (EU, Euratom) 2019/629 of the European Parliament and of the Council of 17 April 2019 amending Protocol No 3 on the Statute of the Court of Justice of the European Union [2019] OJ L111/1.

2 Rules of Procedure of the Court of Justice [2012] OJ L 265/1, with amendments published in [2013] OJ L173/65, [2016] OJ L217/69 and [2019] OJ L111/73; Rules of Procedure of the General Court [2015] OJ L 105/1, with amendments published in [2016] OJ L217/71 and [2018] OJ L240/67.

3 See ch 1, paras [1–05] to [1–09].

4 See Protocol No 8 to the TEU and TFEU and Declaration No 2 annexed to the Final Act of the Intergovernmental Conference which adopted the Lisbon Treaty; Opinion 2/13 *(Accession to the ECHR)* EU:C:2014:2454, 18 December 2014; Johan Callewaert, "Do We Still Need Article 6(2) TEU? Considerations on the Absence of EU Accession to the ECHR and its Consequences" (2018) 55 *Common Market Law Review* 1685; Jörg Polakiewicz, "Accession to the European Convention on Human Rights (ECHR) – An Insider's View Addressing One by One the CJEU's Objections in Opinion 2/13" (2016) 36 *Human Rights Law Review* 10; Síofra O'Leary, "Courts, Charters and Conventions: Making Sense of Fundamental Rights in the EU" (2016) 56 *Irish Jurist*

[8–02] Article 19 TEU provides that the CJEU shall ensure that "in the interpretation and application of the Treaties the law is observed", while the Member States shall provide "remedies sufficient to ensure effective legal protection in the fields covered by Union law".[5] This wording hints at an important division of labour between the CJEU and national courts. Since EU law is an integral part of the national law of the Member States, it falls to their domestic courts to apply EU law in the cases before them on a daily basis. As the Court of Justice has described, both it and the national courts of the Member States are the "guardians of [the Union's] legal order and judicial system" and the "tasks attributed to the national courts and to the Court of Justice respectively are indispensable to the preservation of the very nature of the law established by the Treaties".[6] What, then, is the role of the CJEU?

[8–03] First, through a form of "indirect action" known as the preliminary reference procedure, the Court of Justice may answer a question of EU law posed by a national court in order to assist in resolving a case before it. It is known as an indirect action because, in this procedure, the Court of Justice does not determine the outcome of the case but merely answers the legal question asked, in light of which the national court will then proceed to finalise its deliberations and issue a judgment. The principal rationale behind the preliminary reference procedure is to ensure a uniform application of EU law throughout the Union by allowing national courts faced with a question as to the proper interpretation of EU law to refer the matter to the Court of Justice, rather than to attempt an interpretation of their own.

[8–04] In distinction to indirect actions, "direct actions" involve contentious cases that begin and end before the CJEU. Clearly, in addition to EU law being applied by national courts on a daily basis, there is a need for a separate judicial body to enforce EU law obligations against a Member State in the event that they are in default. These are known alternatively as "enforcement" or "infringement actions" and they arise:

(i) under Art 258 TFEU, where the Commission brings an action against a Member State for failing to fulfil an obligation under the Treaties, having first been called upon to do so;

(ii) under Art 259 TFEU, where one Member State brings an action against another

---

4; Graham Butler, "The Ultimate Stumbling Block? The Common Foreign and Security Policy and Accession of the European Union to the European Convention on Human Rights" (2016) 39 *Dublin University Law Journal* 229; Thomas Ackermann (*et al*), editorial comments, "The EU's Accession to ECHR – A 'NO' from ECJ!" (2015) 52 *Common Market Law Review* 1; Sarah Lambrecht, "The Sting is in the Tail: CJEU Opinion 2/13 Objects to Draft Agreement on Accession of the EU to the European Convention on Human Rights" (2015) *European Human Rights Law Review* 185; Piet Eeckhout, "Opinion 2/13 on EU Accession to the ECHR and Judicial Dialogue: Autonomy or Autarky" (2015) 38 *Fordham International Law Journal* 955; Louise Halleskov Storgaard, "EU Law Autonomy versus European Fundamental Rights Protection – On Opinion 2/13 on EU Accession to the ECHR" (2015) 15 *Human Rights Law Review* 485; Daniel Halberstam, "It's the Autonomy Stupid! A Modest Defense of Opinion 2/13 on EU Accession to the ECHR, and the Way Forward" (2015) 16 *German Law Journal* 105; Eleanor Spaventa, "A Very Fearful Court? The Protection of Fundamental Rights in the European Union after Opinion 2/13" (2015) 22 *Maastricht Journal of European and Comparative Law* 35.

5 See Koen Lenaerts, "The Rule of Law and the Coherence of the Judicial System of the European Union" (2007) 44 *Common Market Law Review* 1625.

6 Opinion 1/09 *(European Patent Court)* EU:C:2011:123, paras 66 and 85. See Kieran Bradley, "International and other apex courts: Dublin viewed from Luxembourg" (2019) 1 *Irish Supreme Court Review* 31.

Member State for failing to fulfil an obligation under the Treaties, having first brought the matter to the attention of the Commission; and

(iii) under Art 260 TFEU, where the Commission brings an action against a Member State for failing to comply with an earlier judgment of the CJEU in which the Member State was found to have failed to fulfil an obligation under the Treaties.

[8–05] Similarly, where it is alleged that an EU institution has infringed the Treaties by failing to act as it ought to have done in some particular way, an enforcement action may be brought against it by another institution or by a Member State pursuant to Art 265 TFEU. As with enforcement actions against Member States, it is appropriate that a centralised EU court should consider any allegation that a Union institution has infringed the Treaties by failing to act.

[8–06] In addition to these enforcement actions, proceedings may be brought before the Court of Justice seeking to have the legality of an EU act judicially reviewed. In other words, an applicant may seek to have an EU act annulled on the grounds that there was a lack of competence to adopt the act or a misuse of powers in its adoption, or that its adoption involved an infringement of the Treaties, any rule of law relating to the Treaties, or of an essential procedural requirement. Such proceedings are governed by Art 263 TFEU and are known as "annulment" actions. An important point to note about annulment actions is that they must be brought within two months of the publication of the challenged measure. In addition, while the Member States and the institutions have general standing to seek the annulment of a measure, a private individual may only challenge an act that is either: (i) addressed specifically to them; (ii) of "direct and individual concern to them"; or (iii) a regulatory act which is of direct concern to them and does not entail implementing measures. The Court has interpreted the criteria of "direct and individual concern" very narrowly, such that it is only in highly particular circumstances that an individual will have the necessary standing required to seek the annulment of an EU act under this procedure.

[8–07] In practice, it may be more likely that an individual will raise the validity of an EU act in national court proceedings and request that court to make a preliminary reference to the Court of Justice. Using this route may be a way of side-stepping the strict two-month time limit for annulment actions, as well as the high threshold required in order to have the standing to bring such actions. Another indirect route is provided by Art 277 TFEU, which allows the inapplicability of a measure to be raised on Art 263 grounds in proceedings in which an EU act of general application is otherwise at issue, regardless of whether the two-month time limit has expired.

[8–08] In addition to enforcement actions, annulment actions and preliminary references, the CJEU also has jurisdiction in respect of claims for damages against the Union on foot of a non-contractual liability, such as a tort committed by the Union.[7] Employment disputes arising from the EU civil service and challenges to decisions of the EU Intellectual Property Office, such as a refusal to grant a trade mark, also comprise a significant part of the case load of the General Court. The Court of Justice can also be conferred with a role in resolving disputes between Member States which relate to the subject matter of the EU Treaties. Under Art 273 TFEU, the Court has jurisdiction in respect of any such dispute that is submitted to it "under a special agreement between

7 Arts 268 and 340 TFEU.

the parties".[8] After first providing an overview of the Court of Justice and the General Court, this chapter will examine the preliminary reference procedure. Chapter 15 considers enforcement actions against Member States, while proceedings against the EU in the form of annulment actions, failure to act claims, indirect challenges and actions for damages are dealt with in Chapter 16.

[8–09] Since the Lisbon Treaty, the jurisdiction of the CJEU extends to all matters of EU law with the exception of the Common Foreign and Security Policy (CFSP). In relation to this area, the Court only has jurisdiction to monitor compliance with Art 40 TEU, which governs the relationship between CFSP and other parts of EU policy,[9] as well as to review the legality of restrictive measures (ie sanctions) adopted on the basis of Chapter 2 of Title V TEU.[10] The most significant expansion of the Court's jurisdiction has been with respect to the Area of Freedom, Security and Justice (AFSJ). Prior to the Lisbon Treaty, the Court's jurisdiction in respect of AFSJ matters was limited, with no enforcement action by the Commission available, limits on the review of the legality of an EU measure and no actions for damages. In addition, a preliminary reference relating to an AFSJ matter could only be received from those Member States that had made a declaration accepting the Court's jurisdiction in this regard. Ireland never made a declaration to this effect.[11] A transitional period allowed for the continuation of this right to opt in to the Court's preliminary reference jurisdiction over AFSJ up until 1 December 2014, from which point the special treatment for this area of EU law was brought to an end, subject to one exception.[12] Reflecting their sensitivity for Member States, the TFEU expressly provides that the CJEU shall have no jurisdiction to review the validity or proportionality of operations carried out by the police or law enforcement services of a Member State, or the exercise by a Member State of its responsibilities for the maintenance of law and order and safeguarding of internal security.[13]

B. Court of Justice

[8–10] The Court of Justice is comprised of one judge from each Member State who is appointed for a renewable six-year term by "common accord of the governments of

[8] See Case C-648/15 *Austria v Germany* EU:C:2017:664, 12 September 2017.

[9] Art 24(1) TEU. See Case C-658/11 *Parliament v Council (Mauritius)* EU:C:2014:2025, 24 June 2014, para 73; Case 263/14 *Parliament v Council (Tanzania)* EU:C:2016:435, paras 68–85; Case C-244/17 *Commission v Council (Kazakhstan)* EU:C:2018:662, 4 September 2018, paras 41–47; Panos Koutrakos, "Judicial Review in the EU's Common Foreign and Security Policy" (2018) 67 *International and Comparative Law Quarterly* 1; Graham Butler, "The Coming of Age of the Court's Jurisdiction in the Common Foreign and Security Policy" (2017) 13 *European Constitutional Law Review* 673; Peter Van Elsuwege, "Upholding the Rule of Law in the Common Foreign and Security Policy: *H v Council*" (2017) 54 *Common Market Law Review* 841; Luigi Lonardo, "The Political Question Doctrine as Applied to Common Foreign and Security Policy" (2017) 22 *European Foreign Affairs Review* 571; Graham Butler, *Constitutional Law of the EU's Common Foreign and Security Policy* (Hart, 2019).

[10] Art 275 TFEU. See Paul James Cardwell, "The Legalisation of European Union Foreign Policy and the Use of Sanctions" (2015) 17 *Cambridge Yearbook of European Legal Studies* 287.

[11] See *O'Sullivan v Chief Executive of the Irish Prison Service* [2010] 4 IR 562, 583; Elaine Fahey, "Being a Third Pillar Guardian of Fundamental Rights? The Irish Supreme Court and the European Arrest Warrant" (2008) 33 *European Law Review* 563.

[12] Protocol No 36 to the TEU and TFEU, Art 10.

[13] Art 276 TFEU.

the Member States".[14] Since the Lisbon Treaty, a nominated candidate for judicial office must first have his or her suitability assessed by a panel made up of former judges of the CJEU, members of national supreme courts and lawyers of recognised competence, one of whom shall be proposed by the European Parliament.[15]

[8–11] The Court of Justice may sit in chambers of three or five judges, or as a Grand Chamber of 15 judges presided over by the President of the Court. The Court shall sit in a Grand Chamber when a Member State or a Union institution that is party to the proceedings so requests, as Ireland did, for example, in the case of *Smith v Meade*.[16] The Court's Statute prescribes four instances where a Full Court of all judges shall be convened, relating to the Court's role in relieving the European Ombudsman, a Commissioner or a member of the Court of Auditors of their duties. Otherwise, a Full Court may be convened where a case is considered to be of "exceptional importance". This is a very rare occurrence but may arise where, pursuant to a procedure provided for in Art 218 TFEU, the Court is requested to provide an opinion on whether an international agreement proposed to be entered into by the Union is compatible with the Treaties. For example, a Full Court considered the draft agreement providing for the EU's accession to the European Convention on Human Rights and found aspects of the agreement to be incompatible with the Treaties.[17] A Full Court also delivered an opinion on a Free Trade Agreement with Singapore that provided important clarification as to the scope of the EU's exclusive competence under the Common Commercial Policy post the Lisbon Treaty, and sat to consider whether the dispute settlement provisions of the Comprehensive Economic and Trade Agreement with Canada were compatible with the Treaties.[18] A rare example of a preliminary reference being dealt with by a Full Court is *Pringle v Ireland*, referred by the Irish Supreme Court, which concerned the validity of the European Stability Mechanism Treaty.[19] By way of illustration, of the judgments delivered in 2018, 300 were by a five-judge chamber, 153 by a three-judge chamber, 76 by a Grand Chamber and just one was by a Full Court.[20]

[8–12] Unlike the practice in Ireland, the Court of Justice delivers only one judgment, representing the agreed view of the Court as a whole, with no dissenting judgments. This need for consensus naturally affects the manner in which judgments are written. Overall, judgments tend to be relatively short with brisk reasoning and a repetition of agreed language from earlier case law. That said, while the Court strives for a high degree of consistency with its earlier judgments, there is no formal system of binding precedent, such that the Court remains free to depart from previous case law.

[8–13] Another key distinction between the Court of Justice and the Irish courts is that the Court of Justice is usually assisted in its deliberations by a separate opinion

---

14 Art 263 TFEU.

15 Art 255 TFEU.

16 Art 16 of the Statute of the Court. Case C-122/17 *Smith v Meade* EU:C:2018:631, 7 August 2018. See ch 12, paras [12–70] to [12–75].

17 Opinion 2/13 *(Accession to the ECHR)* EU:C:2014:2454, 18 December 2014. See para [8–01] above.

18 Opinion 2/15 *(Singapore Free Trade Agreement)* EU:C:2017:376, 16 May 2017; Opinion 1/17 *(CETA)* EU:C:2019:341, 30 April 2019.

19 Case C-370/12 *Pringle v Ireland* EU:C:2012:756, 27 November 2012. See ch 27, paras [27–45] to [27–58].

20 *Court of Justice of the European Union Annual Report 2018, Judicial Activity*, 2019, 129.

that is prepared by an Advocate General. If the Court considers that a case raises no new point of law, it may decide to dispense with the need for an opinion. There are 11 Advocates General, with the UK, France, Germany, Spain, Italy and Poland having a permanent entitlement to a position. The remaining five positions are rotated amongst the other Member States. Until recently, Mr Justice Nial Fennelly had been Ireland's only Advocate General.[21] Mr Justice Gerard Hogan took up position as Ireland's second Advocate General in September 2018. Advocates General are appointed for a six-year term on the same basis as judges of the Court.

[8–14] The opinion of an Advocate General is published in advance of the Court's judgment and is intended to offer guidance to the Court in its own deliberations. An opinion is not binding upon the Court although, in practice, it will be followed more often than not. Accordingly, in important cases, the publication of the Advocate General's opinion can garner significant attention in its own right. In addition, since the judgments of the Court are a collective view of all the judges hearing a case without the author being identified, an Advocate General who delivers a number of influential opinions may become more associated with a specific development of the law than individual judges themselves. This is particularly the case given that the opinions of Advocates General are typically more detailed, and engage in lengthier discursive reasoning, than judgments of the Court. For example, whereas an opinion might set out alternative ways in which a particular provision might be interpreted and the pros and cons of each, judgments tend to pronounce upon the correct interpretation, often without a detailed rationale as to why this option was chosen. For example, in *Ruiz Zambrano,* an important case concerning the residence rights of an EU citizen child, neither of whose parents were EU citizens, an opinion of the Advocate General containing over 100 paragraphs of legal analysis was followed by a judgment containing just 15 sentences devoted to the Court's core reasoning.[22] As a result, when the Court does agree with the opinion of an Advocate General, it may be that the opinion will provide useful insights into the Court's reasoning, although care must be taken not to simply assume that the same reasoning has been used in both.

[8–15] The approach of the Court of Justice to interpretation is usually described as "purposive" or "teleological". As opposed to adhering strictly to a literal interpretation of the language used, a teleological interpretation involves the Court examining the "whole context in which a particular provision is situated, and giv[ing] the interpretation most likely to further what the Court considers that provision sought to achieve".[23] In this context, Paul Craig and Gráinne de Búrca make the insightful observation that the Court's case law reflects the fact that the EEC Treaty's *travaux préparatoires* – preparatory documents used during a treaty's negotiation and subsequently used as an aid in its interpretation – were not made available for 30 years, and so the Court was unable to be guided by them even if it was desired.[24] The Court's purposive approach

---

21 See Nial Fennelly, "Reflections of an Irish Advocate General" (1996) *Irish Journal of European Law* 4; Síofra O'Leary, "Courts, Judges, Lawyers and Legal Principles: Ireland's Contribution to European Courts and European Case Law" (2018) 41 *Dublin University Law Journal* (forthcoming).

22 Case C-34/09 *Ruiz Zambrano* [2011] ECR I-1177.

23 Paul Craig and Gráinne de Búrca, *EU Law* (6th ed, Oxford University Press, 2015) 64. See Nial Fennelly, "Legal interpretation at the European Court of Justice" (1996) 20 *Fordham International Law Journal* 656.

24 *ibid*, 63. See Samuli Miettinen and Merita Kettunen, "*Travaux* to the EU Treaties: Preparatory Work as a Source of EU Law" (2015) 17 *Cambridge Yearbook of European Legal Studies* 145.

has lain behind its development of numerous fundamental concepts that have been said to have constitutionalised the European Union, such as supremacy, direct effect and state liability for breaches of EU law. During the period of "Euro-sclerosis" in the seventies and early eighties, in which the need for unanimity within the Council greatly slowed down the rate of positive integration aimed at completing the Single Market, the Court was particularly active in achieving the same objective through the means of negative integration. Yet, in reply to the frequent accusations of unwarranted judicial activism made against the Court, Niamh Nic Shuibhne has responded that, whilst it is true that many of the Court's judgments have resulted in an outcome that best fits with a preference for deeper European integration, it is also true that:

> those decisions have often required very sparse or ambiguous Treaty provisions to be 'interpreted'. In having resort to the *stated* political ambition of moving towards an 'ever closer Union', can the Court really be criticised for furthering that objective through its case law too? Is this furthering really a displacement of political preferences? And all the more in the enlarged Court, in which 'the Court' is itself an elusive phenomenon, can the Court be said even to have a particular or agreed institutional vision anyway? [25]

[8–16] In terms of the workload of the Court of Justice, during the period from 2014 to 2018, 68 per cent of cases brought before it were requests for preliminary reference rulings, an average of 460 per year.[26] Appeals from the General Court accounted for 20 per cent of the Court's caseload, while direct actions represented just 8 per cent of cases, an average of 58 per year.[27] In 2018, a record 849 new cases were brought before it, with the average duration of proceedings being 16 months. Of the 760 cases completed the most common subject matter was the Internal Market / freedoms of movement and establishment, on which there were 77 judgments, followed by the Area of Freedom, Security and Justice (74); intellectual property (74); taxation (58); social law (42); and competition and state aid (41).[28]

C. General Court

[8–17] Provision for the creation of a court of first instance was included within the Single European Act of 1986 and it became operational in 1989. In 2015, it was decided to merge the seven judges of the Civil Service Tribunal (a specialised court) into the General Court, in addition to appointing 21 new judges, such that from 2019 onwards the General Court comprises 56 judges, or two per each Member State.[29] This was done in order to address a large increase in the workload of the General Court,

[25] Niamh Nic Shuibhne, "The Court of Justice of the European Union" in John Peterson and Michael Shackleton (eds), *The Institutions of the European Union* (3rd ed, Oxford University Press, 2012) 148, 162. See Takis Tridimas, "The Court of Justice and Judicial Activism" (1997) 22 *European Law Review* 199; Thomas Horsley, "Reflections on the Role of the Court of Justice as the 'Motor' of European Integration: *Legal* Limits to Judicial Lawmaking" (2013) 50 *Common Market Law Review* 931; Thomas Horsley, *The Court of Justice of the European Union as an Institutional Actor* (Cambridge University Press, 2018); Joseph Weiler, "The Transformation of Europe" (1991) 100 *Yale Law Journal* 2403; Federico Mancini, "The Making of a Constitution for Europe" (1989) 26 *Common Market Law Review* 595; Eric Stein, "Lawyers, Judges and the Making of a European Constitution" (1981) 75 *American Journal of International Law* 1.

[26] *Court of Justice of the European Union Annual Report 2018, Judicial Activity*, 2019, 127.

[27] *ibid.*

[28] *Court of Justice of the European Union Annual Report 2018*, 2019, 43.

[29] Regulation (EU, Euratom) 2015/2422 of the European Parliament and of the Council of 16 December

whose number of new cases rose from just under 600 in 2010 to over 900 in 2014. This reform perhaps marks a move away from specialised courts, with a Council document explaining the decision not to opt for creating additional specialised courts as follows:

> Specialised courts are not flexible: if the number of cases increases substantially, the court is likely to be unable to cope with them. Specialised courts would also increase the risk of inconsistency of EU law since there would always be three courts that might be seized of similar issues: one by way of the preliminary ruling procedure (Court of Justice), one by way of an appeal (General Court) and one by way of direct actions (the specialised court). Specialised courts also add complexity. Finally, specialised courts would be unnecessarily costly: each requires a President and his or her Cabinet, a registry and other fixed costs.[30]

[8–18] Judges of the General Court are appointed on the same basis and in the same manner as judges of the Court of Justice. Usually, the General Court will sit as a three-judge chamber, but it also sits with five judges or as a Grand Chamber or a Full Chamber. Unlike the Court of Justice, the General Court may sit as a single judge, although it rarely does so.[31] While there are no dedicated Advocates General in the General Court, a judge of the Court may be called upon to carry out this function where it is considered that the legal difficulty or factual complexity of the case so requires, in which case he or she will not participate in the chamber hearing the case.[32]

[8–19] Over the years, the jurisdiction of the General Court has been expanded to include most of the "contentious jurisdiction" of the CJEU, but it still does not receive indirect actions in the form requests for preliminary rulings. While the possibility of the General Court dealing with preliminary references in specific areas laid down by the Court's Statute is provided for, no such designation has yet been made.[33] When provision was made in 2015 for a doubling of the members of the General Court, the regulation required that by December 2017 a report would be drawn up by the Court of Justice for the Parliament, Council and Commission on possible changes to the distribution of competence for preliminary references.[34] In its report, the Court of Justice did not recommend that jurisdiction to hear preliminary references be conferred on the General Court.[35] Rather, it was considered that:

> References for a preliminary ruling constitute the keystone of the judicial system of

---

2015 amending Protocol No 3 on the Statute of the Court of Justice of the European Union [2015] OJ L341/14.

30 Press Release 497/15, "Q&A on the Reform of the General Court", 23 June 2015. See Alberto Alemanno and Laurent Pech, "Thinking Justice Outside the Dock: A Critical Assessment of the Reform of the EU's Court System" (2017) 54 *Common Market Law Review* 129; Daniel Sarimento, "The Reform of the General Court: An Exercise in Minimalist (but Radical) Institutional Reform" (2017) 19 *Cambridge Yearbook of European Legal Studies* 236.

31 By way of illustration, of the judgments delivered in 2018, 546 were by a three-judge chamber, 84 by a five-judge chamber and 5 by a judge sitting alone. *Court of Justice of the European Union Annual Report 2018, Judicial Activity*, 2019, 240.

32 Art 49 of the Statute of the CJEU and Art 30 of the Rules of Procedure of the General Court.

33 Art 256(3) TFEU.

34 Art 3(2) of Regulation (EU, Euratom) 2015/2422 of the European Parliament and of the Council of 16 December 2015 amending Protocol No 3 on the Statute of the Court of Justice of the European Union [2015] OJ L341/14.

35 Court of Justice of the European Union, Report submitted pursuant to Art 3(2) of Regulation (EU, Euratom) 2015/2422 of the European Parliament and of the Council amending Protocol No 3 on the Statute of the Court of Justice of the European Union, 14 December 2017.

> the Union and are dealt with expeditiously, and consequently a transfer to the General Court of jurisdiction to hear and determine questions referred for a preliminary ruling, in specific areas laid down by the Statute of the Court of Justice of the European Union, is at present not necessary.[36]

[8–20] Nevertheless, the report concluded that the possibility of a future transfer of such jurisdiction cannot be ruled out, in certain specific areas, if the number and complexity of requests for a preliminary ruling submitted to the Court of Justice were to be such that the proper administration of justice required it. In such circumstances, it would be necessary to undertake an amendment of the General Court's rules of procedure in order to set out detailed rules for dealing with preliminary references and in order to forestall, as far as possible, the risks of divergent case law.

[8–21] Accordingly, the General Court currently deals with direct actions, such as actions by private individuals or entities seeking to annul an EU legal act, an action claiming that an EU institution has been called upon to act but has failed to do so, or a claim for damages against the EU in respect of a non-contractual liability. The jurisdiction of the General Court does not, however, include: (i) infringement actions brought against a Member State by the Commission (Arts 258 and 260); (ii) infringement actions brought by one Member State against another (Art 259); (iii) actions for annulment or failure to act brought by an institution against the Council, Parliament or Commission, or (iv) actions for annulment or failure to act brought by a Member State against the Council or Parliament.[37]

[8–22] A judgment of the General Court may only be appealed to the Court of Justice on points of law that are limited to claims that the General Court lacked competence, committed a breach of procedure or infringed EU law (such as by making an error of law).[38] From 2006 to 2016 a specialised court operated in the form of the EU Civil Service Tribunal, which heard employment disputes involving EU staff members. A right of appeal existed to the General Court, with an exceptional further right of appeal to the Court of Justice where there was "a serious risk of the unity or consistency of Union law being affected".[39] In 2019, an amendment was made to the Court's Statute in order to restrict the circumstances in which a further (second) appeal can be brought from the General Court, relating to an appeal from a decision of a board of appeal of an EU office or agency. From now on, an appeal brought against a decision of the General Court concerning a decision of a board of appeal of the EU Intellectual Property Office, the Community Plant Variety Office, the European Chemicals Agency or the EU Aviation Safety Agency – or of any other independent board of appeal set up after 1 May 2019 within any other Union office or agency – shall only proceed if the Court of Justice first decides that is should do so on the basis that it "raises an issue that is significant with respect to the unity, consistency or development of Union law".[40]

---

36 Regulation (EU, Euratom) 2019/629 of the European Parliament and of the Council of 17 April 2019 amending Protocol No 3 on the Statute of the Court of Justice of the European Union [2019] OJ L111/1, recital (2).

37 Art 256 TFEU and Art 51 of the Statute of the CJEU. Exceptions are made for acts or decisions made by the Council under Arts 108(2), 207 and 291 TFEU. The General Court does not have jurisdiction in respect of a Member State action against an act of or failure to act by the Commission under the first paragraph of Art 331 TFEU concerning enhanced cooperation.

38 Art 58 of the Statute of the CJEU.

39 Art 256(2) TFEU.

40 Art 58(a) of the Statute of the CJEU, as inserted by Art 1(2) of Regulation (EU, Euratom) 2019/629

[8–23] Bearing in mind that the General Court does not receive requests for preliminary references, in 2018 35 per cent of completed cases related to decisions of the European Intellectual Property Office, 12 per cent concerned state aid and competition law, while 11 per cent related to staff disputes.[41] One well-known example of state aid litigation before the General Court is Ireland's action for the annulment of the Commission's 2016 decision which required Apple to pay Ireland €13 billion on the basis that the tax regime that had applied to it amounted to state aid.[42]

[8–24] As mentioned above, the decision to subsume the role of the Civil Service Tribunal within the work of the General Court signals a move away from the use of specialised courts. This has been added to by the fact that the newly created Unified Patent Court stands separate from the CJEU and has been established through the combined means of enhanced cooperation and an international agreement signed in 2013 amongst the 25 EU Member States that are taking part (ie all bar Spain, Italy and Croatia).[43] Upon its entry into force, the Unified Patent Court will be considered a shared court that forms part of the national judicial systems of each participating Member State and so, like a national court, it will be able and, in certain circumstances, required to make preliminary references to the Court of Justice. Ireland has signed the Agreement establishing the Court but, as a constitutional amendment will be required before ratification, a referendum must first be held. The Government have announced an intention that, should Ireland proceed with ratification, a local division of the Unified Patent Court will be established in Ireland.[44]

D. Preliminary Reference Procedure

[8–25] In 2018, 67 per cent of new cases brought before the Court of Justice were references by national courts or tribunals for a preliminary ruling pursuant to Art 267 TFEU.[45] This mechanism allows for a question to be asked concerning the interpretation of the TEU or TFEU, or the validity and interpretation of acts of the EU institutions, bodies, offices or agencies. As such, the preliminary reference procedure is a key part of the EU's judicial architecture and plays a critical role in ensuring the uniform interpretation of EU law throughout all Member States. This is aided by the fact that, under the Court's Statute, in addition to the general entitlement to intervene in a case,

of the European Parliament and of the Council of 17 April 2019 amending Protocol No 3 on the Statute of the Court of Justice of the European Union [2019] OJ L111/1. See also Amendments to the Rules of Procedure of the Court of Justice [2019] OJ L111/73.

41 *Court of Justice of the European Union Annual Report 2018, Judicial Activity*, 2019, 237.

42 Case T–778/16 *Ireland v Commission (Apple Case)* [2017] OJ C38/35 (ongoing).

43 Agreement on a Unified Patent Court done at Brussels on 19 February 2013 [2013] OJ C175/1; Regulation (EU) No 1257/2012 of the European Parliament and of the Council of 17 December 2012 implementing enhanced cooperation in the area of the creation of unitary patent protection [2012] OJ L361/1. See Tuomas Mylly, "Hovering between Intergovernmentalism and Unionization: The Shape of Unitary Patents" (2017) 54 *Common Market Law Review* 1381; Noel Travers, "From *Merck v Stephar* to the Unitary Patent Regulations and Court: Reflections on the Incremental Development of an EU Patent Law and Legal System" in Kieran Bradley, Noel Travers and Anthony Whelan (eds), *Of Courts and Constitutions. Liber Amicorum in Honour of Nial Fennelly* (Hart, 2014) 155.

44 "Government to Establish Local Division of International Patent Court in Ireland", Press Release, Minister for Jobs, Enterprise and Innovation, 13 November 2014, available at <www.dbei.gov.ie>.

45 *Court of Justice of the European Union Annual Report 2018, Judicial Activity*, 2019, 122.

the registrar of the Court must inform all Member States of a request having been made for a preliminary reference, with the Member States having two months in which to submit their observations to the Court.[46] Given the strict time limits and onerous rules on standing that apply to direct actions, Art 267 became the vehicle through which the Court developed much of its landmark case law, including on the principles of supremacy and direct effect, and has been described as a "veritable cornerstone" of the Internal Market.[47]

[8–26] Article 267 differentiates between two distinct scenarios. First, where a question of EU law is raised before a court or tribunal against whose decision there is a judicial remedy (eg an appeal) under national law, that court or tribunal *may* make a reference if it considers that a decision on the question is necessary to enable it to give judgment. In contrast, where any such question is raised before a court or tribunal against whose decision there is no judicial remedy under national law, that court or tribunal *shall* bring the matter before the Court of Justice. While either party to a case may request that a reference be made, the decision whether or not to do so is ultimately for the national court or tribunal to make. Indeed, a national court may decide of its own motion to make a preliminary reference.[48] While the practice amongst judges will vary, when making a reference frequently the Irish courts will seek an agreed statement of facts, as well as possibly draft questions, from the parties, which will then be considered by the Court.[49] The domestic proceedings stand adjourned until a reply is received from the Court of Justice.[50]

[8–27] Another notable distinction within Art 267 is that as between questions on the correct *interpretation* of EU law and questions as to the *validity* of an act of an EU institution. Given the significance of questioning whether an EU act is invalid – where the need for uniformity across the Member States has been described as particularly vital in order not to jeopardise the very unity of the EU legal order – there are certain differences in how national courts should assess whether to make such a reference and in how they should respond to a ruling by the Court of Justice on the validity of an act. The nature of these differences will be highlighted below.

[8–28] In providing a preliminary ruling, the role of the Court of Justice is confined to giving an interpretation of EU law or ruling on its validity. Its role does not extend to applying that law to the factual situation underlying the main proceedings, which remains the task of the national court or tribunal. It is not, therefore, for the Court of Justice either to decide issues of fact raised in the main proceedings or to resolve any differences of opinion on the interpretation or application of rules of national law. The Court has stated that, while it makes every effort to give a reply which will be of

---

[46] Art 23 of the Statute of the Court of Justice of the European Union.

[47] "The Proceedings of the Court of Justice and Court of First Instance of the European Communities", No 15/95, para 11, cited in Alan Dashwood, Michael Dougan, Barry Rodger, Eleanor Spaventa and Derrick Wyatt, *Wyatt and Dashwood's European Union Law* (6th ed, Hart, 2011) 210.

[48] For example, Joined Cases 36/80 and 70/80 *Irish Creamery Milk Suppliers v Ireland* [1981] ECR 735, where Barrington J referred questions on his own motion.

[49] Elaine Fahey, *Practice and Procedure in Preliminary References to Europe: 30 Years of Article 234 EC Case Law from the Irish Courts* (Firstlaw, 2007) 20; Anthony M Collins and James O'Reilly, *Civil Proceedings and the State* (2nd ed, Thomson Round Hall, 2004) 318.

[50] See *Data Protection Commissioner v Facebook Ireland Ltd* [2019] IESC 46, 31 May 2019, Clarke CJ, discussed below at paras [8–70] to [8–75].

assistance in resolving the dispute in the main proceedings, it is for the referring court or tribunal to draw specific conclusions from that reply, if necessary by disapplying the rule of national law in question.[51] As described by Barr J in *McNamara v An Bord Pleanála*:

> The use of the word 'preliminary' implies that the national court which receives such a ruling from the European Court has not completed its function by delivering final judgment, but will do so, *inter alia*, in the light of the ruling received from the Court of Justice.
>
> … the purpose of [Art 267] is to provide a consultative procedure whereby national courts may obtain rulings on matters of European law from the Court of Justice. It is not an appeal procedure but is consultative only. In short, the purpose of such rulings is to guide national courts of the European Union on matters of European law in cases pending before such courts, *i.e.* a procedure has been put in place the purpose of which is to ensure, as far as possible, that European law is uniformly interpreted and applied by national courts in their judgments.[52]

[8–29] Once the Court of Justice has provided the requested interpretation of EU law, it is then for the national court to apply that ruling when taking up the case again in order to bring it to a final conclusion. It is this feature which gives rise to the titles *preliminary* ruling and *indirect* action. In this way, it can be seen that the preliminary reference procedure is quite different from an appeal to a higher court. Whilst media references to the Court of Justice might suggest otherwise, it is important to remember that there is no right of appeal from decisions of national courts to the Court of Justice. The closest one might get to an "appeal" to Luxembourg is by seeking an interpretation of EU law which must then be applied by the relevant national court. As a result, it is sometimes said that the relationship between national courts and the Court of Justice is collaborative rather than hierarchical, with each having a distinct role to play in ensuring a uniform application of EU law. According to Trevor Hartley, for instance, the preliminary reference procedure puts the Court "in a weaker position than would be normal for the supreme court in a federation. It suggests that the national courts are not subordinate to the European Court, but co-equal; the relationship is not one of hierarchy, but one of co-operation".[53] In *Irish Creamery Milk Suppliers Association v Ireland*, the Court of Justice described the relationship established by Art 267 as being:

> a framework for close cooperation between the national courts and the Court of Justice based on the assignment to each of different functions. The second paragraph of that article makes it clear that it is for the national court to decide at what stage in the proceedings it is appropriate for that court to refer a question to the Court of Justice for a preliminary ruling.
>
> The need to provide an interpretation of [EU] law which will be of use to the national court makes it essential … to define the legal context in which the interpretation requested should be placed. From that aspect it might be convenient, in certain circumstances, for the facts in the case to be established and for questions of purely national law to be settled

---

[51] Recommendations to national courts and tribunals in relation to the initiation of preliminary ruling proceedings [2012] OJ C338/1, para 8.

[52] *McNamara v An Bord Pleanála* [1998] 3 IR 453, 457, 458. See *Data Protection Commissioner v Facebook Ireland Ltd* [2019] IESC 46, 31 May 2019, paras 2.7–2.9 (Clarke CJ); *Eurofood IFSC Ltd (No 2)* [2006] 4 IR 307.

[53] Trevor Hartley, *The Foundations of European Union Law* (8th ed, Oxford University Press, 2014) 281.

> at the time the reference is made to the Court of Justice so as to enable the latter to take cognisance of all the features of fact and of law which may be relevant to the interpretation of [EU] law which it is called upon to give.
>
> However, those considerations do not in any way restrict the discretion of the national court, which alone has a direct knowledge of the facts of the case and of the arguments of the parties, which will have to take responsibility for giving judgment in the case and which is therefore in the best position to appreciate at what stage in the proceedings it requires a preliminary ruling from the Court of Justice.
>
> Hence it is clear that the national court's decision when to make a reference under Article [267] must be dictated by considerations of procedural organisation and efficiency to be weighed by that court.[54]

[8–30] While the distinction between the interpretation of EU law by the Court of Justice and its subsequent application by a national court may be easily understood in theory, in practice it can occasionally become somewhat blurred. This can arise particularly where the preliminary reference is aimed at determining whether a national measure is compatible with EU law. For example, in the area of free movement of goods, it is permissible for a Member State to maintain a non-discriminatory measure that has the effect of restricting imports from other Member States provided that it is necessary to achieve a legitimate public interest objective and is proportionate to that aim. Typically, the Court of Justice will reply to a request for a preliminary ruling by setting out the law and leaving it to the national court to determine whether or not the measure is proportionate in light of the facts available to it.

[8–31] Such a question arose in relation to restrictions on Sunday-trading hours kept by retailers in the UK in *Torfaen Borough Council v B&Q*.[55] In its preliminary ruling, the Court of Justice set out the general approach to be taken, but left it to the national court to determine whether the measure was unnecessarily restrictive of trade in light of the public interest objective being pursued. However, when this test was applied by a number of national courts in different cases, contrasting conclusions were arrived at as to whether or not the measure was proportionate. As a result, in the subsequent case of *Stoke-on-Trent v B&Q*, the Court of Justice proceeded to express its own view on the proportionality assessment. In so doing, the Court concluded that,

> it had all the information necessary for it to rule on the question of the proportionality of such rules and that it had to do so in order to enable national courts to assess their compatibility with [EU] law in a uniform manner since such an assessment cannot be allowed to vary according to the findings of fact made by individual courts in particular cases.[56]

[8–32] This has been identified as one instance where the Court crossed the line between interpreting the Treaties and applying them to the facts of a particular case.[57] Another example might be considered to be that of *Köbler v Austria* referred to below, in which, rather than leaving it to the Austrian courts to apply the criteria set out in its

---

[54] Joined Cases 36/80 and 71/80 *Irish Creamery Milk Suppliers Association v Ireland* [1981] ECR 735, 747–748.

[55] Case C-145/88 *Torfaen Borough Council v B&Q* [1989] ECR 3851.

[56] Case 169/91 *Stoke-on-Trent v B&Q* [1992] ECR I-6635, 6657.

[57] Robert Schütze, *EU Law* (Cambridge University Press, 2015) 380.

ruling, the Court of Justice expressed its own view as to whether the national court of last instance had incurred liability by failing to make a preliminary reference.[58]

[8–33] As a general principle, the interpretation provided by the Court of Justice applies from the time that the relevant EU law first entered into force, and so should be applied to legal relationships entered into before the ruling was delivered.[59] As stated in *Commission v Ireland*, the interpretation which the Court gives to a rule of EU law:

> clarifies and defines, where necessary, the meaning and scope of that rule as it must be or ought to have been understood and applied from the time of its coming into force. In other words, a preliminary ruling does not create or alter the law, but is purely declaratory, with the consequence that in principle it takes effect from the date on which the rule interpreted entered into force.[60]

[8–34] There, infringement proceedings were brought against Ireland for the incorrect transposition of a directive relating to the process for the award of tender contracts. Although the meaning of certain provisions of the directive had been clarified by an earlier preliminary ruling, the Court rejected Ireland's argument to the effect that, as a preliminary reference had been required in order to confirm the proper interpretation of the directive, the directive must be viewed as having lacked sufficient clarity prior to the preliminary ruling so as to excuse Ireland's incorrect transposition.

[8–35] In certain exceptional circumstances, however, the Court will limit the temporal effects of a preliminary ruling. In the 1976 case of *Defrenne v Sabena*, for example, a preliminary ruling clarified that a provision of the EEC Treaty guaranteeing equal pay for equal work among men and women was capable of having direct effect.[61] Ireland argued that to confer the article with direct effect retroactively to 1 January 1973 would be to impose a burden on the Irish economy which it was not in a position to support. The Court of Justice accepted that important considerations of legal certainty affecting all the interests involved made it impossible in principle to reopen the question as regards the past. As a result, the temporal effect of the ruling was limited by providing that the article's direct effect could not be relied on in order to support claims concerning pay periods prior to the date of the judgment, except as regards those workers who had already brought legal proceedings or made an equivalent claim.

[8–36] Historically, Irish courts have made relatively few preliminary references. As of the beginning of 2019, among the first 15 Member States, Ireland ranks as having made the second fewest references, with a total of 115 requests:[62]

---

58 Case C-224/01 *Köbler v Austria* [2003] ECR I-10290, discussed further in paras [8–53] to [8–54] below. See Seán O'Reilly, "*Köbler* in the Common Law Courts: *Cooper v Attorney General*" (2014) 17 *Irish Journal of European Law* 87.

59 Case C-453/00 *Kühne and Heitz* [2004] ECR I-837.

60 Case C-455/08 *Commission v Ireland* [2009] ECR I-225, para 39.

61 Case 43/75 *Defrenne v Sabena* [1976] ECR 455. See Gerard Hogan, "Declarations of Incompatibility, Inapplicability and Invalidity: Rights, Remedies and the Aftermath" in Kieran Bradley, Noel Travers and Anthony Whelan (eds), *Of Courts and Constitutions. Liber Amicorum in Honour of Nial Fennelly* (Hart, 2014) 233.

62 *Court of Justice of the European Union Annual Report 2018, Judicial Activity*, 2019, 143. For a detailed study of the years 1973 to 2003, see Elaine Fahey, *Practice and Procedure in Preliminary References to Europe: 30 Years of Article 234 EC Case Law from the Irish Courts* (Firstlaw, 2007). See also Elaine Fahey, *EU Law in Ireland* (Clarus Press, 2010) 71–76; Elaine Fahey, "An Analysis

Germany	2,527	Denmark	195
Italy	1,513	Portugal	189
Netherlands	1,048	Greece	185
France	1,020	Sweden	141
Belgium	881	Finland	121
UK	637	Ireland	115
Austria	556	Luxembourg	96
Spain	527		

[8–37] That said, there has been a very marked increase in the number of references from Ireland in recent years. Whereas just 55 references were made between joining in 1973 and 2010, over 60 have been made since then, with a whopping 24 requests made in 2017-2018 alone. This is attributable in part to the extension of the Court's jurisdiction over the Area of Freedom, Security and Justice, with a significant proportion of recent Irish references relating to the European Arrest Warrant and the areas of asylum and immigration. In order to dispel the myth that the Irish courts are reluctant referrers of questions, noteworthy preliminary references from Ireland include:

- *Campus Oil v Minister for Industry and Energy*, where the Court found that a requirement that importers were to purchase a certain proportion of petroleum products from a refinery situated in Ireland constituted a measure having equivalent effect to a quantitative restriction on imports, albeit one that was capable of being justified on public security grounds[63];
- *Groener v Minister for Education*, where the Court held that a full-time post of lecturer in a vocational education institution was of such a nature as to justify an Irish language requirement provided that the linguistic requirement was part of a policy for the promotion of the national language and was applied in a proportionate and non-discriminatory manner[64];
- *SPUC v Grogan,* in which it was held that medical termination of pregnancy was a service within the meaning of the EEC Treaty but that it was not contrary to EU law for Ireland to prohibit student associations from distributing information as to clinics in another Member State where those clinics had no involvement in distributing the information[65];
- *Bosphorous Hava v Minister for Transport*, where the Court clarified that, under sanctions measures relating to Yugoslavia, the Irish authorities had been correct to impound an aircraft owned by an entity based in or operating from Yugoslavia,

of Patterns and Trends in the Irish Courts of Practice and Procedure in 30 Years of Article 234 Preliminary References" (2004) 11 *Irish Journal of European Law* 408; Nial Fennelly, "Preliminary Reference Procedure: A Factual and Legal Review" (2006) 13 *Irish Journal of European Law* 55; Morten Broberg and Niels Fenger, "Variations in Member States' Preliminary References to the Court of Justice – Are Structural Factors (Part of) the Explanation?" (2013) 19 *European Law Journal* 488; Graham Butler, "Standing the Test of Time: Reference for a Preliminary Ruling" (2017) 20 *Irish Journal of European Law* 103.

63 Case C-72/83 *Campus Oil v Minister for Industry and Energy* [1984] ECR 2727.

64 Case C-379/87 *Groener v Minister for Education* [1989] ECR 3967.

65 Case C-159/90 *SPUC v Grogan* [1991] ECR I-4685.

notwithstanding that the aircraft was leased to an entity that was not based in or operating from Yugoslavia[66];

- *Metock v Minister for Justice*, where it was held that the Citizens Directive precluded national law from requiring a third-country national, who is the spouse of an EU citizen residing in a Member State but not possessing its nationality, to have previously been lawfully resident in another Member State before arriving in the host Member State in order to benefit from the Citizens Directive[67];
- *Pringle v Ireland*, in which the Court upheld the validity of both the European Stability Mechanism Treaty and the first ever use of the simplified treaty revision procedure to provide for the Stability Mechanism in Art 136 TFEU[68];
- *Digital Rights Ireland v Minister for Communications*, where the Data Retention Directive was found to be invalid due to its disproportionate interference with the right to privacy, contrary to the Charter of Fundamental Rights[69];
- *Schrems v Data Protection Commissioner*, in which the Court declared a Commission Decision relating to the sharing of data with the United States (the "Safe Harbour" agreement) to be invalid[70];
- *Farrell v Whitty*, which required the Court to clarify the "emanation of the state" doctrine for the purposes of determining whether a directive was capable of having direct effect[71];
- *Smith v Meade*, in which the Court clarified the extent to which a directive that had been incorrectly transposed by a Member State can impose obligations on private parties[72];
- *Minister for Justice and Equality v Workplace Relations Commission*, in which the Court confirmed that, as a matter of EU law, the Workplace Relations Commission must have the power to disapply national law which is incompatible with EU law in order that an effective remedy is provided[73];
- *Minister for Justice and Equality v O'Connor*[74] and *MA v International Protection Appeals Tribunal*, where the Court clarified the impact of the UK's withdrawal

---

66 Case C-84/95 *Bosphorus Hava v Minister for Transport* [1996] ECR I-3953.

67 Case C-127/08 *Metock v Minister for Justice* [2008] ECR I-6241.

68 Case C-370/12 *Pringle v Ireland* EU:C:2012:756, 27 November 2012.

69 Joined Cases C-293/12 and C-594/12 *Digital Rights Ireland v Minister for Communications* EU:C:2014:238, 8 April 2014.

70 Case C-362/14 *Schrems v Data Protection Commissioner* EU:C:2015:650, 6 October 2015. A subsequent reference was made by the High Court in the related case of Case C-311/18 *Data Protection Commissioner v Facebook Ireland Ltd* [2018] OJ C249/15 (ongoing); [2017] IEHC 545, 3 October 2017, Costello J, which concerned the validity of further Commission decisions relating to the transfer of data to the United States, including the adequacy of certain remedies under the EU–US Privacy Shield Decision in light of the guarantee in Art 47 of the Charter of Fundamental Rights to an effective remedy before an independent tribunal.

71 Case C-413/15 *Farrell v Whitty* EU:C:2017:745, 10 October 2017; *Farrell v Whitty* [2015] IESC 39, 12 May 2015.

72 Case C-122/17 *Smith v Meade* EU:C:2018:631, 7 August 2018.

73 Case C-378/17 *Minister for Justice and Equality v Workplace Relations Commission* EU:C:2018:979, 4 December 2018.

74 Case C-327/18 PPU *Minister for Justice and Equality v RO* EU:C:2018:733, 19 September 2018; *Minister for Justice and Equality v O'Connor (No 2)* [2018] 2 ILRM 199; *Minister for Justice, Equality and Law Reform v RO* [2018] 2 ILRM 209.

from the EU on a request for surrender to the UK pursuant to a European Arrest Warrant and the allocation of a claim for international protection to the UK under the Dublin III Regulation respectively[75];

- *Minister for Justice and Equality v Celmer*, in which the Court gave guidance as to the test to be applied in deciding whether to allow a surrender for trial pursuant to a European Arrest Warrant when the national court of the requested state had found there to have been a breach of the common value of the rule of law in the requesting state[76], and *Minister for Justice and Equality v OG*, in which it was held that German public prosecutor's offices were not sufficiently independent to constitute a "judicial authority" competent to issue a European Arrest Warrant[77];
- *Horgan v Minister for Education and Skills*, where the Court confirmed that the introduction of lower salary scales for new entrant teachers while leaving unaltered the pay of those teachers already in employment did not amount to indirect discrimination on grounds of age within the meaning of the Equal Treatment Directive.[78]

[8–38] The expansion of the Court's jurisdiction so as to include AFSJ matters has naturally contributed to a growing number of preliminary references generally, with a record number of 568 requests made in 2018.[79] In turn, this high volume inevitably results in a period of time before rulings can be delivered, with the average duration being 16 months. In order to reconcile this with the obligation in Art 267(4) to act with minimum delay where a question is raised in a case regarding a person in custody, the Statute of the Court was amended so as to provide for an urgent procedure, known as the PPU ("procedure prejudicial d'urgence").[80] Out of 19 requests for use of the urgent procedure in 2018, 12 were granted, in which rulings were delivered in three months on average.[81] This procedure is typically applied in cases involving imprisoned individuals who are the subject of a European Arrest Warrant[82] or the custody of a child.[83]

[75] Case C-661/17 *MA v International Protection Appeals Tribunal* EU:C:2019:53, 23 January 2019; *MA v International Protection Appeals Tribunal* [2017] IEHC 677, 11 August 2017, Humphreys J.

[76] Case C-216/18 *Minister for Justice and Equality v LM* PPU EU:C:2018:586, 25 July 2018; *Minister for Justice and Equality v Celmer (No 1)* [2018] IEHC 119, 12 March 2018, Donnelly J; *Minister for Justice and Equality v Celmer (No 2)* [2018] IEHC 153, 23 March 2018, Donnelly J. See Theodore Konstadinides, "Judicial independence and the Rule of Law in the context of non-execution of a European Arrest Warrant: *LM*" (2019) 56 *Common Market Law Review* 743.

[77] Joined Cases C-508/18 and C-82/19 PPU *Minister for Justice and Equality v OG* EU:C:2019:456, 27 May 2019.

[78] Case C-154/18 *Horgan v Minister for Education and Skills* EU:C:2019:113, 14 February 2019.

[79] *Court of Justice of the European Union Annual Report 2018, Judicial Activity*, 2019, 143.

[80] Art 23a of the Statute of the CJEU and Arts 107–114 of the Rules of Procedure of the Court of Justice. See Catherine Barnard, "The PPU: Is it Worth the Candle? An Early Assessment" (2009) 34 *European Law Review* 281.

[81] *Court of Justice of the European Union Annual Report 2018, Judicial Activity*, 2019, 138, 134.

[82] Case C-237/15 PPU *Minister for Justice and Equality v Lanigan* EU:C:2015:474, 16 July 2015; Case C-216/18 PPU *Minister for Justice and Equality v ML* EU:C:2018:586, 25 July 2018; Joined Cases C-508/18 and C-82/19 PPU *Minister for Justice and Equality v OG* EU:C:2019:456, 27 May 2019.

[83] Case C-92/12 PPU *HSE v SC* EU:C:2012:255, 26 April 2012; Case C-400/00 PPU *JMcB v LE* [2010] ECR I-8965.

An expedited procedure was also introduced for possible use in all Court proceedings including preliminary references, which was used, for example, in the *Pringle* case.[84]

[8–39] Four distinct questions arise in relation to the making of a preliminary reference, each of which will be considered in turn. First, what types of question may be referred to the Court of Justice and which aspects of EU law may be the subject of a reference? Secondly, what courts or tribunals either *may* make a reference or are *obliged* to make a reference? Third, how should a national court or tribunal exercise its discretion as to whether to make a reference? And, finally, in what circumstances might the Court of Justice decline to take up a request for a reference? The Court of Justice has issued guidance in relation to some of these questions in Recommendations to national courts and tribunals in relation to the initiation of preliminary ruling proceedings, a number of which are referred to below.[85]

(i) Questions that May Be Referred

[8–40] Article 267 first allows for questions to be referred concerning "the interpretation of the Treaties". Naturally, this includes the TEU and the TFEU, albeit that a preliminary reference may not be referred in respect of the Common Foreign and Security Policy given its general exclusion from the jurisdiction of the Court under Art 275 TFEU. The reference to "the Treaties" also includes accession and amending treaties, protocols to the Treaties and the Charter of Fundamental Rights.

[8–41] Secondly, a reference may be made as to either the validity or the interpretation of an act of the EU institutions, bodies, offices or agencies. Since becoming an EU institution under the Lisbon Treaty, this includes acts of the European Council. It is not necessary that the act be legally binding, and so a reference can concern soft law instruments such as recommendations and opinions. Nor is it necessary that the act have direct effect in order to be made the subject of a reference. An act of the EU institutions also includes international agreements entered into by the EU, including mixed agreements entered into by both the Union and its Member States.[86] For example, in *Christian Dior*, a preliminary reference concerned the interpretation of Art 50 of the WTO Agreement on Trade Related Aspects of Intellectual Property Rights (TRIPs).[87] Article 50 required that the judicial authorities of the contracting parties have the necessary powers to grant provisional measures to prevent an infringement of intellectual property rights from occurring. A question arose as to whether a preliminary reference could be made in respect of Art 50 of TRIPS generally, or whether it could only be made where the underlying dispute concerned a matter of EU law, for example trade marks. Given that Art 50 enshrined a procedural rule that could apply both within, and

---

84 Art 23a of the Statute of the CJEU and Arts 105 and 106 of the Rules of Procedure of the Court of Justice. By way of illustration, the expedited procedure was granted in nine out of 33 requests decided in 2018. *Court of Justice of the European Union Annual Report 2018, Judicial Activity*, 2019, 137. See Melchior Wathelet, "Accelerated Procedures before the Court of Justice of the European Union" in Kieran Bradley, Noel Travers and Anthony Whelan (eds), *Of Courts and Constitutions. Liber Amicorum in Honour of Nial Fennelly* (Hart, 2014) 33.

85 [2012] OJ C338/1.

86 See, for example, Case C-265/19 *Recorded Artists Actors Performers Ltd v Phonographic Performance (Ireland) Ltd* [2019] OJ C206/33 (ongoing) where the High Court has requested a ruling concerning the World Intellectual Property Organisation Performances and Phonograms Treaty 1996.

87 Joined Cases C-300/98 and C-392/98 *Christian Dior* [2000] ECR I-11307.

outside, the scope of EU law, the Court of Justice emphasised the need for a uniform interpretation of the article, regardless of the context in which it was being applied. Since the TRIPS agreement had been concluded by the Union and its Member States as a matter of joint competence, it followed that:

> where a case is brought before the Court in accordance with the provisions of the [TFEU], in particular Article [267] thereof, the Court has jurisdiction to define the obligations which the [Union] has thereby assumed and, for that purpose, to interpret TRIPs.
>
> In particular, the Court has jurisdiction to interpret Article 50 of TRIPs in order to meet the needs of the courts of the Member States when they are called upon to apply national rules with a view to ordering provisional measures for the protection of rights arising under [EU] legislation falling within the scope of TRIPs.
>
> Likewise, where a provision such as Article 50 of TRIPs can apply both to situations falling within the scope of national law and to situations falling within that of [EU] law, as is the case in the field of trade marks, the Court has jurisdiction to interpret it in order to forestall future differences of interpretation.
>
> In that regard, the Member States and the [Union] institutions have an obligation of close cooperation in fulfilling the commitments undertaken by them under joint competence when they concluded the WTO Agreement, including TRIPs.
>
> Since Article 50 of TRIPs constitutes a procedural provision which should be applied in the same way in every situation falling within its scope and is capable of applying both to situations covered by national law and to situations covered by [EU] law, that obligation requires the judicial bodies of the Member States and the Community, for practical and legal reasons, to give it a uniform interpretation.
>
> Only the Court of Justice acting in cooperation with the courts and tribunals of the Member States pursuant to Article [267] of the Treaty is in a position to ensure such uniform interpretation.
>
> The jurisdiction of the Court of Justice to interpret Article 50 of TRIPs is thus not restricted solely to situations covered by trade-mark law.
>
> The answer to the first question … must therefore be that, where the judicial authorities of the Member States are called upon to order provisional measures for the protection of intellectual property rights falling within the scope of TRIPs and a case is brought before the Court of Justice in accordance with the provisions of the Treaty, in particular Article [267] thereof, the Court of Justice has jurisdiction to interpret Article 50 of TRIPs.[88]

[8–42] In other words, the necessity to have the ability to ensure a uniform interpretation throughout the Member States was held to justify the Court of Justice having jurisdiction to hear a preliminary reference concerning the interpretation of a procedural rule within an international agreement to which the EU was a party, even where the circumstances of the particular proceedings did not involve the application

[88] *ibid*, 11357–11359. See Silvère Lefèvre, "The Interpretation of Community Law by the Court of Justice in Areas of National Competence" (2004) 29 *European Law Review* 501; Joni Heliskoski, "Joined Cases C-300/98, *Parfums Christian Dior SA v Tuk Consultancy BV*, and C-392/98, *Assco Gerüste GmbH and R van Dijk v Wilhelm Layher GmbH & Co KG and Layher BV*" (2002) 39 *Common Market Law Review* 159.

of EU law. Otherwise, left to their own devices, national courts might reach a different conclusion when interpreting the provision when being applied outside the scope of EU law, leading to a fragmentation in the law.

[8–43] A similar situation arises where a Member State chooses to extend the application of a particular EU law to situations not directly covered by it. As the Court of Justice has recently described, it may provide a preliminary ruling:

> on questions concerning provisions of EU law in situations in which, even if the facts of the case in the main proceedings do not fall within the field of application of EU law directly, provisions of EU law have been rendered applicable by domestic law due to a renvoi [ie cross-reference or link] made by that law to the content of those provisions.
>
> In such circumstances, it is clearly in the interest of the European Union that, in order to forestall future differences of interpretation, provisions taken from EU law should be interpreted uniformly.
>
> Thus, an interpretation by the Court of provisions of EU law in situations not falling within the scope of EU law is warranted where such provisions have been made applicable to such situations by national law directly and unconditionally, in order to ensure that those situations and situations falling within the scope of EU law are treated in the same way.[89]

[8–44] For example, in order to avoid "reverse discrimination", whereby an EU citizen who exercises the right of free movement has greater rights than a citizen who has always resided in their home Member State, Belgium provided that the spouse of a Belgian national was to be treated as a person who had moved from another EU Member State. In other words, by virtue of Belgian law, a body of EU rules on free movement were to apply to a category of person not in fact covered by EU law as such. In *Dzodzi v Belgium*, a preliminary reference was made concerning the interpretation of EU law on the free movement of persons which applied to Mrs Dzodzi by virtue of its extension under Belgian law. The Court of Justice rejected Belgium's argument that a preliminary reference could only be made in respect of an EU act that was directly at stake. According to the Court,

> It does not appear either from the wording of Article [267] or from the aim of the procedure introduced by that article that the authors of the Treaty intended to exclude from the jurisdiction of the Court requests for a preliminary ruling on a [EU] provision in the specific case where the national law of a Member State refers to the content of that provision in order to determine rules applicable to a situation which is purely internal to that State.
>
> On the contrary, it is manifestly in the interest of the [EU] legal order that, in order to forestall future differences of interpretation, every [EU] provision should be given a uniform interpretation irrespective of the circumstances in which it is to be applied.
>
> Since the jurisdiction of the Court under Article [267] is designed to ensure uniform interpretation in all Member States of the provisions of [EU] law, the Court merely deduces from the letter and the spirit of those provisions the meaning of the [EU] rules at issue. Thereafter it is for the national courts alone to apply the [EU] provisions thus interpreted in the light of the factual and legal circumstances of the case before them.

---

89 Case C-380/17 *K and B* EU:C:2018:877, 7 November 2018, paras 34–36; Case C-635/17 *E* EU:2019:192, 13 March 2019, paras 32–43.

> Consequently, in accordance with the division of judicial tasks between the national courts and the Court of Justice pursuant to Article [267], the Court gives its preliminary ruling without, in principle, having to look into the circumstances in which the national courts were prompted to submit the questions and envisage applying the provision of [EU] law which they have asked the Court to interpret.
>
> ... Where [EU] law is made applicable by national provisions, it is for the national court alone to assess the precise scope of that reference to [EU] law. If it takes the view that the content of a provision of [EU] law is applicable, by virtue of that reference, to the purely internal situation underlying the dispute brought before it, the national court is entitled to request the Court for a preliminary ruling on the terms laid down by the provisions of Article [267] ... [90]

(ii) Courts or Tribunals that May Refer and that Must Refer

[8–45] It is for the Court of Justice to determine, as a matter of EU law, whether a national body seeking to make a reference is a "court or tribunal" within the meaning of Art 267. In line with its purposive approach to interpreting the Treaties, the Court has given the phrase "court or tribunal" a broad, functional meaning rather than a narrow, literal one. Accordingly, it is not necessary that the body be considered, or described as, a court or tribunal within the relevant Member State. As a corollary, a court or tribunal will not be treated as a court or tribunal for the purpose of Art 267 in respect of any mere administrative function it may carry out in connection with a case pending before it, as opposed to its judicial function. In *Dorsch Consult* the Court identified six criteria to be considered when deciding whether a body ought to be regarded as a court or tribunal, namely whether: (i) it is established by law; (ii) it is permanent; (iii) it is independent; (iv) it applies rules of law; (v) its jurisdiction is compulsory; and (vi) its procedure is inter partes.[91]

[8–46] So, for example, an arbitrator appointed under a private contract will not be regarded as a court or tribunal. In contrast, in *Broekmeulen*, it was held that an Appeals Committee for General Medicine was a court or tribunal notwithstanding that it was a professional body established under private law and was not considered a court or tribunal under Dutch law. There, a Belgian doctor was refused registration in the Netherlands and appealed to the Appeals Committee. The Committee was established by the Royal Society for the Promotion of Medicine, registration with which was required in order to practice in the Netherlands. While the Society was a private organisation, it was indirectly recognised under Dutch law. The Committee followed an adversarial procedure, allowed legal representation and issued decisions which were recognised as final. Furthermore, it was understood by the Court of Justice to operate with the consent of the relevant public authorities and with their cooperation. In light of these factors, the Court concluded that it was a court or tribunal for the purpose of Art 267. In doing so, the Court observed that:

> it is incumbent upon Member States to take the necessary steps to ensure that within their own territory the provisions adopted by the [EU] institutions are implemented in their entirety. If, under the legal system of a Member State, the task of implementing

---

[90] Joined Cases C-297/88 and C-197/89 *Dzodzi v Belgium* [1990] ECR I-3763, 3794–3795. See Anthony Arnull, "The Evolution of the Court's Jurisdiction under Article 177 EEC" (1993) 18 *European Law Review* 129.

[91] Case C-54/96 *Dorsch Consult* [1997] ECR I-4961, 4992.

such provisions is assigned to a professional body acting under a degree of governmental supervision, and if that body, in conjunction with the public authorities concerned, creates appeal procedures which may affect the exercise of rights granted by [EU] law, it is imperative, in order to ensure the proper functioning of [EU] law, that the Court should have an opportunity of ruling on issues of interpretation and validity arising out of such proceedings.[92]

[8–47] Preliminary references from Ireland tend to be made by the superior courts, with references made less frequently by the Circuit or District Courts.[93] So, of the 115 references requested by Ireland up to the end of 2018, the High Court and the Supreme Court both made 38 requests each, while the remaining 39 requests were by all of the other courts and tribunals.[94] For example, the Dublin Metropolitan District Court made a reference seeking clarification on whether the closure of airspace due to a volcanic eruption in Iceland was a "super extraordinary circumstance" within the meaning of an EU regulation on compensation for air passengers, such as would absolve airlines from having to cover accommodation expenses. Having received submissions from the Commission, Council, Parliament and four Member States, the Court of Justice ruled that the eruption was not a super extraordinary circumstance and so airlines were liable to cover certain costs incurred by delayed passengers.[95] References have also been made by the Labour Court,[96] the Equality Tribunal,[97] the Revenue Appeals Commissioners[98] and the International Protection Appeals Tribunal.[99]

[8–48] Applying the *Dorsch Consult* criteria to any particular body is highly fact-specific and will depend on the nature of that body within the legal system in which it is located. For example, a UK immigration adjudicator and social security commissioner,[100] a Swedish university appeals board,[101] an Italian Bar Council[102] and a Basque administrative board of contract appeals[103] have all been held to be a court or tribunal capable of making a reference. It does not necessarily follow, however, that comparable bodies under Irish law would have the same qualifying characteristics.

[8–49] Whereas courts or tribunals against whose decision there is a right of appeal have a discretion as to whether to make a reference, courts or tribunals against whose

92 Case 246/80 *Broekmeulen* [1981] ECR 2311, 2328.

93 For a discussion of the other Irish bodies that may be capable of making a reference, see Anthony M Collins and James O'Reilly, *Civil Proceedings and the State* (2nd ed, Thomson Round Hall, 2004) 314; Elaine Fahey, *Practice and Procedure in Preliminary References to Europe: 30 Years of Article 234 EC Case Law from the Irish Courts* (Firstlaw, 2007) 39–40.

94 *Court of Justice of the European Union Annual Report 2018, Judicial Activity*, 2019, 144.

95 Case C-12/11 *McDonagh v Ryanair Ltd* EU:C:2013:43, 31 January 2013. For an example of an unsuccessful request for a reference from the District Court, see Case C-321/16 *Pardue* EU:C:2016:871, 10 November 2016.

96 For example, Case C-443/15 *Parris v Trinity College Dublin* EU:C:2016:897, 24 November 2016; Case C-154/18 *Horgan v Minister for Education and Skills* EU:C:2019:113, 14 February 2019.

97 For example, Case C-363/12 *Z* EU:C:2014:159, 18 March 2014.

98 For example, Case C-344/15 *National Roads Authority v Revenue Commissioners* EU:C:2017:28, 19 January 2017.

99 Case C-385/19 *RAT and DS* [2019] OJ C220/21 (ongoing).

100 Case C-416/96 *El-Yassini* [1999] ECR I-1209; Case C-237/94 *O'Flynn v Adjudication Officer* [1996] ECR I-2617.

101 Case C-407/98 *Abrahamsson* [2000] ECR I-5539.

102 Case C-55/94 *Gebhard* [1995] ECR I-1209.

103 Case C-546/16 *Montte* EU:C:2018:752, 20 September 2018, paras 20–25.

decision there is no right of appeal must make a reference whenever there is a question of EU law that requires guidance. This obligation is designed to ensure that, ultimately, a party to proceedings who wishes to rely on a relevant point of EU law has an avenue to the Court of Justice in Luxembourg. It also operates so as to prevent the development within any Member State of a line of national case law that is not in accordance with EU law. An example of the High Court declining to make a reference, followed by the Supreme Court deciding to do so, is *Karen Millen Ltd v Dunnes Stores*.[104] There, Finlay Geoghegan J, in the High Court, included as a relevant consideration in making her decision the fact that a right of appeal was available to the parties:

> This Court, as a court from whom there is an appeal, has a discretion as to whether it should or should not make a reference to the European Court of Justice pursuant to Article [267 TFEU], even where questions of interpretation of the Regulation arise. I have determined that I should not make a reference to the ECJ prior to determining this claim. The primary reasons for which I have taken this view are as follows. The proceedings raise a significant number of issues. Both parties have a right of appeal from my decision on every issue of law to the Supreme Court. The submissions do not identify any discrete issue on the interpretation of the Regulation … which would itself determine the claim. Insofar as it has been necessary to construe … the Regulation, the view I have formed appears the only one consistent with the terms of the article and the scheme of the Regulation. There is no issue of interpretation of the Regulation on which I have formed a view different from that expressed by [the Office for Harmonisation in the Internal Market] or a Community design court in another Member State in any of the authorities opened to me.[105]

[8–50] The reference in Art 267 to a court or tribunal against whose decision there is no right of appeal does not mean, in an Irish context, that it is only the Supreme Court that is ever obliged to request a preliminary ruling. Rather, the obligation to refer arises whenever there is no further judicial remedy from a particular court due to the avenues of appeal having been exhausted. For example, the obligation may rest on the Circuit Court whenever it is delivering an appeal from a decision of the District Court.

[8–51] The Court of Justice has clarified that the fact that an appellant must apply for leave to appeal, without having an automatic right of appeal, or that an appeal may only be made on points of law, does not mean that the judgment sought to be appealed has been delivered by a court of final instance within the meaning of Art 267. In doing so, however, the Court emphasised the need for the national appellate court to be cognisant of its obligation under Art 267 when deciding on admissibility. For instance, according to the Swedish judicial system, an appeal can be declared admissible if it is important for guidance as to the application of the law that the appeal be examined by the higher court. In *Lyckeskog*, in accepting that the lower court was not a court against whose decision there was no appeal, the Court of Justice noted that uncertainty as to the interpretation of the applicable law, including EU law, may give rise to review, at last instance, by the Swedish Supreme Court. The Court went on to observe that if a question arose as to the interpretation or validity of a rule of EU law, the Supreme Court would be under an obligation to refer a question to the Court of Justice for a preliminary ruling either at the stage of the examination of admissibility or at a later

---

104 *Karen Millen Ltd v Dunnes Stores* [2007] IEHC 449, 21 December 2007, Finlay Geoghegan J. See also *An Taoiseach v Commissioner for Environmental Information* [2013] 2 IR 510, 547–548; [2011] 1 ILRM 508, 539.

105 *ibid*, 48.

stage.[106] The Irish courts have applied the judgment in *Lyckeskog* to confirm that the Court of Appeal is not a court of final appeal within the meaning of Art 267 merely because the Constitution establishes a threshold in accordance with which the Supreme Court may grant leave to appeal.[107]

[8–52] The approach of the Irish Supreme Court to its obligation under Art 267 when considering an application for leave to appeal was recently set out in *Minister for Justice and Equality v O'Connor*.[108] There, an accused who was wanted for surrender to the UK pursuant to a European Arrest Warrant had unsuccessfully sought a preliminary reference from the High Court on the question of whether the UK's withdrawal from the EU impacted on the request for surrender. He sought to appeal this refusal by a direct or "leapfrog" appeal to the Supreme Court. As provided for in Art 34.5 of the Constitution, the Supreme Court has appellate jurisdiction from a decision of the Court of Appeal if it is satisfied that the decision involves a matter of general public importance or, in the interests of justice, it is necessary that there be an appeal to the Supreme Court. The Supreme Court also has appellate jurisdiction from a decision of the High Court if the Supreme Court is satisfied that there are exceptional circumstances warranting a direct appeal to it, which must include that the decision involves a matter of general public importance and/or that it is in the interests of justice. In acceding to the request for a reference, Clarke CJ explained how the Supreme Court would seek to balance its EU law obligations with the procedural rules governing the Irish courts when considering requests for leave to appeal. While the judgment refers to the *CILFIT* case law and *acte clair* doctrine which will be discussed below, it is worth quoting here the relevant portion in full:

> Where a party seeks leave to appeal to this Court … this Court becomes, by definition, a court of final appeal as that term is used in European law, as the refusal gives rise to a situation where there would be no judicial remedy available under Irish law. It follows in turn that this Court may consider it appropriate to grant leave to appeal in certain cases if for no other reason that that it may be considered necessary to make a preliminary reference to the Court of Justice.
>
> It would certainly be a prudent course of action, having regard to the obligations of this Court as a matter of European law, to grant leave to appeal in a case where it was likely that a reference would be required under the *CILFIT* jurisprudence. In that context, it seems to the Court that any issue of European law which would require a reference under that jurisprudence must necessarily be a matter of general public importance for the purposes of the constitutional threshold. However, that being said, it is also clear that the obligations on this Court to refer a matter to the Court of Justice arise only where the issue concerned can be said properly to arise in the case, is necessary to determine the potential appeal before this Court and further will not arise if the relevant issue of European law is *acte clair*.
>
> Where, therefore, an issue of European law is asserted on an application for leave to appeal as being the basis or one of the bases for suggesting that the constitutional threshold is

---

[106] Case C-99/00 *Lyckeskog* [2002] ECR I-4839, 4886.

[107] *Sony Music Entertainment (Ireland) Ltd v UPC Communications Ireland Ltd* [2016] IECA 231, 28 July 2016, Hogan J, paras 94–100; *Byrne v Ó Conbhuí* [2018] IECA 57, 9 March 2018, Hogan J, paras 36–39.

[108] *Minister for Justice and Equality v O'Connor* [2018] IESC 3, 1 February 2018; [2018] IESC 19, 12 March 2018.

> met, this Court will be required to consider whether the issue of European law concerned properly arises on the appeal and whether it can be said that the resolution of the issue will be necessary for the resolution of the appeal. For example, the facts as found by the High Court or affirmed or determined by the Court of Appeal may be such that an issue of European law which might otherwise have arisen can no longer be properly said to remain open on any potential appeal. Furthermore, the ordinary procedural rules which apply in this jurisdiction concerning the extent to which points can be raised on appeal having regard to the manner in which the proceedings were pursued in a lower court or lower courts also apply, so that a point sought to be raised on an appeal to this Court may not be admissible by reason of the failure to raise the point, or at least a sufficiently analogous point, in the courts below. Other examples could be given.
>
> It follows that the mere fact that a party asserts that a point of European law arises which might require to be referred to the Court of Justice does not, of itself, entitle that party to leave to appeal. This Court must assess whether, having regard to considerations such as those just identified, the point truly and properly arises and is necessary to determine the issues which properly arise on the appeal.[109]

[8–53] The degree to which there is an obligation on courts of final instance to refer a question of EU law is highlighted by the decision in *Köbler*, which concerned an Austrian professor who had spent part of his career working in Germany.[110] An Austrian court of last resort regarded as compatible with EU law a measure that deprived Mr Köbler of a bonus to which he would have been entitled had he spent all of his career in Austria. Not only did the Austrian court err in its assessment of compatibility, it further erred in considering that the matter was so obvious that there was no need to make

---

[109] *ibid*, paras 3.4–3.6. In *Dowling v Minister for Finance* [2018] IESCDET 72, 15 May 2018, the Supreme Court observed that the fact that Art 267 distinguishes between courts against whose decisions an appeal lies, and those against whose decision there is no appeal, is not itself a ground for permitting a leapfrog appeal. Nevertheless, "[i]t might be that in some cases that it is apparent that the central issue is one of European law and that that will dispose of the case, and it may be desirable in some cases to give leave to appeal and make an immediate reference" (para 9). The Irish courts have also acknowledged that the application of rules in relation to standing should also take into account when points of EU law are at issue. In *Digital Rights Ireland Ltd v Minister for Communications, Marine and Natural Resources* [2010] 3 IR 251, 276–277, McKechnie J considered it to be clear that: "where issues of European law arise in litigation, the courts may be required to take a more liberal approach to the issue of standing so that a person's rights thereunder are not unduly hampered or frustrated. The rules on standing should be interpreted in a way which would avoid making it 'virtually impossible' or 'excessively difficult' or which impedes or makes 'unduly difficult', the capacity of a litigant to challenge European measures of general application under Article 267 … That is not to say that where questions of European law are raised and a preliminary reference requested, the court is automatically precluded from refusing a plaintiff standing. However, … if the court would be otherwise minded to allow standing in relation to the questions raised, but for a strict application of the national rules on *locus standi*, the court should nonetheless grant standing where to do otherwise would render the plaintiff's [EU] rights effectively enforceable."

[110] Case C-224/01 *Köbler v Austria* [2003] ECR I-10290. See Bjoern Beutler, "State Liability for Breaches of Community Law by National Courts: Is the Requirement of a Manifest Infringement of the Applicable Law an Insurmountable Obstacle?" (2009) 46 *Common Market Law Review* 773; Georgios Anagnostaras, "Erroneous Judgments and the Prospect of Damages: The Scope of the Principle of Governmental Liability for Judicial Breaches" (2006) 31 *European Law Review* 735; Jonathan Buttimore, "State Liability for Judicial Error: A Bridge Too Far?" (2004) 11 *Irish Journal of European Law* 446; Sara Drake, "State Liability under Community Law for Judicial Error" (2004) 11 *Irish Journal of European Law* 34; Georgios Anagnostaras, "The Principle of State Liability for Judicial Breaches: The Impact of European Community Law" (2001) 7 *European Public Law* 281.

a reference. Separate proceedings were then instituted seeking damages against the Austrian state for its breach of EU law (a particular EU law remedy known as *Francovich* damages).[111] The Austrian court hearing these proceedings made a preliminary reference asking whether such damages could be sought where the state institution at fault was the judiciary. The Court of Justice replied that they could, reasoning as follows:

> In the light of the essential role played by the judiciary in the protection of the rights derived by individuals from [EU] rules, the full effectiveness of those rules would be called in question and the protection of those rights would be weakened if individuals were precluded from being able, under certain conditions, to obtain reparation when their rights are affected by an infringement of [EU] law attributable to a decision of a court of a Member State adjudicating at last instance.
>
> It must be stressed, in that context, that a court adjudicating at last instance is by definition the last judicial body before which individuals may assert the rights conferred on them by [EU] law. Since an infringement of those rights by a final decision of such a court cannot thereafter normally be corrected, individuals cannot be deprived of the possibility of rendering the State liable in order in that way to obtain legal protection of their rights.
>
> Moreover, it is, in particular, in order to prevent rights conferred on individuals by [EU] law from being infringed that under the third paragraph of Article [267] a court against whose decisions there is no judicial remedy under national law is required to make a reference to the Court of Justice.
>
> Consequently, it follows from the requirements inherent in the protection of the rights of individuals relying on [EU] law that they must have the possibility of obtaining redress in the national courts for the damage caused by the infringement of those rights owing to a decision of a court adjudicating at last instance.[112]

[8–54] Whilst a usual requirement for *Francovich* damages is that the breach of EU law must be "sufficiently serious", the Court of Justice considered that a higher threshold was required in order to reflect the specific nature of the judicial function and the legitimate requirements of legal certainty. Accordingly, liability would only be incurred in the exceptional case where a court of final instance had manifestly infringed the applicable law. In order to determine whether that condition is satisfied, the national court hearing a claim for reparation would have to take account of all relevant factors including the degree of clarity and precision of the rule infringed, whether the infringement was intentional, whether the error of law was excusable or inexcusable and non-compliance by the court with its obligation to make a reference for a preliminary ruling under Art 267. Taking these factors into account, the Court of Justice concluded that the error was not manifest, and so not sufficiently serious, on the basis that the Austrian court had in good faith mistakenly thought that the matter had been addressed in a previous judgment of the Court of Justice. Given that *Köbler* requires a lower court to make the difficult decision of ruling negatively on the actions of a superior court, it has been suggested that the judgment is more important for what

[111] See ch 14, paras [14–42] to [14–71].

[112] Case C-224/01 *Köbler v Austria* [2003] ECR I-10290, 10306. See also Case C-168/15 *Tomášová v Slovakia* EU:C:2019:602, 28 July 2016.

it symbolises – a comprehensive system for the administration of justice which has the Court of Justice at its apex.[113]

[8–55] More recently, in infringement proceedings brought by the Commission against France, the Court of Justice held, for the very first time, that the failure to make a preliminary reference amounted to a breach of a Member State's obligations under Art 267, such as to amount to an infringement of the Treaties.[114] The Court recalled that a court of final instance is required to make a reference unless it finds that: (i) the question raised is irrelevant; (ii) the provision of EU law in question has already been interpreted by the Court of Justice; or (iii) the correct application of EU law "is so obvious as to leave no scope for any reasonable doubt, and the existence of such a possibility must be assessed in the light of the specific characteristics of EU law, the particular difficulties to which its interpretation gives rise and the risk of divergences in judicial decisions within the European Union".[115] Having been required in proceedings before it to interpret earlier case law of the Court of Justice, the Conseil d'État chose to depart from a judgment of the Court on the ground that the British tax scheme at issue in that case was different from the contested French tax credit. Crucially, however, the Conseil d'État "could not be certain that its reasoning would be equally obvious" to the Court of Justice.[116] In the view of the Court of Justice:

> the absence of a reference for a preliminary ruling on the part of the Conseil d'État … led that court to adopt, in those judgments, a solution based on an interpretation of the provisions of Articles 49 and 63 TFEU which is at variance with that of the present judgment, which implies that the existence of reasonable doubt concerning that interpretation could not be ruled out when the Conseil d'État delivered its ruling.
>
> Consequently, … it must be held that it was for the Conseil d'État, as a court or tribunal against whose decisions there is no judicial remedy under national law, to request a preliminary ruling from the Court of Justice on the basis of the third paragraph of Article 267 TFEU in order to avert the risk of an incorrect interpretation of EU law.[117]

[8–56] The failure to make a reference in such circumstance was, for the first time, deemed an infringement of the Treaties by a Member State.

[8–57] Although not appearing in the wording of Art 267, the Court of Justice has established the principle that *all* courts or tribunals, not just those against whose decision there is no appeal, must make a reference if they have doubts as to the validity of an EU act. This principle is now included within the Court's Recommendations to national courts and tribunals in relation to the initiation of preliminary ruling proceedings.[118] In *Foto–Frost* the Court clarified that if the arguments put forward before a national court in support of invalidity are unfounded, the national court may reject them, concluding that the act is completely valid.[119] On the other hand, where the national court considers that one or more arguments for invalidity put forward by the parties or, as the case

---

113 Damian Chalmers, Gareth Davies and Giorgio Monti, *European Union Law* (3rd ed, Cambridge University Press, 2014) 187.

114 Case C-416/17 *Commission v France* EU:C:2018:811, 4 October 2018.

115 *ibid*, para 110.

116 *ibid*, para 111.

117 *ibid*, paras 112–113.

118 [2012] OJ C338/1, para 16.

119 Case 314/85 *Foto-Frost* [1987] ECR 4199, 4230.

may be, raised by it of its own motion, are well founded, it is incumbent upon it to stay proceedings and to make a reference to the Court of Justice for a preliminary ruling.[120]

[8–58] It follows that a national court may not make its own determination that an EU act is invalid. Rather, this is a question that must be referred to the Court of Justice. This is the case even where an analogous EU act has already been declared invalid since, "even in cases which at first sight are similar, careful examination may show that a provision whose validity is in question is not comparable to a provision which has already been declared invalid because, for instance, it has a different legal or factual context, as the case may be".[121] However, according to the Court's recommendations, if a national court has serious doubts about the validity of an EU act on which a national measure is based, it may exceptionally suspend application of that national measure temporarily or grant other interim relief with respect to it. It must then refer the question of validity to the Court of Justice, stating the reasons for which it considers the act to be invalid.[122]

[8–59] A number of important references have been made from Irish courts concerning the validity of EU measures in the field of data protection. In *Digital Rights Ireland Ltd v Minister for Communications, Marine and Natural Resources*, the High Court questioned the validity of the Data Retention Directive – which governed the retention of electronic data by communications services providers and networks for use in criminal investigations – in light of certain rights guaranteed by the Treaties and the Charter of Fundamental Rights, resulting in a finding of invalidity.[123] In another case, *Schrems v Data Protection Commissioner*, although proceedings in the High Court did not directly challenge the validity of a Commission decision under the Data Protection Directive that the United States ensured an adequate level of data protection (the "Safe Harbour" decision), the High Court's reference did lead the Court of Justice to declare the decision to be invalid.[124] As the Court of Justice observed, the High Court "seems essentially to share" the doubts expressed by Mr Schrems concerning the validity of the decision. In the circumstances, and "in order to give the referring court a full answer", the Court of Justice proceeded to examine the validity of the decision and found that it failed to meet the requirements of the Data Protection Directive, read in the light of the Charter of Fundamental Rights.[125]

[8–60] More recently, a reference was made in somewhat unusual circumstances in

---

[120] Case C-344/04 *International Air Transport Association* [2006] ECR I-403, 462.

[121] Case C-461/03 *Gaston Schul* [2005] ECR I-10513, 10548.

[122] Recommendations to national courts and tribunals in relation to the initiation of preliminary ruling proceedings [2012] OJ C338/1, para 17. See also Joined Cases C-143/88 and C-92/89 *Zuckerfabrik* [1991] ECR I-415; Case C-465/93 *Atlanta* [1995] ECR I-3761; Case C-334/95 *Krüger* [1997] ECR I-4517.

[123] *Digital Rights Ireland Ltd v Minister for Communications, Marine and Natural Resources* [2010] 3 IR 251; Joined Cases C-293/12 and C-594/12 *Digital Rights Ireland Ltd v Minister for Communications, Marine and Natural Resources* EU:C:2014:238, 18 April 2014. See Orla Lynskey, "The Data Retention Directive Is Incompatible with the Rights to Privacy and Data Protection and Is Invalid in its Entirety: *Digital Rights Ireland*" (2014) 51 *Common Market Law Review* 1789.

[124] *Schrems v Data Protection Commissioner* [2014] 3 IR 75.

[125] Case C-362/14 *Schrems v Data Protection Commissioner* EU:C:2015:650, 5 October 2015, para 67. See Loïc Azoulai and Marijn van der Sluis, "Institutionalizing Personal Data Protection in Times of Global Institutional Distrust: *Schrems*" (2016) 53 *Common Market Law Review* 1343.

Data Protection Commissioner v Facebook Ireland Ltd.[126] Here, the Data Protection Commissioner instituted High Court proceedings for the specific purpose of seeking a reference on the validity of Commission decisions on standard contractual clauses (SCC) for the transfer of personal data to third countries. Although the Data Protection Commissioner considered the reference to be necessary in order to deal with a complaint concerning Facebook Ireland's transfer of personal data to the United States, both the complainant and Facebook argued against the necessity of a preliminary reference. Nevertheless, Costello J accepted the central issue for resolution in the proceedings was the validity of the Commission's SCC decisions, and that this could only be resolved by the Court of Justice. In her assessment:

> This court lacks jurisdiction to pronounce upon the validity of the SCC decisions. The [Data Protection Commissioner] says that she needs to know whether or not they are valid, given her concerns that they are not valid ... There are two options open to the court: it can make the reference sought by the [Commissioner] to the CJEU or it can refuse to make the reference and dismiss the proceedings as no other relief is sought. In that event the court in effect will be endorsing the validity of the decisions and require the [Commissioner] to conclude her investigation into Mr Schrem's complaint on the basis that the SCC decisions are valid.
>
> I have formed the view that I concur with the [Commissioner] that there are well founded grounds for believing that the SCC decisions are invalid and furthermore that it is extremely important that there be uniformity in the application of the [Data Protection] Directive throughout the Union on this vitally important issue. This requires that there be consistency and clarity. On that basis, I believe that a reference is necessary and appropriate.[127]

(iii) Exercise of the Discretion to Refer

[8–61] As mentioned above, the preliminary reference procedure is intended to operate within the context of a collaborative relationship between national courts and the Court of Justice, both of which have the obligation to ensure that EU law is properly applied. This partnership involves an allocation of labour as between national courts and the Court in Luxembourg, according to which it is for the national court to decide upon the need to make a preliminary reference in the first instance. Under the doctrine known as "*acte clair*", where it is clear how the national court should act in interpreting EU law, it is not necessary for it to submit a reference to the Court of Justice. Before developing this doctrine in the 1980s, the Court first addressed one particular instance where the interpretation of EU law will be sufficiently clear, namely where the Court has already answered the question that it is intended to refer.

[8–62] Formally, a preliminary ruling by the Court of Justice is binding on the referring national court as to the interpretation of the provision of EU law at issue. What account, therefore, should a national court take of a relevant precedent ruling from the Court of Justice in deciding upon whether to make a reference? This first arose in the early 1960s when, in *Da Costa*, the Court of Justice was asked the same question as it had already addressed in the landmark case of *Van Gend en Loos*. As there was no new

[126] *Data Protection Commissioner v Facebook Ireland Ltd* [2017] IEHC 545, 3 October 2017, Costello J.

[127] *ibid*, paras 337–338. See paras [8–72] to [8–75] below.

factor in the case, the Court simply referred the national court to its earlier judgment. In doing so, the Court made the general observation that:

> Although the third paragraph of Article [267] unreservedly requires courts or tribunals of a Member State against whose decisions there is no judicial remedy under national law … to refer to the Court every question of interpretation raised before them, the authority of an interpretation under Article [267] already given by the Court may deprive the obligation of its purpose and thus empty it of its substance. Such is the case especially when the question raised is materially identical with a question which has already been the subject of a preliminary ruling in a similar case.[128]

[8–63] The existence of a relevant precedent takes on a slightly different complexion when the EU law point at issue concerns the validity of an EU act, rather than a question of interpretation. In *International Chemical Corporation*, an Italian court asked whether a regulation that had been declared void in an earlier reference from a Dutch court was to be considered void in any subsequent litigation, or whether that preliminary ruling was only of relevance to the Dutch court that had posed the question.[129] The Court of Justice commented that when a preliminary reference relates to the validity of an EU act, there are particularly imperative requirements concerning legal certainty involved, in addition to those concerning the uniform application of EU law.[130] It followed from the very nature of a declaration of invalidity that a national court "may not apply the act declared to be void without once more creating serious uncertainty as to the [EU] law applicable".[131] As a result, although a preliminary ruling finding an EU act to be invalid was directly addressed only to the national court that made the reference, it was "sufficient reason for any other national court to regard that act as void for the purpose of a judgment which it has to give".[132] Whilst a national court remained free to request a further reference, particularly if there were questions regarding the scope or consequences of the earlier ruling, in the absence of any such questions national courts were "entirely justified in determining the effect on the cases brought before them of a judgment declaring an act void given by the Court in an action between other parties".[133]

[8–64] The Court of Justice significantly expanded the discretion afforded to national courts not to make a reference in the 1982 case of *CILFIT*.[134] In this landmark case, the Court responded to a request to clarify the nature of the obligation on courts of final instance to make a preliminary reference by developing the *acte clair* doctrine. The Court first confirmed that the mere fact that a party contends that a dispute gives rise to a question concerning the interpretation of EU law does not mean that the national court concerned is compelled to consider that a question has been raised within the meaning of Art 267. Secondly, the Court clarified that courts of final instance enjoy the

---

[128] Joined Cases 28–32/62 *Da Costa* [1963] ECR 31, 38.

[129] Case 66/80 *International Chemical Corporation* [1981] ECR 1191.

[130] *ibid*, 1215.

[131] *ibid*.

[132] *ibid*.

[133] *ibid*, 1216.

[134] Case 283/81 *CILFIT* [1982] ECR 3415. See Hjalte Rasmussen, "The European Court's *Acte Clair* Strategy in *CILFIT* or: '*Acte Clair*, Of Course!' but What Does it Mean?" (1984) 9 *European Law Review* 242; Morten Broberg, "*Acte Clair* Revisited: Adapting the *Acte Clair* Criteria to the Demands of the Times" (2008) 45 *Common Market Law Review* 1383; Niels Fenger and Morten Broberg, "Finding Light in the Darkness: On the Actual Application of the *Acte Clair* Doctrine" (2011) 30 *Yearbook of European Law* 180.

same discretion as lower courts to determine whether the question of EU law is relevant to the case at hand, in the sense of having a bearing on the outcome of the case. Next, the Court recalled its decision in *Da Costa*, which related to a preliminary reference being sought on an identical question to a reference already replied to. It clarified that the same effect, as regards the limits on the obligation laid down by Art 267, may be produced where previous decisions of the Court of Justice have already dealt with the point of law in question, irrespective of the nature of the proceedings which led to those decisions, and even though the questions at issue are not strictly identical. In other words, the Court loosened the principle established in *Da Costa* by making clear that the precedent being relied upon need not have arisen from a preliminary reference, nor need the question raised be strictly identical. Finally, and most significantly, the Court accepted that in certain situations:

> the correct application of [EU] law may be so obvious as to leave no scope for any reasonable doubt as to the manner in which the question raised is to be resolved. Before it comes to the conclusion that such is the case, the national court or tribunal must be convinced that the matter is equally obvious to the courts of the other Member States and to the Court of Justice. Only if those conditions are satisfied, may the national court or tribunal refrain from submitting the question to the Court of Justice and take upon itself the responsibility for resolving it.
>
> However, the existence of such a possibility must be assessed on the basis of the characteristic features of [EU] law and the particular difficulties to which its interpretation gives rise.
>
> To begin with, it must be borne in mind that [EU] legislation is drafted in several languages and that the different language versions are all equally authentic. An interpretation of a provision of [EU] law thus involves a comparison of the different language versions.
>
> It must also be borne in mind, even where the different language versions are entirely in accord with one another, that [EU] law uses terminology which is peculiar to it. Furthermore, it must be emphasized that legal concepts do not necessarily have the same meaning in [EU] law and in the law of the various Member States.
>
> Finally, every provision of [EU] law must be placed in its context and interpreted in the light of the provisions of [EU] law as a whole, regard being had to the objectives thereof and to its state of evolution at the date on which the provision in question is to be applied.[135]

[8–65] The *acte clair* doctrine is now summarised in the Court's Recommendations as follows:

> [C]ourts or tribunals against whose decisions there is no judicial remedy under national law must bring … a request before the Court, unless the Court has already ruled on the point (and there is no new context that raises any serious doubt as to whether that case-law may be applied in that instance), or unless the correct interpretation of the rule of law in question is obvious.
>
> Thus, a national court or tribunal may, in particular when it considers that sufficient guidance is given by the case-law of the Court of Justice, itself decide on the correct interpretation of European Union law and its application to the factual situation before

135 *ibid*, 3430.

it. However, a reference for a preliminary ruling may prove particularly useful when there is a new question of interpretation of general interest for the uniform application of European Union law, or where the existing case-law does not appear to be applicable to a new set of facts.[136]

[8–66] In this way, the national courts act as a filtering system, ensuring that the Court of Justice is only requested to provide a preliminary ruling where it is genuinely needed. A national court may decide not to make a reference where it considers that the question: (i) is irrelevant; (ii) has already been answered by the Court (or is awaiting answer following a reference from another court[137]); or (iii) is so obvious that there is no scope for any reasonable doubt as to the manner in which the question raised is to be resolved.[138] As set out in *CILFIT*, however, the threshold for relying on the last of these options is a stringent one. In *Intermodal Transports*, the Court laid emphasis on the fact that, in order to rely on this option, the national court must be convinced that the matter is equally obvious to the courts of the other Member States and to the Court of Justice. On the other hand, "such a court cannot be required to ensure that, in addition, the matter is equally obvious to bodies of a non-judicial nature such as administrative authorities".[139] As seen above, the failure of the Conseil d'État to correctly apply this third limb of the *acte clair* doctrine led to a finding that France had infringed its obligations under the Treaties.[140] In so finding, the Court observed that in assessing whether the correct application of EU law was so obvious as to leave no scope for any reasonable doubt, due regard must be had to the "specific characteristics of EU law, the particular difficulties to which its interpretation gives rise and the risk of divergences in judicial decisions within the European Union".[141]

[8–67] The academic reaction to *CILFIT* was decidedly mixed, with many highlighting the extent to which, although appearing to expand the discretion of national courts, the strict criteria in fact only served to reinforce the obligation to refer. Nevertheless, while a number of Advocates General have recommended a change in approach, the Court has remained loyal to its 1982 decision.

[8–68] The manner in which the *CILFIT* criteria are applied by Irish courts varies, depending on the approach of individual judges or the nature of the EU law point at

---

136 Recommendations to national courts and tribunals in relation to the initiation of preliminary ruling proceedings [2012] OJ C338/1, paras 12–13.

137 *JTI Ireland Ltd v Minister for Health* [2015] IEHC 481, 7 July 2015, Cregan J.

138 Elaine Fahey has identified as cases where a reference was refused, but arguably might have justifiably been made, *United States Tobacco v Ireland* [1993] 1 IR 241, *Brides v Minister for Agriculture* [1998] 4 IR 250 and *McBride v Galway Corporation* [1998] 1 IR 485: Elaine Fahey, *Practice and Procedure in Preliminary References to Europe: 30 Years of Article 234 EC Case Law from the Irish Courts* (Firstlaw, 2007) 46–49. Other examples of the Irish courts finding a reference to be unnecessary include *Sony Music Entertainment (Ireland) Ltd v UPC Communications Ireland Ltd* [2016] IECA 231, 28 July 2016, Hogan J; *People over Wind Environmental Alliance v An Bord Pleanála* [2015] IECA 272, 20 November 2015, Hogan J; *TD v Minister for Justice, Equality and Law Reform* [2014] 4 IR 277, 363; *An Taoiseach v Commissioner for Environmental Information* [2013] 2 IR 510, 547–548; [2011] 1 ILRM 508, 539; *DT v FL* [2009] 1 IR 434, 462; *Martin v An Bord Pleanála* [2008] 1 IR 336, 386; *Dunne v Minister for the Environment, Heritage and Local Government* [2007] 1 IR 194, 220; *McNamara v An Bord Pleanála* [1998] 3 IR 453; *Emerald Meats Ltd v Minister for Agriculture* [1997] 1 IR 1, 18.

139 Case C-495/03 *Intermodal Transports* [2005] ECR I-8151, 8208.

140 Case C-416/17 *Commission v France* EU:C:2018:811, 4 October 2018.

141 *ibid*, para 110.

issue. In *Pesca Valentia Ltd v Minister for Fisheries (No 2)*, Keane J (as he then was) indicated that unless satisfied that "no serious doubt existed" as to the interpretation of EU law, it would be appropriate to request a preliminary ruling.[142] In *Ryanair Ltd v Aer Rianta*, having applied the criteria, Keane CJ similarly concluded that the correct application of the regulation at issue was not "so obvious in this case as to leave no scope for any reasonable doubt as to the correct construction", and so a reference was required.[143] The existence of conflicting case law from another Member State can prove to be decisive in demonstrating that a reference is required in order to preserve the uniformity of the relevant EU law in question.[144] In other instances, the differences of opinion or lack of clarity as regards a point of EU law may be so significant as to make it unnecessary to engage with the *CILFIT* criteria in any meaningful way.[145] On occasion, the courts have also expressed the view that a reference should only be made on a point of EU law if the proceedings cannot otherwise be determined through the application of Irish law. So, for example, in *Doyle v An Taoiseach*, Henchy J opined that:

> just as it is generally undesirable to decide a case by bringing provisions of the Constitution into play for the purpose of invalidating an impugned law when the case may be decided without thus invoking constitutional provisions, so also, in my opinion, should [EU] law, which also has the paramount force and effect of constitutional provisions, not be applied save where necessary for the decision in the case.[146]

[8–69] In its 1983 judgment in *Campus Oil v Minister for Industry and Energy*, the Irish Supreme Court adopted a position that strongly supported the discretion of lower courts to decide to make a reference, holding that such a decision was not capable of being appealed.[147] As explained by Walsh J, the decision to make a reference was the exercise by a court of a non-contentious right, conferred by the EU Treaties, to request an interpretation of EU law from the Court of Justice:

> The national judge, by virtue of this power conferred upon him by the Treaty, exercises a function under Irish law in making such a request. The power is conferred upon him by the Treaty without any qualification, express or implied, to the effect that it is capable of being overruled by any other national court. It is not within the power of the Oireachtas, or of any rule-making authority, to give any national court the power to modify or to control the unqualified jurisdiction conferred upon the national judge by Article [267] of the Treaty. The national judge has an untrammelled discretion as to whether he will or will not refer questions for a preliminary ruling under Article [267]. In doing so, he is not in any way subject to the parties or to any other judicial authority.
>
> In so far as any reliance is sought to be placed upon Article 34 of the Constitution (which gives a right of appeal to this Court from all decisions of the High Court, subject to such exceptions as are permitted by law), in my view the reference [for a preliminary ruling]

---

142 [1990] 2 IR 305, 317.

143 [2003] 2 IR 143, 150.

144 For example, *MM v Minister for Justice, Equality and Law Reform* [2012] IEHC 547, 18 May 2012, Hogan J.

145 For example, *Minister for Justice and Equality v Celmer (No 1)* [2018] IEHC 119, 12 March 2018, Donnelly J; *Ogieriakhi v Minister for Justice and Equality* [2013] IEHC 133, 5 March 2013, Hogan J; *Metock v Minister for Justice, Equality and Law Reform* [2008] IEHC 77, 14 March 2008, Finlay Geoghegan J.

146 [1986] ILRM 693, 714, applied in *Attorney General v X* [1992] 1 IR 1, 61–62; [1992] ILRM 401, 432.

147 [1983] IR 82.

made by Mr Justice Murphy in this case is not a decision within the meaning of Article 34. He made no order having any legal effect upon the parties to the litigation. If and when he comes to apply the Treaty provisions to the case before him, then he will have made a decision which can be appealed to this Court. This Court would then have to decide whether or not the Treaty provisions in question were applicable to the case. However, even if the reference of questions to the Court of Justice were a decision within the meaning of Article 34 of the Constitution, I would hold that, by virtue of the provisions of Article 29 s.4, sub-s.[6], of the Constitution, the right of appeal to this Court from such a decision must yield to the primacy of Article [267] of the Treaty. That article, as a part of Irish law, qualifies Article 34 of the Constitution in the matter in question. It is a matter of Irish law that Article [267] confers upon an Irish national judge an unfettered discretion to make a preliminary reference to the Court of Justice for an interpretation of the Treaty … The very purpose of that provision … is to enable the national judge to have direct and unimpeded access to the only court which has jurisdiction to furnish him with such interpretation. To fetter that right, by making it subject to review on appeal, would be contrary to both the spirit and the letter of Article [267] of the Treaty. [148]

[8–70] The judgment in *Campus Oil* became the well-established position and has been identified as the reason why the Rules of the Superior Courts do not regulate the making of a request for a preliminary ruling.[149] It should be noted, however, that at the time when it was delivered, the approach of the Supreme Court was not replicated in all other Member States, some of which did allow for the possibility of an appeal. As Costello J pointed out in *Data Protection Commissioner v Facebook Ireland Ltd*, this was known to the Supreme Court when making its decision, it being "fully apprised of the fact that other Member States allowed appeals to higher courts against decisions to refer questions under Article [267] by national judges".[150]

[8–71] Over two decades later, in *Cartesio* and then in *Pohotovost*, the Court of Justice clarified that although, in principle, national law could allow for an appeal to be made to a higher court from a decision to request a preliminary ruling, this was subject to a highly significant limitation.[151] Namely, it is for the referring (lower) court to draw the proper inferences from a judgment delivered on an appeal against its decision to refer and, in particular, to come to a conclusion as to whether it is appropriate to maintain the reference for a preliminary ruling, or to amend it or to withdraw it. A court which is not ruling at final instance must be free, if it considers that a higher court's legal ruling could lead it to give a judgment contrary to EU law, to refer to the Court of Justice questions which concern it.[152] So, for example, in *Elchinov*, a Bulgarian lower court disagreed with findings of EU law made by a higher court, which had then referred the matter

[148] *ibid*, 86–87. See, David O'Keeffe, "Preliminary Deference: The Supreme Court and Community Law" (1983) 5 *Dublin University Law Journal* 286; David O'Keeffe, "Appeals Against an Order to Refer under Art.177 of the EEC Treaty" (1984) 9 *European Law Review* 87; Finbarr Murphy, "Campus Oil v Minister for Industry and Energy" (1984) 21 *Common Market Law Review* 741; Gerard Hogan and Anthony Whelan, *Ireland and the European Union* (Sweet and Maxwell, 1995) 17–20; Elaine Fahey, *Practice and Procedure in Preliminary References to Europe: 30 Years of Article 234 EC Case Law from the Irish Courts* (Firstlaw, 2007) 98–104.

[149] Anthony M Collins and James O'Reilly, *Civil Proceedings in the State* (2nd ed, Thomson RoundHall, 2004) 316–317.

[150] [2018] IEHC 236, 5 February 2018, Costello J, para 13.

[151] Case C-210/06 *Cartesio* [2008] ECR I-9641, para 96; Case C-470/12 *Pohotovost* EU:C:2014:101, 27 February 2014, para 31. See Morten Broberg and Niels Fenger, "Preliminary References as a Right – But for Whom?" The Extent to which Preliminary Reference Decisions can be Subject to Appeal" (2011) 36 *European Law Review* 276.

[152] Case C-173/09 *Elchinov* [2010] ECR I-8889, para 27.

back to the lower court for a determination on the facts.[153] In reply to a preliminary reference from the lower court asking whether it was obliged to accept the interpretation of EU law adopted by its superior court, the Court of Justice concluded that a rule of national law that bound lower courts by legal rulings of a higher court, could not take away from those lower courts the discretion to make a preliminary reference on the same question of EU law.

[8–72] Notwithstanding the longevity of the judgment in *Campus Oil*, the Supreme Court recently granted leave for an appeal to be brought before it in *Data Protection Commissioner v Facebook Ireland Ltd.*[154] In doing so, Clarke CJ observed that while it was undoubtedly the case that *Cartesio* imposed "significant limits on the ability of a national appellate court to interfere with the important freedom, which every national court enjoys, to make a reference to the CJEU" there may nevertheless be "questions as to the precise extent of that limit".[155] As has been noted above, the nature of the proceedings were unusual in that they had been instituted by the Data Protection Commissioner for the particular purpose of obtaining a reference on the validity of certain Commission decisions relating to the transfer of personal data to third countries. As a result, unlike a reference aimed at clarifying a point of EU law, "the matter will not come back to the Irish courts to deal with any subsequent matter of substance", with the result that there would be no possibility for any subsequent appeal within the Irish legal system.[156] An exceptional feature of these proceedings was said to be that the referring court was required to make a series of findings of fact in relation to the concerns expressed by the Data Protection Commissioner, the only purpose of which was to feed into the Court of Justice's analysis of the validity of the Commission decisions. The combined effect of these two features meant that, in practice, there could be no appeal from the High Court's findings of fact, since the Court of Justice will have made a definitive determination on the validity of the Commission decisions on the basis of those factual findings.[157]

[8–73] In opposing leave for appeal, the Data Protection Commissioner accepted that, as matter of Union law, *Cartesio* permitted, with significant limitations, an appeal process in a Member State notwithstanding that a reference from a lower court is pending before the CJEU. She argued, however, that the only form of appeal which *Cartesio* would permit "is an appeal which is not recognised, and therefore is not possible, in the Irish appellate structure. The argument is to the effect that the only form of appeal which is recognised in the Irish appellate structure is one where the appeal court has the power to reverse or overturn any decision of the lower court which is the subject of a successful appeal. It is said that the limitations imposed by *Cartesio* do not permit such an appeal."[158]

[8–74] In delivering the judgment of the Supreme Court on the appeal, Clarke CJ concluded that the effect of *Cartersio* and *Pohotovost* was that there could be no

---

[153] *ibid.*

[154] [2018] IESC 38, 31 July 2018. See Elaine Fahey, "The Supreme Court Preliminary Reference in *DPC v Facebook and Schrems*: Putting National and European Judicial Independence at Risk?" (2019) 1 *Irish Supreme Court Review* 125.

[155] *ibid*, para 3.14.

[156] *ibid*, para 3.6.

[157] [2019] IESC 46, 31 May 2019, para 6.14.

[158] [2018] IESC 38, 31 July 2018, para 3.15.

appeal against the decision of the High Court to make a reference, nor could there be an appeal against the terms of the questions posed. On the other hand, nothing in EU law prohibited the Supreme Court from hearing an appeal against a finding of fact, or of national law, which formed part of the process leading to a reference.[159] In this context it was noted that, while Walsh J in *Campus Oil* did not regard the order to make a reference as a "decision" of a lower court that could be the subject of an appeal, that was in circumstances where the referring court had not made any determinations on matters of fact or of national law.[160] Such determinations of fact or of national law were "decisions" of a lower court that could, in principle, be appealed notwithstanding that a reference by that lower court remained pending. Accordingly, the Supreme Court concluded that:

> as a matter of Irish law, a decision of this Court overturning a finding of fact by the High Court would be binding on the High Court. However, it is equally clear that, as a matter of Union law, the fact that such a decision by this Court would be binding on the High Court cannot remove from the High Court the entitlement which it, and it alone, enjoys to decide whether to continue with, withdraw or amend the reference. But it equally follows that there is no barrier in Union law to this Court overturning decisions of fact or of national law of the High Court, notwithstanding that a reference remains pending.[161]

[8–75] In the end, it was found that the criticisms made by Facebook against the decision of the High Court did not relate to findings of fact as such, but rather involved either the proper characterisation of underlying facts or were directly concerned with the analysis of the High Court as to whether it shared the concerns of the Data Protection Commissioner, such as to be "inextricably linked with the decision to refer and … not a matter which can properly be pursued on appeal".[162]

(iv) Court of Justice's Discretion to Decline a Request

[8–76] Initially, keen to encourage the making of references, the Court of Justice adopted an open-door policy towards requests from national courts. The Court emphasised that the division of labour as between it and national courts left it to the national court to determine whether a reference was needed on the facts of the case before it. Furthermore, the Court expressed a willingness to extract from an imperfectly formulated question, a question as to the interpretation of EU law that it could usefully answer.

[8–77] This liberal approach was significantly altered in the landmark 1980 and 1981 judgments in *Foglia v Novello No 1* and *No 2*.[163] The case involved the unusual situation whereby one Member State sought a preliminary reference questioning the compatibility with EU law of the law of another Member State.[164] In addition, the circumstances were such as to suggest that the dispute between the parties had been deliberately engineered as a vehicle through which to seek a reference. When Ms

---

159 [2019] IESC 46, 31 May 2019, para 6.14.
160 *ibid*, para 6.4.
161 *ibid*, para 6.17.
162 *ibid*, para 12.3.
163 Case 104/79 *Foglia v Novello* [1980] ECR 745; Case 244/80 *Foglia v Novello (No 2)* [1981] ECR 3045.
164 See the opinion of Advocate General Szpunar in Case C-268/17 *AY* EU:C:2018:317, 16 May 2018.

Novello contracted to purchase wine from Mr Foglia, a clause in the contract stipulated that she would not be liable for any taxes levied by France that were contrary to EU law. Mr Foglia had concluded a contract with a separate company for the transport of the wine, which included a similar clause. Although France levied a tax which was passed on to Mr Foglia by the transport company, he paid it without having recourse to his contractual clause. When he subsequently sought to pass on the tax to Ms Novello she refused to pay and the matter was litigated before the Italian courts, which sought a reference as to whether the French tax was contrary to EU law.

[8–78] Noting that the pleadings of both parties concerning the tax were almost identical, the Court of Justice refused to give a ruling. The Court considered that the parties were seeking to obtain a ruling on the French tax through the "expedient of proceedings before an Italian court between two private individuals who are in agreement as to the result to be attained and who have inserted a clause in their contract in order to induce the Italian court to give a ruling on the point".[165] This was underlined by the fact that Mr Foglia had failed to rely on his contractual clause in order to dispute paying the tax to the transport company. The Court highlighted that its duty under Art 267 was to supply the courts of the Member States with an interpretation of EU law whenever "necessary to enable them to settle genuine disputes which are brought before them". If the Court was obliged to provide a preliminary ruling in contrived circumstances such as this, it would "jeopardise the whole system of legal remedies available to private individuals to enable them to protect themselves against tax provisions which are contrary to the Treaty".[166] The Court would apply special vigilance where, as here, the reference was from a court in one Member State seeking to question the compatibility of another Member State's legislation with EU law.

[8–79] Seemingly unsatisfied with the Court's refusal to consider the request, the Italian court submitted a second reference seeking clarification as to the respective powers of the Court of Justice and the national court in relation to the evaluation of all matters of fact and law relevant to the dispute and the wording of any request for a preliminary ruling. The Court replied that, by reason of the fact that it is the national court that is seised of the dispute and must bear responsibility for the decision taken, it is for the national court to assess the need to obtain a preliminary reference. In exercising that power, however, the national court was fulfilling a duty entrusted to it to ensure the proper application of EU law. Accordingly, any problems that might arise in making that assessment, or in the relationship between the national court and the Court of Justice, are governed exclusively by EU law.[167] Having established this initial position, the Court then swiftly moved to set out the principle that it is ultimately for it to control the suitability of a reference. Without disregarding the duties assigned to it, the Court of Justice could not remain indifferent to the assessment made by a national court in the exceptional case in which such assessment may affect the proper working of Art 267. Furthermore, the duty assigned to the Court under that article,

> was not that of delivering advisory opinions on general or hypothetical questions but of assisting in the administration of justice in the Member States. It accordingly does not have jurisdiction to reply to questions of interpretation which are submitted to it within the framework of procedural devices arranged by the parties in order to induce the Court

[165] Case 104/79 *Foglia v Novello* [1980] ECR 745, 759.

[166] *ibid*, 760.

[167] Case 244/80 *Foglia v Novello (No 2)* [1981] ECR 3045, 3062.

to give its views on certain problems of [EU] law which do not correspond to an objective requirement inherent in the resolution of a dispute. A declaration by the Court that it has no jurisdiction in such circumstances does not in any way trespass upon the prerogatives of the national court but makes it possible to prevent the application of the procedure under Article [267] for purposes other than those appropriate for it.

… whilst the Court of Justice must be able to place as much reliance as possible upon the assessment by the national court of the extent to which the questions submitted are essential, it must be in a position to make any assessment inherent in the performance of its own duties in particular order to check, as all courts must, whether it has jurisdiction.[168]

[8–80] The main substantive grounds on which the Court of Justice will decline to consider a request for a preliminary reference are where the question is hypothetical, is not relevant to a resolution of the dispute at hand or does not arise within the context of a genuine dispute.[169] For instance, in one unusual case the Court declined to provide a ruling on the compatibility with the Company Law Directive of a German court judgment concerning the rights of shareholders to obtain certain company information. The case arose from litigation brought by a company law professor who had sought information from a company in which he was a small shareholder. Very extensive questions referred to the Court of Justice had appeared in a book written by him on the subject. The Court considered that it was being asked to give a ruling on a hypothetical problem without having before it the matters of fact or law necessary to give a useful answer to the questions submitted. To give a ruling in such circumstances would be exceeding the limits of the function entrusted to it by Art 267.[170]

[8–81] More recently, in *Mahmood v Minister for Justice and Equality*, the Irish Court of Appeal had sought a preliminary ruling on whether the need to carry out background and security checks was a sufficient reason to justify a period of over 12 months to process a visa for the purposes of family unification under the Citizens Directive.[171] When the Court of Justice became aware that the decisions had been taken, and appeals decided, in each of the cases from which the preliminary reference arose, it sought confirmation from the Court of Appeal that the reference was not devoid of purpose and that a response was still necessary for the resolution of the dispute pending before it. The Court of Appeal replied that, although an answer was not necessary for the applicants in the proceedings, it nonetheless wished to maintain the request since a ruling would have implications for thousands of cases that were being processed. According to the Court of Justice, however:

The justification for a reference for a preliminary ruling is not that it enables advisory opinions on general or hypothetical questions to be delivered, but rather that it is necessary for the effective resolution of a dispute.

… Since, however, all of the visa applications at issue in the main proceedings were the subject of negative decisions, which were contested by means of court actions which were

---

168 *ibid*, 3062–3063.

169 See Case C-612/18 *Wightman v Secretary of State for Exiting the European Union* EU:C:2018:99, 10 December 2018, paras 20–36; Nils Wahl and Luca Prete, "The Gatekeepers of Article 267 TFEU: On Jurisdiction and Admissibility of References for Preliminary Rulings" (2018) 55 *Common Market Law Review* 511.

170 Case C-83/91 *Meilicke* [1992] ECR I-4919, 4935.

171 Case C-169/18 *Mahmood v Minister for Justice and Equality* EU:C:2019:5, 10 January 2019.

not upheld, and since the referring court has noted that the Court's answer can no longer benefit the applicants in the main proceedings, … the dispute in the main proceedings has become devoid of purpose and, consequently, an answer to the questions referred appears to be no longer necessary.

Accordingly, even though the request for a preliminary ruling has not been withdrawn by the referring court, which, in principle, is responsible for drawing the consequences of the decisions refusing visas and, in particular, for reaching a conclusion on whether it is appropriate to maintain the request for a preliminary ruling, to amend it or to withdraw it, it must be held that, in the present case, there is no need to give a ruling on that request.[172]

[8–82] If the Court of Justice is to form its own assessment as to the necessity and relevance of a reference, it follows that it will require some explanation from the national court as to why a request has been made. As stated in *Foglia v Novello (No 2)*, where it is not self-evident from the file, it is necessary for a national court to explain why it considers that a reference is necessary in order for it to give judgment.[173] Accordingly, an insufficiently clear factual narrative may in itself be cause for the Court to decline a request. The Court has emphasised the need for national courts to define the factual and legislative context of the questions posed, or at least explain the factual circumstances on which the questions are based. In this regard, the Recommendations to national courts provide the following guidance:

Owing to the need to translate it into all the official languages of the European Union, the request for a preliminary ruling should therefore be drafted simply, clearly and precisely, avoiding superfluous detail.

About 10 pages is often sufficient to set out in a proper manner the context of a request for a preliminary ruling. That request must be succinct but sufficiently complete and must contain all the relevant information to give the Court and the interested persons entitled to submit observations a clear understanding of the factual and legal context of the main proceedings. In accordance with Article 94 of the Rules of Procedure, the request for a preliminary ruling must contain, in addition to the text of the questions referred to the Court for a preliminary ruling:

- a summary of the subject-matter of the dispute and the relevant findings of fact as determined by the referring court or tribunal, or, at least, an account of the facts on which the questions referred are based;
- the tenor of any national provisions applicable in the case and, where appropriate, the relevant national case-law;
- a statement of the reasons which prompted the referring court or tribunal to inquire about the interpretation or validity of certain provisions of European Union law, and the relationship between those provisions and the national legislation applicable to the main proceedings.

The European Union law provisions relevant to the case should be identified as accurately as possible in the request for a preliminary ruling, which should include, if need be, a brief summary of the relevant arguments of the parties to the main proceedings.

If it considers itself able to do so, the referring court or tribunal may, finally, briefly state its view on the answer to be given to the questions referred for a preliminary ruling. That

[172] *ibid*, paras 23–26.

[173] Case 244/80 *Foglia v Novello (No 2)* [1981] ECR 3045, 3062. See also Joined Cases C-320/90 to C-322/90 *Telemarsicabruzzo* [1993] ECR I-393; Case C-378/93 *La Pyramide* [1994] ECR I-3999.

> information may be useful to the Court, particularly where it is called upon to give a preliminary ruling in an expedited or urgent procedure.
>
> … The questions themselves should appear in a separate and clearly identified section of the order for reference, preferably at the beginning or the end. It must be possible to understand them on their own terms, without referring to the statement of the grounds for the request, which will however provide the necessary background for a proper understanding of the implications of the case.[174]

[8–83] The final basis on which the Court of Justice might decline a request is where the question referred is itself so unclear that the Court is unable to extrapolate an intended question from it. Even where a question is clearly phrased, on occasion the Court will choose to reformulate or supplement a question if it considers that this is necessary to provide the national court "with all the elements of interpretation of European Union law which may be of assistance in adjudicating on the case before it, whether or not that court has specifically referred to them in the questions".[175] For example, in *McCarthy*, the UK Supreme Court asked whether a dual Irish and British national, who was born and lived in the UK all her life, was a beneficiary of the Citizens Directive.[176] Although the question referred was confined to the proper interpretation of the Directive, the Court reformulated the reference so as to include an examination of whether Art 21 TFEU, on the right of Union citizens, was applicable to Mrs McCarthy.

[8–84] In this connection, an interesting issue arose in two preliminary references from Ireland where the Court of Justice answered questions that had not been directly asked of it. Both concerned the manner in which Ireland arranged for the processing of claims for subsidiary protection as provided for in EU law. At the time, the procedure in Ireland was a two-step process. First, a claim for refugee status was considered. If this proved unsuccessful a request for subsidiary protection could be made. In assessing the subsidiary protection claim, reliance could be placed on the earlier assessment that had rejected the refugee claim.

[8–85] A provision of the Qualification Directive provided that, "in cooperation with the applicant", it is the duty of the Member State to assess the relevant elements of the application. In *MM v Minister for Justice*, a preliminary reference asked whether, before a decision to refuse was made, the specific requirement to cooperate meant that an applicant for subsidiary protection was to be supplied with the results of an assessment so as to enable him or her to address the negative aspects. The Court of Justice replied that the duty to cooperate did not in fact require this. Nevertheless, "[i]n order to provide the referring court with a useful answer", the Court proceeded to give its view on the extent to which, where a two-step procedure was applied as in Ireland, the applicant had a right to be heard in the course of the subsidiary protection claim.[177] When the case returned to the High Court, the parties argued for different interpretations of the Court's ruling and whether or not it required the holding of an oral hearing in order to vindicate the applicant's right to be heard. In the view of Hogan J:

---

[174] Recommendations to national courts and tribunals in relation to the initiation of preliminary ruling proceedings [2012] OJ C338/1, paras 21–26.

[175] Case C-434/09 *McCarthy* [2011] ECR I-3375, para 24.

[176] *ibid.*

[177] Case C-277/11 *MM v Minister for Justice and Equality* EU:C:2012:744, 22 November 2012, para 76.

> just as the European Court of Justice will not seek to challenge or in some way look behind findings of fact made by the national court in the context of an Article 267 reference …, I consider that a similar principle should operate in reverse. It would not, I think, be seemly or appropriate for this court to challenge – whether directly or indirectly – the analysis of my judgment or the order for reference which was conducted by the European Court of Justice. The duty of loyal cooperation between the national courts and the European Court of Justice requires no less.[178]

[8–86] Whilst Hogan J determined the proceedings on the basis of his interpretation of the Court's ruling, on appeal to the Supreme Court it was concluded that, as there were then three different interpretations of the preliminary ruling, a further reference was required.[179] In the view of O'Donnell J, the decision of the Court of Justice to proceed to make further observations was the point at which "two aspects of the intersection between Irish proceedings, and those before the European Court of Justice combined to cause potential misunderstanding", namely the limited nature of pleadings in a judicial review and the meaning of the "right to be heard" in a common law jurisdiction.[180] The case, therefore, illustrated

> perhaps negatively, the difficulties of communication between different legal systems, and perhaps more positively and optimistically, the substantial achievements of the European Union in achieving the degree of understanding and comprehension between the legal systems of the Member States and between those systems and the legal system of the European Union which it has.[181]

[8–87] A similar situation arose in *Danqua v Minister for Justice and Equality*.[182] There, a preliminary reference from the Court of Appeal asked whether a time limit of 15 days in which to make an application for subsidiary protection was contrary to the EU law principle of equivalence, given that the same time limit did not apply to an application for asylum which, it was said, could be made both within the scope of EU law and of Irish law. The Court of Justice, however, considered that in the proceedings before it, both the application for asylum and the application for subsidiary protection had been made on the basis of EU law. As a result, the principle of equivalence was irrelevant.[183] Rather than end its ruling there, however, the Court of Justice went on to note that:

> according to settled case-law, in the procedure laid down by Article 267 TFEU, providing for cooperation between national courts and the Court of Justice, it is for the latter to provide the referring court with an answer which will be of use to it and enable it to determine the case before it. With this in mind, the Court may have to reformulate the questions referred to it.
>
> Furthermore, it is for the Court to provide the national court with all those elements for the interpretation of EU law which may be of assistance in adjudicating on the case pending before it, whether or not the referring court has specifically referred to them in its questions.

[178] *MM v Minister for Justice* [2013] 1 IR 370, 383.
[179] Case C-560/14 *MM v Minister for Justice and Equality* EU:C:2017:101, 9 February 2017.
[180] *MM v Minister for Justice* [2018] 1 ILRM 361, 366.
[181] *ibid*, 370.
[182] Case C-429/15 *Danqua v Minister for Justice and Equality* EU:C:2016:789, 20 October 2016.
[183] *ibid*, para 35.

> In this case, and to that end, the two questions referred by the Court of Appeal must be understood as asking whether the *principle of effectiveness* must be interpreted as precluding a national procedural rule, such as that at issue in the main proceedings, which requires an application for subsidiary protection status to be made within a period of 15 working days of notification, by the competent authority, that the applicant whose asylum application has been rejected may make an application for subsidiary protection.[184]

[8–88] The Court proceeded to reply that the principle of effectiveness precluded the Irish procedural rule which required an application for subsidiary protection to be made within 15 days. This arose due to the principle of effectiveness being raised in submissions by the Commission, which considered that the time limit was not in accordance with the principle. The Court then corresponded with the parties and requested them to reply to the Commission's suggestion regarding the principle of effectiveness.

[8–89] When the matter returned to the Court of Appeal, it was argued on behalf of the Minister that the Court ought not to consider itself bound by the preliminary ruling, given that the Court of Justice "has been pleased to answer a question not posed by the referring court and when the issue in question to which the answer refers had not previously been raised in the domestic proceedings".[185] It was claimed that the practical effect of having re-formulated the referred question was that the Court of Justice was then "free to address the question of effectiveness, even though it had not formed any part of the proceedings to date", in either the High Court or the Court of Appeal.[186] Referring to the duty of sincere cooperation enshrined in Art 4 TEU and the duty on national courts to interpret national law in light of EU law, the Court of Appeal concluded that the preliminary ruling was to be regarded as binding upon it. The unusual situation prompted the Court of Appeal to analyse the nature of the relationship between a referring court and the Court of Justice, such that it is worth quoting the judgment of Hogan J (on behalf of the Court) at length:

> It seems to me that the decision [of the Court of Justice] cannot realistically be regarded as other than an express finding that the 15 working day rule is inconsistent with EU law which must therefore be disapplied by national courts by reference to standard *Simmenthal* principles. Inasmuch, therefore, as the *Simmenthal* doctrine requires all national courts to disapply the national rule in question which has been found to be inconsistent with EU law, the Court of Justice's findings to such effect accordingly have a general *erga omnes* application. It is, of course, true that the Court of Justice does not enjoy any formal jurisdiction to annul or otherwise positively invalidate national laws or practices. The practical effect nonetheless of a decision of this nature is in many respects akin to that of a finding of unconstitutionality in our own legal system, given that national courts are called upon to disapply that national law in consequence of that finding on the ground that it is inconsistent with the superior ranking EU law.
>
> While under the *Simmenthal* doctrine the inconsistent national law is simply suspended by the disapplication of that law by the national courts in reliance upon the decision of the Court of Justice rather than formally annulled (as would happen with a declaration of unconstitutionality under Art 34.3.2° of the Constitution under our own legal system), the key point in both instances is nonetheless that the national rule is now no longer legally

[184] *ibid*, paras 36–38. Emphasis added.
[185] *Danqua v Minister for Justice and Equality* [2017] IECA 20, 6 February 2017, Hogan J, para 1.
[186] *ibid*, para 19.

operative and, specifically, it can no longer form the basis of any administrative decision which pre-supposes that the rule in question has full force and effect.

The effective invalidity … of the 15 working day rule as a matter of EU law crystallised with the decision of the Court of Justice in the present case. Accordingly, it seems to me that this Court is entirely bound to apply that decision as part of its duty of sincere co-operation with the Court of Justice as an institution of the European Union in the manner provided for Art 4(3) TEU. …

The decision of the Court of Justice on the Art 267 reference is itself an act of an institution of the Union. It is, accordingly, the task of this Court, discharging as it is the juridical functions of Ireland qua Member State of the Union, to take the appropriate measures to give effect to that decision. This Court discharges that task by simply giving effect to the decision of the Court of Justice.

… While one can certainly sympathize with the Minister's position – in that she has now lost by reference to an issue which had heretofore never formed part of the proceedings and which had never been the subject of any formal finding or determination by either the High Court or this Court prior to the reference to the Court of Justice – I do not see how this Court can in any way look behind the judgment of the Court of Justice, even if some might regard the fact that the Court went beyond the scope of the questions posed in the original Art 267 reference by addressing an entirely new question as unsatisfactory.

The Court of Justice concluded that its function was to give this Court 'with all those elements for the interpretation of EU law which may be of assistance in adjudicating on the case pending before it', irrespective of whether this Court had made reference to these issues in the Art 267 reference. It was on this basis that the Court of Justice elected to address the effectiveness issue on the basis that it had both the jurisdiction and (by implication) the duty to do so. The Court of Justice concluded that it was necessary as part of its functions under the Art 267 reference procedure for it to give this assistance to this Court.

Given that that Court has elected to take that step, it would not be appropriate for this Court to conclude that this approach was unnecessary or that the pronouncements of that Court on the effectiveness issue were merely in the way of pure *obiter dicta* which were not binding on this Court. All of this is yet another way of saying once again that this Court's duty – both by reference to Art 4(3) TEU and Art 267 TFEU itself – is to give effect to the decision of the Court of Justice and not to look behind the basis of that judgment, however tempting it may seem to do so.[187]

[8–90] In the passage above, the Court of Appeal makes a significant statement of a general nature as regards the relationship between a referring court and the Court of Justice, and how this in turn relates to a Member State's duty of sincere cooperation and the nature of EU law more generally. The doctrine of "harmonious interpretation", as developed by the Court of Justice in *Simmenthal*, is discussed in Chapter 12. The duty of national courts to disapply any domestic law that is contrary to EU law is known as the doctrine of supremacy, or primacy, of Union law and is the subject of Chapter 13.

[187] *ibid*, paras 23–25 and 36–38.

PART THREE

CHAPTER 9

UNION COMPETENCE

A. INTRODUCTION

[9–01] The EU has what is known as *attributed competence*. In contrast to the unlimited competence typically enjoyed by national parliaments, the Union has those competences that have been conferred on it by the Member States, but no others. This is also known as the principle of conferral. For the Union to adopt a legal act that is beyond its competence is to act *ultra vires*, rendering that act invalid. The means by which it is checked whether the EU is competent to adopt a legal act is through the identification of a particular legal base that expressly or implicitly permits that action. The legal base will take the form of one or more articles of the Treaties. Given the nature of the TEU and TFEU, most legal bases are found in the TFEU. In order to provide a clear statement of the legal base, a legal act usually begins with a recital along the following lines: "Having regard to the Treaty on the Functioning of the European Union, and in particular Article … thereof".

[9–02] As an example of the approach taken in the Treaties to conferring competence, one important element of the Single Market is the freedom to establish a business anywhere in the EU. Article 49 TFEU first establishes the core principle that restrictions on the freedom of establishment in the territory of another Member State shall be prohibited. Article 50 TFEU then goes on to provide that "[i]n order to attain freedom of establishment as regards a particular activity, the European Parliament and the Council, acting in accordance with the ordinary legislative procedure and after consulting the Economic and Social Committee, shall act by means of directives". Article 50, therefore, confers a particular legislative competence and is the legal base for Union acts regulating the freedom of establishment. In addition to conferring this competence on the Union, the article prescribes both the particular legislative procedure to be used and the form of legal act that may be adopted.

[9–03] Since the Lisbon Treaty, Arts 3, 4 and 6 TFEU set out a categorisation of exclusive, shared and supporting competences. The lists of five exclusive competences in Art 3 and seven supporting competences in Art 6 are exhaustive. In contrast, Art 4 sets out an illustrative list of 11 areas of shared competence and establishes as a default rule that, where the Treaties confer a competence which does not relate to the areas in Arts 3 and 6, the Union shall share that competence with the Member States.

[9–04] While the principle of conferral points to a situation whereby the Member States are firmly in control of the powers exercised by the Union, in practice the Union often succeeds in expanding its powers beyond those as originally envisaged by the Member States. This phenomenon of an incremental expansion of the Union's powers is known as "competence creep".[1] It generally comes about in one of three ways: (i) the use of the residual legal bases provided by Arts 114 and 352 TFEU; (ii) the application of the Court of Justice's purposive or teleological approach to the question of competence; and (iii) the development by the Court of parallelism and pre-emption to afford the EU various external competences.

[9–05] First, the Treaties have long provided for two residual or "catch all" powers that may be used as a default legislative basis if no specific base is otherwise provided for – Arts 114 and 352 TFEU. Article 114 TFEU relates to the establishment of the Internal Market as defined in Art 26 TFEU and provides that:

> *Save where otherwise provided in these Treaties*, the following provisions shall apply for the achievement of the objectives set out in Article 26. The European Parliament and the Council shall, acting in accordance with the ordinary legislative procedure and after consulting the Economic and Social Committee, adopt the measures for the approximation of the provisions laid down by law, regulation or administrative action in Member States which have as their object the establishment and functioning of the internal market.[2]

[9–06] Secondly, Art 352 TFEU provides a much broader default power that extends to the whole breadth of the Treaties' objectives with the exception of CFSP. The use of this power is confined, however, by the fact that unanimity is required within the Council in order to make use of it and the article cannot be used for the adoption of measures aimed at the harmonisation of Member States' laws. It reads:

> If action by the Union should prove necessary, within the framework of the policies defined in the Treaties, to attain one of the objectives set out in the Treaties, *and the Treaties have not provided the necessary powers*, the Council, acting unanimously on a proposal from the Commission and after obtaining the consent of the European Parliament, shall adopt the appropriate measures.[3]

[9–07] As a safeguard, the Commission is specifically required to draw any proposal with Art 352 as its legal base to the attention of national parliaments. In addition, the Intergovernmental Conference that adopted the Lisbon Treaty included a declaration on the use of Art 352 in which it underlined that, in accordance with the principle of conferral, Art 352 "cannot serve as a basis for widening the scope of Union powers beyond the general framework created by the provisions of the Treaties as a whole and, in particular, by those that define the tasks and the activities of the Union".[4] While

---

1 See Stephen Weatherill, "Competence Creep and Competence Control" (2004) 23 *Yearbook of European Law* 1.

2 Emphasis added.

3 Emphasis added.

4 Declaration No 42.

the use of Art 114 will be considered further below, for now it can be noted that, as "flexibility clauses", both articles inevitably represent a weakening of the principle of conferral. This weakening is taken further due to the fact that the Court of Justice adopts a teleological or purposive approach to interpreting the Treaties, including these two articles. This can result in a high "elasticity" or "mobility" of Union competences.[5]

[9–08] It is this purposive approach that also gives rise to the second means by which competence creep can occur. Even when dealing with a specific legal base such as Art 50 TFEU above, the Court of Justice may be called upon to identify the outer limits of its scope. A good example of this is the *Working Time Directive* case, which concerned a directive having as its legal base a Treaty article mandating the adoption of measures for improvements "especially in the working environment, as regards the health and safety of workers".[6] The Directive required the introduction of minimum rest periods and a maximum working week of 48 hours, a matter regarded by the UK as going beyond the scope of regulating the health, safety and working environment of workers. In particular, the UK argued that the reference within the Treaty article to working environment indicated that the legal base was confined to the adoption of measures to address the physical conditions and risks within a workplace. In rejecting the UK's arguments the Court took a purposive approach, reasoning as follows:

> There is nothing in the wording of [the Article] to indicate that the concepts of 'working environment', 'safety' and 'health' as used in that provision should, in the absence of other indications, be interpreted restrictively, and not as embracing all factors, physical or otherwise, capable of affecting the health and safety of the worker in his working environment, including in particular certain aspects of the organization of working time. On the contrary, the words 'especially in the working environment' militate in favour of a broad interpretation of the powers which [the Article] confers upon the Council for the protection of the health and safety of workers. Moreover, such an interpretation of the words 'safety' and 'health' derives support in particular from the preamble to the Constitution of the World Health Organization to which all the Member States belong. Health is there defined as a state of complete physical, mental and social well-being that does not consist only in the absence of illness or infirmity.[7]

[9–09] More generally, in the field of establishing the Internal Market through negative harmonisation, the Court of Justice is often described as having acted as a "motor of integration", particularly in the period before the extension of the use of Qualified Majority Voting (QMV). As just one example, the famous *Dassonville* formula involved the Court giving an interpretation to the concept of a measure having an equivalent effect to a quantitative restriction on imports.[8] Member States are prohibited by Art 34 TFEU from applying such measures. The Court adopted an extremely broad definition, encompassing all trading rules that were capable of hindering, directly or indirectly, actually or potentially, trade between Member States. This had the knock-on effect of potentially expanding the Union's competence to adopt harmonising measures over a range of different areas that might otherwise have seemed far removed from the original

---

5 Robert Schütze, "EU Competences: Existence and Exercise" in Anthony Arnull and Damian Chalmers (eds), *The Oxford Handbook of European Union Law* (Oxford University Press, 2015) 75, 78.

6 Case C-84/94 *United Kingdom v Council (Working Time Directive)* [1996] ECR I-5755. The legal basis for the Directive was Art 118a of the EEC Treaty, now Art 154 TFEU.

7 *ibid*, 5800.

8 Case 8/74 *Dassonville* [1974] ECR 837. See ch 19, paras [19–31] to [19–37].

idea of a quantitative restriction on imports. As Gerard Conway has remarked, the twin principles of conferral and subsidiarity sit uneasily with, and can be opposed to the "conceptual pull" of, the two Internal Market principles of abolition of obstacles to free movement and undistorted competition.[9]

[9–10] The third way in which the Union's competence has been expanded has been through the doctrines of "parallelism" and "pre-emption" in the field of the EU's external competence. Parallelism refers to the principle developed by the Court of Justice that, where it is necessary in order for the Union to be able to effectively exercise its internal competence that it also act internationally, there will be an implicit parallel external competence to do so. As described by the Court, whenever EU law has created for the institutions powers within its internal system for the purpose of attaining a specific objective, the EU has competence to enter into the international commitments necessary for the attainment of that objective even in the absence of an express provision to that effect.[10] The Court of Justice was also responsible for developing the doctrine of pre-emption, whereby once the EU has laid down common rules implementing a common policy envisaged by the Treaties, the Member States no longer have the right to undertake obligations with third countries which may affect those rules.[11] In such circumstances, the Union alone has the competence to enter into international agreements within the particular field of activity. Both of these principles are now codified within the definition of exclusive external competence in Art 3(2) TFEU, as introduced by the Lisbon Treaty.

B. Categories of Competence

[9–11] Prior to the entry into force of the Lisbon Treaty on 1 December 2009, the division of competence as between the Union and the Member States, and the different nature of Union competences, was not set out in the Treaties and was heavily influenced by the Court's jurisprudence. From Chapter 3 it will be recalled that, dissatisfied with the level of reforms that were being introduced by the Nice Treaty, in an accompanying Declaration on the Future of the Union, the European Council committed to considering initiatives on further reform, including how to establish and monitor a more precise delimitation of powers between the EU and the Member States, reflecting the principle of subsidiarity. Subsidiarity is the idea that a central authority should perform only those tasks which cannot be performed effectively at a more immediate or local level. First introduced by the Maastricht Treaty, it is a commitment to confining Union action to those areas where action at Member State level is in some way inadequate or inefficient and can be better undertaken by the Union. The following year, the Laeken Declaration of 2001 set out a series of questions that initiatives on reform might address in order to improve the delimitation of EU competence:

> Citizens often hold expectations of the European Union that are not always fulfilled. And vice versa – they sometimes have the impression that the Union takes on too much in areas where its involvement is not always essential. Thus the important thing is to clarify, simplify and adjust the division of competence between the Union and the Member States

[9] Gerard Conway, *EU Law* (Routledge, 2015) 269.

[10] Case 3/76, 4/76 and 6/76 *Kramer* [1976] ECR 1279, 1309; Opinion 1/76 *European Laying-up Fund for Inland Waterway Vessels* [1977] ECR 741, 755.

[11] Case 22/70 *Commission v Council (ERTA)* [1971] ECR 263, 274. See Merijn Chamon, "Implied Exclusive Powers in the ECJ's post-Lisbon Jurisprudence: The Continued Development of the *ERTA* Doctrine" (2018) 55 *Common Market Law Review* 1101.

in the light of the new challenges facing the Union. This can lead both to restoring tasks to the Member States and to assigning new missions to the Union, or to the extension of existing powers, while constantly bearing in mind the equality of the Member States and their mutual solidarity.

A first series of questions that needs to be put concerns how the division of competence can be made more transparent. Can we thus make a clearer distinction between three types of competence: the exclusive competence of the Union, the competence of the Member States and the shared competence of the Union and the Member States? At what level is competence exercised in the most efficient way? How is the principle of subsidiarity to be applied here? And should we not make it clear that any powers not assigned by the Treaties to the Union fall within the exclusive sphere of competence of the Member States? And what would be the consequences of this?

The next series of questions should aim, within this new framework and while respecting the "acquis communautaire", to determine whether there needs to be any reorganisation of competence. How can citizens' expectations be taken as a guide here? What missions would this produce for the Union? And, vice versa, what tasks could better be left to the Member States? What amendments should be made to the Treaty on the various policies? How, for example, should a more coherent common foreign policy and defence policy be developed? … Do we want to adopt a more integrated approach to police and criminal law cooperation? How can economic policy coordination be stepped up? How can we intensify cooperation in the field of social inclusion, the environment, health and food safety? But then, should not the day-to-day administration and implementation of the Union's policy be left more emphatically to the Member States and, where their constitutions so provide, to the regions? Should they not be provided with guarantees that their spheres of competence will not be affected?

Lastly, there is the question of how to ensure that a redefined division of competence does not lead to a creeping expansion of the competence of the Union or to encroachment upon the exclusive areas of competence of the Member States and, where there is provision for this, regions. How are we to ensure at the same time that the European dynamic does not come to a halt? In the future as well, the Union must continue to be able to react to fresh challenges and developments, and must be able to explore new policy areas.[12]

[9–12] Paul Craig and Gráinne de Búrca have categorised these questions as being driven by four principal forces: (i) *conferral*, in the sense that the Union should be granted the power to take actions best taken at EU level; (ii) *clarity*, reflecting the desire to simplify and make transparent a complex picture that had developed mainly through the case law of the Court; (iii) *consideration* of the EU's existing competences and whether these were necessary or were in need of enhancement; and (iv) *containment*, based on a concern held by some that the Union had too much power and tended to stretch its existing competences beyond their proper limits.[13]

[9–13] Picking up from the work carried out by the Constitutional Convention, the Lisbon Treaty introduced a number of important amendments that aimed to address these concerns. Article 5 TEU now sets out that the Union's competences are governed

[12] Annex I to the Presidency Conclusions of the Laeken European Council, 14 and 15 December 2001.

[13] Paul Craig and Gráinne de Búrca, *EU Law* (6th ed, Oxford University Press, 2015) 74. See Paul Craig, "Competence: Clarity, Conferral, Containment and Consideration" (2004) 29 *European Law Review* 323; Francis J Conte, "Reinforcing Democracy, Sovereignty and Union Efficacy: Supremacy and Subsidiarity in the European Union" (2004) 24 *Dublin University Law Journal* 1.

by the principles of conferral, subsidiarity and proportionality. First, the Union shall only act within the limits of the competences conferred upon it by the Member States in the Treaties. Competences not so conferred remain with the Member States. Given the number of references to conferral introduced by the Lisbon Treaty (Arts 3, 4 and 5 TEU, Art 7 TFEU and Art 51 of the Charter) it has been remarked that it seems to have become almost an obsession amongst the negotiators, revealing the degree to which the Member States had become distrustful of the institutions.[14]

[9–14] Secondly, under the principle of subsidiarity, in areas which do not fall within its exclusive competence, the Union shall act only if and in so far as the objectives of the proposed action cannot be sufficiently achieved by the Member States, but can rather, by reason of the scale or effects of the proposed action, be better achieved at Union level. Finally, under the principle of proportionality, the content and form of Union action shall not exceed what is necessary to achieve the objectives of the Treaties. It is often said that conferral governs the *limits* of Union competence (ie whether there is a competence), while subsidiarity and proportionality govern the *use* of Union competence (ie how a conferred competence should be used). Although the Treaties contain no statement of competences retained by the Member States, the Lisbon Treaty did introduce a new explicit acknowledgment of the important roles performed by Member States in the form of Art 4(2) TEU:

> The Union shall respect the equality of Member States before the Treaties as well as their national identities, inherent in their fundamental structures, political and constitutional, inclusive of regional and local self-government. It shall respect their essential State functions, including ensuring the territorial integrity of the State, maintaining law and order and safeguarding national security. In particular, national security remains the sole responsibility of each Member State.[15]

[9–15] The most innovative change introduced by the Lisbon Treaty was to both define and categorise the three principal types of EU competence as: (i) exclusive; (ii) shared; and (iii) supporting, coordinating or supplementing. There are, however, two additional competences that do not fall neatly within one of these three categories. First, the Union has competence to define and implement a Common Foreign and Security Policy (CFSP), including the progressive framing of a common defence.[16] Secondly, the TFEU provides that the Member States shall coordinate their economic and employment policies within arrangements as determined by the TFEU, "which the Union shall have competence to provide".[17] For example, the Member States agree to coordinate their economic policies according to broad guidelines adopted by the Council. The Union

---

14 Lucia Serena Rossi, "Does the Lisbon Treaty Provide a Clearer Separation of Competences between EU and Member States?" in Andrea Biondi, Piet Eeckhout and Stefanie Ripley (eds), *EU Law after Lisbon* (Oxford University Press, 2012) 85, 93, 94. See Christiaan Timmermans, "The Competence Divide of the Lisbon Treaty Six Years After" in Sacha Garben and Inge Govaere (eds), *The Division of Competences between the EU and the Member States* (Hart, 2017) 19.

15 See Barbara Guastaferro, "Beyond the *Exceptionalism* of Constitutionalism Conflicts: The *Ordinary* Functions of the Identity Clause" (2012) 31 *Yearbook of European Law* 263; Armin von Bogdandy and Stephan Schill, "Overcoming Absolute Primacy: Respect for National Identity under the Lisbon Treaty" (2011) 48 *Common Market Law Review* 1417; Neil Murphy, "Article 4(2) TEU: A Blow to the Supremacy of Union Law?" (2017) 20 *Trinity College Law Review* 94.

16 Art 2(4) TFEU.

17 Art 2(3) TFEU.

may also take measures, including by defining guidelines, to ensure the coordination of employment policies, and may take initiatives to ensure coordination of social policies.[18]

(i) Exclusive Competence

[9–16] For the first time, Art 2 TFEU provides a definition of exclusive EU competence. According to Art 2(1), when the Treaties confer on the Union exclusive competence in a specific area, only the Union may legislate and adopt legally binding acts, the Member States being able to do so themselves only if so empowered by the Union or for the implementation of acts of the Union. Article 3(1) then sets out an exhaustive list of the five areas of exclusive competence as:

- the Customs Union;
- the establishing of competition rules necessary for the functioning of the Internal Market;
- monetary policy for the Member States whose currency is the euro;
- the conservation of marine biological resources under the Common Fisheries Policy; and
- Common Commercial Policy.

[9–17] Two noteworthy aspects of this list are, first, the omission of the Internal Market (other than in respect of competition rules), which is a matter of shared competence. The dividing line between the *exclusive* competence to establish competition rules necessary for the Internal Market and the *shared* competence to establish the Internal Market itself, can give rise to dispute, as can the line demarcating the Customs Union from the Internal Market. Secondly, it will be noted that exclusive competence in respect of monetary policy only applies in respect of those Member States whose currency is the euro, highlighting one particular instance of differentiated integration.

[9–18] Article 3(2) goes on to provide that the competence of the Union to conclude an international agreement shall be exclusive in three distinct situations, reflecting the earlier case law of the Court of Justice:

- when conclusion of the agreement is provided for in a legislative act of the Union;
- when conclusion of the agreement is necessary to enable the Union to exercise its internal competence; or
- in so far as conclusion of the agreement may affect common rules or alter their scope.[19]

(ii) Shared Competence

[9–19] As the following definition contained in Art 2(2) TFEU demonstrates, the category of shared competence is something of a misnomer. Competences falling within this category may be exercised by either the Union or the Member States, but only until such time as the Union exercises its competence in the area. Thereafter, the Member States may only exercise their competence if the Union decides to cease its own exercise of the competence:

[18] Art 5 TFEU. The Union's exercise of competence in the area of Economic and Monetary Union is discussed in ch 27.

[19] See Case C-600/14 *Germany v Commission (OTIF)* EU:C:2017:935, 5 December 2017, paras 43-73.

> When the Treaties confer on the Union a competence shared with the Member States in a specific area, the Union and the Member States may legislate and adopt legally binding acts in that area. The Member States shall exercise their competence to the extent that the Union has not exercised its competence. The Member States shall again exercise their competence to the extent that the Union has decided to cease exercising its competence.

[9–20] The concept whereby the Member States lose their right to exercise a shared competence due to the Union's exercise of the competence is known as "pre-emption". It is also referred to as the Union "occupying the field". An additional detail of the manner in which pre-emption operates is provided in Protocol No 25 to the Treaties, which specifies that "when the Union has taken action in a certain area, the scope of this exercise of competence only covers those elements governed by the Union act in question and therefore does not cover the whole area". This reinforces the reference in Art 2(2) TFEU to the fact that Member States may exercise their competence "*to the extent that* the Union has not exercised its competence". In other words, the fact that the Union exercises its competence in a given area does not necessarily mean that that entire field of activity has been occupied by the Union. However, it has rightly been noted that the pre-emptive effect of an EU measure "will ultimately depend on its scope and is a matter of interpretation. The Protocol introduces a presumption against field pre-emption but does not preclude it."[20]

[9–21] The situation whereby the Member States might regain a competence due to the Union ceasing to exercise it is taken up in Declaration No 18 to the Treaties, which notes that:

> When the Treaties confer on the Union a competence shared with the Member States in a specific area, the Member States shall exercise their competence to the extent that the Union has not exercised, or has decided to cease exercising, its competence. The latter situation arises when the relevant EU institutions decide to repeal a legislative act, in particular better to ensure constant respect for the principles of subsidiarity and proportionality. The Council may, at the initiative of one or several of its members (representatives of Member States) and in accordance with Article 241 of the Treaty on the Functioning of the European Union, request the Commission to submit proposals for repealing a legislative act. The Conference welcomes the Commission's declaration that it will devote particular attention to these requests.

[9–22] The presence of both the Protocol and the Declaration is a testament to the sensitivity that surrounds the issue of shared competence. It is this sensitivity that originally gave rise to the principle of subsidiarity which, as will be seen below, applies to areas of shared and supporting competence, but not to exclusive competences. As an exception to the principle of pre-emption, Art 4 TFEU provides that in two specific areas the Union shall have shared competence, the exercise of which shall not result in the Member States being prevented from exercising theirs: (i) research, technological development and space; and (ii) development cooperation and humanitarian aid. As a result, these have been described as "parallel" competences.

[9–23] Article 4(1) TFEU establishes shared competence as the default rule when it states that the Union shall share competence with the Member States where the

---

[20] Takis Tridimas, "Competence after Lisbon: The Elusive Search for Bright Lines" in Diamond Ashiagbor, Nicola Countoutis and Ioannis Lianos (eds), *The European Union after the Treaty of Lisbon* (Cambridge University Press, 2012) 47, 65.

Treaties confer on it a competence which does not relate to the areas referred to in Art 3 (exclusive competences) or Art 6 (supporting competences). As referred to above, CFSP is dealt with separately in Art 2(4) TFEU, which does not specify whether this competence is exclusive, shared or supporting. As a result, there is some ambiguity as to whether CFSP ought to be regarded as a shared competence, as the default rule in Art 4(1) would appear to suggest. Derrick Wyatt and Alan Dashwood suggest that CFSP may be considered a variant within the category of shared competence, albeit one whose political sensitivity for the Member States led the Treaty drafters to highlight its special character.[21] Paul Craig and Gráinne de Búrca, however, note that CFSP does not readily fit within the frame of shared competence, particularly as regards the pre-emption of Member State action, while Robert Schütze points to the fact that the adoption of legislative acts is excluded within CFSP in support of the conclusion that it is a *sui generis* competence.[22] Declarations No 13 and No 14 to the Treaties are of relevance in assessing the nature of CFSP competence and, once again, are testament to the particular sensitivities involved. In Declaration No 13, the Intergovernmental Conference which adopted the Lisbon Treaty underlined that the provisions of the TEU covering CFSP did not affect the responsibilities of the Member States for the formulation and conduct of their foreign policy, nor of their national representation in third countries and international organisations. Declaration No 14 went on to add that the provisions on CFSP would not affect the existing legal basis, responsibilities, and powers of each Member State in relation to the formulation and conduct of its foreign policy, its national diplomatic service, relations with third countries and participation in international organisations, nor did they give new powers to the Commission to initiate decisions or increase the role of the European Parliament.

[9–24] This same ambiguity arises in relation to the stand-alone competence conferred on the Union by Art 5 TFEU to coordinate the economic, employment and social policies of the Member States. This separate competence derives from political disagreement within the Constitutional Convention, where some wished to place it within the category of shared competence, while others regarded it as a supporting competence. As a result of its specific nature, it was felt that it merited a separate provision given that, politically, the "importance of the coordination done by the EU in this area made it difficult to make it appear as a mere 'complementary' competence".[23] Technically, therefore, it might be seen as a variant of shared competence albeit that pre-emption does not apply and substantive competence remains with the Member States, with the Union playing a coordinating role.

(iii) Supporting/Coordinating/Supplementing Competence

[9–25] Article 6 TFEU identifies six areas where the Union has competence to carry out actions to support, coordinate or supplement the actions of the Member States. These are: protection and improvement of human health; industry; culture; tourism; education, vocational training, youth and sport; and civil protection. The distinguishing features of this supporting, coordinating or supplemental competence are that, first,

---

21 Alan Dashwood, Michael Dougan, Barry Rodger, Eleanor Spaventa and Derrick Wyatt, *Wyatt and Dashwood's European Union Law* (6th ed, Hart, 2011) 105.

22 Paul Craig and Gráinne de Búrca, *EU Law* (6th ed, Oxford University Press, 2015) 90; Robert Schütze, "EU Competences: Existence and Exercise" in Anthony Arnull and Damian Chalmers (eds), *The Oxford Handbook of European Union Law* (Oxford University Press, 2015) 75, 88–89.

23 Jean-Claude Piris, *The Lisbon Treaty* (Cambridge University Press, 2010) 77.

Union action does not operate to supersede or pre-empt the competence of the Member States and, secondly, the competence cannot be used by the Union to adopt measures aimed at harmonising the laws of the Member States.

Exclusive Competence	Shared Competence	Supporting Competence
– Customs Union; – Establishing competition rules necessary for functioning of Internal Market; – Monetary policy for Member States whose currency is the euro; – Conservation of marine biological resources under the common fisheries policy; – Common commercial policy; – For the conclusion of an international agreement: (i) provided for in an EU legislative act; (ii) necessary to enable the Union to exercise its internal competence; or (iii) in so far as conclusion of the agreement may affect common rules or alter their scope.	– Internal Market; – Social policy, for TFEU aspects; – Economic, social and territorial cohesion; – Agriculture and fisheries (other than conservation of marine biological resources); – Environment; – Consumer protection; – Transport; – Trans-European networks; – Energy; – Area of Freedom, Security and Justice; – Common safety concerns in public health matters, for TFEU aspects. *Without giving rise to pre-emption:* – Research, technological development and space; – Development cooperation and humanitarian aid. *Separate, sui generis competences:* – Coordination of economic, employment and social policies; – Common Foreign and Security Policy.	– Protection and improvement of human health; – Industry; – Culture; – Tourism; – Education, vocational training, youth and sport; – Civil protection; – Administrative cooperation.

C. Disputes as to Legal Basis

[9–26] The correct use of the proper legal base is a matter of constitutional importance within the EU legal order, with the failure to do so rendering a measure liable to be declared invalid by the Court of Justice.[24] This section will look at three types of dispute that may arise as to the use of a legal base. First, there may be a disagreement as to the scope of action that a particular legal base allows. Secondly, there may be different views as to which of one or more legal bases is the most appropriate to be used. Thirdly, the very general nature of the legal base afforded by Art 114 TFEU renders its use particularly susceptible to legal challenge.

[24] See Marcus Klamert, "Conflicts of Legal Basis: No Legality and No Basis but a Bright Future under the Lisbon Treaty?" (2010) 35 *European Law Review* 497.

(i) Disputes as to the Scope of a Legal Base

[9–27] Because the description of legal competence within the Treaties tends to be drawn in general terms, disagreement can arise as to what measures the Union can adopt in pursuit of broad policy objectives. This can be described as a dispute as to the *scope* of a legal base. In other words, is a particular activity to be regarded as being among the powers intended within a conferral of a given competence. For example, in the *Working Time Directive* case referred to above, the UK was unsuccessful in arguing that a reference within a legal base to improving the working environment should be interpreted as being confined to the adoption of measures to address the physical conditions and risks within a workplace.[25] The Court of Justice disagreed and favoured a broader interpretation, which included an authorisation to adopt EU measures regulating conditions such as mandatory rest periods and a maximum working week.

[9–28] Another example of such a dispute arose in the *Migration Policy* case, in which a number of Member States challenged the adoption of a decision by the Commission that required Member States to inform the Commission and other Member States of any draft measures or agreements relating to the immigration of workers from outside the EU and their integration into social and cultural life.[26] As this was long before the introduction of a specific competence in the area of migration, the decision was based on a Treaty article that conferred on the Commission the task of "promoting close cooperation between Member States in the social field" and, to that end, mandated the Commission to act in close contact with the Member States by "making studies, delivering opinions and arranging consultations".

[9–29] The Member States first argued that migration remained an area of Member State competence and that the legal base's reference to the "social field" could not be interpreted as extending to migration from third countries. The Court rejected this argument, pointing to three earlier resolutions of the Council in which it was recognised that the migration policies pursued by the Member States affected the Community's social policy, in particular the employment market and working conditions. Accordingly,

> it must be observed that the employment situation and, more generally, the improvement of living and working conditions within the Community are liable to be affected by the policy pursued by the Member States with regard to workers from non-member countries. In the preamble to [the challenged Decision] the Commission rightly considers that it is important to ensure that the migration policies of Member States in relation to non-member countries take into account both common policies and the actions taken at Community level, in particular within the framework of Community labour market policy, in order not to jeopardize the results.
>
> … It must therefore be held that the argument that migration policy in relation to non-Member States falls entirely outside the social field, in respect of which [the relevant Treaty Article] provides for cooperation between the Member States, cannot be accepted.[27]

[9–30] Secondly, the Member States argued that the conferral of a power to "arrange

---

25 Case C-84/94 *United Kingdom v Council (Working Time Directive)* [1996] ECR I-5755.

26 Joined Cases 281/85, 283-285/85 and 287/85 *Commission v Germany (Migration Policy)* [1987] ECR 3203.

27 *ibid*, 3251–3252.

consultations" could not be interpreted to include a power to adopt binding decisions. The Court rejected this argument also, reasoning that:

> where an article of the EEC Treaty … confers a specific task on the Commission it must be accepted, if that provision is not to be rendered wholly ineffective, that it confers on the Commission necessarily and per se the powers which are indispensable in order to carry out that task. Accordingly, the [reference in the article to "arranging consultations"] must be interpreted as conferring on the Commission all the powers which are necessary in order to arrange the consultations. In order to perform that task of arranging consultations the Commission must necessarily be able to require the Member States to notify essential information, in the first place in order to identify the problems and in the second place in order to pinpoint the possible guidelines for any future joint action on the part of the Member States; likewise it must be able to require them to take part in consultations.
>
> Indeed, the collaboration between Member States required by [the relevant article] is only possible within the framework of organized consultations. In the absence of any action to initiate it that collaboration might remain a dead letter, even though provision is made for it in the Treaty. Since the Commission was specifically given the task of promoting such collaboration and arranging it, it is entitled to initiate consultation procedures within the social field referred to …[28]

(ii) Disputes as to Choice of Legal Base

[9–31] The Treaties specify a large number of legal bases for Union action across a multitude of policy areas. As a result, issues frequently arise regarding the choice of legal base where a particular Union measure straddles more than one policy area, or where the object of a measure can be categorised in a variety of ways. Disputes are especially prone to occur where one of the proposed legal bases is of a broad nature – such as Art 114 TFEU which allows for the adoption of harmonisation measures necessary for the functioning of the Internal Market – and a possible alternative legal base is more specific, such as, for example, the protection of the environment. If a harmonising measure addresses, say, the waste treatment sector with a view to facilitating the operation of a single market in that sector, should that be categorised as a measure aimed at harmonisation or a measure aimed at addressing environmental concerns? The significance of the choice of legal base is often heightened by the fact that it has knock-on implications for the roles afforded to the institutions or the voting method to be used. Clearly, the Parliament's interpretation of the most appropriate legal base is likely to be influenced by the fact that one legal base may grant it a greater degree of involvement than another. Similarly, if one of two legal bases requires unanimity within the Council, Member States may prefer for it to be used. Through successive treaty reforms, the use of QMV has been progressively extended and the ordinary legislative procedure is now established as the default rule. As a result, disputes as to the choice of legal base should, in theory, be lessening in number.

[9–32] An example of such a dispute arose in the *Waste Shipments* case.[29] There, a regulation was adopted on the basis of a Treaty article relating to the protection of the environment. The regulation dealt with establishing procedures and control regimes for the shipment of waste both between Member States and between Member States and third countries. The Commission challenged the regulation on the ground that a

---

[28] *ibid*, 3253–3254.

[29] Case C-411/06 *Commission v Parliament and Council (Waste Shipments)* [2009] ECR I-7585.

dual legal basis ought to have been used, combining the environmental legal base with the Treaty article providing for the Common Commercial Policy (now Art 207 TFEU).

[9–33] The Court of Justice first restated its well-established position that the choice of legal basis for an EU measure must rest on objective factors which are amenable to judicial review, including in particular the aim and the content of the measure. In addition, the legal basis for an act must be determined having regard to its own aim and content and not to the legal basis used for the adoption of other EU acts which might display similar characteristics.[30]

[9–34] Secondly, if examination of an EU measure reveals that it pursues a twofold purpose or that it has a twofold component and if one of these is identifiable as the main or predominant purpose or component, whereas the other is merely incidental, the act must be based on the single legal basis of that required by the main or predominant purpose or component. This is known alternatively as the *predominant purpose* or *centre of gravity* test. Exceptionally, if it is established that an act simultaneously pursues a number of objectives or has several components that are inseparably linked, without one being secondary and indirect in relation to the other, the act will have to be founded on the various corresponding legal bases.[31] This will not be possible, however, where the procedures laid down for each legal basis are incompatible with each other.[32]

[9–35] In this case, the Court had to consider whether the regulation had components falling within the Common Commercial Policy which were inseparably linked to environmental protection-related components of such importance that it ought to have had a dual legal basis. After examining the objective and content of the regulation, the Court concluded that the Parliament and the Council had been correct to regard the protection of the environment as the regulation's predominant purpose. The purpose of the regulation was not to define those characteristics of waste which would enable it to circulate freely within the Internal Market or as part of commercial trade with third countries, but to provide a harmonised set of procedures whereby movements of waste could be limited in order to secure protection of the environment. In particular, the Court considered that it would not be coherent to regard the procedures prescribed by the regulation as having an environmental purpose when applied between Member States, but as having a Common Commercial Policy purpose when applied between Member States and a third country.

[9–36] A further example is found in the *Philippines* case, which related to a Council decision authorising the Union to sign a Partnership and Cooperation Agreement with the Philippines. Given the broad scope of the agreement, the Council insisted on adding to the development cooperation and Common Commercial Policy legal bases proposed by the Commission, additional bases concerning the readmission of third-country nationals, transport and the environment. The Commission brought proceedings challenging the inclusion of these extra bases. The readmission of third-country nationals falls within Title V of Part Three of the TFEU concerning the Area of Freedom, Security

30 *ibid*, paras 45, 77.

31 *ibid*, paras 46–47. See also Case C-263/14 *Parliament v Council (Tanzania)* EU:C:2016:435, 14 June 2016, para 44; Case C-377/12 *Commission v Council (Philippines)*, EU:C:2014:1903, 11 June 2014, para 34.

32 Cases C-164/97 and C-165/97 *Parliament v Council (Titanium Dioxide)* [1999] ECR I-1139, 1163. See also Case C-155/07 *Parliament v Council* [2008] ECR I-8103.

and Justice (AFSJ). According to Protocol No 21 to the Treaties, Ireland has a right to decide whether to opt-in to any measures adopted under a Title V, Part Three legal base. As a result, Ireland intervened in the case in support of the Council's inclusion of this additional legal base.

[9–37] The Court of Justice followed its earlier case law to conclude that the proper approach was to examine whether the agreement's provisions relating to the readmission of third-country nationals, transport and the environment contributed to the pursuit of the objectives of development cooperation and, if so, whether those provisions nevertheless contained obligations so extensive that they constituted distinct objectives that were neither secondary nor indirect in relation to the objectives of development cooperation.[33] In doing so the Court looked at both the approach taken in the TEU and TFEU to development cooperation and the overall framework of the agreement with the Philippines. In addition, the Court examined the conception of development cooperation reflected in secondary EU legislation, as well as in a 2006 joint statement on EU development policy, the "European Consensus", adopted by the Council and the representatives of the governments of the Member States meeting within the Council, the European Parliament and the Commission. Reviewing the European Consensus, the Court observed that:

> migration, transport and the environment are integrated into the development policy defined in the European Consensus. … both migration and the environment and sustainable management of natural resources are among the many development activities envisaged in order to achieve the Millennium Development Goals agenda and to take account of the economic, social and environmental dimensions of poverty eradication in the context of sustainable development. Migration is viewed … as being a positive factor for development contributing to poverty reduction, and development is viewed … as being the most effective long-term response to forced and illegal migration. The environment and transport are included … among the main areas of European Union action in order to respond to the needs of partner countries.[34]

[9–38] In light of this, the Court concluded that the provisions of the agreement relating to readmission of third-country nationals, transport and the environment contributed to the pursuit of the objectives of development cooperation. Furthermore, those provisions did not contain obligations so extensive that they could be considered to constitute objectives distinct from those of development cooperation that were neither secondary nor indirect in relation to those objectives. As a result, no separate legal base was warranted in respect of these three policy areas.

[9–39] The Court did not address the argument made by Ireland that a specific legal base ought to be included in relation to the readmission of third-country nationals in order to give effect to Ireland's right to choose to opt-in under Protocol No 21. It was, however, addressed by Advocate General Mengozzi, who considered that if any future agreement were to be concluded to implement the provision on readmission, "firmly and unequivocally" this could not be concluded on the basis of development cooperation but must be concluded on the basis of an AFSJ provision. It was whenever

---

[33] Case C-377/12 *Commission v Council (Philippines)*, EU:C:2014:1903, 11 June 2014, para 48.
[34] *ibid*, para 49.

such a possible future agreement was concluded that the full effectiveness of Protocol No 21, and the rights of Ireland under it, would be ensured.[35]

[9–40] A related argument was made by Ireland in relation to the EU's conclusion of a Free Trade Agreement with Singapore but was similarly unsuccessful. Finding that Protocol No 21 did not apply as there was no AFSJ legal base in the decision to conclude the agreement, the Court observed that "it is the aim and the content of the measure in question which determine the protocols that may be applicable, and not vice versa".[36] Advocate General Sharpston expressed the same view in her opinion, observing that Protocol No 21 was "not capable of having any effect on the question of the correct legal basis for adopting a decision of the Council concluding an international agreement. It is the legal basis for a measure that determines the protocols to be applied, not the other way round".[37] Given that Art 207 TFEU on the Common Commercial Policy was revised by the Lisbon Treaty, the Court's opinion on the Singapore Free Trade Agreement is, more generally, a highly significant analysis of the distribution of competences between the Union and the Member States when concluding "new generation" trade agreements.[38]

[9–41] The same argument was raised again by Ireland when an opinion was sought from the Court on the proper legal basis for a proposed Passenger Name Record (PNR) Agreement which would allow for the sharing of data on air passengers travelling between the EU and Canada (*EU–Canada PNR Agreement*).[39] Wishing to ensure the application of Protocol No 21, Ireland argued that the agreement's predominant purpose was to facilitate police cooperation and so it should have a legal base taken from Title V of Part Three of the TFEU, dealing with AFSJ. In contrast, the Parliament claimed that the predominant purpose of the agreement was to protect personal data that was transferred to Canada, such that Art 16 TFEU on data protection was the appropriate

---

35 Opinion of Advocate General Mengozzi, EU:C:2014:29, 23 January 2014, para 77. This is reflected in a recital paragraph that is frequently included in mixed international agreements entered into by the Union and its Member States. For example, in the Partnership Agreement on Relations and Cooperation with New Zealand, a recital notes that "in case the Parties decided, within the framework of this Agreement, to enter into specific agreements in the area of freedom, security and justice which were to be concluded by the Union pursuant to Title V of Part Three of the [TFEU], the provisions of such future agreements would not bind the United Kingdom and/or Ireland unless the Union, simultaneously with the United Kingdom and/or Ireland as regards their respective previous bilateral relations, notifies New Zealand that the United Kingdom and/or Ireland has/have become bound by such agreements as part of the Union in accordance with Protocol No 21 … Likewise, any subsequent Union internal measures which were to be adopted pursuant to the above mentioned Title V to implement this Agreement would not bind the United Kingdom and/or Ireland unless they have notified their wish to take part or accept such measures in accordance with Protocol No 21." [2016] OJ L312/3, 4.

36 Opinion 2/15 (*Singapore Free Trade Agreement*) EU:C:2017:376, 2017, para 218.

37 Opinion of Advocate General Sharpston, EU:C:2016:992, 31 December 2016, para 203.

38 The *Singapore* opinion is discussed further in ch 18, paras [18–77] to [18–80]. See Marise Cremona, "Shaping EU Trade Policy post-Lisbon: Opinion 2/15 of 16 May 2017: ECJ, 16 May 2017, Opinion 2/15 *Free Trade Agreement with Singapore*" (2018) 14 *European Constitutional Law Review* 231; Dylan Geraets, "Changes in EU Trade Policy After Opinion 2/15" (2018) 13 *Global Trade and Customs Journal* 13.

39 Opinion 1/15 *EU–Canada Passenger Name Record Agreement*, EU:C:2017:592, 26 July 2017. See Christopher Docksey, "Opinion 1/15: Privacy and Security, Finding the Balance" (2017) 24 *Maastricht Journal of European and Comparative Law* 768.

legal base. The Court concluded that this was an instance where a combined legal basis was required:

> Having regard both to its aims and its content, the envisaged agreement … has two components, one relating to the necessity of ensuring public security and the other to the protection of PNR data.
>
> As regards which of those two components is the preponderant one, it should be observed that, admittedly, the transfer of PNR data by air carriers to Canada and the use of that data by the Canadian Competent Authority are justified, in themselves, only by the objective of ensuring public security in that non-member country and in the European Union.
>
> However, the content of the envisaged agreement largely consists of detailed rules to ensure that the transfer of PNR data to Canada, with a view to its use for the purposes of the protection of public security and safety, takes place under conditions consistent with the protection of personal data.
>
> In this connection, it must be pointed out that the transfer of personal data, such as PNR data, from the European Union to a non-member country is lawful only if there are rules in that country which ensure a level of protection of fundamental rights and freedoms that is essentially equivalent to that guaranteed within the European Union.
>
> It follows that the two components of the envisaged agreement are inextricably linked. They must, therefore, both be considered to be fundamental in nature.[40]

[9–42] In reaching this conclusion, the Court reaffirmed its earlier case law that Protocol No 21 was not capable of having any effect whatsoever on the question of the correct legal basis.[41] In assessing whether the procedures prescribed by the two legal bases were compatible, the Court noted that as both Ireland and the UK had notified of their intention to opt-in to the Council Decision on the conclusion of the agreement, Protocol No 21 would not affect the voting rules within the Council.

(iii) Article 114 TFEU: A Residual Competence to Harmonise

[9–43] Throughout the 1970s and early 1980s, the EEC fell behind in the goal of creating a common market through the adoption of legislative measures aimed at harmonising relevant laws of the Member States. An important factor that contributed to this lack of progress was the need for unanimity within the Council in order to adopt a harmonising measure pursuant to the residual competence provided by Art 100 of the Treaty of Rome. To overcome this obstacle, the Single European Act introduced Art 100a which allowed for qualified majority voting in respect of certain harmonising measures, a legislative competence now found in Art 114 TFEU. As set out above, Art 114 provides a legal base for the adoption of EU measures for the approximation of Member State laws which have as their object the establishment and functioning of the Internal Market. This residual base may only be used, however, where no specific legal base is available.

[9–44] The use of Art 114 gives rise to important constitutional questions regarding the balance of power between the Union and the Member States (and as between the EU

---

40 *ibid*, paras 90–94.

41 *ibid*, para 108. See also Opinion 2/15 (*Singapore Free Trade Agreement*) EU:C:2017:376, 16 May 2017, para 218.

institutions) when it comes to regulating aspects of the Internal Market. As Advocate General Fennelly observed in *Tobacco Advertising I*, to interpret Art 114 as giving *carte blanche* to the EU legislature to "harmonise any national rule that meets the eye … would risk transferring general Member State regulatory competence to the [EU] if recourse to [it] … were not subject to some test of the reality of the link between such measures and internal market objectives".[42] In its judgment in the case, delivered in 2000, the Court of Justice for the first time annulled a legislative harmonisation measure, agreeing with Germany that incorrect use had been made of Art 114.

[9–45] As tobacco advertising on television had already been dealt with in an earlier directive, the Tobacco Advertising Directive sought to ban other forms of advertising including sports sponsorship, magazine and cinema adverts and branded goods such as ashtrays, parasols and posters. In order to justify reliance on Art 114, it was claimed that the aim of the Directive was to reduce obstacles to free movement and distortions in competition resulting from variations in national rules on tobacco advertising. For example, it was said that advertising firms and sporting teams, events and competitions in Member States that allowed such advertising enjoyed an advantage over firms, teams and events based in other Member States. Similarly, an obstacle to the free movement of goods arose from the fact that magazines that included tobacco advertising could be sold in some Member States, but not in others.

[9–46] Germany, however, argued that there were no appreciable obstacles to inter-state trade in tobacco advertising, nor any distortions in competition, that would be addressed by the Directive. Rather, according to Germany, the Directive was in reality a health protection measure. The issue was further complicated by the fact that Art 168(5) TFEU, which provides a legislative basis for EU action aimed at the protection of public health, including regarding tobacco, expressly excludes from its scope the adoption of harmonisation measures.

[9–47] In describing its general approach to the use of Art 114 the Court established the criteria that, in order for a measure to be adopted having Art 114 as its legal base, it must genuinely have as its object the improvement of the conditions for the establishment and functioning of the Internal Market. In this regard,

> [i]f a mere finding of disparities between national rules and of the abstract risk of obstacles to the exercise of fundamental freedoms or of distortions of competition liable to result therefrom were sufficient to justify the choice of Article [114] as a legal basis, judicial review of compliance with the proper legal basis might be rendered nugatory.[43]

[9–48] While the Court accepted that Art 114 could be used in order to prevent the emergence of *future* obstacles to trade resulting from the development of separate national laws, the "emergence of such obstacles must be likely and the measure in question must be designed to prevent them".[44]

---

[42] Case C-376/98 *Germany v Parliament and Council (Tobacco Advertising I)* [2000] ECR I-8419, 8462.

[43] Case C-376/98 *Germany v Parliament and Council (Tobacco Advertising I)* [2000] ECR I-8419, 8524. See Christophe Hillion, "Tobacco Advertising: If You Must, You May" (2001) 60 *Cambridge Law Journal* 486 (2001); Scott Crosby, "The New Tobacco Control Directive: An Illiberal and Illegal Disdain for the Law" (2002) 27 *European Law Review* 177.

[44] *ibid.*

[9–49] As regards, first, obstacles to the free movement of goods and services, the Court accepted that it was probable that such obstacles would arise in the future, given the trend in Member State laws regarding magazine and newspaper advertising. However, it was unprepared to accept that the Directive could be characterised as facilitating trade in cinema advertising or advertising on parasols, ashtrays and posters, given the lack of existing obstacles and the fact that the proposed prohibition could not be said to further facilitate trade in such products.

[9–50] Turning then to distortions of competition, the Court held that in order for a reasonable limit to be placed on the use of Art 114, any distortion in competition invoked as the basis for its use would need to be "appreciable". Distortion would not be regarded as appreciable if it related merely to the "smallest distortions in competition" that can arise from differences in national laws.[45] The Court considered the effects of different Member State rules relating to tobacco on advertising agencies and producers of advertising media to be "remote and indirect" and so not appreciable. In contrast, it accepted that the effect on sporting teams, events and competitions was appreciable and so may have justified recourse to Art 114 for the adoption of a directive aimed solely at addressing that issue.

[9–51] A revised and more limited directive, addressing only print and radio advertising and international sporting competitions, was the subject of *Tobacco Advertising II*, in which the Court reaffirmed that Art 114 could be relied upon:

> when there are obstacles to trade, or it is likely that such obstacles will emerge in the future, because the Member States have taken, or are about to take, divergent measures with respect to a product or class of products, which bring about different levels of protection and thereby prevent the product or products concerned moving freely within the Community.[46]

[9–52] In upholding the use of Art 114 in this instance, the Court confirmed that removing either an obstacle to free movement, or a distortion of competition, was a sufficient reason to invoke the article. It also confirmed that the fact that harmonisation measures were excluded from the scope of Art 168(5), dealing with the protection of health, did not preclude incidental harmonisation in the field of human health within the context of the Internal Market.

[9–53] In subsequent cases, the Court of Justice has accepted the use of Art 114 as an appropriate legal base for measures aimed at regulating mobile phone roaming charges,[47] vitamin food supplements,[48] as well as for an outright ban on the marketing of a product, such as snus, a form of tobacco powder that is placed on the lip.[49] The Court has also confirmed that the addressees of measures adopted under Art 114 need not necessarily be the Member States themselves and has upheld the use of Art 114 in order to establish EU agencies, including the European Supervisory Authorities such as

---

45 *ibid*, 8511, 8530.

46 Case C-380/03 *Germany v European Parliament* [2006] ECR I-11573, 11645. See also Case C-210/03 *R v Secretary of State for Health ex parte Swedish Match* [2004] ECR I-11893; Case C-66/04 *United Kingdom v Parliament (Smoke Flavourings)* [2005] ECR I-10553; Case C-151/17 *Swedish Match v Secretary of State for Health* EU:C:2018:938, 22 November 2018.

47 Case C-58/08 *Vodafone v Secretary of State* [2010] ECR I-4999.

48 Joined Cases C-154/04 and C-155/04 *Alliance for Natural Health* [2005] ECR I-6451.

49 Case C-210/03 *R v Secretary of State ex parte Swedish Match* [2004] ECR I-11893.

the European Banking Authority (EBA).[50] For instance, in order to rationalise the use of Art 114 as a legal base, recitals to the Regulation establishing the EBA set out the following connections between the creation of the new Authority and the establishment and functioning of the Internal Market:

> The financial and economic crisis has created real and serious risks to the stability of the financial system and the functioning of the internal market. Restoring and maintaining a stable and reliable financial system is an absolute prerequisite to preserving trust and coherence in the internal market, and thereby to preserve and improve the conditions for the establishment of a fully integrated and functioning internal market in the field of financial services. Moreover, deeper and more integrated financial markets offer better opportunities for financing and risk diversification, and thus help to improve the capacity of the economies to absorb shocks.
>
> ... The Authority should act with a view to improving the functioning of the internal market, in particular by ensuring a high, effective and consistent level of regulation and supervision taking account of the varying interests of all Member States and the different nature of financial institutions ...
>
> ... The purpose and tasks of the Authority – assisting competent national supervisory authorities in the consistent interpretation and application of Union rules and contributing to financial stability necessary for financial integration – are closely linked to the objectives of the Union acquis concerning the internal market for financial services. The Authority should therefore be established on the basis of Article 114 TFEU.[51]

[9–54] A rather different example of reliance on Art 114 arose in *Parliament v Council (EU–US PNR Agreement)*.[52] There, the European Parliament challenged the use of the article as the basis for a Council Decision on the conclusion of an agreement between the EU and the United States on the transfer of data relating to air passengers collected by airlines. In seeking to defend the use of Art 114, the Council unsuccessfully contended that the agreement was

> intended to eliminate any distortion of competition, between the Member States' airlines and between the latter and the airlines of third countries, which may result from the requirements imposed by the United States, for reasons relating to the protection of individual rights and freedoms. The conditions of competition between Member States' airlines operating international passenger flights to and from the United States could have been distorted because only some of them granted the United States authorities access to their databases. The Agreement is designed to impose harmonised obligations on all the airlines concerned.[53]

[9–55] Annulling the Decision, the Court concluded that the rules governing the

---

50 Case C-217/04 *United Kingdom v European Parliament (European Network and Information Security Agency)* [2006] ECR I-3771.

51 Regulation (EU) No 1093/2010 of the European Parliament and of the Council of 24 November 2010 establishing a European Supervisory Authority (European Banking Authority), amending Decision No 716/2009/EC and repealing Commission Decision 2009/78/EC [2015] OJ L 331/12, recitals 7, 11 and 17. See Elaine Fahey, "Does the Emperor Have Financial Crisis Clothes? Reflections on the Legal Basis of the European Banking Authority" (2011) 74 *Modern Law Review* 581.

52 Joined Cases C-317/047 and C-318/04 *Parliament v Council (EU-US PNR Agreement)* [2006] ECR I-4721.

53 *ibid*, 4830.

transfer of data in fact concerned public security and the activities of the state in the areas of criminal law.

[9–56] Ireland sought to rely on this judgment in its challenge to the use of Art 114 for the adoption of the Data Retention Directive in *Ireland v Parliament*.[54] According to the Directive's recitals, several Member States had adopted legislation providing for the retention of data by service providers for the prevention, investigation, detection and prosecution of criminal offences, and these national provisions varied considerably. The legal and technical differences in national laws presented "obstacles to the internal market for electronic communications, since service providers are faced with different requirements regarding the types of traffic and location data to be retained and the conditions and periods of retention".[55] Accordingly, the aim of the Directive was set out in Art 1 as being to:

> harmonise Member States' provisions concerning the obligations of the providers of publicly available electronic communications services or of public communications networks with respect to the retention of certain data which are generated or processed by them, in order to ensure that the data are available for the purpose of the investigation, detection and prosecution of serious crime, as defined by each Member State in its national law.

[9–57] The contention of Ireland was that the Directive's sole objective, and therefore its centre of gravity, was to facilitate the investigation, detection and prosecution of crime. As a result, rather than Art 114, it was argued that the Directive ought to have had a legal base from within the (pre-Lisbon) Third Pillar, concerning justice matters. Even if it could be said that part of the Directive's aim was to prevent distortions or obstacles to the Internal Market, Ireland claimed that this aim was purely incidental to the main or predominant objective of combatting crime.

[9–58] The Court distinguished its earlier decision on the EU–US Passenger Name Records Agreement on the basis that it had concerned a transfer of personal data within a framework instituted by the public authorities in order to ensure public security. The Data Retention Directive, in contrast, covered the "activities of service providers in the internal market and does not contain any rules governing the activities of public authorities for law-enforcement purposes".[56] In reaching this conclusion, the Court observed that:

- as was apparent from the recitals, the EU legislature started from the premise that there were legislative and technical disparities between the national provisions governing the retention of data by service providers;
- the evidence submitted to the Court confirmed that following terrorist attacks, several Member States, realising that data relating to electronic communications constitute an effective means for the detection and prevention of crimes, adopted measures

[54] Case C-301/06 *Ireland v Parliament and Council* [2009] ECR I-593. See Sara Poli, "The Legal Basis of Internal Market Measures with a Security Dimension" (2010) 6 *European Constitutional Law Review* 137; Theodore Konstadinides, "Wavering between Centres of Gravity: Comment on *Ireland v Parliament and Council*" (2010) 35 *European Law Review* 88.

[55] Directive 2006/24/EC of the European Parliament and of the Council of 15 March 2006 on the retention of data generated or processed in connection with the provision of publicly available electronic communications services or of public communications networks [2006] OJ L105/54, recital 6.

[56] *ibid*, para 91.

pursuant to an existing directive with a view to imposing obligations on service providers concerning the retention of such data;
- it was clear that the obligations relating to data retention had significant economic implications for service providers in so far as they may involve substantial investment and operating costs;
- the evidence submitted to the Court showed that the national measures adopted pursuant to the existing directive differed substantially, particularly in respect of the nature of the data retained and the periods of data retention;
- it was entirely foreseeable that the Member States which did not yet have rules on data retention would introduce rules which were likely to further accentuate the differences between the various existing national measures;
- it was apparent that the differences between the various national rules adopted on the retention of data relating to electronic communications were liable to have a direct impact on the functioning of the Internal Market, and foreseeable that that impact would become more serious with the passage of time;
- such a situation justified the EU legislature in pursuing the objective of safeguarding the proper functioning of the Internal Market through the adoption of harmonised rules;
- the provisions of the Data Retention Directive were designed to harmonise national laws on the obligation to retain data, the categories of data to be retained, the periods of retention of data, data protection and data security and the conditions for data storage;
- service providers were to retain only data generated or processed in the course of the provision of the relevant communication services, and such data was closely linked to the exercise of the commercial activity of those service providers;
- the measures provided for by the Directive did not, in themselves, involve intervention by the police or law-enforcement authorities of the Member States;
- the Directive regulated operations which were independent of the implementation of any police and judicial cooperation in criminal matters. It harmonised neither the issue of access to data by the competent national law-enforcement authorities nor that relating to the use and exchange of those data between those authorities;
- the substantive content of the Directive was directed essentially at the activities of service providers in the relevant sector of the Internal Market and so it related predominantly to the functioning of the Internal Market.

[9–59] Stephen Weatherill has offered a forceful critique of the approach of the Court of Justice in cases challenging the use of Art 114. Examining judgments such as that in *Ireland v Parliament*, he suggests that the Court's inquiry:

> has a weary feel and it scarcely extends beyond the perfunctory. It draws on the evidence of those directly and partially implicated in the adoption of the measure in the first place – the Commission, the Council and states who had voted in favour of the measure in Council, the Parliament, and the European Data Protection Supervisor. The Court skips lightly over the legal threshold and the factual appraisal: the Directive is valid.[57]

[9–60] Weatherill has suggested that, in effect, the criteria developed by the Court offer the institutions a "drafting guide", highlighting the particular terminology and phrases to use in order to tie a regulatory dimension sufficiently tightly to the market-making function of harmonisation. This is not difficult to achieve, he suggests, "partly because the Court is generous in its interpretation of the scope of the legislative grant

[57] Stephen Weatherill, "The Limits of Legislative Harmonisation Ten Years after *Tobacco Advertising*: How the Court's Case Law has become a 'Drafting Guide'" (2011) 12 *German Law Journal* 827, 840.

[in Article 114] but mainly because the Treaty, and the concept of internal market in particular, simply is broad".[58] Although the criteria set out by the Court purport to establish an objective standard, which is not intended to be reliant on the subjective views of the legislative institutions, he suggests that the language used by the Court has the potential to undermine this by setting up general tests which the institutions can then use to deliberately frame their legislative approach, and supporting documentation, in order to fulfil. He explains his argument as follows:

> The Court places enormous weight on slippery adjectives and adverbs in its attempts to define the limits of Article 114 TFEU in a more sophisticated manner than does the Treaty. The object of a measure must *genuinely* be to improve the conditions for the establishment and functioning of the internal market. Conversely, an *abstract* risk of infringements of fundamental freedoms or distortion of competition is not sufficient to justify reliance on Article 114 TFEU; differences must have a *direct* effect on the functioning of the internal market or cause an *appreciable* distortion of competition. Preventive harmonization – targeted at obstacles to trade resulting from future divergent development of national law – is allowed but emergence of such obstacles must be *likely*.
>
> These words carry immense constitutional weight. Find that an effect on the market is *direct*, a distortion of competition *appreciable* or emergence of obstacles *likely* and the diversity between national laws is of sufficient magnitude to impact on the functioning of the internal market: the matter falls within the limits of Article 114 TFEU in particular and of the EU generally. Take away that crucial quality of directness or appreciability or likelihood and the matter rests with the Member States, for it is legislative diversity of a type that does not harm the EU's market-making project.[59]

[9–61] In addition, he points to the fact that while the threshold criteria can be easily manipulated by those politically responsible for their application (ie the legislative institutions), in contrast the Court faces practical difficulties in developing "any means to find independent evidence for claimed appreciable distortions or likely emergence of new obstacles".[60]

[9–62] Aspects of Weatherill's criticism as to the general and subjective nature of the Court's approach can be seen to have been at issue in *Inuit Tapiriit Kanatami*.[61] There, a challenge was brought to the use of Art 114 as the legal base for a regulation that banned the marketing of all seal products, with the exception of those resulting from hunts traditionally conducted by Inuit and other indigenous communities and which contributed to their subsistence. The recitals to the regulation noted that, as a result of the animal welfare concerns of consumers, several Member States had adopted or intended to adopt legislation regulating trade in seal products by prohibiting the import and production of such products, while in other Member States no restrictions were placed on trade in these products. According to the recitals, these differences,

> adversely affect the operation of the internal market in products which contain or may contain seal products, and constitute barriers to trade in such products.
>
> The existence of such diverse provisions may further discourage consumers from buying products not made from seals, but which may not be easily distinguishable from similar

[58] *ibid*, 834.
[59] *ibid*, 832–833.
[60] *ibid*, 838–839.
[61] Case T–526/10 *Inuit Tapiriit Kanatami v Commission*, EU:T:2013:215, 25 April 2013.

goods made from seals, or products which may include elements or ingredients obtained from seals without this being clearly recognisable, such as furs, Omega–3 capsules and oils and leather goods.

[9–63] The applicants, who represented Inuit communities, argued that the primary objective of the regulation was not the functioning of the Internal Market, but rather the protection of animal welfare. In the course of the hearing, the Commission pointed out that at the time of the adoption of the regulation, four Member States had imposed bans on seal products, two had published draft legislation to that effect and three had made known their intention to adopt a ban in the absence of EU measures. As a result, the General Court found that the Union legislature correctly concluded that, in the absence of action at EU level, more Member States were likely to impose a ban, giving rise to an obstacle to trade. The fact that the trade of seal products within the EU may have been small, or largely confined to those Member States that had already imposed a ban, did not detract from this conclusion, particularly given that diverse national provisions might further discourage consumers from buying products not easily distinguishable from seal products.

[9–64] In appealing the judgment, the applicants argued that the recitals to the regulation were not sufficient to justify recourse to Art 114 in that they failed to identify the Member States that had adopted, or intended to adopt, a ban and contained "only vague and general assertions as to the disparities between national rules and the risk of infringements of fundamental freedoms or of distortion of competition".[62] The Court of Justice rejected this argument, finding it sufficient that the recital had indicated the general situation which led to the adoption of the regulation and the general objectives which it was intended to achieve. It was unnecessary, therefore, for the recitals to go so far as to specify the number and identity of the Member States whose national provisions had led to the regulation. The Court of Justice also confirmed the view of the General Court that recourse to Art 114 did not require that there be a "relatively sizeable" trade in the products concerned.[63]

D. Subsidiarity

[9–65] In the very first article of the TEU, the Treaty is described as marking a new stage in the process of creating an ever-closer union among the peoples of Europe, in which decisions are taken as openly as possible and *as closely as possible to the citizen.* This final phrase captures the essence of subsidiarity, or the idea that "public powers should normally be located at the lowest tier of government where they can be exercised effectively".[64] The principle applies to areas of shared and supporting competence, but not to the Union's exclusive competence. As per Art 5(3) TEU, subsidiarity requires

[62] Case C-398/13 P *Inuit Tapiriit Kanatami v Commission*, EU:C:2015:535, September 2015, para 19.

[63] *ibid*, para 41.

[64] Alan Dashwood, Michael Dougan, Barry Rodger, Eleanor Spaventa and Derrick Wyatt, *Wyatt and Dashwood's European Union Law* (6th ed, Hart, 2011) 115. See Gareth Davies, "Subsidiarity: The Wrong Idea, in the Wrong Place, at the Wrong Time" (2006) 43 *Common Market Law Review* 63; Robert Schütze, "Subsidiarity after Lisbon: Reinforcing the Safeguards of Federalism" (2009) 68 *Cambridge Law Journal* 525; Paul Craig, "Subsidiarity: A Legal and Political Analysis" (2012) 50 *Journal of Common Market Studies* 72; Katarzyna Granat, *The Principle of Subsidiarity and its Enforcement in the EU Legal Order* (Hart, 2018).

that in matters of shared or supporting competence, the Union shall only act if and in so far as the objectives of the proposed action: (i) cannot be sufficiently achieved by the Member States, either at central, regional or local level but rather, (ii) by reason of the scale of effects of the proposed action, can be better achieved at Union level. Further detail is provided in Protocol No 2 to the Treaties on the application of the principles of Subsidiarity and Proportionality, which is to be followed by the EU institutions when applying the principle of subsidiarity, and by national parliaments in ensuring compliance with the principle.

[9–66] When preparing a draft legislative act, the Protocol on Subsidiarity and Proportionality requires that the Commission must consult widely and take account of the need to minimise any administrative or financial burden falling upon the Union, national governments, regional or local authorities, economic operators or citizens, which must be kept commensurate with the objective to be achieved. Draft legislative acts are required to be accompanied by a detailed statement that makes it possible to appraise compliance with subsidiarity and proportionality, including some assessment of the proposal's financial impact. In particular, the reasons for concluding that an objective can be better achieved at Union level is to be substantiated by qualitative and, wherever possible, quantitative indicators. This requirement to provide a written account of the consideration of subsidiarity and proportionality is now further enhanced through the regular use of Impact Assessment Reports, on which the Commission has issued dedicated Guidelines.[65] According to these Guidelines, when assessing subsidiarity the Impact Assessment should address the following five questions:

(i) Does the issue being addressed have transnational aspects which cannot be dealt with satisfactorily by action by Member States?
(ii) Would actions by Member States alone, or the lack of Union action, conflict with the requirements of the Treaty?
(iii) Would actions by Member States alone, or the lack of Union action, significantly damage the interests of Member States?
(iv) Would action at Union level produce clear benefits compared with action at the level of Member States by reason of its scale?
(v) Would action at Union level produce clear benefits compared with action at the level of Member States by reason of its effectiveness?[66]

[9–67] In 2015, the Commission issued *Better Regulation Guidelines* which set out further detail as to how an Impact Assessment analysis should verify whether Member States alone could resolve a problem sufficiently and whether the Union has the competence to act and would be best placed to do so.[67] According to these Guidelines, the Impact Assessment:

> should verify whether EU action in areas outside its exclusive competence is compatible with the principle of subsidiarity. This is not to be taken for granted and it is important to remember that, pursuant to the Treaty of Lisbon, the respect of the principle of subsidiarity is closely scrutinised by the other EU institutions and by national Parliaments and that Union acts can be annulled by the Court for non-respect of the principle.

---

65 Impact Assessment Guidelines, SEC(2009) 92, 15 January 2009.

66 *ibid*, para 5.2.

67 Commission Staff Working Document, Better Regulation Guidelines, SWD(2017) 350 final, 7 July 2017. See Sacha Garben and Inge Govaere eds, *The EU Better Regulation Agenda: A Critical Assessment* (Hart, 2018).

> The following key questions should be reviewed when assessing whether or not the subsidiarity principle is respected: whether the problem addressed has transnational aspects which cannot be adequately addressed by action by Member States and whether action at EU level would produce greater benefits compared with action at the level of Member States due to its scale or effectiveness.
>
> This assessment is likely to be an iterative process. Preliminary analyses in the inception impact assessment and early in the [Impact Assessment] process should clarify the legal basis and indicate whether advancing further at EU level would make sense. A final verification of compliance with the subsidiarity principle will only be possible once all relevant information is collected and the analysis of impacts is completed. In addition, the assessment of whether an initiative is proportionate is clearly linked to the assessment of subsidiarity and the need to match the nature and intensity of a given measure to the identified problem.
>
> Assessing subsidiarity necessarily involves elements of political judgement, particularly when evidence is inconclusive and/or stakeholder views diverge. All elements should, therefore, be presented objectively in the [Impact Assessment] Report, providing the basis for a political appreciation by the College. General statements and circular reasoning should be avoided in favour of concrete arguments, specific to the issues being analysed and substantiated with qualitative, and where possible, quantitative evidence.[68]

[9–68] First convened in 2018, a dedicated Task Force has been established on Subsidiarity, Proportionality and "Doing Less More Efficiently", charged with examining ways to better apply the principles of subsidiarity and proportionality in the work of the institutions, particularly as regards the preparation and implementation of Union legislation and policies. The Task Force has also been asked to identify any policy areas where, over time, decision-making and/or implementation could be re-delegated in whole or in part or definitively returned to the Member States, as well as ways to better involve regional and local authorities in the preparation and the follow-up of Union policies. Among the conclusions reached in its first report, the Task Force identified the need for a:

> new way of working to improve the current policymaking processes and to allow the Union to use it more efficiently. It will allow local and regional authorities and national Parliaments to make a more effective contribution to policymaking, to the design of (new) legislation and to ensuring respect for the principles of subsidiarity and proportionality.
>
> This new way of working requires a common understanding of subsidiarity and proportionality and a greater participation of all stakeholders and particularly national, local and regional authorities who often have a specific role in implementing Union legislation on the ground. Such "active subsidiarity" should promote greater ownership and understanding of what the Union does by those involved.
>
> A model grid should be used to assess subsidiarity and proportionality more consistently by the European Commission, the national and regional Parliaments, the European Committee of the Regions and the European Parliament and the Council throughout the decision-making process.[69]

---

[68] *ibid*, 19. See also ch 2 of the Better Regulation Toolbox ("How to Carry out an Impact Assessment", Tool Nos 8 to 18), available at <https://ec.europa.eu/info/better-regulation-toolbox_en>.

[69] "Active Subsidiarity: A New Way of Working", Report of the Task Force on Subsidiarity, Proportionality and "Doing Less More Efficiently", 10 July 2018, 4. See also Commission Communication, "The principles of subsidiarity and proportionality: Strengthening their role in the EU's policymaking", COM(2018) 703 final, 23 October 2018.

[9–69] In order to foster a shared understanding of subsidiarity amongst those involved in assessing compliance with the principle, the Task Force has developed a model assessment grid which is set out as an annex to the report. This model assessment grid highlights the concept of "European added value, which is the key factor that determines whether the Union should act, and is also a concept more easily understood by the general public".[70] The report suggests that the assessment grid could be useful to the Court of Justice, be used as the foundation for discussion amongst the EU institutions and the national parliaments and, in the longer term, be incorporated in a future revision of the Inter-Institutional Agreement on Better Law-Making to provide a more structured basis for its use by the Parliament, Council and Commission.[71]

[9–70] Protocol No 2 to the TEU and TFEU establishes a dedicated mechanism designed to enhance the ability of national parliaments to scrutinise compliance with the principle of subsidiarity. First, the Commission is required to forward all draft legislative acts to national parliaments at the same time as they are provided to the institutions. Similarly, upon their adoption the European Parliament and the Council are obliged to forward all legislative resolutions or positions to national parliaments. By way of a response, within eight weeks a national parliament or, where there is more than one chamber, any chamber of a national parliament, may send a reasoned opinion stating why it considers that the draft does not comply with the principle of subsidiarity. Such a reasoned opinion is to be "taken account of" by the Union institutions.

[9–71] Secondly, the Protocol provides for what is known as the "yellow card" procedure.[72] Each national parliament is given two votes, with bicameral parliaments such as the Oireachtas allocating a vote to each chamber. Where the number of reasoned opinions submitted amounts to one-third of the allocated votes, the draft legislative act must be reviewed. Reflecting its sensitivity for Member States, as an exception, this threshold is reduced to just a quarter of the allocated votes in respect of acts based on Art 76 TFEU relating to judicial cooperation in criminal matters and police cooperation. In response, the Commission or other relevant institution may decide to maintain, amend or withdraw the draft legislative act, giving reasons for its decision.

[9–72] The yellow card was first engaged in 2012 in response to a proposed regulation that addressed the relationship between the right to strike, on the one hand, and the freedom of establishment and to provide services on the other. The proposal prompted reasoned opinions from 12 national parliaments (which did not include Ireland), most of which questioned the use of Art 352 TFEU as a legal base for the proposed measure. In its response, the Commission concluded that the subsidiarity principle had not been breached, but nonetheless went on to withdraw the proposal. The second use of the yellow card came in 2013 and related to the proposed establishment of a European Public Prosecutor's Office that would investigate and prosecute crimes against the EU budget and VAT fraud. On this occasion, both Houses of the Oireachtas submitted a

---

70 *ibid*, 10.

71 Interinstitutional Agreement between the European Parliament, the Council of the European Union and the European Commission of 13 April 2016 on Better Law-Making [2016] OJ L123/1.

72 See, for example, Federico Fabbrini and Katarzyna Granat, "'Yellow Card, but no Foul': The Role of the National Parliaments under the Subsidiarity Protocol and the Commission proposal for an EU Regulation on the Right to Strike" (2013) 50 *Common Market Law Review* 115; Philip Kiiver, "The Early-Warning System for the Principle of Subsidiarity: The National Parliament as a Conseil d'État for Europe" (2011) 36 *European Law Review* 98.

reasoned opinion in which they argued that: (i) the investigation and prosecution of all fraud, including against the EU, was primarily a duty of national authorities; (ii) the Commission had not demonstrated that Member States were taking inadequate action in response to EU-related fraud; (iii) inadequate consideration had been given to the option of strengthening existing mechanisms, and (iv) greater emphasis ought to have been placed on improving cooperation between Member States and existing organisations such as the European Anti-Fraud Office. The Public Prosecutor's Office was subsequently established by means of the enhanced cooperation procedure with Ireland among those opting not to participate.[73] The yellow card procedure was invoked for a third time in 2016 in response to a proposed Posted Workers Directive, on foot of reasoned opinions from 11 national parliaments (which did not include Ireland).

[9–73] Thirdly, the Protocol provides for a more forceful "orange card" procedure which may be employed where the ordinary legislative procedure is being used. Where reasoned opinions on non-compliance with subsidiarity are submitted by a simple majority of the allocated votes, the proposal must be reviewed and the Commission may decide to maintain, amend or withdraw it. If, however, the Commission chooses to maintain the proposal it is required to provide a reasoned opinion justifying how the proposal complies with subsidiarity. This opinion, together with those of the national parliaments, is submitted to the European Parliament and the Council for consideration before concluding the first reading. If either the Council (by a majority of 55 per cent of its members) or the European Parliament (by a majority of the votes cast) is of the opinion that the proposal is not compatible with subsidiarity, it shall not be given further consideration.

[9–74] Fourthly, the Protocol provides that infringement proceedings under Art 263 TFEU may be brought before the Court of Justice by a Member State, or notified by a Member State in accordance with its legal order on behalf of its national parliament or a chamber thereof, in respect of an alleged infringement of the principle of subsidiarity by a legislative act. This is provided for in s 7(4) of the European Union Act 2009 according to which, where either House of the Oireachtas is of the opinion that an EU act infringes the principle of subsidiarity and wishes that a review of the act be sought from the Court of Justice, it shall notify the Minister for Foreign Affairs and Trade who shall, as soon as may be after being so notified, arrange for Art 263 proceedings to be brought.[74]

[9–75] Finally, the Commission is required to publish an annual report on the Protocol's operation.[75] These reports reveal that the level of engagement by national parliaments can vary from year to year, partly in response to the level of legislative activity within the Union. For example, while 21 reasoned opinions on subsidiarity were received in 2014, and eight in 2015, the number jumped to 65 in 2016, the third largest since the mechanism's introduction. Over the period 2010 to 2018, the number of subsidiarity reasoned opinions submitted by the Oireachtas has averaged two a year as follows:

[73] Council Regulation (EU) 2017/1939 of 12 October 2017 implementing enhanced cooperation on the establishment of the European Public Prosecutor's Office [2017] OJ L283/1.

[74] See Standing Order 116 of the Standing Orders relative to Public Business, Dáil Éireann, 2016.

[75] European Commission, *Annual Report 2017 on Subsidiarity and Proportionality* COM(2018) 490 final, 23 October 2018. For details of all opinions submitted by national parliaments, see <http://ec.europa.eu/dgs/secretariat_ general/relations/relations_other/npo/index_en.htm>.

	Total Oireachtas Opinions	Oireachtas Subsidiarity Opinions	Total Subsidiarity Opinions received by Parliament, Council and Commission	Subject of Oireachtas Subsidiarity Reasoned Opinion
2018	8	4	—	o Proposals for a Council Directive laying down rules relating to the Corporate Taxation of a Significant Digital Presence and a Council Directive on the Common System of a Digital Services Tax on revenues resulting from the provision of certain digital services o Proposal for a Regulation on Streamlining Measures for Advancing the Realisation of the Trans-European Network o Proposal for a Regulation on establishing a framework for interoperability between EU information systems (borders and visa) o Proposal for a Directive on the quality of water intended for human consumption
2017	7	2	52	o Proposed Directive on preventive restructuring frameworks, second chance and measures to increase the efficiency of restructuring, insolvency and discharge procedure o Proposal to amend Regulation 1073/2009 on common rules for access to the international market for coach and bus services
2016	5	2	65	o Common Consolidated Corporate Tax Base o Proposal to amend Directive 2013/34/EU as regards disclosure of income tax information by certain undertakings and branches
2015	9	0	8	
2014	8	0	21	
2013	12	3	70	o Framework for maritime spatial planning and integrated coastal management o Establishment of a European Public Prosecutor's Office o Measures concerning the European single market for electronic communications and to achieve a Connected Continent
2012	7	0	84	

	Total Oireachtas Opinions	Oireachtas Subsidiarity Opinions	Total Subsidiarity Opinions received by Parliament, Council and Commission	Subject of Oireachtas Subsidiarity Reasoned Opinion
2011	1	1	64	o Common Consolidated Corporate Tax Base
2010	3	0	34	

(i) Judicial Review of Subsidiarity

[9–76] Because the principle of subsidiarity involves elements of political judgment, an obvious question that arises is how the Court of Justice should approach reviewing a decision of the Union legislature on the ground of subsidiarity. In particular, what level of intensity should judicial review on the ground of subsidiarity take? One of the first occasions on which the Court addressed subsidiarity was in the *Working Time Directive* case.[76] Among the grounds for seeking the Directive's annulment, the UK argued that: (i) the Union had not fully considered or adequately demonstrated that there were transnational elements which could not be adequately addressed at national level; and (ii) the principle of subsidiarity should not allow the adoption of a directive in such wide and prescriptive terms, given that the way in which working time was regulated within the Member States varied widely. The Court reacted to this argument with a succinct and "light-touch" response that has been said to have structured the judicial vision of the principle ever since.[77] The relevant paragraph of the judgment reads:

> [I]t should be noted that it is the responsibility of the Council, under [the relevant Treaty Article] to adopt minimum requirements so as to contribute, through harmonization, to achieving the objective of raising the level of health and safety protection of workers which … is primarily the responsibility of the Member States. Once the Council has found that it is necessary to improve the existing level of protection as regards the health and safety of workers and to harmonize the conditions in this area while maintaining the improvements made, achievement of that objective through the imposition of minimum requirements necessarily presupposes [EU]-wide action, which otherwise, as in this case, leaves the enactment of the detailed implementing provisions required largely to the Member States. The argument that the Council could not properly adopt measures as general and mandatory as those forming the subject-matter of the directive will be examined below in the context of the plea alleging infringement of the principle of proportionality.[78]

[9–77] A subsidiarity challenge was also mounted in *Vodafone* concerning a regulation that imposed caps on the wholesale and retail charges that mobile phone operators could charge for the provision of roaming services on calls between Member States.[79] In particular, it was claimed that the imposition of a ceiling not only for wholesale charges

[76] Case C-84/94 *United Kingdom v Council (Working Time Directive)* [1996] ECR I-5755.

[77] Robert Schütze, "EU Competences: Existence and Exercise" in Anthony Arnull and Damian Chalmers (eds), *The Oxford Handbook of European Union Law* (Oxford University Press, 2015) 75, 92.

[78] Case C-84/94 *United Kingdom v Council (Working Time Directive)* [1996] ECR I-5755, 5808–5809.

[79] Case C-58/08 *Vodafone* [2010] ECR I-4999.

per minute, but also for retail charges, was contrary to the principle of subsidiarity. The Court rejected this argument, reasoning that:

> [T]he [Union] legislature, wishing to maintain competition among mobile telephone network operators, has, in adopting [the Regulation] introduced a common approach, in order in particular to contribute to the smooth functioning of the internal market, allowing those operators to act within a single coherent regulatory framework.
>
> As is clear from … the preamble to the regulation, the interdependence of retail and wholesale charges for roaming services is considerable, so that any measure seeking to reduce retail charges alone without affecting the level of costs for the wholesale supply of [EU]-wide roaming services would have been liable to disrupt the smooth functioning of the [EU]-wide roaming market. For that reason, the [Union] legislature decided that any action would require a joint approach at the level of both wholesale charges and retail charges, in order to contribute to the smooth functioning of the internal market in those services.
>
> That interdependence means that the [Union] legislature could legitimately take the view that it had to intervene at the level of retail charges as well. Thus, by reason of the effects of the common approach laid down in [the Regulation], the objective pursued by that regulation could best be achieved at [EU] level.[80]

[9–78] Thus far, the case law of the Court of Justice has demonstrated a significant degree of deference to the political judgment of the legislative institutions when it comes to assessing the comparative efficiency of action taken at the Union level. As a result, it has been suggested that judicial review on subsidiarity grounds is "likely to be confined to examining whether the assessment reached by the responsible institution has been vitiated by manifest error or abuse of powers, or whether the institution has manifestly exceeded the limits of its discretion".[81] Much of Stephen Weatherill's criticism of the Court's approach to adjudicating on the use of Art 114 TFEU, discussed above, might be said to apply equally to its approach to subsidiarity. Some, such as Craig and de Búrca, see a possible answer in a heightened duty to provide reasons. By requiring the Commission to disclose greater qualitative and quantitative data to justify its reasoning, the Court would have more to go on than as compared to its present reliance on the relatively cursory explanations set out in the recitals to a contested measure.[82] In this regard, the greater detail provided in the *Better Regulation Guidelines*, and the related components of the accompanying "Tool Box", on how to address subsidiarity within an Impact Assessment Report is likely to enable the Court to conduct a more thorough review whenever a measure is challenged on subsidiarity grounds.[83]

E. Proportionality

[9–79] Of the two principles included within Art 5 TEU for guiding the use of EU competence, the second is that of proportionality. In accordance with Art 5 TEU, the institutions shall apply the principle of proportionality as laid down in Protocol No 2

---

80 *ibid*, paras 76–78.

81 Alan Dashwood, Michael Dougan, Barry Rodger, Eleanor Spaventa and Derrick Wyatt, *Wyatt and Dashwood's European Union Law* (6th ed, Hart, 2011) 119.

82 Paul Craig and Gráinne de Búrca, *EU Law* (6th ed, Oxford University Press, 2015) 100.

83 Commission Staff Working Document, Better Regulation Guidelines, SWD(2017) 350 final, 7 July 2017; ch 2 of the Better Regulation Toolbox ("How to Carry out an Impact Assessment", Tool Nos 8 to 18), available at <https://ec.europa.eu/info/better-regulation-toolbox_en>.

in order to ensure that "the content and form of Union action shall not exceed what is necessary to achieve the objectives of the Treaty". Unlike subsidiarity, which was specifically introduced in the Treaties by the Member States as a means of restraining competence creep by the Union, proportionality is among the oldest of the general principles of EU law developed by the Court of Justice and is of broad application across a range of areas.[84] Here, we are concerned with proportionality as a constitutional principle aimed at limiting the use of Union competence. Another distinction is that, unlike subsidiarity, proportionality applies to all Union acts, including those within the EU's exclusive competence. Furthermore, whereas the procedural requirements in Art 5 of Protocol No 2 apply to proportionality (eg the requirement to accompany draft legislative acts with a detailed statement making it possible to appraise compliance with the principle), the special role afforded to national parliaments by Arts 6, 7 and 8 of the Protocol (ie the yellow and orange card procedures and recourse to the Court of Justice through the relevant Member State) are confined to ensuring compliance with subsidiarity only and do not extend to proportionality. That said, given their close relationship, a concern as to the proportionality of a proposed legislative measure can readily feed in to an objection on the ground of subsidiarity.

[9–80] Proportionality has been described by the Court as requiring that, first, an EU measure must not exceed the limits of what is appropriate and necessary in order to attain the objectives legitimately pursued by the legislation in question. Secondly, when there is a choice between several appropriate measures, recourse must be had to the least onerous. Thirdly, the disadvantages caused by the measure must not be disproportionate to the aims pursued.[85] The *Better Regulation Guidelines* outline four questions that are to be considered when addressing proportionality as part of an Impact Assessment report:

(i) Whether the option goes beyond what is necessary to achieve the objectives satisfactorily;
(ii) Whether the scope of the option is limited to those aspects that Member States cannot achieve satisfactorily on their own, and where the Union can do better;
(iii) Whether costs for the Union, national governments, regional or local authorities, economic operators or citizens, are minimised in relation to the objective to be achieved;
(iv) Whether the form of action (choice of instrument) is as simple as possible, and coherent with satisfactory achievement of the objective and effective enforcement.[86]

[9–81] In the *Working Time Directive* case, the Court's review on the grounds of proportionality can reasonably be described as low-intensity. There, proportionality was condensed into two essential components: whether the means employed were suitable for the purpose of achieving the desired objective and, secondly, whether the means employed went beyond what was necessary to achieve the objective. According to the Court, where the EU legislative institutions are required to make social policy choices that involve carrying out complex assessments, they must be allowed a wide

[84] See Wolf Sauter, "Proportionality in EU Law: A Balancing Act?" (2013) 13 *Cambridge Yearbook of European Legal Studies* 439; Tor-Inge Harbo, "The Function of the Proportionality Principle in EU Law" (2010) 16 *European Law Journal* 158; Gráinne de Búrca, "The Principle of Proportionality and its Application in EC Law" (1993) 13 *Yearbook of European Law* 105.

[85] Case C-310/04 *Spain v Council (Cotton Subsidies)* [2006] ECR I-7318, 7346.

[86] Commission Staff Working Document, Better Regulation Guidelines, SWD(2017) 350 final, 7 July 2017, 28–29.

discretion. Moreover, judicial review of the exercise of that discretion must be limited to examining whether it has been vitiated by manifest error or misuse of powers, or whether the institution concerned has manifestly exceeded the limits of its discretion.[87] So, as regards the first condition, it sufficed to note that the measures in the Working Time Directive contributed directly to improving protection for the health and safety of workers within the meaning of the relevant Treaty article and so could not be regarded as unsuited to the purpose of achieving that objective. The Court conducted a more detailed analysis as to whether the same objective may have been achieved by less restrictive means. Here, it had regard to the various derogations and transitional periods that were available to Member States in relation to issues such as mandatory rest periods, maximum working weeks and minimum annual leave entitlements. In light of these, the Court concluded that no manifest error had been committed by the institutions in taking the view that the objective of harmonising national legislation on the health and safety of workers, while maintaining improvements made, could not be achieved by any less restrictive measures.

[9–82] In *Vodafone*, the Court of Justice confirmed that the criterion to be applied in assessing proportionality was not whether a measure was the only or the best possible measure, but rather whether the measure was manifestly inappropriate having regard to the objective being pursued.[88] There, it was alleged that the measure was disproportionate in that it did not confine itself to imposing a cap on wholesale roaming charges, but also imposed a cap on retail charges. It was claimed that a less intrusive and more proportionate approach would have been to regulate wholesale charges only, while allowing competition in retail markets to bring retail prices down according to the normal rules of supply and demand, leaving national regulatory authorities free to intervene in cases where the markets were not functioning properly. The Court noted that before introducing its proposal, the Commission had carried out an exhaustive study which examined various options including regulating only retail charges or wholesale charges, or both, and assessed the economic impact of these various options. This study was reflected in the impact assessment report, which recommended that: (i) as the dynamics of the roaming markets were complex and in the process of changing, there was a risk that a reduction in wholesale charges would not be reflected in retail charges; (ii) as the regulation of wholesale charges alone would not have a direct and immediate effect for consumers, only the regulation of retail charges could improve the situation of consumers directly; and (iii) it would be more prudent to regulate retail charges at the same time as wholesale charges. The Court concluded that

> [i]n those circumstances, and particularly in the light of the broad discretion which the [Union] legislature has in the area at issue, which involves choices to be made of an economic nature, requiring complex assessments and evaluations, it could legitimately take the view that regulation of the wholesale market alone would not achieve the same result as regulation … which covers at the same time the wholesale market and the retail market, and that the latter was therefore necessary.[89]

[9–83] Similarly, in *Inuit Tapiriit Kanatami*, the General Court rejected an argument that a labelling requirement would have been a less-restrictive means of achieving the same objective as an outright ban on seal products with an exception for hunts

87 Case C-84/94 *United Kingdom v Council (Working Time Directive)* [1996] ECR I-5755, 5811.
88 Case C-58/08 *Vodafone* [2010] ECR I-4999.
89 *ibid*, para 68.

traditionally carried out by indigenous communities that contributed to their subsistence. From the recitals to the regulation, it was clear that consideration had been given to a labelling requirement that would allow only products from humanely killed seals to be placed on the market, but that this had not been favoured by the institutions. The recitals stated that, given the conditions in which seal hunting occurs, consistent verification and control of hunters' compliance with animal welfare requirements was either not feasible in practice or very difficult to achieve in an effective way. The recitals also stated that labelling requirements would not achieve the same result and that requiring manufacturers to label products that were derived partially from seals would impose a significant burden and be disproportionately costly in cases where seal products represented only a minor part of the product. The measures contained in the regulation would, according to its recitals, be easier to comply with, whilst also reassuring consumers. On the basis of this, the General Court found that the applicants had failed to establish that the legislature had been in error in concluding that a general ban on seal products was the best means of guaranteeing the free movement of goods.

[9–84] If the institutions can be shown to have committed an error in the manner in which they have assessed the proportionality of a proposed measure, such as by failing to take into account a relevant consideration, the measure may be vulnerable to challenge. The *Cotton Subsidies* case (*Spain v Council)* is a rare example of a legal act being annulled due to an infringement of the principle of proportionality.[90] There, a regulation was introduced reforming the calculation of subsidies to cotton farmers under the Common Agricultural Policy. The objective of the regulation was to ensure economic conditions which, in regions which lend themselves to cotton farming, enable that activity to continue and so prevent cotton from being driven out by other crops. Under the regulation, the amount to be paid represented 35 per cent of the payment that had been made under the previous regime. Spain, which carried out a number of studies of its own on the likely economic effects of the measure, argued that the institutions had failed to take account of labour costs when assessing the future profitability of cotton farmers in receipt of the reduced subsidy. The specific nature of the alleged failing in the proportionality assessment gave the Court something unusually concrete to review, reasoning as follows:

> the [Union] legislature's broad discretion, which implies limited judicial review of its exercise, applies not only to the nature and scope of the measures to be taken but also, to some extent, to the finding of the basic facts.
>
> However, even though such judicial review is of limited scope, it requires that the [Union] institutions which have adopted the act in question must be able to show before the Court that in adopting the act they actually exercised their discretion, which presupposes the taking into consideration of all the relevant factors and circumstances of the situation the act was intended to regulate.
>
> It follows that the institutions must at the very least be able to produce and set out clearly and unequivocally the basic facts which had to be taken into account as the basis of the contested measures of the act and on which the exercise of their discretion depended.
>
> … it is apparent from the information provided by the Commission at the hearing that certain labour costs were not included and were thus not taken into consideration in the comparative study of the foreseeable profitability of cotton growing under the new

[90] Case C-310/04 *Spain v Council (Cotton Subsidies)* [2006] ECR I-7318.

support scheme which was used as the basis of the determination of the amount of the specific aid for cotton.

The Spanish Government submits, however, relying on studies giving figures, that those costs can be calculated, that they are significant, and that taking them into account creates serious doubts as to the profitability of cotton growing under the new support scheme.

Without it being necessary to take a decision on the correctness of the figures produced by the various parties, it must be said that the relevance of the labour costs in question for the purposes of calculating the production costs of cotton and the foreseeable profitability of that crop appears in itself to be scarcely deniable. The circumstance relied on by the Commission that obtaining that information would have raised certain technical problems cannot call into question its relevance.

Moreover, it must be observed that the Council and the Commission have not put forward specific arguments to disprove the Spanish Government's assertion that the inclusion of those costs entails an increase in the production costs of cotton such that adequate profitability of that crop under the new support scheme is not ensured, so that that crop, or at least a substantial part of it, is liable to be given up or in some cases driven out by other crops.[91]

[9–85] In contrast, some proportionality challenges do not point to a particular failing in the assessment carried out by the legislature, but rather claim in a broad sense that a measure taken is disproportionate. Here, the Court tends to examine whether the measure is "manifestly inappropriate" or, in other words, whether it was possible for the legislature to take the view that it did without going beyond the bounds of the discretion which it enjoys in the area. So, for example, in a challenge to the *Tobacco Advertising Directive*, it was claimed that a ban on the use of terms such as "low-tar", "light" and "ultra-light" and an increase in the portion of a cigarette packet that was to be given over to health warnings were disproportionate.[92] This required the Court to consider, in essence, the coherence of the legislature's reasoning on matters such as whether the term "light" was liable to mislead consumers, or whether it had overstepped the bounds of its discretion by reducing the space available for affixing a trade mark. In each case, the Court found the principle of proportionality not to have been infringed.

[9–86] In this context it is worth noting that, in addition to a constitutional principle governing the relationship between Union and Member State competences, proportionality also arises in the context of EU human rights law. According to Art 52 of the Charter of Fundamental Rights, any limitations on the rights and freedoms recognised by the Charter are subject to the principle of proportionality and may only be made if they are necessary and genuinely meet objectives of general interest recognised by the Union. As a result, a proportionality challenge may combine arguments that a measure goes beyond what is necessary to achieve a stated objective from a constitutional perspective, as well as that it infringes upon Charter rights in a manner that is disproportionate.

---

[91] *ibid*, 7352.

[92] Case C-491/01, *R v Secretary of State for Health, ex parte British American Tobacco* [2002] ECR I-11543.

F. Oireachtas Scrutiny

[9–87] In June 2001, the Irish people broke with a consistent pattern of voting in favour of EU Treaties by rejecting Ireland's ratification of the Nice Treaty. One particular element of a disparate "No" campaign centred round a lack of understanding as to the Treaty's content, related to which was a further argument that the Oireachtas had become increasingly sidelined in the context of legislation emerging from the EU institutions.[93] Prior to the second referendum, the European Union (Scrutiny) Act 2002 was introduced, with its final version enacted just four days after a "Yes" vote was secured in October 2002.[94]

[9–88] The Act introduced three requirements. First, Oireachtas scrutiny of proposed EU measures was to be facilitated by relevant ministers laying new proposals before both Houses, together with an information note, with the minister required to have regard to any recommendations made. Secondly, each Government minister was to report to both Houses not less than twice yearly in relation to any EU measures, proposed measures or other developments relevant to his or her department. As a consequence of this new requirement, it was considered appropriate to reduce the existing obligation on the Government to report to the Houses twice yearly on EU developments, under s 5 of the European Communities Act 1972, to reporting on an annual basis. Thirdly, the Joint Committee on EU Affairs is required to make an annual report on the operation of the Act.

[9–89] The scrutiny procedure requires that, as soon as practicable after a proposed measure is presented by the Commission, the relevant minister must lay a copy of the proposal before both Houses of the Oireachtas, together with an accompanying statement outlining the content, purpose and likely implications for Ireland (known as an "Oireachtas Scrutiny Information Note"). Guidelines to departments indicate that

[93] In Gavin Barrett (ed), *National Parliaments and the European Union* (Clarus Press, 2008) see Gavin Barrett, "Oireachtas Control over Government Activity at European Union Legal: Reflections on the Historical Context and the Legal Framework" 145, 158–159; Michael McDowell, "Democratic Control over Governmental Action in European Matters: The Example of Justice and Home Affairs" 179, 191–192; Lia O'Hegarty, "Parliamentary Scrutiny of European Affairs in Ireland – The European Affairs Committee, the Scrutiny Committee, and the European Union (Scrutiny) Act 2002" 273, 281. On the topic of Oireachtas scrutiny more generally, see Gavin Barrett, *The Evolving Role of National Parliaments in the European Union: Ireland as a Case Study* (Manchester University Press, 2018); Noel Travers, "The Reception of Community Legislation into Irish Law and Related Issues Revisited" (2003) 37 *Irish Jurist* 58; Elaine Fahey, "Reflecting on the Scope of the European Union (Scrutiny) Act, 2002 and Parliamentary Scrutiny in the Draft Constitutional Treaty as to European Integration and the Irish Legal Order" (2007) 13 *European Public Law* 85; Elaine Fahey, *EU Law in Ireland* (Clarus Press, 2010) ch 8; Dermot Walsh, "Irish Parliamentary Scrutiny of EU Measures on the Free Movement of Persons: Going Through the Motions?" (2005) 40 *Irish Jurist* 261; Dermot Walsh, "Parliamentary Scrutiny of EU Criminal Law in Ireland" (2006) 32 *European Law Review* 48; Alice Walsh, "Oireachtas Scrutiny of EU Legislation: Still a Work in Progress after 40 Years" (2013) 50 *Irish Jurist* 138; Gavin Barrett, *The Oireachtas and the European Union: The Evolving Role of a National Parliament in European Affairs* (Houses of the Oireachtas, 2013); Patricia Conlan, "Ireland: Enhanced Parliamentary Scrutiny of European Affairs: But Is It Effective" in John O'Brennan and Tapio Raunio (eds), *National Parliaments within the Enlarged European Union* (Rutledge, 2007) 178; Eunan O'Halpin, "Irish Parliamentary Culture and the European Union: Formalities to be Observed" in Philip Norton (ed), *National Parliaments and the European Union* (Frank Cass, 1996) 124.

[94] As a result, the Act was required to be amended by s 2 of the European Communities (Amendment) Act 2002 in order to take account of the amendment to Art 29 of the Constitution.

Notes should be provided within 20 days of the Commission presenting a new proposal, and 426 Information Notes were submitted by departments in 2018.[95] As amended by the European Union Act 2009, a measure is defined as:

- (i) a regulation or directive adopted under the TFEU;
- (ii) a decision adopted under Art 28 or 29 TEU (ie a CFSP decision);
- (iii) any other act that requires the prior approval of both Houses pursuant to Art 29.4.7°, namely:
  - – a decision to participate in enhanced cooperation pursuant to Art 20 TEU;
  - – a decision to opt-in to a measure pursuant to Protocol No 19 concerning the Schengen acquis;
  - – a decision to opt-in to a measure pursuant to Protocol No 21 (concerning AFSJ); or Art 29.4.8°, namely:
    - o a decision to authorise the Council to act otherwise than by unanimity or to allow the use of the ordinary legislative procedure (general *passerelle* clause);
    - o a measure identifying other aspects of criminal procedure that may be subject to a directive establishing minimum rules (Art 82.2(d) TFEU);
    - o a measure identifying other areas of crime that may be subject to a directive establishing minimum rules concerning the definition of criminal offences and sanctions (Art 83.1 TFEU);
    - o a measure establishing, or extending the powers of, the European Public Prosecutor's Office (Art 86(1) or (4) TFEU).

[9–90] Although not expressly included within the scope of the Act, in practice, Scrutiny Information Notes are also provided in respect of green and white papers and Council decisions. If, in the opinion of the minister, there is insufficient time for the Oireachtas to consider the matter, the proposal is laid after its adoption together with a "Post Adoption Information Note". If the minister considers a proposal to be confidential he or she may make such report as is deemed appropriate in the circumstances. Oireachtas scrutiny has been aided by the fact that, since 2006, the Commission transmits legislative proposals to national parliaments at the same time as they are sent to the Council and European Parliament. Also in 2006, a dedicated website, the Interparliamentary EU Information Exchange (IPEX), was established in order to facilitate the swift transmission of documents to national parliaments, as well as the exchange of views between parliaments and the institutions.

[9–91] Under s 2(2) of the Act, the minister is obliged to have regard to any recommendation on a proposed measure that is made by either House, or by a relevant committee. As Lia O'Hegarty has described, although this requirement is expressed as a legal rule, it is best understood as a political reality: "the Minister must take account of and recognise the parliamentary recommendations in some sense. The Parliamentary recommendations do not actually bind the Minister, however. In other words, there is no kind of legal veto at issue here."[96]

[9–92] As currently organised, it is for each Oireachtas Joint Committee to examine EU proposals that fall within their remit. During the general elections of 2011 and 2016,

---

[95] Joint Committee on European Union Affairs, "Annual Report on the Operation of the European Union (Scrutiny) Act 2002, 1 January 2018 to 31 December 2018", March 2019, 8.

[96] Lia O'Hegarty, "Parliamentary Scrutiny of European Affairs in Ireland – The European Affairs Committee, the Scrutiny Committee, and the European Union (Scrutiny) Act 2002" in Gavin Barrett (ed), *National Parliaments and the European Union* (Clarus Press, 2008) 273, 283.

a transitional committee was established to carry out this purpose pending the formation of new Joint Committees. Indeed, the first subsidiarity opinion issued by the Oireachtas was prepared by the 2011 transition committee, and related to the Common Consolidated Corporate Tax Base. The Orders of Reference for sectoral Joint Committees provide that they shall each consider, in respect of the relevant department or departments:

- (i) EU draft legislative acts referred to them, including the compliance of such acts with the principle of subsidiarity;
- (ii) other proposals for EU legislation and related policy issues, including programmes and guidelines prepared by the Commission as a basis of possible legislative action;
- (iii) non-legislative documents published by any EU institution in relation to EU policy matters; and
- (iv) matters listed for consideration on the agenda for meetings of the relevant Council and the outcome of such meetings.

[9–93] The Joint Committee of EU Affairs is mandated to consider such matters arising from Ireland's EU membership and adherence to the TEU and TFEU as it may select and which are not referred to any other Committee.[97] In particular, as well as the preparation of an annual report on the operation of the 2002 Act, the Joint Committee is tasked with considering:

- (i) the Commission's strategic planning documents, including the Commission Work Programme;
- (ii) cross-sectoral developments at EU level;
- (iii) matters listed for consideration at the General Affairs Council and the outcome of such meetings;
- (iv) such regulations under the European Communities Acts, and other Acts, necessitated by EU membership as the Committee may select;
- (v) as referred by the Dáil, any proposal to authorise the Council to act otherwise than by unanimity or to allow the use of the ordinary legislative procedure (general *passerelle* clause);
- (vi) any proposals received from the European Council to amend the Treaties; and
- (vii) any applications for EU membership received from the European Council.

[9–94] The Joint Committee also represents the Oireachtas at the Conference of Community and European Affairs Committees of Parliaments of the EU (COSAC) and reports back to both Houses. Although not having a right to vote, members of the European Parliament from Irish constituencies, including Northern Ireland, and members of the Irish delegation to the Council of Europe's Parliamentary Assembly may participate in proceedings of the Joint Committee, while other members of the European Parliament may be invited to do so. The same entitlement applies to sectoral Joint Committees whenever they are considering the EU matters listed above.

[9–95] As seen above, the Lisbon Treaty introduced important reforms aimed at strengthening the role of national parliaments in the EU legislative process, most noticeably through the introduction of the yellow and orange card procedures for subsidiarity in Protocol No 2.[98] In addition to this, for the first time the Treaties

---

[97] See Katherine Meenan, "What is the Role of a Committee on European Affairs?" in Gavin Barrett (ed), *National Parliaments and the European Union* (Clarus Press, 2008) 309.

[98] See Gavin Barrett, "The King Is Dead: Long Live the King: The Recasting by the Reform Treaty of the Provisions of the Constitutional Treaty Concerning National Parliaments" (2008) 33 *European Law Review* 66.

themselves expressly acknowledge that "national parliaments contribute actively to the good functioning of the Union". Article 12 TEU proceeds to identify eight means by which this contribution is made, namely by: considering draft legislative acts; monitoring subsidiarity; participating in the evaluation of AFSJ policies (Art 70 TFEU); participating in the evaluation of Eurojust's activities (Art 85 TFEU); participating in the political monitoring of Europol (Art 88 TFEU); participating in the procedures for revising the Treaties; considering applications to join the EU and by taking part in inter-parliamentary cooperation between national parliaments and with the European Parliament.

[9–96] Article 12 TEU is supplemented by Protocol No 1 on the Role of National Parliaments in the EU, which provides greater detail on how information exchanges and inter-parliamentary cooperation is to take place. It provides that, in addition to sending draft legislative acts, the Commission will also send green and white papers, communications and the annual legislative programme to national parliaments at the same time as it sends them to the European Parliament and Council. Agendas for, and the outcome of, meetings of the Council are also provided directly to national parliaments at the same time as to governments. Importantly, the Protocol requires that, except in cases of urgency, eight weeks should elapse between sending a draft legislative act to national parliaments and it being placed on a Council agenda for its adoption or for adoption of a position under a legislative procedure.

[9–97] As seen above, however, it is the Protocol on Subsidiarity and Proportionality that introduced a practical means of allowing national parliaments to influence the course of EU legislative proposals. This is given effect to by s 7(3) of the European Union Act 2009, which provides that either House of the Oireachtas may, not later than eight weeks after the transmission of the draft legislative act, send to the Presidents of the European Parliament, the Council and the European Commission a reasoned opinion on subsidiarity if the House concerned passes a resolution authorising the House to do so.[99] Since 2010, the Oireachtas has issued 60 opinions as part of general political dialogue, of which 12 have been reasoned opinions on the principle of subsidiarity. As one of its own-initiative political contributions, in 2015 the Oireachtas submitted its views on how the role of national parliaments could be improved at EU level, which provides useful insights into the ways in which Irish parliamentarians see their role and how it might be enhanced.[100] No use has yet been made of the power within s 7(4) of the Act for the Oireachtas to notify the Minister for Foreign Affairs and Trade of its opinion that annulment proceedings should be brought against a measure on the ground that it infringes upon subsidiarity.

[9–98] Finally, with regard to the consultation with national parliaments envisaged by Art 48.7 TEU on any proposed use of the general *passerelle* clauses (to switch from unanimity to QMV or the special legislative procedure to the ordinary legislative procedure), s 7(1) of the 2009 Act introduces what is referred to in the Dáil Standing Orders as a "red card" procedure.[101] Article 48.7 requires that any initiative by the European Council to use either of the two *passerelle* clauses be notified to national

---

[99] See Standing Order 114 of the Standing Orders relative to Public Business, Dáil Éireann, 2016.

[100] Joint Committee on European Affairs, "Five Years Post the Lisbon Treaty: How Can the Role of the National Parliaments at EU Level Be Improved?", January 2015, available at <http://ec.europa.eu/dgs/secretariat_general /relations/relations_other/npo/index_en.htm>.

[101] See Standing Order 115 of the Standing Orders relative to Public Business, Dáil Éireann, 2016.

parliaments and that, if a national parliament makes known its opposition within six months, the decision shall not be adopted. Section 7(1) provides that either House may adopt a resolution opposing a proposal under Art 48.7, in which case the European Council shall be informed accordingly.[102] Section 7(2) provides for the same procedure to be used in respect of the consultation mandated by Art 81.3 TFEU relating to any proposed measure concerning family law with cross-border implications. In the event of either House passing a resolution of opposition, the Council is to be informed accordingly.

[102] A negative resolution procedure is used in s 7(1) notwithstanding that Art 29.4.8° of the Constitution indicates that the State may agree to the use of the general *passerelle* clauses "subject to the prior approval of both Houses of the Oireachtas", which suggests that a positive resolution may be required.

Chapter 10

SOURCES OF EU LAW

A. Introduction

[10–01] The term "*acquis communautaire*" is used to describe the entire body of EU law in all its various guises. The term is commonly heard in the context of accession negotiations, where reference is made to comparing the laws of the candidate state with those of the EU *acquis* so as to ensure that there is equivalence. The elements that make up the *acquis* can be divided in a very rudimentary way into three categories: primary, secondary and tertiary EU law.

[10–02] Primary EU law is made up of the constitutive treaties of the Union, as interpreted by the Court of Justice. Secondary law takes the form of secondary legislation that the Union institutions may adopt pursuant to the Treaties. Article 288 TFEU sets out the five types of act that may be adopted by the institutions, three of which are legally binding – regulations, directives and decisions – while two – recommendations and opinions – do not have binding force. A fourth form of legally binding act is provided for in Art 295 TFEU in the shape of inter-institutional agreements between the Parliament, the Commission and the Council, such as for example the Interinstitutional Agreement on Better Law-Making.[1] These agreements may be of a binding nature depending on the intention of the institutions in each particular case. Finally, tertiary sources of EU law include the case law of the Court of Justice and international agreements entered into by the EU. As will be seen below, to describe these sources as tertiary is not to suggest that they are the lowest ranking in terms of hierarchy, but merely that they are the third in three separate categories of sources. Other sources of law, while not originating from the EU itself, may be relied upon by the Court of Justice when interpreting EU law, such as the national law of the Member States or international agreements to which the Member States are a party.

[10–03] While these three categories of primary, secondary and tertiary sources provide a general framework for understanding the building blocks of EU law, when

---

1 Interinstitutional Agreement between the European Parliament, the Council of the European Union and the European Commission of 13 April 2016 on Better Law-Making [2016] OJ L123/1.

it comes to considering the hierarchy in which these sources are ranked the picture becomes more nuanced. In particular, while international agreements can be regarded as a tertiary source of EU law, they rank above secondary law in the sense that secondary EU law must comply with international law binding on the EU. Similarly, while in a general sense the case law of the Court of Justice may be regarded as a tertiary source of law, case law that clarifies the interpretation of primary law, including through the elaboration of general principles, has the same ranking as the primary law that it interprets.

[10–04] The foundational element of EU law is the Treaties themselves, which are said to constitute primary EU law, reflecting the fact that they are of a constitutional status and that, in the hierarchy of the sources of EU law, they are the pinnacle. As stated in Art 1 TEU, the Union shall be founded on the Treaty on European Union (TEU) and the Treaty on the Functioning of the European Union (TFEU), both of which shall have the same legal value. Article 6 TEU provides that the Charter of Fundamental Rights of the European Union shall have the same legal value as the Treaties, and so it too constitutes primary EU law. Just as an Act of the Oireachtas will be invalidated if it is found to contravene a provision of the Constitution, a secondary form of EU law will be held to be invalid if it contravenes a provision of primary EU law.

[10–05] In addition to the Treaties and the Charter, primary EU law can also take the form of general principles of law. Similar to the role played by natural justice and unenumerated rights in interpreting the Irish Constitution, the concept of general principles of EU law is fluid and not clearly defined. Some guidance, however, is found in Art 2 TEU, which provides that:

> The Union is founded on the values of respect for human dignity, freedom, democracy, equality, the rule of law and respect for human rights, including the rights of persons belonging to minorities. These values are common to the Member States in a society in which pluralism, non-discrimination, tolerance, justice, solidarity and equality between women and men prevail.

[10–06] In addition, Art 19 TEU establishes that, in the interpretation and application of the Treaties, the Court of Justice shall ensure that "the law is observed". The broad and open-ended nature of these concepts provide the Court with the necessary flexibility to make use of generally accepted legal norms and principles when assessing the validity of secondary EU law. On occasion, recourse to general principles of law may allow the Court to avoid countenancing a clear illegality merely because the Treaties have not expressly regulated the precise matter. As a result, general principles of law that are of fundamental importance may be regarded as forming part of primary EU law and as coming second in the hierarchy of sources of EU law, after the Treaties. This high ranking is justified because general principles of EU law may lead, not only to the annulment of secondary and other lower-ranking legal rules, but are also used to interpret the provisions of primary EU law.[2]

[10–07] After general principles of EU law comes international law, in the form of customary rules of international law or international agreements to which the EU is a party. The Court of Justice has confirmed that not only is the EU bound to respect international law in the exercise of its powers, but further, and as a consequence of this,

2 Nigel Foster, *EU Law* (5th ed, Oxford University Press, 2016) 111.

EU legal acts must be interpreted in the light of any relevant rules of international law.[3] This hierarchical relationship does not extend, however, to the EU Treaties themselves, as illustrated by the fact that under Art 218 TFEU, the Court of Justice may be asked for an opinion as to whether a proposed international agreement is compatible with the Treaties. Where it is found not to be, the "agreement envisaged may not enter into force unless it is amended or the Treaties are revised". The Court has confirmed that any proposed international agreement must also be compatible with the general principles of EU law, such that in terms of hierarchy, international law ranks third after the EU Treaties and the general principles of law that constitute EU primary law.

[10–08] In summary, therefore, the three highest ranking sources of EU law might be ordered as follows:

1	**EU Treaties** – TEU, TFEU and Charter of Fundamental Rights (Treaty of Rome, SEA, Maastricht Treaty, Amsterdam Treaty, Nice Treaty, Lisbon Treaty, Accession Treaties, Merger Treaty, Budget Treaties), as well as Protocols and Declarations	Primary Law
2	**General principles of EU law** that are regarded as amounting to primary law and/or are reflected within provisions of the Treaties	Primary Law
3	**International law** binding on the EU, such as customary international law or international agreements to which the EU is a party	A source of law with which the secondary law of the EU must comply

B. General Principles of EU Law

[10–09] As set out above, Art 2 TEU provides that the EU is founded on the values of respect for human dignity, freedom, democracy, equality, the rule of law and respect for human rights, while Art 19 TEU charges the Court of Justice with ensuring that "in the interpretation and application of the Treaties the law is observed". In line with its broad, teleological approach, the Court has understood the concept of observance of the law in an expansive manner and as reflecting the values set out in Art 2.[4] This arises most frequently in the context of the Court having to assess actions seeking the annulment of an EU act under Art 263 TFEU, or a request for a preliminary ruling on the validity of an EU act, where an act may be challenged on the grounds of lack of competence, misuse of powers, infringement of an essential procedural requirement and infringement of the Treaties "or of *any rule of law* relating to their application". In granting the Court jurisdiction to hear actions relating to the non-contractual liability of the Union, Art 340(2) TFEU provides a similar steer, mandating the Court to determine liability "in accordance with the *general principles common to the laws of the Member States*".

[10–10] These open-ended references to the rule of law and general principles of law common to the Member States have permitted the Court to look to the law of the Member States in order to elaborate a distinct body of general principles of EU law.[5] Long before the adoption of the Charter of Fundamental Rights, these principles

---

3 See Case C-228/06 *Soysal* [2009] ECR I-1031, para 59.

4 See Case C-64/16 *Associação Sindical dos Juízes Portugueses* EU:C:2018:117, 27 February 2018, paras 30–44. See ch 14, para [14–02].

5 For a comprehensive account see Takis Tridimas, *The General Principles of EU Law* (3rd ed, Oxford University Press, 2018). See also Editorial, "The Scope of Application of the General Principles

included fundamental rights that, although not expressly provided for in the Treaties, were nonetheless held to form part of EU law. This is now acknowledged in Art 6(3) TEU, which states that fundamental rights, as guaranteed by the European Convention on Human Rights and as they result from the constitutional traditions common to the Member States, shall constitute general principles of the Union's law.

[10–11] Principles that have been found to be general principles of EU law include the equal treatment of like situations unless there is an objective justification for a difference in treatment (equality/non-discrimination), proportionality, legal certainty, *res judicata*, the non-retroactivity of penal provisions, legitimate expectation, legal professional privilege, the precautionary principle and the right to due process/natural justice, which may include the right to a hearing and to be given reasons for a decision taken.

[10–12] In terms of the hierarchy of the sources of EU law, it is important to remember that general principles have been described by the Court as having a "constitutional status", and they may be seen as unenumerated principles that derive from, and supplement, the provisions of the TEU and TFEU themselves.[6] They have been neatly explained as a set of rules that overarch the Union legal order and which act both as a guide to interpret Treaty provisions and legislative enactments, and as a measure against which EU law is judged and national implementation of EU law is assessed.[7]

C. International Law

[10–13] Reflecting the commitment expressed in Art 3 TEU that the Union shall contribute to the strict observance of international law, the Court of Justice has confirmed that the EU must respect international law in the exercise of its powers, including acting in compliance with rules of customary international law.[8] As described by the Court, "when it adopts an act, [the Union] is bound to observe international law in its entirety, including customary international law, which is binding upon the institutions".[9] For example, in *Front Polisario* the Court held that, pursuant to the international law principle of the right to self-determination, an agreement between the EU and Morocco could only apply to the non-self-governing territory of Western Sahara, over which Morocco exercised control, if the consent of the people of that territory had first

of Union Law: An Ever-Expanding Union?" (2010) 47 *Common Market Law Review* 1589; Koen Lenaerts and Jose Guttiérez-Fons, "The Constitutional Allocation of Powers and General Principles of EU Law" (2010) 47 *Common Market Law Review* 1629.

6 Case C-101/08 *Audiolux v Groupe Bruxelles Lambert* [2009] ECR I-9823, para 63.

7 Margot Horspool, Matthew Humphreys and Michael Wells-Greco, *European Union Law* (9th ed, Oxford University Press, 2016) 122.

8 For example, Case C-286/90 *Poulsen* [1992] ECR I-6019 (the right to control fishing within territorial waters); Case C-162/96 *Racke* [1998] ECR I-3655 (fundamental change of circumstances as a ground for suspending a treaty); Case C-386/08 *Firma Brita* [2010] ECR I-1289 (the relative effect of treaties and non-imposition of obligations on third parties); Case C-366/10 *Air Transport Association of America* [2011] ECR I-13755 (no state may extend its jurisdiction over the High Seas). See Gráinne de Búrca, "International Law before the Courts: The EU and the US Compared" (2015) 55 *Virginia Journal of International Law* 685; Jed Odermatt, "The Court of Justice of the European Union: International or Domestic Court?" (2014) 3 *Cambridge Journal of International and Comparative Law* 696; Inge Govaere and Sacha Garben (eds), *The Interface between EU and International Law: Contemporary Reflections* (Hart, 2019).

9 Case C-366/10 *Air Transport Association of America* [2011] ECR I-13755, para 101.

been obtained. As it had not been demonstrated that such consent had been given, the agreement could not be regarded as applying to Western Sahara.[10]

[10–14] The relationship between EU law and international law was put to the test in the landmark case of *Kadi I*.[11] There, Mr Kadi challenged the validity of an EU regulation that implemented sanctions adopted by the United Nations Security Council that required the freezing of assets belonging to named persons who were believed to have some involvement in terrorism. Article 103 of the UN Charter provides that in the event of a conflict between the obligations of UN members under the Charter and their obligations under any other international agreement, their obligations under the Charter shall prevail. The General Court took the view that, as a result of Art 103, the obligation on EU Member States to carry out decisions of the Security Council prevailed over any other obligation that they may have entered into in an international agreement, including the EU Treaties.[12] It followed that the General Court did not have jurisdiction to review the lawfulness of the UN sanctions according to the fundamental rights standard of protection recognised by the EU legal order.

[10–15] In a Grand Chamber judgment, the Court of Justice disagreed with the conclusion reached by the General Court.[13] First, the Court of Justice recalled that the Union must respect international law in the exercise of its powers and that an EU act must be interpreted, and its scope limited, in the light of the relevant rules of international law. Nevertheless, the Court observed that an international agreement cannot affect the allocation of powers fixed by the EU Treaties or, consequently, the autonomy of the EU legal system. Part of the very foundations of the Union was the exclusive jurisdiction of the Court of Justice to ensure the proper observance of this allocation of powers. Secondly, fundamental rights formed an integral part of the general principles of law whose observance the Court ensures. For that purpose, the Court drew inspiration from the constitutional traditions common to the Member States and from the guidelines supplied by international human rights instruments on which the Member States have collaborated or to which they are signatories, with the European Convention on Human Rights having a special significance. Thirdly, obligations imposed by an international agreement cannot have the effect of prejudicing the constitutional principles of the Treaties, which include the principle that respect for fundamental rights is a condition of the lawfulness of EU acts which it is for the Court to review.

[10–16] In terms of reviewing the lawfulness of the regulation that implemented the UN sanctions within the Union, the Court sought to draw a distinction between a review of the internal EU act, which was required, and a review of the Security Council resolution itself. According to the Court, the primacy of a Security Council resolution

---

10 Case C-104/16 P *Council v Front Polisario* EU:C:2016:973, 21 December 2016. See Eva Kassoti, "The ECJ and the Art of Treaty Interpretation: *Western Sahara Campaign UK*" (2019) 56 *Common Market Law Review* 209; Eva Kassoti, "The EU and Western Sahara: An Assessment of Recent Developments" (2018) 43 *European Law Review* 751; Enzo Cannizzaro, "In Defence of *Front Polisario*: The ECJ as a Global Jus Cogens Maker" (2018) 55 *Common Market Law Review* 569. See also Case C-308/06 *Intertanko* [2008] ECR I-4057; Eileen Denza, "A Note on *Intertanko*" (2008) 33 *European Law Review* 870.

11 Joined Cases C-402/05P and 415/05P *Kadi v Council* [2008] ECR I-6351.

12 Case T–315/01 *Kadi v Council* [2005] ECR II–3649.

13 Joined Cases C-402/05P and 415/05P *Kadi v Council* [2008] ECR I-6351. See also Joined Cases C-584/10P, 593/10P and 595/10P *Commission v Kadi* (*Kadi II*) EU:C:2013:518, 18 July 2013.

in international law would not be challenged by any finding it was to make that an EU measure intended to give effect to the resolution was contrary to a higher rule of law in the EU legal order. The Court went on to reason as follows:

> it is not a consequence of the principles governing the international legal order under the United Nations that any judicial review of the internal lawfulness of the contested regulation in the light of fundamental freedoms is excluded by virtue of the fact that that measure is intended to give effect to a resolution of the Security Council adopted under Chapter VII of the Charter of the United Nations.
>
> What is more, such immunity from jurisdiction for a [EU] measure like the contested regulation, as a corollary of the principle of the primacy at the level of international law of obligations under the Charter of the United Nations … cannot find a basis in the [Treaties].
>
> … an immunity from jurisdiction for the contested regulation with regard to the review of its compatibility with fundamental rights, arising from the alleged absolute primacy of the resolutions of the Security Council to which that measure is designed to give effect, [cannot] find any basis in the place that obligations under the Charter of the United Nations would occupy in the hierarchy of norms within the [EU] legal order if those obligations were to be classified in that hierarchy.
>
> … [supposing the UN Charter to be binding on the Union, the Charter] would have primacy over acts of secondary [EU] law.
>
> That primacy at the level of [EU] law would not, however, extend to primary law, in particular to the general principles of which fundamental rights form part.[14]

[10–17] The judgment in *Kadi I* is a stark illustration of the fact that while secondary EU law measures may be reviewed in the light of international law, the obligations imposed by international law cannot have the effect of prejudicing the constitutional principles of the EU Treaties, which include the principle that all Union acts must respect fundamental rights. Indeed, adherence to fundamental rights is a condition of the validity of Union acts, including acts adopted in order to implement UN Charter obligations, which it is for the CJEU to review in the framework of the complete system of legal remedies established by the Treaty. As a result, in the hierarchy of the sources of EU law, international law ranks below the EU Treaties and the general principles of EU law, but above secondary EU law.

[10–18] The *Kadi I* judgment caused shockwaves and led to much commentary, particularly due to its challenge to the orthodox supremacy of the UN Charter as a source of legal obligation in international law. For example, Jennifer Hendry has written of how the judgment can be seen to represent

> a marked departure for the CJEU from its "traditional embrace of international law" and a reorientation towards a more pluralist approach to the issue of the "multiplication, overlap and conflict of normative orders in the global realm". … the *Kadi* case appears to have been selected intentionally as the platform for the Court's "you shall not pass" moment, whereby it asserted the EU's distinctiveness and separation from the international order. It appears that the opportunity presented itself in *Kadi* for a clear statement of EU autonomy in the international realm and this chance was seized upon by the CJEU. From a systems-theoretical perspective, the points of interest here are this robust assertion of autonomy

[14] *ibid*, paras 299–308.

on the part of the CJEU and its result in generating a situation of overt plurality within international (multi-level) governance.[15]

(i) International Agreements

[10–19] International agreements concluded by the Union are, in accordance with Art 216 TFEU, binding on the institutions and the Member States and have been held to form an "integral part" of EU law.[16] Where an international agreement is entered into by the Union only, it will bind the Member States as a matter of EU law, even though the Member States have not themselves assumed obligations under international law. Where the Union and the Member States together become party to an international agreement (known as a "mixed" agreement, reflecting the fact that it involves a mixture of EU and Member State competence), the Member States will be bound both as a matter of EU law and international law. As with rules of customary international law, the primacy of international agreements concluded by the Union over provisions of secondary EU law means that such provisions must, so far as possible, be interpreted in a manner that is consistent with those international agreements.[17]

[10–20] Finally, the EU may also be bound by an international agreement to which it itself is not a party, but where the Member States became a party to the agreement and the EU subsequently assumes the powers that were previously exercised by the Member States in the area governed by that agreement. The best-known example of this arose in respect of the 1947 General Agreement on Tariffs and Trade (GATT), which was held in *International Fruit Company* to bind the Union on this basis.[18] As the field covered

---

15 Jennifer Hendry, "*Kadi* in Sight of Autopoiesis" in Matej Avbelj, Filippo Fontanelli and Giuseppe Martinico (eds), *Kadi on Trial* (Routledge, 2014) 63, 65. See Juliane Kokott and Christoph Sobotta, "The *Kadi* Case – Constitutional Core Values and International Law – Finding the Balance?" (2012) 23 *European Journal of International Law* 1015; Tarcisio Gazzini and Ester Herlin-Karnell, "Restrictive Measures Adopted by the EU from the Standpoint of International and EU Law" (2011) 36 *European Law Review* 798; Gráinne de Búrca, "The European Court of Justice and the International Order after *Kadi*" (2010) 51 *Harvard International Law Journal* 41; Horst G Krenzler and Oliver Landweh, "'A New Legal Order of International Law': On the Relationship between Public International Law and European Union Law after *Kadi*" in Ulrich Fastenrath *et al* (eds), *From Bilateralism to Community Interest: Essays in Honour of Bruno Simma* (Oxford University Press, 2011) 1004; Nikolaos Lavranos, "Protecting European Law from International Law" (2010) 15 *European Foreign Affairs Review* 265; Samantha Besson, "European Legal Pluralism after *Kadi*" (2009) 5 *European Constitutional Law Review* 237; Riccardo Pavoni, "Freedom to Choose the Legal Means for Implementing UN Security Council Resolutions and the ECJ *Kadi* Judgment" (2009) 28 *Yearbook of European Law* 627; Guy Harpaz, "Judicial Review by the ECJ of UN 'Smart Sanctions' against Terrorism" (2009) 14 *European Foreign Affairs Review* 65; Daniel Halberstram and Eric Stein, "The United Nations, the European Union, and the King of Sweden: Economic Sanctions and Individual Rights in a Plural World Order" (2009) 46 *Common Market Law Review* 13; Takis Tridimas and Jose A Gutierrez-Fons, "EU Law, International Law, and Economic Sanctions against Terrorism: The Judiciary in Distress?" (2008) 32 *Fordham International Law Journal* 660; Stefan Griller, "Case Comment: International Law, Human Rights and the European Community's Autonomous Legal Order: Notes on the European Court of Justice Decision in *Kadi*" (2008) 4 *European Constitutional Law Review* 528; Carl Lebeck, "UN Security Council Anti-Terrorism Measures Implemented via EC/EU Law – Constitutional Dilemmas of Multilevel Governance" (2007) 14 *Irish Journal of European Law* 3.

16 Case 181/73 *Haegeman v Belgium* [1974] ECR 449. For a detailed account see David Fennelly, *International Law in the Irish Legal System* (Round Hall, 2014) ch 3.

17 Case C-228/06 *Soysal* [2009] ECR I-1031, para 59.

18 Joined Cases 21/72, 22/72, 23/72, 24/72 *International Fruit Company* [1972] ECR 1219. See Allan

by GATT was brought within the jurisdiction of the EU's Common Commercial Policy, its provisions were binding upon the Union. In contrast, in *Intertanko*, it was held that in the absence of a full transfer to the Union of the powers previously exercised by the Member States, the International Convention for the Prevention of Pollution from Ships could not bind the Union simply because all of the Member States were themselves party to the Convention.[19]

[10–21] A good example of the Court of Justice having to consider the status of international agreements in EU law is *Bosphorus Queen Shipping Ltd.*[20] This case arose from a preliminary reference from Finland that concerned: (i) the UN Convention on the Law of the Sea (the "Montego Bay Convention"), to which the EU was a party; (ii) the International Convention for the Prevention of Pollution from Ships ("the Marpol Convention 73/78"), to which the EU was not a party but all Member States were a party; (iii) the International Convention Relating to Intervention on the High Seas in Cases of Oil Pollution Casualties, to which Finland was a party but the EU and a number of Member States were not; and (iv) a directive which incorporated certain provisions of the Montego Bay Convention into EU law. According to the Court:

> In order to answer the questions from the referring court in the present case, the Court must examine the Montego Bay Convention, the Marpol Convention 73/78 and the Convention Relating to Intervention on the High Seas 1969. Therefore, the status of those conventions with regard to EU law should be set out.
>
> First, with regard to the Montego Bay Convention, which was signed and approved by the EU, its provisions are an integral part of the European Union legal order and is binding on it. Therefore, the Court has jurisdiction to interpret those provisions. Furthermore, that convention has primacy over secondary EU legislation which must be interpreted as far as possible in accordance with those agreements.
>
> Second, as far as concerns the Marpol Convention 73/78, to which the European Union is not a party, but which binds all its Member States, that convention is liable to have consequences for the interpretation of the Montego Bay Convention and, second, the provisions of secondary law which fall within the field of application of the Marpol Convention 73/78, such as those of Directive 2005/35. In view of the customary principle of good faith, which forms part of general international law, and of Article 4(3) TEU, the Court is to interpret the provisions by taking account of the Marpol Convention 73/78.
>
> Third, concerning the Convention Relating to Intervention on the High Seas 1969, it must be observed, first, that the European Union has not acceded to that convention and, second, that the European Union cannot be regarded as having taken the place of the Member State, if only because not all of them are parties to that convention. It follows that that convention is not binding on the European Union and the court does not have jurisdiction to interpret it as such in a reference for a preliminary ruling.
>
> However, … since the Court is requested to interpret the Montego Bay Convention, the Convention Relating to Intervention on the High Seas 1969 must be taken into account since the latter convention is part of the relevant rules for the interpretation of the Montego Bay Convention.

Rosas, "The Status in EU Law of International Agreements Concluded by EU Member States" (2011) 34 *Fordham International Law Journal* 1304.

19 Case C-308/06 *Intertanko* [2008] ECR I-4057, para 49.

20 Case C-15/17 *Bosphorous Queen Shipping Ltd* EU:C:2018:557, 11 July 2018.

> … Fourth, Article 7(2) of Directive 2005/35, which incorporates into EU law the provisions of Article 220(6) of the Montego Bay Convention, and whose wording is almost identical to it, must be interpreted in accordance with the latter. Therefore, the interpretation of Article 220(6) of the Montego Bay Convention must, in principle, be regarded as being applicable to Article 7(2) of Directive 2005/35.[21]

[10–22] So, in respect of the agreement to which the EU was itself a party, it formed an integral part of EU law, the Court of Justice had jurisdiction to interpret it and the agreement had primacy over secondary EU law, which law was to be interpreted as far as possible in accordance with its provisions. An EU directive that incorporated a provision of the agreement into EU law, using almost identical wording, had to be interpreted in accordance with that agreement. Regarding the agreement to which all the Member States were a party, but the EU was not, it had consequences for the interpretation of secondary EU law that fell within the field of application of the agreement, with the international law principle of good faith requiring the Court of Justice to interpret such laws by taking account of the agreement. In contrast, the agreement to which neither the EU nor all the Member States were a party was not binding on the EU and the Court of Justice did not have jurisdiction to interpret it as part of a request for a preliminary ruling.

D. Secondary Legal Acts

[10–23] Secondary legal act is the term used to describe legal acts adopted by the EU institutions. A complication in considering the EU's secondary legal acts is an unusual but important distinction between the *nature* or form of a particular act and its place within the *hierarchy* of EU legal acts. In and of itself, the nature of the instruments available to the Union institutions is set out in a straightforward manner in Art 288 TFEU. There, three instruments with legal force are defined – regulations, directives and decisions – together with recommendations and opinions which have no binding force and are a form of soft law.

[10–24] Intuitively, one might think that a regulation is superior to a directive, which in turn is superior to a decision, but this is not the case. As between regulations, directives and decisions, there is no hierarchy provided for in Art 288. Frequently, a particular matter might be governed by a combination of a regulation, directive and/or decision, with a principal or parent act being further elaborated in one or more supplemental acts. For example, a parent regulation might be supplemented by a directive or a decision. Equally, a parent directive (or decision) might be supplemented by a regulation.

[10–25] In a small number of areas, the relevant Treaty provision will specify the type of legal act that must be used in order to achieve an objective. For instance, Art 50 TFEU prescribes that "in order to attain freedom of establishment as regards a particular activity, the European Parliament and the Council, acting in accordance with the ordinary legislative procedure and after consulting the Economic and Social Committee, shall act by means of directives". More commonly, the Treaty provisions remain silent as to the type of act to be used. In such cases, Art 296 TFEU requires the institutions to make their selection on a case-by-case basis, in compliance with the applicable procedures

[21] *ibid*, paras 43–49.

and with the principle of proportionality. As a result, institutions must opt for the least intrusive form capable of achieving the desired objective.

[10–26] From this it can be seen to follow that, when it comes to considering hierarchy, the status of a secondary legal act is not determined by its particular form. Instead, the ranking of a secondary legal act is governed by the procedure under which it is adopted. Since the entry into force of the Lisbon Treaty, the term "legislative act" is confined by Art 289 TFEU to legal acts that are adopted by either of the two legislative procedures (ordinary or special). If a regulation, directive or decision is adopted by a procedure other than one of the two legislative procedures it is not a legislative act and so can be described as a non-legislative act.

[10–27] Only legislative acts may delegate to the Commission the power to adopt non-legislative acts of general application to amend certain non-essential elements of the legislative act. These are known as Commission Delegated Regulations/Directives/Decisions and provision is made for them in Art 290 TFEU. In contrast, Art 291 TFEU allows *any* legal act to confer on the Commission or, exceptionally, the Council, the power to adopt implementing acts where uniform conditions are needed for implementing that legal act. These are known as Implementing Regulations/Directives/Decisions. As a result, the three legally binding instruments provided for in Art 288 can take a number of forms as: (i) legislative acts; (ii) non-legislative acts adopted directly on the basis of a Treaty provision through what is known as an "innominate non-legislative procedure"; (iii) delegated acts (adopted by the Commission); or (iv) implementing acts (adopted by the Commission and, exceptionally, by the Council). By way of a statistical illustration, while 454 legislative acts were adopted during the first Barroso Commission (2004–2009), 14,522 non-legislative acts were agreed upon.[22]

1	EU legal acts in the form of "legislative acts" adopted pursuant to the Ordinary or Special Legislative procedure: • *Regulation* • *Directive* • *Decision*	Legislative Acts
2	EU legal acts in the form of "non-legislative acts" adopted directly pursuant to a particular provision of the TEU or TFEU (an "innominate non-legislative procedure"): • *Regulation* • *Directive* • *Decision*	Non-Legislative Acts
3	EU legal acts in the form of subordinate *delegated* "non-legislative acts" that may be made by the Commission to supplement or amend certain non-essential elements of a legislative act: • *Commission Delegated Regulation* • *Commission Delegated Directive* • *Commission Delegated Decision*	Non-Legislative Acts "Subordinate" or "Derived" Secondary Legal Acts, also known as Regulatory Acts when of general application

[22] Michael Kaeding and Alan Hardacre, "The European Parliament and the Future of Comitology after Lisbon" (2013) 19 *European Law Journal* 382, 382.

4	EU legal acts in the form of subordinate *implementing* "non-legislative acts" that may be made by the Commission and, in duly justified specific cases and under Arts 24 and 26 TEU relating to CFSP, the Council, to implement legally binding EU acts: • *Commission Implementing Regulation* • *Commission Implementing Directive* • *Commission Implementing Decision* • *Council Implementing Regulation (in duly justified specific cases)* • *Council Implementing Directive (in duly justified specific cases)* • *Council Implementing Decision (in duly justified specific cases)*	Non-Legislative Acts "Subordinate" or "Derived" Secondary Legal Acts, also known as Regulatory Acts when of general application

(i) Regulations

[10–28] As described in Art 288 TFEU, a regulation has general application, is binding in its entirety and is directly applicable in all Member States. The characteristic of having general application means that a regulation is normative in nature, applying to categories of persons in the abstract and as a whole, rather than being concerned with an individual situation or a limited, identifiable group of persons. As they are binding in their entirety and directly applicable in all Member States, regulations have the force of law within each Member State without the need for any national implementation measures. Indeed, the Court of Justice has made clear that Member States should not introduce any implementing measures that would serve to conceal the EU law nature of a regulation,[23] nor should a regulation be subject to any implementing measures other than those required by the regulation itself as this would jeopardise its simultaneous and uniform application throughout the whole of the EU.[24] While direct applicability is now a standard feature of EU law, at the time of the 1957 Treaty of Rome it was entirely innovative. For dualist states such as Ireland, in particular, this was a radical departure from the typical way in which international law would only form part of domestic law if the Oireachtas specifically legislated to this effect. By virtue of regulations, the EU was given the power to directly legislate for all of the Member States. Regulations enter into force on the date specified in them or, in the absence thereof, on the twentieth day following their publication in the Official Journal.

(ii) Decisions

[10–29] Whereas a regulation will, by definition, be of general application, a decision is binding in its entirety but, when it specifies those to whom it is addressed, it is binding only on them. So, it is possible to have a specifically addressed decision which may be addressed to one or more Member States or to private individuals or entities. In the field of competition law, for example, the Commission commonly addresses a decision concerning an anti-competitive practice to a particular company, while decisions concerning state aid are frequently addressed to a particular Member State. While a specifically addressed decision is said to be binding only on the person or entity to

---

23 Case 34/73 *Variola* [1973] ECR 981, 991.

24 Case 39/72 *Commission v Italy* [1973] ECR 101, 114.

which it is addressed, this does not mean that the obligation which it creates cannot be enforced by a third party who is affected by the decision.

[10–30] Although the majority of decisions are addressed to a specific addressee, since the Lisbon Treaty Art 288 allows for the possibility of a non-addressed decision that will be of general application. Non-addressed decisions are typically used for internal, institutional arrangements within the EU, such as adopting rules of procedure or the budget. Decisions authorising the Union to sign or conclude an international agreement are also non-addressed.

[10–31] It can be seen, therefore, that the main distinction between a regulation and a decision is that a regulation is of general application, whereas a decision is typically addressed to a specific addressee. If there is a challenge to the purported nature of a regulation or a decision, the choice of instrument adopted by the institutions will not be determinative. In other words, it is possible to claim that an instrument which is identified as a regulation is in fact a decision, or even that parts of a regulation amount in reality to an individualised decision or a bundle of individual decisions. The Court of Justice will look behind the form of the legal act and consider its substantive content and object in order to determine whether this is the case.[25] Such challenges were more common prior to an amendment to the rules on standing for persons seeking to challenge the validity of an EU act. Before the Lisbon Treaty, one path to establishing standing was to demonstrate that a regulation was, in reality, a series of decisions one of which was of direct and individual concern to the applicant. Changes to the rules on standing have meant that, since 2009, there is less to be gained from arguing that a regulation is, in substance, comprised of a series of decisions.

[10–32] It is worth noting here that a different form of decision arises in the context of the EU's Common Foreign and Security Policy (CFSP). Article 24 TEU makes clear that CFSP is subject to specific rules and procedures and that the adoption of legislative acts is excluded. One way in which CFSP is to be conducted, as set out in Art 25 TEU, is through the adoption of decisions defining: (i) actions to be undertaken by the Union; (ii) positions to be taken by the Union; and (iii) arrangements for the implementation of such actions and positions. It is for the Council to frame CFSP and take the decisions necessary for defining and implementing it on the basis of the general guidelines and strategic lines defined by the European Council. Except where the Treaties provide otherwise, the Council acts by unanimity in adopting such decisions. Under Art 28 TEU, where the international situation requires operational action by the Union, the Council shall adopt decisions laying down objectives, scope, duration and means to be made available to the Union, as well as the conditions for their implementation. Such decisions commit the Member States in the positions they adopt and in the conduct of their activity. In addition, Art 29 TEU envisages the adoption of decisions which define the approach of the Union to a particular matter of a geographical or thematic

[25] Joined Case 41/70, 42/70, 43/70, 44/70 *International Fruit Company v Commission* [1971] ECR 411, 422: "Article 1 of [the] Regulation is not a provision of general application within the meaning of [Article 288], but must be regarded as a conglomeration of individual decisions taken by the Commission under the guise of a regulation …, each of which decisions affects the legal position of each author of an application for a licence."

nature. Member States are required to ensure that their national policies conform to the Union positions.[26]

[10–33] Decisions adopted pursuant to Art 25 TEU are differentiated from Art 288 TFEU decisions by the inclusion of the acronym "CFSP" within the serial number,[27] eg Decision 2013/255/CFSP concerning restrictive measures against Syria. Since a new harmonised system for numbering legal acts was introduced on 1 January 2015, the domain (eg "CFSP") now appears at the beginning of the number in brackets, eg Council Decision (CFSP) 2018/778 concerning restrictive measures against Syria. As the power to grant delegated acts may only be conferred by a legislative act, there are no delegated CFSP decisions. Implementing powers may, however, be conferred by a CFSP decision, giving rise to implementing CFSP decisions, eg Council Implementing Decision (CFSP) 2018/284 of 26 February 2018 implementing Decision 2013/255/CFSP concerning restrictive measures against Syria.

(iii) Directives

[10–34] A directive is binding, as to the result to be achieved, upon each Member State to which it is addressed, but shall leave to the national authorities the choice of form and methods. Unlike a regulation, therefore, a directive does not have to be addressed to all Member States, although they usually are. Directives are a means of setting an overall legislative objective which is to be achieved throughout the Union by a particular date, whilst leaving to each Member State a degree of discretion and flexibility as to how to achieve this objective within the context of their own legal systems and societal characteristics. Member States are required to give effect to, or "transpose", a directive by the prescribed date and to notify the Commission of the transposition measures adopted. As will be seen in Chapter 12, the Court of Justice's conferral of vertical direct effect upon directives that Member States have failed to implement before the end of the prescribed deadline means that, once that deadline has passed, the distinction between a regulation and a directive can become somewhat blurred. An example of a directive that is considered in some detail in this book is the Citizens Directive, the content of which is outlined in Chapter 24, together with the statutory instrument that transposes the Directive into Irish law.[28]

(iv) Recommendations and Opinions

[10–35] Recommendations and opinions are the two forms of non-binding, soft law mentioned in Art 288, although there are others that are used such as guidelines and communications. While not legally binding, relevant recommendations are to be taken into account by national courts in interpreting EU law or national law based on EU law. A soft law instrument such as a guideline or a communication might be issued by the Commission following a very significant judgment by the Court of Justice, setting out its understanding of what change has been made to existing EU law, or how the judgment is to be given effect in practice. For example, the Commission issued a communication

---

[26] See Ramses A Wessel, "Resisting Legal Facts: Are CFSP Norms as Soft as They Seem?" (2015) 20 *European Foreign Affairs Review* 123.

[27] Section C, Annex VI, Council Decision of 1 December 2009 adopting the Council's Rules of Procedure (2009/937/EU) [2009] OJ L 325/35.

[28] See ch 24, paras [24–02] to [24–03].

on the consequences of the landmark judgment in *Cassis de Dijon* concerning the free movement of goods.[29] A particularly well-known use of soft law is what is known as the "Open Method of Coordination", first developed in 2000.[30] This is an alternative to the adoption of legal acts through the legislative process and instead involves:

(i) *fixing guidelines* for the Union combined with *specific timetables* for achieving short, medium and long-term goals;
(ii) establishing *indicators and benchmarks* as a means of comparing best practice;
(iii) translating the guidelines into *national and regional policies* by setting *specific targets and adopting measures*; and
(iv) mutual learning processes through the use of *periodic monitoring, evaluation and peer review*.

[10–36] The European Pillar of Social Rights, which was proclaimed by the Commission, Parliament and Council on 17 November 2017, is another, more recent instance of a soft law document. It sets out 20 principles in the areas of equal opportunities, access to the labour market, fair working conditions, social protection and inclusion. The Pillar is not a legally binding instrument but rather provides a:

> reference framework to screen the employment and social performance of participating Member States, to drive reforms at national level and, more specifically, to serve as a guide for the renewed process of convergence towards better working and living conditions in Europe. … The Pillar reaffirms a number of rights already present in the EU and in the international legal acquis. As such, the Pillar does not affect principles and rights already contained in binding provisions of Union law: by putting together principles and rights which were set at different times, in different ways and in different forms, it seeks to render them more visible, more understandable and more explicit for citizens and for actors at all levels.[31]

E. Legislative Acts and Non-Legislative Acts

[10–37] The classification of legal acts as either a "legislative" or a "non-legislative" act originates in the drafting of a Constitutional Treaty in the early 2000s. One of the aims of this ambitious project was to simplify the many types of legal act and to ensure that "acts with the same legal/political force have the same foundation in terms of democratic legitimacy".[32] To this end, the classification sought to guarantee that

---

[29] Commission Communication concerning the consequences of the judgment given by the Court of Justice on 20 February 1979 in Case 120/78 (*Cassis de Dijon*) [1980] OJ C256/2. See ch 19, paras [19–44] to [19–53].

[30] Presidency Conclusions, Lisbon European Council, 24 March 2000. See Bruno de Witte, "The Place of the OMC in the System of EU Competences and Sources of Law" (2018) 3 *European Papers* 207; Colin Scott, "Governing Without Law or Governing without Government? New-ish Governance and the Legitimacy of the EU" (2009) 15 *European Law Journal* 160; Christian Joerges, "Integration through De-legislation?" (2008) 33 *European Law Review* 291; Erika Szyszczak, "Experimental Governance: The Open Method of Coordination" (2006) 12 *European Law Journal* 486.

[31] European Commission Factsheet, European Pillar of Social Rights – Questions and Answers, Memo 17/1004, 26 April 2017, updated 24 October 2017. See Sacha Garben, "The European Pillar of Social Rights: Effectively Addressing Displacement?" (2018) 14 *European Constitutional Law Review* 210.

[32] Final Report of Working Group IX on Simplification of 29 November 2002, CONV 424/02, 2. See

"an act of a legislative nature must always come from the bodies which represent [the Union's] states and peoples, namely the Council and the Parliament".[33]

[10–38] The idea of an act of a legislative nature is related to the principle of the separation of powers and the difference between the legislative function, where principles of democratic participation are most relevant, and the executive function, where they are less so. Compared to national systems of government, however, the allocation of duties amongst the EU institutions does not fit comfortably with the traditional distinction between legislative and executive functions. As a result, within the EU legal system "legislative acts" are determined not by the identity of the institution responsible for their adoption but on the type of procedure used. The aim was to prescribe the most appropriate procedure for the legislative and executive functions of the institutions. According to the scheme adopted, legislative acts are to set out the essential elements, or basic policy choices, governing an area, and so are to be adopted according to one of the two legislative procedures (ordinary or special). In contrast, executive acts in the form of delegated and implementing acts are not adopted pursuant to a legislative procedure and so are not legislative acts.

[10–39] It is important to note that the definition of a legislative act is a formalistic one, in the sense that it is the procedure used to adopt the act which defines it as a legislative act, rather than the content of the act. As will be seen below, in practice a delegated act may very well be legislative in nature given that it is supplementing or amending certain non-essential elements of a legislative act. This is greatly compounded by the fact that the Lisbon Treaty reforms "made the highly contentious choice" of retaining miscellaneous instances where the Treaties directly allow for the adoption of legal acts by a means other than the ordinary or special legislative procedure, while simply omitting to include any explicit reference to this category of non-legislative act.[34] As a collective term, these have been referred to as "innominate non-legislative procedures", with 28 different TFEU legal bases identified as availing of them in respect of the Council and the Commission alone.[35]

[10–40] In terms of both their content and their applicable scope throughout the Union, acts adopted under an innominate legislative procedure might very much be legislative in nature and so, from a democratic participation perspective, ought to follow the same procedure as applied to legislative acts. For example, in the areas of competition law (Art 103 TFEU) and state aid (Art 109 TFEU), the procedure prescribed is neither the ordinary or the special legislative procedure, such that any regulations or directives adopted thereunder are not legislative acts.[36] Non-legislative acts are also used by the

Jürgen Bast, "New Categories of Acts after the Lisbon Reform: Dynamics of Parliamentarization in EU Law" (2012) 49 *Common Market Law Review* 885.

[33] *ibid.*

[34] Deirdre Curtin and Tatevik Manucharyan, "Legal Acts and Hierarchy of Norms in EU Law" in Anthony Arnull and Damian Chalmers (eds), *The Oxford Handbook of European Union Law* (Oxford University Press, 2015) 103, 122.

[35] Kieran St C Bradley, "Legislating in the European Union" in Catherine Barnard and Steve Peers (eds), *European Union Law* (2nd ed, Oxford University Press, 2017) 97, 124; Edward Best, "Legislative Procedures after Lisbon: Fewer, Simpler, Clearer?" (2008) 15 *Maastricht Journal of European and Comparative Law* 85, 93.

[36] Deirdre Curtin and Tatevik Manucharyan, "Legal Acts and Hierarchy of Norms in EU Law" in Anthony Arnull and Damian Chalmers (eds), *The Oxford Handbook of European Union Law* (Oxford University Press, 2015) 103, 109.

Council in the field of CFSP. As a result, acts adopted in these areas cannot confer a power to make delegated acts. Another consequence is that, whereas the Council is required to meet in public when discussing legislative acts, it is not required to do so when discussing non-legislative acts. Thirdly, the role afforded to national parliaments by Protocols No 2 and No 3 in scrutinising proposals for adherence to the subsidiarity principle is confined to draft legislative acts only. Consequently, it has been said that from the perspective of transparency, accountability and democratic legitimacy, the seriousness of the omission of any explicit Treaty treatment of these non-legislative acts cannot be overstated:

> Given that non-legislative acts adopted directly on the basis of the [TEU and TFEU] constitute a big proportion of the acts adopted by the Union institutions, the failure to include an explicit reference to this category of act is significant. It means that the hierarchy of acts in the Lisbon Treaty, unlike the one found in the [proposed Constitutional Treaty], is incomplete as it fails to account for this second type of non-legislative act.[37]

[10–41] Even where a legislative procedure is used, criticism has been levelled at the application of the legislative act label to acts adopted pursuant to the variant of the special legislative procedure that requires that the Council merely consult the European Parliament. It has been claimed that such acts cannot be considered truly legislative from the perspective of democratic legitimacy or in the sense of the term used on the national level.[38] As a result of these two criticisms it has been suggested that, rather than reflecting any coherent underlying constitutional principle, the Lisbon Treaty's introduction of the term legislative act "seems instead to emerge as a labelling exercise with an essentially pragmatic basis and some rather arbitrary consequences".[39]

F. Delegated Acts

[10–42] As discussed above, the reforms introduced by the Lisbon Treaty sought to reflect a clearer separation as between the Union's legislative and executive powers. Whereas legislative acts were henceforth to be confined to legal acts adopted pursuant to the ordinary or the special legislative procedure, legal acts of the executive in the form of limited rule-making or administrative acts were to take the form of regulatory acts, namely delegated or implementing acts.

[10–43] This distinction between legislative and executive powers is replicated at the level of the subordinate adoption of legal acts, in a new dual categorisation of executive acts. On the one hand, delegated acts involve the exercise of a limited delegation of the *legislative* power to supplement or amend certain non-essential elements of the legislative act that conferred the power. In contrast, implementing acts involve a delegation of the *executive* power in that they "execute the legislative act without amendment or supplementation".[40] Delegated acts are adopted by the Commission. Implementing acts are usually adopted by the Commission but, in duly justified specific

---

37 *ibid*, 122, 105–106.
38 *ibid*, 109–110.
39 Alan Dashwood, Michael Dougan, Barry Rodger, Eleanor Spaventa and Derrick Wyatt, *Wyatt and Dashwood's European Union Law* (6th ed, Hart, 2011) 85.
40 Paul Craig and Gráinne de Búrca, *EU Law* (6th ed, Oxford University Press, 2015) 117.

cases and under Arts 24 and 26 TEU relating to CFSP, may exceptionally be adopted by the Council. Delegated acts are provided for in Art 290 TFEU as follows:

> 1. A legislative act may delegate to the Commission the power to adopt non-legislative acts of general application to supplement or amend certain non-essential elements of the legislative act.
>
> The objectives, content, scope and duration of the delegation of power shall be explicitly defined in the legislative acts. The essential elements of an area shall be reserved for the legislative act and accordingly shall not be the subject of a delegation of power.
>
> 2. Legislative acts shall explicitly lay down the conditions to which the delegation is subject; these conditions may be as follows:
> (a) the European Parliament or the Council may decide to revoke the delegation;
> (b) the delegated act may enter into force only if no objection has been expressed by the European Parliament or the Council within a period set by the legislative act.
>
> For the purposes of (a) and (b), the European Parliament shall act by a majority of its component members, and the Council by a qualified majority.
>
> 3. The adjective "delegated" shall be inserted in the title of delegated acts.

[10–44] From paragraph 1 it can be seen that a key element in limiting the power to make delegated acts is that they must only supplement or amend certain non-essential elements of the legislative act.[41] In a 2009 Communication, the Commission put forward its own interpretation of this phrase.[42] By "amend" it understood any formal amendment that might relate to the text of an article or the text of an annex that legally forms part of the legislative act. In relation to amending an annex, it is said to make little difference whether the annex contains purely technical measures: "as soon as the Commission is empowered to amend an annex containing measures of general application, the regime of delegated acts must be applied".[43] The Commission considered that an act "supplements" a legislative act if it specifically adds new non-essential rules which change the framework of the legislative act, whereas "measures intended only

---

[41] See Anne Pieter Van der Mei, "Delegation of Rulemaking Powers to the European Commission post-Lisbon" (2016) 12 *European Constitutional Law Review* 538; Dominique Ritleng, "The Dividing Line between Delegated and Implementing Acts" (2015) 52 *Common Market Law Review* 243; Merijn Chamon, "How the Concept of Essential Elements of a Legislative Act Continues to Elude the Court" (2013) 50 *Common Market Law Review* 849; Joana Mendes, "Delegated and Implementing Rule Making: Proceduralisation and Constitutional Design" (2013) 19 *European Law Journal* 22; Thomas Christiansen and Mathias Dobbels, "Non-legislative Rule Making after the Lisbon Treaty: Implementing the New System of Comitology and Delegated Acts" (2013) 19 *European Law Journal* 42; Steve Peers and Marios Costa, "Accountability for Delegated and Implementing Acts after the Treaty of Lisbon" (2012) 18 *European Law Journal* 427; Paul Craig, "Delegated Acts, Implementing Acts and the New Comitology Regulation" (2011) 36 *European Law Review* 671; Robert Schütze, "'Delegated' Legislation in the (New) European Union: A Constitutional Analysis" (2011) 74 *Modern Law Review* 661; Herwig Hofmann, "Legislation, Delegation and Implementation under the Treaty of Lisbon: Typology Meets Reality" (2009) 15 *European Law Journal* 482.

[42] Commission Communication, "Implementation of Article 290 of the Treaty on the Functioning of the European Union", COM(2009) 673 final, 9 December 2009.

[43] *ibid*, 4.

to give effect to the existing rules of the basic instrument should not be deemed to be supplementary measures".[44]

[10–45] In a series of cases involving *Dyson Ltd v Commission*, the Court of Justice and the General Court grappled with the question of whether the Commission had infringed a delegated power conferred on it by a directive by disregarding an essential element of the directive. The directive governed the energy labelling of vacuum cleaners. Its objective was set in Art 1 as being to establish a framework for the harmonisation of national measures on end-user information, particularly by means of labelling and standard product information, "on the consumption of energy ... during use". In a delegated regulation setting out the detailed rules for testing and labelling of energy consumption, the Commission required that an energy consumption was to be tested on the basis of an empty vacuum cleaner receptacle. It was argued by Dyson that, in doing so, the Commission had exceeded the delegated power conferred on it by contravening an essential element of the directive, which required testing to reflect normal conditions of use, rather than on the basis of an empty receptacle. According to the Court of Justice:

> the possibility of delegating powers provided for in Article 290 TFEU aims to enable the legislature to concentrate on the essential elements of a piece of legislation and on the non-essential elements in respect of which it finds it appropriate to legislate, while entrusting the Commission with the task of "supplementing" certain non-essential elements of the legislative act adopted or "amending" such elements within the framework of the power delegated to it.
>
> It follows that the essential rules on the matter in question must be laid down in the basic legislation and cannot be delegated.
>
> It must be determined, secondly, whether the requirement that the information supplied to consumers must reflect energy consumption while the machine is in use, as follows from [certain provisions of the Directive], is an essential element of the directive.
>
> The essential elements of basic legislation are those which, in order to be adopted, require political choices falling within the responsibilities of the EU legislature.
>
> Identifying the elements of a matter which must be categorised as essential must be based on objective factors amenable to judicial review, and requires account to be taken of the characteristics and particular features of the field concerned.
>
> In view of the general scheme of [the Directive], it must be considered that the requirement [that the information supplied to consumers must reflect energy consumption while the machine is in use] is an essential element of the directive.
>
> ... In the light of the forgoing, the Commission was thus obliged, in order not to disregard an essential element of [the Directive], to adopt in the regulation at issue a method of calculation which makes it possible to measure the energy performance of vacuum cleaners in conditions as close as possible to actual conditions of use, requiring the vacuum cleaner's receptacle to be filled to a certain level ...[45]

[10–46] Having heard the appeal, the Court of Justice referred the case back to the General Court for determination of certain grounds. The General Court confirmed that

---

[44] *ibid.*

[45] Case C-44/16 P *Dyson Ltd v Commission* EU:2017:357, 11 May 2017, paras 58–63, 68.

the Commission's delegated regulation had failed to adhere to the essential elements of the directive and so was annulled.[46]

[10–47] Given that it is afforded a greater role in the adoption of delegated acts than as compared with implementing acts, the Parliament tends to favour the use of delegated acts while, conversely, the Council favours the use of implementing acts. In an attempt towards reaching an agreed approach, in 2011 the Commission, Council and Parliament concluded a detailed Common Understanding on Delegated Acts, which was subsequently incorporated into the 2016 Agreement on Better Law-Making.[47] The Common Understanding sets out procedural arrangements for a cooperative approach and standard clauses to be used to govern the use of the delegated power.

[10–48] Despite the Common Understanding, the very general nature of the language used in Arts 290 and 291 means that disagreement amongst the institutions can lead to litigation. An early example of this arose in the *Frontex* case.[48] Although the judgment was delivered in 2012, it concerned measures adopted under pre-Lisbon procedures that were the equivalent of delegated acts. There, the Parliament challenged the use of what would now be termed a delegated act to supplement or amend the Schengen Borders Code. In response to a sudden increase in migration in the Mediterranean Sea, the Commission proposed additional rules that were to be applied by Frontex, the EU's external borders agency, in the course of surveillance operations against ships which were suspected of carrying persons intending to circumvent border checks. The Parliament argued that while the Schengen Borders Code had delegated a power to adopt "additional measures", these did not allow the Commission to lay down rules which amended the powers and obligations of Frontex and which had the effect of modifying the regulation by which it was established.

[10–49] In a Grand Chamber judgment, the Court began by recalling that provisions which, in order to be adopted, require political choices falling within the responsibilities of the Union legislature cannot be delegated. Secondly, contrary to what was claimed by the Commission and the Council, ascertaining which elements of a matter must be categorised as essential is not for the assessment of the Union legislature alone, but must be based on objective factors amenable to judicial review and which take account of the characteristics and particularities of the domain concerned. In this case, the Court concluded that:

> the adoption of rules on the conferral of enforcement powers on border guards … entails political choices falling within the responsibilities of the European Union legislature, in that it requires the conflicting interests at issue to be weighed up on the basis of a number of assessments. Depending on the political choices on the basis of which those rules are adopted, the powers of the border guards may vary significantly, and the exercise of those powers require authorisation, be an obligation or be prohibited, for example, in relation to applying enforcement measures, using force or conducting the persons apprehended to a specific location. In addition, where those powers concern the taking of measures against ships, their exercise is liable, depending on the scope of the powers, to interfere with the sovereign rights of third countries according to the flag flown by the

---

46 Case T–544/13 RENV *Dyson Ltd v Commission* EU:T:2018:761, 8 November 2018, paras 61–74.

47 Interinstitutional Agreement of 13 April 2016 on Better Law-Making [2016] OJ L123/1, paras 26–31 and the Annex thereto.

48 Case C-355/10 *Parliament v Council (Frontex)* EU:C:2012:516, 5 September 2012.

> ships concerned. Thus, the adoption of such rules constitutes a major development in the [Schengen Borders Code] system.
>
> Second, it is important to point out that provisions on conferring powers of public authority on border guards – such as the powers conferred in the contested decision, which include stopping persons apprehended, seizing vessels and conducting persons apprehended to a specific location – mean that the fundamental rights of the persons concerned may be interfered with to such an extent that the involvement of the European Union legislature is required.
>
> Thus, the adoption of [the] provisions ... requires political choices to be made ... Accordingly, the adoption of such provisions goes beyond the scope of the additional measures within the meaning of [the Schengen Borders Code] and, in the context of the European Union's institutional system, is a matter for the legislature.
>
> ... In those circumstances, the contested decision must be annulled in its entirety because it contains essential elements of the surveillance of the sea external borders of the Member States which go beyond the scope of the additional measures ... of the [Schengen Borders Code], and only the European Union legislature was entitled to adopt such a decision.[49]

[10–50] While the *Frontex* case involved a dispute as to whether delegated legislation could be used to make the amendments at issue, disagreements as to the choice between delegated and implementing acts have also been litigated. For example, in the *Chemicals Agency* case the Commission argued that an implementing power ought not to have been used to allow the European Chemicals Agency to set the fees to be charged for authorisations for the placing of biocidal products on the market.[50] As this was a quasi-legislative function, the Commission regarded it as a delegated power that ought to have been based on Art 290. According to the Court, the purpose of granting a delegated power was to "achieve the adoption of rules coming within the regulatory framework as defined by the basic legislative act". In contrast, an implementing power is to be used to "provide further detail in relation to the content of a legislative act, in order to ensure that it is implemented under uniform conditions in all Member States".[51]

[10–51] The Court expressed a high degree of deference for what it termed the exercise of the legislature's discretion in choosing as between the two powers. A judicial review of the decision to confer an implementing power was, according to the Court, limited to determining if there had been a manifest error of assessment as to whether the legislature could reasonably have taken the view: (i) that in order to be implemented, the legal framework which it laid down in the regulation needed only the addition of further detail, without its non-essential elements having to be amended or supplemented; and (ii) that the provisions of the regulation require uniform conditions for implementation. As the parent regulation had set down the guiding principles that fees were to be paid to the Agency and were to be set at such a level as to ensure that they were sufficient to cover the cost of the services delivered, the Court was satisfied that the legislature

---

49 *ibid*, paras 76–84. See Maarten Den Heijer and Eljalill Tauschinsky, "Where Human Rights Meet Administrative Law: Essential Elements and Limits to Delegation" (2013) 9 *European Constitutional Law Review* 514; Merijn Chamon, "How the Concept of Essential Elements of a Legislative Act Continues to Elude the Court: *Parliament v Council*" (2014) 50 *Common Market Law Review* 849.

50 Case C-427/12 *Commission v Parliament* EU:C:2014:170, 18 March 2014.

51 *ibid*, paras 38, 39.

had not erred in deciding that the necessary measures could be adopted pursuant to an implementing power.[52]

[10–52] The *Visa Exemption* case involved the opposite scenario. There, the Commission claimed that a delegated power conferred on it ought to have been an implementing power, given that the measures to be adopted implemented the parent regulation, rather than supplementing or amending it.[53] In the event that a third country changed its policy towards the EU such as to impose a requirement for a visa to enter its territory, the Commission was authorised to adopt a delegated act removing that country from the list of visa-exempt countries. The Court rejected the Commission's argument that, as it had no discretion to remove the country from the list, it was merely implementing the regulation rather than amending it. According to the Court:

> neither the existence nor the extent of the discretion conferred on it by the legislative act is relevant for determining whether the act to be adopted by the Commission comes under Article 290 TFEU or Article 291 TFEU. It follows from the wording of Article 290(1) TFEU that the lawfulness of the EU legislature's choice to confer a delegated power on the Commission depends solely on whether the acts the Commission is to adopt on the basis of the conferral are of general application and whether they supplement or amend non-essential elements of the legislative act.
>
> … As to the question whether [the parent regulation] confers power on the Commission to amend that regulation within the meaning of Article 290(1) TFEU, it should be recalled that … nationals of the third countries on the list in Annex I to that regulation must be in possession of a visa when crossing the external borders of the Member States. … nationals of the third countries on the list in Annex II to the regulation are exempt from that requirement for stays of no more than 90 days in any 180-day period.
>
> An act adopted on the basis of [the delegated power] has the effect of reintroducing for a period of 12 or 18 months a visa obligation for all nationals of a third country listed in Annex II to that regulation for stays which, in accordance with Article 1(2) of that regulation, are exempt from that obligation. For all those nationals, the [delegated act] … thus has the effect of amending, if only temporarily, the normative content of the legislative act in question. Apart from their temporary nature, the effects of the act adopted on the basis of that provision are identical in all respects with those of a formal transfer of the reference to the third country concerned from Annex II to Annex I of [the regulation].
>
> … In those circumstances, the EU legislature conferred power on the Commission to amend the normative content of that legislative act within the meaning of Article 290(1) TFEU.[54]

G. Implementing Acts

[10–53] Delegated acts, such as that at issue in the *Visa Exemption* case, are quasi-

[52] *ibid*, paras 40–44. See Dominique Ritleng, "The Dividing Line between Delegated and Implementing Acts: The Court of Justice Sidesteps the Difficulty in *Commission v Parliament and Council (Biocides)*" (2015) 51 *Common Market Law Review* 243.

[53] Case C-88/14 *Commission v Parliament* EU:C:2015:499, 16 July 2015.

[54] *ibid*, paras 32, 42–44. See Merijn Chamon, "The Dividing Line between Delegated and Implementing Acts, Part Two: The Court of Justice Settles the Issue in *Commission v Parliament and Council* (Visa Reciprocity)" (2015) 51 *Common Market Law Review* 1617; Anne Pieter Van der Mei, "Delegation of Rulemaking Powers to the European Commission post-Lisbon" (2016) 12 *European Constitutional Law Review* 538.

legislative in nature, in that they supplement or amend a non-essential element of a legislative act. In contrast, implementing acts are executive in nature, in that they provide for the uniform execution of a legislative act where implementation by the Member States alone would lead to an unacceptable diversity, but without supplementing or amending the act in any way. As a result, the degree of control exercised over the Commission's use of implementing powers is less than in respect of delegated powers. This leads the Council to have a tendency to favour the use of implementing powers, as a greater degree of control is left to the Member States through what are known as the comitology procedures. According to Art 291 TFEU:

> 2. Where uniform conditions for implementing legally binding Union acts are needed, those acts shall confer implementing powers on the Commission, or, in duly justified specific cases and in the cases provided for in Articles 24 and 26 of the Treaty on European Union, on the Council.
>
> 3. For the purposes of paragraph 2, the European Parliament and the Council, acting by means of regulations in accordance with the ordinary legislative procedure, shall lay down in advance the rules and general principles concerning mechanisms for control by Member States of the Commission's exercise of implementing powers.
>
> 4. The word "implementing" shall be inserted in the title of implementing acts.

[10–54] The mechanisms for allowing Member States some control over the Commission's exercise of implementing powers take the form of an "examination procedure" and an "advisory procedure" as provided for in the Comitology Regulation.[55] Under both procedures, draft implementing acts are submitted to a committee made up of Member State representatives. Whereas the Commission must take "utmost account" of a negative opinion of an advisory committee, but nevertheless can proceed to adopt the act, the examination committee can veto an act, which will then go to an appeal committee for a second opinion. If the appeal committee does not favour the adoption of the act, the Commission cannot proceed. The Comitology Regulation provides guidance as to which of the two procedures is to apply in any given case. The advisory procedure is the default choice, while the examination procedure is to be used in relation to implementing acts "of general scope" as well as in relation to implementing acts in important policy areas such as the common agricultural, fisheries and commercial policies and the protection of health and of the environment.

[10–55] The aim of the reforms introduced by the Lisbon Treaty was to reflect, in the distinction between delegated and implementing acts, the difference between a conferred power that was quasi-legislative and one that was more executive in nature. In turn, this distinction would lead to different control mechanisms being applied to each, reflective of the separation of powers within the Union. Whereas the control mechanisms involving the Parliament set out in Art 290 TFEU would apply to delegated acts, the Comitology Regulation involving committees of Member State representatives would apply to implementing acts. As illustrated by the inter-institutional litigation referred to above, the difference between the two procedures has a very real impact on

---

[55] Regulation 182/2011 laying down the rules and general principles concerning mechanisms for control by Member States of the Commission's exercise of implementing powers [2011] OJ L55/13. See Paul Craig, "Delegated Acts, Implementing Acts and the New Comitology Regulation" (2011) 36 *European Law Review* 671. The Commission has put forward a proposal to amend the Regulation, COM(2017) 85 final.

the participation afforded to an institution and so is a matter of considerable concern to them whenever the choice is being made between the two.

[10–56] Given the significance of this choice, there has been criticism that the criteria used to define delegated and implementing acts are "questionable in terms of principle and very difficult to apply" as a matter of practice.[56] The conceptual distinction between delegated and implementing acts has been described as "fragile", with Paul Craig and Gráinne de Búrca pointing out that

> [t]here will inevitably be instances where juxtaposition of acts reveals scant reason as to why the "supplementation" of the legislative act in the one instance should be regarded as a "new" non-essential element, such that a delegated act is required, while in other instances this is not so, such that an implementing act can be used.[57]

[10–57] This difficulty is exacerbated by the fact that the choice as to whether an act is delegated or implementing needs to be made at an early stage in order to know which control mechanism procedure is to be followed – those set out in Art 290 or the Comitology Regulation. Given the subtle nature of the distinction, it may prove challenging to make this call when an act is only in a draft form and may undergo further changes. These difficulties may have influenced the Court's decision in the *Chemicals Agency* case to grant the legislature a high degree of deference in the exercise of its "discretion" in choosing as between delegated and implementing powers.[58] There, the Court indicated that a judicial review of the decision to confer a delegated or implementing power should be confined to determining if there had been a manifest error of assessment by the legislature in the choice that it made. Whilst this high degree of deference has the benefit of discouraging a ready willingness to bring legal challenges on this ground, the downside is that it may be difficult for an institution to enforce its rights should it feel that the proper separation of powers is not being respected in the choice of act to be used.

---

56 Paul Craig and Gráinne de Búrca, *EU Law* (6th ed, Oxford University Press, 2015) 122.

57 *ibid*, 118.

58 Case C-427/12 *Commission v Parliament* EU:C:2014:170, 18 March 2014.

CHAPTER 11

DIRECT EFFECT OF PRIMARY EU LAW

A. INTRODUCTION

[11–01] One of the most striking aspects of the TEU and TFEU is the absence of any reference to the two most fundamental characteristics of EU law: direct effect and supremacy (also known as primacy). While the draft Constitutional Treaty would have addressed this, the compromise approach of the Lisbon Treaty was to annex a short declaration on primacy in which the existing case law of the Court of Justice is briefly recalled. Direct effect, on the other hand, remains without a single mention. This chapter deals with the direct effect of primary EU law, while direct effect of secondary EU law and the doctrine of indirect effect is dealt with in the following chapter. The supremacy of EU law is the subject of chapter 13.

[11–02] In the previous chapter it was seen that Art 288 TFEU defines a regulation as being both binding in its entirety and "directly applicable" in all Member States. In other words, a regulation has the force of law within each Member State without the need for any national implementation measures. Given that it is not precisely defined, different understandings persist as to the exact nature of direct applicability and how it is to be distinguished from direct effect. Some commentators, and certain judgments of the Court of Justice, tend to elide the distinction altogether, treating direct effect and direct applicability as more or less synonymous. In seeking to clarify their separate nature, Robert Schütze describes direct *applicability* as a "federal question", in that it relates to what internal effect an EU norm is to have within the legal systems of the Member States. In this way, direct applicability is concerned with the relationship between EU law and national law and, more particularly, the reception of EU law within the Member States. Direct *effect*, in contrast, is a "separation of powers question", concerned with the individual effect that an EU norm has in a specific case and whether its ability to execute itself means that it must be applied by the legislature or by the executive and judiciary. Direct effect, therefore, refers to the "capacity of Union law to produce *independent* legal effects within the national legal systems".[1] Direct applicability is wider than, and

1 Alan Dashwood, Michael Dougan, Barry Rodger, Eleanor Spaventa and Derrick Wyatt, *Wyatt and Dashwood's European Union Law* (6th ed, 2011, Hart) 244.

is a pre-condition for, direct effect.[2] Whereas the quality of direct applicability means that a regulation is immediately and automatically part of the "law of the land" in each Member State, whether an individual may invoke the regulation before a national court or administrative process in order to advance his or her legal rights is a question of the extent to which the regulation has direct effect.

[11–03] The principle of direct effect developed through a series of cases in which the Court of Justice was required to consider whether a particular source of EU law – the Treaties, the Charter, general principles of EU law, international agreements, regulations, decisions and directives – were capable of having direct effect and, if so, the circumstances under which direct effect can arise. The picture that emerges is a complex mosaic in which each source of EU law needs to be considered separately. This chapter will deal with the direct effect of primary EU law in the form of the Treaties, including the Charter of Fundamental Rights, and general principles of EU law.

[11–04] Before approaching our central question, it is worth introducing a key concept that arises in this area. This is the important distinction between "vertical" and "horizontal" direct effect. Representing the idea that actions by private litigants against the state are actions that are aimed upwards, towards a higher authority, vertical direct effect means that a source of EU law may be invoked in actions against the relevant Member State. Reverse vertical direct effect describes a situation whereby a source of EU law may be relied on by a Member State in an action against a private party. In contrast, representing the idea that actions between private litigants are carried out on an equal plane, horizontal direct effect means that a source of EU law may be invoked in an action by one private party against another private party. In respect of each source of EU law, therefore, two pertinent questions are whether it is capable of having direct effect and, if so, is this confined to vertical direct effect or does it also have horizontal direct effect. Directives, for example, have vertical direct effect but do not have horizontal direct effect.

B. Direct Effect

[11–05] Although the unique nature of EU law is largely taken for granted today, it is important to remember that the 1957 Treaty of Rome was an international agreement under public international law through which six states agreed to "establish amongst themselves a European Economic Community". According to the traditional approach of international law, it is for each state to determine, as a matter of its own constitutional law, the relationship between its domestic law and international law. This choice lies between two alternative approaches known as "monism" and "dualism".

[11–06] A monist approach to international law means that when a state enters into an international agreement, that agreement is automatically rendered part of the state's domestic law. So, for example, the US Constitution provides that all treaties made by the United States "shall be the supreme law of the land; and the judges in every State

[2] Robert Schütze, *European Union Law* (Oxford University Press, 2015) 81, emphasis added. See JA Winter, "Direct Effect and Direct Applicability: Two Distinct and Different Concepts in Community Law" (1972) 9 *Common Market Law Review* 425. For an opposing view, however, see Nigel Foster, *EU Law* (5th ed, Oxford University Press, 2016) 210–211.

shall be bound thereby, any thing in the Constitution or laws of any State to the contrary notwithstanding".[3]

[11–07] Dualism, on the other hand, maintains a strict distinction between international law at the state-to-state level, and domestic law at the national level. When a dualist state enters into an international agreement, the agreement does not automatically form part of domestic law. Rather, to the extent necessary, obligations under the agreement must expressly be given effect to by national law – often referred to as "incorporation" into domestic law. As a dualist state, Art 29.6 of Ireland's Constitution provides that "No international agreement shall be part of the domestic law of the State save as may be determined by the Oireachtas". Robert Schütze puts the matter well by stating that the difference between the two approaches boils down to whether international law is incorporated via a state's constitution (such as the US and France), or whether international treaties need to be validated by a particular parliamentary measure (as in the case of Ireland and the UK).[4]

[11–08] One consequence of the Second World War was a softening of traditional approaches to sovereignty and international governance, given their abject failures, leading to an unprecedented growth of international organisations. Evidencing this trend, the German Basic Law, introduced in 1949, allowed for the transfer of sovereign powers to international organisations. In 1953 the Dutch constitution was amended to enable international agreements to prevail over domestic law, while the constitution of Luxembourg was amended in 1956 so as to allow executive, legislative and judicial powers to be vested in an international organisation.[5]

[11–09] In only its fifth year in force, a Dutch court requested a preliminary ruling from the Court of Justice as to whether an article of the Treaty of Rome had "direct application in national law in the sense that nationals of Member States may on the basis of this Article lay claim to rights which the national court must protect". The resulting 1963 decision in *Van Gend en Loos* remains among the most significant and celebrated of all of the Court's judgments, its fiftieth anniversary being marked by academic conferences and in the pages of the *Irish Times*.[6] As has rightly been said, its importance is difficult to exaggerate.[7] The judgment marks the start of a legal revolution that saw the Court of Justice "setting EU law apart from all other forms of international

---

3 Art VI.

4 Robert Schütze, *An Introduction to European Law* (2nd ed, Cambridge University Press, 2015) 116.

5 Damian Chalmers, Gareth Davies and Giorgi Monti, *European Union Law* (3rd ed, Cambridge University Press, 2014) 201.

6 Case 26/62 *Van Gend en Loos* [1963] ECR 1; "Fifty Years Since *Van Gend en Loos* Judgment", *The Irish Times*, 25 February 2013. See Damian Chalmers and Luis Barroso, "What *Van Gend en Loos* Stands For" (2014) 12 *International Journal of Constitutional Law* 105; Morten Rasmussen, "Revolutionizing European Law: A History of the *Van Gend en Loos* Judgment" (2014) 12 *International Journal of Constitutional Law* 136; Eyal Benvenisti and George W Downs, "The Premises, Assumptions, and Implications of *Van Gend en Loos*: Viewed from the Perspectives of Democracy and Legitimacy of International Institutions" (2015) 25 *European Journal of International Law* 85; Antoine Vauchez, "The Transnational Politics of Jurisprudence. *Van Gend en Loos* and the Making of EU Polity" (2010) 16 *European Law Journal* 1.

7 Nial Fennelly, "Legal Interpretation at the European Court of Justice" (1996) 20 *Fordham International Law Journal* 656, 659.

law" by "defining itself in opposition to, rather than in conformity with, the 'old' legal order of international law".[8]

[11–10] The facts of *Van Gend en Loos* were as follows. When the Treaty of Rome entered into force on 1 January 1958, the duty on imports to the Netherlands of a certain resin material (urea-formaldehyde) was 5 per cent. Article 12 of the Treaty provided that Member States were to refrain from introducing between themselves any new customs duties on imports or exports, or from increasing those already in place. In 1960, the Van Gend en Loos company imported the resin to Netherlands from another Member State, on which, as a result of its reclassification, a higher duty of 8 per cent was imposed. In proceedings before a Dutch court, the company sought reimbursement of the monies paid, arguing that Art 12 of the Treaty of Rome prohibited any such increase in customs duties.

[11–11] A fundamental question arose as to whether or not, just as an applicant might invoke and rely upon a provision of national law, a provision of the Treaty could likewise be directly invoked and relied upon by an individual applicant in domestic court proceedings. As the Court of Justice put it, did Art 12 have direct application in Dutch law in the sense that it could be used by a private individual or company as the basis on which to lay claim to rights which the Dutch court must protect. While the judgment itself refers to "direct application", the EU law terminology for this question is now whether the Treaty, or a certain provision thereof, has "direct effect" within the Member States. *Van Gend en Loos* was the first occasion on which the Court considered this important issue.

[11–12] Of the six EEC Member States at the time, the Netherlands, Belgium and Germany filed written submissions in which they argued against the concept that individual applicants could enforce provisions of the Treaty of Rome in national courts. According to the Netherlands, the question of whether, under Dutch law, Art 12 was directly applicable was one concerning the interpretation of Dutch law, and did not come within the jurisdiction of the Court of Justice. To decide otherwise would "upset the system which the authors of the Treaty intended to establish" and would "put in issue the responsibility of states by means of a procedure which was not designed for this purpose".[9] Belgium, too, considered the question referred to the Court of Justice to be a "typical question of national constitutional law which has nothing to do with the interpretation of an article of the EEC Treaty and is within the exclusive jurisdiction of the Netherlands court, because it can only be answered according to the constitutional principles and jurisprudence of the national law of the Netherlands".[10] Germany did not consider Art 12 to be a directly applicable legal provision that could be invoked by individuals, with the result that in German law, "a legal provision which laid down a customs duty contrary to the provisions of Article 12 would be perfectly valid".[11] Rather, following the traditional approach of international law, Germany regarded Art 12 as imposing on Member States an international obligation, applicable only to the other contracting states, "which must be implemented by national authorities endowed with legislative powers".[12]

---

[8] Piet Eeckhout, *EU External Relations Law* (2nd ed, Oxford University Press 2011) 324.

[9] Case 26/62 *Van Gend en Loos* [1963] ECR 1, 8.

[10] *ibid*, 6.

[11] *ibid*, 8.

[12] *ibid*.

[11–13] By what is now known to have been the slimmest of majorities, the Court of Justice held that Art 12 did in fact produce direct effects and created individual rights which national courts must protect.[13] The Court's reasoning in reaching this ground-breaking conclusion was as follows:

> To ascertain whether the provisions of an international treaty extend so far in their effects [as to have direct application in national law in the sense that nationals of Member States may on the basis of this Article lay claim to rights which the national court must protect] it is necessary to consider the spirit, the general scheme and the wording of those provisions.
>
> The objective of the EEC Treaty, which is to establish a common market, the functioning of which is of direct concern to interested parties in the community, implies that this Treaty is more than an agreement which merely creates mutual obligations between the contracting states. This view is confirmed by the preamble to the Treaty which refers not only to governments but also to peoples. It is also confirmed more specifically by the establishment of institutions endowed with sovereign rights, the exercise of which affects Member States and also their citizens. Furthermore, it must be noted that the nationals of the States brought together in the Community are called upon to cooperate in the functioning of this Community through the intermediary of the European Parliament and the Economic and Social Committee.
>
> In addition the task assigned to the Court of Justice under Article [267 TFEU] the object of which is to secure uniform interpretation of the Treaty by national courts and tribunals, confirms that the States have acknowledged that Community law has an authority which can be invoked by their nationals before those courts and tribunals. The conclusion to be drawn from this is that *the Community constitutes a new legal order of international law for the benefit of which the States have limited their sovereign rights, albeit within limited fields, and the subjects of which comprise not only Member States but also their nationals. Independently of the legislation of Member States, Community law therefore not only imposes obligations on individuals but is also intended to confer upon them rights which become part of their legal heritage. These rights arise not only where they are expressly granted by the Treaty, but also by reason of obligations which the Treaty imposes in a clearly defined manner upon individuals as well as upon the Member States and upon the institutions of the Community.*[14]

[11–14] This passage, and the highlighted portion in particular, is amongst the most famous and momentous of all of the Court's case law. It has been suggested that, implicitly, the judgment conveys the founding myth that the EU "may be seen as a settlement between the peoples of Europe that binds their governments, and not simply as an agreement between the governments of Europe that binds their peoples".[15] It is not surprising, therefore, that the judgment is often cited as an early example of the Court's tendency to adopt a "teleological" or purposive approach to EU law. Despite the absence of any express provision in the Treaty of Rome suggesting that it was to have direct effect within the Member States, the Court was prepared to deduce such a principle from the overall object and purpose of the Treaty. In order to do so, the Court pointed to: (i) preambular language which referred to citizens as well as states; (ii) the ability of individuals to request a national court to seek a preliminary ruling from the Court of Justice; and (iii) the role of the European Parliament and the Economic and

---

13 Morten Rasmussen, "Revolutionizing European law: A History of the *Van Gend en Loos* judgment" (2014) 12 *International Journal of Constitutional Law* 136, 154.

14 *ibid*, 12. Emphasis added.

15 Damian Chalmers, Gareth Davies and Giorgi Monti, *European Union Law* (3rd ed, Cambridge University Press, 2014) 17.

Social Committee even though, at that time, the Parliament was not directly elected but was made up of representatives from national parliaments.

[11–15] When looked at separately, each of these supportive rationales provide a weak basis on which to develop such a fundamental principle, particularly when half of the parties to the Treaty of Rome made clear to the Court that they never intended its articles to be directly effective within their national courts. It is, therefore, the underlying logic of the Court's judgment that is of most importance, rather than the particular elements of the Treaty invoked to bolster this logic. This underlying logic is now referred to as the principle of effectiveness (or *effet utile*). One way of reading the judgment is to view the Court as having adopted a vision of the unique kind of legal community that the founding Member States had created, based on the Treaty as a whole, and of working backwards from there. This vision is set out in the portion of the judgment highlighted above. If this is the objective to be achieved, the principle of effectiveness operates so as to consider the question of direct effect from the lens of how best to create this ambitious new legal community. To permit the Treaty of Rome to have direct effect served the purposes of EU law by providing an effective means of enforceability.

[11–16] Before the Court, it had been argued that the inclusion within the Treaty of Rome of a dedicated enforcement mechanism to be used against Member States for alleged breaches of EU law – to be taken at the Court of Justice by either the Commission (Art 258 TFEU) or another Member State (Art 259 TFEU) – indicated that the Treaty was not intended to be capable of being directly invoked by private litigants before national courts. In the view of the Court, however, this argument was misconceived:

> The fact that [Arts 258 and 259 TFEU] enable the Commission and the Member States to bring before the Court a State which has not fulfilled its obligations does not mean that individuals cannot plead these obligations, should the occasion arise, before a national court ... A restriction of the guarantees against an infringement of Article 12 by Member States to the procedures under Article [258 and 259] would remove all direct legal protection of the individual rights of their nationals. There is the risk that recourse to the procedure under these Articles would be *ineffective* if it were to occur after the implementation of a national decision taken contrary to the provisions of the Treaty.
>
> The vigilance of individuals concerned to protect their rights amounts to an *effective* supervision in addition to the supervision entrusted by Articles [258 and 259] to the diligence of the Commission and of the Member States.[16]

[11–17] The Court's rationale in this passage has been referred to as "dual vigilance", whereby actions brought by individuals before their national courts act as a parallel form of supervision that serves to contribute towards the effectiveness and uniform application of EU law. Indeed, national courts can be seen to act as agents of the EU on a daily basis whenever they apply and interpret EU law in the course of domestic proceedings. By their very nature, the number of enforcement proceedings that may be brought by the Commission against Member States for failing to fulfil their EU law obligations will, as a practical matter, remain relatively small. In comparison, on any given day there will be countless occasions on which national courts throughout the EU will operate as enforcers of EU law at a local level. So, it has been said that:

[16] Case 26/62 *Van Gend en Loos* [1963] ECR 1, 13. Emphasis added.

> all Irish Courts from District to Supreme are trusted partners of the ECJ in the process of enforcement. However, the ECJ can exercise only limited control over the day to day lives of their partners. Ultimately, the extent to which the powerful rhetoric of the ECJ will have meaning is dependent upon whether the national courts themselves take up their role with enthusiastic faithfulness or begrudging acceptance.[17]

[11–18] *Van Gend en Loos* made clear that EU law was different from, and to a degree therefore, independent of, international law. As well as deciding that the subjects of EU law were not just Member States, but also their individual citizens, who were entitled to rely upon the Treaty directly before national courts, the judgment established that it was for the EU legal order itself to determine the effect of EU law within the domestic legal order of its Member States. As Michal Bobek has described:

> By opting for an *objective* test of direct effect, the Court cut the cord with traditional public international law, where the intent of the signatories is relevant for the later interpretation of a treaty. Moreover, by stipulating that EU law is to be directly effective in all Member States' legal systems irrespective of what their individual national constitutions state in relation to the domestic status of international law, the Court *pre-empted* national choices in that regard. By combining both of these points in one stroke, the Court indeed carved out a *new legal order*, independent of both international law as well as national constitutions.[18]

[11–19] The judgment did, however, draw some influence from international law, particularly as regards the criteria that were to be applied in determining whether a Treaty article was sufficiently "self-executing" as to be capable of having direct effect. In holding that Art 12 could be relied upon directly, the Court noted that it: (i) was clear and unconditional; (ii) contained a prohibition on raising customs duties which was not a positive but a negative obligation; and (iii) the obligation was not qualified by any reservation on the part of the Member States that would make its implementation conditional upon a legislative measure being enacted under national law.

[11–20] Through a series of cases the Court of Justice came to significantly relax the criteria for determining whether a Treaty article had direct effect. First, the Court made it clear that direct effect was not confined solely to articles that *prohibited* certain action, but could also apply to positive obligations.[19] Secondly, the Court reconsidered the criterion of no further legislative measure being required. In *Reyners v Belgium*, the Court had to consider whether the freedom of establishment, now found in Art 49 TFEU, had direct effect.[20] There, a Dutch lawyer who had been educated in Belgium was refused admission to the Belgian Bar on the basis that he was not a Belgian national. In 1970, he sought to challenge the refusal in the Belgian courts on the basis that it was contrary to the Treaty right of freedom of establishment. By way of a preliminary reference, the Court of Justice was asked whether the article was capable of having direct effect. The Treaty had provided that freedom of establishment was to be guaranteed by the end of the 12-year transitional period set out in the Treaty of Rome for the creation of the Common Market, which ended in 1969. While the general principle was set out, the Treaty envisaged that further effect would be given to it "within the framework

---

17 Seán O'Reilly, "The Private Enforcement of European Community Law in the Irish Superior Courts" (2009) 31 *Dublin University Law Journal* 324, 325–326.

18 Michal Bobek, "The Effects of EU law in the National Legal Systems" in Catherine Barnard and Steve Peers (eds), *European Union Law* (2nd ed, Oxford University Press, 2017) 143, 147.

19 Case 41/74 *Van Duyn v Home Office* [1974] ECR 1337.

20 Case 2/74 *Reyners v Belgium* [1974] ECR 631.

of the provisions set out below", which provided a legislative basis for the adoption of directives. By 1970, however, the transition period had ended without the intended directives in place. Ireland was among those Member States to argue that, in view of the complexity of the subject, the Treaty article constituted "only the expression of a simple principle, the implementation of which is necessarily subject to a set of complementary provisions, both [EU] and national".[21] It was argued that, as it was not for the courts to exercise a discretionary power reserved to the legislative institutions of the Union and the Member States, the article was incapable of having direct effect.

[11–21] The Court rejected this argument by displaying a willingness to extricate the core general principle – freedom of establishment on an equal basis – from the supplementary provisions of the Treaty of Rome that envisaged further legislative measures. According to the Court:

> The rule on equal treatment with nationals is one of the fundamental legal provisions of the Community.
>
> As a reference to a set of legislative provisions effectively applied by the country of establishment to its own nationals, this rule is, by its essence, capable of being directly invoked by nationals of all the other Member States.
>
> In laying down that freedom of establishment shall be attained at the end of the transitional period, Article [49] thus imposes an obligation to attain a precise result, the fulfilment of which had to be made easier by, but not made dependent on, the implementation of a programme of progressive measures.
>
> The fact that this progression has not been adhered to leaves the obligation itself intact beyond the end of the period provided for its fulfilment.[22]

[11–22] In *Defrenne v Sabena*, the issue was less the need for implementing measures and more to do with the alleged lack of precision and clarity in the relevant Treaty article, which required Member States to ensure the "application of the principle that men and women should receive equal pay for equal work" (now enshrined in Art 157 TFEU).[23] In response to the argument that the concept of a "principle" of equal pay for equal work was so inherently vague as to require implementing measures, the Court was once again willing to extract a core principle that was capable of being applied to straightforward cases of direct discrimination between men and women. In such instances, the Article was held to be capable of having direct effect:

> For the purposes of the implementation of these provisions a distinction must be drawn within the whole area of application of Article [157 TFEU] between, first, direct and overt discrimination which may be identified solely with the aid of the criteria based on equal work and equal pay referred to by the article in question and, secondly, indirect and disguised discrimination which can only be identified by reference to more explicit implementing provisions of a Community or national character.
>
> It is impossible not to recognise that the complete implementation of the aim pursued by Article [157], by means of the elimination of all discrimination, direct or indirect, between men and women workers ... may in certain cases involve the elaboration of criteria whose

21 *ibid*, 648.
22 *ibid*, 651.
23 Case 43/75 *Defrenne v Sabena* [1976] ECR 455.

> implementation necessitates the taking of appropriate measures at Community and national level. ... Among the forms of direct discrimination which may be identified solely by reference to the criteria laid down by Article [157] must be included in particular those which have their origin in legislative provisions or in collective labour agreements and which may be detected on the basis of a purely legal analysis of the situation.
>
> This applies even more in cases where men and women receive unequal pay for equal work carried out in the same establishment or service, whether public or private.
>
> As is shown by the very findings of the judgment making the reference, in such a situation the court is in a position to establish all the facts which enable it to decide whether a woman worker is receiving lower pay than a male worker performing the same tasks.
>
> In such situation, at least, Article [157] is directly applicable and may thus give rise to individual rights which the courts must protect.[24]

[11–23] In summary, therefore, it might be said that while a relatively high threshold for establishing the direct effect of a Treaty provision was originally set in *Van Gend en Loos*, this has subsequently been relaxed and reduced to the key features of whether the provision is sufficiently clear, precise and unconditional.

[11–24] A more recent example of an attempt to invoke the direct effect of a Treaty provision concerned Art 48 TFEU. It provides that the European Parliament and the Council shall make arrangements to secure for migrant workers, for the purpose of acquiring and retaining the right to social security benefits and of calculating the amount of benefits, aggregation of all periods taken into account under the laws of the several countries in which they have worked. In finding that the article was not capable of having direct effect, the Court of Justice observed that:

> Article 48 TFEU does not have the objective of laying down a legal rule which is operative as such. It constitutes a legal basis which allows the European Parliament and Council ... to adopt such measures in the field of social security as are necessary to provide freedom of movement for workers.
>
> That provision thus requires action by the European Union legislature and is for that reason subject in its effects to the adoption of a measure by the institutions of the European Union. It cannot therefore, as such, confer rights on individuals which those individuals might be able to rely on before their national courts.[25]

[11–25] Each Treaty article is dealt with on a case-by-case basis and, given the broad nature in which the criteria are formulated, the Court of Justice enjoys a degree of flexibility in carrying out its assessment. Articles that have been held to have direct effect include those dealing with non-discrimination (Art 18 TFEU), the right of citizens to move and reside freely within the Union (Art 21 TFEU), the free movement of goods (Arts 30, 34, 35 and 110 TFEU), the free movement of workers (Art 45 TFEU), freedom of establishment (Art 49 TFEU), the free movement of services (Art 56 TFEU) and the core competition law rules prohibiting restrictions on competition or abuse of a dominant position (Arts 101 and 102 TFEU). Given that it has the same legal values as the TEU and TFEU, it is clear that the provisions of the Charter of Fundamental Rights are also capable of having vertical direct effect. It has been observed that, given

---

24 *ibid*, 473–474.

25 Case C-379/09 *Maurits Casteels v British Airways* [2011] ECR I-01379, paras 14–15.

the Charter's high level of abstraction, in practice the question is often not whether a provision is capable of direct effect but rather what is the scope of a right's guarantee, and what limitation does it place on a Member State when implementing EU law.[26] Finally, general principles of EU law are also capable of vertical direct effect.

(i) When May Direct Effect Be Relied Upon

[11–26] While the criteria for establishing whether a Treaty article is capable of having direct effect are, by now, relatively settled, an academic debate continues as to the precise nature of direct effect. For some, direct effect means the capacity of a Treaty article (or other instrument of EU law) to be invoked before a national court.[27] For others, however, direct effect is understood in a narrower sense as those Treaty articles that confer rights on individuals which can, in turn, be enforced before a national court.[28] So, while Paul Craig and Gráinne de Búrca suggest that the direct effect of a provision of EU law normally, though not always, means that it is capable of conferring rights on an individual, Robert Schütze is of the view that "direct effect does *not* depend on a European norm granting a subjective right … Direct effect simply means that a norm can be invoked in and applied by a court."[29]

[11–27] In their text, Derrick Wyatt and Alan Dashwood conclude that there now seems to be greater consensus around the proposition that the doctrine of direct effect is capable of applying, in principle, to any provision of Union law that produces independent legal effects, regardless of whether it creates rights.[30] Bruno de Witte has suggested that the reason for this shift from a narrow conception of conferral of rights to a broader notion of provisions that can be invoked was the gradual realisation that, although not having as their object the attribution of a benefit to individuals, many norms of EU law "may very well serve as a standard for reviewing the legality of Member State action when individuals can show a sufficient interest in the outcome of such a review".[31] The result, he suggests, is that the test for direct effect really boils down to a test of justiciability, namely, in any given case, is the norm sufficiently operational in itself to be applied by a court.

(ii) Who May Rely on Direct Effect

[11–28] If a provision of EU law is capable of having direct effect, in that it is sufficiently clear, precise and unconditional and is capable of having its independent

---

26 Michal Bobek, "The Effects of EU Law in the National Legal Systems" in Catherine Barnard and Steve Peers (eds), *European Union Law* (2nd ed, Oxford University Press 2017) 143, 151.

27 For example, Matthias Ruffert, "Rights and Remedies in European Community Law: A Comparative View" (1997) 34 *Common Market Law Review* 307; Michael Dougan, "When Worlds Collide! Competing Visions of the Relationship Between Direct Effect and Supremacy" (2007) 44 *Common Market Law Review* 931.

28 For example, Koen Lenaerts and Tim Corthaut, "Of Birds and Hedges: The Role of Primacy in Invoking Norms of EU Law" (2006) 31 *European Law Review* 287.

29 Paul Craig and Gráinne de Búrca, *EU Law* (6th ed, Oxford University Press, 2015) 222; Robert Schütze, *European Union Law* (Cambridge University Press, 2015) 86–87.

30 Alan Dashwood, Michael Dougan, Barry Rodger, Eleanor Spaventa and Derrick Wyatt, *Wyatt and Dashwood's European Union Law* (6th ed, Hart, 2011) 250.

31 Bruno de Witte, "Direct Effect, Supremacy, and the Nature of the Legal Order" in Paul Craig and Gráinne de Búrca (eds), *The Evolution of EU Law* (2nd ed, Oxford University Press, 2011) 323, 330.

legal effects invoked, a second question that arises is whether the particular individual seeking to rely on the direct effect is entitled to do so. For adherents of a narrow view of direct effect limited to the conferral of rights, it might logically follow that only those on whom rights are conferred by a provision of EU law are in a position to rely on its direct effect. The more widely accepted view, however, is that direct effect can arise in relation to any provision of EU law that produces independent legal effects. Once this is accepted, the test becomes not whether the applicant has benefitted from a conferral of rights, but whether the applicant falls within the intended scope of the provision more generally. Depending on the nature of the provision in question, this might be expressly set out, such as where the personal scope of a regulation or a directive is defined within the instrument itself, or it may require a broader contextual analysis looking at the object and purpose of the provision and the circumstances of the applicant. In addition, the Court of Justice is likely to have regard to the importance of ensuring the effective enforcement of EU law, which may often militate in favour of facilitating domestic reliance on the provision. More particularly, the principle of effectiveness tends to lead the Court to permit reliance on direct effect by a person who is not the primary beneficiary of a measure but who nevertheless: (i) has a sufficiently close relationship with the primary beneficiary or (ii) is acting as a private enforcer of EU regulatory obligations.

[11–29] An example of a sufficiently close relationship is where employers have successfully relied upon the Treaty guarantee of the free movement of workers in order to maximise their ability to hire the employee of their choosing.[32] For instance, a good example of a private enforcer successfully relying on direct effect arose in *Muñoz*, which concerned a company's marketing of grapes in the UK in a manner that was not in compliance with an EU regulation.[33] Muñoz was a competitor that also imported grapes into the UK and made several complaints to the UK inspectorate. When the inspectorate failed to take any action, Muñoz instituted proceedings before the High Court seeking to have its competitor's failure to comply with the regulation brought to an end. While the High Court accepted that grapes were being marketed in breach of the regulation, it did not regard the regulation as giving Muñoz a right to bring a private action of this kind. In reply to a preliminary reference from the Court of Appeal, the Court of Justice upheld the ability of a private enforcer to rely directly on the regulation, reasoning as follows:

> Muñoz submits that it is both necessary and sufficient for a [EU] provision to be relied on in relations between individuals that the obligation it sets out be clear and unconditional. That obligation may be imposed for the benefit of individuals in general, without there being any need to prove that the intent of the [Union] legislature was to benefit any particular class of the public or to confer subjective rights.
>
> The Commission considers that the question whether the relevant provisions confer the right on an individual to bring an action to compel another individual to comply with the obligations imposed on him by the [EU] legislation must be determined in the light of the regulations in question and of the general principles of the common agricultural policy, of which they form part.
>
> … owing to their very nature and their place in the system of sources of [EU] law,

[32] See, for example, Case C-350/96 *Clean Car Autoservice* [1998] ECR I-2521, 2545.

[33] Case C-253/00 *Muñoz* [2002] ECR I-7289. See Andrea Biondi, "Comment, Case C-253/00" (2003) 40 *Common Market Law Review* 1241.

regulations operate to confer rights on individuals which the national courts have a duty to protect.

> The national courts, whose task it is to apply the provisions of [EU] law in areas within their jurisdiction, must ensure that they take full effect.
>
> … [T]he purpose of applying common quality standards is to keep products of unsatisfactory quality off the market, to guide production to meet consumers' requirements, and to facilitate trade relations based on fair competition. That objective is confirmed by the third recital … which states that the classification of goods using common obligatory standards seeks, first, to establish a reference framework that encourages fair trading and market transparency and, second, to eliminate products of unsatisfactory quality from the market. The 20th recital … states that the rules of the common market organisation should be complied with by all operators to whom they apply, since otherwise their impact will be distorted.
>
> Accordingly, the full effectiveness of the rules on quality standards and, in particular, the practical effect of the obligation laid down … imply that it must be possible to enforce that obligation by means of civil proceedings instituted by a trader against a competitor.
>
> The possibility of bringing such proceedings strengthens the practical working of the [EU] rules on quality standards. As a supplement to the action of the authorities designated by the Member States to make the checks required by those rules it helps to discourage practices, often difficult to detect, which distort competition. In that context actions brought before the national courts by competing operators are particularly suited to contributing substantially to ensuring fair trading and transparency of markets in the [Union].[34]

C. Horizontal Direct Effect

[11–30] As has been noted above, the 1976 case of *Defrenne v Sabena* saw the Court of Justice take a more relaxed approach to the criteria for establishing the direct effect of a Treaty article. There, the applicant successfully sought to rely on what is now Art 157 TFEU, which enshrines the principle that men and women should receive equal pay for equal work.[35] Another important aspect of that case was the fact that the action in which the applicant was seeking to rely directly on the Treaty was against her employer, the Belgian airline Sabena, and not a Member State, as had been the case in *Van Gend en Loos*. Ireland supported Belgium and submitted to the Court that Art 157 was fundamentally different to the Treaty articles that had previously been held to have direct effect, given that it related to contractual employment relationships between private parties. Furthermore, the possibility of direct reliance upon Art 157 in a dispute between an employee and employer had been rejected by the authors of the Treaty of Rome, and Ireland's Treaty of Accession, as reflected in the fact that the article expressly referred to the obligation on *Member States* to ensure that the principle was fulfilled.

[11–31] Emphasising the need to ensure the effectiveness of Art 157 in practice, the Court rejected the argument made by Ireland and others that the article was capable of only having vertical direct effect. For the first time, the Court elaborated on the concept of horizontal direct effect. It rationalised this development by observing that the obligation placed upon Member States to give effect to EU law included an obligation

---

[34] *ibid*, 7320–7321.

[35] Case 43/75 *Defrenne v Sabena* [1976] ECR 455.

on their national courts whenever they were adjudicating cases that involved a claim for equal pay. According to the Court:

> [T]he fact that certain provisions of the Treaty are formally addressed to the Member States does not prevent rights from being conferred at the same time on any individual who has an interest in the performance of the duties thus laid down.
>
> The very wording of Article [157] shows that it imposes on States a duty to bring about a specific result to be mandatorily achieved within a fixed period.
>
> The effectiveness of this provision cannot be affected by the fact that the duty imposed by the Treaty has not been discharged by certain Member States and that the joint institutions have not reacted sufficiently energetically against this failure to act.
>
> To accept the contrary view would be to risk raising the violation of the right to the status of a principle of interpretation, a position the adoption of which would not be consistent with the task assigned to the Court by … the Treaty.
>
> Finally, in its reference to 'Member States', Article [157] is alluding to those States in the exercise of all those of their functions which may usefully contribute to the implementation of the principle of equal pay.
>
> Thus, contrary to the statements made in the course of the proceedings this provision is far from merely referring the matter to the powers of the national legislative authorities.
>
> Therefore, the reference to 'Member States' in Article [157] cannot be interpreted as excluding the intervention of the courts in direct application of the Treaty.
>
> Furthermore it is not possible to sustain any objection that the application by national courts of the principle of equal pay would amount to modifying independent agreements concluded privately or in the sphere of industrial relations such as individual contracts and collective labour agreements.
>
> In fact, since Article [157] is mandatory in nature, the prohibition on discrimination between men and women applies not only to the action of public authorities, but also extends to all agreements which are intended to regulate paid labour collectively, as well as to contracts between individuals.
>
> The reply … must therefore be that the principle of equal pay contained in Article [157] may be relied upon before the national courts and that these courts have a duty to ensure the protection of the rights which this provision vests in individuals, in particular as regards those types of discrimination arising directly from legislative provisions or collective labour agreements, as well as in cases in which men and women receive unequal pay for equal work which is carried out in the same establishment or service, whether private or public.[36]

[11–32] The case of *Defrenne* clearly established that Treaty articles are capable of having horizontal direct effect. Since then, the Court of Justice has confirmed that the Treaty guarantees on the free movement of workers, services and of establishment are among those that can have horizontal direct effect, as are the Treaty articles on competition law. So, for example, in *Angonese* a job applicant was held to be entitled to rely on Art 45 TFEU, on the free movement of workers, in order to challenge an Italian bank's insistence that he prove his language ability by obtaining a diploma from a particular Italian province:

[36] *ibid*, 475–476.

> The Court has held that the abolition, as between Member States, of obstacles to freedom of movement for persons would be compromised if the abolition of State barriers could be neutralised by obstacles resulting from the exercise of their legal autonomy by associations or organisations not governed by public law.
>
> Since working conditions in the different Member States are governed sometimes by provisions laid down by law or regulation and sometimes by agreements and other acts concluded or adopted by private persons, limiting application of the prohibition of discrimination based on nationality to acts of a public authority risks creating inequality in its application.
>
> The Court has also ruled that the fact that certain provisions of the Treaty are formally addressed to the Member States does not prevent rights from being conferred at the same time on any individual who has an interest in compliance with the obligations thus laid down. The Court accordingly held, in relation to a provision of the Treaty which was mandatory in nature, that the prohibition of discrimination applied equally to all agreements intended to regulate paid labour collectively, as well as to contracts between individuals. Such considerations must, a fortiori, be applicable to Article [45] of the Treaty, which lays down a fundamental freedom and which constitutes a specific application of the general prohibition of discrimination contained in Article [18 TFEU]. …
>
> Consequently, the prohibition of discrimination on grounds of nationality laid down in Article 48 of the Treaty must be regarded as applying to private persons as well.[37]

[11–33] Until the case of *Fra.bo* in 2012, it had been thought that Treaty provisions on the free movement of goods were not capable of having horizontal direct effect.[38] There, the Court held that Art 34 TFEU must be considered to apply to the standardisation and certification activities of a *private-law body*, where the national legislation considers the products certified by that body to be compliant with national law, which in turn has the effect of restricting the marketing of products which are not certified by that body. This clearly has echoes of the collective pay agreements referred to in *Defrenne*, which could impair the effectiveness of the principle of equal pay were they to be excluded from the article's direct effect. The decision is significant in that it affords Art 34 on the free movement of goods a limited degree of horizontal direct effect for the first time.

(i) General Principles of EU Law

[11–34] Although it is clear that both general principles of EU law and the Charter of Fundamental Rights are capable of having vertical direct effect, the extent to which

---

[37] Case C-281/98 *Angonese* [2000] ECR I-4139, 4172-4173. See Case 36/74 *Walrave and Koch v Union Cycliste Internationale* [1974] ECR 1405; Case C-415/93 *Union Royale Belge des Sociétés de Football Association v Bosman* [1995] ECR I-4921; Case C-453/99 *Courage Ltd v Crehan* [2001] ECR I-6927; Case C-438/05 *International Transport Workers' Federation v Viking Line* [2007] ECR I-10779; Pedro Caro de Sousa, "Horizontal Expressions of Vertical Desires: Horizontal Effect and the Scope of the EU Fundamental Freedoms" (2013) 2 *Cambridge Journal of International and Comparative Law* 479.

[38] Case C-171/11 *Fra.bo v DVGW* EU:C:2012:453, 12 July 2013, para 32. See Herman van Harten and Thomas Nauta, "Towards Horizontal Direct Effect for the Free Movement of Goods? Comment on *Fra.bo*" (2013) 38 *European Law Review* 677; Christoph Krenn, "A Missing Piece in the Horizontal Effect 'Jigsaw': Horizontal Direct Effect and the Free Movement of Goods" (2012) 49 *Common Market Law Review* 177; Harm Schepel, "Constitutionalising the Market, Marketising the Constitution, and To Tell the Difference: On the Horizontal Application of the Free Movement Provisions in EU Law" (2012) 18 *European Law Journal* 177.

they can have horizontal direct effect is considerably more complex. Regarding general principles of EU law, in *Mangold* the Court established that, in a dispute between private parties involving such a principle (in that case, non-discrimination on the grounds of age) it is the responsibility of a national court to provide the "legal protection which individuals derive from the rules of [EU] law and to ensure that those rules are fully effective, setting aside any provision of national law which may conflict with that law".[39] In *Kücükdeveci*, the Court clarified that this obligation on a national court would only arise when the dispute before it concerned a matter that was within the scope of EU law.[40] Accordingly, a general principle of EU law capable of direct effect may be relied upon in a private dispute that falls within the scope of EU law.

[11–35] This approach was followed in the 2016 case of *Dansk Industri (on behalf of Ajos)*.[41] There, the Danish Supreme Court had requested a preliminary ruling concerning a national law under which an employer was not obliged to give severance pay if an employee was entitled to receive an old age pension. In legal proceedings involving two private parties it was claimed that this law was contrary to the general principle of EU law prohibiting discrimination on the grounds of age, as confirmed by the Court of Justice in *Mangold* and *Kücükdeveci*. In making the reference, the Danish Supreme Court expressed its concern that to give horizontal direct effect to the general principle would be contrary to the countervailing principles of legal certainty and the protection of legitimate expectations, suggesting that it would render it impossible for a private party to predict when an unwritten general principle might set aside a national law. The Supreme Court also indicated that the doctrine of *contra legem* would prevent it from giving a harmonious interpretation to the Danish law in line with the general principle, since the national courts had consistently interpreted the relevant law as precluding an entitlement to severance pay. Accordingly, it asked whether it would be consistent with EU law to weigh the general principle of non-discrimination on grounds of age, and the issue of its direct effect, against the principles of legal certainty and the protection of legitimate expectations and to conclude on that basis that the principle of legal certainty must take precedence, such that the employer is, in accordance with national law, relieved of its obligation to pay the severance pay.

[11–36] Sitting as a Grand Chamber, the response of the Court of Justice was to indicate that, in line with its judgments in *Mangold* and *Kücükdeveci*, it was not permissible to preclude an entitlement to severance pay on the basis that an employee also had a right to claim an old age pension.[42] The Danish court had two options by which to achieve this: either interpret Danish law consistently with the general principle or, if that was not considered possible, set aside the conflicting national law. As will be seen in Chapter 13 when examining the doctrine of the supremacy of EU law, the Danish Supreme Court took the unprecedented step of indicating its inability to follow

[39] Case C-144/04 *Mangold* [2005] ECR I-9981, 10040–10041.

[40] Case C-555/07 *Kücükdeveci* [2010] ECR I-365. See Case C-147/08 *Römer* [2011] ECR I-3591; Elise Muir, "Of Ages in – and Edges of – EU Law" (2011) 48 *Common Market Law Review* 39; Laurent Pech, "Between Judicial Minimalism and Avoidance: The Court of Justice's Side-Stepping of Fundamental Constitutional Issues in *Römer* and *Dominquez*" (2012) 49 *Common Market Law Review* 1841.

[41] Case C-441/14 *Dansk Industri (on behalf of Ajos)* EU:C:2016:278, 19 April 2016.

[42] *ibid.*

the Grand Chamber's ruling, finding that Danish law did not envisage general principles of EU law having horizontal direct effect.[43]

[11–37] The 2018 case of *Egenberger*, discussed below in the context of the Charter of Fundamental Rights, also concerned the general principles of EU law.[44] The Court's judgment in that case has been described as coming in the line of *Mangold, Kücükdeveci* and *Dansk Industri (Ajos)*, "reiterating the basic approach of these cases and demonstrating that the reasoning of the ECJ with regard to the general principle of equal treatment is now firmly established".[45] Nevertheless, as the response of the Danish Supreme Court indicates, a certain controversy remains that the inherent vagueness of general principles of EU law may mean that conferring them with horizontal direct effect will serve to undermine legal certainty, in which there is a competing public interest.

[11–38] Both of the two central questions in determining horizontal direct effect – whether a particular general principle of EU law is capable of direct effect and, if so, whether the dispute falls within the scope of EU law – entail a good deal of uncertainty. As a result, unless the matter has already been decided by the Court of Justice, it may be difficult to predict in advance whether a general principle of EU law has horizontal direct effect. A recent example of this arose in the judgment of the UK Supreme Court in *Walker v Innospec Ltd*.[46] There, Mr Walker had entered into a civil partnership with his male partner and asked his employer to confirm that, in the event of his death, his spouse's pension would be paid to his partner on the same basis as if he had a female spouse. When introducing civil partnerships, the UK had amended its Equality Act 2010 so as to provide that it was *not* a contravention of the Act to prevent a person from having access to a benefit which accrued, or was payable in respect of periods of service, before the date of commencement of the Civil Partnership Act. The UK Supreme Court accepted his argument that non-discrimination on grounds of sexual orientation was a general principle of EU law. As a result, to deny a spouse's pension calculated on the basis of all the years of Mr Walker's service would be incompatible with the Equal Treatment Directive and so, on the basis of the principles articulated in *Kücükdeveci*, the relevant provision of the Equality Act had to be disapplied.

---

[43] See ch 13, paras [13–34] to [13–36]. See Helle Krunke and Sune Klinge, "The Danish *Ajos* Case: The Missing Case from *Maastricht* and *Lisbon*" (2018) 3 *European Papers* 157; Rass Holdgaard, Daniella Elkan and Gustav Krohn Schaldemose, "From Cooperation to Collision: The ECJ's *Ajos* Ruling and the Danish Supreme Court's Refusal to Comply" (2018) 55 *Common Market Law Review* 17; Mikael Rask Madsen, Henrik Palmer Olsen and Urška Šadl, "Competing Supremacies and Clashing Institutional Rationalities: The Danish Supreme Court's Decision in the *Ajos* Case and the National Limits of Judicial Cooperation" (2017) 23 *European Law Journal* 140; Urška Šadl and Sabine Mair, "Mutual Disempowerment: Case C-441/14 *Dansk Industri, Acting on Behalf of Ajos A/S v Estate of Karsten Eigil Rasmussen* and Case no. 15/2014 *Dansk Industri (DI) Acting for Ajos A/S v The Estate Left by A*" (2017) 13 *European Constitutional Law Review* 347; Sim Haket, "The Danish Supreme Court's *Ajos* Judgment (Dansk Industri): Rejecting a Consistent Interpretation and Challenging the Effect of a General Principle of EU Law in the Danish Legal Order" (2017) 10 *Review of European Administrative Law* 135.

[44] Case C-414/16 *Egenberger* EU:C:2018:257, 17 April 2018.

[45] Luísa Lourenço, "Religion, Discrimination and the EU General Principles' Gospel: *Egenberger*" (2019) 56 *Common Market Law Review* 193, 200.

[46] *Walker v Innospec Ltd* [2017] UKSC 47, 12 July 2017.

(ii) Charter of Fundamental Rights

[11–39] Until very recently, the position as regards the horizontal direct effect of the Charter of Fundamental Rights was even more uncertain. A series of judgments in 2018 has, however, brought some welcome clarity. In the 2014 case of *Association de Médiation Sociale (AMS)*, for example, the Court of Justice chose not to express a view on whether Art 27 of the Charter, concerning the right of workers to information and consultation with an employer, was capable of having horizontal direct effect as was being claimed. As Art 27 provided that the right was to be "provided for by European Union law and national law and practices", the Court concluded that it was not sufficiently clear, precise and unconditional to be capable of having any direct effect.[47]

[11–40] The Court remained silent on the important question of horizontal direct effect notwithstanding that it had been addressed in some detail by Advocate General Cruz Villalón. In his opinion he had, first, rejected the argument that, because the Charter is stated in Art 51 to be addressed to the Union institutions and to the Member States, it is not addressed to individuals and therefore cannot have horizontal direct effect. According to the Advocate General, there was nothing in the wording of Art 51 to suggest that there was any intention to "address the very complex issue of the effectiveness of fundamental rights in relations between individuals".[48] Instead, in addressing the effect of rights on individuals, an "interpreter of the Charter is faced with the same, often uncertain, prospect that an interpreter of the Constitutions of the Member States generally faces".[49]

[11–41] Although he proceeded to find that Art 27 enshrined a "principle" rather than a "right", and so was judicially cognisable only in the interpretation of other Union acts, the Advocate General concluded that the article was, in principle, capable of horizontal direct effect, reasoning as follows:

> Coming now to the crux of the matter, and in view of certain opinions which are expressed in this regard, it might seem that the idea of horizontal effect was a concept unknown to European Union law, which had to be addressed for the first time as a result of the incorporation of the Charter into European Union primary law. However, the idea that the fundamental freedoms of movement or particular principles such as non-discrimination on grounds of sex are relevant in private legal relations is an old and well-established one. That being so, the idea that the fundamental rights of the Charter other than the fundamental freedoms or the principle of equality could have a system which is separate and, so to speak, of lower status in the Charter as a whole seems highly problematic.
>
> In short, … since the horizontal effect of fundamental rights is not unknown to European Union law, it would be paradoxical if the incorporation of the Charter into primary law actually changed that state of affairs for the worse.

---

47 Case C-176/12 *Association de Médiation Sociale (AMS)* EU:C:2014:2, 15 January 2014. Eleni Frantziou, "The Horizontal Effect of the Charter of Fundamental Rights of the EU: Rediscovering the Reasons for Horizontality" (2015) 21 *European Law Journal* 657; Cian C Murphy, "Using the EU Charter of Fundamental Rights Against Private Parties after *Association de Médiation Sociale*" (2014) *European Human Rights Law Review* 170; Dorota Leczykiewicz, "Horizontal Application of the Charter of Fundamental Rights" (2013) 38 *European Law Review* 479; Nicole Lazzerini, "(Some of) the Fundamental Rights Granted by the Charter may be a Source of Obligations for Private Parties: AMS" (2014) 51 *Common Market Law Review* 907.

48 Case C-176/12 *Association de Médiation Sociale (AMS)* EU:C:2013:491, 18 July 2013, para 31.

49 *ibid*, para 33.

> … For practical purposes, the effectiveness of fundamental rights between individuals becomes relevant when the legal system provides for a specific guarantee of fundamental rights, often a judicial one. In such cases, the inherent nature of fundamental rights is imposed or superimposed on private-law relations by the State body with the most authority to give rulings on fundamental rights. From that perspective, the concept of horizontal effect results in a notable increase in the involvement of judicial interpreters of fundamental rights in the framework of relations governed by private law. The most specific instrument through which that mechanism becomes effective is that of ad hoc procedures for the individual protection of fundamental rights, where they exist.
>
> Finally, the horizontal effect of fundamental rights operates very differently for each right or, more simply, for the various groups of rights. There are rights which, by their very structure, are not addressed to individuals, just as there are rights whose relevance in relationships governed by private law it would be inconceivable to deny …
>
> … It is true that the public authorities (the European Union and the Member States) will be the first to be called upon to 'guarantee' workers the enjoyment of [the right to information and consultation], through adopting and implementing the relevant provisions. However, in complying with the provisions of the public authority, undertakings themselves, and for such purposes the same is true whether they are public or private, must also ensure, on a day-to-day basis, that workers are guaranteed information and consultation at the appropriate levels.
>
> The foregoing leads me to the intermediate conclusion … that Article 27 may be relied on in a dispute between individuals. In other words, that possibility cannot be denied on the basis of the argument that the Charter, as a consequence of the provisions of Article 51(1), has no relevance in relations governed by private law.[50]

[11–42] While Advocate General Cruz Villalón had set out one cogent approach to the horizontal direct effect of the Charter, since it had decided the case on the basis that the provision was, in any event, insufficiently clear, precise and unconditional, it remained to be seen whether such an approach would ultimately find favour with the Court.

[11–43] The first of a series of important judgments delivered in 2018 was that of *Egenberger*.[51] There, the Court of Justice reaffirmed that, as a general principle of EU law that was also enshrined in Art 21 of the Charter, the prohibition of discrimination on the grounds of religion was "sufficient in itself to confer on individuals a right which they may rely on as such in disputes between them in a field covered by EU law".[52] Likewise, both Art 21 and Art 47 of the Charter – on the right to effective judicial protection – were sufficient in themselves and did not need to be made more specific by provisions of EU or national law in order to confer on individuals a right which they may rely on as such.[53]

[11–44] The facts of the case concerned Ms Egenberger, who had applied for a job with a private law, religious body. She attributed the failure of her application to the fact that membership of a church was a condition for the position. In reply to a preliminary reference, the Court of Justice confirmed that, where a national court is hearing a dispute between two individuals and it is not possible for it to interpret the applicable national

50 *ibid*, paras 34–41.
51 Case C-414/16 *Egenberger* EU:C:2018:257, 17 April 2018.
52 *ibid*, para 71.
53 *ibid*, para 78.

law in conformity with the Equal Treatment Directive, the national court was obliged to ensure within its jurisdiction the judicial protection deriving for individuals from Arts 21 and 47 of the Charter and to guarantee the full effectiveness of those articles by disapplying if need be any contrary provision of national law. Perhaps prompted, in part, by criticisms of its *Mangold* judgment by the German Constitutional Court, the Court of Justice took the opportunity to outline the degree of flexibility available to a national court in carrying out such an assessment:

> a court may, in a dispute between individuals, be called on to balance competing fundamental rights which the parties to the dispute derive from the provisions of the [TFEU] or the Charter, and may even be obliged, in the review that it must carry out, to make sure that the principle of proportionality is complied with. Such an obligation to strike a balance between the various interests involved has no effect on the possibility of relying on the rights in question in such a dispute.
>
> Further, where the national court is called on to ensure that Articles 21 and 47 of the Charter are observed, while possibly balancing the various interests involved, such as respect for the status of churches as laid down in Article 17 TFEU, it will have to take into consideration the balance struck between those interests by the EU legislature in [the Equal Treatment Directive], in order to determine the obligations deriving from the Charter in circumstances such as those at issue in the main proceedings.[54]

[11–45] Initial responses to the judgment in *Egenberger* have seen it commended for engaging in a "more discursive form of constitutional reasoning" than the Court's earlier case law in this area, with the suggestion that it offers a "methodology for assessing the application of fundamental rights in disputes between private parties that is capable of reconciling the effectiveness of EU law with national constitutional structures".[55] Ronan McCrea has described the approach of the Court of Justice as having given a "notably constitutionalized interpretation" of the Equal Treatment Directive, by relying on the Charter and general principles of EU law to read a proportionality test into a provision of the Equal Treatment Directive that did not appear in the text.[56] He suggests that the Court has insisted on proportionality as the "framework within which the 'fair balancing' of the autonomy rights of religious employers and equal treatment rights of employees must take place". Regarding the fact that the dispute at issue was as between two private parties, he observes that:

> The Court's insistence that EU non-discrimination law merely codifies a self-executing (and horizontally directly effective) constitutional general principle of non-discrimination law represents a continuation of the controversial line of cases beginning in *Mangold* which has attracted significant criticism, including from national courts given the potential for legal uncertainty that such an approach involves. Here, the Court of Justice has made it clear that the EU's constitutional commitment to proportionality means that religious bodies may only impose discriminatory conditions on employees when it is proportionate to do so and national courts must be empowered to ensure religious employers do not exercise their right to discriminate in a disproportionate way.[57]

---

54 *ibid*, paras 80–81.

55 Eleni Frantziou, "*Mangold* Recast? The ECJ's Flirtation with Drittwirkung in *Egenberger*", *European Law Blog*, 24 April 2018, available at <www.europeanlawblog.eu>. See Luísa Lourenço, "Religion, Discrimination and the EU General Principles' Gospel: *Egenberger*" (2019) 56 *Common Market Law Review* 193.

56 Ronan McCrea, "Salvation Outside the Church? The ECJ Rules on Religious Discrimination in Employment", *EU Law Analysis*, 18 April 2018, available at <www.eulawanalysis.blogspot.com>.

57 *ibid.*

[11–46] It will be recalled from above that the Charter right at issue in *AMS* was that of a worker's right to information and consultation within an undertaking, as guaranteed by Art 27 of the Charter. It provides that "workers or their representatives must, at the appropriate levels, be guaranteed information and consultation in good time *in the cases and under the conditions provided for by Union law and national laws and practices*". Partly due to the highlighted wording, the Court of Justice concluded that this provision was insufficiently clear, precise and unconditional to be capable of direct effect.

[11–47] In three judgments delivered on the same day in November 2018, a German law that appeared to end, upon an employee's termination of employment, the right to be paid in lieu for any unused annual leave, was considered by the Grand Chamber in light of Art 31(2) of the Charter. It provides that every worker shall have the right, inter alia, to an annual period of paid leave.[58] This entitlement is subject to more detailed rules in the Working Time Directive.[59] Unlike the right to information and consultation in Art 27, the right to annual paid leave is expressed in Art 31(2) in unqualified terms. As the Working Time Directive did not have horizontal direct effect, and so could not be relied upon in a dispute between an employee and a private employer over unpaid pay-in-lieu, in two of the cases the question arose as to whether, in proceedings brought against private employers in the German courts, reliance could be placed instead on Art 31(2) of the Charter. Building on the Court's decision in *Egenberger*, in *Max Planck* and in *Bauer* the Grand Chamber ruled that if the German law was not capable of being interpreted in a manner that was compatible with Art 31(2), the national court was obliged to disapply it in order to give full effect to the Charter right.[60] In explaining how this obligation arose in cases involving only private parties, the Grand Chamber's judgment in *Max Planck* reasoned as follows:

> By providing, in mandatory terms, that 'every worker' has 'the right' 'to an annual period of paid leave' without referring in particular in that regard — like, for example, Article 27 of the Charter which led to the judgment [in *AMS*] — to the 'cases' and 'conditions provided for by Union law and national laws and practices', Article 31(2) of the Charter, reflects the essential principle of EU social law from which there may be derogations only in compliance with the strict conditions laid down in Article 52(1) of the Charter and, in particular, the fundamental right to paid annual leave.
>
> The right to a period of paid annual leave, affirmed for every worker by Article 31(2) of the Charter, is thus, as regards its very existence, both mandatory and unconditional in nature, the unconditional nature not needing to be given concrete expression by the provisions of EU or national law, which are only required to specify the exact duration of annual leave and, where appropriate, certain conditions for the exercise of that right. It follows that that provision is sufficient in itself to confer on workers a right that they may actually rely on in disputes between them and their employer in a field covered by EU law and therefore falling within the scope of the Charter.
>
> Article 31(2) of the Charter therefore entails … that the national court must disapply national legislation negating the principle … that a worker cannot be deprived of an acquired right to paid annual leave at the end of the leave year and/or of a carry-over

---

58 Case C-684/16 *Max Planck* EU:C:2018:874, 6 November 2018; Joined Cases C-569/16 and C-570/16 *Bauer* EU:C:2018:871, 6 November 2018 and Case C-619/16 *Kreuziger* EU:C:2018:872, 6 November 2018. See also Case C-609/17 *TSN* [2018] OJ C13/8 (ongoing).

59 Directive 2003/88/EC of the European Parliament and of the Council of 4 November 2003 concerning certain aspects of the organisation of working time [2003] OJ L299/9.

60 Case C-684/16 *Max Planck* EU:C:2018:874, 6 November 2018.

period fixed by national law when the worker has been unable to take his leave, or correspondingly, of the entitlement to the allowance in lieu thereof upon termination of the employment relationship, as a right which is consubstantial with the right to 'paid' annual leave. Under that provision, nor may employers rely on that national legislation in order to avoid payment of the allowance in lieu which they are required to pay pursuant to the fundamental right guaranteed by that provision.

With respect to the effect of Article 31(2) of the Charter on an employer who is a private individual, it should be noted that, although Article 51(1) of the Charter states that the provisions thereof are addressed to the institutions, bodies, offices and agencies of the European Union with due regard for the principle of subsidiarity and to the Member States only when they are implementing EU law, Article 51(1) does not, however, address the question whether those individuals may, where appropriate, be directly required to comply with certain provisions of the Charter and cannot, accordingly, be interpreted as meaning that it would systematically preclude such a possibility.

First of all, ... the fact that certain provisions of primary law are addressed principally to the Member States does not preclude their application to relations between individuals (see, to that effect, [*Egenberger*]).

Next, the Court has, in particular, already held that the prohibition laid down in Article 21(1) of the Charter is sufficient in itself to confer on individuals a right which they may rely on as such in a dispute with another individual ([*Egenberger*]), without, therefore, Article 51(1) of the Charter precluding it.

Finally, as regards, more specifically, Article 31(2) of the Charter, it must be noted that the right of every worker to paid annual leave entails, by its very nature, a corresponding obligation on the employer, which is to grant such periods of paid leave or an allowance in lieu of paid annual leave not taken upon termination of the employment relationship.

In the event that it is impossible to interpret the national legislation at issue in the main proceedings in a manner consistent with Article 31(2) of the Charter, it will therefore be for the referring court ... to ensure within its jurisdiction the judicial protection for individuals flowing from that provision and to guarantee the full effectiveness thereof by disapplying if need be that national legislation.[61]

[11–48] It has been said that the significance of these recent cases lies in the Court's general instruction that the Charter does not preclude horizontal direct effect. While the Court noted that Art 51(1) did not address the question of whether individuals may be directly required to comply with the Charter, "it nevertheless rejected that Article 51(1) systematically precluded such a possibility, thus re-enforcing the increasing recognition of a horizontal direct effect of certain Charter provisions".[62]

[11–49] In addition to cases where an individual seeks to directly rely on a Charter right, the Charter may also impact the outcome of disputes between private parties where it is relied upon by one party to question the validity of an EU measure, or a national measure that is being applied within the scope of EU law. An example of this can be seen in the decision of the UK Supreme Court in *Benkharbouche*.[63] There, Ms

---

[61] *ibid*, paras 73–80.

[62] Emilija Leinarte, "EU Fundamental Rights and their Enforcement" (2019) 78 *Cambridge Law Journal* 31, 33-34.

[63] *Benkharbouche v Secretary of State for Foreign and Commonwealth Affairs* [2017] UKSC 62, 18 October 2017, paras 78–79. See also *Google Inc v Vidal-Hall* [2015] EWCA Civ 311; [2015] 3 WLR 409, where the UK Court of Appeal relied on Arts 7 (right to private and family life) and 8

Benkharbouche brought EU law-based claims for discrimination, harassment and breach of Working Time Regulations against her employer, the Embassy of Sudan. The Embassy sought to rely on provisions of the UK's State Immunity Act that would have rendered it immune to the claims. In response, it was argued that these provisions were contrary to Art 47 of the Charter which guarantees the right to an effective remedy to everyone who has suffered a breach of their EU law rights. As the Supreme Court accepted this argument, it was required to disapply the provisions of the State Immunity Act in the determination of her employment claims, depriving the Embassy of the immunity it otherwise had as a matter of UK law.

D. Direct Effect in Irish Law

[11–50] It will be recalled from Chapter 1 that, in order to provide for Ireland's accession to the EEC, the ECSC and Euratom, the third amendment to the Constitution inserted Art 29.4.3°, which contained an express permission that the State "may become" a member of these three Communities. As we have seen, the limits of this enabling provision were the subject of important Supreme Court decisions in *Crotty* and *Pringle.* In addition, Art 29.4.3° protected from constitutional challenge any acts introduced by the State that were "necessitated by the obligations" that arose from Ireland being a member of the EEC, the ECSC and Euratom. As a result, the only constitutional ground upon which such a measure could be challenged was on the basis that it was not, in fact, necessitated by membership of the Communities. This question will be considered further in Chapter 12.

[11–51] The third and final element of Art 29.4.3° provided that no provision of the Constitution "prevents laws enacted, acts done or measures adopted by the Communities, or institutions thereof, from having the force of law in the State". This aspect was necessary given that Art 29.6 establishes the dualist nature of Ireland's legal system, unequivocally stating that "No international agreement shall be part of the domestic law of the State save as may be determined by the Oireachtas". By the time of Ireland's accession in 1973, *Van Gend en Loos* had made clear that: (i) EEC law was a new legal order of international law; (ii) the subjects of EEC law were not only the Member States, but also their citizens; (iii) independently of the legislation of Member States, EEC law conferred rights upon individuals which became part of their legal heritage; and (iv) to this end, provisions of the Rome Treaty that were sufficiently clear, precise and unconditional were capable of being relied upon directly by individuals before their national courts. Article 29.4.3° now allowed for an exception to be made to Art 29.6, which was done in the form of the accompanying European Communities Act 1972, s 2 of which provided that from 1 January 1973, the treaties governing the European Communities and the existing and future acts adopted by the institutions of the Communities, "shall be binding on the State and shall be part of the domestic law thereof under the conditions laid down in those Treaties".[64] The need for

(protection of data) of the Charter in order to disapply a provision of the Data Protection Act 1998 that expressly limited damages for "pure" distress to certain circumstances that were not applicable in the case before it, which was between two private parties.

64 See John Temple Lang, "Legal and Constitutional Implications for Ireland of Adhesion to the EEC Treaty" (1972) 9 *Common Market Law Review* 167; John Temple Lang, "The Republic of Ireland and the EEC – The Constitutional Position: II" in Maurice E Bathurst et al (eds), *Legal Problems of an Enlarged European Community* (Stevens and Sons, 1972); Mary Robinson, "The

s 2 of the 1972 Act was explained by Barrington J in delivering the judgment of the High Court in *Crotty* as follows:

> Had the Oireachtas not passed the European Communities Act 1972, Ireland might still have been a member of the Community in international law but it would have been in breach of its obligations in international law under the Treaty of Rome and under the Treaty of Accession. This would not have been a matter in relation to which the domestic courts of this country would have had any competence because the Treaty would not have been part of domestic law. The immunity from constitutional challenge conferred by the second sentence of the Third Amendment on laws enacted, acts done, or measures adopted by the Community or its institutions would therefore have been meaningless as these laws, acts or measures would not have been part of the domestic law of this country.[65]

[11–52] As memorably described by Carroll J in *Tate v Minister for Social Welfare*, s 2 of the 1972 Act served as the "conduit pipe" through which EEC law became part of Irish law, albeit that it is "still community law governed by community law but with domestic effect".[66] This dual character is reflected in s 2 itself, which provides that the Treaties and acts of the institutions shall be part of Irish law "under the conditions laid down in those Treaties". According to Costello J in *Pigs and Bacon Commission v McCarren*, the effect of s 2 is that:

> Community law takes legal effect in the Irish legal system in the manner in which Community law itself provides. Thus, if according to Community law a provision of the Treaty is directly applicable so that rights are conferred on individuals which national courts must enforce, an Irish court must give effect to such a rule. And, if according to Community law, the provisions of Community law take precedence over a provision of national law in conflict with it an Irish court must give effect to this rule.[67]

[11–53] There has been a vigorous debate as to the precise nature of the incorporation of EU law within the Irish legal system. According to Gerard Hogan and Anthony

---

Irish European Communities Act 1972" (1973) 10 *Common Market Law Review* 352; Bryan McMahon, "Constitutional Adjustments Necessitated by Community Membership" (1976) 1 *European Law Review* 86; Séamus Henchy, "The Irish Constitution and the EEC" (1977) 1 *Dublin University Law Journal* 20; Brian Walsh, "Reflections on the Effects of Membership of the European Communities in Irish Law" in Francesco Capotorti et al (eds), *Du Droit International au Droit de l'Intégration: Liber Amicorum Pierre Pescatore* (Nomos, 1987); Bryan McMahon and Finbarr Murphy, *European Community Law in Ireland* (Butterworths, 1989) 272–273; Madeline Reid, *The Impact of Community Law on the Irish Constitution* (Irish Centre for European Law, 1990); Anthony M Collins and James O'Reilly, "The Application of Community Law in Ireland 1973–1989" (1992) 1 *Irish Journal of European Law* 38; Paul Gallagher, "The Constitution and Community" (1993) 2 *Irish Journal of European Law* 192; Gerard Hogan and Anthony Whelan, *Ireland and the European Union: Constitutional and Statutory Texts and Commentary* (Sweet and Maxwell, 1995) 7, 156, 165–172; Diarmuid Rossa Phelan, *Revolt or Revolution* (Round Hall Sweet and Maxwell, 1997) 332–334; Diarmuid Rossa Phelan and Anthony Whelan, "National Constitutional Law and European integration: FIDE Report" (1997) 6 *Irish Journal of European Law* 24; Nial Fennelly, "The Effect of European Community Law on Irish Law and the Irish Constitution" in Anthony Arnull, Piet Eeckhout and Takis Tridimas (eds), *Continuity and Change in EU Law, Essays in Honour of Francis Jacobs* (Oxford University Press, 2008) 446; Elaine Fahey, *EU Law in Ireland* (Clarus Press, 2010) 43–47; Maria Cahill, "A Critical Assessment of Irish Scholarship on the Constitutional Reception of European Law" in Thomas Mohr and Jennifer Schweppe (eds), *Thirty Years of Irish Legal Scholarship* (Round Hall, 2011).

65 *Crotty v An Taoiseach* [1987] IR 713, 757.

66 *Tate v Minister for Social Welfare* [1995] 1 IR 418, 437; [1995]1 ILRM 507, 521.

67 *Pigs and Bacon Commission v McCarren*, unreported, High Court, 30 June 1978.

Whelan, two perspectives on the incorporation of EU law persist simultaneously. From the EU law perspective, the EU legal order has its own authority and is supreme and capable of direct effect by virtue of that fact. The EU Treaties "are both a necessary and a sufficient basis for the obligations of [EU] law to be effective throughout the territory governed by its legal order, and require no further national act after that of ratification of the Treaties for them to have constitutional effect".[68] From the national perspective, however, EU law requirements such as supremacy and direct effect are accommodated by special concessions within the national constitutional order, which remains the over-arching source of authority of both national competence and EU competence. According to this view, the Third Amendment to the Constitution and the European Communities Act 1972 "seem to belie by their very existence the constitutional claims of [EU] law".[69] Awareness of this dual perspective is said to be obscured by a "mirror image" principle: while EU law is only operative in the Irish legal order by virtue of the 1972 Act,

> it is sought by that act of incorporation to grant to [EU] law the effect in national legal order which it itself requires. Thus, the daily interaction of national and [EU] law, operating on fundamentally different premises, should be conflict-free. While Costello J's remarks in *Pigs and Bacon Commission v McCarren* on the receipt of [EU] law in Irish law on its own terms are therefore inaccurate, a possible pretence is made of doing so consistently with the Irish constitutional paradigm.[70]

[11–54] An alternative view, put forward by Diarmuid Rossa Phelan, is that it is contrary to EU law, and a state of "permanent disobedience", for Irish courts to rely on a provision of domestic law in order to permit EU law to have direct effect. In this regard, he argues that the meaning of the phrase "the conditions laid down in those Treaties" in s 2 of the 1972 Act must be a matter of Irish constitutional law for the Irish courts to interpret. Given that EU law does not regard its integration within national legal orders as dependent on an act of reception, it would make little sense to ask the Court of Justice for an interpretation of a statute which it regards as irrelevant to the status of EU law in national courts. Accordingly, to ascribe an EU law meaning to the phrase "would make a complete nonsense" of s 2.[71] In reply, Hogan and Whelan claim that this analysis:

> fails to appreciate the operation of the principle of the mirror image in a situation,

---

68 Gerard Hogan and Anthony Whelan, *Ireland and the European Union: Constitutional and Statutory Texts and Commentary* (Sweet and Maxwell, 1995) 7–8. Bryan McMahon and Finbarr Murphy in *European Community Law in Ireland* (Butterworths, 1989) 242 cite Paul Joan George Kapteyn and Pieter Verloren van Themat, *Introduction to the Law of the European Communities* (Sweet and Maxwell, 1973) 25 to similar effect when they write that EU law rules: "have internal effect without reference to the national legal order, viz. in the area that has been created in consequence of the limitation of national sovereignty. In other words, the national constitutional law with regard to the internal effect and the internal order of priority to be given to rules of international law does not apply with reference to rules of [EU] law, because it can apply only within the limits of sovereignty. Beyond these limits, ie within the [EU] legal order, the municipal court without being hampered by constitutional restrictions, may give to the rules of [EU] law the effect desired by the European Court. If the municipal court comes across legal measures conflicting with [EU] law, it must refrain from applying them, not because they are a lower order than [EU] law, but because in such a case the national legislator has acted *ultra vires*."

69 *ibid*, 7.

70 *ibid*, 12.

71 Diarmuid Rossa Phelan, *Revolt or Revolution. The Constitutional Boundaries of the European Community* (Round Hall Sweet and Maxwell, 1997) 334.

> admittedly paradoxical but not intolerably so, where the national legislator wishes to accept [EU] law and all its incidents (including those of primacy and direct effect) with the context of the national legal order. … Before [EU] law is received into national law, by an act of incorporation supported by a constitutional amendment designed to save it from unconstitutionality, it has no foothold in that system; … After reception (if it proceeds on the mirror image principle, as the Irish measures clearly do), [EU] law should operate as if its claims had in fact been accepted after all. The purpose of the act of reception is to ensure that this pretence can be maintained. Thus, it would be contrary to the object of section 2 of the 1972 Act … to read it as permitting national interpretations of the [EU] Treaties other than those adopted by the Court of Justice, even though the section is otiose from the point of view of [EU] law. The section can be said to be self-abnegating, in that its chief purpose is to engender a state of affairs in national law which permits the national judge to act in compliance with the requirements of the [EU] legal order, and thereby to act, as a matter of [EU] law, as if the section did not exist.[72]

[11–55] Although the mirror image principle might work to avoid conflict between the two legal orders on a day-to-day basis, it can come under strain in the event of a clash as between competing fundamental norms or principles. When this occurs, it may become difficult to maintain the pretence that there is no tension as to which of the two orders is the ultimate source of authority. This is considered further in Chapter 13, which looks at the supremacy of EU law over national law.

[11–56] While, amongst Irish writers, this debate was at its height in the 1990s, the issue came to prominence in the UK more recently in the context of the triggering of Art 50 TEU, following a referendum result in June 2016 that favoured leaving the EU. In considering whether a vote of the Westminster Parliament was required in order to trigger Art 50, or whether it was an executive power that could be carried out by the government, the UK Supreme Court had to consider the nature of the UK's own European Communities Act 1972. In concluding that the 1972 Act was a source of domestic law and legal rights, the Supreme Court concluded that the sanction of Parliament was required before an Art 50 letter could be sent to the European Council. Given the parallels to the debates outlined above, as well as the clear exposition of the relationship between EU law and an incorporating act similar to our own, it is worth setting out the relevant portion of the *Miller* judgment in some detail:

> Many statutes give effect to treaties by prescribing the content of domestic law in the areas covered by them. The 1972 Act does this, but it does considerably more as well. It authorises a dynamic process by which, without further primary legislation (and, in some cases, even without any domestic legislation), EU law not only becomes a source of UK law, but actually takes precedence over all domestic sources of UK law, including statutes. This may sound rather dry or technical to many people, but in constitutional terms the effect of the 1972 Act was unprecedented. Indeed, it is fair to say that the legal consequences of the United Kingdom's accession to the EEC were not fully appreciated by many lawyers until the *Factortame* litigation in the 1990s … Of course, consistently with the principle of Parliamentary sovereignty, this unprecedented state of affairs will only last so long as Parliament wishes: the 1972 Act can be repealed like any other statute. For that reason, we would not accept that the so-called fundamental rule of recognition (ie the fundamental rule by reference to which all other rules are validated) underlying UK laws has been varied by the 1972 Act or would be varied by its repeal.

[72] Gerard Hogan and Anthony Whelan, *Ireland and the European Union: Constitutional and Statutory Texts and Commentary* (Sweet and Maxwell, 1995) 14.

In one sense, of course, it can be said that the 1972 Act is the source of EU law, in that, without that Act, EU law would have no domestic status. But in a more fundamental sense and, we consider, a more realistic sense, where EU law applies in the United Kingdom, it is the EU institutions which are the relevant source of that law. The legislative institutions of the EU can create or abrogate rules of law which will then apply domestically, without the specific sanction of any UK institution. It is true that the UK government and UK-elected members of the European Parliament participate in the EU legislative processes and can influence their outcome, but that does not diminish the point. Further, in the many areas of EU competence which are subject to majority decision, the approval of the United Kingdom is not required for its legislation to take effect domestically. It is also true that EU law enjoys its automatic and overriding effect only by virtue of the 1972 Act, and thus only while it remains in force. That point simply reflects the fact that Parliament was and remains sovereign: so, no new source of law could come into existence without Parliamentary sanction – and without being susceptible to being abrogated by Parliament. However, that in no way undermines our view that it is unrealistic to deny that, so long as that Act remains in force, the EU Treaties, EU legislation and the interpretations placed on these instruments by the Court of Justice are direct sources of UK law.

The 1972 Act did two things which are relevant to these appeals. First, it provided that rights, duties and rules derived from EU law should apply in the United Kingdom as part of its domestic law. Secondly, it provided for a new constitutional process for making law in the United Kingdom. These things are closely related, but they are legally and conceptually distinct. *The content of the rights, duties and rules introduced into our domestic law as a result of the 1972 Act is exclusively a question of EU law. However, the constitutional processes by which the law of the United Kingdom is made is exclusively a question of domestic law.*

Under the terms of the 1972 Act, EU law may take effect as part of the law of the United Kingdom in one of three ways. First, the EU Treaties themselves are directly applicable by virtue of section 2(1). Some of the provisions of those Treaties create rights (and duties) which are directly applicable in the sense that they are enforceable in UK courts. Secondly, where the effect of the EU Treaties is that EU legislation is directly applicable in domestic law, section 2(1) provides that it is to have direct effect in the United Kingdom without the need for further domestic legislation. This applies to EU Regulations (which are directly applicable by virtue of article 288 of the TFEU). Thirdly, section 2(2) authorises the implementation of EU law by delegated legislation. This applies mainly to EU Directives, which are not, in general, directly applicable but are required (again by article 288) to be transposed into national law. While this is an international law obligation, failure of the United Kingdom to comply with it is justiciable in domestic courts, and some Directives may be enforced by individuals directly against national governments in domestic courts. Further, any serious breach by the UK Parliament, government or judiciary of any rule of EU law intended to confer individual rights will entitle any individual sustaining damage as a direct result to compensation from the UK government …

Thus, EU law in EU Treaties and EU legislation will pass into UK law through the medium of section 2(1) or the implementation provisions of section 2(2) of the 1972 Act, so long as the United Kingdom is party to the EU Treaties. Similarly, so long as the United Kingdom is party to the EU Treaties, UK courts are obliged (i) to interpret EU Treaties, Regulations and Directives in accordance with decisions of the Court of Justice, (ii) to refer unclear points of EU law to the Court of Justice, and (iii) to interpret all domestic legislation, if at all possible, so as to comply with EU law ... And, so long as the United Kingdom is party to the EU Treaties, UK citizens are able to recover damages from the UK government in cases where a decision of one of the organs of the state based on a serious error of EU law has caused them loss.

In our view, then, although the 1972 Act gives effect to EU law, it is not itself the originating

> source of that law. It is … the "conduit pipe" by which EU law is introduced into UK domestic law. So long as the 1972 Act remains in force, its effect is to constitute EU law an independent and overriding source of domestic law. …
>
> … The EU Treaties as implemented pursuant to the 1972 Act were and are unique in their legislative and constitutional implications. In 1972, for the first time in the history of the United Kingdom, a dynamic, international source of law was grafted onto, and above, the well-established existing sources of domestic law: Parliament and the courts. … [B]efore (i) signing and (ii) ratifying the 1972 Accession Treaty, ministers, acting internationally, waited for Parliament, acting domestically, (i) to give clear, if not legally binding, approval in the form of resolutions, and (ii) to enable the Treaty to be effective by passing the 1972 Act. Bearing in mind this unique history and the constitutional principle of Parliamentary sovereignty, it seems most improbable that those two parties had the intention or expectation that ministers, constitutionally the junior partner in that exercise, could subsequently remove the graft without formal appropriate sanction from the constitutionally senior partner in that exercise, Parliament.[73]

Direct Effect – When and by Whom Traditionally, it was considered that in order to be capable of direct effect, a provision of EU law must confer rights on individuals. Now, the better view is that it suffices that the provision produces independent legal effects that can be invoked before a national court. In order to be able to invoke direct effect, the applicant must fall within the intended scope of the provision. Depending on the nature of the provision, this might be expressly set out, such as where the personal scope of a regulation or a directive is defined within the instrument itself, or it may require a broader contextual analysis looking at the object and purpose of the provision and the circumstances of the applicant. A person who is not the primary beneficiary of a measure may rely on its direct effect if he or she has a sufficiently close relationship with the primary beneficiary. A person who is not the primary beneficiary of a measure may rely on its direct effect if he or she is acting as a private enforcer of EU regulatory obligations.	• *Muñoz* (2002)

[73] *R (ex p. Miller) v Secretary of State for Exiting the European Union* [2017] UKSC 5, 24 January 2017, paras 60–65, 90. See Gavin Phillipson, "EU Law as an Agent of National Constitutional Change: *Miller v Secretary of State for Exiting the European Union*" (2017) 36 *Yearbook of European Law* 46; Alison Young, "*R (Miller) v Secretary of State for Exiting the European Union*: Thriller or Vanilla?" (2017) 42 *European Law Review* 280; Mark Elliott, "The Supreme Court's Judgment in *Miller*: In Search of Constitutional Principle" (2017) 76 *Cambridge Law Journal* 257.

Direct Effect of Treaty Provisions Treaty provisions are capable of direct effect if they are sufficiently clear, precise and unconditional.	• *Van Gend en Loos* (1963) • *Reyners v Belgium* (1974)
In principle, Treaty provisions are capable of both vertical and horizontal direct effect.	• *Defrenne v Sabena* (1976)
Whether a Treaty provision has direct effect and, if so, whether it has horizontal as well as vertical direct effect, is decided on a case-by-case basis.	
Articles that have been held to have direct effect include those dealing with non-discrimination (Art 18 TFEU), the right of citizens to move and reside freely within the Union (Art 21 TFEU), free movement of goods (Arts 30, 34, 35 and 110 TFEU), free movement of workers (Art 45 TFEU), freedom of establishment (Art 49 TFEU), free movement of services (Art 56 TFEU) and core competition law rules prohibiting restrictions on competition or abuse of a dominant position (Arts 101 and 102 TFEU).	
Treaty guarantees on the free movement of workers, services and of establishment have been held to be capable of horizontal direct effect, as have articles on competition law.	• *Angonese* (2000)
Treaty guarantees on the free movement of goods were not considered to be capable of horizontal direct effect. The 2012 judgment in *Fra.bo* did, however, afford a limited degree of horizontal direct effect.	• *Fra.bo* (2012)

Direct Effect of General Principles of EU Law General principles of EU law are capable of vertical direct effect. They are capable of horizontal direct effect in matters falling within the scope of EU law.	• *Mangold* (2005) • *Kücükdeveci* (2010) • *Dansk Industri (Ajos)* (2016) • *Egenberger* (2018) • *Walker v Innospec* (2017)

Direct Effect of the Charter of Fundamental Rights While the Charter's provisions are capable of having vertical direct effect in matters falling with the scope of EU law, the extent to which they have horizontal direct effect was, until recently, unclear. In *AMS*, Advocate General Villalón considered that they should be capable of horizontal direct effect. The Court did not address the question in its judgment. The 2018 judgments in *Egenberger, Max Plank and Bauer* indicate that in horizontal disputes, national courts will have to disapply a national law if it cannot be interpreted in a manner that is compatible with a sufficiently clear Charter right.	• *AMS* (2013) • *Egenberger* (2018) • *Max Planck, Bauer* (2018) • *Benkharbouche* (2017)

Chapter 12

DIRECT EFFECT OF SECONDARY EU LAW AND INDIRECT EFFECT

[12–01] Following on from the examination of the direct effect of primary EU law in the previous chapter, attention will now turn to the direct effect of secondary EU law in the form of international agreements, regulations, decisions and directives. A distinguishing feature of directives is that, given their nature, they have been held by the Court of Justice to be incapable of having horizontal direct effect. Clearly, this means that a directive may have very different legal effects depending on whether it is being relied upon against a state entity or a private party. A number of innovative ways have been found to mitigate the absence of a directive's horizontal direct effect, including: (i) a liberal approach to defining emanations of the state for the purpose of applying vertical direct effect and (ii) the possibility of directives having *incidental* horizontal effects. In Chapter 14 it will be seen that a further important means of compensating for the lack of horizontal direct effect is provided by the possibility of claiming damages as a result of a Member State's failure to fulfil its EU law obligations, including the obligation to implement a directive by the end of the period allowed for its transposition. A fourth way in which the exclusion of horizontal direct effect is softened is through the doctrine of indirect effect or harmonious interpretation, which applies to all sources of EU law and not just to directives. This chapter will conclude by examining the mechanisms in Irish law for ensuring the efficient implementation of secondary EU law.

A. Direct Effect of International Agreements

[12–02] International agreements entered into by the EU are capable of having direct effect within the Member States. This is the case for both "EU-only" agreements, to which the Union alone is a party, and for "mixed" agreements, to which both the Union and the Member States are a party.[1] The criteria for establishing the direct effect of

---

[1] See, for example, Case 87/75 *Bresciani* [1976] ECR 129, 140–142; Case 12/86 *Dermirel* [1987] ECR 3719, 3751, where the Court of Justice rejected an argument that it did not have jurisdiction to interpret provisions of a mixed agreement that concerned Member State competence. The Court reiterated that, in ensuring respect for commitments arising from an agreement concluded by the Union, the Member States fulfil, within the EU system, an obligation in relation to the Union, which has assumed responsibility for the due performance of the agreement.

international agreements are more exacting than those that apply to the EU Treaties themselves. More specifically, where the terms of an agreement do not expressly state whether it is intended to have direct effect, in addition to assessing whether a particular provision of an international agreement is sufficiently clear, precise and unconditional, the Court of Justice will examine the overall structure and nature of the agreement as a whole in order to determine whether the agreement ought to be regarded as being capable of having direct effect.[2] Indeed, it has been suggested that the very concept of direct effect has certain differences when applying "externally" to the question of the relationship between an international agreement and EU law.[3]

[12–03] An illustration of the development of, and rationale for, the Court's approach to the direct effect of international agreements can be seen from two cases relating to an "EU-only" free trade agreement between the EEC and Portugal prior to its accession to the Community: *Polydor v Harlequin Record Shops* and *Kupferberg*, with the latter providing a key and oft-repeated statement of the test to be applied. In *Polydor v Harlequin Record Shops*, Polydor sought to prevent Harlequin Record Shops from importing records from Portugal to the UK, which it claimed was in breach of its copyright.[4] In proceedings before the English courts, by way of a defence Harlequin Record Shops sought to rely directly on an article of the agreement that prohibited quantitative restrictions on imports or measures having an equivalent effect. The Court of Justice compared the object and purpose of the Treaty of Rome – which was to "create a single market reproducing as closely as possible the conditions of a domestic market" – with that of the agreement with Portugal, which had the more limited aim to "consolidate and to extend the economic relations existing between the Community and Portugal and to ensure, with due regard for fair conditions of competition, the harmonious development of their commerce for the purpose of contributing to the work of constructing Europe".[5] Although the prohibition on measures equivalent to quantitative restrictions closely mirrored the same prohibition in the Treaty of Rome, the instruments which the EEC had at its disposal in order to achieve the uniform application of Community law and the progressive abolition of legislative disparities within the Common Market had no equivalent in the context of the relations between the EEC and Portugal. As a result, the Court held that the provision of the agreement with Portugal could not be relied upon directly.

[12–04] Later in the same year, in *Kupferberg* an importer of port from Portugal to Germany sought to rely directly on an article of the free trade agreement that prohibited

2 See Szilárd Gáspár-Szilágyi, "The 'Primacy' and 'Direct Effect' of EU International Agreements" (2015) 21 *European Public Law* 343; Francesca Martines, "Direct Effect of International Agreements of the European Union" (2014) 25 *European Journal of International Law* 129; Simon Marsden, "Invoking Direct Application and Effect of International Treaties by the ECJ: Implications for International Environmental Law in the EU" (2011) 60 *International and Comparative Law Quarterly* 737; Mario Mendez, "The Legal Effects of Community Agreements: Maximalist Treaty Enforcement and Judicial Avoidance Techniques" (2010) 21 *European Journal of International Law* 83; Nadine Zipperle, *EU International Agreements: An Analysis of Direct Effect and Judicial Review Pre- and Post-Lisbon* (Springer, 2017); David Fennelly, *International Law in the Irish Legal System* (Round Hall, 2014) 135–154; Yuji Iwasawa, "Domestic Application of International Law" (2016) 378 *Recuil des Cours* 9, 111–118.

3 See Piet Eeckhout, *EU External Relations Law* (2nd ed, Oxford University Press, 2011) 330; Robert Schütze, *European Union Law* (Cambridge University Press, 2015) 111.

4 Case 270/80 *Polydor v Harlequin Record Shops* [1982] ECR 329.

5 *ibid*, 347, citing the preamble to the agreement.

internal fiscal measures that discriminated as between domestically produced goods and Portuguese goods.[6] A number of Member States intervened before the Court of Justice arguing against the agreement having direct effect. In addition to pointing to the overall object and purpose of the agreement, they highlighted the fact that the reciprocal nature of the agreement would become one-sided if it were to have direct effect within the Member States but not within Portugal. Secondly, they argued that the agreement had established its own institutional framework through which disputes between Portugal and the EEC were to be settled, suggesting that this was the means of seeking redress rather than relying on the direct effect of the agreement before a national court. Thirdly, it was claimed that the inclusion of safeguard clauses that allowed Member States to derogate from certain provisions within the agreement also militated against the agreement having direct effect. The Court rejected each of these three arguments as follows:

> The Treaty establishing the Community has conferred upon the institutions the power not only of adopting measures applicable in the Community but also of making agreements with non-member countries and international organizations in accordance with the provisions of the Treaty. According to Article [216(2)] these agreements are binding on the institutions of the Community and on Member States. Consequently, it is incumbent upon the Community institutions, as well as upon the Member States, to ensure compliance with the obligations arising from such agreements.
>
> … In ensuring respect for commitments arising from an agreement concluded by the Community institutions the Member States fulfil an obligation not only in relation to the non-member country concerned but also and above all in relation to the Community which has assumed responsibility for the due performance of the agreement. That is why the provisions of such an agreement … form an integral part of the Community legal system.
>
> It follows from the Community nature of such provisions that their effect in the Community may not be allowed to vary according to whether their application is in practice the responsibility of the Community institutions or of the Member States and, in the latter case, according to the effects in the internal legal order of each Member State which the law of that State assigns to international agreements concluded by it. Therefore it is for the Court [of Justice], within the framework of its jurisdiction in interpreting the provisions of agreements, to ensure their uniform application throughout the Community.
>
> The governments which have submitted observations to the Court do not deny the Community nature of the provisions of agreements concluded by the Community. They contend, however, that the generally recognized criteria for determining the effects of provisions of a purely Community origin may not be applied to provisions of a free-trade agreement concluded by the Community with a non-member country.
>
> In that respect the governments base their arguments in particular on the *distribution of powers* in regard to the external relations of the Community, the *principal of reciprocity* governing the application of free-trade agreements, the *institutional framework* established by such agreements in order to settle differences between the contracting parties and *safeguard clauses* allowing the parties to derogate from the agreements.
>
> It is true that the effects within the Community of provisions of an agreement concluded by the Community with a non-member country may not be determined without taking account of the international origin of the provisions in question. In conformity with the principles of public international law Community institutions which have power to negotiate and conclude an agreement with a non-member country are free to agree with that country

[6] Case 104/81 *Kupferberg* [1982] ECR 3641.

> what effect the provisions of the agreement are to have in the internal legal order of the contracting parties. *Only if that question has not been settled by the agreement does it fall for decision by the courts having jurisdiction in the matter, and in particular by the Court of Justice within the framework of its jurisdiction under the Treaty, in the same manner as any question of interpretation relating to the application of the agreement in the Community.*
>
> According to the general rules of international law there must be bona fide performance of every agreement. Although each contracting party is responsible for executing fully the commitments which it has undertaken it is nevertheless free to determine the legal means appropriate for attaining that end in its legal system unless the agreement, interpreted in the light of its subject-matter and purpose, itself specifies those means. Subject to that reservation the fact that the courts of one of the parties consider that certain of the stipulations in the agreement are of direct application whereas the courts of the other party do not recognize such direct application is not in itself such as to constitute a *lack of reciprocity* in the implementation of the agreement.
>
> … The mere fact that the contracting parties have established a *special institutional framework* for consultations and negotiations inter se in relation to the implementation of the agreement is not in itself sufficient to exclude all judicial application of that agreement. The fact that a court of one of the parties applies to a specific case before it a provision of the agreement involving an unconditional and precise obligation and therefore not requiring any prior intervention on the part of the joint committee does not adversely affect the powers that the agreement confers on that committee.
>
> As regards the *safeguard clauses* which enable the parties to derogate from certain provisions of the agreement it should be observed that they apply only in specific circumstances and as a general rule after consideration within the joint committee in the presence of both parties. Apart from specific situations which may involve their application, the existence of such clauses … is not sufficient in itself to affect the direct applicability which may attach to certain stipulations in the agreement.
>
> It follows from all the foregoing considerations that neither the nature nor the structure of the Agreement concluded with Portugal may prevent a trader from relying on the provisions of the said Agreement before a court in the Community.[7]

[12–05] Having established that the overall structure and nature of the agreement was such that its provisions could, in principle, have direct effect, the Court then moved on to consider whether the particular article at issue was sufficiently precise and unconditional as to be capable of being relied on directly. It began by noting that, for this assessment, it was necessary to analyse the article in light of both the object and purpose of the agreement and its context.

> The purpose of the Agreement is to create a system of free trade in which rules restricting commerce are eliminated in respect of virtually all trade in products originating in the territory of the parties, in particular by abolishing customs duties and charges having equivalent effect and eliminating quantitative restrictions and measures having equivalent effect.
>
> Seen in that context … Article 21 of the Agreement seeks to prevent the liberalization of the trade in goods through the abolition of customs duties and charges having equivalent effect and quantitative restrictions and measures having equivalent effect from being rendered nugatory by fiscal practices of the Contracting Parties. That would be so if the

[7] *ibid*, 3662–3665. Emphasis added.

> product imported of one party were taxed more heavily than the similar domestic products which it encounters on the market of the other party.
>
> It appears from the foregoing that … Article 21 of the Agreement imposes on the Contracting Parties an unconditional rule against discrimination in matters of taxation, which is dependent only on a finding that the products affected by a particular system of taxation are of like nature, and the limits of which are the direct consequence of the purpose of the Agreement. As such this provision may be applied by a court and thus produce direct effects throughout the Community.[8]

[12–06] Turning then to mixed agreements to which both the Union and the Member States are a party, a prominent example of such an agreement being held to have direct effect is the case of *Sevince*.[9] There, Mr Sevince successfully sought to rely directly on a decision of an Association Council established under the Association Agreement between the EEC and its Member States and Turkey. Mr Sevince was a Turkish national who had been living and working in the Netherlands but was refused a renewal of his residence permit when his circumstances changed. The decision of the Association Council provided that Turkish workers who had been in legal employment for five years in a Member State were to enjoy free access in that Member State to any paid employment of their choice. The Court of Justice held that the same criteria for determining direct effect applied to a decision of the Association Council as to a provision of an agreement with a third country itself, namely if, having regard to its wording and the purpose and nature of the agreement, the provision contains a clear and precise obligation which is not subject, in its implementation or effects, to the adoption of any subsequent measure.

[12–07] Examining the decision, the Court concluded that it upheld "in clear, precise and unconditional terms, the right of a Turkish worker, after a number of years' legal employment in a Member State, to enjoy free access to any paid employment of his choice".[10] The overall object and purpose of the Association Agreement also supported a finding of direct effect given that its aim was to "promote the continuous and balanced strengthening of trade and economic relations" between Turkey and the EEC by establishing an association that provided for a preparatory stage to enable Turkey to strengthen its economy with aid from the Community, a transitional stage for the progressive establishment of a customs union and for the alignment of economic policies, and a final stage based on the customs union and entailing close coordination of economic policies.[11]

[12–08] As the Court of Justice will examine the object and purpose of provisions which it is claimed are capable of direct effect, it is possible for the Union to preclude direct effect by making this intention clear within the text of the agreement itself, or in a Council decision relating to the signature or conclusion of the agreement. For example, Art 17.15 of the EU–Singapore free trade agreement is simply titled "No Direct Effect" and states that nothing in the agreement "shall be construed as conferring rights or imposing obligations on persons, other than those created between the Parties under public international law".[12] Similarly, Art 8 of the Council Decision on the signing

---

8 *ibid*, 3665.

9 Case C-192/89 *Sevince* [1990] ECR I-3461.

10 *ibid*, 3502.

11 *ibid*, 3502–3503.

12 See Aliki Semertzi, "The Preclusion of Direct Effect in the Recently Concluded EU Free Trade

of a free trade agreement between the EU, and its Member States, and the Republic of Korea, provides that the agreement "shall not be construed as conferring rights or imposing obligations which can be directly invoked before Union or Member State courts and tribunals", with like wording found in Art 30.6 of the EU's Comprehensive Economic and Trade Agreement with Canada.[13] It should also be noted that, given the nature of CFSP agreements, combined with the unique treatment of CFSP within the EU legal order, they are unlikely to be held to have direct effect.[14]

[12–09] The direct effect of a bilateral, mixed EU agreement was at issue before the Irish Supreme Court in *GAG v Minister for Justice*, which concerned the right of establishment as contained in Association Agreements between the European Communities and their Member States, of the one part, and the Czech Republic and Romania, of the other part.[15] Following earlier decisions of the Court of Justice that had confirmed that such provisions enjoyed direct effect, the Supreme Court accepted without any elaboration that the right of establishment could be relied upon by individuals before the Irish courts. As David Fennelly has observed,

> notwithstanding the fact that in the normal course such an international agreement concluded by the State would require positive legal action in order to take effect in the Irish legal system in accordance with Art 29.6 of the 1937 Constitution, the fact that the agreement was one which had been concluded by the European Communities and which the Court of Justice had held to have direct effect is sufficient to circumvent the normal constitutional procedures without further comment or consideration. In this decision, therefore, the Supreme Court showed the same ready acceptance of the direct effect of the mixed agreements concluded by the EU as it has shown in respect of the primary and secondary law of the EU more generally.[16]

[12–10] All of the international agreements referred to thus far have taken the form of bilateral agreements entered into with a third country by either the EU, or the EU and its Member States. When it comes to considering the direct effect of a multilateral agreement to which the EU is a party, the Court of Justice has adopted a distinctly more cautious approach. For example, certain obligations under the Aarhus Convention on Access to Information, Public Participation in Decision-making and Access to Justice in Environmental Matters have been held to require the adoption of subsequent measures in order to ensure their implementation, thereby preventing their direct effect.[17] Provisions of the UN Convention on the Law of the Sea were considered not to directly confer rights on individuals and so were not capable of direct effect, while provisions of the Kyoto Protocol[18] and the UN Convention on the Rights of Persons with Disabilities were

---

Agreements" (2014) 51 *Common Market Law Review* 1125.

13 Council Decision 2011/265/EU of 16 September 2010 on the signing, on behalf of the European Union, and provisional application of the Free Trade Agreement between the European Union and its Member States, of the one part, and the Republic of Korea, of the other part [2011] OJ L 127/1.

14 See David Fennelly, *International Law in the Irish Legal System* (Round Hall, 2014) 119; Robert Schütze, *European Union Law* (Cambridge University Press, 2015) 112.

15 [2003] 3 IR 442.

16 David Fennelly, *International Law in the Irish Legal System* (Round Hall, 2014) 155.

17 Case C-240/09 *Lesoochranárske (Slovak Brown Bears* case) [2011] ECR I-1255. See Marcus Klamert, "Dark Matter – Competence, Jurisdiction and 'the Area Largely Covered by EU Law': Comment on *Lesoochranárske*" (2012) 37 *European Law Review* 340; Mariolina Eliantonio, "Case C-240/09, *Lesoochranárske*" (2012) 49 *Common Market Law Review* 767.

18 Case C-308/06 *Intertanko* [2008] ECR I-4057; Case C-366/10 *Air Transport Association of America* [2011] ECR I-13755. See Esa Paasivirta, "The European Union and the United Nations Convention

not sufficiently precise and unconditional.[19] The provisions of the General Agreement on Tariffs and Trade (GATT) and the WTO Agreement have likewise been held not to have direct effect.[20] As Piet Eeckhout has outlined:

> In the light of the broad scope of WTO law, covering trade in goods, trade in services, and intellectual property law, and bearing in mind its many connections with EU law, the recognition of the direct effect of WTO law provisions would have opened up large avenues for claims based on WTO law, claims no doubt often directed at invalidating or setting aside either EU or national legislation. At a political level, the Council and the Commission clarified from the outset that they were opposed to the recognition of direct effect. Their position was reflected in two legal documents. First, the Schedule of Commitments of the Community and its Member States under GATS [General Agreement on Trade in Services] states in an introductory note that the rights and obligations arising from GATS, including the Schedule of Commitments, shall have no self-executing effect and thus confer no rights directly on individual natural persons or juridical persons. Secondly, the Council Decision concluding the WTO Agreement on behalf of the EC states, in its preamble, that by its nature the agreement, including the annexes, is not susceptible to being directly invoked in Community or Member States courts.[21]

[12–11] An example of a provision of a multilateral agreement having direct effect is the Protocol for the Protection of the Mediterranean Sea against Pollution from Land-based Sources. Having examined the overall object and purpose of the Protocol and the precision and conditionality of the provision in question, the Court of Justice concluded that:

> By establishing a system of prior authorisation by the competent national authorities for the discharge of the substances listed in Annex II to the Protocol, [the] Article contributes to the elimination by Member States of pollution from land-based sources in the area covered by the Protocol. Recognition of the direct effect of the provision in question can only serve the purpose of the Protocol … and reflect the nature of the instrument, which is intended, inter alia, to prevent pollution resulting from the failure of public authorities to act.[22]

[12–12] The Irish courts have also been called upon to consider the direct effect of provisions of multilateral mixed competence agreements, such as in *MX v Health Service Executive*.[23] There, MX sought to rely before the High Court on Art 12 of the UN Convention on the Rights of Persons with Disabilities – a mixed competence

---

on the Law of the Sea" (2015) 38 *Fordham International Law Journal* 1045; Eileen Denza, "Case Comment: A Note on *Intertanko*" (2008) 33 *European Law Review* 870.

19 Case C-363/12 *Z v A Government Department* EU:C:2014:159, 18 March 2014. See Garrett De Baere, "Shall I be mother? The prohibition on sex discrimination, the UN Disability Convention, and the right to surrogacy leave under EU law" (2015) 74 *Cambridge Law Journal* 44; Connie Healy, "Once more with 'sympathy' but no resolution for intended mothers: the EU, Ireland and the surrogacy dilemma" (2017) 39 *Journal of Social Welfare and Family Law* 504.

20 Cases 21–24/72 *International Fruit Company* [1972] ECR 1219; Case C-149/96 *Portugal v Council* [1999] ECR I-8395. See Hélène Ruiz Fabri, "Is There a Case – Legally and Politically – for Direct Effect of WTO Obligations?" (2014) 25 *European Journal of International Law* 151; Pieter Jan Kuijper and Marco Bronckers, "WTO Law in the European Court of Justice" (2005) 42 *Common Market Law Review* 1313; Francis Snyder, "The Gatekeepers: The European Court and WTO Law" (2003) 40 *Common Market Law Review* 313; Maria Cahill, "What Do We Want? When Do We Want It? Direct Effect and the World Trade Organisation" (2002) 5 *Trinity College Law Review* 77.

21 Piet Eeckhout, *EU External Relations Law* (2nd ed, Oxford University Press, 2011) 345–346.

22 Case C-213/03 *Pêcheurs de l'étang de Berre* [2004] ECR I-7357, 7374.

23 [2012] 3 IR 254.

international agreement that, at the time, had been ratified by the Union but not by Ireland – in order to challenge certain medical treatment decisions that had been taken on her behalf. Article 12 of the Convention requires that the legal capacity of persons with disabilities be respected. MacMenamin J explained that, in order to establish that Art 12 had the force of law in Ireland, the plaintiff would have to show that it, first, fell within an EU competence which had been exercised to a large degree or was an integral part of EU law and, secondly, was sufficiently clear, precise and unconditional as to be capable of itself directly regulating the legal position of individuals.[24] As the matter covered by Art 12 fell within the exclusive competence of the Member States, Art 12 was found not to be capable of having direct effect in Irish law by virtue of the EU's ratification of the Convention on the Rights of Persons with Disabilities.[25]

[12–13] More recently, the Supreme Court has considered the same question in the context of the Aarhus Convention, a mixed-competence international agreement to which both the Union and Ireland are a party. One aspect of *Conway v Ireland* concerned the extent to which the applicant could place reliance on the Aarhus Convention in order to claim legal aid for an appeal that was said to involve an alleged omission by a public authority in relation to national environmental law.[26] While the Supreme Court was not satisfied that the facts of the case fell within the scope of the Aarhus Convention, in delivering the Court's judgment Clarke J (as he then was) nevertheless considered the question of whether the provisions of the Convention were capable of having direct effect in Irish law. Clarke J began his analysis by quoting from the *Slovak Brown Bears* judgment of the Court of Justice, in which it was held that provisions of the Aarhus Convention were, in principle, capable of direct effect.[27] According to the Court of Justice in that case, which concerned the direct effect of Art 9(3) of the Convention,

> [s]ince the Aarhus Convention was concluded by the Community and all the Member States on the basis of joint competence, it follows that where a case is brought before the Court in accordance with the provisions of the … [TEU and TFEU], … the Court has jurisdiction to define the obligations which the Community has assumed and those which remain the sole responsibility of the Member States in order to interpret the Aarhus Convention.
>
> Next, it must be determined whether, in the field covered by Article 9(3) of the Aarhus Convention, the European Union has exercised its powers and adopted provisions to implement the obligations which derive from it. If that were not the case, the obligations deriving from Article 9(3) of the Aarhus Convention would continue to be covered by the national law of the Member States. In those circumstances, it would be for the courts of those Member States to determine, on the basis of national law, whether individuals could rely directly on the rules of that international agreement relevant to that field or whether the courts must apply those rules of their own motion. In that case, EU law does not require or forbid the legal order of a Member State to accord to individuals the right to rely directly on a rule laid down in the Aarhus Convention or to oblige the courts to apply that rule of their own motion.
>
> However, if it were to be held that the European Union has exercised its powers and adopted provisions in the field covered by Article 9(3) of the Aarhus Convention, EU law

24 *ibid*, 272.
25 *ibid*, 276.
26 [2017] 1 IR 53.
27 Case C-240/09 *Lesoochranárske* [2011] ECR I-1255. See footnote 17 above.

> would apply and it would be for the Court of Justice to determine whether the provision of the international agreement in question has direct effect.[28]

[12–14] The particular provision of the Aarhus Convention at issue in the *Slovak Brown Bears* case was found by the Court of Justice not to have direct effect, as it failed to fulfil the established criteria. Notwithstanding this, the Court noted the existence of an obligation on national courts to interpret, "to the fullest extent possible", relevant national laws in such a way as to give effect to the objectives of the Convention.[29] For Clarke J, the implication of the judgment was that it was

> at least possible in principle that provisions of the Aarhus Convention may be directly effective in Member States or be required to be implemented as far as practicable by a conforming interpretation of national procedural rules but it is also clear that not every provision of the Convention is directly effective or capable of such implementation. Thus, in respect of any particular provision sought to be relied on, it will be necessary to determine whether it met the relevant criteria.[30]

B. Direct Effect of Regulations and Decisions

[12–15] In Chapter 10 it was seen that regulations are defined in Art 288 TFEU as having general application, are binding in their entirety and are directly applicable in all Member States. It has already been noted, however, that direct applicability is a broader concept than direct effect.[31] In the early 1970s, the Court of Justice confirmed in *Leonesio* that because of its nature and its purpose within the system of sources of EU law, a regulation may have direct effect in the sense of being capable of creating individual rights which national courts must protect.[32] There, a regulation aimed at reducing Europe's "milk lake" had encouraged farmers to slaughter their dairy herds by offering them a financial subsidy for doing so subject to certain conditions. Having had her herd slaughtered and meeting the conditions, Mrs Leonesio applied to the Italian authorities for the subsidy but was informed that payment would have to await the adoption of certain measures by the Italian parliament. A preliminary reference asked whether the regulation created individual rights which the national courts must protect. Having examined the regulation, the Court of Justice concluded that it created pecuniary rights against the state which arose once the conditions set out in the regulation are complied with. As a result, it was not possible at a national level to render the exercise of the rights subject to implementing provisions other than those which might be required by the regulation itself.

[12–16] While it is usually the case that a regulation has direct effect, it cannot be presumed that every provision of every regulation, merely by virtue of its status, has such an effect. For example, in another Italian preliminary reference concerning a regulation governing farming, *Azienda Agricole*, the Court of Justice had to consider

---

28 *ibid*, 1301–1302.

29 *ibid*, 1307.

30 [2017] 1 IR 53, 65. See also *Byrne v Ó Conbhuí* [2018] IECA 57, unreported, Court of Appeal, 9 March 2018, Hogan J, paras 26–34; *McCoy v Shillelagh Quarries Ltd* [2015] 1 IR 627, 634–638; *Kimpton Vale Ltd v An Bord Pleanála* [2013] 2 IR 767, 773–776.

31 See ch 11, para [11–02].

32 Case 93/71 *Leonesio* [1972] ECR 287, 293. In an Irish context, see the discussion in *Campbell v Minister for Agriculture* [1999] 2 IR 245, 252–254.

whether the regulation had direct effect in circumstances where the regulation left it to Member States to define, for the purposes of the regulation, what was meant by the expression a "farmer practising farming as his main occupation".[33] Italian law defined the term as a farmer at least two-thirds of whose income is derived from farming and two-thirds of his or her working time is devoted to farming. The law made no mention of whether a legal entity (as opposed to an individual) could be a farmer for the purpose of the regulation. The preliminary reference inquired as to whether a company could rely directly on the regulation before the Italian courts. The Court noted that although regulations "*generally* have immediate effect in the national legal systems without it being necessary for the national authorities to adopt measures of application, some of their provisions may none the less necessitate, for their implementation, the adoption of measures of application by the Member States".[34] In the light of the discretion enjoyed by the Member States in implementing certain provisions of the regulation, it could not be held that individuals derived rights from those provisions in the absence of measures of application adopted by the relevant Member State.

[12–17] As exemplified by the case of *Muñoz* referred to in the previous chapter, where a private enforcer was permitted to rely on a regulation governing the marketing of grapes against a competitor, regulations are capable of having horizontal as well as vertical direct effect.[35]

[12–18] According to Art 288 TFEU, a decision is binding in its entirety, while a decision which specifies to whom it is addressed is binding only on them. This wording, introduced by the Lisbon Treaty, is a slight change to what had gone before, whereby a decision was said to be binding in its entirety on those to whom it was addressed. The revised wording more clearly envisages decisions that apply to the world at large, without any specific addressee. As early as 1970 the Court of Justice confirmed, in *Grad*, that a decision was capable in principle of having direct effect, reasoning as follows:

> the provision according to which decisions are binding in their entirety on those to whom they are addressed enables the question to be put whether the obligation created by the decision can only be invoked by the Community institutions against the addressee or whether such a right may possibly be exercised by all those who have an interest in the fulfilment of this obligation. It would be incompatible with the binding effect attributed to decisions by Article [288] to exclude in principle the possibility that persons affected may invoke the obligation imposed by a decision. Particularly in cases where, for example, the Community authorities by means of a decision have imposed an obligation on a Member State or all the Member States to act in a certain way, the effectiveness ("*l'effet utile*") of such a measure would be weakened if the nationals of that State could not invoke it in the courts and the national courts could not take it into consideration as part of Community law. Although the effects of a decision may not be identical with those of a provision contained in a regulation, this difference does not exclude the possibility that the end result, namely the right of the individual to invoke the measure before the courts, may be the same as that of a directly applicable provision of a regulation.[36]

[12–19] Where a decision is addressed to a Member State and is sufficiently clear, precise and unconditional in conferring a right or an interest on an individual, that

---

33 Case C-403/98 *Azienda Agricole* [2001] I–103.
34 *ibid*, 131.
35 Case 253/00 *Muñoz* [2002] ECR I-7289. See ch 11, para [11–29].
36 Case 9/70 *Grad* [1970] ECR 825.

decision is capable of having vertical direct effect. For example, in *Dellway Investments Ltd v National Asset Management Agency* it was claimed that a Commission Decision,[37] addressed to Ireland, on the compliance with state aid rules of the establishment of NAMA, had direct effect, such that certain limitations on the operation of NAMA set out in the Decision could be relied upon in Irish proceedings.[38] Having closely examined the terms of the decision, the Supreme Court concluded that there was:

> no term of the Commission Decision, invoked by the applicants, which meets the requirements for the Decision to have direct effect by conferring rights on the applicants capable of being relied upon before this court. The Decision did not purport to lay down any requirement and certainly not one which was unconditional, clear and precise.[39]

[12–20] A decision addressed to a Member State is generally not capable of having horizontal direct effect, however. In contrast, a decision that imposes an obligation on a private party can be enforced against that party by the relevant Member State (reverse vertical direct effect) or by another private party who has a sufficient interest in its enforcement (horizontal direct effect).

[12–21] Gerard Conway proposes an interesting way of thinking about the nature of EU law, particularly from the perspective of a dualist state like Ireland, suggesting that it pushes national systems towards a form of monism. Whilst a dualist state will remain dualist as regards primary EU law (ie the Treaties and any protocols thereto), once having so ratified and incorporated those Treaties, it becomes monist towards secondary EU law: "once secondary legislation is adopted in Brussels, it can be invoked (assuming certain conditions are met) in a national court without implementing legislation, once the conditions for direct effect are satisfied, irrespective of whether a Member State is monist or dualist towards 'ordinary' international law".[40]

C. Direct Effect of Directives

[12–22] Given that the very nature of a directive is that it is dependent upon the adoption of implementation measures by the Member States, one might reasonably assume that directives are not capable of having direct effect. Certainly, the drafters of the Treaty of Rome would have been surprised to learn that direct reliance could be placed on an instrument that was specifically designed so as to leave to each Member State the choice of form and methods to achieve the prescribed result. If directives had direct effect, a legitimate question would arise as to why Art 288 draws a distinction between a regulation and a directive in the first place.

[12–23] This question was first examined by the Court of Justice in the 1974 case of *Van Duyn v Home Office*.[41] Ms Van Duyn had sought to move to the United Kingdom

[37] Commission Decision in Case N 725/09, Ireland – Establishment of a National Asset Management relief scheme for banks in Ireland – NAMA [2010] OJ C94/10.

[38] [2011] 4 IR 1, 176–181.

[39] *ibid*, 181.

[40] Gerard Conway, *EU Law* (Routledge, 2015) 216. See Gerard Hogan, Gerry Whyte, David Kenny and Rachel Walsh, *Kelly: The Irish Constitution* (5th ed, Bloomsbury Professional, 2018) 619–620.

[41] Case 41/74 *Van Duyn v Home Office* [1974] ECR 1337. See Morten Rasmussen, "How to Enforce European Law? A New History of the Battle Over the Direct Effect of Directives, 1958–1987" (2017) 23 *European Law Journal* 290; Julie Dickson, "Directives in EU Legal Systems: Whose

from another Member State in order to take up a position as secretary with the Church of Scientology, of which she was a member. Since the UK regarded scientology as socially harmful, it refused her permission to enter the UK as a matter of public policy. At the time, a relevant directive on the free movement of workers provided that permission to enter a Member State could be withheld on grounds of public policy provided, however, that the decision was "based exclusively on the personal conduct of the individual concerned". Ms Van Duyn sought to rely on this provision of the directive before the UK courts. Upon a preliminary reference being made to the Court of Justice, the UK argued that Art 288 draws a clear distinction between regulations and directives, with different effects ascribed to each. Prima facie, therefore, in not issuing a regulation the EU legislature must have intended that the directive should have an effect other than that of a regulation and accordingly should not be binding in its entirety and not be directly applicable in all Member States. These arguments were rejected by the Court in the following, complex passage:

> If … by virtue of the provisions of Article [288] regulations are directly applicable and, consequently, may by their very nature have direct effects, it does not follow from this that other categories of acts mentioned in that Article can never have similar effects. It would be incompatible with the binding effect attributed to a directive by Article [288] to exclude, in principle, the possibility that the obligation which it imposes may be invoked by those concerned. In particular, where the Community authorities have, by directive, imposed on Member States the obligation to pursue a particular course of conduct, the useful effect of such an act would be weakened if individuals were prevented from relying on it before their national courts and if the latter were prevented from taking it into consideration as an element of [EU] law. Article [267], which empowers national courts to refer to the Court questions concerning the validity and interpretation of all acts of the Community institutions, without distinction, implies furthermore that these acts may be invoked by individuals in the national courts. It is necessary to examine, in every case, whether the nature, general scheme and wording of the provision in question are capable of having direct effects on the relations between Member States and individuals.
>
> By providing that measures taken on grounds of public policy shall be based exclusively on the personal conduct of the individual concerned, [the] Directive … is intended to limit the discretionary power which national laws generally confer on the authorities responsible for the entry and expulsion of foreign nationals. First, the provision lays down an obligation which is not subject to any exception or condition and which, by its very nature, does not require the intervention of any act on the part either of the institutions of the Community or of Member States. Secondly, because Member States are thereby obliged, in implementing a clause which derogates from one of the fundamental principles of the Treaty in favour of individuals, not to take account of factors extraneous to personal conduct, legal certainty for the persons concerned requires that they should be able to rely on this obligation even though it has been laid down in a legislative act which has no automatic direct effect in its entirety.[42]

[12–24] As with *Van Gend en Loos*, where the Court of Justice first established the direct effect of Treaty provisions, the Court's reasoning for conferring direct effect on a directive is noticeably weak and places much reliance on the overall importance of

---

Norms Are They Anyway?" (2011) 17 *European Law Journal* 349; Paul Craig, "The Legal Effects of Directives: Policy, Rules and Exceptions" (2009) 34 *European Law Review* 349; Alan Dashwood, "From *Van Duyn* to *Mangold* via *Marshall*: Reducing Direct Effect to Absurdity" (2006–2007) 9 *Cambridge Yearbook of European Legal Studies* 81; Michael Dougan, "The 'Disguised' Vertical Direct Effect of Directives" (2000) 59 *Cambridge Law Journal* 586.

42 *ibid*, 1348.

ensuring EU law's *effet utile*. Regarding the argument that it would be incompatible with the binding effect attributed to a directive in Art 288 to exclude the possibility of its direct effect, this has been dismissed as an unsound "sleight of hand" since "it is quite possible for a measure to be fully binding at the international level without its being enforced in national courts by private individuals", in which case it could still be enforced in proceedings before the Court of Justice brought by the Commission or another Member State.[43] Similarly, no particular inference can be drawn from the nature of the Art 267 procedure given that a national court may equally request a preliminary ruling on a provision of EU law that is not directly effective. Just as it was in *Van Gend en Loos*, the true rationale for conferring the directive with direct effect was the policy imperative to ensure the overall effectiveness of EU law. In order not to weaken the useful effect of directives, it was necessary that they were capable of being directly relied upon before national courts.

[12–25] The decision in *Van Duyn* was subject to much criticism along the lines that the Court had engaged in an intolerable degree of judicial activism that stretched the wording of Art 288 beyond its breaking point. As one account recalls:

> Making directives immediately enforceable poses, however, a formidable problem. Unlike Regulations and the Treaty provisions dealt with by *Van Gend en Loos*, Directives resemble international treaties, in so far as they are binding only on the States and only as to the results to be achieved. It is understandable therefore that, whereas the *Van Gend en Loos* doctrine established itself within a relatively short time, its extension to Directives met with bitter opposition in many quarters. For example, the French Conseil d'État and the German Bundesfinanzhof [Federal Fiscal Court] bluntly refused to abide by it and Professor Rasmussen, in a most un-Danish fit of temper, went so far as to condemn it as a case of "revolting judicial behaviour".[44]

[12–26] The Court of Justice quickly responded to these criticisms by introducing an additional and quite different rationale for the direct effect of directives in the case of *Ratti*.[45] Mr Ratti ran a firm that packaged and sold solvents and varnishes. A directive governed the sale of solvents and the deadline for its transposition had passed. A directive also governed the sale of varnishes but the deadline for its transposition remained outstanding. Italy had not yet transposed either directive. The firm had decided to market its products in compliance with both directives, but was then prosecuted for its failure to adhere to Italian law. In relation to the first directive, whose deadline for transposition had passed, the Court of Justice confirmed that it had direct effect but did so on the basis of a rationale that did not appear in *Van Duyn*. According to the Court:

> It would be incompatible with the binding effect which Article [288] ascribes to directives to exclude on principle the possibility of the obligations imposed by them being relied on by persons concerned.
>
> Particularly in cases in which the Community authorities have, by means of directive, placed Member States under a duty to adopt a certain course of action, the effectiveness of such an act would be weakened if persons were prevented from relying on it in legal

---

43 Robert Schütze, *European Union Law* (Cambridge University Press, 2015) 97; Trevor C Hartley, *The Foundations of European Union Law* (8th ed, Oxford University Press, 2014) 219.

44 Federico Mancini, "The Making of a Constitution for Europe" (1989) 26 *Common Market Law Review* 595, 602.

45 Case 148/78 *Ratti* [1979] ECR 1629.

proceedings and national courts prevented from taking it into consideration as an element of Community law.

Consequently a Member State which has not adopted the implementing measures required by the directive in the prescribed periods may not rely, as against individuals, on its own failure to perform the obligations which the directive entails.

It follows that a national court requested by a person who has complied with the provisions of a directive not to apply a national provision incompatible with the directive not incorporated into the internal legal order of a defaulting Member State, must uphold that request if the obligation in question is unconditional and sufficiently precise.[46]

[12–27] The argument that a Member State may not rely on its own failure to perform the obligation which a directive entails is essentially an estoppel or legitimate expectation argument for justifying the ability of a private party to rely upon a benefit or entitlement in an unimplemented directive against a Member State. In other words, it allows a plaintiff to use the unimplemented directive as a "sword" in proceedings against a state entity. Alternatively, as in this case, the argument may be used to defend oneself against an action by a Member State based on a national law that, in fact, ought to have been amended in order to implement a directive. In other words, it allows a defendant to use the unimplemented directive as a "shield". In essence, had the Member State done what it was supposed to do in fulfilment of EU law, the individual would have been entitled to rely on the directive. Given that the Member State is at fault for failing to bring this situation about, it cannot rely on its own failure to argue that the individual does not yet have such an entitlement. The consequences of this new rationale became evident in *Ratti* when the Court of Justice proceeded to consider the second directive, whose transposition period was yet to expire:

It follows that, for the reasons expounded [above] … it is only at the end of the prescribed period and in the event of the Member State's default that the directive … will be able to have the effects described in the answer to the first question.

Until that date is reached the Member States remain free in that field.

… In conclusion, since a directive by its nature imposes obligations only on Member States, it is not possible for an individual to plead the principle of 'legitimate expectation' before the expiry of the period prescribed for its implementation.

Therefore the … [second] Directive … cannot bring about with respect to any individual who has complied with the provisions of the said directive before the expiration of the adaptation period prescribed for the Member State any effect capable of being taken into consideration by national courts.[47]

[12–28] While the judgment speaks here of a Member State remaining "free in that field" pending the deadline for transposition, in subsequent case law the Court has clarified that during the period for implementation there is an obligation on Member States to refrain from adopting any measure that is liable to seriously compromise the result which the directive aims to achieve.[48]

---

46 *ibid*, 1642.

47 *ibid*, 1645–1646.

48 Case C-192/96 *Inter-Environment Wallonie* [1997] ECR I-7411; Case C-268/06 *IMPACT V Minister for Agriculture and Food* [2008] ECR I-2483, para 92.

[12–29] The adoption of an estoppel rationale has two critical implications for the direct effect of directives. First, direct effect only commences once the period for transposition has expired. Secondly, since direct effect arises due to the responsibility of the Member State for failing to implement the directive, direct effect may only be relied upon against a Member State. In other words, directives are capable of having *vertical* direct effect but do not have *horizontal* direct effect. As the Court made clear in *Marshall v Southampton Area Health Authority*, under Art 288 the binding nature of a directive exists only in relation to each Member State to which it is addressed, and so a directive may not directly impose obligations on, or be relied upon against, an individual.[49]

[12–30] It has been pointed out that the Court's fidelity to the text of Art 288 in *Marshall* is in stark contrast to its purposive approach in cases such as *Van Gend en Loos* and *Defrenne*, where the Court was happy to establish that Treaty provisions, entered into by Member States, were capable of horizontal direct effect. In a number of cases, Advocates General have recommended to the Court that the principles of equality and effectiveness ought to take precedence over the principle of legal certainty, such that horizontal direct effect be extended to directives. In *Faccini Dori*, however, the Court once again reaffirmed its existing position.[50] There, Ms Dori had bought a language-learning course in Milan railway station which she later sought to cancel. A directive that provided for a "cooling-off" period in such circumstances would have permitted cancellation, had it been implemented. The Court of Justice declined to follow the suggestion of the Advocate General Lenz that, following the entry into force of the Maastricht Treaty and the completion of the Internal Market, the interests of the uniform and effective application of EU law should mean that it develops "so as to recognise the general applicability of precise, unconditional provisions in directives in order to respond to the legitimate expectations nurtured by citizens of the Union".[51] Instead, the Court confirmed that the effect of extending the direct effect of directives to private litigation "would be to recognise a power in the [EU] to enact obligations for individuals with immediate effect, whereas it has competence to do so only where it is empowered to adopt regulations".[52] This continues to be the position.

[12–31] Accordingly, when considering the direct effect of directives there are five criteria to assess: is the relevant provision sufficiently clear, precise and unconditional; has the deadline for transposition passed; and can it be said that the directive is being sought to be relied upon against a Member State.[53] Perhaps the best-known instance of direct effect being afforded to a directive in Irish law arose in the case of *McDermott v*

---

49 Case 152/84 *Marshall v Southampton Area Health Authority* [1986] ECR 723, 749.

50 Case C-91/92 *Faccini Dori* [1994] ECR I-3325.

51 *ibid*, 3346.

52 *ibid*, 3356.

53 Examples of the application of the criteria in an Irish context include *Abbeydrive Developments Ltd v Kildare County Council* [2010] 2 ILRM 461, 467–470; *Friends of the Curragh Environment Ltd v An Bord Pleanála* [2009] 4 IR 451, 471–473; *Sweetman v An Bord Pleanála* [2008] 1 IR 277; *Coppinger v Waterford County Council* [1998] 4 IR 220, 227. See Eamonn Conlon, "Vertical and Horizontal Effect of Directives: Recent Irish Cases" (2018) 21 *Irish Journal of European Law* 91; Seán O'Reilly, "The Private Enforcement of European Community Law in the Irish Superior Courts" (2009) 31 *Dublin University Law Journal* 324, 331–337; Bríd Moriarty, "Direct Effect, Indirect Effect and State Liability: An Overview" (2007) 14 *Irish Journal of European Law* 97; Elaine Fahey, *EU Law in Ireland* (Clarus Press, 2010) 25–27.

Minister for Social Welfare[54] and the follow-on judgment in *Tate v Minister for Social Welfare*.[55] In *McDermott*, the Court of Justice confirmed that a directive on the equal treatment of men and women in matters of social security was capable of having direct effect. The case had been referred from the High Court in proceedings in which two married women argued that their entitlement to unemployment benefit would have been greater had they been either single or male, a situation that would not have pertained had Ireland implemented the directive in the time allowed.

[12–32] It is important to note that the fact that a Member State has implemented a directive does not operate so as to preclude any future direct reliance upon it. First, if the Member State has failed to implement the directive correctly, an applicant may continue to invoke its direct effect. Secondly, even where a Member State has correctly implemented a directive, if it is not applying that directive correctly in practice, direct reliance may be placed on the directive. As the Court of Justice explained in the case of *Marks & Spencer*:

> the adoption of national measures correctly implementing a directive does not exhaust the effects of the directive. Member States remain bound *actually to ensure full application of the directive* even after the adoption of those measures. Individuals are therefore entitled to rely before national courts, against the State, on the provisions of a directive which appear, so far as their subject-matter is concerned, to be unconditional and sufficiently precise whenever the full application of the directive is not in fact secured, that is to say, not only where the directive has not been implemented or has been implemented incorrectly, but also where the national measures correctly implementing the directive are not being applied in such a way as to achieve the result sought by it.
>
> … it would be inconsistent with the [Union] legal order for individuals to be able to rely on a directive where it has been implemented incorrectly but not to be able to do so where the national authorities apply the national measures implementing the directive in a manner incompatible with it.[56]

[12–33] While academic debate continues as to the need to extend the direct effect of directives to horizontal situations, the position remains that unimplemented directives are only capable of having vertical direct effect.[57] As will be seen below, there are a number of ways in which the harshness of this rule can be mitigated.

[12–34] First, where an unimplemented directive encapsulates a general principle of EU law, such as in the area of non-discrimination, an applicant may be able to rely directly on the general principle in a horizontal situation to the same effect, provided that the matter is within the scope of EU law. So, for example, both *Mangold* and *Kücükdeveci*, referred to in the previous chapter, involved applicants seeking to rely on general principles of EU law in circumstances where the Equal Treatment Directive was not capable of having horizontal direct effect.[58]

---

[54] Case 286/85 *McDermott v Minister for Social Welfare* [1987] ECR 1453.

[55] [1995] 1 IR 418; [1995] 1 ILRM 507.

[56] Case C-62/00 *Marks & Spencer* [2002] ECR I-6325, 6358-6359. Emphasis added. See Sara Drake, "Vouchers and VAT: Issues of Direct Effect and National Time-Limits Raised by the *Marks and Spencer* Case" (2003) 28 *European Law Review* 418.

[57] See Garrett O'Brolchain, "Unimplemented Directives – Re-examining the Need for Horizontal Direct Effect" (2003) 3 *University College Dublin Law Review* 92.

[58] Case C-144/04 *Mangold* [2005] ECR I-9981; Case C-555/07 *Kücükdeveci* [2010] ECR I-365. See ch 11, paras [11–34] to [11–37].

[12–35] Secondly, the Court of Justice has adopted a very broad approach to determining what constitutes the "state" for the purpose of vertical direct effect. In addition, a directive may be relied upon as against a state entity regardless of whether it was acting in that capacity in the circumstances of the particular case. For example, an unimplemented directive relating to employment matters may be relied upon by the employees of a state entity, placing them in a privileged position as compared with private-sector employees.

[12–36] Thirdly, it has been held that an unimplemented directive can have "incidental" horizontal effects. This can arise where an action is taken against a Member State but, in practice, the outcome of the proceedings will impact on the rights of a private third party. For example, if an unimplemented directive required the carrying out of an environmental impact assessment report prior to the grant of planning permission and a permission was quashed for a failure to adhere to this, the real effect of the judgment will be felt by the private party who had intended to carry out the development on foot of the permission. Another example of incidental horizontal effect arises in the application of Directive 2015/1535, which requires Member States to inform the Commission in advance of any proposed new technical regulations.[59] A failure to do so may require that the national regulation be disapplied by the national courts. Clearly, this may have the result of altering the legal position of private parties that had relied upon, or acted in accordance with, the national regulation.

[12–37] A further important means of compensating for the lack of horizontal direct effect is provided by the possibility of claiming damages as a result of a Member State's failure to fulfil its EU law obligations. As will be seen in Chapter 14, such an action for damages can arise due to a Member State failing to transpose a directive by the end of the prescribed period.

[12–38] A fifth and final way in which the lack of horizontal direct effect of directives is mitigated is through the doctrine of "indirect effect". This requires that, in hearing a case between private parties (as well as proceedings involving the state) a national court is obliged, when applying the provisions of domestic law adopted for the purpose of transposing obligations laid down by a directive, to consider the whole body of rules of national law and to interpret them, so far as possible, in light of the wording and purpose of the directive in order to achieve an outcome consistent with the objective pursued by the directive.

(i) Emanation of the State

[12–39] Since directives are only capable of having vertical direct effect, an important question arises as to what constitutes "the state" for the purpose of relying directly upon a directive. In the *Marshall* case, referred to above, Ms Marshall was required by UK law to retire from the Southampton Area Health Authority at a younger age than her male colleagues. She sought to rely directly on the Equal Treatment Directive in order to challenge the validity of this difference in treatment. The Court of Justice declared that, "where a person involved in legal proceedings is able to rely on a directive as

[59] Directive (EU) 2015/1535 of the European Parliament and of the Council of 9 September 2015 laying down a procedure for the provision of information in the field of technical regulations and of rules on Information Society services [2015] OJ L241/1.

against the State he may do so regardless of the capacity in which the latter is acting, whether employer or public authority. In either case it is necessary to prevent the State from taking advantage of its own failure to comply with [EU] law."[60] In response to the UK's argument that this would give rise to an arbitrary and unfair distinction between the rights of state employees and those of private employees, the Court had a ready answer: "such a distinction may easily be avoided if the Member State concerned has correctly implemented the directive in national law".[61]

[12–40] In *Foster v British Gas*, which concerned precisely the same issue as in *Marshall*, a preliminary reference requested guidance from the Court as to whether, as a nationalised company, British Gas was an emanation of the UK for the purpose of the doctrine of vertical direct effect.[62] The Court established criteria for determining this issue in paragraph 20 of its judgment, namely that:

> a body, whatever its legal form, which has been made responsible, pursuant to a measure adopted by the State, for providing a public service under the control of the State and has for that purpose special powers beyond those which result from the normal rules applicable in relations between individuals is included in any event among the bodies against which the provisions of a directive capable of having direct effect may be relied upon.[63]

[12–41] When these four criteria were subsequently applied by the House of Lords it held that British Gas was an emanation of the state as it had been given a monopoly on the supply of gas, had been conferred by statute with the duty of maintaining an efficient system of gas supply for Great Britain and a government minister had authority to issue it with directions.[64] The fact that the government did not enjoy day-to-day control over the company was held not to be relevant.

[12–42] A complication arose, however, in applying the *Foster v British Gas* test due to the fact that in paragraph 18 of its judgment, the Court of Justice had used a broader formulation than the four criteria set out in paragraph 20. There, the Court indicated that the direct effect of a directive could be invoked against any organisation or body that was either "subject to the authority or control of the State or had special powers beyond those which result from the normal rules applicable to relations between individuals". It was only in the 2017 case of *Farrell v Whitty*, referred from the Irish Supreme Court, that the Court of Justice confirmed that paragraph 20 was not intended to formulate a general test to cover all situations in which a body may be considered an emanation of the state for the purpose of direct effect. Rather, it was sufficient if the organisation or body met *either* of the two criteria set out in paragraph 18, namely that it is subject to the authority or control of the state or, alternatively, possesses special powers beyond those which result from normal rules applicable to relations between individuals.[65] According to the Court:

---

60 Case 152/84 *Marshall v Southampton Area Health Authority* [1986] ECR 723, 749.

61 *ibid*, 749.

62 Case C-188/89 *Foster v British Gas* [1990] ECR I-3313.

63 *ibid*, 3348–3349. In an Irish context see, for example, *Ahmed v Health Service Executive* [2007] 2 IR 106, 125; *Catholic University School v Dooley* [2011] 4 IR 517, 533; *Browne v An Bord Pleanála* [1991] 2 IR 209, 216–220; *Friends of the Curragh Environment Ltd v An Bord Pleanála* [2009] 4 IR 451, 471; *Sweetman v An Bord Pleanála* [2008] 1 IR 277, 288.

64 [1991] AC 306.

65 Case C-413/15 *Farrell v Whitty* EU:C:2017:745, 10 October 2017, para 33.

> Such organisations or bodies can be distinguished from individuals and must be treated as comparable to the State, either because they are legal persons governed by public law that are part of the State in the broad sense, or because they are subject to the authority or control of a public body, or because they have been required, by such a body, to perform a task in the public interest and have been given, for that purpose, such special powers.
>
> Accordingly, a body or an organisation, even one governed by private law, to which a Member State has delegated the performance of a task in the public interest and which possesses for that purpose special powers beyond those which result from the normal rules applicable to relations between individuals is one against which the provisions of a directive that have direct effect may be relied upon.[66]

[12–43] *Farrell v Whitty* concerned the Motor Insurance Bureau of Ireland (MIBI), a company limited by guarantee that was entirely funded by its members, in the form of insurers operating in the motor insurance market in Ireland, and was established following an agreement between the Department of Local Government and the participating motor insurers. Pursuant to a later agreement with the Minister for the Environment, it was provided that legal proceedings could be brought against the MIBI by any person seeking compensation from an uninsured or unidentified driver, and that compensation would be paid by the MIBI to the victims of uninsured or unidentified drivers. A directive on motor insurance also required Member States to set up or authorise a body with the task of providing compensation for personal injuries caused by an unidentified or uninsured vehicle. In finding that the MIBI was an emanation of the Irish State, against whom the directive could be relied upon, the Court of Justice reasoned as follows:

> the task that a compensation body such as MIBI is required by a Member State to perform, a task that contributes to the general objective of victim protection pursued by the EU legislation relating to compulsory motor vehicle liability insurance, must be regarded as a task in the public interest that is inherent, in this case, in the obligation imposed on the Member States by … the Second Directive.
>
> … As regards the MIBI, it must be added that … the Irish legislature made membership of that organisation compulsory for all insurers who carry on motor vehicle insurance in Ireland. In doing so, the Irish legislature conferred on the MIBI special powers beyond those which result from the normal rules applicable to relations between individuals, in that, on the basis of that statutory provision, that private organisation has the power to require all those insurers to become members of it and to contribute funds for the performance of the task conferred on it by the Irish State.
>
> The provisions of a directive that are unconditional and sufficiently precise may consequently be relied upon against an organisation such as the MIBI.[67]

[12–44] The ruling of the Court of Justice clarified an important aspect of the direct effect of directives and brought to an end a long series of cases in which the Irish courts had come to differing conclusions as to whether or not the MIBI ought to be regarded as an emanation of the State.[68]

---

[66] *ibid*, paras 34–35.

[67] *ibid*, paras 36–41.

[68] See *Farrell v Whitty* [2015] IESC 39, 12 May 2015; *Farrell v Whitty* [2008] IEHC 124, Birmingham J, 31 January 2008; *De Largy v Minister for the Environment and Local Government* [2005] IEHC 94, Murphy J, 18 March 2005; *Dublin Bus v MIBI*, Circuit Court, unreported, McMahon J, 29 October 1999; *Withers v Delaney*, Circuit Court, unreported, McMahon J, 7 February 2003;

(ii) Incidental Horizontal Effect

[12–45] Adopting an expansive definition of an emanation of the state was one way in which to mitigate the harshness of the rule whereby directives were incapable of having horizontal direct effect. A second means has arisen whereby the Court of Justice has permitted directives to be relied upon against state institutions even where the practical effects of doing so is borne by a private party. So, for example, an unsuccessful applicant for a government procurement contract or an individual whose objection to planning permission was not upheld may be able to challenge the award of the contract or the grant of planning permission if it failed to comply with an unimplemented directive, notwithstanding that it is the right of a private party that will be most affected.[69] In the view of Derrick Wyatt and Alan Dashwood, "for the Court to accept so willingly that the enforcement of an unimplemented directive vertically against the Member State may legitimately produce 'incidental effects' for a third (private) party does threaten to make its reasoning [in *Marshall* and *Faccini Dori*] appear rather more formalistic than deeply principled".[70]

[12–46] Situations such as these are known as the "incidental" horizontal effect of directives, or disguised direct effect.[71] A more obvious use of incidental horizontal effect has arisen in the context of Directive 2015/1535 on the provision of information in the field of technical regulations.[72] This important Directive is considered further in Chapter 15. A key focus of the Directive is on technical specifications, which are defined broadly as a specification contained in a document which lays down the characteristics required of a product such as levels of quality, performance, safety or dimensions, including the requirements applicable to the product as regards the name under which the product is sold, terminology, symbols, testing and test methods, packaging, marking or labelling and conformity assessment procedures. Notifications of proposed technical regulations are required to be submitted to the Commission for consideration by it and by the other Member States.

[12–47] Directive 2015/1535 has been given further "bite" by virtue of the fact that, in conjunction with the doctrine of the supremacy of EU law, directives of this kind have been held to be capable of giving rise to an incidental form of horizontal effect.

Eamonn Conlon, "Vertical and Horizontal Effect of Directives: Recent Irish Cases" (2018) 21 *Irish Journal of European Law* 91; Elaine Fahey, *EU Law in Ireland* (Clarus Press, 2010) 33–36; Bríd Moriarty, "Direct Effect, Indirect Effect and State Liability: An Overview" (2007) 14 *Irish Journal of European Law* 97, 144–150; John Gaffney, "Pleading EC Law in Irish Litigation: A Case Study" (2005) 5 *Judicial Studies Institute Journal* 153, 188–193.

69 Case 103/88 *Fratelli Costanzo* [1989] ECR 1839; Case C-201/02 *Wells* [2004] ECR I-723.

70 Alan Dashwood, Michael Dougan, Barry Rodger, Eleanor Spaventa and Derrick Wyatt, *Wyatt and Dashwood's European Union Law* (6th ed, Hart, 2011) 264.

71 See Michael Dougan, "The 'Disguised' Vertical Direct Effect of Directives" (2000) 59 *Cambridge Law Journal* 586; Takis Tridimas, "Black, White and Shades of Grey: Horizontality of Directives Revisited" (2002) 21 *Yearbook of European Law* 327.

72 Directive (EU) 2015/1535 of the European Parliament and of the Council of 9 September 2015 laying down a procedure for the provision of information in the field of technical regulations and of rules on Information Society services [2015] OJ L241/1. In an Irish context see, for example, the discussion in *McNally v Ireland* [2011] 4 IR 431, 450–451 and *James Elliott Construction Ltd v Irish Asphalt Ltd* [2014] IESC 74, unreported, Supreme Court, 2 December 2014, paras 156–184 and Case C-613/14 *James Elliott Construction Ltd v Irish Asphalt Ltd* EU:C:2016:821, 27 October 2016, paras 63–72 (where the national measure at issue was held not to be a technical regulation within the meaning of the Directive).

In *CIA Security*, an application was brought to restrain CIA Security from selling an alarm system on the basis that it had not received the necessary prior authorisation required under Belgian law.[73] In response, CIA Security argued that the relevant Belgian law had not been notified to the Commission pursuant to an earlier version of Directive 2015/1535. The Court of Justice considered that, as there was an obligation on Member States to notify draft technical regulations to the Commission before they were adopted, which was "unconditional and sufficiently precise in terms of [its] content", the Directive could be relied on by individuals before their national courts. Although Germany, the UK and the Netherlands argued that the Directive ought to be regarded as solely concerning relations between Member States and the Commission, and as merely creating procedural obligations for the Member States, the Court concluded that:

> the effectiveness of [Union] control will be that much greater if the Directive is interpreted as meaning that breach of the obligation to notify constitutes a substantial procedural defect such as to render the technical regulations in question *inapplicable to individuals*.[74]

[12–48] Accordingly, the Belgian law which ought to have been notified to the Commission could not be invoked by the private party in order to restrain CIA Security from selling unauthorised alarm systems. As the Court put it, an individual could rely on Directive 2015/1535 in a private action "before the national court which must decline to apply a national technical regulation which has not been notified in accordance with the directive".[75] In the following chapter it will be seen that the obligation upon a national court to disapply a national law that is incompatible with EU law lies at the heart of the doctrine of supremacy.

[12–49] A similar result emerged in *Unilever v Central Food* in relation to an Italian law that confined the use of the term "Italian" when marketing olive oil to produce that had been harvested, produced, processed and packaged in Italy.[76] The law was enacted despite the fact that the Commission had called upon Italy to postpone its enactment for 12 months, as it intended to introduce a harmonising measure in the area. Unilever had provided olive oil to Central Foods pursuant to a contract that expressly required the goods to be labelled in accordance with Italian law. When Central Foods refused to accept them on the basis that they were, under the Italian law, incorrectly labelled "Italian", the Court of Justice held that the relevant law could not be relied upon as it had not been notified to the Commission prior to its adoption. According to the Court, while it was true that, as per *Faccini Dori*, of itself a directive cannot impose obligations on an individual and so cannot be relied upon, as such, against an individual, that did not apply where non-compliance with (what is now) Directive 2015/1535 renders a national technical regulation inapplicable. In the eyes of the Court, failure to comply with the Directive amounted to a "substantial procedural defect".[77] The Court distinguished its earlier case law concerning the non-transposition of a directive by stating that Directive 2015/1535 did not create rights or obligations for individuals and did not "in any way

---

[73] Case C-194/94 *CIA Security International* [1996] ECR I-2201.

[74] *ibid*, 2247. See Michael Dougan, "Community Directives: Explaining *CIA Security*?" (2001) 60 *Cambridge Law Journal* 231.

[75] *ibid.*

[76] Case C-443/98 *Unilever v Central Food* [2000] ECR I-7535.

[77] *ibid*, 7585.

define the substantive scope of the legal rule on the basis of which the national court must decide the case before it".[78]

[12–50] In both *CIA Security* and *Unilever*, it can be said that the incidental horizontal effect given to a directive had the effect of *excluding* the application of a national law that would otherwise have applied. This is known as an "exclusionary effect" and can be seen as deriving from the supremacy of EU law. Bearing in mind the reasons why directives are not afforded horizontal direct effect, incidental effects do not go so far as to substitute EU law for a national law or, in other words, cannot have "substitutionary effect". As has been pointed out, however, this distinction is based on a questionable assumption that "to 'exclude' national law that is inconsistent with a directive is somehow less intrusive or less far-reaching in its consequences for the individual than 'substitution' of something new within the national legal order".[79]

[12–51] The Court's reasoning in *CIA Security* and *Unilever* has been subject to criticism. In relation to *Unilever* in particular, it is unclear what the significance is of the Court's characterisation of Italy's failure to comply with Directive 2015/1535 as a "substantial procedural defect". In stating that the Directive did not create rights or obligations for individuals, the Court may have meant that it was the contract itself, and not the Directive, that required the goods to be labelled in accordance with Italian law. Nevertheless, in both cases the legal situation of the parties was reversed as a result of the effect given to the Directive. Were it not for the effect given to the Directive, CIA Security would not have been entitled to sell its alarm system in Belgium as it failed to comply with Belgian law. Similarly, were it not for the Directive, Central Food would have been entitled to refuse to accept the olive oil provided by Unilever, as it was not labelled in accordance with Italian law. More generally, it might be said that in both cases the Court of Justice prioritised enhancing the effectiveness of Directive 2015/1535 over the principle of legal certainty. By excluding the application of a national technical regulation that was not adopted in compliance with the Directive, the Court strengthened the need to comply with the Directive at the expense of a private party whose legal position was altered due to the failure of the Member State. As Stephen Weatherill has commented in relation to *Unilever*:

> Although one may accept the Court's analysis that the Directive did not impose an obligation directly on Central Foods, nevertheless the injection into the proceedings of the consequences of Italy's failure to suspend its laws as required by the directive entirely changed the circumstances in which the pattern of rights and obligations arising under the contract fell to be judged. Goods which could have been refused under domestic law now had to be accepted. This is not horizontal direct effect according to its classic meaning, but it is not so very far away in its effect on the legal position of private parties. An unimplemented directive has exerted a powerful impact on a private party; it has altered Central Food's contractual position. It is troubling that the Court of Justice feels justified in loading immense constitutional significance on to such a narrow distinction.[80]

[12–52] In a subsequent case, *Sapod Audic*, the Court of Justice has sought to temper the rigidity of *CIA Security* and *Univiler* by emphasising that the conclusions to be

[78] *ibid*

[79] Paul Craig and Gráinne de Búrca, *EU Law* (6th ed, Oxford University Press, 2015) 220.

[80] Stephen Weatherill, "Breaches of Directives and Breach of Contract" (2001) 26 *European Law Review* 177, 183. For the relationship between incidental horizontal direct effect of this kind, and the supremacy of EU law, see ch 13, paras [13–16] to [13–22].

drawn from the inapplicability of the national regulation is a question to be governed by the national law governing contracts.[81] Accordingly, in deciding on the implications in any particular case, the national court should include within its consideration any rules of contract law that limit or adjust the sanction for non-performance "in order to render its severity proportionate to the particular defect found".[82]

D. Indirect Effect

[12–53] The doctrine of indirect effect was first developed in the context of considering what account should be taken of a directive that was not sufficiently clear, precise and unconditional to be capable of direct effect but that had not been adequately implemented into national law. Like the emanation of the state doctrine and incidental horizontal effect, indirect effect serves to lessen the harshness of the rule whereby directives may be capable of being relied upon against a Member State, but not in disputes as between private parties. Indirect effect is also known as the duty of harmonious interpretation and is now understood to apply to all sources of EU law, and not just directives.[83] It does, however, have a particular pertinence when interpreting national measures that have been introduced for the very purpose of implementing a directive.[84] In the case of directives, the duty of harmonious interpretation does not fully apply until the period for transposition has ended. Prior to that time, to the extent possible national courts must refrain from interpreting national law in a way that might seriously compromise the attainment of the directive's objective.[85]

[12–54] The indirect effect of directives was first established in the seminal 1984 case of *Von Colson*.[86] Ms Von Colson had applied for a job as a social worker in a prison but was unsuccessful, with the position offered to a male candidate. A German court accepted that she had been denied the job due to her sex but held that, under German law implementing the Equal Treatment Directive, the only compensation available was that equalling the expenses incurred in applying and attending for interview. Ms Colson sought to rely directly on a provision of the Directive that required Member States to ensure that persons discriminated against had recourse to an effective judicial remedy. In replying to a preliminary reference, the Court of Justice held that this provision was not sufficiently precise to be capable of direct effect. Nevertheless, the Court went on to state:

> the Member States' obligation arising from a directive to achieve the result envisaged by the directive and their duty under Article [4 TEU] to take all appropriate measures, whether general or particular, to ensure the fulfilment of that obligation, is binding on all the authorities of Member States including, for matters within their jurisdiction, the courts. It follows that, in applying the national law and in particular the provisions of a national

---

81 Case C-159/00 *Sapod Audic* [2002] ECR I-5031.

82 *ibid*, 5078.

83 For example, in Case C-60/02 *Rolex* [2004] ECR I-651 a duty of harmonious interpretation was held to apply in the context of interpreting a regulation.

84 See Marcus Klammert, "Judicial Implementation of Directives and Anticipatory Indirect Effect: Connecting the Dots" (2006) 43 *Common Market Law Review* 1251; Ninon Colneric, "Interpretation of Community Law and Interpretation in Conformity with Community Law" (2005) 12 *Irish Journal of European Law* 142.

85 Case C-212/04 *Adeneler* [2006] ECR I-6057, 6134.

86 Case 14/83 *Von Colson* [1984] ECR 1891.

> law specifically introduced in order to implement [the] Directive ... national courts are required to interpret their national law in the light of the wording and the purpose of the directive in order to achieve the result referred to in the third paragraph of Article [288].
>
> It should ... be pointed out to the national court that although [the] Directive ..., for the purpose of imposing a sanction for the breach of the prohibition of discrimination, leaves the Member States free to choose between the different solutions suitable for achieving its objective, it nevertheless requires that if a Member States chooses to penalize breaches of that prohibition by the award of compensation, then in order to ensure that it is effective and that it has a deterrent effect, that compensation must in any event be adequate in relation to the damage sustained and must therefore amount to more than purely nominal compensation such as, for example, the reimbursement only of the expenses incurred in connection with the application. It is for the national court to interpret and apply the legislation adopted for the implementation of the directive in conformity with the requirements of [EU] law, in so far as it is given discretion to do so under national law.[87]

[12–55] The doctrine of indirect effect was further developed by the case of *Marleasing*, where it was established that the obligation applies to all national legislation, not just legislation enacted in order to implement a directive.[88] Indeed, the obligation applies to legislation that pre-dates the adoption of a directive. *Marleasing* also clarified that the obligation of harmonious interpretation applies to horizontal situations between two private parties, in this case one Spanish company seeking to have the incorporation of another Spanish company declared void. Under Spanish law, a contract without a cause had no legal effect. It was claimed that, by way of a sham transaction, a company was formed for the purpose of defrauding creditors. A directive on company law, however, provided an exhaustive list of the grounds on which an incorporation could be declared void, and this did not include a lack of cause. As the directive had not yet been implemented in Spain, there was a conflict between it and Spanish law. The Court of Justice repeated the obligation, expressed in *Von Colson*, on national courts to interpret national law in conformity with the requirements of EU law, "in so far as it is given discretion to do so under national law". It followed that,

> in applying national law, *whether the provisions in question were adopted before or after the directive*, the national court called upon to interpret it is required to do so, *as far as possible*, in the light of the wording and the purpose of the directive in order to achieve the result pursued by the latter and thereby comply with the third paragraph of Article [288] of the Treaty.
>
> It follows that the requirement that national law must be interpreted in conformity with [the] Directive ... precludes the interpretation of provisions of national law relating to public limited companies in such a manner that the nullity of a public limited company may be ordered on grounds other than those exhaustively listed in ... the directive in question.[89]

[12–56] A more recent restatement of the obligation of harmonious interpretation was provided by the Court in *Pfeiffer*.[90] There, employees of the German Red Cross sought to rely on a directive governing health and safety at work that set 48 hours as the maximum working week. The employees argued that the manner in which their working

---

87 *ibid*, 1909.

88 Case C-106/89 *Marleasing* [1990] ECR I-4135.

89 *ibid*, 4159, emphasis added. See Gráinne de Búrca, "Giving Effect to European Community Directives" (1992) 52 *Modern Law Review* 215; Nick Maltby, "*Marleasing*: What is all the Fuss About?" (1993) 109 *Law Quarterly Review* 301.

90 Joined Cases C-397/01 to C-403/01 *Pfeiffer* [2004] ECR I-8835.

hours were calculated under the German transposing law was contrary to the directive. The Court placed the obligation of harmonious interpretation within the context of the framework of EU law as a whole, and not just the duty of sincere cooperation under Art 4 TEU, commenting that:

> The requirement for national law to be interpreted in conformity with [EU] law is inherent in the system of the Treaty, since it permits the national court, for the matters within its jurisdiction, to ensure the full effectiveness of [EU] law when it determines the dispute before it.
>
> Although the principle that national law must be interpreted in conformity with [EU] law concerns chiefly domestic provisions enacted in order to implement the directive in question, it does not entail an interpretation merely to those provisions but requires the national court to consider national law as a whole in order to assess to what extent it may be applied so as not to produce a result contrary to that sought by the directive.
>
> In that context, if the application of interpretative methods recognised by national law enables, in certain circumstances, a provision of domestic law to be construed in such a way as to avoid conflict with another rule of domestic law or the scope of that provision to be restricted to that end by applying it only in so far as it is compatible with the rule concerned, the national court is bound to use those methods in order to achieve the result sought by the directive.
>
> ... Accordingly, ... when hearing a case between individuals, a national court is required, when applying the provisions of domestic law adopted for the purpose of transposing obligations laid down by a directive, to consider the whole body of rules of national law and to interpret them, so far as possible, in light of the wording and purpose of the directive in order to achieve an outcome consistent with the objective pursued by the directive.[91]

[12–57] There was, therefore, a duty on the German court to "do whatever lies within its jurisdiction" to ensure that the directive was effective in preventing the maximum 48-hour working week from being exceeded. This concept of the national court's obligation being "to the extent possible" points to the inherent tension between ensuring that a provision of EU law is effective, while at the same time acting within the limits of national law. As Stephen Weatherill has described:

> An enduring tension lies embedded within this line of case law. On the one hand, there is a concern to enhance the "full effectiveness" of EU law, which is promoted by requiring national judiciaries to adapt national provisions in order to achieve the objectives set out by the Treaty and legislation adopted thereunder. On the other hand, there is a concern that such adaptation, which in some circumstances may fall little short of judicial re-writing of national law which does not conform to EU law, generates uncertainty and unpredictability in the law and inflicts potential unfairness on private parties who happen to find apparently reliable rules of national law set aside by a court, not a legislature.
>
> ... Although the principle of legal certainty is unequivocally part of EU law and serves to protect private parties, it will often be difficult for a national court to determine how much momentum it carries when it collides with the principle of conform-interpretation to which national judges are subject. The Court of Justice frequently seems concerned to avoid clarifying in concrete terms what limits on creative judicial interpretation are envisaged by the proviso that interpretation be conducted 'so far as possible'.[92]

---

[91] *ibid*, 8918–8919.

[92] Stephen Weatherill, *Cases and Materials on EU Law* (10th ed, Oxford University Press, 2012) 136, 137.

[12–58] This tension is particularly evident when one considers that, similar to the incidental horizontal effect of directives, harmonious interpretation can result in the legal position of a private party being altered where they believe themselves to have acted in conformity with national law. In *Centrosteel*, for example, when one company sought to enforce a commercial agency contract against another, the defendant argued that the contract was void as it was not in compliance with the requirement under Italian law that it be registered.[93] Had the relevant Italian law applied without the need to interpret it in conformity with EU law, this argument would have been decisive. In response, however, Centrosteel successfully argued that the Italian law must be given a harmonious interpretation with an EU directive that required only that such contracts be in writing in order to be valid, thereby reversing the outcome of the case.

[12–59] In order to achieve some balance as between these competing tensions, the Court of Justice has placed three limitations on the obligation to interpret national law in a manner that is in conformity with EU law. These limitations derive from general principles of EU law concerning legal certainty and non-retroactivity. First, the obligation of harmonious interpretation does not require the national court to contravene its own domestic law, or to give a provision of domestic law an interpretation that it simply cannot bear (ie an interpretation *contra legem*). As described by Murray CJ:

> If national legislation, having been interpreted as far as possible in conformity with [EU] legislation to which it purports to give effect, but still falls short of what is required by the latter, a national court must, as a general principle, apply that legislation as interpreted although there may be other consequences for a Member State which has failed to fully implement a directive or framework decision.[94]

[12–60] Secondly, the obligation is not intended to operate so as to impose or increase the criminal liability of an individual.[95] Thirdly, the obligation should not result in legislation being granted retrospective effect where this was not intended.

[12–61] Careful consideration of these limitations was displayed in *IMPACT v Minister for Agriculture and Food*, where the Court of Justice went further than usual in providing guidance as to how the referring court should exercise its discretion.[96] There, a directive on fixed-term contracts of employment was implemented in Irish law by the Protection of Employees (Fixed-Term Work) Act 2003. Although the directive was to be transposed by July 2001, the Act only entered into force in July 2003. In making a claim for equal treatment with established civil servants, it was submitted that a number of workers had had successive fixed-term contracts renewed during the period from July 2001 to July 2003, when the directive ought to have been transposed but was not. In making a preliminary reference, the Labour Court noted that while Irish law generally precludes the retrospective application of legislation, there was nothing in the 2003 Act to prevent it from being applied retrospectively. It asked, therefore, whether the obligation of harmonious interpretation meant that the 2003 Act could be applied retrospectively so as to impose civil liability on Irish government departments, in their capacity as an employer, for acts contrary to the provisions of the directive

---

93 Case C-456/98 *Centrosteel* [2000] ECR I-6007.

94 *Minister for Justice, Equality and Law Reform v Altaravicius* [2006] 3 IR 148, 156.

95 Case 80/86 *Kolpinghuis Nijmegen* [1987] ECR 3969; Case C-168/95 *Arcaro* [1996] ECR I-4705; Case C-105/03 *Pupino* [2005] ECR I-5285; Case C-403/02 *Berlusconi* [2005] ECR I-3565.

96 Case C-268/06 *IMPACT v Minister for Agriculture and Food* [2008] ECR I-2483.

which occurred at a time when that directive ought to have been transposed. In addition to setting out the general principles to be applied, the Court of Justice was unusually explicit as to how it foresaw their application in Irish law:

> The referring court states … that, while it is true that the wording of section 6 of the 2003 Act does not expressly preclude a retrospective construction, a domestic rule of construction does preclude the retrospective application of legislation unless there is a clear and unambiguous indication to the contrary.
>
> In that regard, when applying domestic law and, in particular, legislative provisions specifically adopted for the purpose of implementing the requirements of a directive, national courts are bound to interpret that law, so far as possible, in the light of the wording and the purpose of the directive in order to achieve the result sought by it and thus to comply with the third paragraph of Article [288].
>
> The requirement that national law be interpreted in conformity with [EU] law is inherent in the system of the … Treaty, since it permits national courts, for the matters within their jurisdiction, to ensure the full effectiveness of [EU] law when they determine the disputes before them.
>
> However, the obligation on a national court to refer to the content of a directive when interpreting and applying the relevant rules of domestic law is limited by general principles of law, particularly those of legal certainty and non-retroactivity, and that obligation cannot serve as the basis for an interpretation of national law *contra legem*.
>
> The principle that national law must be interpreted in conformity with [EU] law none the less requires national courts to do whatever lies within their jurisdiction, taking the whole body of domestic law into consideration and applying the interpretative methods recognised by domestic law, with a view to ensuring that the directive in question is fully effective and achieving an outcome consistent with the objective pursued by it.
>
> In the present case, since, … domestic law appears to include a rule that precludes the retrospective application of legislation unless there is a clear and unambiguous indication to the contrary, it is for the referring court to ascertain whether there is a provision in that legislation, in particular in the 2003 Act, which contains such an indication capable of giving retrospective effect to section 6 of the 2003 Act.
>
> In the absence of such a provision, [EU] law – in particular the requirement for national law to be interpreted in conformity with [EU] law – cannot be interpreted as requiring the referring court to give … the 2003 Act retrospective effect to the date by which [the] Directive should have been transposed, as the referring court would otherwise be constrained to interpret national law *contra legem*.
>
> In the light of the foregoing, the answer … must be that, in so far as the applicable national law contains a rule that precludes the retrospective application of legislation unless there is a clear and unambiguous indication to the contrary, a national court hearing a claim based on an infringement of a provision of national legislation transposing [the] Directive is required, under [EU] law, to give that provision retrospective effect to the date by which that directive should have been transposed only if that national legislation includes an indication of that nature capable of giving that provision retrospective effect.[97]

[12–62] In the recent case of *Minister for Justice and Equality v Vilkas*, the Supreme Court overturned a decision of the Court of Appeal which had found that a provision

---

97 *ibid*, paras 97–104.

of the European Arrest Warrant Act 2003 was capable of being given a harmonious interpretation with the EAW Framework Decision.[98] Mr Vilkas had frustrated his surrender from Ireland by twice refusing to board commercial flights. A question arose as to whether the terms of the 2003 Act permitted an agreement with the requesting state on a new surrender date on more than one occasion. Following a preliminary ruling from the Court of Justice which established that the Framework Decision did permit more than one extension of the surrender date, the Court of Appeal interpreted the 2003 Act in a harmonious fashion.[99] In overturning this on appeal, McKenchnie J made the following general observations in delivering the judgment of the Supreme Court:

> Often the case law of the CJEU will simply refer to the prohibition on a *contra legem* interpretation without elaborating on what precisely this means. However, the meaning of the concept is somewhat intuitive although generally well understood at a surface level: it is that a court cannot adopt an interpretation which goes against the express wording of a provision. Put differently where it is not reasonably possible to construe a national measure in conformity with its EU counterpart, to do so would be against the law. If a conflict of that scale exists, a court must give preference to its domestic provisions.
>
> A good description of the rule was that as stated by AG Bobek in his Opinion in Case C 220/15 *European Commission v Federal Republic of Germany*, where he said that "the clear wording of a provision is the outer limit of any interpretative endeavour". The same Advocate General also defined the principles thus in his Opinion in Case C–441/14 *Dansk Industri, acting on behalf of Ajos* ... :
>
>> "A *contra legem* interpretation must, to my mind, be understood as being an interpretation that contradicts the very wording of the national provision at issue. In other words, a national court is confronted by the obstacle of *contra legem* interpretation when the clear, unequivocal wording of a provision of national law appears to be irreconcilable with the wording of a directive. The Court has acknowledged that *contra legem* interpretation represents a limit on the obligation of consistent interpretation, since it cannot require national courts to exercise their interpretative competence to such a point that they substitute for the legislative authority." (para. 68)
>
> As alluded to in this passage, the interpretive limit provided by the *contra legem* principle is tied to the separation of powers, insofar as it ensures that a court will not assume the mantle of a legislature and interpret a provision contrary to the clear meaning of its express terms. To interpret *contra legem* is to surpass the limits of the judicial function, for the judge must be bound by statute. The concept is also connected to the principles of legality and legal certainty, in that it is important that the law should be certain and its application foreseeable, which understandably would not be the case if judges could freely adopt interpretations *contra legem*, as just defined.[100]

[12–63] When interpreting EU legal acts, or Irish legislation implementing EU legal acts, the Irish courts have deemed it appropriate to adopt a teleological approach, aimed at achieving the purpose of the act in question.[101] This is combined with the doctrine of harmonious interpretation, which has been applied by the Irish courts

---

98 [2018] IESC 69, unreported, Supreme Court, 5 December 2018.

99 [2018] IECA 33, unreported, Court of Appeal, 15 February 2018.

100 [2018] IESC 69, unreported, Supreme Court, 5 December 2018, McKechnie J, paras 79–81.

101 See *NAMA v Commissioner for Environmental Information* [2015] 4 IR 626, 637; *OCS One Complete Solutions Ltd v Dublin Airport Authority* [2015] IESC 6, unreported, Supreme Court, 30 January 2015; *O'Connell v Environmental Protection Agency* [2003] 1 IR 530, 555; *Bosphorus Hava v Minister for Transport* [1994] 2 ILRM 551, 558.

in a wide range of areas, including with regard to directives concerning the Aarhus Convention,[102] animal health,[103] asylum and subsidiary protection,[104] data protection,[105] electronic communications and services,[106] environmental impact assessments,[107] equal treatment,[108] free movement of persons,[109] genetically modified organisms,[110] milk quotas,[111] health and safety of workers,[112] intellectual property rights,[113] misleading advertising,[114] organisation of working time,[115] package holidays,[116] public procurement,[117] VAT,[118] and waste management and disposal.[119] The doctrine has also been applied in connection with other EU legal acts, such as regulations[120] and, to a prominent extent, the European Arrest Warrant Framework Decision.[121]

---

102 *NAMA v Commissioner for Environmental Information* [2015] 4 IR 626; [2015] 2 ILRM 165; *Right to Know CLG v An Taoiseach* [2019] 1 ILRM 270.

103 *Albatross Feeds Ltd v Minister for Agriculture* [2007] 1 IR 221, 244–245.

104 *MST v Minister for Justice, Equality and Law Reform* [2009] IEHC 529, unreported, High Court, Cooke J, 4 December 2009, para 27; *Izevbekhai v Minister for Justice and Equality* [2010] IESC 44, unreported, Supreme Court, 9 July 2010, paras 82–87; *WA v Minister for Justice and Equality* [2012] IEHC 251, unreported, High Court, Cooke J, 25 June 2012, para 33; *NN (Cameroon) v Minister for Justice and Equality* [2014] 3 IR 396, 417; *LH v Minister for Justice, Equality and Law Reform* [2011] 3 IR 700, 711–712.

105 *Collins v FBD Insurance plc* [2013] IEHC 137, unreported, High Court, Feeney J, 14 March 2013, para 3.6.

106 *Eircom Ltd v Commission for Communications Regulation* [2007] 1 IR 1, 24–25.

107 *Maher v An Bord Pleanála* [1999] 2 ILRM 198, 213–214; *O'Connell v Environmental Protection Agency* [2003] 1 IR 530, 555 (Fennelly J); *Usk and District Residents Association Ltd v An Bord Pleanála* [2010] 4 IR 113, 178-179, 182; *Environmental Protection Agency v Harte Peat Ltd* [2015] 1 IR 462.

108 *Nathan v Bailey Gibson* [1998] 2 IR 162; *Telecom Éireann v O'Grady* [1998] 3 IR 432.

109 *IB v Minister for Justice, Equality and Law Reform* [2009] IEHC 447, unreported, High Court, 15 October 2009 Cooke J; *Lahyani v Minister for Justice* [2013] 2 IR 131, 149; *KP v Minister for Justice and Equality* [2017] IEHC 95, unreported, High Court, Humphreys J, 20 February 2017, paras 30–33.

110 *Watson v Environmental Protection Agency* [2000] 2 IR 454, 477.

111 *Dowling v Ireland* [1991] 2 IR 379, 383; *Lawlor v Minister for Agriculture* [1990] I IR 356, 374–376.

112 *Thompson v Dublin Bus* [2016] 2 IR 156, 169–184.

113 *Duhan v Radius Television Productions Ltd* [2008] 1 IR 506, 522.

114 *Dunnes Stores Ltd v Mandate* [1996] 1 IR 55.

115 *Coastal Line Container Terminal Ltd v SIPTU* [2000] 1 IR 549, 559–561.

116 *Scaife v Falcon Leisure Group (Overseas) Ltd* [2008] 2 IR 359, 373.

117 *OCS One Complete Solutions Ltd v Dublin Airport Authority* [2015] IESC 6, unreported, Supreme Court, 30 January 2015, paras 5.1–5.5, 9.22–9.24.

118 *Crawford (Inspector of Taxes) v Centime Ltd* [2006] 2 IR 106, 113; *Cadbury Ireland Pension Trust Ltd v Revenue Commissioners* [2007] 4 IR 334, 340.

119 *Wicklow County Council v Fenton (No 2)* [2002] 4 IR 44, 62–63, 68; *Brady v Environmental Protection Agency* [2007] 3 IR 232, 248; *Environmental Protection Agency v Neiphin Trading Ltd* [2011] 2 IR 575, 614–620, 634–637; *Laois County Council v Scully* [2006] 2 IR 292, 295.

120 *Bosphorus Hava v Minister for Transport* [1994] 2 ILRM 551, 557–558 (concerning EU sanctions); *Popley v Popley* [2006] 4 IR 356, 364 (concerning the jurisdiction and recognition and enforcement of civil and commercial judgments).

121 *Dundon v Governor of Cloverhill Prison* [2006] 1 IR 518, 531, 547; *Minister for Justice, Equality and Law Reform v Altaravicius* [2006] 3 IR 148, 156; *O Fallúin v Governor of Cloverhill Prison* [2007] 3 I.R. 414, 420; *Minister for Justice, Equality and Law Reform v Stapleton* [2008] 1 IR 669, 684; *Minister for Justice, Equality and Law Reform v Desjatnikovs* [2009] 1 IR 618, 635; *Minister for Justice, Equality and Law Reform v Gotszlik* [2007] IEHC 369, unreported, High Court (Peart J) 2 November 2007; [2009] 3 IR 390, 403–404 (Supreme Court); *SMR v Governor of Wheatfield Prison* [2010] 1 IR 141, 156, 166; *Minister for Justice, Equality and Law Reform v Murphy* [2010] 3 IR 77, 92–93; *Minister for Justice v Dillon* [2011] 3 IR 536, 544; *Minister for*

[12–64] A useful illustration of how the harmonious interpretation doctrine operates in practice is to compare the two judgments in *Nathan v Bailey Gibson Ltd* and *Telecom Éireann v O'Grady*, which concern Ireland's implementation of the Equal Treatment Directive through the Employment Equality Act 1977. When her colleague retired as a machine operator, Ms Nathan applied for the position but was informed that the company operated a "closed shop" whereby members of the Irish Print Union had the first opportunity to fill available vacancies. The membership of the Irish Print Union was overwhelmingly male and the position was filled by an unemployed male. In the High Court, the terms of the Employment Equality Act were held to require a "causal connection" as between the sex of a person and the treatment afforded to him or her, such that the Act did "not deem discrimination to have occurred merely because historical factors (other than sex or marital status) have limited the eligible candidates to a pool which contains a larger number of the members of one sex than the other".[122] In the Supreme Court, having cited *Von Colson* and *Marleasing*, Hamilton CJ described the obligation on national courts as being to interpret the Act "as far as possible, in the light of the wording and purpose of the directive in order to achieve the result pursued by the directive viz. establishing that there shall be no discrimination on grounds of sex either directly or indirectly".[123] As the directive clearly prohibited indirect discrimination, the Act was to be interpreted to similar effect. Consequently, a requirement relating to employment which was not an essential requirement for the position and in respect of which the proportion of persons of the other sex able to comply was substantially higher, could amount to indirect discrimination.

[12–65] By way of contrast, in *Telecom Éireann v O'Grady*, Telecom Éireann sought to rely on a saving provision of the Employment Equality Act which provided that nothing in the Act shall make it unlawful for an employer to arrange for special treatment to be given to women in connection with pregnancy or childbirth.[124] When Telecom Éireann refused Mr O'Grady adoptive leave upon his adoption of a child, he successfully claimed that this amounted to unlawful discrimination that was not permitted by the derogation for pregnancy or childbirth. In the Supreme Court, Telecom Éireann argued that the term "childbirth" ought to be interpreted teleologically rather than literally in order to give full effect to the Equal Treatment Directive, pointing to the fact that the Court of Justice had confirmed that the terms "pregnancy and maternity", as used in the Directive, could include adoptive leave. The Supreme Court rejected the argument, holding that the exemption provided for in the 1977 Act was "clearly confined to biological motherhood and its consequences and cannot, giving the words their ordinary meaning, be extended to leave for adoptive mothers".[125] This conclusion was said to become irresistible when account was taken of the fact that the drafters of the 1977 Act must be presumed to have been aware that the term "maternity" had been used in the Directive, rather than "childbirth". Furthermore, the interpretation suggested by Telecom Éireann would not further the overall objective of the Directive of achieving equality between men and women, but rather in the context of adoptive leave would frustrate it. Finally, it was unsustainable to suggest that the failure of the Oireachtas to make full use of exemptions permitted by the Directive in any sense frustrated

Justice v Tobin [2012] 4 IR 147, 264–266; *Minister for Justice and Equality v Skiba* [2018] IESC 68, unreported, Supreme Court, 5 December 2018, paras 67–74.

[122] [1998] 2 IR 162, 170.

[123] *ibid*, 175.

[124] [1998] 3 IR 432.

[125] *ibid*, 449.

the purpose of the Directive.[126] Rather, in providing an exception for pregnancy and childbirth "the Oireachtas was exercising the discretion conferred on Member States by the Directive and it is not for this Court to extend such protection".[127]

[12–66] A further example of the principle of *contra legem* precluding an argument for harmonious interpretation is *Albatross Feeds Ltd v Minister for Agriculture*.[128] There, the Minister for Agriculture sought to argue that a statutory instrument adopted so as to transpose a directive on the control of animal feed ought to be understood as conferring a power to order the detention and seizure of feed containing unauthorised substances. While no such express power was included in the statutory instrument, it was argued that this logically followed from requirements in related directives to carry out inspections and to prevent the marketing of unauthorised feed. In delivering the judgment of the Supreme Court, Fennelly J held that it would do "too much violence to language" to interpret a reference to "inspections" as including powers of detention and seizure.[129] This was particularly the case given that the powers that were being claimed entailed "a drastic incursion into the fundamental property rights of the affected trader. Such action must be justified, if at all, by clear words".[130]

[12–67] The need for harmonious interpretation has been considered more recently by the High Court in *Environmental Protection Agency v Harte Peat Ltd*, which concerned the need for an environmental impact assessment in respect of the extraction of peat "in the course of business which involves an area exceeding 50 hectares".[131] Two companies, with common shareholders and some common directors and secretaries, carried out peat extraction. The first company leased 44 hectares to the second company for peat extraction and, in adjacent lands, carried out its own works relating to peat extraction. A question of interpretation arose as to whether it was proper to aggregate the lands in order to apply the threshold of 50 hectares. Barrett J observed that in cases such as this one, which concerned the interpretation of Irish law having its provenance in EU law, statutory interpretation must be done in the context of, and in compliance with, the requirements of EU law. In order to give effect to the purpose of the relevant directive, it was proper that the two areas of land be counted together for the purposes of applying the threshold. This "interpretive genuflection by the Irish courts" towards EU law could be viewed:

> less as an aspect of the supremacy of European Union law and more as a particular, though particularly important, dimension of the general and longstanding rule of statutory interpretation whereby the Oireachtas, when it enacts domestic legislation, is presumed to intend to comply with its international legal obligations ... The difference between this traditional presumption and the applicable European law requirements is perhaps the depth and detail of the latter requirements and of course that conformity with European Union law interpretative requirements is demanded of the court in cases where European Union law comes into play.[132]

[12–68] Naturally, in seeking to interpret an implementation measure harmoniously

---

[126] *ibid*, 451.
[127] *ibid*, 447.
[128] [2007] 1 IR 221.
[129] *ibid*, 244.
[130] *ibid.*
[131] [2015] 1 IR 462.
[132] *ibid*, 470.

with a directive, it will be of relevance if the directive, in turn, has been interpreted by the Court of Justice. For instance, in *NAMA v Commissioner for Environmental Information*, the Supreme Court had to consider whether NAMA was a "public authority" within the meaning of a statutory instrument that transposed a directive which gave effect in EU law to provisions of the Aarhus Convention.[133] In holding that it was such a public authority, the Supreme Court noted that had the law stood as it was at the time of the High Court decision, it would have requested a preliminary ruling from the Court of Justice. In the interim, however, the Court of Justice had provided a ruling on the point in a reference from the United Kingdom. As the ruling "provides an authoritative interpretation of the Directive, and moreover does so in the context of a common law system", it was clear that NAMA was to be considered a public authority exercising public administrative functions.[134]

[12–69] Although the doctrine of indirect effect plays an important role in compensating for the absence of the horizontal direct effect of directives, it has been noted that it has always been a doctrine of uncertain effect: "[w]hile in practice the doctrine that national courts turn to first, it is to some extent unreliable as it depends on the scope the national court has in interpretation".[135] According to Stephen Weatherill, there are enduring difficulties in defining the proper scope of the obligation of harmonious interpretation, and these difficulties are multiplied by the number of Member States, each of whose courts must grapple with the issue.[136] As will be seen in Chapter 14, in its landmark 1991 judgment in *Francovich*, the Court of Justice added a further element to the toolkit for ensuring the full effectiveness of EU law.[137] According to this judgment, the effectiveness of EU law would be impaired if individuals were unable to obtain redress when their rights are infringed by a breach of EU law for which a Member State is responsible. As a result, where a Member State has failed to take all the measures necessary to achieve the result prescribed by a directive, there should be a right to reparation provided that three conditions are fulfilled: (i) the result prescribed by the directive should entail the grant of rights to individuals; (ii) it should be possible to identify the content of those rights on the basis of the provisions of the directive; and (iii) there is a causal link between the breach of the Member State's obligation and the loss and damage suffered by the injured party.

[12–70] These issues came together in the case of *Smith v Meade* which, like *Farrell v Whitty*, concerned Ireland's implementation of the Third Motor Insurance Directive.[138] At the time that an insurance policy was entered into between FBD Insurance and the owner of a van (Mr Meade), Irish law implementing the Directive permitted the inclusion of a clause that limited insurance cover to include only passengers seated in the fixed passenger seat at the front of the van. As a matter of Irish law, therefore, it was lawful to drive a van with a passenger in the back, without a fixed seat, who was not covered by the van's insurance policy. Mr Smith was travelling as a passenger in the rear of the van, without a fixed passenger seat, when he was seriously injured in an accident. Relying on the *Marleasing* principle, the High Court held that the relevant

---

133 [2015] 4 IR 626; [2015] 2 ILRM 165.

134 *ibid*, 657; 191.

135 Lorna Woods and Philippa Watson, *Steiner and Woods EU Law* (12th ed, Oxford University Press, 2014) 136.

136 Stephen Weatherill, *Cases and Materials on EU Law* (10th ed, Oxford University Press, 2012) 139.

137 Joined Cases C-6/90 and C-9/90 *Francovich v Italy* [1991] ECR I-5357, 5413–5415.

138 Case C-122/17 *Smith v Meade*.

Irish law was capable of being interpreted in line with the Directive by ignoring the permission to include an exclusion clause of this kind in an insurance policy.[139] As a result, the clause to that effect in FBD's policy of insurance was to be regarded as void, such that FBD was required to pay out on the passenger's claim. Following the High Court judgment, a settlement was reached whereby FBD paid Mr Smith €3 million.

[12–71] In considering an appeal, the Court of Appeal differed from the High Court in concluding that to interpret the Irish legislation by ignoring the express permission to include such a clause would be *contra legem* and so was not a remedy available to it. According to Hogan J:

> It is, of course, correct to say that … the *Marleasing* interpretative obligation applies with particular force where – as here – the national law was expressly amended with the declared intention of giving effect to the Directive in question. Yet both national provisions are in themselves pellucidly clear and are entirely free from any ambiguity whatever: both expressly exclude cases such as the present one where the passenger was travelling in a part of a mechanically propelled vehicle which did not have fixed seating.
>
> These exclusions clearly represent what must have been understood at the time to have been a legislative policy choice in that they were plainly quite deliberate and are obviously not the product of some legislative oversight. Private parties (such as FBD) quite obviously acted on foot of these excluding provisions. There can, moreover, be little doubt but that the cost of the insurance policy written by FBD in the present case reflected what it legitimately understood to be the limits of its insurance risks and those risks did not extend to passengers travelling in vans which did not have fixed seats.
>
> In these circumstances, I must respectfully disagree with the view taken of this issue of interpretation by … the High Court. I consider that it is simply not possible to interpret these provisions in a manner which would be compatible with the requirements of the Third Directive, as to do otherwise would be to adopt an interpretation which would be *contra legem* and which would do violence to the actual wording of both provisions.[140]

[12–72] The Court of Appeal next considered whether, since an earlier preliminary reference had found the manner in which Ireland had implemented the Third Directive to be contrary to EU law, it was required to disapply the relevant provision and thereby deem unlawful the clause included in the insurance policy concluded between FBD and the owner of the van. The Court of Appeal requested a preliminary ruling from the Court of Justice as to whether the obligation to disapply required such a result in this case, or whether this would effectively amount to a form of horizontal direct effect of a Directive against a private party in a manner not provided for in EU law. As emphasised by Hogan J:

> The importance of these questions cannot be overstated so far as this appeal is concerned. If this Court is obliged to disapply the exclusion clause in the insurance policy, then it follows that the plaintiff could properly have recovered as against the first defendants and FBD would in turn have been obliged to indemnify these defendants. Alternatively, if there is no such obligation on the national court, FBD would be free to seek to recover from the State the €3m it paid out to the plaintiff by way of settlement by means of appropriate legal proceedings (which might include a *Francovich* claim).[141]

[139] *Smith v Meade* [2009] 3 IR 335.
[140] *Smith v Meade* [2016] IECA 389, 16 December 2016, paras 49–51.
[141] *ibid*, para 69.

[12–73] In its ruling, the Court of Justice reaffirmed that a directive cannot of itself impose obligations on an individual and cannot therefore be relied upon as such against an individual.[142] As it previously stated in *Faccini Dori*, if the possibility of relying on a provision of a directive that has not been transposed, or has been incorrectly transposed, were to be extended to the sphere of relations between individuals, that would amount to recognising an EU power to enact obligations for individuals with *immediate* effect, whereas it has competence to do so only where it is empowered to adopt regulations.[143] Accordingly, even a clear, precise and unconditional provision of a directive seeking to confer rights, or impose obligations, on individuals cannot of itself apply in a dispute exclusively between private persons. Nor could a directive be relied on in a dispute between private individuals for the purpose of setting aside legislation of a Member State that is contrary to that directive. As a result,

> A national court is obliged to set aside a provision of national law that is contrary to a directive only where that directive is relied on against a Member State, the organs of its administration, such as decentralised authorities, or organisations or bodies which are subject to the authority or control of the State or which have been required by a Member State to perform a task in the public interest and, for that purpose, possess special powers beyond those which result from the normal rules applicable to relations between individuals.
>
> … a national court, hearing a dispute between private persons, which finds itself unable to interpret provisions of its national law in a manner that is compatible with a directive, is not obliged, solely on the basis of EU law, to disapply the provisions of its national law which are contrary to those provisions of that directive that fulfil all the conditions required for them to produce direct effect and thereby to extend the possibility of relying on a provision of a directive that has not been transposed, or that has been incorrectly transposed, to the sphere of relationships between private persons.[144]

[12–74] With regard to its earlier judgments in *CIA Security* and *Unilever*, the Court of Justice observed that those cases had seen national technical regulations declared inapplicable in a dispute between individuals on the ground that: (i) non-compliance with the obligations stemming from (what is now) Directive 2015/1535 constituted a "substantial procedural defect" that had vitiated the adoption of those technical regulations by the states concerned and (ii) Directive 2015/1535 created neither rights nor obligations for individuals and did not determine the substantive content of the legal rule on the basis of which the national court had to decide the case before it. Consequently, the Court's case law to the effect that a directive that has not been transposed may not be relied upon in horizontal disputes between one individual against another was not relevant to the situation in either of those cases.

[12–75] In contrast, the relevant provision of the Third Motor Insurance Directive at issue here, which required that there be insurance cover for all passengers in a vehicle, defined "the substantive content of a rule of law and falls, consequently, within the scope of the case-law to the effect that a directive that has not been transposed or has been incorrectly transposed may not be relied on by one individual against another".[145] It followed, therefore, that the Irish courts were not obliged by EU law to disapply the

[142] Case C-122/17 *Smith v Meade* EU:C:2018:631, 7 August 2018.
[143] *ibid*, para 42.
[144] *ibid*, paras 45, 49.
[145] *ibid*, para 54.

incompatible provision of national law, or the contractual clause in the FBD insurance policy that was based on that provision. Rather, as pointed out by the Court of Justice, a party adversely affected by the incompatibility of Irish law with the Third Motor Insurance Directive could rely on the *Francovich* case law in order to obtain from the State, if appropriate, compensation for any loss sustained.[146]

E. Implementation of Secondary EU Law in Irish Law

[12–76] The reception of EU law into Irish law is facilitated by Art 29.4.6° of the Constitution, which reads:

> No provision of this Constitution invalidates laws enacted, acts done or measures adopted by the State, before, on or after the entry into force of the Treaty of Lisbon, that are *necessitated by the obligations of membership of the European Union* … or of the European Atomic Energy Community, or prevents laws enacted, acts done or measures adopted by—
> i the said European Union or the European Atomic Energy Community, or institutions thereof,
> ii the European Communities or European Union existing immediately before the entry into force of the Treaty of Lisbon, or institutions thereof, or
> iii bodies competent under the treaties referred to in this section,
> from having the force of law in the State.[147]

[12–77] In addition to shielding EU legal acts from a constitutional challenge, Art 29.4.6° similarly protects laws enacted, acts done or measures adopted by the State that are necessitated by the obligations of EU membership. The key phrase here is "necessitated by", as this establishes the test by which the conferral of a constitutional immunity is to be judged. Article 29.4.6° must be read in conjunction with the European Communities Act 1972, as amended.[148] Section 2 of the Act provides that, as well as the EU treaties, acts adopted by the EU institutions shall also be binding on the State and be part of Irish law, with the exception of CFSP acts. It reads:

> (1) The following shall be binding on the State and shall be part of the domestic law thereof under the conditions laid down in the treaties governing the European Union:
> (a) the treaties governing the European Union;
> (b) acts adopted by the institutions of the European Union (other than acts to which the first paragraph of Article 275 of the Treaty on the Functioning of the European Union applies [ie "the provisions relating to the common foreign and security policy nor with respect to acts adopted on the basis of those provisions"]);
> (c) acts adopted by the institutions of the European Communities in force immediately before the entry into force of the Lisbon Treaty; and
> (d) acts adopted by bodies competent under those treaties (other than acts to which the first paragraph of the said Article 275 applies).

---

146 *ibid*, para 56.

147 Emphasis added. See Maria Cahill, "Constitutional Exclusion Clauses, Article 29.4.6°, and the Constitutional Reception of European Law" (2011) 34 *Dublin University Law Journal* 74; Elaine Fahey, *EU Law in Ireland* (Clarus Press, 2010) 43–62; Cathryn Costello, "European Community Judicial Review in the Irish Courts – Scope, Standards and the Separation of Powers" in Mary Catherine Lucey and Cathrina Keville (eds), *Irish Perspectives on EC Law* (Round Hall, 2003) 17; Gerard Hogan, Gerry Whyte, David Kenny and Rachel Walsh, *Kelly: The Irish Constitution* (Bloomsbury Professional, 5th ed, 2018) 591–609.

148 A consolidated version of the Act is available at <http://revisedacts.lawreform.ie/revacts/alpha>.

(2) Without prejudice to subsection (1) of this section, from the coming into force of the EEA Agreement, the provisions of that Agreement and the acts to be adopted by institutions established by that Agreement which, pursuant to the treaties governing the European Communities, will be binding on the State and an integral part of the legal order of those Communities, shall have the force of law in the State on the conditions laid down in those treaties and in that Agreement.

(3) Without prejudice to subsection (1) of this section, from the coming into force of the Agreements (within the meaning of the European Communities and Swiss Confederation Act, 2001), the provisions of those Agreements and the acts to be adopted by the institutions established by those Agreements which, pursuant to the treaties governing the European Communities, will be binding on the State and an integral part of the legal order of those Communities, shall have the force of law in the State on the conditions laid down in those treaties and in those Agreements.

[12–78] In order to enable s 2 to have full effect, s 3 empowers government ministers to make regulations by way of statutory instrument. These regulations may contain "such incidental, supplementary and consequential provisions" as appear to be necessary for the purposes of the regulations. A particularly striking feature of this power is that s 3 expressly provides that a regulation may include provisions repealing or amending any other law, including primary legislation, with the exception of the 1972 Act itself. Clearly, this power cuts across the separation of powers as regards the legislative function set out in Art 15.2.1°, which vests the "sole and exclusive power of making laws for the State" in the Oireachtas and confirms that "no other legislative authority has power to make laws for the State". As has been described by Denham CJ:

> To provide that a law may be amended by statutory instrument as in the European Communities Act 1972, is an exceptional power given by the Oireachtas, pursuant to the Constitution, to a minister. It was necessitated by obligations of membership of the European Communities, which itself gave rise to a high volume of technical regulations based on Community law. Such power would, in general, be an impermissible delegation of legislative powers, without the specific legislative and constitutional foundation. ... Such power is a delegation of the legislative power only constitutionally sound because it is necessitated by the obligations of the European Community.[149]

[12–79] The constitutionality of this ability to amend primary legislation by statutory instrument was affirmed by the Supreme Court in the important case of *Meagher v Minister for Agriculture and Food*.[150] There, two statutory instruments were made under the 1972 Act in order to implement a directive on the control of hormonal products in animals. While the Petty Sessions Ireland Act 1851 provided for a six-month period in which to issue a summons for the prosecution of summary offences, this was amended by the statutory instruments to allow for a two-year period in respect of prosecutions for a breach of their rules.

[12–80] In the High Court, Johnson J was of the view that any power given to a minister to amend or repeal primary legislation by way of a statutory instrument was

---

149 *Quinn v Ireland* [2007] 3 IR 395, 412.

150 [1994] 1 IR 329; [1994] 1 ILRM 1. Earlier High Court judgments considering the use of s 3 of the 1972 Act include *Lawlor v Minister for Agriculture* [1990] 1 IR 356; *Greene v Minister for Agriculture* [1990] 2 IR 17; *Condon v Minister for Agriculture* unreported, High Court, 12 October 1990, Lynch J. See Anthony Whelan, "Article 29.4.3 and the Meaning of 'Necessity'" (1992) 2 *Irish Student Law Review* 60.

contrary to Art 15 of the Constitution, and so he held that, to that extent, s 3 of the 1972 Act was unconstitutional. More generally, Johnson J observed that, in deciding whether to implement a directive by either enacting a law, doing an act or adopting a measure (as referred to in s 3 of the 1972 Act), a minister did not have a free discretion. Rather, a minister was obliged to examine the directive and determine the correct means of implementation, having regard to the fact that

> [q]uite clearly it was envisaged by the Constitution that one of the means of implementation of such measures in the appropriate case would be the enactment of legislation. Indeed it is the first of the three different means mentioned, and therefore the Minister should have looked, having regard to the whole of the Constitution, as to when, in the implementation of the measures which he considered necessary, it was required, having regard to the other Articles in the Constitution, to enact laws. The Minister argued … that it was basically a matter of choice for him. This I do not accept, and where it is appropriate for the purposes of the directives and their implementation that, in regard to Article 15 of the Constitution, legislation be introduced and Acts enacted, then this should be done. In my view, any power given to a Minister to make regulations for the purposes of amending or repealing laws is unconstitutional.[151]

[12–81] Gerard Hogan and Anthony Whelan have observed that implicit in this analysis is a presumption that, of itself, EU law does not require that any particular means of implementation is used within a Member State, so long as it is effective. In other words, all that is necessitated is the implementation: "the method of it is a choice to be made by the State within its own national law framework, and must be consistent with the Constitution".[152] As a result of this presumption, the minister is unable to rely on a necessity argument to claim constitutional immunity on the basis of Art 29.4.6°, and instead is forced to interpret that article in harmony with the Constitution's other provisions, including Art 15.2.1°. Accordingly, the idea of what is an appropriate implementation of EU law "is built upon an appreciation of the Irish constitutional context; and the status of national implementing measures can hardly be divorced from that context".[153]

[12–82] On appeal, the Supreme Court delivered two judgments. The first, delivered by Finlay CJ, addressed the constitutional validity of s 3 of the 1972 Act. Separately, Blayney and Denham JJ delivered judgments on the lawfulness of the two particular statutory instruments at issue (with which the rest of the Supreme Court agreed). In upholding the validity of s 3 of the Act and overturning the decision of the High Court, the Supreme Court adopted a more pragmatic and purposive approach, considering in a broad way the kind of "mechanism" that was required in order to enable Ireland to meet its obligations as an EU Member State. According to Finlay CJ (delivering judgment for the Court):

> The power to make regulations contained in section 3, sub-s.1 of the Act of 1972 is exclusively confined to the making of regulations for one purpose, and one purpose only, that of enabling s.2 of the Act to have full effect. Section 2 of the Act which provides for the application of the [EU] law and acts as binding on the State and as part of the domestic law subject to conditions laid down in the Treaty which, of course, include its primacy,

---

151 *ibid*, 343–344; 11.

152 Finlay CJ (summarising the basis of the challenge to the validity of s 3 of the 1972 Act), *ibid*, 350; 14.

153 Gerard Hogan and Anthony Whelan, *Ireland and the European Union: Constitutional and Statutory Texts and Commentary* (Sweet and Maxwell, 1995) 59.

is the major or fundamental obligation necessitated by membership of the [Union]. The power of regulation-making, therefore, contained in s.3 is prima facie a power which is part of the necessary machinery which became a duty of the State upon its joining the [EU] and therefore necessitated by that membership.

The Court is satisfied that, having regard to the number of [EU] laws, acts done and measures adopted which either have to be facilitated in their direct application to the law of the State or have to be implemented by appropriate action into the law of the State, the obligation of membership would necessitate facilitating of these activities, in some instances, at least, and possibly in a great majority of instances, by the making of ministerial regulation rather than legislation of the Oireachtas.

The Court is accordingly satisfied that the power to make regulations in the form in which it is contained in s.3, sub-s.2 of the Act of 1972 is necessitated by the obligations of membership by the State … of the Union and is therefore by virtue of Article [29.4.6°] immune from constitutional challenge.

In so far as it may be possible to point to hypothetical instances of certain types of laws, measures or acts of the Community or Union which in their implementation or application within the national law might not, as to the method of implementation or application, be necessarily carried out by ministerial regulation, but rather should have been carried out by enactment of law by the Oireachtas, the Court is satisfied, without deciding that such instances do occur, that the principles laid down by this Court in the decision of *East Donegal Co-Operative Livestock Marts Ltd v Attorney General* [1970] IR 317, must be applied to the construction of the impugned subsection ... That principle is that it must be implied that the making of regulations by the Minister, as is permitted by the section, is intended by the Oireachtas to be conducted in accordance with the principles of constitutional justice, and therefore that it is to be implied that the Minister shall not in exercising the power of making regulations pursuant to the section, contravene any provisions of the Constitution.

If therefore in such an instance challenge were to be made to the validity of a ministerial regulation having regard to the absence of necessity for it to be carried out by regulation instead of legislation and having regard to the nature of the content of such regulation it would have to be a challenge made on the basis that the regulation was invalid as ultra vires being an unconstitutional exercise by the Minister of the power constitutionally conferred upon him by the section.[154]

[12–83] The essential premise behind this portion of the judgment has been described as being that, because of the Oireachtas timetable and the excessive quantities of primary legislation which would otherwise be entailed, there is simply no alternative to this statutory mechanism if Ireland is to avoid falling behind in its duty to implement directives on time.[155] The judgment has been criticised for taking an overly generous and general approach to the concept of measures necessitated by EU membership. According to Gerard Hogan and Anthony Whelan:

The patent necessity of *some* machinery for applying and implementing [EU] law in Ireland can hardly mean that *any* machinery will do. The Supreme Court appears to employ no qualitative criterion in assessing our machinery other than that of administrative facility. That criterion alone would leave the State free to comply with the obligations of membership of the [EU] by recognising some fantastic implementing authority in Irish law,

[154] [1994] 1 IR 329, 351–353; [1994] 1 ILRM 1, 15–16.

[155] Gerard Hogan and David Gwynn Morgan, *Administrative Law in Ireland* (4th ed, Round Hall, 2010) 22.

> such as edicts of the Irish Permanent Representative to the [EU] (whose staff would, after all, be among the best informed in the State's service about the [EU] measures involved). More realistically, it could permit the State to confer binding authority on instruments which at present lack that quality, such as administrative circulars, for the purposes solely of implementing [EU] law. One imagines that neither of these was countenanced by the Supreme Court, but the judgment of the court does not reveal why such unsatisfactory implementing devices should not be permitted. In short, the Supreme Court's test of necessity fails because it does not tell us what we need to know.[156]

[12–84] For others, however, the judgment can be seen as an appropriate balancing between the constitutional demand for a separation of powers, as required by Art 15.2.1°, and the practical reality of having to accommodate a new and plentiful source of law deriving from EU membership. More recently, it has been noted that the growing number of obligations arising under EU law means that the number of statutory instruments made under s 3 of the 1972 Act has become increasingly common, representing, for example, 20 per cent of all SIs made in 2015, or 134 instruments.[157] As of 2016, it was calculated that just under 2,000 SIs made pursuant to s 3 of the 1972 were currently in force, out of a total of 15,000 SIs that were in force (or appeared to remain in force).[158]

[12–85] Having found that s 3 of the 1972 Act was constitutionally valid, Finlay CJ proceeded to caution that notwithstanding the constitutional shield afforded by Art 29.4.6°, the use of s 3 in any particular instance may be challenged as being *ultra vires* if it goes beyond what is in fact necessary in order to implement an EU legal act. The manner in which this judicial control was to be exercised formed the subject of the judgments of Blayney and Denham JJ, which are concerned with whether the particular use of s 3 in this case was justified or whether it was *ultra vires* the Minister for Agriculture.

[12–86] In his judgment, Blayney J highlighted evidence submitted on behalf of the Minister outlining the time required to carry out scientific tests or to cooperate with other Member States in preparing a prosecution. This led Blayney J to conclude that, if the power of prosecution was to be effective, the existing six-month period was too short and so it was necessary to extend it.[159] Since the directive required that offences be created, it followed that it had to be possible for them to be prosecuted effectively, and so the implementation of the directive required that the statutory instrument should provide for an adequate time for the preparation of prosecutions. It was not necessary, in his view, that the directive should itself fix a time period for prosecutions, but rather

156 Gerard Hogan and Anthony Whelan, *Ireland and the European Union: Constitutional and Statutory Texts and Commentary* (Sweet and Maxwell, 1995) 60. See Gerard Hogan, "The Implementation of European Union Law in Ireland: The *Meagher* Case and the Democratic Deficit" (1994) 2 *Irish Journal of European Law* 190; Anthony Whelan, "Constitutional Law – *Meagher v Minister for Agriculture*" (1994) 15 *Dublin University Law Journal* 152; Elaine Fahey, *EU Law in Ireland* (Clarus Press, 2010) 51–54; Gerard Hogan and David Gwynn Morgan, *Administrative Law in Ireland* (4th ed, Round Hall, 2010) 21–23; Noel Travers, "The Constitutionality of the Implementation of EC Directives into Irish Law" (1994) 88 *Gazette of Incorporated Law Society of Ireland* 99; Noel Travers, "The Implementation of Directives into Irish Law" (1995) 20 *European Law Review* 103; Jonathan Tomkin, "Implementing Community Legislation into National Law: The Demands of a New Legal Order" (2004) 4 *Judicial Studies Institute Journal* 130.

157 Law Reform Commission, *Accessibility, Consolidation and Online Publication of Legislation* (Issues Paper 11, 2016) 12.

158 *ibid*, 12–13.

159 [1994] 1 IR 329, 359; [1994] 1 ILRM 1, 21.

it was a matter for the State to decide. He concluded, therefore, that since the State was obliged to implement the directive, it was equally obliged to:

> choose a method of implementation and, provided the method it chooses is appropriate for the purpose of satisfying the obligation of the State and the measures it incorporates do not go beyond what is required to implement the directive, it is correctly categorised as being necessitated by the directive. In any instance where the method was not appropriate, or its measures went beyond what was required, it would not be necessitated and would be open to constitutional challenge. This is not such a case.[160]

[12–87] In contrast, Denham J engaged in a more explicit balancing exercise that sought to harmonise the clear tension that existed as between the constitutional licence in Art 29.4.6° and the restriction in Art 15.2.1°. This was achieved by invoking the "principles and policies" test that had been developed by the Supreme Court in the seminal case of *Cityview Press v An Chomhairle Oiliúna*.[161] According to this test, in order not to infringe Art 15.2.1°, the making of a statutory instrument as part of a delegated power must not do more than give effect to the principles and policies contained in a parent act. In other words, delegated law-making by statutory instrument is permitted provided that the "law is laid down in the statute and details only are filled in or completed by the designated Minister".[162]

[12–88] In assessing whether or not the statutory instruments in *Meagher* were in fact "necessitated" within the meaning of Art 29.4.6°, Denham J effectively substituted a principles and policies test. Her reasoning for this was that the trigger for requiring the use of an Act of the Oireachtas – as opposed to secondary legislation – was if the directive left to the Member States matters of principle or policy. Where the principles and policies are already established in the directive, it is a valid choice for a minister to choose to implement this by way of secondary legislation. Furthermore, such secondary legislation may include elements that exceed the principles and policies set out in the directive, provided that they are, in the words of s 3 of the 1972 Act, "incidental, supplementary or consequential" thereto. Denham J concluded by placing this reasoning within the wider doctrine of the separation of powers:

> In the directives herein the policies and principles have been determined. Thus there is no role of determining policies or principles for the Oireachtas. While the directive must be implemented there is no policy or principle which can be altered by the Oireachtas, it is already binding as to the result to be achieved.
>
> That being the case the role of the Oireachtas in such a situation would be sterile. To require the Oireachtas to legislate would be artificial. It would be able solely to have a debate as to what has already been decided, which debate would act as a source of information. Such a sterile debate would take up Dáil and Seanad time and act only as a window on [EU] directives for the members of the Oireachtas and the Nation. That is not a role envisaged for the Oireachtas in the Constitution.
>
> Consequently, solely because the Minister is making a regulation which repeals a statute, does not of itself invalidate the regulation which as a vehicle, as a choice, can be intra vires the Constitution under Article 29.4. To say that the regulations breach Article 15.2.1°

160 *ibid* 360; 22.
161 [1980] IR 381.
162 *ibid*, 399.

simply because it repeals or amends a statute is to hold the false premise that the Minister is determining principles or policy.

The regulations in this case being within the policies and principles of the directives the substance of the regulation is within the directives. There are no policies and principles enunciated in the regulations that are not within the directives. There are no policies and principles in the regulations additional to the directive.

Consequently, to state that such an action – effectively an administrative implementation of policies and principles of a directive – is superior legislation as envisaged in Article 15.2.1° is a misnomer. Superior legislation involves a decision on policies and principles by the legislature and an implementation thereof in the form of a statute. Here what is at issue in essence is subordinate legislation as delegated under [EU] law.[163]

[12–89] This approach of applying a "principles and policies" test to determining whether it is valid to use a secondary law measure to implement an EU law obligation was confirmed by the Supreme Court in the similarly named *Maher v Minister for Agriculture*.[164] There, a challenge was brought against a statutory instrument made by the Minister for Agriculture in order to implement an EU regulation governing milk quotas. It was argued that in exercising certain discretions permitted by the regulation, the Minister had made substantial policy choices and so had effectively been legislating contrary to Art 15.2.1°. The Supreme Court clarified that the choice as between primary or secondary legislation could not, of itself, be described as being necessitated by EU membership, which merely required that EU law be given effective implementation, whatever the choice of form or method.[165] In particular, the fact that the use of a statutory instrument was "convenient" or "desirable" was insufficient to deem it necessitated by EU membership.[166] In applying, by analogy, the principles and policies test to the use of s 3 of the 1972 Act, Keane CJ observed that there is:

manifestly a significant difference between a directive or regulation, which is applicable throughout the … Member States of the European Union, and an Act of the Oireachtas the effect of which is confined to a relatively small and homogeneous area within the European Union. In the case of a regulation which is intended to apply in a number of different regions throughout the European Union in which the conditions of the dairying industry may vary widely, it is not surprising to find that the regulation, in specified areas, leaves choices as to the nature of the implementing measures to be introduced by the Member State. The issue in this case is as to whether the choice of the appropriate measures can be regarded as involving no determination of policy or principle, as that expression has been used in previous decisions of this Court.[167]

[12–90] Applying the test to any particular use of s 3 of the 1972 Act will, naturally,

---

[163] [1994] 1 IR 329, 367; [1994] 1 ILRM 1, 27–28.

[164] [2001] 2 IR 139; [2001] 2 ILRM 481. See Barry Doherty, "Land, Milk and Freedom – Implementing Community Law in Ireland" (2004) 11 *Irish Journal of European Law* 141; Elaine Fahey, *EU Law in Ireland* (Clarus Press, 2010) 54–58; Cathryn Costello, "European Community Judicial Review in the Irish Courts – Scope, Standards and the Separation of Powers" in Mary Catherine Lucey and Cathrina Keville (eds), *Irish Perspectives on EC Law* (Round Hall, 2003) 17, 37–39; Jonathan Tomkin, "Implementing Community Legislation into National Law: The Demands of a New Legal Order" (2004) 4 *Judicial Studies Institute Journal* 130; Gerard Hogan and David Gwynn Morgan, *Administrative Law in Ireland* (4th ed, Round Hall, 2010) 23–24.

[165] *ibid*, 181; 517.

[166] *ibid*, 182; 517–518.

[167] *ibid*, 185; 520.

be heavily fact-specific and will depend on the precise provisions of the directive or other EU measure to which effect is being given. Even bearing in mind his observation as to the nature of EU legal acts, Keane CJ admitted to experiencing difficulty in deciding on whether the statutory instrument in *Maher* did more than give effect to the principles and policies set out in the EU regulation. Indeed, he commented that, once it is acknowledged that the discretions afforded to the Member States by the EU regulation

> may be implemented in a manner requiring parliamentary scrutiny and that implementation by ministerial regulation is not necessitated by our membership of the European Union, it gives rise to natural misgivings to find that there is no role for the democratically elected institutions of the State, other than the limited one under s.4 of the 1972 Act.[168]

[12–91] On balance, however, Keane CJ was persuaded that on close inspection of the EU regulation, the "choices as to policy available to the Member States have, in truth, been reduced almost to vanishing point".[169] The Milk Levy scheme at issue was "essentially the creation of the European Union", with the relevant principles and policies contained in the EU legal acts establishing the Common Agricultural Policy. As a result, the use of a statutory instrument to implement the regulation, including making choices as between certain discretions within it, was permissible and did not fall foul of Art. 15.2.1°.[170] In his own analysis of the regulation (which was relied upon by Keane CJ) Fennelly J observed that in exercising discretions permitted by the regulation, Member States were constrained by the general principles of EU law, suggesting that this may serve to narrow the scope of a discretion as it may otherwise appear from a straightforward reading of the EU legal act.[171]

[12–92] The Supreme Court has recently had cause to consider this case law in *O'Sullivan v Sea Fisheries Protection Authority*, which concerned a statutory instrument made by the Minister for Agriculture, Food and Marine in order to implement EU regulations preventing illegal, unreported and unregulated ("IUU") fishing.[172] According to a 2008 regulation, Member States were required to put in place "effective, proportionate and dissuasive" administrative and/or criminal sanctions to prevent IUU fishing. A 2009 regulation bolstered the earlier regulation by providing that the establishment of administrative and/or criminal sanctions should be "complemented by a point system for serious infringements on the basis of which a fishing licence should be suspended if a certain number of points have been attributed to the holder of a fishing licence *following* the imposition of sanctions for serious infringements".[173] In the Supreme Court it was argued that a statutory instrument made pursuant to s 3 of the 1972 Act went beyond the power of the Minister to give effect to EU law in that the additional policy choice was made not to make the point system contingent upon a prior criminal sanction (no scheme of administrative sanction having been introduced). This, it was argued, represented the introduction of a "stand alone" penalty point system,

[168] *ibid.*

[169] *ibid.*

[170] *ibid*, 185–186; 520.

[171] *ibid*, 258; 585. See also *Sam McCauley Chemists (Blackpool) Ltd v Pharmaceutical Society of Ireland* [2008] 1 IR 16 (High Court); Case C-221/05 *Sam McCauley Chemists (Blackpool) Ltd v Pharmaceutical Society of Ireland* [2006] ECR I-6869.

[172] [2017] 3 IR 751; [2018] 1 ILRM 245. See also *Crayden Fishing Co Ltd v Sea Fisheries Protection Authority* [2017] 3 IR 785; [2018] 1 ILRM 225.

[173] Recital 40 of Council Regulation (EC) 1224/2009, quoted *ibid*, 760; 251. Emphasis added.

something that the EU regulations did not require. Accordingly, it was said that any such system ought to have been introduced by primary legislation.

[12–93] In delivering the judgment of the Supreme Court, O'Donnell J observed that, although the principles and policies test was regularly invoked, it remained somewhat elusive and was difficult to apply to the facts before it.[174] On the one hand, the two EU regulations – which between them contained 127 recitals – were "replete with policy ... giving cumulatively, a very clear view of the overall thrust of the provisions and the principles and policies embodied in them".[175] On the other hand, the regulations deliberately left to Member States the choice of method for establishing a system for the allocation of penalty points. In doing so, the regulations required the national authorities to make choices that, at one level, involved policy choices "since presumably the choice is made on the basis that a particular provision is considered more effective, convenient, compatible or simply better".[176] In other words, in certain areas, the *policy* of the regulations themselves was to leave certain choices to the national authorities. But, according to O'Donnell J, a "choice does not imply a capacity to determine policy", since "every delegate must make some choice".[177] In his analysis:

> If the parent legislation dictated the outcome, then there would be no benefit gained by the delegation of the task to the subordinate: the parent legislation could, and therefore should, include the provision in the first place. Thus the entire concept of subordinate regulation depends upon and contemplates decisions being made between a range of options. Any decision involves consideration of what the decision-maker considers is the best solution in the circumstances. The question is the scope of the decision making left to the subordinate rule maker.[178]

[12–94] Having established this general starting point, O'Donnell J suggested that the test be approached negatively by asking whether the delegated rule-making was so broad as to trespass onto the domain reserved to the Oireachtas by Art 15.2.1°. This would require consideration of a number of factors such as the function of the parent legislation, the area in which a freedom of action was granted and the width of that freedom or the defined parameters in which it was to operate. Applying this approach in the instant case:

> the most striking feature of the legislative scheme is not just the regulatory straitjacket that applies to Member States, but the detailing on the garment. Uniformity in the rules, and so far as possible in their application as between Member States, is a clear and specific objective of the European Regulations. The fundamental decisions, that IUU fishing is a serious threat to the Common Fisheries Policy; that existing methods of enforcement were not sufficient to discourage and prevent such fishing; that those methods of enforcement require to be supplemented by a system of points allocation on licences; the particular transgressions requiring points allocations; the number of points to be applied once a breach is established; the number of points which can be accumulated before suspension; the initial and subsequent periods of suspension; the level of the infringement giving rise to loss of a licence; the requirement that points transfer with the licence; the possibility of erasing all accumulated points; the period necessary to do so and many other features of the scheme are all specified by the European Regulations. Indeed, it might be said

174 [2017] 3 IR 751, 776; [2018] 1 ILRM 245, 265.
175 *ibid.*
176 *ibid.*
177 *ibid*, 779, 777; 267, 265.
178 *ibid*, 777; 265.

> that the only substantive matter left to Member States in this regard is a decision as to whether an infringement is serious, and even then the factors to which regard may be had are themselves prescribed.
>
> What is left to Member States therefore is the establishment of a process for the allocation of the points in practice. It is to be noted that every other step in the process is prescribed by the European Regulations. Whatever the vehicle chosen it must address the same issue in the same way with the same consequences. Even then, that choice is constrained by the requirement that the system be effective and dissuasive, and the overriding obligation in both national and European law that any process be fair. Viewed in this way it can be fairly said that the 2014 Regulations [made by the Minister] are indeed incidental, supplemental and consequential to the European Regulations. While the Regulations of 2014 certainly involve a choice or a range of choices on the part of the Minister, those choices are severely limited in terms of the overall regulatory scheme. The points system whether laid down as a stand-alone regime, or consequential on a determination made in other proceedings, will operate in exactly the same way. The procedure is required to be determined by the Member States and raises no issue of broad policy that requires a determination by the Oireachtas.
>
> A useful comparison may be drawn with the decision in *Maher v Minister for Agriculture*. There the decisions to be made by the Member State had undeniable significance for individuals concerned (and indeed the dairy industry more generally) but as Keane CJ put it, the choice of policy in the field available to the Minister had been reduced almost to vanishing point, and as Fennelly J put it, the Minister was acting as the delegate of the Community. In other words the area of delegation was small and constrained. In the same way the area of policy left to the Member State here is also severely reduced. A choice does not imply a capacity to determine policy. The matters dealt with in the Regulations were incidental, supplemental and consequential to the provisions of the European Regulations. Accordingly, I do not consider that in principle the establishment of procedures under the 2014 Regulations contravened Art. 15.2.1°, and I would allow the appeal in that respect.[179]

[12–95] Accordingly, notwithstanding that neither of the two EU regulations had required the creation of a *stand alone* penalty point system, the fact that they had set the objective of establishing effective and persuasive deterrents, and had prescribed in some detail aspects of a penalty point system that was to complement criminal and/or administrative sanctions, meant that the use of s 3 of the 1972 Act had not gone beyond what was permitted applying the approach of a principles and policies test as developed in *Meagher* and *Maher*. It is worth noting that the statutory instrument was nevertheless declared to be invalid on the separate ground that it breached the right to fair procedures by allowing certain presumptions to reverse the onus of proof should a licence-holder wish to appeal the issuing of penalty points.[180]

[12–96] The merits of Art 29.4.6° and s 3 of the 1972 Act were considered by the Constitutional Review Group in its 1996 report. Whilst recognising the utility and necessity for a provision such as s 3, the Review Group nevertheless did not regard the situation as entirely satisfactory. According to its report:

> The extensive use of statutory instruments to implement directives has meant that hundreds of statutory provisions, some important, have been expressly or impliedly repealed by statutory instruments often with a minimum of publicity. The use of statutory instruments

[179] *ibid*, 778–779; 266–267.

[180] See Laurie O'Keeffe, "The Point System for Fishing Vessels – Dead in the Water?" (2016) 39 *Dublin University Law Journal* 429.

> ensures speedy and effective implementation of [EU] law but often at the expense of publicity and debate which attends the processing of legislation through the Oireachtas. In this respect the operation of the 1972 Act might be said to contribute to an "information deficit" and possibly a "democratic deficit". The Review Group recognises, of course, that following the judgments of the Supreme Court in the *Meagher* case, and in particular the judgment of Denham J, the use of statutory instruments to implement [EU] directives is confined to circumstances where the policies and principles have been determined in the [EU] directive. Thus in many instances there may not be choices available which would warrant an Oireachtas debate. However, the Review Group draws attention to this problem which results from the inapplicability of Article 15 by reason of Article [29.4.6°] to legislative amendments or provisions necessitated by [EU] directives.[181]

[12–97] On occasion, the Supreme Court has also recently expressed some criticism as to the manner in which statutory instruments are being used to transpose directives. In *One Complete Solutions Ltd v Dublin Airport Authority*, Clarke J (as he then was) spoke of an all-too-frequent problem whereby the courts were faced with implementing measures that closely follow the wording of a directive "but use Irish legal terminology in circumstances where the precise way in which the requirements of the relevant directive will need to fit within Irish procedural machinery have not been properly worked out".[182] A particular instance of this can be seen in *NAMA v Commissioner for Environmental Information*, where the Supreme Court was required to consider the meaning of a "public authority" within a statutory instrument used to transpose a directive giving effect to parts of the Aarhus Convention in EU law.[183] In delivering the Court's judgment, it was noted by O'Donnell J that, with minor exceptions, the definition of a "public authority" in the directive was "functionally identical" to the definition found in the Aarhus Convention. The statutory instrument, however, combined this general definition, as set out in three sub-paragraphs (a)–(c), with an additional list of Irish-specific bodies or offices. After repeating the definition in sub-paragraphs (a)–(c) the provision stated that the definition also includes the bodies or offices listed (i)–(vii). It was the addition of this list that proved problematical.[184] O'Donnell J observed that, if the directive had been implemented by primary legislation, the difficulty in interpretation might have been lessened, since a primary act may have been interpreted as being more extensive than as required by the directive (which permitted Member States to adopt more demanding requirements). As the directive had been implemented by a statutory instrument made under s 3 of the 1972 Act, however, interpretation of the SI was constrained by the fact that it was only permitted to faithfully implement the directive. As a result, there was:

> a specific importance in Irish law in understanding the extent and terms of a directive, where implemented by secondary legislation. In addition to the obvious benefits therefore of democratic oversight that implementation by primary legislation would entail, that route would also avoid some of the difficulties of interpretation which arose in this case.[185]

[12–98] There are, O'Donnell J suggested, two broad options open to a Member State in transposing a directive: it can simply adopt the provisions of the directive as they are, "in effect placing the national emblem on what is and remains European

[181] *Report of the Constitutional Review Group* (Government Publications, 1996) 115.
[182] [2015] IESC 6, unreported, Supreme Court, 30 January 2015, para 9.20.
[183] [2015] 4 IR 626; [2015] 2 ILRM 165.
[184] *ibid*, 635; 171.
[185] *ibid*, 635; 172.

language", or, if confident as to the scope and interpretation of the directive, it can use its own language to implement it, translating the European provisions into the language and concepts of the national legal system. While either approach has its attractions, in the view of O'Donnell J the hybrid method used in this instance posed real problems of interpretation:

> Subparagraphs (a) to (c) reproduce the terms of [the] Directive ... (and therefore the Convention) with no material change. Subparagraphs (i) to (vi) are therefore clearly matters of national law but cannot, or at least should not, materially extend (or indeed reduce) the scope of the provision. The problem of interpretation posed in this case calls to mind the observations of the Caliph of Baghdad on the burning of the library in Alexandria ... : if it contained nothing that was not in the Koran it was superfluous, and if it contained something different it was dangerous. In the same way it can be said that if subparas. (i) to (vi) say something different to subparas. (a) to (c) then they are possibly dangerous and certainly difficult.[186]

[12–99] Prior to the enactment of an amendment to s 3 of the 1972 Act in 2007, the Act precluded the creation of an indictable offence by a statutory instrument made under the Act. In the cases of *Browne v Attorney General*[187] and *Kennedy v Ireland*[188] the Supreme Court confirmed that the express exclusion of this power in the 1972 Act had the effect of precluding reliance upon the power to make delegated legislation in other primary acts in order to create indictable offences that were required by EU legal acts. The Oireachtas responded to these judgments by enacting the European Communities Act 2007, which amended s 3 of the 1972 Act so as to permit the creation of indictable offences subject to a maximum fine of €500,000 and a maximum term of imprisonment of three years.[189] In *O'Connor v DPP*, it was held that the Minister for the Arts, Heritage and the Gaeltacht was entitled to create an indictable offence by SI relating to actions likely to have a significant effect on certain listed environmental sites.[190] This was said to be done in order to implement the Habitats Directive, which obliged Member States to take appropriate steps to avoid the deterioration of natural habitats. The Directive, however, did not expressly require the creation of criminal offences. According to O'Malley J in the High Court, the principles and policies of the Habitats Directive obliged the State to take all appropriate steps to prevent deterioration in listed sites:

> There is no dispute as to the obligation of the State to implement effectively the objectives of the Habitats Directive, or as to the status of the bog in question as a protected site. Further, there has been no challenge to the evidence adduced on behalf of the respondents either as to the damage being caused by turf-cutting on raised bogs, or as to the efforts

---

186 *ibid*, 636; 172–173.

187 [2003] 3 IR 205.

188 [2007] 2 IR 45; [2005] 2 ILRM 401. See also *Quinn v Ireland* [2007] 3 IR 395; *Hayes v Ireland* [2010] 4 IR 702. See Elaine Fahey, "*Browne v Attorney General* and *Kennedy v Attorney General* – the Current State of the Ultra Vires Doctrine and the 'Necessitated' Clause" (2005) 23 *Irish Law Times* 258; Elaine Fahey, "The European Communities Bill, 2006" (2007) 12 *Bar Review* 4; Gerard Hogan and David Gwynn Morgan, *Administrative Law in Ireland* (4th ed, Round Hall, 2010) 23–26.

189 See also, for example, s 14 of the Communications Regulations (Amendment) Act 2007, which inserted s 46A into the Communications Regulations Act 2002 in order to allow for indictable offences to be created by ministerial statutory instrument for the purpose of giving effect to a provision of the EU treaties or an act, or provision of an act, adopted by a Union institution.

190 [2015] 2 IR 71. The judgment of O'Malley J was upheld by the Court of Appeal ([2017] IECA 101, unreported, 20 March 2017), from which decision the Supreme Court declined to hear a further appeal ([2018] IESCDET 92, 29 June 2018).

> made by the State, dating back to the 1990s, to halt the practice by means of persuasion and/or compensation. It is also clear that those efforts have not been fully successful and that cutting continues on protected sites, with the associated damage thereby entailed.
>
> In those circumstances, it seems to me that the introduction of criminal sanctions, almost 20 years after the Habitats Directive came into being, can fairly be said to have been necessary for the proper implementation of that directive. The fact that it does not, in terms, call for the creation of criminal offences is not, in my view, decisive, since directives by their nature leave the choice of implementation methods to the member states. No authority has been referred to which might suggest that criminal sanctions cannot be created unless the "parent" directive calls for them. Other measures to bring a stop to the deterioration of raised bogs have been tried. If they have not succeeded, as appears to be the case, then the choices of the State as to how the Habitats Directive is to be implemented may narrow down to the point where the criminal law has to be invoked. In my view that situation has been reached in relation to this issue. It is not open to the State to stand by and permit further damage to be done – that would be a breach of its legal obligations under the Habitats Directive.[191]

[12–100] As an additional check on the use of this power, s 3A was inserted into the 1972 Act. It provides that any statutory instrument made under the Act which establishes an indictable offence shall be laid before each House of the Oireachtas after it is made and, if a resolution annulling the SI is passed by *either* House within the next 21 sitting days, it shall be annulled. This is a stronger power of annulment than applies to SIs made pursuant to the Act more generally. According to the default rule, if the Joint Committee on European Affairs recommends to the Houses of the Oireachtas that any SI be annulled and a resolution annulling the SI is passed by *both* Houses within one year after it is made, the statutory instrument is annulled.[192] An exceptionally rare use of the annulment power occurred in 2018 when the Dáil voted to annul the European Union (Common Fisheries Policy) Point System Regulations 2018 (SI No 89 of 2018) that had been introduced to replace the statutory instrument that was found to be invalid by the Supreme Court in *O'Sullivan v Sea Fisheries Protection Authority* referred to above.[193]

[12–101] In addition to allowing for the creation of indictable offences under the 1972 Act, the European Communities Act 2007 also introduced a new power to make delegated legislation for the purposes of implementing EU law obligations under *other* primary legislation. According to s 4 of the 2007 Act, a power to make a statutory instrument conferred on a Minister by a provision of a statute may be exercised for the purpose of giving effect to a European act if the obligations imposed on the State under the European act relate, in whole, to matters to which that provision relates. The SI, or its preamble or recital, is required to specify the European act to which it gives effect. Any such statutory instrument may contain incidental, supplementary and consequential provisions that appear to the Minister to be necessary for the purposes of the SI, including provisions that repeal, amend or apply any other law, with the exception of the 2007 Act itself, the 1972 Act and the provision of the statute under which the SI is made.[194]

---

191 *ibid*, 92–93.

192 Section 4(1)(b) of the European Communities Act 1972, as inserted by s 1 of the European Communities (Amendment) Act 1973.

193 See Dáil Éireann debate, 23 May 2018, Vol 969, No 5. See Laurie O'Keeffe, "The Point System for Fishing Vessels – Dead in the Water?" (2016) 39 *Dublin University Law Journal* 429.

194 See, for example, s 46A(3) of the Communication Regulations Act 2002, as inserted by s 14 of

Direct Effect of International Agreements	
International agreements (whether "mixed" or "EU only") entered into with a third country are capable of having direct effect if the Court establishes that that was the intention having examined the overall object and purpose of the agreement. The relevant provision must be sufficiently clear, precise and unconditional.	• *Polydor v Harlequin Record Shops* (1982) • *Kupferberg* (1982) • *Sevince* (1990) • *GAG v Minister for Justice* (2003)
Multilateral agreements to which the EU is a party may also, in principle, be capable of having direct effect, however the Court of Justice has adopted a cautious approach with a number of agreements found not to have direct effect.	• *Pêcheurs de l'étang de Berre* (2004) • *Intertanko* (2008) • *Slovak Brown Bears* (2011) • *MX v HSE* (2012) • *Conway v Ireland* (2017)

Direct Effect of Regulations and Decisions	
Regulations generally have direct effect. It cannot be presumed, however, that every provision of every regulation, merely by virtue of its status, has such an effect. If a regulation leaves a particular discretion to Member States that provision may lack the clarity, precision and/or unconditionality to be directly effective.	• *Leonesio* (1972) • *Azienda Agricole* (2001)
Regulations are capable of both vertical and horizontal direct effect.	• *Muñoz* (2002)
Decisions are capable of having direct effect.	• *Grad* (1970)
A decision addressed to a Member State that is sufficiently clear, precise and unconditional in conferring a right or an interest on an individual is capable of having vertical direct effect. A decision addressed to a Member State is generally not capable of having horizontal direct effect. A decision that imposes an obligation on a private party can be enforced against that party by the relevant Member State (reverse vertical direct effect) or by another private party who has a sufficient interest in its enforcement (horizontal direct effect).	• *Dellway Investments Ltd v NAMA* (2011)

the Communications Regulations (Amendment) Act 2007, and the European Communities (Postal Services) (Amendment) Regulations 2008 (SI No 135 of 2008).

Direct Effect of Directives A provision of a directive that is sufficiently clear, precise and unconditional may be relied upon directly against a state entity based on the rationale that a Member State ought not to be able to benefit from its own failure to transpose the directive by the prescribed deadline. As a result, the direct effect of a directive only arises following the expiry of the transposition period and is vertical only.	• *Van Duyn v Home Office* (1970) • *Ratti* (1974) • *Marshall* (1983) • *McDermott v Minister for Social Welfare* (1987) • *Faccini Dori* (1994)
Following transposition of a directive, if the Member State has failed to implement the directive correctly an applicant may continue to invoke its direct effect. Even where a Member State has correctly implemented a directive, if it is not actually applying that directive correctly in practice, direct reliance may be placed on the directive.	• *Marks & Spencer* (2002)
There are four ways in which the lack of horizontal effect is mitigated:	
(i) if a directive encapsulates general principles of EU law these may be capable of being relied upon in a horizontal situation;	• *Mangold* (2005) • *Kücükdeveci* (2010)
(ii) through the "emanation of the state" doctrine, the Court of Justice has adopted a broad approach to defining the state for the purpose of vertical direct effect;	• *Marshall* (1983) • *Foster v British Gas* (1990) • *Farrell v Whitty* (2017)
(iii) in triangular situations, a directive may have incidental horizontal effects or a directive may have an exclusionary effect where it requires the disapplication of a national rule (eg Directive 2015/1535);	• *CIA Security* (1996) • *Unilever v Central Food* (2000) • *Sapod Audic* (2002)
(iv) the doctrine of indirect effect allows for directives to influence the interpretation of national law even in horizontal situations.	

Indirect Effect The doctrine of indirect effect or the duty of "harmonious interpretation" first emerged out of situations where a directive was incapable of having direct effect (either because it was a horizontal situation or the provision was not sufficiently clear, precise and unconditional). It has since developed into a general doctrine that applies to all sources of EU law and to all national law, not just laws enacted to transpose a directive. Nevertheless, the doctrine retains a particular pertinence when a national court is interpreting a law that is intended to give effect to a directive. The doctrine applies in both vertical and horizontal situations.	• *Von Colson* (1984) • *Marleasing* (1990)
Originally, the doctrine of indirect effect was said to derive from Art 4 TEU according to which Member States are obliged to take any appropriate measure, general or particular, to ensure fulfilment of the obligations arising out of the Treaties or resulting from the acts of the institutions of the Union. More recently, the Court has described the requirement for national law to be interpreted in conformity with EU law as being inherent in the system of the Treaty, since it permits the national court, for the matters within its jurisdiction, to ensure the full effectiveness of EU law when it determines the dispute before it.	• *Pfeiffer* (2004) • *Nathan v Bailey Gibson Ltd* (1998) • *Environmental Protection Agency v Harte Peat Ltd* (2015) • *NAMA v Commissioner for Environmental Information* (2015)
When applied in horizontal situations, the doctrine of indirect effect can alter the rights of private parties who may have acted in conformity with national law. As a result, there is a tension between ensuring the full effectiveness of EU law and the principles of legal certainty and non-retroactivity.	• *Centrosteel* (2000)
There are limitations on the duty to interpret national law in conformity with EU law, such that the duty on the national court is to do so only to the extent possible: (i) the national court is not required to give a national law an interpretation that it cannot bear (ie an interpretation *contra legem*); (ii) the doctrine cannot lead to the imposition of a criminal liability, or an increase in criminal liability, on an individual; and (iii) the doctrine should not give rise to retrospective effect where this was not intended.	• *IMPACT* (2008) • *Smith v Meade* (2017) • *Telecom Éireann v O'Grady* (1998) • *Albatross Feeds Ltd v Minister for Agriculture* (2007) • *Minister for Justice and Equality v Vilkas* (2018)

Use of s 3 of European Communities Act 1972, as amended Section 3 of the 1972 Act derogates from the normal rule in Art 15.2.1° of the Constitution whereby the sole law-making power for the State is vested in the Oireachtas. In order to be considered "necessitated by the obligations" of EU membership, such that an SI could be used rather than primary legislation, the SI must do no more than give effect to the principles and policies established in a directive, or other EU act.	• *Meagher v Minister for Agriculture* (1994) • *Maher v Minister for Agriculture* (2001) • *O'Sullivan v Sea Fisheries Protection Authority* (2017)
The Supreme Court has commented on certain difficulties that can arise when the language of a directive is combined with Irish legal terminology in an SI.	• *NAMA v Commissioner for Environmental Information* (2015) • *One Complete Solutions Ltd* (2015)
The 1972 Act originally contained an express exclusion of the power to create indictable offences by SI. This was held to mean that indictable offences could not be created by delegated legislation adopted under other primary legislation in order to give effect to EU obligations. In 2007, the 1972 Act was amended to allow for the creation of indictable offences, as well as to allow the making of SIs under other legislation in order to implement EU law obligations that relate to that legislation.	• *Browne v Ireland* (2003) • *Kennedy v Attorney General* (2005) • *O'Connor v DPP* (2015)

Chapter 13

SUPREMACY OF EU LAW

A. The Development of Supremacy

[13–01] As will be recalled from Chapter 11, in 1963 the Court of Justice delivered a landmark judgment in the case of *Van Gend en Loos*.[1] Notwithstanding the absence of any explicit textual basis in the Treaty of Rome and opposition from three of the six Member States, the Court established the principle that provisions of the EU's primary Treaties are capable of having direct effect and can be relied upon before national courts. Pointing to the specific reference to citizens as well as states in the Treaty's preamble, the ability of individuals to request a national court to seek a preliminary ruling from the Court of Justice and the role of the European Parliament and the Economic and Social Committee, the Court famously concluded that the EEC constituted:

> a new legal order of international law for the benefit of which the States have limited their sovereign rights, albeit within limited fields, and the subjects of which comprise not only Member States but also their nationals. Independently of the legislation of Member States, Community law therefore not only imposes obligations on individuals but is also intended to confer upon them rights which become part of their legal heritage. These rights arise not only where they are expressly granted by the Treaty, but also by reason of obligations which the Treaty imposes in a clearly defined manner upon individuals as well as upon the Member States and upon the institutions of the Community.[2]

[13–02] The Court's judgment in *Van Gend en Loos* was confined to the question of direct effect and did not inquire as to whether it was national law or EU law that had primacy or supremacy in the event of a conflict. This was due to the fact that the Dutch constitution itself provided that a self-executing treaty prevailed over any conflicting national law. Once the Court of Justice had confirmed the ability of the relevant Treaty provision to have direct effect, Dutch constitutional law determined that the Treaty of Rome would take precedence over a conflicting national law that had reclassified certain resin materials in such a way as to increase the rate of customs duty to be paid. It was clear, however, that having proclaimed the creation of a "new legal order of international law for the benefit of which the Member States had limited their sovereign rights",

---

1 Case 26/62 *Van Gend en Loos* [1963] ECR 1.
2 *ibid*, 12.

an obvious question arose as to what this would mean in the event of a clash between national law and EU law. The following year, in *Costa v ENEL*, the Court of Justice delivered a second judgment of equal significance that addressed this fundamental issue.[3] Although the Court consistently favours the term "primacy", writers on EU law tend to use the more suggestive "supremacy", and that is the description used here. The two terms are, however, interchangeable.

[13–03] *Costa v ENEL* began rather mundanely with the refusal to pay a small electricity bill. At a time when the Treaty of Rome had already entered into force, an Italian law was passed nationalising a number of electricity companies, including ENEL. Mr Costa was the unhappy shareholder of another electricity company affected by the nationalisation who refused to pay a bill owed to ENEL. When proceedings were instituted against him for non-payment of the bill, he successfully requested the court to make a preliminary reference concerning the compatibility of the nationalisation with the Treaty's provisions on competition law. Italy argued that the reference should be deemed inadmissible on the basis that, as the Italian court was obliged to apply the relevant national law, the possibility of seeking a preliminary reference should not have been open to it. In response to this provocative claim, the Court of Justice elaborated one of its most important and well-known passages. In a further striking example of its teleological approach, the Court enunciated a doctrine of the supremacy of EU law, based on the following reasoning:

> By contrast with ordinary international treaties, the EEC Treaty has created its own legal system which, on the entry into force of the Treaty, became an integral part of the legal systems of the Member States and which their courts are bound to apply.
>
> By creating a Community of unlimited duration, having its own institutions, its own personality, its own legal capacity and capacity of representation on the international plane and, more particularly, real powers stemming from a limitation of sovereignty or a transfer of powers from the States to the Community, the Member States have limited their sovereign rights, albeit within limited fields, and have thus created a body of law which binds their nationals and themselves.
>
> The integration into the laws of each Member State of provisions which derive from the Community, and more generally the terms and spirit of the Treaty, make it impossible for the states, as a corollary, to accord precedence to a unilateral and subsequent measure over a legal system accepted by them on the basis of reciprocity. Such a measure cannot therefore be inconsistent with that legal system. The executive force of Community law cannot vary from one State to another in deference to subsequent domestic laws, without jeopardising the attainment of the objectives of the Treaty … and giving rise to discrimination …
>
> The obligations undertaken under the Treaty establishing the Community would not be unconditional, but merely contingent, if they could be called into question by subsequent legislative acts of the signatories …
>
> The precedence of Community law is confirmed by [Article 288] whereby a regulation "shall be binding" and "directly applicable in all Member States". This provision, which is subject to no reservation, would be quite meaningless if a State could unilaterally nullify its effects by means of a legislative measure which could prevail over Community law.
>
> It follows from all these observations that the law stemming from the Treaty, an independent source of law, could not, because of its special and original nature, be overridden by

[3] Case 6/64 *Costa v ENEL* [1964] ECR 585.

> domestic legal provisions, however framed, without being deprived of its character as Community law and without the legal basis of the Community itself being called into question.
>
> The transfer by the states from their domestic legal system to the Community legal system of the rights and obligations arising under the Treaty carries with it a permanent limitation of their sovereign rights, against which a subsequent unilateral act incompatible with the concept of the Community cannot prevail.[4]

[13–04] The Court's reasoning in this passage can legitimately be described as highly purposive. As in *Van Gend en Loos*, the principle of effectiveness is clearly evident. In addition to stressing the unique nature of EU law, the Court emphasises its special purpose: the executive force of EU law cannot vary from one Member State to another without jeopardising the attainment of the objectives of the Treaty of Rome. Indeed, for some, the only decisive argument for supremacy is that of *effet utile*, with none of the other grounds put forward being particularly convincing by themselves.[5] Arguably, there is a distinct circularity to the Court's reasoning, which might be said to claim that the "special and original nature of the new Community requires the Community to have these special and original characteristics".[6]

[13–05] By 1970, in *Internationale Handelsgesellschaft*, the Court of Justice made clear that the supremacy of EU law applied to all forms of national law, including even the constitutional rules of a Member State.[7] There, it was claimed that a regulation which provided for the forfeiture of a deposit in the event that goods were not exported within a certain time was contrary to fundamental rights guarantees enshrined in the German constitution relating to the protection of property. The Court confirmed that the validity of an EU measure could not be affected by allegations that it ran counter to fundamental rights as found within a Member State's constitution or constitutional order. As the Court explained:

> Recourse to the legal rules or concepts of national law in order to judge the validity of measures adopted by the institutions of the Community would have an adverse effect on the uniformity and efficacy of Community law. The validity of such measures can only be judged in the light of Community law. In fact, the law stemming from the Treaty, an independent source of law, cannot because of its very nature be overridden by rules of national law, however framed, without being deprived of its character as Community law and without the legal basis of the Community itself being called in question.[8]

[13–06] Over a short space of time, through its judgments in *Van Gend en Loos* (1963), *Costa v ENEL* (1964) and *Internationale Handelsgesellschaft* (1970), the Court of Justice utterly transformed the nature of EU law. In addition to distinguishing it from international law by conferring it with the ability to have direct effect within the Member States in certain circumstances – regardless of whether they had a monist or a dualist legal system – EU law was also afforded primacy over all of a Member State's

---

4 *ibid*, 593–594.

5 Bruno de Witte, "Direct Effect, Supremacy, and the Nature of the Legal Order" in Paul Craig and Gráinne de Búrca (eds), *The Evolution of EU Law* (2nd ed, Oxford University Press, 2011) 323, 329.

6 Michal Bobek, "The Effects of EU Law in the National Legal Systems" in Catherine Barnard and Steve Peers (eds), *European Union Law* (2nd ed, Oxford University Press, 2017) 143, 162.

7 Case 11/70 *Internationale Handelsgesellschaft* [1970] ECR 1125.

8 *ibid*, 1134.

national law, including its constitution. This transformation of the Treaty of Rome from a traditional agreement under international law to a new legal order has been identified as the key "creation story" in EU law.[9] As Michal Bobek has described:

> To provide for both principles in almost one breath was a defining moment for EU law. Similarly to Christopher Columbus and his egg, the Court elegantly redefined the nature of the problem. It is said that when challenged that his journey to the Americas was no great accomplishment, Columbus asked his critics to try and make an egg balance on its tip. After they failed to do so, Columbus tapped the egg and made it stand on the crack. In a similar vein, instead of trying to explain to the Member States in future individual cases what is and what is not an effective enforcement of their international obligations, the Court pre-empted any national choice in this matter. It cracked national constitutional choices and gave EU law the same effects everywhere. Thus, in all the Member States, EU law is to have the same type of primacy over national law, irrespective of what the national constitution states with respect to the status of international law obligations in the national legal order. The choice made in *Costa* and *Van Gend en Loos* … was certainly a courageous choice which became *the* key element of the entire EU legal system.[10]

[13–07] The doctrine of supremacy was further strengthened a few years later in the 1978 judgment in *Simmenthal*.[11] Here, the Court of Justice addressed both the *nature* of the obligation on national courts to respect the supremacy of EU law and the *addressees* of that obligation within Member States. When importing beef into Italy, the Simmenthal company had been charged a levy which was designed to cover the cost of border veterinary inspections. On foot of a preliminary ruling which found the levy to be contrary to EU law, an Italian court ordered the relevant national authorities to repay the sums collected. The authorities refused to do so, however, arguing that only the higher-level Italian constitutional court could declare the law unconstitutional, leading to a repayment. As a result, the Italian court felt the need to make a second reference, asking whether the supremacy of EU law required that a conflicting national measure must, forthwith, be disregarded without waiting until the measure has either been repealed by the national legislature or declared unconstitutional by a court specifically authorised to do so under the Member State's constitutional order.

[13–08] The Court of Justice first confirmed that, by virtue of the principle of supremacy, upon its entry into force an EU law measure renders "automatically *inapplicable* any conflicting provision of current national law", regardless of whether that law was adopted before or after the EU measure.[12] It is important to note here that the adjective used by the Court to describe the effect of incompatibility on the national law is that it renders it "inapplicable", rather than say "void" or "annulled". The duty on the national court is to *disapply* the relevant national law in the particular case before it. Supremacy, therefore, can be understood as a "conflict rule, indicating which norm should be applied where two inconsistent norms collide".[13] This does not, however,

---

9 Michael Dougan, "The Vicissitudes of Life at the Coalface: Remedies and Procedures for Enforcing Union Law before the National Courts" in Paul Craig and Gráinne de Búrca (eds), *The Evolution of EU Law* (2nd ed, Oxford University Press, 2011) 406, 409.

10 Michal Bobek, "The Effects of EU Law in the National Legal Systems" in Catherine Barnard and Steve Peers (eds), *European Union Law* (2nd ed, Oxford University Press, 2017) 143, 163.

11 Case 106/77 *Simmenthal* [1978] ECR 629.

12 *ibid*, 643. Emphasis added.

13 Monica Claes, "The Primacy of EU Law in European and National Law" in Anthony Arnull and Damian Chalmers (eds), *The Oxford Handbook of European Union Law* (Oxford University Press, 2015) 178, 182.

have the effect of rendering the national law non-existent, and it may be that a national law can continue to have an application in other situations that do not have an EU law element.[14] In such a situation, however, there is an onus on the relevant competent body to remove the legal uncertainty that affects rights deriving from EU law.[15] In addition, the principle of supremacy was said by the Court of Justice to preclude the adoption of any new national laws that would be incompatible with the EU measure.

[13–09] Turning then to the question of whether the lower-level Italian court should, of itself, disapply the national law, or whether it was permitted to await such a ruling by the Italian constitutional court, the Court of Justice once again relied upon the principle of effectiveness to clarify that the obligation is to be exercised by *all* national courts having jurisdiction to apply the national law in question. This, it considered, flowed from the logic of Art 267 TFEU, whereby any national court or tribunal may seek a preliminary ruling from the Court of Justice. Since every national court can request a preliminary ruling, it followed that:

> every national court must, in a case within its jurisdiction, apply [EU] law in its entirety and protect rights which the latter confers on individuals and must accordingly set aside any provision of national law which may conflict with it, whether prior or subsequent to the [EU] rule.
>
> Accordingly any provision of a national legal system and any legislative, administrative or judicial practice which might impair the effectiveness of [EU] law by withholding from the national court having jurisdiction to apply such law the power to do everything necessary at the moment of its application to set aside national legislative provisions which might prevent [EU] rules from having full force and effect are incompatible with those requirements which are the very essence of [EU] law.
>
> This would be the case in the event of a conflict between a provision of [EU] law and a subsequent national law if the solution of the conflict were to be reserved for an authority with a discretion of its own, other than the court called upon to apply [EU] law, even if such an impediment to the full effectiveness of [EU] law were only temporary.[16]

[13–10] So, for example, the Court of Justice has held that the Italian competition authority and the Belgian institute for administering social insurance to self-employed persons ought to have disapplied a national law that was not in conformity with an EU measure.[17] More recently, the Court of Justice has found that it would be contrary to the supremacy of EU law if a body such as the Workplace Relations Commission, established by Irish law in order to ensure the enforcement of EU law in a particular area – in this case the Equal Treatment Directive – lacked the jurisdiction to decide to disapply a rule of national law that is contrary to EU law.[18] In the next chapter it will be seen that the related "principle of effectiveness" builds upon the reasoning in *Simmenthal* in holding that national rules and procedures governing litigation, remedies and the enforcement of claims should not operate so as to impair the proper effectiveness of EU law rights.

---

14 Joined Case C-10/97 to C-22/97 *IN.CO.GE.* [1998] ECR I-6307, 6333.

15 Case C-264/96 *Imperial Chemical Industries v Colmer* [1998] ECR I-4695, 4725.

16 Case 106/77 *Simmenthal* [1978] ECR 629, 644.

17 Case C-198/01 *CIF* [2003] ECR I-8055; Case C-118/00 *Larsy* [2001] ECR I-5063.

18 Case C-378/17 *Minister for Justice and Equality v Workplace Relations Commission* EU:C:2018:979, 4 December 2018.

[13–11] Despite the many reforms introduced by the Lisbon Treaty there still remains no reference to the supremacy of EU law within the TEU or the TFEU themselves. The draft Constitutional Treaty included a provision that would have stated that both it, and the law adopted by the Union institutions, have primacy over the law of the Member States. This provision was among those elements of the draft Constitutional Treaty deemed responsible for its rejection in referendums in France and the Netherlands for having been too akin to a national constitution. The Lisbon Treaty did, however, annex a new declaration to the TEU and TFEU, Declaration 17, which comprises the following single sentence: "The Conference recalls that, in accordance with well settled case law of the Court of Justice of the European Union, the Treaties and the law adopted by the Union on the basis of the Treaties have primacy over the law of Member States, under the conditions laid down by the said case law." The inclusion of the declaration helps counter any potential argument that the decision to drop the primacy provision in the draft Constitutional Treaty is indicative of a weakening of the supremacy doctrine. Unusually, it was also decided to annex to the Final Act of the Intergovernmental Conference that adopted the Lisbon Treaty a short 2007 opinion by the Council Legal Service, which is set out beneath Declaration 17 and reads as follows:

> It results from the case-law of the Court of Justice that primacy of EC law is a cornerstone principle of Community law. According to the Court, this principle is inherent to the specific nature of the European Community. At the time of the first judgment of this established case-law (*Costa/ENEL …*) there was no mention of primacy in the treaty. It is still the case today. The fact that the principle of primacy will not be included in the future treaty shall not in any way change the existence of the principle and the existing case-law of the Court of Justice.

[13–12] Another more significant change brought about by the Lisbon Treaty was the granting of legal effect to the Charter of Fundamental Rights, which now has the same legal value as the TEU and TFEU. When discussing the Charter in Chapter 3, reference was made to the well-known case of *Melloni*, in which the Court of Justice was called upon to interpret Art 53 of the Charter.[19] According to that article, nothing in the Charter shall be interpreted as restricting or adversely affecting human rights and fundamental freedoms as recognised, in their respective fields of application, by Union law, international law, international agreements to which the Union or all the Member States are party, and, most importantly here, by the Member States' constitutions. In *Melloni*, a European Arrest Warrant (EAW) request was made by Italy for the return of an individual from Spain who had been convicted in Italy *in absentia*. The EAW Framework Decision provided that the fact of having been convicted *in absentia* was not a valid ground on which to refuse surrender. Indeed, an amendment to the Framework Decision had introduced specific rules aimed at harmonising an approach to surrender in such cases. As the Spanish constitutional court thought that surrender in the circumstances would breach Spanish constitutional guarantees of the right to a fair trial, it requested a preliminary ruling from the Court of Justice as to whether Art 53 of the Charter allowed it to apply this higher standard of protection.

[13–13] For Advocate General Bot, to allow whichever was the higher of the two standards to prevail would infringe the supremacy of EU law since, in certain cases, it would mean giving national constitutions primacy over EU law. As he explained:

---

[19] Case C-399/11 *Melloni* EU:C:2013:107, 23 February 2013.

> it is settled case-law that recourse to provisions of national law, even of a constitutional order, to limit the scope of European Union law would have the effect of impairing the unity and efficacy of that law and consequently cannot be accepted.
>
> In my view, Article 53 of the Charter is not to be regarded as a clause designed to regulate a conflict between, on the one hand, a provision of secondary law which, interpreted in the light of the Charter, sets a given level of protection for a fundamental right and, on the other hand, a provision drawn from a national constitution which provides a higher level of protection for the same fundamental right. In such a situation, that article has neither the objective nor the effect of giving priority to the more protective rule deriving from a national constitution. To accept otherwise would be tantamount to disregarding the settled case-law of the Court concerning the primacy of European Union law.
>
> I would point out, in that regard, that it is by no means apparent from the wording of Article 53 of the Charter that it is to be considered as establishing an exception to the principle of the primacy of European Union law. On the contrary, it may be argued that the words "in their respective fields of application" were chosen by the drafters of the Charter in order not to infringe that principle. Moreover, that principle as it derives from the Court's case-law is confirmed in the declarations annexed to the final act of the Intergovernmental Conference which adopted the Treaty of Lisbon signed on 13 December 2007.[20]

[13–14] Sitting as a Grand Chamber, the Court of Justice came to the same conclusion, albeit with a somewhat more focused attention on the terms of the EAW Framework Decision itself. According to the Court, the interpretation proposed by the Spanish court would:

> allow a Member State to make the execution of a European arrest warrant issued for the purposes of executing a sentence rendered in absentia subject to conditions intended to avoid an interpretation which restricts or adversely affects fundamental rights recognised by its constitution, even though the application of such conditions is not allowed under [the] Framework Decision …
>
> Such an interpretation of Article 53 of the Charter cannot be accepted.
>
> That interpretation … would undermine the principle of the primacy of EU law inasmuch as it would allow a Member State to disapply EU legal rules which are fully in compliance with the Charter where they infringe the fundamental rights guaranteed by that State's constitution.
>
> It is settled case-law that, by virtue of the principle of primacy of EU law, which is an essential feature of the EU legal order, rules of national law, even of a constitutional order, cannot be allowed to undermine the effectiveness of EU law on the territory of that State.
>
> It is true that Article 53 of the Charter confirms that, where an EU legal act calls for national implementing measures, national authorities and courts remain free to apply national standards of protection of fundamental rights, provided that the level of protection provided for by the Charter, as interpreted by the Court, and the primacy, unity and effectiveness of EU law are not thereby compromised.
>
> However, … [the] Framework Decision … does not allow Member States to refuse to execute a European arrest warrant when the person concerned is in one of the situations provided for therein.
>
> … Consequently, allowing a Member State to avail itself of Article 53 of the Charter to

---

[20] Case C-399/11 *Melloni* EU:C:2012:600, 2 October 2012, paras 98–100.

> make the surrender of a person convicted in absentia conditional upon the conviction being open to review in the issuing Member State … in order to avoid an adverse effect on the right to a fair trial and the rights of the defence guaranteed by the constitution of the executing Member State, by casting doubt on the uniformity of the standard of protection of fundamental rights as defined in that framework decision, would undermine the principles of mutual trust and recognition which that decision purports to uphold and would, therefore, compromise the efficacy of that framework decision.[21]

[13–15] While the Court's judgment was perhaps to be expected, and may be seen as flowing from the specific terms of the EAW Framework Decision as amended, it did spark a fair deal of critical commentary.[22] Rather than accepting a degree of pluralism amongst the human rights standards of Member States and the Union, which would allow the highest standard to prevail, *Melloni* can be understood as an "unequivocal reassertion of the primacy of EU law over national constitutional rights".[23] It is a forceful affirmation of *Internationale Handelsgesellschaft* for the post-Lisbon age, notwithstanding the margin of flexibility that Art 53 of the Charter had appeared to promise the Member States.

B. Relationship between Supremacy and Direct Effect

[13–16] It has already been seen in Chapter 11 that there continues to be a debate concerning the precise circumstances in which the direct effect of EU law can arise. For some, it is necessary that the relevant provision of EU law confer a right on individuals that can be invoked before national courts in order for it to have direct effect. For others, to be directly effective it is sufficient that a provision produces independent legal effects that can be invoked before a national court, without necessarily entailing the conferral of rights.

[13–17] When considering, in Chapter 12, the incidental horizontal effect that may be attributed to a directive, it was also seen that a distinction is often drawn between granting a directive an *exclusionary* effect, whereby a national law must be disapplied, and the more expansive *substitutionary* effect, where an EU rule not only knocks out a national law but also takes the further step of moving in to replace it, thereby allowing direct reliance on EU law.

[13–18] Both of these debates resurface when one comes to look at the related question of whether, in order for the supremacy of EU law to apply in a particular case, the relevant EU rule in question must first have direct effect. In a well-known article on the topic, Michael Dougan labels two contrasting approaches to this question as

---

21 Case C-399/11 *Melloni* EU:C:2013:107, 23 February 2013, paras 56–63.

22 See Asterios Pliakos and Georgios Anagnostaras, "Fundamental Rights and the New Battle over Legal and Judicial Supremacy: Lessons from *Melloni*" (2015) 34 *Yearbook of European Law* 97; Leonard FM Besselink, "The Parameters of Constitutional Conflict after *Melloni*" (2014) 39 *European Law Review* 531; Nik de Boer, "Addressing Rights Divergences under the Charter: *Melloni*" (2013) 50 *Common Market Law Review* 1083; Daniel Sarmiento, "Who's Afraid of the Charter? The Court of Justice, National Courts and the New Framework of Fundamental Rights Protection in Europe" (2013) 50 *Common Market Law Review* 1267.

23 Paul Craig and Gráinne de Búrca, *EU Law* (6th ed, Oxford University Press, 2015) 400.

the "primacy" and the "trigger" models.[24] According to the primacy model, because supremacy is a fundamental constitutional principle of the EU legal order, it is capable of producing legal effects within a Member State independently of direct effect. The argument in favour of the primacy model has been summarised by Paul Craig as follows:

> It is clear in terms of principle and positive domestic law that there can be legal rules that do not give rise to individual rights, but which nonetheless impose obligations or empower organs of the State. This is equally true for EU law. A legal norm may not have direct effect because it is not for the benefit of individuals, or it is not sufficiently certain or precise. The Member State may nonetheless have failed to fulfil its obligations under such a norm, with the consequence that primacy would dictate that the inconsistent national law should fall. It is true that the relevant EU provision must be cognizable by the national court before there can be conflict with the applicable national rules. This can, however, occur in a number of ways: it might be argued that the EU provision meets the requirements of direct effect; that it does not do so, but nonetheless satisfies the conditions for indirect effect; or that it comes before the national court in some other way, for example as an action between different institutional organs of the same State. There is then no logical bar to primacy applying even in the absence of direct effect. [25]

[13–19] Support for the primacy model can be seen to come from the judgment of the Court of Justice in *Pupino*, a pre-Lisbon Treaty case concerning a framework decision on the standing of victims in criminal proceedings.[26] Mrs Pupino was a nursery school teacher who was accused of inflicting injuries on her pupils. Given the young age of the victims, a request was made for special procedures to be applied that were provided for under the framework directive. The national court was unable to accede to the request, however, as Italian law had not been amended to provide for such procedures. A question arose as to whether a duty of harmonious interpretation applied in the circumstances, notwithstanding the fact that framework decisions – a particular instrument used before the Lisbon Treaty in the third pillar covering police and judicial cooperation in criminal matters – were not capable of having direct effect. In holding that a duty of harmonious interpretation did apply, the Court of Justice had recourse, once again, to the principle of *effet utile* and observed that:

> It would be difficult for the Union to carry out its task effectively if the principle of loyal cooperation, requiring in particular that Member States take all appropriate measures … to ensure fulfilment of their obligations under European Union law, were not also binding in the area of police and judicial cooperation in criminal matters, which is moreover entirely based on cooperation between Member States and the institutions.[27]

[13–20] Michael Dougan suggests that the primacy model can have a particular resonance with regard to exclusionary effects, given that the doctrine of supremacy requires the disapplication of any conflicting national law. So, for example, proponents of the primacy model may see cases such as *CIA Security*[28] and *Unilever*[29] – where the

---

24 Michael Dougan, "When Worlds Collide! Competing Visions of the Relationship between Direct Effect and Supremacy" (2007) 44 *Common Market Law Review* 931.

25 Paul Craig, *The Lisbon Treaty: Law, Politics, and Treaty Reform* (Oxford University Press, 2010) 432. See Koen Lenaerts and Tim Corthaut, "Of Birds and Hedges: The Role of Primacy in Invoking Norms of EU Law" (2006) 31 *European Law Review* 287.

26 Case C-105/03 *Pupino* [2005] ECR I-5283.

27 *ibid*, 5327–5328.

28 Case C-194/94 *CIA Security International* [1996] ECR I-2201.

29 Case C-443/98 *Unilever v Central Food* [2000] ECR I-7535.

failure to notify the Commission of national measures under what is now Directive 2015/1535 led to their disapplication – as being less about the incidental direct effect of a directive or a "substantial procedural defect", and more about the supremacy of EU law in a constitutional sense. For them, these two judgments "were no flash in the pan whose legal relevance should be limited to the exceptional category of 'procedural' measures" such as Directive 2015/1535.[30] Rather than being understood as a giving the Directive a form of incidental horizontal direct effect – as proponents of the trigger model would conceptually understand the judgments – viewed through the lens of the primacy model, the exclusionary effect in those cases can be seen as deriving from the "principle of supremacy *in and of itself*".[31]

[13–21] Whereas the primacy model is premised on a view of supremacy as a foundational constitutional principle of the EU legal order, the trigger model has a very different perspective. It sees supremacy in a narrower sense, treating it as a conflict rule whose purpose is to provide a remedy in situations of conflict between EU law and national law. As a result, under the trigger model supremacy only comes into the picture once a directly effective rule has come up against an incompatible rule of national law. The trigger model "places direct effect in the driving seat, with supremacy being the remedial manifestation of using directly effective EU rights in national courts".[32] In contrast, the primacy model "places supremacy in the driving seat, with direct effect being relevant only in relation to substitution effects".[33]

[13–22] Ever since the old pillar structure was done away with by the Lisbon Treaty, the debate between the primacy and trigger models of supremacy has lost much of its practical relevance, save perhaps for an unresolved question regarding the applicability of direct effect to CFSP measures. It does continue, however, to divide academic opinion and can account for different theoretical understandings of the jurisprudence of the Court of Justice, such as we have seen with *CIA Security* and *Unilever*. For Monica Claes, the exact link between direct effect and supremacy remains unclear. Nevertheless, she suggests that supremacy is most effective when used in connection with direct effect, and carries less weight when direct effect is absent. Depending on the nature of the measure involved and the obligation it imposes, the supremacy of a non-directly effective EU measure may result in an obligation of harmonious interpretation, state liability for infringement of a Treaty obligation and possibly also in the setting aside of any inconsistent national law (ie an exclusionary effect).[34]

C. The Member State View of Supremacy

[13–23] The description of supremacy outlined thus far has been from the perspective

---

[30] See Alan Dashwood, Michael Dougan, Barry Rodger, Eleanor Spaventa and Derrick Wyatt, *Wyatt and Dashwood's European Union Law* (6th ed, Hart, 2011) 281–282.

[31] *ibid*, 282.

[32] Paul Craig and Gráinne de Búrca, *EU Law* (6th ed, Oxford University Press, 2015) 277. See Alicia Hinarejos, "On the Legal Effect of Framework Decisions and Decisions: Directly Applicable, Directly Effective, Self-Executing, Supreme?" (2008) 14 *European Law Journal* 620.

[33] *ibid.*

[34] Monica Claes, "The Primacy of EU Law in European and National Law" in Anthony Arnull and Damian Chalmers (eds), *The Oxford Handbook of European Union Law* (Oxford University Press, 2015) 178, 183.

of the Court of Justice in Luxembourg and its own understanding of the EU legal order. So, for example, we have seen that in its judgment in *Melloni*, the Court took the opportunity to reaffirm the importance of the supremacy, effectiveness and uniform interpretation of EU law notwithstanding the reference in Art 53 of the Charter of Fundamental Rights to human rights standards mandated by national constitutions. There is, however, another perspective on supremacy, and that is the view as seen from the Member States themselves and, in particular, their national courts who deal with the relationship between domestic constitutional norms and EU law. As Daniel Sarimento has described:

> For many years, the Court of Justice of the European Union and the constitutional courts of the Member States have lived under the illusion of unilateral supremacy. According to the Court of Justice, EU law has primacy over national Constitutions, whilst national supreme jurisdictions have repeatedly stated that EU law's ultimate source of legitimacy lies in the Constitution of the Member State, thus subjecting EU law to constitutional review. The illusion played the trick and it has bound this odd couple happily together for more than forty years.[35]

[13–24] Similarly, Monica Claes suggests that virtually no Member State unconditionally accepts the principle of supremacy as propounded by EU law. Rather, both continue to claim the ultimate authority, and to claim that the other will eventually have to give way, with the result that there is, in fact, a "plurality of conceptions as to how they interrelate and how conflicts are to be resolved. There is not *one* principle of primacy, but many in operation".[36] Bruno de Witte shares this assessment, colourfully describing what Sarimento calls the "illusion of unilateral supremacy" as follows:

> A benign interpretation is that national courts must necessarily find a way to recognise those principles and to achieve the result imposed by the European Court on them. A stronger interpretation would be that national courts have no choice and that they simply cannot resist the authority of EU law. The latter reading implies that national courts, when acting on the duties imposed on them by the European Court, are exercising a jurisdiction attributed to them directly by Union law, and not a jurisdiction given to them by their own constitutions. This was adopted by many European Community law scholars ... but there is hardly any evidence of national courts adopting this radical approach. National courts see themselves as organs of their state, and try to fit their European mandate within the framework of the powers attributed to them by their national legal system. For them ... the idea that EU law can claim its primacy within the national legal system on the basis of its own authority seems as implausible as Baron von Munchhausen's claim that he had lifted himself from the sand by pulling on his bootstraps. The national courts ... see EU law as rooted in their constitution, and seek a foundation for the primacy and direct effect of EU law in that constitution.[37]

[13–25] While the manner in which Member States accept the supremacy of EU law

---

[35] Daniel Sarmiento, "Who's Afraid of the Charter? The Court of Justice, National Courts and the New Framework of Fundamental Rights Protection in Europe" (2013) 50 *Common Market Law Review* 1267.

[36] Monica Claes, "The Primacy of EU Law in European and National Law" in Anthony Arnull and Damian Chalmers (eds), *The Oxford Handbook of European Union Law* (Oxford University Press, 2015) 178, 199.

[37] Bruno de Witte, "Direct Effect, Supremacy, and the Nature of the Legal Order" in Paul Craig and Gráinne de Búrca (eds), *The Evolution of EU Law* (2nd ed, Oxford University Press, 2011) 323, 350. See also Mrs Justice Susan Denham and Genevieve Burke, "Constitutional Courts and the Lisbon Treaty" (2009) 16 *Irish Journal of European Law* 93, 113.

varies, it has been suggested that the spectrum of views has begun to coalesce around a position of *qualified* or *conditional* supremacy.[38] For example, in the *HS2* case the UK Supreme Court observed that certain of the arguments being made by the appellants raised a question as to the extent to which established constitutional principles governing the relationship between Parliament and the courts, as reflected in the Bill of Rights of 1689, may have been qualified by the European Communities Act 1972. Contrary to the appellants' submissions, the Supreme Court considered that such a question

> cannot be resolved simply by applying the doctrine developed by the Court of Justice of the supremacy of EU law, since the application of that doctrine in our law itself depends upon the 1972 Act. If there is a conflict between a constitutional principle, such as that embodied in … the Bill of Rights, and EU law, that conflict has to be resolved by our courts as an issue arising under the constitutional law of the United Kingdom.[39]

(i) The View from Germany and Denmark

[13–26] A principal and forceful proponent of conditional or qualified supremacy is the Bundesverfassungsgericht, the German Federal Constitutional Court (FCC) or "Karlsruhe" court, from the city in which it sits. Given the influence of its judgments, an overview of the Federal Constitutional Court's take on the supremacy of EU law will be outlined here. Over a lengthy period of time, the Court has delivered a series of judgments in which it has emphasised that the source of the Union's authority "are the peoples of Europe with democratic constitutions in their states". Accordingly, the EU is understood to be a "derived fundamental order", while the Member States "permanently remain the masters of the Treaties".[40]

[13–27] We have already seen in Chapter 10 that, in the case of *Kadi I*, the Court of

---

38 Damian Chalmers, Gareth Davies and Giorgio Monti, *European Union Law* (3rd ed, Cambridge University Press, 2014) 223.

39 *R (HS2 Action Alliance Ltd) v Secretary of State for Transport* [2014] UKSC 3; [2014] 1 WLR 324, para 79 (Lord Reed).

40 2 BvE 2/08, judgment on the Treaty of Lisbon, 30 June 2009, para 231. See Wolfgang Heusel, "Preserving National Identity: The Bundesverfassungsgericht between National Constitutional Constraints and an Ever Closer European Union" in Kieran Bradley, Noel Travers and Anthony Whelan (eds), *Of Courts and Constitutions: Liber Amicorum in Honour of Nial Fennelly* (Hart, 2014) 375; Erich Vranes, "German Constitutional Foundations of, and Limitations to, EU Integration: A Systematic Analysis" (2013) 14 *German Law Journal* 75; Christian Calliess, "The Future of the Eurozone and the Role of the German Federal Constitutional Court" (2012) 31 *Yearbook of European Law* 402; Mehrdad Payandeh, "Constitutional Review of EU Law after *Honeywell*: Contextualising the Relationship between the German Constitutional Court and the EU Court of Justice" (2011) 48 *Common Market Law Review* 9; Asterios Pliakos and Georgios Anagnostaras, "Who is the Ultimate Arbiter? The Battle over Judicial Supremacy in EU law" (2011) 36 *European Law Review* 109; Philipp Kiiver, "The *Lisbon* Judgment of the German Constitutional Court: A Court-Ordered Strengthening of the National Legislature in the EU" (2010) 16 *European Law Journal* 578; Christoph Schönberger, "Lisbon in Karlsruhe: Maastricht's Epigones at Sea" (2010) 10 *German Law Journal* 1201; Dimitrios Doukas, "The Verdict of the German Federal Constitutional Court on the Lisbon Treaty: Not Guilty, but Don't Do It Again!" (2009) 34 *European Law Review* 866; Daniel Thym, "In the Name of Sovereign Statehood: A Critical Introduction to the *Lisbon* judgment of the German Constitutional Court" (2009) 46 *Common Market Law Review* 1795; Joseph H Weiler, "Does Europe Need a Constitution? Reflections on Demos, Telos and the German *Maastricht* Decision" (1995) 1 *European Law Journal* 219; Matthias Herdegen, "*Maastricht* and the German Constitutional Court: Constitutional Restraints for an Ever Closer Union" (1993) 31 *Common Market Law Review* 235.

Justice's Grand Chamber delivered a landmark judgment dealing with the relationship between EU law and international law.[41] There, the Court of Justice asserted its own responsibility to ensure that Union measures adopted pursuant to binding obligations imposed by the UN Security Council were compatible with EU law, notwithstanding the primacy afforded to the UN Charter in Art 103 of the Charter. In a judgment on the compatibility of the Lisbon Treaty with the German Constitution, the Federal Constitutional Court drew an analogy with the approach of the Court of Justice in *Kadi*, which it described as placing, in a borderline case, "the assertion of its own identity as a legal community above the [UN Charter] commitment that it otherwise respects".[42] If used constructively, the FCC regarded this legal construct as having an application in the relationship between Member States and the Union, which was a political order "not structured according to strict hierarchy". Accordingly, it was deemed consistent with the German constitution's commitment to the Union and openness to EU law that, "exceptionally, and under special narrow circumstances", the Federal Constitutional Court might declare EU law inapplicable in Germany.[43]

[13–28] One of the exceptional grounds on which the FCC might declare EU law to be inapplicable is on the basis that the Union institutions have "manifestly" acted beyond their competences (*ultra vires*) in such a way that entails a "structurally significant shift in the allocation of powers to the detriment of the Member States", and in circumstances where the Court of Justice has first been given an opportunity to adjudicate on the matter. So, for example, in the 2014 case of *Gauweiler*, the FCC gave serious consideration to a challenge to the establishment of an Outright Monetary Transactions (OMT) programme by the European Central Bank, on the basis that it went beyond the powers conferred on the Bank. For the first and, to date, only one of two occasions, the Federal Constitutional Court requested a preliminary ruling from the Court of Justice, affording it the opportunity to consider the issues raised.[44] In doing so, however, the FCC made clear that it was reserving to itself the ultimate right to consider the Court's ruling in light of the requirements of the German constitution.

[13–29] The Court of Justice upheld the lawfulness of the ECB's establishment of the OMT programme, but did so on the basis that the programme would be operated in accordance with certain conditions.[45] Of particular interest is the fact that the Luxembourg court did not rise to the bait presented by the provocative manner in which the request for a ruling had been issued from Karlsruhe. Instead, the Court of Justice:

> wisely did not question the national rules governing the judicial review of the OMT measures nor the organisation of the domestic judicial proceedings. It did not express any views on the FCC's reserve power, merely confining itself to a simple statement that preliminary rulings are binding on the national courts. Notably, it went on to give clear answers to the questions referred without discussing directly the FCC's analysis, in contrast to Advocate General Cruz Villalón, who examined the alleged consequences of the OMT programme to Germany's constitutional identity. One may say that, if the

---

41 Joined Cases C-402/05P and 415/05P *Kadi v Council* [2008] ECR I-6351. See ch 10, paras [10–14] to [10–18].

42 2 BvE 2/08, judgment on the Treaty of Lisbon, 30 June 2009, para 340.

43 *ibid.*

44 The second reference from the FCC came in Case C-493/17 *Weiss* EU:C:2018:1000, 11 December 2018, which concerned the ECB's Public Sector Asset Purchase Programme. The Court of Justice, sitting as a Grand Chamber, upheld the validity of the Programme.

45 Case C-62/14 *Gauweiler v Deutscher Bundestag* EU:C:2015:400, 16 June 2015.

Court of Justice's ruling is read in isolation from the reference and the Advocate General's Opinion, it would not be easy to see the peculiarities of the FCC's request or the underlying controversial constitutional debate. As a result, it is now the FCC that bears the burden of deciding whether to reconsider its analysis or realise its threat. In essence, the Court of Justice responded that it retained the exclusive competence to determine the legality of an EU act and that it was not willing to negotiate.[46]

[13–30] The stand-off eventually came to an end on 21 June 2016 (two days before the UK's referendum on EU membership), when the Federal Constitutional Court determined that if the OMT programme was administered in accordance with the interpretations and conditions set out in the judgment of the Court of Justice, it did not "manifestly" exceed the competences attributed to the European Central Bank, nor did it present a constitutionally relevant threat to the German Federal Parliament's right to decide on budgetary matters.[47]

[13–31] One particular aspect of the *ultra vires* limitation developed by the Karlsruhe court is the principle that the German constitution does not allow the transfer of sovereign powers in such a way that the exercise of those powers can independently establish other EU competences. Accordingly, the FCC will not allow the transfer of competence to the EU to decide upon its own competence – a power that is known as *Kompetenz-Kompetenz*. When assessing the compatibility of the Lisbon Treaty with the German constitution, the FCC was therefore required to consider changes to Art 352 TFEU, the "flexibility clause". This significant provision grants a residual competence that allows the Union to take action necessary to attain a Treaty objective where the Treaties have not otherwise provided the requisite powers. The FCC pointed to the fact that the newly worded Art 352 made it possible to substantially amend the treaty foundations of the EU without the constitutive participation of the Member States' legislative bodies. The obligation on the Commission to inform national parliaments of any proposed use of Art 352 as a legal base was deemed not to be a sufficient safeguard. Rather, in order for the use of Art 352 to be constitutional, ratification by the Federal Parliament (Bundestag) and Federal Council (Bundesrat) representing the sixteen *länder* was required. In assessing the Lisbon Treaty to be compatible with the constitution, the FCC required that the German representative in the Council not

46 Takis Tridimas and Napoleon Xanthoulis, "A Legal Analysis of the *Gauweiler* Case: Between Monetary Policy and Constitutional Conflict" (2016) 23 *Maastricht Journal of European and Comparative Law* 17, 36. See Vestert Borger, "Outright Monetary Transactions and the Stability Mandate of the ECB: *Gauweiler*" (2016) 53 *Common Market Law Review* 139; Paul Craig and Menelaos Markakis, "*Gauweiler* and the Legality of Outright Monetary Transactions" (2016) 41 *European Law Review* 4; Dariusz Adamski, "Economic Constitution of the Euro Area after the *Gauweiler* Preliminary Ruling" (2015) 52 *Common Market Law Review* 1451; Federico Fabbrini, "After the OMT Case: The Supremacy of EU Law as the Guarantee of the Equality of the Member States" (2015) 16 *German Law Journal* 1003; Thomas Beukers, "The Bundesverfassungsgericht Preliminary Reference on the OMT Programme: 'In the ECB We Do Not Trust. What About You?'" (2014) 15 *German Law Journal* 343; Editorial, "An Unintended Side-Effect of Draghi's Bazooka: An Opportunity to Establish a More Balanced Relationship between the ECJ and Member States' Highest Courts" (2014) 51 *Common Market Law Review* 375; Henning Detters, "National Constitutional Jurisprudence in a Post-National Europe: The ESM Ruling of the German Federal Constitutional Court and the Disavowal of a Conflict" (2014) 20 *European Law Journal* 204.

47 2 BvE 13/13, 21 June 2016. See also 2 BvR 1390/12, *European Stability Mechanism Treaty*, 12 September 2012.

express any formal approval to the use of Art 352 unless the Bundestag and Bundesrat had first given their consent.[48]

[13–32] As well as subjecting the acceptance of EU law to adherence with German constitutional identity and the limits of the Union's competence, in earlier cases the FCC had made clear that in the event of a conflict between EU law and the guarantee of fundamental rights in the German constitution, the national rights guarantees would prevail for so long as the conflict of norms was not removed by the EU institutions. This was first established in a case in which the FCC was required to consider the landmark ruling of the Court of Justice in *Internationale Handelsgesellschaft*, which had concerned a clash between an EU regulation and the protection of property rights under the German constitution. The judgment of the FCC is known as *Solange I*, from the German for "so long as".[49] Over a decade later, in 1986, the FCC delivered a judgment known as *Solange II*, in which it revised its earlier assessment in light of the strengthening of fundamental rights protections within EU law, including the establishment of direct elections to the European Parliament.[50] According to this revised approach, so long as the EU, and the Court of Justice in particular, ensures an effective protection of fundamental rights which is substantially similar to the protection required by the German constitution, the FCC will no longer exercise its jurisdiction to review EU legal acts by the rights standards prescribed by the constitution. This was because, since the Constitutional Court had first given judgment in *Solange I*:

> a measure of protection of fundamental rights has been established in the meantime within the sovereign jurisdiction of the European Communities which in its conception, substance and manner of implementation is essentially comparable with the standards of fundamental rights provided fore in the [German constitution]. All the main institutions of the Community have since acknowledged in a legally significant manner that in the exercise of their powers and the pursuit of the objectives of the Community they will be guided as a legal duty by respect for fundamental rights, in particular as established by the constitutions of Member States and by the European Convention on Human Rights. There are no decisive factors to lead one to conclude that the standard of fundamental rights which has been achieved under Community law is not adequately consolidated and is only of a transitory nature.[51]

[13–33] While the Federal Constitutional Court is here expressing very significant deference towards the EU in view of its comparable standards of human rights

---

[48] 2 BvE 2/08, judgment on the Treaty of Lisbon, 30 June 2009, para 328.

[49] *Internationale Handelsgesellschaft (Solange I)* [1974] CMLR 540.

[50] *Re Wünsche Handelsgesellschaft (Solange II)* [1987] CMLR 225.

[51] *ibid*, 259. The European Court of Human Rights applies a presumption of a similar nature to EU legal order, which is often referred to as the doctrine of equivalent protection or the "*Bosphorus* presumption", from a case involving Ireland's impounding of an aircraft pursuant to EU sanctions. See *Bosphorus Hava v Ireland*, European Court of Human Rights, 30 June 2005, Application No 45036/98 (2006) 42 EHRR 1; *Michaud v France*, European Court of Human Rights, 6 December 2012, Application No 12331/11 (2014) 59 EHRR 9; *Avotiņš v Latvia*, European Court of Human Rights, 23 May 2016, Application No 17502/07; Síofra O'Leary, "A Tale of Two Cities: Fundamental Rights Protection in Strasbourg and Luxembourg" (2018) 20 *Cambridge Yearbook of European Legal Studies* 3; Tony Marguery, "Je t'aime moi non plus: The *Avotiņš v Latvia* Judgment: An Answer from the ECrtHR to the CJEU" (2017) 10 *Review of European Administrative Law* 113; Paul De Hert and Fisnik Korenica, "The Doctrine of Equivalent Protection: Its Life and Legitimacy Before and After the European Union's Accession to the European Convention on Human Rights" (2012) 13 *German Law Journal* 874.

protection, it is important not to lose sight of the fact that, ultimately, the FCC is reserving to itself the power to assess the applicability of EU law in light of the level of protection afforded at EU level and how that compares with the rights guarantees in the German Constitution. As occurred in the *Gauweiler* case, one way in which to minimise the possibility of divergent views may be for a national court to seek a preliminary ruling before expressing its own opinion as regards the validity of an EU measure in light of domestic constitutional norms. The fact that, since 2009, the Charter of Fundamental Rights has legally binding force clearly facilitates this. As Monica Claes has observed:

> The recent Data Retention Directive saga provides an excellent illustration. The constitutional and supreme courts of Romania, Germany, Cyprus, and the Czech Republic, and several Parliaments were struggling with the directive, which they considered to be at odds with fundamental rights. Their attempts to salvage these rights were limited to trying to use the discretion provided by the directive in accordance with national constitutional rights. It was only when the Irish Supreme Court and the Austrian [Constitutional Court] made references to the ECJ challenging the validity of the directive itself that the Court of Justice was able actually to declare the directive invalid on the basis of the Charter. The decision of the Court illustrates that using the EU system involving the Charter and preliminary references to the European Court can be more effective in protecting fundamental rights than procedures challenging the primacy of EU law before national courts based on national Constitutions. It also shows how the "self-cleansing" capacity of the EU legal system in terms of fundamental rights protection can operate.[52]

[13–34] A preliminary ruling failed to prevent a clash, however, in *Dansk Industri (on behalf of Ajos)*, a reference from the Danish Supreme Court concerning the extent to which horizontal direct effect could be given to general principles of EU law.[53] Under Danish law, an employer was not obliged to give severance pay if an employee was entitled to receive an old age pension. In Danish legal proceedings involving two private parties it was claimed that this law was contrary to the general principle of EU law prohibiting discrimination on the ground of age, as confirmed by the Court of Justice in *Mangold* and *Kücükdeveci*.[54] In requesting a preliminary reference, the Danish Supreme Court expressed its concern that to give horizontal direct effect to the general principle would be contrary to the countervailing principles of legal certainty and the protection of legitimate expectations, suggesting that it would render it impossible for a private party to predict when an unwritten general principle might set aside a national law. The

---

[52] Monica Claes, "The Primacy of EU Law in European and National Law" in Anthony Arnull and Damian Chalmers (eds), *The Oxford Handbook of European Union Law* (Oxford University Press, 2015) 178, 199.

[53] Case C-441/14 *Dansk Industri (on behalf of Ajos)* EU:C:2016:278, 19 April 2016. See Helle Krunke and Sune Klinge, "The Danish *Ajos* Case: The Missing Case from *Maastricht* and *Lisbon*" (2018) 3 *European Papers* 157; Rass Holdgaard, Daniella Elkan and Gustav Krohn Schaldemose, "From Cooperation to Collision: The ECJ's *Ajos* Ruling and the Danish Supreme Court's Refusal to Comply" (2018) 55 *Common Market Law Review* 17; Mikael Rask Madsen, Henrik Palmer Olsen and Urška Šadl, "Competing Supremacies and Clashing Institutional Rationalities: The Danish Supreme Court's Decision in the *Ajos* Case and the National Limits of Judicial Cooperation" (2017) 23 *European Law Journal* 140; Urška Šadl and Sabine Mair, "Mutual Disempowerment: Case C-441/14 *Dansk Industri, acting on behalf of Ajos A/S v Estate of Karsten Eigil Rasmussen* and Case no. 15/2014 *Dansk Industri (DI) acting for Ajos A/S v The estate left by A*" (2017) 13 *European Constitutional Law Review* 347; Sim Haket, "The Danish Supreme Court's *Ajos* Judgment (Dansk Industri): Rejecting a Consistent Interpretation and Challenging the Effect of a General Principle of EU Law in the Danish Legal Order" (2017) 10 *Review of European Administrative Law* 135.

[54] Case C-144/04 *Mangold* [2005] ECR I-9981; Case C-555/07 *Kücükdeveci* [2010] ECR I-365. See ch 11, paras [11–34] to [11–37].

Supreme Court also indicated that the doctrine of *contra legem* would prevent it from giving a harmonious interpretation to the Danish law in line with the general principle, since the national courts had consistently interpreted the relevant law as precluding an entitlement to severance pay. Accordingly, it asked whether it would be consistent with EU law to weigh the general principle of non-discrimination on the ground of age, and the issue of its direct effect, against the principles of legal certainty and the protection of legitimate expectations and to conclude on that basis that the principle of legal certainty must take precedence, such that the employer is, in accordance with national law, relieved of its obligation to provide the severance pay.

[13–35] Unsurprisingly, the response of the Court of Justice was to indicate that, in line with its judgments in *Mangold* and *Kücükdeveci*, it was not permissible to preclude an entitlement to severance pay on the basis that an employee also had a right to claim an old age pension.[55] The Danish court had two options by which to achieve this: either interpret Danish law consistently with the general principle or, if that was not considered possible, set aside the conflicting national law.

[13–36] The Danish Supreme Court's reception of the ruling has been described as the "first time in recent EU law history that the highest national court in a Member State so openly and in such general terms declared that it is unable – within its mandate as a court of law – to comply with an ECJ judgment".[56] The Court examined the preparatory materials to Denmark's Accession Act (equivalent to Ireland's European Communities Act 1972) and concluded that it had not foreseen that general principles of EU law, without a basis in the Treaties, would be conferred with direct effect in disputes between private parties. The Court then considered the fact that the general principle of non-discrimination on the ground of age was, since the Lisbon Treaty, also found in Art 21 of the Charter of Fundamental Rights. However, while the Charter was binding on the EU institutions and the Member States, it was not considered to impose legal obligations on individuals. Accordingly, the Supreme Court concluded that general principles of EU law did not have horizontal direct effect in Danish law and that, for the position to be otherwise, an amendment would need to be made to Denmark's Accession Act. In terms of judicial dialogue, the exchange is of interest for what has been described as the "regrettably short and cold reasoning" of the Court of Justice, in which it questioned the premise of the Danish Supreme Court on *contra legem* and reminded it of the Court of Justice's own "apparently flawless and unquestionable case law (on direct applicability of general principles), dismissing in effectively one sentence the [Supreme Court's] attempt to compromise and completely discarding, almost disregarding, the [Supreme Court's] concerns for legal certainty".[57] More particularly, the Court of Justice passed up on the opportunity to address the genuine criticisms presented of the implications of *Mangold* and *Kücükdeveci*.

(ii) Supremacy as Viewed by the Irish Courts

[13–37] The Irish courts have never, to date, displayed the robustness of approach typical of the German Constitutional Court, or adopted by the Danish Supreme Court

---

55 Case C-441/14 *Dansk Industri (on behalf of Ajos)* EU:C:2016:278, 19 April 2016.

56 Rass Holdgaard, Daniella Elkan and Gustav Krohn Schaldemose, "From Cooperation to Collision: The ECJ's *Ajos* Ruling and the Danish Supreme Court's Refusal to Comply" (2018) 55 *Common Market Law Review* 17, 18.

57 *ibid*, 42–43.

in *Dansk Industri (on behalf of Ajos)*. Rather, save for one notable exception, the Irish courts have been said to have "unhesitatingly acknowledged" the supremacy of EU law.[58] The commonly held view would appear to be that, as described by Elaine Fahey in 2010:

> While not impossible, it seems most unlikely that the current Supreme Court would make an intervention into European constitutionalism in the same way as the German Constitutional Court. This much can be deduced from, firstly, the largely *communautaire* nature of the existing case-law; secondly, the tendency of the Court to cooperate with the Court of Justice, to avoid conflict with its responsibilities as a matter of EU law and to seek its assistance regularly pursuant to Article 267 TFEU; and thirdly, its tendency to readily apply the duty of co-operation incumbent upon national courts.[59]

[13–38] Naturally, in approaching the question of the supremacy of EU law, Irish courts take as their starting point Art 29.4.6° of the Constitution. Since the decision of the Court of Justice in *Costa v ENEL* was almost a decade old by the time of Ireland's accession in 1973, it followed that the necessary steps would need to be taken to facilitate the reception of Community law into the Irish legal system in a manner that was consistent with the demands of the Luxembourg court. The method by which it was chosen to do this was to create a constitutional licence or "exclusion clause" whereby, in accordance with (what is now) Art 29.4.6°, no provision of the Constitution prevents laws enacted, acts done or measures adopted by the European Union or its institutions from having the force of law in the State.[60] This is supplemented by s 2 of the European Communities Act 1972, which provides that EU Treaties and the acts of the institutions shall be binding on the State and shall be part of domestic Irish law under the conditions laid down in those treaties. As early as 1978, the effect of these provisions was described by Costello J in *Pigs and Bacon Commission v McCarren* as meaning that "if, according to Community law, the provisions of Community law take precedence over a provision of national law in conflict with it an Irish court must give effect to this rule".[61]

[13–39] Although the rationale behind the conclusion was contested, the 1983 decision of Supreme Court in *Campus Oil Ltd v Minister for Industry and Energy* has often been held up as an indication that the Irish courts were willing to be "more *communautaire* than the Community".[62] There, Walsh J held that it would be contrary to what is now Art 267 TFEU to allow for a right of appeal from a decision by a lower

---

[58] Gerard Hogan, Gerry Whyte, David Kenny and Rachel Walsh, *Kelly: The Irish Constitution* (5th ed, Bloomsbury Professional, 2018) 613.

[59] Elaine Fahey, *EU Law in Ireland* (Clarus Press, 2010) 18.

[60] See Maria Cahill, "Constitutional Exclusion Clauses, Article 29.4.6°, and the Constitutional Reception of European Law" (2011) 34 *Dublin University Law Journal* 74, who highlights the unusual nature of Art 29.4.6° from a comparative perspective. See also Elaine Fahey, *EU Law in Ireland* (Clarus Press, 2010) 13–23; Gerard Hogan, Gerry Whyte, David Kenny and Rachel Walsh, *Kelly: The Irish Constitution* (5th ed, Bloomsbury Professional, 2018) 600–608; Gerard Hogan and Anthony Whelan, *Ireland and the European Union: Constitutional and Statutory Texts and Commentary* (Sweet and Maxwell, 1995) 7–16; Paul Gallagher, "The Constitution and the Community" (1993) 2 *Irish Journal of European Law* 129; Diarmuid Rossa Phelan, *Revolt or Revolution* (Round Hall, 1997) 338–349; David O'Keefe, "Preliminary Deference: The Supreme Court and Community Law" (1983) 5 *Dublin University Law Journal* 286.

[61] [1978] *Journal of the Irish Society of European Law* 87, 126; unreported, High Court, Costello J, 30 June 1978.

[62] [1983] IR 82.

court to request a preliminary ruling from the Court of Justice, even though there is nothing in the TFEU itself to preclude the possibility of such appeals. In the view of Walsh J (with whom the rest of the Supreme Court agreed), as a result of Art 29.4.6°, the right to an appeal guaranteed by Art 34 of the Constitution "must yield to the primacy" of Art 267 which "as part of Irish law, qualifies Article 34 of the Constitution".[63] A *communautaire* approach was similarly displayed in the 1985 case of *Pesca Valentia Ltd v Minister for Fisheries and Forestry*, in which the Supreme Court was willing to grant interlocutory injunctive relief where it was claimed that a nationality condition for the issuing of fishing licences was contrary to the Treaty of Rome.[64] In contrast, the House of Lords considered it necessary to refer the same matter to the Court of Justice in the well-known *Factortame* case.[65]

[13–40] An acceptance of supremacy was also expressed by the Supreme Court in its landmark 1987 decision in *Crotty v An Taoiseach*.[66] In delivering the Court's judgment on the constitutionality of the European Communities (Amendment) Act 1986, Finlay CJ acknowledged that decisions of the Court of Justice on the "interpretation of the Treaty and on questions covering its implementation take precedence, in case of conflict, over the domestic law and the decisions of national courts of Member States", and that decisions of the Council "have primacy over domestic law".[67] As one further example, when the Court of Justice provided a preliminary ruling in *Murphy v Bord Telecom Éireann*[68] to the effect that the failure of Ireland's Anti-Discrimination (Pay) Act 1974 to provide a remedy for women who were paid less than their male counterparts, for work of a greater value, was contrary to EU law, the High Court readily accepted that

> [w]here such a conflict exists, national law must yield primacy to [EU] law. The exclusive role of the making of laws assigned to the Oireachtas by the Constitution has been expressly modified by [Art 29.4.6°] so as to enable [EU] law to have the force of law in the State. Where such a conflict arises, the national law is, accordingly, inapplicable.[69]

[13–41] Although the general disposition of the Irish courts towards the supremacy of EU law is undoubtedly one of broad acceptance, there are two caveats to this. The first relates to the obligation on national courts to disapply any national law that is contrary to EU law, where the Irish courts have applied a somewhat conservative approach when it comes to considering the ability of statutory tribunals to disapply national law in particular. As described by Cooke J in *Saleem v Minister for Justice, Equality and Law Reform*, the principle in *Simmenthal* is:

> concerned with confirming the jurisdiction of a national court to refuse to apply a provision of national law which is incompatible with a directly applicable provision of European

---

63 *ibid*, 87. See ch 8, paras [8–69] to [8–70]; *Data Protection Commissioner v Facebook Ireland Ltd* [2018] IESC 38, 31 July 2018; [2019] IESC 46, 31 May 2019; Elaine Fahey, "The Supreme Court Preliminary Reference in *DPC v Facebook and Schrems*: Putting National and European Judicial Independence at Risk?" (2019) 1 *Irish Supreme Court Review* 125.

64 [1985] IR 193.

65 Case C-213/89 *R v Secretary of State for Transport ex p. Factortame Ltd* [1990] ECR I-2433.

66 [1987] IR 713.

67 *ibid*, 769. See Gerard Hogan, Gerry Whyte, David Kenny and Rachel Walsh, *Kelly: The Irish Constitution* (5th ed, Bloomsbury Professional, 2018) 600.

68 Case 157/86 *Murphy v Bord Telecom Éireann* [1988] ECR 673.

69 [1989] ILRM 53, 59.

> Union law. The jurisdiction of this court in that regard is not in doubt. The principle was adopted and applied thirty years ago in *Pigs & Bacon Commission v McCarren.*[70]

[13–42] In *Simmenthal*, the Court of Justice declared that, "in a case within its jurisdiction", every national court must apply EU law in its entirety and protect rights which it confers on individuals by setting aside any provision of national law which may conflict with it, whether prior or subsequent to the EU rule.[71] Accordingly, any provision of a national legal system and any legislative, administrative or judicial practice which might impair the effectiveness of EU law by "withholding from the national court having jurisdiction to apply such law the power to do everything necessary at the moment of its application to set aside national legislative provisions which might prevent [EU] rules from having full force and effect are incompatible with those requirements which are the very essence of [EU] law".[72] Having noted that *Simmenthal* had long been accepted by the Irish courts, Cooke J went on to emphasise the limitation imposed by the clause "in a case within its jurisdiction". In his view, the principle only applied where a national court is "called upon to give effect to directly applicable European Union law and thereby disregard an incompatible provision of national law in a case where the matter comes within its jurisdiction".[73] In judicial review proceedings, for instance, it was noted that the jurisdiction of the High Court was limited to the grounds upon which leave had been granted.

[13–43] The ability of Irish statutory bodies to disapply national law has arisen in two recent cases, the later of which has resulted in the Irish courts receiving a clear confirmation of the position in EU law from the Court of Justice. In *An Taoiseach v Commissioner for Environmental Information*, the Commissioner had disapplied aspects of the statutory instrument under which her office had been established.[74] The SI had been introduced in order to implement a directive governing public access to environmental information. An issue arose as to whether the SI had correctly transposed the directive in allowing for an exemption from public release for records of Cabinet discussions relating to emissions into the environment. Having received representations from both sides in respect of an application for Cabinet records, the Commissioner decided that, in providing for such an exemption, the SI was incompatible with the directive and so the relevant provision should be disapplied.

[13–44] On appeal to the High Court, Ó Néil J characterised the problem in the case as not one of "securing supremacy or primacy of [EU] law over domestic law, but discerning the correct procedural means for doing this".[75] This relates to the principle known as "national procedural autonomy", which is explored further in Chapter 14. On behalf of the Commissioner it was submitted that disapplication of the SI would not mean that it was deemed invalid, but merely that in the discrete circumstances of the present case it would not be applied. According to Ó Néil J, however:

> This outcome could be seen as the worst of all worlds, in that a law or rule which is said to be inconsistent with a superior European Union law is not declared invalid by a court of

70 [2011] 2 IR 386, 394.
71 Case 106/77 *Simmenthal* [1978] ECR 629, 644.
72 *ibid.*
73 [2011] 2 IR 386, 395.
74 [2013] 2 IR 510; [2011] 1 ILRM 508.
75 *ibid*, 537; 531.

competent jurisdiction but remains in force where its validity and enforceability is in doubt, there being circumstances in which it cannot apply and perhaps others where it can. It is to be envisaged that over time and with the expanding role of the European Union in so many areas of life and commerce, the national legal landscape would become littered with the moribund remains of hitherto valid national laws. Such a state of affairs would greatly undermine the clarity and certainty that are necessary and fundamental to the integrity of legal systems in societies and communities based on the rule of law. In effect the vast array of administrative bodies across the entire spectrum of public administration could claim, or have imposed on them, a jurisdiction to hear and determine all questions of law and fact relating to the application or enforcement of European Union rights, in preference to national laws, once European Union rights were asserted by a party to a dispute.

Manifestly under our domestic law this could not occur as disputes of this nature are reserved exclusively to the courts and issues such as arose in this case, i.e. the consistency of the [Statutory Instrument] of 2007 with the Directive, could only be litigated in the High Court at first instance. The problem with all this, apart from the violence done to the judicial architecture of the State, is that the party who may wish to rely on domestic law, either as a protection of his rights or as establishing a binding duty, will be denied a hearing of his case in a forum, i.e. the courts, established by law for that purpose and which, by virtue of such, over time have acquired the professional expertise, experience and competence to deal with these matters with the constitutional guarantee of independence and impartiality. As the focus of the concern of many of these public bodies, many of whom are purely administrative in character, would be the enforcement of the European Union rights relying on the supremacy of European Union law, attaining that supremacy might too easily be achieved by the suppression of rights and duties based on national laws, without adequate or appropriate consideration of correct constitutional and legal tests and balances.

... Whilst there can be no doubt but that where there is a conflict between a European Union law and a national law the European Union law must prevail, the question must be asked whether it is necessary to ensure the supremacy of European Union law to undermine national systems of law, which would be the inevitable outcome if the respondent's submission is correct, or do the relevant judgments of the European Court of Justice demand such a response from national legal systems.[76]

[13–45] Having considered the case law of the Court of Justice, some of which suggested that it was the duty of all public bodies to disapply conflicting national law, Ó Néil J concluded that it was left to the Member States within the architecture of their own legal systems to determine procedures for the enforcement of EU law.[77] This freedom was subject to the twin principles of equivalence and effectiveness, which are the subject of the following chapter. Ó Néil J was satisfied that neither of these principles were contravened by the requirement to pursue an appeal to the High Court in order to have an adjudication of a claim of incorrect transposition.

[13–46] A similar issue confronted the Supreme Court in *Minister for Justice, Equality and Law Reform v Workplace Relations Commission*.[78] There, an issue arose as to whether the Equality Tribunal (now the Workplace Relations Commission) was permitted to consider the compatibility with EU law of an SI that established a maximum recruitment age for joining the gardaí, such that it might disapply the relevant provision if it was found to be contrary to the Equal Treatment Directive. In delivering

[76] *ibid*, 538–539, 540; 531–532, 533.
[77] *ibid*, 541; 534.
[78] [2017] IESC 43, unreported, Supreme Court, 15 June 2017.

the Supreme Court's judgment, Clarke J (as he then was) noted that the question of jurisdiction first had to be addressed as a matter of Irish law and, if the answer was no, then as a matter of EU law. As a matter of Irish law,

> it cannot be said that there is anything even remotely resembling an express jurisdiction conferred on the Tribunal to set aside or disapply general measures of secondary legislation (that is measures other than registered employment agreements). This would suggest that the Tribunal could not provide any relief to the notice parties for the only means by which any relief could be given would be if the Tribunal did have a jurisdiction to disapply the Regulations.
>
> It should be said that that position in national law stems from fundamental constitutional provisions which require that important or significant legal questions are determined by courts established under the Constitution rather than by statutory bodies or Tribunals. It is also worth recording, in that context, an important aspect of the way in which, as a matter of national law, Irish law interacts with European Union law in this area. The Irish courts fully recognise and seek to implement the obligations placed on them by European Union law to seek to ensure that rights guaranteed by Union law are vindicated by an appropriate remedy. Where, however, and subject to the principles of equivalence and effectiveness … there may be two ways of ensuring the vindication of European Union law rights, the Irish Constitution mandates that the solution to be found is the one which most closely accords with the Irish constitutional legal order.[79]

[13–47] Turning, then, to the question from an EU law perspective, Clarke J accepted that, in an appropriate case, EU law might require that a statutory body such as the Equality Tribunal would have jurisdiction to disapply a measure of national law if that tribunal was the only body which had any competence to deal with the relevant issue. In his view, therefore, the question was essentially a procedural one that turned on whether or not it was permissible to require an employment equality claim of this kind to be commenced in the High Court, rather than before the Equality Tribunal. According to the Tribunal, while it was accepted that Ireland did not have to choose the procedural model which it did and thereby create the Tribunal, nonetheless, having done so, EU law mandated that the Tribunal have the power to disapply secondary legislation. In contrast, the Minister argued that EU law did not require that the entire jurisdiction in relation to employment equality matters governed by EU law be conferred on a single body. There was, therefore, no reason in principle why jurisdiction in respect of one type of case could not be conferred on a statutory body with another type of case being exclusively reserved to the courts established in accordance with the Constitution. Faced with these opposing views, the Supreme Court considered that the answer to the question was not *acte clair* and so requested a preliminary ruling from the Court of Justice.[80]

[13–48] In delivering its ruling, the Grand Chamber began by distinguishing between the power to disapply, in a specific case, a provision of national law that is contrary to EU law, and the power to strike down such a provision, "which has the broader effect that the provision is no longer valid for any purpose".[81] While it is for the Member States to designate which of their courts are empowered to review the validity of national law, and the remedies available, in contrast:

---

[79] *ibid*, paras 5.11–5.12.

[80] C-378/17 *Minister for Justice and Equality v Workplace Relations Commission* EU:C:2018:979, 4 December 2018.

[81] *ibid*, para 34.

> the primacy of EU law means that the national courts called upon, in the exercise of their jurisdiction, to apply provisions of EU law must be under a duty to give full effect to those provisions, if necessary refusing of their own motion to apply any conflicting provision of national law, and without requesting or awaiting the prior setting aside of that provision of national law by legislative or other constitutional means.[82]

[13–49] Secondly, the Grand Chamber noted that the duty to disapply national legislation that is contrary to EU law is owed by all organs of the state, including administrative authorities, called upon within the exercise of their respective powers, to apply EU law. The Oireachtas had chosen to confer the specific power of ensuring compliance with the Equal Treatment Directive on the Workplace Relations Commission. This was in fulfilment of a specific obligation in the Directive itself to ensure that judicial and/or administrative procedures were available to individuals for the enforcement of obligations. From these principles it followed that:

> if the Workplace Relations Commission, as a body upon which the national legislature has conferred the power to ensure enforcement of the principle … of non-discrimination in respect of employment and occupation, has before it a dispute involving observance of that principle, the principle of primacy of EU law requires it to provide, within the framework of that power, the legal protection which individuals derive from EU law and to ensure that EU law is fully effective, disapplying, if need be, any provision of national legislation that may be contrary thereto.
>
> Indeed, it would be contradictory if an individual were able to rely upon the provisions of EU law in a particular area before a body upon which national law has conferred jurisdiction over disputes in that area but that body were under no obligation to apply those provisions by refraining from applying provisions of national law which conflict with them.
>
> Furthermore, in so far as the Workplace Relations Commission must be considered to be a "court or tribunal" within the meaning of Article 267 TFEU, it may refer to the Court, pursuant to that article, questions of interpretation of relevant provisions of EU law and, as it is bound by the judgment in which the Court gives a preliminary ruling, it must forthwith apply that judgment, disapplying, if necessary, of its own motion conflicting provisions of national legislation.
>
> If a body such as the Workplace Relations Commission, entrusted by law with the task of ensuring that the obligations stemming from the implementation of [the Equal Treatment Directive] are implemented and complied with, were unable to find that a national provision is contrary to that directive and, consequently, were unable to decide to disapply that provision, the EU rules in the area of equality in employment and occupation would be rendered less effective.
>
> Rules of national law, even constitutional provisions, cannot be allowed to undermine the unity and effectiveness of EU law.[83]

[13–50] It can be seen that the position under EU law, deriving from the principle of supremacy and as clearly set out in the relatively short judgment of the Grand Chamber, differs significantly from the views expressed by Ó Néil J in *An Taoiseach v Commissioner for Environmental Information*. Whereas Ó Néil J had sought to respect the supremacy of EU law, while at the same time not doing anything to "undermine national systems of law", the Grand Chamber did not concern itself with any such

82 *ibid*, para 35.
83 *ibid*, paras 45–49.

dichotomy. In its view, Member States were free to assign amongst their courts, howsoever they saw fit, the power to declare invalid a national law. In contrast, Member States were not free to confine the power to disapply national law that was contrary to EU law to only certain courts. Rather, the principle of supremacy precluded any national law which prevented a statutory body established in order to ensure the enforcement of EU law in a particular area from having the jurisdiction to disapply national law that was contrary to EU law.

[13–51] The second caveat relates to the potential scenario of a conflict arising between EU law and a fundamental rights provision of the Constitution. The case of *Society for the Protection of Unborn Children (SPUC) v Grogan* is well known for a statement by Walsh J in the Supreme Court to the effect that "[i]n the last analysis only this Court can decide finally what are the effects of the interaction of the 8th Amendment of the Constitution [on the right to life of the unborn] and the 3rd Amendment [on Ireland's accession to the EEC]".[84] This arose in the context of an application by the Society for an injunction preventing student unions from distributing information on clinics providing abortion in another EU Member State. The High Court requested a preliminary ruling from the Court of Justice as to whether abortion was a service within the meaning of EU law and, if so, whether a Member State could prohibit the distribution of information on abortion clinics operating in other Member States. Pending the outcome of the preliminary reference, the High Court declined to grant an interlocutory injunction. The decision not to grant an injunction was appealed to the Supreme Court, which delivered its judgment before the Court of Justice provided its ruling.

[13–52] In each of the three judgments delivered by the Supreme Court, it is possible to read a statement of intent regarding the respective roles of that Court and the Court of Justice in resolving any conflict as between applicable norms. According to Finlay CJ, the application for an interlocutory injunction sought to:

> restrain an activity which has been clearly declared by this Court to be unconstitutional and therefore unlawful and which could assist and is intended to assist in the destruction of the right to life of an unborn child, a right acknowledged and protected under the Constitution. That constitutionally guaranteed right must be fully and effectively protected by the courts.
>
> If and when a decision of the Court of Justice of the European Communities rules that some aspect of European Community law affects the activities of the defendants impugned in this case, the consequence of that decision on these constitutionally guaranteed rights and their protection by the courts will then fall to be considered by these courts.[85]

[13–53] According to McCarthy J:

> The sole authority for the construction of the Constitution lies in the Irish courts, the final authority being this Court. Article [29.4.6°] may exclude from constitutional invalidation some provision of the Treaty of Rome the enforcement of which is necessitated by the obligations of membership of the European Communities; it may be that in enacting the 8th Amendment to the Constitution … the People of Ireland did so in breach of the Treaty to which Ireland had acceded in 1973.[86]

---

84 [1989] IR 753, 768–769; [1990] ILRM 350, 361.
85 *ibid*, 764–765; 356.
86 *ibid*, 770; 362.

[13–54] While both of these statements are ambiguous and open to interpretation, the sentiment expressed by Walsh J was more emphatic:

> When the present matter came before the High Court it was clear beyond all doubt that the activities complained of were contrary to the Constitution. The decision of the High Court judge to adopt the course which she did namely, to leave the matter undecided [by declining to grant an interlocutory injunction], was in effect to suspend the provisions of the 8th Amendment of the Constitution for an indefinite period. It is not open to any judge to do anything which in effect suspends any provisions of the Constitution for any period whatsoever …
>
> … It is the undoubted duty of this Court to ensure that the protection guaranteed by the 8th Amendment is not put in abeyance. …
>
> … It has been sought to be argued in the present case that the effect of the amendment of Article 29 of the Constitution, which was necessary to permit our adhesion to the treaties of the European Communities, is to qualify all rights including fundamental rights guaranteed by the Constitution. The 8th Amendment of the Constitution is subsequent in time, by several years, to the amendment of Article 29. That fact may give rise to the consideration of the question of whether or not the 8th Amendment itself qualifies the amendment to Article 29. Be that as it may any answer to the reference received from the Court of Justice of the European Communities will have to be considered in the light of our own constitutional provisions. In the last analysis only this Court can decide finally what are the effects of the interaction of the 8th Amendment of the Constitution and the 3rd Amendment of the Constitution.
>
> … The fact that particular activities even grossly immoral ones, may be permitted to a greater or lesser extent in some Member States does not mean that they are considered to be within the objectives of the treaties of the European Communities, particularly the Treaty of Rome … A *fortiori* it cannot be one of the objectives of the European Communities that a Member State should be obliged to permit activities which are clearly designed to set at nought the constitutional guarantees for the protection within the State of a fundamental human right.[87]

[13–55] The potential clash between EU law and Art 40.3.3° was defused when the Court of Justice ruled that, although lawful abortion did constitute a service within the meaning of the Treaty of Rome, the fact that there was no commercial relationship between the student unions and the abortion clinics meant that Ireland was permitted to prohibit their distribution of information.[88] When considering the Supreme Court's judgment in *SPUC v Grogan* it is important to remember that its distinguishing feature is its exceptionality. As the authors of *Kelly: The Irish Constitution* note, the remarks "must be regarded as isolated ones and entirely confined to an area of great sensitivity

---

87 *ibid*, 768–769; 359–361.

88 Case C-159/90 *Society for the Protection of the Unborn Child (Ireland) Ltd v Grogan* [1991] ECR I-4685. See Diarmuid Rossa Phelan, "Right to Life of the Unborn v Promotion of Trade in Services: The European Court of Justice and the Normative Shaping of the European Union" (1992) 55 *Modern Law Review* 670; Síofra O'Leary, "The Court of Justice as a Reluctant Constitutional Adjudicator: An Examination of the Abortion Information Case" (1992) 16 *European Law Review* 138; Deirdre Curtin, "Case C-159/90, *The Society for the Protection of Unborn Children Ireland Ltd v Grogan*, Judgment of 4 October 1991" (1992) 29 *Common Market Law Review* 585; Cathleen M Colvin, "Irish Abortion Law and the Free Movement of Services in the European Community" (1991–1992) 15 *Fordham International Law Journal* 476; James Kingston and Anthony Whelan, "The Protection of the Unborn in Three Legal Orders" 10 *Irish Law Times* 93 (Part I) and 104 (Part II).

and it is unlikely that they would nowadays be followed".[89] Others, however, have not ruled out entirely the possibility of a conflict emerging and being addressed by the Irish courts. According to Diarmuid Rossa Phelan and Anthony Whelan:

> It is probably only in situations of profound normative conflict, which threatens directly the Constitution's fundamental principles or legitimation, that the Irish Courts will consider the non-application of a [EU] law rule as part of domestic law. It is difficult to place total reliance in such situations on a statute coupled with a provision, like Article [29.4.6°], of the very Constitution which is fundamentally threatened.[90]

[13–56] In their consideration of the judgment, Anthony Collins and James O'Reilly have commented that the Irish Courts "jealously guard their jurisdiction over those rights as are recognised by the Constitution", and would appear to be of the view that the interpretation of the scope of such rights is a matter exclusively within their jurisdiction, notwithstanding any possible conflict with EU law.[91] More recently, another open-ended remark by the Supreme Court has the possibility of suggesting that a vestige of *SPUC v Grogan* remains. In *Rea v Ireland*, leave was sought to challenge the result of the second referendum on the Lisbon Treaty. The grounds of challenge referred, in part, to the Protocol on the Concerns of the Irish People, the substance of which was agreed upon before the holding of the second referendum. As part of this Protocol, it was provided that nothing in the Lisbon Treaty attributing legal status to the Charter of Fundamental Rights, or in the provisions of the Lisbon Treaty in the area of Freedom, Security and Justice, "affects in any way the scope and applicability of the protection of the right to life in Articles 40.3.1, 40.3.2 and 40.3.3, the protection of the family in Article 41 and the protection of the rights in respect of education in Articles 42 and 44.2.4 and 44.2.5 provided by the Constitution of Ireland". In dismissing an appeal from a refusal to grant leave, Denham CJ observed:

> This Protocol, as do the others, respects the Constitution of Ireland. The Supreme Court of Ireland has the duty and obligation to interpret and apply the Constitution of Ireland.
>
> The Court is satisfied that it is for the Supreme Court of Ireland to interpret the Constitution of Ireland.
>
> The Court understands that the power and duty of the Supreme Court of Ireland to interpret the Constitution of Ireland would be respected by institutions of the European Union, including the European Court of Justice.[92]

[13–57] As this passage is somewhat enigmatic it must be read in the context in which it was made and not be over-interpreted. Nonetheless, it arguably does hint that the Irish courts, like many of their European counterparts, believe that, when it comes to applying national constitutional norms, the perspective from Luxembourg is not the only way in which to view the principle of supremacy.

---

89 Gerard Hogan, Gerry Whyte, David Kenny and Rachel Walsh, *Kelly: The Irish Constitution* (5th ed, Bloomsbury Professional, 2018) 615.

90 Diarmuid Rossa Phelan and Anthony Whelan, "National Constitutional Law and European Integration: FIDE Report" (1997) 6 *Irish Journal of European Law* 24, 45.

91 Anthony M Collins and James O'Reilly, "The Application of Community Law in Ireland 1973–1989" (1992) 1 *Irish Journal of European Law* 38, 45.

92 [2016] IESC 19, unreported, Supreme Court, 9 May 2016, paras 16–18.

Chapter 14

NATIONAL PROCEDURAL AUTONOMY AND EFFECTIVE JUDICIAL PROTECTION

A. National Procedural Autonomy

[14–01] From earlier chapters, it will be recalled that the underlying rationale for the development of the doctrine of supremacy by the Court of Justice was the need to ensure the uniformity and effectiveness of EU law throughout the Member States. On the other hand, we have also seen that the routine administration of EU law is operated on a decentralised basis, whereby it is for each court and tribunal within each Member State to apply EU law whenever relevant to the proceedings before it, seeking guidance from the Court of Justice by way of a preliminary reference where necessary. This burden-sharing relationship is reflected in Art 19 TEU. Having first assigned to the CJEU the task of ensuring that in the interpretation and application of the Treaties the law is observed, Art 19(1) goes on to impose upon Member States the responsibility for providing "remedies sufficient to ensure effective legal protection in the fields covered by Union law". This is bolstered by the right, enshrined in Art 47 of the Charter of Fundamental Rights, of every person whose rights and freedoms guaranteed by EU law are violated, to have access to an effective remedy before a tribunal. A useful description of the nature of this burden-sharing between national and EU courts was recently provided by Advocate General Bot in Opinion 1/17 *(EU–Canada Comprehensive Economic Trade Agreement)* as follows:

> As the Court [of Justice] stated in Opinion 2/13, "in order to ensure that the specific characteristics and the autonomy of [the EU legal order] are preserved, the Treaties have established a judicial system intended to ensure consistency and uniformity in the interpretation of EU law".
>
> In that context, "it is for the national courts and for the Court of Justice to ensure the full application of EU law in all Member States and to ensure judicial protection of an individual's rights under that law".
>
> The Court's mission is to "ensure that in the interpretation and application of the Treaties the law is observed", as provided for in Article 19(1) TEU. That function of the Court

entails responsibility to "ensure respect for the autonomy of the European Union legal order thus created by the Treaties".

In Opinion 1/09, the Court pointed out that it shares that responsibility with the national courts. The Court stated that, "as is evident from Article 19(1) TEU, the guardians of that legal order and the judicial system of the European Union are the Court of Justice and the courts and tribunals of the Member States".

The Court also takes Article 4(3) TEU as the basis for its finding that "the Member States are obliged, by reason, inter alia, of the principle of sincere cooperation set out in the first subparagraph of Article 4(3) TEU, to ensure, in their respective territories, the application of and respect for EU law".

The Court also pointed out that "the national court, in collaboration with the Court of Justice, fulfils a duty entrusted to them both of ensuring that in the interpretation and application of the Treaties the law is observed".

In particular, "the judicial system as thus conceived has as its keystone the preliminary ruling procedure provided for in Article 267 TFEU, which, by setting up a dialogue between one court and another, specifically between the Court of Justice and the courts and tribunals of the Member States, has the object of securing uniform interpretation of EU law …, thereby serving to ensure its consistency, its full effect and its autonomy as well as, ultimately, the particular nature of the law established by the Treaties".

The Court has thus firmly asserted "the importance of cooperation between the European Union judicature and the national courts and tribunals of the Member States in order to guarantee the constitutional structure of the [EU legal] system".

That specific relationship between the Court and the national courts and tribunals, which is characterised by constant dialogue, both gives expression to and protects the specific legal order, namely the EU legal order. It is for that reason that the Court seeks to protect that relationship from anything which might affect it.[1]

[14–02] The importance of national courts within the EU's judicial system was also emphasised in *Associação Sindical dos Juízes Portugueses*.[2] There, a preliminary reference asked whether the principle of judicial independence enshrined in Art 19 TEU and Art 47 of the Charter precluded a temporary reduction in the pay of Portuguese judges as part of wider pay cuts in the public sector aimed at reducing Portugal's excessive budget deficit. Sitting as a Grand Chamber, the Court ruled that Art 19 TEU did not preclude such a measure. In doing so, however, the Grand Chamber stressed the importance of judicial independence at the national level to the nature of the EU as a Union that is based on the rule of law, as set out in Art 2 TEU. In turn, Art 19 "gives concrete expression to the value of the rule of law", entrusting "responsibility for ensuring judicial review in the EU legal order not only to the Court of Justice but also to national courts and tribunals".[3]

1 Opinion 1/17 *(EU–Canada Comprehensive Economic and Trade Agreement)* EU:C:2019:72, 29 January 2019, paras 50–58.

2 Case C-64/16 *Associação Sindical dos Juízes Portugueses* EU:C:2018:117, 27 February 2018. See Matteo Bonelli and Monica Claes, "Judicial Serendipity: How Portuguese Judges Came to the Rescue of the Polish Judiciary" (2018) 14 *European Constitutional Law Review* 622; Laurent Pech and Sébastien Platon, "Judicial Independence under Threat: The Court of Justice to the rescue in the *ASPJ* case" (2018) 55 *Common Market Law Review* 1827.

3 *ibid*, para 32.

[14–03] Since, in conjunction with the Court of Justice, national courts fulfil a duty of ensuring that in the interpretation and application of the EU Treaties the law is observed, it is for each Member State to establish a system of legal remedies and procedures that will ensure effective judicial protection in the fields covered by EU law.[4] As described by the Grand Chamber, the "very existence of effective judicial review designed to ensure compliance with EU law is the very essence of EU law".[5] The principle of effective judicial protection of individuals' rights as referred to in Art 19 TEU and Art 47 of the Charter is a general principle of EU law stemming from the constitutional traditions common to the Member States and enshrined in the European Convention on Human Rights. Accordingly, as a matter of EU law, national courts operating in the fields covered by EU law must meet the requirements of effective judicial protection, such that the "guarantee of independence, which is inherent in the task of adjudication, is required not only at EU level as regards the Judges of the Union and the Advocates-General of the Court of Justice, ... but also at the level of the Member States as regards national courts".[6]

[14–04] Notwithstanding these high-level statements of the obligations placed upon national courts, when it comes to more precise *procedural* matters the default principle is that, in the absence of EU procedural rules having been established by either the Union's legislative institutions or the Court of Justice, it is for each Member State to apply its own national legal system to disputes involving EU law. In other words, except where specific uniform or harmonised rules have been established, it is not intended that new remedies be created by national courts to ensure the observance of EU law, but rather reliance should be placed on those existing remedies already laid down in national law. This is known as the principle of "national procedural autonomy". Some examples of uniform rules having been established in sectoral areas include regulations dealing with insolvency proceedings or the recognition and enforcement of judgments in civil and commercial matters. Harmonised rules have been introduced by directives dealing with matters such as asylum procedures, the European Arrest Warrant, enforcement of intellectual property rights and the review of public works contracts.

[14–05] The principle of national procedural autonomy, and its limitations, was first established by the Court of Justice in two seminal judgments delivered on the same day in 1976 dealing with largely identical facts: *Rewe-Zentralfinanz* (where a refund was sought) and *Comet* (where a right of set-off was claimed). In *Rewe-Zentralfinanz* levies for the inspection of apples had been imposed by Germany contrary to EU law.[7] When the importer sought repayment of the sums charged, the authorities sought to rely on the fact that the limitation period for claims under German law had expired. A preliminary reference asked whether the importer was entitled to a refund even if, under the German rules of procedure, the time limit for contesting the validity of the administrative measure had passed. In its ruling, the Court of Justice began by deferring to the rules of the domestic legal system of each Member State. Importantly, however, the Court subjected this freedom to two caveats. First, the national rule cannot treat claims based on EU law any less favourably than claims based on national law. This is known as the principle of equivalence. Secondly, the national rules cannot make it

4 *ibid*, para 34.
5 *ibid*, para 36.
6 *ibid*, para 42.
7 Case 33/76 *Rewe-Zentralfinanz* [1976] ECR 1989; Case C-637/17 *Cogeco Communications Inc* EU:C:2019:263, 28 March 2019.

practically impossible to bring an EU law claim, which is referred to as the principle of effectiveness. As explained by the Court:

> in the absence of [EU] rules on this subject, it is for the domestic legal system of each Member State to designate the courts having jurisdiction and to determine the procedural conditions governing actions at law intended to ensure the protection of the rights which citizens have from the direct effect of [EU] law, it being understood that such conditions *cannot be less favourable than those relating to similar actions of a domestic nature*.
>
> … In the absence of … measures of harmonization the right conferred by [EU] law must be exercised before the national courts in accordance with the conditions laid down by national rules.
>
> The position would be different only if the conditions and time-limits *made it impossible in practice* to exercise the rights which the national courts are obliged to protect. This is not the case where reasonable periods of limitation of actions are fixed. The laying down of such time-limits with regard to actions of a fiscal nature is an application of the fundamental principle of legal certainty protecting both the tax-payer and the administration concerned.[8]

[14–06] The judgment in *Comet* was to the same effect, finding that a limitation period could be relied upon against the applicant, provided that the procedural rules applicable to the EU law claim were not less favourable than those governing the same right of action concerning an internal matter.[9] As will be seen below, the principle that national rules must not make it impossible in practice to exercise EU law rights has been broadened into a more general principle of effectiveness, such that the national rule will fall foul of EU law if it merely makes the exercise of EU law rights excessively difficult. Arguably, the operation of these twin principles renders the doctrine of national procedural *autonomy* something of a misnomer. As Michal Bobek explains, all national procedural rules may, in fact,

> be subject to the dual requirement of equivalence and/or effectiveness, provided that EU law is involved in the individual case at hand. They may involve any part of the national judicial process: from rules on jurisdiction through access to court, fees, representation, to finality of judgments and their binding force. Seen from this perspective, it might be somewhat misplaced to refer to the original national procedural choice as "national procedural autonomy", at least if we understand "autonomy" in its dictionary sense as the ability to act and make decisions without being controlled by anyone else.[10]

[14–07] Michael Dougan explains the interplay between national procedural autonomy, on the one hand, and the limitations imposed upon it, on the other, as an attempt to strike an appropriate balance between legitimate Union concerns about its own legal effectiveness and uniformity, and the equally legitimate – and varied – Member State conceptions of how best to organise the administration of justice.[11]

---

8 *ibid*, 1997–1998.

9 Case 45/76 *Comet* [1976] ECR 2043.

10 Michal Bobek, "The Effects of EU Law in the National Legal Systems" in Catherine Barnard and Steve Peers (eds), *European Union Law* (2nd ed, Oxford University Press, 2017) 143, 169.

11 Michael Dougan, "The Vicissitudes of Life at the Coalface: Remedies and Procedures for Enforcing Union Law before the National Courts" in Paul Craig and Gráinne de Búrca (eds), *The Evolution of EU Law* (2nd ed, Oxford University Press, 2011) 406, 411. See Anthony M Collins, "Community Law as a Source of Rights and Remedies in the Irish Legal Order" (1994) 3 *Irish Journal of European Law* 173.

(i) Principle of Equivalence

[14–08] The principle of equivalence is a form of non-discrimination rule aimed at ensuring that reliance upon EU law rights is not made any more difficult than reliance upon national law. It requires that, *with respect to the same type of claims*, national procedural rules apply without distinction to actions alleging an infringement of EU law and to those alleging infringement of national law. In the case of *Jőrös*, for instance, it was held that the principle of equivalence required that where a national appellate court was permitted to raise of its own motion, even where the point had not been raised in the first instance proceedings, the validity of a legal measure in light of *national rules of public policy*, it must also be permitted to raise of its own motion the question of whether a contractual term falling within the scope of the Unfair Terms Directive was unfair.[12]

[14–09] While the principle of equivalence might at first seem relatively innocuous and as relating to technical procedural matters, it does have the potential to intrude quite significantly into how Member States arrange their own domestic legal systems. As Michael Dougan has described, the principle:

> carries significant integrative potential, not only for the purposes of embedding Union rights into the domestic legal orders on an equal basis with national rights, but also in questioning the overall coherence of national choices about remedies and procedural rules: particularly when a given Union claim might be compared to several distinct national actions, each of which attracts rather different standards of judicial protection, the equivalence assessment can challenge each Member State to revisit the inherited but possibly rather incoherent structures of its own legal system.[13]

[14–10] Equivalence does not require, however, that a Member State extend its most favourable rules governing a particular type of claim under national law to all actions of the same type alleging a breach of EU law.[14] The Court of Justice accepts that there may be objective policy reasons for having different procedural rules applying to certain causes of action, and so the key element in determining whether the principle of equivalence has been breached usually lies in the identification of a national law claim that can serve as an appropriate comparator to the claim based on EU law. So, for example, in *Edis*, the national law provided different limitation periods for seeking refunds depending on whether the return of the money was sought from a private party or a public body. An attempt was made to argue that the principle of equivalence required the application of the longer limitation period that applied to private parties. The Court of Justice rejected this, holding that as a matter of EU law it was permissible for a Member State to apply stricter rules to certain types of claim; it would only be if those stricter rules applied solely to actions based on EU law that the principle of equivalence would be infringed.[15]

---

[12] Case C-397/11 *Jőrös* EU:C:2013:340, 30 May 2013, paras 29–30. See also C-93/12 *Agrokonsulting* EU:C:2013:432, 27 June 2013, [2014] 1 CMLR 3; Case C-246/09 *Bulicke* [2010] ECR I-7003; Case C-326/96 *Levez v Jennings* [1998] ECR I-7835; Case C-261/95 *Palmisani v INPS* [1997] ECR I-4025.

[13] Michael Dougan, "The Vicissitudes of Life at the Coalface: Remedies and Procedures for Enforcing Union Law before the National Courts" in Paul Craig and Gráinne de Búrca (eds), *The Evolution of EU Law* (2nd ed, Oxford University Press, 2011) 406, 423.

[14] Case C-231/96 *Edis* [1998] ECR I-4951.

[15] *Ibid*, 4991.

[14–11] The application of the principle of equivalence in any individual case is often complex as it requires a careful assessment of the factual circumstances and the applicable procedural rules in order to determine whether there is a sufficiently similar national comparator based on their respective objectives and essential characteristics. This can be a particularly difficult task for the Court of Justice, given that it will be unfamiliar with the detailed procedural rules of each Member State. Accordingly, the Court has repeatedly stated that:

> In order to verify whether the principle of equivalence has been complied with … it is for the national court, which alone has direct knowledge of the procedural rules governing actions in the field of domestic law, to verify whether the procedural rules intended to ensure that the rights derived by individuals from [EU] law are safeguarded under domestic law comply with that principle and to consider both the purpose and the essential characteristics of allegedly similar domestic actions.[16]

[14–12] It follows that many preliminary references on the topic conclude by calling on the national court to carry out its own assessment in light of the general guidance provided by the Court of Justice. Indeed, in *TD v Minister for Justice, Equality and Law Reform*, Fennelly J referred to this stance in declining to make a request for a preliminary ruling. In delivering the majority judgment in the Supreme Court, Fennelly J noted that, in addition to the fact that the principles governing the exercise by the national courts of their application of the principle of equivalence had been clearly laid down in settled case law of the Court of Justice, it was also "abundantly clear that it is for the national court to form its own judgement as to whether the national rules infringe the principle for the very reason that only that court has the capacity to know and understand the operation of the national rules within the context of the system as a whole".[17] In addition to being heavily fact-specific, in less clear-cut cases the concept of a sufficiently similar comparator will inevitably involve a judgement call that, in the end, will require an element of subjectivity. As Derrick Wyatt and Alan Dashwood observe:

> a test of comparability based on the "objectives" and "essential characteristics" of the relevant claims is capable of operating at several different levels of abstraction. For example, a claim for financial benefits wrongly withheld from an employee in breach of the principle of equal pay between men and women might be said to have the purpose of enforcing the general principle of non-discrimination, and thus to be comparable to domestic claims based on other forms of unlawful prejudice. Alternatively, such a claim might be understood to pursue the objective of recovering remuneration properly due to a worker by his/her employer, and thus properly to be compared with domestic actions or arrears of wages or breach of the employment contract.[18]

---

16 Case C-78/98 *Preston v Wolverhampton NHS Healthcare Trust* [2000] ECR I-3201, 3261.

17 [2014] 4 IR 277, 363.

18 Alan Dashwood, Michael Dougan, Barry Rodger, Eleanor Spaventa and Derrick Wyatt, *Wyatt and Dashwood's European Union Law* (6th ed, Hart Publishing, 2011) 293–294. See Case C-234/17 *XC* EU:C:2018:853, 24 October 2018, where a Grand Chamber ruling held that an Austrian procedural rule that permitted a rehearing of criminal proceedings, closed by a national decision having the force of *res judicata*, in the event of an infringement of the European Convention on Human Rights did not have to be extended to infringements of fundamental rights under EU law, including the Charter of Fundamental Rights, by virtue of the principles of equivalence and effectiveness. In the view of the Grand Chamber, the differences between the Austrian procedure for relying on infringements of the ECHR, on the one hand, and actions for protecting rights which individuals derive from EU law, on the other hand, were such that the two actions could not be regarded as similar.

[14–13] The judgments of Hogan J in the High Court, Fennelly J for the majority of the Supreme Court and Murray J (as he then was) dissenting in *TD v Minister for Justice, Equality and Law Reform* illustrate the difficulty of identifying the appropriate comparator. Here, it was argued that a 14-day time limit for seeking judicial review of an asylum decision was contrary to the principle of equivalence.[19] In the High Court, Hogan J considered that it was not sufficient that s 5 of the Illegal Immigrants (Trafficking) Act 2000 set a 14-day time limit for all judicial review proceedings relating to the asylum process, regardless of whether the grounds of challenge was based on Irish law or EU law. Rather, he felt obliged to take a "broader view of what constitutes equivalence for this purpose and that the comparison must also be made with other broadly similar actions in the sphere of judicial review", such as in planning and environmental matters.[20] The majority of the Supreme Court, however, considered this approach to be overly broad in that it failed to limit the comparator by having regard to a similar underlying subject matter, area of law or ground of complaint. Rather, it was considered that Hogan J had chosen to "define the subject matter by reference to the limitation periods themselves".[21] Fennelly J expressed the majority view in the Supreme Court as follows:

> Only the national court is in a position to understand and appreciate the multitudes of national rules and jurisdictions and how they relate to and affect each other. This court, as the national court applying EU law, must conscientiously give full effect to the principles laid down by the European Court of Justice, but, in performing that duty, it applies its own special knowledge of the national legal system.
>
> The court must determine whether the 14 day time limit infringes the principle of equivalence by treating claims based on EU law less favourably than equivalent or similar claims based on national law. Quite obviously, the 14 day limit is more exacting and less favourable than the six month limit (now three months) which applies generally to applications for judicial review. The answer to the question comes down essentially to whether the relevant national law, i.e., s.5(1) of the Act of 2000 picks out a list of subjects of claim under EU law which must be brought within a special period of 14 days, which is shorter than the period applied to equivalent claims under national law.
>
> I would interpret the references by the European Court of Justice to cause of action and special characteristics as referring to the subject matter of claims. When referring to judicial review, the subject matter could be broadly defined so as to encompass all claims for review of administrative decisions of every type or it could relate to the underlying subject matter of the decisions which may be challenged.
>
> The decisions of the European Court of Justice do not make any distinction on these grounds. The court must, it is clear, take a broad view and examine the system in its entirety. The subject matter of an application for judicial review is related to both the underlying area of law to which the decision relates, whether it be employment, planning, immigration or anything else and the relief sought in the claim, such as certiorari of an administrative decision. Judicial review concerns both the decision under challenge and whatever the decision is about.
>
> It is easy, at one level to show lack of equivalent treatment. An asylum decision is subject to the 14 day limit and a challenge to any administrative decision, where no special limit is laid down, was six months at the relevant time. But that analysis is insufficient and is

---

19 [2014] 4 IR 277.
20 *ibid*, 358.
21 *ibid*, 359.

> not required by EU law. As the European Court of Justice has repeatedly stated, national law is not required to accord its most favourable time limits to EU law claims. Regard must be had to the essential nature of the subject matter of the claim.
>
> The court should look at the substance of the rule whose compatibility is under scrutiny to see whether it is discriminatory. One looks at its essential scope and area of operation. This brings us back to s.5(1) of the Act of 2000. I am satisfied that s.5(1) covers all decisions related to immigration and the entry or refusal of entry of non-nationals into the national territory of the State, whether those decisions are based on EU law or not. … While it is true that asylum decisions concern important and fundamental rights of those affected, the same can be said of decisions, made by national authorities outside the scope of EU law. Those decisions also concern the fundamental rights of those affected. In addition they relate to the fundamental right and duty of the State to police its own frontiers.
>
> It is my opinion that s.5(1) of the Act of 2000 applies without distinction both to claims based on EU law and to those made under national law. Consequently, s.5(2) of the same Act does not discriminate between claims based on EU law and those based on national law. It does not infringe the principle of equivalence.[22]

[14–14] As well as comparing the objectives, cause of action and essential characteristics of the EU law claim and comparator national claim, a national court must also take into account: (i) the role played by the impugned provision in the procedure as a whole; (ii) the operation and any special features of that procedure before different national courts; and (iii) whether reliance on the EU law claim incurs additional costs or delay as compared with the comparator national claim.[23] While these factors are to be placed in their general context, rather than examined in isolation, the examination is intended to involve an "objective comparison, in the abstract, of the procedural rules at issue".[24]

[14–15] Given their closely related nature, it is common to find a challenge to a national procedural rule being mounted on the basis that it is contrary to both the principle of equivalence and the principle of effectiveness, with a degree of overlap occasionally occurring between the two grounds. In the Irish case of *Danqua*, for example, the Court of Appeal requested a preliminary ruling as to whether a 15-day time limit for the making of an application for subsidiary protection was contrary to the principle of equivalence, given that the same time limit did not apply to applications for asylum which, it was said, could be made both within the scope of EU law and of Irish law. The Court of Justice, however, considered that the application for asylum and the application for subsidiary protection at issue in the proceedings were both based on EU law. As a result, it did not consider the principle of equivalence to be relevant. Nonetheless, the Court of Justice went on to interpret the question referred as if it had addressed the principle of effectiveness instead.[25]

---

22 *ibid*, 361–362.

23 Case C-326/96 *Levez v Jennings Ltd* [1998] ECR I-7385, 7870-7871. See also Case C-378/10 *Vale* EU:C:2012:440, 12 July 2012, paras 54–57; Case C-246/09 *Bulicke* [2010] ECR I-7003, paras 24–34; Joined Cases C-391/04 and C-422/04 I–21 *Germany* [2006] ECR I-8559, 8608-8611; Case C-147/01 *Weber's Wine World* [2003] ECR I-11365, 11414–11415.

24 Case C-78/98 *Preston v Wolverhampton NHS Healthcare Trust* [2000] ECR I-3201, 3264.

25 Case C-429/15 *Danqua v Minister for Justice and Equality* EU:C:2016:789, 20 October 2016, para 35.

(ii) Principle of Effectiveness

[14–16] Accounts of the principle of effectiveness typically begin by recalling that there are three distinct phases in the Court of Justice's development of the principle.[26] First, in the early phase lasting until the mid 1980s, the Court displayed restraint and largely deferred to national procedural rules. As exemplified by the *Rewe* and *Comet* cases, the standard for effectiveness was low and was satisfied so long as the national rule did not make the enforcement of EU law virtually impossible.

[14–17] Lasting until the mid 1990s, the second phase saw a more robust approach, where the Court of Justice was willing to apply a higher standard of effectiveness. Two important cases that have already been encountered provide examples of this more demanding attitude. When examining the indirect effect of directives in Chapter 12, the case of *Von Colson* was considered.[27] Ms Von Colson had applied for a job as a social worker in a prison but was unsuccessful, with the position offered to a male candidate. A German court accepted that she had been denied the job due to her sex but held that, under German law implementing the Equal Treatment Directive, the only compensation available was that corresponding to the expenses incurred in applying for the job and attending for interview. Ms Von Colson sought to rely directly on a provision of the Directive that required Member States to ensure that persons discriminated against had recourse to an effective judicial remedy. In replying to a preliminary reference, the Court of Justice held that this provision was not sufficiently precise to be capable of direct effect. Nevertheless, the Court went on to state that:

> although [the] Directive …, for the purpose of imposing a sanction for the breach of the prohibition of discrimination, leaves the Member States free to choose between the different solutions suitable for achieving its objective, it nevertheless requires that if a Member State chooses to penalize breaches of that prohibition by the award of compensation, then in order to ensure that it is effective and that it has a deterrent effect, that compensation must in any event be *adequate in relation to the damage sustained* and must therefore amount to more than purely nominal compensation such as, for example, the reimbursement only of the expenses incurred in connection with the application. It is for the national court to interpret and apply the legislation adopted for the implementation of the Directive in conformity with the requirements of [EU] law, in so far as it is given discretion to do so under national law.[28]

[14–18] Another important case concerning direct effect is *Marshall v Southampton Area Health Authority*, in which the Court of Justice clarified the emanation of the state doctrine in relation to Ms Marshall's employer.[29] When Ms Marshall subsequently had her equal pay claim assessed by an industrial tribunal, it was calculated that she was due over £18,000, which included a sum of almost £8,000 in interest. Under the applicable UK law, however, the maximum compensation allowable was just over £6,000 and it was unclear whether interest could be awarded. A second preliminary reference was

[26] See Michael Dougan, "The Vicissitudes of Life at the Coalface: Remedies and Procedures for Enforcing Union Law before the National Courts" in Paul Craig and Gráinne de Búrca (eds), *The Evolution of EU Law* (2nd ed, Oxford University Press, 2011) 406, 412–421; Robert Schütze, *European Union Law* (Cambridge University Press, 2015) 404–410.

[27] Case 14/83 *Von Colson* [1984] ECR 1891. See ch 12, para [12–54].

[28] *ibid*, 1909. Emphasis added.

[29] Case 152/84 *Marshall v Southampton Area Health Authority* [1986] ECR 723. See ch 12, para [12–39].

made, this time asking whether the limited compensation available was contrary to the requirement for an effective remedy under the Equal Treatment Directive.[30]

[14–19] The Court of Justice emphasised that, as the objective of the Equal Treatment Directive was to arrive at real equality of opportunity, it was necessary to have appropriate measures in place to restore such equality when it has not been observed. Repeating its stance from *Von Colson,* this required national measures that guaranteed "real and effective judicial protection and have a real deterrent effect on the employer".[31] In the event of a discriminatory dismissal, equality could only be restored by either reinstatement or financial compensation for the loss sustained. In the event of the latter, financial compensation must be "adequate, in that it must enable the loss and damage actually sustained … to be made good *in full* in accordance with the applicable national rules".[32] As a result, it was inconsistent with the Equal Treatment Directive for a national law to fix an upper limit on the damages that could be awarded. Furthermore, the award of interest, in accordance with applicable national rules, was to be regarded as an essential component of compensation for the purpose of restoring real equality of treatment.

[14–20] The third and current phase has seen the Court of Justice retreat from the height of its interventionist stance. The Court's approach is now characterised by a more determined effort to strike a balance between the legitimate interests underlying the national procedural rule at issue and the effectiveness of Union law. The Court regularly emphasises the need to analyse the role of the national rule at issue "in the procedure, its progress and its special features, viewed as a whole, before the various national instances".[33] Basic principles of the domestic judicial systems – such as the protection of the rights of defence, the principle of legal certainty and the proper conduct of procedure – must be taken into consideration. In *Van Schijndel*, for example, the Court had to consider whether a Dutch rule that prevented an appellate court from raising a point of EU law of its own motion was contrary to the principle of effectiveness.[34] The rule was aimed at keeping a court's deliberations to the subject matter of the dispute at hand and ensuring that its decision was based on the facts as pleaded by the parties. The Court of Justice considered that such a limitation was

> justified by the principle that, in a civil suit, it is for the parties to take the initiative, the court being able to act of its own motion only in exceptional cases where the public interest requires its intervention. That principle reflects conceptions prevailing in most of the Member States as to the relations between the State and the individual; it safeguards the rights of the defence; and it ensures proper conduct of proceedings by, in particular, protecting them from the delays inherent in examination of new pleas.
>
> In those circumstances, … [EU] law does not require national courts to raise of their own motion an issue concerning the breach of provisions of [EU] law where examination of that issue would oblige them to abandon the passive role assigned to them by going beyond the ambit of the dispute defined by the parties themselves and relying on facts

---

30 Case C-271/91 *Marshall v Southampton Area Health Authority* [1993] ECR I-4367.
31 *ibid*, 4407.
32 *ibid*, 4408, emphasis added.
33 Joined Cases C-430/93 and C-431/93 *Van Schijndel* [1995] ECR I-4705, 4738.
34 *ibid.*

> and circumstances other than those on which the party with an interest in application of those provisions bases his claim.[35]

[14–21] It has been sought to rely on the principle of effectiveness in respect of a range of procedural rules including discovery,[36] *res judicata*,[37] time limits/limitation periods and their extension,[38] rules of evidence,[39] the rule in *Foss v Harbottle*,[40] the rule in *Henderson v Henderson*,[41] limitations on the right to appeal,[42] and the ability of a court to raise a matter of its own motion or for matters to be introduced on appeal where they had not been raised at first instance. In *Danqua*, for example, the Court of Justice considered a 15-day period from the date of refusal of refugee status in which to apply for subsidiary protection to be inadequate. The Court accepted that it was for each Member State to establish time limits, taking account of factors such as the complexities of the legislation and procedures to be applied, the significance of the decisions to be taken for the parties concerned, the number of persons who may be affected and any other public or private interests which must be taken into consideration. Nevertheless,

> the procedure for examining applications for subsidiary protection is of particular importance inasmuch as it enables applicants for international protection to safeguard their most basic rights by the grant of such protection.
>
> In that context, taking account of the difficulties such applicants may face because of, inter alia, the difficult human and material situation in which they may find themselves, it must be held that a [15-day] time limit … is particularly short and does not ensure, in practice, that all those applicants are afforded a genuine opportunity to submit an application for subsidiary protection and, where appropriate, to be granted subsidiary protection status. Therefore, such a time limit cannot reasonably be justified for the purposes of ensuring the proper conduct of the procedure for examining an application for that status.
>
> … Accordingly, it must be held that a national procedural rule, such as [a 15-day time limit], is capable of compromising the ability of applicants for subsidiary protection actually to avail themselves of the rights conferred on them by [the] Directive.[43]

[14–22] A rule concerning the disclosure of information was at issue in *Kelly v*

---

[35] *ibid*, 4738. See Sacha Prechal, "Community Law in National Courts: The Lessons from Van Schijndel" (1998) 35 *Common Market Law Review* 681.

[36] *Framus Ltd v CRH plc* [2004] 2 IR 20, 47–48.

[37] Case C-505/14 *Klausner* EU:C:2015:742, 11 November 2015. See Alexander Kornezov, "*Res Judicata* of National Judgments Incompatible with EU Law: Time for a Major Rethink?" (2014) 51 *Common Market Law Review* 809.

[38] *TD v Minister for Justice, Equality and Law Reform* [2014] 4 IR 277; *Veolia Water UK v Fingal Co Co (No 1)* [2007] 1 IR, 701–702; *Dekra Erin Ltd v Minister for the Environment* [2002] 2 ILRM 30.

[39] Case C-55/06 *Arcor* [2008] ECR I-2931; Case C-264/08 *Digital Parcel Distribution Belgium* [2010] ECR I-731; Case C-437/13 *Unitrading* EU:C:2014:2318, 23 October 2014.

[40] *O'Neill v Ryan* [1990] 2 IR 200, 208–209 (High Court); [1993] ILRM 557, 571 (Supreme Court). According to the rule in *Foss v Harbottle*, the proper plaintiff in an action against a third party for injury to a company is the company itself, and not its shareholders.

[41] *Arklow Holidays Ltd v An Bord Pleanála* [2012] 2 IR 99, 127–128. According to the rule in *Henderson v Henderson*, a party is ordinarily precluded from raising in subsequent proceedings grounds which could and should have been raised in earlier proceedings on the same subject matter but which were not so raised.

[42] *McNamara v An Bord Pleanála* [1998] 3 IR 453, 467.

[43] Case C-429/15 *Danqua v Minister for Justice and Equality* EU:C:2016:789, 20 October 2016, paras 45–48.

National University of Ireland.[44] Mr Kelly had unsuccessfully applied to undertake a course in University College Dublin and subsequently brought a claim to the Equality Tribunal under Equal Treatment Directives, arguing that he was better qualified than the least qualified successful female candidate. When he sought disclosure of the applications and scoring sheets relating to other candidates, the High Court considered that the University was not obliged to disclose them as a matter of Irish law. The High Court nevertheless made a reference to the Court of Justice, inquiring as to whether EU law required that disclosure be available in these circumstances. Under the Directive, Member States were required to take such measures as were necessary to ensure that, when persons who consider themselves to have been discriminated against establish facts from which it may be presumed that there has been discrimination, it shall be for the respondent to prove that they have not, in fact, been discriminatory. The Court of Justice first determined that the Directive, as such, did not entitle an applicant such as Mr Kelly to information on other candidates in order that he could establish facts from which it could be presumed that there had been discrimination. The Court went on to find, however, that it could not be ruled out that a refusal of disclosure by the University, in the context of establishing such facts, could risk compromising the achievement of the objective pursued by that Directive and thus depriving it of its effectiveness. This was a matter for the Irish court to ascertain in the particular proceedings before it.

[14–23] A further example is *Impact v Minister for Agriculture and Food.*[45] Ireland's transposition of the Fixed-Term Workers Directive involved the conferral of a jurisdiction on the Rights Commissioner and the Labour Court to hear complaints arising from the date of the commencement of Ireland's implementing legislation. While the deadline for transposition was July 2001, the relevant legislation did not come into force until July 2003. A question arose as to whether the principle of effectiveness required the Rights Commissioner and the Labour Court to also have jurisdiction in respect of complaints under the Directive (which was capable of having direct effect) arising between July 2001, when the Directive ought to have been transposed, and July 2003, when it was in fact transposed. The Court of Justice provided a somewhat equivocal answer as follows:

> where the national legislature has chosen to confer on specialised courts jurisdiction to hear and determine actions based on the legislation transposing [the] Directive ..., the obligation which would be placed on individuals in the situation of the complainants ... to bring at the same time a separate action before an ordinary court to assert the rights which they can derive directly from that directive in respect of the period between the deadline for transposing it and the date on which the transposing legislation entered into force, would be contrary to the principle of effectiveness if – which is for the referring court to ascertain – it would result in procedural disadvantages for those individuals, in terms, inter alia, of cost, duration and the rules of representation, such as to render excessively difficult the exercise of rights deriving from that directive.
>
> At the hearing, Ireland claimed that the jurisdiction given to the Rights Commissioners and the Labour Court ... is optional and therefore does not prevent individuals from bringing a single action, based partly on national law and partly on [EU] law, before an ordinary court.
>
> Even if that is so, the fact remains that where individuals intended ... to rely on the, albeit

---

[44] Case C-104/10 *Kelly v National University of Ireland* EU:C:2011:506, 21 July 2011. See also Case C-415/10 *Meister v Speech Design* EU:C:2012:217, 19 April 2012.

[45] Case C-268/06 *Impact v Minister for Agriculture and Food* [2008] ECR I-2483.

> optional, jurisdiction which the national legislature, when transposing [the] Directive ..., conferred on those specialised courts to hear and determine disputes ..., the principle of effectiveness requires that those individuals should also be able to seek before the same courts the protection of the rights which they can derive directly from the directive itself, if it should emerge from the checks undertaken by the referring court that the obligation to divide their action into two separate claims and to bring the claim based directly on the directive before an ordinary court leads to procedural complications liable to render excessively difficult the exercise of those rights conferred on the parties by [EU] law.
>
> If the referring court were to find such an infringement of the principle of effectiveness, it would be for that court to interpret the domestic jurisdictional rules in such a way that, wherever possible, they contribute to the attainment of the objective of ensuring effective judicial protection of an individual's rights under [EU] law.[46]

[14–24] The Labour Court, which had referred the question, determined that the principle of effectiveness did require that its jurisdiction date back to the date on which the Fixed-Term Workers Directive ought to have been transposed.

[14–25] Issues similar to those in *IMPACT* arose in two cases relating to the disapplication of national law considered in the previous chapter. In *An Taoiseach v Commissioner for Environmental Information* and *Minister for Justice and Equality v Workplace Relations Commission*, it was argued that the *Simmenthal* principle required statutory bodies – such as the Commissioner for Environmental Information and the Equality Tribunal – to be able to disapply a provision of national law should they find it to be contrary to EU law. In addition, however, it was also argued that it would be contrary to the principle of effectiveness to require a claim of incompatibility with EU law to be commenced before the High Court. In *An Taoiseach v Commissioner for Environmental Information*, Ó Néil J rejected an argument that the principle of effectiveness would be breached if the notice party, who was seeking the release of Cabinet records relating to emissions into the environment, was required to litigate his right to disclosure in the High Court.[47] In support of this conclusion, Ó Néil J referred to the fact that, in its access to justice provision, the Directive on Public Access to Environmental Information itself provided for a review procedure to a court of law or an independent impartial body established by law.[48]

[14–26] A more detailed analysis of the effectiveness argument was conducted by the Supreme Court in *Minister for Justice and Equality v Workplace Relations Commission*.[49] There, Clarke J (as he then was) observed that the Court of Justice typically calls upon a national court to apply its knowledge of its own procedural rules and structures to determine whether the principle of effectiveness has been breached. First, it was to be noted that even if the Equality Tribunal were entitled to disapply a provision of national law, such a decision would, in practice, be likely to be appealed to the High Court. It followed that,

> as matter of national procedural structure, cases, such as those which are the subject of these proceedings, are highly likely to end up before the High Court in any event and might, indeed, involve further appeals within the courts system. On one view the fact that

46 *ibid*, paras 51–54.
47 [2013] 2 IR 510; [2011] 1 ILRM 508.
48 *ibid*, 539-540; 532.
49 [2017] IESC 43, unreported, Supreme Court, 15 June 2017.

> such a case might commence before the [Equality] Tribunal could give rise to additional layers of hearing and thus, if anything, make the process more complicated, lengthy and potentially expensive.[50]

[14–27] Secondly, there was an argument that the additional cost of High Court proceedings infringed the principle of effectiveness. In response to this, Clarke J reiterated the observation that, in practice, were the Equality Tribunal to disapply a provision of national law, an appeal to the High Court would be likely. The recent jurisprudence of the Court of Justice also indicated that while, at the level of principle, it was possible that excessive costs may breach the principle of effectiveness, the costs concerned were not found to render the process excessively difficult.[51] For Clarke J, another consideration in this context was the fact that, while a losing party may have costs awarded against them in the High Court, equally a successful party will have costs awarded in their favour. This provided a:

> form of litigation support which has proved, in practice, effective in ensuring legal representation in cases where it is needed. The fact that costs are not awarded before the Tribunal does, obviously, mean that a complainant to the Tribunal is not at risk of having an award of costs against them but also means that the complainant does not have the benefit of possibly obtaining an order for costs in the event of being successful. Thus a complainant who feels that legal assistance may be to their advantage in pursuing a complaint may find it more difficult to obtain the services of the necessary lawyers precisely because of the absence of any potentiality to award costs.[52]

[14–28] Thirdly, while an argument could be made that the Equality Tribunal had a degree of specialist expertise that could be brought to bear on employment equality claims, by allowing for an appeal on a point of law the Employment Equality Acts had effectively left the final decision to the courts rather than the Tribunal. Once again, in practice, any decision as to the disapplication of national law would be likely to end up before the High Court, and there was no reason in principle why the Equality Tribunal could not be involved as a notice party so that their expertise could be brought to bear on the case. Fourthly, in light of the broad powers of the High Court as regards disclosure of documents, etc, it could not be said that the ability to establish the facts would be any less in a case commenced before the High Court as opposed to a case commenced before the Equality Tribunal. The fact that the procedure in the High Court was adversarial, as opposed to the inquisitorial nature of the Tribunal, "can hardly be said to show that the vindication of European Union law rights would be excessively difficult particularly where, as here, the High Court would enjoy the entitlement to ensure that all necessary facts and documents can be procured so as to come to an appropriate resolution of the case".[53] Had the range of remedies available been more limited in the High Court, as compared with the Tribunal, that might have been a factor that would have gone towards effectiveness, however the Supreme Court found that in fact this was not the case. Accordingly, Clarke J concluded that it was

> worth recording that the test which must be applied under the jurisprudence of the Court of Justice in determining whether a measure of national procedural law breaches the principle of effectiveness does not require that the procedure be perfect or that there might

---

[50] *ibid*, para 7.6.
[51] *ibid*, para 7.7.
[52] *ibid*, para 7.8.
[53] *ibid*, para 7.12.

> not be ways in which the procedure might be improved. Rather the test is as to whether the procedure which national law would require to be followed might render the vindication of Union rights excessively difficult.
>
> The Tribunal has not, in my view, pointed to any aspect of the regime which would require to be followed in the event that national law is applied and proceedings of this type are required to be brought before the High Court, which would render the vindication of Union employment equality rights in the High Court excessively difficult. ... It is difficult to see how the fact that the proceedings are adversarial renders the pursuit of a vindication of Union rights excessively difficult particularly where those same adversarial procedures allow any party to require, under compulsion, the disclosure of any facts or documents which might potentially be relevant to the factual issues in the case. So far as cost is concerned there might be some circumstances in which there would be a greater exposure to cost before the High Court but it might equally follow that there would be disadvantages in being required to pursue a case in circumstances where the costs incurred in bringing the complaint before a body such as the Tribunal could not be recovered even if the proceedings were successful.[54]

[14–29] The Supreme Court requested a preliminary ruling from the Court of Justice on whether the *Simmenthal* principle required that the Equality Tribunal be empowered to disapply national law. In so doing, however, the Supreme Court noted that in its assessment, the existing remedy available from the High Court complied with the principles of effectiveness and equivalence.[55] In a Grand Chamber ruling, the Court of Justice relied on the doctrine of supremacy of EU law to find that Irish law must allow the Equality Tribunal (now the Workplace Relations Commission) to disapply national law, given that it is the body established by national law in order to ensure the enforcement of EU law in a particular area. As a result, although the Supreme Court's assessment of effectiveness has not been contradicted by the Court of Justice's judgment, it is best read in light of that important ruling.

[14–30] The picture that emerges from the recent judgments of the Court of Justice is an approach based on an individualised, fact-based assessment, rather than the application of generic rules.[56] Indeed, when parties before the Court have sought to rely on earlier judgments that appear to support their arguments, the Court has pointed out that such judgments are "merely the result of assessments on a case by case basis, taking account of each case's own factual and legal context as a whole, which cannot be applied mechanically in fields other than those in which they were made".[57] Rather, in each case, the question of whether a national procedural rule renders the application of EU law excessively difficult must be analysed by reference to the role of that provision in the procedure, its progress and its special features, viewed as a whole, before the various national instances. One benefit of this is that it has allowed for a flexible standard of effectiveness, with vulnerable applicants – such as those seeking subsidiary protection or consumers alleging unfair contractual terms – often afforded a greater degree of protection. On the other hand, this "contextual and *ad hoc* approach"

---

[54] *ibid*, paras 7.14–7.15.

[55] C-378/17 *Minister for Justice and Equality v Workplace Relations Commission* EU:C:2018:979, 4 December 2018.

[56] Michael Dougan, "The Vicissitudes of Life at the Coalface: Remedies and Procedures for Enforcing Union Law before the National Courts" in Paul Craig and Gráinne de Búrca (eds), *The Evolution of EU Law* (2nd ed, Oxford University Press, 2011) 406, 419.

[57] Case C-473/00 *Cofidis* [2002] ECR I-10875, 10911.

has caused Michael Dougan to concede that it can give rise to serious difficulties of predictability and consistency, noting that for some the Court:

> surely spends a disproportionate amount of its scarce judicial energy delving into the nitty-gritty of the national legal systems, in a way unbefitting what is (in effect) a federal constitutional court surrounded by more pressing legal issues to resolve, and with few tangible benefits in terms of improving the effectiveness or uniform application of Union law to show for all its trouble. … [Some] have called for the delivery in this field of some sort of "remedies equivalent" to the *Keck* judgment as regards the free movement of goods, so that the great majority of national remedies and procedural rules are simply acknowledged not to endanger any fundamental Union interest, or at least not to do so in any fundamental way, and are therefore pushed outside the scope of Union law altogether.[58]

B. Effective Judicial Protection

[14–31] Article 4 TEU imposes on the Member States an obligation to take any appropriate measure, general or particular, to ensure fulfilment of the obligations arising out of the Treaties or resulting from acts of the Union institutions. This obligation provides the bedrock for another principle that is similar to, but distinct from, the principle of effectiveness and runs in parallel to it. This is the principle of "effective judicial protection", or what are also known as autonomous EU actions. Just as the need to confer EU law with direct effect and supremacy was originally rooted in ensuring that the law was effective, or had *effet utile*, the concept of effective judicial protection is based on the premise that the full effectiveness of EU law would be equally impaired if a national law could prevent domestic courts seised of disputes governed by EU law from granting the relief necessary to ensure the full effect of their judgments on matters of EU law. We have already seen that the default position under the presumption of national procedural autonomy is that EU law does not require Member States to create new national remedies. Autonomous EU actions based on the need to ensure effective judicial protection are therefore not understood to be "mediated through the *Rewe/Comet* presumption of national procedural autonomy subject to the principles of equivalence and effectiveness", but rather they are "deemed by the Court to derive from the Treaty itself, inherently and directly".[59] Put another way, as described by

---

58 Michael Dougan, "The Vicissitudes of Life at the Coalface: Remedies and Procedures for Enforcing Union Law before the National Courts" in Paul Craig and Gráinne de Búrca (eds), *The Evolution of EU Law* (2nd ed, Oxford University Press, 2011) 406, 420–421. See Pieter van Cleynenbreugel, "Judge Made Standards of National Procedure in the post-Lisbon Constitutional Framework" (2012) 37 *European Law Review* 90; Andrea Biondi, "The European Court of Justice and Certain National Procedural Limitations: Not Such a Tough Relationship" (1999) 36 *Common Market Law Review* 1271; Chris Himsworth, "Things Fall Apart: The Harmonisation of Community Judicial Procedural Protection Revisited" (1997) 22 *European Law Review* 291.

59 Michael Dougan, "The Vicissitudes of Life at the Coalface: Remedies and Procedures for Enforcing Union Law before the National Courts" in Paul Craig and Gráinne de Búrca (eds), *The Evolution of EU Law* (2nd ed, Oxford University Press, 2011) 406, 426. See Jasper Krommendijk, "Is There Light on the Horizon? The Distinction between 'Rewe Effectiveness' and the Principle of Effective Judicial Protection in Article 47 of the Charter after Orizzonte" (2016) 53 *Common Market Law Review* 1395; Anthony Arnull, "The Principle of Effective Judicial Protection in EU Law: An Unruly Horse?" (2011) 36 *European Law Review* 51; Paolisa Nebbia, "The Double Life of Effectiveness" (2007/2008) 10 *Cambridge Yearbook of European Legal Studies* 287; Cathrina Keville, "The Principle of Effectiveness and the Development of a System of Remedies at European Community Law" in Mary Catherine Lucey and Cathrina Keville (eds), *Irish Perspective on EC Law* (Thomson Round Hall, 2003) 1.

Murray J (as he then was) in *TD v Minister for Justice, Equality and Law Reform*, the requirements of equivalence and effectiveness "embody the general obligation on the Member States to ensure judicial protection of an individual's rights derived from the law of the European Union".[60]

(i) Damages for Breach of EU Law by Private Party

[14–32] The most well known and significant of autonomous EU actions is the principle that a Member State may be held liable for a breach of EU law committed by it. Before considering this, however, two other actions deserve brief mention. The first is the ability, in certain instances, for private parties to ground a claim for damages in the Treaties themselves. A seminal expression of this principle is the case of *Courage Ltd v Crehan*.[61] There, an English brewery brought proceedings for unpaid deliveries of beer against a publican, Mr Crehan, with whom it had a "beer-tie" lease, obliging the publican to sell only its product. Mr Crehan contested the action by contending that the beer-tie was contrary to the prohibition on anti-competitive practices enshrined in Art 101 TFEU. Not only that, he also counter-claimed for damages, contending that the brewery sold its beers to independent pubs at substantially lower prices than to those subject to a beer-tie lease.

[14–33] The Court of Appeal of England and Wales felt bound by the fact that: (i) English law did not allow a party to an illegal agreement to claim damages from the other party and (ii) it had previously held that Art 101 TFEU was intended to protect third-party competitors or consumers, and not parties to the prohibited agreement itself. Accordingly, it made a reference to the Court of Justice asking whether Art 101 could be relied upon by a party to a prohibited agreement to recover damages alleged to arise as a result of his adherence to the agreement and, if so, whether a rule of national law which prevented a person from relying on his own illegal actions to recover damages was consistent with EU law. After confirming that even a party to a contract that is liable to restrict or distort competition can rely on a breach of Art 101 TFEU before a national court, the Court of Justice went on to address the ability of such a party to claim damages:

> it should be remembered from the outset that, in accordance with settled case-law, the national courts whose task it is to apply the provisions of [EU] law in areas within their jurisdiction must ensure that those rules take full effect and must protect the rights which they confer on individuals.
>
> The full effectiveness of Article [101] of the Treaty and, in particular, the practical effect of the prohibition laid down in Article [101(1)] would be put at risk if it were not open to any individual to claim damages for loss caused to him by a contract or by conduct liable to restrict or distort competition.

---

[60] [2014] 4 IR 277, 289.

[61] Case C-453/99 *Courage Ltd v Crehan* [2001] ECR I-6297. See Case C-724/17 *Skanska* EU:C:2019:204, 14 March 2019; Dorota Leczykiewicz, "Private Party Liability in EU Law: In Search of the General Regime" (2009–10) 12 *Cambridge Yearbook of European Legal Studies* 257; Norbert Reich, "Horizontal Liability in EC Law: Hybridization of Remedies for Compensation in Case of Breaches of EC Rights" (2007) 44 *Common Market Law Review* 705; Sara Drake, "Scope of *Courage* and the Principle of 'Individual Liability' for Damages: Further Development of the Principle of Effective Judicial Protection by the Court of Justice" (2006) 31 *European Law Review* 841.

> Indeed, the existence of such a right strengthens the working of [EU] competition rules and discourages agreements or practices, which are frequently covert, which are liable to restrict or distort competition. From that point of view, actions for damages before the national courts can make a significant contribution to the maintenance of effective competition in the [Union].
>
> There should not therefore be any absolute bar to such an action being brought by a party to a contract which would be held to violate the competition rules.[62]

[14–34] Outside the field of competition law, the extent to which a claim for damages in a private dispute can be grounded in EU law remains contested. Given the importance of competition law to the functioning of the Internal Market, it was considered that the existence of differing national rules governing damages claims for breaches of competition law could lead to an uneven playing field amongst the Member States. Harmonising rules were introduced to address this concern in a 2014 Directive.[63] As the recitals to the Directive set out the rationale for both an autonomous EU action for damages, and the need to harmonise and limit national procedural autonomy in this area, they are worth quoting at length:

> Articles 101 and 102 TFEU produce direct effects in relations between individuals and create, for the individuals concerned, rights and obligations which national courts must enforce. National courts thus have an equally essential part to play in applying the competition rules (private enforcement). When ruling on disputes between private individuals, they protect subjective rights under Union law, for example by awarding damages to the victims of infringements. The full effectiveness of Articles 101 and 102 TFEU, and in particular the practical effect of the prohibitions laid down therein, requires that anyone – be they an individual, including consumers and undertakings, or a public authority – can claim compensation before national courts for the harm caused to them by an infringement of those provisions. …
>
> The right in Union law to compensation for harm resulting from infringements of Union and national competition law requires each Member State to have procedural rules ensuring the effective exercise of that right. The need for effective procedural remedies also follows from the right to effective judicial protection as laid down in the second subparagraph of Article 19(1) of the Treaty on European Union (TEU) and in the first paragraph of Article 47 of the Charter of Fundamental Rights of the European Union. Member States should ensure effective legal protection in the fields covered by Union law.
>
> … Undertakings established and operating in various Member States are subject to differing procedural rules that significantly affect the extent to which they can be held liable for

[62] *ibid*, 6323–6324. See Erling Hjelmeng, "Competition Law Remedies: Striving for Coherence of Finding New Ways" (2013) 50 *Common Market Law Review* 1007; Katri Havu, "Horizontal Liability for Damages in EU Law – The Changing Relationship of EU and National Law" (2012) 18 *European Law Journal* 407; Norbert Reich, "Horizontal Liability in EU Law: Hybridization of Remedies for Compensation in Case of Breach of EC Rights" (2007) 44 *Common Market Law Review* 705; Sara Drake, "Scope of *Courage* and the Principle of 'Individual Liability' for Damages" (2006) 26 *European Law Review* 841; Assimakis P Komninos, "New Prospects for Private Enforcement of EC Competition Law: *Courage v Crehan* and the Community Right to Damages" (2002) 39 *Common Market Law Review* 447.

[63] Directive 2014/104/EU of the European Parliament and of the Council of 26 November 2014 on certain rules governing actions for damages under national law for infringements of the competition law provisions of the Member States and of the European Union [2014] OJ L349/1. See Niamh Dunne, "Courage and Compromise: The Directive on Antitrust Damages" (2015) 40 *European Law Review* 581.

infringements of competition law. This uneven enforcement of the right to compensation in Union law may result not only in a competitive advantage for some undertakings which have infringed Article 101 or 102 TFEU but also in a disincentive to the exercise of the rights of establishment and provision of goods or services in those Member States where the right to compensation is enforced more effectively. As the differences in the liability regimes applicable in the Member States may negatively affect both competition and the proper functioning of the internal market, it is appropriate to base this Directive on the dual legal bases of Articles 103 and 114 TFEU.

... In the absence of Union law, actions for damages are governed by the national rules and procedures of the Member States. According to the case-law of the Court of Justice of the European Union, any person can claim compensation for harm suffered where there is a causal relationship between that harm and an infringement of competition law. All national rules governing the exercise of the right to compensation for harm resulting from an infringement of Article 101 or 102 TFEU, including those concerning aspects not dealt with in this Directive such as the notion of causal relationship between the infringement and the harm, must observe the principles of effectiveness and equivalence. This means that they should not be formulated or applied in a way that makes it excessively difficult or practically impossible to exercise the right to compensation guaranteed by the TFEU or less favourably than those applicable to similar domestic actions. Where Member States provide other conditions for compensation under national law, such as imputability, adequacy or culpability, they should be able to maintain such conditions in so far as they comply with the case-law of the Court of Justice, the principles of effectiveness and equivalence, and this Directive.

... The right to compensation is recognised for any natural or legal person – consumers, undertakings and public authorities alike – irrespective of the existence of a direct contractual relationship with the infringing undertaking, and regardless of whether or not there has been a prior finding of an infringement by a competition authority.[64]

(ii) Interim Relief to Protect Against Breach of EU Law

[14–35] The principle of effectiveness has also led the Court of Justice to declare that national courts must be in a position to grant interim relief, such as an interlocutory injunction, where it is alleged that the operation of an incompatible national law is infringing EU law rights. Whilst the Irish courts had already acknowledged the need for such a remedy,[65] in the well-known case of *Factortame*, the House of Lords did not consider itself permitted, as a matter of national law, to grant an interim injunction to suspend the application of rules under the Merchant Shipping Act that required boats to be at least 75 per cent British-owned in order to be included on the ship register. In reply to a preliminary reference, the Court of Justice recalled that it is for the national courts, in application of the principle of sincere cooperation, to ensure the legal protection which persons derive from the direct effect of EU law.[66] Just as in *Simmenthal*, where the effectiveness of the doctrine of supremacy would have been undermined if a national court had to await a decision of a constitutional court, in *Factortame* it was held that:

the full effectiveness of [EU] law would be just as much impaired if a rule of national law could prevent a court seised of a dispute governed by [EU] law from granting interim relief

64 *ibid*, recitals 3, 4, 8, 11, 13.

65 *Pesca Valentia v Minister for Fisheries and Forestry* [1985] IR 193. See also the discussion in *Kingdom of Belgium v Ryanair Ltd* [2009] 3 IR 417; *Martin v An Bord Pleanála* [2002] 2 IR 655, 661–663; *RTÉ v Magill* [1988] IR 97.

66 Case C-213/89 *R v Secretary of State for Transport, ex parte Factortame* [1990] ECR I-2433.

> in order to ensure the full effectiveness of the judgment to be given on the existence of the rights claimed under [EU] law. It follows that a court which in those circumstances would grant interim relief, if it were not for a rule of national law, is obliged to set aside that rule.
>
> That interpretation is reinforced by the system established by Article [267 TFEU] whose effectiveness would be impaired if a national court, having stayed proceedings pending the reply by the Court of Justice to the question referred to it for a preliminary ruling, were not able to grant interim relief until it delivered its judgment following the reply given by the Court of Justice.
>
> Consequently, … [EU] law must be interpreted as meaning that a national court which, in a case before it concerning [EU] law, considers that the sole obstacle which precludes it from granting interim relief is a rule of national law must set aside that rule.[67]

[14–36] A similar issue arose in the more recent case of *Melki*.[68] There, the French constitution required that questions as regards the constitutionality of any measure, including its compatibility with EU law, be sent as a matter of priority to the French constitutional court. The Court of Justice held that for such a rule to be permissible, it must allow for the lower court to remain free to adopt any measure necessary to ensure the provisional judicial protection of the rights conferred under EU law and, second, to disapply, at the end of such an interlocutory procedure, the national legislative provision if that court holds it to be contrary to EU law.[69]

[14–37] The Court of Justice has taken a different approach to the granting of interim relief by national courts depending on whether the measure being challenged is a national law or an EU legal act. In the case of a national law, the Court established in *Unibet* that it is to be left to national procedural rules to determine the relevant criteria and thresholds for the granting of interim relief, subject to the principles of equivalence and effectiveness.[70] As the uniform application of EU law would risk being undermined by the frequent granting of interim relief by national courts, a higher threshold – and one set by EU law – is prescribed where the validity of an EU legal act is at issue. In the cases of *Zuckerfabrick* and *Atlanta* the Court set out the following four criteria that are to be fulfilled before a national court suspends the application of an EU act on an interim basis, pending a ruling from the Court of Justice: (i) the national court must be satisfied that serious doubt exists as to the validity of the measure; (ii) there must be a degree of urgency, arising from the likelihood of irreparable damage to the applicant if interim relief is not granted (with purely financial damage not being regarded, in principle, as irreparable); (iii) that urgency must be balanced against the possibility of irreparable damage to the Union should the applicant's challenge fail; and (iv) regard should be had to the potential cumulative effect of a large number of courts granting interim relief for similar reasons.[71]

[14–38] Both *Zuckerfabrick* and *Atlanta* were relied upon by the plaintiff in *Pringle v*

---

67 *ibid*, 2474.

68 Joined Cases C-188/10 and C-189/10 *Melki* [2010] ECR I-5667. See also Case C-314/08 *Filipiak* [2009] ECR I-11049.

69 *ibid*, para 53.

70 Case C-432/05 *Unibet* [2007] ECR I-2271. See Anthony M Collins and James O'Reilly, *Civil Proceedings and the State* (2nd ed, Thomson Round Hall, 2004) 301–304.

71 Joined Cases C-143/88 and C-92/89 *Zuckerfabrick* [1991] ECR I-415, 542–544; Case C-465/93 *Atlanta* [1995] ECR I-3761, 3793.

Ireland in requesting that the Supreme Court grant an interlocutory injunction preventing Ireland's ratification of the Treaty establishing the European Stability Mechanism (ESM) pending the Court of Justice's ruling on EU law questions concerning the Treaty's validity.[72] In his judgment, O'Donnell J noted that some doubt had been expressed as to whether the test set out in these cases differed in substance from the established test for an injunction in Irish law found in *Campus Oil v Minister for Industry (No 2)*.[73] While conceding that there may be cases in which it would be necessary to address whether some higher threshold should be established before an injunction is granted restraining the implementation of an EU measure that is claimed to be invalid, O'Donnell J considered that the present application was capable of being resolved by reference to the balance of convenience.[74] Clarke J (as he then was) agreed that another case might usefully explore the extent to which there were differences between the two tests. He, however, saw it as at least arguable that, in requiring that a court must "entertain serious doubts", the *Atlanta* test needed the strength of a case to be established to a higher degree than *Campus Oil,* which requires only that it be established that there is a fair issue to be tried.[75]

[14–39] In applying the balance of convenience test, O'Donnell J noted that an affidavit submitted by the State swore to irreparable harm being caused to the national interest, and that of the EU, were Ireland not to be in a position to ratify the Treaty as soon as possible. Secondly, a key distinction with the case of *Crotty v An Taoiseach,* where an injunction had been granted restraining Ireland from ratifying the Single European Act, was that the issue there was one of Irish constitutional law, rather than EU law.[76] In contrast, for Ireland to proceed with ratification pending the conclusion of the present case would not put the ESM Treaty beyond effective challenge at the level of EU law. As a result, it could not be said that irreparable harm would be caused to the plaintiff if an injunction was not granted. Thirdly, O'Donnell J observed that, although the EU law points at issue were, in theory, applicable in every Member State, an injunction would only prevent ratification by Ireland and would not prevent the Treaty's entry into force. This, in his view, would

> produce the worst of all outcomes even if temporary: it would run the risk of causing the harm to the State's interests which they apprehend without benefiting the plaintiff's interest in any material way. If the plaintiff were ultimately to succeed, that would have the same impact across the Eurozone. Pending such a decision there is no compelling reason why Ireland should not be in the same position as its European partners.[77]

[14–40] Fourthly, in line with *Zuckerfabrick*, it was necessary to consider the interests of the EU. For O'Donnell J, the Irish law concept of the balance of convenience was sufficiently flexible to take such a consideration into account. In his assessment, it was

> apparent that the interests of the EU weigh heavily against the grant of an injunction at

---

72 [2013] 3 IR 1.

73 [1983] IR 88. According to this test, a court must decide whether it has been shown that there is a fair issue to be tried. If so, the court considers whether damages would be an adequate remedy. Where damages would not be an adequate remedy, the court must consider where the balance of convenience lies.

74 [2013] 3 IR 1, 118.

75 *ibid*, 171.

76 [1987] 1 IR 713. See ch 2, paras [2–14] to [2–28].

77 *ibid*, 121–122.

> this stage, since the only certain consequence of such an order is further uncertainty in an already volatile financial world. Furthermore it does not appear that any other citizen of the EU has commenced a challenge to the ESM on grounds of EU law. The citizenry of the EU have interests and rights which would be affected, perhaps severely, by the grant of an injunction. In circumstances where the plaintiff's case is not compelling, and where the outcome of any order is unpredictable, I consider that the interests of the EU lie against any temporary order under which the interests of the wider citizenry of the EU and the euro zone in particular might be affected, without the possibility of representation in the proceedings, or remedy should the proceedings ultimately fail.[78]

[14–41] Accordingly, the Supreme Court declined to grant an injunction and Ireland's instrument of ratification was deposited the following day.

(iii) State Liability for a Breach of EU Law

[14–42] The third and final autonomous EU action to be considered is the most well-known and significant of the three. This is the principle of state liability for breaches of EU law, or what are known as *Francovich* damages. In its landmark 1991 judgment in that case, the Court of Justice established that a Member State which had failed to properly implement a directive would be obliged to provide compensation for the loss suffered as a result if: (i) the directive conferred rights on individuals; (ii) the content of those rights could be identified from the directive's provisions; and (iii) there was a causal link between the state's failure and the damage suffered by the applicants.[79]

[14–43] The case involved the failure by Italy to implement a directive that sought to establish a system whereby unpaid wages owed to employees in the event of their employer becoming insolvent would be guaranteed. Infringement proceedings had already resulted in a finding that Italy had infringed its Treaty obligations by failing to transpose the directive on time. Subsequently, a number of affected employees brought proceedings before the Italian courts seeking to rely on the unimplemented directive through the doctrine of direct effect. Alternatively, they made the novel argument that, should reliance on direct effect not be possible, Italy should be liable to compensate the employees for the loss suffered by them as a result of the state's failure. In replying to a request for a preliminary ruling, the Court of Justice first concluded that the directive was insufficiently clear, precise and unconditional to have direct effect. It then turned to the question of whether Italy could be held liable for the losses sustained, noting that this was a question that needed to be considered in the light of the general system of the Treaties and its fundamental principles.

---

78 *ibid*, 122.

79 Joined Cases C-6/90 and C-9/90 *Francovich v Italy* [1991] ECR I-5357. See Michael Dougan, "Addressing Issues of Protective Scope within the *Francovich* Right to Reparation" (2017) 13 *European Constitutional Law Review* 124; Tobias Lock, "Is Private Enforcement of EU Law through State Liability a Myth? – An Assessment 20 Years after *Francovich*" (2012) 49 *Common Market Law Review* 1675; Björn Beutler, "State liability for breaches of Community law by national courts: Is the requirement of a manifest infringement of applicable law an insurmountable obstacle? (2009) 46 *Common Market Law Review* 773; Takis Tridimas, "Liability for Breach of Community Law: Growing Up and Mellowing Down?" (2001) 38 *Common Market Law Review* 301; Georgios Anagnostaras, "The Allocation of Responsibility in State Liability Actions for Breach of Community Law: A Modern Gordian Knot?" (2001) 26 *European Law Review* 139; Paul Craig, "Once More Unto the Breach: The Community, The State and Damages Liability" (1997) 113 *Law Quarterly Review* 67; Carol Harlow, "*Francovich* and the Problem of the Disobedient State" (1996) 2 *European Law Journal* 199.

[14–44] Recalling its judgments in *Van Gend en Loos* and *Costa v ENEL* on direct effect and supremacy, the Court emphasised that the subjects of the EU legal order included individuals as well as states, upon whom had been conferred rights that had become part of their legal patrimony. Secondly, as had been stated in *Simmenthal*, it was for national courts to ensure that, in applying the provisions of EU law, the rights conferred on individuals take full effect. The Court then turned to the principle of effectiveness or *effet utile* and considered whether this would go so far as to require a principle of state liability in the event that a Member State failed to fulfil its obligation to transpose a directive. According to the Court:

> The full effectiveness of [EU] rules would be impaired and the protection of the rights which they grant would be weakened if individuals were unable to obtain redress when their rights are infringed by a breach of [EU] law for which a Member State can be held responsible.
>
> The possibility of obtaining redress from the Member State is particularly indispensable where, as in this case, the full effectiveness of [EU] rules is subject to prior action on the part of the State and where, consequently, in the absence of such action, individuals cannot enforce before the national courts the rights conferred upon them by [EU] law.
>
> It follows that the principle whereby a State must be liable for loss and damage caused to individuals as a result of breaches of [EU] law for which the State can be held responsible is inherent in the system of the Treaty.
>
> A further basis for the obligation of Member States to make good such loss and damage is to be found in Article [4(3) TEU], under which the Member States are required to take all appropriate measures, whether general or particular, to ensure fulfilment of their obligations under [EU] law. Among these is the obligation to nullify the unlawful consequences of a breach of [EU] law.
>
> It follows from all the foregoing that it is a principle of [EU] law that the Member States are obliged to make good loss and damage caused to individuals by breaches of [EU] law for which they can be held responsible.[80]

[14–45] It is worth pausing here to note that, just as with the principles of direct effect and supremacy, the principle of state liability is not provided for in the Treaties. Rather, through the use of a teleological approach that gives paramount importance to ensuring the overall effectiveness of EU law, the principle of state liability is one that the Court of Justice derives from the general system of the Treaties and the fundamental principles of EU law. As described by the Court in *Francovich*, although state liability was not referred to in the Treaty of Rome, it was nevertheless "inherent in the system of the Treaty". For this reason, Stephen Weatherill has described the judgment as among the Court's most remarkable, in which the Court presides over the development of a type of EU "common law". As well as creating a remedy defined by criteria under EU law which must be absorbed into the national legal system of each Member State, the judgment "represents a statement of the Court of Justice's readiness to appeal to the 'system of the Treaty' as a basis for establishing a system of judicial remedies that will further the cause of effective protection of EU law rights".[81] This is all the more remarkable when one bears in mind that it was not until the following year, with the signing of the Maastricht Treaty in 1992, that provision was made to allow the Court

80 *ibid*, 5414–5415.

81 Stephen Weatherill, *Cases and Materials on EU Law* (10th ed, Oxford University Press, 2012) 143.

of Justice to impose a lump sum or penalty payment on a Member State for failing to implement a judgment of the Court which found an infringement of EU law.

[14–46] Having established that EU law requires a principle of state liability, the Court then turned to consider the conditions under which such liability will arise, observing that this would depend on the nature of the breach of EU law giving rise to the loss:

> Where, as in this case, a Member State fails to fulfil its obligation under [Article 288] to take all the measures necessary to achieve the result prescribed by a directive, the full effectiveness of that rule of [EU] law requires that there should be a right to reparation provided that three conditions are fulfilled.
>
> The first of those conditions is that the result prescribed by the directive should entail the grant of rights to individuals. The second condition is that it should be possible to identify the content of those rights on the basis of the provisions of the directive. Finally, the third condition is the existence of a causal link between the breach of the State's obligation and the loss and damage suffered by the injured parties.
>
> Those conditions are sufficient to give rise to a right on the part of individuals to obtain reparation, a right founded directly on [EU] law.[82]

[14–47] Each of these three conditions was fulfilled by the particular circumstances in *Francovich.* Of critical importance is the fact that not included amongst the three criteria is any requirement for the directive to be capable of having direct effect. As a result, the development of the principle of state liability can be regarded as one further means by which the Court of Justice has softened the distinction, in practice, between the vertical and horizontal effect of a directive.

[14–48] Finally, the Court sought to integrate this new principle with its general approach to national procedural autonomy. Whilst it had now been established that *EU law* required that compensation be made available in accordance with the principle of state liability, it was on the basis of the rules of *national law* on liability that Member States were obliged to make reparation for the consequences of the loss and damage caused. In the absence of harmonising legislation at the EU level, it was for each Member State to designate the competent courts and lay down the detailed procedural rules for legal proceedings intended fully to safeguard the rights which individuals derive from EU law – provided that they were in accordance with the principles of equivalence and effectiveness.

[14–49] In cases such as *Byrne v Ireland* and *Crowley v Ireland*, it had already been established as a matter of Irish law that the Irish State could be held liable in damages for the tortious act of one of its servants, or for the breach of a constitutional right.[83] Indeed, a few months prior to the judgment in *Francovich*, the High Court had held in *Emerald Meats v Minister for Agriculture* that the plaintiff was entitled to special damages to compensate for the loss of a meat import quota arising from the Minister's breach of a Commission regulation. On appeal, the Supreme Court declined to request a preliminary reference, noting that the principles established in *Francovich* in the interim "must be applied by the courts of every Member State and it is clear from them that Emerald is entitled to claim compensation from the State for the Department of

---

[82] Joined Cases C-6/90 and C-9/90 *Francovich v Italy* [1991] ECR I-5357, 5415.

[83] *Byrne v Ireland* [1972] 2 IR 241; *Crowley v Ireland* [1980] IR 102.

Agriculture's failure to carry out the obligation imposed on it by [the] Regulation".[84] Comparing the breach of the directly effective regulation to a breach of statutory duty, the Supreme Court found there to be no reason why the plaintiff should not be entitled to claim general damages, as well as special damages.

[14–50] The Irish courts were required to consider the precise nature of this novel remedy in *Tate v Minister for Social Welfare*.[85] There, a claim for damages was brought in respect of unpaid social welfare benefits arising from Ireland having implemented an equal treatment directive two years late (at the end of 1986 rather than by 23 December 1984). Before Carroll J in the High Court, it was argued on behalf of the plaintiffs that as there was, as yet, no national rules relating to damages for a breach by the State of its obligations under EU law, the State's failure to implement the directive ought to be regarded as a breach of the State's guarantee under Art 40.3 of the Constitution to "respect and as far as practicable by its laws to defend and vindicate the personal rights of the citizen" and, in the case of injustice done, to vindicate their property rights. It was contended that the right acquired by an individual at the end of the implementation period was either a personal right or a property right within the meaning of Art 40.3 and that, in addition, the Minister for Social Welfare owed a duty of care to transpose the directive before the end of the prescribed deadline. The Minister, in contrast, argued that the plaintiffs' rights derived from the directive itself, together with the EU Treaties as interpreted by the Court of Justice, and was not grounded in either constitutional rights or any duty of care. This was the view favoured by Carroll J. Commenting that "we are concerned here with a whole new legal order", she reasoned as follows:

> The Constitution was amended to enable accession to the Community, the European Communities Act 1972 was passed and the Treaty of Accession was agreed, and thereby the whole body of Community law, past, present and future was incorporated into domestic law. But community law did not thereby become constitutional law or statute law. It is still community law governed by community law but with domestic effect. And it is in that form that it is part of domestic law.
>
> … Therefore the rights of the plaintiffs in this case come from the Directive which had direct effect as from the 23 December 1984, because the State failed in its obligation to implement the Directive under Article 5 of the Treaty of Rome.
>
> In my opinion, the concept of the duty of care under the law of negligence is not applicable. The plaintiffs' claim does not arise as a breach of constitutional right. The plaintiffs' right to sue the State derives from the Directive itself once the date for implementation had passed and this right must be interpreted in accordance with Community law as enunciated by the European Court of Justice.

---

[84] *Emerald Meats Ltd v Minister for Agriculture (No 2)* [1997] 1 IR 1, 17.

[85] *Tate v Minister for Social Welfare* [1995] 1 IR 418; [1995] 1 ILRM 507. See also *X v Minister for Justice and Equality (No 2)* [2019] IEHC 226, 4 March 2019, Barrett J; *Glegola v Minister for Social Protection* [2019] 1 ILRM 225; *Ogieriakhi v Minister for Justice and Equality* [2017] 2 ILRM 340; *P v Chief Superintendent of the Garda National Immigration Bureau* [2015] IEHC 222, 15 April 2015 and 10 June 2015, O'Malley J; *Maxwell v Minister for Agriculture* [1999] 2 IR 474; *Coppinger v Waterford County Council* [1998] 4 IR 220; Anthony M Collins and James O'Reilly, *Civil Proceedings in the State* (2nd ed, Thomson RoundHall, 2004) 304–306 and annexes 10.8 and 10.9; Seán O'Reilly, "The Private Enforcement of European Community Law in the Irish Superior Courts" (2009) 31 *Dublin University Law Journal* 324, 350–355; Bríd Moriarty, "Direct Effect, Indirect Effect and State Liability: An Overview" (2007) 14 *Irish Journal of European Law* 97, 117–135.

> Therefore, as from the 23 December 1984, the plaintiffs were entitled to rely on the provisions of the Directive to preclude the application of any national provision inconsistent with … the Directive.
>
> That being so, what was the nature of the wrong committed by the State in failing to implement the Directive within the time limited? Here again the wrong belongs to the new order.
>
> In my opinion, the wrong committed by the State in continuing the discrimination by failing to fully implement the Directive is a wrong arising from Community law which has domestic effect. It is not a breach of constitutional rights; it is not a breach of statutory duty and it is not a breach of the duty of care. It is a breach of duty to implement the Directive and it approximates to a breach of constitutional duty. Every type of action which would be available in the national domestic law to ensure the observance of national law is available to ensure observance of the Directive once it took on the mantle of direct effect.[86]

[14–51] The State's liability arising from its failure to implement the directive has been estimated to have exceeded €325 million.[87]

[14–52] *Francovich* dealt with one particular type of breach of EU law – a Member State's failure to implement a directive – and the Court of Justice made clear that the *conditions* under which state liability may arise depends upon the nature of the breach involved in each case. Whereas the failure to transpose a directive relates to a particular obligation that it imposed on Member States alone, more generally the Court has indicated that the approach to liability for breaches of EU law should be the same for Member States as it is for the Union. These matters first received detailed treatment by the Court of Justice in the joined cases of *Brasserie du Pêcheur/Factortame*.[88]

[14–53] *Brasserie du Pêcheur* concerned German beer purity laws, which imposed strict conditions on the ingredients that could be used in an alcoholic beverage in order for it to be marketed as beer. A French exporter of beer claimed to have suffered losses as a result of the German law, which was subsequently found by the Court of Justice to be contrary to Art 34 TFEU on the free movement of goods. When the French company brought its claim before the German courts, it was considered that no claim for damages lay in German law. Accordingly, a preliminary reference was made asking whether the principle of state liability established in *Francovich* applied where the breach comprised a failure to adapt national laws to the higher-ranking rules of EU law. The second of the two joined cases followed on from an earlier Court of Justice ruling in *Factortame*. There, it was held that a nationality requirement that prevented the Spanish applicants from being entered onto the UK's shipping register was contrary to EU law. The UK court sought a ruling from the Court of Justice as to whether EU law required that there be an entitlement to compensation for loss suffered due to a state's infringement of the Treaties.

[14–54] Ireland was among those Member States to argue that the entitlement to *Francovich* damages only arose where the provisions breached were *not* directly effective, as had been the situation in that case. By introducing this remedy, it was argued, the Court of Justice had simply sought to fill a lacuna in the system for safeguarding

---

86 *ibid*, 437–438; 521–522.

87 TP Kennedy (ed), *European Law* (5th ed, Oxford University Press, 2011) 88.

88 Joined Cases C-46/93 and C-48/93, *Brasserie du Pêcheur/Factortame* [1996] ECR I-1029.

the rights of individuals. In contrast, in so far as national law afforded individuals a right of action enabling them to assert their rights under directly effective provisions of EU law, it was unnecessary, where such provisions were breached, to also grant them a right to reparation founded directly on EU law.

[14–55] The Court of Justice rejected this argument, observing that the right of individuals to rely on the directly effective provisions of the Treaty before national courts was only a *minimum guarantee* and was not sufficient in itself to ensure the full and complete implementation of the Treaty. Direct effect could not, in every case, secure for individuals the benefit of the rights conferred on them by EU law and, in particular, avoid their sustaining damage as a result of a breach of EU law attributable to a Member State. Indeed, compared to the failure to transpose a directive, it was even more so the case that the full effectiveness of EU law would be impaired if individuals were unable to obtain redress in respect of an infringement of a right directly conferred by EU law upon which individuals are entitled to rely before the national courts. In that event, the "right to reparation was the necessary corollary of the direct effect of the [EU] provision whose breach caused the damage sustained".[89] The principle of state liability applied, therefore, in any case in which a Member State breaches EU law, whatever be the organ of the state whose act or omission was responsible for the breach – even the legislature.[90] As was seen in Chapter 8, state liability for a breach of EU law can also arise due to a failure by the judiciary. A higher threshold applies to a judicial failing, however, with liability only being incurred in the exceptional case where a court of final instance has manifestly infringed the applicable EU law.[91]

[14–56] Having established that state liability can, in principle, arise from any breach of EU law by any state organ, the Court of Justice next turned its attention to explaining the conditions under which state liability will arise. It began by noting that its existing case law on the non-contractual liability of the Union under Art 340 TFEU is of particular relevance, given the close analogy between the two. Moreover, the conditions under which a *Member State* may incur liability for damage caused to individuals by a breach of EU law cannot, in the absence of particular justification, differ from those governing the liability of the *Union* in like circumstances. This is based on the principle that the protection of the rights which individuals derive from EU law cannot vary depending on whether it is a national authority or an EU authority that is responsible for the damage.[92]

[14–57] As will be seen further in Chapter 16, the non-contractual liability of the Union is governed by Art 340(2) TFEU. It provides that in the case of non-contractual liability, the Union shall, in accordance with the general principles common to the laws of the Member States, make good any damage caused by its institutions or by its servants in the performance of their duties. Well before the decision in *Francovich*, the Court had developed what became known as the *Schöppenstedt* formula which applied to damage caused by *legislative* action by the Union involving measures of economic policy.[93] The distinction drawn here was as between non-discretionary acts, such as administrative acts, and discretionary acts, such as legislative acts. In respect

[89] *ibid*, 1143.
[90] *ibid*, 1145.
[91] See ch 8, paras [8–53] to [8–54].
[92] *ibid*, 1147.
[93] Case 5/71, *Schöppenstedt v Council* [1971] ECR 975.

of administrative/non-discretionary acts, it was sufficient to demonstrate that the breach of an EU law that granted rights to individuals had resulted in real and certain loss. On the other hand, because discretionary acts, such as legislative acts, were regarded as involving complex policy choices, it was considered appropriate to apply a higher threshold of wrongfulness. This higher threshold was achieved in part by requiring that the breach be "sufficiently flagrant" or serious.

[14–58] In *Brasserie du Pêcheur/Factortame*, the Court of Justice recalled that the rules for establishing Union liability for a legislative act under Art 340 took account of the complexity of the situation to be regulated, difficulties in the interpretation of the texts and the margin of discretion available to the author of the act in question. This approach, the Court explained, was based on two considerations. First, the exercise of the legislative function ought not to be hindered by the prospect of actions for damages when the general interest of the Union required legislative measures to be adopted which may adversely affect individual interests. Secondly, where a legislative choice was required to be made by an EU institution in the Union's interest, involving a wide discretion, the Union ought not to incur liability unless the institution had "manifestly and gravely disregarded the limits on the exercise of its powers".[94]

[14–59] As the principles for incurring liability were to be the same for Union and Member State institutions, it followed that a Member State should enjoy the benefit of the same approach to liability where it was acting in a field in which it enjoyed a wide discretion – as was the case in respect of the decisions by the German and UK legislatures regarding beer purity laws and the registration of merchant shipping vessels respectively, given the absence of harmonising EU measures at the time. The three conditions to be applied in order for liability to be incurred were: (i) the rule of law infringed must be intended to confer rights on individuals; (ii) the breach must be *sufficiently serious*, in the sense that the institution concerned has "manifestly and gravely disregarded the limits on the exercise of its powers"; and (iii) there must be a direct causal link between the breach of the obligation resting on the Member State and the damage sustained by the injured parties.[95] The Court identified a list of factors that may be taken into account by a national court in deciding whether a breach is sufficiently serious as follows:

- the clarity and precision of the rule breached;
- the measure of discretion left by that rule to the national or Union authorities;
- whether the infringement and the damage caused was intentional or involuntary;
- whether any error of law was excusable or inexcusable;
- the fact that the position taken by the Union institutions may have contributed towards the omission;
- the adoption or retention of national measures or practices contrary to EU law;
- if the breach has persisted despite a judgment finding an infringement to have been established; and
- if a preliminary ruling or settled case law of the Court of Justice makes clear that the conduct amounted to an infringement.

[14–60] As regards Germany's decision to maintain its beer purity laws, the Court indicated that it would be difficult to regard the breach of Art 34 TFEU as an excusable

[94] Joined Cases C-46/93 and C-48/93, *Brasserie du Pêcheur/Factortame* [1996] ECR I-1029, 1147–1148.

[95] *ibid*, 1149.

error, given that the incompatibility of those laws with Art 34 was manifest in light of the Court's earlier case law. Aspects of the UK's Merchant Shipping Act were less clear-cut, and here the Court of Justice suggested that regard be had to the legal disputes relating to particular features of the common fisheries policy, the attitude of the Commission, which had made its position known to the UK in good time, and the assessments as to the state of certainty of EU law made by the national courts in the interim proceedings in which injunctions were sought by individuals affected by the Merchant Shipping Act. The House of Lords ultimately decided that the breach was sufficiently serious (with a settlement of £55 million eventually being reached).[96]

[14–61] Another instance of a breach of the Treaties leading to state liability is *Hedley Lomas (Ireland) Ltd.*[97] There, the UK was found to have breached Art 35 TFEU, which prohibits any quantitative restriction on exports unless permitted under one of the grounds provided for in Art 36 TFEU. The UK banned the export of live sheep to Spain on the ground that Spain was not obliging its slaughterhouses to comply with relevant EU directives. The Commission had raised the matter with Spain and had decided not to initiate infringement proceedings. Importantly, the Court of Justice noted that the UK was not in a position to produce any proof of non-compliance with the directive by the slaughterhouse to which the animals for which the export licence was sought were destined. The Court concluded that where, as in this case, at the time when it committed the infringement, a Member State was not called upon to make any legislative choices and had only considerably reduced or even no discretion, the mere infringement of EU law may be sufficient to establish the existence of a sufficiently serious breach.[98]

[14–62] Examples of where a Member State has escaped liability for the *incorrect* transposition of a directive include *British Telecom.*[99] There, a directive on public procurement had intended to allow certain economic operators, such as British Telecom, to make their own decision as to which contracts within its sector would require a public tendering process. When transposing the directive, the UK incorrectly designated the types of contracts within the implementing legislation itself, thereby depriving British Telecom of the choice it was meant to have and causing it to suffer a loss. Although the assessment of whether a breach is sufficiently serious is usually a matter for the national court to determine, in this case the Court of Justice deemed there to be enough information before it for it to make its own determination as follows:

> [the provision of the Directive] is imprecisely worded and was reasonably capable of bearing, as well as the construction applied to it by the Court in this judgment, the interpretation given to it by the United Kingdom in good faith and on the basis of arguments which are not entirely devoid of substance. That interpretation, which was also shared by other Member States, was not manifestly contrary to the wording of the directive or to the objective pursued by it.
>
> Moreover, no guidance was available to the United Kingdom from case-law of the Court as to the interpretation of the provision at issue, nor did the Commission raise the matter when the [UK] Regulations were adopted.

---

96 Stephen Weatherill, *Cases and Materials on EU Law* (10th ed, Oxford University Press, 2012) 154.

97 Case 5/94 *R v Ministry of Agriculture, Fisheries and Food, ex parte Hedley Lomas (Ireland) Ltd* [1996] ECR I-2553.

98 *ibid*, 2613.

99 Case C-392/93 *British Telecom* [1996] ECR I-1631.

> In those circumstances, the fact that a Member State, when transposing the directive into national law, thought it necessary itself to determine which services were to be excluded from its scope in implementation of [the relevant provision], albeit in breach of that provision, cannot be regarded as a sufficiently serious breach of [EU] law of the kind intended by the Court in its judgment in *Brasserie du Pêcheur* and *Factortame.*[100]

[14–63] Whether a Member State's incorrect transposition of a directive is a sufficiently serious breach so as to give rise to liability is one of the most difficult aspects of the doctrine to apply in practice. In principle, a Member State has no discretion, as such, in whether or not it implements a directive. In certain cases, therefore, the Court has indicated that the non-implementaton of a directive in order to achieve the result it prescribes is, of itself, a sufficiently serious breach to give rise to liability.[101] As against this, it has been suggested:

> The principal reason for limiting liability under *Francovich* is not because Member States' "discretion" in implementing Union law must not be unfettered, but because the rules of Union law are often not clear. To hold them liable in damages for "mere infringements" of such rules, thereby introducing a principle akin to strict liability, would not only be politically dangerous, it would be contrary to the principle of legal certainty, itself a respected principle of Union law.[102]

[14–64] The relationship between the breadth of discretion afforded to Member States in implementing a directive, and the precision and clarity of the provisions of the directive, is seen in the cases of *Robins v Secretary of State for Work and Pensions*[103] and *Glegola v Minister for Social Protection.*[104] Like *Francovich,* both of these cases concerned EU directives on the protection of employees in the event of insolvency. In *Robins*, the UK courts made a preliminary reference inquiring as to the extent to which a provision of a directive that obliged Member States to protect certain pension benefits in the event of insolvency, required those benefits to be fully guaranteed. If the manner in which the UK had transposed the directive was held to be incorrect, it was further asked whether this failing was a sufficiently serious breach as to give rise to liability. The Court noted that, unlike the provisions of the same directive that were in issue in *Francovich*, the relevant provision of the directive at issue here did not contain elements which would make it possible to establish with any precision the minimum level required in order to "protect" pension benefits within the meaning of the directive. It was found, however, that a protection level of less than 50 per cent, as provided for in the UK's implementing measures, was less than the directive had intended. Turning, then, to the question of state liability, the Court did not answer the question directly but did provide the following guidance to the national court:

> The discretion enjoyed by the Member State … constitutes an important criterion in determining whether there has been a sufficiently serious breach of [EU] law.
>
> That discretion is broadly dependent on the degree of clarity and precision of the rule infringed. … [O]n account of the general nature of the wording of [the provision] of the

---

[100] *ibid*, 1669.

[101] Joined Cases C-178/94, C-188/94, C-189/94 and C-190/94 *Dillenkofer* [1996] ECR I-4845.

[102] Lorna Woods and Philippa Watson, *Steiner and Woods EU Law* (12th ed, Oxford University Press, 2014) 215.

[103] Case C-278/05 *Robins v Secretary of State for Work and Pensions* [2007] ECR I-1053.

[104] [2019] 1 ILRM 225.

> Directive, that provision allows the Member States considerable discretion for the purposes of determining the level of protection of entitlement to benefits.
>
> Accordingly, the liability of a Member State by reason of incorrect transposition of that provision is conditional on a finding of manifest and serious disregard by that State for the limits set on its discretion.
>
> In order to determine whether that condition is satisfied, the national court hearing a claim for reparation must take account of all the factors which characterise the situation put before it.
>
> Those factors include, in particular, in addition to the clarity and precision of the rule infringed and the measure of discretion left by that rule to the national authorities, whether the infringement or the damage caused was intentional or involuntary, whether any error of law was excusable or inexcusable, and the fact that the position taken by a [Union] institution may have contributed towards the adoption or maintenance of national measures or practices contrary to [EU] law. In the present case the national court will have to take into account the clarity and precision of [the provision] of the Directive with regard to the level of protection required.
>
> In that respect, it is to be emphasised that the parties in the main proceedings, the Member States which have submitted observations and the Commission have none of them been able to suggest with precision the minimum degree of protection that in their view is required by the Directive, if it should be considered that the latter does not impose a full guarantee.
>
> Furthermore, ... neither [the relevant provision] of the Directive nor any other provision therein contains anything that makes it possible to establish with any precision the minimum level required in order to protect entitlement to benefits.
>
> The national court may also take into consideration Commission report ... of 15 June 1995, concerning the transposition of the Directive by the Member States, ... in which the Commission had then concluded: "The abovementioned rules [adopted by the United Kingdom] appear to meet the requirements of Article 8 [of the Directive]". ... [T]hat wording may, although careful, have reinforced the view of the Member State concerned with regard to the transposition of the Directive into domestic law.
>
> The answer ... must therefore be that, if [the provision] of the Directive has not been properly transposed into domestic law, the liability of the Member State concerned is contingent on a finding of manifest and grave disregard by that State for the limits set on its discretion.[105]

[14–65] In *Glegola*, the provision at issue concerned the definition of an employer's state of insolvency and, in particular, whether or not the directive was intended to apply to a situation of informal insolvency (ie. where a determination is made that a company has ceased trading and is insolvent, but no winding up order is made, or liquidator appointed, due to a lack of assets). As the transposing Irish legislation had not provided for access to the Social Insurance Fund in such a situation, Ms Glegola claimed to have suffered a financial loss. In delivering the judgment of the Supreme Court, O'Donnell J cautioned that:

> It is necessary to be alive to the fact that the meaning of particular provisions of a Regulation or Directive may be unclear and open to a spectrum of possible reasonable interpretations. In this case, it is said that the approach taken by Ireland, even if incorrect,

[105] Case C-278/05 *Robins v Secretary of State for Work and Pensions* [2007] ECR I-1053, 1102–1104.

> was a reasonable one, since the United Kingdom had not made a separate provision for informal insolvencies at least until relatively recently, and the European institutions, and in particular the Commission, had not expressed any criticism or disapproval of the manner in which the 2008 Directive had been implemented in the law of both Ireland and the United Kingdom.[106]

[14–66] In support of her argument, the Minister placed reliance on the fact that a number of academic writings did not consider a procedure for informal insolvency to be required by the directive, nor had a Commission report on Ireland's implementation of the directive raised any issue with the absence of such a procedure. Nevertheless, the Supreme Court came to the view that, on close analysis, it was not possible to advance any reasonable interpretation of the relevant provision other than that it required that the protection under the directive to extend to informal insolvencies. As explained by O'Donnell J:

> It does not appear to me that there is a scope for any interpretative discretion in that regard. Further, it is obvious that the 2008 Directive is intended to secure important benefits for citizens. In this case, I do not think it is appropriate or permissible to treat the limited implementation of the 2008 Directive as excusable or understandable because of the absence of complaint by the Commission and the views expressed in certain academic articles, referred to above. That, in my view, would be to apply too low a standard. The Commission's 2011 report … does not address the question of informal insolvencies in Ireland at all. Accordingly, the weight to be attached to it is limited, given that what is relied on is the absence of any observation on the Irish position with regard to informal insolvencies, rather than a positive endorsement of it. It is also the case that the length of time during which Irish law, and it appears the law in the United Kingdom, remained unchanged is not compelling, in circumstances where the [Minister has] not shown before this court that the issue arose or the law was in fact tested and found capable of surviving judicial scrutiny either here or in the United Kingdom.[107]

[14–67] The complexity of applying the *Brasserie du Pêcheur* test in practice is keenly illustrated by the series of judgments in *Ogieriakhi v Minister for Justice and Equality*. This case concerned not the manner of transposition *per se*, but rather the way in which the Irish authorities interpreted a provision of the Citizens Directive dealing with the right to permanent residence, and the implementing measures based on that provision. It was held by the High Court that the Minister's incorrect interpretation of the relevant provision was a serious breach of EU law such as to give rise to damages.[108] Given that Mr Ogieriakhi was let go from his employment as a result of the residence decision, the High Court awarded damages for the loss he incurred. As an interesting aside, in dealing with the substantive issue the High Court made a reference to the Court of Justice, as part of which it asked whether, if there was held to be an infringement of EU law, the fact that a national court had found it necessary to seek a preliminary ruling on the question ought to be regarded as a decisive factor in determining whether there had been an obvious infringement by the Member State. The Court replied that it ought not to be regarded as a relevant factor, as to do so would compromise the purpose and characteristics of the preliminary reference procedure. This was due to the Court's fear that the discretion of national courts to make a reference if they consider it necessary to obtain an interpretation of EU law, "would undoubtedly be limited if the exercise

---

106 [2019] 1 ILRM 225, 241.

107 *ibid*, 246.

108 *Ogieriakhi v Minister for Justice and Equality* [2015] 1 ILRM 344.

of that discretion were a decisive factor in determining whether or not there had been an obvious infringement of EU law" for the purposes of assessing state liability.[109]

[14–68] On appeal, the Court of Appeal held that the State's "inadvertent error" in interpreting the Citizens Directive was not such as to give rise to a *Brasserie du Pêcheur/Factortame* claim given the lack of clarity and precision in the relevant provision.[110] The Court of Appeal had regard to the fact that: (i) prior to a judgment from the Court of Justice clarifying the proper interpretation of the Directive, there had been substantial uncertainty about the issue; (ii) the judgment of the Court of Justice had demonstrated the complexity of the matter; (iii) it was relevant that Ireland was not alone in its interpretation; and (iv) the Commission had not commented adversely on the manner of Ireland's implementation. In the circumstances, the Court of Appeal found that, since the Minister's interpretation of the relevant provision was not "bizarre or eccentric", it was:

> difficult to understand how there could be a finding that the State manifestly and gravely disregarded the limits on its discretion when all the relevant personnel were working honestly to implement the Directive ... The most that can be said, and the worst that can be said, is that the State made a mistake. And insofar as it did so, it was not alone ...
>
> ... in the case of an honest mistake or an honestly differing interpretation that is not actuated by any wrongful motive, it would be absurd to declare that the State on the "losing" side manifestly and gravely disregarded the limits of its discretion.[111]

[14–69] While the decision of the Court of Appeal was upheld by the Supreme Court, it disagreed with parts of its reasoning. According to the Supreme Court (O'Malley J), under the *Brasserie du Pêcheur/Factortame* criteria:

> it is not sufficient for an aggrieved person to establish as a fact that the State misunderstood or misapplied a provision of EU law and that he or she suffered loss as a result. On the other hand, it does not suffice for a successful defence to a claim of this nature that officials acted honestly on foot of a misapprehension that was not "bizarre or eccentric". Having regard to para.2 of the conclusions in *Brasserie du Pêcheur* those considerations cannot be all that is required to establish excusability, and in my view the decision of the Court of Appeal lays too great an emphasis on them. Good faith is certainly relevant to the extent that a finding of improper motivation would probably be decisive as against the State ... However, good faith and honest misapprehension cannot be sufficient to excuse the State from liability in an appropriate case. Similarly, a mistake as to the true meaning of a legal measure might be shared with the authorities of one or more other Member States, and yet, objectively, be clearly wrong.
>
> ... In my view both of [the matters of incorrect interpretation] gave rise to complex considerations that were not expressly covered by the terms of the Directive. While the rulings of the Court of Justice in *Lassal* and in this case are clearly determinative of the issues it cannot, in my opinion, be said that the answers to the questions were obvious, or that the Directive was so clear and precise as to render the error on the part of the State authorities "grave and manifest" or "inexcusable". It is relevant to note that the Commission, in its correspondence and its communication to the Parliament, appears to

[109] *Ogieriakhi v Minister for Justice and Equality* ECLI:EU:C:2014:2068, 10 July 2014, paras 54–55.
[110] *Ogieriakhi v Minister for Justice and Equality* [2016] 1 ILRM 504.
[111] *ibid*, 518–519.

have taken the position at least at some stage that, if the facts of the case were as they ultimately turned out to be, the appellant did not have a valid claim.[112]

[14–70] One further instance of the doctrine of state liability being applied by the Irish courts is the judgment of the High Court in *BUPA Ireland Ltd v Health Insurance*.[113] This followed on from a finding that a Risk Equalisation Scheme introduced by the Minister for Health to govern the health insurance market was *ultra vires* her powers under the relevant legislation. The Supreme Court remitted the matter to the High Court for an assessment of damages where, *inter alia*, *Francovich* damages were sought on the basis that the scheme had infringed an applicable directive. In setting out the criteria for an award of damages, Cooke J paid particular attention to the need for an alleged breach of EU law to be sufficiently serious. Cooke J described the purpose of this condition as being to:

> draw a distinction between loss or damage which flows from the mere exercise of policy choices on the part of Union institutions or state authorities and loss or damage resulting from a manifest and grave disregard by the institution or authority on the limits of exercise of its powers. One of the factors to be taken into account in determining whether there has been such a manifest and grave disregard of the limits on the exercise of an institution's powers is whether the institution was acting in circumstances where it had a wide degree of discretion, as opposed to a very reduced or even no discretion. A further element which is of relevance in assessing this aspect of the condition is whether the irregularity identified in the act or conduct of the institution or state authority is one which, in comparable circumstances, would not have been committed by a normally prudent and diligent administration. Such a finding may lead to the conclusion that the conduct concerned was of sufficiently serious illegality to give rise to liability. It is relevant, also, to take into account the complexity of the situation with which the institution or authority was dealing, and any difficulties in the application or interpretation of legislation.[114]

[14–71] Applying this approach to the facts of the case, Cooke J held that, having regard to the nature and complexity of the subject matter involved, it could not reasonably be said that in adopting the scheme the Minister was culpable of a manifest and grave disregard of the margin of appreciation available to the State under the directive. The history of this legislative process demonstrated that the decision to initiate the scheme was "not reached in a manner which could be characterised as in any sense careless, arbitrary or lacking in preparation or planning".[115] Rather, the Minister had consulted extensively with experts, commissioned reports and published a white paper, all of which "clearly contradict any suggestion that careful consideration was not given to the exercise of the powers available to the Minister".[116] Secondly, in addition to these expert reports, the expert evidence, legal submissions and detailed judgments in both the High Court and Supreme Court made clear that the matter at hand was of "very considerable complexity, from the point of view of the technicalities of insurance underwriting, the equilibrium of the private health insurance market and the interpretation of both the Directive and national law".[117] Thirdly, the fact that the draft scheme had been notified to the European Commission under state aid rules and that the Minister had the benefit of the analysis and approval of the Commission, "must

---

112 *Ogieriakhi v Minister for Justice and Equality* [2017] 2 ILRM 340, 365–366.
113 [2014] 2 IR 67.
114 *ibid*, 113.
115 *ibid*, 116.
116 *ibid*.
117 *ibid*, 117.

weigh heavily in negating any possible finding that there has been a manifest and grave disregard on her part".[118] Accordingly, Cooke J concluded that the introduction of the Scheme could not be described as "action or conduct which a normally prudent and diligent administration would not have undertaken".[119]

[118] *ibid.*
[119] *ibid.*

PART FOUR

CHAPTER 15

ENFORCEMENT ACTIONS AGAINST MEMBER STATES

A. INTRODUCTION

[15–01] As it is the role of the Commission to act as the "guardian of the Treaties", it makes sense that it should be given a particular function in ensuring the enforcement of EU law against any Member State that is in default of its obligations. Reflecting the status of the TEU and TFEU as multilateral treaties under international law, it is also to be expected that where one Member State considers that another is in breach of EU law, it should have a legal mechanism available to it through which it can seek to reinstate reciprocal adherence to mutual legal obligations. Such enforcement mechanisms are provided for in Arts 258 and 259 TFEU, while Art 260 allows for the Court of Justice to impose a lump sum or penalty payment on a Member State should it fail to comply with a judgment of the Court issued on foot of enforcement proceedings.

[15–02] Under Art 258 TFEU, if the Commission considers that a Member State has failed to fulfil an obligation under the Treaties, it shall deliver a reasoned opinion on the matter after giving the Member State the opportunity to submit its observations. If the Member State does not comply with the opinion within the period laid down by the Commission, the Commission may bring the matter before the Court of Justice. Such proceedings are known as "infringement proceedings" and are a form of direct action.[1]

[15–03] Article 259 TFEU provides that a Member State which considers that another Member State has failed to fulfil its obligations under the Treaties may bring the matter before the Court of Justice, provided that it first brings the matter to the attention of the Commission. After each state has been given the opportunity to submit observations, the Commission shall deliver a reasoned opinion. If, however, the Commission fails

1 See Luca Prete and Ben Smulders, "The Coming of Age of Infringement Proceedings" (2009) 47 *Common Market Law Review* 9.

to deliver a reasoned opinion within three months, the matter may be brought before the Court of Justice by the Member State.

[15–04] By way of derogation from the general rule in Arts 258 and 259, separate provision is made for more direct recourse to the Court by the Commission or a Member State in cases involving state aid[2] or the misuse by a Member State of its power to derogate from Internal Market harmonisation measures.[3] For example, the Commission may directly bring an action before the Court where it is claimed that a Member State has failed to comply with a Commission decision in relation to state aid within the prescribed timeframe, as occurred in respect of Ireland's compliance with the Commission's decision that it recover tax payments of €13 billion from Apple by January 2017.[4]

[15–05] Infringement proceedings by one Member State against another pursuant to Art 259 are exceedingly rare, with only eight having been brought to date. Interestingly, the first such case was initiated by Ireland against France in 1977, the only occasion on which Ireland has sought to use procedure. This concerned a French restriction on imports of lamb, although the matter did not proceed to judgment and was superseded by separate proceedings brought by the Commission.[5] Judgments have been given in inter-state cases involving sea fisheries (*France v UK*),[6] the naming of wines according to their place of production (*Belgium v Spain*),[7] the extension of European Parliament voting rights to Gibraltar (*Spain v UK*)[8] and a refusal by Slovakia to allow the Hungarian president to enter the country in order to attend an event.[9] Following a decision by the Commission to terminate its own infringement proceedings, in 2017 Austria successfully brought an action against Germany in respect of the imposition of motorway charges for which the owners of German registered vehicles could claim a tax relief.[10] In 2018, an action was brought by Slovenia alleging that Croatia's failure to implement the decision of an arbitral tribunal on a boundary dispute between the two countries infringes EU law.[11] Given the infrequency with which Art 259 is used, this chapter will focus on enforcement actions brought by the Commission under Art 258.

[15–06] Each year, the Commission publishes an annual report on Monitoring the

---

2 Art 108(2) TFEU: "If, after giving notice to the parties concerned to submit their comments, the Commission finds that aid granted by a State or through State resources is not compatible with the internal market having regard to Article 107, or that such aid is being misused, it shall decide that the State concerned shall abolish or alter such aid within a period of time to be determined by the Commission. If the State concerned does not comply with this decision within the prescribed time, the Commission or any other interested State may, in derogation from the provisions in Articles 258 and 259, refer the matter to the Court of Justice of the European Union direct."

3 Art 114(9): "By way of derogation from the procedure laid down in Articles 258 and 259, the Commission and any Member State may bring the matter directly before the Court of Justice of the European Union if it considers that another Member State is making improper use of the powers provided for in this Article." See ch 17, paras [17–53] to [17–58].

4 Case C-678/17 *Commission v Ireland* (ongoing) [2018] OJ C22/31.

5 Case 58/77 *Ireland v France* [1977] OJ C142/8 (application); [1978] OJ C76/8 (removal from register). See Case 232/78 *Commission v France* [1979] ECR 2729.

6 Case 141/78 *France v UK* [1979] ECR 2923.

7 Case C-388/95 *Belgium v Spain* [2000] ECR I-3123.

8 Case C-145/04 *Spain v UK* [2006] ECR I-7917.

9 Case C-364/10 *Hungary v Slovakia* EU:C:2012:630, 16 October 2012.

10 Case C-591/17 *Austria v Germany* EU:C:2019:504, 18 June 2019.

11 Case C-457/18 *Slovenia v Croatia* (ongoing) [2018] OJ C399/19.

Application of EU Law, providing detailed information on the enforcement proceedings undertaken.[12] Twenty-nine new infringement procedures were opened against Ireland in 2017, which was just above the EU average of 26.[13] As will be seen below, a large majority of infringement procedures are resolved before the Commission takes the final step of litigating the matter before the Court of Justice. In terms of the total number of outstanding procedures at the end of 2017, Ireland fares slightly better with 56, which is exactly the EU average.[14] Half of these outstanding procedures relate to Ireland's alleged late transposition of directives. To provide some context, the figure of 56 outstanding procedures is a six-year high for Ireland, with just 35 having been outstanding at the end of 2015. Up to the end of 2018, in respect of the first 12 Member States, the number of infringement proceedings that ended up being brought before the Court of Justice was as follows:[15]

Italy	652	Germany	293	Portugal	203
France	419	Luxembourg	273	Netherlands	148
Greece	411	Spain	255	UK	143
Belgium	388	Ireland	211	Denmark	41

B. Failure to Fulfil an Obligation

[15–07] Although Art 258 TFEU refers to a failure by a Member State "to fulfil an obligation under the Treaties", infringement proceedings may be brought not just in respect of breaches of a Treaty provision, but any rule of EU law, whether that is to be found in secondary EU law, general principles of EU law or an international agreement. In very general terms it might be said that, the longer the EU legal order has been established and the longer a Member State has been in the EU, the more likely it is that any necessary amendments will have been made to national laws so as to ensure full respect for core Treaty obligations. For example, the early years of Ireland's membership saw a number of infringement proceedings concerning infringement of Treaty provisions that would seem unlikely to arise in more recent times, some of which are discussed below. As against this, the interpretation of certain provisions of the Treaties have continued to evolve and, where they cover complex factual situations, may lead to states being found in error. For example, in 2017 Ireland was held to have infringed Art 56 TFEU on the freedom to provide services.[16] This arose out of the Irish system of vehicle registration tax, which required that the full amount due be paid upon permanent registration. The failure to take account of the limited duration for which vehicles rented or leased from a company established in another Member State would be used in Ireland was held to infringe Ireland's obligations under Art 56. Contemporary infringement proceedings more typically arise as a result of a failure

[12] 2017 Annual Report on Monitoring the Application of EU Law, COM(2018) 540 final, 12 July 2018.

[13] Commission Staff Working Document, General Statistical Overview 2017, Part 1, SWD(2018) 377, 12 July 2018, 10.

[14] *ibid*, 12.

[15] *Court of Justice of the European Union Annual Report 2018, Judicial Activity 2019*, 147.

[16] Case C-552/15 *Commission v Ireland (Vehicle Registration Tax)* EU:C:2017:698, 19 September 2017.

to properly implement, apply or enforce secondary EU law. As a 2017 Commission Communication on the matter describes:

> Effective enforcement of EU rules – from the fundamental freedoms, food and product safety to air quality to the protection of the single currency – matters to Europeans and affects their daily lives. It serves the general interest. Often, when issues come to the fore – car emission testing, water pollution, illegal landfills, transport safety and security – it is not the lack of EU legislation that is the problem but rather the fact that the EU law is not applied effectively. That is why a robust, efficient and effective enforcement system is needed to ensure that Member States fully apply, implement and enforce EU law and provide adequate redress for citizens.[17]

[15–08] Arising from the duty of sincere cooperation enshrined in Art 4(3) TEU, Member States are to take "any appropriate measure, general or particular, to ensure fulfilment of the obligations arising out of the Treaties or resulting from the acts of the institutions of the Union". So, for example, a large proportion of infringement proceedings relate to the failure of a Member States to notify of its implementation of a directive within the deadline set down for transposition. Indeed, of the 1,559 infringement procedures that remained open at the end of 2017, 808 concerned the late transposition of a directive.[18]

(i) Breach of a Treaty Obligation

[15–09] Examples of a failure to abide by a Treaty obligation can be seen from five cases brought by the Commission against Ireland during the early years of its membership. In order to protect the local potato crop, Ireland maintained a licensing regime where potatoes from non-EU Member States could only be imported on foot of a licence. Crucially, however, the requirement to have a licence applied even where potatoes had been imported into another Member State and so were already in free circulation within the EU. The Commission argued that the licencing regime was contrary to the prohibition on restrictions on imports from Member States, now found in Art 34 TFEU. Among the defences put forward by Ireland was that the importation of potatoes would have such disastrous consequences for the disposal of the Irish potato crop that protection of the domestic market became a matter of public policy which, it was claimed, permitted a derogation from the prohibition on restrictions. The Court adhered to its earlier case law to the effect that the public policy ground could not be relied upon by a Member State to protect its economic interests, and found that Ireland had failed to fulfil its express Treaty obligation.[19]

[15–10] In another case, Ireland was found to have breached the prohibition on discrimination in the application of internal taxes as between imports and domestic goods, now found in Art 110 TFEU. While the same rate of taxation applied, the process for payment was more lenient for domestic producers, who were afforded a period of time in which to pay, than for importers, who were required to pay at the time of importation.[20]

---

[17] Commission Communication, "EU Law: Better Results through Better Application" (2017/C 18/02) [2017] OJ C18/10.

[18] Commission Staff Working Document, General Statistical Overview 2017, Part 1, SWD(2018) 377, 12 July 2018, 12, 15.

[19] Case 283/83 *Commission v Ireland* [1985] ECR 1761.

[20] Case 55/79 *Commission v Ireland* [1980] ECR 481.

[15–11] A third case involved a requirement that imported souvenir products containing any motif suggesting that they were from Ireland bear a clear indication that they had, in fact, been made elsewhere. Ireland sought to argue that purchasers would be misled if a souvenir bought in Ireland was actually manufactured somewhere else. Given this difference in the nature of the products, it was claimed that the Irish measure was not discriminatory. The Court, however, considered that the essential characteristic of the souvenirs was that they constituted a pictorial reminder of the place visited, which did not by itself mean that they must be manufactured in the country of sale. In addition, manufacturers of Irish goods were free to indicate that their products had been made in Ireland. As a result, by maintaining the relevant statutory instrument, Ireland was found to have breached its Art 34 TFEU obligation.[21] Another breach of this article arose due to the Government's support for a "Buy Irish" campaign that promoted the purchase of Irish goods over imports.[22] Finally, a further breach of Art 34 was found to arise as a result of a tender contract advertised by Dundalk Urban District Council for the laying of a water supply system which specified that a pipe of certain certification must be used. It so happened that the only manufacturer of that particular pipe was located in Ireland, albeit that other pipes manufactured in other Member States would be of the same quality. In proceedings brought by the Commission it was held that by allowing the inclusion of the clause Ireland had breached its obligation under the Treaty to prohibit restrictions on imports.[23]

[15–12] A different and more recent instance of Ireland being found to have infringed a Treaty obligation occurred on foot of arbitral proceedings instituted by Ireland against the UK concerning environmental obligations arising out of the operation of the MOX plant which forms part of the Sellafield nuclear facility. The arbitral proceedings were brought pursuant to the UN Convention on the Law of the Sea. By doing so, in circumstances where aspects of the proceedings were held to concern EU law, Ireland was found to have breached what is now Art 344 TFEU, according to which Member States are not to submit a dispute concerning the interpretation or application of the Treaties to any method of settlement other than those provided for in the EU Treaties.[24]

(ii) Failure to Implement EU Law in National Law

[15–13] A very significant proportion of infringement proceedings arise due to the failure of a Member State to notify the Commission that it has transposed a directive into its national law within the time period set down by the directive. In such circumstances, an infringement will be found even if, in practice, national law is applied as if the directive had been transposed. This occurred in Ireland, for example, in relation to a directive governing the breeding of cattle. The Court rejected Ireland's defence that,

---

21 Case C-113/80 *Commission v Ireland* [1981] ECR 1625.

22 Case 249/81 *Commission v Ireland (Buy Irish)* [1982] ECR 4005.

23 Case 45/87 *Commission v Ireland (Dundalk Water)* [1988] ECR 4929.

24 Case C-459/03 *Commission v Ireland* (*Mox Plant*) [2006] ECR I-4635. See Paul Sreenan, "The State in International Litigation – The Capacity to Sue other Member States of the EU before International Tribunals – The Mox Litigation" in Blathna Ruane, David Barniville and James O'Callaghan (eds), *Law and Government: A Tribute to Rory Brady* (Thomson Reuters, 2014) 89; Patrick T Eicher, "International Forum Shopping: The MOX Plant Case and the ECJ" (2008) 30 *Dublin University Law Journal* 367; Robin Churchill and Joanne Scott, "The Mox Plant Litigation: The First Half-Life" (2004) 53 *International and Comparative Law Quarterly* 643; Case C-284/16 *Slovakia v Achmea* EU:C:2018:158, 6 March 2018.

pending the adoption of the necessary legislation, the rules laid down by the directive were observed in practice, noting that "mere administrative practices, which by their nature are alterable at will by the authorities and are not given the appropriate publicity, cannot be regarded as constituting the proper fulfilment" of the obligation to transpose a directive by the prescribed deadline.[25]

[15–14] A breach might also arise where a Member State, either deliberately or inadvertently, has transposed a directive in an inadequate or incorrect manner. In this case, it is the lack of proper adherence to EU law that itself constitutes the infringement, rather than there having to be some form of harm caused as a result. So, for example, in a case against Ireland for failing to properly implement a directive on environmental impact assessments, it was claimed that Ireland had provided for an overly generous threshold that would serve to exempt certain developments from the requirement of an impact assessment, when they ought properly to have been subject to the requirement. In response, Ireland pointed to the fact that, in practice, the threshold had not been relied upon in respect of any development and so no infringement had occurred. This was rejected by the Court of Justice, which observed that:

> the alleged infringement has to do with the way in which the Directive has been transposed into Irish law and not with the actual result of the application of the transposing legislation.
>
> In order to prove that the transposition of a directive is insufficient or inadequate, it is not necessary to establish the actual effects of the legislation transposing it into national law: it is the wording of the legislation itself which harbours the insufficiencies or defects of transposition.
>
> There is, therefore, nothing to prevent the Commission from demonstrating that transposition is defective or insufficient without waiting for the application of the transposing legislation to produce harmful effects.[26]

[15–15] In addition to the late or improper transposition of directives, the inadequate implementation of EU law might also arise due to the fact that national law has not been sufficiently amended or revoked so as to bring it into line with EU law. For instance, an infringement was upheld against France in circumstances where, although the relevant authorities had been instructed to treat EU nationals as French nationals, a law nevertheless remained on the books that required a certain percentage of ship crews to be of French nationality. The failure to amend national law had resulted in an ambiguous state of affairs by creating uncertainty as to the possibilities available to EU crew members of relying on EU law.[27]

[15–16] Finally, it is worth highlighting that the obligation to implement EU law can also extend to international agreements which form part of EU law. An example of an infringement arising from a breach of an international agreement arose in a case brought against Ireland for its failure to become a party to the Berne Convention for the Protection of Artistic and Literary Works. A commitment to become a party to the Convention by 1 January 1995 was included in the European Economic Area (EEA) Agreement, which is a mixed agreement to which the EU and Ireland are a party. Although Ireland was progressing legislation to enable its accession to the Convention,

---

[25] Case C-236/91 *Commission v Ireland* [1992] ECR I-5933, 5940.

[26] Case C-392/96 *Commission v Ireland* [1999] ECR I-5929, 5949–5950.

[27] Case 167/73 *Commission v France* [1974] ECR 359.

as it had failed to become a party by the deadline set by the Commission's reasoned opinion, the Court found that an infringement had occurred.[28]

(iii) Failure to Apply or Enforce EU Law

[15–17] An infringement can also arise due to the failure to adequately apply or enforce EU law as intended, notwithstanding that national law has been amended so as to implement the relevant law onto its statute books. This can result from an administrative practice that is general and consistent in nature. For instance, proceedings were brought against Greece on the grounds that, in tendering for medical devices, its hospitals were excluding certain medical devices that met EU standards. Greece was found to be in breach even though it had adequately transposed the relevant directive into national law, and the government had sent a circular to hospitals reminding them of the legal position.[29] The Court of Justice confirmed that an administrative practice can give rise to a breach if: (i) there is sufficiently documented and detailed proof of the alleged practice and (ii) the practice is, to some degree, of a consistent and general nature. However, the Court also held that in determining whether the practice is consistent and general, reliance may not be placed on any presumption. In that case, the number of hospitals involved, their wide geographical spread and their variety in terms of size and areas of specialisation pointed to an administrative practice that was general and consistent in nature.

[15–18] Although a presumption cannot be adopted of a general and consistent practice, where a pattern emerges concerning facts which should be within the power of the Member State's authorities to ascertain, the Commission may succeed in shifting the burden of proof on to the Member State, requiring it to demonstrate that it has taken adequate steps to enforce EU law. This principle was first elaborated by the Court of Justice in a case concerning Ireland's implementation of the Waste Directive.[30] Having demonstrated 12 individual instances of non-compliance, the Commission not only sought a declaration of a breach in respect of each one of these, but also successfully requested the Court to find a general and persistent breach of the Directive. The Court justified its relaxation of the general rule as follows:

> The Irish Government has also contended that the Commission is not justified in drawing general conclusions from the examination of those specific complaints by presuming alleged systemic failures by Ireland to fulfil its obligations.
>
> It is to be remembered that in proceedings under Article [258] for failure to fulfil obligations it is incumbent upon the Commission to prove the allegation that the obligation has not been fulfilled. It is the Commission's responsibility to place before the Court the information needed to enable the Court to establish that the obligation has not been fulfilled, and in so doing the Commission may not rely on any presumption.
>
> However, the Member States are required, under Article [4 TEU], to facilitate the achievement of the Commission's tasks, which consist in particular … in ensuring that the provisions of the Treaty and the measures taken by the institutions pursuant thereto are applied.

---

[28] Case 13/00 *Commission v Ireland (Berne Convention)* [2002] ECR I-2943.

[29] Case C-489/06 *Commission v Greece (Medical Devices)* [2009] ECR I-1797. See also Case C-427/17 *Commission v Ireland (Urban Waste Water)* EU:C:2019:269, 28 March 2019.

[30] Case C-494/01 *Commission v Ireland (Waste Directive)* [2005] ECR I-3331.

> In this context, account should be taken of the fact that, where it is a question of checking that the national provisions intended to ensure effective implementation of the directive are applied correctly in practice, the Commission which … does not have investigative powers of its own in the matter, is largely reliant on the information provided by any complainants and by the Member State concerned.
>
> It follows in particular that, where the Commission has adduced sufficient evidence of certain matters in the territory of the defendant Member State, it is incumbent on the latter to challenge in substance and in detail the information produced and the consequences flowing therefrom.
>
> In such circumstances, it is indeed primarily for the national authorities to conduct the necessary on-the-spot investigations, in a spirit of genuine cooperation and mindful of each Member State's duty … to facilitate the general task of the Commission.
>
> Thus, where the Commission relies on detailed complaints revealing repeated failures to comply with the provisions of the directive, it is incumbent on the Member State to contest specifically the facts alleged in those complaints.
>
> Likewise, where the Commission has adduced sufficient evidence to show that a Member State's authorities have developed a repeated and persistent practice which is contrary to the provisions of a directive, it is incumbent on that Member State to challenge in substance and in detail the information produced and the consequences flowing therefrom.[31]

[15–19] Exceptionally, the Commission may initiate infringement proceedings for a violation of EU law through the commission of a single administrative act, although these have been confined to cases concerning the residence or expulsion of non-nationals or public procurement. In the case of residence or expulsion, important civil liberties may be at issue, while with large public procurement contracts, the "particularity of each tender would always make it difficult to identify a general practice".[32] For example, Ireland was found to have breached a directive on public works contracts due to a failure to notify an unsuccessful tenderer of the result of a competition for a motorway bypass of Dundalk, who then made a complaint to the Commission.[33] The Court rejected Ireland's argument that, as it had properly transposed the directive into Irish law, a single failure to notify could not justify a finding that it had failed to fulfil its obligations under EU law. Rather than provide an expansive reasoning, the Court simply noted that according to its existing case law, an action for failure to fulfil obligations makes possible not only an examination of the compatibility of a Member State's laws, regulations and administrative provisions with EU law, but also a determination that there has been an infringement of EU law by the national bodies in a specific individual case.

---

[31] *ibid*, 3397–3398. This is, however, an exception to the Court's general approach, which is to be cautious when it comes to accepting the use of presumptions. In Case C-507/03 *Commission v Ireland* [2007] ECR I-9777, 9808, the Court was unwilling to presume that the award of a contract for the provision of services relating to the payment of social welfare payments was of a cross-border interest, such that it should have been advertised in a way that it was brought to the attention of service providers in other Member States. The contract was awarded to An Post. The Court concluded that no evidence of a cross-border interest had been provided by the Commission, and that a "mere statement by it that a complaint was made to it in relation to the contract in question is not sufficient to establish that the contract was of certain cross-border interest and that there was therefore a failure to fulfil obligations". See also Case C-399/17 *Commission v Czech Republic* EU:C:2019:200, 14 March 2019, referred to in fn 61 below.

[32] Damian Chalmers, Gareth Davies and Giorgi Monti, *European Union Law* (3rd ed, Cambridge University Press, 2014) 342.

[33] Case C-456/08 *Commission v Ireland* [2010] ECR I-859.

(iv) Acts for which the Member State is Responsible

[15–20] Similar to the position in international law, the Art 258 infringement procedure views Member States as "unitary states", in the sense that a Member State will be declared liable for an infringement committed by any state agency, whether it be at national, regional or local level, and regardless of whether that body operates in a manner that is constitutionally independent from the government. For example, the Court of Justice did not consider it necessary to scrutinise the nature or legal status of Dundalk Urban District Council in circumstances where a breach of Art 34 TFEU was claimed to have arisen in the awarding of a tender contract and where, as a final stage in the tender process, approval by the Department of the Environment was required before the contract could be awarded.[34]

[15–21] This approach tends to make it difficult for a Member State to raise arguments that might seek to explain away an infringement since, ultimately, the buck stops with it. Accordingly, the internal situation within a Member State will generally not absolve responsibility for an infringement, such as when a government genuinely seeks to pass necessary legislation but is prevented from doing so by parliament. For instance, infringement proceedings were brought against Ireland for its failure to comply with a requirement, set down in a regulation, to notify the Commission every two weeks of the market price of certain fish.[35] In addition to the representative ports at which information was to be gathered, Irish inspectors were required to monitor some 900 ports and landing places. Ireland argued that it was simply not possible to deploy its limited number of fisheries inspectors at the representative ports for the purpose of gathering the pricing information and submitting it to the Commission every two weeks. The Court rejected this argument, observing that it was well established that a Member State may not plead internal circumstances in order to justify a failure to comply with EU law obligations and time-limits, and that practical difficulties which appear at the stage when an EU measure is put into effect cannot permit a Member State to unilaterally opt out of fulfilling its obligations.[36]

[15–22] Whilst it would have a natural reluctance to reach such a finding, the Court has indicated that even the activities of the judicial branch may be held to have caused a Member State to breach its EU law obligations. This might particularly be the case in the event of an incorrect position that was a "widely-held judicial construction which has not been disowned by the supreme court, but rather confirmed by it", as compared with "isolated or numerically insignificant judicial decisions in the context of case law taking a different direction, or still more a construction disowned by a national supreme court".[37] Indeed in 2018 the Court of Justice held, for the very first time, that the failure of a court of final instance to make a preliminary reference amounted to a breach of a Member State's obligations under Art 267 TFEU, such as to amount to an infringement of the Treaties.[38]

---

[34] Case 45/87 *Commission v Ireland (Dundalk Water)* [1988] ECR 4929.

[35] Case C-39/88 *Commission v Ireland (Fish Prices)* [1990] ECR I-4271.

[36] *ibid*, 4282–4283.

[37] Case C-129/00 *Commission v Italy* [2003] ECR I-14637, 14686–14687. See Maciej Taboroski, "Infringement Proceedings and Non-Compliant National Courts" (2012) 49 *Common Market Law Review* 1881.

[38] Case C-416/17 *Commission v France* EU:C:2018:811, 4 October 2018. See ch 8, paras [8–55] to [8–56].

[15–23] As well as bearing responsibility for its various agencies, the activities of a private entity may be attributable to a Member State where it is subject to overall direction or control by the state. In the *Buy Irish* case, the campaign under challenge was run by the Irish Goods Council which had been established by amalgamating existing state bodies through the creation of a company limited by guarantee. A government minister appointed the company's chairman and board members, and the minister's approval was required for any amendment to the company's Memorandum or Articles of Association.[39] Financially, the company was subsidised by both the State and by private industry. Ireland had argued that the Irish Goods Council was not a public authority, but merely an arrangement whereby various Irish industries could cooperate for their common good, that its activities were not based on any official enactment, and that the involvement of the Government consisted exclusively of financial aid and moral support. The Court of Justice took a holistic view of the State's involvement in the campaign and was unwilling to accept the argument that the separate legal status of the Goods Council meant that responsibility for the campaign could not be attributed to the State.

[15–24] An example of where a Member State's omission to stop the acts of private individuals amounted to a breach of an obligation is found in the *Spanish Strawberries* case.[40] There, infringement proceedings were brought against France arising out of the "passivity" of its authorities, over a number of years, towards protests by French farmers against imported agricultural products. The actions of the famers included intercepting lorries transporting goods into France and destroying their load, damaging goods on display in French shops, threatening wholesalers and retailers in order to induce them to stock exclusively French products and organising checks to verify whether they had complied with instructions given to them. The Court accepted that, as a matter of principle, a Member State's failure to adopt adequate measures to prevent obstacles to the free movement of goods created by the actions of private individuals may be caught by Art 34 TFEU. It concluded that the French authorities had "manifestly and persistently abstained from adopting appropriate and adequate measures to put an end to the acts of vandalism which jeopardize the free movement on its territory of certain agricultural products originating in other Member States and to prevent the recurrence of such acts".[41] As a result of its failure to adopt "all necessary and proportionate measures in order to prevent the free movement of fruit and vegetables from being obstructed by actions by private individuals", France had failed to fulfil its obligations under Art 34.[42]

C. Steps in the Procedure

[15–25] An Art 258 infringement procedure begins life when a potential breach of a Member State obligation is first detected by the Commission. This might arise due to the Commission's own investigations. For example, databases are now maintained through which Member States are to notify of their transposition of directives. Once the deadline set for transposition has passed, the Commission will automatically know whether any Member State is in default. In 2017, the Commission launched 139

---

39 Case 249/81 *Commission v Ireland (Buy Irish)* [1982] ECR 4005.
40 Case C-265/95 *Commission v France (Spanish Strawberries)* [1997] ECR I-6959.
41 *ibid*, 7005.
42 *ibid*.

investigations on its own initiative under the EU Pilot mechanism and opened 694 infringement procedures by directly sending a letter of formal notice.[43]

[15–26] The other means by which a potential breach is detected is through complaints received from individuals, which might include lobbying groups and NGOs, with 3,786 complaints received by the Commission in 2017.[44] It has been noted, for instance, that the campaign group, Friends of the Irish Environment, has "consistently brought information about environmental infringements in Ireland to the attention of the Commission, leading to the initiation of several important infringement proceedings".[45] The three main areas of complaint, which made up roughly half of all complaints received, were justice and consumer matters, the environment and employment. The vast majority of complaints received, however, do not result in an investigation either because an initial assessment reveals that no EU law has been broken, the correspondence does not qualify as a complaint or the Commission has no power to act, or the complaint is withdrawn. So, while the Commission handled just over 3,600 complaints in 2017, only around 150 of these led to an investigation.[46]

[15–27] Even where a complaint is well founded, the Commission has discretion as to whether or not to commence infringement proceedings. Various legal challenges which have sought to oblige the Commission to initiate an infringement procedure on foot of a complaint have failed, with the Court of Justice consistently upholding the Commission's freedom of action in the exercise of its discretion.[47] As a result, the Commission is entitled to allow policy considerations to influence its use of Art 258 in order to achieve certain goals. Indeed, the Commission has emphasised the importance of using its discretionary power in a strategic way to focus and prioritise its efforts on the most important breaches of EU law affecting the interests of citizens and business. Most recently, it has indicated that it will act firmly on infringements which obstruct the implementation of important EU policy objectives, or which risk undermining the four fundamental freedoms, giving priority to cases where Member States have: (i) failed to communicate transposition measures or where those measures have incorrectly transposed directives; (ii) failed to comply with a judgment of the Court of Justice; (iii) caused serious damage to EU financial interests; or (iv) violated any of the EU's exclusive competences.[48]

[15–28] In response to criticism from the European Ombudsman and others, the Commission has put in place improved procedures governing its communications with complainants, including an online standard complaint form. Updated administrative procedures for handling complaints are included as an annex to a 2017 Commission Communication on the matter, which provide that the Commission will inform the

[43] Commission Staff Working Document, General Statistical Overview 2017, Part 1, SWD(2018) 377, 12 July 2018, 6.

[44] *ibid.*

[45] Paul Craig and Gráinne de Búrca, *EU Law* (6th ed, Cambridge University Press, 2015) 432. See Richard Rawlings, "Engaged Elites: Citizen Action and Institutional Attitudes in Commission Enforcement" (2000) 6 *European Law Journal* 4.

[46] Commission Staff Working Document, General Statistical Overview 2017, Part 1, SWD(2018) 377, 12 July 2018, 7.

[47] See Ernõ Várnay, "Discretion in the Articles 258 and 260(2) TFEU Procedures" (2015) 22 *Maastricht Journal of European and Comparative Law* 836.

[48] Commission Communication, "EU Law: Better Results through Better Application" (2017/C 18/02) [2017] OJ C18/10.

complainant in writing if, following registration, a complaint is examined further in cooperation with the Member State concerned.[49] If infringement procedures are launched, the Commission will inform complainants in writing of each procedural step (letter of formal notice, reasoned opinion, referral to the Court of Justice or closure of the case). Where a number of complaints are lodged in relation to the same grievance, this written correspondence may be replaced by the publication of a notice on the Europa website. At any point during the procedure complainants may ask to explain or clarify to the Commission, at its premises and at the complainants' own expense, the grounds for their complaint.

[15–29] Once the Commission has decided to initiate an infringement action, there are three steps that are gone through in a pre-litigation stage before a case might eventually be lodged with the Court of Justice: the EU Pilot mechanism, a letter of formal notice and a reasoned opinion. These stages involve progressive degrees of formality and are designed to ensure that, if it all possible, a potential breach is resolved without the need to seek a declaration from the Court.

(i) EU Pilot Mechanism

[15–30] Introduced in 2008 to replace administrative letters that had previously been sent by the Commission, the somewhat oddly named "EU Pilot" mechanism involves both the Commission and national governments using an online database and communication tool to share information on the details of particular cases. The Commission will send an initial query and request for information to a national government via the database, giving the Member State seven weeks in which to reply. In turn, the Commission then has ten weeks in which to assess the reply. If the Member State's response is unsatisfactory, the Commission will formally start the infringement procedure by issuing a letter of formal notice. In 2017, 77 per cent of cases in which the EU Pilot mechanism was deployed were closed following a satisfactory response from the Member State.[50]

[15–31] Until 2017, the default position was that the EU Pilot mechanism would be used unless urgency or another overriding interest required the immediate launching of an infringement procedure. Anxious to avoid the mechanism becoming a cause for delay rather than expedition, this position has now been reversed such that the Commission will launch infringement procedures without relying on the EU Pilot Mechanism, unless recourse to it is seen as useful in a given case. This has resulted in a dramatic drop in the use of the mechanism, falling from 790 instances in 2016 to just 178 in 2017.[51]

(ii) Letter of Formal Notice

[15–32] Article 258 provides that, if the Commission considers that a Member State has failed to fulfil its obligations under the Treaties, it shall deliver a reasoned opinion on the matter *after giving the Member State the opportunity to submit its observations.* The means by which the Commission gives effect to this principle of natural justice

---

[49] *ibid*, 18.

[50] Commission Staff Working Document, General Statistical Overview 2017, Part 1, SWD(2018) 377, 12 July 2018, 8.

[51] *ibid.*

is through issuing a letter of formal notice that sets out what the alleged breach is, thereby defining the terms of reference for the procedure beyond which the Commission cannot go. The letter of formal notice both delimits the subject matter of the dispute and informs the Member State of the aspects of the alleged breach so as to allow it to prepare its defence.

[15–33] The letter of formal notice will put forward a defined period of time within which the Member State is to reply. The length of time set will depend on what is reasonable in the particular circumstances, although two months is the general rule of thumb. Where, for example, the Member State is already well aware of the Commission's views and there is a particular urgency to the matter, it may be considered reasonable to set a shorter period of time. As with the EU Pilot mechanism, the aim is for a dialogue to take place on foot of the letter of formal notice that will satisfactorily resolve the matter. So, for instance, in 2017, the Commission sent 716 letters of formal notice, 29 of which were to Ireland (slightly above the EU average of 26).[52] In contrast, only 275 reasoned opinions were issued, 12 of which were to Ireland (slightly above the EU average of 10), reflecting the degree to which resolutions were achieved following the receipt of a letter of formal notice.[53]

(iii) Reasoned Opinion

[15–34] If discussions on foot of a letter of formal notice fail to result in a resolution, the Commission has the option to proceed to issue a more detailed "reasoned opinion" on the matter. As the subject of the dispute has already been established by the letter of formal notice, the reasoned opinion must be based on the same complaints as were set out therein, albeit that account can be taken of certain changes in circumstances. In addition, as the letter of formal notice is an initial setting out of an alleged breach, it is permissible for the reasoned opinion to set the complaints out in a greater level of detail. The reasoned opinion must contain a cogent and detailed exposition of the reasons which led the Commission to conclude that the Member State was in breach of its obligations, taking account of any observations submitted by the Member State on foot of the letter of formal notice. If failure to adopt a particular measure is intended to form the subject of possible Court proceedings, the reasoned opinion must indicate the necessity to adopt such a measure; otherwise, however, the general position is that the Commission is not required to spell out what steps are required in order to remedy a breach.

[15–35] If the Commission institutes Court proceedings, its submissions are not required to be identical to the reasoned opinion, but they must be essentially the same. The Commission can, however, respond to additional arguments or defences raised by the Member State in its response to the reasoned opinion. The only circumstance in which the subject matter of a dispute brought before the Court may include events that took place after the reasoned opinion is if they are of the same kind and constitute the same conduct as the events referred to in the opinion, or if the subsequent events are being referred to in order to support an argument that the facts set out in the reasoned

[52] *ibid*, 10

[53] *ibid*, 11.

opinion form part of a general and persistent practice, as occurred for example in the case against Ireland concerning implementation of the Waste Directive.[54]

[15–36] The Court of Justice has clarified that a reasoned opinion is not a binding act of the Commission that is capable of being challenged under Art 263 TFEU, but rather is a step in the overall infringement proceedings. In general, both letters of formal notice and reasoned opinions are kept confidential, at least until the end of Court proceedings. As the Court has described, the disclosure of documents concerning an infringement procedure during its pre-litigation stage would be likely to change the nature and progress of the procedure, "given that, in those circumstances, it could prove even more difficult to begin a process of negotiation and to reach an agreement between the Commission and the Member State concerned putting an end to the infringement alleged".[55] The Commission has, however, developed the practice of issuing press releases and memorandums in respect of reasoned opinions and maintains a dedicated webpage on which information concerning infringement decisions is set out.[56] By way of illustration, the Commission indicates that the following steps were taken with respect to Ireland in 2017:

Formal Notices (29)
Late adoption of 2nd round of River Basin Management Plans under Water Framework Directive
Non-reporting of Flood Risk Management Plans
Non-transposition of Directive on disclosure of non-financial and diversity information by certain large undertakings
Non-transposition of Directive on markets in financial instruments (Mifid II)
Failure to fulfil reporting obligations under INSPIRE Directive
Implementation of Schengen Information System
Compliance with reporting obligations under Waste Shipments Regulation, Waste Framework Directive and the Packaging Waste Directive
Directive on deployment of alternative fuels infrastructure (1st)
Directive on deployment of alternative fuels infrastructure (2nd)
Directive on reduction of national emissions of certain atmospheric pollutants
Directive on periodic roadworthiness tests for motor vehicles and their trailers and repealing
Directive on registration documents for vehicles
Directive laying down for certain road vehicles the maximum authorised dimensions in national and international traffic and the maximum authorised weights in international traffic
Directive on driving licences
Directive on prevention of the use of the financial system for the purposes of money laundering or terrorist financing
Directive on certain rules governing actions for damages under national law for infringements of the competition law

54 Case C-494/01 *Commission v Ireland (Waste Directive)* [2005] ECR I-3331.

55 Joined Cases C-514/11P and C-605/11P *LPN and Finland v Commission* EU:C:2013:738, 14 November 2013, para 63. The same has been held in relation to EU Pilot documents: Case C-562/14P *Sweden v Commission* EU:C:2017:356, 11 May 2017.

56 <http://ec.europa.eu/atwork/applying-eu-law/infringements-proceedings/infringement_decisions>.

Directive on technical roadside inspection of the roadworthiness of commercial vehicles
Directive on assessment of the effects of certain public and private projects on the environment
Directive facilitating cross-border exchange of information on road-safety-related traffic offences
Directive on deployment of alternative fuels infrastructure
Directive amending annexes on the laying down of rules concerning reference methods, data validation and location of sampling points for the assessment of ambient air quality
Commission Delegated Directive as regards the list of restricted substances
Commission Implementing Directive on specific requirements for the genus and species of fruit plants
Commission Implementing Directive on marketing of seed of oil and fibre plants
Commission Implementing Directive on requirements for the labelling, sealing and packaging of fruit plant propagating material
Commission Implementing Directive on registration of suppliers and of varieties and the common list of varieties
Commission Implementing Directive on characteristics to be covered as a minimum by the examination and the minimum conditions for examining certain varieties of agricultural plant species
Directive amending certain directives as regards seafarers
Delays in conducting Market reviews
Reasoned Opinions (12)
Transposition of Directive on taking-up and pursuit of the business of Insurance and Reinsurance (Solvency II)
Transposition of Directive on powers of the European Insurance and Occupational Pensions Authority and the European Securities and Markets Authority
Non-compliance with Prüm Decisions
Non-transposition of Directive on disclosure of non-financial and diversity information by certain large undertakings
Operation of Irish Marine Casualty Investigation Board in implementation of Directive on the investigation of accidents in the maritime transport sector
Directive on recreational craft and personal watercraft
Directive on deployment of alternative fuels infrastructure (17 May)
Directive on deployment of alternative fuels infrastructure (13 July)
Directive on marine equipment
Directive on harmonisation of laws relating to lifts and safety components for lifts
Directive on harmonisation of laws relating to equipment intended for use in potentially explosive atmospheres
Directive on Rights of Victims of Crime
Decision to Institute Court Proceedings (1)
Transposition of Directive on annual financial statements, consolidated financial statements and related reports of certain types of undertakings
Institution of Court Proceedings (2)
Application of minimum levels of taxation applicable to motor fuels under Directive on taxation of energy products (Case C–504/17)
Application of Directive concerning urban waste water treatment (Case C–427/17)

Closure of Cases (27)
Transposition of Directive on over-reliance on credit ratings
Directive on marine equipment
Directive on recreational craft and personal watercraft
Directive on harmonisation of laws relating to electromagnetic compatibility
Directive on recognition of professional qualifications and administrative cooperation through the Internal Market Information System
Directive on list of defence-related products
Directive as regards language requirements
Directive on harmonisation of laws relating to the making available on the market and supervision of explosives for civil uses
Directive on common system of taxation applicable in the case of parent companies and subsidiaries of different Member States
Commission Implementing Directive on specific requirements for the genus and species of fruit plants
Commission Implementing Directive on marketing of seed of oil and fibre plants
Commission Implementing Directive on registration of suppliers and of varieties and the common list of varieties
Commission Implementing Directive on requirements for the labelling, sealing and packaging of fruit plant propagating material
Directive on attacks against Information Systems
Directive on harmonisation of laws relating to lifts
Directive on harmonisation of laws relating to equipment intended for use in potentially explosive atmospheres
Directive on harmonisation of the laws relating to the making available on the market of pressure equipment
Commission Delegated Directive as regards the list of restricted substances (chemicals)
Commission Directive laying down rules concerning reference methods, data validation and location of sampling points for the assessment of ambient air quality
Commission Directive on driving licences
Directive on reduction of national emissions of certain atmospheric pollutants
Directive facilitating cross-border exchange of information on road-safety-related traffic offences
Commission Implementing Directive on minimum conditions for examining certain varieties of agricultural plant species
Directive on deployment of alternative fuels infrastructure
Failure to fulfil reporting obligations under INSPIRE Directive and Reporting and Monitoring Decision (sharing of environmental information)
Compliance with reporting obligations under the waste legislation
Incorrect application of Directive on Mutual Recognition of Seafarer's Certificates issued by the Member State

[15–37] The nature and significance of a reasoned opinion was the subject of discussion in *Cromane Seafoods Ltd v Minister for Agriculture*, where a majority of the Supreme Court held that the circumstances of the case could not give rise to a claim of negligence against the Minister in relation to the implementation of the Habitats

Directive.[57] In a dissenting judgment, however, Clarke J (as he then was) considered that such a claim could be made out arising from a failure to collect scientific data in relation to activities within a conservation area as required by the Directive. Critical to this finding was the fact that a reasoned opinion from the Commission was deemed relevant in determining the existence of foreseeability and a consequent duty of care owed to the plaintiffs. According to Clarke J, upon receiving the reasoned opinion, "it must at least have been clear to the Minister that the Commission had not been persuaded by Ireland's arguments and was of the view that Ireland was in breach of a range of obligations including the one concerning appropriate assessment which is at the heart of this case".[58] Whilst acknowledging that the Commission will not always be right, and that a Member State is free to argue their case before the Court of Justice, Clarke J observed that a reasoned opinion was not in the same category as speculation or an allegation by a private individual, but represented:

> the considered view of the body which, under the Union treaties, is charged, amongst other things, with ensuring that Union law is properly transposed and implemented in Member States. The duty of care which I suggest requires to be analysed is, therefore, one which arises in a specific timeframe and operates against the backdrop of a formal contention on the part of the Commission that an appropriate assessment (requiring, necessarily, appropriate scientific data) would be required to allow for the continuance of traditional activities.
>
> … The Minister simply got it wrong in taking the view that traditional activities could be authorised to continue without an appropriate assessment.
>
> In particular, the Minister got it wrong by failing to put in place measures to secure the appropriate scientific data to enable an appropriate assessment to be carried out long after it had become clear, by reason of the position adopted by the Commission, that there was, to put it at its mildest, a significant doubt as to whether the Minister's position was correct.
>
> The failure of the Minister was in omitting to take any steps towards assembling the necessary scientific data to allow an appropriate assessment to be carried out at least after his position had been significantly questioned by the Commission. A similar failure by a private individual in an analogous situation would, in my view, be likely to lead to the court imposing a duty of care and finding that private individual negligent in failing to comply with the duty of care in question.[59]

(iv) Court Proceedings

[15–38] If a Member State fails to ensure compliance by the time set down by the Commission in its reasoned opinion, the Commission may take the final step of instituting proceedings in the Court of Justice.[60] An important feature of this stage of

---

57 [2016] 2 ILRM 81.

58 *ibid*, 157.

59 *ibid*, 158, 162.

60 If the circumstances are such that a Member State cannot ensure compliance by the end of the prescribed period due to the fact that a certain breach cannot be undone, that does not mean that infringement proceedings cannot be brought. As stated in Case C-620/16 *Commission v Germany (OTIF)* EU:C:2019:256, 27 March 2019, para 57, "a Member State cannot be allowed to rely upon a *fait accompli* of which it is itself the author so as to evade proceedings brought before the Court for failure to fulfil obligations a Member State cannot be allowed to rely upon a fait accompli of which it is itself the author so as to evade proceedings brought before the Court for failure to fulfil obligations".

the process is that, once the deadline set out in the reasoned opinion has passed, the Member State cannot avoid or defend the proceedings by subsequently remedying the breach. The time at which the Court will assess whether an obligation has been fulfilled is at the expiry of the prescribed deadline. From the perspective of the Commission, this clearly enhances the effectiveness of the Art 258 procedure and avoids a situation whereby a Member State might leave it until the institution of court proceedings before taking steps to remedy a breach. In addition, a declaration by the Court of a failure to fulfil EU law obligations may be of considerable assistance to any private parties that have suffered loss as a result of the infringement and who may wish to seek *Francovich* damages against the Member State at fault.

[15–39] If the Court is satisfied that the Commission has demonstrated a breach of EU law obligations, it will issue a declaration to that effect.[61] While the Court does not set out precisely what the Member State must do to remedy the breach, Art 260 obliges the Member State to take the necessary measures to comply with the Court's judgment, which are expected to be undertaken as soon as possible. A declaration that a national law infringes upon an EU obligation does not have the effect of annulling that law, but rather the obligation is on the Member State to quickly bring the infringement to an end by legislating appropriately.

D. Financial Penalties

[15–40] There is only one situation in which the Commission may directly seek the imposition of a lump sum or a penalty payment within the Art 258 infringement proceedings themselves, and that is where a Member State has failed to fulfil its obligation to notify measures transposing a directive adopted under a legislative procedure. Article 260(3) provides that in such circumstances, if the Court finds that there is an infringement it may impose a lump sum or penalty payment not exceeding the amount specified by the Commission, with the payment obligation taking effect on the date set by the Court. This opportunity for the Commission to directly seek a financial penalty for non-transposition was first introduced by the Lisbon Treaty as a means of enhancing and streamlining the enforcement procedure and of further incentivising Member States to transpose directives on time. In 2017, the Commission sought financial penalties in seven cases, while in five other cases the Commission took a decision to institute proceedings but the Member States adopted the transposition measures before the application was sent to Court. In a recent judgment, the Court of Justice was required to interpret Art 260(3) for the first time. In *Commission v Belgium*, Belgium argued that, given that it had notified the Commission of transposition measures, Art 260(3) ought not to have been used.[62] In the view of Belgium (and of Ireland, intervening), the dispute at issue concerned the adequacy of transposition, rather than a failure to

---

[61] For an example of the Commission being found to have failed to have established a breach of EU law see Case C-399/17 *Commission v Czech Republic* EU:C:2019:200, 14 March 2019, where it was held that the Commission had failed to prove that a shipment of a substance derived from petroleum refining from the Czech Republic to Poland was in fact "waste" within the meaning of the Waste Shipments Regulation. Although the Regulation provided that the subject matter of a shipment is presumed to be waste when, as here, the competent authorities of dispatch and of destination cannot agree on its classification, in the context of infringement proceedings the Court held that it was for the Commission to establish the existence of the alleged failure, without relying on any presumption.

[62] Case C-543/17 *Commission v Belgium* EU:C:2019:573, 8 July 2019.

notify of transposing measures. The Court rejected this argument. It found that the obligation to notify required the Member States to disclose sufficiently clear and precise information on the national measures transposing each provision of the directive. While it was not for the Court of Justice to consider, in Art 260(3) proceedings, whether the national measures correctly transposed a directive, the Commission could bring such proceedings on the basis that it considered the transposition measures to be clearly lacking or they that did not cover the entire national territory, as was found to be the case with the Belgian measures.

[15–41] Although the wording of Art 260 refers to the imposition of a lump sum *or* a penalty payment, the Court has held that both may be imposed together, particularly where the breach has persisted for a long time and is likely to continue into the future.[63] In doing so, it explained that financial penalties should be determined by taking account of the degree of persuasion needed in order for the Member State to alter its conduct. In its 2017 Communication, the Commission announced a change to its practice as set out in an earlier 2011 Communication as follows:

> In the light of experience, the Commission will now adjust its practice … by systematically asking the Court to impose a lump sum as well as a periodic penalty payment. When determining the amount of the lump sum in accordance with its practice, the Commission will take into account the extent of transposition when determining the seriousness of the failure to transpose.
>
> The logical consequence of the approach concerning the lump sum payment is that, in cases where a Member State rectifies the infringement by transposing the directive in the course of the court proceedings, the Commission will no longer withdraw its action for that reason alone. The Court of Justice cannot take a decision to impose a penalty payment because such a decision would no longer serve a useful purpose. However, it can impose a lump sum payment penalising the duration of the infringement up to the time the situation was rectified because this aspect of the case has not lost its purpose.[64]

[15–42] Where a Member State has been found by the Court to have failed to fulfil its EU law obligations and the Commission subsequently considers that it has not taken the necessary measures to comply with that judgment, Art 260(2) allows for the Commission to bring the matter before the Court for a second time, in a separate set of proceedings, after giving the Member State an opportunity to submit its observations by way of issuing a formal letter of notice.[65] On foot of a change introduced by the Lisbon Treaty, in order to speed up these proceedings the Commission no longer issues a reasoned opinion. As indicated above, it is now the practice of the Commission to seek a lump sum payment, and so the fact that the Member State may remedy the breach before the case is heard will not necessarily mean that the Commission will withdraw the case. In 2016, the Court imposed fines in two cases. In the first, a lump sum payment of €3 million and a daily penalty of €8,000 was imposed on Portugal for its failure to comply with a 2009 judgment that found it to have not properly implemented the

---

63 Case C-304/02 *Commission v France* [2005] ECR I-6263, 6345.

64 Commission Communication, "EU Law: Better Results through Better Application" (2017/C 18/02) [2017] OJ C18/10; Commission Communication, "Implementation of Article 260(3) of the Treaty" (2011/C 12/01) [2011] OJ C12/1.

65 See Brian Jack, "Article 260(2) TFEU: An Effective Judicial Procedure for the Enforcement of Judgments?" (2013) 19 *European Law Journal* 404; Pål Wennerås, "Sanctions Against Member States under Article 260 TFEU: Alive, But Not Kicking?" (2012) 49 *Common Market Law Review* 145.

Waste Water Treatment Directive.[66] In the second, Greece was required to make a lump sum payment of €10 million and pay a daily penalty of €30,000 for having failed to implement a 2009 judgment concerning its treatment of hazardous waste in accordance with EU directives.[67] Only one fine was imposed under Art 260(2) in 2017, in which Spain was obliged to make a lump sum payment of €3 million for failing to comply with a 2014 judgment concerning Spanish rules that restricted freedom of establishment in the cargo-handling business at Spanish ports.[68]

[15–43] An example involving Ireland arose out of the failure to give full effect to a judgment of October 2009 in which Ireland was found to have inadequately implemented the Waste Directive by addressing the discharge of domestic waste waters in the countryside through septic tanks.[69] When the Commission brought a second case seeking the imposition of financial penalties Ireland argued that the Commission's action should be dismissed on the basis that 21 months was an insufficient time in which to expect full compliance with the judgment, taking into account the difficulties involved in the adoption of legislation in a particularly complex area. The Court recalled that, even though Art 260(1) does not specify the period within which a judgment must be complied with, the importance of immediate and uniform application of EU law meant that the process of compliance must be initiated at once and completed as soon as possible. While the implementation of the judgment involved complex operations, the Court regarded 21 months as sufficient time in the circumstances of the case.

[15–44] In deciding whether to impose a penalty payment, the Court noted that although legislation had been enacted, further implementing measures were required, a national inspection plan was still to be developed and a definitive deadline had yet to be set for the registration of individual water treatment systems. In these circumstances, the imposition of a penalty payment constituted an appropriate financial means to ensure full compliance with the Court's earlier judgment. In calculating the appropriate daily amount to be €12,000, the Court reasoned as follows:

> [T]he criteria which must be taken into account in order to ensure that a penalty payment has coercive force with a view to the uniform and effective application of European Union law are, in principle, the duration of the infringement, its degree of seriousness and the ability of the Member State concerned to pay. For the purpose of applying those criteria, the Court is required to have regard in particular to the effects of non-compliance on the public and private interests at issue and to the urgency of compliance by the Member State concerned with its obligations.
>
> In the present case, the failure to fulfil obligations identified in the judgment … concerns the incomplete transposition of [the] Directive … which provided for a transposition period expiring no later than 1 April 1993. Since, more than 19 years after that date, Ireland has still not complied with all of its obligations under that directive – the principal objectives

[66] Case C-557/14 *Commission v Portugal* EU:C:2016:471, 22 June 2016.

[67] Case C-584/14 *Commission v Greece* EU:C:2016:636, 7 September 2016.

[68] Case C-388/16 *Commission v Spain* EU:C:2017:548, 13 July 2017.

[69] Case C-374/11 *Commission v Ireland (Septic Tanks)* EU:C:2012:827, 19 December 2012. See also Case C-261/18 *Commission v Ireland (Wind Farm)* [2018] OJ C240/25 (ongoing), where the Commission seeks: (i) a penalty payment of €12,264 per day from the date of the Court's judgment (on the matter of the financial penalty) to the date of compliance by Ireland with the earlier judgment finding an infringement and (ii) a lump sum of €1,343 multiplied by the number of days between the judgment finding an infringement and the earlier of compliance by Ireland with that judgment or judgment on the matter of the financial penalty, with a minimum lump sum of €1,685,000.

of which are the protection of human health and of the environment – the Court cannot but confirm the particularly lengthy character of an infringement which, in the light of such objectives, is also a matter of indisputable gravity.

While Ireland claims that the delay in its compliance with the judgment ... was attributable to internal difficulties connected with the complexity of the implementation of [the] Directive ..., it must be pointed out that a Member State cannot plead provisions, practices or situations prevailing in its domestic legal order to justify the failure to observe obligations arising under European Union law.

Account must, however, be taken of the adoption of the Water Services (Amendment) Act 2012 and of significant measures such as, in particular, those designed to establish a national register of [individual water treatment systems] and to ensure the training of inspectors of those systems, which demonstrate the efforts made by the Irish authorities since the delivery of the judgment ... with a view to full compliance therewith.

In addition, Ireland has committed itself to implementing the final steps necessary for the full implementation of that judgment in close collaboration with the Commission. Ireland also states, inter alia, that the recruitment of the inspectors is underway and that the national inspection plan should be finalised by 31 December 2012.[70]

[15–45] In further suggesting that the Court also impose a lump sum, the Commission adopted its standard approach of taking a base daily rate to be multiplied by three coefficients reflecting: (i) seriousness (1 to 20); (ii) duration (1 to 3); and (iii) a factor specific to each Member State based on its Gross Domestic Product and number of votes in the Council, aimed at reflecting its capacity to pay.[71] Once this daily rate is obtained, the lump sum figure is derived by multiplying the daily rate with the duration between the delivery of the first and second judgments. Taking account of the importance of the rules that were the subject of the infringement, which were intended to protect human health and the environment, the large number of individual waste water treatment systems concerned, and the extent of the risk of pollution, the Commission proposed a seriousness coefficient of 8 out of 20, which led it to propose a lump sum penalty based upon €4,700 per day since the judgment. In doing so, the Commission argued that "account must be taken of Ireland's repeated engagement in infringing conduct which has given rise to the delivery by the Court of several judgments ... for failure to fulfil its obligations in environmental matters".[72]

[15–46] In contrast, Ireland suggested a seriousness coefficient of 3 out of 20 in view of the difficulties encountered by the Irish legislature, the existence in Irish law of provisions which could not have been taken into account by the Court in 2009, the establishment by the Environmental Protection Agency of stricter criteria regarding drinking water and the sincere cooperation of the Irish authorities with the Commission throughout the process. The Court set out its own reasoning as follows:

---

70 *ibid*, paras 37–41.

71 See Commission Communication, "Updating of data used to calculate lump sum and penalty payments to be proposed by the Commission to the Court of Justice in infringement proceedings" C(2018) 5851 final, 18 September 2018, which establishes a standard flat-rate amount for calculating the penalty payment proposed by the Commission as €690 per day, a standard flat-rate amount for the lump sum payment as €230 per day, a minimum lump sum for Ireland of €1,723,000 (as compared with €11,835,000 for Germany) and a special "n" factor for Ireland of 3.02 (as compared with 20.74 for Germany).

72 *ibid*, para 25.

> The imposition of a lump sum payment must, in each individual case, depend on all the relevant factors relating both to the characteristics of the infringement established and to the conduct of the Member State involved in the procedure initiated under Article 260 TFEU. In that respect, that provision confers a wide discretion on the Court in deciding whether or not to impose such a penalty.
>
> With regard to the present case, the Court takes the view that all the legal and factual circumstances pertaining to the infringement established indicate that effective prevention of future repetition of similar infringements of European Union law requires the adoption of a deterrent measure, such as the imposition of a lump sum payment.
>
> Indeed, other than the failure to comply with the judgment … which has given rise to the present proceedings, a finding of a failure on the part of Ireland to fulfil its obligations under European Union law as regards water quality was made, as the Commission points out, in the judgments in Case C–316/00 *Commission v Ireland* [2002] ECR I–10527, Case C–396/01 *Commission v Ireland* [2004] ECR I–2315 and Case C–282/02 *Commission v Ireland* [2005] ECR I–4653. Such a situation reflects the persistent avoidance by that Member State of its European Union obligations in that area.
>
> If the Court decides to order a lump sum payment, it must, in the exercise of its discretion, set that payment in such a way that it is, first, appropriate to the circumstances and, secondly, proportionate both to the infringement that has been established and to the ability of the Member State concerned to pay.
>
> The relevant factors to be taken into account in that regard include, in particular, factors such as how long the breach of obligations has persisted since the judgment which initially established it was delivered and the public and private interests involved.[73]

[15–47] In light of these factors, including earlier infringement declarations concerning Ireland's protection of the environment, the Court imposed a lump sum payment of €2 million (roughly €1,700 per day from the date of the earlier judgment to the second judgment). In calculating both the lump sum and penalty payment, the Court accepted data provided by Ireland which demonstrated that its capacity to pay was reduced in the context of the economic crisis being experienced at the time.

(i) Interim Measures

[15–48] Finally, it is worth noting that Art 279 TFEU provides that the Court of Justice may, in any case before it, prescribe any interim measures. It has been held that this provision confers on the Court the power to prescribe any interim measures that it deems necessary in order to ensure that the final decision is fully effective. Such a measure can include a requirement for a penalty payment to be imposed should the Court's order not be respected. This arose in infringement proceedings brought against Poland arising from the felling of trees in a well-known natural forest that was protected under both the Habitats Directive and the Birds Directive.[74] A provisional order was made, pending a hearing for interim measures, requiring that all logging be stopped. Four months later, an interim order was made to the same effect. At that point, the Commission further sought an order that a penalty payment be imposed if Poland failed

[73] *ibid*, paras 47–51.

[74] Case C-441/17 R *Commission v Poland* EU:C:2017:877, 20 November 2017. See Pål Wannerås, "Saving a forest and the rule of law: *Commission v Poland*" (2019) 56 *Common Market Law Review* 541.

to respect the interim order. This was sought on the basis of evidence presented by the Commission to suggest that the provisional order had not been complied with, giving rise to a doubt as to whether the interim order would be respected. The Court, sitting as a Grand Chamber, ordered that details be provided within 15 days of the measures taken to comply with the interim order. If the Court was then not satisfied that it had been complied with, it would make a new order imposing a penalty payment of at least €100,000 per day. In response to Poland's argument that Art 260 TFEU was the only basis on which the Court could impose financial penalties, the Grand Chamber reasoned as follows:

> [O]nce the matter is before it, the Court hearing the application for interim measures must satisfy itself that the measures that it is minded to order are sufficiently effective to achieve their aim. It is specifically for that purpose that Article 279 TFEU grants the Court a broad discretion, in the exercise of which it is empowered, inter alia, having regard to the circumstances of each case, to specify the subject matter and the scope of the interim measures requested, and also, if it deems appropriate, to adopt, where necessary of its own motion, any ancillary measure intended to guarantee the effectiveness of the interim measures that it orders.
>
> In particular, the Court hearing an application for interim measures must be able to ensure the effectiveness of an order directed at a party pursuant to Article 279 TFEU, by adopting any measure intended to ensure that the interim order is complied with by that party. Such a measure may entail, inter alia, provision for a periodic penalty payment to be imposed should that order not be respected by the relevant party.
>
> ... first, a periodic penalty payment cannot, in the circumstances of the present case, be seen as a punishment and, second, the Republic of Poland's interpretation of the system of legal remedies under EU law in general, and of proceedings for interim measures in particular, would have the effect of considerably reducing the likelihood of those proceedings achieving their objective in the event of the Member State concerned failing to comply with the interim measures ordered against it. The purpose of seeking to ensure that a Member State complies with interim measures adopted by the Court hearing an application for such measures by providing for the imposition of a periodic penalty payment in the event of non-compliance with those measures is to guarantee the effective application of EU law, such application being an essential component of the rule of law, a value enshrined in Article 2 TEU and on which the European Union is founded.
>
> Thus, while it is true that the scope of proceedings for interim measures under Article 279 TFEU is limited by their ancillary nature vis-à-vis the main action and by the provisional nature of the measures that may be adopted in those proceedings, a feature of that scope is nonetheless the breadth of the powers which are afforded to the Court hearing an application for interim measures in order to enable it to guarantee the full effectiveness of the final decision.
>
> To that end, if the Court hearing an application for interim measures considers that the circumstances of the case require additional measures to be taken in order to ensure the effectiveness of the measures requested, it has power under Article 279 TFEU, inter alia, to provide for a periodic penalty payment to be imposed on a Member State in the event that that Member State fails to comply with the interim measures ordered.
>
> Since the prospect of a periodic penalty payment being imposed in such a situation encourages the relevant Member State to comply with the interim measures ordered, it

enhances the effectiveness of those measures and guarantees the full effectiveness of the final decision, thus falling entirely within the ambit of the objective of Article 279 TFEU.[75]

[75] *ibid*, paras 99–105.

CHAPTER 16

PROCEEDINGS AGAINST THE EU

A. INTRODUCTION

[16–01] This chapter is concerned with the four distinct avenues of legal redress in respect of acts of the European Union. Two of these relate to questioning the validity of an EU act. This can take the form of an annulment action under Art 263 TFEU, or an indirect challenge to the applicability of an EU act under Art 277 TFEU. The third means of redress involves a claim that an EU institution has infringed the Treaties by failing to act, having first been called upon to do so, and is provided for in Art 265 TFEU. Finally, it is possible to bring a claim for damages against the Union arising from an alleged breach of contract or commission of a tort.

[16–02] The first avenue of redress is found in Art 263 TFEU which provides that, within two months of its publication, a direct action may be brought seeking to review the legality of an EU act. This is known as an "annulment action", in that successful proceedings will result in the act's annulment by the Court. In Irish law terms, the equivalent action may be judicial review proceedings in which an order of *certiorari* is sought in respect of a particular decision or measure, or the bringing of a constitutional challenge to legislation by way of plenary summons. The four grounds on which the Court of Justice may be asked to review the legality of an EU act are: (i) lack of competence; (ii) infringement of an essential procedural requirement; (iii) infringement of the Treaties or of any rule of law relating to their application; or (iv) misuse of powers. As will be seen, an important procedural limitation on this ground of action arises from the rather stringent and complex rules that govern the required standing in order to be able to institute proceedings.

[16–03] A second, related means of redress allows for an *indirect* challenge to be made to an EU act of general application in separate proceedings in which that act is in issue. Such a challenge, however, is confined to arguing that the act should be considered inapplicable in the particular circumstances of the case, rather than seeking the annulment of the act more generally. This is provided for in Art 277 TFEU. It provides that, in proceedings relating to an EU act of general application, notwithstanding the expiry of the two-month period provided for in Art 263, a party may nevertheless plead any of the four grounds listed in Art 263.

[16–04] An important feature of the system of legal redress against the EU is that a complete system of legal protection is said to be provided through a combination of, on the one hand, the annulment procedure under Art 263 supplemented by the ability to bring an indirect challenge under Art 277 and, on the other hand, the possibility of raising the invalidity of an EU act in domestic proceedings before a national court. As will be recalled from Chapter 8, the two avenues of redress in Arts 263 and 277 TFEU operate in parallel to the possibility of raising the validity of an EU act before national courts. This, in turn, might lead to the question of the EU act's validity being the subject of a preliminary reference to the Court of Justice under Art 267 TFEU. In establishing this combination of Luxembourg and Member State based mechanisms, the Court of Justice has described the Treaties as providing a "complete system of legal remedies and procedures designed to permit the Court of Justice to review the legality of measures adopted by the institutions".[1] This reflects the fact that the Union is "based on the rule of law, inasmuch as neither its Member States nor its institutions can avoid a review of the question whether the measures adopted by them are in conformity with the basic constitutional charter, the Treaty".[2] Article 47 of the Charter of Fundamental Rights copper-fastens this commitment by providing that everyone whose rights and freedoms guaranteed by the law of the Union are violated has the right to an effective remedy before a tribunal.

[16–05] It is worth highlighting, however, that an individual or private entity seeking to challenge the validity of an EU act via the preliminary reference procedure may face a difficulty if they knew of the measure before the expiry of the two-month period in which to bring an annulment action, and it was undoubtedly the case that they would have had the necessary standing to challenge the measure directly under Art 263 TFEU. In such a situation, the applicant may essentially be regarded as being estopped from seeking to indirectly challenge the measure's validity by way of a preliminary reference.[3]

[16–06] In the *Pringle* case, for example, Ireland argued that the request for a preliminary reference from the Supreme Court was inadmissible on the basis that Mr Pringle ought to have instituted direct annulment proceedings in Luxembourg under Art 263 within the two-month time period allowed.[4] The question referred concerned the validity of a decision of the European Council amending the TFEU so as to allow for the establishment of a stability mechanism to ensure the financial stability of the Euro Area. It was claimed that, as a member of Dáil Éireann, Mr Pringle could contend that the use of the simplified revision procedure in this way affected his rights as a national parliamentarian. The Court of Justice rejected Ireland's argument on the basis that it could not be said, without doubt, that Mr Pringle would have had the necessary standing to bring a direct action for annulment. The Court explained that:

---

1 Case 294/83 *Les Verts v Parliament* [1986] ECR 1339, 1365.

2 *ibid.* See ch 14, paras [14–01] to [14–03].

3 See Case C-188/92 *TWD* [1994] ECR I-833 and Case C-241/95 *Accrington Beef* [1996] ECR I-6691 (establishing the basic principle); Case C-408/95 *Eurotunnel v Sea France* [1997] ECR I-6315 and Case C-494/09 *Bolton Alimentari* [2011] ECR I-647 (clarifying the principle's application). See also Roland Schwensfeier, "The *TWD* Principle Post-Lisbon" (2012) 37 *European Law Review* 156.

4 Case C-370/12 *Pringle v Government of Ireland* EU:C:2012:756, 27 November 2012.

> any party has the right, in proceedings before the national courts, to plead, before the court hearing the case, the invalidity of an act of the Union and to ask that court, which has no jurisdiction itself to declare the act invalid, to put that question to the Court [of Justice] by means of a reference for a preliminary ruling. It must be emphasised that under indent (b) of the first paragraph of Article 267 TFEU the admissibility of a reference for a preliminary ruling made on the basis of that provision is not subject to a condition that such a party has complied with a time-limit within which a case challenging the validity of the Union act concerned must be brought before the national court or tribunal with jurisdiction. In the absence of regulation by the Union, time-limits for the introduction of actions before national courts are to be determined by the national rules of procedure and it is exclusively for the courts and tribunals of the Member States to assess whether such time-limits have been respected in the main proceedings.
>
> … [T]he point must be made that the recognition of a party's right to plead the invalidity of an act of the Union presupposes that that party did not have the right to bring, under Article 263 TFEU, a direct action for the annulment of that act. Were it to be accepted that a party who *beyond doubt* had standing to institute proceedings under the fourth paragraph of Article 263 TFEU for the annulment of an act of the Union could, after the expiry of the time-limit for bringing proceedings laid down in the sixth paragraph of Article 263 TFEU, challenge before the national courts the validity of that act, that would amount to enabling the person concerned to circumvent the fact that that act is final as against him once the time-limit for his bringing an action has expired.
>
> In the present case, it is not evident that the applicant in the main proceedings had *beyond doubt* standing to bring an action for the annulment of [the] Decision under Article 263 TFEU.[5]

[16–07] The third avenue of redress against the EU is provided by Art 265 TFEU. Under it, an action may be brought claiming that an EU institution or body has infringed the Treaties as a result of its failure to act, having first been called upon to do so. Finally, a claim may be brought alleging a liability of the Union arising from either a breach of contract (Art 340(1) TFEU) or from any non-contractual (ie tortious) damage caused by the Union's institutions or servants in the performance of their duties (Arts 268 and 340(2) TFEU). Each of these four procedures – annulment actions, indirect challenges, actions for a failure to act and a claim for damages – will be considered in turn, with a particular focus on actions for the annulment of an EU act, given the overall significance of such actions and the complexity of the rules governing standing to bring such a claim.

B. Annulment Actions – Article 263 TFEU

[16–08] Article 263 TFEU is critically important in contributing to the fundamental value which the EU places on the rule of law. For, it is this article which provides the mechanism whereby acts of the EU institutions having legal effect may be subject to judicial review and, if the action is well founded, declared void.[6] As they are each

---

5 *ibid*, paras 39–42. Emphasis added.

6 See Albertina Albors-Llorens, "Remedies Against the EU Institutions after Lisbon: An Era of Opportunity?" (2012) 71 *Cambridge Law Journal* 507; Steve Peers and Marios Costa, "Judicial Review of EU Acts after the Treaty of Lisbon" (2012) *European Constitutional Law Review* 82; Alexander Türk, "Oversight of Administrative Rulemaking: Judicial Review" (2013) 19 *European Law Journal* 126; Anthony Arnull, "Judicial Review in the European Union" in Anthony Arnull and Damian Chalmers (eds), *The Oxford Handbook of European Union Law* (Oxford University

significant and deal with separate issues, the six paragraphs of Art 263 are set out below and numbered for ease of reference:

1. The Court of Justice of the European Union shall review the legality of legislative acts, of acts of the Council, of the Commission and of the European Central Bank, other than recommendations and opinions, and of acts of the European Parliament and of the European Council intended to produce legal effects vis-à-vis third parties. It shall also review the legality of acts of bodies, offices or agencies of the Union intended to produce legal effects vis-à-vis third parties.
2. It shall for this purpose have jurisdiction in actions brought by a Member State, the European Parliament, the Council or the Commission on grounds of lack of competence, infringement of an essential procedural requirement, infringement of the Treaties or of any rule of law relating to their application, or misuse of powers.
3. The Court shall have jurisdiction under the same conditions in actions brought by the Court of Auditors, by the European Central Bank and by the Committee of the Regions for the purpose of protecting their prerogatives.
4. Any natural or legal person may, under the conditions laid down in the first and second paragraphs, institute proceedings against an act addressed to that person or which is of direct and individual concern to them, and against a regulatory act which is of direct concern to them and does not entail implementing measures.
5. Acts setting up bodies, offices and agencies of the Union may lay down specific conditions and arrangements concerning actions brought by natural or legal persons against acts of these bodies, offices or agencies intended to produce legal effects in relation to them.
6. The proceedings provided for in this Article shall be instituted within two months of the publication of the measure, or of its notification to the plaintiff, or, in the absence thereof, of the day on which it came to the knowledge of the latter, as the case may be.

[16–09] Paragraph 1 deals with the types of EU act that may be subject to an annulment action. In addition to "legislative acts" (ie regulations, directives and decisions adopted under the legislative procedure) and acts "intended to produce legal effects vis-à-vis third parties", paragraph 4 refers to a third category of act, namely "regulatory acts". As will be seen, since the term "regulatory act" was introduced by the Lisbon Treaty without a definition, it has required judicial interpretation, as has the accompanying phrase "that does not entail implementing measures".

[16–10] Paragraphs 2, 3 and 4 each deal with a particular class of person or entity defined by their standing to bring annulment proceedings, namely "privileged", "semi-privileged" and "non-privileged" applicants. The privileged category comprises the Member States, the European Parliament, the Commission and the Council, each of which has a general entitlement to bring proceedings (curiously, the European Council is not a privileged applicant). Those with semi-privileged status – the Court of Auditors, the European Central Bank and the Committee of the Regions – have standing which is confined to the purpose of protecting their own prerogatives. Paragraph 4 serves to limit the extent to which natural or legal persons may bring an annulment action and

---

Press, 2015) 376; Koen Lenaerts and Tim Corthaut, "Judicial Review as a Contribution to the Development of European Constitutionalism" (2002) 22 *Yearbook of European Law* 1; David Bailey, "Scope of Judicial Review under Article 81 EC" (2004) 41 *Common Market Law Review* 1327; Renato Nazzini, "Administrative Enforcement, Judicial Review and Fundamental Rights in EU Competition Law: A Comparative, Contextual-Functionalist Perspective" (2012) 49 *Common Market Law Review* 971.

so renders them non-privileged. There are three ways in which a natural or legal person may bring such an action, namely:

(i) if the challenged act is actually addressed to that person or entity, such as for example a decision of the Commission relating to competition law or state aid rules;
(ii) if the challenged act is of direct and individual concern to them; or
(iii) if the challenged act is a regulatory act which is of direct concern to them and does not entail implementing measures (without having to be of individual concern to them).

[16–11] As will be seen below, this threshold, and the requirement for an act to be of individual concern in particular, makes it extremely difficult for a natural person or legal entity to have the necessary standing to bring a direct action challenging the validity of an EU act that is not addressed to them.

[16–12] In addition to setting out the status of privileged applicant, paragraph 2 also describes the four grounds on which an annulment action may be brought. Finally, paragraph 6 establishes that any annulment action must be instituted within two months of the publication of the measure or its notification to the plaintiff. If neither of these occurred, the deadline is two months from the date on which the plaintiff became aware of the measure.[7]

[16–13] As provided for in the Statute of the CJEU, certain annulment actions bypass the General Court and are brought directly to the Court of Justice, namely actions brought by an EU institution and actions brought by a Member State against an act of the European Parliament or the Council, subject to certain exceptions for particular acts of the Council of an executive nature.[8] In contrast, annulment actions by natural or legal persons are brought before the General Court, with a limited right of appeal on points of law to the Court of Justice.

(i) Grounds of Challenge

[16–14] Although four distinct grounds of challenge are listed in Art 263 – lack of competence, infringement of an essential procedural requirement, infringement of the Treaties or of any rule of law relating to their application, and misuse of powers – they overlap to a large extent and the Court of Justice does not draw technical or rigid distinctions between them.

---

7 This must be read in light of Arts 50 and 51 of the Rules of Procedure of the Court of Justice and Arts 59 and 60 of the Rules of Procedure of the General Court, which provide that: (i) where the time-limit allowed for initiating proceedings against a measure adopted by an institution runs from the publication of that measure, that time-limit shall be calculated from the end of the 14th day after publication of the measure in the Official Journal and (ii) procedural time-limits shall be extended on account of distance by a single period of 10 days. Rules of Procedure of the Court of Justice [2012] OJ L 265/1, with amendments published in [2013] OJ L173/65, [2016] OJ L217/69 and [2019] OJ L111/73; Rules of Procedure of the General Court [2015] OJ L 105/1, with amendments published in [2016] OJ L217/71 and [2018] OJ L240/67.

8 Art 256 TFEU and Art 51 of the Statute of the CJEU. Exceptions are made for challenges to acts or decisions made by the Council under Arts 108(2), 207 and 291 TFEU, which may be brought before the General Court. A challenge by a Member State to a Commission act under Art 331(1) TFEU concerning enhanced cooperation is to be brought directly before the Court of Justice.

[16–15] Of the four, it is exceedingly rare for the concept of misuse of powers to be raised successfully. By its nature, it demands a high threshold, requiring an applicant to demonstrate that the predominant purpose for which an act was adopted was other than its stated objective or, alternatively, that it was adopted in order to evade the proper procedure prescribed by the Treaties. As a variant of a misuse of powers, it might be alleged that an institution has committed a manifest error of assessment in making a decision, although this may also be viewed as coming under the headings of infringing the Treaties or infringing an essential procedural requirement. For example, if an institution were to take a decision that was clearly based on insufficient, incomplete or inconsistent evidence, it may be susceptible to a challenge under Art 263. The level of intensity of the review undertaken by the Court is likely to vary, depending on the nature of the decision at issue and the field to which it relates, and the Court will be anxious to avoid substituting its own assessment for that of the relevant institution.[9]

[16–16] The ground of lack of competence was considered in Chapter 9. In addition to lacking competence in terms of not having an appropriate legal base, this ground may be seen as encompassing the doctrine of *ultra vires* more generally.[10] In *Boyle v Commission*, for example, the Commission was found to have exceeded the powers conferred on it by a delegating parent regulation.[11] The regulation concerned funding for the modernisation of national fishing fleets, requests for which were to be considered by the Commission on the basis that they were not to lead to an overall increase in the national fishing capacity. The Commission adopted a decision setting out a number of criteria to guide its assessment, one of which was to require that vessels be at least five years old before any alterations could begin. On foot of a challenge from a number of Irish fishermen, the General Court ruled that while there was nothing to stop the Commission from assessing, on a case-by-case basis, whether a new vessel increased fishing capacity, by adopting a decision with a criterion not included in the parent regulation (ie that a vessel be at least five years old) the Commission had exceeded its powers.

[16–17] The infringement of an essential procedural requirement may take the form of an institutional failing, such as the use of the wrong voting procedure or omitting to consult with an institution as required. Article 296 TFEU obliges all legal acts to state the reasons on which they are based, and a failure to do so will amount to the infringement of an essential procedural requirement. While the level of detail required will depend on the nature of the act in question, it must disclose in a clear and unequivocal fashion the reasoning followed by the institution which adopted the measure, in such a way as to make those concerned aware of the reasons for the measure and to enable the Court to exercise its power of review.[12]

[16–18] As it is for the Court to decide on what amounts to an essential procedural requirement, this category is relatively open-ended and the Court has taken it to include

9 See Case C-12/03 P *Commission v Tetra Laval* [2005] ECR I-987; Case T-13/99 *Pfizer Animal Health v Council* [2002] ECR II–3305; Alexander Fritzsche, "Discretion, Scope of Judicial Balance and Institutional Review in European Law" (2010) 47 *Common Market Law Review* 361.

10 See Paul Craig, "The ECJ and Ultra Vires Action: A Conceptual Analysis" (2011) 48 *Common Market Law Review* 395.

11 Joined Cases T-218/03 to T-240/03 *Boyle v Commission* [2006] ECR II–1699.

12 Joined Cases C-27/00 and C-122/00 *R v Secretary of State for the Environment, ex parte Omega Air* [2002] ECR I-2569, 2617.

a number of due process rights, particularly in the context of individualised decisions. This is now reinforced by Art 41 of the Charter of Fundamental Rights, which enshrines the right of every person to: (i) have his or her affairs handled impartially, fairly and within a reasonable time; (ii) be heard before any individual measure which would affect him or her adversely is taken; (iii) have access to his or her file; and (iv) be given reasons for a decision.

[16–19] Where a decision is liable to negatively affect an individual or a legal entity, such as the imposition of a penalty or the refusal of a permission, the right to due process forms part of a category of rights known as the rights of defence.[13] This has proved to be a common ground on which those subject to EU restrictive measures (ie sanctions) seek to challenge their inclusion on a list of sanctioned persons. For example, in the important case of *Kadi II*, the Court of Justice considered a decision by the Commission to retain Mr Kadi on an EU sanctions list relating to international terrorism.[14] The EU list was for the purposes of implementing United Nations sanctions, and the decision to retain him on the list was based on a statement of reasons provided by the relevant UN sanctions committee. In upholding Mr Kadi's challenge to his listing, the Court outlined the due process requirements as follows:

> [R]espect for the rights of the defence and the right to effective judicial protection requires that the competent Union authority disclose to the individual concerned the evidence against that person available to that authority and relied on as the basis of its decision, that is to say, at the very least, the summary of reasons provided by the [UN] Sanctions Committee, so that that individual is in a position to defend his rights in the best possible conditions and to decide, with full knowledge of the relevant facts, whether there is any point in bringing an action before the Courts of the European Union.
>
> When that disclosure takes place, the competent Union authority must ensure that that individual is placed in a position in which he may effectively make known his views on the grounds advanced against him.
>
> ... When comments are made by the individual concerned on the summary of reasons, the competent European Union authority is under an obligation to examine, carefully and impartially, whether the alleged reasons are well founded, in the light of those comments and any exculpatory evidence provided with those comments.
>
> ... Lastly, without going so far as to require a detailed response to the comments made by the individual concerned, the obligation to state reasons laid down in Article 296 TFEU entails in all circumstances, not least when the reasons stated for the European Union measure represent reasons stated by an international body, that that statement of reasons identifies the individual, specific and concrete reasons why the competent authorities consider that the individual concerned must be subject to restrictive measures.
>
> ... The effectiveness of the judicial review guaranteed by Article 47 of the Charter also requires that, as part of the review of the lawfulness of the grounds which are the basis of the decision to list or to maintain the listing of a given person ..., the Courts of the European Union are to ensure that that decision, which affects that person individually,

---

13 See Case C-276/12 *Sabou* EU:C:2013:678, 22 October 2013, para 38; Case C-413/06P *Bertelsmann AG v Impala* [2008] ECR I-4951, para 61; Thorsten Käseberg, "Case C-413/06 P, *Bertelsmann AG and Sony Corporation of America v Independent Music Publishers and Labels Association (Impala)*" (2009) 46 *Common Market Law Review* 255.

14 Joined Cases C-584/10P, C-593/10P and C-595/10P *Commission v Kadi* EU:C:2013:518, 18 July 2013.

is taken on a sufficiently solid factual basis. That entails a verification of the factual allegations in the summary of reasons underpinning that decision, with the consequence that judicial review cannot be restricted to an assessment of the cogency in the abstract of the reasons relied on, but must concern whether those reasons, or, at the very least, one of those reasons, deemed sufficient in itself to support that decision, is substantiated.

To that end, it is for the Courts of the European Union, in order to carry out that examination, to request the competent European Union authority, when necessary, to produce information or evidence, confidential or not, relevant to such an examination.

That is because it is the task of the competent European Union authority to establish, in the event of challenge, that the reasons relied on against the person concerned are well founded, and not the task of that person to adduce evidence of the negative, that those reasons are not well founded.

For that purpose, there is no requirement that that authority produce before the Courts of the European Union all the information and evidence underlying the reasons alleged in the summary provided by the Sanctions Committee. It is however necessary that the information or evidence produced should support the reasons relied on against the person concerned.[15]

[16–20] A claim of infringement of the rights of defence can also frequently arise in relation to competition or state aid decisions adopted by the Commission. For instance, in *United Parcel Service* the Commission had used an econometric analysis in reaching a decision to refuse permission for UPS to acquire TNT Express.[16] A decisive factor in its decision was that the analysis indicated that the acquisition would lead to a risk of increased prices in the majority of markets concerned. In challenging the refusal, UPS argued that the final version of the econometric model used by the Commission differed significantly from the version that was disclosed to it during the administrative procedure that preceded the decision, thereby depriving it of the opportunity to make submissions on the changes made. In upholding the judgment of the General Court that had found an infringement of the rights defence, the Court of Justice reasoned that:

Observance of the rights of the defence before the adoption of a decision relating to merger control ... requires the notifying parties to be put in a position in which they can make known effectively their views on the accuracy and relevance of all the factors that the Commission intends to base its decision on.

As regards the econometric models used in merger control procedures, it should be recalled that the necessary prospective analysis consists of an examination of how a concentration might alter the factors determining the state of competition on the markets affected. Such an analysis makes it necessary to envisage various chains of cause and effect with a view to ascertaining which of them are the most likely.

To that end, the use of econometric models allows better understanding of the planned operation by identifying and, where relevant, quantifying some of its effects, and thus contributes to the quality of the Commission's decisions. It is therefore necessary that,

[15] *ibid*, paras 111–122. See Zahra Al-Rikabi, "*Kadi II*: The Right to Effective Judicial Review Triumphs Yet Again" (2013) 6 *European Human Rights Law Review* 631; Armin Cuyvers, "'Give me one good reason': The Unified Standard of Review for Sanctions after *Kadi II*" (2014) 51 *Common Market Law Review* 1759. On *Kadi I* (Joined Cases C-402 and 415/05P *Kadi v Council* [2008] ECR I-6351) see Gráinne de Búrca, "The European Court of Justice and the International Legal Order After *Kadi*" (2010) 51 *Harvard International Law Journal* 1.

[16] Case C-265/17P *Commission v United Parcel Express* EU:C:2019:23, 16 January 2019.

> where the Commission intends to base its decision on such models, the notifying parties are able to submit their observations in that regard.
>
> The disclosure of such models and methodological choices underlying their development is all the more necessary as it contributes ... to ensuring that the procedure is fair, in accordance with the principle of good administration enshrined in Article 41 of the Charter of Fundamental Rights of the European Union.[17]

[16–21] The Commission had also argued that, even if the failure to disclose amounted to an infringement of the rights of defence, it ought not lead to an annulment of the decision unless there was no other evidence, of which UPS had been made aware, that could form the basis for the decision. The Court of Justice did not favour this argument. Instead, it upheld the approach of the General Court that the decision ought to be annulled if UPS could make out that disclosure of the final methodology would have given UPS "even a slight chance that it would have been better able to defend itself". As explained by the Court:

> Given the importance of econometric models for the prospective analysis of the effects of a merger, raising the standard of proof required to cancel a decision due to an infringement of the rights of the defence resulting ... from failure to disclose the methodological choices, especially as regards statistical techniques, which are inherent to those models, as is advocated, in essence, by the Commission, would run counter to the objective of encouraging it to show transparency in the development of econometric models used in merger control procedures and undermine the effectiveness of subsequent judicial review of its decisions.
>
> It follows from the above that the General Court did not err in law when it held ... that "the applicant's rights of defence were infringed, with the result that the [decision at issue] should be annulled, provided that it has been sufficiently demonstrated by the applicant not that, in the absence of that procedural irregularity, the [decision at issue] would have been different in content, but that there was even a slight chance that it would have been better able to defend itself".[18]

[16–22] The fourth ground of illegality is also open-ended, comprising infringements of the Treaties or of *any rule of law* relating to their application. These rules of law are not confined to secondary law enacted by the institutions but include general principles of law as developed by the Court of Justice including proportionality, legal certainty, non-retroactivity, legitimate expectations, non-discrimination and respect for fundamental rights. So, for example, Ireland successfully challenged a decision of the Commission calculating funds connected to the use of fishing quotas.[19] It was claimed that in reaching its decision, the Commission relied upon a position that did not take the form of a legally binding decision, but rather was set out in a declaration by the Commission that formed part of the minutes of a Council meeting. In upholding Ireland's challenge to the decision on the ground that it breached the principle of legal certainty, the Court observed that EU legislation "must be certain and its application foreseeable by those subject to it. That requirement of legal certainty must be observed all the more strictly in the case of rules liable to entail financial consequences, in order

---

[17] *ibid*, paras 31–34.

[18] *ibid*, paras 55–56.

[19] Case 325/85 *Ireland v Commission (Fishing Quotas)* [1987] ECR 5041.

that those concerned may know precisely the extent of the obligations which they impose on them".[20]

[16–23] The principle of legitimate expectation arises where an EU institution offers a sufficiently precise and unconditional assurance that may be said to give rise to a legitimate expectation on the part of those to whom it is addressed, and there is no countervailing public interest that overrides that expectation.[21] Applying this test in practice means that, of necessity, the judgments of the Court are highly fact-specific.

[16–24] An illustration of the multiple alternative grounds on which the validity of an EU act may be questioned can be seen in *Irish Farmers Association v Minister for Agriculture, Food and Forestry*.[22] There, the validity of regulations governing the market in milk were challenged on the basis that they breached the principles of: (i) legitimate expectation; (ii) the fundamental right to property; (iii) proportionality; and (iv) non-discrimination or equal treatment. In addition, it was claimed that the relevant regulation had failed to provide a statement of reasons, as required by Art 296 TFEU.

[16–25] In order to deal with surpluses of milk, a regulation imposed a levy on milk that was delivered in excess of a "reference quantity" determined for each producer. In 1987 and 1988 further regulations temporarily reduced the reference quantity by a certain percentage and, in return for this temporary suspension, compensation was made available. This was continued until 1992. By way of a new regulation, from 1993 onwards the suspended percentage was excluded from the reference quantity altogether, such that the compensation also came to an end. The plaintiff farmers argued that as each regulation from 1987 to 1993 had provided for a temporary and provisional suspension of part of the reference quantity, they could have legitimately expected that, in the event that the temporary withdrawal became permanent, the quantities withdrawn would be restored or their permanent loss would be compensated. The Court of Justice rejected this ground of invalidity, reasoning as follows:

> in the sphere of the common organisation of the markets, whose purpose involves constant adjustments to meet changes in the economic situation, economic operators cannot legitimately expect that they will not be subject to restrictions arising out of future rules of market or structural policy. The principle of the protection of legitimate expectations may be invoked as against [EU] rules only to the extent that the [EU] itself has previously created a situation which can give rise to a legitimate expectation
>
> However, the Council and the Commission did not create a situation in which milk producers could legitimately expect restoration of the reference quantities temporarily withdrawn, or compensation if the reduction of 4.5% of the reference quantities became permanent.
>
> It is certainly possible that the description of the suspension … as temporary may have instilled the idea that the suspended quantity would be restored. None the less, it was

[20] *ibid*, 5088.

[21] See Case 120/86 *Mulder v Minister van Landbouw* [1988] ECR 2321; Case C-313/90 *CIRFS v Commission* [1993] ECR I-1125; Case T–347/03 *Branco v Commission* [2005] ECR II–255; Case T–264/07 *CSL Behring v Commission* [2010] ECR II–4469; Redmond Arigho, "Legitimate Expectations in Irish and EU law – Lessons for Ireland?" (2016) 19 *Irish Journal of European Law* 76.

[22] Case C-22/94 *Irish Farmers Association v Minister for Agriculture, Food and Forestry* [1997] ECR I-1809.

> provided that the arrangements for temporary withdrawal would expire, initially after two periods ... and, after an extension, at the end of three further periods ..., on the dates on which the reference quantities arrangements were themselves to end. The duration of the arrangements for temporary withdrawal was therefore intrinsically linked, from its entry into force as well as from its renewal, to the duration of the additional levy scheme.
>
> Milk producers could not expect that, on the indicated dates, the quantities which had been withdrawn until then would be restored or that their permanent loss would be compensated. Even before the date on which the withdrawal arrangements ... were to expire, the withdrawal arrangements were extended ... in the context of the extension of the levy scheme. Finally, when the schemes thus extended expired, that is to say, on 31 March 1992, the Irish milk producers could not have been unaware of the continuing surplus in milk production and, therefore, of the need to maintain the levy scheme.
>
> Even if the ... [prior] regulations ... made no mention, in view of the continuing surpluses on the milk market, of the consequences of the expiry both of the additional levy scheme in general and of the temporary withdrawal in particular, it should be observed that the debate on the reform of the Common Agricultural Policy had begun some time before that expiry and that the Commission had submitted on 11 November 1991, in the context of its proposals on the reform of the Common Agricultural Policy, [a proposal for a regulation which] provides in particular in the fourth recital in the preamble that "because of persisting surpluses the suspension of 4.5% of the reference quantities for deliveries must be converted to a definitive reduction in the guaranteed total quantities".
>
> ... The Court has consistently held that any trader in regard to whom an institution has given rise to justified hopes may rely on the principle of the protection of legitimate expectations. On the other hand, if a prudent and discriminating trader could have foreseen the adoption of a [EU] measure likely to affect his interests, he cannot plead that principle if the measure is adopted. In view of the foregoing considerations, the plaintiffs ... had sufficient information to enable them to anticipate, particularly in view of the continuing surpluses on the market, the subsequent reductions, the gradual decrease in compensation and the Commission's proposal for a regulation of 11 November 1991 to adopt the measures which appear in [the] Regulations.[23]

[16–26] The plaintiffs were no more successful in their other grounds. Whilst it was accepted that the right to property was one of the fundamental rights whose observance the Court ensured, the right to property was not absolute and had to be considered in relation to its social function. Restrictions could be imposed on the exercise of the right, in particular in the context of a common organisation of the markets, provided that those restrictions corresponded to Union objectives of general interest and did not constitute, with regard to the aim pursued, a disproportionate and intolerable interference, impairing the very substance of those rights. The Court concluded that the reduction in the reference quantity without compensation did not affect the actual substance of the right inasmuch as the Irish producers were able to continue to pursue their trade as milk producers. Moreover, the reduction in milk production led to an increase in prices, thus partially compensating for the loss suffered.

[16–27] Similarly, it was found that, in view of the limited size of the reduction of the reference quantity (4.5 per cent), and the fact that farmers had received compensation for five years, the conversion of the temporary reduction into a permanent reduction without compensation was not disproportionate to the overall aim being pursued. Finally,

[23] *ibid*, 1837–1839.

it was argued that the regulations were invalid due to the fact that they breached the principle of non-discrimination or equal treatment. First, the plaintiffs pointed to the fact that farmers who permanently ceased milk production received compensation in respect of all of their reference quantity, including the 4.5 per cent which had been temporarily withdrawn. Secondly, it was claimed that unlike other Member States, such as those on the Mediterranean, milk production constituted a considerable proportion of Ireland's overall agricultural production and so was of particular importance. In respect of both of these claims, the Court was unwilling to accept that like situations were being treated differently, pointing to the fact that Ireland's unique situation was taken into account when the reference quantities were first set.

[16–28] In relation to the separate ground of failing to state reasons, the Court recalled that that question must be assessed with regard not only to the wording of the relevant act, but also to its context and to all the legal rules governing the matter in question. Accordingly, while a legitimate criticism might be made of the reasons set out in certain of the regulations, the circumstances in which the regulation was adopted – namely, the temporary nature of the compensation provided for as part of the reduction programmes and the possibility of renewing the levy scheme on a permanent basis under the conditions indicated in the Commission's proposal for a regulation of 11 November 1991 – enabled the plaintiffs to know the reasons for the adoption of the challenged measures.

(ii) Standing to Bring a Challenge

[16–29] As set out in Art 263(4), as non-privileged applicants, a natural or legal person may institute annulment proceedings against an act addressed to that person. Secondly, if the act is not addressed to them a challenge may be brought if the act is nevertheless of direct and individual concern to them. Thirdly, if the act in question is a "regulatory act" and does not entail implementing measures, a challenge may be brought if the act is of direct concern to that person, and it is not necessary to show that it is of individual concern. This third category of "regulatory act" was introduced by the Lisbon Treaty as a means of lowering the standing requirement for non-privileged applicants. Although not expressly stated in Art 263(4), a non-privileged applicant must also be able to show that they have an interest in the annulment of the act being challenged.

(a) "Direct Concern"

[16–30] To be considered of direct concern to the applicant, an act must *directly* affect that person's legal situation. Accordingly, direct concern relates to the "immediacy of the contested measure's impact on the applicant".[24] If the act leaves to the addressees of the act a discretion as to how to implement it, it is likely that the chain of causation between the act and the change in the applicant's legal situation will be considered to be broken. In contrast, an act is likely to be considered of direct concern to an applicant if its implementation is automatic and does not rely on any additional intermediate rules. So, for example, in *International Fruit Company v Commission*, a regulation limited the import of apples from third countries for a period of three months.[25] Member States

---

24 Anthony Arnull, "Judicial Review in the European Union" in Anthony Arnull and Damian Chalmers (eds), *The Oxford Handbook of European Union Law* (Oxford University Press, 2015) 376, 387.

25 Joined Cases 41–44/70 *International Fruit Company v Commission* [1971] ECR 411.

were, however, entitled to issue licenses for the import of apples. In order to do so, each Member State was to notify the Commission on a weekly basis of the quantities for which licences had been requested. The Commission would then adopt a decision authorising the issuance of certain licences. When a challenge was made to one such decision, the Court was satisfied that the Member States enjoyed no discretion as to whether to issue a licence, but rather merely collected the weekly data and then adopted the national measures needed to give effect to the Commission's decision. Accordingly, the act whereby the Commission decided on the issuance of import licences was regarded as directly affecting the legal position of the applicant.

[16–31] A theoretical discretion on the part of the Member State may not be sufficient to break the chain of causation if the applicant can show that, in practice, there was never any real doubt as to how that discretion would be exercised. This arose in *Piraiki-Patraiki v Commission*, which involved a system of Commission authorisation for the taking of safeguard measures in connection with Greece's accession to the EEC.[26] In seeking to protect its own cotton industry, France requested the Commission to extend an authorisation which allowed French restrictions to be placed on the import of cotton from Greece. The Commission acceded to this request by way of a decision. When a challenge was brought to the decision by a number of Greek cotton manufacturers, the Commission argued that the decision was not of direct concern to the applicants as it merely authorised the imposition of restrictions, which France was free to avail of if it so wished by introducing implementing measures. Rejecting this argument, the Court was satisfied that, as there was no doubt as to the intention of the French authorities to apply the decision, the possibility that France would decide not to avail of the authorisation granted to it was entirely theoretical.

(b) "Individual Concern"

[16–32] The test for determining whether an act is of individual concern to an applicant is named after the judgment of the Court of Justice in *Plaumann v Commission*.[27] There, Germany requested the Commission to suspend the tariff applicable to clementines imported from third countries. The Commission's decision, which was addressed to Germany, refused the request. The applicant company, which sought the annulment of the decision, was an importer of fruits, including clementines. In holding that the applicant was not individually concerned by the decision, the Court established the following test:

> Persons other than those to whom a decision is addressed may only claim to be individually concerned if that decision affects them by reason of certain attributes which are peculiar to them or by reason of circumstances in which they are differentiated from all other persons and by virtue of these factors distinguishes them individually just as in the case of the person addressed. In the present case the applicant is affected by the disputed decision as an importer of clementines, that is to say, by reason of a commercial activity which may at any time be practised by any person and is not therefore such as to distinguish the applicant in relation to the contested decision as in the case of the addressee.[28]

[16–33] So, for example, in *Calpak*, the applicants were producers of a particular type

---

[26] Case 11/82 *Piraiki-Patraiki v Commission* [1985] ECR 207.

[27] Case 25/62 *Plaumann v Commission* [1963] ECR 95.

[28] *ibid*, 107.

of pear who sought to challenge a regulation altering the way in which production aid was to be calculated.[29] They argued that they formed part of a closed group that was identifiable to the Commission. As in *Plaumann*, the Court held that the applicants lacked standing, observing that the challenged regulation "applies to objectively determined situations and produces legal effects with regard to categories of persons described in a generalised and abstract manner".[30] This characteristic was not called into question "by the mere fact that it is possible to determine the number or even identity of the producers to be granted the aid" who were affected by the regulation.[31]

[16–34] In *Greenpeace v Commission*, private individuals who claimed to be affected by a decision to provide funding for two power stations in the Canary Islands were similarly found not to have standing on the basis that they could not be said to be individually concerned in a manner that was different from other inhabitants on the islands.[32] As the individuals were not individually concerned, neither was the representative association acting on their behalf. As one further example, in *Altadis v Commission*, it was held that a company that had benefited from a tax arrangement that was found by the Commission to constitute state aid did not have standing to challenge the decision. Noting that, "in order for the contested measure to be of individual concern to the applicant, the latter must establish that it belongs to a closed class, that is to say, a group which can no longer be extended after the contested measure has been adopted", the General Court held that only those companies that had been ordered to repay the benefit obtained from the arrangement could be said to have been individually concerned by the decision.[33]

[16–35] The approach of the Court of Justice to individual concern can be described from two different perspectives. From a negative perspective, an act is unlikely to be of individual concern if it applies to objectively determined situations and produces legal effects with regard to categories of persons that are described in a generalised and abstract manner. From a positive perspective, an act is likely to be of individual concern if it creates, or applies to, a closed category of persons. So, in *International Fruit Company*, as the category of potential applicants was confined to those who had requested an import licence for apples in the previous week, the challenged act was held to be of individual concern to them.[34] Similarly, in *Piraiki-Patraiki*, the Court was able to identify a closed group by confining potential applicants to those who, before the adoption of the contested Commission decision, entered into contracts for the supply of cotton that were to be performed while the act was in force.[35]

[16–36] Paul Craig and Gráinne de Búrca suggest that the *Plaumann* test is vulnerable to criticism on both practical and conceptual terms. Practically, it may not be realistic to imagine that if, say, there was an increase in the demand for clementines, new importers could quickly join the existing group of traders within the lifetime of a contested act. Importers already operating in the sector will have an advantage and might simply choose to import more in order to meet a growing demand. The test, they

[29] Joined Cases 789/79 and 790/79 *Calpak v Commission* [1980] ECR 1949.
[30] *ibid*, 1961.
[31] *ibid*
[32] Case C-321/95P *Greenpeace v Commission* [1998] ECR I-1651.
[33] Case T-400/11 *Altadis v Commission* EU:T:2013:490, 9 September 2013, para 39.
[34] Joined Cases 41–44/70 *International Fruit Company v Commission* [1971] ECR 411.
[35] Case 11/82 *Piraiki-Patraiki v Commission* [1985] ECR 207.

claim, "ignores the practical economics that determine those who supply a product".[36] Conceptually, the test makes it likely that challenges can only be brought to acts with retrospective effect, where the category of persons affected is closed, rendering acts with a future impact immune from challenge. Although the question of an applicant's standing is determined when the proceedings are brought, the assessment of whether the applicant belongs to a group that is open or closed is determined with reference to some future point in time. As a result, the "possibility of *locus standi* is like a mirage in the desert, ever receding and never capable of being grasped".[37] They suggest that the fact that it is possible that others might acquire the attributes of a group should not mean that they are regarded as presently part of that group, as this possibility might often be more theoretical than a practical likelihood.

[16–37] The merits of the *Plaumann* test were thoroughly debated in the two cases of *Unión de Pequeños Agricultores* and *Jégo-Quéré* in an exchange that went as follows. In March 2002, Advocate General Jacobs delivered an opinion in *Unión de Pequeños Agricultores* in which he identified the shortcomings of *Plaumann* and recommended a new, more liberal test. The General Court followed this new approach in *Jégo-Quéré* in May 2002, however, when the Court of Justice gave judgment in *Unión de Pequeños Agricultores* two months later it disagreed with Advocate General Jacobs and reaffirmed the *Plaumann* test. Finally, in 2004, the Court of Justice set aside the decision of the General Court in *Jégo-Quéré* in favour of the approach adopted in its own earlier judgment.

[16–38] *Unión de Pequeños Agricultores* involved an association of small farmers that were seeking to challenge a regulation governing the market in olive oil.[38] Advocate General Jacobs identified a number of reasons why the Court's long-established case law on standing should be departed from. First, in many borderline cases the case law was not stable, and had become relaxed in more recent years, resulting in increasingly complex and unpredictable decisions on admissibility. Secondly, the case law was increasingly out of line with more liberal developments in the Member States. Thirdly, the establishment of the General Court, and the transfer to that court of all actions brought by individuals, made it increasingly appropriate to enlarge the standing of individuals to challenge general measures. Finally, the Court's case law on the principle of effective judicial protection in national courts made it increasingly difficult to justify narrow restrictions on standing before the Union courts.[39]

[16–39] The argument that the preliminary reference procedure provided an effective judicial protection against general measures was, in the view of the Advocate General, also open to serious objection. Under the preliminary reference procedure: (i) the applicant has no right to decide whether a reference is made, which measures are referred or what grounds of invalidity are raised, and so has no right of access to the Court of Justice; (ii) the national court cannot itself grant the desired remedy to declare the general measure invalid; and (iii) there are procedural disadvantages relating to delay, costs, award of interim measures, the participation of the institutions which adopted the measures and the possibility of third-party intervention. More fundamentally, it may be difficult or impossible for an applicant to challenge a general measure where

---

[36] Paul Craig and Gráinne de Búrca, *EU Law* (6th ed, Oxford University Press, 2015) 520.

[37] *ibid.*

[38] Case C-50/00P *Unión de Pequeños Agricultores v Council* [2002] ECR I-6677.

[39] *ibid*, 6717.

there are no implementing measures or where the applicant would have to break the law in order to challenge ensuing sanctions. In his view, the principle of legal certainty favoured allowing a general measure to be reviewed as soon as possible and not only after implementing measures have been adopted.

[16–40] In light of these factors, Advocate General Jacobs recommended that the Court of Justice alter its approach so as to recognise that an applicant is individually concerned by an EU measure where the measure has, or is liable to have, a substantial adverse effect on that person's interests. Such an approach would avoid cases of possible denial of access to justice by allowing direct access to a court which can grant the most appropriate remedy. It would also remove the anomaly under *Plaumann* whereby the greater the number of persons affected by a measure the less likely it is that effective judicial review is available.

[16–41] Two months after the delivery of the *Unión* opinion, the General Court gave judgment in *Jégo-Quéré*.[40] This case involved a challenge by a French fishing company to a regulation that limited the size of fishing nets that could be used off the coast of Ireland in order to preserve stocks of hake. The company argued that given the unique nature of its activities, including the size of its vessels and the nature of its catches, of which the Commission would have been aware, it ought to be regarded as being individually affected. The General Court rejected this, but went on to consider an alternative argument to the effect that, if it were denied standing, the applicant would be denied any legal remedy enabling it to challenge the legality of the contested act. Since the regulation did not provide for the adoption of any implementing measures by the Member States, the applicant maintained that it would have no right of action before the national courts. In reply, the Commission argued that the applicant remained free to bring an action for non-contractual liability pursuant to Art 268 TFEU. Placing reliance on the opinion of AG Jacobs in *Unión de Pequeños Agricultores*, the General Court considered that:

> as regards proceedings before a national court giving rise to a reference to the Court of Justice for a preliminary ruling under Article [267 TFEU], it should be noted that, in a case such as the present, there are no acts of implementation capable of forming the basis of an action before national courts. The fact that an individual affected by a [Union] measure may be able to bring its validity before the national courts by violating the rules it lays down and then asserting their illegality in subsequent judicial proceedings brought against him does not constitute an adequate means of judicial protection. Individuals cannot be required to breach the law in order to gain access to justice.
>
> The procedural route of an action for damages based on the non-contractual liability of the [Union] does not, in a case such as the present, provide a solution that satisfactorily protects the interests of the individual affected. Such an action cannot result in the removal from the [Union] legal order of a measure which is nevertheless necessarily held to be illegal. Given that it presupposes that damage has been directly occasioned by the application of the measure in issue, such an action is subject to criteria of admissibility and substance which are different from those governing actions for annulment, and does not therefore place the [Union] judicature in a position whereby it can carry out the comprehensive judicial review which it is its task to perform. In particular, where a measure of general application, such as the provisions contested in the present case, is challenged in the context of such an action, the review carried out by the [Union] judicature does not cover all the factors

40 Case T-177/01 *Jégo-Quéré v Commission* [2002] ECR II–2365.

which may affect the legality of that measure, being limited instead to the censuring of sufficiently serious infringements of rules of law intended to confer rights on individuals.

On the basis of the foregoing, the inevitable conclusion must be that the procedures provided for in, on the one hand, Article [267 TFEU] and, on the other hand, Article [268 TFEU] can no longer be regarded, in the light of Articles 6 and 13 of the ECHR and of Article 47 of the Charter of Fundamental Rights, as guaranteeing persons the right to an effective remedy enabling them to contest the legality of [EU] measures of general application which directly affect their legal situation.

… In the light of the foregoing, and in order to ensure effective judicial protection for individuals, a natural or legal person is to be regarded as individually concerned by a [Union] measure of general application that concerns him directly if the measure in question affects his legal position, in a manner which is both definite and immediate, by restricting his rights or by imposing obligations on him. The number and position of other persons who are likewise affected by the measure, or who may be so, are of no relevance in that regard.

In the present case, obligations are indeed imposed on Jégo-Quéré by the contested provisions. The applicant, whose vessels are covered by the scope of the regulation, carries on fishing operations in one of the areas in which, by virtue of the contested provisions, such operations are subjected to detailed obligations governing the mesh size of the nets to be used.

It follows that the contested provisions are of individual concern to the applicant.[41]

[16–42] A further two months after this judgment, however, the Court of Justice firmly rejected the call by Advocate General Jacobs to depart from its existing case law. In its judgment in *Unión de Pequeños Agricultores*, the Court of Justice observed that while it was possible to envisage an alternative system of judicial review, it would be for the Member States to bring this about by introducing the necessary Treaty reforms.[42] The Court closely adhered to the long-held view that the Treaties establish a complete system of legal remedies designed to ensure judicial review of the legality of Union acts. Under that system, where a person does not meet the admissibility criteria to challenge an act of general application, they may either indirectly plead the invalidity of the act under Art 277 or request a national court to seek a preliminary ruling on the validity of the act. In this regard, the Court underlined the obligation that is imposed on national courts "so far as possible, to interpret and apply national procedural rules governing the exercise of rights of action in a way that enables natural and legal persons to challenge before the courts the legality of any decision or other national measure relative to the application to them of [an EU] act of general application, by pleading the invalidity of such an act".[43]

[16–43] This dialogue came to its predictable conclusion with the 2004 judgment of

---

41 *ibid*, paras 44–47, 51–53. See Marie-Pierre Granger, "Towards a Liberalisation of Standing Conditions for Individuals Seeking Judicial Review of Community Acts: *Jégo-Quéré et Cie SA v Commission* and *Unión de Pequeños Agricultores v Council*" (2003) 66 *Modern Law Review* 124.

42 Case C-50/00P *Unión de Pequeños Agricultores v Council* [2002] ECR I-6677, 6735–6736. See Filip Ragolle, "Access to Justice for Private Applicants in the Community Legal Order: Recent (R)evolutions" (2003) 28 *European Law Review* 90; John Temple Lang, "Actions for Declarations that Community Regulations Are Invalid: The Duties of National Courts under Article 10 EC" (2003) 28 *European Law Review* 102.

43 *ibid*, 6735.

the Court of Justice in *Jégo-Quéré*, in which it overturned the judgment of the General Court by following its own 2002 decision in *Unión de Pequeños Agricultores*. According to the Court of Justice:

> it is not appropriate for an action for annulment before the [Union] Court to be available to an individual who contests the validity of a measure of general application, such as a regulation, which does not distinguish him individually in the same way as an addressee, even if it could be shown, following an examination by that Court of the particular national procedural rules, that those rules do not allow the individual to bring proceedings to contest the validity of the [EU] measure at issue. Such an interpretation would require the [Union] Court, in each individual case, to examine and interpret national procedural law. That would go beyond its jurisdiction when reviewing the legality of [EU] measures.
>
> Accordingly, an action for annulment before the [Union] Court should not on any view be available, even where it is apparent that the national procedural rules do not allow the individual to contest the validity of the [EU] measure at issue unless he has first contravened it.[44]

[16–44] Tasked with developing a constitutional treaty for the EU, the Convention on the Future of Europe was sitting when the Court of Justice delivered its judgment in *Unión de Pequeños Agricultores*, and the judgment has been described as a public invitation to the Convention to consider whether the standing rules should in fact be reformed.[45] The deliberations resulted in what is now the third category set out in Art 263(4), namely challenges to "regulatory acts" that do not entail implementing measures and which directly concern the applicant, without having to be of individual concern.[46]

(c) Regulatory Acts that Do Not Entail Implementing Measures

[16–45] In the case of *Inuit Tapiriit Kanatami*, the Court of Justice was required to consider for the first time the meaning of the third category of acts listed in Art 263(4), and so was called upon to interpret the scope of the reform that had been introduced as part of the Lisbon Treaty.[47] The case concerned a challenge by a number of associations of seal hunters to the validity of a regulation, adopted pursuant to the ordinary legislative procedure, governing trade in seal products. In seeking to establish their standing, the associations argued that the regulation was a regulatory act that did not entail implementing measures, and so they were only required to demonstrate direct concern, as opposed to both direct and individual concern.

[16–46] As the term "regulatory act" is not defined in the Treaties, and might be said to sit rather uncomfortably with the dichotomy between legislative acts and delegated/implementing acts, the Court of Justice was required to choose between contrasting interpretations of the term. For the applicants, a teleological interpretation of "regulatory act" that included both legislative and non-legislative acts was in line with the original concern of the authors of the proposed treaty establishing a Constitution for Europe and

---

[44] Case C-263/02P *Commission v Jégo-Quéré* [2004] ECR I-3425, 3458–3459.

[45] Anthony Arnull, "Judicial Review in the European Union" in Anthony Arnull and Damian Chalmers (eds), *The Oxford Handbook of European Union Law* (Oxford University Press, 2015) 376, 390.

[46] See Stephan Balthasar, "Locus Standi Rules for Challenges to Regulatory Acts by Private Applicants: The New Article 263(4) TFEU" (2010) 35 *European Law Review* 542.

[47] Case C-583/11P *Inuit Tapiriit Kanatami v Parliament and Council* EU:C:2013:625, 3 October 2013.

of the Lisbon Treaty, who wanted to fill the lacunae which had been clearly identified in *Unión de Pequeños Agricultores* and *Jégo-Quéré*. In contrast, the General Court and the Advocate General had concluded that regulatory acts meant acts other than legislative acts, a position supported by the Parliament, Council and Commission. The institutions presented their view that "regulatory act" was intended to include various categories of legal acts that were *not* legislative acts, including delegated acts and implementing acts of general application which constitute the overwhelming majority of EU legal acts. The Commission added that the term also covered non-legislative acts of general application adopted on specific legal bases, and also acts of general application adopted by the various other EU bodies, offices or agencies.

[16–47] The Court of Justice upheld the interpretation of the General Court in ruling that regulatory acts did not include legislative acts, concluding that if it were otherwise the case there would, in effect, be no distinction between acts and regulatory acts. In doing so, the Court placed some significant reliance on the *travaux préparatoires* of the Constitution for Europe, notwithstanding that that proposed treaty was never in fact adopted. The Court began by noting that, in interpreting a provision of EU law, it is necessary to take account not only of its wording and the objectives it pursues, but also its context and the provisions of EU law as a whole. Not only that, but the origins of a provision of EU law "may also provide information relevant to its interpretation".[48] The Court then proceeded to reason as follows:

> The first paragraph of Article 263 TFEU identifies the European Union acts which may be the subject matter of an action for annulment before the Courts of the European Union, namely (i) legislative acts and (ii) … other binding acts intended to produce legal effects vis-à-vis third parties, and the latter may be individual acts or acts of general application …
>
> … First, it must be stated that the first two limbs of the fourth paragraph of Article 263 TFEU correspond with those which were laid down, before the entry into force of the Treaty of Lisbon, by the EC Treaty, in the fourth paragraph of Article 230 thereof.
>
> Given the reference to "acts" in general, the subject matter of those limbs of Article 263 is any European Union act which produces binding legal effects. That concept therefore covers acts of general application, legislative or otherwise, and individual acts. …
>
> Secondly, by means of the Treaty of Lisbon, there was added to the fourth paragraph of Article 263 TFEU a third limb which relaxed the conditions of admissibility of actions for annulment brought by natural and legal persons. Since the effect of that limb is that the admissibility of actions for annulment brought by natural and legal persons is not subject to the condition of individual concern, it renders possible such legal actions against "regulatory acts" which do not entail implementing measures and are of direct concern to the applicant.
>
> As regards the concept of "regulatory act", it is apparent from the third limb of the fourth paragraph of Article 263 TFEU that its scope is more restricted than that of the concept of "acts" used in the first and second limbs of the fourth paragraph of Article 263 TFEU, in respect of the characterisation of the other types of measures which natural and legal persons may seek to have annulled. The former concept cannot … refer to all acts of general application but relates to a more restricted category of such acts. To adopt an interpretation to the contrary would amount to nullifying the distinction made between the term "acts" and "regulatory acts" by the second and third limbs of the fourth paragraph of Article 263 TFEU.

---

48 *ibid*, para 50.

> Further, it must be observed that the fourth paragraph of Article 263 TFEU reproduced in identical terms the content of Article III–365(4) of the proposed treaty establishing a Constitution for Europe. It is clear from the *travaux préparatoires* relating to that provision that while the alteration of the fourth paragraph of Article 230 EC was intended to extend the conditions of admissibility of actions for annulment in respect of natural and legal persons, *the conditions of admissibility laid down in the fourth paragraph of Article 230 EC relating to legislative acts were not however to be altered*. Accordingly, the use of the term "regulatory act" in the draft amendment of that provision made it possible to identify the category of acts which might thereafter be the subject of an action for annulment under conditions less stringent than previously, while maintaining "a restrictive approach in relation to actions by individuals against legislative acts (for which the 'of direct and individual concern' condition remains applicable)".
>
> In those circumstances, it must be held that that the purpose of the alteration to the right of natural and legal persons to institute legal proceedings, laid down in the fourth paragraph of Article 230 EC, was to enable those persons to bring, under less stringent conditions, actions for annulment of acts of general application *other than legislative acts*.[49]

[16–48] In response to the applicants' claim that such an interpretation was contrary to their right to an effective judicial remedy as guaranteed by Art 47 of the Charter of Fundamental Rights, the Court repeated its established view that the combination of the Art 267 preliminary reference procedure and the indirect plea of illegality under Art 277 means that, even if an individual does not have standing to challenge a measure directly under Art 263, he or she nevertheless does have adequate judicial protection against the application of such a measure. As explained by the Court:

> Where responsibility for the implementation of those acts lies with the European Union institutions, those persons are entitled to bring a direct action before the Courts of the European Union against the *implementing measures* under the conditions stated in the fourth paragraph of Article 263 TFEU, and to plead, pursuant to Article 277 TFEU, in support of that action, the illegality of the general act at issue. Where that implementation is a matter for the Member States, such persons may plead the invalidity of the European Union act at issue before the national courts and tribunals and cause the latter to request a preliminary ruling from the Court of Justice, pursuant to Article 267 TFEU.
>
> In that context, it must be emphasised that, in proceedings before the national courts, individual parties have the right to challenge before the courts the legality of any decision or other national measure relative to the application to them of a European Union act of general application, by pleading the invalidity of such an act.
>
> It follows that requests for preliminary rulings which seek to ascertain the validity of a measure constitute, like actions for annulment, means for reviewing the legality of European Union acts.[50]

[16–49] As Robert Schütze has put it, in *Inuit* the Court "justified its restrictive stance on the *direct* review of European law by pointing to its expansive stance on the *indirect* review of European law".[51] While this might be said to flow from the unique nature of

---

49 *ibid*, paras 51–60. Emphasis added. See Pieter-Augustijn van Malleghem and Niels Baeten, "Before the Law Stands a Gatekeeper – Or, What Is a 'Regulatory Act' in Article 263(4) TFEU?" (2014) 51 *Common Market Law Review* 1187; Alexander Kornezov, "Shaping the New Architecture of the EU System of Judicial Remedies: Comment on *Inuit*" (2014) 39 *European Law Review* 251.

50 *ibid*, paras 93–95. Emphasis added.

51 Robert Schütze, *European Union Law* (Cambridge University Press, 2015) 363.

the EU legal order, it is hard to deny that at a certain level it does seem counter-intuitive. From his own review of the *travaux préparatoires*, Schütze considers the drafting history to be inconclusive as between the two opposing interpretations of "regulatory act", nor does he consider a textual argument to clearly favour one interpretation over another. Teleological arguments, on the other hand, "point in both directions – depending which *telos* one prefers".[52] Anthony Arnull is less circumspect in his assessment, describing the decision in *Inuit* as

> a remarkable judgment for a court not generally noted for its restraint. Absent was any trace of the spirit that animated *Van Gend en Loos* and its progeny. The Court could have taken as its starting point the observation … that the final clause of Article 263 "pursues an objective of opening up the conditions for bringing direct actions…". Instead it resorted to a narrow conservativism jerry-built on the presumed intentions of the authors of the Treaty of Lisbon, the explanations accompanying the Charter and the *travaux préparatoires* of the Convention on the Future of Europe. … [I]t led the Court to a conclusion which it accepted might sometimes prove inadequate to guarantee respect for the fundamental right to effective judicial protection, a general principle of law having constitutional status. The result was to leave the Union dependent on the national courts to ensure full respect for that principle, one which seems to impose greater burdens on them that it does on the Union Courts.[53]

[16–50] The narrowing of the third category in Art 263(4) did not end with the decision in *Inuit*. While that judgment provided a relatively restrictive interpretation of regulatory acts, in contrast, the Court of Justice has interpreted the concept of "implementing acts" in an expansive manner, thereby reducing the scope of the third category even further. It will be recalled that this third category relates to challenges to regulatory acts that *do not* entail implementing measures and so, the broader the definition of implementing measures, the narrower the third category becomes. The logic behind the introduction of such a category was to avoid the situation whereby the absence of any implementing acts to challenge would force an individual to have to infringe an EU act in order to have the grounds to challenge it. In *Telefónica v Commission*, the applicant was held not to have standing as the contested Commission decision was comprised of a declaration that certain financial schemes made available by the Spanish Government amounted to state aid.[54] The Court noted that the declaration contained within the Commission's decision did not set out the consequences for those who had availed of the scheme. Rather, those consequences would have to be established by means of an administrative document, such as a tax notice, which would be an implementing act that was entailed by the contested regulatory act. As described by the Court:

> where a regulatory act entails implementing measures, judicial review of compliance with the European Union legal order is ensured irrespective of whether those measures are adopted by the European Union or the Member States. Natural or legal persons who are unable, because of the conditions governing admissibility laid down in the fourth paragraph of Article 263 TFEU, to challenge a regulatory act of the European Union directly before the European Union judicature are protected against the application to them of such an act by the ability to challenge the implementing measures which the act entails.
>
> Where responsibility for the implementation of such acts lies with the institutions, bodies,

[52] *ibid*, 360.

[53] Anthony Arnull, "Judicial Review in the European Union" in Anthony Arnull and Damian Chalmers (eds), *The Oxford Handbook of European Union Law* (Oxford University Press, 2015) 376, 398.

[54] Case C-274/12P *Telefónica v Commission* EU:C:2013:852, 19 December 2013.

offices or agencies of the European Union, natural or legal persons are entitled to bring a direct action before the European Union judicature against the implementing acts under the conditions stated in the fourth paragraph of Article 263 TFEU, and to plead in support of that action, pursuant to Article 277 TFEU, the illegality of the basic act at issue. Where that implementation is a matter for the Member States, those persons may plead the invalidity of the basic act at issue before the national courts and tribunals and cause the latter to request a preliminary ruling from the Court of Justice, pursuant to Article 267.[55]

[16–51] This narrow approach was reaffirmed in *T&L Sugars Ltd*, which concerned an action seeking the annulment of a Commission regulation and implementing regulations governing the release of out-of-quota sugar onto the Union market at reduced levies.[56] The regulations provided that, in order to benefit from the permission to release additional amounts of sugar, producers had to apply to the competent authority within their Member State. The competent authorities were to decide on the admissibility of the applications based on criteria set down in the regulations, and pass on this information to the Commission. Based on the decisions taken by the Commission, every week, the national authorities would issue certificates granting a reduction of the levy in respect of the applications notified to the Commission the preceding week, according to a template certificate annexed to the regulation.

[16–52] The General Court held that the regulations could not produce their legal effects vis-à-vis the operators concerned without the intermediary step of measures first being taken by the competent national authorities. Such measures were held to constitute implementing measures within the meaning of Art 263(4), with the General Court rejecting the applicants' argument that those measures were "automatic and mandatory".[57] On appeal, the applicants argued that "every detail of the contested regulations was determined by the Commission and the only role left to the Member States was to act merely as a 'mail box'".[58] They claimed that the General Court had erred in law in holding that the degree of discretion enjoyed by Member States is irrelevant for the purposes of ascertaining whether a regulatory act "entails implementing measures". According to the applicants, in order to determine whether a measure taken by a Member State in fact added anything to the EU act under which it was taken, the existence of a discretion was a relevant criterion. Sitting as a Grand Chamber, the Court of Justice rejected this line of argument and shared the position of the General Court. In its view, the Commission regulations:

> produce their legal effects vis-à-vis the appellants only through the intermediary of acts taken by the national authorities following the submission of applications for certificates on the basis of Implementing Regulation No 302/2011. The decisions of the national authorities granting such certificates, which apply the coefficients fixed by Implementing Regulation No 393/2011 to the operators concerned, and the decisions refusing such certificates in full or in part therefore constitute implementing measures within the meaning of the final limb of the fourth paragraph of Article 263 TFEU.
>
> That conclusion is not called into question by the allegedly mechanical nature of the measures taken at national level.

---

[55] *ibid*, paras 28–29.

[56] Case C-456/13 P *T&L Sugars Ltd v Commission* EU:C:2015:284, 28 April 2015. See Camilla Buchanan and Luca Bolzonello, "Towards a Definition of 'Implementing Measures' under Article 263, Paragraph 4, TFEU" (2015) 6 *European Journal of Risk Regulation* 671.

[57] Case T-279/11 *T&L Sugars Ltd v Commission* EU:T:2013:299, 6 June 2013.

[58] Case C-456/13 P *T&L Sugars Ltd v Commission* EU:C:2015:284, 28 April 2015.

> As the General Court rightly held ..., that question is irrelevant in ascertaining whether those regulations entail implementing measures within the meaning of the final limb of the fourth paragraph of Article 263 TFEU.[59]

[16–53] In response to more general arguments based on Art 47 of the Charter of Fundamental Rights and the right to effective judicial protection, the Grand Chamber repeated the position that, as regards persons or entities that do not meet the standing requirement in Art 263(4), "it is for the Member States to establish a system of legal remedies and procedures which ensure respect for the fundamental right to effective judicial protection".[60] More particularly, the Grand Chamber emphasised once again that in proceedings before the national courts, "individual parties have the right to challenge before the courts the legality of any decision or other national measure relative to the application to them of a European Union act of general application, by pleading the invalidity of such an act".[61] Accordingly, just like annulment actions, preliminary references on validity constitute means for reviewing the legality of EU acts.

C. Indirect Challenges – Article 277 TFEU

[16–54] Article 277 TFEU provides that, notwithstanding the expiry of the two-month period laid down in Art 263, in proceedings in which an EU act of general application is at issue, any party may plead the four grounds specified in Art 263 in order to invoke the inapplicability of that act.[62] Accordingly, Art 277 is not an independent cause of action. Rather, Art 277 allows for an indirect form of challenge, in the sense that it can only be relied upon in proceedings brought on the basis of another Treaty article. Crucially, a declaration that an act is inapplicable will deprive any act adopted under it of its legal basis. More generally, a declaration of inapplicability has been described as "tantamount in practical terms to a declaration of invalidity, for the institutions will immediately cease to apply the measure and the Union courts will thenceforth treat it as invalid".[63]

[16–55] A typical manner in which Art 277 is relied upon is where, say, a decision has been adopted pursuant to a "parent" regulation. The two-month time limit might have precluded any Art 263 annulment challenge to the regulation, but, as it has been adopted more recently, an Art 263 action has been brought seeking the annulment of the decision. In addition, whereas the decision may be of direct and individual concern to the applicant, giving the necessary standing to bring a challenge, the regulation may not, ruling out a direct challenge under Art 263. By virtue of Art 277 it is nonetheless permissible, in such proceedings, to rely on the four Art 263 grounds in order to challenge the applicability of the parent regulation. As the Court of Justice has described, Art 277

> gives expression to a general principle conferring upon any party to proceedings the right to challenge, for the purpose of obtaining the annulment of a decision of direct and

---

59 *ibid*, paras 40–42.

60 *ibid*, para 49.

61 *ibid*, para 46.

62 See Matthias Vogt, "Indirect Judicial Protection in EC Law: The Case of the Plea of Illegality" (2006) 31 *European Law Review* 364.

63 Alan Dashwood, Michael Dougan, Barry Rodger, Eleanor Spaventa and Derrick Wyatt, *Wyatt and Dashwood's European Union Law* (6th ed, Hart, 2011) 202.

> individual concern to that party, the validity of previous acts of the institutions which form the legal basis of the decision which is being attacked, if that party was not entitled under Article [263] of the Treaty to bring a direct action challenging those acts by which it was thus affected without having been in a position to ask that they be declared void.
>
> … This wide interpretation of Article [277] derives from the need to provide those persons who are precluded by the second paragraph Article [263] from instituting proceedings directly in respect of general acts with the benefit of judicial review of them at the time when they are affected by implementing decisions which are of direct and individual concern to them.[64]

[16–56] The General Court has similarly explained that, since the legality of a contested measure must be assessed on the basis of the elements of fact and law existing at the time when the measure was adopted, the legality of a legal act which forms the legal basis for that measure must also be assessed at that time, rather than the time at which it itself was adopted.[65]

[16–57] An example of reliance on Art 277 can be seen in the case of *Inuit*, referred to above. It having been held that the applicants did not have the necessary standing to challenge a regulation governing the trade in seal products, a second set of Art 263 proceedings were instituted, this time seeking to challenge a subsequent regulation laying down detailed rules for the implementation of the basic regulation. In those proceedings, via Art 277, the applicants were able to raise arguments as to the inapplicability of the basic regulation that they had been found to lack the standing to challenge in the first set of proceedings.[66]

D. Failure to Act – Article 265 TFEU

[16–58] Under Art 265 TFEU, an action may be brought against a Union institution, body, office or agency other than the Court of Justice or the Court of Auditors if, in infringement of the Treaties, it fails to act having first been called upon to do so.[67] Once called upon to act, the institution has two months within which to "define its position",

---

64 Case 92/78 *Simmenthal v Commission* [1979] ECR 777, 800.

65 Joined Cases T-177/94 and T-377/94 *Altmann v Commission* [1996] ECR II-2041, 2092.

66 Case T-526/10 *Inuit Tapiriit Kanatami v Commission* EU:T:2013:215, 25 April 2013; Case C-398/13 P *Inuit Tapiriit Kanatami v Commission* EU:C:2015:535, 3 September 2015. It might be noted that the General Court decided to deal with the merits of the case first and, having dismissed the applicants' claims, it was unnecessary to consider whether each of the applicants had the necessary standing. The Court of Justice upheld the judgment of the General Court.

67 See, for example, Case T-521/14 *Sweden v Commission* EU:T:2015:976, 16 December 2015; Apolline JC Roger, "Endocrine Disrupting Chemical Wars: The Saga Continues: The Court Found the Commission in Failure to Act (and May Need to Strike Back Later)" (2016) 7 *Journal of European Risk Regulation* 629. See Ole Due, "Legal Remedies for the Failure of European Community Institutions to Act in Conformity with EEC Treaty Provisions" (1990) 14 *Fordham International Law Journal* 341; John Temple Lang and Colin Raftery, "Remedies for the Commission's Failure to Act in 'Comitology' Cases" (2011) 36 *European Law Review* 264. In the ongoing case of *Czech Republic v Commission*, the alleged failure to act is, unusually, the Commission not having brought proceedings against the Czech Republic for failure to fulfil obligations. Having conditionally paid a sum into the Commission's account in 2015 in respect of tradition own resources, it is claimed by the Czech Republic that the Commission ought to either have returned the sum or instituted infringement proceedings. Case T-13/19 *Czech Republic v Commission* (ongoing) [2019] OJ C103/48.

failing which an action may be brought within a further two-month period. In turn, while the definition of the institution's position – such as, for example, that it does not consider that any action is warranted – rules out the possibility of an action for failure to act, it itself may be subject to an annulment action under Art 263.[68] Although Art 265 does not prescribe any time limit as to when a complaint must first be made regarding a failure to act, the Court of Justice has indicated that it should be made within a reasonable period once it has become clear that the institution has decided not to take action. The institution whose failure to act has been declared contrary to the Treaties is required, within a reasonable period of time, to take the necessary measures to comply with the Court's judgment.

[16–59] A failure to act action may be brought by a Member State, an EU institution, agency or body, or by a natural or legal person in respect of a failure "to address to that person any act other than a recommendation or an opinion". Although the terms of Art 265 require that the act which it is claimed ought to have been adopted be *addressed* to the applicant, the Court has held that the possibility for individuals to assert their rights should not depend upon whether the institution concerned has acted or has failed to act. In other words, the same test for determining standing to seek the annulment of an act under Art 263 will also apply to an individual alleging a failure to act. A private applicant will have standing, therefore, if it can demonstrate that the act would have been of direct and individual concern to it, or that the act would have comprised a regulatory act that did not entail implementing measures and was of direct concern to it.[69]

[16–60] There is a close relationship between an annulment action under Art 263 and an action for a failure to act under Art 265, which have been described as providing complementary remedies. That said, relatively few cases have succeeded in establishing a failure to act and so the overall significance of this remedy is somewhat less than that of an annulment action. The interaction between the two can be seen from *Irish Cement Ltd v Commission*, in which Irish Cement lodged a complaint with the Commission in April 1985 alleging that aid granted to Sean Quinn Quarries Ltd by the Northern Irish Development Board for the building of a plant in Fermanagh, amounted to unlawful state aid.[70] By a letter of May 1985, the Commission replied that the aid had been granted in accordance with the relevant rules. In March 1986, Irish Cement wrote again to the Commission, further outlining why it considered the grant to be unlawful and requesting the Commission to open a state aid procedure. By a letter of July 1986, the Commission replied that, "as has already been stated in the previous letter … dated 14 May 1985 the grant to Sean Quinn Quarries Ltd to build a cement manufacturing plant in Northern Ireland falls under an aid system which the Commission has deemed to be compatible with the common market … The Commission is therefore unable to intervene in the award of this aid".[71]

[16–61] Irish Cement brought an action under Art 265 alleging the failure of the Commission to open a procedure as it had requested the Commission to do. Shortly afterward, Irish Cement brought a second set of proceedings in which it sought to challenge, pursuant to Art 263, the validity of the Commission's decision of July 1986 not to open a procedure. In these second proceedings, it also sought a declaration,

68 See, for example, Case C-192/12 *Commission v Council* EU:C:2013:753, 19 November 2013.
69 See Case T-395/04 *Air One v Commission* [2006] ECR II–1343.
70 Joined Cases 166/86 and 220/86 *Irish Cement Ltd v Commission* [1988] ECR 6473.
71 *ibid*, 6501.

pursuant to Art 265, that the Commission had still failed to define its position on all the points raised in the applicant's letter of March 1986. The Court of Justice concluded that the May 1985 letter constituted a decision by the Commission rejecting the complaint, which had definitive legal effects as far as the applicant was concerned. That decision had not been referred to the Court within the two-month time limit and so was no longer open to challenge. As the July 1986 decision merely confirmed the earlier decision it, too, was not open to challenge. As regards the alleged failure to act, the Court reiterated that such an action refers to failure to act in the sense of failure to take a decision or to define a position, and not the adoption of a measure different from that desired or considered necessary by the persons concerned. As the Commission had defined its position in its letter of May 1985, this action was also dismissed.

[16–62] In order to establish that a failure to act has infringed the Treaties, it is necessary to demonstrate that the EU institution had an obligation to act in the particular circumstances. A mere failure to exercise a discretion to act will not suffice. So, for example, in *Star Fruit v Commission* a Belgian importer and exporter of fruit alleged that the market in France was being operated in a manner that was not compatible with the Treaties and called upon the Commission to launch infringement proceedings under Art 258.[72] When the Commission failed to bring such proceedings, an Art 265 action was brought, but rejected by the Court as follows:

> it is clear from the scheme of Article [258] of the Treaty that the Commission is not bound to commence the proceedings provided for in that provision but in this regard has a discretion which excludes the right for individuals to require that institution to adopt a specific position.
>
> It is only if it considers that the Member State in question has failed to fulfil one of its obligations that the Commission delivers a reasoned opinion. Furthermore, in the event that the State does not comply with the opinion within the period allowed, the institution has in any event the right, but not the duty, to apply to the Court of Justice for a declaration that the alleged breach of obligations has occurred.
>
> It must also be observed that in requesting the Commission to commence proceedings pursuant to Article [258] the applicant is in fact seeking the adoption of acts which are not of direct and individual concern to it ... and which it could not therefore challenge by means of an action for annulment in any event.[73]

[16–63] Similarly, in *Parliament v Council*, the Parliament alleged that the Council had failed to introduce a common transport policy by a certain deadline as required by a provision of the EEC Treaty, and that it had failed to introduce measures to secure freedom to provide transport services, as also required by certain provisions of the Treaty.[74] The Court of Justice held that whereas the obligation to secure the freedom of transport services was sufficiently well defined to be the subject of a finding of a failure to act, the same could not be said of the introduction of a common transport policy more generally. In order for acts to be subject to Art 265 proceedings their scope would have to be sufficiently defined so as to enable them to be identified individually and adopted in compliance with the Court's judgment. In relation to the common transport policy,

72 Case 247/87 *Star Fruit v Commission* [1989] ECR 291.
73 *ibid*, 301.
74 Case 13/83 *Parliament v Council* [1985] ECR 1513.

> the Council's argument that it has a discretion must, in principle, be accepted. Although it is true that the discretion is limited by the requirements which stem from the establishment of the common market and by certain precise provisions in the Treaty such as those laying down time-limits, the fact remains that under the system laid down by the Treaty it is for the Council to determine, in accordance with the rules of procedure provided for in the Treaty, the aims of and means for implementing a common transport policy.
>
> As part of its obligation to introduce a common transport policy the Council is required to make all the decisions necessary for the gradual introduction of such a policy, but the substance of those decisions is not determined by the Treaty. Thus, for example, the Treaty leaves it to the Council to decide whether action in the transport sector must deal first with relations between the railways and the public authorities or with competition between road and rail. It is also for the Council to determine what priorities are to be observed in harmonizing the laws and administrative practices in the sector and to decide what matters such harmonization must cover. In that respect the Treaty gives the Council a discretion.
>
> ... the absence of a common policy which the Treaty requires to be brought into being does not in itself necessarily constitute a failure to act sufficiently specific in nature to form the subject of an action under Article [265]. That observation applies in the present case notwithstanding the fact that progress towards the achievement of a common transport policy ... must continue, or the fact that a substantial part of that work ought ... to have been completed before the expiry of the transitional period.[75]

[16–64] In contrast, in relation to the specific Treaty obligation to introduce the freedom to provide transport services, such as through the elimination of discrimination on the grounds of nationality, the Council did not have the same discretion as that on which it could rely in other areas of the common transport policy. In the Court's view, therefore, these more specific obligations were "sufficiently well-defined for disregard of them to be the subject of a finding of failure to act" pursuant to Art 265.[76]

E. Action for Damages – Article 340 TFEU

[16–65] The contractual liability of the Union is, in accordance with Art 340(1) TFEU, governed by the law applicable to the contract in question and the Treaties confer no specific role on the CJEU in respect of it. Rather, Art 274 TFEU clarifies that national courts are competent to hear claims of contractual liability against the Union.[77] However, as provided for in Art 272 TFEU, the CJEU may have jurisdiction to give judgment pursuant to any arbitration clause contained in a contract concluded by or on behalf of the Union, whether that contract be governed by public or private law.

[16–66] In contrast, Art 268 TFEU confers jurisdiction on the CJEU over disputes relating to claims for damages arising out of non-contractual liability under Art 340(2)

---

75 *ibid*, 1596, 1597.

76 *ibid*, 1600.

77 According to Art 274 TFEU, "save where jurisdiction is conferred on the [CJEU] by the Treaties, disputes to which the Union is a party shall not on that ground be excluded from the jurisdiction of the courts or tribunals of the Member States". Article 78(3) of the Rules of Procedure of the General Court provides that any application submitted under Art 272 TFEU pursuant to an arbitration clause in a contract shall be accompanied by a copy of the contract which contains that clause. Rules of Procedure of the General Court [2015] OJ L 105/1, with amendments published in [2016] OJ L217/71 and [2018] OJ L240/67.

TFEU. Article 340(2) provides that in the case of non-contractual liability, the Union shall, in accordance with the general principles common to the laws of the Member States, make good any damage caused by its institutions or by its servants in the performance of their duties. The broad phrase "non-contractual liability" reflects the fact that the different legal systems within the Member States will include various forms of liability for wrongful acts.

[16–67] Where an action for damages is brought by an individual it is heard by the General Court, whereas an action by a Member State goes directly to the Court of Justice. The Statute of the Court provides for a five-year limitation period for actions for non-contractual liability, which runs from the occurrence of the event giving rise to the alleged liability.[78] The Court has interpreted this to mean that the time period only begins to run once all the requirements for liability have materialised, including damage. So, for example, if the action relates to an administrative act, the time may begin when the applicant becomes aware of the damage arising rather than the moment at which the act was adopted.[79]

[16–68] Although the Court initially viewed Art 340(2) as a supplementary cause of action that was dependent on the prior success of another cause of action, such as annulment, it quickly altered its position and declared Art 340(2) to be an "independent form of action with a particular purpose to fulfil within the system of actions and subject to conditions for its use, conceived with a view to its specific purpose".[80] As a result, there are no standing requirements and any person who claims to have suffered damage due to a Union act may bring an action. Where the Union's liability arises from an act of one of its institutions, the proceedings are brought against that particular institution.

(i) Wrongful Acts

[16–69] In order to make out a claim for damages it is necessary to show that a wrongful act of the Union, its institutions or servants has caused the applicant to suffer a loss. A small number of cases have been brought seeking to establish a claim for damages where the relevant EU act is not unlawful – such as where the EU required the imposition of an asset freeze pursuant to a UN sanctions measure,[81] or where the EU's position in a trade dispute led to the WTO authorising the United States to impose retaliatory measures, causing a loss to a trader.[82] While both of these claims were unsuccessful, the Court appears not to have entirely ruled out the possibility that an action for damages may be brought in respect of lawful activity of the Union that causes a loss, but only if the damage is "unusual", in that it affects a particular group of economic operators in a disproportionate manner, as compared with others, and "special", in that the damage exceeds the economic risks inherent in operating in the sector concerned.[83] Although the legal systems of some Member States include such a principle, there is no consensus on the matter and so the Court of Justice has remained extremely cautious when addressing such a claim and has not yet found such a principle

78 Statute of the Court of Justice, Art 46.
79 Case C-282/05 *Holcim (Deutschland) v Commission* [2007] ECR I-2941, 2987.
80 Cases 4/69 *Lütticke v Commission* [1971] ECR 325, 336.
81 Case T-184/95 *Dorsch Consult v Council* [1998] ECR II-667.
82 Case C-120/06P *FIAMM v Council* [2008] ECR I-6513.
83 Case T-184/95 *Dorsch Consult v Council* [1998] ECR II-667, 696.

to exist as part of EU law. The current position, therefore, is that an action for damages is confined to loss that is suffered as a result of a wrongful act of the Union.

[16–70] At its most simple, a wrongful act might take the form of a negligent act of a servant of an EU institution in the performance of official duties, such as might cause someone to suffer a personal injury. In the case of *Adams v Commission*, the Commission was found to have breached a duty of confidentiality and a duty of care owed to Mr Adams, who had acted as a whistle-blower in respect of anti-competitive practices being carried out by his employer.[84] The Commission inadvertently made documents available to his employer which enabled his identification. On foot of a complaint by his employer to Swiss authorities, Mr Adams was prosecuted and convicted of industrial espionage. Whilst awarding damages, the Court found Mr Adams to have been 50 per cent contributory negligent in that he failed to make inquiries before returning to Switzerland and had failed to inform the Commission that it was possible to identify him from the documents.

[16–71] A wrongful act might also arise due to the adoption of an invalid act that has legal effect, such as a legislative act. Finally, wrongful acts can occur in the context of the duty of the institutions to exercise good administration. Generally, the distinction here is between legislative acts which have a broad application to people or entities at large, and administrative acts which tend to be of a more individualised nature. Administrative failures that could amount to wrongful acts include failing to follow proper procedures, failing to act without undue delay, making a decision based on incorrect facts or providing inaccurate information.[85] Whereas legislative acts will usually require the institution to exercise a considerable degree of discretion in making relevant policy choices and weighing up competing viewpoints, administrative acts will typically involve a much lesser degree of discretion, and possibly no discretion, although this is not always the case. An example of an administrative failure is seen in *Richez Parise*, where the Commission incorrectly interpreted rules governing staff pension entitlements, leading to misinformation being provided to staff.[86] While the Court considered that only in exceptional circumstances would an incorrect interpretation amount to a wrongful act, the same could not be said of the failure to rectify the information within a reasonable period of the error becoming known.

[16–72] The Court's case law on the nature or degree of wrongfulness required has developed over time. Initially, following the landmark judgment in *Schöppenstedt*, it was understood that a distinction was drawn between non-discretionary acts, such as administrative acts, and discretionary acts, such as legislative acts.[87] In respect of administrative / non-discretionary acts, it is sufficient to demonstrate that the breach of an EU law that grants rights to individuals has resulted in real and certain loss. This might include the matters mentioned above such as breach of fair procedures or a duty of confidentiality.

[16–73] Because discretionary acts, such as legislative acts, were regarded as involving complex policy choices, it was considered appropriate to apply a higher threshold of

---

[84] Case C-145/83 *Adams v Commission* [1985] ECR 3539.

[85] For example, Case T-292/15 *Vakakis kai Synergates v Commission* EU:T:2018:103, 28 February 2018; EU:T:2019:84, 12 February 2019.

[86] Joined Cases 19/69, 20/69, 25/69 and 30/69 *Richez Parise v Commission* [1970] ECR 325.

[87] Case 5/71 *Schöppenstedt v Council* [1971] ECR 975.

wrongfulness.[88] In *Schöppenstedt*, it was claimed that a regulation governing the pricing policy for sugar was discriminatory and that this, in itself, was the cause of a loss to the applicant. The Court ruled that in order for a legislative action involving measures of economic policy to amount to a wrongful act, there would need to be "a sufficiently flagrant violation of a superior rule of law for the protection of the individual".[89] Accordingly, the *Schöppenstedt* formula entailed three separate elements: (i) it applied to "legislative action involving measures of economic policy"; (ii) it required that the unlawfulness arose out of a breach of a "superior rule of law for the protection of the individual"; and (iii) it required that the breach be "sufficiently flagrant" or serious.

[16–74] The idea of legislative action involving measures of economic policy was interpreted broadly, so as to include a wide range of EU acts that entailed the exercise of discretionary policy choices. So too was the concept of a superior rule of law for the protection of the individual. Whereas rules governing competence, for example, could not be said to relate to the protection of the individual, general principles of EU law such as proportionality, non-discrimination, fundamental rights, procedural rights and legitimate expectations could, as could a relevant provision within a regulation. The most variable and complex of the three criteria was the requirement that the breach be sufficiently serious. The greater the level of discretion involved in the policy decision, the more serious a breach would be required, with the result that actions for damages relating to legislative acts or the exercise of discretionary powers by the institutions were rarely successful.

[16–75] A significant development in the approach to actions for damages arose out of the 1996 judgment in *Brasserie du Pêcheur*, in which the Court of Justice clarified the liability of Member States for failing to adhere to EU law.[90] In the course of it judgment, the Court observed that where a Member State acts in a field in which it enjoys a wide discretion, comparable to that of the EU institutions in implementing Union policies, the "conditions under which it may incur liability must, in principle, be the same as those under which the [EU] institutions incur liability in a comparable situation".[91] This was so as to ensure that the protection of the rights of individuals under EU law did not vary depending on whether a national authority or an EU institution was responsible for the damage. The test established in *Brasserie du Pêcheur* was that there must be a sufficiently serious breach of a rule of law intended to confer rights on individuals, with a sufficiently serious breach being said to arise where the Member State "manifestly and gravely disregarded the limits on its discretion".[92]

[16–76] In 2000, in the case *Bergaderm*, the Court of Justice was required to consider the nature of a Commission directive that had banned the use of certain substances in cosmetics on the basis that they were potentially carcinogenic, a matter that was of some scientific controversy.[93] In practice, the directive only affected the applicant, who

---

88 See Chris Hilson, "The Role of Discretion in EC Law on Non-Contractual Liability" (2005) 42 *Common Market Law Review* 677.

89 Case 5/71 *Schöppenstedt v Council* [1971] ECR 975, 984.

90 Joined Cases C-46/93 and C-48/93 *Brasserie du Pêcheur v Germany* [1996] ECR I-1029.

91 *ibid*, 1148.

92 *ibid*, 1150.

93 Case C-352/98P *Bergaderm v Commission* [2000] ECR I-5291. See Kathleen Gutman, "The Evolution of the Action for Damages against the European Union and its Place in the System of Judicial Protection" (2011) 48 *Common Market Law Review* 695; Takis Tridimas, "Liability for

used the prohibited substance in manufacturing sun tan oil. In its action for damages, the applicant argued that the directive was in the nature of an administrative act and that, as a result, it was only required to demonstrate that the directive breached an EU law that grants rights to individuals, namely that the adoption of the directive had involved a manifest error of assessment, breach of the principle of proportionality and procedural errors. The Commission, on the other hand, argued that the directive was of general legislative scope and concerned the applicants as manufacturers of sun protection products by reason of a business activity which may be pursued at any time by any person. Consequently, the Commission contended that the *Schöppenstedt* formula should apply, requiring a sufficiently flagrant breach of a superior rule of law for the protection of the individual.

[16–77] Having recalled the decision in *Brasserie du Pêcheur*, the Court suggested that the test to be followed in respect of actions against both Member States and Union institutions was whether there had been a manifest and grave disregard of the limits on the discretion to be exercised. Critically, the Court held that whether the measure taken by an institution was of a general or an individual nature was not a decisive criterion for identifying the limits of the discretion enjoyed by the institution.[94] This new *Bergaderm* formula indicated that the old distinction between legislative and administrative acts was to be replaced by a unified approach that mirrored the one taken by the Court in *Brasserie de Pêcheur*. As Lorna Woods and Philippa Watson have described:

> The new approach, in the wake of *Bergaderm*, therefore marks a departure from *Schöppenstedt* in three main respects: first, it is no longer necessary to consider whether the rule infringed was a "superior rule of law"; instead, the rule infringed has to be one intended to confer rights on individuals. Secondly, in establishing whether a breach is sufficiently serious, the criteria listed in ... *Brasserie de Pêcheur* are now applied, rather than the cases on the effects of the breach and harm to the claimant. ... Finally, the focus has also shifted away from the question of whether the act complained about was administrative or legislative; instead what matters now is the degree of discretion for the Union institution.[95]

[16–78] In addition to the level and complexity of the discretion being exercised, other factors relevant to determining the severity of a breach include the "relative clarity of the rule which has been breached; the measure of discretion left to the relevant authorities; whether the error of law was excusable or not; and whether the breach was intentional or voluntary".[96] For example, in *MyTravel* a successful annulment action was brought against a decision of the Commission which had found that a corporate acquisition by Airtours plc of First Choice plc would lead to a dominant position and was contrary to competition rules. The Commission's decision was annulled on the basis that it had made errors in assessing the impact of the acquisition on the market in short-haul package holidays. A subsequent action for damages was rejected by the General Court on the basis that the wrongfulness was not sufficiently serious, in that the error of assessment

Breach of Community Law: Growing Up and Mellowing Down?" (2001) 38 *Common Market Law Review* 301; Chris Hilson, "The Role of Discretion in EC Law on Non-Contractual Liability" (2005) 42 *Common Market Law Review* 677.

94 *ibid*, 5325.

95 Lorna Woods and Philippa Watson, *Steiner and Woods EU Law* (3rd ed, Oxford University Press, 2014) 313.

96 Paul Craig and Gráinne de Búrca, *EU Law* (6th ed, Oxford University Press, 2015) 589.

did not involve a manifest and grave infringement of the discretion being exercised. According to the General Court:

> Where, as in the present case, the unlawfulness of a legal measure is relied on as a basis for an action for damages, that measure, in order to be capable of causing the [Union] to incur non-contractual liability, must constitute a sufficiently serious breach of a rule of law intended to confer rights on individuals. The decisive criterion in that regard is whether the [Union] institution concerned manifestly and gravely disregarded the limits on its discretion.
>
> The system of rules which the Court of Justice has worked out with regard to the non-contractual liability of the [EU] takes into account, inter alia, the complexity of the situations to be regulated, difficulties in the application or interpretation of the texts and, more particularly, the margin of discretion available to the author of the act in question.
>
> Where the institution in question has only a considerably reduced, or even no, discretion, the mere infringement of [EU] law may be sufficient to establish the existence of a sufficiently serious breach of [EU] law. The same applies where the defendant institution improperly applies the relevant substantive or procedural rules.
>
> … the parties recognised that it is clear from the case-law that the concept of a sufficiently serious breach does not comprise all errors or mistakes which, even if of some gravity, are not incompatible with the normal conduct of an institution responsible for overseeing the application of competition rules, which are complex, delicate and subject to a considerable degree of discretion.
>
> When questioned on that point at the hearing …, the applicant also stated that the fact that the Court had annulled the Airtours decision – considering that the prospective analysis of the competitive situation set out in it, far from being based on cogent evidence, was vitiated by a series of errors of assessment as to factors fundamental to any assessment of whether a collective dominant position might be created – was not of itself sufficient to give rise to non-contractual liability on the [Union's] part, in so far as additional criteria were required by the case-law relating to actions for damages.
>
> To accept that the position was otherwise, by equating, without further analysis, the annulment established in *Airtours v Commission* with a sufficiently serious breach within the meaning of *Bergaderm*, would risk compromising the capacity of the Commission fully to function as regulator of competition, a task entrusted to it by the [TFEU], as a result of the inhibiting effect that the risk of having to bear the losses alleged by the undertakings concerned might have on the control of concentrations.
>
> Because of the need to have regard to such an effect, which is contrary to the general [Union] interest, a failure to fulfil a legal obligation, which, regrettable though it may be, can be explained by the objective constraints to which the institution and its officials are subject in the control of concentrations, cannot be held to constitute a breach of [EU] law which is sufficiently serious to give rise to the non-contractual liability of the [Union]. Conversely, the right to compensation for damage resulting from the conduct of the institution becomes available where such conduct takes the form of action manifestly contrary to the rule of law and seriously detrimental to the interests of persons outside the institution and cannot be justified or accounted for by the particular constraints to which the staff of the institution, operating normally, are objectively subject.[97]

[97] Case T-212/04 *MyTravel Group plc v Commission* [2008] ECR II-1967, paras 37–43. See also Case C-45/15 P *Safa Nicu Sepahan v Council* EU:C:2017:402, 30 May 2017, paras 29–31; Case T-434/15 *Islamic Republic of Iran Shipping Lines v Council* EU:T:2019:307, 8 May 2018, paras

[16–79] In general, the Court takes a restrictive approach to assessing the amount that is required to "make good any damage caused" by placing the applicant in the position that he or she would have been in had the wrongful act not occurred. The amount sought must be certain, specific, proven and quantifiable, but may also include imminent foreseeable damage. Non-material damage is compensated for on an exceptional basis.[98] In addition, in order for a loss to be considered to have been "caused" by the EU act, within the meaning of Art 340(2) TFEU, there must be a "sufficiently direct causal nexus between the conduct of the EU institutions and the damage, the burden of proof of which rests on the applicant, so that the conduct complained of must be the determining cause of the damage".[99]

[16–80] By way of illustration, an interesting recent case involved an award of damages made by the General Court based on the Court's own failure to adjudicate on proceedings within a reasonable time. In the case of *Gascogne*, a Commission decision had found a company to be participating in a cartel and imposed a fine.[100] The company instituted annulment proceedings against the decision in February 2006. The actions were eventually dismissed by the General Court in November 2011. A subsequent appeal was dismissed by the Court of Justice in November 2013.

[16–81] In a claim for damages brought against the EU, represented by the CJEU, the General Court awarded the company non-material damages of €5,000. In addition, the General Court awarded €47,000 in material damages to compensate for the fact that Gascogne had paid bank charges in respect of a guarantee for the fines owed on foot of the Commission decision. Rather than pay the fine, the company had provided this guarantee while the litigation was ongoing. On appeal, the Court of Justice found that the decision of the company to maintain the bank guarantee broke the causal link between the delay and the costs incurred. As explained by the Court of Justice:

> Nothing prevents, as a matter of EU law, that undertaking from terminating, at any time, the bank guarantee that it has provided and paying the fine imposed, where, in view of the evolution of the circumstances in relation to those existing on the date when that guarantee was provided, that undertaking deems that option more advantageous for it. That might be the case, in particular, where the conduct of the proceedings before the General Court leads the undertaking in question to take the view that the judgment will be delivered at a date later than that which it had initially envisaged and that, consequently, the cost of the bank guarantee will be higher than the cost that it had initially envisaged when providing that guarantee.[101]

[16–82] It followed that the breach of the obligation to adjudicate the proceedings within a reasonable time could not be regarded as the "determining cause" of the damage suffered by the company as a result of paying bank guarantee charges during the period which was deemed to be excessive. Rather, this damage was a consequence of the

50–58; Case T-37/17 *Bank Tejarat v Council* EU:T:2019:337, 16 May 2019; Case T-399/17 *Dalli v Commission* EU:T:2019:384, 6 June 2019.

[98] See Case T-558/15 *Iran Insurance Company v Council* EU:T:2018:945, 13 December 2018, paras 123–135.

[99] Joined Cases C-138/17 P and C-146/17 P *European Union v Gascogne Sack* EU:C:2018:1013, 13 December 2018, para 22. See also Case T-406/15 *Mahmoudian* EU:T:2019:468, 2 July 2019; Case T-405/15 *Fulmen* EU:T:2019:469, 2 July 2019.

[100] *ibid*

[101] *ibid*, para 29.

company's own decision to maintain the bank guarantee throughout the proceedings, despite the financial consequences which that entailed. In awarding material damages, the General Court had erred in misinterpreting the notion of "causal link".

[16–83] As regards non-material damage, in the General Court the company had sought an amount of €500,000 by way of compensation for matters such as harm to the company's reputation, uncertainty in decision-making, difficulties in managing the business and anxiety and inconvenience experienced by the members of the company's executive bodies and employees. As the proceedings were in the name of the company only, the claim in respect of its executives and employees was held to be inadmissible, as well as being unfounded in terms of the evidence produced. As the proceedings had lasted five years and nine months, the General Court accepted that the company had been placed "in a position of uncertainty greater than that normally engendered by court proceedings. That prolonged state of uncertainty inevitably had an impact on decision-making and the running of those businesses and therefore constituted non-material damage".[102]

[16–84] In assessing the proper amount to be awarded, the General Court followed existing case law according to which,

> having regard to the need to ensure that the competition rules of EU law are complied with, the Court of Justice cannot allow an appellant to reopen the question of the validity or amount of a fine, on the sole ground that there was a failure to adjudicate within a reasonable time, where all of its pleas directed against the findings concerning the amount of that fine and the conduct that it penalises have been rejected.
>
> It follows that the failure to adjudicate within a reasonable time when examining a legal action brought against a Commission decision imposing a fine on an undertaking for infringing the EU law competition rules cannot lead to the annulment, in whole or in part, of the fine imposed by that decision.
>
> Given the extent of it, the compensation sought by the applicants as reparation for the non-material damage they have suffered would, if awarded, have the effect of reopening the question of the amount of the fine imposed ..., even though it has not been established that the failure to adjudicate within a reasonable time ... had any bearing on the amount of that fine.
>
> Thus, the amount sought by the applicants cannot be regarded as a relevant criterion for the purposes of assessing the amount of compensation that they are entitled to claim.[103]

[16–85] In the assessment of the General Court, the appropriate award to compensate for non-material damage was €5,000, an assessment that was upheld by the Court of Justice on appeal.[104]

[16–86] Finally, complex situations can arise where both an EU institution and a Member State might share concurrent liability for a wrongful act, such as where a Member State implements an EU act that is found to be unlawful. The general rule of thumb is that where proceedings before a national court will provide an effective means

---

102 Case T-577/14 *Gascogne Sack v European Union* EU:T:2017:1, 10 January 2017, para 157.

103 *ibid*, paras 161–164.

104 Joined Cases C-138/17 P and C-146/17 P *European Union v Gascogne Sack* EU:C:2018:1013, 13 December 2018, paras 50–51.

of protecting the applicant's interests, the claim should be brought within the Member State. So, for example, a claim for the return of money paid to a national authority, even if the money is then passed on to form part of EU funds, should be brought within the Member State, as should a claim for a payment that is alleged to be unlawfully withheld.

Annulment Actions, Art 263	
• Grounds for Annulment	*Boyle v Commission* *Kadi II* *United Parcel Service* *Ireland v Commission (Fishing Quotas)* *Irish Farmers Association v Minister for Agriculture*
• "Direct Concern"	*International Fruit Company* *Piraiki-Patraiki*
• "Individual Concern"	*Plaumann* *Calpak* *Greenpeace* *Altadis* *International Fruit Company* *Piraiki-Patraiki* *Unión de Pequeños Agricultores* *Jégo-Quéré*
• Regulatory Acts	*Inuit Tapiriit*
• Implementing Measures	*Telefónica v Commission* *T&L Sugars Ltd v Commission*
Indirect Challenges, Art 277	*Inuit Tapiriit*
Failure to Act, Art 265	*Irish Cement Ltd v Commission* *Star Fruit v Commission* *Parliament v Council (Common Transport Policy)*
Action for Damages, Art 340	*Adams v Commission* *Richez Parise* *Schöppenstedt* *Brasserie du Pêcheur* *Bergaderm* *MyTravel* *Gascogne*

PART FIVE

Chapter 17

THE INTERNAL MARKET

A. Introduction

[17–01] Over time, successive treaties have added many important new areas to the substantive law of the EU. This ought not to obscure the fact, however, that the cornerstone of the European Union is, and always has been, the Internal Market (also known as the "Common Market" or "Single Market"). In 1957, the Treaty of Rome established the European Economic Community with the more narrowly defined task of promoting a "harmonious development of economic activities, a continuous and balanced expansion, an increase in stability, an accelerated raising of the standard of living and closer relations between the States belonging to it". These five goals were to be achieved through the creation of a "common market" and by progressively approximating the economic policies of the Member States. Having set out, in Art 2, the task of the EEC and the means by which to achieve it, Art 3 of the Treaty of Rome listed 11 specific activities that were to be included amongst those of the Community as:

(a) the elimination, as between Member States, of customs duties and of quantitative restrictions on the import and export of goods, and of all other measures having equivalent effect;
(b) the establishment of a common customs tariff and of a common commercial policy towards third countries;
(c) the abolition, as between Member States, of obstacles to freedom of movement for persons, services and capital;
(d) the adoption of a common policy in the sphere of agriculture;
(e) the adoption of a common policy in the sphere of transport;
(f) the institution of a system ensuring that competition in the common market is not distorted;
(g) the application of procedures by which the economic policies of Member States can be co-ordinated and disequilibria in their balances of payments remedied;
(h) the approximation of the laws of Member States to the extent required for the proper functioning of the common market;
(i) the creation of a European Social Fund in order to improve employment opportunities for workers and to contribute to the raising of their standard of living;

(j) the establishment of a European Investment Bank to facilitate the economic expansion of the Community by opening up fresh resources;
(k) the association of the overseas countries and territories in order to increase trade and to promote jointly economic and social development.

[17–02] Although the term "common market" was not defined in the Treaty of Rome, a description of what it entailed can be taken from the influential Spaak Report, whose language found its way into Art 2 of the Treaty:

> The objective of a common European market must be to create a vast zone of common economic policy, constituting a powerful unit of production, and making possible continuous growth, an increase in stability, an accelerated raising of the standard of living and the development of harmonious relations between the States which it unites. … However, these advantages of a common market can only be achieved if time is granted and means are collectively made available to permit necessary adaptations to be made, if practices which distort competition between producers are ended and if co-operation between the States is established in order to ensure monetary stability, economic growth and social progress. This is the basic reason why, where in theory liberalization of trade at a world wide level appears to be desirable, a true common market can in the end only be realized between a limited group of States, which one would wish to be as broad as possible.[1]

[17–03] An examination of the activities of the EEC set out in Art 3 of the Treaty of Rome illustrates that the Community was more than merely a free trade area or a customs union but was a common market, with additional aims that put it firmly on the road towards a future economic union.

[17–04] First, Art 3(a) provided for free trade between the Member States, requiring the elimination of customs duties and quantitative restrictions on the import and export of goods, and of all other measures having an equivalent effect. Whereas a free trade area would end here, a customs union goes further in that it provides for a common commercial policy towards third countries and a common customs tariff on imports into the EU, as set out in Art 3(b). As they are formally distinct from the Internal Market, the Customs Union and the Common Commercial Policy are considered separately in the following chapter.

[17–05] A common market, in contrast, adds a further, hugely significant dimension to a customs union by providing for the free mobility not just of goods themselves, but also of the factors of production – persons, services and capital – as described in Art 3(c). As well as this, Art 3(d) and (e) included the adoption of common policies in the spheres of agriculture and transport. Article 3(h) called for the approximation of the laws of the Member States to the extent required for the proper functioning of the Common Market, while Art 3(f) envisaged the institution of a system for ensuring that competition in the Common Market was not distorted.

[17–06] An economic union goes a step beyond a common market by agreeing a common monetary and fiscal policy, the first traces of which could be seen with the inclusion in Art 3 of the activity of applying "procedures by which the economic policies of Member States can be co-ordinated and disequilibria in their balances of

1 Cited in (and translated by) Keimal Mortelmans, "The Common Market, the Single Market and the Internal Market, What's in a Market?" (1998) 35 *Common Market Law Review* 101, 102–103.

payments remedied" and the establishment of a European Investment Bank.[2] While all of the Member States are now part of the Economic and Monetary Union, 19 are also members of the Euro Area, sharing the euro as their common currency.

[17–07] The closest equivalent to Art 3 of the Treaty of Rome is now Art 3 of the TEU, and in particular paragraphs 3 and 4 thereof, which read as follows:

> 3. The Union shall establish an internal market. It shall work for the sustainable development of Europe based on balanced economic growth and price stability, a highly competitive social market economy, aiming at full employment and social progress, and a high level of protection and improvement of the quality of the environment. It shall promote scientific and technological advance. It shall combat social exclusion and discrimination, and shall promote social justice and protection, equality between women and men, solidarity between generations and protection of the rights of the child. It shall promote economic, social and territorial cohesion, and solidarity among Member States. It shall respect its rich cultural and linguistic diversity, and shall ensure that Europe's cultural heritage is safeguarded and enhanced.
>
> 4. The Union shall establish an economic and monetary Union whose currency is the euro.

[17–08] A number of features stand out, most obviously the extent to which the scope of the EU's stated tasks and activities have extended beyond those listed in Arts 2 and 3 of the Treaty of Rome. From the relatively narrow economic focus of 1957, the objectives of the Union now include such matters as the protection of the environment and of cultural heritage, scientific and technological advancement, social justice and economic and monetary union.

[17–09] Secondly, it will be noted that the term "common market" has been replaced by "internal market". From the entry into force of the Single European Act in 1987 up until the Lisbon Treaty reforms in 2009, both terms co-existed within the Treaties. Now, only the term internal market is used. Although there is a suggestion that common market was the slightly broader of the two terms, more clearly including within its remit the common commercial policy and competition policy, the more widespread view is that there is no practical difference between the two phrases, such that they are interchangeable.[3] Notwithstanding its absence from the TEU and TFEU, the term "single market" is also very frequently used, and is perhaps now the most popular way in which to refer to the Internal Market in English, at least in a non-technical context. So, while a 1985 Commission White Paper was entitled "Completing the Internal Market", there is now a Single Market Strategy, a Single Market Act and a Single Market Forum, albeit that there remains a Commissioner and Directorate General for the Internal Market. Accordingly, these two terms would also appear to be largely synonymous, albeit

---

2 See Pieter verLoren van Themaat, "Some Preliminary Observations on the IGC: The Relations between the Concepts of a Common Market, a Monetary Union, an Economic Union, a Political Union and Sovereignty" (1991) 28 *Common Market Law Review* 291.

3 Lorna Woods and Philippa Woods, *EU Law* (11th ed, Oxford University Press, 2012) 327; Pierre Pescatore, "Some Critical Remarks on the 'Single European Act'" (1987) 24 *Common Market Law Review* 9, 11: "For the well-balanced and complex notion of a 'Common Market', the Single [European] Act substitutes the one-sided notion of an 'internal market' based on an arbitrary selection of the Treaty objectives, ignoring essential features such as the rules on competition, freedom of current payments, economic policy, commercial policy, taxation, non-discrimination etc." See also Keimal Mortelmans, "The Common Market, the Single Market and the Internal Market, What's in a Market?" (1998) 35 *Common Market Law Review* 101.

that internal market is the only one to appear in the Treaties. Indeed, as early as 1982 the Court appeared to foretell the interchangeability of these terms, using all three in describing the concept of a *common* market as involving "the elimination of all obstacles to intra-Community trade in order to merge the national markets into a *single* market bringing about conditions as close as possible to those of a genuine *internal* market".[4]

[17–10] Finally, it is worth considering Art 3 TEU in conjunction with Arts 3 and 4 TFEU, which set out the division of exclusive and shared competences as between the EU and the Member States. In accordance with Art 3 TFEU, the Customs Union, the establishing of competition rules necessary for the functioning of the Internal Market,[5] monetary policy for those states whose currency is the euro and the Common Commercial Policy are all matters of exclusive Union competence. In contrast, under Art 4 TFEU, the Internal Market more generally is an area of shared competence between the Union and the Member States. As an area of shared competence, the Member States may exercise their competence only to the extent that the Union has not exercised its competence or has decided to cease exercising its competence.

[17–11] Part III of the TFEU deals with the Union's policies and internal actions, and it is here that are found the provisions on the Internal Market and the four fundamental freedoms. The central provision is Art 26 TFEU, first introduced by the Single European Act of 1986, in which the Internal Market is defined as comprising "an area without internal frontiers in which the free movement of goods, persons, services and capital is ensured in accordance with the provisions of the Treaties". The Union is tasked with adopting measures with the aim of either *establishing* or *ensuring the functioning* of the Internal Market. On a proposal from the Commission, the Council is to determine the guidelines and conditions necessary to ensure balanced progress in all of the sectors concerned. A certain qualification is provided for in the following article, where an instruction is given to the Commission that, when drawing up its proposals, it is to take account of the "extent of the effort that certain economies showing differences in development will have to sustain for the establishment of the internal market". In light of this, the Commission may propose appropriate provisions. However, if these provisions take the form of derogations, they must be both temporary and cause the least possible disturbance to the functioning of the Internal Market.

[17–12] An essential element of the Internal Market is the removal of *physical* barriers such as customs checkpoints between the Member States. The inspection of goods themselves, or the documentation that may be required to accompany goods, undermines any advanced concept of the free movement of goods and creates significant additional costs to trading within the EU.

[17–13] Other barriers to trade are *fiscal* in nature, such as the imposition of tariffs or duties on imports or exports, or other charges on goods crossing a border that, although not formally termed a "tariff" or a "duty", have an equivalent effect. A fiscal barrier may also come about due to certain discriminatory treatment within the internal tax regime of a Member State where domestic goods or capital are treated favourably, giving them a competitive advantage, or imported goods or capital are treated less favourably, making it more difficult or less attractive for importers to trade, or investors

[4] Case 15/81 *Gaston Schul Douane Expediteur* [1982] ECR 1409, 1431–1432.

[5] See also Protocol No 27 to the TEU and TFEU on the Internal Market and Competition.

to invest, in that market.[6] So, even where taxation remains a matter of Member State competence, national taxes must be imposed in a manner that is compatible with EU law.[7] In proceedings brought by the Commission against Ireland, for instance, it was found that by requiring vehicle registration tax to be paid on imported cars – even where those cars had been leased or rented for a defined period in another Member State – Ireland had infringed the freedom to provide services as guaranteed by Art 56 TFEU.[8] According to the Court of Justice, the obligation to pay in advance the full amount of registration tax was "liable to deter both Irish residents from calling on vehicle rental or leasing services offered by service providers established in other Member States and those service providers from offering vehicle rental or leasing services to Irish residents".[9] The fact that vehicle taxation had not been harmonised at EU level and so fell within Ireland's competence could not justify the restriction on the freedom to provide services, since the exercise of that competence had to be in compliance with EU law. Whilst the Court accepted that the protection of the environment, by discouraging the rental or leasing of vehicles with heavy fuel consumption, may be an overriding public-interest objective, it was not satisfied that the Irish rules were a proportionate measure to achieve that objective.

[17–14] A third form of barrier comprises *regulatory* standards, restrictions and controls, primarily on goods. Here, it is the diversity among rules governing the manufacture and sale of products within each Member State that makes it difficult to operate within the Internal Market as if it were one, single marketplace, as is intended. Whereas the elimination of physical and fiscal barriers can be seen as part of the essential infrastructure of an internal market and a prerequisite to ensuring a basic level of openness and fairness, regulatory barriers are more complex, in that they will usually involve a competing policy objective against which the desire for free movement must be balanced, such as consumer protection, public health or the protection of the environment. As Art 3(3) of the TEU provides, it is the aim of the Union to establish a highly competitive *social market* economy.[10] This gives rise to delicate questions such as: (i) which state should be permitted to apply their own national rules – the home state of manufacture of a good or the host state in which the good is sold; and (ii) should Member States be allowed to make their own rules as to the appropriate standards to be applied or should such rules be harmonised at the EU level, so as to have a common approach throughout the entire Single Market.

[17–15] The approach taken by the Treaties to establishing an internal market without frontiers, in which the free movement of goods, persons, services and capital is ensured, is one which combines a number of different but complementary elements. Among these elements, the two principal methods used are negative integration, led by the Court of Justice, and positive integration, led by the Commission bringing forward

---

6 See Suzanne Kingston, "The Boundaries of Sovereignty: The ECJ's Controversial Role Applying Internal Market Law to Direct Tax Measures" (2006–2007) 9 *Cambridge Yearbook of European Legal Studies* 287.

7 Case C-451/99 *Cura Anlagen v Auto Service Leasing* [2002] ECR I-3193, 3230.

8 Case C-552/15 *Commission v Ireland* EU:C:2017:698, 19 September 2017. See Yannis Schlüter, "Towards a Court Mandated Harmonization of National Tax Rules Case 552/15, *Commission v Ireland*" (2018) 45 *Legal Issues of Economic Integration* 413.

9 *ibid*, para 82.

10 See Case C-201/15 *AGET Iraklis* EU:C:2016:972, 21 December 2016, paras 76–77.

legislative proposals aimed at the harmonisation of national laws. These twin methods of integration will be discussed below.

[17–16] Although they are not dealt with in this book, it is important to bear in mind that additional elements of EU law also serve to maintain and protect a functioning internal market. In particular, by prohibiting anti-competitive behaviour by private actors (Art 101 TFEU on restrictive practices and Art 102 TFEU on abuse of a dominant position), EU competition law has amongst its objectives the prevention of the partitioning of the Single Market, typically along Member State lines, "rendering more difficult the interpenetration of trade which the Treaty is intended to create".[11] Similarly, in relation to the law on state aids, Art 107 TFEU provides that any aid granted by a Member State which distorts or threatens to distort competition by favouring certain undertakings or the production of certain goods shall, in so far as it affects trade between Member States, be incompatible with the Internal Market.[12] A 2012 Commission Communication on *State Aid Modernisation* observes that:

> [r]obust State aid control is ... essential to ensure a well functioning single market. Such robust control goes hand in hand with the effective implementation of EU internal market rules and is of particular relevance in markets that have only recently been opened and where large incumbents aided by the State still play a major role, such as transport, postal services or, in more limited cases, energy. State aid modernisation can improve the functioning of the internal market through a more effective policy aimed at limiting distortions of competition, preserving a level playing field and combating protectionism.[13]

[17–17] Finally, the EU has a trade defence policy which, in accordance with World Trade Organisation rules, can deploy certain mechanisms in order to counter anti-competitive practices by third countries, such as the "dumping" of goods within the EU at below cost price, or below the sales price within the domestic market, or the granting of state subsidies that have trade distorting effects. A Trade Defence Instruments Committee, made up of representatives of the Member States, assists the Commission in the exercise of its implementation powers, guidance in relation to which is now provided by two 2016 regulations on protection against dumped imports, and protection against subsidised imports, from non-EU countries.[14]

B. Negative Integration

[17–18] In addition to the Customs Union and common competition law and state aid rules, the creation of the conditions necessary for an internal market can be seen as involving two parallel, but different strategies which are termed "negative integration" and "positive integration". Negative integration is so called because it functions by way of overriding or disapplying national rules which are found to be incompatible with the

---

[11] Case 56/65 *Société Technique Minière* [1966] ECR 234, 249.

[12] See Andrea Biondi, "State Aid is Falling Down, Falling Down: An Analysis of the Case Law on the Notion of Aid" (2013) 50 *Common Market Law Review* 1719.

[13] Commission Communication, *State Aid Modernisation*, COM(2012) 209 final, 8 May 2012.

[14] Regulation (EU) 2016/1036 of the European Parliament and of the Council of 8 June 2016 on protection against dumped imports from countries not members of the European Union [2016] OJ L176/21 and Regulation (EU) 2016/1037 of the European Parliament and of the Council of 8 June 2016 on protection against subsidised imports from countries not members of the European Union [2016] OJ L176/55.

TFEU's guarantee of the free movement of goods, persons, services or capital. In other words, negative integration is de-regulatory in that it results in the removal of national rules which either discriminate against goods, persons, services or capital from other Member States, or otherwise hinder their access to some part of the Internal Market, in a manner that infringes EU law.

[17–19] So, for instance, Art 34 TFEU provides that quantitative restrictions on imports and all measures having an equivalent effect shall be prohibited between Member States. Article 45 TFEU provides that the freedom of movement for workers shall be secured within the Union, which shall entail the abolition of any discrimination based on nationality as regards employment, remuneration and other conditions of work and employment. Article 49 TFEU prohibits restrictions on the freedom of establishment of nationals of a Member State in the territory of another Member State. Similarly, Art 56 TFEU provides that restrictions on the freedom to provide services within the Union shall be prohibited in respect of nationals of Member States who are established in a Member State other than that of the person for whom the services are intended. Each of these provisions has been held to have vertical direct effect (with the position as regards horizontal direct effect being more nuanced), such that they can be directly relied upon in domestic courts in order to challenge national rules or administrative practices that are alleged to violate the primary law guarantees of free movement. As a result, both national courts and the Court of Justice have had a central role to play in driving negative integration.

[17–20] In the following chapters, each of the four freedoms will be examined in greater detail, including the question of the *scope* of the prohibition on restrictions to free movement and what kinds of restriction are caught by the prohibition. It will be seen that a number of common themes emerge. First, in order to be caught by the prohibition, a restriction need not be *directly* discriminatory, but may discriminate against goods, persons, services or capital from another Member State in an *indirect* manner. In other words, a restriction will be caught even if, formally, it applies equally to both national goods and goods from other Member States but where, in practice, it has a greater effect on the goods from other Member States as compared with domestic goods. Moreover, it is also possible for *non-discriminatory* measures to be caught by the prohibition. Academic debates continue as to the proper rationale for prohibiting a particular restriction, such as whether it ought to entail some form of difference in treatment as between the Member State imposing the measure and another Member State, or rather whether, instead of difference in treatment, the essential question is whether or not a national measure restricts or hinders access to a part of the Internal Market. This latter view was famously summed up by Advocate General Jacobs in *Leclerc-Siplec* as involving the guiding principle that:

> all undertakings which engage in a legitimate economic activity in a Member State should have unfettered access to the whole [EU] market, unless there is a valid reason for denying them full access to a part of that market... If the principle is that all undertakings should have full unfettered access to the whole of the [EU] market, then the appropriate test in my view is whether there is a substantial restriction on that access.[15]

[17–21] In addition to the principle of "market access", this quotation hints at two

[15] Case C-412/93 *Société d'Importation Edouard Leclerc-Siplec v TF1 Publicité* [1995] ECR I-179, 195.

further concepts that are central to EU law on the free movement of goods. The first is that of "mutual recognition", or the idea that a product lawfully marketed in one Member State should be free to be sold in any other Member State. Mutual recognition is at the heart of Court's approach to negative integration, and can be seen to entail a transfer of regulatory control in the sense that the Member State in which a good is sold is no longer free to impose its own standards on it, but rather must accept those which are applied by the Member State in which the good is produced. This, in turn, may prompt regulatory competition, whereby Member States compete with each other in order to have the most attractive regulatory regime for manufacturers choosing where to locate their business. From a more critical perspective, this is often referred to as the "regulatory race to the bottom".[16]

[17–22] Advocate General Jacobs' remark does, however, refer to potentially valid reasons for denying full access to a Member State's market. This second concept serves to mitigate the possible adverse effects of regulatory competition and to ensure that a balance is maintained as between market-driven demands and societal interests. The prohibition on restrictions is not absolute, therefore, in that the TFEU sets out limited grounds on which a Member State may derogate from the freedom of movement. In respect of all four freedoms, derogations may be justified on the ground of public policy or public security. Derogations on the ground of public health are permitted in respect of persons and services, while restrictions on the movement of goods may be justified for human, animal or plant health protection, as well as to protect public morality, national treasures possessing artistic, historic or archaeological value or industrial or commercial property. Secondly, in respect of a non-discriminatory restriction on the free movement of goods (which, in principle, might be said to be less bad than a discriminatory restriction), in addition to the derogations expressly permitted by the TFEU, a Member State may seek to justify a restriction on the basis of what is known alternatively as a "mandatory requirement" or "the rule of reason", a judicial concept developed by the Court of Justice in a series of landmark judgments. In order to be permitted, as well as being non-discriminatory, the Member State will need to demonstrate that the restriction is necessary in order to achieve an imperative requirement in the public interest, that it is suitable for achieving that objective and that it is proportionate, in that it does not go beyond what is necessary in order to do so.

[17–23] Much of the case law discussed in the following chapters will involve an assessment of: (i) whether or not a national restriction on free movement ought to be regarded as having been "caught" by the prohibition in Arts 34, 45, 49 or 56 TFEU; (ii) if it is caught, is the restriction discriminatory, in which case it may only be justified on the basis of the limited grounds expressly provided for in the relevant Treaty article, or is it non-discriminatory, in which case it may also be justified on the basis of a more open-ended category of public interests; and (iii) has the Member State seeking to justify the measure provided sufficiently persuasive evidence and argumentation to demonstrate that the restriction is necessary, suitable to achieving the stated aim and proportionate.

[16] See Catherine Barnard, "Social Dumping Revisited: Lessons from Delaware" (2000) 25 *European Law Review* 57.

C. Positive Integration

[17–24] Positive integration is achieved, not through de-regulation, but by the "approximation" or "harmonisation" of diverse national laws into one, common EU standard. Accordingly, positive integration is driven by the Commission, which brings legislative proposals to the Council and the Parliament.

[17–25] As the Internal Market is an area of shared competence, Member States retain a regulatory competence to the extent that the EU has not legislated in respect of a particular matter – often phrased as the EU having "pre-empted" the Member State's ability to act or, more informally, having "occupied the field". There are two distinct aspects to assessing this. First, it is necessary to identify the *scope* of the legal act, in the sense of defining the particular field at issue. Secondly, once the field is determined, it is necessary to examine the *intensity* of harmonisation within that field. Since the somewhat vague notion of a subject matter having been pre-empted or occupied by an EU legal act can have significant implications in terms of the division of competence between the EU and its Member States, the application of these criteria can often become a contentious and politicised affair.

[17–26] The case law of the Court of Justice illustrates that, rather than simply adopting a broad categorisation of a given area, a detailed examination of EU measures will be carried out when assessing the extent to which harmonisation has taken place. A good example of this can be seen from *Crespelle*.[17] There, France successfully sought to invoke the protection of animal and human health grounds for a derogation in respect of measures it retained on the treatment of imported bovine semen for use in insemination. The French measures required that imports be delivered only to certain designated centres in France. The Court of Justice accepted that, although two directives harmonised certain rules to do with the import of animal semen, including rules on the *processing* of semen in the Member State of dispatch and *transport* to the state of destination, there was no provision dealing specifically with its *storage or use* in the state of destination. Accordingly, it followed that:

> *health conditions* in intra-[EU] trade in bovine semen have not yet been fully harmonized at [EU] level in relation to the *State for which the semen is destined*. Member States may therefore rely on health grounds in impeding the free movement of bovine semen, provided that the restrictions on intra-[EU] trade are in proportion to the aim in view.[18]

(i) Total, Optional and Minimum Harmonisation

[17–27] It is possible to identify three different approaches to harmonisation based on varying levels of intensity. The first may be termed "total" or "exhaustive" or "complete" harmonisation. Total harmonisation occurs where an EU measure leaves no room for any divergent action by a Member State. This arises where the EU measure contains both a "free movement clause", requiring that goods complying with the measure are freely allowed to be imported and sold in each Member State, and an "exclusivity clause", prohibiting the sale of any goods that do not comply with the measure, even if the goods are manufactured and sold within a single Member State. So, for example, when a directive specified an exhaustive list of lights to be used in

---

[17] Case C-323/93 *Crespelle* [1994] ECR I-5077.

[18] *ibid*, 5108. Emphasis added.

motor vehicles, in infringement proceedings brought by the Commission, the Court of Justice held that the UK was no longer permitted to require cars to have a particular type of light not included on the list, namely dim-dip headlights.[19] As stated by the Court, the Member States could not unilaterally require manufacturers who had complied with the harmonised technical requirements set out in the directive to "comply with a requirement which is not imposed by that directive, since motor vehicles complying with the technical requirements laid down therein must be able to move freely within the common market".[20]

[17–28] Total harmonisation is the most intense form of harmonisation and operates so as to pre-empt the area to which it applies, occupying the field to the exclusion of any Member State competence. One important consequence of this is that a Member State can no longer seek to rely on the express Treaty grounds for derogation in order to defend a national regulation, such as for example the UK seeking to justify a requirement for dim-dip headlights on the ground of protecting human health. As the Court has described, recourse to the exemptions set out in Art 36 TFEU in respect of the free movement of goods

> ceases to be justified only if … directives provide for the complete harmonisation of national laws. It must therefore be accepted that where the approximation of the laws of the Member States has not yet been achieved in a given field the corresponding national laws may place obstacles in the way of the principle of free movement in so far as the obstacles in question are justified by one of the grounds set out in [Article 36] of the Treaty or by imperative requirements.[21]

[17–29] The second approach, which is rarely used, is "optional harmonisation", in that it sets out a common EU standard which manufacturers may choose to apply, guaranteeing them access to the entire EU market, or they may choose to adhere to their own national standard. Finally, "minimum harmonisation" involves the EU establishing minimum requirements while permitting Member States to apply higher standards provided that they are compatible with the Treaties.[22] The higher national standards may only apply, however, within that Member State and cannot be applied to imported goods that meet the minimum EU standard, or extra-territorially by purporting to restrict exports to Member States that do not meet the higher standard. For instance, under a Tobacco Control directive, warnings on cigarette packets had to cover at least 4 per cent of the surface. The UK went further than this, requiring its manufacturers to have a warning covering no less than 6 per cent of the surface. The Court of Justice rejected an argument by UK cigarette manufacturers that the advantage enjoyed by imported cigarette brands amounted to an impermissible form of reverse

---

19 Case 60/86 *Commission v UK* [1988] ECR 3921. See also Case 150/88 *Parfürmerie-Fabrik v Provide* [1989] ECR 3891.

20 *ibid*, 3935.

21 Case C-39/90 *Denkavit Futtermittel* [1991] ECR I-3069, 3107. See also Case 278/85 *Commission v Denmark* [1987] ECR 4069.

22 See Amedeo Arena, "The *ERTA* Pre-Emption Effects of Minimum and Partial Harmonisation Directives: Insights from Opinion 3/15 on the Competence to Conclude the Marrakesh Treaty" (2018) 43 *European Law Review* 770; Francesco de Cecco, "Room to Move? Minimum Harmonisation and Fundamental Human Rights" (2006) 43 *Common Market Law Review* 9; Peter Rott, "Minimum Harmonisation for the Completion of the Internal Market? The Example of Consumer Sales Law" (2003) 40 *Common Market Law Review* 1107; Michael Dougan, "Minimum Harmonisation and the Internal Market" (2000) 37 *Common Market Law Review* 853.

discrimination.[23] Similarly, when a directive laid down minimum standards, including housing space, for the protection of fattening calves, the UK applied stricter standards. The Court of Justice confirmed that this could not extend to a ban on the exporting of calves for rearing in veal crates in a Member State that applied the minimum EU standard, but did not meet the higher standard imposed within the UK.[24] It can be seen, therefore, that unlike total harmonisation, optional and minimum harmonisation do not completely occupy the field but leave Member States with some limited legislative competence in the area.

(ii) The "New Strategy" and "New Approach" to Harmonisation

[17–30] Despite its name, the "New Approach" to harmonisation dates from the mid 1980s and has its origins in the Commission's seminal 1985 White Paper, *Completing the Internal Market*.[25] The New Approach grew out of the fact that the use of highly technical and specific directives, dealing with very particular types of goods, required extensive and lengthy consultations and so could not keep pace with constant changes in the nature of products, or with new rules and regulations introduced by Member States in order to address such changes. Between 1968 and 1983, on average only around 10 technical directives were adopted each year. The combination of an increase in the bureaucratic regulatory capacity of Member States and their growing preference for environmental and consumer protection meant that the adoption of new rules and regulations by Member States far exceeded the annual output of highly specific EU directives.[26] As a result, positive harmonisation was failing to achieve a general improvement in market access, prompting the European Council to request the Commission to prepare a detailed programme for completing the Common Market by the end of 1992.

[17–31] The resulting White Paper recommended Treaty amendments that would see the Single European Act of 1986 introduce a definition of the Internal Market and set 31 December 1992 as a deadline for its achievement (now Art 26 TFEU). A proposal by the Commission that Art 26 ought to have direct effect once the 1992 deadline had expired was resisted by Member States as too ambitious, and a declaration to the Single European Act made clear that the deadline did not confer Art 26 with automatic legal effect. As the Single Market is now seen as a continuous and ever-evolving project, the reference to a deadline for completion (and the consequent declaration) has been dropped from the Treaties. A further proposal saw the introduction of a new legislative competence in respect of Internal Market harmonisation measures that, critically, required only a qualified majority within the Council rather than the unanimous agreement of all the Member States (now Art 114 TFEU). The White Paper also outlined both a "New Strategy" on *what* to harmonise and a "New Approach" on *how* to harmonise.

[17–32] In parallel with the difficulties faced by positive harmonisation, impetus for the new approach came from developments in the case law of the Court of Justice,

[23] Case C-11/92 *Gallaher* [1993] ECR I-3545.

[24] Case C-1/96 *Compassion in World Farming* [1998] ECR I-1251.

[25] European Commission, "Completing the Internal Market: White Paper from the Commission to the European Parliament", COM/85/0310 FINAL, 28 June 1985.

[26] Jacques Pelkmans, "The New Approach to Technical Harmonization and Standardization" (1986–1987) 25 *Journal of Common Market Studies* 249, 251.

and its landmark 1979 judgment in *Cassis de Dijon* in particular.[27] The issue in that case was whether a German law requiring fruit liqueurs to have an alcohol volume of at least 25 per cent, which was higher than that found within a French liqueur that was being sought to be imported, constituted a restriction on the free movement of goods contrary to Art 34 TFEU. In finding that the German requirement did fall foul of Art 34, the Court established the important doctrine of "mutual recognition", according to which each Member State is to accept that a product deemed suitable for marketing and consumption within one Member State is capable of being marketed and sold within all of them.

[17–33] Given the radical and far-reaching nature of mutual recognition, the Court simultaneously introduced a tool to temper its effects, where necessary, in the form of the parallel doctrine of "mandatory requirements", otherwise known as the "rule of reason" or "overriding public interests". Both mutual recognition and mandatory requirements – which have been described as among the most important legal developments since the Union's foundation – are introduced in paragraph 8 of the judgment.[28] While the first sentence establishes the principle of mutual recognition, the second sentence immediately pulls back to rein it in by allowing a Member State to seek to rely on mandatory requirements in order to justify a national measure that restricts a good's freedom of movement:

> In the absence of common rules relating to the production and marketing of alcohol ... it is for the Member States to regulate all matters relating to the production and marketing of alcohol and alcoholic beverages on their own territory. Obstacles to movement within the [Union] resulting from disparities between the national laws relating to the marketing of the products in question must be accepted in so far as those provisions may be recognized as being necessary in order to satisfy mandatory requirements relating in particular to the effectiveness of fiscal supervision, the protection of public health, the fairness of commercial transactions and the defence of the consumer.[29]

[17–34] The first point to note about the principle of mutual recognition is that it applies where a particular area has not yet been harmonised at EU level. In this way, the principle of mutual recognition can be seen as "auxiliary" to, or a "second-best" option in the absence of, positive integration.[30] Secondly, where it applies, the principle replaces dual regulation by both a home state of manufacture and a host state of sale, with regulation by the home state only. Thus, it has been said that *Cassis de Dijon* elevated the principle of home state control to a general constitutional principle of the Internal Market, such that, except where mandatory requirements apply, goods are subject to the law of the home Member State and should not be subjected to the requirements of the host state.[31]

[17–35] From the point of view of harmonisation, the effect of *Cassis de Dijon* can be seen as prohibiting host state regulations, such as quality standards, that cannot be said to be necessary in order to protect a mandatory requirement. In doing so, the judgment

[27] Case 120/78 *Rewe-Zentral* ("*Cassis de Dijon*") [1979] ECR 649. See ch 19, paras [19–44] to [19–53].

[28] Damian Chalmers, Gareth Davies and Giorgio Monti, *European Union Law* (3rd ed, Cambridge University Press, 2014) 775.

[29] *ibid*, 662.

[30] Robert Schütze, *European Union Law* (Cambridge University Press, 2015) 557.

[31] *ibid.*

vastly broadened the net cast by Art 34 TFEU. Henceforth, negative integration operated to prohibit a far greater range of national measures, thereby narrowing the areas in need of positive integration through harmonisation. Within a year of the judgment, the Commission issued a communication to Member States on its consequences, in which it explained:

> Whereas Member States may, with respect to domestic products and in the absence of relevant [EU] provisions, regulate the terms on which such products are marketed, the case is different for products imported from other Member States.
>
> Any product imported from another Member State must in principle be admitted to the territory of the importing Member State if it has been lawfully produced, that is, conforms to rules and processes of manufacture that are customarily and traditionally accepted in the exporting country, and is marketed in the territory of the latter.
>
> This principle implies that Member States, when drawing up commercial or technical rules liable to affect the free movement of goods, may not take an exclusively national viewpoint and take account only of requirements confined to domestic products. The proper functioning of the common market demands that each Member State also give consideration to the legitimate requirements of the other Member States.
>
> Only under very strict conditions does the Court accept exceptions to this principle; barriers to trade resulting from differences between commercial and technical rules are only admissible: if the rules are necessary, that is appropriate and not excessive, in order to satisfy mandatory requirements (public health, protection of consumers or the environment, the fairness of commercial transactions, etc).[32]

[17–36] As a result of *Cassis de Dijon*, in its 1985 White Paper the Commission set out a new strategy towards the matters to be addressed by positive integration. Henceforward, the Commission's work on harmonisation would be directed "mainly at national laws having an impact on the functioning of the common market where barriers to trade to be removed arise from the national provisions *which are admissible under the criteria set by the Court*", or in other words, national laws aimed at addressing mandatory requirements such as public health and consumer protection.[33] Although the White Paper is famous for having included an Annex listing 279 legislative measures that were to be enacted by the end of 1992, it has been commented that its real merit lay in the "renunciation of more than 1,000 directives which would have been necessary according to the traditional internal market strategies".[34]

[17–37] In addition to the new strategy on what to harmonise, the White Paper also endorsed a new approach on how to harmonise according to which:

> where barriers to trade are created by justified divergent national regulations concerning the health and safety of citizens and consumer and environmental protection, legislative harmonisation will be confined to laying down the *essential requirements*, conformity to which will entitle a product to free movement within the [EU].[35]

---

32 Commission Communication concerning the consequences of the judgment given by the Court of Justice on 20 February 1979 in Case 120/78 (*Cassis de Dijon*) [1980] OJ C256/2.

33 *ibid*, para 16.

34 Schmitt von Sydow, "The Basic Strategies of the Commission's White Paper" in Roland Bieber, Renaud Dehousse, John Pinder and Joseph Weiler (eds), *1992: One European Market* (Nomos, 1988) 91, cited in Robert Schütze, *European Union Law* (Cambridge University Press, 2015) 558.

35 European Commission, "Completing the Internal Market: White Paper from the Commission to

[17–38] Further details were set out in an annex to a 1985 Council Resolution on a New Approach to Technical Harmonisation and Standards, which identified the following four principles as the basis for the new approach:

(i) legislative harmonisation is limited to the adoption, by means of Directives … of the *essential safety requirements* (or other requirements in the general interest) with which products put on the market must conform, and which should therefore enjoy free movement throughout the [EU];

(ii) the task of drawing up the *technical specifications* needed for the production and placing on the market of products conforming to the essential requirements established by the Directives, while taking into account the current stage of technology, is entrusted to organisations competent in the standardisation area;

(iii) these technical specifications are not mandatory and maintain their status of voluntary standards;

(iv) but at the same time national authorities are obliged to recognise that products manufactured in conformity with harmonised standards … are presumed to conform to the "essential requirements" established by the Directive. (This signifies that the producer has the choice of not manufacturing in conformity with the standards but that in this event he has an obligation to prove that his products conform to the essential requirements of the Directive.)[36]

[17–39] It can be seen from this that the New Approach takes a more minimalist approach to harmonisation, not seeking to impose common quality standards on particular goods, but rather seeking to guarantee that "essential safety requirements" are met in respect of a broad category of goods. The New Approach affords Member States flexibility as to how they regulate so as to ensure the minimum standards are met, and does not require that the same precise rules are followed in each state. The 2009 Directive on the Safety of Toys is a good example of this.[37] It requires that certain minimum, broadly defined criteria are met, such as that "toys must be designed and manufactured in such a way as not to present any risk or only the minimum risk inherent to their use which could be caused by movement of their parts".[38]

[17–40] Although, under the New Approach, the legislation itself does not prescribe precise standards, specialist standardisation agencies may be mandated by the Commission to elaborate detailed rules, such as the European Committee for Standardisation (CEN), the European Committee for Electrotechnical Standardisation (CENELEC) and the European Telecommunication Standards Institute (ETSI).[39] This is referred to in paragraph (ii) quoted above, where it is provided that the task of drawing up the technical specifications needed to conform to the essential requirements established by a directive will be entrusted to organisations competent in the standardisation area. Such delegation allows for a quicker and more nimble reaction to changes in the design and manufacture of goods, as compared with having to go through the entire legislative process in order to amend a directive.

---

the European Council", COM/85/0310 FINAL, 28 June 1985, para 68.

[36] Council Resolution of 7 May 1985 on a New Approach to Technical Harmonisation and Standards, Annex, [1985] OJ C136/1. Emphasis added.

[37] Directive 2009/48/EC of the European Parliament and of the Council of 18 June 2009 on the safety of toys [2009] OJ L170/1.

[38] *ibid*, Annex II, para 3.

[39] See General Guidelines for the Cooperation between CEN, CENELEC and ETSI and the European Commission and EFTA, [2003] OJ C91/7.

[17–41] As stated in paragraph (iii) quoted above, the technical standards developed by specialist agencies such as CEN and CENELEC are not mandatory. Rather, instead of complying with the prescribed standards, a manufacturer may choose to meet the essential requirements in a different way, in which case the goods will need to be submitted for testing. Each directive will specify how such testing is to be carried out and whether it needs to be done by a third party or may be done by manufacturers themselves. Certain directives require that "conformity assessment bodies" must be used, which have been designated by the Member States by notifying the Commission. The idea behind providing for this alternative approach is to encourage continued innovation by manufacturers, and to avoid a situation whereby the development of technical standards by specialist agencies results in a rigid uniformity that prevents creativity and new innovative approaches to satisfying essential requirements.

[17–42] Goods which have followed either of these methods of production may have applied to them the "CE" (Communauté européenne) marking, which gives rise to a presumption that the goods conform to the essential requirements set out in the relevant directive, allowing free circulation throughout the EU.

(iii) Market Surveillance

[17–43] A vitally important component of the New Approach is the obligation on Member States to take appropriate enforcement measures, including through what is known as market surveillance, to make sure that goods that fail to comply with essential requirements are withdrawn from the market. Guidance in this regard is set out in the "RAMS" Regulation on the Requirements for Accreditation and Market Surveillance relating to the marketing of products.[40] Under Art 16 of the Regulation, Member States are to organise and carry out market surveillance that will ensure

> that products covered by [EU] harmonisation legislation which, when used in accordance with their intended purpose or under conditions which can be reasonably foreseen and when properly installed and maintained, are liable to compromise the health or safety of users, or which otherwise do not conform to applicable requirements set out in [EU] harmonisation legislation are withdrawn or their being made available on the market is prohibited or restricted and that the public, the Commission and the other Member States are informed accordingly.

[17–44] In order to achieve this objective, Art 19 establishes that, taking account of established principles of risk assessment, complaints and other information, market surveillance authorities shall perform appropriate checks on the characteristics of products on an adequate scale, by means of documentary checks and, where appropriate, physical and laboratory checks on the basis of adequate samples.

[17–45] In accordance with the principle of mutual recognition, a host Member State must assume that a certificate issued by a conformity assessment body in the home

---

[40] Regulation (EC) No 765/2008 of the European Parliament and of the Council of 9 July 2008 setting out the requirements for accreditation and market surveillance relating to the marketing of products and repealing Regulation (EEC) No 339/93 [2008] OJ L218/30; Regulation (EU) 2019/1020 of the European Parliament and of the Council of 20 June 2019 on market surveillance and compliance of products and amending Directive 2004/42/EC and Regulations (EU) No 765/2008 and (EU) No 305/2011 [2019] OJ L169/1.

Member State is of an equivalent standard and trustworthiness as a certificate issued by one of its own assessment bodies. In practice, however, difficulties arose due to different Member States and their assessment bodies adopting differing interpretations of technical standards, giving rise to a lack of confidence in the certifications provided in some instances. In order to address this, the RAMS Regulation requires Member States to establish a national accreditation body that, when requested by a conformity assessment body, will evaluate whether it is competent to carry out a specific conformity assessment activity and, if so, issue it with an accreditation certificate to that effect. The accreditation body is to monitor the performance of assessment bodies that it has certified and, where it ascertains that an assessment body is no longer competent to carry out a specific conformity assessment activity or has committed a serious breach of its obligations, it shall take all appropriate measures within a reasonable timeframe to restrict, suspend or withdraw the accreditation certificate. In 2010, the Irish National Accreditation Board, which is a committee of the Health and Safety Authority, was notified to the Commission as Ireland's sole accreditation body for the purposes of the RAMS Regulation.[41]

[17–46] A further market surveillance tool is the RAPEX rapid information exchange system for dangerous products, other than medical devices, pharmaceutical products and food. RAPEX is established pursuant to the General Product Safety Directive,[42] with a Commission Decision laying down detailed guidelines on the management of the system.[43] The Irish national contact point for RAPEX is the Competition and Consumer Protection Commission, which is responsible for receiving and disseminating EU-wide alerts on unsafe products. More generally, responsibility for monitoring goods falls to a number of different agencies depending on the nature of goods, including: (a) the Competition and Consumer Protection Commission in respect of toys, domestic electrical, electronic and gas appliances and personal protective equipment used by consumers such as bicycle helmets, sunglasses, swimming armbands; (b) the Health and Safety Authority for machinery and personal protective equipment, such as hard hats, used in the workplace; (c) the Health Products Regulatory Authority for medical devices, cosmetics and pharmaceuticals; (d) the Food Safety Authority of Ireland regarding food; and (e) the Commission for Communications Regulation for mobile phones.

(iv) Directive 2015/1535 on Provision of Information in the Field of Technical Regulations

[17–47] Since 1983, an EU directive has imposed an obligation on each Member State to inform the Commission, in advance of its adoption, of any draft technical regulation that it proposes to introduce. As well as this, the Member State is required to operate a "standstill period" of at least three months, in order to allow the Commission and other Member States time to consider the proposal (unless grounds exist for the Member State to invoke an "urgency procedure"). If the Commission wishes to propose a measure

---

41 See Part 7 of the Industrial Development (Dissolution of Forfás) Act 2014, which amends the Safety, Health and Welfare at Work Act 2005.

42 Directive 2001/95/EC of the European Parliament and of the Council of 3 December 2001 on general product safety [2002] OJ L11/4.

43 Commission Decision 2010/15/EU of 16 December 2009 laying down guidelines for the management of the Community Rapid Information System 'RAPEX' established under Art 12 and of the notification procedure established under Art 11 of Directive 2001/95/EC, [2010] OJ L22/1.

of its own dealing with the issue, the Member State must postpone the introduction of its national measure for 12 months.

[17–48] These rules are now provided for in Directive 2015/1535 on the provision of information in the field of technical regulations.[44] This important Directive applies to industrially manufactured products, agricultural products and certain "information society" or electronic services. A key focus of the Directive is on technical specifications, which are defined broadly as any:

> specification contained in a document which lays down the characteristics required of a product such as levels of quality, performance, safety or dimensions, including the requirements applicable to the product as regards the name under which the product is sold, terminology, symbols, testing and test methods, packaging, marking or labelling and conformity assessment procedures.[45]

[17–49] Technical specifications also include production methods and processes used in respect of: (i) agricultural products (ie products of the soil, of stockfarming and of fisheries and products of first-stage processing directly related to these products); (ii) products intended for human and animal consumption; (iii) medicinal products as defined in Art 1 of Directive 2001/83/EC on the Community code relating to medicinal products for human use[46]; and (iv) production methods and processes relating to other products, where these have an effect on their characteristics.

[17–50] Notifications of proposed technical regulations are submitted to the Commission via its public Technical Regulations Information System (TRIS) database, in respect of which the National Standards Authority of Ireland is the national contact point.[47] During the standstill period, the Commission and other Member States may ask questions or make comments on the proposed measure, which the Member State is obliged to take into account as far as possible in the subsequent preparation of the technical regulation. If it is considered that the proposed measure may create an obstacle to the free movement of goods, services or establishment, the Commission or a Member State may issue a "detailed opinion", which will extend the standstill period to six months and require a response from the proposing Member State, detailing why the measure is still deemed to be necessary. If the Commission informs that it intends to propose a harmonisation measure on the matter, the Member State must postpone adopting its own measure for a further nine months. As detailed in the table below, the TRIS database indicates that in recent years Ireland has made notifications relating to such matters as standardised tobacco packaging, restrictions on alcohol advertising and

---

44 Directive (EU) 2015/1535 of the European Parliament and of the Council of 9 September 2015 laying down a procedure for the provision of information in the field of technical regulations and of rules on Information Society services [2015] OJ L241/1. On what is captured by the term "technical regulation" see Case C-137/17 *Van Gennip* EU:C:2018:771, 26 September 2018, paras 36–45; Case C-303/15 *M and S* EU:C:2016:771, 13 October 2016, paras 18–21. In an Irish context see, for example, the discussion in *McNally v Ireland* [2011] 4 IR 431, 450–451; *James Elliott Construction Ltd v Irish Asphalt Ltd* [2014] IESC 74, unreported, Supreme Court, 2 December 2014, paras 156–184; and Case C-613/14 *James Elliott Construction Ltd v Irish Asphalt Ltd* EU:C:2016:821, 27 October 2016, paras 63–72 (where the national measure at issue was held not to be a technical regulation within the meaning of the Directive).

45 *ibid*, Art 1(c).

46 Directive 2001/83/EC of the European Parliament and of the Council of 6 November 2001 on the Community code relating to medicinal products for human use [2001] OJ L311/67.

47 Available at <http://ec.europa.eu/growth/tools-databases/tris/en/search/>.

alcohol pricing, the provision of health information concerning sunbeds, the provision of food allergen information on non-prepacked food, the regulation of retail pharmacies and a licensing regime for remote betting services.

2018	• Draft Technical Guidance Document L – Conservation of Fuel and Energy for Dwellings • Draft Technical Guidance Document F – Ventilation • Public Health (Alcohol) Bill 2015 (in so far as it relates to additional specifications to labelling, advertising and broadcast watershed)
2017	• Sugar Sweetened Beverages Tax – Finance Bill 2017 • Air Pollution Act (Marketing, Sale, Distribution and Burning of Specified Fuels) Regulations 2017 • Road Traffic (Construction and Use of Vehicles) (Amendment No 2) Regulations 2017 • An Act to amend and extend the law relating to the assaying and hallmarking of articles of precious metal • Technical Guidance Document L – Conservation of Fuel and Energy for Buildings other than Dwellings • Proposed Orders and Regulations under the Misuse of Drugs Acts 1977 to 2016 to amend the level of control placed upon certain substances and to control a number of additional substances
2016	• Microchipping of Dogs Regulations 2017 • Public Health (Alcohol) Bill 2015 • An Act to amend and extend the law relating to the assaying and hallmarking of articles of precious metal • Health (Provision of Mandatory Food Information to Consumers in respect of certain Non-Packaged Meats) Regulations 2017 • Draft Building Regulations (Part L Amendment) Regulations 2016 • Draft Technical Guidance Document L – Conservation of Fuel and Energy – Dwellings • Draft Technical Guidance Document B – Fire Safety – Dwelling Houses • Notification of Technical Specification of Bovine Identification Tags
2015	• Draft Public Health (Standardised Packaging of Tobacco) Regulations • Safety, Health and Welfare at Work (General Application) (Amendment) Regulations 2015
2014	• Public Health (Sunbeds) (Health Information) Regulations 2015 • Mineral Oil Tax (Amendment) Regulations 2014 • Health (Provision of Food Allergen Information to Consumers in respect of Non-Prepacked Food) Regulations 2014 • Betting (Amendment) Bill 2013 • Public Health (Standardised Packaging of Tobacco) Bill 2014 • Regulation of Retail Pharmacy Businesses (Amendment) Regulations 2014

[17–51] Directive 2015/1535 is given further "bite" by virtue of the fact that it has been held to be capable of giving rise to an "incidental" form of horizontal direct effect.[48] In *CIA Security*, an application was brought to restrain CIA Security from selling an alarm system on the basis that it had not received the necessary prior authorisation required under a particular Belgian law.[49] In response, CIA Security argued that the relevant Belgian law had not been notified to the Commission pursuant to an earlier version of Directive 2015/1535. The Court of Justice considered that, as there was an obligation on a Member State to notify draft technical regulations to the Commission

[48] See ch 12, paras [12–45] to [12–52].
[49] Case C-194/94 *CIA Security International* [1996] ECR I-2201.

before they were adopted, which was "unconditional and sufficiently precise in terms of [its] content", the Directive could be relied on by individuals before their national courts. Although Germany, the UK and the Netherlands argued that the Directive ought to be regarded as solely concerning relations between the Member States and the Commission, and as merely creating procedural obligations for the Member States, the Court concluded that the "effectiveness of [EU] control will be that much greater if the Directive is interpreted as meaning that breach of the obligation to notify constitutes a substantial procedural defect such as to render the technical regulations in question *inapplicable to individuals*".[50] Accordingly, the Belgian law could not be invoked by the private party in order to restrain CIA Security from selling unauthorised alarm systems.

[17–52] A similar result emerged in *Unilever* in relation to an Italian law that confined the use of the term "Italian" when marketing olive oil to produce that had been harvested, produced, processed and packaged in Italy.[51] Unilever had provided olive oil pursuant to a contract that required the goods to be labelled in accordance with Italian law. When the purchaser of the goods refused to accept them because they were, under the Italian law, incorrectly labelled "Italian", the Court of Justice held that the relevant law could not be relied upon as it had not been notified prior to its adoption. These two judgments led to a significant increase in the number of notifications made by Member States, jumping from 751 in 2000 to 1,525 in 2010, causing Catherine Barnard to note that, as with *Cassis de Dijon*, the old allies of the Commission and the Court worked together to ensure the effective application of EU law.[52]

(v) Article 114 TFEU: A Residual Competence to Harmonise

[17–53] It was described above how, throughout the 1970s and early 1980s, the EEC fell behind in its goal of creating a common market through the means of positive integration. An important factor that contributed to this was the need for unanimity within the Council when seeking to adopt a harmonising measure pursuant to the residual competence provided for in Art 100 of the Treaty of Rome. To overcome this obstacle, the Single European Act introduced Art 100a, which crucially allowed for qualified majority voting (QMV) in respect of certain harmonising measures. The introduction of an additional, more generous, residual competence was a major milestone in the establishment of the Internal Market, freeing up a long period of legislative deadlock in which the role of driving integration was, by default, left to the Court of Justice. This significant legislative competence is now found in Art 114 TFEU as follows:

> 1. Save where otherwise provided in the Treaties, the following provisions shall apply for the achievement of the objectives set out in Article 26. The European Parliament and the Council shall, acting in accordance with the ordinary legislative procedure and after consulting the Economic and Social Committee, adopt the measures for the approximation of the provisions laid down by law, regulation or administrative action in Member States which have as their object the establishment and functioning of the internal market.
> 2. Paragraph 1 shall not apply to *fiscal provisions*, to those relating to the *free movement of persons* nor to those relating to the *rights and interests of employed persons*.
> 3. The Commission, in its proposals envisaged in paragraph 1 concerning *health, safety, environmental protection* and *consumer protection*, will take as a base a high level of

---

50 *ibid*, 2247.

51 Case C-443/98 *Unilever v Central Food* [2000] ECR I-7535.

52 Catherine Barnard, *The Substantive Law of the EU* (4th ed, Oxford University Press, 2013) 116.

protection, taking account in particular of any new development based on scientific facts. Within their respective powers, the European Parliament and the Council will also seek to achieve this objective.

4. If, after the adoption of a harmonisation measure … a Member State deems it necessary to maintain national provisions on grounds of major needs referred to in Article 36 [ie public morality, public policy or public security; the protection of health and life of humans, animals or plants; the protection of national treasures possessing artistic, historic or archaeological value; or the protection of industrial and commercial property], or relating to the *protection of the environment* or *the working environment*, it shall notify the Commission of these provisions as well as the grounds for maintaining them.
5. Moreover, without prejudice to paragraph 4, if, after the adoption of a harmonisation measure … a Member State deems it necessary to introduce national provisions based on new scientific evidence relating to the *protection of the environment* or the *working environment* on grounds of a problem specific to that Member State arising after the adoption of the harmonisation measure, it shall notify the Commission of the envisaged provisions as well as the grounds for introducing them.
6. The Commission shall, within six months of the notifications as referred to in paragraphs 4 and 5, approve or reject the national provisions involved after having verified whether or not they are a means of arbitrary discrimination or a disguised restriction on trade between Member States and whether or not they shall constitute an obstacle to the functioning of the internal market. In the absence of a decision by the Commission within this period the national provisions referred to in paragraphs 4 and 5 shall be deemed to have been approved. …
7. When, pursuant to paragraph 6, a Member State is authorised to maintain or introduce national provisions derogating from a harmonisation measure, the Commission shall immediately examine whether to propose an adaptation to that measure.
8. When a Member State raises a specific problem on *public health* in a field which has been the subject of prior harmonisation measures, it shall bring it to the attention of the Commission which shall immediately examine whether to propose appropriate measures to the Council.
9. By way of derogation from the procedure laid down in Articles 258 [reasoned opinion] and 259 [infringement proceedings], the Commission and any Member State may bring the matter directly before the Court of Justice of the European Union if it considers that another Member State is making improper use of the powers provided for in this Article.
10. The harmonisation measures referred to above shall, in appropriate cases, include a safeguard clause authorising the Member States to take, for one or more of the *non-economic reasons referred to in Article 36* [ie public morality, public policy or public security; the protection of health and life of humans, animals or plants; the protection of national treasures possessing artistic, historic or archaeological value; or the protection of industrial and commercial property], provisional measures subject to a Union control procedure.[53]

[17–54] The old Art 100 of the Treaty of Rome is now found in Art 115 TFEU, according to which the Council, acting *unanimously* in accordance with a special legislative procedure and after consulting the European Parliament and the Economic and Social Committee, may issue directives for the approximation of such laws, regulations or administrative provisions of the Member States as directly affect the establishment or functioning of the Internal Market. In contrast with Art 114, Art 115 requires unanimity rather than a qualified majority, and only empowers the adoption of directives, rather than EU measures more generally.

[53] Emphasis added.

[17–55] It can be seen from the ten paragraphs of Art 114 that, while Member States were willing to allow the use of QMV in order to quicken the pace of positive integration, they remained concerned that this might allow them to be out-voted in respect of sensitive matters of public importance. Accordingly, paragraph (2) excludes from Art 114 altogether fiscal provisions, the free movement of persons and the rights and interests of employed persons. Where a proposal relates to health, safety, environmental protection or consumer protection, paragraph (3) mandates the Commission to adopt a high level of protection.

[17–56] Paragraph (4) is particularly generous to Member States, allowing them to maintain existing national provisions considered necessary for the protection of the six grounds set out in Art 36, as well as the environment or the working environment (albeit not allowing them to apply *new* provisions, as had been the case prior to the Amsterdam Treaty). Around the time of its introduction, this clause was said to go "back to the fact that the United Kingdom, and later Ireland, wished to safeguard certain special measures connected with their island status against the threat of majority voting. Neither country was satisfied with the safeguard offered by paragraph (3)".[54] In practice, however, paragraph (4) is rarely invoked; when it is, the grounds for doing so may be judicially reviewed by the Court of Justice.

[17–57] The introduction by a Member State of new national provisions, subsequent to an EU-wide harmonising measure, is dealt with in paragraph (5). The ability to do so is limited to where the protection of the environment or the working environment is at issue, secondly, new scientific evidence in relation to that problem has come to light and, thirdly, the problem is specific to that Member State. As with paragraph (4), the decision of the Commission on whether or not to accept a Member State's derogation may be judicially reviewed. The Court of Justice has adopted a strict approach, requiring the Member State to clearly demonstrate how each of the three requirements set out in paragraph (5) have been met.[55]

[17–58] Finally, paragraph (10) makes an exception to the general rule that, once a matter is harmonised at EU level, a Member State is no longer able to invoke any of the six grounds for derogation set out in Art 36 TFEU in order to defend a restriction on the free movement of goods. Paragraph (10) allows for the possibility that a harmonisation measure may expressly permit the Member States to take provisional measures in order to protect one or more of the Art 36 grounds subject, however, to EU control.

[17–59] As a residual provision, Art 114 should only be used where a more specific legislative competence is not provided for in the Treaties. In addition, Art 114(1) refers to the introduction of measures "for the approximation of laws", and accordingly Art 114 may only be used for the purposes of harmonisation, rather than for some other objective. That said, where the purpose of a measure is for the approximation of laws in order to ensure the functioning of the Internal Market, the fact that another purpose,

---

54 Claus Dieter Ehlermann, "The Internal Market Following the Single European Act" (1987) 24 *Common Market Law Review* 361, 389.

55 See Cases C-439/05P and C-454/05P *Land Oberösterreich v Commission* [2007] ECR I-7141, 7205; Case C-512/99 *Commission v Germany* [2003] ECR I-845; Michael Doherty, "Challenging a Commission Refusal to Allow the Introduction of 'More Stringent National Measures'" (2004) 6 *Environmental Law Review* 122.

such as the protection of human health or of animal welfare, was a "decisive factor" in the legislative choices made, does not prevent reliance on Art 114.

[17–60] While arguments as to the appropriate choice of legal base may at first seem technical and somewhat academic, in practice the use of Art 114 gives rise to important constitutional questions regarding the balance of power between the Union and the Member States (and as between the EU institutions) when it comes to regulating aspects of the Internal Market. As Advocate-General Fennelly observed in *Tobacco Advertising I*, to interpret Art 114 as giving *carte blanche* to the EU legislator to "harmonise any national rule that meets the eye … would risk transferring general Member State regulatory competence to the [EU] if recourse to [it] … were not subject to some test of the reality of the link between such measures and internal market objectives".[56] In its judgment in that case, delivered in 2000, the Court of Justice for the first time annulled a legislative harmonisation measure, agreeing with Germany that incorrect use had been made of Art 114. This aspect of Art 114 is considered more fully in Chapter 9.[57]

D. The Contemporary Single Market

[17–61] Unlike in the past – when 31 December 1992 had been set as a target date – the TEU and TFEU do not include any deadline for the completion of the Internal Market. This reflects a contemporary understanding of the Internal Market as an ever-evolving project responding to changing needs, rather than as something capable of obtaining definitive completion. In addition, the functioning of the Internal Market is now often considered as an important component of the overall economic, industrial, social and employment policies of the Union. For instance, discussion of contemporary challenges facing the Single Market and proposals for future action are included within the Commission's 2010 communication, "Europe 2020: A Strategy for Smart, Sustainable and Inclusive Growth" as follows:

> Every day businesses and citizens are faced with the reality that bottlenecks to cross-border activity remain despite the legal existence of the single market. They realise that networks are not sufficiently inter-connected and that the enforcement of single market rules remains uneven. Often, businesses and citizens still need to deal with 27 different legal systems for one and the same transaction. Whilst our companies are still confronted with the day-to-day reality of fragmentation and diverging rules, their competitors from China, the US or Japan can draw full strength from their large home markets.
>
> The single market was conceived before the arrival of the Internet, before information and communication technologies became one of the main drivers of growth and before services became such a dominant part of the European economy. The emergence of new services (eg content and media, health, smart energy metering) shows huge potential, but Europe will only exploit this potential if it overcomes the fragmentation that currently blocks the flow of on-line content and access for consumers and companies. To gear the single market to serve the Europe 2020 goals requires well-functioning and well-connected markets where competition and consumer access stimulate growth and innovation. An open single market for services must be created on the basis of the Services Directive, whilst at the same time ensuring the quality of services provided to consumers. …

[56] Case C-376/98 *Germany v Parliament and Council (Tobacco Advertising I)* [2000] ECR I-8419, 8462.

[57] See ch 9, paras [9–43] to [9–64].

> Access for [small and medium sized enterprises] to the single market must be improved. Entrepreneurship must be developed by concrete policy initiatives, including a simplification of company law (bankruptcy procedures, private company statute, etc.), and initiatives allowing entrepreneurs to restart after failed businesses. Citizens must be empowered to play a full part in the single market. This requires strengthening their ability and confidence to buy goods and services crossborder, in particular on-line.
>
> … The Commission will propose action to tackle bottlenecks in the single market by:
> - Reinforcing structures to implement single market measures on time and correctly, including network regulation, the Services Directive and the financial markets legislative and supervision package, enforce them effectively and when problems arise, resolve them speedily;
> - Pressing ahead with the Smart Regulation agenda, including considering the wider use of regulations rather than directives, launching ex-post evaluation of existing legislation, pursuing market monitoring, reducing administrative burdens, removing tax obstacles, improving the business environment, particularly for [small and medium sized enterprises], and supporting entrepreneurship;
> - Adapting EU and national legislation to the digital era so as to promote the circulation of content with high level of trust for consumers and companies. This requires updating rules on liability, warranties, delivery and dispute resolution;
> - Making it easier and less costly for businesses and consumers to conclude contracts with partners in other EU countries, notably by offering harmonised solutions for consumer contracts, EU model contract clauses and by making progress towards an optional European Contract Law;
> - Making it easier and less costly for businesses and consumers to enforce contracts and to recognise court judgments and documents in other EU countries.[58]

[17–62] In 2011, the Commission published an ambitious communication, *The Single Market Act*, setting out "twelve key actions and 50 complementary actions to boost growth and strengthen confidence".[59] This was followed up in 2012 by a communication on *Better Governance for the Single Market*[60] and a second *Single Market Act II*, which identified four drivers of new growth and proposals for pursuing them, namely:

(i) developing fully integrated rail, maritime, aviation and energy networks in the Single Market;
(ii) fostering mobility across borders of citizens (eg the improvement of tools to match job-seekers with job offers across the EU; the mobility of supplementary social security rights) and businesses (eg modernising EU insolvency rules);
(iii) supporting the digital economy across Europe (eg supporting online services by making payment services in the EU more efficient; reducing the cost and increasing efficiency in the deployment of high speed communication infrastructure; making electronic invoicing the standard invoicing mode for public procurement); and
(iv) strengthening social entrepreneurship, cohesion and consumer confidence (eg by improving the safety of products circulating in the EU through better coherence and enforcement of product safety and market surveillance rules; by giving all EU citizens

---

[58] Commission Communication, "Europe 2020: A Strategy for Smart, Sustainable and Inclusive Growth", COM(2010) 2020, 3 March 2010, 20–21.

[59] Commission Communication, "Single Market Act. Twelve Levers to Boost Growth and Strengthen Confidence: Working Together to Create New Growth", COM(2011) 206, 13 April 2011. See also Commission Staff Working Document, "Delivering the Single Market Act: State of Play", SWD(2012) 12, 15 February 2012.

[60] Commission Communication, "Better Governance for the Single Market", COM(2012) 259, 8 June 2012.

access to a basic payment account, ensuring bank account fees are transparent and comparable, and making it easier to switch bank accounts; and by focussing attention on the issue of co-operatives and employee share-ownership).[61]

[17–63] As well as examining new areas that might benefit from positive integration, there is an awareness amongst the institutions that EU legal acts can be difficult to find or to follow and can impose additional regulatory burdens on businesses and individuals. Accordingly, beginning in 1996, a programme was launched aimed at the Simplification of Legislation in the Internal Market (SLIM), which has been followed by a series of multi-annual programmes with similar aims. The need to cut "red-tape" has become a constant refrain, prompting the Commission's 2015 communication "Better Regulation for Better Results".[62] As the Communication describes:

> The natural tendency of politicians is to focus on new initiatives. However, the EU is judged not just on new political initiatives, but on the benefits and the burden of existing EU legislation. As such, actively managing existing EU legislation is just as important politically as preparing new initiatives. Over time, even well-designed legislation may become out of date, more burdensome than it needs to be, or ceases to achieve its objectives. For example, changes in the market may mean a law is no longer useful, relevant, or serving its purpose. Changing technology may offer the opportunity to deliver the policy goal in a better way – for example, allowing a form to be submitted online. Lessons learned from implementing a policy through better monitoring and evaluation may also provide fresh evidence about which policy solution is the best.[63]

[17–64] An important part of the *Better Regulation* agenda is the Regulatory Fitness and Performance Programme (REFIT), described as a lasting commitment to keeping the body of EU law lean and healthy by removing red tape and lowering costs without compromising policy objectives. Progress is monitored by way of a REFIT scoreboard. An inter-institutional agreement on Better Law-Making, entered into in April 2016 between the European Parliament, the Council and the Commission, includes a commitment to cooperate in order to update and simplify legislation and to avoid overregulation and administrative burdens for citizens and businesses, while ensuring that the objectives of the legislation are met.[64] As part of the REFIT programme, the Commission has undertaken to present an annual overview, including a burden survey, of the results of the Union's efforts to simplify legislation and to avoid overregulation and reduce administrative burdens. Wherever possible, the Commission will also aim to quantify the regulatory burden reduction or savings potential of individual proposals or legal acts.

---

61 Commission Communication, "Single Market Act II: Together for New Growth", COM(2012) 573, 3 October 2012.

62 Commission Communication, "Better Regulation for Better Results: An EU Agenda", COM(2015) 215, 19 May 2015. See Mariolina Eliantonio and Aneta Spendzharova, "The European Union's New 'Better Regulation' Agenda: Between Procedures and Politics" (2017) 19 *European Journal of Law Reform* 3; Mark Dawson, "Better Regulation and the Future of EU Regulatory Law and Politics" (2016) 53 *Common Market Law Review* 1209; Sacha Garben and Inge Govaere, *The EU Better Regulation Agenda* (Hart 2018).

63 *ibid*, 10.

64 [2016] OJ L123/1, para 48.

CHAPTER 18

THE CUSTOMS UNION AND COMMON COMMERCIAL POLICY

A. INTRODUCTION

[18–01] In this chapter, an introduction will be provided to the Customs Union and the Common Commercial Policy, with a focus on how they contribute to the removal of physical and fiscal barriers on the free movement of goods. Although they are closely interrelated, the Customs Union is an internal policy of the EU, whereas the Common Commercial Policy is an external policy. As a result, they are dealt with in different parts of the TFEU. The Customs Union is provided for in Part III of the TFEU on Union Policies and Internal Actions, within Title II dealing with the free movement of goods. In contrast, the Common Commercial Policy makes up Title II of Part V of the TFEU on External Action.

[18–02] Since its inception, EU law has provided for a common customs union with respect to the movement of goods. This is now enshrined in Art 28(1) TFEU as follows:

> The Union shall comprise a customs union which shall cover all trade in goods and which shall involve the prohibition between Member States of customs duties on imports and exports and of all charges having equivalent effect, and the adoption of a common customs tariff in their relations with third countries.

[18–03] From this it can be seen that the Customs Union has both an internal and external dimension. Within the EU, goods are to flow freely as between the Member States without (i) customs duties on imports; (ii) customs duties on exports; and (iii) charges having an equivalent effect to customs duties on imports or exports. This is reaffirmed in Art 30 TFEU, which states that customs duties on imports and exports, and charges having equivalent effect, shall be prohibited between Member States.

[18–04] There are seven very small parts of the EU that, for geographical or historical reasons, are outside the Customs Union, namely Gibraltar (a British Overseas Territory to which the Treaties apply), the German town of Büsingen (an enclave in Switzerland), Campione d'Italia (an Italian enclave in Switzerland), the Italian town of Livigno (historically duty-free), the autonomous Spanish cities of Ceuta and Melilla on the north African coast and the VAT-exempt German islands of Heligoland. These seven areas are also excluded from the EU VAT area. The only non-EU Member States that participate in both the Customs Union and the Single Market are the three micro-states of Andorra and San Marino (through bilateral agreements with the EU) and Monaco (through a bilateral agreement with France).

[18–05] Although the Customs Union is sometimes described as being an essential element in the functioning of the Single Market, the European Economic Area (EEA) states of Norway, Iceland and Liechtenstein participate in the Single Market but are outside of the Customs Union. It is also possible to participate in *a* customs union with the EU without participating in the Single Market, as is the case with Turkey. The 1963 Association Agreement between the EU and Turkey committed to the creation of a customs union between the two parties, with Turkey undertaking to adopt the EU's common customs tariff in its trade relations with third countries.[1] Following an Additional Protocol agreed in 1970, the EU dropped all tariffs and quotas on Turkish industrial goods, while Turkey agreed to follow suit, and to implement the common customs tariff, over a 22-year period.[2] By an important 1995 decision of the Association Council established pursuant to the Agreement, rules were laid down for the final implementation of the customs union.[3]

[18–06] Pursuant to Art 31 TFEU, imports into the EU from third countries are subject to a common customs tariff (CCT) upon crossing the Union's external border. This is sometimes referred to as the common external tariff. In accordance with Arts 28(2) and 29 TFEU, once inside the EU, imported goods that have complied with the relevant formalities, including the payment of customs duties or charges, are in "free circulation", benefiting from the same rules as apply to EU-made goods. As described by the Court of Justice, such imports are thereafter "definitively and wholly assimilated to products originating in Member States".[4] This is known as the principle of assimilation. According to the Court:

> Products in free circulation are to be understood as meaning those products which, coming from third countries, were duly imported into any one of the Member States in accordance with the requirements laid down by [the TFEU].

---

1 Association Agreement between the European Economic Community and its Member States and Turkey, 12 September 1963 [1964] OJ L217, Art 10(2).

2 Additional Protocol to the Association Agreement [1972] OJ L293/4.

3 Decision No 1/95 of the EC-Turkey Association Council of 22 December 1995 on implementing the final phase of the Customs Union [1996] OJ L35/1. See Steve Peers, "Living in Sin: Legal Integration under the EC-Turkey Customs Union" (1996) 7 *European Journal of International Law* 411; Fadi Hakura, "EU–Turkey Customs Union: Prospects for Modernization and Lessons for Brexit" (Royal Institute of International Affairs, 2018).

4 Case C-83/89 *Openbaar Ministerie v Houben* [1990] ECR I-1161, 1177.

> … as regards free circulation of goods within the [Union], products entitled to "free circulation" are definitively and wholly assimilated to products originating in Member States.
>
> The result of this assimilation is that the provisions of Article [34 TFEU] concerning the elimination of quantitative restrictions and all measures having equivalent effect are applicable without distinction to products originating in the [Union] and to those which were put into free circulation in any one of the Member States, irrespective of the actual origin of these products.[5]

[18–07] An example of the principle of assimilation in action is the well-known case of *Dassonville*, which concerned a measure equivalent to a quantitative restriction imposed by Belgium on imports from France.[6] The import at issue, however, was Scotch whisky that had been imported into France from the UK at a time when the UK had yet to join the EEC. As the whisky had been imported into the EEC in accordance with the relevant rules, it was thereafter in free circulation as between the Member States, and so benefited from the Treaty rules on the free movement of goods when moving from France to Belgium. The principle of assimilation is reflected in the definition of "Union goods" found within the Union Customs Code. For the purposes of the Code, Union goods can comprise: (a) goods wholly obtained in the EU and not incorporating goods imported from countries outside the customs territory of the Union; (b) goods brought into the EU from countries outside the customs territory of the Union and released for free circulation; and (c) goods obtained or produced in the EU, either solely from goods referred to in (a) or from goods referred to in (a) and (b).[7]

[18–08] It is the addition of the external dimension in the form of the Common Customs Tariff that transforms what would otherwise be a free trade area between participating states into a customs union. In a free trade area, although customs duties and quantitative restrictions *between* states are eliminated, each participating state remains free to decide its own external trade policy, including the customs or restrictions it imposes on imports coming from states that are not part of the area. As Nigel Foster describes, this limitation means that, from the perspective of seeking to build a single market for goods, a free trade area is "regarded as of little use, because third countries may target the country with the lowest external duties".[8] This is known as trade deflection. Since any goods entering a free trade area will compete with domestically produced goods, the competitive advantage that could be garnered through trade deflection is often addressed by requiring goods to be accompanied by certificates of origin, so as to identify whether they are internally produced or have been imported from outside of the area. Such a certification system is, however, difficult and expensive to administer and requires checks to take place on goods in order to determine their country of origin. A customs union builds upon a free trade area by adding a common customs policy towards the rest of the world such that, as seen from the outside, the EU is one cohesive unit when it comes to trade matters. Once goods have been imported into a customs union and paid the common customs tariff, they can then move freely within that union without the need for each participating state to carry out checks of its

---

5 Case 41/76 *Donckerwolke v Procureur de la République* [1976] ECR 1921, 1935.

6 Case 8/74 *Procureur du Roi v Dassonville* [1974] ECR 837. See ch 19, paras [19–31] to [19–37].

7 Regulation (EU) No 952/2013 of the European Parliament and of the Council of 9 October 2013 laying down the Union Customs Code [2013] OJ L269/1, Art 5(23).

8 Nigel Foster, *Foster on EU Law* (Oxford University Press, 2015) 257.

own. As a result, certifications of origin are no longer required when imported goods move from one state to another within a customs union.

[18–09] The practical difference between membership of a free trade area and membership of a customs union has been brought into sharp relief by the UK's withdrawal from the EU, and the devising of a solution to avoid a hard border on the island of Ireland in particular. For example, frequent comparisons have been made to the border between Sweden, as an EU Member State, and Norway, as a state outside of the Customs Union but within a free trade area with the EU, in the form of the European Economic Area. Crucially, the application of country of origin rules and other checks throughout the external frontier of the Customs Union means that commercial traffic crossing the Norway–Sweden border is subject to controls, even though that border lies within a free trade area. In assessing a hypothetical scenario in which the UK were to join the EEA following its withdrawal from the EU, the Swedish National Board of Trade concluded that, although this would mean an exemption from customs duty or tariff reductions for goods covered by the EEA Agreement, customs formalities would have to be completed for goods crossing the border, and it would be necessary to present proof of the goods' origin to avail of exemption from, or reduced, customs duty. In its assessment, whereas businesses trading within the EU, "are accustomed to trade flowing without any special administration … and consumers are accustomed to being able to order goods without having to fill in import and/or export documentation and pay various fees in the form of customs duty, VAT etc", were the UK to leave the Customs Union and join the EEA, "in order to benefit from exemption from customs duty under the agreement, the bureaucracy would be significant".[9]

[18–10] The creation of a customs union (or a free trade area) is expressly accommodated for in Art XXIV, paragraph (5) of the General Agreement on Trade and Tariffs (GATT). This provides that nothing in the Agreement shall prevent the formation of a customs union provided that the duties and other regulations of commerce imposed at the institution of the union, in respect of trade with GATT states outside of the union, shall not on the whole be higher or more restrictive than the general incidence of the duties and regulations applicable in the participating states prior to the formation of the union. Such a provision is necessary due to what is known as the "Most Favoured Nation" clause, found in Art 1 of the GATT. It requires that any advantage granted to a product originating in (or destined for) any other country shall be accorded "immediately and unconditionally" to the like products of all other contracting parties. Article XXIV sets out the rationale for departing from the Most Favoured Nation clause by recognising, provided a customs union does not raise barriers to trade between states outside of the union, the desirability of "increasing free trade by the development, through voluntary agreements, of closer integration between economies of the countries parties to such agreements". Article 206 TFEU reciprocates this sentiment in stating that, by establishing a customs union, the EU "shall contribute, in the common interest, to the harmonious development of world trade, the progressive abolition of restrictions on international trade and on foreign direct investment, and the lowering of customs and other barriers".

---

[9] Swedish National Board of Trade, "Brexit – Options for a Future Regulatory Framework for Trade in Services and Customs and Trade Procedures between the EU and the UK", 15 March 2017, 8–9. See Arno Hantzsche and Garry Young, "The Economic Impact on the United Kingdom of a Customs Union Deal with the European Union", National Institute of Economic and Social Research, 2019.

[18–11] Given their nature, it is unsurprising that the Customs Union and the Common Commercial Policy are two of the five areas of exclusive Union competence listed in Art 3(1) TFEU. Individual Member States, therefore, are no longer free to enter into bilateral trade agreements with third countries. As the Court of Justice described in *Aprile*:

> it must be borne in mind that the Customs Union, which ... is to cover all trade in goods, incorporates a Common Customs Tariff intended to bring about equalization of the charges borne at the external frontiers of the [EU] by products imported from non-member countries, in order to ensure that trade with such countries is not diverted and that the free movement of products between Member States and the conditions of competition between economic agents are not distorted.
>
> As regards the common commercial policy, based ... on uniform principles, particularly in regard to changes in tariff rates, the conclusion of tariff and trade agreements and the achievement of uniformity in measures of liberalization, it implies that national disparities of a fiscal and commercial nature affecting trade with non-member countries must be abolished.
>
> Both the unicity of the [Union] customs territory and the uniformity of the common commercial policy would be seriously undermined if the Member States were authorized unilaterally to impose charges having equivalent effect to customs duties on imports from non-member countries.
>
> It has thus been consistently held that the Member States have no right unilaterally to add national charges to the duties payable under the [EU] rules, otherwise such rules might be deprived of the requisite uniformity.
>
> In order to ensure that taxation has a uniform impact in all the Member States on trade with non-member countries, it is therefore the responsibility of the [EU] alone to determine and, if necessary, change the level of duties and taxes payable on products from those countries.
>
> It follows that the Member States may not impose, by way of national legislation alone, charges having equivalent effect in trade with non-member countries.[10]

[18–12] What the Court is describing here is known as the principle of uniformity, which entails that the "unicity" of the Customs Union is guaranteed by each Member State applying a fully uniform regime for imports and exports. The principle can be seen to flow in large part from the requirements of Art XXIV of the GATT.[11] In order for a customs union to be permissible under GATT rules, it must constitute a single customs territory where "substantially the same duties and other regulations of commerce are applied by each of the members of the union" to countries outside of the union.[12] The principle of uniformity is now enshrined in Art 207 TFEU which provides that the Common Commercial Policy shall be based, *inter alia*, on uniform principles, particularly with regard to changes in tariff rates.

[18–13] Related to the prohibition on customs duties and charges having an equivalent effect, the TFEU also provides for certain rules at EU level in order to ensure that the *internal* tax system of a Member State in relation to goods does not operate so as to

---

10 Case C-125/94 *Aprile* [1995] ECR I-2919, 2950–2951.

11 See Piet Eeckhout, *EU External Relations Law* (2nd ed, Oxford University Press, 2011) 441.

12 Article XXIV:8(a) of the General Agreement on Trade and Tariffs.

favour domestic products over imports.[13] So, Art 110 TFEU prohibits Member States from applying their tax system in such a way that leads to either direct or indirect discrimination against imported goods that are in free circulation within the EU, or to otherwise affording indirect protection to domestic products that are in competition with imported goods. In addition, Art 113 TFEU provides the Union with a legislative competence to harmonise legislation concerning turnover taxes, excise duties and other forms of indirect taxation on products, such as VAT, "to the extent that such harmonisation is necessary to ensure the establishment and the functioning of the internal market and to avoid distortion of competition". The limited nature of the EU's competence with respect to such tax matters has been well described as follows:

> Articles 110–113 TFEU serve to dissolve the latent tension between the preservation of national tax sovereignty to the greatest possible degree and the aim of ensuring that the European internal market continues to function with a minimum of disruption. However, it has to be taken into account that tax diversity and the resulting competition for locational advantages are not per se incompatible with the internal market objective. ... Until today, tax law harmonisation or even unification has still not become an autonomous objective of the Union but it is always functionally related to the internal market objective and factually limited by the scope of this objective... However, because of the primacy of Union law, Member States must always exercise their generally enduring sovereignty in tax matters (including matters of direct taxation) "consistently with Community [now Union] law".[14]

[18–14] The contribution of Arts 110 and 113 TFEU to the functioning of the Customs Union is considered in Sections C and D below.

[18–15] Since the Customs Union is described in Art 28 TFEU as covering all trade in goods, a preliminary question arises as to what is meant by the term "goods", which is not defined in the Treaties. The Court of Justice has interpreted the term very broadly as meaning "products which can be valued in money and which are capable, as such, of forming the subject of commercial transactions".[15] So, diverse items such as artistic and archaeological treasures and electricity have been held to be goods.[16] Where the predominant element of a transaction relates to a good, with an element of service connected thereto, the transaction will be considered to be one involving goods. For example, the Court has found that non-recyclable waste is a good, and subsequently held that the depositing of waste at a waste disposal facility was also a good.[17]

B. Customs Duties – Article 30 TFEU

[18–16] As between Member States, Art 30 TFEU prohibits all customs duties on imports and exports and charges having equivalent effect. In equally robust terms, the Court of Justice has made clear that in order for a customs duty or charge to be prohibited by Art 30, it is not necessary that it be designed with the traditional purpose

13 See Jukka Snell, "Non-Discriminatory Tax Obstacles in Community Law" (2007) 56 *International and Comparative Law Quarterly* 339.

14 Daniel-Erasmus Khan and Nadine Lichtblau in Rudolf Geiger, Daniel-Erasmus Khan and Markus Kotzur (eds), *European Union Treaties* (CH Beck, 2015) 110.

15 Case 7/68 *Commission v Italy (Art Treasures)* [1968] ECR 423, 428.

16 See Case C-305/17 *FENS v Slovakia* EU:C:2018:986, 6 December 2018, paras 34–35.

17 Case C-2/90 *Commission v Belgium (Walloon Waste)* [1992] ECR I-4431; Case C-221/06 *Stadtgemeinde Frohnleiten* [2007] ECR I-9643.

of protecting domestic goods from imports. Rather, customs duties are prohibited "independently of any consideration of the purpose for which they are introduced and the destination of the revenue obtained therefrom".[18] In other words, the Court is not concerned with the *purpose* behind a charge, but rather the *effect* that it has on trade. In *Sociaal Fonds*, for example, the fact that Belgium did not have a diamond mining industry of its own to protect was immaterial in considering the permissibility of a levy imposed on imported diamonds which went towards a social fund for workers in the industry.[19] Given that the focus is on the effect of a charge rather than its purpose, it is not surprising that Art 30 has no equivalent to the six grounds in Art 36 TFEU that permit a derogation from the prohibition on quantitative restrictions on the free movement of goods found in Art 34 TFEU.

[18–17] In the *Artistic Treasures* case, the Court of Justice effectively dismissed as irrelevant the argument made by Italy that a charge on the export of artistic treasures did not make any significant budgetary contribution, but rather was designed to protect against the loss of Italian cultural objects. According to the Court, the charge was prohibited "by reason of the fact that export trade in the goods in question is hindered by the pecuniary burden which it imposes on the price of the exported articles".[20] Soon afterwards, in the *Statistical Levy* case, the Court rejected an attempt by Italy to rationalise a levy imposed on exports on the basis that it funded the maintenance of statistical data on trade patterns. The Court re-emphasised that Art 30 was not only concerned with preventing protectionist duties, but was "based on the fact that any pecuniary charge, however small, imposed on goods by reason of the fact that they cross a frontier constitutes an obstacle to the movement of such goods".[21] Accordingly,

> any pecuniary charge, however small and whatever its designation and mode of application, which is imposed unilaterally on domestic or foreign goods by reason of the fact that they cross a frontier, and which is not a customs duty in the strict sense, constitutes a charge having equivalent effect … even if it is not imposed for the benefit of the State, is not discriminatory or protective in effect and if the product on which the charge is imposed is not in competition with any domestic product.[22]

[18–18] An alternative argument put forward by Italy was that the levy should be seen as consideration for a service rendered, given that the exactness of the statistical information was of a benefit to importers and exporters and was in the nature of a *quid pro quo*. As any such advantage was "so general, and so difficult to assess", the Court held that the levy could not be regarded as the "consideration for a specific benefit actually conferred".[23]

[18–19] Italy attempted this same "consideration for services rendered" argument in *Bresciani*, but was met with a similar result.[24] There, it sought to defend a charge that was imposed for the laboratory inspection of cowhides imported into Italy, where the charge was proportionate to the cost of the inspection. According to the Court, a state activity "intended to maintain a public health inspection imposed in the general

---

18 Case 24/68 *Commission v Italy (Statistical Levy)* [1969] ECR 193, 200.
19 Cases 2/69 and 3/69 *Sociaal Fonds* [1969] ECR 211.
20 Case 7/68 *Commission v Italy (Artistic Treasures)* [1968] ECR 423, 429.
21 Case 24/68 *Commission v Italy (Statistical Levy)* [1969] ECR 193, 200.
22 *ibid*, 201.
23 *ibid*, 202.
24 Case 87/75 *Bresciani* [1976] ECR 129.

interest cannot be regarded as a service rendered to the importer", such as to justify a charge.[25] Rather, the cost of such inspections was to be met by the general public which, as a whole, benefited from the free movement of goods within the Union. Two further arguments put forward by Italy also failed. First, the Court did not regard it as being relevant that the charge imposed was calculated in proportion to the quantity of the goods, rather than their value. Secondly, in response to Italy's argument that the charge ought to be permitted due to the fact that a similar charge was imposed on domestic producers, the Court outlined that, for this to be the case, the two respective charges must be "applied according to the same criteria and at the same stage of production, thus making it possible for them to be regarded as falling within a general system of internal taxation applying systematically and in the same way to domestic and imported products".[26]

[18–20] From *Statistical Levy* and *Bresciani* it can be seen that, in principle, a charge that is consideration for a service actually rendered, and that is for an amount commensurate with that service, will not be considered to be a customs duty. In practice, however, this is difficult to establish given the Court's reluctance to accept that the facilitation of imports is a service provided for the benefit of a particular importer. So, for example, in the *Warehousing Case (Commission v Belgium)*, the Court was required to consider whether the imposition of a fee for the use of warehousing facilities made available by Belgium, not at its frontiers – where there was no charge for completing customs formalities – but at interior locations, constituted a charge having an equivalent effect or a genuine service of direct benefit to importers.[27] Belgium argued that a service was being provided to importers in that an importer was enabled to have its goods declared through customs near the places for which they were bound. This, it was claimed, relieved an importer of the necessity of either having its own premises suitable for goods clearance or having recourse to private premises, the use of which was more expensive than that of the public warehouses.[28] The Court accepted that where an importer chose to leave imported goods in storage in the public warehouse for a period of time, a service was being provided for which a charge could be imposed. Where, however, the warehouse was used solely for the purpose of completing customs formalities it could not be said that a service was being provided. Accordingly, in those circumstances, any fee was a charge having an equivalent effect to a customs duty.

[18–21] In addition to a charge for a genuine service rendered, the other circumstance in which a charge will not be prohibited is where it covers the cost of an inspection or other service that is *required* as a matter of EU law or by virtue of an international agreement to which the Member State and/or the EU is a party. It is not sufficient that the inspection is required as a matter of national law, nor is it sufficient if the inspection is merely permitted under EU law or an international agreement, as opposed to being required. The charge must not exceed the actual cost of the inspection, and the inspection must be: (i) prescribed by EU law in the general interest of the Union; (ii) obligatory and uniform for all the products concerned in the EU; and (iii) promote the free movement of goods, in particular by neutralising obstacles which could arise from unilateral inspections applied by Member States in accordance with Art 36.[29]

---

25 *ibid*, 138–139.
26 *ibid*, 139.
27 Case 132/82 *Commission v Belgium (Warehousing Case)* [1983] ECR 1649.
28 *ibid*, 1659.
29 Case 18/87 *Commission v Germany* [1988] ECR 5427.

C. Internal Taxation – Article 110 TFEU

[18–22] As mentioned above, in *Bresciani* Italy argued that a charge for the inspection of imported cowhides ought to be permitted given that a similar charge was imposed on domestic producers.[30] The Court of Justice responded that, for this to be the case, the two charges must be applied "according to the same criteria and at the same stage of production, thus making it possible for them to be regarded as falling within a general system of internal taxation applying systematically and in the same way to domestic and imported products".[31] So, while a customs duty or a charge having an equivalent effect is characterised by the fact that it is placed on imports or exports as a result of their crossing of a frontier, a tax relates to a "general system of internal duties applied systematically to categories of products in accordance with objective criteria irrespective of the origins of the products".[32]

[18–23] There is a close relationship between the prohibition on customs duties found in Art 30 TFEU, and the rules governing Member States' regimes of internal taxation found in Art 110 TFEU in particular. Article 110 provides that:

> No Member State shall impose, directly or indirectly, on the products of other Member States any internal taxation of any kind in excess of that imposed directly or indirectly on similar domestic products.
>
> Furthermore, no Member State shall impose on the products of other Member States any internal taxation of such a nature as to afford indirect protection to other products.

[18–24] Article 110 is concerned with indirect taxes, which are imposed on goods themselves or the use of such goods, but not with the direct taxation of the profits earned by the producer of goods. Its aim is to ensure that, in order not to distort competition within the Single Market, the internal tax regimes of Member States adopt a position of "complete neutrality" as regards domestic products and imported products. In other words, in order not to violate Art 110, a tax system must "exclude any possibility of imported products being taxed more heavily than similar domestic products".[33] Although it refers only to imports, Art 110 has been held to apply to exports. In addition, while it refers to the "products of *other Member States*", the Court has confirmed that Art 110 also applies to imports from third countries that, having complied with formalities at the external border, are in free circulation within the EU.

[18–25] Clearly, the effect of prohibiting customs duties on imports would be significantly undermined if Member States were nonetheless free to impose internal taxes, or higher rates of tax, specifically on imported goods, thereby giving domestic producers a competitive advantage. It is important to note, however, that despite having a close relationship and a shared objective, Arts 30 and 110 TFEU are mutually exclusive, in the sense that a measure imposed by a Member State can be either (i) a customs duty or charge having an equivalent effect or (ii) a form of internal taxation, but it cannot be both.[34] As a result, where a challenge is being brought to such a measure,

---

[30] Case 87/75 *Bresciani* [1976] ECR 129.

[31] *ibid*, 139.

[32] Case 90/79 *Commission v France (Reprographic Machines)* [1981] ECR 283, 301.

[33] Case C-302/00 *Commission v France (Dark Tobacco)* [2002] ECR I-2055, 2087.

[34] Case 305/17 *FENS v Slovakia* EU:C:2018:986, 6 December 2018, paras 36–48.

both articles will often be invoked, leaving it for the relevant court to determine which of the two is applicable.

[18–26] A particular instance of where this distinction is difficult to discern concerns a levy that is imposed on both domestic producers and importers (or goods for the domestic market and goods for the export market), suggesting that it is not a customs duty, but where the money raised from the levy is used only to benefit domestic producers (or those selling on the domestic market), such as by promoting the industry within that Member State. These are known as "para-fiscal charges". In *Capolongo*, for example, Italy imposed a levy on both domestically produced and imported paper, cardboard and cellulose (which is used in the production of paper and cardboard).[35] The monies raised from the levy were used solely to promote cellulose production in Italy, including through the granting of subsidies to national manufacturers. An importer challenging the levy argued that it was a charge having an equivalent effect to a customs duty prohibited by Art 30. Italy, on the other hand, argued that since the levy applied to both domestic and imported goods, it ought to be judged under Art 110. The Court of Justice agreed that the overall effect was that the levy was a charge on imports, reasoning that:

> when such a financial charge or duty is intended exclusively to support activities which specifically profit taxed domestic products, it can follow that the general duty levied according to the same criteria on the imported product and the domestic product nevertheless constitutes for the former a net supplementary tax burden, whilst for the latter it constitutes in reality a set-off against benefits or aids previously received.
>
> Consequently, a duty within the general system of internal taxation applying systematically to domestic and imported products according to the same criteria, can nevertheless constitute a charge having an effect equivalent to customs duty on imports, when such contribution is intended exclusively to support activities which specifically benefit the taxed domestic product.[36]

[18–27] In contrast, if the monies raised by the charge are only partially used to help domestic producers, so that their tax burden is not fully offset by a benefit received, the measure is considered part of internal taxation and falls to be assessed in accordance with Art 110.[37]

(i) Direct and Indirect Discrimination

[18–28] Given the clarity of the prohibition, it is relatively infrequent for a Member State's tax regime to be found to directly discriminate against imports. In addition to the rate of tax imposed, direct discrimination can also come about through a difference in the procedures governing how a tax is collected. In the late 1970s, for example, the Commission instituted proceedings against Ireland on the basis that the manner in which excise duty was imposed on spirits favoured domestic producers, who were permitted to pay the duties within a certain period after which they had been put on the market, compared to importers, from whom duties were collected at the point of importation.[38] The Court of Justice rejected Ireland's contention that Art 110 only

[35] Case 77/72 *Capolongo* [1973] ECR 611.
[36] *ibid*, 623.
[37] Case C-234/99 *Nygård* [2002] ECR I-3657.
[38] Case 55/79 *Commission v Ireland* [1980] ECR 481.

concerned discrimination in the *rate* of the duty imposed. Instead, the Court held that it was necessary to

> take into consideration the provisions relating to the basis of assessment and the detailed rules for levying the various duties in addition to the rate of tax. In fact the decisive criterion of comparison for the purposes of the application of Article [110] is the actual effect of each tax on national production on the one hand and on imported products on the other, since even where the rate of tax is equal the effect of that tax may vary according to the detailed rules for the basis of assessment and levying thereof applied to national production and imported products respectively.[39]

[18–29] The fact that, in order to avail of the option of deferred payment, domestic producers of spirits needed to fulfil certain requirements, such as the payment of a security, was not a justification for the difference in treatment, given that these additional obligations were "trifling" and could have equally been imposed on importers in order to give them the choice of making a deferred payment. Nor was the Court persuaded by the argument that account should be taken of the disadvantage faced by Irish whiskey producers compared with producers of Scotch whisky given divergent exchange rates. In its view, if the "Irish authorities consider that the exchange rates in question were not fixed appropriately, they should seek the remedy for that situation by the appropriate means. A monetary situation cannot be corrected by means of discriminatory tax provisions."[40]

[18–30] Whereas direct discrimination openly differentiates on the basis of the origin of the goods, indirect discrimination does not make such a distinction as a matter of law but, when applied in practice, has such an effect as a matter of fact. A good example of this is the *Dark Tobacco* case (*Commission v France*).[41] There, infringement proceedings were brought against France as a result of its different treatment of light and dark tobacco, with dark tobacco, which was almost exclusively produced in France, taxed at a lower rate. In contrast, light tobacco was essentially an imported product. Although the tax code did not expressly differentiate on the basis of the origin of the tobacco, the effect of the distinction between light and dark tobacco was to tax French-produced tobacco at a more favourable rate. Accordingly, the Court found a violation of Art 110, reasoning that:

> Although [the tax] does not establish any formal distinction according to the origin of the products, it adjusts the system of taxation in such a way that the cigarettes falling within the most favourable category come almost exclusively from domestic production whereas almost all imported products come within the least advantageous category. Those features of the system are not nullified by the fact that a very small fraction of imported cigarettes come within the most favourable category, whereas, conversely, a certain proportion of domestic production come within the same tax category as imported cigarettes. It appears, therefore, that the system of taxation is designed in such a way as to benefit domestic product and handicaps imported cigarettes to the same extent.[42]

---

39 *ibid*, 491.

40 *ibid*, 492.

41 Case C-302/00 *Commission v France (Dark Tobacco)* [2002] ECR I-2055.

42 *ibid*, 2088.

(ii) Similar Products v Other Competing Products

[18–31] A close reading of Art 110 reveals that it in fact contains two quite distinct prohibitions. The first paragraph prohibits the direct or indirect imposition of any tax on imported goods that is *in excess* of that imposed on *similar* domestic products. In contrast, the second paragraph prohibits the imposition of any internal tax on imports that *indirectly protects other* (domestic) products. In other words, the second prohibition is aimed at ensuring equal tax treatment of imported and domestic products that, although not similar, still compete against each other, usually as substitutes. The Court of Justice has described the prohibition in the first paragraph as the "basic rule", while the function of the second paragraph is:

> to cover, in addition, all forms of indirect tax protection in the case of products which, without being similar within the meaning of the first paragraph, are nevertheless in competition, even partial, indirect or potential, with certain products of the importing country ...
>
> Whilst the criterion indicated in the first paragraph of Article [110] consists in the comparison of tax burdens, whether in terms of the rate, the mode of assessment or other detailed rules for the application thereof, in view of the difficulty of making sufficiently precise comparisons between the products in question, the second paragraph of that article is based upon a more general criterion, in other words the protective nature of the system of internal taxation.[43]

[18–32] The line between products that are "similar" and products that are not similar but nonetheless compete against one another is often difficult to draw. There is, however, a clear difference in both the application of the two paragraphs, and the consequences of a violation. In order to establish a violation of paragraph (1) of Art 110 it is necessary to show that the products are similar, which then allows a direct comparison to be made as between the applicable tax rates and, if there is a difference, a violation will have been established (unless, in the case of indirect discrimination, the Member State can point to an objective justification for applying the criteria that gives rise to the different treatment).

[18–33] In contrast, under paragraph (2) it is not necessary to show that the products are similar. This means, however, that a direct comparison as between the two products cannot be made. As a result, it is necessary to show that the tax has a protectionist effect in order to establish a violation of paragraph (2). Flowing from these two approaches, there is a corresponding difference in the consequences of a finding of a violation. Since paragraph (1) targets taxes *in excess* of those on domestic goods, a finding of a violation will require that the taxes be equalised. In contrast, paragraph (2) targets taxes with a protectionist effect, and so a finding of a violation will only require that that protectionist effect be removed, which may not necessarily entail an equalisation of the taxes.

[18–34] That said, on occasion the Court of Justice adopts a global approach to Art 110, in that it does not identify which of the two paragraphs it is applying. This typically arises where it is clear that the goods are in competition with each other and that the tax has a protectionist effect, such that it is not necessary for the Court to take the extra step of deciding whether they are in fact "similar" within the meaning of Art 110(1).

[43] Case 168/78 *Commission v France (Spirits)* [1980] ECR 347, 360.

In *Humblot*, for example, an instance of indirect discrimination was alleged against a French tax on cars that, up to a certain horsepower, increased gradually, but after that point jumped to a significantly larger, fixed rate that was almost five times the highest rate under the gradual rating.[44] It so happened that no French-made cars exceeded the horsepower from which the higher rate applied, whereas cars imported from other Member States did. In defending the tax regime, France argued that the cars of a higher horsepower were luxury cars that were not "similar" to the French produced cars, such that Art 110(1) did not apply. While France conceded that the cars could be regarded as being in competition, it argued that the tax did not have a protectionist effect within the meaning of Art 110(2). The Commission, on the other hand, took the view that cars, regardless of their horsepower, were to be regarded as "similar" products for the purposes of Art 110(1). In its judgment, the Court considered paragraphs (1) and (2) of Art 110 together without dwelling on their differences or deciding whether luxury cars were "similar" to cars with a lower horsepower. It held that, although the French tax

> embodies no formal distinction based on the origin of products it manifestly exhibits discriminatory or protective features contrary to Article [110], since the power rating determining liability to the special tax has been fixed at a level such that only imported cars, in particular from other Member States, are subject to the special tax whereas all cars of domestic manufacture are liable to the distinctly more advantageous differential tax.[45]

[18–35] Likewise, in a case involving France's imposition of a higher rate of tax on spirits made from grain, such as gin and vodka, which it generally did not produce, than on spirits made from fruit, such as cognac, which it did produce, the Court satisfied itself that the various spirits had "sufficient characteristics in common with other spirits to constitute at least in certain circumstances an alternative choice for consumers", such that "the protective nature of the tax system criticised by the Commission is clear".[46] In these circumstances, it did not consider it necessary to decide whether each of the relevant spirits were similar. The more recent case law of the Court, however, has seen a greater adherence to the two-step approach set out in Art 110.

(iii) Similar Products – Article 110(1)

[18–36] Direct or indirect discrimination in the tax treatment of "similar products" is prohibited by Art 110(1). The approach of the Court of Justice to deciding whether two products are similar is nuanced and fact-specific, involving the application of a number of criteria to the characteristics of a good and the use to which it is put. It set out its starting position in the *Spirits* case (*Commission v France*) as follows:

> [Article 110(1)] must be interpreted widely so as to cover all taxation procedures which conflict with the principle of the equality of treatment of domestic products and imported products; it is therefore necessary to interpret the concept of "similar products" with sufficient flexibility ... [I]t is necessary to consider as "similar" products which have similar characteristics and meet the same needs from the point of view of consumers. It is therefore necessary to determine the scope of the paragraph of [Article 110] on the basis not of the criterion of the strictly identical nature of the product but on that of their similar and comparable use.[47]

---

[44] Case 112/84 *Humblot* [1985] ECR 1367.

[45] *ibid*, 1379.

[46] Case 168/78 *Commission v France (Spirits)* [1980] ECR 347, 369–370.

[47] *ibid*, 359–360.

[18–37] In *Dark Tobacco*, for example, it was readily apparent that light and dark tobacco were similar products. The Court noted that, given their similar properties, the two types of tobacco were able to satisfy the same needs of consumers, in that they would both be typically used in cigarettes. The fact that the average age of consumers of dark tobacco was higher than that of light tobacco did not, in the Court's assessment, cast doubt on that finding.[48] In response to the allegation that it was applying different rates of tax to similar products, thereby indirectly discriminating against imported tobacco, France was unable to point to any objective justification for the distinction drawn between the two types of tobacco.

[18–38] An example of the Court finding products not to be similar includes a decision in *Italian Fruits (Commission v Italy)* that bananas are not similar to water-based fruits, such as apples and peaches, for the purposes of Art 110(1). Italy, which produces many water-based fruits but not bananas, placed a tax on bananas that was significantly higher than that placed on other fruits. As explained by the Court:

> the higher water content of pears and other fruit typically grown in Italy give them thirst-quenching properties which bananas do not possess. Moreover, the observation of the Italian Government, which has not been challenged by the Commission, that the banana is regarded, at least on the Italian market, as a foodstuff which is particularly nutritious, of a high energy content and well-suited for infants must be accepted. It must therefore be held that those two categories of fruit are not similar within the meaning of the first paragraph of Article [110].[49]

[18–39] Other products that have been held not to be similar include whiskey and liqueur wines, given that whiskey has twice the alcohol content, and sherry and wine, given the difference in alcohol content and the fact that sherry is usually consumed as an aperitif.[50] Indeed, many of the cases concerning Art 110 concern alcoholic drinks given the high taxes commonly applied to them.

(iv) Other Competing Products – Article 110(2)

[18–40] Where two products are not considered to be similar within the meaning of Art 110(1), a difference in tax treatment may nevertheless be prohibited by Art 110(2) if that treatment is shown to afford "indirect protection" to domestic products. This usually arises where goods that are not similar, in the Art 110(1) sense, nevertheless have a competitive relationship such that where the price of one increases, demand for the other product is likely to go up. As Catherine Barnard has pointed out, the approach of the Court of Justice to other competing products is ultimately impressionistic, involving an overall assessment as to whether, in view of its inherent characteristics, "a given tax mechanism [is] *likely* to bring about the protective effect referred to by Article 110(2)".[51] For example, in *Italian Fruits*, although not considered to be "similar", bananas and water-based fruits were found to be in competition with each other within the meaning of Art 110(2).[52] The higher rate of tax was held to be in violation of Art 110(2) since bananas were a substitute for other fruits and the rate of tax "influences

---

48 Case C-302/00 *Commission v France (Dark Tobacco)* [2002] ECR I-2055, 2088.

49 *ibid.*

50 Case 243/84 *John Walker & Sons* [1986] ECR 833; Joined Cases C-367/93 to C-377/93 *FG Roders BV* [1995] ECR I-2229.

51 Catherine Barnard, *The Substantive Law of the EU* (4th ed, Oxford University Press, 2013) 62.

52 Case 184/85 *Commission v Italy (Italian Fruit)* [1987] ECR 2013.

the market in the products in question by reducing the potential consumption of the imported products".[53]

[18–41] The most well-known case involving Art 110(2) is the 1980 *Wine and Beer* case (*Commission v UK)*.[54] There, the Commission alleged that by imposing an excise duty on wine, which was mostly imported, almost five times that imposed on beer, which was mainly domestically produced, the UK was in violation of Art 110(2). In addition to pointing to their different tastes, ingredients and alcohol contents, the UK argued that wine and beer did not compete against one another in that beer was mainly consumed in pubs or in connection with work and was rarely consumed at home or with meals. In contrast, as a matter of social custom, wine was commonly associated with special occasions. In response to this line of argument, the Court of Justice made an important observation of a general nature, commenting that for the purposes of assessing whether one product may act as a substitute for another or is in a competitive relationship within the meaning of Art 110(2),

> it is necessary to consider not only the present state of the market but also the possibilities for development within the context of free movement of goods at the [EU] level and the further potential for the substitution of products for one another which may be revealed by intensification of trade, so as fully to develop the complementary features of the economies of the Member States in accordance with the objectives laid down by Article [3 TEU].
>
> … [i]t is impossible to restrict oneself to consumer habits in a Member State or in a given region. In fact, those habits, which are essentially variable in time and space, cannot be considered to be a fixed rule; the tax policy of a Member State must not therefore crystallise given consumer habits so as to consolidate an advantage acquired by national industries concerned to comply with them.[55]

[18–42] Given the wide varieties of wine in terms of quality and price, the Court concluded that it could not be said that all wines were in competition with beer, which was a popular and widely consumed beverage. Rather, the appropriate competitor was the lightest and cheapest wines that were the most accessible to the public at large and which sold in significant quantities. Upon comparing those wines with beer, it became apparent that they were subject to a considerably higher tax burden, such that:

> the United Kingdom's tax system has the effect of subjecting wine imported from other Member States to an additional burden so as to afford protection to domestic beer production. … Since such production is most marked in the case of the most popular wines, the effect of the United Kingdom tax system is to stamp wine with the hallmarks of a luxury product which, in the view of the tax burden which it bears, can scarcely constitute in the eyes of the consumer a genuine alternative to the typically produced domestic beverage.[56]

[18–43] In a more recent case involving Sweden's taxation of wine and beer, the Court acknowledged that it would not be possible in all such cases to require that the protective effect be shown statistically, but rather it would be enough to show that "a given tax mechanism is likely, in view of its inherent characteristics, to bring about such an effect".[57] There, because the price difference between comparator wines and beers

---

53 *ibid*, 2026.
54 Case 170/78 *Commission v United Kingdom (Wine and Beer)* [1980] ECR 417.
55 *ibid*, 432, 434.
56 Case 170/78 *Commission v United Kingdom (Wine and Beer)* [1983] ECR 2265, 2292.
57 Case C-167/05 *Commission v Sweden (Wine and Beer)* ECR I-2127, para 60.

before tax was largely the same as that after tax, the Court was not satisfied that the Commission had shown that the different tax treatment was likely to have a protectionist effect. As a result, there was found to be no violation of Art 110(2).

D. Excise Duty and Value Added Tax

[18–44] In addition to the two prohibitions on different tax treatment contained in Art 110 TFEU, Art 113 TFEU provides that the Council shall, acting unanimously in accordance with a special legislative procedure and after consulting the European Parliament and the Economic and Social Committee, adopt provisions for the harmonisation of legislation concerning turnover taxes, excise duties and other forms of indirect taxation to the extent that such harmonisation is necessary to ensure the establishment and the functioning of the Internal Market and to avoid distortion of competition. Differences in indirect taxes on goods may hamper the functioning of the Single Market by creating incentives to purchase goods in one Member State, where taxes are lower, rather than another. In addition, disparities in levels of taxation require administrative mechanisms to be in place in order to take account of cross-border transactions, which in turn impose a regulatory burden on intra-EU trade.

(i) Excise Duty

[18–45] A number of separate directives provide for a partial degree of harmonisation of excise duty imposed upon alcohol,[58] tobacco[59] and energy products,[60] including an obligation on Member States to impose minimum rates of excise duty on such goods. The manner in which excise duty is collected and may be temporarily suspended in respect of cross-border transactions is also harmonised.[61]

[18–46] Where a private individual buys excise goods for their own use, excise duty is paid in the Member State where the goods are bought, even if the goods are then brought to another Member State. For example, an Irish person buying permitted amounts of wine in France and bringing them to Ireland will pay excise duty in France at the French rate. However, where a private individual buys excise goods for private use from another Member State online or by phone (ie "distance selling"), where those

58 Council Directive 92/83/EEC of 19 October 1992 on the harmonisation of the structures of excise duties on alcohol and alcoholic beverages [1992] OJ L316/21 and Council Directive 92/84/EEC of 19 October 1992 on the approximation of the rates of excise duty on alcohol and alcoholic beverages [1992] OJ L316/29. See European Commission, "Study on Council Directive 92/83/EEC on the structures of excise duty on alcohol and alcoholic beverages", June 2018.

59 Council Directive 2011/64/EU of 21 June 2011 on the structure and rates of excise duty applied to manufactured tobacco [2011] OJ L176/24. See European Commission, "Study on Council Directive 2011/64/EU on the Structure and Rates of Excise Duty Applied to Manufactured Tobacco", May 2017.

60 Council Directive 2003/96/EC of 27 October 2003 restructuring the Community framework for the taxation of energy products and electricity [2003] OJ L283/51.

61 Council Directive 2008/118/EC of 16 December 2008 concerning the general arrangements for excise duty [2009] OJ L9/12; Commission Regulation (EC) No 684/2009 of 24 July 2009 implementing Council Directive 2008/118/EC as regards the computerised procedures for the movement of excise goods under suspension of excise duty [2009] OJ L197/24; Council Regulation (EU) No 389/2012 of 2 May 2012 on administrative cooperation in the field of excise duties [2012] OJ L121/1.

goods have already been released for consumption in that state (for example, ordering wine online from a French wine-seller for delivery to Ireland), the excise duty is paid in the Member State of destination at the time of the delivery of the goods. The vendor is liable to pay the excise duty in the state of destination but, to avoid double payment of the duty, the vendor is reimbursed the excise duty levied in the home Member State.

[18–47] Finally, for commercial transactions, excise duty is generally paid in the Member State of consumption. This is facilitated by allowing excise goods to be transported from one Member State to another under "duty suspension" until they reach their final destination. According to a 2016 report, almost 99 per cent of all intra-EU movements of excise goods take place under duty suspension, amounting to approximately 3.5 million individual movements of alcohol, tobacco and energy products each year, with a total financial value of €270 billion and associated excise duty of €90 billion.[62] Under duty suspension, a registered consignor or authorised warehouse-keeper can move excise goods from a tax warehouse, or place of importation into the EU, to a registered (or exempt) consignee, another tax warehouse or to a point of export from the EU. A sophisticated computerised system (the Excise Movements and Control System or EMCS) is used to track goods moving under duty suspension so as to ensure that the duty is paid in the Member State of destination. The EMCS aims at a paperless administration of excise duties throughout the EU. This involves an electronic Administrative Document being issued by the original consignor, setting out information on the consignment and the planned movement within the EU. This is validated in the Member State of dispatch, which uses an EU register of economic operators to check the excise numbers of the consignor and consignee, and then transmits it electronically to the Member State of destination, who in turn forwards it to the consignee. Upon receiving the goods, the consignee submits a report of receipt. The report of receipt is sent to the consignor who can then recover the financial guarantees they had to make for the excise goods.

[18–48] As with distance selling to private individuals, where commercial consignments that have already been released for consumption in one Member State with the duty having been paid are transported to another Member State as the final destination, double taxation is avoided through a system of reimbursement.

(ii) Value Added Tax

[18–49] The most significant harmonising measure adopted on the basis of Art 113 TFEU is a series of VAT Directives that establish a common system of value added tax. The current version – Directive 2006/112 – is a recast of the original Sixth VAT Directive of 1977.[63] VAT also forms part of the EU's "own resources", or budget, with a rate of

[62] European Commission, "Evaluation of Current Arrangements for the Holding and Moving of Excise Goods under Excise Duty Suspension", January 2016, 6.

[63] Council Directive 2006/112/EC of 28 November 2006 on the common system of value added tax [2006] OJ L347/1. See also Council Directive (EU) 2018/1910 of 4 December 2018 amending Directive 2006/112/EC as regards the harmonisation and simplification of certain rules in the value added system for the taxation of trade between Member States [2018] OJ L311/3; Council Implementing Regulation (EU) No 282/2011 of 15 March 2011 laying down implementing measures for Directive 2006/112/EC on the common system of value added tax [2011] OJ L77/1; Council Regulation (EU) No 904/2010 of 7 October 2010 on administrative cooperation and combating fraud in the field of value added tax [2010] OJ L268/1; Council Directive 2008/9/EC

0.3 per cent levied on the VAT base of each Member State (which, for 2014–2020, is applied at 0.15 per cent for Germany, the Netherlands and Sweden).

[18–50] VAT is an indirect tax in which the "taxable person" is the seller of the goods in question, such as a manufacturer or retailer. Taxable persons must register for VAT purposes and keep records both of the VAT which they have paid to suppliers and the VAT they have passed on when selling their own goods or services. The tax burden, however, is ultimately borne by the final purchaser or customer, even though they themselves do not make any direct tax payment to the tax collection authorities. The amount of VAT paid by the final customer represents the total sum of VAT that has been added-on at each stage of production and distribution. The two defining characteristics of VAT, therefore, are that it has a distinctly self-policing character and is based on a system of fractionated payments. Ireland introduced VAT in 1971 in preparation for joining the EEC in 1973.

[18–51] The VAT Directive provides a form of partial harmonisation by requiring Member States to apply a standard rate of VAT of not less than 15 per cent, while permitting them to apply two reduced rates of not less than 5 per cent. Ireland's standard rate is 23 per cent, with a reduced rate of 13.5 per cent applied to fuel, construction, housing, hotels and restaurants, etc. A reduced rate of 9 per cent applies to sports facilities and newspapers. Ireland applies a "super" reduced rate of 4.8 per cent to farm livestock. This is permitted by virtue of Art 110 of the Directive, which allows Member States to continue to apply a reduced rate lower than 5 per cent where such a rate applied on 1 January 1991. This article also allows Ireland to continue to apply a "zero rate" to food, children's clothes and shoes and certain medicines. A zero rate differs from VAT exempt goods in that, whereas the manufacturer of a zero-rated good may reclaim VAT paid on supplies used to make the product, the manufacturer of an exempted good may not do so. As the zero rate is not expressly provided for in the Directive, Art 110 is essentially a derogation for those Member States that applied such a rate on 1 January 1991.

[18–52] Given that taxation remains a matter over which Member States are anxious to retain control, harmonisation of VAT has proceeded slowly and gradually since it was first introduced at EU level in 1967. Within its recitals, the VAT Directive observes that:

> The attainment of the objective of establishing an internal market presupposes the application in Member States of legislation on turnover taxes that does not distort conditions of competition or hinder the free movement of goods and services. It is therefore necessary to achieve such harmonisation of legislation on turnover taxes by means of a system of value added tax, such as will eliminate, as far as possible, factors which may distort conditions of competition, whether at national or [EU] level.[64]

[18–53] While this marks the height of the ambition, the recitals go on to propose that even if rates and exemptions are not fully harmonised, the common system of VAT should nevertheless result in neutrality in competition, such that within the territory of each Member State similar goods and services bear the same tax burden, whatever

---

of 12 February 2008 laying down detailed rules for the refund of value added tax, provided for in Directive 2006/112/EC, to taxable persons not established in the Member State of refund but established in another Member State [2008] OJ L44/23.

64 Recital 4.

the length of the production and distribution chain. Technically, therefore, the VAT Directive continues to provide for a transitional period, with Art 402 making clear that the arrangements for trade between Member States are "transitional and shall be replaced by definitive arrangements based in principle on the taxation in the Member State of origin of the supply of goods or services". Despite a number of proposals over the years, agreement has yet to be reached on the principle of taxation at origin. The reasons for this are, first, close harmonisation of VAT rates would be needed in order to prevent differences in applicable rates from influencing decisions on where to buy. Secondly, a clearing system would be needed to ensure that VAT receipts accrue to the Member State of consumption. Thirdly, Member States would have to rely on each other to collect a substantial part of their VAT revenue.[65]

[18–54] Until then, the general rule governing intra-EU trade is that VAT is charged at the rate applicable in the Member State of *destination*. In order to achieve this, the exporting Member State will "zero-rate" the VAT by not collecting VAT on the export transaction, but instead give the exporter a rebate of the VAT already paid. The Member State to which the goods are being imported will then "reverse charge" the VAT by requiring the importer to pay the applicable VAT rate in that Member State. This creates a risk of fraud, in that false VAT returns may be made, asserting that goods are being exported and so entitled to benefit from zero-rating, when in fact they are sold on the domestic market. It is estimated that cross-border VAT fraud amounts to €50 billion of lost revenue each year.[66] In order to apply for zero-rating, the exporter must be able to check that their customer in another Member State is a taxable person and holds a valid VAT identification number. In order to enable this, a computerised VAT Information Exchange System (VIES) has been established, with a web-portal maintained by the Commission, which allows businesses to verify the VAT number of a customer in another Member State by sending a request through a secure connection to the relevant national database to check if the given number is recorded there, with a return generated indicating whether the number is valid or invalid.

[18–55] A certain exception to this general rule is provided for in respect of distance selling by phone or internet to purchasers who are not registered for VAT. Unless prescribed annual thresholds are reached, an online supplier of goods will be liable for VAT in their own Member State. The annual threshold for goods being shipped to Ireland is €35,000, after which point a supplier in another Member State must register for VAT in Ireland and must account for VAT at the appropriate Irish rates. The supplier also has the option to register in Ireland and pay Irish rates of VAT even before the annual threshold is met. Member States have a choice as between €35,000 and €100,000 in setting the applicable annual threshold, with only Germany, Luxembourg and the

---

65 European Commission, *Green Paper on the Future of VAT: Towards a Simpler, More Robust and Efficient VAT System* COM(2010) 695, 1 December 2010, 6–7.

66 European Commission Communication, *On an Action Plan on VAT: Towards a Single EU VAT Area – Time to Decide* COM(2016) 148, 7 April 2016, 3. See Council Directive 2013/42/EU of 22 July 2013 amending Directive 2006/112/EC on the common system of value added tax, as regards a Quick Reaction Mechanism against VAT fraud [2013] OJ L201/1; European Commission, *Report on the Effects of Articles 199a and 199b of Council Directive 2006/112/EC on Combatting Fraud* COM(2018) 118, 8 March 2018; Council Directive 2018/1695 of 6 November 2018 amending Directive 2006/112/EC on the common system of value added tax as regards the period of application of the optional reverse charge mechanism in relation to supplies of certain goods and services susceptible to fraud and of the Quick Reaction Mechanism against VAT fraud [2018] OJ L282/5.

Netherlands choosing the highest figure, and the UK applying a threshold of £70,000.[67] Similarly, an Irish supplier making distance sales to customers in another Member State who are not VAT registered is liable for VAT in Ireland unless the threshold in that other Member State is reached, or unless the supplier opts to register for VAT in the other Member State before the threshold is reached.

[18–56] Since 2015, particular rules apply to the cross-border supply to non-taxable customers (ie private individuals not engaged in business) of telecommunications, broadcasting and e-services, which are known as "TBE services".[68] For these services, the place of supply is deemed to be the place where the customer is established, requiring the supplier to register and account for VAT in that Member State. In order to facilitate this, a "Mini-One Stop Shop" (MOSS) has been established for suppliers of TBE services.[69] Rather than register in each Member State in which they supply services, the MOSS system allows businesses to opt to account for VAT due on supplies via a web-portal in one just Member State, known as the Member State of identification. The supplier electronically submits quarterly MOSS returns via the web-portal in respect of its supplies to non-taxable customers in Member States of consumption, along with the VAT due to each state. The Member State of identification submits these returns, together with the VAT paid, to the relevant Member States of consumption via a secure network. As part of a recent VAT e-commerce package, from 1 January 2019 an annual threshold of €10,000 has been introduced before a supplier of TBE services is required to register either in the Member State of the customer or via MOSS. Where the total value of TBE services supplied to other Member State does not exceed €10,000 (exclusive of VAT), the place of supply is considered to be the Member State in which the supplier is established.[70]

[18–57] In 2016, the Commission published a communication in which it called for the creation of a "genuine single EU VAT area" for the Single Market, announcing its intention to present a legislative proposal to put in place a definitive VAT system based on the principle of taxation in the country of destination of the goods. This would depart from the objective, set out in Art 402 of the VAT Directive, to eventually move to a system based on taxation in the country of origin. It would mean that, in place of the current system of zero-rating and reverse charges for cross-border trade, the domestic practice of suppliers collecting VAT directly from their customers would be

---

67 See <https://ec.europa.eu/taxation_customs/business/vat/eu-country-specific-information-vat_en>.

68 See Council Directive 2008/8/EC of 12 February 2008 amending Directive 2006/112/EC as regards the place of supply of services [2008] OJ L44/11; Council Regulation (EU) No 967/2012 of 9 October 2012 amending Implementing Regulation (EU) No 282/2011 as regards the special schemes for non-established taxable persons supplying telecommunications services, broadcasting services or electronic services to non-taxable persons [2012] OJ L290/1; Council Implementing Regulation (EU) No 1042/2013 of 7 October 2013 amending Implementing Regulation (EU) No 282/2011 as regards the place of supply of services [2013] OJ L284/1, given effect in Irish law by the European (Value Added Tax) Regulations 2014 (SI No 340 of 2014), amending the VAT Consolidation Act 2010.

69 See <https://ec.europa.eu/taxation_customs/business/vat/telecommunications-broadcasting-electronic-services/>.

70 Council Directive (EU) 2017/2455 of 5 December 2017 amending Directive 2006/112/EC and Directive 2009/132/EC as regards certain value added tax obligations for supplies of services and distance sales of goods [2017] OJ L348/7; Council Implementing Regulation (EU) 2017/2459 of 5 December 2017 amending Implementing Regulation (EU) No 282/2011 laying down implementing measures for Directive 2006/112/EC on the common system of value added tax [2017] OJ L348/32.

extended to cross-border transactions. As the Commission Communication explains, the current system:

> splits every cross-border transaction into an exempted cross-border supply and a taxable cross-border acquisition. It is like a customs system, but lacks equivalent controls and is therefore the root of cross-border fraud.
>
> Such fraud occurs when a supplier pretends to have transported the goods to another Member State but the goods are in fact consumed VAT-free locally or especially when a client of a cross-border transaction purchases goods or services VAT-free and charges VAT without remitting it to tax authorities while his/her customer can deduct it.
>
> It is now high time to adopt a unified approach to tackling such fraud that is fully compatible with the requirements of the single market. …
>
> A robust single European VAT area would treat cross-border transactions in the same way as domestic transactions, putting an end to the endemic weakness of the system, and would integrate the management and enforcement of VAT through closer cooperation between tax administrations.
>
> … Under a generalised reverse charge system, VAT is "suspended" along the whole economic chain and is charged only to consumers. This means that total VAT collection is shifted to the retail stage. Such a system does not have the self-policing nature of the current VAT system (ie under the principle of fractionated payment), which ensures that a small number of fairly large, reliable taxable persons in the economic chain account for most of VAT.
>
> In addition, other types of fraud can arise, eg fraudsters claiming to be taxable persons to obtain goods intended for final consumption VAT-free. There is therefore a high built-in risk that fraud and untaxed private consumption would soar, particularly in view of EU countries' high VAT rates (up to 27%).
>
> The Commission's conclusion from this work is therefore that the best option for the EU as a whole would be to tax [business to business] supplies of goods within the EU in the same way as domestic supplies, thus fixing the great flaw of the [current] transitional arrangements while keeping the underlying features of the VAT system intact.
>
> Such a system of taxation of cross-border supplies will ensure consistent treatment of domestic and cross-border supplies along the entire chain of a production and distribution, and re-establish the basic features of the VAT in cross-border trade, ie the fractionated payments system with its self-policing character.
>
> Therefore, this change should reduce cross-border fraud by about €40 billion (80%) a year in the EU. The intermediate and final consumption of the goods will continue to be taxed where the goods are transported to, which is a reliable proxy of the place of consumption. Such an objective criterion would make it difficult for taxable persons to engage in tax planning or commit fraud. …
>
> Some significant simplification measures will be taken to accompany this change. For instance, the One Stop Shop that already exists for telecommunication, broadcasting and electronic services and which is due to be extended to all e-commerce transactions, will be even more widely implemented and rebooted, so as to fully exploit the opportunities presented by digital technology to simplify, standardise and modernise processes. Businesses will need to register for VAT purposes in the Member States where they were established only. Collectively, businesses should save an average of around EUR 1 billion.

Such a system would require more trust and cooperation between tax administrations as the Member State where the goods arrive would have to rely on the Member State of departure to collect the VAT due on the cross-border supply.[71]

E. The Common Customs Tariff

[18–58] The prohibition on customs duties as between Member States (Art 30 TFEU), the prohibition on discrimination within internal taxation (Art 110 TFEU) and the harmonisation of indirect taxes such as VAT and excise duty (Art 113 TFEU) all primarily relate to intra-EU trade between the Member States. In contrast, the Common Customs Tariff (CCT) comprises the Customs Union's external dimension and is concerned with trade between the EU and the rest of the world. Imposed on goods entering into the Customs Union, the CCT forms part of the EU's "own resources" or income. Including sugar levies, in 2017 the CCT amounted to 15 per cent of the EU's total revenue. Since the 2014 Council Decision on own resources, Member States are entitled to retain 20 per cent of CCT duties in order to cover the costs of collection, down from the former figure of 25 per cent.[72] So, in 2017, Ireland collected €356m in duties and provided €285m of this to the EU.[73] A Convention on Centralised Customs Clearance, concerning the allocation of national collection costs retained when traditional own resources are made available to the EU budget, entered into force in January 2019. The Convention has been given the force of law in Ireland by s 43 of the Customs Act 2015.

[18–59] In addition to contributing to the financial interests of the Union as a source of revenue and serving as an important trade policy tool, the Member States also have their own vested interest in maintaining the standardised application of the CCT and related customs controls across all of the EU's territory. This is because discrepancies in the application of customs controls could give rise to a competitive advantage to using a particular entry or exit point into or out of the EU, causing trade deflection. In other words, any lack of uniformity in the operation of the Customs Union could impact on the Single Market by making some Member States more attractive as a gateway to the EU market than others. As the Court of Justice has described,

> the Common Customs Tariff is intended to achieve an equalization of customs charges levied at the frontiers of the [Union] on products imported from non-member countries, in order to avoid any deflection of trade in relations with those countries and any distortion of free internal circulation or of competitive conditions, and the definition of uniform principles for the common commercial policy involves, as does the common tariff itself, the elimination of national disparities, whether in the field of taxation or of commerce, affecting trade with non-member countries.[74]

---

[71] European Commission Communication, *On an Action Plan on VAT: Towards a Single EU VAT Area – Time to Decide*, COM(2016) 148, 7 April 2016, 9–10. See Council Directive (EU) 2018/1910 of 4 December 2018 amending Directive 2006/112/EC as regards the harmonisation and simplification of certain rules in the value added system for the taxation of trade between Member States [2018] OJ L311/3; Commission Amended proposal for a Council Regulation amending Regulation (EU) No 904/2010 as regards measures to strengthen administrative cooperation in the field of value added tax COM(2017) 706 final, 30 November 2017.

[72] Council Decision of 26 May 2014 on the system of own resources of the European Union (2014/355/EU, Euratom) [2014] OJ L168/105.

[73] European Commission, *EU Budget 2017, Financial Report* (2018) 32.

[74] Case 51/87 *Commission v Council* [1988] ECR 5459, 5478.

(i) Union Customs Code

[18–60] The Customs Union was first completed in 1968. As of 1 May 2016, the Union Customs Code (UCC), set down in Regulation 952/2013,[75] is the comprehensive consolidation of the law governing this area, as supplemented by an important Delegated Regulation[76] and Implementing Regulation.[77] The Union Customs Code has as its stated aim to reduce the administrative burden on importers and exporters by simplifying and streamlining processes and procedures throughout the EU Member States. To allow for the roll-out of new IT systems, the Code is being introduced over a transitional period that will last until 31 December 2020.[78] Nevertheless, the default rule established by Art 6 of the Code is that all exchanges of information, such as declarations, applications or decisions, between economic operators and customs authorities, and the storage of such information, shall be made using electronic data-processing techniques.

[18–61] As the EU does not have a customs agency of its own, it relies on the customs authorities of each Member State to regulate the Union's external border. Under the Customs Code, it is the national customs authorities that are primarily responsible for the supervision of international trade, "thereby contributing to fair and open trade, to the implementation of the external aspects of the internal market, of the common trade policy and of the other common Union policies having a bearing on trade, and to overall supply chain security".[79] In particular, customs authorities are required to put measures in place in order to: protect the financial interests of the EU and its Member States; protect the EU from unfair and illegal trade while supporting legitimate business activity; ensure the security and safety of the EU and its residents, and the protection of the environment, and maintain a proper balance between customs controls and facilitation of legitimate trade. As Catherine Barnard has described, the abolition

---

[75] Regulation (EU) No 952/2013 of the European Parliament and of the Council of 9 October 2013 laying down the Union Customs Code [2013] OJ L269/1. See Tom Walsh, *European Union Customs Code* (Wolters Kluwer, 2015); Kathrin Limbach, *Uniformity of Customs Administration in the European Union* (Hart, 2015). With regard to controls on imports into the Union of animals and related products see Regulation (EU) 2017/625 of the European Parliament and of the Council of 15 March 2017 on official controls and other official activities performed to ensure the application of food and feed law, rules on animal health and welfare, plant health and plant protection products [2017] OJ L95/1 (which applies in general from 14 December 2019).

[76] Commission Delegated Regulation (EU) 2015/2446 of 28 July 2015 supplementing Regulation (EU) No 952/2013 of the European Parliament and of the Council as regards detailed rules concerning certain provisions of the Union Customs Code [2015] OJ L343/1.

[77] Commission Implementing Regulation (EU) 2015/2447 of 24 November 2015 laying down detailed rules for implementing certain provisions of Regulation (EU) No 952/2013 of the European Parliament and of the Council laying down the Union Customs Code [2015] OJ L343/558.

[78] See Commission Implementing Regulation (EU) 2019/1026 of 21 June 2019 on technical arrangements for developing, maintaining and employing electronic systems for the exchange of information and for the storage of such information under the Union Customs Code [2019] OJ L167/3; Commission Delegated Regulation (EU) 2016/341 of 17 December 2015 supplementing Regulation (EU) No 952/2013 of the European Parliament and of the Council as regards transitional rules for certain provisions of the Union Customs Code where the relevant electronic systems are not yet operational and amending Delegated Regulation (EU) 2015/2446 [2016] OJ L69/1; Commission Implementing Decision (EU) 2016/578 of 11 April 2016 establishing the Work Programme relating to the development and deployment of the electronic systems provided for in the Union Customs Code [2016] OJ L99/6; European Court of Auditors, "Special Report: A Series of Delays in Customs IT Systems: What Went Wrong?" (2018).

[79] Regulation (EU) No 952/2013 of the European Parliament and of the Council of 9 October 2013 laying down the Union Customs Code [2013] OJ L269/1, Art 3.

of internal frontier controls has increased the importance of controls at the external borders which, in the past, were largely physical. Today, however, the "emphasis is on computerization, post-import and audit controls, and risk analysis which allows the selection of those consignments which constitute the greatest risk, while physical controls are often carried out at the trader's premises. Frontier controls are largely devoted to combating smuggling and fraud".[80] This change is reflected in the Union Customs Code, which notes how:

> The completion of the internal market, the reduction of barriers to international trade and investment and the reinforced need to ensure security and safety at the external borders of the Union have transformed the role of customs authorities giving them a leading role within the supply chain and, in their monitoring and management of international trade, making them a catalyst to the competitiveness of countries and companies. The customs legislation should therefore reflect the new economic reality and the new role and mission of customs authorities.[81]

[18–62] The focus of the Union Customs Code is to pursue the two objectives of facilitating legitimate trade and combatting fraud. In order to minimise any delays that may be caused, use is made of standardised customs procedures and modern information technology (IT). Indeed, the Code has the ultimate aim of creating a paperless customs environment in which all transactions are handled electronically and economic operators are provided with the same IT systems for customs operations in each Member State. Further efficiency is achieved by granting the status of "authorised economic operators" to trustworthy operators once certain conditions are met. Authorised operators can then benefit from simplified procedures, such as fewer physical inspections or document-based controls. Related to this, the Code calls for the establishment of a risk management framework common to all Member States, and for the application of risk-based controls by national customs authorities. In addition, the Code replaces a wide variety of national customs documents with a Single Administrative Document (SAD). It also introduces common approaches to warehousing procedures and provides for centralised customs clearance at the place where an economic operator is located, rather than having to make customs declarations at the place where the goods are located.

[18–63] To ensure a uniform application of the Common Customs Tariff, the Code sets down comprehensive rules on how national customs authorities are to calculate the tariff amount due based on where the goods are from, what the goods are and their value. As the tariff will depend, in part, on where the goods are being imported from, rules are also prescribed for determining the country of origin of goods.

[18–64] Secondly, the applicable tariff rate will depend on what the goods are, and for this the EU has its own "Combined Nomenclature". This is a detailed list of goods classified into various categories and assigned individual codes, which is set out in Council Regulation 2658/87 and updated annually.[82] The Combined Nomenclature is based on the Harmonised Commodity Description and Coding System (the "HS"),

---

80 Catherine Barnard, *The Substantive Law of the EU* (4th ed, Oxford University Press, 2013) 43.

81 Regulation (EU) No 952/2013 of the European Parliament and of the Council of 9 October 2013 laying down the Union Customs Code [2013] OJ L269/1, recital 16.

82 Council Regulation (EEC) No 2658/87 of 23 July 1987 on the tariff and statistical nomenclature and on the Common Customs Tariff [1987] OJ L256/1; Commission Implementing Regulation (EU) 2018/1602 of 11 October 2018 amending Annex I to Council Regulation (EEC) No 2658/87 on the tariff and statistical nomenclature and on the Common Customs Tariff [2018] OJ L273/1.

which is maintained by the World Customs Organisation (WCO). The Combined Nomenclature reproduces the HS six-digit headings and subheadings, while adding seventh and eighth figures that create further subheadings which are specific to it. The specificity given to the description of a categorised good may vary, with an example of a detailed description being as follows[83]:

Description	Code	Reasons
A product consisting of glitter for toothpaste in the form of dark blue particles which dissolve when brushing the teeth and give a blue colour to the foam formed by the toothpaste. The colouring matter adheres to the cleaned teeth, allowing a reflection of blue light from the teeth enamel, thereby causing the teeth to appear whiter for a limited period of time. The product is composed of the following ingredients (% by weight): hydroxypropyl methylcellulose approx 55, propylene glycol approx 21, blue pigment approx 17, polysorbate 80 approx 4, red dye approx 3. The blue pigment and the red dye serve as colouring matter. The product is presented in bulk.	3204 19 00	Classification is determined by general rules 1, 3(b) and 6 for the interpretation of the Combined Nomenclature and the wording of CN codes 3204, and 3204 19 00. Classification under heading 3912 as cellulose and its chemical derivatives, not elsewhere specified or included, in primary forms, is excluded as the hydroxypropyl methylcellulose, although predominant by weight, serves only as a carrier for the colouring matter but does not give the product its essential character. The blue pigment and the red dye, serving as colouring matter, give the product its essential character. Therefore, the product is to be classified in CN code 3204 19 00 as a preparation based on a mixture of colouring matter of two or more of the subheadings 3204 11 to 3204 19.

[18–65] Disputes as to how a particular good ought to be categorised can lead to litigation and preliminary references to the Court of Justice that require very precise examination of the nature of goods as compared with the description set out in the Combined Nomenclature. For example, the Court has been asked to determine whether medical implant screws intended for use in the human body were to be categorised in the same way as ordinary screws,[84] or whether a camera capable of capturing a large number of photographs per second and storing them in a "volatile" internal memory so long as the camera remained switched on and no new images were captured, was a "digital camera" or a "television camera", as had been found by the Rotterdam customs authorities.[85] The Court has outlined the approach it takes to such interpretative questions as being that

> in the interests of legal certainty and ease of verification, the decisive criterion for the tariff classification of goods is in general to be sought in their objective characteristics and properties, as defined in the wording of the relevant [Combined Nomenclature] CN heading and of the notes to the sections or chapters.

The Court has also held that the Explanatory Notes drafted by the Commission, in respect

[83] Commission Implementing Regulation (EU) 2016/2033 of 17 November 2016 concerning the classification of certain goods in the Combined Nomenclature [2016] OJ L314/1.

[84] Case C-51/16 *Stryker EMEA Supply Chain Services* EU:C:2017:298, 26 April 2017. See also Case C-227/17 *Medtronic* EU:C:2018:247, 12 April 2018; Case C-547/13 *Oliver Medical* EU:C:2015:139, 4 March 2015.

[85] Case C-372/17 *Vision Research Europe* EU:C:2018:708, 13 September 2018.

> of the CN, and those adopted by the [World Customs Organisation], in respect of the HS, are an important aid for interpreting the scope of the various tariff headings but do not have legally binding force. The Explanatory Notes to the CN do not take the place of those of the HS but should be regarded as complementary to them and consulted jointly with them.[86]

[18–66] Finally, in accordance with WTO rules, the Customs Code provides that the value of the goods shall be based, primarily, on their transaction value, being the "price actually paid or payable for the goods when sold for export to the customs territory of the Union, adjusted where necessary".[87] The Code sets out certain matters that are to be included within the transaction value, and items that are to be excluded such as the cost of transporting the goods, or their maintenance or assembly, after they have entered the EU customs territory.

[18–67] The Customs Code also includes rules that facilitate the movement of goods in "customs transit".[88] This is where goods cross borders en route to their final destination under "customs control", allowing charges payable to be secured but suspended and collected by the customs authorities of the Member State of destination, rather than the Member State in which they first enter the Customs Union. The transit procedure involves traders inputting data via the New Computerised Transit System (NCTS), on foot of which they will receive a hardcopy Transit Accompanying Document at the customs office of departure. Although the European Economic Area states of Iceland, Liechtenstein and Norway participate in the Internal Market, the Customs Union does not extend to them, or to Switzerland (the other European Free Trade Area state) with whom the EU has a series of bilateral agreements including in relation to the free movement of goods.[89] The EU and EFTA states have, however, agreed a Convention on a Common Transit Procedure[90] and a Convention on the Simplification of Formalities in Trade in Goods[91] which provides for the use of a "Single Administrative Document" regardless of the kind and origin of the goods being transferred, to which Turkey, North Macedonia and Serbia are also a party. In preparation for its withdrawal from the EU, the UK has acceded to both Conventions, albeit that their entry into force in respect of the UK is suspended until it ceases to be an EU Member State.

[18–68] Finally, as part of the EU's Import Control System, the Customs Code requires that all goods brought into the Union's customs territory are to be covered by an Entry Summary Declaration that is to be lodged by the carrier at the customs office of first entry within a specific time-limit before the goods arrive. The Entry Summary Declaration is to contain the "particulars necessary for risk analysis for security and safety purposes".[92] Within specified time-limits, and on the basis of the Entry Summary Declaration, the customs office of first entry is required to carry out a risk analysis

---

86 *ibid*, paras 22–23.

87 Union Customs Code, Art 70.

88 See European Commission, *Transit Manual*, TAXUD/A2/TRA/003/2016-EN, 27 April 2016.

89 Stephan Breitenmoser, "Sectoral Agreements between the EC and Switzerland: Contents and Context" (2003) 40 *Common Market Law Review* 1137.

90 Convention between the European Economic Community, the Republic of Austria, the Republic of Finland, the Republic of Iceland, the Kingdom of Norway, the Kingdom of Sweden and the Swiss Confederation, on a Common Transit Procedure [1987] OJ L226/2.

91 Convention between the European Economic Community, the Republic of Austria, the Republic of Finland, the Republic of Iceland, the Kingdom of Norway, the Kingdom of Sweden and the Swiss Confederation on the Simplification of Formalities in Trade in Goods [1987] OJ L134/2.

92 Union Customs Code, Art 127(5).

primarily for security and safety purposes, and take the necessary measures based on the results of that risk analysis.[93] The requirement for an Entry Summary Declaration is waived for goods coming from Norway and Switzerland on foot of agreements with those countries.[94]

F. The Common Commercial Policy

[18–69] The Common Commercial Policy (CCP) allows for the Union to act at the international level in conducting the EU's trade policy. One area that is excluded, however, is transport, which continues to be governed by the external competence that is implicit in the Union's separate transport policy.[95] The CCP is provided for in Title II of Part V of the TFEU, which comprises of just Arts 206 and 207. Article 206 sets out the overall objective that, by establishing a Customs Union, the EU shall contribute, "in the common interest, to the harmonious development of world trade, the progressive abolition of restrictions on international trade and on foreign direct investment, and the lowering of customs and other barriers". The general orientation and aims of the CCP are then described in a non-exhaustive fashion in Art 207(1) as follows:

> The common commercial policy shall be based on uniform principles, particularly with regard to changes in tariff rates, the conclusion of tariff and trade agreements relating to trade in goods and services, and the commercial aspects of intellectual property, foreign direct investment, the achievement of uniformity in measures of liberalisation, export policy and measures to protect trade such as those to be taken in the event of dumping or subsidies. The common commercial policy shall be conducted in the context of the principles and objectives of the Union's external action.

[18–70] From this list it can be seen that the conclusion of international agreements with third countries forms a central part of the CCP. As the Court of Justice has described, however, the CCP is "in fact made up by the combination and interaction of internal and external measures, without priority being taken by one over the others".[96] Internal Union measures are often described as being unilateral or autonomous. In accordance with Art 207(1), it is for the European Parliament and the Council, acting by means of regulations in accordance with the ordinary legislative procedure, to adopt the measures defining the framework for implementing the CCP.

(i) International Agreements

[18–71] In negotiating and concluding international trade agreements, the general rules on treaty-making in Art 218 TFEU apply, subject to certain specific provisions of Art 207 TFEU. The process begins by the Commission making a recommendation to the Council. The Council can then decide to authorise the Commission to open negotiations

---

93 *ibid*, Art 128.

94 Agreement between the European Community and the Swiss Confederation on the simplification of inspections and formalities in respect of the carriage of goods and on customs security measures [2009] OJ L199/24; Decision of the EEA Joint Committee No 76/2009 of 30 June 2009 amending Protocol 10 on simplification of inspections and formalities in respect of carriage of goods and Protocol 37 containing the list provided for in Article 101 [2009] OJ L232/40.

95 Title VI, Part Three, TFEU (Arts 90–100); Art 207(5) TFEU. See Opinion 2/15 (*Singapore Free Trade Agreement*) EU:C:2017:376, 16 May 2017, paras 57–68.

96 Opinion 1/75 (*Local Cost Standard*) [1975] ECR 1355, 1363.

by giving it a defined mandate for doing so. The Council will also appoint a "special committee" to assist the Commission with the negotiations, with whom the Commission is required to consult. The Commission must report regularly on the progress of the negotiations to both the special committee and the European Parliament. Generally, the Council acts by qualified majority voting when deciding on the negotiation or conclusion of trade agreements. As an exception to this, unanimity is required for the negotiation or conclusion of an association agreement or an agreement:

(i) that covers a field for which unanimity is required for the adoption of a Union act;
(ii) in the fields of trade in services and the commercial aspects of intellectual property, as well as foreign direct investment, that includes provisions for which unanimity is required for the adoption of internal rules;
(iii) in the field of trade in cultural and audiovisual services, where it risks prejudicing the Union's cultural and linguistic diversity;
(iv) in the field of trade in social, education and health services, where it risks seriously disturbing the national organisation of such services and prejudicing the responsibility of Member States to deliver them.

[18–72] Since the entry into force of the Lisbon Treaty, the Union's exclusive competence with respect to the CCP is expressly stated in Art 3 TFEU. Prior to this, the exclusive nature of the Union's competence in this area had required clarification through a series of important judgments of the Court of Justice.[97]

[18–73] The categorisation of the EU's various trade agreements is complex due to the fact that, in addition to agreements dedicated solely to trade, significant trade elements can be included in broader framework agreements that establish an overall relationship between the EU and a third country, the terminology and practice in relation to which has evolved over time. The Commission distinguishes between three main groups of agreement.[98] The first is a customs union, in which customs duties are eliminated for bilateral trade and a joint customs tariff established for foreign imports. The EU has such an agreement with Turkey, San Marino and Andorra.

[18–74] The second group is the most complex as it comprises not only free trade agreements, but also broader political agreements that include trade elements that remove or reduce customs tariffs in bilateral trade. So, for example, the EU has negotiated free trade agreements with Japan, Canada, Colombia, Ecuador, Peru, the Republic of Korea, Ukraine, Vietnam and Singapore, and is negotiating agreements with Australia, Indonesia, Mexico, New Zealand and the Philippines. This second category also includes "Association Agreements", such as with Georgia, Moldova, Morocco, Egypt and Israel, "Stabilisation Agreements" such as with Albania, Kosovo, Montenegro and Serbia, and "Economic Partnership Agreements", such as with South Africa and Kazakhstan.

---

[97] Opinion 1/75 (*Local Cost Standard*) [1975] ECR 1355; Opinion 1/78 (*Natural Rubber*) [1979] ECR 2871; Case 45/86 *Commission v Council* (*Generalised Tariff Preferences*) [1987] ECR 1493; Opinion 1/94 (*WTO Agreement*) [1994] ECR I-5267; Case C-360/93 *Parliament v Council* (*Public Procurement*) [1996] ECR I-1195; Opinion 1/2008 (*GATS Schedules*) [2009] ECR I-11129. See Piet Eeckhout, *EU External Relations Law* (2nd ed, Oxford University Press, 2011) 13–35; Panos Koutrakos, *EU International Relations Law* (2nd ed, Hart, 2015) 19–30; Marise Cremona, "Balancing Union and Member State Interests: Opinion 1/2008, Choice of Legal Base and the Common Commercial Policy Under the Treaty of Lisbon" (2010) 35 *European Law Review* 678.

[98] See <http://ec.europa.eu/trade/policy/countries-and-regions/negotiations-and-agreements/>.

[18–75] The third category is made up of "Partnership and Cooperation Agreements", such as with Armenia, Cuba and Iraq. These agreements provide a general framework for bilateral economic relations but leave customs tariffs as they are. Finally, the EU is a party to the European Economic Area Agreement, together with Iceland, Liechtenstein and Norway, while its relationship with the remaining EFTA state – Switzerland – is governed by a series of many bilateral agreements.

[18–76] An alternative categorisation is to distinguish between "first generation" trade agreements, "deep and comprehensive" trade agreements, such as those with Ukraine, Georgia and Moldova, and "new generation" trade agreements, such as those agreed with Japan, Canada, Colombia, Ecuador, Peru and the Republic of Korea.[99]

[18–77] The scope of the CCP was at issue in an important 2017 opinion delivered by the Court of Justice, sitting as a Full Court, concerning a proposed free trade agreement (FTA) with Singapore.[100] There, the Court was requested to clarify whether, as claimed by the Commission, the Union had the competence to conclude the FTA on its own, as an "EU-only" agreement. To do so, the Court was asked to identify the provisions of the agreement that fell within: (i) the Union's exclusive competence; (ii) the Union's shared competence; and (iii) the exclusive competence of the Member States (if any). Here, it is worth recalling that in addition to being expressly conferred with exclusive external competences by the Treaties, under the *ERTA* doctrine the Union has exclusive competence to enter into an international agreement in so far as its conclusion may affect common rules or alter their scope.[101] This is now enshrined in Art 3(2) TFEU.

[18–78] The Court found that all chapters of the free trade agreement fell within the Union's exclusive external competence – either by virtue of the CCP or the *ERTA* doctrine – with the exception of those concerning non-direct investment and investor-state dispute settlement, as well as certain governance provisions in so far as they related to these chapters. The chapters that were confirmed as falling within the CCP covered: (i) national treatment and market access for goods; (ii) trade remedies, including anti-dumping and countervailing measures; (iii) technical barriers to trade; (iv) sanitary and phytosanitary measures; (v) customs and trade facilitation; (vi) services, establishment and electronic commerce, including the recognition of qualifications; (vii) government

99 European Commission, "Report on Implementation of EU Free Trade Agreements, 1 January 2017 – 31 December 2017" (2018) 4. See also Commission Staff Working Document, "Individual Reports and Info Sheets on Implementation of EU Free Trade Agreements" SWD(2018) 454 final, 31 October 2018. The agreement with Canada was the subject of an opinion of the Full Court in Opinion 1/17 (*Comprehensive and Economic Trade Agreement with Canada*) EU:C:2019:341, 30 April 2019, in which the provisions on investor-state dispute settlement were held to be compatible with EU law.

100 Opinion 2/15 (*Singapore Free Trade Agreement*) EU:C:2017:376, 16 May 2017. See Marise Cremona, "Shaping EU Trade Policy post-Lisbon: Opinion 2/15 of 16 May 2017" (2018) 14 *European Constitutional Law Review* 231; Dylan Geraets, "Changes in EU Trade Policy After Opinion 2/15" (2018) 13 *Global Trade and Customs Journal* 13; Charlotte Beaucillon "Opinion 2/15: Sustainable Is the New Trade: Rethinking Coherence for the New Common Commercial Policy" (2017) 2 *European Papers* 819.

101 Case 22/70 *Commission v Council* (*European Road Transport Agreement*) [1971] ECR 263. See Merijn Chamon, "Implied Exclusive Powers in the ECJ's Post-Lisbon Jurisprudence: The Continued Development of the *ERTA* Doctrine" (2018) 55 *Common Market Law Review* 1101; Amedeo Arena, "The ERTA Pre-Emption Effects of Minimum and Partial Harmonisation Directives: insights from Opinion 3/15 on the Competence to Conclude the Marrakesh Treaty" (2018) 43 *European Law Review* 770.

procurement; (viii) intellectual property; (ix) provisions on competition law; (x) sustainable development; and (xi) direct investment.

[18–79] The Lisbon Treaty brought to an end a "15-year long 'saga' of treaty changes and disputes between the Member States and the EU's institutions" regarding the scope of the CCP concerning trade in services.[102] The *Singapore* opinion copper-fastened this by allowing the Full Court to affirm the current regime of exclusive Union external competence in respect of services, and to elaborate on the elements that this entails. The Lisbon Treaty also extended the CCP to include foreign direct investment, and the opinion offered the Court its first opportunity to interpret the meaning of this term within the context of Art 207 TFEU. The Court applied its existing case law in the field of free movement of capital to distinguish between foreign *direct* investment, which enables "effective management or control of a company carrying out an economic activity", and non-direct or "portfolio" investment.[103] Portfolio investment, in contrast, can take place "in the form of the acquisition of company securities with the intention of making a financial investment without any intention to influence the management and control of the undertaking".[104] Whereas foreign direct investment fell within the CCP, non-direct investment remained outside of the Policy and so is a competence that is still shared with the Member States.

[18–80] In response to the Court's opinion, the Commission made known its intention to recommend, for future free trade agreements, splitting those parts of the agreement covering exclusive Union competence on the one hand, which would be entered into by the Union on its own, and a separate "mixed" investment agreement to be concluded by both the Union and the Member States. The Council took note of this new approach in its conclusions to the Foreign Affairs Council of May 2018.[105] Where a trade agreement is mixed, such that Ireland is a party to the agreement, and the agreement involves a charge on public funds within the meaning of Article 29.5.2° of the Constitution, the approval of the Dáil is required before Ireland may ratify the agreement. This was the case, for example, with the free trade agreement concluded with the Republic of Korea, and will be done with respect to the trade agreement that has been signed with Canada.[106]

(ii) Unilateral EU Measures

[18–81] In addition to international agreements with third countries, the Union implements the CCP through a number of unilateral measures. These unilateral measures are set down in EU legal acts and address three main areas: (i) general rules

[102] Markus Krajewski, "The Reform of the Common Commercial Policy" in Andrea Biondi, Piet Eeckhout and Stefanie Ripley (eds), *EU Law After Lisbon* (Oxford University Press, 2012) 292, 300. See also Gonzalo Villalta Puig and Bader Al-Haddab, "The Common Commercial Policy after Lisbon: An Analysis of the Reforms" (2011) 36 *European Law Review* 289.

[103] Opinion 2/15 (*Singapore Free Trade Agreement*) EU:C:2017:376, 16 May 2017, para 82. See Philip Hainbach, "The CJEU's Opinion 2/15 and the Future of EU Investment Policy and Law-Making" (2018) 45 *Legal Issues of Economic Integration* 199; Rumiana Yotova, "Opinion 2/15 of the CJEU: Delineating the Scope of the New EU Competence in Foreign Direct Investment" (2018) 17 *Cambridge Law Journal* 29.

[104] *ibid*, para 227.

[105] Council Conclusions on the negotiation and conclusion of EU trade agreements, 22 May 2018, 8622/18; Press Release No 266/18, "New Approach on Negotiating and Concluding EU Trade Agreements Adopted by Council", 22 May 2018.

[106] Dáil Debates, 21 July 2011, Vol 739, No 4; Dáil Debates, 20 July 2016, Vol 919, No 1.

as regards imports to and exports from the Union, including the circumstances in which "safeguard measures" can be adopted to address serious injury to Union producers; (ii) the Generalised System of Preferences, whereby favourable trading conditions are unilaterally afforded to developing and lower-income countries; and (iii) "trade defence instruments", which are the means by which the Union can respond to the imposition of trade barriers by third countries or the importation of "dumped" or subsidised goods, as well as implement reports of the WTO Dispute Settlement Body.

[18–82] Common rules for imports are set down in a regulation, with a separate regulation prescribing specific rules for imports from certain third countries that do not operate on a market economy basis, such as Turkmenistan and North Korea.[107] These regulations deal with the manner in which the EU can respond where the flow of a particular import causes, or threatens to cause, serious injury to Union producers in the form of a "significant overall impairment" in their position. This derives from the WTO Agreement on Safeguards, which permits a WTO member, following an investigation, to

> apply a safeguard measure to a product only if that Member has determined ... that such product is being imported into its territory in such increased quantities, absolute or relative to domestic production, and under such conditions as to cause or threaten to cause serious injury to the domestic industry that produces like or directly competitive products.[108]

[18–83] The regulations set out: (i) an investigation procedure that may be initiated by the Commission, which results in a report being submitted to a Committee on Safeguards; (ii) a system of surveillance that may be put in place where the trend in imports of a product threatens to cause injury to Union producers, and where the interests of the Union so require; and (iii) the circumstances in which safeguard measures may be temporarily adopted, such as a quota on imports. Separately, there is a regulation governing the import of cultural goods into the Union.[109]

[18–84] There is also a regulation establishing common rules for exports, which provides that exports to third countries shall not be subject to any quantitative restrictions other than those that may be applied in conformity with the regulation.[110] If, as a result of any unusual developments on the market, a Member State considers that protective measures might be necessary, it is to notify the Commission, which then advises all other Member States. After an examination procedure and having consulted the Committee on Safeguards, the Commission may make the export of a product subject to the production of an export authorisation where this is considered necessary "in order to prevent a critical situation from arising on account of a shortage of essential products, or to remedy such a situation, and where Union interests call for immediate

---

[107] Regulation (EU) 2015/478 of the European Parliament and of the Council of 11 March 2015 on common rules for imports [2015] OJ L83/16; Regulation (EU) 2015/755 of the European Parliament and of the Council of 29 April 2015 on common rules for imports from certain third countries [2015] OJ L123/33. See also Regulation (EU) 2019/287 of the European Parliament and of the Council of 13 February 2019 implementing bilateral safeguard clauses and other mechanisms allowing for the temporary withdrawal of preferences in certain trade agreements concluded between the European Union and third countries [2019] OJ L53/1.

[108] Art 1.

[109] Regulation (EU) 2019/880 of the European Parliament and of the Council of 17 April 2019 on the introduction and import of cultural goods [2019] OJ L151/1.

[110] Regulation (EU) 2015/479 of the European Parliament and of the Council of 11 March 2015 on common rules for exports [2015] OJ L83/34.

intervention".[111] In addition, a separate regulation establishes an EU regime for the control of exports of dual-use items, which are defined as "items, including software and technology, which can be used for both civil and military purposes, and shall include all goods which can be used for both non-explosive uses and assisting in any way in the manufacture of nuclear weapons or other nuclear explosive devices".[112] The EU also frequently adopts "restrictive measures" or sanctions as part of its Common Foreign and Security Policy that may include prohibitions on the import or export of goods.[113] Such measures do not form part of the CCP under Art 207 TFEU, but rather have their own legal base in Art 215 TFEU, which provides that:

> Where a decision, adopted in accordance with Chapter 2 of Title V [on CFSP] of the Treaty on European Union, provides for the interruption or reduction, in part or completely, of economic and financial relations with one or more third countries, the Council, acting by a qualified majority on a joint proposal from the High Representative of the Union for Foreign Affairs and Security Policy and the Commission, shall adopt the necessary measures. It shall inform the European Parliament thereof.

[18–85] Originating out of a recommendation of the UN Conference of Trade and Development, the EU operates an autonomous measure known as the generalised scheme of preferences (GSP), which is set down in a regulation.[114] Aiming at promoting sustainable development within developing countries, the regulation establishes three different trade preference arrangements known as "Standard GSP", "GSP+" and "Everything But Arms". The standard tariff preference grants tariff reductions on around two-thirds of all products to low income or lower-middle income countries that do not benefit from other preferential trade access to the EU market. GSP+ grants full duty suspension in respect of the same products as a special incentive to commit to sustainable development and good governance goals. Beneficiary countries must become a party to, and effectively implement, 27 international agreements listed in the regulation relating to human rights, environmental protection, good governance and the protection of workers. Finally, Everything But Arms grants to Least Developed Countries full duty-free access for all products except arms and ammunition. In 2016–2017, 49 countries benefited from EBA, 10 from GSP+ and 23 from the Standard GSP.[115]

[18–86] As well as rules governing imports to, and exports from, the EU, a series of three regulations provide the Union with what are known as "trade defence instruments". These regulations set out the means by which the EU can respond to a third country that imposes trade barriers,[116] engages in the "dumping" of imports at less than their

---

111 Art 5.

112 Council Regulation (EC) No 428/2009 of 5 May 2009 setting up a Community regime for the control of exports, transfer, brokering and transit of dual-use items [2009] OJ L134/1, Art 2(1).

113 See <www.sanctionsmap.eu> for details of the EU sanctions regimes that are in place.

114 Regulation (EU) No 978/2012 of the European Parliament and of the Council of 25 October 2012 applying a scheme of generalised tariff preferences and repealing Council Regulation (EC) No 732/2008 [2012] OJ L303/1.

115 European Commission, "Report on the Generalised Scheme of Preferences Covering the Period 2016–2017" COM(2018) 36 final, 19 January 2018, 1–2. See also European Commission, "Mid-Term Evaluation of the EU's Generalised Scheme of Preferences (GSP)", 2018.

116 Regulation (EU) 2015/1843 of the European Parliament and of the Council of 6 October 2015 laying down Union procedures in the field of the common commercial policy in order to ensure the exercise of the Union's rights under international trade rules, in particular those established under the auspices of the World Trade Organization [2015] OJ L272/1.

normal value[117] or the importation of subsidised products.[118] A fourth regulation details the measures that the Union may take following a report adopted by the WTO Dispute Settlement Body concerning anti-dumping and anti-subsidy matters.[119]

[18–87] Under the Trade Barriers Regulation, a procedure is set out that allows a written complaint to be submitted to the Commission on behalf of a Union industry or enterprise which considers that it has suffered injury as a result of obstacles to trade imposed by a third country that have an effect on the market of the Union. The complaint is required to set out sufficient evidence of the existence of the obstacles to trade and the resulting injury. A Member State may also bring a matter to the attention of the Commission in a similar way. Assisted by a Trade Barriers Committee, the Commission may decide to open an examination procedure to investigate further. If it is concluded that action is necessary in the interests of the Union in order to "ensure the exercise of the Union's rights under international trade rules, with a view to removing the injury or the adverse trade effects resulting from obstacles to trade that are adopted or maintained by third countries", appropriate commercial policy measures may be adopted. If, however, the Union's international obligations require the use of a dispute settlement mechanism, this avenue must first be availed of. Subject to its international obligations, commercial policy measures may involve:

(a) suspension or withdrawal of any concession resulting from commercial policy negotiations;
(b) the raising of existing customs duties or the introduction of any other charge on imports;
(c) the introduction of quantitative restrictions or any other measures modifying import or export conditions or otherwise affecting trade with the third country concerned.[120]

[18–88] A response to dumping or subsidised imports usually involves the levying of a duty that would seek to counteract the price differential.[121] In order to determine

---

117 Regulation (EU) 2016/1036 of the European Parliament and of the Council of 8 June 2016 on protection against dumped imports from countries not members of the European Union [2016] OJ L176/21; Regulation (EU) 2017/2321 of the European Parliament and of the Council of 12 December 2017 amending Regulation (EU) 2016/1036 on protection against dumped imports from countries not members of the European Union and Regulation (EU) 2016/1037 on protection against subsidised imports from countries not members of the European Union [2017] OJ L338/1.

118 Regulation (EU) 2016/1037 of the European Parliament and of the Council of 8 June 2016 on protection against subsidised imports from countries not members of the European Union [2016] OJ L176/55; Regulation (EU) 2017/2321 of the European Parliament and of the Council of 12 December 2017 amending Regulation (EU) 2016/1036 on protection against dumped imports from countries not members of the European Union and Regulation (EU) 2016/1037 on protection against subsidised imports from countries not members of the European Union [2017] OJ L338/1.

119 Regulation (EU) 2015/476 of the European Parliament and of the Council of 11 March 2015 on the measures that the Union may take following a report adopted by the WTO Dispute Settlement Body concerning anti-dumping and anti-subsidy matters [2015] OJ L83/6.

120 Regulation (EU) 2015/1843 of the European Parliament and of the Council of 6 October 2015 laying down Union procedures in the field of the common commercial policy in order to ensure the exercise of the Union's rights under international trade rules, in particular those established under the auspices of the World Trade Organization [2015] OJ L272/1, Art 13(3).

121 See, for example, Commission Implementing Regulation (EU) 2018/140 of 29 January 2018 imposing a definitive anti-dumping duty and collecting definitively the provisional duty imposed on imports of certain cast iron articles originating in the People's Republic of China and terminating the investigation on imports of certain cast iron articles originating in India [2018] OJ L25/6; Commission Implementing Regulation (EU) 2019/67 of 16 January 2019 imposing safeguard

the existence of dumping it is necessary to carry out a detailed price analysis in order to demonstrate that goods are being imported at less than their normal value. This is particularly difficult in respect of imports from non-market economies, and so the regulation provides for special rules to apply in such circumstances. As part of its accession to the WTO in 2001, for example, it was agreed that China would have 15 years in which to assimilate to normal market economy conditions. The reluctance of the EU to accept China's market economy status from 2016 onwards led China to lodge a dispute with the WTO dispute settlement body, claiming that the EU's continued application of non-market economy rules for determining the value of Chinese imports is contrary to WTO rules.[122]

(iii) Scope of Article 207 as a Legal Base

[18–89] Like the residual competence conferred by Art 114 TFEU relating to the Internal Market, the broad nature of the competence provided for in Art 207 TFEU has led to a number of inter-institutional disputes as to the scope of this competence, and how it interacts with more precise legal bases. The test that has been developed by the Court of Justice to define the scope of Art 207 goes as follows: the fact that an act of the EU, such as an international agreement concluded by it, is liable to have implications for international trade is not enough for that act to be classified as falling within the CCP. Rather, in addition to the condition that such an act must be essentially intended to promote, facilitate or govern international trade, "it must also have direct and immediate effects on such trade".[123]

[18–90] Inter-institutional tension between the Council and the Commission in this area is understandable given that the CCP is an exclusive Union competence. This often means that the Commission will regard Art 207 as a sufficient legal base that does not need to be supplemented by another legal base, which may entail a shared competence that would involve a greater role for the Member States. As an example of such disputes, in each of the following four cases the Commission instituted proceedings relating to the interplay between Art 207 and the Union's competence in environmental matters. These concerned, respectively, the Cartagena Protocol on Biosafety, the Energy Star Agreement with the United States, the Rotterdam Convention on the Prior Informed Consent Procedure for certain hazardous chemicals and pesticides in international trade and the Waste Shipments Regulation. The issue was also among the many areas of competence considered by the Court of Justice in its recent opinion on the EU–Singapore free trade agreement.

[18–91] In the first of these four cases, the Commission sought an opinion from

measures with regard to imports of Indica rice originating in Cambodia and Myanmar/Burma [2019] OJ L15/5.

[122] DS516 *European Union — Measures Related to Price Comparison Methodologies*. See Commission Staff Working Document on Significant Distortions in the Economy of the People's Republic of China for the Purposes of Trade Defence Investigations SWD(2017) 483 final/2, 20 December 2017; Laura Puccio, "Granting Market Economy Status to China" (European Parliamentary Research Service, 2017); Meadhbh Costello, "China's Market Economy Status: A Political Issue" (Institute of International and European Affairs, 2016).

[123] Case C-389/15 *Commission v Parliament (Appellations of Origin)* EU:C:2017:798, 25 October 2017, para 65; Opinion 2/15 (*Singapore Free Trade Agreement*) EU:C:2017:376, 16 May 2017, para 36.

the Court of Justice as to whether the Council was correct in its position that an environmental legal base was sufficient for a decision that the Union become a signatory to the Cartagena Protocol on Biosafety, which was a protocol to the Convention on Biological Diversity.[124] The aim of the Protocol was to regulate the safe transfer, handling and use of living modified organisms (LMOs) resulting from biotechnology, specifically focusing on transboundary movements. The Court rejected the Commission's argument that the Protocol ought to be regarded as falling within the CCP. In the Court's view:

> it is true that, in the very words of Article 1 of the Protocol, the "adequate level of protection" sought concerns in particular the "transfer" of LMOs and that the "focus" must be placed on "transboundary movements" of LMOs. It is also true that numerous provisions of the Protocol relate specifically to control of those movements, in particular where LMOs are intended for direct use as food or animal feed or for processing, in order to enable the national authorities to prevent or reduce the risks which they entail for biological diversity or human health. However, even if, as the Commission maintains, the control procedures set up by the Protocol are applied most frequently, or at least in terms of market value preponderantly, to trade in LMOs, the fact remains that … the Protocol is, in the light of its context, its aim and its content, an instrument intended essentially to improve biosafety and not to promote, facilitate or govern trade.[125]

[18–92] In reaching this conclusion, the Court emphasised that the definition of transboundary movements set out in the Protocol included not only movements for commercial reasons but also "illegal and 'unintentional' transboundary movements, movements for charitable or scientific purposes and movements serving the public interest".[126]

[18–93] The *Energy Star Agreement* case followed soon afterward and involved a similar dispute.[127] There, the Commission challenged the Council's choice of an environmental legal base for the signing of an agreement with the United States on a common labelling system for office equipment that would indicate levels of efficiency in energy consumption. In this case, however, the Commission was successful in arguing that Art 207 was the proper and sufficient legal base. The Court began by recalling its existing case law to the effect that, if examination of a measure reveals that it pursues a twofold purpose and if one is identifiable as the main or predominant purpose, whereas the other is merely incidental, the measure must be founded on the single legal basis of that required by the main or predominant purpose. By way of exception, if it is established that the measure simultaneously pursues several objectives which are inseparably linked without one being secondary and indirect in relation to the other, the measure must be founded on the corresponding legal bases.[128] Since the Court regarded the Energy Star Agreement as pursuing both a commercial and an environmental policy objective, it was necessary to determine if one was predominant over the other. In the Court's assessment:

> It is clear from the terms in which the Energy Star Agreement is couched … that the Energy Star labelling program is essentially intended to enable manufacturers to use, in accordance with a procedure for the mutual recognition of registrations, a common

---

[124] Opinion 2/00 (*Cartagena Protocol*) [2001] ECR I-9713.
[125] *ibid*, 9762.
[126] *ibid*, 9762–9763.
[127] Case C-281/01 *Commission v Council (Energy Star Agreement)* [2002] ECR I-12049.
[128] *ibid*, 12086.

> logo to identify for consumers certain products complying with a common set of energy efficiency specifications which they intend to sell on the American and [EU] markets. An instrument having a direct impact on trade in office equipment is therefore involved.
>
> It is true that in the long term, depending on how manufacturers and consumers in fact behave, the programme should have a positive environmental effect as a result of the reduction in energy consumption which it should achieve. However, that is merely an indirect and distant effect, in contrast to the effect on trade in office equipment which is direct and immediate.[129]

[18–94] The choice between Art 207 and an environmental legal base was again at issue in the *Rotterdam Convention* case.[130] The stated aim of the Convention was to promote shared responsibility and cooperative efforts among states in the international trade of certain hazardous chemicals in order to protect human health and the environment. This was to be achieved through facilitating the exchange of information about hazardous chemicals, by providing for a national decision-making process on their import and export (a "prior informed consent" procedure) and by informing states parties of those decisions. While the Court accepted that the protection of human health and the environment was the uppermost concern in the minds of the signatories, equally the commercial aspects of the Convention were not "purely incidental" given that it contained rules "governing trade in hazardous chemicals and having direct and immediate effects on such trade".[131] As a result, the Court reached the conclusion that the Rotterdam Convention included:

> both as regards the aims pursued and its contents, two indissociably linked components, neither of which can be regarded as secondary or indirect as compared with the other, one falling within the scope of the common commercial policy and the other within that of protection of human health and the environment. … the decision approving that Convention on behalf of the [Union] should therefore have been based on the two corresponding legal bases.[132]

[18–95] Finally, the *Waste Shipments* case concerned an argument by the Commission that Art 207 ought to have been included alongside an environmental legal base to adopt a regulation governing the shipments of waste within, into and out of the EU.[133] Like the Rotterdam Convention, the regulation imposed a system of prior consent. The Commission argued that given that parts of the regulation governed exports of waste to, and imports from, third countries, Art 207 ought to have been added as a legal base. As with the Cartagena Protocol on Biosafety, the Court was not convinced by the Commission's argument and instead considered the regulation's predominant purpose to be the protection of the environment. In the view of the Court:

> It should be borne in mind … that the prior written notification and consent procedure applies to all shipments of waste, irrespective of any commercial context in which they might take place. The term "shipment" is defined … in a neutral manner as "the transport of waste destined for recovery or disposal …". The term "transport", in turn, is defined … as "the carriage of waste by road, rail, air, sea or inland waterways". "Import" and "export"

[129] *ibid*, 12088.

[130] Case C-94/03 *Commission v Council (Rotterdam Convention)* [2006] ECR I-1.

[131] *ibid*, 46.

[132] *ibid*, 49–50.

[133] Case C-411/06 *Commission v European Parliament and Council (Waste Shipments)* [2009] ECR I-7585.

> are also defined ... in neutral terms, as "any entry of waste into the Community ..." and "the action of waste leaving the Community ..." respectively. The contested regulation thus emphasises the carriage of waste with a view to its treatment rather than carriage thereof for commercial purposes. Even if waste is shipped in the context of commercial trade, the fact remains that the prior written notification and consent procedure is aimed solely at protecting against risks to human health and the environment arising from such shipments and not to promote, facilitate or govern commercial trade.
>
> Moreover, a broad interpretation of the concept of common commercial policy is not such as to call into question the finding that the contested regulation is an instrument falling principally under environmental protection policy. As the Court has held, a [Union] act may fall within that area, even when the measures provided for by that act are liable to affect trade.
>
> A [Union] act falls within the exclusive competence in the field of the common commercial policy provided for in [Art 207 TFEU] only if it relates specifically to international trade in that it is essentially intended to promote, facilitate or govern trade and has direct and immediate effects on trade in the products concerned.
>
> That is clearly not the situation in the present case. ... [T]he aim of the contested regulation is not to define those characteristics of waste which will enable it to circulate freely within the internal market or as part of commercial trade with third countries, but to provide a harmonised set of procedures whereby movements of waste can be limited in order to secure protection of the environment.[134]

[18–96] The relationship between the CCP and environmental protection was also among the many competence issues considered by the Full Court in its opinion on the EU–Singapore free trade agreement. There, the proposed agreement included a chapter on sustainable development, in which protection of the environment and protection of workers were said to be mutually reinforcing components. The Court noted that, as introduced by the Lisbon Treaty, Art 207 now includes the express instruction that the CCP is to be conducted "in the context of the principles and objectives of the Union's external action".[135] As specified in the TEU, these principles and objectives include sustainable development linked to the preservation and improvement of the quality of the environment. In addition, Art 3 TEU obliges the Union's external relations to contribute to "free and fair" trade. As a result, the Court concluded that the objective of sustainable development now forms an integral part of the CCP.[136]

[18–97] In line with its earlier case law, the test for establishing whether or not a matter fell within the CCP was defined by the Court as being whether the matter relates specifically to international trade, "in that it is essentially intended to promote, facilitate or govern such trade and has direct and immediate effect on it".[137] The provisions of the agreement relating to environmental protection were characterised as mutual commitments by the EU and Singapore that the trade between them would take place in compliance with relevant international agreements to which they were a party. Consequently, the relevant provisions were held not to regulate environmental protection in their respective territories, but rather to govern trade between them "by making liberalisation of that trade subject to the condition that the Parties comply

---

134 *ibid*, paras 69–72.

135 Opinion 2/15 (*Singapore Free Trade Agreement*) EU:C:2017:376, 16 May 2017, para 142.

136 *ibid*, para 147.

137 *ibid*, para 36.

with their international obligations".[138] The environmental provisions of the free trade agreement, therefore, did fall within the scope of the CCP and so were matters for which the Union had exclusive external competence.

[138] *ibid*, para 166.

Chapter 19

RESTRICTIONS ON THE FREE MOVEMENT OF GOODS

A. Introduction – Articles 34 and 36 TFEU

[19–01] Within Part Three of the TFEU, dealing with the EU's policies and internal actions, Title II provides for the free movement of goods. In turn, Chapter 3 of Title II (Arts 34–37) is dedicated to the prohibition of quantitative restrictions between Member States. For present purposes, Art 37, dealing with state monopolies of a commercial character, is of less importance and the focus here is on Arts 34, 35 and 36, and the manner in which the prohibition of quantitative restrictions guarantees the free movement of goods.

[19–02] Article 34 TFEU prohibits not only quantitative restrictions on imports between Member States, but also all measures having an *equivalent effect* to quantitative restrictions on imports between Member States. Article 35 provides for the same prohibition in respect of exports. Whilst, in the past, treatment of Arts 34 and 35 by the Court of Justice differed to a significant extent, it has now been reconciled and the focus here will be on the more commonly applied restrictions on imports. Generally, Member States do not have an economic interest in placing restrictions on exports leaving their territory.[1]

[19–03] Although a fundamental Treaty guarantee, it is important to remember that the free movement of goods under EU law is not absolute. Article 36 TFEU

---

1 See Case C-205/07 *Gysbrechts* [2008] ECR I-9947.

details six exceptional grounds under which, by way of derogation from Art 34 or 35, a Member State is allowed to place a restriction on the free movement of goods. Provided that they are not used as a means of arbitrary discrimination or a disguised restriction on trade between Member States, restrictions may be justified on the grounds of (i) public morality; (ii) public policy; (iii) public security; (iv) the protection of health and life of humans, animals or plants; (v) the protection of national treasures possessing artistic, historic or archaeological value; or (vi) the protection of industrial and commercial property. In accordance with the general principles of EU law, to be permissible a national restriction that is being defended on the basis of Art 36 must also be proportionate, in the sense of not going beyond what is necessary in order to achieve the stated policy objective.

[19–04] A quantitative restriction on an import might take the form of an outright ban or a quota limiting the permitted number of imports of a product such as, for example, no more than 1,000 imported cars per year.[2] As the prohibition on quantitative restrictions is clear and definitive, little difficulty arises as to its application in practice and it is rare to come across a Member State attempting to impose a quantitative restriction on either imports or exports.

[19–05] In stark contrast, the term "measure having an equivalent effect to a quantitative restriction" (MEQR) is not defined in Art 34 or elsewhere in the Treaties. As a result, its meaning has been developed through the case law of the Court of Justice, with some important guidance being derived from Directive 70/50 of 1969 on the abolition of measures which have an effect equivalent to quantitative restrictions on imports.[3] This somewhat innocuous phrase lies at the heart of the creation of a single market in goods and has given rise to a complex line of landmark jurisprudence and endless academic commentary. This jurisprudence and commentary often turns on discrete concepts and categorisations that have been developed in order to explain certain economic rationales and theories relating to the free movement of goods, some of which are worth introducing at the outset.

[19–06] First, it will be seen that a crucial distinction is drawn between *distinctly* applicable MEQRs (also referred to as discriminatory MEQRs), which openly treat imports less favourably than domestic goods without any objective justification for doing so, and *indistinctly applicable* MEQRS, which, as a matter of law, treat imports and domestic goods the same but, as a matter of fact, pose a greater burden to imports than to domestic goods. The significance of this difference lies in the fact that whereas distinctly applicable MEQRs may be defended only on the basis of the six grounds listed in Art 36, indistinctly applicable MEQRs may, in addition, be defended on the basis of an open-ended set of grounds that have been developed by the Court of Justice. These additional grounds are known alternatively as "mandatory requirements", the "rule of reason" or, more simply, as overriding public interests.

[19–07] A further distinction is drawn as between indistinctly applicable MEQRs, such as *product requirements*, that relate to the character of a good, such as its shape or

2 See, for example, Case 34/79 *R v Henn and Darby* [1979] ECR 3795; Case C-170/04 *Rosengren* [2007] ECR I-4071.

3 Directive 70/50 on the abolition of measures which have an effect equivalent to quantitative restrictions on imports and are not covered by other provisions adopted in pursuance of the EEC Treaty [1970] OJ L13/29.

size, and rules governing the *market circumstances* under which a good is sold, such as where it can be sold, when it can be sold, how it can be sold or marketed (eg through advertising or promotional offers) and by whom it can be sold (eg only by holders of a particular licence or qualification). Generally, product requirement rules can be said to impose a *dual burden* in that, as manufacturers are required to comply with the law of the home state of manufacture and the host state of sale, changes will be required to be made to the product depending on the market in which it is being sold. Market circumstances rules, in contrast, typically do not impose a dual burden in this way as they do not require a change to be made to the product itself, and are therefore described as *equal burden* measures.

[19–08] A final distinction worth noting is that market circumstances rules governing where, when and by whom a good can be sold or marketed are described as *static*, in distinction to rules governing how a good may be sold or marketed, which are described as *dynamic*. This internal distinction amongst market circumstances rules is based on the idea that rules governing how a good may be sold or marketed, such as what advertising or promotional activities can be used, tend to be much more closely related to the nature of a particular product, and therefore variable, than rules governing when, where and by whom goods may be sold, which tend to be of a general and stable nature. In addition, whereas static rules usually affect retailers of products, dynamic rules tend to affect importers or manufacturers of products and are more likely to give rise to an element of dual burden. Dynamic rules, therefore, might be seen as occupying a space somewhere between product requirements and market circumstances rules.

B. Vertical and Horizontal Direct Effect

[19–09] Both Arts 34 and 35 TFEU have been held to have vertical direct effect.[4] As they are addressed to the Member States, in general they do not have horizontal direct effect. A certain degree of horizontal effectiveness can, however, arise in two ways: by taking a broad view of what constitutes a state entity for the purpose of vertical direct effect, and by imposing a form of vicarious responsibility on a Member State for the actions of private individuals.

(i) A Broad View of State Entities

[19–10] First, the Court of Justice has tended to adopt an expansive view of what constitutes a state entity for the purpose of deciding against whom the direct effect of Arts 34 and 35 can be invoked. An early instance of this arose in the *Buy Irish* case (*Commission v Ireland*), where the Commission successfully argued that the activities of the Irish Goods Council were attributable to the State. The Irish Goods Council had been established by amalgamating existing state bodies by creating a company limited by guarantee to which a government minister appointed the chairman and board members. The minister's approval was required for any amendment to the company's Memorandum or Articles of Association. Financially, the Council was subsidised by both the State and by private industry.[5] Ireland had argued that the Goods Council was not a public authority, but merely an arrangement whereby various Irish industries

---

4 Case 74/76 *Ianelli and Volpi v Meroni* [1977] ECR 595.

5 Case 249/81 *Commission v Ireland (Buy Irish)* [1982] ECR 4005.

could cooperate for their common good, that its activities were not based on any official enactment, and that the involvement of the Government consisted exclusively of financial aid and moral support.[6] As will be seen below when considering the meaning of "measures" as referred to in Art 34, the Court took a holistic view of the State's involvement in the Buy Irish campaign and was unwilling to accept the argument that the separate legal status of the Irish Goods Council meant that responsibility for the campaign could not be attributed to the State. In another case involving Ireland, the Court of Justice did not consider it necessary to scrutinise the nature of Dundalk Urban District Council as a state body in circumstances where a breach of Art 34 was claimed to have arisen in the awarding of a tender contract, where, as a final stage in the tender process, approval by the Department of the Environment was required before the contract could be awarded.[7]

[19–11] Similarly, it has been held that a code of ethics issued by the Royal Pharmaceutical Society of Great Britain constituted a "measure" within the meaning of Art 34 in circumstances where the Society had been established by royal charter in the 1800s, was referred to in legislation, and whose disciplinary committee had conferred on it by law the power to remove an individual from the professional register.[8] This was taken a step further in the significant case of *Fra.bo*, which concerned a decision of a German private-law body, the DVGW, that carried out certifications of fittings to be used in the gas and water sector.[9] When an Italian company whose copper fittings were refused certification alleged a breach of Art 34, the DVGW claimed that, as it was not a state body, it could not be held to have infringed Art 34, nor was there anything to prevent it from drawing up technical standards which went beyond those in place in Member States other than Germany and to apply them to its certification activities. Although the DVGW did not receive any state funding, German law did provide that products certified by it were to be deemed compliant with national legislation. Moreover, while an alternative verification procedure was open to the Italian company (which, the Court found, would involve administrative difficulties and additional expense), there was no other body that could certify the fittings for the purpose of German law. As a result, the Court of Justice concluded that Art 34 must be considered to apply to "standardisation and certification activities of a *private-law body*, where the national legislation considers the products certified by that body to be compliant with national law and that has the effect of restricting the marketing of products which are not certified by that body".[10]

---

6 *ibid*, 4018.

7 Case 45/87 *Commission v Ireland (Dundalk Water)* [1988] ECR 4929.

8 Joined Cases 266/87 and 267/87 *R v Royal Pharmaceutical Society of Great Britain* [1989] ECR 1295.

9 Case C-171/11 *Fra.bo v DVGW* EU:C:2012:453, 12 July 2012, para 32, emphasis added. See Herman van Harten and Thomas Nauta, "Towards Horizontal Direct Effect for the Free Movement of Goods? Comment on *Fra.bo*" (2013) 38 *European Law Review* 677; Alex Crespo van de Kooij, "The Private Effect of the Free Movement of Goods: Examining Private-Law Bodies' Activities under the Scope of Article 34 of the Treaty of the Functioning of the European Union" (2013) 40 *Legal Issues of Economic Integration* 363; Christoph Krenn, "A Missing Piece in the Horizontal Effect 'Jigsaw': Horizontal Direct Effect and the Free Movement of Goods" (2012) 49 *Common Market Law Review* 177; Harm Schepel, "Constitutionalising the Market, Marketising the Constitution, and to Tell the Difference: On the Horizontal Application of the Free Movement Provisions in EU Law" (2012) 18 *European Law Journal* 177 (2012).

10 *ibid*, para 32, emphasis added.

(ii) Indirect State Responsibility

[19–12] The second way in which a degree of horizontal direct effect can arise is that a Member State may be held responsible for the acts of private individuals where it is considered that the state ought to have prevented or stopped their activity, or otherwise bears some indirect responsibility for their actions. Put another way, given its importance as a fundamental freedom, there is a positive obligation on Member States to take all necessary and appropriate measures to ensure that the free movement of goods is respected on their territory.

[19–13] In the *Spanish Strawberries* case (*Commission v France*), the Commission successfully brought infringement proceedings against France arising out of the "passivity" of its authorities, over a number of years, towards protests by French farmers against imported agricultural products.[11] The actions of the famers included intercepting lorries transporting goods into France and destroying their load, damaging goods on display in French shops, threatening wholesalers and retailers in order to induce them to stock exclusively French products and organising checks to verify whether they had complied with instructions given to them.

[19–14] The Court accepted that, as a matter of principle, a Member State's failure to adopt adequate measures to prevent obstacles to the free movement of goods created by the actions of private individuals may be caught by Art 34. It concluded that the French authorities had "manifestly and persistently abstained from adopting appropriate and adequate measures to put an end to the acts of vandalism which jeopardize the free movement on its territory of certain agricultural products originating in other Member States and to prevent the recurrence of such acts".[12] As a result of its failure to adopt all necessary and proportionate measures to prevent the free movement of fruit and vegetables from being obstructed by the actions of private individuals, France had failed to fulfil its obligations under Art 34.

[19–15] In a subsequent case, *Austrian Motorways*, it was similarly held that the failure of Austria to prevent an environmental protest from blocking a motorway amounted to a restriction caught by Art 34.[13] The Court accepted that the principle established in *Spanish Strawberries* could be applied "without the need to distinguish between cases where such acts affect the flow of imports or exports and those affecting merely the transit of goods".[14] Accordingly, the Austrian authorities were required to take adequate steps to ensure the free movement of goods even if those goods were merely passing through Austria en route for Italy or Germany, rather than being imported into Austria itself. The decision by Austria not to ban the demonstration, resulting in the closure of a major transit motorway for 30 hours, constituted an MEQR caught by Art 34 which, therefore, required a justification in order to be permitted. On the facts of the case, however, taking into account the value of the freedoms of expression and assembly and the relatively limited nature of the disruption, the Court of Justice held that the failure to ban the demonstration did not amount to a breach of Art 34.

[19–16] Following the *Spanish Strawberries* case, a regulation was introduced in

---

11 Case C-265/95 *Commission v France (Spanish Strawberries)* [1997] ECR I-6959.
12 *ibid*, 7005.
13 Case C-112/00 *Schmidberger v Austria (Austrian Motorways)* [2003] ECR I-5659.
14 *ibid*, 5714.

order to provide an intervention mechanism to safeguard against obstacles to the free movement of goods within the Single Market (known alternatively as the "Strawberry" or "Monti" Regulation).[15] The Regulation defines an "obstacle" to the free movement of goods as any obstacle attributable to a Member State, whether arising from its action or inaction, that: (a) leads to serious disruption of the free movement of goods by physically or otherwise preventing, delaying or diverting their import into, export from or transport across a Member State; (b) causes serious loss to the individuals affected; and (c) requires immediate action in order to prevent any continuation, increase or intensification of the disruption or loss in question. More particularly, "inaction" is defined as covering a situation where the "competent authorities of a Member State, in the presence of an obstacle caused by actions taken by private individuals, fail to take all necessary and proportionate measures within their powers with a view to removing the obstacle and ensuring the free movement of goods in their territory".

[19–17] Where an obstacle threatens to occur, the Commission may request information from the relevant Member State, which is obliged to respond as soon as possible outlining the action it intends to take. Where an obstacle does occur, the Member State is required to take all necessary and proportionate measures so that the free movement of goods is assured in its territory and inform the Commission accordingly, which in turn immediately transmits that information to the other Member States. In Ireland, the administrative formalities provided for in the Regulation are dealt with by the Internal Market Unit of the Department of Business, Enterprise and Innovation, which is responsible for forwarding notifications in relation to the Regulation to contact points in various business and government bodies for onward transmission to their relevant contacts.

C. MEQR – Measures Equivalent to a Quantitative Restriction

[19–18] The concept of a measure having an equivalent effect to a quantitative restriction (an "MEQR") is a cornerstone of the law on free movement of goods. The fact that it is described in Art 34 TFEU in only very general terms has allowed the concept to be interpreted by the Court of Justice in a flexible manner. This flexibility has enabled the Court to adapt its approach in response to the changing practices of Member States when it comes to regulating the production and marketing of goods.

[19–19] There are, in fact, two different sources of ambiguity within the concept of an MEQR. First, what exactly is meant by a "measure", and what form is it intended that a measure must take in order for it to fall within the scope of the Article – a law or regulation of a Member State, or a broader definition that can include an administrative practice or procedure adopted by a state that restricts the import of goods? The second ambiguity arises from the inherently imprecise notion of a measure that is *equivalent to* a quantitative restriction. This is a complex question that has long dominated the law in relation to the free movement of goods and so requires close examination.

---

[15] Regulation 2679/98 of 7 December 1998 on the functioning of the internal market in relation to the free movement of goods among the Member States [1998] OJ L337/8.

(i) "Measures" within the Meaning of Article 34

[19–20] As exemplified by *Spanish Strawberries* and *Austrian Motorways*, discussed above, the nature of a "measure" that may have an equivalent effect to quantitative restrictions within the meaning of Art 34 can take a wide variety of forms and is not limited solely to national laws or regulations. A consistent administrative practice may breach Art 34, such as the necessary prior approval for postal franking machines being given, by the French Post Office, to French-made machines only, and not those produced in the UK.[16] The actions of individual state officials may also amount to measures within the meaning of the prohibition, such as where a Finnish ministry expert stated on a national television news programme that lifts made by an Italian company were unsafe and could present an immediate danger.[17] The lifts had been certified as conforming with a relevant EU safety directive, which provided that Member States were not to restrict or impede the placing on the market of machinery that complied with the directive. As reports of the statement were widely circulated, the Court of Justice was satisfied that the actions of the official were capable of hindering, at least indirectly and potentially, imports of the lifts.

[19–21] A good early example of this broad approach to defining measures for the purposes of Art 34 may be seen in the *Buy Irish* case (*Commission v Ireland*), in which the Court of Justice considered a campaign to promote the purchase of Irish goods to be a "national practice introduced by the Irish government and prosecuted with its assistance".[18] The campaign, which included placing a "Guaranteed Irish" symbol on Irish produced goods, an advertising campaign promoting Irish goods and an exhibition space reserved exclusively for such goods, received financial assistance from the State and was assisted by the Irish Goods Council. In addition to claiming that the activities of the Goods Council were not attributable to the State, Ireland argued that it had not enacted any "measure" within the meaning of Art 34 and that, in any event, the campaign had had no restrictive effect on the free movement of goods in that, during its lifetime, the proportion of Irish-made goods sold in Ireland actually fell from 49 to 43 per cent. The Court rejected these arguments, noting that:

> Regardless of the means used to implement it, the campaign is a reflection of the Irish Government's considered intention to substitute domestic products for imported products on the Irish market and thereby to check the flow of imports from other Member States.
>
> It must be remembered here that a representative of the Irish Government stated when the campaign was launched that it was a carefully thought-out set of initiatives constituting an integrated programme for promoting domestic products; that the Irish Goods Council was set up at the initiative of the Irish Government a few months later; and that the task of implementing the integrated programme as it was envisaged by the government was entrusted, or left, to that Council.
>
> Whilst it may be true that the two elements of the programme which have continued in effect, namely the advertising campaign and the use of the "Guaranteed Irish" symbol, have not had any significant success in winning over the Irish market to domestic products, it is not possible to overlook the fact that, regardless of their efficacity, those two activities

---

16 Case 21/84 *Commission v France* [1985] ECR 1355.

17 Case C-470/03 *AGM-COS.MET* [2007] ECR I-2749.

18 Case 249/81 *Commission v Ireland (Buy Irish)* [1982] ECR 4005, 4023. See Janja Hojnik, "Free Movement of Goods in a Labyrinth: Can *Buy Irish* Survive the Crisis?" (2010) 49 *Common Market Law Review* 291.

> form part of a government programme which is designed to achieve the substitution of domestic products for imported products and is liable to affect the volume of trade between Member States.
>
> … In the circumstances the two activities in question amount to the establishment of a national practice, introduced by the Irish Government and prosecuted with its assistance, the potential effect of which on imports from other Member States is comparable to that resulting from government measures of a binding nature.
>
> Such a practice cannot escape the prohibition laid down by Article [34 TFEU] solely because it is not based on decisions which are binding upon undertakings. Even measures adopted by the government of a Member State which do not have binding effect may be capable of influencing the conduct of traders and consumers in that State and thus of frustrating the aims of the [Union].[19]

[19–22] Another instance of Irish conduct being regarded as a "measure" caught by Art 34 arose in *Dundalk Water* (*Commission v Ireland*).[20] These proceedings were brought by the Commission on foot of a contract tender issued by Dundalk Urban District Council relating to an improvement of the town's water supply. One condition for the award of a contract was that pipes certified in accordance with a particular Irish standard were to be used. The only pipes certified in accordance with the Irish standard were made by a company based in Ireland. The matter had been brought to the Commission's attention by an Irish company that had unsuccessfully competed for the tender using Spanish pipes that, whilst not having been certified with the Irish standard, had been certified in accordance with relevant international standards. The Commission argued that by allowing the inclusion of such a clause in the tender contract, and by not allowing for the possibility of awarding the contract to a firm using pipes of an equivalent standard and suitability, Ireland had breached Art 34. In response, Ireland argued that the clause was necessary in order to ensure that the pipes used were compatible with the existing pipe network. The Court rejected Ireland's argument, holding that the failure to allow for a process whereby the compatibility and suitability of other pipes could be verified amounted to an impermissible restriction on the free movement of goods.

(ii) Having an "Equivalent" Effect to a Quantitative Restriction

[19–23] The case law on MEQRs is among the most intricate of all of the jurisprudence of the Court of Justice. As a result, a first encounter can benefit from adopting an overall framework within which to consider this long line of cases. Although it may involve some generalisation, a broad overview of the evolution in judicial thinking can be gained from categorising the case law into four thematic groups. These groups roughly correlate to a sequence of four chronological periods, as follows:

(i) the umbrella definition or *Dassonville* formula – 1974
(ii) product requirements (*Cassis de Dijon*) – 1979
(iii) selling arrangements (*Keck and Mithouard*) – 1993
(iv) restrictions on use/market access (*Italian Trailers, Mickelsson and Roos)* – 2009.[21]

---

19 *ibid*, 4022.
20 Case 45/87 *Commission v Ireland (Dundalk Water)* [1988] ECR 4929.
21 This categorisation is based upon that adopted by Gareth Davies in Damian Chalmers, Gareth Davies and Giorgio Monti, *European Union Law* (3rd ed, Cambridge University Press, 2014) 754; and Robert Schütze in *European Union Law* (Cambridge University Press, 2015) 499.

[19–24] In this section, a compressed summary of these four categories or periods of case law is provided by way of an introduction and guide to the four sections that follow. The remainder of this chapter will then take each of these periods in turn, examining the evolving case law in some detail.

[19–25] First, there may be said to be a general or "umbrella" definition of an MEQR that derives from the 1974 *Dassonville* case and is known as the "*Dassonville* formula". This umbrella definition famously describes an MEQR as including "all trading rules enacted by a Member State which are capable of hindering, directly or indirectly, actually or potentially, intra-community trade".[22] The *Dassonville* formula renders the scope of the prohibition in Art 34 TFEU extremely broad such that a national measure which, on the face of it, does not appear to constitute a restriction on imports may, nevertheless, be caught. In particular, an indistinctly applicable measure, in the sense of a measure that applies both to imports and domestic goods, can come within the scope of the *Dassonville* formula if it has the effect, or merely potentially has the effect, of hindering trade between Member States, even if this effect is an indirect consequence of the measure.

[19–26] The second category of cases relates to what are termed "product requirements" or "product standards". Initially, the *Dassonville* formula was not understood to capture national rules prescribing a particular standard or requirement that a product must meet in order to be sold within a Member State, provided that the same rules also applied to domestically produced products (ie provided that the measure was "indistinctly applicable"). So, for example, a German law that required all drinks sold as liqueurs to have an alcohol content of at least 25 per cent was not, at first, considered to constitute an MEQR as defined by the Court in *Dassonville*, as it applied equally to both German-made drinks and imported drinks. The 1979 case of *Cassis de Dijon* altered this by introducing the principle of mutual recognition. According to this principle, there is "no valid reason why, provided that they have been lawfully produced and marketed in one of the Member States, alcoholic beverages should not be introduced into any other Member State".[23] The rationale for treating a product requirement as a MEQR lay partly in the fact that it was said to create a "dual burden" for importers, which placed them at a disadvantage to domestic producers. Whereas exporters, having complied with their own national laws in designing and manufacturing a product, would have to go to the additional expense of complying with a second set of regulations in each Member State to which it exported goods, domestic producers only had to comply with a single set of rules.

[19–27] As will be seen, the far-reaching nature of the principle of mutual recognition led the Court of Justice to moderate its effect in certain respects by simultaneously introducing a more flexible and generous approach to allowing a Member State to seek to justify an indistinctly applicable restriction on the free movement of goods on the basis of what are termed "mandatory requirements", otherwise known as the "rule of reason" or "overriding public interests". It is important to remember, however, that while mandatory requirements broaden the grounds on which a Member State may justify a restriction, *Cassis de Dijon* also greatly expanded the scope of the net cast by Art 34 by further adding to the type of measure that can constitute an MEQR. The 1979 judgment,

[22] Case 8/74 *Procureur du Roi v Dassonville* [1974] ECR 837, 852.

[23] Case 120/78 *Cassis de Dijon* [1979] ECR 649, 664.

therefore, had the effect of making it much more likely that a national restriction would be deemed to be an MEQR, thereby requiring the Member State to mount a defence of the measure on the basis that it was justified by a mandatory requirement.

[19–28] The third category of cases relates to "selling arrangements", or rules that do not govern goods themselves but rather "market circumstances", or the manner in which goods are marketed and sold. In the 1993 case of *Keck and Mithouard*, the Court of Justice took the very rare step of departing from its earlier reasoning in *Cassis de Dijon*. It did so in order to establish that a national restriction on selling arrangements would not constitute an MEQR, and so henceforth would fall outside the scope of Art 34, provided that the restriction: (i) applied to all relevant traders operating within the Member State; and (ii) affected in the same manner, in law and in fact, the marketing of domestic products and those imported from another Member State.[24]

[19–29] *Keck* is commonly seen as a necessary correction to an overly broad approach in *Cassis de Dijon* that was leading to many creative cases being brought before the Court of Justice, successfully arguing that a national measure constituted an MEQR, but ultimately failing in that the Court would accept that the measure was justified by a mandatory requirement. Nevertheless, the judgment in *Keck* created its own difficulties due to the complexity of demarcating between selling arrangements and product requirements. In addition, there is a clear line of judicial thought which suggests that the discriminatory effect required by the second condition of the *Keck* test (ie that, in order not to be deemed an MEQR, a selling arrangement must affect domestic and imported products in the same manner, in law and in fact) is unnecessary. According to this view, rather than examining whether there is any discriminatory effect, it is more appropriate to take a holistic approach to assessing a restriction on free movement, such that the overall question to be asked is whether the national measure hinders, impedes or creates an obstacle to trade between Member States. This approach has particularly arisen in cases involving a more recently developed fourth category of restriction, namely rules limiting the *use* of a product such as a ban on the use of trailers on motorbikes (*Italian Trailers*)[25] or a rule restricting the use of personal watercraft to certain designated navigable waterways only (*Mickelsson and Roos*).[26]

[19–30] Accordingly, when considering the development of the law in relation to MEQRs it is useful to bear the following four categorisations in mind:

(i) the general or umbrella definition of an MEQR as a measure that is capable of hindering, directly or indirectly, actually or potentially, trade between member states (*Dassonville*);
(ii) following from the principle of mutual recognition, an MEQR may take the form of a product requirement. A product requirement is caught by Article 34 TFEU and so is presumed to be unlawful. However, indistinctly applicable MEQRs, such as product requirements, may be defended by a Member State not only on the basis of the six grounds listed in Art 36 TFEU, but also on the basis of open-ended mandatory requirements, otherwise know as the "rule of reason" (*Cassis de Dijon*);
(iii) a restriction on a selling arrangement that is applied to all relevant traders within a Member State and affects in the same manner, in law and in fact, the marketing of domestic products and those imported from another Member State will not constitute

[24] Joined Cases C-267/91 and C-268/91 *Keck and Mithouard* [1993] ECR I-6097.
[25] Case C-110/05 *Commission v Italy (Italian Trailers)* [2009] ECR I-519.
[26] Case C-142/05 *Mickelsson and Roos* [2009] ECR I-4273.

an MEQR. There is a presumption, therefore, that selling arrangements are lawful and are not caught by Art 34 TFEU, unless these two conditions are not fulfilled. As a result, the onus is on the person seeking to challenge such a restriction to demonstrate that one of these two conditions is not fulfilled. If this is successfully done, the onus will then shift onto the Member State to justify the measure on the basis of one of the six Art 36 TFEU grounds or a mandatory requirement (*Keck and Mithouard*);

(iv) in some cases, particularly those concerning restrictions on the use to which a product can be put, the Court of Justice has not looked for a discriminatory effect on imports but rather has assessed whether the measure hinders, impedes or imposes an obstacle to goods seeking to access the market of another Member State (*Italian Trailers; Mickelsson and Roos*). There remains a degree of uncertainty, and differing views, as to whether a unified market access test has come to replace *Keck*, or whether the market access test ought to be regarded as a third category, residual to those of product requirements and selling arrangements.

D. The *Dassonville* Formula

[19–31] The first landmark case interpreting Art 34 TFEU is that of *Dassonville*, delivered in 1974.[27] Under Belgian law, it was a criminal offence to import or sell any spirit that bore a designation of origin adopted by the Belgian Government, such as "Scotch whisky", unless the spirits were accompanied by a certificate of origin certifying the right to bear such a designation. At the time, the UK had not yet joined the EEC and so was a third country outside of the Customs Union. Mr Dassonville imported into Belgium bottles of "Johnnie Walker" Scotch whisky from France where, having complied with the relevant customs requirements upon import from the UK, they were in free circulation (the certificate of origin having then been removed from the goods). In France, such goods were not required to display a certificate of origin, and Mr Dassonville did not obtain a certificate of origin from the UK authorities. As a result, a prosecution was brought alleging a violation of the Belgian criminal law.

[19–32] As part of his defence, Mr Dassonville argued that the Belgian requirement to obtain a certificate of origin was contrary to Art 34 in that it rendered impossible imports into Belgium from any country other than that in which the goods originate, "in the case where the country concerned has no rules similar to those operating in Belgium with regard to certificates of origin. These rules involve a strict walling-off of markets or, at the very least, discrimination or a disguised restriction on trade between Member States".[28] In supporting the Belgian law, the UK argued that the concept of an MEQR did not cover measures that were only potentially liable to have an effect on trade. In contrast, in what became known as the *Dassonville* formula, the Court of Justice established that:

> All trading rules enacted by Member States which are capable of hindering, directly or indirectly, actually or potentially, intra-community trade are to be considered as measures having an effect equivalent to quantitative restrictions.[29]

[19–33] In many respects, this single sentence that comprises the *Dassonville* formula is of greater significance than the outcome of the case itself, which turned on the fact

---

27 Case 8/74 *Procureur du Roi v Dassonville* [1974] ECR 837.

28 *ibid*, 840.

29 *ibid*, 852.

that the Belgian law made it more difficult to import goods from an EU Member State in which they were in free circulation, having been imported from their country of manufacture, than to import them directly from their country of manufacture. It was this fact that led the Court to hold that the Belgian law prohibiting the sale of goods bearing a designation of origin without a certificate of origin amounted to an MEQR prohibited by the Treaty. It is somewhat ironic, therefore, that while the *Dassonville* formula is seen as supporting an interpretation of Art 34 that places overall importance on whether a measure *hinders market access* in a general sense, rather than whether it specifically *discriminates against imports*, the particular restriction at issue in the judgment did effectively discriminate as between direct imports and imports from a Member State in which the goods were in free circulation having been already imported from another Member State. Nevertheless, the fact that the Court chose not to expressly categorise the problem as one of discrimination, but rather as a hindrance to intra-community trade in a broader sense, opened the door to a line of jurisprudence that has now eventually culminated in a general market access approach. As Paul Craig and Gráinne de Búrca have described, by focusing on the effect of a restriction, rather than on requiring it to have a discriminatory intent, the *Dassonville* formula "sowed the seeds which bore fruit" in *Cassis de Dijon*.[30]

[19–34] As a consequence of the *Dassonville* formula's broad nature, it became relatively easy for apparently internal situations to be covered by EU rules on the free movement of goods, on the basis that there was a potential effect on trade with other Member States, even if the facts of a particular case did not directly involve imports or exports.[31] Indeed, the Court of Justice has elaborated on the formula by noting that the "mere fact that an importer might be dissuaded from introducing or marketing the products in question in the Member State concerned constitutes a restriction on the free movement of goods for the importer".[32] As Gareth Davies has pointed out, the breadth of the *Dassonville* formula can, therefore, be seen as the Court extending the reach of its jurisdiction:

> By making Article 34 broad, the Court is granting itself equally broad powers to supervise national measures via the preliminary reference procedure, even if in some cases it will find those measures compatible with the Treaty [by virtue of the exceptions in Article 36 or mandatory requirements / the rule reason]. This was particularly important in a time where the internal market was in its infancy and national protectionist traditions were well-entrenched, while national judges were still often unfamiliar with EU law.[33]

[19–35] A good modern example of the breadth of the *Dassonville* formula can be seen in the case of *Alfa Vita*, which concerned a Greek law that required bakeries to hold a licence, a requirement for which was the maintenance of specified equipment and a minimum space for baking.[34] Certain supermarkets operating in Greece sold "bake-off" bread products without holding a bakery licence and were ordered to cease this activity. The bake-off products comprised of ready-made doughs that required re-heating and were then sold as finished baked goods. The supermarkets would not have been entitled to a bakery licence as they did not meet the necessary equipment

---

30 Paul Craig and Gráinne de Búrca, *EU Law* (6th ed, Oxford University Press, 2015) 668.

31 See Case C-321/94 *Pistre* [1997] ECR I-2343.

32 Case C-171/11 *Fra.bo v DVGW* EU:C:2012:453, 12 July 2013, para 22.

33 Damian Chalmers, Gareth Davies and Giorgio Monti, *European Union Law* (3rd ed, Cambridge University Press 2014) 758.

34 Joined Cases C-158/04 and C-159/04 *Alfa Vita* [2006] ECR I-8135.

and space requirements. A preliminary reference asked whether the requirement for a bakery licence to sell bake-off products constituted an MEQR contrary to Art 34. Given the nature of the alleged restriction, the reference also asked whether there was a link to EU law given that the requirement for a licence applied equally to domestically produced bake-off products as to imported products.

[19–36] What is striking about the Court's approach is that, not only does it decide to address the questions posed together, but it does not engage in any detailed analysis or reasoning as to how the restriction hinders the importation of goods, but rather treats it as self-evident that the restriction will have this effect. According to the Court:

> It is common ground that the principal characteristic of "bake-off" products is that they are delivered at sales outlets after the main stages of preparation of those products have been completed. At those sales outlets, only a brief thawing and reheating or final baking are carried out. In those circumstances, requiring vendors of "bake-off" products to comply with all of the requirements imposed on traditional bakeries, including, in particular, the requirement of having a flour store, an area for kneading equipment and a solid-fuel store, does not take the specific nature of those products into account and entails additional costs, thereby making the marketing of those products more difficult. That legislation therefore constitutes a barrier to imports ...[35]

[19–37] As has already been seen in the Section C above, although the *Dassonville* formula refers to "all *trading rules enacted* by Member States", the requirement for an MEQR to amount to a "trading rule" or to have been "enacted" by a Member State has been dropped by the Court, which now applies the formula "in a very pragmatic and non-theoretical way".[36]

E. Product Requirements

(i) Directive 70/50

[19–38] While the *Dassonville* formula continues to carry great weight, it is important to remember that the application of the formula has evolved over time. To understand its historical significance, it is necessary to recall the particular context in which the judgment was delivered in 1974. In this regard, it is useful to bear in mind that in 1970, the Commission's view on MEQRs was set out in Directive 70/50 on the abolition of measures which have an effect equivalent to quantitative restrictions on imports.[37] Although the Directive only applied for a transitional period during which the rules on the free movement of goods were to be introduced, it continues to provide guidance as to the meaning of MEQRs.

[19–39] Significantly, Directive 70/50 drew a distinction between "equally" or "indistinctly" applicable measures that applied to both imports and domestic goods, on the one hand, and "distinctly" applicable measures that applied to imported goods only, on the other. According to the Directive, distinctly applicable measures included:

---

35 *ibid*, 8163.

36 Damian Chalmers, Gareth Davies and Giorgio Monti, *European Union Law* (3rd ed, Cambridge University Press, 2014) 760.

37 [1970] OJ L13/29.

> those which make access of imported products to the domestic market, at any marketing stage, subject to a condition which is not laid down for domestic products or to a condition differing from that laid down for domestic products, and more difficult to satisfy, so that a burden is thus placed on imported products only … [and] those which, at any marketing stage, grant to domestic products a preference, other than an aid, to which conditions may or may not be attached, and where such measures totally or partially preclude the disposal of imported products.[38]

[19–40] In contrast, indistinctly applicable measures tend to concern attributes of the goods themselves, or "product requirements", such as the shape, size, weight, composition, labelling, packaging or presentation of a product.

[19–41] The approach taken by the Directive might be categorised as one in which distinctly applicable measures are viewed as more offending than indistinctly applicable measures. Whereas distinctly applicable measures "hinder imports which could otherwise take place, and thus have an effect equivalent to quantitative restrictions on imports", in contrast, the effect on the free movement of goods of measures which relate to the marketing of products and which apply equally to domestic and imported products "*are not as a general rule* equivalent to those of quantitative restrictions, since such effects are normally inherent in the disparities between rules applied by Member States in this respect".[39]

[19–42] Put simply, because the Directive views indistinctly applicable measures as significantly less bad than distinctly applicable ones, it differentiates in its approach to each. Accordingly, whereas Art 2 of the Directive required Member States to abolish distinctly applicable measures that hindered imports that could otherwise take place, the requirement to abolish indistinctly applicable measures, under Art 3, was limited only to circumstances where the "restrictive effect of such measures on the free movement of goods exceeds the effects intrinsic to trade rules". Such excessive effect was considered to arise, in particular, where the "restrictive effects on the free movement of goods are out of proportion to their purpose" or the "same objective can be attained by other means which are less of a hindrance to trade".

[19–43] Although the Court's judgment in *Dassonville* did not distinguish between distinctly and indistinctly applicable measures, it has been suggested that it should be understood as a "judicial complement" to Directive 70/50, particularly given that the measure at issue in that case was an international trading rule.[40] In this regard, it is important to remember that although the requirement has subsequently been dropped, such that the *Dassonville* formula now applies to all measures, as originally enunciated the formula was aimed at governing "all trading rules", a category did not encompass indistinctly applicable measures such as product requirements. Seen in this way, notwithstanding the very broad wording of the *Dassonville* formula itself, the judgment in its originally intended form ought to be regarded as confined to distinctly applicable trading rules, and not to extend to indistinctly applicable rules such as rules governing product requirements.

---

38 Recitals 6 and 7.

39 Recitals 8 and 9, emphasis added.

40 Robert Schütze, *European Union Law* (Cambridge University Press, 2015) 502.

(ii) Cassis de Dijon

[19–44] The argument that an indistinctly applicable product requirement could amount to an MEQR was considered by the Court of Justice in the landmark 1979 case *Cassis de Dijon*.[41] This, amongst the Court's most well-known and important judgments, concerned a German law that governed the sale of alcohol, according to which a fruit liqueur was required to have a minimum alcohol content of 25 per cent in order to be sold as a liqueur. As the law in France was satisfied by a lower minimum alcohol content, the German law operated so as to prevent the sale in Germany of fruit liqueur lawfully sold in France which had an alcohol content of less than 25 per cent. Here, it is useful to think of France as the "home state" or country of origin where the product is manufactured, and Germany as the "host state" or country of destination where the product is being sold and consumed.

[19–45] Although the Commission had submitted a proposal for a regulation on alcohol to the Council in 1976, it had not yet been approved by the Council and so there was no applicable harmonisation measure. In response to the claim that the minimum alcohol requirement amounted to an MEQR, Germany argued:

> Until such time as the national rules relating to manufacture and marketing have been harmonised, Article [34] ... is to be applied only in so far as those provisions lead to discrimination against imported goods in relation to domestic goods. Measures which are applicable without distinction to domestic products and imported products do not, according to Directive No 70/50, have effects equivalent to those of quantitative restrictions and do not therefore, in principle, fall within the scope of Article [34]. The conditions regarding minimum quantities in force in [Germany] quite clearly do not involve different treatment for imported goods and there can therefore be no question of the application of Article [34].[42]

[19–46] The Court's judgment developed two crucially important principles of EU law: "mandatory requirements" and "mutual recognition". While the two principles will be presented here in the sequence in which they appear in the judgment, it is generally recognised that it is more intuitive to think of mutual recognition as the default principle, and so should be considered first, to which mandatory requirements can be seen as a form of exception, and therefore coming second.

[19–47] The Court's judgment first confirms that, in the absence of common rules relating to the production and marketing of a product, it is for the Member States to regulate all matters relating to the production and marketing of that product on their own territory. According to the Court, obstacles to the free movement of goods within the EU resulting from disparities between national laws relating to the marketing of products (ie indistinctly applicable measures) must be accepted "in so far as those provisions may be recognised as being necessary in order to satisfy *mandatory requirements* relating in particular to the effectiveness of fiscal supervision, the protection of public health, the fairness of commercial transactions and the defence of the consumer".[43] This confirmation can be seen as building on Art 3 of Directive 70/50, albeit that the Court has introduced the entirely new concept of "mandatory requirements" (otherwise known as the "rule of reason") as a framework within which Member States can seek

---

[41] Case 120/78 *Cassis de Dijon* [1979] ECR 649.

[42] *ibid*, 655.

[43] *ibid*, 662, emphasis added.

to justify an indistinctly applicable MEQR. Further reflecting Art 3 of the Directive, in *Rau* the Court subsequently confirmed that in order to be justified by a mandatory requirement, an indistinctly applicable MEQR must also be proportionate to the objective to be achieved, in the sense of not going beyond what is required in order to achieve that objective.[44]

[19–48] The judgment in *Cassis de Dijon* then assessed the two mandatory requirements put forward by Germany – public health and the protection of consumers against unfair commercial practices – and found both to be inadequate to justify the restriction. Unlike the list of six grounds set out in Art 36 TFEU, the concept of mandatory requirements is open-ended, with the four objectives identified by the Court essentially forming a non-exhaustive or illustrative list. On the other hand, mandatory requirements may only be relied upon in respect of indistinctly applicable measures; in order to justify a directly discriminatory measure, a Member State may only have recourse to the six grounds listed in Art 36.

[19–49] Secondly, and just as important as the concept of mandatory requirements, the Court then proceeded to establish that, as a matter of principle: "there is no valid reason why, provided that they have been lawfully produced and marketed in one of the Member States, [a good] should not be introduced into any other Member State".[45] Although the Court does not use the term in its judgment, this fundamental principle is known as the "principle of mutual recognition".[46]

[19–50] Having started out extolling the freedom of Member States, in the absence of harmonising measures, to regulate goods sold on their territory according to mandatory requirements, the Court shifts radically in the opposite direction in order to establish as the fundamental starting point when considering indistinctly applicable measures a principle of equivalence, or mutual recognition. According to this principle, each host state must accept as adequate the regulation imposed on manufacturers by their home state. In this case, this meant that Germany could no longer subject the sale of fruit liqueurs within its territory to a national rule that required a minimum alcohol content. Rather, Germany had to allow the sale of liqueurs with a lower alcohol content, since such products were lawfully sold in another Member State. In terms of progressing towards the creation of a Single Market, the significant contribution of the judgment is clear.

[19–51] It can be seen that the two new principles introduced by *Cassis de Dijon* – mutual recognition and mandatory requirements – operate in a combined way so as to balance the interests of a host state, which will wish to legislate in order to control what is sold on its territory and consumed by its citizens, and those of a home state, which will wish to see its exporters free to sell their products throughout the EU. By establishing mutual recognition as the default position, which a host state may seek to rebut by relying on a mandatory requirement, the judgment can be said to replace regulation by both a home state and a host state with regulation by the home state alone, subject to exceptional measures that will require justification in accordance with the rule

---

44 Case 261/81 *Rau* [1982] ECR 3961.

45 Case 120/78 *Cassis de Dijon* [1979] ECR 649, 664.

46 See Jacques Pelkmans, "Mutual Recognition in Goods: On Promises and Disillusions" (2007) 14 *Journal of European Public Policy* 699; Christine Janssens, *The Principle of Mutual Recognition in EU Law* (Oxford University Press, 2013).

of reason. In this way, the judgment reverses the presumption of legality of indistinctly applicable measures originally found in Art 3 of Directive 70/50. As Robert Schütze has described, the judgment implicitly overruled

> the substantive presumption that trade restrictions flowing from disparities between equally applicable product requirements would only *exceptionally* qualify as [MEQRs]. From now on, a different logic applied: *unless* there are mandatory requirements in the general interest, the host State is *not* entitled to impose its domestic product standards on imported goods.[47]

[19–52] In other words, the principle of mutual recognition "turns the presumption of legality for product requirements – established by Directive 70/50 – into a presumption of illegality".[48] On the other hand, the fact that a host state can seek to rely on mandatory requirements where it considers that an important public interest is at stake operates so as to limit what might otherwise turn into a "regulatory race to the bottom" – a scenario whereby manufacturers might choose to make their product in whichever Member State has the least onerous rules, thereby giving them a competitive advantage.

[19–53] The many cases in which the Court of Justice has had to consider whether an indistinctly applicable measure is prohibited by Art 34 TFEU can be seen as essentially involving a balancing exercise between the principle of mutual recognition, guaranteeing free movement, and an attempt by a Member State to rely on a mandatory requirement in order to justify a certain restriction on the right to free movement in order to protect a particular public interest. As will be seen in Chapter 20, very often, although an MEQR will be considered, in principle, to be capable of being justified by a mandatory requirement, the Member State falls short in satisfying the Court that the restriction is proportionate, in the sense of being the least restrictive means of achieving the stated public interest objective.

(iii) Equal Burden v Dual Burden

[19–54] Two good examples of indistinctly applicable product requirements amounting to MEQRs are found in *Rau* and *Mars*. In *Rau*, the Court of Justice considered a Belgian law that required all margarine products be sold in a cube shape.[49] This was to enable consumers to easily distinguish margarine products from butter, which were traditionally sold in a different shape. Belgium argued that, whereas the restriction at issue in *Cassis de Dijon* prevented the sale of a product altogether if it did not meet the minimum alcohol content level, its requirement in relation to margarine only necessitated a change to be made to the external presentation of the product. The Court rejected this argument, stating that:

> Although the requirement that a particular form of packaging must also be used for imported products is not an absolute barrier to the importation into the Member State concerned of products originating in other Member States, nevertheless it is of such a nature as to render the marketing of those products more difficult or more expensive either by barring them from certain channels of distribution or owing to the additional costs

[47] Robert Schütze, *European Union Law* (Cambridge University Press, 2015) 503.

[48] *ibid.*

[49] Case 261/81 *Rau* [1982] ECR 3961.

brought about by the necessity to package the products in question in special packs which comply with the requirements in force on the market of their destination.[50]

[19–55] In *Mars*, the restriction at issue was a German law on unfair competition that prohibited a "plus 10%" marking on products that exceeded 10 per cent of the surface area of the product, lest consumers be led to believe that the size of the marking corresponded to the increase in the size of the product.[51] Mars manufactured its chocolate bars in France and exported them throughout the EU, including Germany. As part of an EU-wide marketing campaign, a "plus 10%" marking had been placed on the bars. The Court held the restriction to be an MEQR since,

> Although it applies to all products without distinction, a prohibition ... which relates to the marketing in a Member State of products bearing the same publicity markings as those lawfully used in other Member States, is by nature such to hinder intra-Community trade. It may compel the importer to adjust the presentation of his products according to the place where they are to be marketed and consequently to incur additional packaging and advertising costs.[52]

[19–56] Both of these quotations from *Rau* and *Mars* address what is often termed the "dual burden" that is imposed by certain indistinctly applicable measures. This is the idea that such national measures impose an additional burden on importers, as compared with domestic producers. Importers, having already complied with the rules of their home state, are required to modify their products in order to comply with the different rules of each host state into which they import. In contrast, measures of "equal burden" might limit the sale of a product, but do not affect imports any more than they do domestic products; in other words, "both the application of the rules *and* the consequential burden [is] felt equally" by imports and by domestic goods.[53] An example of an equal burden measure might be a minimum age requirement for the purchase of a certain good.

[19–57] At a theoretical level, there are different views as to how to conceptualise the Court's approach to indistinctly applicable measures. For some, the imposition of a dual burden on importers is a form of indirect discrimination that serves to protect domestic producers, with the result that it can be said that the prohibition in Art 34 TFEU is, as a whole, based on a premise of discriminatory action by a Member State against imports. According to this view:

> [g]oods which have been produced in one Member State under a given legal regime have to submit themselves to a different set of regulations, those of the State of importation, in order to be marketable in that State. Trading rules therefore have a disparate impact on imported goods and domestic goods, which results in additional costs for the imported goods, such as repackaging or reprocessing costs, that are not borne by domestic goods. This disparate impact of trading rules means that the mere imposition of national requirements on goods imported from other Member States always constitutes indirect discrimination.[54]

---

[50] *ibid*, 3972–3973.

[51] Case C-470/93 *Mars* [1995] ECR I-1923.

[52] *ibid*, 1941.

[53] Stephen Weatherill, *Cases and Materials on EU Law* (10th ed, Oxford University Press, 2012) 326.

[54] Nicolas Bernard, "Discrimination and Free Movement in EC Law" (1996) 45 *International and Comparative Law Quarterly* 82, 92. See also Niamh Nic Shuibhne, "The Free Movement of Goods and Article 28 EC: An Evolving Framework" (2002) 27 *European Law Review* 408.

[19–58] For others, however, the effect of *Cassis de Dijon* was that the discrimination rationale for identifying MEQRs became "sidelined" or "disappeared".[55] This was particularly the case during the decade prior to 1993 when the Court was willing to regard not only dual burden measures, but also equal burden measures, as being caught by Art 34. Equal burden measures often take the form of what are termed "market circumstances rules", which have been described as rules that govern the who, how, when and where of the sale and marketing of goods.[56]

[19–59] For example, in *Cinéthèque*, a French law aimed at supporting film production by requiring one year to pass before a film could be released on video was held to constitute an MEQR caught by Art 34, albeit that it was found to be justified by a mandatory requirement.[57] While the Court acknowledged that the measure was not discriminatory, nor did it aim to favour national film production over that of other Member States, nevertheless, the "application of such a system may create barriers to intra-Community trade in video-cassettes because of the disparities between the systems operated in the different Member States and between the conditions for the release of cinematographic works in the cinemas of those States".[58]

[19–60] A key issue, therefore, became whether indistinctly applicable measures, and in particular equal burden measures such as market circumstances rules

> should be held to fall within Article 34, subject to a possible justification, or whether they should be deemed to be outside Article 34 altogether. The result may be the same, in that the rule may be held lawful. This choice is nonetheless important. If these rules are within Article 34 they are *prima facie* unlawful, and the burden is on those seeking to uphold the rule to show the objective justification.[59]

[19–61] As illustrated by a series of UK cases involving Sunday trading rules, in practice it often proved difficult for national courts to apply mandatory requirements to a regulatory measure imposed by the state, especially when it came to assessing the measure's proportionality in light of the overriding public interest at stake. In *Torfaen Borough Council v B&Q* a preliminary reference asked whether a ban on retailers opening on a Sunday, reducing B&Q's total sales – approximately 10 per cent of which were goods imported from other Member States – amounted to an MEQR.[60] The Borough Council denied that the ban was an MEQR on the ground that it applied to domestic and imported products alike and did not put imported products at any disadvantage. The Court of Justice, following *Cinéthèque*, considered the restriction an MEQR, notwithstanding that the ban did not make the marketing of imported products more difficult than the marketing of domestic products. Regarding the application of the rule of reason, the Court noted that Sunday trading rules

> reflect certain political and economic choices in so far as their purpose is to ensure that working and non-working hours are so arranged as to accord with national or regional

55 Robert Schütze, *European Union Law* (Cambridge University Press, 2015) 503; Lorna Woods and Philippa Watson, *EU Law* (Oxford University Press, 2014) 392.

56 Kamiel Mortelmans, "Article 30 of the EEC Treaty and Legislation Relating to Market Circumstances: Time to Consider a New Definition" (1991) 28 *Common Market Law Review* 115.

57 Joined Cases 60/84 and 61/84 *Cinéthèque* [1985] ECR 2605.

58 *ibid*, 2626.

59 Paul Craig and Gráinne de Búrca, *EU Law* (6th ed, Oxford University Press, 2015) 679.

60 Case 145/88 *Torfaen Borough Council v B&Q* [1989] ECR 3851.

> socio-cultural characteristics, and that, in the present state of Community law, is a matter for the Member States. … [I]t is necessary to ascertain whether the effects of such national rules exceed what is necessary to achieve the aim in view. … The question whether the effects of specific national rules do in fact remain within that limit is a question of fact to be determined by the national court.[61]

[19–62] In a series of cases, different UK courts reached contrasting conclusions as to whether Sunday trading restrictions were proportionate to the aim to be achieved. Whereas one judgment, taking the "socio-cultural characteristic" in question to be the protection of workers who did not wish to work on Sunday, considered the restriction to be disproportionate, another upheld the measure as proportionate on the basis that its aim was to preserve the traditional character of the British Sunday. Ultimately, in a further preliminary reference from the UK, the Court of Justice confirmed that Sunday trading restrictions were capable of being justified by the rule of reason and so were not prohibited by Art 34.[62]

F. Selling Arrangements

[19–63] As exemplified by the Sunday trading cases, the expansive breadth of the *Cassis de Dijon* approach to MEQRs was having the effect of encouraging challenges to all manner of national rules that could be said, in some way or another, to limit the marketing of products. From the perspective of the Court's own efficacy, this raised certain questions. Was it worthwhile to encourage liberal recourse to legal challenges in which, at the first hurdle, a national rule may easily be held to be caught by Art 34, only for it to go on to have a reasonable likelihood of being justified, in the end, by a mandatory requirement? As Gareth Davies describes, "[a]ll that was happening was that many creative cases were being brought, but they were not being won. Such a broad reading of the Treaty was not therefore opening up the internal market or increasing trade. It was just increasing work for the Court".[63] In addition, Member States were naturally uncomfortable with their regulation of social matters, such as Sunday trading hours, being assessed by the Court of Justice on the basis of a tangential impact on the free movement of goods.

[19–64] Recognising that its case law in the 1980s and early 1990s had gone too far, in the 1993 case of *Keck and Mithouard* the Court took the unprecedented step of acknowledging that, in view of the increasing tendency to invoke Art 34 as a means of challenging any rules that limited commercial freedom even where such rules were not aimed at products from other Member States, it was necessary for the Court to re-examine and clarify its case-law on the matter.[64]

---

[61] *ibid*, 3889.

[62] Case C-169/91 *Stoke-on-Trent City Council v B&Q* [1992] ECR I-6635.

[63] Damian Chalmers, Gareth Davies and Giorgio Monti, *European Union Law* (3rd ed, Cambridge University Press, 2014) 786.

[64] Joined Cases C-267/91 and C-268/91 *Keck and Mithouard* [1993] ECR I-6097, 6131. See Eyad Maher Dabbah, "The Dilemma of *Keck*: The Nature of the Ruling and the Practical Implications of the Judgment" (1999) 8 *Irish Journal of European Law* 84; Imelda Higgins, "The Free and Not So Free Movement of Goods Since *Keck*" (1997) 6 *Irish Journal of European Law* 166; Noel Travers, "The *Keck* Legacy: The Scope of Article 30 Revisited" (1995) 13 *Irish Law Times* 39; Noel Travers, "Regulating Community Restrictions on Trade: The Scope of Article 30 EC Revisited" (1994) 12 *Irish Law Times* 57; Damian Chalmers, "Repackaging the Internal Market – The Ramifications of

[19–65] In re-examining the approach in *Cassis de Dijon*, the judges of the Court of Justice had a wealth of academic commentary, much of it critical, to draw upon.[65] From this, a number of different approaches could be identified. For example, the Court might have:

- drawn a clear line between distinctly and indistinctly applicable measures, as originally found in Directive 70/50;
- differentiated between measures that imposed a dual burden on manufacturers and those that imposed an equal burden;
- distinguished between product requirement rules that regulated the characteristics of a good itself and market circumstances rules that regulated the conditions under which goods were sold; or
- within the category of market circumstances rules, distinguished between rules relating to *static* conditions of sale and rules relating to *dynamic* conditions of sale. Rules governing the general conditions of when, where and by whom goods may be sold, such as Sunday-trading rules, are said to relate to static conditions of sale. In contrast, rules governing the way in which a particular product may be marketed, such as through a particular promotional technique or form of advertising, relate to dynamic conditions of sale. It is considered that the dividing line between product requirements and market circumstances rules is more blurred when dealing with dynamic conditions of sale concerning a particular product, than with static conditions of sale, which tend to be of a more general and fixed nature.

(i) The Decision in *Keck*

[19–66] In *Keck*, the Court of Justice chose to draw a clear distinction between "product requirements" relating to the characteristics of a good itself, and which would continue to be governed by *Cassis de Dijon*, and what it termed "certain selling arrangements", which regulated the manner in which a good was sold and to which a new test would now be applied. Provided that certain prescribed conditions were fulfilled, this new test served to take selling arrangements outside the scope of Art 34 altogether.

[19–67] In its judgment, the Court was required to assess a French law that prohibited retailers from selling goods at a loss. Like Sunday trading rules, while a prohibition on "loss-leaders" might reduce the overall volume of goods sold, and by implication reduce imports, it is an equal burden measure that does not relate to goods themselves, but the circumstances in which they can be sold. Wishing to narrow the definition of MEQRs, and rein in the expansive approach taken in cases like *Cinéthèque* and *Torfaen v B&Q,* the Court set out the following rationale for departing from its earlier position and for creating a special rule for "certain selling arrangements":

> 12. National legislation imposing a general prohibition on resale at a loss is not designed to regulate trade in goods between Member States.

---

the *Keck* Judgment" (1994) 19 *European Law Review* 385; Sarah Moore, "Quantitative Restrictions and Measures Having Equivalent Effect – Re-visiting the Limits of Article 30 EEC" (1994) 19 *European Law Review* 195; Miguel Poiares Maduro, "*Keck*: The End? The Beginning of the End? Or Just the End of the Beginning?" (1994) 3 *Irish Journal of European Law* 30; Norbert Reich, "The 'November Revolution' of the European Court of Justice: *Keck*, *Meng* and *Audi* Revisited" (1994) 31 *Common Market Law Review* 459.

[65] For example, Eric L White, "In Search of the Limits of Article 30 of the EEC Treaty" (1989) 26 *Common Market Law Review* 235.

13. Such legislation may, admittedly, restrict the volume of sales, and hence the volume of sales of products from other Member States, in so far as it deprives traders of a method of sales promotion. But the question remains whether such a possibility is sufficient to characterise the legislation in question as a measure having equivalent effect to a quantitative restriction on imports.

14. In view of the increasing tendency of traders to invoke Article [34] of the Treaty as a means of challenging any rules whose effect is to limit their commercial freedom even where such rules are not aimed at products from other Member States, the Court considers it necessary to re-examine and clarify its case-law on this matter.

15. It is established by the case-law beginning with *Cassis de Dijon* … that, in the absence of harmonisation of legislation, obstacles to free movement of goods which are the consequence of applying, to goods coming from other Member States where they are lawfully manufactured and marketed, rules that lay down requirements to be met by such goods (such as those relating to designation, form, size, weight, composition, presentation, labelling, packaging) constitute measures of equivalent effect prohibited by Article [34]. This is so even if those rules apply without distinction to all products unless their application can be justified by a public-interest objective taking precedence over the free movement of goods.

16. By contrast, contrary to what has previously been decided, the application to products from other Member States of national provisions restricting or prohibiting certain selling arrangements is not such as to hinder directly or indirectly, actually or potentially, trade between Member States within the meaning of the *Dassonville* judgment …, so long as those provisions apply to all relevant traders operating within the national territory and so long as they affect in the same manner, in law and in fact, the marketing of domestic products and of those from other Member States.

17. Provided that those conditions are fulfilled, the application of such rules to the sale of products from another Member State meeting the requirements laid down by that State is not by nature such as to prevent their access to the market or to impede access any more than it impedes the access of domestic products. Such rules therefore fall outside the scope of Article [34] of the Treaty.[66]

[19–68] The judgment's two key elements can be summarised as the "paragraph 16 conditions" and the "paragraph 17 rationale". As set out in paragraph 16, the effect of the judgment is to distinguish certain national restrictions on "selling arrangements" from other restrictions such as product requirements that come within the *Dassonville* formula and the approach set out in *Cassis de Dijon*. From now on, national measures relating to selling arrangements are a special case, and are not to be regarded as MEQRs falling within Article 34, provided that the restriction: (i) applies to all relevant traders within the Member State and (ii) affects in the same manner, both as a matter of law and as a matter of fact, the marketing of domestic products and those from other Member States ("the paragraph 16 conditions").

[19–69] This means that, whereas there is a presumption in respect of product requirements that they do fall within Art 34 and so are unlawful unless a Member State can meet the burden of defending them, the presumption in respect of selling arrangements is the opposite. Selling arrangements are presumed to fall outside Art 34 and to be lawful, unless a challenge to the measure can demonstrate that either of the two conditions in paragraph 16 is not met.

66 Joined Cases C-267/91 and C-268/91 *Keck and Mithouard* [1993] ECR I-6097, 6130–6131.

[19–70] In practical terms, the significance of distinguishing restrictions governing selling arrangements from product requirements is that it determines on whom the onus is placed whenever a measure is challenged. In respect of product requirements, it is the Member State that is faced with the onus of defending the measure on the basis of an Art 36 ground or a mandatory requirement. In respect of selling arrangements, it is the challenger of a measure who must demonstrate precisely how either of the two paragraph 16 conditions is not met. In practice, this usually means demonstrating how, *as a matter of fact*, the measure affects imports more than it does domestic goods.

[19–71] Another way of thinking about this is to observe that, whereas *Cassis de Dijon* may be said to have done away with the need for a discriminatory effect in respect of product requirements, *Keck* reintroduces such a requirement for restrictions on selling arrangements.

[19–72] As the second key element of the judgment, paragraph 17 of *Keck* is interesting for the manner in which it provides an explicit rationale for the test set out in paragraph 16. Where a selling arrangement rule fulfils the two paragraph 16 conditions, the reason why it then falls outside Art 34 is because its application to imported products is "not by nature such as to prevent their access to the market" nor does it "impede access any more than it impedes the access of domestic products". Whereas the second limb of this rationale – that such a rule is non-discriminatory – clearly follows from the paragraph 16 conditions, the first does not appear to follow directly, namely that the rule does not *prevent access* to the market, in a more straightforward sense. As discussed in the following section, in subsequent cases the Court has on occasion relied on this "market access" test as a standalone criteria by which to judge certain measures that do not fall squarely within the idea of a selling arrangement.

(ii) Applying the Paragraph 16 Conditions

[19–73] In addition to national rules regulating the opening hours of retailers, or the maximum or minimum prices at which goods can be sold, rules dictating where goods can be sold have also been held to be a "selling arrangement" falling outside Art 34. In the *Baby Milk* case, a law requiring that processed milk for infants be sold only in pharmacies was found to be a selling arrangement that fulfilled the paragraph 16 conditions and so fell outside of Art 34.[67] In contrast, however, in both *DocMorris* and *Ker-Optika*, German and Hungarian rules requiring medicines and contact lenses to be sold in pharmacies or specialist medical accessory shops, thereby prohibiting their sale via the internet, were held, as a matter of fact, not to affect in the same manner imports and domestic products.[68] In so deciding, the Court of Justice focused on examining whether, as a matter of fact, the rules affected imports to a greater extent than domestic goods:

> A prohibition such as that at issue in the main proceedings is more of an obstacle to pharmacies outside Germany than to those within it. Although there is little doubt that as a result of the prohibition, pharmacies in Germany cannot use the extra or alternative method of gaining access to the German market consisting of end consumers of medicinal products, they are still able to sell the products in their dispensaries. However, for pharmacies not established in Germany, the internet provides a more significant way to

[67] Case C-391/92 *Commission v Greece (Baby Milk)* [1995] ECR I-1621.

[68] Case C-322/01 *DocMorris* [2003] ECR I-14887; Case C-108/09, *Ker-Optika* [2010] ECR I-12213.

gain direct access to the German market. A prohibition which has a greater impact on pharmacies established outside German territory could impede access to the market for products from other Member States more than it impedes access for domestic products.

Accordingly, the prohibition does not affect the sale of domestic medicines in the same way as it affects the sale of those coming from other Member States.[69]

[19–74] As the restrictions were not selling arrangements within the meaning of *Keck*, they were MEQRs that, in order to be lawful, required justification by Germany and Hungary on the basis of an Art 36 ground or a mandatory requirement. In a more recent case involving DocMorris, *DPV*, Germany had subsequently permitted the sale of prescription drugs by mail order, but continued to apply a system of fixed sales prices for such medicines.[70] Operating from the Netherlands, DocMorris ran a bonus system whereby rewards were given on purchases made, but was ordered to stop applying the scheme to Germany as it contravened the fixed-prices rule. In considering whether the German prohibition was an MEQR, the Court of Justice accepted the argument that the fixed-prices rule had a greater impact on pharmacies established in other Member States, and so it impeded market access for importers more than it did for domestic pharmacies. According to the Court:

traditional pharmacies are, in principle, better placed than mail-order pharmacies to provide patients with individually-tailored advice given by the staff of the dispensary and to ensure a supply of medicinal products in cases of emergency. In so far as mail-order pharmacies cannot, given the limited services that they offer, adequately replace such services, it must be held that price competition is capable of providing a more important factor of competition for mail-order pharmacies than for traditional pharmacies, since price competition lays the basis for their potential to access the German market directly and to continue to be competitive in it.

Consequently, and in so far as sales by mail order constitute a more important means of accessing the German market directly for pharmacies established in Member States other than Germany ... the national legislation at issue in the main proceedings does not affect the sale of national medicinal products in the same way as it affects the sale of medicinal products originating in other Member States.[71]

[19–75] Similarly, in *Heimdienst*, the Court was required to consider whether an Austrian rule that bakers, butchers and grocers could only carry out door-to-door sales rounds in the administrative district where they had a permanent establishment, or districts adjacent thereto, amounted to a rule governing a selling arrangement such as to fall outside Art 34. While, prima facie, the rule related to selling arrangements for certain goods, the rule failed to fulfil the paragraph 16 conditions in that it did not affect in the same manner the marketing of domestic products and that of products from other Member States:

Such legislation imposes an obligation on bakers, butchers and grocers who already have a permanent establishment in another Member State and who wish to sell their goods on rounds in a particular [Austrian] administrative district … to set up or purchase another permanent establishment in that administrative district or in an adjacent municipality, whilst local economic operators already meet the requirement as to a permanent establishment.

---

[69] Case C-322/01 *DocMorris* [2003] ECR I-14887, 14987.

[70] Case C-148/15 *Deutsche Parkinson Vereinigung (DPV)* EU:C:2016:776, 19 October 2016.

[71] *ibid*, paras 24–25.

> Consequently, in order for goods from other Member States to enjoy the same access to the market of the Member State of importation as domestic goods, they have to bear additional costs.[72]

(iii) Criticisms and Difficulties

[19–76] Catherine Barnard vividly describes the reception received by *Keck* as involving "brickbats and bouquets in equal measure".[73] Member States naturally welcomed the Court's decision to rein in the excesses of *Cassis de Dijon* by shielding selling arrangements with a presumption of legality, thereby shifting the onus of proof off the Member States and onto the challengers of such arrangements. Many critics, however, "bemoaned the introduction of a new formulistic classification … which, unlike well-established legal concepts such as direct and indirect discrimination, had never before seen the legal light of day".[74] A common complaint was the fact that, although the Court acknowledged that it was departing from earlier case law, it failed to identify the particular cases that it had in mind. More fundamentally, many considered that the distinction between a selling arrangement and a product requirement was not always clear. A good illustration of this can be seen by comparing the two cases of *Morellato* and *Alfa Vita*.

[19–77] In *Morellato*, an Italian law required that bread products that were not freshly baked, but resulted from re-heating partially baked products, were to be packaged before being sold with a label indicating the particular nature of the product.[75] Mr Morellato imported partially baked breads from France and received a fine for failing to comply with the Italian law. Within his bakery, all types of bread were displayed loose and unpackaged. When a partially baked product was sold, it was placed in a paper bag, with the appropriate labelling attached. The Italian authorities insisted that the packaging and labelling was required to be placed on the bread from the moment at which it was put on sale, rather than when it was sold. The Commission submitted that this requirement for prior packaging should be considered as affecting the bread manufacturing process and so amount to an MEQR relating to a specific characteristic of the product. The Court of Justice, however, took a different view, finding the requirement to be a selling arrangement that, prima facie, fell outside of Art 34:

> [I]t should be remembered that the need to alter the packaging or the labelling of imported products prevents such requirements from constituting selling arrangements within the meaning of the judgment in *Keck and Mithouard*.
>
> Accordingly, legislation of a Member State which prohibits a product that is lawfully manufactured and marketed in another Member State from being put on sale in the first Member State without being subjected to new packaging of a specific type that complies with the requirements of that legislation cannot be held to concern selling arrangements within the meaning of *Keck and Mithouard*.
>
> … The distinctive feature of the main proceedings is that the product put on sale by Mr Morellato was imported at a stage when its production process was not yet finished. In

72 Case C-254/98 *Heimdienst* [2000] ECR I-151, 170.
73 Catherine Barnard, *The Substantive Law of the EU* (4th ed, Oxford University Press, 2013) 128.
74 *ibid*, 129.
75 Case C-416/00 *Morellato* [2003] ECR I-9343.

order to be able to market the product in Italy as bread ready for consumption, it was necessary to complete the baking of the pre-baked bread imported from France.

> The fact that a product must, to a certain extent, be transformed after importation does not in itself preclude a requirement relating to its marketing from falling within the scope of application of Article [34] of the Treaty. It is possible that, as in the main proceedings, the imported product is not simply a component or ingredient of another product but in reality constitutes the product that is intended for marketing as soon as a simple transformation process has been carried out.
>
> In such a situation, the relevant question is whether the requirement for prior packaging laid down in the legislation of the Member State of import *makes it necessary to alter the product* in order to comply with that requirement.
>
> In the present case, nothing in the file indicates that it was necessary for the pre-baked bread, as imported into Italy, to be altered in order to comply with that requirement.
>
> In those circumstances, the requirement for prior packaging, since it relates only to the marketing of the bread which results from the final baking of pre-baked bread, is in principle such as to fall outside the scope of Article [34] of the Treaty, provided that it does not in reality constitute discrimination against imported products.[76]

[19–78] In finding that the Italian measure was not a product requirement, the Court focused on the fact that as the production of the bread was not yet completed when it was imported into Italy, the Italian law did not require for the product to be *changed* in order to be sold there. As a result, the law could not be said to impose a dual burden on importers, as compared to a single burden on domestic producers. Here, the requirement to add the packaging fell on the retailers of the good, and the Court was satisfied that it was a selling arrangement that, prima facie, fell outside of Art 34.

[19–79] In *Alfa Vita*, on the other hand, a Greek law required bakeries to hold a licence, a requirement for which was the maintenance of certain equipment and a minimum space for baking.[77] A number of supermarkets operating in Greece were ordered to stop selling "bake-off" bread products as they did not hold a bakery licence. As in *Morellato*, bake-off products comprised ready-made doughs that required re-heating and were then sold as finished goods. As they did not meet the necessary equipment and space requirements, the supermarkets would not have been entitled to a bakery licence. While Greece sought to argue that the requirement for a licence was a selling arrangement, the Court disagreed, finding that the rules related to the nature of the products themselves:

> It is common ground that the principal characteristic of "bake-off" products is that they are delivered at sales outlets after the main stages of preparation of those products have been completed. At those sales outlets, only a brief thawing and reheating or final baking are carried out. In those circumstances, requiring vendors of "bake-off" products to comply with all of the requirements imposed on traditional bakeries, including, in particular, the requirement of having a flour store, an area for kneading equipment and a solid-fuel store, *does not take the specific nature of those products into account* and entails additional costs, thereby making the marketing of those products more difficult. That legislation therefore constitutes a barrier to imports which cannot be regarded as establishing a selling arrangement as contemplated in *Keck and Mithouard.*[78]

---

76 *ibid*, 9370. Emphasis added.
77 Joined Cases C-158/04 and C-159/04 *Alfa Vita* [2006] ECR I-8135.
78 *ibid*, 8163. Emphasis added.

[19–80] Although, as in *Morellato*, those directly affected by the Greek measure were retailers rather than manufacturers, here the Court of Justice took the view that the application of a licensing requirement to bake-off products went to the nature of the products themselves, making it less attractive for retailers to import bake-off products, thereby affecting in substance the manufacturers of the goods. Accordingly, the Court regarded the application of the licensing requirement as a product requirement that fell within Art 34 and so required justification by Greece on the basis of an Art 36 ground or a mandatory requirement.

[19–81] A further example of this difficulty in distinguishing product requirements from selling arrangements is seen in *Dynamic Medien*, in which German law prohibited mail order or online sales, to children, of DVDs that had not been given an age classification by a German authority.[79] In intervening in the case, Ireland supported Germany in arguing that the restriction was a selling arrangement that applied equally to importers and domestic sellers, and so fell outside the scope of Art 34. The Court, however, held that the need to adapt the DVDs to the rules in force in the Germany, by the addition of a label, prevented the requirements from being treated as selling arrangements and they were, therefore, an MEQR that required justification by Germany.

(iv) *Keck* and Dynamic Rules

[19–82] The cases of *Morellato*, *Alfa Vita* and *Dynamic Medien* demonstrate that the distinction between product requirements and selling arrangements introduced by *Keck* may not be as clear-cut as that judgment would suggest. This is particularly the case when dealing with "dynamic" market circumstances rules, as opposed to static rules. Given their nature, matters governed by dynamic rules tend to be more closely entwined with a product itself than matters governed by static rules, such as when or where a good may be sold.

[19–83] A good example of this is *Familiapress*, in which an Austrian law prohibited publishers of magazines from including prize competitions within their publications.[80] Austria argued that the possibility of offering readers of a magazine the chance to take part in a prize competition was merely a method of promoting sales and hence a selling arrangement within the meaning of *Keck.* The Court of Justice disagreed, holding that even though the law was directed against a method of sales promotion, "in this case it bears on the actual content of the products, in so far as the competitions in question form an integral part of the magazine in which they appear".[81] In order to be sold in Austria, publishers of such magazines in other Member States would be required to alter their contents, thereby impairing their access to the Austrian market and hindering free movement of goods. As a result, the law was an MEQR falling within Art 34.

[19–84] Given that his discussion of this point is more expansive, it is useful to consider the opinion of Advocate General Tesauro in *Familiapress*. He recalled that the Court in *Keck* had referred only to "certain", and not to all, selling arrangements, without being more specific. In his view:

---

[79] Case C-244/06 *Dynamic Medien* [2008] ECR I-505.

[80] Case C-368/95 *Familiapress* [1997] ECR I-3689.

[81] *ibid*, 3714.

it is relevant to bear in mind that, again in *Keck and Mithouard*, it was held that, where the conditions laid down by the Court are fulfilled, "the application of such rules [on selling arrangements] to the sale of products from another Member State meeting the requirements laid down by that State is not by nature such as to prevent their access to the market or to impede access any more than it impedes the access of domestic products".

In this case, it is clear that the impugned measure prohibits the access to the market of periodicals having the characteristics of the weekly magazine "Laura". *Even if one regards it as having to do with selling arrangements, it is still the case that the measure in question, by preventing the access to the market of the product in question, does not fall within the scope of the* Keck and Mithouard *case-law*.

It is also instructive to recall the measures which the Court has hitherto held to relate to "selling arrangements" and thus to fall outside the scope of Article [34]. In addition to the prohibition on below-cost selling considered in *Keck and Mithouard*, other measures deemed to come within this category have included: a prohibition on selling at a very low profit margin; rules governing the opening hours of shops and filling stations; a prohibition on selling infant formula otherwise than in pharmacies; a retailing system for manufactured tobacco products; a prohibition on pharmacists advertising quasi-pharmaceutical products outside pharmacies; a prohibition on television advertising by distribution companies. These national measures, as can easily be seen, are clearly not by nature such as to "affect directly the access to the market" of the relevant product.

At a general level then I think it can reasonably be inferred that the only measures excluded from the scope of Article [34] are those which are absolutely general in nature, which apply — needless to say — without distinction, which do not impede imports and which might lead at most to a (hypothetical) reduction in the volume of imports only as a consequence of an equally hypothetical reduction in the overall volume of sales. Moreover, the Court itself has not hesitated to emphasise, and indeed has laid down as a basic premise underlying this approach, that "the fact that national legislation may restrict the volume of sales generally, and hence the volume of sales of products from other Member States, is not sufficient to characterise such legislation as a measure having an equivalent effect to a quantitative restriction".

Returning to the measure at issue in this case, I therefore take the view that although it applies without distinction it does directly affect the marketing of the relevant product and obliges the trader concerned to alter its presentation and content. In contrast to *Keck and Mithouard* and subsequent cases decided similarly, the prohibition in question is not in any way linked to a hypothetical reduction in the volume of imports as part of a more general contraction in the overall volume of sales.[82]

[19–85] Although the Court chose to focus on the fact that the Austrian measure, in substance, related to the product itself and so was an MEQR, Advocate General Tesauro developed an alternative line of argument. In his opinion he suggested that even if it was accepted that, as a limitation on marketing methods, the Austrian law related to selling arrangements, it nevertheless fell afoul of the paragraph 17 rationale in *Keck* in that it operated so as to prevent access to the Austrian market. It might be said that the paragraph 17 rationale is here applied as an additional criteria to the two conditions in paragraph 16, rather than as a mere rationale underpinning them.

[19–86] By reviewing the various measures that, within the Court's case law, had been found to be selling arrangements within the meaning of *Keck*, Advocate General Tesauro

[82] *ibid*, 3696–3698.

identified as their common features that they: (i) are absolutely general in nature; (ii) apply without distinction; and (iii) do not impede imports but, at most, might lead to a hypothetical reduction in the volume of imports only as a consequence of an equally hypothetical reduction in the overall volume of sales.

[19–87] Like promotional techniques, the question of advertising is another dynamic market circumstances rule that does not fit as comfortably with the *Keck* concept of selling arrangements as static rules. This is less because advertising is closely entwined with the product, as in *Familiapress*, and more to do with the relationship between advertising and access to the market, as emphasised by Advocate General Tesauro, and access to new markets in particular. In three well-known cases, *Leclerc-Siplec*, *De Agostini* and *Gourmet International*, the Court accepted that restrictions on advertising were, in principle, selling arrangements provided that the paragraph 16 conditions are fulfilled. *Leclerc-Siplec*, however, is better known for the opinion of Advocate General Jacobs in which he expressed his dislike of *Keck* and set out an alternative approach. In *De Agostini*, the Court left it to the national court to determine whether the second paragraph 16 condition was fulfilled, while hinting heavily that it was not. In *Gourmet International*, the Court bit the bullet and declared that the impact of the advertising ban was more severely felt by importers than by the makers of domestic goods.

[19–88] The 1995 judgment in *Leclerc-Siplec* arose out of the wish of a French chain of petrol stations to advertise on television.[83] A French law, motivated by a desire to protect regional newspapers by requiring certain sectors to advertise with them, prohibited TV advertising by some sectors. The Court of Justice was satisfied that the restriction was a selling arrangement and so fell outside the scope of Art 34. Advocate General Jacobs agreed that, if the *Keck* approach was to be applied, the restriction would fulfil the two paragraph 16 conditions and so be lawful. However, in cogent and, what transpired to be, influential terms, he expressed his preference for applying a different approach, stemming in part from the particular role that he saw advertising as playing in accessing new markets, thereby helping to create a genuine Single Market. In his opinion, he reasoned that:

> Advertising plays a particularly important part in the launching of new products. It is by means of advertising that consumers can be induced to abandon their existing brand loyalties and make a sample purchase of a different manufacturer's goods. Without advertising consumers would tend to go on buying the goods that they are familiar with and it would be difficult for manufacturers to persuade retailers to stock unknown brands that could not be promoted by means of advertising. Without advertising it would be much easier for established manufacturers to retain their existing market share, because prospective market entrants would find it difficult to gain a foothold. In short, advertising injects greater fluidity and mobility into the economy and enhances competitiveness. A ban on advertising tends to crystallize existing patterns of consumption, to ossify markets and to preserve the status quo.
>
> These findings have important implications for the basic freedoms created by [EU] law. In markets that are still, notwithstanding the process of economic integration initiated by the Treaty, to a large extent divided and compartmentalised along the lines of national frontiers, it is likely that the established brands will predominantly belong to domestic producers. Without advertising it would be extremely difficult for a manufacturer located in one Member State to penetrate the market in another Member State where his products

[83] Case C-412/93 *Leclerc-Siplec* [1995] ECR I-179.

> have not previously been sold and so enjoy no reputation among consumers. Thus measures that prohibit or severely restrict advertising tend inevitably to protect domestic manufacturers and to disadvantage manufacturers located in other Member States. Such measures prevent the interpenetration of markets and are inimical to the very concept of a single market. The Court should therefore be extremely vigilant when appraising the compatibility with [EU] law of restrictions on advertising.[84]

[19–89] As will be discussed further in the following section, the important role played by advertising in enabling importers to break into new markets clearly prompted Advocate General Jacobs to question the reasoning behind the *Keck* approach. How could it be that a national ban on advertising, even if, as a matter of fact, it affected domestic goods and imports in the same way, could fall outside of Art 34 if it nonetheless had the effect of preventing importers from accessing a new market? Finding this result unacceptable, Advocate General Jacobs suggested an alternative "single test formulated in the light of the purpose of Article [34]", namely: does the non-discriminatory measure substantially restrict access to the market?[85]

[19–90] *De Agostini* and *Gourmet International* also saw the Court of Justice accept that, in principle, restrictions on advertising constituted selling arrangements. Unlike *Leclerc-Siplec*, however, in both of these preliminary references the Court concluded that the restrictions either may (*De Agostini*) or did (*Gourmet International*), as a matter of fact, affect imports to a greater extent than domestic goods, so as to be caught by Art 34.

[19–91] In *De Agostini*, the Court accepted that a Swedish ban on TV advertising aimed at children under 12 was a selling arrangement.[86] Nevertheless, the Court observed that it could not be excluded that an outright ban of a type of promotion for a product might have a greater impact on imports from other Member States. Indeed, while leaving it for the national court to determine, the Court went so far as to note, without demurring, that "de Agostini stated that television advertising was the only effective form of promotion enabling it to penetrate the Swedish market since it had no other advertising methods for reaching children and their parents".[87]

[19–92] Similarly, in *Gourmet International* the Court had to address a Swedish ban on the advertising of alcoholic drinks on television, radio or in magazines other than trade magazines.[88] Here, the Court was so convinced of the advertising ban's unequal effect on imports that it provided its own conclusion on the matter in the course of giving its preliminary ruling:

> It is apparent that [the] prohibition on advertising … not only prohibits a form of marketing a product but in reality prohibits producers and importers from directing any advertising messages at consumers, with a few insignificant exceptions.
>
> Even without its being necessary to carry out a precise analysis of the facts characteristic of the Swedish situation, which it is for the national court to do, the Court is able to conclude that, in the case of products like alcoholic beverages, the consumption of which is linked to traditional social practices and to local habits and customs, a prohibition of

---

84 *ibid*, 186–187.
85 *ibid*, 194, 198.
86 Joined Cases C-34/95, C-35/96 and C-36/96 *De Agostini* [1997] ECR I-3843.
87 *ibid*, 3890.
88 Case C-405/98 *Gourmet International* [2001] ECR I-1795.

> all advertising directed at consumers in the form of advertisements in the press, on the radio and on television, the direct mailing of unsolicited material or the placing of posters on the public highway is liable to impede access to the market by products from other Member States more than it impedes access by domestic products, with which consumers are instantly more familiar.
>
> … A prohibition on advertising such as that at issue in the main proceedings must therefore be regarded as affecting the marketing of products from other Member States more heavily than the marketing of domestic products and as therefore constituting an obstacle to trade between Member States caught by Article [34] of the Treaty.[89]

G. Measures that Hinder Market Access

[19–93] The opinions in *De Agostini* and *Gourmet International* were both written by Advocate General Jacobs and, in one way, his overall concern regarding market access may be seen to have been incorporated via the Court's application of the second paragraph 16 condition and how it determined whether a national measure affected domestic goods and imports in the same manner, in law and in fact. Nevertheless, in the earlier case of *Leclerc-Siplec* he spelt out two specific reasons why he did not favour the approach in *Keck*. First, he disliked the drawing of a clear distinction between product requirements and rules governing selling arrangements. In his view, this distinction was rather artificial given that, in practice, the severity of a restriction is one of degree that depends upon its effects, rather than on some "a priori" categorisation. As he put it:

> it is inappropriate to make rigid distinctions between different categories of rules, and to apply different tests depending on the category to which particular rules belong. The severity of the restriction imposed by different rules is merely one of degree. Measures affecting selling arrangements may create extremely serious obstacles to imports. For example, a rule permitting certain products to be sold only in a handful of small shops in a Member State would be almost as restrictive as an outright ban on importation and marketing. … [I]t would be more appropriate to measure restrictions against a single test formulated in the light of the purpose of Article [34].[90]

[19–94] Secondly, Advocate General Jacobs did not support *Keck's* reintroduction of a discrimination test in respect of rules governing selling arrangements, such that rules that fulfilled the paragraph 16 condition by affecting domestic goods and imports in the same manner, in law and in fact, would fall outside Art 34. In his view:

> The central concern of the Treaty provisions on the free movement of goods is to prevent unjustified obstacles to trade between Member States. If an obstacle to inter-State trade exists, it cannot cease to exist simply because an identical obstacle affects domestic trade. I have difficulty in accepting the proposition that a Member State may arbitrarily restrict the marketing of goods from another Member State, provided only that it imposes the same arbitrary restriction on the marketing of domestic goods. If a Member State imposes a substantial barrier on access to the market for certain products – for example, by providing that they may be sold only in a very limited number of establishments – and a manufacturer of those products in another Member State suffers economic loss as a result, he will derive little consolation from the knowledge that a similar loss is sustained by his competitors in the Member State which imposes the restriction.

---

89 *ibid*, 1823–1825.

90 Case C-412/93 *Leclerc-Siplec* [1995] ECR I-179, 194.

> Equally, from the point of view of the Treaty's concern to establish a single market, discrimination is not a helpful criterion: from that point of view, the fact that a Member State imposes similar restrictions on the marketing of domestic goods is simply irrelevant. The adverse effect on the [EU] market is in no way alleviated; nor is the adverse effect on the economies of the other Member States, and so on the [EU] economy. Indeed the application of the discrimination test would lead to the fragmentation of the [EU] market, since traders would have to accept whatever restrictions on selling arrangements happened to exist in each Member State, and would have to adapt their own arrangements accordingly in each State. Restrictions on trade should not be tested against local conditions which happen to prevail in each Member State, but against the aim of access to the entire [EU] market. A discrimination test is therefore inconsistent as a matter of principle with the aims of the Treaty.[91]

[19–95] Having explained these two key objections, Advocate General Jacobs proceeded to set out an alternative approach to determining whether or not an indistinctly applicable measure falls within the scope of Art 34. Despite inconsistencies within the reasoning of certain Court judgments, he identified one common "guiding principle" that provided an appropriate test: that all undertakings which engage in a legitimate economic activity in a Member State should have unfettered access to the whole of the EU market, unless there is a valid reason for denying them full access to a part of that market. If this is accepted as a guiding principle, then the test should be whether there is a *substantial restriction* on unfettered access to the EU market, or a part thereof. Introducing a "substantial restriction" test would, he conceded, involve introducing a *de minimis* test into Art 34, which would need to be defined carefully and applied with caution. Nevertheless,

> Once it is recognised that there is a need to limit the scope of Article [34] in order to prevent excessive interference in the regulatory powers of the Member States, a test based on the extent to which a measure hinders trade between Member States by restricting market access seems the most obvious solution.
>
> … The impact on access to the market of measures applicable without distinction may vary greatly, depending on the nature of the measure in issue. Where such a measure prohibits the sale of goods lawfully placed on the market in another Member State (as in *"Cassis de Dijon"*), it may be presumed to have a substantial impact on access to the market, since the goods are either denied access altogether or can gain access only after being modified in some way; the need to modify goods is itself a substantial barrier to market access.
>
> Where, on the other hand, a measure applicable without distinction simply restricts certain selling arrangements, by stipulating when, where, how, by whom or at what price goods may be sold, its impact will depend on a number of factors, such as whether it applies to certain goods …, or to most goods (as in *Torfaen*), or to all goods (as in *Keck*), on the extent to which other selling arrangements remain available, and on whether the effect of the measure is direct or indirect, immediate or remote, or purely speculative and uncertain. Accordingly, the magnitude of the barrier to market access may vary enormously: it may range from the insignificant to a quasi-prohibition. Clearly, this is where a *de minimis* test could perform a useful function. The distinction recognised in *Keck* between a prohibition of the kind in issue in *"Cassis de Dijon"* and a mere restriction on certain selling arrangements is therefore valuable: the former inevitably creates a substantial barrier to trade between Member States, whereas the latter may create such a barrier. But it cannot be maintained that the latter type of measure is not capable of hindering trade contrary to Article [34] in the absence of discrimination. It should therefore be recognised

[91] *ibid*, 194–195.

> that such measures, unless overtly discriminatory, are not automatically caught by Article [34], as are measures of the type at issue in *"Cassis de Dijon"*, but may be caught if the restriction which they cause on access to the market is substantial.
>
> … In *Keck* itself, the result is consistent with the view taken above. A law which prohibits all retailers of all goods from reselling goods at less than cost price is unlikely to have a significant impact on the marketing of imported goods. It has no significant effect on the global volume of imports and it does not prevent a trader in another Member State from enjoying full access to the market. The same will normally be true of legislation which restricts the opening hours of shops, at least if it is of general application and does not arbitrarily restrict marketing opportunities for a limited range of goods. Such legislation may lead to a slight reduction in the total volume of sales of goods, including imported goods, but it is unlikely to restrict substantially market access for any specific trader's goods, since its impact will be spread across the whole range of goods.
>
> Accordingly, I reach the conclusion that Article [34] should be regarded as applying to non-discriminatory measures which are liable substantially to restrict access to the market.[92]

[19–96] The opinion of Advocate General Jacobs in *Leclerc-Siplec* has remained influential. In particular, his preference for a more general market access approach came to the fore in a series of cases involving national restrictions on the use to which a good may be put. Since a restriction on the use of a good is neither clearly a product requirement nor a selling arrangement, the cases required fresh consideration of whether the approach in *Keck* ought to be extended so as to include such rules.

[19–97] The first judgment came in *Tinted Windows*, in which the Court did regard a Portuguese ban on the placing of tinted film on car windows as an MEQR.[93] The Court did not explore whether the *Keck* criteria ought to apply to such a restriction, and reasoned succinctly as follows:

> It must be held that potential customers, traders or individuals have practically no interest in buying them in the knowledge that affixing such film to the windscreen and windows alongside passenger seats in motor vehicles is prohibited.
>
> … The contested provision therefore affects the marketing in Portugal of almost all tinted film legally manufactured and sold in other Member States or in States party to the EEA Agreement intended to be affixed to the windows of motor vehicles.
>
> It follows that the ban … constitutes a measure having equivalent effect to quantitative restrictions within the meaning of Article [34] … That provision is incompatible with the obligations arising from those provisions, unless it may be objectively justified.[94]

[19–98] The analysis in two subsequent cases is of particular interest given the different views taken by Advocates General Kokott and Bot. Whereas in her December 2006 opinion in *Mickelsson and Roos*,[95] Advocate General Kokott found a Swedish law restricting the use of watercraft to certain, authorised navigable waters to be a selling arrangement, in July 2008 (shortly after the Court's judgment in *Tinted Windows*) Advocate General Bot advised against extending *Keck* to an Italian law prohibiting

---

92 *ibid*, 195–197.

93 Case C-265/06 *Commission v Portugal (Tinted Windows)* [2008] ECR I-2245.

94 *ibid*, paras 33–36.

95 Case C-142/05 *Mickelsson and Roos* [2009] ECR I-4273, EU:C:2006:782, 14 December 2006, paras 25–28.

the towing of trailers by mopeds.[96] The judgments of the Court were delivered in the reverse order, with *Italian Trailers* coming first in February 2009 and *Mickelsson and Roos* following in June of the same year. In both judgments, the Court favoured a general market access approach rather than applying *Keck* to rules on the use of goods (ie the approach advocated by Advocates General Jacobs and Bot and favoured by the Court in *Tinted Windows*).

[19–99] In his opinion to a Grand Chamber of the Court in *Italian Trailers*, Advocate General Bot advised that the *Keck* criteria ought not to be extended to rules governing the use of products. He put forward a number of reasons for this. First, the drawing of distinctions between different categories of rules was not appropriate, as it was an artificial approach that could be a source of confusion for national courts. The traditional judicial analysis laid down in *Dassonville* and *Cassis de Dijon* was satisfactory and there was no reason to depart from it. Secondly, extending *Keck* to rules governing use would result in the introduction of a new category of exemption from the application of Art 34, in circumstances where it was unclear that the reasons which prompted the Court to exclude selling arrangements also existed in the case of rules governing use. Thirdly, to exclude rules on use from the scope of Art 34 would be contrary to the Treaty's objectives of creating a single and integrated market and would undermine the useful effect of Art 34, since it would once again allow Member States to legislate in areas that were intended to be harmonised. Fourthly, in order to ensure that national courts are not prompted to exclude too many measures from Art 34, the term "restriction" should be viewed in broad terms. Finally, by its very nature, a ban on the use of a product was an impediment to the free movement of goods. Even if the ban applied in the same way to domestic and imported products, it prevented access to the market and so should be examined under Art 34 rather than being excluded from it.[97]

[19–100] In its judgment, the Grand Chamber confined its assessment to trailers that had been specifically designed for use with mopeds. It applied to them the principle that Art 34 captures any measure which hinders access of products originating in one Member State to the market of another. According to the Court:

> [A] prohibition on the use of a product in the territory of a Member State has a considerable influence on the behaviour of consumers, which, in its turn, affects the access of that product to the market of that Member State.
>
> Consumers, knowing that they are not permitted to use their motorcycle with a trailer specially designed for it, have practically no interest in buying such a trailer. Thus, … the [Italian] Highway Code prevents a demand from existing in the market at issue for such trailers and therefore hinders their importation.
>
> It follows that the prohibition laid down in … the Highway Code, to the extent that its effect is to hinder access to the Italian market for trailers which are specially designed for motorcycles and are lawfully produced and marketed in Member States other than the Italian Republic, constitutes a measure having equivalent effect to quantitative restrictions on imports within the meaning of Article [34], unless it can be justified objectively.[98]

[96] Case C-110/05 *Commission v Italy (Italian Trailers)* [2009] ECR I-519, EU:C:2006:646, 8 July 2006.

[97] *ibid*, paras 88–106.

[98] Case C-110/05 *Commission v Italy* [2009] ECR I-519, EU:C:2009:66, 10 February 2009, paras 56–58. See Eleanor Spaventa, "Leaving *Keck* Behind? The Free Movement of Goods after the Rulings in *Commission v Italy* and *Mickelsson and Roos*" (2009) 34 *European Law Review* 914;

[19–101] Some months later, in *Mickelsson and Roos*, the Court decided not to follow the opinion prepared for it by Advocate General Kokott. Instead, the Court followed the approach that had since been taken by the Grand Chamber in *Italian Trailers* in holding that any measure which hinders access of products originating in one Member State to the market of another is an MEQR. Even though the Swedish measure merely restricted the use of watercraft to certain waterways, rather than prohibiting a use entirely as in *Italian Trailers*, the Court closely followed the reasoning of the earlier case in holding as follows:

> It is apparent from the file ... that, at the material time, no waters had been designated as open to navigation by personal watercraft, and thus the use of personal watercraft was permitted on only general navigable waterways. However, the accused in the main proceedings and the Commission ... maintain that those waterways are intended for heavy traffic of a commercial nature making the use of personal watercraft dangerous and that, in any event, the majority of navigable Swedish waters lie outside those waterways. The actual possibilities for the use of personal watercraft in Sweden are, therefore, merely marginal.
>
> Even if the national regulations at issue do not have the aim or effect of treating goods coming from other Member States less favourably, which is for the national court to ascertain, the restriction which they impose on the use of a product in the territory of a Member State may, depending on its scope, have a considerable influence on the behaviour of consumers, which may, in turn, affect the access of that product to the market of that Member State.
>
> Consumers, knowing that the use permitted by such regulations is very limited, have only a limited interest in buying that product.
>
> In that regard, where the national regulations for the designation of navigable waters and waterways have the effect of preventing users of personal watercraft from using them for the specific and inherent purposes for which they were intended or of greatly restricting their use, which is for the national court to ascertain, such regulations have the effect of hindering the access to the domestic market in question for those goods and therefore constitute, save where there is a justification pursuant to Article [36] or there are overriding public interest requirements, measures having equivalent effect to quantitative restrictions on imports prohibited by Article [34].[99]

[19–102] It is clear that the judgments in *Italian Trailers* and *Mickelsson and Roos* have established "market access" as a relevant principle when applying Art 34, such that in addition to measures that discriminate against imports and product requirements, measures that otherwise hinder access to the market will be considered an MEQR. In this way, what first appeared in paragraph 17 of *Keck* as a rationale for the paragraph 16 conditions has now been elevated to an MEQR criteria in its own right.

[19–103] What is less clear, however, is the relationship between the market access test and the other approaches to MEQRs. To read the opinion of Advocate General Jacobs

---

Catherine Barnard, "Trailing a New Approach to Free Movement of Goods" (2009) 68 *Cambridge Law Journal* 288; Jukka Snell, "The Notion of Market Access: A Concept or a Slogan?" (2010) 47 *Common Market Law Review* 437; Peter Oliver, "Of Trailers and Jet-Skis: Is the Case Law on Article 34 TFEU Hurtling in a New Direction?" (2010) 33 *Fordham Journal of International Law* 1423; Stefan Enchelmaier, "Moped Trailers, *Mickelsson and Roos*, *Gysbrechts*: The ECJ's Case Law on Goods Keeps on Moving" (2010) 29 *Yearbook of European Law* 190.

99 Case C-142/05 *Mickelsson and Roos* [2009] ECR I-4273, EU:C:2009:336, 4 June 2009, paras 25–28.

in *Leclerc-Siplec*, one gets the impression that market access is the one overarching or guiding principle that is found within all of the various strands of case law on MEQRs, such that categories such as discriminatory measures or product requirements are just subsets of this broader principle. In the *Minimum Alcohol Pricing* case, for instance, the Court of Justice did not analyse whether a Scottish proposal to impose minimum prices for alcohol was a selling arrangement, but rather went directly to an assessment of market access, observing that:

> the fact that the legislation … prevents the lower cost price of imported products being reflected in the selling price to the consumer means, by itself, that that legislation is capable of hindering the access to the United Kingdom market of alcoholic drinks that are lawfully marketed in Member States other than the United Kingdom …, and constitutes therefore a measure having an effect equivalent to a quantitative restriction within the meaning of Article 34 TFEU.[100]

[19–104] Similarly, in *DPV*, concerning a German fixed-price regime for prescription drugs, the Court examined the effect of the regime on imports as compared with domestic sales and, finding that there was a greater impact on imports, held the measure to be a hindrance to accessing the German market and so it constituted an MEQR. Whilst this involves applying the essence of the second paragraph 16 condition, combined with the paragraph 17 rationale, in its judgment the Court does not refer to *Keck,* nor to the category of "selling arrangement".[101] In contrast, although describing it as "arguably the most contested judgment in the domain of free movement of goods", in his opinion for the Court, Advocate General Szpunar noted that although the instances in which the *Keck* exception was found to apply had grown rare, "*Keck* is still alive and must be examined in the case at issue".[102] Evidently, the Court felt differently, considering it unnecessary to apply the *Keck* approach to selling arrangements in express terms, favouring a more general market access rationale.

[19–105] In other cases, however, the Court has continued to first consider whether a measure is discriminatory or a product requirement and, only after excluding these possibilities, goes on to assess whether the measure otherwise hinders access to the market.[103] This has led Catherine Barnard, for example, to conclude that the market access test has not subsumed the other tests but rather is a residual, catch-all category. Pointing to an "increasing inconsistency among the Court's chambers (and its Advocates General)" and a "marked absence of a common intellectual frame within the Court; or at least, a lamentable deficiency in the articulation of all the dogmatic elements within its chain of reasoning", Robert Schütze has called for the adoption of a single unitary approach.[104] Subjecting all national measures to a market access test would, he suggests, give the Court's jurisprudence "dogmatic clarity and casuistic flexibility",

---

[100] Case C-333/14 *Scotch Whisky Association v Lord Advocate, Advocate General of Scotland* EU:C:2015:845, 23 December 2015, para 32.

[101] Case C-148/15 *Deutsche Parkinson Vereinigung (DPV)* EU:C:2016:776, 19 October 2016.

[102] Case C-148/15 *Deutsche Parkinson Vereinigung (DPV)* EU:C:2016:394, 2 June 2016, paras 21 and 23.

[103] Case C-456/10 *ANETT* EU:C:2012:241, 26 April 2012.

[104] Robert Schütze, "Of Types and Tests: Towards a Unitary Doctrinal Framework for Article 34 TFEU?" (2016) 41 *European Law Review* 826, 841–842. See also Laurence Gormley, "Inconsistencies and Misconceptions in the Free Movement of Goods" (2015) 40 *European Law Review* 925.

while dropping the category approach would "remove the sharp conceptual edges inherent in subjecting different types of measures to different tests".[105]

[19–106] As seen in the case of *DPV*, a separate but related question is whether the *Keck* exclusion of selling arrangements from Art 34 continues to survive the more recent case law on market access. Academic opinion is divided on the matter, with some declaring *Keck* to be no longer relevant, whereas others point to the fact that it has never been abandoned by the Court and remains a pillar of its case law.[106] The nuanced position is perhaps summed up nicely by Laurence Gormley when he describes how:

> Although *market access* plays the central role in the argumentation [in *Tinted Windows, Italian Trailers* and *Mickelsson*] the intention of the ECJ is not to revise its view of the certain selling arrangements as expressed in *Keck*, nor to revise the conditions under which it declares Article 34 TFEU inapplicable. On the other hand, the exceptional status of those measures which do satisfy the *Keck* criteria is more and more anomalous. Perhaps the truth is that the ECJ is not thinking in terms of grand theory, but is actually simply deciding, on a case-by-case basis, the reasonableness of national measures. The ECJ does not particularly have an eye to theoretical considerations, and it is worth recalling that judges are more concerned with sorting out disputes than forming a coherent doctrine, even though they try to be consistent as much as possible. If the approach in *Keck* was a reaction to management concerns about the ECJ being flooded out by litigants seeking to challenge any national rule which prevented them from trading quite as they wished, the cases on the *use of goods* … signal the end of the slippery slope approach of allowing an expansion of the type of measures which the ECJ will accept as not being caught by Article 34.[107]

[19–107] Finally, one further question left unanswered from *Italian Trailers* is the extent to which the market access test involves applying a *de minimis* rule to Art 34. Traditionally, the Court of Justice has rejected any attempts to subject breaches of Art 34 to a *de minimis* requirement, with the prevailing view being that, first, the free movement of goods is a fundamental freedom and so any national restriction should require justification and, secondly, a *de minimis* requirement would introduce legal uncertainty and prove difficult to be applied by national courts in practice.[108] On the other hand, in setting out an alternative analysis in *Leclerc-Siplec*, Advocate General Jacobs spoke of cautiously applying a *de minimis* requirement when assessing whether or not there is a "substantial hindrance" to market access, taking into account factors such as: whether the measure applies to certain goods, most goods, or to all goods; the extent to which other selling arrangements remain available, and whether the effect of the measure is direct or indirect, immediate or remote, or purely speculative and uncertain. Catherine Barnard suggests that it may, perhaps, continue to be the case that no *de minimis* requirement arises in the context of discriminatory measures or product requirements, but that it does arise when applying the residual, market access test.[109]

---

[105] *ibid*, 841.

[106] Eleanor Spaventa, "Leaving *Keck* Behind? The Free Movement of Goods after the Rulings in *Commission v Italy* and *Mickelsson and Roos*" (2009) 34 *European Law Review* 914; Lorna Woods and Philippa Watson, *EU Law* (Oxford University Press, 2014) 395; Damian Chalmers, Gareth Davies and Giorgio Monti, *European Union Law* (3rd ed, Cambridge University Press, 2014) 790.

[107] Laurence Gormley, "Free Movement of Goods and their Use – What Is the Use of It?" (2010) 33 *Fordham Journal of International Law* 1589, 1626–1627. Emphasis added.

[108] See Peter Oliver, "Some Further Reflections on the Scope of Article 28–34 (ex Article 30–36) EC" (1999) 36 *Common Market Law Review* 783.

[109] Catherine Barnard, *The Substantive Law of the EU* (4th ed, Oxford University Press, 2013) 107.

Even if not expressly referred to by the Court, it is hard to imagine that the factors identified by Advocate Jacobs are not part of any assessment as to whether or not a particular measure imposes a hindrance to importers seeking access to a part of the Single Market.

Overview of Case Law

Degree of Horizontal Effect through Broad View of State Entities and Indirect State Responsibility	*Buy Irish (Commission v Ireland)*	1982
	Dundalk Water (Commission v Ireland)	1988
	Fra.bo	2013
	Spanish Strawberries (Commission v France)	1997
	Austrian Motorways	2003
"Measures" within Meaning of Art 34 TFEU	*Buy Irish (Commission v Ireland)*	1982
	Dundalk Water (Commission v Ireland)	1988
	Spanish Strawberries (Commission v France)	1997
	Austrian Motorways	2003
Umbrella Definition of a MEQR	*Dassonville*	1974
Product Requirements	*Cassis de Dijon*	1979
	Rau	1982
	Mars	1995
Selling Arrangements	*Cinéthèque*	1985
	Torfaen Borough Council v B&Q	1989
	Keck and Mithouard	1993
	Baby Milk (Commission v Greece)	1995
	Heimdienst	2000
	DocMorris	2003
	Morellato	2003
	Alfa-Vita	2006
	Dynamic Medien	2008
	Ker-Optika	2010
	DPV	2016
Dynamic Rules	*Leclerc-Siplec (including Opinion of AG Jacobs)*	1995
	Familiapress (including Opinion of AG Tesauro)	1997
	De Agostini	1997
	Gourmet International	2001
Market Access / Rules Governing Use	*Tinted Windows (Commission v Portugal)*	2008
	Italian Trailers (including Opinion of AG Bot)	2009
	Micklesson and Roos (including Opinion of AG Kokott)	2009
	Minimum Alcohol Pricing	2015
	DPV (including Opinion of AG Spuznar)	2016

See Max Jansson and Harry Kalimo, "De Minimis Meets Market Access: Transformation in the Substance – and the Syntax – EU Free Movement Law" (2014) 51 *Common Market Law Review* 523; Hojnik Janja, "De Minimis Rule Within the Internal Market: Towards a More Mature and Legitimate Market" (2013) 6 *European Journal of Legal Studies* 25.

CHAPTER 20

DEFENDING RESTRICTIONS ON THE FREE MOVEMENT OF GOODS

A. INTRODUCTION

[20–01] The six grounds upon which a Member State can seek to justify a restriction on the free movement of goods are set out in Art 36 TFEU. It provides that the provisions of Arts 34 and 35 shall not preclude prohibitions or restrictions on imports, exports or goods in transit that are justified on grounds of: public morality; public policy; public security; the protection of health and life of humans, animals or plants; the protection of national treasures possessing artistic, historic or archaeological value; and the protection of industrial or commercial property. Such prohibitions or restrictions shall not, however, constitute a means of arbitrary discrimination or a disguised restriction on trade between Member States.

[20–02] These are the only grounds that may be relied upon by a Member State in seeking to justify a *discriminatory* or *distinctly applicable* restriction on the free movement of goods. The grounds have been interpreted strictly by the Court of Justice. The Court has also emphasised that what is, in reality, a budgetary or economic concern cannot be invoked by a Member State in order to justify a discriminatory measure merely because it is related to one of the six grounds such as, for example, a funding concern that is related to the protection of public health.

[20–03] It is important to bear in mind that the six grounds for exemption listed in Art 36 do not confer on Member States a competence reservation with respect to these areas. Instead, the grounds for exemption are available to a Member State in order to defend a particular restriction on the free movement of goods. The burden is on the Member State to make out this justification and, ultimately, it is for the Court of Justice to determine, on a case-by-case basis, whether the argument put forward is sufficiently persuasive. Meanwhile, the EU retains a competence to harmonise in respect of these six public interest areas should it be considered necessary. If there is total harmonisation by the EU in respect of a particular product or area, a Member State will no longer be able to rely on the relevant Art 36 ground. If the harmonisation is only partial, the ability of a Member State to rely on the Art 36 ground will be limited to that extent.

[20–04] So, for example, in *Hedley Lomas (Ireland) Ltd* a company wishing to export live sheep to Spain for slaughter was refused an export licence on the ground that the UK authorities were not satisfied that Spanish slaughterhouses were complying with an animal welfare directive on stunning before slaughter.[1] In addition, the UK pointed to the fact that the directive did not prescribe any monitoring requirements to ensure that the rules were being adhered to, or any penalties in the event of a breach of the rules. The UK accepted that the refusal of an export licence amounted to an MEQR, but sought to justify it on the basis of Art 36. In answering a preliminary reference, the Court of Justice made clear that recourse to Art 36 was no longer possible where a directive had provided for harmonisation of the measures necessary to achieve the specific objective which was said to justify the national measure that restricted free movement. This was unaffected by the fact that the directive did not lay down a monitoring regime, or provide for penalties in the event of breach. Since all Member States were under an obligation to guarantee the application and effectiveness of EU law, it followed that they "must rely on trust in each other to carry out inspections on their respective territories".[2]

[20–05] In addition to having to show that a distinctly applicable measure is necessitated by one of the six grounds, Art 36 also requires a Member State to demonstrate that the measure is not a disguised restriction on trade or a means of arbitrary discrimination. Through its case law, the Court of Justice has added one further important test, namely that the restriction must be proportionate to the objective being pursued, in the sense that there is no less restrictive means available of achieving the same objective. The case law demonstrates that whatever margin of appreciation is, in principle, afforded to Member States by the terms of Art 36, in practice it is significantly narrowed by the Court's application of the proportionality requirement in a strict manner. In conducting this proportionality assessment, the Court of Justice is effectively carrying out its own balancing exercise as between the fundamental Treaty guarantee of the free movement of goods and the competing public interest that falls within the Art 36 ground. The Court has, however, indicated that the burden of proof on Member States to demonstrate proportionality cannot be so extensive as to require them to prove, positively, that no other conceivable measure could enable that objective to be attained under the same conditions.[3] Where the proceedings are by way of a preliminary reference, the Court of Justice will typically set out the general principles governing the case, but leave it to the national court to make a factual assessment as to whether the restriction is proportionate to the aim being pursued.

[20–06] The situation is different when it comes to defending an *indistinctly* applicable measure that restricts trade in goods but is not deliberately discriminatory. From the previous chapter it will be recalled that, in *Cassis de Dijon*, the Court balanced the introduction of the principle of mutual recognition – which greatly limited the ability

1 Case C-5/94 *R v Minister for Agriculture, Food and Fisheries ex p Hedley Lomas (Ireland) Ltd* [1996] ECR I-2553.
2 *ibid*, 2611.
3 Case C-110/05 *Commission v Italy (Italian Trailers)* [2009] ECR I-519, para 66.

of a host state to regulate what is sold and marketed in its territory – by elaborating the concept of "mandatory requirements", also known as the "rule of reason".[4] Mandatory requirements are an open-ended category of imperative requirements, or overriding public interests, that a Member State may rely upon in order to defend an indistinctly applicable measure. In *Cassis de Dijon*, the Court identified as four examples of mandatory requirements the effectiveness of fiscal supervision, fairness of commercial transactions, consumer protection and public health. This list has been much added to since then.

[20–07] As can be seen, a mandatory requirement may overlap with an Art 36 ground, such as the protection of public health. On a number of occasions, where the ground invoked by a Member State is both an Art 36 ground and a mandatory requirement, the Court of Justice has not placed great emphasis on determining whether the national measure is distinctly or indistinctly applicable. More generally, although the traditional approach has been that only Art 36 grounds can be relied upon in defending a distinctly applicable measure, this rigid distinction has been described as coming "under increasing strain in recent years" and as "breaking down".[5] As Paul Craig and Gráinne de Búrca have convincingly argued:

> It would be best for the same justifications to be available in principle, irrespective of whether the measure is discriminatory or indistinctly applicable, although greater justification might be required for discriminatory measures. It might be argued that this is not possible, given the wording of Article 36. There is however no reason why phrases within Article 36, such as the protection of the health and life of humans, could not be interpreted to include consumer protection and the environment. … [I]f it was legitimate in *Cassis* to create an open-ended list of mandatory exceptions, not mentioned in the Treaty, then it is difficult to see why it would not be legitimate for the ECJ to read Article 36 to include matters such as the environment or consumer protection.[6]

(i) Mutual Recognition Regulation

[20–08] Before turning to the defences themselves, it is worth noting that Regulation No 764/2008 – known as the Mutual Recognition Regulation – imposes important procedural obligations on Member States whenever they wish to apply national technical rules to products lawfully marketed in another Member State.[7] This Regulation applies to certain administrative decisions taken by national authorities that are addressed to economic operators in respect of any product lawfully marketed in another Member State, where the direct or indirect effect of the decision is: (i) the prohibition of the placing of the product on the market; (ii) the modification or additional testing of the product before it can be placed or kept on the market; or (iii) the withdrawal of the product from the market.

[20–09] The administrative decisions to which the Regulation relates are those based on national technical rules, governing a non-harmonised area, which either prohibit the

---

4 See ch 19, paras [19–44] to [19–53].

5 Paul Craig and Gráinne de Búrca, *EU Law* (6th ed, Oxford University Press, 2015) 705; Catherine Barnard, *The Substantive Law of the EU* (4th ed, Oxford University Press, 2013) 171.

6 Paul Craig and Gráinne de Búrca, *EU Law* (6th ed, Oxford University Press, 2015) 705.

7 Regulation (EC) No 764/2008 of the European Parliament and of the Council of 9 July 2008 laying down procedures relating to the application of certain national technical rules to products lawfully marketed in another Member State [2008] OJ L218/21.

marketing of a product, or require compliance with the rules in order for the product to be marketed on the national territory, and which lay down either:

(i) the characteristics required of the product such as quality, performance, safety, testing and test methods, the name under which it is sold, dimensions, packaging, marking or labelling; or

(ii) any other requirement which is imposed on the product for the purposes of protecting consumers or the environment, and which affects the life-cycle of the product after it has been placed on the market, such as conditions of use, recycling, reuse or disposal, where such conditions can significantly influence the composition, nature or marketing of the product.

[20–10] Where a competent authority of a Member State intends to adopt such an administrative decision, it must send the economic operator a written notice specifying the technical rule on which the decision is to be based and setting out technical or scientific evidence to the effect that the intended decision is: (i) justified on one of the grounds of public interest set out in Art 36 TFEU or by reference to other overriding reasons of public interest and (ii) appropriate for the purpose of achieving the objective pursued and does not go beyond what is necessary in order to attain that objective. Following a period during which the economic operator may make representations, of which the competent authority is required to "take due account", any decision made must be notified to the economic operator and to the Commission, stating the grounds and technical and scientific evidence on which it is based, including the reasons for rejecting any arguments that had been put forward. If a competent authority fails to notify an economic operator of a relevant decision the product shall be deemed to be lawfully marketed in the Member State insofar as the application of its technical rules is concerned.

[20–11] The Regulation also establishes a network of "Product Contact Points" within each Member State who, at the request of any economic operator, are to provide information on: (i) the national technical rules applicable to a specific type of product; (ii) whether that type of product is subject to a requirement for prior authorisation under national law; and (iii) information concerning the principle of mutual recognition and the application of the Regulation in the particular Member State. The Irish Product Contact Point is the National Standards Authority of Ireland.

B. Defending Discriminatory Measures – Article 36 TFEU

[20–12] In this section, each of the six grounds provided for in Art 36 TFEU will be considered in turn. It will be seen that much greater reliance has been placed on the protection of health and life of humans, animals and plants than the grounds of public morality, public policy, public security or the protection of national treasures. The protection of industrial and commercial property is closely related to the body of intellectual property law more generally. As this is a complex area, only the broad nature of this ground will be outlined here.

(i) Public Morality

[20–13] In the early case of *Henn and Darby*, the Court of Justice established the principle that it was for each Member State, in accordance with its own scale of values, to determine the requirements of public morality in its territory. Indeed, in finding it permissible that the UK had imposed a restriction on the importation of pornography, the Court did not consider it necessary to inquire in detail as to the restrictions imposed by the UK on domestic goods of a similar nature.[8]

[20–14] Some years later, however, in *Conegate*, the Court was more rigorous in assessing whether the challenged restriction treated imported goods less favourably than domestic goods.[9] On this occasion, the UK was seeking to justify the confiscation of life-sized inflatable dolls upon importation. The equivalent domestic product could not be sold by post or publicly displayed for sale, but was not subject to an outright ban and could be manufactured and sold, under certain conditions, within the UK. As a result, the Court found that the ground of public morality could not be relied upon. Although EU law left it to each Member State to make their own assessment of the indecent or obscene character of a good, the fact that a good caused offence could not be regarded as sufficiently serious to justify a restriction on its free movement where the Member State did not adopt, with respect to the same good marketed within its territory, "penal measures or other serious and effective measures intended to prevent the distribution of such goods in its territory".[10]

(ii) Public Policy

[20–15] The ground of public policy has been interpreted very strictly by the Court of Justice, and it has rarely succeeded as a stand-alone ground. It was relied upon by the UK in an early case involving a prohibition on the export of silver coins, where the Court accepted that the minting of coinage was traditionally regarded as involving the fundamental interests of the state.[11] In a more recent case, the Court agreed that a Finnish ban on the importation, without a licence, of alcoholic drinks of over 80 per cent proof, sought to combat alcohol abuse which was both a health and a public policy concern recognised by Art 36.[12] It was left for the national court to determine whether a less restrictive means was available of achieving the same objective. Not uncontroversially, the House of Lords accepted a public policy with regard to maintaining order and the proper allocation of police resources as justification for a decision to police just two sailings of live animal cargo a week from a particular port in the UK that was experiencing protests by animal rights groups.[13]

[20–16] Whilst, from a common law perspective, the term "public policy" might be regarded as open-ended, or indeed as a concept close to that of "mandatory requirements" developed by the Court of Justice in *Cassis de Dijon*, for the purposes of Art 36 TFEU the term is not understood in this broad fashion. For example, in the *Irish Souvenirs* case (*Commission v Ireland*) Ireland sought to justify a requirement that imported jewellery bearing motifs of Ireland, such as a shamrock, must bear a mark of origin indicating that it was not made in Ireland.[14] This requirement, it was argued, was justifiable on the grounds of public policy or the protection of industrial or commercial

[8] Case 34/79 *R v Henn and Darby* [1979] ECR 3795.

[9] Case 121/85 *Conegate Ltd v Commissioners of Customs and Excise* [1986] ECR 1007.

[10] *ibid*, 1022.

[11] Case 7/78 *R v Thompson* [1978] ECR 2247.

[12] Case C-434/04 *Ahokainen and Leppik* [2006] ECR I-9171.

[13] *R v Chief Constable of Sussex ex p International Trader's Ferry Ltd* [1999] 1 All ER 129.

[14] Case 113/80 *Commission v Ireland (Irish Souvenirs)* [1981] ECR 1625.

property as it served to protect the consumer from being misled into buying souvenirs of Ireland that were not, in fact, Irish-made goods. The Court firmly rejected this suggestion by emphasising that, since Art 36 constitutes a derogation from the basic rule that all obstacles to the free movement of goods are to be eliminated, it must be interpreted strictly. As a result, the Art 36 grounds "cannot be extended to cases other than those specifically laid down. In view of the fact that neither the protection of consumers nor the fairness of commercial transactions is included amongst the exceptions set out in Article 36, those grounds cannot be relied upon as such in connection with that article".[15]

(iii) Public Security

[20–17] The public security ground covers both a state's internal and external security. The most frequently cited instance of the Court of Justice accepting it as a defence to a national measure is *Campus Oil Ltd v Minister for Industry and Energy*.[16] This concerned an Irish requirement that importers of petroleum products were to purchase a certain percentage of their needs from a State-owned oil refinery at a fixed price based on the costs incurred by the refinery. The Court accepted that, because of the exceptional importance of petrol products to a state's economy, essential public services and the survival of its citizens, an interruption of supply could seriously affect the public security that Art 36 permitted a Member State to protect. The requirement on importers to purchase a percentage of their needs from Ireland's only oil refinery allowed the refinery to remain viable, thereby guaranteeing a source of domestic supply.

(iv) Health and Life of Humans, Animals or Plants

[20–18] In contrast to the grounds of public morality, public policy and public security, the need to protect human health has been successfully relied upon in numerous cases. A key aspect of the approach of the Court of Justice is an acceptance that Member States will differ in their approaches to the protection of human health, particularly where there is a degree of uncertainty as to the scientific evidence. A good example of this is *Sandoz*, which concerned a Dutch law that prevented the sale of foods that contained added vitamins without a prior authorisation.[17] The law had been applied to imports of muesli bars lawfully sold in other Member States. The Court reasoned that uncertainties did exist as to the scientific assessment of the potential benefit and harm of added vitamins. Secondly, although added vitamins may not pose a danger in themselves, over-consumption could be detrimental to a person's health. On the other hand, there may be circumstances where added vitamins do meet a real technical or nutritional need. In the Court's view, whereas a Member State would enjoy a margin of appreciation or discretion to decide how to protect against the risk of excessive consumption of added vitamins, any restrictive measure must be proportionate and, in particular, should allow for the sale of added vitamins where they meet a real technical or nutritional need. According to the Court, therefore:

> In so far as there are uncertainties at the present state of scientific research it is for the Member States, in the absence of harmonization, to decide what degree of protection of the health and life of humans they intend to assure, having regard however for the requirements of the free movement of goods within the [EU].

---

15 *ibid*, 1638.
16 Case 72/83 *Campus Oil Ltd v Minister for Industry and Energy* [1984] ECR 2727.
17 Case 174/82 *Sandoz* [1983] ECR 2445.

Those principles also apply to substances such as vitamins which are not as a general rule harmful in themselves but may have special harmful effects solely if taken to excess as part of the general nutrition, the composition of which is unforeseeable and cannot be monitored. In view of the uncertainties inherent in the scientific assessment, national rules prohibiting, without prior authorization, the marketing of foodstuffs to which vitamins have been added are justified on principle within the meaning of Article 36 of the Treaty on grounds of the protection of human health.

Nevertheless the principle of proportionality which underlies the last sentence of Article 36 of the Treaty requires that the power of the Member States to prohibit imports of the products in question from other Member States should be restricted to what is necessary to attain the legitimate aim of protecting health. Accordingly, national rules providing for such a prohibition are justified only if authorizations to market *are granted* when they are compatible with the need to protect health.

Such an assessment is, however, difficult to make in relation to additives, such as vitamins, the abovementioned characteristics of which exclude the possibility of foreseeing or monitoring the quantities consumed as part of the general nutrition and the degree of harmfulness of which cannot be determined with sufficient certainty. Nevertheless, although in view of the present stage of harmonization of national laws at the [EU] level a wide discretion must be left to the Member States, *they must, in order to observe the principle of proportionality, authorize marketing when the addition of vitamins to foodstuffs meets a real need*, especially a technical or nutritional one.[18]

[20–19] Although not using the term, the judgment in *Sandoz* pre-empts the development of the precautionary principle, which has been expressly referred to in later case law. Indeed, in conferring the Union with a residual competence to harmonise with respect to ensuring the functioning of the Internal Market, Art 114 TFEU provides that any Commission proposal concerning health will take as a base a high level of protection, taking account in particular of any new development based on scientific facts. Article 35 of the Charter of Fundamental Rights also guarantees that a "high level of human health protection shall be ensured in the definition and implementation of all the Union's policies and activities". More particularly, Art 191 TFEU expressly states that the Union's environmental policy, which shall contribute to the protection of human health, shall be based on the precautionary principle. A Commission Communication on the precautionary principle highlights that, although it is only explicitly mentioned in the Treaties in the context of environmental protection,

its scope is far wider and covers those specific circumstances where scientific evidence is insufficient, inconclusive or uncertain and there are indications through preliminary objective scientific evaluation that there are reasonable grounds for concern that the potentially dangerous effects on the environment, human, animal or plant health may be inconsistent with the chosen level of protection.[19]

[20–20] Consistent with the conclusion in *Sandoz*, in infringement proceedings brought by the Commission against France, national rules governing the sale of foodstuffs with added nutrients were found to be in breach of Art 34 (*Red Bull*).[20] The

[18] *ibid*, 2463–2464. Emphasis added.

[19] Commission Communication on the Precautionary Principle, COM(2000) 1, 2 February 2000. See also Joined Cases C-487/17 to C-489/17 *Verlezza* EU:C:2019:270, 28 March 2019, paras 55–62.

[20] Case 24/00 *Commission v France (Red Bull)* [2004] ECR I-1277. See Malcolm A Jarvis, "Cases C-24/00, *Commission v France*, C-95/01 *Greenham and Abel* and C-270/02 *Commission v Italy*" (2004) *Common Market Law Review* 1395.

first breach arose from the fact that France had failed to provide a simplified procedure for including, on its national list of authorised nutrients, those added to foodstuffs for daily consumption, and foodstuffs intended for particular nutritional uses, which were lawfully manufactured or marketed in another Member State. Secondly, the French rules were held to hinder the marketing of certain foodstuffs, such as food supplements and confectionery products to which nutrients had been added, without establishing that the marketing of such foodstuffs entailed a real risk for public health.

[20–21] The Court was also required to consider whether a ban on the caffeine drink, Red Bull, could be justified on the ground of protecting human health. This aspect of the Commission's claim was dismissed by the Court on the basis of the Art 36 defence put forward by France. The Court reasoned as follows:

> A decision to prohibit the marketing of a fortified foodstuff, which is in fact the most restrictive obstacle to trade in products lawfully manufactured and marketed in other Member States, can be adopted only if the alleged real risk for public health appears to be sufficiently established on the basis of the latest scientific data available at the date of the adoption of such decision. In such a context, the object of the risk assessment to be carried out by the Member State is to appraise the degree of probability of harmful effects on human health from the addition of certain nutrients to foodstuffs and the seriousness of those potential effects.
>
> It is clear that such an assessment of the risk could reveal that scientific uncertainty persists as regards the existence or extent of real risks to human health. In such circumstances, it must be accepted that a Member State may, in accordance with the precautionary principle, take protective measures without having to wait until the existence and gravity of those risks are fully demonstrated. However, the risk assessment cannot be based on purely hypothetical considerations.[21]

[20–22] In support of the ban's introduction, a French public health authority had provided an opinion recommending that the drink should not be authorised due to an excessive caffeine content that was higher than that authorised in France, the risk of excessive caffeine consumption, in particular among pregnant women, a misleading claim concerning the "energy-enhancing" character of the product and the risk of positive drug tests among sportsmen. In light of this opinion, the Court considered that the onus had shifted to the Commission, which had "not adduced evidence sufficient to call into question the French authorities' analysis as regards the dangers which those drinks pose to public health".[22]

[20–23] Although involving a legal challenge of a different nature, it might be noted that in *R ex p Philip Morris v Secretary of State for Health (Plain Tobacco Packaging)*, a preliminary reference required the Court to consider the validity of a directive on the presentation of tobacco products in light of the principle of proportionality.[23] In particular, it was argued that standardised packaging requirements and a requirement that health warnings cover a certain percentage of the front and back of cigarette packets was

[21] *ibid*, 1323–1324.
[22] *ibid*, 1327.
[23] Case C-547/14 *R ex p Phillip Morris v Secretary of State for Health (Plain Tobacco Packaging)* EU:C:2016:325, 4 May 2016. See Katharina Ó Cathaoir, "Court of Justice Upholds the Tobacco Products Directive 2014" (2016) 7 *European Journal of Risk Regulation* 623.

disproportionate to the public health objective being pursued, particularly having regard to the right to freedom of expression guaranteed by the Charter of Fundamental Rights.

[20–24] In response, the Court noted that both the Charter and the Treaties require that a high level of human health protection be ensured in the definition and implementation of all of the Union's policies and activities. In its view, the protection of human health, "in an area characterised by the proven harmfulness of tobacco consumption, by the addictive effects of tobacco and by the incidence of serious diseases caused by the compounds those products contain that are pharmacologically active, toxic, mutagenic and carcinogenic", outweighed corporate interests in freedom of expression.[24] In upholding the proportionality of the directive, the Court went on to observe that a high level of protection of human health, especially for young people, requires that "consumers of tobacco products, who are a particularly vulnerable class of consumers because of the addictive effects of nicotine, should not be encouraged to consume those products by means of, albeit factually accurate, information, which they may interpret as meaning that the risks associated with their habits are reduced or that the products have certain benefits".[25]

[20–25] Regarding the protection of animal health, an interesting example is provided by the response of the United Kingdom and Ireland to incidence of Newcastle Disease amongst poultry in the 1980s, which resulted in infringement proceedings by the Commission. With respect to a UK ban on the importation of turkeys from certain Member States, including France, the Court of Justice concluded that the measure was, in fact, a disguised restriction on trade that went beyond what was necessary in order to protect the UK's poultry population. According to the Court:

> Certain established facts suggest that the real aim of the 1981 measures was to block, for commercial and economic reasons, imports of poultry products from other Member States, in particular from France. The United Kingdom Government had been subject to pressure from British poultry producers to block these imports. It hurriedly introduced its new policy with the result that French Christmas turkeys were excluded from the British market for the 1981 season. It did not inform the Commission and the Member States concerned in good time, as the letter in which the Commission was informed of the new measures — which took effect on 1 September 1981 — was dated 27 August 1981. It did not find it necessary to discuss the effects of the new measures on imports with the Community institutions, with the Standing Veterinary Committee or with the Member States concerned.
>
> It should be noted, in this context, that when the United Kingdom abandoned, in 1964, the policy of non-vaccination and compulsory slaughter conducted till then in Great Britain, in order to adopt a policy of control of Newcastle disease by vaccination, this change of policy was thoroughly prepared by an elaborate report of a committee of experts, by various studies and by prolonged discussions among veterinary experts. The evidence available in the present case does not suggest that any comparable effort was made before the Government decided, in 1981, to reintroduce the policy which it had applied before 1964. The deduction must be made that the 1981 measures did not form part of a seriously considered health policy.[26]

[20–26] In addition, a licensing requirement for the import of poultry into Great

---

24 *ibid*, para 156.

25 *ibid*, para 144.

26 Case 40/82 *Commission v United Kingdom (Newcastle Disease)* [1982] ECR 2793, 2825–2826.

Britain was held to exceed what was necessary in order to protect animal health and so was not exempted by virtue of Art 36.

[20–27] Unlike within Great Britain, however, in Northern Ireland a policy of compulsory slaughter rather than vaccination had been continuously applied, meaning that the poultry population there was healthier, but more susceptible to infection should an outbreak occur. The UK successfully argued that this, together with the high density of the poultry population in Northern Ireland and its relative importance to the local economy, justified the operation of an import licensing requirement in respect of this territory. In considering the situation in Northern Ireland, the Court accepted that the question of whether or not a national measure on animal health may include an import licensing system without infringing Art 36 "depends upon the relationship in an individual case between, on the one hand, the inconvenience caused by the administrative and financial burdens imposed under such a system and, on the other hand, the dangers and risks for animal health resulting from the imports in question".[27] Similarly, in proceedings against Ireland, where the same policy of compulsory slaughter had been pursued, the Court observed that the question of whether or not national measures on animal health may include an import licensing system without infringing Art 36 "cannot be answered uniformly in every case".[28] In view of the risk posed to the Irish poultry population, an import licence regime was held to be justifiable, in distinction to the Court's finding with respect to Great Britain.

(v) National Treasures of Artistic, Historic or Archaeological Value

[20–28] This rather discrete ground for an exemption, which relates to the export of cultural goods much more than to imports, has not been successfully relied upon before the Court. The issue is also the subject of a directive on the return of cultural objects unlawfully removed from the territory of a Member State,[29] a regulation on the export of cultural goods from the EU to a third country,[30] and a regulation on the import of cultural goods into the Union.[31]

(vi) Industrial or Commercial Property

[20–29] Of the six grounds contained in Art 36, the protection of industrial or commercial property is, by some way, the most complex, in that it is, essentially, a cross-reference to the separate body of intellectual property law.[32] In addition, Art 36 must be read in light of the guarantee in Art 345 TFEU that the Treaties "shall in no way prejudice the rules in Member States governing the system of property ownership". The tension between the free movement of goods and the protection of intellectual

---

27 Case 40/82 *Commission v United Kingdom (Newcastle Disease)* [1984] ECR 283, 301.

28 Case 74/82 *Commission v Ireland (Newcastle Disease)* [1984] ECR 317, 346.

29 Directive 2014/60/EU of the European Parliament and of the Council of 15 May 2014 on the return of cultural objects unlawfully removed from the territory of a Member State and amending Regulation (EU) No 1024/2012 (Recast) [2014] OJ L159/1.

30 Council Regulation (EC) No 116/2009 of 18 December 2008 on the export of cultural goods [2009] OJ L39/1.

31 Regulation (EU) 2019/880 of the European Parliament and of the Council of 17 April 2019 on the introduction and import of cultural goods [2019] OJ L151/1.

32 See Charlotte Waelde, Abbe Brown, Smita Kheria, and Jane Cornwell, *Contemporary Intellectual Property: Law and Policy* (4th ed, Oxford University Press, 2016) ch 20.

property rights can be seen from the facts of the early case of *Deutsche Grammophon*.[33] There, a German music company sought to rely on German copyright laws in order to prevent records it had exported to France from being reimported back into Germany. As described by the Court of Justice:

> If a right related to copyright is relied upon to prevent the marketing in a Member State of products distributed by the holder of the right or with his consent on the territory of another Member State on the sole ground that such distribution did not take place on the national territory, such a prohibition, which would legitimize the isolation of national markets, would be repugnant to the essential purpose of the Treaty, which is to unite national markets into a single market. That purpose could not be attained if, under the various legal systems of the Member States, nationals of those States were able to partition the market and bring about arbitrary discrimination or disguised restrictions on trade between Member States.
>
> Consequently, it would be in conflict with the provisions prescribing the free movement of products within the common market for a manufacturer of sound recordings to exercise the exclusive right to distribute the protected articles, conferred upon him by the legislation of a Member State, in such a way as to prohibit the sale in that State of products placed on the market by him or with his consent in another Member State solely because such distribution did not occur within the territory of the first Member State.[34]

[20–30] Having regard to Art 345 TFEU, the Court drew an important distinction between the *existence* of an intellectual property right, which was a matter for the law of the Member States, and the *exercise* of that right in such a way as to impinge upon the right of free movement guaranteed by Art 34, which was legitimately a matter of EU law.

[20–31] A further distinction introduced by the Court in *Deutsche Grammophon* was to establish that Art 36 could only provide an exemption from Art 34 to the extent that the impugned measure was "justified for the purpose of safeguarding rights which constitute *the specific subject-matter*" of the intellectual property right. What constitutes the "specific subject-matter" of an intellectual property right will vary depending on whether it is a patent, copyright, trade mark etc that is in issue. In essence, however, it entails the right to place an intellectual property protected product onto the market for the first time and to enjoy the benefits of the *de facto* monopoly situation to which that gives rise. According to what is known as the doctrine of "exhaustion of rights", once the owner has benefited from this situation, however, his or her rights have become exhausted, in the sense that they cannot seek to prevent the importation of the product into another Member State. Through the application of the two concepts of specific subject matter and exhaustion of rights, the Court has sought to balance the protection of intellectual property rights with the proper functioning of the Single Market.

C. Mandatory Requirements

[20–32] Mandatory requirements are unusual in that, although they are defences available to Member States in order to justify a restriction on the free movement of

[33] Case 78/70 *Deutsche Grammophon* [1971] ECR 487. See Robert S Smith, "The Unresolved Tension between Trademark Protection and Free Movement of Goods in the European Community" (1992) 3 *Duke Journal of Comparative and International Law* 89.

[34] *ibid*, 500.

goods, no reference to them is to be found within the Treaties. Rather, mandatory requirements formed part of the novel approach developed by the Court of Justice in *Cassis de Dijon* in order to address indistinctly applicable measures.[35] By establishing the principle of mutual recognition, the Court rendered an indistinctly applicable measure such as a product requirement, previously thought to have fallen outside of Art 34, to be an MEQR. This had the effect of greatly reducing the legislative competence of Member States to control the nature of imported goods sold and marketed on their territory. In recognition of this, and having regard to the fact that – provided they are not discriminatory[36] – indistinctly applicable measures are less inherently "bad", from a Single Market perspective, than distinctly applicable measures, the Court offered Member States some consolation by creating the open-ended category of mandatory requirements.

[20–33] So, when seeking to defend an indistinctly applicable measure, in addition to the six grounds listed in Art 36, a Member State may present a case based on any imperative requirement or overriding public interest such as:

- *protection of the environment*, such as in *Mickelsson and Roos* where it was held that national regulations restricting the use of watercraft to certain designated navigable waterways could, in principle, be regarded as proportionate provided that: (i) the competent national authorities were required to adopt the necessary implementing measures; (ii) those authorities had actually made use of the power conferred on them and designated the waters which satisfy the conditions provided for by the national regulations; and (iii) such measures had been adopted within a reasonable period after the entry into force of those regulations. This was a factual matter for the national court to determine.[37] Protection of the environment was also successfully relied upon in *Walloon Waste (Commission v Belgium)*, where the Court rejected the Commission's claim that Belgium had infringed Art 34 by banning the importation of waste into the region of Wallonia. Having first accepted that waste, even if non-recyclable, may constitute a "good" for the purpose of Art 34, the Court went on to find that "in view of the abnormal large-scale inflow of waste from other regions for tipping in Wallonia, there was a real danger to the environment, having regard to the limited capacity of that region", such that the ban was justified.[38]
- *protection of children*, such as in *Dynamic Medien*, where the Court accepted this ground as justifying a German requirement that all mail-order or online sales of DVDs to children must first be examined by a German authority and affixed with an age-appropriate classification.[39] In assessing the proportionality of the measure, it was relevant that such goods could be imported where an adult had made contact with the seller in order to arrange the sale. The proportionality of

[35] Case 120/78 *Cassis de Dijon* [1979] ECR 649. See ch 19, paras [19–44] to [19–53].

[36] As Paul Craig and Gráinne de Búrca point out, the traditional view was that mandatory requirements could only be used in respect of rules that were not discriminatory. Over time, this distinction has come under strain, including where it is necessary to distinguish between an indistinctly applicable rule and indirect discrimination, which can become a matter of degree that is difficult to assess. Paul Craig and Gráinne de Búrca, *EU Law* (6th ed, Oxford University Press, 2015) 705.

[37] Case C-142/05 *Mickelsson and Roos* [2009] ECR I-4273.

[38] Case C-2/90 *Commission v Belgium (Walloon Waste)* [1992] ECR I-4431, 4479. See also Case C-463/01 *Commission v Germany (Waste Packaging)* [2004] ECR I-11705.

[39] Case C-244/06 *Dynamic Medien* [2008] ECR I-505.

the measure also required that the examination procedure in Germany be readily accessible, completed within a reasonable period, and that any refusal be open to challenge before the courts (which were all factual matters for the national court to determine). It has been commented that, given that it was the protection of children that was at stake, the Court afforded Germany a generous margin of appreciation, as compared with other cases, and "gave only the most cursory examination of the proportionality principle".[40]

- *road safety*, such as in *Italian Trailers* where it was held that a prohibition on motorcycles towing trailers that had been specially designed for such a use was justified. While it was possible to envisage alternative measures that could guarantee a certain level of road safety for the combination of a motorcycle and a trailer, the fact remained that Member States could not be denied the possibility of attaining an objective such as road safety by the introduction of general and simple rules which would be easily understood and applied by drivers and easily managed and supervised by the competent authorities.[41] In *Commission v Finland*, the Court accepted that, in principle, Finland could seek to rely on road safety as a mandatory requirement that might potentially justify a requirement that cars imported into Finland first undergo a "transfer licence" registration procedure.[42] Finland claimed that the registration procedure provided up-to-date information that assisted in investigating traffic violations or accidents. On the facts, however, the Court was not satisfied that the procedure had been designed with the aim of road safety in mind. In addition, the Court was unconvinced of its necessity given that all other Member States maintained their own car-registration systems, from whom identifying information could be sought in the event of an accident or a traffic violation.

- *preventing crime*, such as in *Tinted Windows*, where it was held that a ban on the sale of tinted film to be placed on car windows was excessive and therefore disproportionate. Portugal had claimed that the ban was necessary to assist in the fight against crime and to detect whether seat belts were being worn. Portugal did not, however, ban cars being sold with tinted windows, undermining the justification put forward. In addition, the Court noted that tinted film was sold in a range of opacity, with some being close to transparency.[43]

- *socio-cultural characteristics*, such as in *Torfaen Borough Council v B&Q*, where it was held that it was for the national courts to determine whether the effects of Sunday trading rules were excessive to the aims being pursued. National courts in the UK reached different conclusions, depending on whether the "socio-cultural characteristic" was considered to be the protection of workers who did not wish to work on Sunday (disproportionate) or to preserve the traditional character of the British Sunday (proportionate). Ultimately, in a further preliminary reference it was held that such rules were proportionate.[44]

- *promoting cultural activities*, such as in *Cinéthèque*, where it was held that a requirement that one year pass before a cinema release was made available on

[40] Catherine Barnard, *The Substantive Law of the EU* (4th ed, Oxford University Press, 2013) 179.

[41] Case C-110/05 *Commission v Italy (Italian Trailers)* [2009] ECR I-519.

[42] Case C-54/05 *Commission v Finland* [2007] ECR I-2473.

[43] Case C-265/06 *Commission v Portugal (Tinted Windows)* [2008] ECR I-2245.

[44] Case 145/88 *Torfaen Borough Council v B&Q* [1989] ECR 3851; Case C-169/91 *Stoke-on-Trent City Council v B&Q* [1992] ECR I-6635.

video was justified in order to promote cinema-going and protect film production.[45] The Court has also accepted that the protection of books and small booksellers can constitute a mandatory requirement. On the facts, however, it was held that an Austrian minimum sales price regime for books was disproportionate, as there were less restrictive means of achieving this objective.[46]

- *press diversity*, such as in *Familiapress*, where it was held that it was for the national court to determine whether a ban on publications containing competitions with the chance of winning a prize was proportionate to the objective of maintaining press diversity. In so deciding, the national court was to have regard to: (i) whether newspapers offering the chance of winning a prize were, in fact, in competition with small newspaper publishers who were deemed to be unable to offer comparable prizes; (ii) whether the prospect of winning a prize was liable to bring about a shift in demand; and (iii) the fact that the national prohibition must not constitute an obstacle to the marketing of newspapers which, even though containing prize competitions open to readers in other Member States, did not give readers residing in the host Member State the opportunity to win a prize.[47]
- *fundamental rights*, such as the freedom of expression, as in *Austrian Motorways*, where it was held that a decision by the Austrian authorities to allow an environmental protest that closed a motorway for 30 hours was justified, having regard to the fact that citizens were exercising their fundamental rights by manifesting in public an opinion which they considered to be of importance to society.[48]

[20–34] The two most commonly invoked mandatory requirements, however, are consumer protection and the protection of public health.

(i) Consumer Protection

[20–35] Famously, in *Cassis de Dijon* itself, Germany sought to defend its requirement for a minimum alcohol content in order for a drink to be sold as a liqueur on the basis that this was necessary so as to prevent consumers from being misled into buying drinks with a lower alcohol content than that which they would expect of such a product.[49] To address this consumer-protection concern, the Court replied, it was a "simple matter to ensure that suitable information is conveyed to the purchaser by requiring the display of an indication of origin and of the alcohol content on the packaging of products".[50] This same robust approach to consumers was evident in the *Beer Purity* case, concerning a German law that confined drinks that could be sold as "beer" to those made from just barley, hops, yeast and water.[51] According to Germany, in its consumers' minds the term "beer" was inseparably linked to a drink made from these four ingredients only. The Court of Justice reaffirmed its position that suitable labelling ought to be sufficient to adequately inform consumers. In rejecting Germany's contention, the Court also made

---

45 Joined Cases 60/84 and 61/84 *Cinéthèque* [1985] ECR 2605.
46 Case C-513/07 *Fachverband der Buch* [2009] ECR I-3717.
47 Case C-368/95 *Familiapress* [1997] ECR I-3689.
48 Case C-112/00 *Schmidberger v Austria (Austrian Motorways)* [2003] ECR I-5659.
49 Case 120/78 *Cassis de Dijon* [1979] ECR 649.
50 *ibid*, 664.
51 Case 178/84 *Commission v Germany (Beer Purity)* [1987] ECR 1227.

an important general observation regarding the expectations of consumers within the Single Market:

> [C]onsumers' conceptions which vary from one Member State to the other are also likely to evolve in the course of time within a Member State. The establishment of the common market is, it should be added, one of the factors that may play a major contributory role in that development. Whereas rules protecting consumers against misleading practices enable such a development to be taken into account, legislation [such as in this case] prevents it from taking place. … [T]he legislation of a Member State must not "crystallize given consumer habits so as to consolidate an advantage acquired by national industries concerned to comply with them".[52]

[20–36] The Court's high regard for consumer awareness is seen again in *Rau*, where Belgium insisted on margarine being sold in cubes in order to distinguish it from butter,[53] and in *Mars*, where Germany prohibited the use of labelling such as "plus 10%" where the label exceeded 10 per cent of the surface of the good. According to the Court, "[r]easonably circumspect consumers may be deemed to know that there is not necessarily a link between the size of publicity markings relating to an increase in a product's quantity and the size of that increase".[54] Similarly, in *Clinique*, the Court was not convinced of the need for the application to cosmetic products branded as "Clinique" of a German law prohibiting misleading names.[55] Although Germany argued that the brand was so close to the word "clinic" that the products could be mistaken to have medicinal properties, the Court responded by noting that the "products are ordinarily marketed in other countries under the name 'Clinique' and the use of that name apparently does not mislead consumers".[56] The Court is, however, willing to moderate its approach to consumers where there are particular grounds for doing so, such as where the market for a product is highly specialised and well informed, or is likely to be less well informed than the average consumer. So, for example, the Court accepted a French law preventing door-to-door selling of educational materials, partly due to the fact that the product in question was aimed at vulnerable consumers who were "behind with their education and are seeking to catch up".[57]

(ii) Protection of Human Health

[20–37] The Court of Justice will closely scrutinise a defence put forward by a Member State on protection of human health grounds, considering the scientific evidence in support of the restriction, the practice in other Member States, as well as the overall coherence of the state's health policy. In *Cassis de Dijon*, for example, Germany sought to justify the minimum alcohol content requirement in order for drinks to be sold as liqueur by arguing that this served to prevent the proliferation of drinks on the market with a low alcohol content which "may more easily induce a tolerance towards alcohol than more highly alcoholic beverages".[58] The Court rejected this argument by noting that the "consumer can obtain on the market an extremely wide range of weakly or moderately alcoholic products and furthermore a large proportion of alcoholic beverages

52 *ibid*, 1270–1271.
53 Case 261/81 *Rau* [1982] ECR 3961.
54 Case C-470/93 *Mars* [1995] ECR I-1923, 1944.
55 Case C-315/92 *Clinique Laboratories* [1994] ECR I-317.
56 *ibid*, 337.
57 Case 382/87 *Buet* [1989] ECR 1235, 1252.
58 Case 120/78 *Cassis de Dijon* [1979] ECR 649, 663.

with a high alcohol content freely sold on the German market is generally consumed in a diluted form".[59] Similarly, in the *Beer Purity* case, Germany failed to convince the Court of the human health need for a ban on additives in beer when it did not prohibit the use of additives in other drinks.[60]

[20–38] Three further cases demonstrating the Court's rigorous approach in this area are *DocMorris, Ker-Optika* and *DPV*. In *DocMorris*, a German ban on the sale of medicinal products online was held to be justified on public health grounds in relation to prescription drugs.[61] According to the Court:

> Given that there may be risks attaching to the use of these medicinal products, the need to be able to check effectively and responsibly the authenticity of doctors' prescriptions and to ensure that the medicine is handed over either to the customer himself, or to a person to whom its collection has been entrusted by the customer, is such as to justify a prohibition on mail-order sales. As the Irish Government has observed, allowing prescription medicines to be supplied on receipt of a prescription and without any other control could increase the risk of prescriptions being abused or inappropriately used. Furthermore, the real possibility of the labelling of a medicinal product bought in a Member State other than the one in which the buyer resides being in a language other than the buyer's may have more harmful consequences in the case of prescription.[62]

[20–39] In contrast, a ban was held not to be justified in the case of non-prescription medicines, with the Court having regard to inherent reduced risk to health and to the fact that any risk that did exist could be lessened "through an increase in the number of on-line interactive features which the customer must use before being able to proceed to a purchase".[63]

[20–40] In *Ker-Optika,* Hungary sought to defend a law that required contact lenses to be sold only in shops specialising in medical devices, preventing their sale online, on the ground that it was necessary to protect human health.[64] In particular, it was said to be necessary to require customers to take delivery of contact lenses in specialist shops because they must have access to an optician who could carry out the necessary physical examinations, undertake checks and give instructions on the wearing of the lenses.

[20–41] The Court reiterated its settled case law to the effect that: (i) account must be taken of the fact that the health and life of humans rank foremost among the interests protected by the Treaty; (ii) it is for the Member States to determine the level of protection which they wish to afford to public health and the way in which that level is to be achieved; (iii) since the level may vary from one Member State to another, Member States should be allowed a measure of discretion; but nevertheless (iv) for a national provision to be exempt under Art 36 it must be appropriate for securing the attainment of the objective pursued and must not go beyond what is necessary in order to attain the objective.

---

59 *ibid.*

60 Case 178/84 *Commission v Germany (Beer Purity)* [1987] ECR 1227.

61 Case C-322/01 *DocMorris* [2003] ECR I-14887.

62 *ibid*, 15000.

63 *ibid*, 14998.

64 Case 108/09 *Ker-Optika* [2010] ECR I-12213. See Pedro Caro de Sousa, "Through Contact Lenses, Darkly: Is Identifying Restrictions to Free Movement Harder than Meets the Eye? Comment on *Ker-Optika*" (2012) 37 *European Law Review* 79.

[20–42] Applying this logic to the facts before it, the Court first accepted that, in principle, a Member State may seek to reduce the risks inherent in wearing contact lenses by requiring that they be sold by qualified staff who will: alert the customer to those risks; carry out an examination of the customer and recommend or advise against the wearing of lenses; invite them to obtain the advice of an ophthalmologist where necessary; determine the most appropriate type of lenses; check the positioning of the lenses on the eyes and provide information on the correct use and care of the lenses. On the other hand, in order to meet the test of proportionality, it was necessary that there be no other measures less restrictive of the free movement of goods by which the same public health objectives could be achieved. It was here that the Hungarian legislation was found to exceed the discretion afforded to Member States.

[20–43] First, as there was no legal requirement that, on each occasion when contact lenses were supplied, the customer was to undergo an eye exam or to confirm that medical advice had been obtained, undergoing such an exam or obtaining such advice was optional, with the customer having the primary responsibility to make use of them. Before supplying contact lenses via the internet, advice could be provided by means of interactive features on the website, the use of which could be made mandatory before the customer could proceed to purchase the lenses. Secondly, whereas Member States could require that the determination of the most appropriate type of contact lenses should be undertaken by an optician under an obligation to check the positioning of the lenses on the customer's eyes and to advise on the correct use and care of the lenses, those services were generally required only when contact lenses were first supplied. At the time of subsequent supplies, it sufficed that the customer informed the seller of the type of lenses which were first supplied. Thirdly, a Member State could require a seller to make available a qualified optician with the task of giving customers, at a distance, individualised information and advice on the use and care of the contact lenses. In the view of the Court, the "provision of such information and advice at a distance may, moreover, offer advantages, since the lens user is enabled to submit questions which are well thought out and pertinent, and without the need to go out".[65] As a result, the Court concluded that Hungary's objective could be achieved by less restrictive means, "namely measures which subject to certain restrictions only the first supply of lenses and which require the economic operators concerned to make available a qualified optician to the customer".[66]

[20–44] What is striking about the Court's analysis is the manner in which it seeks to suggest alternative means by which the public health risks might be minimised whilst allowing sales via the internet, even going so far as to highlight related advantages to such alternative approaches. The judgment illustrates how the margin of appreciation initially granted to states by Art 36 is significantly reduced by the Court's strict and detailed approach to proportionality.

[20–45] This was seen more recently in *DPV*, where Germany, having revoked its earlier ban on mail-order sales of prescription drugs, continued to apply a regime of fixed sales prices for prescription drugs.[67] This prevented a Dutch mail-order firm from

---

[65] *ibid*, para 73.

[66] *ibid*, para 74.

[67] Case C-148/15 *Deutsche Parkinson Vereinigung (DPV)* EU:C:2016:776, 19 October 2016. See Simon López Artetxe, "Is Health *Really* the First Thing in Life?" (2017) 44 *Legal Issues of Economic Integration* 315.

operating a bonus scheme, where rewards were received on the basis of purchases made. According to Germany, the fixed pricing system was necessary so as to ensure that mail-order pharmacies did not engage in "ruinous price competition which would result in the closure of traditional pharmacies, especially in rural or underpopulated areas which are less attractive areas for traditional pharmacies to set up business. The German Government insists that such pharmacies alone are capable of ensuring safe and high-quality supplies, especially in cases of emergency, tailored advice and effective checks on the medicinal products supplied".[68]

[20–46] The Court, however, was unconvinced, concluding that Germany had not shown the fixed-price system to be an appropriate and proportionate means of attaining the objectives relied on. The Court began by setting out its general approach to such cases, noting that it was, in each case, for the national authorities to provide the necessary evidence of proportionality, with reasons that must be "accompanied by an analysis of the appropriateness and proportionality of the measure adopted by that State, and by specific evidence substantiating its arguments".[69] Whenever a national court is required to consider the protection of human health as an Art 36 ground, it must:

> examine objectively, through statistical or ad hoc data or by other means, whether it may reasonably be concluded from the evidence submitted by the Member State concerned that the means chosen are appropriate for the attainment of the objectives pursued and whether it is possible to attain those objectives by measures that are less restrictive of the free movement of goods.[70]

[20–47] Regarding the case before it, the Court concluded that there was no evidence to substantiate the contention that the fixed-price regime was necessary to ensure a uniform supply of prescription medicines for essential medical purposes throughout Germany. The general nature of the contentions made had failed to demonstrate how setting fixed prices allowed for a better geographical allocation of traditional pharmacies in Germany. Indeed, "[q]uite to the contrary, certain factors on which the Commission relies tend to suggest that increased price competition between pharmacies would be conducive to a uniform supply of medicinal products by encouraging the establishment of pharmacies in regions where the scarcity of dispensaries allows for higher prices to be charged".[71]

[20–48] Similarly, Germany had failed to demonstrate how the absence of a fixed-price regime would enable mail-order pharmacies to compete in terms of price in such a way that essential services, such as emergency care, could no longer be ensured in Germany due to a consequential fall in the number of dispensing pharmacies. Instead, the Court reiterated that competition factors other than price "could potentially allow traditional pharmacies, faced with competition from mail-order sales, to remain competitive in the German market".[72] Nor had it been shown how price competition for prescription medicine would adversely affect traditional pharmacies in performing certain activities in the general interest, such as producing prescription medicinal products or maintaining a given stock and selection of medicinal products. On the

---

68 *ibid*, para 33.
69 *ibid*, para 35.
70 *ibid*, para 36.
71 *ibid*, para 38.
72 *ibid*, para 39.

contrary, the Court pointed to the possibility that, "faced with price competition from mail-order pharmacies, traditional pharmacies will be encouraged to improve such activities".[73]

[20–49] Regarding an argument by Germany that a patient in poor health ought not to be required to carry out a market analysis in order to determine which pharmacy offers the medicinal product sought at the most attractive price, the Court was dismissive in its response, pointing out that the existence of a genuine risk to human health,

> must be measured, not according to the yardstick of general conjecture, but on the basis of relevant scientific research. Such general conjecture made in that regard does not in any way suffice to prove that the possibility for the consumer to seek to acquire prescription-only medicinal products at lower prices poses an actual risk to public health.[74]

[20–50] Indeed, rather than posing a risk to public health, the Court viewed price competition as potentially benefiting the patient in so far as it would allow for prescription medicines to be offered at more attractive prices than those that were being imposed by Germany. According to the Court, the effective protection of human health "demands, inter alia, that medicinal products be sold at reasonable prices".[75]

[20–51] As in *Ker-Optika*, *DPV* demonstrates the Court's willingness to engage in a robust policy dialogue with Member States, challenging their assumptions and putting forward alternative rationales and arguments of its own. This rigorous approach can be seen too in the Court's approach to evidence in the *Minimum Alcohol Pricing* case.[76] There, a preliminary reference questioned whether the protection of public health could justify a Scottish law that provided for the imposition of a minimum price per unit of alcohol. Draft secondary legislation proposed to set a minimum price of 50 pence per unit. A question arose as to whether, when considering the proportionality of a national measure, the moment in time at which the relevant evidence was to be assessed was: (i) when the measure was decided upon by the national authority, confining the scientific evidence to that which was available to the national authority at the time, or (ii) whenever the proportionality assessment is being carried out by the relevant court, allowing that court to consider evidence that was not available to the national authority when it made its decision. Consistent with the overall stance adopted in earlier case law, it was held that a national court was not to be confined to examining only information, evidence or material available to the national legislature when it adopted a measure, but rather the compatibility of a measure with EU law must be reviewed on the basis of the information, evidence or material available to the national court on the date on which it gives its ruling.

[20–52] It was, therefore, for the national court to determine, "having regard to a detailed analysis of all the relevant factors", whether the Scottish Parliament had rejected a measure that would have obtained the same objective by a less restrictive means,

---

[73] *ibid*, para 40.
[74] *ibid*, para 42.
[75] *ibid*, para 43.
[76] Case 333/14 *Scotch Whisky Association v Lord Advocate (Minimum Alcohol Pricing)* EU:C:2015:845, 23 December 2015. See Albertina Albors-Llorens, "The Alcohol (Minimum-Pricing) (Scotland) Act 2012 and the Collision between Single-Market Objectives and Public-Interest Requirements" (2017) 76 *Cambridge Law Journal* 25.

namely an increase in excise duties rather than a fixed, minimum-pricing regime.[77] In carrying out this proportionality assessment, the Court of Justice identified as relevant factors the existence of scientific uncertainty as to the actual effects of the legislation and the fact that the legislation would be subject to review after six years to see whether it had affected the consumption of alcohol, as well as its impact on other EU policies.[78] Ultimately, the proportionality of the measure was upheld by the UK Supreme Court, which found that minimum unit pricing was a more targeted means of changing the behaviour of those most at risk, than compared with an increase in excise duty, which would have had a greater impact on moderate drinkers who were not, in fact, at risk.[79] The Public Health (Alcohol) Act 2018 has introduced a similar system of minimum unit pricing in Ireland.[80]

---

77 *ibid*, para 65.

78 *ibid*, paras 57–58.

79 *Scotch Whisky Association v The Lord Advocate* [2017] UKSC 76, 15 November 2017, para 37.

80 No 24 of 2018. See Ollie Bartlett, "The Compatibility of Ireland's Public Health (Alcohol) Bill with EU Law", 13 October 2018, available at <http://eulawanalysis.blogspot.com/2018/10/the-compatibility-of-irelands-public.html>.

Chapter 21

FREEDOM OF ESTABLISHMENT

A. Introduction

[21–01] Within Part Three of the TFEU covering "Union Policies and Internal Actions", Title IV concerns the free movement of persons, services and capital. It comprises four separate chapters dealing with: (i) workers; (ii) the right of establishment; (iii) services; and (iv) capital and payments. Depending on the particular activity being pursued, an economic migrant exercising the right of free movement falls within the scope of one of the first three chapters, either as a worker, a self-employed "established" person, or as the provider or the recipient of a service in a Member State other than his or her own. Whereas this used to be the end of the matter, the Citizens Directive (Directive 2004/38) now provides for certain common rules to apply to the right to move and reside freely in a Member State other than of one's own nationality, irrespective of the specific economic activity that is being pursued, including rights pertaining to family members.[1] The conditions and limitations governing the exercise of these rights are dealt with in Chapter 24.

[21–02] Despite the common rules found within the Citizens Directive, the law governing the movement of workers, the self-employed and service providers or recipients continues to be supplemented by more specific rules and principles particular to each category. These rules relate to matters such as: the definition of a "worker", "established" person, "service provider" or "recipient"; whether the Treaty provisions have vertical and horizontal direct effect; the scope of the right to equal treatment; whether, to be prohibited, a restriction on free movement must involve direct or

---

[1] Directive 2004/38/EC of the European Parliament and of the Council of 29 April 2004 on the right of citizens of the Union and their family members to move and reside freely within the territory of the Member States [2004] OJ L158/77.

indirect discrimination, or may also include non-discriminatory measures, and the grounds on which a Member State may be permitted to place restrictions on the right to equal treatment. In addition to these Treaty-based rules, which primarily relate to establishing and maintaining the Single Market through *negative* integration, within each category *positive* integration has been advanced through the adoption of important secondary legal acts. The law in relation to the free movement of economic migrants can thus be seen to involve a patchwork of specific rules which are supplemented by both a shared bundle of rights set out in the Citizens Directive and shared underlying principles, with common trends and approaches to the respective Treaty guarantees being easily identifiable.

[21–03] Within Title IV of Part Three of the TFEU, the freedom of establishment is provided for in Chapter 2, comprising Arts 49–55. First, the guarantee of the right to establish oneself as a self-employed person, or as a business, in another Member State, is set out in Art 49, together with a prohibition on restrictions on the exercise of that right by the nationals or companies of another Member State. Article 49 guarantees the right to be able to carry on (or "establish") a business in another Member State without discrimination, whether as a self-employed person or in the form of a company, and whether as the primary business operation ("primary establishment") or as a branch or subsidiary of a larger operation based in a different Member State ("secondary establishment"). It states that:

> Within the framework of the provisions set out below, restrictions on the freedom of establishment of nationals of a Member State in the territory of another Member State shall be prohibited. Such prohibition shall also apply to restrictions on the setting up of agencies, branches or subsidiaries by nationals of any Member State established in the territory of any Member State.
>
> Freedom of establishment shall include the right to take up and pursue activities as self-employed persons and to set up and manage undertakings, in particular companies and firms within the meaning of the second paragraph of Article 54, under the conditions laid down for its own nationals by the law of the country where such establishment is effected, subject to the provisions of the Chapter relating to capital.

[21–04] The vertical and horizontal direct effect of Art 49 mirrors that of Art 45 TFEU on the free movement of workers. That is, while it has been clearly established that Art 49 has vertical direct effect,[2] and that it has *some* horizontal direct effect, the precise scope of its horizontal direct effect has yet to be clearly established. In the *Viking* and *Laval* cases, the Court of Justice was satisfied that Art 49 could be relied upon against a trade union or an association of trade unions, and that its direct applicability was not confined merely to "quasi-public organisations or to associations exercising a regulatory task and having quasi-legislative powers".[3] The extent to which horizontal direct effect may be relied upon against an individual private entity, however, remains unclear.

[21–05] So as to allow the principal Treaty guarantee to be supplemented by secondary legislation, Art 50 confers on the Union a competence to adopt directives, by way of the ordinary legislative procedure, in order to attain the freedom of establishment in relation to a particular activity. In acknowledging that it may be legitimate to treat certain

---

2 Case 2/74 *Reyners v Belgium* [1974] ECR 631.

3 Case C-438/05 *International Transport Workers' Federation v Viking Line* [2007] ECR I-10779, 10831; Case C-341/05 *Laval* [2007] ECR I-11767.

state activities in a distinct manner, Art 51 excludes from the scope of the Treaty rules activities which, even occasionally, are connected with the exercise of official authority within a Member State, and allows the Parliament and the Council, acting in accordance with the ordinary legislative procedure, to exclude other activities from the application of Chapter 2. As with the other fundamental freedoms, by way of an exception to the general prohibition on restrictions to the exercise of the right of establishment, Art 52 permits national measures providing for special treatment for foreign nationals on the grounds of public policy, public security or public health.

[21–06] A second conferral of legislative competence is then provided for in Art 53. In order to make it easier for individuals to take up and pursue activities as a self-employed person, it confers on the Union a competence to adopt directives, by way of the ordinary legislative procedure, for the mutual recognition of diplomas, certificates and other evidence of formal qualifications, and for the coordination of Member State laws in the area. In the case of the medical and pharmaceutical professions, however, the progressive abolition of restrictions is made dependent upon coordination of the conditions for their exercise in the Member States. A major piece of legislation in this area is the Recognition of Professional Qualifications Directive.[4] Although the regimes established by the Directive are somewhat complex, a summary of the Directive and how it operates is set out in Section G below.

[21–07] As regards the exercise of the right of establishment by corporate entities, Art 54 provides that, for the purposes of Chapter 2, companies established within the EU are to be treated in the same manner as EU nationals. This means that a company or firm constituted under civil or commercial law in accordance with the law of a Member State (including a cooperative society or other legal person governed by public or private law), and having its registered office, central administration or principal place of business within the Union, shall be treated for the purposes of Chapter 2 in the same way as a national of a Member State. Excluded from this definition are non-profit-making entities. Accordingly, an individual can exercise the right of establishment by virtue of participation in a company that is also exercising that right through, for example, being a director or a shareholder in the company. As stated by the Court of Justice in *Baars*,

> It is clear from the second paragraph of Article [49] of the Treaty that freedom of establishment includes the right to set up and manage undertakings, in particular companies or firms, in a Member State by a national of another Member State. So, a national of a Member State who has a holding in the capital of a company established in another Member State which gives him definite influence over the company's decisions and allows him to determine its activities is exercising his right of establishment.[5]

[21–08] Finally, in accordance with Art 55, Member States are required to treat the nationals of other Member States the same way as their own nationals as regards participation in the capital of companies.

[21–09] A useful overview of what is entailed by the freedom of establishment was provided by the Grand Chamber in its 2016 judgment in *AGET Iraklis*, which will be

[4] Directive 2005/36/EC of the European Parliament and of the Council of 7 September 2005 on the recognition of professional qualifications [2005] OJ L255/22.

[5] Case C-251/98 *Baars* [2000] ECR I-2728, 2815.

encountered further below.[6] There, the objective of Art 49 TFEU was described as being to:

> allow nationals of a Member State or legal persons established in that Member State to set up a secondary establishment in another Member State in order to carry on their business there and thus to promote economic and social interpenetration within the European Union in the sphere of economic activity other than as an employee. To that end, freedom of establishment is intended to allow such nationals or legal persons of the European Union to participate, on a stable and continuing basis, in the economic life of a Member State other than their State of origin and to profit therefrom by actually pursuing, in the host Member State, an economic activity through a fixed establishment for an indefinite period.
>
> The concept of establishment consequently presupposes actual establishment of the company concerned in that State and the pursuit of genuine economic activity there.
>
> Actual exercise of freedom of establishment thus entails, in particular, as a necessary adjunct to that freedom, that the subsidiary, agency or branch set up by a legal person established in another Member State must be able, where relevant, and if the activity which it proposes to carry out in the host Member State so requires, to take on workers in that Member State.
>
> Such exercise also entails, in principle, the freedom to determine the nature and extent of the economic activity that will be carried out in the host Member State, in particular the size of the fixed establishments and the number of workers required for that purpose, and also … the freedom subsequently to scale down that activity or even the freedom to give up, should it so decide, its activity and establishment.[7]

B. Meaning of "Establishment"

[21–10] Just as the term "worker" is not defined in Art 45 TFEU and was left to the Court of Justice to determine, there is no Treaty or secondary law definition of the term "establishment". As with workers, the concept of establishment has been given a broad interpretation by the Court, with an emphasis placed on the duration and the stable and consistent nature of the activity engaged in. It has also been defined largely in contrast with the concept of the provision of services.

[21–11] In *Factortame*, the Court described establishment as the "actual pursuit of an economic activity through a fixed establishment in another Member State for an indefinite period".[8] There, a question arose as to whether, in and of itself, the seeking, by Spanish owners, to have their fishing vessels entered onto the British shipping register constituted an exercise of the right of establishment. Whilst the Court accepted that the mere registration of a vessel, of itself, did not constitute establishment, nevertheless,

> where the vessel constitutes an instrument for pursuing an economic activity which involves a fixed establishment in the Member State concerned, the registration of that vessel cannot be dissociated from the exercise of the freedom of establishment. It follows that the conditions laid down for the registration of vessels must not form an obstacle to freedom of establishment.[9]

---

6 Case C-201/15 *AGET Iraklis* EU:C:2016:972, 21 December 2016.

7 *ibid*, paras 50–53.

8 Case C-221/89 *R v Secretary of State for Transport ex p. Factortame* [1991] ECR I-3905, 3965.

9 *ibid.*

[21–12] As a result, the Court held that a requirement that to be included on the register a ship must be owned by a British national, or by a UK registered company with at least 75 per cent British ownership, was in breach of Art 49 TFEU.[10] A similar finding was subsequently made against Ireland in relation to vessels other than fishing vessels.[11]

[21–13] A key judgment on the freedom of establishment remains that delivered in the 1995 case of *Gebhard*.[12] It concerned a German lawyer with a chambers in Germany who simultaneously established a chambers in Milan, where he used the Italian title "avvocato". His use of the title without having being registered led to his suspension from the Milan Bar. In considering whether or not Mr Gebhard was exercising the right of establishment in Italy, as opposed to providing services, the Court of Justice described the right of establishment as allowing an EU national to participate "on a stable and continuous basis, in the economic life of a Member State other than his State of origin and to profit therefrom, so contributing to the economic and social inter-penetration within the [Union] in the sphere of activities as self-employed persons".[13] The key characteristic of establishment, therefore, is that the economic activity is conducted on a stable and continuous basis. This is to be contrasted with the provision of services, which envisages activities of a temporary nature, taking into account not only the duration of the provision of the service but also its "regularity, periodicity or continuity".[14]

[21–14] Although Mr Gebhard had lived and practised as a lawyer in Italy for a number of years, the Milan Bar Association argued that unless he belonged to the relevant Italian professional body or, at least, pursued his activity in collaboration with persons belonging to that body, he ought to be regarded as a provider of services rather than as having established himself in Italy. This argument was rejected by the Court, which noted that the Treaty provisions relating to the right of establishment cover both the *taking-up* and the *pursuit* of activities. Accordingly, whilst membership of a professional body could be a condition of taking up and pursuing a particular activity, "[i]t cannot itself be constitutive of establishment. It follows that the question whether it is possible for a national of a Member State to exercise his right of establishment and the conditions for exercise of that right must be determined in the light of the activities which he intends to pursue on the territory of the host Member State."[15]

[21–15] Whilst the pursuit of an activity on an indefinite basis or the complete transfer of a business from one Member State to another is likely to be regarded as establishment rather than the provision of services, the distinction between the two is not always clear, particularly given that the Court confirmed in *Gebhard* that: (i) the right of establishment can be carried out simultaneously in more than one Member State and (ii) the fact that the provision of services is temporary does not mean that the provider cannot equip him or herself with some form of infrastructure in the host Member State insofar as it is necessary for the purpose of performing the services, such as an office, chambers or consulting rooms. Furthermore, in relation to companies, the Court has held that the

---

10 *ibid*, 3966.

11 Case C-151/96 *Commission v Ireland* [1997] ECR I-3327.

12 Case 55/94 *Gebhard* [1995] ECR I-4165, 4195. See also Case C-470/11 *Garkalns* EU:C:2012:505, 19 July 2012; Malcolm Jarvis, "Case Comment: Freedom of Establishment and Freedom to Provide Services – Lawyers on the Move?" (1996) 21 *European Law Review* 247.

13 *ibid*, 4198.

14 *ibid*, 4195.

15 *ibid*, 4196.

requirement for a continuous presence in a Member State need not necessarily take for the form of a "branch" or "agency", but can be met by having an office there, even if the office is managed for the company by an independent person.[16] Finally, in *Schnitzer* the Court complicated matters further by stressing that the mere fact that a business supplied identical or similar services in a repeated or more or less regular manner for a number of years (in that case, a Portuguese construction company operating in Germany for three years) was not sufficient to be regarded as being established in circumstances where it did not have "infrastructure there enabling it to pursue a professional activity there on a stable and continuous basis and, from the infrastructure, to hold itself out to, amongst other, nationals of the second Member State".[17]

[21–16] The nature of this grey area is fittingly described by Derrick Wyatt and Alan Dashwood's observation that it "seems that the provision of services from one Member State to another on a regular basis, accompanied by the use of an office or similar facility in the host state, may shade imperceptibility into establishment. But offering the services from an established professional base in the host Member State is essential if a person is to be regarded as established in that Member State".[18] In contrast, given that the definition of a worker requires a person to work under the direction of an employer, it is unsurprising that the Court considers the categories of worker and establishment to be "mutually exclusive".[19] In light of the above, it can be seen that any assessment of whether an activity fulfils the definition of establishment will be heavily fact-dependent.

C. Direct and Indirect Discrimination

[21–17] The prohibition in Art 49 TFEU on restrictions on the freedom of establishment has been held to preclude direct and indirect forms of discrimination on the grounds of nationality, both as regards the taking up of such activities, and their ongoing pursuit in a broad sense (for instance, rules relating to the renting of commercial property). Examples of direct discrimination include *Reyners v Belgium*, where admission to the Belgian Bar was confined to persons of Belgian nationality, *Factortame*, where inclusion on the British register of vessels was confined to those owned by British nationals or British-controlled companies, and *Steinhauser v City of Biarritz*, where only French artists were entitled to rent beach huts as gallery spaces.[20]

[21–18] A typical form of indirect discrimination is a residence requirement. Examples include *Stöber*, where child benefit for self-employed persons in Germany was conditional on the child being habitually resident in Germany, or *Engelmann,* where an Austrian law required the operators of casinos to have their seat in Austria.[21] Indirect

---

16 Case 205/84 *Commission v Germany* [1986] ECR 3755.

17 Case C-215/01 *Schnitzer* [2003] ECR I-14847, 14883.

18 Alan Dashwood, Michael Dougan, Barry Rodger, Eleanor Spaventa and Derrick Wyatt, *Wyatt and Dashwood's European Union Law* (6th ed, Hart, 2011) 533–534.

19 Case 55/94 *Gebhard* [1995] ECR I-4165, 4194.

20 Case 2/74 *Reyners v Belgium* [1974] ECR 631; Case C-221/89 *R v Secretary of State for Transport ex p Factortame* [1991] ECR I-3905; Case 197/84 *Steinhauser v City of Biarritz* [1985] ECR 1819. See also Joined Cases C-458/14 and C-67/15 *Promoimpresa* EU:C:2016:558, 14 July 2016, paras 58–74.

21 Case 4/95 *Stöber* [1997] ECR I-511; Case C-64/08 *Engelmann* [2010] ECR I-8219.

discrimination can also arise from a requirement that only a national qualification will suffice. In the 1977 case of *Thieffry*, a Belgian lawyer with a Belgian doctorate in law and who had practised as an advocate in Belgium, obtained recognition from a French university that his qualifications were equivalent to a French law degree, as well as a certificate of aptitude for the profession of advocate in France. Notwithstanding this, the fact that he did not have a French law degree was used as the basis for refusing his admission to a training stage at the Paris Bar.

[21–19] The Court of Justice held that, despite the then absence of harmonising measures at EU level, such a requirement breached Art 49 TFEU. The Court began by observing that, since the practical enjoyment of the freedom of establishment can, in certain situations, depend on the national practice or legislation of a host Member State, it was incumbent on national authorities, including recognised professional bodies, to ensure that such practices or laws were applied in accordance with the Treaty objective of ensuring the freedom of establishment. To this end, within each Member State, it was necessary that, to the full extent compatible with the observance of the professional requirements, recognition be given to evidence of a professional qualification for the purposes of establishment. In particular, it would amount to an unjustified restriction on the freedom of establishment for a Member State to refuse admission to a profession to a person who (i) held a diploma which had been recognised as an equivalent qualification by the competent authority of the host Member State and (ii) fulfilled the conditions on professional training in the host Member State, solely on the basis that he or she did not possess the *national* diploma corresponding to the diploma from another Member State which had been recognised as an equivalent qualification. Accordingly,

> it is for the competent national authorities, taking account of the requirements of [EU] law ..., to make such assessments of the facts as will enable them to judge whether a recognition granted by a university authority can, in addition to its academic effect, constitute valid evidence of a professional qualification.
>
> The fact that a national legislation provides for recognition of equivalence only for university purposes does not of itself justify the refusal to recognise such equivalence as evidence of a professional qualification.
>
> This is particularly so when a diploma recognised for university purposes is supplemented by a professional qualifying certificate obtained according to the legislation of the country of establishment.
>
> In these circumstances, ... when a national of one Member State desirous of exercising a professional activity such as the profession of advocate in another Member State has obtained a diploma in his country of origin which has been recognised as an equivalent qualification by the competent authority under the legislation of the country of establishment and which has thus enabled him to sit and pass the special qualifying examination for the profession in question, the act of demanding the *national* diploma prescribed by the legislation of the country of establishment constitutes, even in the absence of the directives provided for in Article [53 TFEU], a restriction incompatible with the freedom of establishment guaranteed by Article [49 TFEU].[22]

[21–20] The logic of *Thieffry* was extended a step further in *Vlassopoulou*, a 1991 case concerning a Greek lawyer who had practised in Germany for a number of years, but

[22] Case 71/76 *Thieffry* [1977] ECR 765, 778–779, emphasis added. See also Case 222/86 *Heylens* [1987] ECR 4097.

whose application to the Bar was refused on the basis that she had not passed the relevant German exams.[23] Whereas in *Thieffry*, a French university had certified the equivalence of his Belgian law degree, Ms Vlassopoulou had obtained no such declaration, and her difficulty arose in particular due to the fact that, in addition to not having studied law at a German university, she had not sat the state examinations required in order to be called to the Bar. Germany argued that, in the absence of directives on the mutual recognition of educational qualifications, a Member State was entitled to make admission to a Bar dependent on the fulfilment of non-discriminatory conditions laid down by national law. In rejecting this argument, the Court of Justice required a host Member State: (i) to carry out a thorough assessment of the equivalence of educational qualifications obtained in another Member State; (ii) if there were any gaps in the qualification, to examine whether they had been made up through work experience gained since then; and (iii) to afford the individual procedural rights in carrying out the assessment, including the provision of reasons for the decision and the opportunity to seek judicial review. In addition to explaining its reasoning, the Court set out in considerable detail the steps that national authorities are required to undertake in order not to pose an obstacle to the exercise of the right of establishment by failing to have due regard to a person's qualifications, knowledge and experience acquired in another Member State:

> [E]ven if applied without any discrimination on the basis of nationality, national requirements concerning qualifications may have the effect of hindering nationals of the other Member States in the exercise of their right of establishment guaranteed to them by Article [49]. That could be the case if the national rules in question took no account of the knowledge and qualifications already acquired by the person concerned in another Member State.
>
> Consequently, a Member State which receives a request to admit a person to a profession to which access, under national law, depends upon the possession of a diploma or a professional qualification must take into consideration the diplomas, certificates and other evidence of qualifications which the person concerned has acquired in order to exercise the same profession in another Member State by making a comparison between the specialised knowledge and abilities certified by those diplomas and the knowledge and qualifications required by the national rules.
>
> That examination procedure must enable the authorities of the host Member State to assure themselves, on an objective basis, that the foreign diploma certifies that its holder has knowledge and qualifications which are, if not identical, at least equivalent to those certified by the national diploma. That assessment of the equivalence of the foreign diploma must be carried out exclusively in the light of the level of knowledge and qualifications which its holder can be assumed to possess in the light of that diploma, having regard to the nature and duration of the studies and practical training to which the diploma relates.
>
> In the course of that examination, a Member State may, however, take into consideration objective differences relating to both the legal framework of the profession in question in the Member State of origin and to its field of activity. In the case of the profession of lawyer, a Member State may therefore carry out a comparative examination of diplomas, taking account of the differences identified between the national legal systems concerned.
>
> If that comparative examination of diplomas results in the finding that the knowledge and qualifications certified by the foreign diploma correspond to those required by the

[23] Case 340/89 *Vlassopoulou* [1991] ECR 2357. See Julian Lonbay, "Picking Over the Bones: Rights of Establishment Reviewed" (1991) 16 *European Law Review* 507; Torsten Stein, "Case 340/89 *Vlassopoulou*" (1992) 29 *Common Market Law Review* 625.

> national provisions, the Member State must recognise that diploma as fulfilling the requirements laid down by its national provisions. If, on the other hand, the comparison reveals that the knowledge and qualifications certified by the foreign diploma and those required by the national provisions correspond only partially, the host Member State is entitled to require the person concerned to show that he has acquired the knowledge and qualifications which are lacking.
>
> In this regard, the competent national authorities must assess whether the knowledge acquired in the host Member State, either during a course of study or by way of practical experience, is sufficient in order to prove possession of the knowledge which is lacking.
>
> If completion of a period of preparation or training for entry into the profession is required by the rules applying in the host Member State, those national authorities must determine whether professional experience acquired in the Member State of origin or in the host Member State may be regarded as satisfying that requirement in full or in part.
>
> Finally, it must be pointed out that the examination made to determine whether the knowledge and qualifications certified by the foreign diploma and those required by the legislation of the host Member State correspond must be carried out by the national authorities in accordance with a procedure which is in conformity with the requirements of [EU] law concerning the effective protection of the fundamental rights conferred by the Treaty on [Union] subjects. It follows that any decision taken must be capable of being made the subject of judicial proceedings in which its legality under [EU] law can be reviewed and that the person concerned must be able to ascertain the reasons for the decision taken in his regard.[24]

[21–21] There can be a thin line between a qualification requirement that is indirectly discriminatory, as it will inevitably be more easily met by one's own nationals, and such a requirement that is non-discriminatory, in that it can be said not to benefit the host Member State's nationals over any others. It is interesting to note, therefore, the Court's observation above that "even if applied without any discrimination on the basis of nationality, national requirements concerning qualifications may have the effect of hindering nationals of the other Member States in the exercise of their right of establishment".[25] The Court expressed an openness to non-discriminatory measures being caught by Art 49, and did so by referencing restrictions having the "effect of hindering" the freedom of establishment, suggesting a test based on whether a measure restricts access to the market. As will be seen in Section G below, significant harmonisation measures have since been introduced governing the recognition of professional qualifications.

D. Derogations from the Freedom of Establishment

[21–22] Mirroring the three grounds for limiting the free movement of persons and of services, Art 52 TFEU provides that the rules in relation to the freedom of establishment "shall not prejudice the applicability of provisions laid down by law, regulation or administrative action providing for special treatment for foreign nationals on grounds of public policy, public security or public health". As is the case with each of the four freedoms, the Court of Justice takes a restrictive approach to the interpretation and application of these grounds of derogation.

---

24 *ibid*, 2383–2385.
25 *ibid*, 2383.

[21–23] In the unusual circumstances of *Commission v UK (Open Skies)*, the Commission took issue with the conclusion and application of a bilateral air services agreement between the UK and the United States due to the fact that a clause within the agreement permitted the suspension of traffic rights in respect of airlines designated by the UK but which were not owned and controlled by UK nationals.[26] This, argued the Commission, had the result that an airline established in the UK but owned or controlled by a Member State other than the UK, or by nationals of such a Member State, was prevented from receiving the same treatment as that reserved for airlines owned and controlled by the UK or its nationals.

[21–24] As one line of defence, the UK argued that the clause was justifiable on the basis of the public policy in ensuring that a reciprocal suspension of traffic rights could be invoked in respect of an airline designated by the United States but not owned and controlled by US nationals. According to the UK, the implications of the loss of such a power went "beyond the purely economic aspects and encompass foreign policy, safety and security considerations".[27] The Court responded to this claim by following its approach when dealing with the free movement of persons. It first noted that the invocation of an Art 52 ground "presupposes the need to maintain a discriminatory measure in order to deal with a genuine and sufficiently serious threat affecting one of the fundamental interests of society".[28] Secondly, as is required when seeking to exclude an individual, "there must be a direct link between that threat, which must, moreover, be current, and the discriminatory measure adopted to deal with it".[29] Here, the clause within the agreement did not limit the power of suspension solely to circumstances where an airline represented a threat to the public policy of the party granting an authorisation or permission. Moreover, there was no direct link between the "purely hypothetical" threat to the UK's public policy and generalised discrimination against airlines from other EU Member States. As a result, the UK failed in its attempt to rely on the public policy ground as a justification for the measure.

[21–25] A further example of an unsuccessful attempt to rely on Art 52 is *Commission v Italy (Data Processing Services)*.[30] There, the Commission challenged an Italian law that required companies providing data processing services to public authorities to have at least a majority of their shares in public or state ownership, given the confidential nature of the data involved. The Court rejected this, finding that the nature of the aims pursued by the data processing systems was not sufficient to establish that there would be any threat to public policy if companies from other Member States were awarded contracts for the operation of those systems. In addition, the confidential nature of the data processed by the systems could be protected by a duty of secrecy, without there being any need to restrict freedom of establishment.[31]

[21–26] One slight difference between the free movement of persons and the freedom of establishment arises in respect of "employment in the public service", as referred to

---

[26] Case C-466/98 *Commission v UK* [2002] ECR I-9496. See Liz Heffernan and Conor McAuliffe, "External Relations in the Air Transport Sector: The Court of Justice and the Open Skies Agreements" (2003) 26 *European Law Review* 601.

[27] *ibid*, 9514.

[28] *ibid*, 9515.

[29] *ibid.*

[30] Case 3/88 *Commission v Italy (Data Processing Services)* [1989] ECR 4035.

[31] *ibid*, 4060.

in Art 45 TFEU. The equivalent provision in relation to establishment is found in Art 51 TFEU. It provides that the Treaty rules shall not apply to activities within a Member State which are "connected, even occasionally, with the exercise of official authority".

[21–27] The Court's approach to Art 51, which is particularly restrictive, was first elaborated in *Reyners v Belgium*, in which Belgium unsuccessfully sought to argue that the profession of avocat (similar to a barrister) involved the exercise of official authority.[32] The Court was satisfied that the overall objective of Art 51 would be sufficiently met if it were "limited to those activities which, taken on their own, constitute a *direct and specific* connection with the exercise of official authority".[33] Accordingly, an extension of the exception to a whole profession would be possible "only in cases where such activities were linked with that profession in such a way that freedom of establishment would result in imposing on the Member State concerned the obligation to allow the exercise, even occasionally, by non-nationals of functions appertaining to official authority".[34] Such an extension would not be permitted where the "activities connected with the exercise of official authority are separable from the professional activity in question taken as a whole"[35]. The Court has gone on to find that notaries and court translators are similarly not exempted from the freedom of establishment by virtue of Art 51.[36]

[21–28] A further constraint on the official authority exemption was developed by the Court in *Thijssen*, where it was held that although the position of Insurance Inspectorate in Belgium did fall within Art 51, the subordinate position of Insurance Commissioner did not.[37] The reasoning for this was that, as the commissioner performed his duties under the supervision of the inspectorate and as his duties were "auxiliary and preparatory", they could not be said have a direct and specific connection with the exercise of official authority, as referred to by the Court in *Reyners*.[38]

E. Non-Discriminatory Restrictions

[21–29] Just as with the free movement of goods and of workers, in *Gebhard* the Court of Justice confirmed that a non-discriminatory restriction that is "liable to hinder or make less attractive" the exercise of the freedom of the establishment may by caught by the prohibition in Art 49. Once caught, the measure will require justification along the "rule of reason" lines set out in *Cassis de Dijon*, or on the grounds of public policy, public security or public health as provided for in Art 52.[39] In other words, in order to be permitted the restriction must be: (i) non-discriminatory; (ii) justified by an imperative requirement or overriding reason in the general interest; (iii) suitable for attaining the pursued objective; and (iv) proportionate, in that it does not go beyond

32 Case 2/74 *Reyners v Belgium* [1974] ECR 631.
33 *ibid*, 654. Emphasis added.
34 *ibid.*
35 *ibid.*
36 Case C-54/08 *Commission v Germany* [2011] ECR I-4355; Joined Cases C-372/09 and C-373/09 *Peñarroja* [2011] ECR I-1785; Case C-575/16 *Commission v Czech Republic* EU:C:2018:186, 15 March 2018.
37 Case C-42/92 *Thijssen* [1993] ECR I-4047.
38 *ibid*, 4073.
39 Case 120/78 *Cassis de Dijon* [1979] ECR 649.

what is necessary to achieve the objective. In addition, there must be no harmonisation at EU level providing for measures necessary to ensure that the interest is protected. So, for instance, in *Memoria*, an Italian law that required cremation urns to be kept in a private dwelling or in a municipal cemetery only was found to be caught by Art 49 since it prohibited EU nationals from providing a safekeeping service for the custody of urns.[40] As a result, it hindered EU nationals from establishing themselves in Italy for the purpose of performing a safekeeping service, and so the law was liable to hinder the exercise of the freedom of establishment guaranteed by the Treaty. Although a number of public interest reasons for the measure were presented, the Court considered the absolute restriction to go beyond what was necessary to achieve those objectives.

[21–30] An example of an assessment of justifications put forward in defence of a non-discriminatory restriction arose in *Commission v France (Bovine Centres)*.[41] There, the Commission had brought infringement proceedings in respect of a French measure that restricted the establishment of bovine artificial insemination centres to just one licensed centre for each prescribed geographical region. The Court reaffirmed that, as Art 49 requires the elimination of restrictions on the freedom of establishment, "all measures which prohibit, impede or render less attractive the exercise of that freedom must be regarded as restrictions within the meaning of that article".[42] France sought to justify the measure on the basis of the overriding public interest in improving the bovine genetic stock. It argued that the limit of one centre per region was the only means of guaranteeing accurate and comprehensive genetic information on bovine animals, which was essential to the continued genetic improvement of the stock. It was also said that the measures were necessary in order to centralise within a single body in each area all data on the inseminations carried out. The Court found this purported justification to be neither proportionate nor necessary, as an alternative would have been simply to impose an obligation on all operators to provide the information to a body designated for that purpose, thereby collecting the data centrally without restricting the freedom of establishment.

[21–31] France also argued that the measure was necessary in order to conserve agricultural activity in the greater part of France, most of which consisted of areas that were sparsely populated with livestock or were mountainous. It submitted that preserving cattle breeds adapted to the climate and terrain had allowed livestock rearing to be maintained in regions threatened with depopulation on account of their climate or geographical characteristics. This argument was rejected by the Court on the basis that France had failed to substantiate it with any statistical information or data, and had failed to establish that the measure was necessary to ensure that an insemination service was offered throughout France. In addition, the justification could not be relied upon in respect of those areas of France that did not have an unfavourable climate or geographical characteristics.

[21–32] A second example of the Court's strict approach to restrictions on the right of establishment is to be found in *Hartlauer*.[43] Hartlauer was a German company

---

[40] Case C-342/17 *Memoria* EU:C:2018:906, 14 November 2018.

[41] Case C-389/05 *Commission v France (Bovine Centres)* [2008] ECR I-5337.

[42] *ibid*, para 52.

[43] Case C-169/07 *Hartlauer* [2009] ECR I-1721. See Leigh Hancher and Wolf Sauter "One Step Beyond? From *Sodemare* to *Docmorris*: The EU's Freedom of Establishment Case Law Concerning Healthcare" (2010) 47 *Common Market Law Review* 117.

that had sought permission to open a dental clinic in Vienna. Permission was refused pursuant to an Austrian law which provided that new health institutions could only be opened where the local authority considered there to be a health need to do so. As will be seen, the Court placed considerable emphasis on the fact that a similar restriction was not imposed on group practices of independently practising dentists. Different local authorities applied a different test to assess whether or not there was a health need. In Vienna, the assessment was on the basis of the ratio of inhabitants to existing dental practitioners. The local authority found that dental care was already adequately taken care of, such that the proposed clinic would "not have the effect of substantially accelerating, intensifying or improving the provision of dental medical care for patients resident in Vienna".[44] The Court first explained why the non-discriminatory measure was to be regarded as a restriction that was caught by Art 49, necessitating an examination as to whether it could be objectively justified. According to the Court:

> A national rule under which the establishment of an undertaking from another Member State is subject to the issue of a prior authorisation constitutes a restriction within the meaning of Article [49], since it is capable of hindering the exercise by that undertaking of freedom of establishment by preventing it from freely carrying on its activities through a fixed place of business.
>
> First, that undertaking may have to bear the additional administrative and financial costs involved in any grant of such an authorisation. Second, the national legislation reserves the pursuit of self-employed activity to certain economic operators who satisfy predetermined requirements, compliance with which is a condition for the issue of that authorisation.
>
> Moreover, the Court has already held that national legislation under which the pursuit of an activity is subject to a condition linked to the economic or social need for that activity constitutes a restriction in that it tends to limit the number of providers of services. …
>
> … [The Austrian law] deters or even prevents undertakings from other Member States from pursuing their activities on the territory of the Republic of Austria through a health institution designed as a fixed place of business. In the present case, its application had the effect of depriving Hartlauer altogether of access to the market in dental care in Austria.
>
> Consequently, the legislation constitutes a restriction of freedom of establishment within the meaning of Article [49] notwithstanding the alleged absence of discrimination on grounds of the nationality of the persons concerned.[45]

[21–33] Austria sought to justify the restriction on the ground of protecting public health by arguing that, in a sector that was not governed by the law of supply and demand, it ensured a high quality medical service accessible to all, as well as the "financial balance of the social security system in that it enables social security institutions to control expenditure by adapting it to planned needs".[46] It further claimed that to allow private institutions to freely open without limitation would risk undermining the position of practitioners who participated in publicly funded schemes.

[21–34] Although the Court accepted that a prior authorisation requirement could, in principle, be permitted in order to achieve a particular objective relating to public health, in order for this to be the case the restriction would have to be applied in a consistent

---

[44] *ibid*, para 18.
[45] *ibid*, paras 34–39.
[46] *ibid*, para 41.

and systematic manner. A critical failing in the Austrian law was that it inconsistently imposed a prior authorisation regime on outpatient dental clinics, whatever their size, whereas the setting up of new group practices was not subject to any system of authorisation, regardless of their size. This was the case even though

> the premises and equipment of group practices and those of outpatient dental clinics may have comparable features and that in many cases the patient will not notice any difference between them.
>
> Moreover, group practices generally offer the same medical services as outpatient dental clinics and are subject to the same market conditions.
>
> … Since those two categories of providers of services may have comparable features and a comparable number of practitioners and provide medical services of equivalent volume, they may therefore have a similar impact on the market in medical services, and are thus liable to affect in an equivalent manner the economic situation of contractual practitioners in certain geographical areas and, in consequence, the attainment of the planning objectives pursued by the competent authorities.
>
> That inconsistency also affects the attainment of the objective of preventing a risk of serious harm to the financial balance of the national social security system. Even supposing that the uncontrolled establishment of independent outpatient dental clinics may lead to a considerable increase in the volume of medical services at constant prices to be paid for by that system, the Austrian Government has not put forward anything capable of explaining why the establishment of those clinics but not of group practices could have such an effect.
>
> … In those circumstances, it must be concluded that the national legislation … does not pursue the stated objectives in a consistent and systematic manner, since it does not make the setting up of group practices subject to a system of prior authorisation, as is the case with new outpatient dental clinics.[47]

[21–35] In addition, the Court found that the prior authorisation regime fell foul of the principle, developed in its earlier case law, that any such regime must not render legitimate "discretionary conduct on the part of the national authorities which is liable to *negate the effectiveness* of provisions of [EU] law, in particular those relating to a fundamental freedom" such as the right of establishment.[48] In order to be permissible, a prior authorisation regime must be based on objective, non-discriminatory criteria known in advance, in such a way as to adequately circumscribe the exercise of the national authorities' discretion. In this case, the discretion of the relevant Austrian authorities was not adequately circumscribed, nor were the criteria sufficiently known in advance, in that different local authorities applied different tests in assessing the existence of a health need. Whereas some local authorities based their decision on the ratio of inhabitants to practitioners, others looked to appointment waiting times, whilst one went by the answers given by practitioners in the catchment area of the proposed new clinic, "even though they are potential direct competitors of that clinic. Such a method is liable to affect the objectivity and impartiality of the treatment of the application for authorisation."[49] As a result of these two separate failings, the restriction on the freedom of establishment had not been justified by Austria and so was found to be in breach of Art 49 TFEU.

---

47 *ibid*, paras 57–63.
48 *ibid*, para 64.
49 *ibid* para 69.

[21–36] Both *Commission v France* and *Hartlauer* illustrate the rigorous approach that the Court of Justice has taken to assessing whether a non-discriminatory restriction on the freedom of establishment is capable of being defended on the basis of a competing public interest. In particular, in each case the arguments put forward by the Member State suffered from a lack of statistical information to substantiate the claims being made, and from internal inconsistencies in the rationales put forward. This in-depth analysis by the Court has prompted Catherine Barnard to observe:

> While the restrictions approach has proved effective in attacking a wide range of rules which impede access to the market … it can reach too deeply into the national systems and force a whole range of national rules to be justified where their effect on inter-state trade is in fact too remote or insubstantial. There are some signs that the Court is beginning to recognise this as a problem and place limits on the reach of the restrictions approach by introducing a threshold requirement.[50]

[21–37] Finally, it is worth noting that in the controversial cases of *Viking* and *Laval*, the Court of Justice ruled that collective action by trade unions, in the form of strikes, was capable of falling within the scope of Art 49 where it was aimed at inducing an undertaking to enter into a collective agreement, the terms of which were liable to deter it from exercising its right to freedom of establishment.[51] This was held to be the case even though Art 153 TFEU, which confers on the Union a supporting competence in respect of working conditions, expressly excludes the right to strike. In these cases, it had been sought to change the registration of passenger ferries from Finland to Estonia in order to be able to hire crew at a lower rate of pay. It was left to the national court to determine whether the resultant strike action was capable of being justified as a proportionate and necessary means of protecting the rights of workers.

[21–38] More recently, in *AGET Iraklis* the Court considered whether a Greek law that required the permission of the Minister of Labour for certain collective redundancies was contrary to the freedom of establishment, as well as the freedom of conduct of business as enshrined in Art 16 of the Charter of Fundamental Rights.[52] AGET Iraklis was a Greek company whose principal shareholder was a French multinational group. It operated three cement plants in Greece. Due to a contraction in the construction industry and surplus capacity, it decided to consolidate by closing one of these plants. As required by Greek law, it sought the authority of the Minister of Labour for collective redundancies but was refused. Given that the decision to effect collective redundancies was a "fundamental decision in the life of an undertaking", the Court, sitting as a Grand Chamber, readily accepted that the requirement for Ministerial approval was "liable to constitute a serious obstacle to the exercise of freedom of establishment in Greece".[53] As explained by the Court, the law constituted a significant interference in the freedoms which economic operators generally enjoy. These included:

---

[50] Catherine Barnard, *The Substantive Law of the EU* (4th ed, Oxford University Press, 2013) 310.

[51] Case C-438/05 *International Transport Workers' Federation v Viking Line* [2007] ECR I-10779; Case C-341/05 *Laval* [2007] ECR I-11767. See Ciarán O'Mara, "Judgments in Case 438/05 *Viking* and Case C-341/05 *Laval*" (2008) 5 *Irish Employment Law Journal* 39; Brian Bercusson, "The Trade Union Movement and the European Union: Judgment Day" (2007) 13 *European Law Journal* 279; Mark R Freedland and Jeremias Prassl (eds), *Viking, Laval and Beyond* (Hart, 2014).

[52] Case C-201/15 *AGET Iraklis* EU:C:2016:972, 21 December 2016; Menelaos Markakis, "Can Governments Control Mass Layoffs by Employers? Economic Freedoms vs Labour Rights in Case C-201/15 *AGET Iraklis*" (2017) 13 *European Constitutional Law Review* 724.

[53] *ibid*, paras 54, 57.

> the freedom of economic operators to enter into contracts with workers in order to be able to carry out their activities or the freedom, for their own reasons, to bring the activity of their establishment to an end, and their freedom to decide whether and when they should formulate plans for collective redundancies on the basis, in particular, of factors such as a cessation or reduction of the activity of the undertaking or a decline in demand for the product which they manufacture, or as a result of new working arrangements within an undertaking unconnected with its level of activity.
>
> National legislation such as that at issue in the main proceedings is thus such as to render access to the Greek market less attractive and, following access to that market, to reduce considerably, or even eliminate, the ability of economic operators from other Member States who have chosen to set up in a new market to adjust subsequently their activity in that market or to give it up, by parting, to that end, with the workers previously taken on.[54]

[21–39] As well as being a restriction on the freedom of establishment, the law was also an interference in the exercise of the freedom to conduct a business within the meaning of Art 16 of the Charter. That said, in terms of considering any justification for the measure put forward by Greece, it was important to bear in mind that the aim of the EU was not only to establish the Internal Market but also to

> work for the sustainable development of Europe, which is based, in particular, on a highly competitive social market economy aiming at full employment and social progress, and it is to promote, inter alia, social protection.
>
> Since the European Union thus has not only an economic but also a social purpose, the rights under the provisions of the Treaty on the free movement of goods, persons, services and capital must be balanced against the objectives pursued by social policy, which include … the promotion of employment, improved living and working conditions, so as to make possible their harmonisation while the improvement is being maintained, proper social protection, dialogue between management and labour, the development of human resources with a view to lasting high employment and the combating of exclusion.[55]

[21–40] The Grand Chamber concluded that, as a matter of principle, a measure such as that imposed by Greece was capable of being regarded as a proportionate restriction aimed at ensuring a legitimate overriding public interest. Nevertheless, as in *Hartlauer*, the specific terms of the Greek law failed to satisfy the Court's earlier case law to the effect that, where powers of intervention of a public authority are not qualified by any condition, save for criteria formulated in general terms, without any indication of the specific objective circumstances in which those powers are to be exercised, this results in serious interference with the freedom of establishment which may have the effect of excluding that freedom altogether. In this regard, the Greek law did state that the power of a public authority to permit collective redundancies must be exercised by analysing the documents in the file, taking into account the situation of the undertaking and the conditions in the labour market, and must result in a reasoned decision. Nevertheless, in the view of the Grand Chamber:

> it is clear that, in the absence of details of the particular circumstances in which the power in question may be exercised, the employers concerned do not know in what specific objective circumstances that power may be applied, as the situations allowing its exercise are potentially numerous, undetermined and indeterminable and leave the authority concerned a broad discretion that is difficult to review. Such criteria which are

54 *ibid*, paras 55–56.
55 *ibid*, paras 76–77.

> not precise and are not therefore founded on objective, verifiable conditions go beyond what is necessary in order to attain the objectives stated and cannot therefore satisfy the requirements of the principle of proportionality.[56]

[21–41] As a result of failing to comply with the principle of proportionality, the measure was found to be in breach of both Art 49 TFEU and Art 16 of the Charter.

F. Establishment by Companies

[21–42] Article 54 TFEU guarantees that companies formed in accordance with the law of a Member State and having their registered office, central administration or principal place of business within any of the Member States, shall be treated in the same way as an EU national. In other words, a company formed in accordance with the law of any EU Member State may not be discriminated against on the basis of the location of its registered office, central administration or principal place of business. So, in *Überseering*, a German law that had the effect of requiring companies whose central administration was in Germany to be incorporated there in order to have legal capacity was held to be in violation of Art 49.[57] In that case, a Dutch incorporated company with a central administration in Germany was unable to bring legal proceedings there as it was not considered to have legal capacity. As the company was lawfully incorporated in one Member State, Germany was required to give effect to this, including by recognising its legal capacity.

[21–43] Although there are a number of EU directives governing company law, harmonisation is far from complete. In particular, just as it is for each Member State to define its own citizenship rules, the existence of a company as a legal entity remains to be determined by national law. The law of each Member State will, therefore, prescribe matters such as the technical requirements to be fulfilled in order to register as a company, and the connections required, if any, with that Member State in order to be registered there. For example, whereas some Member States may make it a precondition for incorporation under their law that the company maintain its central administration, or "real head office", in that state, others may deem it sufficient that they merely keep a registered office in the state.

[21–44] The significance of this variation in company law was considered by the Court of Justice in the *Daily Mail* case.[58] Although the *Daily Mail* wished to remain a UK registered company, it decided to move its central management to the Netherlands in order to sell certain shares without being subject to UK capital gains tax. The law of the UK provided that only with the prior consent of the Treasury could a company move its central management out of the UK but retain its UK registration. The Court rejected the *Daily Mail*'s argument that the rule breached Arts 49 and 54 TFEU. This was because the rule was not concerned with preventing a UK company from moving to another Member State, but rather sought to define what it meant to be a UK company, which was a matter for the UK to decide. According to the Court, Arts 49 and 54 could not be interpreted as conferring on companies incorporated in one Member State a

---

[56] *ibid*, para 100.

[57] Case C-208/00 *Überseering* [2002] ECR I-9919.

[58] Case 81/87 *R v HM Treasury ex parte Daily Mail* [1988] ECR 5483. See AV Gill, "Migration of Companies and the Right of Establishment under EC Law" (1989) 7 *Irish Law Times* 59.

right to transfer their central administration to another Member State while retaining their status as companies incorporated under the legislation of the first Member State.

[21–45] While the *Daily Mail* judgment dates from 1988, it was confirmed in 2008 in *Cartesio*, in which Hungarian law did not allow a company incorporated in Hungary to transfer its seat to Italy and to remain subject to Hungarian law. The Court reaffirmed that a Member State:

> has the power to define both the connecting factor required of a company if it is to be regarded as incorporated under the law of that Member State and, as such, capable of enjoying the right of establishment, and that required if the company is to be able subsequently to maintain that status. That power includes the possibility for that Member State not to permit a company governed by its law to retain that status if the company intends to reorganise itself in another Member State by moving its seat to the territory of the latter, thereby breaking the connecting factor required under the national law of the Member State of incorporation.[59]

[21–46] It is, however, worth comparing the judgment in *Cartesio* with that in *Vale*, which concerned the reverse situation of an Italian incorporated company seeking to end its incorporation in Italy and incorporate in Hungary by way of a conversion (ie where a company ceases to exist and a new company is formed which is recorded in the register as the successor of the former company).[60] Although Hungarian law permitted the conversion of Hungarian companies, it did not permit cross-border conversions, with the result that if the new company were to be established in Hungary it could not do so on the basis of being the successor to the former Italian company. The Court found the difference in treatment between domestic and cross-border conversions to be a restriction on the freedom of establishment within the meaning of Art 49 TFEU which, therefore, required justification. Given the absolute nature of the ban on cross-border conversions, the restriction was held to go beyond what was necessary to protect against legitimate difficulties that may arise in certain instances. As explained by the Court:

> in so far as the national legislation … provides only for conversion of companies which already have their seat in the Member State concerned, that legislation treats companies differently according to whether the conversion is domestic or of a cross-border nature, which is likely to deter companies which have their seat in another Member State from exercising the freedom of establishment laid down by the Treaty and, therefore, amounts to a restriction within the meaning of Articles 49 TFEU and 54 TFEU.
>
> In so far as concerns possible justification for the restriction at issue, it is true that the Court recognised … that cross-border mergers pose specific problems, which is also true of cross-border conversions. Indeed, such conversions presuppose the consecutive application of two national laws.
>
> The Court notes, at the outset, that differences in treatment depending on whether a domestic or cross-border conversion is at issue cannot be justified by the absence of rules laid down in secondary European Union law. Even though such rules are indeed useful for facilitating cross-border conversions, their existence cannot be made a precondition

---

59 Case C-210/06 *Cartesio* [2008] ECR I-9641, para 110. See Marek Szydło, "Case C-210/06 *Cartesio*" (2009) 46 *Common Market Law Review* 703.

60 Case C-378/10 *Vale* EU:C:2012:440, 12 July 2012. See Thomas Biermeyer, "Shaping the Space of Cross-Border Conversions in the EU: Between Right and Autonomy" (2013) 50 *Common Market Law Review* 571; Oliver Mörsdorf, "The Legal Mobility of Companies within the European Union through Cross-Border Conversions" (2012) 49 *Common Market Law Review* 629.

> for the implementation of the freedom of establishment laid down in Articles 49 TFEU and 54 TFEU.
>
> In so far as concerns justification on the basis of overriding reasons in the public interest, such as protection of the interests of creditors, minority shareholders and employees, the preservation of the effectiveness of fiscal supervision and the fairness of commercial transactions, it is established that such reasons may justify a measure restricting the freedom of establishment on the condition that such a restrictive measure is appropriate for ensuring the attainment of the objectives pursued and does not go beyond what is necessary to attain them.
>
> However, such justification is lacking in the present case. Hungarian law precludes, in a general manner, cross-border conversions, with the result that it prevents such operations from being carried out even if the interests, mentioned in the preceding paragraph, are not threatened. In any event, such a rule goes beyond what is necessary to protect those interests.
>
> In those circumstances, ... Articles 49 TFEU and 54 TFEU must be interpreted as precluding national legislation which enables companies established under national law to convert, but does not allow, in a general manner, companies governed by the law of another Member State to convert to companies governed by national law by incorporating such a company.[61]

[21–47] Similarly, in the case of *Polbud*, a Polish company sought to move its registered office to Luxembourg by way of a conversion.[62] Having become established in Luxembourg, it then sought to have the previous legal entity removed from the Polish commercial register. Under Polish law, however, the company could not be removed without going through a liquidation process. In line with its judgments in *Daily Mail* and *Cartesio*, the Court confirmed that the fact that the company's activities or real head office were not being moved to Luxembourg did not mean that Art 49 was not engaged, or that the move could be regarded as an abuse of rights. This followed from the fact that, as EU law currently stands, "each Member State has the power to define the connecting factor required of a company if that company is to be regarded as incorporated in accordance with its national legislation".[63] The Court was satisfied that a requirement to go through liquidation was likely to impede a cross-border conversion and so was a restriction on the freedom of establishment. This was because the process of liquidation would require the "completion of current business, recovery of debts owed to the company, performance of its obligations and sale of its assets, satisfaction or securing of its creditors, submission of a financial statement on the conduct of that process and indication of where the books and documents of the company in liquidation are to be deposited".[64] By way of a justification, it was claimed that the liquidation of the company was necessary in order to protect the interests of its creditors, minority shareholders and employees. This was rejected by the Court on the basis that the requirement for liquidation went beyond what was necessary to achieve these objectives, given that it gave:

---

61 *ibid*, paras 36–41.

62 Case C-106/16 *Polbud* EU:C:2017:804, 25 October 2017. See Marek Szydło, "Cross-Border Conversion of Companies under Freedom of Establishment: *Polbud* and Beyond" (2018) 55 *Common Market Law Review* 1549; Stephan Rammeloo, "Cross-Border Company Migration in the EU: Transfer of Registered Office (Conversion) – The Last Piece of the Puzzle? Case C-106/16 *Polbud*" (2018) 25 *Maastricht Journal of European and Comparative Law* 87.

63 *ibid*, para 43.

64 *ibid*, para 50.

no consideration of the actual risk of detriment to the interests of creditors, minority shareholders and employees and no possibility of choosing less restrictive measures capable of protecting those interests. As regards, in particular, the interests of creditors, … the provision of bank guarantees or other equivalent guarantees could offer adequate protection of those interests.

Second, the Polish Government relies on the objective of preventing abusive practices in order to justify the national legislation at issue in the main proceedings.

In that regard, it is open to the Member States to adopt any appropriate measure for preventing or penalising fraud.

However, … the fact that either the registered office or real head office of a company was established in accordance with the legislation of a Member State for the purpose of enjoying the benefit of more favourable legislation does not, in itself, constitute abuse.

Moreover, the mere fact that a company transfers its registered office from one Member State to another cannot be the basis for a general presumption of fraud and cannot justify a measure that adversely affects the exercise of a fundamental freedom guaranteed by the Treaty.

Since a general obligation to implement a liquidation procedure amounts to establishing a general presumption of the existence of abuse, the Court must hold that legislation, such as that at issue in the main proceedings, which imposes such an obligation, is disproportionate.[65]

[21–48] Cases such as *Daily Mail* and *Cartesio* demonstrate the extent to which the Court will allow each Member State to regulate the incorporation of companies within their own national legal system. In contrast, the Court has sought to strengthen the freedom of establishment when it comes to a company setting up a *secondary* form of establishment, as was the case in Überseering, referred to above. The judgment most regularly cited in this connection is that of *Centros*, in which two Danish nationals deliberately sought to avoid the minimum share capital requirement for limited liability companies in Denmark (100,000 kroner) by incorporating their company in the UK, where there was no such requirement.[66] Most of the company's business was to be conducted in Denmark. However, when they sought to register a branch there the Danish authorities refused on the basis that, in reality, Denmark was the principal country of establishment. It was argued that incorporation in the UK was merely an abuse of the right of establishment in order to avoid Danish company law.

[21–49] The Court of Justice rejected the argument that the fact that the company did not conduct any business in the UK, and all of its business in Denmark, demonstrated fraudulent or abusive conduct. Rather,

the fact that a national of a Member State who wishes to set up a company chooses to form it in the Member State whose rules of company law seem to him the least restrictive and to set up branches in other Member States cannot, in itself, constitute an abuse of the right of establishment. The right to form a company in accordance with the law of a Member

65 *ibid*, paras 58–64.

66 Case C-212/97 *Centros* [1999] ECR I-1459. See Case C-167/01 *Inspire Art Ltd* [2003] ECR I-10155; Karsten Engsig Sørensen, "The Fight Against Letterbox Companies in the Internal Market" (2015) 52 *Common Market Law Review* 85.

> State and to set up branches in other Member States is inherent in the exercise, in a single market, of the freedom of establishment guaranteed by the Treaty.[67]

[21–50] Whereas, in *Daily Mail*, the lack of harmonisation at EU level had been a critical factor in favour of allowing Member States to regulate the incorporation of companies within their territory, here the lack of harmonisation was said to be of "little consequence" to the argument put forward by Denmark, with the Court noting that Art 50 TFEU provided the Council with the legislative competence to achieve complete harmonisation if it wished.

[21–51] For some, the judgment in *Centros* was seen to encourage regulatory competition amongst Member States, thereby giving the "green light to a Delaware-style race to the bottom coming to the EU in the field of company law".[68] This may be of greater significance to countries such as France and Germany, whose company law apply a "real seat" doctrine, than to those such as Ireland and the Netherlands, who apply a "state of incorporation" rule. Zoe Adams and Simon Deakin have summed up the combined effect of the Court's jurisprudence as follows:

> The upshot of the post-*Centros* case law, then, is that while Member States retain the capacity to tax and regulate companies falling under their jurisdiction, they may not prevent them leaving for other jurisdictions which offer a different mix of regulatory controls; nor may they refuse to admit foreign companies which meet local conditions for incorporation. As a result, the European Union has moved several steps closer to realising the conditions for a market for incorporations. …
>
> … The effect of *Cartesio* is that a company must accept the package of regulatory norms which are attached to incorporation in a given Member State: it can only escape them by exiting the jurisdiction entirely. However, given this exit option, many regulations will become at best semi-mandatory "default rules". A degree of "negative harmonisation" can be expected to follow.[69]

G. The Professional Qualifications Directive

[21–52] As was seen above, in cases such as *Thieffry* and *Vlassopoulou* the Court of Justice established that national rules regarding the recognition of professional qualifications may amount to indirect discrimination that is contrary to the guarantee of the freedom of establishment if they fail to take account of the knowledge and qualifications already acquired by an individual in another Member State. In addition, and for some time now, the recognition of qualifications has been the subject of secondary legislation aimed at positive integration. Subject to a proviso in relation to the medical and pharmaceutical professions, Art 53 TFEU confers a competence on the Union to adopt directives on the mutual recognition of formal qualifications and for the coordination of national provisions concerning the taking-up and pursuit of activities

---

67 *ibid*, 1493.

68 Catherine Barnard, *The Substantive Law of the EU* (4th ed, Oxford University Press, 2013) 339.

69 Zoe Adams and Simon Deakin, "Freedom of Establishment and Regulatory Competition" in Anthony Arnull and Damian Chalmers (eds), *The Oxford Handbook of European Law* (Oxford University Press, 2015) 537, 547. In relation to tax, see Wolfgang Schön, "Playing Different Games? Regulatory Competition in Tax and Company Law Compared" (2005) 42 *Common Market Law Review* 331; Case C-446/03 *Marks & Spencer* ECR I-10837; Case C-196/04 *Cadbury's Schweppes* [2006] ECR I-7995.

as self-employed persons. This initially took the form of "sectoral harmonisation", whereby particular professions such as doctors, nurses, midwives, dentists, pharmacists, vets and architects were the subject of standalone directives. These were consolidated and replaced by the Professional Qualifications Directive 2005/36 (the "Qualifications Directive").[70] This important Directive establishes rules that apply where a Member State makes access to, or the pursuit of, a "regulated profession" subject to the holding of a specific professional qualification. In accordance with the Directive, for the purposes of a Union citizen accessing and pursuing that profession, Member States are to recognise qualifications obtained in another Member State.

[21–53] In 2010, as part of the Single Market Act project aimed at further consolidating Europe's economy, the Commission identified the need to modernise the law in this area. The EU Citizenship report of the same year also underlined the need to lighten the administrative burden linked to the recognition of professional qualifications. This led to the introduction of a series of reforms in Directive 2013/55/EU, the most significant of which will be highlighted below.[71] As a result of these changes, it is worthwhile consulting a consolidated version of the Qualifications Directive. The two directives have been transposed into Irish law by the European Union (Recognition of Professional Qualifications) Regulations 2017.[72]

[21–54] The Qualifications Directive applies irrespective of whether a profession is being pursued as an employee or on a self-employed basis, with Title II dealing with the provision of services and Title III covering the freedom of establishment. Once a qualification is recognised pursuant to the Directive, the holder is entitled to gain access to the "same profession" in the host Member State as that for which he or she is qualified in their home state. Professions are to be regarded as "the same" if the activities engaged in are comparable.[73] The holder of a recognised qualification is also entitled to pursue the profession under the same conditions as nationals of the host state.

[21–55] For the purposes of the Directive, a "regulated profession" is defined as a professional activity that, by virtue of legislative, regulatory or administrative provisions, access to which or the pursuit of which is either directly or indirectly subjected to the holding of a specific professional qualification.[74] This includes the situation where the use of a particular professional title is made dependent on having a certain professional qualification. Although it is for each Member State to determine whether or not to regulate a profession, the definition of what constitutes a regulated profession is, like the definition of a worker, of necessity a matter of EU law. A regulated profession is defined in the Irish Regulations as either: (i) a profession or professional activity in the State listed in Schedule 1 to the Regulations or (ii) an activity in the State

---

[70] Directive 2005/36/EC of the European Parliament and of the Council of 7 September 2005 on the recognition of professional qualifications [2005] OJ L255/22. See also Commission Delegated Decision (EU) 2019/608 of 16 January 2019 amending Annex V to Directive 2005/36 [2019] OJ L104/1.

[71] Directive 2013/55/EU of the European Parliament and of the Council of 20 November 2013 amending Directive 2005/36/EC on the recognition of professional qualifications and Regulation (EU) No 1024/2012 on administrative cooperation through the Internal Market Information System [2013] OJ L354/132.

[72] SI No 8 of 2017.

[73] Art 4.

[74] Art 3(1)(a).

listed in Annex IV to the Directive, access to or the pursuit of which is contingent upon possession of general, commercial or professional knowledge and aptitudes. Schedule 1 lists just over 190 professions or professional activities as follows:

Aircraft Maintenance Engineer	Speech and Language Therapist
Architect	Advanced Paramedic
Archaeologist	Emergency Medical Technician
Auditing company accounts	Paramedic
Barrister	Primary School Teacher
Building Energy Rating Assessor	Post-Primary School Teacher
Building Surveyor	Further Education Teacher
Quantity Surveyor	Employees of pre-school service providers working directly with children
Construction:	Workers on Ships [32 eg Chief Engineer, Chief Mate, Master, etc]
Scaffolding — basic	Dentist/Dental Practitioner
Scaffolding — advanced	Dental Hygienist
Mobile tower scaffold	Dental Nurse
Tower crane operation	Clinical Dental Technician
Self-erecting tower crane operation	Orthodontic Therapist
Slinging/ signalling	Dispensing Optician Optometrist
Telescopic handler operation	Doctor/Medical Practitioner
Tractor dozer operation	Door Supervisor
Mobile crane operation	Security Guard
Crawler crane operation	Driving Instructor
Articulated dumper operation	Liquidator
Site dumper operation	Examiner
180° excavator operation	Personal Insolvency Practitioner
Mini-digger operation	Approved Intermediary
360° excavator operation	Property Service Provider
Roof and wall cladding/sheeting	Inspector of Air Accidents
Built-up roof felting	Medical Scientist
Signing, lighting and guarding on roads	Patent Agent
Locating underground services	Trade Mark Agent
Shotfiring	Pharmacist
Health and Safety at Roadworks	Physiotherapist
Quarrying [14, eg Explosives Supervision]	Midwife/Registered Midwife
Chartered Engineer	Nurse/Registered Nurse
Audiologist	Pesticide Advisor
Environmental Health Officer	Pesticide Equipment Inspector
Clinical Biochemist	Pesticide Distributor
Orthoptist	Pesticide Professional User/Sprayer Operator
Podiatrist	Social Worker
Psychologist	Solicitor
Dietician	Veterinary Practitioner
Occupational Therapist	Veterinary Nurse
Radiation Therapist	
Radiographer	

[21–56] The Qualifications Directive also provides that professions practised by members of certain organisations or associations, listed in Annex I of the Directive, shall be treated as regulated professions. These organisations promote and maintain a high standard in the professional field and are

> recognised in a special form by a Member State and award evidence of formal qualifications to their members, ensure that their members respect the rules of professional conduct

which they prescribe, and confer on them the right to use a title or designatory letters or to benefit from a status corresponding to those formal qualifications.[75]

[21–57] Only Ireland and the UK have added organisations to Annex I, with eight Irish organisations listed.[76]

[21–58] The Qualifications Directive can only be relied upon where the profession is "regulated" in the host Member State. Accordingly, a person with a professional qualification from one Member State, in which a particular profession is regulated, will be unable to avail of the Directive if they seek to pursue that profession in a Member State in which the profession is not regulated within the meaning of the Directive. Instead, the host Member State will be obliged to follow the approach set out in *Vlassopoulou* in order to determine whether the qualification fulfils an assessment of equivalence.[77] This was confirmed in *Aranitis*, a case concerning a Greek geologist, with a university qualification in geology and many years professional experience, who on moving to Germany was categorised by the local employment office as an "unskilled assistant".[78] The German authorities took the view that as geology was not a regulated profession within Germany, Mr Aranitis was not entitled to use the relevant professional title. While finding that Germany was correct in arguing that it did not treat geology as a regulated profession, the Court of Justice noted that in respect of unregulated professions

> the competent authorities of the host Member State responsible for classifying the nationals of other Member States, which will affect their chances of finding work on the territory of the host Member State, are required when carrying out that classification to take into consideration the diplomas, knowledge, qualifications and other evidence of qualifications that the person concerned has obtained in order to pursue a profession in the Member State of origin or from which he comes.[79]

[21–59] In relation to the establishment of a professional in another Member State, Title III of the Qualifications Directive provides for three separate regimes of recognition, a structure that derives from the earlier directives that it consolidated and replaced. The regimes are as follows, each of which will be considered in turn:

(a) a general system for the recognition of evidence of training (Chapter I);
(b) recognition of professional experience (Chapter II); and
(c) recognition on the basis of coordination of minimum training conditions (Chapter III).

[21–60] Whereas the general system of recognition calls for the application of an

---

75 Art 3(2).

76 The eight organisations are: Institute of Chartered Accountants; Institute of Certified Public Accountants; Association of Certified Accountants; Institute of Incorporated Public Accountants; Institution of Engineers of Ireland; Irish Planning Institute; Institute of Chemistry of Ireland and the Irish Taxation Institute. Nine of the 59 UK organisations listed in Annex I are identified as also having Irish members: Institute of Chartered Accountants in England and Wales; Institute of Chartered Accountants in Scotland; Institute of Actuaries; Faculty of Actuaries; Chartered Institute of Managements Accountants; Institute of Chartered Secretaries and Administrators; Royal Town Planning Institute; Royal Institute of Chartered Surveyors; Chartered Institute of Building.

77 See para [21–20] above.

78 Case C-164/94 *Aranitis* [1996] ECR I-135.

79 *ibid*, 157–158.

assessment of equivalence based on five levels of competence, and is open-ended as to the professions that may fall within its scope, the second and third regimes provide for a degree of automatic recognition of qualifications in respect of an exhaustive list of professions once the prescribed conditions are fulfilled. Certain common provisions apply to all three regimes, including Art 53 of the Directive (as amended), which provides that a professional benefiting from the recognition of a professional qualification shall have a knowledge of languages necessary for practising the profession in the host Member State. In relation to professions with patient safety implications, the host Member State has a general freedom to carry out proportionate controls to ensure sufficient language knowledge; in respect of all other professions, controls may be imposed where there is a serious and concrete doubt about the sufficiency of the professional's language knowledge.

(i) General System for the Recognition of Evidence of Training

[21–61] The "General System" for the recognition of evidence of training can be used in relation to all regulated professions that do not fall within either of the two other regimes – ie industrial, craft and commercial activities (the second regime) and the seven professions for which there are coordinated minimum standards, namely doctors, nurses, health care workers, pharmacists, midwives, vets and architects (the third regime) – as well as the few professions that continue to be regulated by stand-alone directives, such as lawyers, or are otherwise excluded from the Qualifications Directive, such as notaries. In addition, if an individual does not meet the criteria to be granted "automatic" recognition under the relevant specialised regime, an application can be made under the General System.

[21–62] The General System operates on the basis of five levels of qualification, set out in Art 11, paragraphs (a) to (e). The levels begin with an attestation of competence having been issued by a competent authority on the basis of: a training course; an exam without prior training; three years full-time professional experience, or general knowledge acquired through primary or secondary education (Level A). They end with certification of completion of either a three-year (Level D) or a four-year (Level E) course in a university or other third-level institution, together, where appropriate, with completion of any professional training required.[80] The General System distinguishes

[80] **Level A** – an attestation of competence issued by a competent authority on the basis of: (i) a training course not forming part of a certificate or diploma; (ii) a specific examination without prior training; (iii) full-time pursuit of a profession for three consecutive years or for an equivalent duration on a part-time basis during the previous 10 years; or (iv) general primary or secondary education, attesting that the holder has acquired general knowledge.
Level B – a certificate attesting to a successful completion of a secondary course either general in character, and supplemented by a course of study or professional training and/or by the probationary or professional practice required in addition to that course, or technical or professional in character, supplemented where appropriate by a course of study or professional training and/or by the probationary or professional practice required in addition to that course.
Level C – a diploma certifying successful completion of either (i) training at post-secondary level of a duration of at least one year or of an equivalent duration on a part-time basis, one of the conditions of entry of which is, as a general rule, the successful completion of the secondary course required to obtain entry to university or higher education, as well as the professional training which may be required in addition to that post-secondary course; or (ii) education and training and/or vocational training with a special structure, with competences going beyond what is provided for Level 2, equivalent to the level of training provided for under (i), if such training

between where an activity is a regulated profession in both the home state and host state, and where it is regulated in just the host state. Where regulated in both, the host state is to allow an individual access to the profession, under the same conditions as apply to its nationals, if they possess the qualification required by the home Member State in order to access the profession there. The only exception to this is where the host state requires the highest of the five levels (Level E) and the individual's qualification is at the lowest level (Level A).

[21–63] Where the profession is only regulated in the host state, access is to be granted where the individual has pursued the profession on a full-time basis for one year (or for an equivalent duration on a part-time basis over the previous 10 years) and has one or more formal qualifications that attest that he or she has been prepared to pursue the profession. If the formal qualifications certify regulated education and training, the one year experience may not be required. Once again, the only exception is where the host state requires a Level E qualification and the individual has a Level A.

[21–64] In both of these situations, the host state can require the individual to take "compensatory measures" in order to make up for the fact that either: (i) the training received covers *substantially different matters* than those covered by the formal qualifications required in the host state or (ii) the regulated profession in the host state comprises one or more activities which do not exist in the corresponding profession in the home state, and the training required in the host state covers *substantially different matters* from those covered by the individual's formal qualifications.[81]

[21–65] Compensatory measures can take the form of either an aptitude test, testing the "professional knowledge, skills and competences of the applicant" and to be made available for sitting within six months, or an "adaptation period", during which the individual may pursue the profession in the host state "under the responsibility of a qualified member of that profession".[82] This supervisory period can be accompanied by further training and is the subject of an assessment. Compensatory measures must be applied proportionally and a decision imposing either measure must provide an express justification including: (i) the level of qualification required in the host state and the level of qualification held by the applicant, using the Art 11 scale of A to E, and (ii) the "substantially different matters" in the respective training or professional activity in the two states and the "reasons for which those differences cannot be compensated by knowledge, skills and competences acquired in the course of professional experience or through lifelong learning formally validated to that effect by a relevant body".[83]

---

provides a comparable professional standard and prepares the trainee for a comparable level of responsibilities and functions.

Level D – a diploma certifying successful completion of training at post-secondary level of at least three years and not more than four years' duration, or an equivalent duration on a part-time basis, at a university or establishment of higher education level and, where appropriate, successful completion of additional professional training required.

Level E – a diploma certifying successful completion of a post-secondary course of a least four years' duration, or an equivalent duration on a part-time basis, at a university or establishment of higher education level and, where appropriate, successful completion of additional professional training required.

[81] Art 14(1).

[82] Art 14(2) and Art 3(g) and (h).

[83] Art 14(5).

[21–66] Generally, an applicant is to be afforded the choice as between an aptitude test or an adaptation period. A Member State can, however, seek to derogate from this right to choose in respect of professions that require "precise knowledge of national law and in respect of which the provision of advice and/or assistance concerning national law is an essential and constant aspect of the professional activity".[84] It can also derogate where the holder of a Level A qualification seeks to exercise a profession requiring, in the host state, a Level C qualification, or where the holder of a Level B qualification seeks to exercise a profession requiring a Level D or E. Indeed, both types of measure may be imposed where the holder of a Level A qualification seeks to carry out a profession requiring a Level D.[85] The only other circumstance in which a host state can deviate from offering a choice as between the two measures is where it has informed the Commission of its intention in advance, together with a sufficient justification, and the Commission has not requested the state to refrain from doing so.[86]

[21–67] The application of compensatory measures was considered by the Court of Justice in *Colegio de Ingenieros*, which concerned an Italian civil engineer with a specialist degree in hydraulics.[87] The Spanish Colegio de Ingenieros appealed against the recognition of his qualification on the ground that it only covered one aspect of the much broader engineering degree required within Spain. The Spanish court had found that, such were the differences between the specialist Italian degree and the Spanish degree in civil engineering, the application of compensatory measures "would in effect amount to requiring the party concerned to complete a fresh, complete programme of education and training".[88]

[21–68] Although the judgment of the Court of Justice relates to an earlier qualifications directive, the principles enunciated continue to apply. The Court began by noting that the directive did not expressly prohibit the *partial* recognition of a qualification, observing that although the directive treated a regulated profession as a whole, it nevertheless recognised that there were, in reality, separate professional activities and corresponding education and training. It followed that a case-by-case approach, tailored to each of the professional activities covered by a regulated profession, was not contrary to or beyond the scope of the general scheme of the directive.[89] Expressly adopting a teleological approach, the Court went on to comment that compensatory measures must be restricted to what is proportionate in order to achieve the objective being pursued:

> In other words, although those measures are expressly authorised, they may, in certain cases, be a highly dissuasive factor for a national of a Member State exercising his rights under the Directive. An adaptation period and an aptitude test both call for considerable time and effort on the part of the party concerned. A non-application of those measures might be significant, and even decisive, for a national of one Member State wishing to take up a regulated profession in another Member State. In cases such as those at issue in the main proceedings, partial taking-up of the profession in question, granted at the request of the party concerned, dispensing that party from having to comply with the compensatory

[84] Art 14(3).
[85] Art 14(3).
[86] Art 14(2).
[87] Case C-330/03 *Colegio de Ingenieros de Caminos, Canales y Puertos* [2006] ECR I-801, 842. See also Case C-575/11 *Nasiopoulos* EU:C:2013:430, 27 June 2013.
[88] *ibid*, 842.
[89] *ibid*, 836.

> measures and allowing him to take up immediately professional activities for which he is already qualified, would be in keeping with the objectives pursued by the Directive.
>
> … It could of course be argued … that such partial taking-up could entail a risk of multiplication of the professional activities pursued independently by nationals of other Member States, thereby giving rise also to a certain degree of confusion in the minds of consumers. However, that potential risk does not lead to a finding that partial recognition of professional qualifications is incompatible with the Directive. There are sufficient ways of remedying that problem, such as the possibility of requiring the persons concerned to mention the names and locations of the establishments or examining boards which awarded their academic titles. Likewise, the host Member State can always require the persons concerned to use, in all of their legal and commercial dealings in its territory, the respective academic title or professional title in the original language and form, as well as the translation into the language of the host Member State, in order to ensure that it is understood and to avoid all risk of confusion. …
>
> … When the activity in question may objectively be separated from the rest of the activities covered by the profession in question in the host Member State, the conclusion is that the dissuasive effect caused by the preclusion of any possibility of partial recognition of the professional qualification in question is too serious to be offset by the fear of potential harm to recipients of services. In such a case, the legitimate objective of protection of consumers and other recipients of services may be achieved through less restrictive means, particularly the obligation to use the professional title of origin or the academic title both in the language in which it was awarded and in its original form, and in the official language of the host Member State.[90]

[21–69] Following its amendment in 2013, the granting of partial access on a case-by-case basis is now expressly provided for in Art 4f of the Qualifications Directive, provided that the professional activity can objectively be separated from other activities falling under the regulated profession in the host Member State. Partial access may be rejected where justified by overriding reasons of general interest, suitable for securing the attainment of the objective pursued, which do not go beyond what is necessary to attain the objective. As noted in the recitals to the Directive, this may particularly be the case for health professions if there are patient safety implications.[91]

[21–70] According to figures maintained by a dedicated European Commission database, between 1997 and 2017, recognition was granted by Ireland under the General Scheme in 12,503 cases, 10,343 of which did not require any compensation measures.[92] An aptitude test was used prior to granting recognition in 1,272 cases, while an adaptation period was applied in 888 cases. Eighty-seven per cent of recognitions related to UK qualifications, with the next highest, Poland, representing 4 per cent.

(ii) Recognition of Professional Experience

[21–71] The second system operated by the Qualifications Directive provides for the recognition of professional experience and relates to industrial, craft and commercial activities. In respect of the activities listed in Annex IV of the Directive, if a Member State makes access to or pursuit of such an activity contingent upon possession of general, commercial or professional knowledge and aptitudes, it shall automatically

90 *ibid*, 838–839.

91 Directive 2013/55, Recital 7.

92 See <http://ec.europa.eu/growth/tools-databases/regprof/index.cfm>.

recognise previous pursuit of the activity in another Member State as sufficient proof of such knowledge and aptitudes.[93] Annex IV includes a large list of activities, including manufacturing of industrial products, food products and artisan products, the chemical industry, construction, decoration, transport, electrical engineering, the repair of electrical equipment, the repair motor vehicles, etc. The Annex is broken down into three lists, with different durations of experience ranging from two to six years being required depending on the applicable conditions such as the seniority of the position held and amount of training provided.

(iii) Recognition Based on Coordination of Minimum Training Conditions

[21–72] The third regime is confined to just seven professions that had previously been the subject of stand-alone directives that prescribed EU-wide minimum standards. The seven professions are doctors, nurses, midwives, dentists, veterinary surgeons, pharmacists and architects. Each of these professions now receives separate treatment in Chapter III of Title III of the Qualifications Directive, which coordinates minimum qualification requirements across all the Member States. For example, it is provided that basic medical training for doctors shall comprise of at least five years of study, consisting of at least 5,500 hours of theoretical and practical training provided by, or under the supervision of, a university. Certain compulsory areas of study are set out, including a requirement that students undergo clinical experience in hospitals under appropriate supervision.[94] Given the harmonisation of training requirements for these professions, a qualification granted by one Member State is to be automatically recognised by all other Member States.[95] The approach of this regime has, therefore, been summed up as involving unqualified mutual recognition combined with partial harmonisation of training requirements.[96]

[21–73] For the period between 1997 and 2017, the Commission's database indicates the following number of recognitions were granted in Ireland pursuant to this automatic system: 3,181 nurses; 2,726 doctors; 1,538 pharmacists; 685 veterinary surgeons; 439 midwives; 173 architects; and 172 dentists.[97] Recognition may also be granted in respect of qualifications in these areas pursuant to the General System. The importance of these seven professions is evident when reviewing the top 15 professions for which qualifications were recognised for the purpose of establishment both in Ireland and in the EU as a whole, from 1997 to 2017:

93 Art 16.

94 Art 24.

95 Art 23. See Case C-675/17 *Ministero della Salute v Preindl* EU:C:2018:990, 6 December 2018.

96 Catherine Barnard, *The Substantive Law of the EU* (4th ed, Oxford University Press, 2013) 323.

97 See <http://ec.europa.eu/growth/tools-databases/regprof/index.cfm>.

In Ireland		**In all EU Member States**	
Nurse	3,989	Secondary school teacher	88,929
Primary school teacher	2,897	*Nurse*	85,215
Doctor	2,738	*Doctor*	82,527
Lawyer/Barrister/Solicitor	1,772	Physiotherapist	27,742
Pharmacist	1,542	*Dentist*	18,434
Engineer	1,146	*Architect*	12,784
Social worker	1,090	Primary school teacher	12,325
Physiotherapist	984	Lawyer/Barrister/Solicitor	11,149
Secondary school teacher	852	*Veterinary Surgeon*	10,997
Occupational therapist	811	Second level nurse	10,423
Radiographer/Radiotherapist	795	*Pharmacist*	8,999
Veterinary Surgeon	727	Social worker	6,850
Midwife	497	*Midwife*	4,699
Nursery school teacher	451	Psychologist	4,537
Associate engineer	377	Occupational therapist	4,362

(iv) European Professional Card

[21–74] From January 2016, five professions – general care nurses, pharmacists, physiotherapists, real estate agents and mountain guides – can use an EU online procedure, the "Internal Market Information System", in order to obtain an electronic certificate to be used in recognising their qualifications, known as a European Professional Card. The Card was first provided for by the 2013 amendment of the Qualifications Directive, with further details set out in a Commission Implementing Regulation.[98] It is intended that the Card will be extended to other professions in relation to which: (i) there is significant mobility or potential for significant mobility; (ii) there is sufficient interest expressed by relevant stakeholders; and (iii) the profession, or the education and training geared to the pursuit of the profession, is regulated in a significant number of Member States.

[21–75] Strict time limits are imposed within which the competent authorities of the Member States must act, such that an application must be acknowledged within a week and, by the end of a further month, a decision must be made. Assuming that no further documentation or information is sought from the applicant, a failure by the competent authority to make a decision within that time period will result in a Card being deemed to be issued, which will be automatically sent to the applicant by the Internal Market Information System.[99]

(v) Lawyers

[21–76] In addition to the framework for recognition in the Qualifications Directive, lawyers continue to receive separate treatment by way of the Lawyers' Establishment Directive, Directive 98/5.[100] It allows for the establishment of lawyers with the right

[98] Commission Implementing Regulation (EU) 2015/983 of 24 June 2015 on the procedure for issuance of the European Professional Card and the application of the alert mechanism pursuant to Directive 2005/36/EC, [2015] OJ L159/27.

[99] Art 4d(5).

[100] Directive 98/5/EC to facilitate practice of the profession of lawyer on a permanent basis in a Member State other than that in which the qualification was obtained [1998] OJ L77/36. See Colm Hagan, "The Free Movement of Lawyers" (2003) 11 *Irish Student Law Review* 149; Case

to use the professional title gained in their home Member State, provided that they register with the competent authority of the host Member State on the basis of their registration in their home state and comply with the professional and ethical rules of both the home and host states. Whilst free to provide legal advice, the Directive permits Member States to require lawyers representing clients in court proceedings to work in conjunction with a lawyer who practices before the relevant judicial authority and is answerable to it. In Irish law, this is provided for in Regulation 10(2) of European Communities (Lawyers' Establishment) Regulations 2003, according to which:

> In any proceedings before a judicial authority where the professional activities in question may, but for these Regulations, be lawfully provided only by a practising barrister or a solicitor qualified to practise, a registered lawyer shall act in conjunction with such a barrister or solicitor who practises before the judicial authority concerned and who would, where necessary, be answerable to that authority.[101]

[21–77] A recent judgment of the Court of Justice in the *Monk Irenaeus* case illustrates how the Lawyers' Establishment Directive operates in practice.[102] There, a monk who was registered as a lawyer in Cyprus was refused registration, under his home-state professional title, with the Athens Bar. This was on the basis of Greek law, which deemed practice as a lawyer incompatible with the status of being a monk. This was because a monk was unable to provide certain guarantees that were required to be made by lawyers practising in Greece – such as independence from church authorities, the ability to devote oneself entirely to practice of the profession of lawyer and the ability to handle contentious cases. The relevant Greek authority considered that it would automatically have to find an infringement of these professional conduct rules were Monk Irenaeus to be registered as a lawyer in Greece. A preliminary reference inquired as to whether it was contrary to the Directive not to register Monk Irenaeus on this basis. The Court ruled that it was contrary to the Directive, given that the only condition for registration in a host state was the presentation of a certificate attesting to registration within the home state. Nevertheless, the Court went on to explain that:

> A distinction should be drawn between, on the one hand, registration with the competent authority of the host Member State of a lawyer who wishes to practise in that Member State under his home-country professional title … and, on the other, the practice itself of the profession of lawyer in that Member State, in respect of which that lawyer is subject … to the rules of professional conduct applicable in that Member State.
>
> Those rules, unlike the rules concerning the preconditions for such registration, have not been harmonised and may therefore differ considerably from those in force in the home Member State. Moreover, as … Directive 98/5 confirms, failure to comply with those rules is liable to lead to application of the penalties provided for in the law of the host Member State. Those penalties may, where appropriate, include removal from the register of the relevant bar in that Member State.

C-168/98 *Luxembourg v European Parliament* [2000] ECR I-9131; Case C-506/04 *Wilson* [2006] ECR I-8613 and Case C-359/09 *Ebert* [2011] ECR I-269. Although concerning the conditions of access to vocational training in the form an exemption from entrance exams for law graduates from Northern Irish universities, the approach of Laffoy J in *Bloomer v Incorporated Law Society of Ireland* [1995] 3 IR 14 is of interest from the perspective of the establishment of lawyers.

[101] See the European Communities (Lawyers' Establishment) Regulations 2003 (SI No 732 of 2003) and the Solicitors Acts 1954 to 2002 (Apprenticeship and Education) (Recognition of Qualifications) Regulations 2004 (SI No 717 of 2004). SI No 752 of 2004, SI No 96 of 2008 and SI No 46 of 2015 extended the 2003 Regulations to new Member States following their accession to the EU.

[102] Case C-431/17 *Monachos Eirinaios ("Monk Irenaues")* EU:C:2019:368, 7 May 2019.

In the present instance, it is apparent from the information provided by the referring court that, according to the competent authority of the host Member State, practice of the profession of lawyer by a monk would not be consistent with the guarantees … which, under the law of that Member State, are required for practice of that profession.

In that regard, it should be pointed out that it is permissible for the national legislature to prescribe such guarantees provided that the rules laid down for that purpose do not go beyond what is necessary in order to attain the objectives pursued. In particular, the absence of conflicts of interest is essential for practice of the profession of lawyer and requires, inter alia, that lawyers should be in a situation of independence vis-à-vis the authorities, by which they must never be influenced.

This power available to the national legislature nevertheless does not allow it to supplement the preconditions for registration with the competent authority of the host Member State — which … have been fully harmonised — by adding further conditions that relate to compliance with requirements of professional conduct. If a lawyer wishing to practise in the host Member State under his home-country professional title were refused registration with the competent authorities of that Member State solely on the ground that he has the status of monk, that would effectively add a registration condition to those set out in … Directive 98/5, whereas such addition is not permitted by that provision.

Furthermore, … in order for the rules of professional conduct applicable in the host Member State to be in compliance with EU law, they must in particular comply with the principle of proportionality, which means that they are not to go beyond what is necessary in order to attain the objectives pursued. It is for the referring court to carry out the necessary checks in respect of the rule regarding incompatibility at issue in the main proceedings.[103]

[21–78] If a lawyer wishes to take the further step of taking on the professional title of the host Member State – in other words, to become, in Ireland, a solicitor or barrister – provided that he or she has effectively and regularly practised in the host state, and in the law of that state, for three years, he or she can apply to avail of an exemption from the requirements of the Qualifications Directive, eg having to sit an aptitude test or undergo an adaptation period. If this route is not available to them, a lawyer can sit an exam which, for solicitors, is the Qualified Lawyers Transfer Test administered by the Law Society of Ireland, and for barristers, an aptitude test administered by the Council of the King's Inns.

[21–79] A further alternative means of obtaining recognition arises where a lawyer, practising under his home-country professional title, has effectively and regularly pursued a professional activity in the host state for a period of at least three years but for a lesser period in the law of that Member State. Upon an application being made, the competent authority must consider: (i) the professional activity pursued; (ii) any knowledge and professional experience of the law of the host state; and (iii) any attendance at lectures or seminars on the law of the host state, including the rules regulating professional practice and conduct. Assessment of the lawyer's experience and capacity is to be carried out by means of an interview.

[21–80] The matter of lawyers seeking to provide legal services on a temporary basis in a Member State other than the one in which they qualified is dealt with separately in the Lawyers' Services Directive.[104] It prescribes rules governing the conditions on

[103] *Ibid*, paras 30-35.

[104] Council Directive 77/249/EEC to facilitate the effective exercise by lawyers of freedom to provide

which certain lawyers may provide legal services on a temporary basis in another Member State, including the title they should use and the applicable regulatory and professional rules.

H. The Services Directive

[21–81] While it may not be immediately apparent from its title, it is important to recall that the Services Directive, Directive 2006/123, includes a chapter dedicated to the freedom of establishment for service providers.[105] The Directive is outlined more fully in Chapter 22, however, it is worth noting here the key features of its provisions on establishment, which relate to the manner in which authorisation systems may be imposed by Member States for establishment by a service provider and secondly, certain other requirements which are either prohibited or must be evaluated by Member States. In respect of both authorisation schemes and other requirements, Member States are required to report to the Commission outlining how the continuation of such schemes and requirements is considered to be justifiable.

(i) Authorisation Schemes

[21–82] In Chapter III of the Services Directive, dealing with the freedom of establishment, Art 9 provides that a Member State shall not make the exercise of a service activity subject to any form of authorisation scheme, requiring a decision from a competent authority, unless: (a) the authorisation scheme does not discriminate against the provider; (b) the need for such a scheme is justified by an overriding reason relating to the public interest; and (c) the objective pursued cannot be attained by means of a less-restrictive measure, in particular because a subsequent inspection would take place too late to be genuinely effective. An "overriding reason relating to the public interest" (ORRPI) is defined in Art 4 in a broad and non-exhaustive manner as meaning reasons recognised as such in the case law of the Court of Justice, including the following grounds:

> public policy; public security; public safety; public health; preserving the financial equilibrium of the social security system; the protection of consumers, recipients of services and workers; fairness of trade transactions; combating fraud; the protection of the environment and the urban environment; the health of animals; intellectual property; the conservation of the national historic and artistic heritage; social policy objectives and cultural policy objectives.

[21–83] Recital 40 adds to the air of generality by noting that the concept of an ORRPI has been developed by the Court "and may continue to evolve", before going on to note that it covers "at least" a series of grounds then listed, which, in addition to those set out in Art 4, include: the maintenance of order in society; social policy objectives; the prevention of fraud and unfair competition; the protection of creditors; safeguarding the sound administration of justice; road safety; cultural policy objectives, including

services [1977] OJ L78/7, implemented by the European Communities (Freedom to Provide Services) (Lawyers) Regulations 1979 (SI No 58 of 1979), as amended by SI No 197 of 1981, SI No 226 of 1986, SI No 132 of 1999, SI No 753 of 2004 and SI No 45 of 2015.

[105] Directive 2006/123/EC of the European Parliament and of the Council of 12 December 2006 on services in the internal market [2006] OJ L376/36.

safeguarding the freedom of expression; the need to ensure a high level of education; the maintenance of press diversity and promotion of the national language, and veterinary policy. Nevertheless, whilst the grounds that may constitute an ORRPI are extensive and open-ended, Art 10 imposes additional restrictions on the use of authorisation schemes, requiring that they must also be: (i) proportionate; (ii) clear and unambiguous; (iii) objective; (iv) made public in advance; (v) transparent and accessible; and (vi) not duplicate requirements and controls which are equivalent or essentially comparable as regards their purpose to which the provider is already subject in another Member State or in the same Member State.

[21–84] The Services Directive also prescribes conditions on the procedure to be applied when operating an authorisation system, requiring that the procedure not be dissuasive or unduly complicate or delay the provision of the service. Any charges imposed shall be reasonable and not exceed the cost of the procedure. A reasonable period for processing applications shall be fixed and made public in advance which, when justified by the complexity of the issue, may be extended once. If an application is not processed within the fixed time period, it shall be deemed to have been granted.

(ii) Other Requirements that Are Prohibited or Must Be Evaluated

[21–85] Articles 14 and 15 of the Services Directive deal with certain other forms of restriction on establishment by service providers that, from the case law of the Court of Justice, have been identified as either being so egregious as to be incapable of being justified by an ORRPI, or are less egregious but nonetheless give rise to such concern that they ought to be closely examined by Member States to see whether they ought to be continued. Article 14 lists eight restrictions that are prohibited, including discriminatory requirements, a ban on having an establishment or being enrolled with a professional body in more than one Member State, a requirement to locate a primary establishment within the state or making the granting of authorisation subject to proof of the existence of an economic need or market demand.

[21–86] Article 15 lists eight further restrictions that Member States must examine in order to ensure that they are compatible with the requirements of non-discrimination, necessity in order to ensure an ORRPI and proportionality, such as: (i) quantitative or territorial restrictions in the form of limits fixed according to population or a minimum geographical distance between providers or (ii) an obligation for the establishment to take a specific legal form or to have a particular shareholding or minimum number of employees.[106] From December 2006, Member States were not to introduce any new restrictions unless they met the three criteria of non-discrimination, necessity and proportionality, and are required to report the introduction of any measure, and the reasons for it, to the Commission. Within three months, the Commission will examine its compatibility with EU law and, where appropriate, will adopt a decision requesting that the restriction cease to be applied.

[106] See Case C-171/17 *Commission v Hungary* EU:C:2018:881, 7 November 2018.

Overview of Case Law

Nature of Establishment	*Baars* *AGET Iraklis* *Factortame* *Gebhard* *Schitzner*
Direct Discrimination	*Reyners v Belgium* *Factortame* *Steinhauser v City of Biarritz*
Indirect Discrimination *Qualifications*	*Stöber* *Engelmann* *Thieffry* *Vlassopoulou* *Aranitis*
Derogations – Art 52 TFEU	*Commission v UK (Open Skies)* *Commission v Italy (Data Processing Services)* *Reyners v Belgium*
Non-Discriminatory Restrictions	*Memoria* *Commission v France (Bovine Centres)* *Hartlauer* *Viking and Laval* *AGET Iraklis*
Establishment by Companies	*Überseering* *Daily Mail* *Cartesio* *Vale* *Polbud* *Centros*
Qualifications Directive	*Colegio de Ingenieros*

Chapter 22

FREEDOM TO PROVIDE AND TO RECEIVE SERVICES

A. Introduction

[22–01] Within Part Three of the TFEU on the Union's Policies and Internal Actions, Title IV concerns Persons, Services and Capital. Chapter 3 of this Title comprises Arts 56–62 and deals with the freedom of services. Article 56 enshrines the key rule that restrictions on the freedom to provide services shall be prohibited in respect of EU nationals (including EU-based companies) who are established in a different Member State from the person for whom the services are intended. Accordingly, there must be a cross-border element in order for the prohibition on restrictions to apply.

[22–02] Although Art 56 TFEU refers only to the freedom to *provide* services, in addition to a provider temporarily leaving its own Member State in order to provide a service, the cross-border element can also come about through a recipient travelling to another Member State in order to receive a service. As the Court of Justice confirmed in *Luisi and Carbone*, the freedom to *receive* services is a "necessary corollary" of the freedom to provide services.[1] There, the Court held that the imposition of a fine on two Italians for having taken currency out of the country, contrary to national regulations, in order to travel to another Member State as a tourist and for medical treatment respectively, amounted to a restriction on the freedom of services. More generally, the freedom to provide services was found to include the freedom for the recipient of a service, such as those travelling for business, tourism, education or medical treatment, to go to another Member State for that purpose without being obstructed by restrictions.

[22–03] A well-known example of this is *Cowan v Le Trésor Public*, where the right to receive services was the avenue by which EU law was engaged.[2] A British tourist in Paris was violently assaulted leaving a metro station. Because he was not a French national or in possession of a resident card, he was not entitled to avail of a statutory compensation scheme for the victims of crime. Mr Cowan claimed that his inability

1 Joined Cases 286/82 and 26/83 *Luisi and Carbone* [1984] ECR 377, 402–403.
2 Case 186/87 *Cowan v Le Trésor Public* [1989] ECR 195.

to avail of the scheme was contrary to (what is now) Art 18 TFEU, which prohibits discrimination on the grounds of nationality "within the scope of application of the Treaties". Referring to *Luisi and Carbone*, without elaboration the Court's judgment readily accepted that as a tourist visiting Paris, Mr Cowan was exercising the freedom to receive services and so his claim for compensation fell within the scope of the Treaties. Similarly, in *Commission v Spain*, a rule that Spanish citizens, foreigners resident in Spain and EU nationals under the age of 21 could visit museums for free, was held to be contrary to Arts 18 and 56 as it conferred preferential treatment on Spanish citizens over other EU nationals above the age of 21 with regard to the receipt of services.[3]

[22–04] In the case of *Alpine Investments*, involving unsolicited telephone calls being made from one Member State to another offering financial services, it was confirmed that the cross-border element can also be met where it is the service itself that travels to another Member State without any movement by the service provider or recipient, for example telephone or online services.[4] The fact that movement by the service can fulfil the cross-border element greatly widens the possibility for providers to challenge their own national laws on the basis that they restrict their freedom to provide a service in another Member State. This is particularly the case given that it is not necessary for there to be an identifiable recipient of the service who has been put off by the restriction. Rather, it suffices to be able to identify potential recipients in another Member State who may be so affected.

[22–05] Article 56 TFEU has vertical direct effect. As established in *Walrave and Koch*, it is also capable of horizontal direct effect at least in relation to self-regulating, collective entities such as sporting bodies (in that case, the International Cycling Union) or trade unions (as in the case of *Laval*).[5] Just as with the freedom of establishment, the precise scope of this horizontal direct effect has yet to be clearly established.

[22–06] Following the principal prohibition in Art 56, Art 57 then sets out a definition of services according to which, first, services are normally provided for remuneration, "insofar as they are not governed by the provisions relating to freedom of movement for goods, capital and persons". In order to qualify as a service, therefore, it is necessary that remuneration be provided, although it is not necessary that the recipient of the service is the one who provides the remuneration. In *SPUC v Grogan*, for instance, it was held that the distribution by student unions in Ireland of information on abortion services in the UK did not come within the definition set out in Art 57 as no remuneration was provided in return for distributing the information.[6] As considered below, the issue of remuneration has led to a series of cases involving the sensitive question of whether certain public services, such as health care and education, fall within the scope of Art 56.

[22–07] Historically, the reference within the Art 57 definition to "insofar as they are not governed by the provisions relating to freedom of movement for goods, capital and persons" had led to a perception that the free movement of services was in some way of a lesser significance than the other three freedoms. It is true that the Court of Justice has indicated that, for the purposes of definition, services are a form of residual

---

3 Case C-45/93 *Commission v Spain* [1994] ECR I-00911.

4 Case C-384/93 *Alpine Investments* [1995] ECR I-1141.

5 Case 36/74 *Walrave and Koch* [1974] ECR 1405; Case C-341/05 *Laval* [2007] ECR I-11767.

6 Case C-159/90 *Society for the Protection of the Unborn Child (Ireland) Ltd v Grogan* [1991] ECR I-4685. See ch 13, paras [13–51] to [13–55].

category that "covers services which are not governed by other freedoms, in order to ensure that all economic activity falls within the scope of the fundamental freedoms".[7] In doing so, however, the Court was equally adamant that this did not establish any order of priority as between the freedom to provide services and the other freedoms. Rather, the Court applies a centre of gravity assessment, such that where a national measure simultaneously relates to the freedom to provide services and another freedom, it will consider the extent to which the exercise of the freedom is affected and whether one of them prevails over the other. In principle, if it appears on the facts that one of the two freedoms is entirely secondary to the other and may be considered together with it, the Court will examine the disputed measure in the light of the predominant freedom only.

[22–08] Secondly, in somewhat outdated terminology, the definition provides that services shall, in particular, include activities of an industrial or commercial character and activities of craftsmen and of the professions. This must now be read in light of the more expansive and contemporary list of activities set out in recital 33 of the Services Directive.[8] It describes how the services covered by the Directive "concern a wide variety of ever-changing activities" including: (i) business services, such as management consultancy, office management, recruitment services and commercial agents; (ii) services provided to both consumers and to business, such as legal or fiscal advice, real estate services, construction, architects, car rental and travel agencies; and (iii) consumer services such as tourism, leisure services, sports centres and household support services such as help for the elderly.

[22–09] Lastly, the person providing a service may, in order to do so, temporarily pursue his activity in the Member State where the service is provided, under the same conditions as are imposed by that state on its own nationals. The case of *Gebhard* considered the distinction between establishment and services, concentrating on the "stable and continuous basis" of establishment, as compared with the pursuit of an activity in another Member State "on a temporary basis" when providing a service, albeit that a service provider may equip him or herself with some form of necessary infrastructure in the host Member State, such as an office of consulting rooms.[9] In *Schnitzer*, the Court of Justice stressed that the mere fact that a business supplied identical or similar services in a repeated or more or less regular manner for a number of years (in that case, a Portuguese construction company operating in Germany for three years) was not sufficient to be regarded as being established, as opposed to providing a service, in circumstances where it did not have "infrastructure there enabling it to pursue a professional activity there on a stable and continuous basis and, from the infrastructure, to hold itself out to, amongst other, nationals of the second Member State".[10]

[22–10] Article 58 TFEU is simply an exclusionary provision which provides that the freedom to provide services in the field of transport shall be governed by the Treaty provisions relating to transport, whilst the liberalisation of banking and insurance services connected with movements of capital shall be effected "in step with the liberalisation of movement of capital".

---

7 Case C-452/04 *Fidium Finanz* [2006] ECR I-9521, 9576.

8 Recital 33 of Directive 2006/123/EC of the European Parliament and of the Council of 12 December 2006 on services in the internal market [2006] OJ L376/36.

9 Case C-55/94 *Gebhard* [1995] ECR I-4165. See ch 21, paras [21–13] to [21–15].

10 Case C-215/01 *Schnitzer* [2003] ECR I-14847, 14883.

[22–11] Article 59 TFEU confers a legislative competence on the Parliament and the Council, acting in accordance with the ordinary legislative procedure and after consulting the Economic and Social Committee, to issue directives aimed at achieving the liberalisation of specific services, with priority to be given to those services which directly affect production costs or the liberalisation of which helps to promote trade in goods. This Union competence is then buttressed in Art 60 by a commitment that the Member States shall endeavour to undertake the liberalisation of services, beyond the extent required by any EU directives, if their general economic situation and the situation of the relevant economic sector permit. The Commission is tasked with making recommendations as to what action might suitably be taken by Member States so as to achieve this further liberalisation.

[22–12] As long as certain restrictions on the freedom to provide services have not been abolished, Art 61 TFEU requires that any such restrictions be applied without distinction on grounds of nationality or residence. Finally, by way of a cross-reference to the relevant provisions of the TFEU on the freedom of establishment, Art 62 provides that the following rules also apply to services: (i) the exemption in relation to the exercise of official authority within a Member State; (ii) the permission for a Member State to apply restrictions on the grounds of public policy, public security or public health; (iii) the conferral of an EU competence to adopt directives for the mutual recognition of qualifications; and (iv) for the purposes of the Chapter on services, companies established within the EU are to be treated in the same manner as EU nationals.

[22–13] The rules in Arts 56, 57 and 61 TFEU requiring equal treatment of service providers has led to *negative* integration through the case law of the Court of Justice. In addition, the conferral of legislative competence on the Union has enabled a significant degree of *positive* integration through a series of directives dealing with particular sectors, such as the Lawyers' Services Directive,[11] the Audiovisual Media Services Directive,[12] the Patients' Rights Directive,[13] the Energy Efficiency Directive,[14] the Payment Services Directive[15] and the Markets in Financial Instruments Directive.[16] In 2006, a year after the adoption of the Professional Qualifications Directive, a broadly comprehensive Services Directive was adopted, said to be the "most widely

[11] Council Directive 77/249/EEC of 22 March 1977 to facilitate the effective exercise by lawyers of freedom to provide services [1977] OJ L78/71.

[12] Directive 2010/13/EU of the European Parliament and of the Council of 10 March 2010 on the coordination of certain provisions laid down by law, regulation or administrative action in Member States concerning the provision of audiovisual media services [2010] OJ L95/1. See also the Proposal for a Directive of the European Parliament of the Council amending Directive 2010/13/EU on the coordination of certain provisions laid down by law, regulation or administrative action in Member States concerning the provision of audiovisual media services in view of changing market realities, COM/2016/0287 final, 25 May 2016, together with the European Parliament's legislative resolution thereon of 2 October 2018.

[13] Directive 2011/24/EU of the European Parliament and of the Council of 9 March 2011 on the application of patients' rights in cross-border healthcare [2011] OJ L88/45.

[14] Directive 2012/27/EU of the European Parliament and of the Council of 25 October 2012 on energy efficiency [2012] OJ L315/1.

[15] Directive (EU) 2015/2366 of the European Parliament and of the Council of 25 November 2015 on payment services in the internal market [2015] OJ L337/35.

[16] Directive 2014/65/EU of the European Parliament and of the Council of 15 May 2014 on markets in financial instruments. See also the European Union (Markets in Financial Instruments) Regulations 2017 (SI No 375 of 2017) and the European Union (Markets in Financial Instruments) (Amendment) Regulations 2017 (SI No 614 of 2017).

and passionately discussed" of all of the EU's legislative measures.[17] The Directive has been transposed into Irish law by the European Union (Provision of Services) Regulations 2010.[18]

B. The Sensitive Nature of Services

[22–14] The difficulty in agreeing on a Services Directive arose in part due to the complex and varied nature of services themselves, which can encompass services as diverse as dog grooming to laser eye surgery, computer programming to quantity surveying. Services can also straddle grey areas between both establishment, where the service provider sets up in another Member State for a significant period of time, and goods, where the provision of a service entails making certain physical items available, such as CDs and text books provided on a language learning course. E-books, for example, are a service, whereas the supply of electricity is a good.[19]

[22–15] In this context it is interesting to recall that in the first case to establish the direct effect of Art 56, *Van Binsbergen*, which followed soon after *Reyners* had established the direct effect of the freedom of establishment, Ireland was among a number of intervening Member States to argue against extending the approach in *Reyners* to services.[20] In addition to pointing to the need for directives to harmonise particular sectors, Ireland argued that the removal of restrictions on the freedom to provide services necessitated the resolution of problems which arose from different applicable laws and regulations, from the different conditions in which services were rendered in the Member States and from the fact that Member States required different educational and professional qualifications, particularly with regard to the legal profession. Services now account for over 70 per cent of the euro area economy and, after a slow start, have become one of the most progressive freedoms, with their importance to the Internal Market evident for all to see.[21] Nevertheless, Damian Chalmers, Gareth Davies and Giorgio Monti observe that the way in which services require active interaction with individuals makes them more in need of regulation than goods. This, in turn, makes Art 56 "constitutionally dangerous" in that:

> [i]f all law affecting a service provider imposes costs on her somehow, then all law deters her activities to some extent, and Article 56 might become a tool for a general review of national legislative proportionality. One of the central issues of the free movement of services is … how to define its limits in a way reflecting the right balance between purposive market-creation, and practical, attribution-respecting, limits to EU law. The Court of Justice has not yet created a *Keck* for services, a case which is accepted to draw such lines, perhaps partly because the type of restrictions which impact on services are less easy to categorise than is the case for goods. Rather, the Court uses a variety of formulas

---

17 Directive 2006/123/EC of the European Parliament and of the Council of 12 December 2006 on services in the internal market [2006] OJ 2006 L376/36. Vassilis Hatzopoulos, "Assessing the Services Directive 2006/123" (2007–2008) 10 *Cambridge Yearbook of European Legal Studies* 215, 236.

18 SI No 533 of 2010. See John Biggins and Catherine Donnelly, "Transposition of the Directive on Services in the Internal Market (2006/123/EC) in Ireland" in Michael Mirschberger (ed), *The Implementation of the Services Directive in EU Member States* (TMC Asser Press, 2012) 309.

19 Gareth Davies, "The Law of the Free Movement of Services" in Anthony Arnull and Damian Chalmers (eds), *The Oxford Handbook of European Law* (Oxford University Press, 2015) 563.

20 Case 33/74 *Van Binsbergen* [1974] ECR 1299, 1303.

21 Robert Schütze, *European Union Law* (Cambridge University Press, 2015) 633.

> and phrases to sum up the scope of Article 56, not all of which are entirely consistent with each other. In particular, it is unclear whether regulation which has an entirely equal impact on domestic and cross-border services, and which merely impose costs rather than actually preventing service provision, is caught by the Treaty.[22]

[22–16] The following three examples of national laws being challenged on the basis of Art 56 in somewhat unusual circumstances demonstrate the very wide reach of the prohibition on restrictions. In *De Coster*, a Belgian local authority imposed a yearly tax on satellite dishes in order to discourage their "uncontrolled proliferation".[23] In responding to a preliminary reference, the Court of Justice confirmed that Art 56 applied not only to directly or indirectly discriminatory measures, but also to non-discriminatory measures, such as the satellite dish tax, which were liable to prohibit or further impede the activities of a service provider established in another Member State. Whereas Belgian broadcasters enjoyed unlimited access to cable transmission, broadcasters from other Member States were more reliant on satellite transmission. The Court considered that the tax would dissuade customers in the local authority's area from choosing television services broadcast from another Member State, and would also "hinder the activities of operators in the field of satellite transmission by imposing a charge on the reception of programmes transmitted by such operators which does not apply to the reception of programmes transmitted by the national cable distributors".[24] Accordingly, the tax was found to be caught by Art 56 on the basis that it was liable to impede more the activities of broadcasters established outside Belgium, while giving an advantage to Belgian broadcasters. Although restrictions on the use of satellite dishes were capable of being justified on public policy grounds, the tax was considered to be disproportionate in that less restrictive measures, such as regulations governing the size and placement of satellite dishes, could have achieved the same goal.

[22–17] *Josemans* concerned an effort by the city of Maastricht to prevent drug tourism by introducing a residence criterion whereby any "coffee-shop" (where cannabis was sold, together in some cases with non-alcoholic food and drink) was prohibited from admitting non-Dutch residents.[25] It was estimated that the city's 14 coffee shops attracted 10,000 visitors a day, 70 per cent of whom came from outside the Netherlands. Following reports that two non-Dutch residents had been admitted, Mr Josemans' coffee-shop was temporarily closed. In considering a preliminary reference, the Court held that given the general prohibition across the EU on drugs such as cannabis, coffee-shop owners were unable to rely on the freedom to provide services in respect of this aspect of their trade. Such owners were, however, entitled to invoke Art 56 with respect to the provision of food and drink (notwithstanding that the Dutch Government estimated that no more than 7 per cent of coffee-shop trade related to such services). As a result, the restriction imposed by the city of Maastricht was caught by Art 56 and required justification. Having regard to factors such as the difficulty in monitoring what non-resident customers consumed on the premises and the availability of other cafés and restaurants in the city, the Court was satisfied that the measure was justified by the objective of combating drug tourism and the accompanying public nuisance.

---

[22] Damian Chalmers, Gareth Davies and Giorgio Monti, *European Union Law* (3rd ed, Cambridge University Press, 2014) 800–801.

[23] Case C-17/00 *De Coster* [2001] ECR I-9445.

[24] *ibid*, 9501.

[25] Case C-137/09 *Josemans* [2010] ECR I-13019.

[22–18] The final case is that of *R v Human Fertilisation and Embryology Authority ex p Blood*, and involved litigation brought by Mrs Blood seeking permission to undergo artificial insemination in Belgium following the death of her husband.[26] Mr and Mrs Blood had been trying to start a family when he fell ill and entered a coma. Mrs Blood wished to use sperm samples taken before his death but was refused permission by the relevant UK authority on the basis that the donor's written consent was required in order to bring the sperm abroad for treatment. In judicial review proceedings before the English Court of Appeal, it was successfully argued that the Authority's imposition of such a requirement infringed her EU law right to receive medical services in another Member State. In particular, the Authority's decision was held to be flawed in that it had failed to be properly advised as to the importance of the EU law right to treatment in Belgium:

> In coming to its decision the authority was required to take into account that to refuse permission to export would impede the treatment of Mrs Blood in Belgium and to ask whether in the circumstances this was justified. The material which was placed before the authority in order to assist them to perform this task is known. Unfortunately it makes no mention of this requirement. … The authority must balance [the importance of consent in the UK Act] against Mrs Blood's cross-border rights as a [Union] citizen. … [R]eferring to the fact that Mrs Blood has no prior connection with any country to which she wishes to export the sperm, ignores the fact that she has the right to receive treatment in Belgium and that Parliament has placed no restriction on the authority's discretion to permit this. … If the authority is to reconsider their decision it will have to direct itself correctly as to the law, that is the law including European law. This will involve starting from the premise that to refuse to allow the export of the sperm is contrary to Article [56] unless there are appropriate reasons to justify this. The onus is therefore on the authority to provide reasons which meet the standards set by European law.[27]

[22–19] In deciding on the matter again, the Authority permitted Mrs Blood to travel for the treatment. As well as these cases, it will be recalled that in *SPUC v Grogan* the Court of Justice side-stepped the direct question of whether an abortion, legally carried out in a Member State other than Ireland, was a service to which Art 56 applied, by focusing on the absence of remuneration or any commercial relationship between the student unions and the abortion clinics. In taking a different approach, Advocate General Van Gerven was in "no doubt" that the lawful termination of a pregnancy amounted to a service, albeit that he considered the Irish restrictions on its freedom to be justifiable on public policy grounds.[28] As part of the negotiations on the Maastricht Treaty, Ireland succeeded in having a short Protocol concluded (now Protocol No 35 to the TEU and TFEU) that confirmed that nothing in the Treaties, or in any acts modifying or supplementing the Treaties, "shall affect the application in Ireland of Article 40.3.3° of the Constitution of Ireland". Wording to similar effect was also included in the Protocol on the Concerns of the Irish People on the Treaty of Lisbon. Following a referendum in May 2018, Art 40.3.3° was replaced with a statement that "[p]rovision may be made by law for the regulation of termination of pregnancy".

---

26 [1997] 2 CMLR 591.

27 *ibid*, 606–608.

28 Case C-159/90 *SPUC v Grogan* [1991] ECR I-4685, 4707. See Diarmuid Rossa Phelan, "The Right to Life of the Unborn v Promotion of Trade in Services: The European Court of Justice and the Normative Shaping of the European Union" (1992) 55 *Modern Law Review* 670; Síofra O'Leary, "The Court of Justice as a Reluctant Constitutional Adjudicator: An Examination of the Abortion Information Case" (1992) 17 *European Law Review* 138.

C. Non-Discriminatory Restrictions

[22–20] As seen above in the cases of *De Coster*, involving a tax on satellite dishes, and *Alpine Investments*, involving a Dutch ban on cold-calling for financial services, whether within the Netherlands or to Member States where such cold-calling was not prohibited, Art 56 TFEU's prohibition of restrictions on the freedom to provide services applies not only to directly and indirectly discriminatory measures, but can also apply to non-discriminatory measures.

[22–21] Mirroring developments in the field of free movement of goods in landmark cases such as *Dassonville* and *Cassis de Dijon*, in its 1986 judgment in *Commission v Germany (Insurance Services)* the Court of Justice confirmed that Art 56 requires the removal "not only of all discrimination against a provider of a service on the grounds of his nationality but also all restrictions on his freedom to provide services imposed by reason of the fact that he is established in a Member State other than that in which the service is to be provided".[29] At a time when there were only 10 Member States, five intervened in support of Germany (including Ireland, against whom similar infringement proceedings were pending), whilst traditional supporters of the freedom of services, the UK and the Netherlands, supported the Commission.

[22–22] The action concerned a requirement that insurance providers in Germany have a permanent establishment there, and receive prior authorisation from the German authorities to offer insurance services. The Court considered that, as these restrictions increased the cost of providing insurance services in Germany for insurers from outside of Germany, in particular where an insurer conducted business there only occasionally, they were caught by Art 56 and so required justification. It explained the approach it would take to assessing Germany's defence of the measures as follows:

> the freedom to provide services, as one of the fundamental principles of the Treaty, may be restricted only by provisions which are justified by the general good and which are applied to all persons or undertakings operating within the territory of the State in which the service is provided in so far as that interest is not safeguarded by the provisions to which the provider of a service is subject in the Member State of his establishment. In addition, such requirements must be objectively justified by the need to ensure that professional rules of conduct are complied with and that the interests which such rules are designed to safeguard are protected. …
>
> … [The] requirements may be regarded as compatible with Articles [56 and 57 TFEU] only if it is established that in the field of activity concerned there are imperative reasons relating to the public interest which justify restrictions on the freedom to provide services, that the public interest is not already protected by the rules of the State of establishment and that the same result cannot be obtained by less restrictive rules. …
>
> … [T]he insurance sector is a particularly sensitive area from the point of view of the protection of the consumer both as a policy-holder and as an insured person. … It therefore appears that in the field in question there are imperative reasons relating to the public interest which may justify restrictions on the freedom to provide services, provided, however, that the rules of the State of establishment are not adequate in order to achieve

---

[29] Case 205/84 *Commission v Germany* [1986] ECR 3755, 3803. See Vassilis Hatzopoulos, "The Court's Approach to Services (2006–2012): From Case Law to Case Load?" (2013) 50 *Common Market Law Review* 459; Stefan Enchelmaier, "Always at Your Service (within Limits): The ECJ's Case Law on Article 56 TFEU 2006–11" (2011) 36 *European Law Review* 615.

> the necessary level of protection and that the requirements of the State in which the service is provided do not exceed what is necessary in that respect.[30]

[22–23] With regard to the requirement of establishment within Germany, the Court held that this was not capable of being justified as it went beyond what was necessary to achieve the goal of regulating insurance providers. In contrast, when examined in the light of EU law governing the insurance sector at the time, the separate prior authorisation requirement was regarded as having been justified by Germany as the only effective means of ensuring adequate supervision for the protection of consumers.

[22–24] The key case which is often cited as establishing the Court's approach to non-discriminatory restrictions on services remains that of *Säger*.[31] This involved a UK company that provided a patent monitoring service, whereby it would notify its clients whenever one of their patents became due for renewal. The company had clients in Germany for whom it monitored patents, but it did not hold a patent agent licence as required by German law. At issue was whether the German requirement for such a licence was a restriction on services caught by Art 56 and, if so, whether it was justified. The Court of Justice confirmed that Art 56 prohibits not only direct discrimination, but also requires

> the abolition of any restriction, even if it applies without distinction to national providers of services and to those of other Member States, when it is liable to prohibit or otherwise impede the activities of a provider of services established in another Member State where he lawfully provides similar services. In particular, a Member State may not make the provision of services in its territory subject to compliance with all the conditions required for establishment and thereby deprive of all practical effectiveness the provisions of the Treaty whose object is, precisely, to guarantee the freedom to provide services. Such a restriction is all the less permissible where ... the service is supplied without its being necessary for the person providing it to visit the territory of the Member State where it is provided. It should next be stated that national legislation which makes the provision of certain services on the national territory by an undertaking established in another Member State subject to the issue of an administrative licence for which the possession of certain professional qualifications is required constitutes a restriction on the freedom to provide services within the meaning of Article [56] of the Treaty. By reserving the provision of services in respect of the monitoring of patents to certain economic operators possessing certain professional qualifications, national legislation prevents an undertaking established abroad from providing services to the holders of patents in the national territory and also prevents those holders from freely choosing the manner in which their patents are to be monitored.[32]

[22–25] In finding that the restriction was disproportionate, the Court noted that the UK company providing the notification service did not advise clients as to the implications of any decision, since the clients were themselves often patent agents or undertakings which employed qualified patent experts. Rather, the service was confined to alerting when renewal fees had to be paid in order to prevent a patent from lapsing, requesting instructions as to whether to renew the patent and, if so, paying the corresponding fees. In the view of the Court, those tasks were "essentially of a straightforward nature and do not call for specific professional aptitudes" as indicated

---

30 *ibid*, 3803.

31 Case C-76/90 *Säger* [1991] ECR I-4221.

32 *ibid*, 4243.

by the high level of computerisation involved.[33] As a result, the German requirement for a patent licence was not proportionate to the objective of protecting the interests of patent holders and so was contrary to Art 56.

[22–26] Shortly afterwards, in the important freedom of establishment case of *Gebhard*, the Court of Justice confirmed in general terms that all national measures "liable to hinder or make less attractive the exercise of fundamental freedoms" were to be regarded as restrictions on free movement.[34] The principle underlying the approach in *Säger* can be described as one of mutual recognition, similar to that applied to the free movement of goods. Whereas a person or company exercising the freedom of establishment on a permanent basis is required to comply with the laws of the host Member State, the provision of services can be seen to be closer to cross-border trade in goods, such that in principle, compliance with the laws of the home state should suffice. As Advocate General Jacobs explained in his opinion, the principle should be that:

> if an undertaking complies with the legislation of the Member State in which it is established it may provide services in another Member State, even though the provision of such services would not normally be lawful under the laws of the second Member State. Restrictions imposed by those laws can only be applied against the foreign undertaking if they are justified by some requirement that is compatible with the aims of the Community.[35]

[22–27] Another example of a non-discriminatory restriction caught by Art 56 arose in *Commission v Italy*, in which infringement proceedings were brought in respect of an Italian law that required all motor vehicle insurers to provide third-party liability insurance to any customer that wished to enter into such a policy (termed an "obligation to contract").[36] The measure was primarily designed to address difficulties faced by certain categories of driver – namely drivers in the south of Italy and young drivers – in obtaining car insurance. The Court, sitting as a Grand Chamber, reasoned as follows in concluding that the obligation was a restriction within the meaning of Art 56:

> It is settled case-law that the term "restriction" within the meaning of [Art 56] covers all measures which prohibit, impede or render less attractive … the freedom to provide services.
>
> As regards the question of the circumstances in which a measure applicable without distinction, such as the obligation to contract at issue in the present case, may come within that concept, it should be borne in mind that rules of a Member State do not constitute a restriction within the meaning of the [TFEU] solely by virtue of the fact that other Member States apply less strict, or more commercially favourable, rules to providers of similar services established in their territory.
>
> By contrast, *the concept of restriction covers measures taken by a Member State which, although applicable without distinction, affect access to the market for undertakings from other Member States and thereby hinder intra-[EU] trade.* …
>
> … the imposition by a Member State of an obligation to contract such as that at issue

---

33 *ibid*, 4245.

34 Case C-55/94 *Gebhard* [1995] ECR I-4165, 4197. See ch 21, paras [21–13] to [21–15].

35 Case C-76/90 *Säger* [1991] ECR I-4221, 4235. See Wulf-Henning Roth, "Case C-76/90, *Manfred Säger v Dennemeyer & Co Ltd*" (1993) 30 *Common Market Law Review* 145.

36 Case C-518/06 *Commission v Italy* [2009] ECR I-3491.

constitutes a substantial interference in the freedom to contract which economic operators, in principle, enjoy.

In a sector like that of insurance, *such a measure affects the relevant operators' access to the market*, in particular where it subjects insurance undertakings not only to an obligation to cover any risks which are proposed to them, but also to requirements to moderate premium rates.

Inasmuch as it obliges insurance undertakings which enter the Italian market to accept every potential customer, that obligation to contract is likely to lead, in terms of organisation and investment, to significant additional costs for such undertakings.

If they wish to enter the Italian market under conditions which comply with Italian legislation, such undertakings will be required to re-think their business policy and strategy, inter alia, by considerably expanding the range of insurance services offered.

Inasmuch as it involves changes and costs on such a scale for those undertakings, the obligation to contract renders access to the Italian market less attractive and, if they obtain access to that market, reduces the ability of the undertakings concerned to compete effectively, from the outset, against undertakings traditionally established in Italy.

Therefore, the obligation to contract restricts the freedom of establishment and the freedom to provide services.[37]

[22–28] Taking into account that it remained open to insurers to charge higher premiums for geographical areas with high levels of claims, the Court considered that the measure was objectively justifiable and proportionate. From the extract above, it can be seen that in considering whether the obligation to contract amounted to a restriction on the freedom to provide services, the Court focused on the effect it had on service providers seeking to "access the market" in another Member State. Although the obligation to contract applied to all insurance providers, it was likely to require new entrants to the market to "moderate premium rates", incur additional costs "in terms of organisation and investment" and to "re-think their business policy and strategy" by considerably expanding the range of services offered", all of which had the effect of making Italy a less attractive market and reducing the ability of new entrants to compete effectively.

[22–29] A useful elaboration on the Court's approach to non-discriminatory measures was provided in *Mobistar*, in which it was argued that a tax imposed on telecommunications pylons was a restriction on the freedom of services.[38] The Court concluded that the tax was not such a restriction, explaining that:

measures, the only effect of which is to create additional costs in respect of the service in question and which affect in the same way the provision of services between Member States and that within one Member State, do not fall within the scope of Article [56] of the Treaty.

As regards the question whether the levy by municipal authorities of taxes … amounts to a restriction incompatible with Article [56], it is necessary to point out that such taxes *apply without distinction to all owners of mobile telephone installations within the commune*

[37] *ibid*, paras 62–71. Emphasis added.

[38] Case C-544/03 *Mobistar* [2005] ECR I-7723. See also Case C-134/03 *Viacom Outdoor* [2005] ECR I-1167.

in question, and that foreign operators are not, either in fact or in law, more adversely affected by those measures than national operators.

Nor do the tax measures in question make cross-border service provision more difficult than national service provision. Admittedly, introducing a tax on pylons, masts and antennae can make tariffs for mobile telephone communications to Belgium from abroad and vice versa more expensive. However, national telephone service provision is, to the same extent, subject to the risk that the tax will have an impact on tariffs.

It is appropriate to add that there is nothing in the file to suggest that the cumulative effect of the local taxes compromises freedom to provide mobile telephony services between other Member States and the Kingdom of Belgium.

… Article [56] of the Treaty must be interpreted as not precluding the introduction … of a tax on mobile and personal communications infrastructures used to carry on activities provided for in licences and authorisations, which applies without distinction to national providers of services and to those of other Member States and affects in the same way the provision of services within one Member State and the provision of services between Member States.[39]

[22–30] Gareth Davies suggests that the judgment in *Mobistar* applies to services "essentially the same approach as taken in the free movement of goods, where *Keck* exempts a category of measures which the Court considers, like the cost burden in *Mobistar*, to have no trade-diverting effect. Just as *Keck* modified (or interprets), the apparently all-encompassing language of *Dassonville*, *Mobistar* and phrases such as that in *Commission v Italy* give nuance to the apparent breadth of *Gebhard*."[40] Elsewhere, Davies explains the "very solid policy" behind the Court's approach:

If a mere cost burden that has an equal impact on domestic and foreign trade is a restriction on services, then almost every tax or regulation relevant to a service industry will fall within Article 56 TFEU. This is undesirable and unrealistic, and an unconvincing reading of the intention of Article 56. It is very reminiscent of the situation in goods pre-*Keck*. Thus, it is suggested that *Mobistar* is likely to be followed in similar situations, and should, like *Keck*, be treated as a specific exception to the general rule. Mere cost burdens, like selling-arrangements, if they have an equal impact on national and foreign, domestic and cross-border, are not restrictions on trade. … However, experience with *Keck* indicates that this exception may shrink with time. Serious factual investigation often reveals unequal effects even where rules are apparently neutral, and the discussion of business models in *Commission v Italy* indicates a certain judicial preparedness to engage with this commercial reality.[41]

[22–31] It is possible to detect some support for this approach within the Services Directive, which uses the term "requirements" defined very broadly as "any obligation, prohibition, condition or limit provided for in the laws, regulations or administrative provisions of the Member States …".[42] The ninth recital, however, describes how the Directive applies

---

39 *ibid*, 7749–7750. Emphasis added.

40 Gareth Davies, "The Law of the Free Movement of Services" in Anthony Arnull and Damian Chalmers (eds), *The Oxford Handbook of European Law* (Oxford University Press, 2015) 574.

41 Damian Chalmers, Gareth Davies and Giorgio Monti, *European Union Law* (3rd ed, Cambridge University Press, 2014) 811, 813.

42 Article 4(7), Directive 2006/123/EC of the European Parliament and of the Council of 12 December 2006 on services in the internal market [2006] OJ L376/36.

> only to requirements which affect the access to, or the exercise of, a service activity. Therefore, it does not apply to requirements, such as road traffic rules, rules concerning the development or use of land, town and country planning, building standards ... which does not specifically regulate or specifically affect the service activity but have to be respected by providers in the course of carrying out their economic activity in the same way as by individuals acting in their private capacity.

[22–32] A final form of non-discriminatory restriction worth highlighting is that of controls on advertising. In *Gourmet International*, the Court was satisfied that a Swedish ban on adverts for alcohol within magazines was a restriction on the freedom to provide advertising services, particularly given the international nature of the advertising market for alcoholic drinks.[43] In the context of the preliminary reference, it was left to the national court to determine whether the measure was a justified and proportionate means of protecting public health. Similarly, under French law, indirect advertising of alcohol on television was prohibited. A code of conduct required French broadcasters of sporting events to take certain steps in order to avoid such advertising being transmitted, for example by showing hoardings at sports grounds or by way of sponsorship of team strips. In *Bacardi*, the drinks company sought to challenge the law as a restriction contrary to Art 56. Once again, the Court accepted that these measures did fall within the scope of Art 56, but were capable of justification on grounds of public health provided that they did not go beyond what was necessary to achieve that objective.[44] Finally, in *Vanderborght*, a complete ban on advertising dental care services in Belgium was found to be contrary to Art 56 due to its lack of proportionality.[45] Notwithstanding the large degree of discretion afforded to Member States in protecting public health, the objectives pursued by the advertising ban "could be attained through the use of less restrictive measures supervising, closely if necessary, the form and manner which the communication tools used by dentists may legitimately have, without imposing on them a general and absolute prohibition of any form of advertising".[46]

D. Grounds for Justifying Restrictions

[22–33] By virtue of Art 62 TFEU, both Arts 51 and 52 on exceptions to the freedom of establishment apply equally to services. Accordingly, as per Art 51, the rules on the freedom to provide services shall not apply to activities connected, even occasionally, with the exercise of official authority. The concept of official authority has, however, been given a very narrow interpretation by the Court of Justice, requiring a direct and specific connection with official authority.[47] Read together with Art 52, Art 62 allows for the imposition of restrictions on the freedom to provide or to receive services on the grounds of public policy, public security or public health. A Member State may also seek to justify non-discriminatory restrictions on services on the basis of an overriding public interest objective. It will be necessary to demonstrate that any restriction is proportionate, in the sense that there is no less restrictive means available of achieving the same objective.

---

43 Case C-405/98 *Gourmet International* [2001] ECR I-1795. See Andrea Biondi, "Advertising Alcohol and the Free Movement Principle: The *Gourmet* Decision" (2001) 26 *European Law Review* 616.

44 Case C-429/02 *Bacardi* [2004] ECR I-6613. See Jules Stuyck, "Case C-262/02, *Commission v France* and Case C-429/02, *Bacardi*" (2005) 42 *Common Market Law Review* 783.

45 Case C-339/15 *Vanderborght* EU:C:2017:335, 4 May 2017.

46 *ibid*, para 75.

47 See ch 21, paras [21–26] to [21–28].

[22–34] As will be seen in the following section, in a number of cases involving health care treatment the Court of Justice has recognised the importance of the public health ground. This has resulted in Member States being afforded a degree of latitude with regard to how they ensure the maintenance of a balanced hospital service open to all, even if this objective is intrinsically linked to broader aims such as the method of financing a state's social security system or ensuring proper planning and cost efficiencies. Nevertheless, when it comes to assessing a justification put forward on the basis of this ground, the Court has applied a close and exacting examination. For example, in *Corporación Dermoestética*, the Court accepted that the public health ground could be relied upon to defend an Italian law that prohibited advertisements on national television channels for medical treatments by private health-care clinics. Nevertheless, by introducing a measure resulting in a prohibition on advertising medical and surgical treatments on national television networks while at the same time making it possible to broadcast such advertisements on local television networks, such rules were found to "exhibit an inconsistency which the Italian Government has not attempted to justify and cannot therefore properly attain the public health objective which they seek to pursue".[48]

[22–35] In addition to the cases of *De Coster* and *Josemans* referred to above – concerning restriction on satellite dishes and "coffee-shops" respectively – the public policy ground has been invoked in unusual circumstances in *Omega*, where a German company was ordered to withdraw a laser-shooting game in which participants could "play at killing" by aiming at their opponents.[49] As the equipment was provided by a British company, it was claimed that the prohibition on the activity amounted to a restriction on the freedom to provide services. In response, the restriction was claimed to be justified on the public policy ground that the commercial exploitation of games involving simulated killing infringed human dignity, a fundamental value enshrined in the German constitution. Whilst confirming that the public policy ground may be relied on only if there is a genuine and sufficiently serious threat to a fundamental interest of society, the Court of Justice went on to note that the "specific circumstances which may justify recourse to the concept of public policy may vary from one country to another and from one era to another. The competent national authorities must therefore be allowed a margin of discretion within the limits imposed by the Treaty."[50] As the ban imposed was limited to the particular type of laser equipment used for aiming at human targets, it was held that the restriction was proportionate and justifiable.

[22–36] An illustration of an overriding public interest being invoked in order to defend a non-discriminatory measure is found in infringement proceedings brought against Ireland concerning the manner in which vehicle registration tax was collected on rental vehicles.[51] The Commission argued that, by requiring the payment of the full amount of vehicle registration tax on rental vehicles that were to be brought into Ireland for use over a limited duration, Ireland was in breach of Art 56 TFEU. This was because the obligation to pay the full amount – with the opportunity to avail of a refund mechanism at the end of the period of use – was liable to render the rental of a vehicle from a company established in another Member State more onerous than rental

48 Case C-500/06 *Corporación Dermoestética*, [2008] ECR I-5785, para 39.

49 Case C-36/02 *Omega* [2004] ECR I-9609.

50 *ibid*, 9652.

51 Case C-552/15 *Commission v Ireland (Vehicle Registration Tax)* EU:C:2017:698, 19 September 2017.

from a company established in Ireland. Having determined that the requirement was a restriction on the freedom to provide services, the Court of Justice accepted that the protection of the environment through discouraging the rental of vehicles with heavy fuel consumption may have a public interest objective. However, reasoning as follows, the Court was not convinced that the requirement was a proportionate means of attaining this objective, with the result that Ireland was found to be in breach of Art 56:

> [A]t the time of registration, the Irish system of registration tax seeks to achieve the objective of protecting the environment principally by means of applying a rate of taxation which depends on the level of carbon dioxide emissions. To that extent, such a system is appropriate for attaining that objective, by discouraging the rental or leasing of vehicles with heavy fuel consumption.
>
> On the other hand, at the time of registration, the amount of registration tax is determined without regard to the duration of the use of the vehicle and, in the case of vehicles imported from another Member State, irrespective of whether they are imported permanently or temporarily.
>
> That being so, so far as concerns vehicles rented or leased from a company established in another Member State for a period that is determined and known in advance, the obligation to pay the full amount of registration tax goes beyond what is necessary in order to achieve the objective of protecting the environment. Those vehicles, whose use in Ireland is envisaged for a limited period, are taxed at the time of registration on the basis of their potential polluting impact as if they were vehicles used permanently and over a long period in Ireland. Since the duration of their use in Ireland is limited and known in advance, a less restrictive measure could consist in levying, at the time of their registration, a registration tax proportionate to the duration of that use.
>
> ... the introduction of an additional factor corresponding to the duration of use envisaged in Ireland at the time of initial payment of the registration tax would enable the objective of protecting the environment that is pursued to be achieved by means of a less restrictive measure, without calling into question the basis of taxation constituted by the vehicle's open market value and its level of carbon dioxide emissions.
>
> ... Thus, by making it obligatory to pay the full amount of registration tax in advance, Irish law, despite the fact that it provides for part of the tax paid to be refunded, goes beyond what is necessary in order to achieve the objective of protecting the environment and, in particular, in order to deter the rental or leasing of vehicles with heavy fuel consumption.[52]

E. Publicly Funded Services

[22–37] Given that the definition of services in Art 57 TFEU explicitly refers to the need for an exchange of payment, a question arises as to whether publicly funded services, provided by a Member State, are to fall within the scope of Art 56. Whilst it might at first appear straightforward that services, such as education and hospital care, that do not require direct payment are not to be governed by the relevant Treaty rules, the picture becomes more complicated when it is remembered that it is not necessary that the remuneration be provided by the receiver of the service, but may come from elsewhere.

---

[52] *ibid*, paras 97–99, 102 and 107.

(i) Education

[22–38] The 1988 case of *Belgium v Humbel* saw a relatively uncomplicated approach to the question of whether secondary schooling in Belgium, which required non-Belgian students to pay an annual fee, was a service within the meaning of Art 56 TFEU.[53] The Court of Justice held that it was not, reasoning as follows:

> The essential characteristic of remuneration thus lies in the fact that it constitutes consideration for the service in question, and is normally agreed upon between the provider and the recipient of the service.
>
> That characteristic is, however, absent in the case of courses provided under the national education system. First of all, the State, in establishing and maintaining such a system, is not seeking to engage in gainful activity but is fulfilling its duties towards its own population in the social, cultural and educational fields. Secondly, the system in question is, as a general rule, funded from the public purse and not by pupils or their parents.
>
> The nature of the activity is not affected by the fact that pupils or their parents must sometimes pay teaching or enrolment fees in order to make a certain contribution to the operating expenses of the system. A fortiori, the mere fact that foreign pupils alone are required to pay a [fee] can have no such effect.[54]

[22–39] In a subsequent case, however, the Court clarified that although the exception from Art 56 outlined in *Humbel* could also apply to third-level courses, it would not apply to education services provided by institutions "financed essentially out of private funds, in particular by students or their parents, and which seek to make an economic profit. When courses are given in such establishments, they become services within the meaning of Article [57] of the Treaty. Their aim is to offer a service for remuneration."[55]

[22–40] This approach was followed in *Schwarz*, in which a German family sent their children to a private school in Scotland for specially gifted children.[56] Under German law, a tax deduction was available in respect of fees paid to private schools in Germany, but not for fees paid to such schools outside Germany. The Court responded to a preliminary reference by noting that "where taxpayers of a given Member State send their children to a private school established in another Member State which may be regarded as providing services for remuneration, that is to say which is essentially financed by private funds", Art 56 was engaged.[57] The difference in tax treatment amounted to an obstacle to the free movement of services which, given its absolute exclusion of non-German schools, was disproportionate to any public policy aim being pursued and so was impermissible.

(ii) Medical Services

[22–41] A number of cases dealing with the provision of medical treatment have required consideration to be given to the situation where a patient pays for a service abroad, only to subsequently seek reimbursement from their home state. In *Kohll*, one of the first cases to address this issue, Mr Kohll applied under the Luxembourg

---

53 Case 263/86 *Belgium v Humbel* [1988] ECR 5365.
54 *ibid*, 5388.
55 Case C-109/92 *Wirth* [1993] ECR I-6447, 6469.
56 Case C-76/05 *Schwarz* [2007] ECR I-6849.
57 *ibid*, 6893.

health-insurance scheme for authorisation to arrange for orthodontic treatment for his daughter in Germany.[58] Such prior authorisation was required if treatment obtained outside Luxembourg was to be covered by the scheme. Approval was declined on the basis that the treatment was not urgent and there was no need to travel abroad to receive it. In replying to a preliminary reference, the Court observed that the prior authorisation rules served to "deter insured persons from approaching providers of medical services established in another Member State and constitute, for them and their patients, a barrier to freedom to provide services".[59] On the case presented by Luxembourg, the Court was not satisfied that the restriction was justified on the basis of either protecting public health or maintaining a balanced social security system. It has been said that the historic contribution of *Kohll* "resides in the fact that for the first time, the Court applied [the freedom to provide services] to care covered by social security", subjecting national rules requiring prior authorisation for the reimbursement of expenses incurred to the judicial doctrines of the Internal Market.[60] As a result, any such rules may be scrutinised in order to determine whether they are: (i) justified on the grounds of protecting public health or some other overriding reason of general interest; (ii) proportionate and necessary to achieve the objective; and (iii) non-discriminatory and based on objective criteria that are known in advance.

[22–42] A similar scenario was considered in *Geraets-Smits and Peerbooms*.[61] Here, however, the Dutch public health-insurance scheme was specifically for those below a certain income, with the scheme's fund made up of state contributions, individual premiums and subsidisation from private insurers. The scheme was one of benefits in kind, under which an insured person was entitled, not to reimbursement of costs incurred for medical treatment, but to free treatment. Treatment under the scheme was organised on the basis of a system of agreements made between sickness funds and healthcare providers. Prior authorisation was required in order to obtain the treatment abroad, which to be approved had to be deemed both necessary and "normal in the professional circles concerned".

[22–43] The two applicants had received hospital treatment abroad without having obtained prior authorisation. They subsequently applied to the insurance scheme for reimbursement of the costs incurred. Ms Geraets-Smits, who suffered from Parkinson's Disease, was refused on the basis that the treatment received in Germany was not normal within the relevant Dutch professional circle and, secondly, it was not regarded as necessary. Mr Peerbooms, who was in a coma, received treatment in Austria that, in the Netherlands, was regarded as experimental and was only applied to patients under the age of 25.

58 Case C-158/96 *Kohll* [1998] ECR I-1931. See also Case C-120/95 *Decker* [1998] ECR I-1831; Pedro Cabral, "Cross-Border Medical Care in the European Union – Bringing Down a First Wall" (1999) 24 *European Law Review* 387; AP Van der Mei, "Cross-Border Access to Medical Care within the European Union – Some Reflections on the Judgments in *Decker* and *Kohll*" (1998) 5 *Maastricht Journal of European and Comparative Law* 277.

59 *ibid*, 1946.

60 Stephane de la Rosa, "The Directive on Cross-Border Healthcare or the Art of Codifying Complex Case Law" (2012) 49 *Common Market Law Review* 15, 19.

61 Case C-157/99 *Geraets-Smits and Peerbooms* [2001] ECR I-5473. See Elies Steygen, "National Health Care Systems Under Fire (But not too Heavily)" (2002) 29 *Legal Issues of Economic Integration* 97; Vassilis Hatzopoulos, "Killing National Health and Insurance Systems but Healing Patients? The European Market for Health Care Services after the Judgments of the ECJ in *Vanbraekel* and *Peerbooms*" (2002) 36 *Common Market Law Review* 683.

[22–44] Ireland was among twelve Member States which, in their interventions, emphasised that "by comparison with medical services provided by practitioners in their surgeries or at the patient's home, medical services provided in a hospital take place within an infrastructure with … certain very distinct characteristics".[62] In particular, along the lines of *Humbel*, it was argued that there was no remuneration within the meaning of Art 57 TFEU where a patient receives care in a hospital infrastructure without having to pay for it him or herself, or where all or part of the amount paid is reimbursed.

[22–45] The Court repeated its earlier case law that medical treatment, including hospital care, can fall within the scope of Art 56 TFEU. In this case, rather than payment being provided pursuant to an insurance scheme, the treating hospitals in Germany and Austria had been paid directly by the patients. Crucially, the Court held that a "medical service provided in one Member State and paid for by the patient should not cease to fall within the scope of the freedom to provide services guaranteed by the Treaty merely because reimbursement of the costs of the treatment involved is applied for under another Member State's sickness insurance legislation which is essentially of the type which provides for benefits in kind".[63] This was the case, even though hospital treatment was financed directly by the Dutch sickness insurance fund on the basis of contractual agreements and pre-set scales of fees. Although the payments made by the fund under these arrangements were set at a flat rate, they were nonetheless consideration for the hospital services and "unquestionably represent remuneration for the hospital which receives them and which is engaged in an activity of an economic character".[64] Following *Kohll*, it was found that the dual requirements that the treatment be "normal" and "necessary" for prior authorisation to be granted "deter, or even prevent, insured persons from applying to providers of medical services established in another Member State and constitute, both for insured persons and service providers, a barrier to freedom to provide services", thereby requiring justification.[65]

[22–46] All the intervening Member States emphasised the possible risk of seriously undermining the financial balance of a given social security system. This, they argued, constituted an overriding reason in the general interest capable of justifying a barrier to the freedom to provide services. In addition to accepting this, the Court also confirmed that the maintenance of a balanced hospital service open to all, even if intrinsically linked to the method of financing the social security system, may fall within the derogation on grounds of public health provided for in Art 52 TFEU. In order to ensure proper planning and cost efficiencies, it was accepted that a requirement for prior authorisation could be regarded as necessary and reasonable. A second question, therefore, was whether the particular criteria of "normal" and "necessary" were proportionate. Although ultimately concluding that such criteria were potentially permissible, the Court closely scrutinised their application, reasoning as follows:

> [EU] law cannot in principle have the effect of requiring a Member State to extend the list of medical services paid for by its social insurance system: the fact that a particular type of medical treatment is covered or not covered by the sickness insurance schemes of other Member States is irrelevant in this regard.

---

62 *ibid*, 5534.
63 *ibid*, 5529.
64 *ibid*.
65 *ibid*, 5532.

None the less, … in exercising that power the Member State must not disregard [EU] law.

… [A] scheme of prior authorisation cannot legitimise discretionary decisions taken by the national authorities which are liable to negate the effectiveness of provisions of [EU] law, in particular those relating to a fundamental freedom such as [the freedom to provide services]. Therefore, in order for a prior administrative authorisation scheme to be justified even though it derogates from such a fundamental freedom, it must, in any event, be based on objective, non-discriminatory criteria which are known in advance, in such a way as to circumscribe the exercise of the national authorities' discretion, so that it is not used arbitrarily. Such a prior administrative authorisation scheme must likewise be based on a procedural system which is easily accessible and capable of ensuring that a request for authorisation will be dealt with objectively and impartially within a reasonable time and refusals to grant authorisation must also be capable of being challenged in judicial or quasi-judicial proceedings.[66]

[22–47] Applying this logic to the two criteria, it was concluded that the requirement that the treatment be "normal" must be construed as meaning that authorisation will be granted where the treatment is sufficiently tried and tested by *international* medical science, and not merely assessed according to the prevailing professional view within the Netherlands. Regarding "necessity", authorisation could only be refused if the same or equally effective treatment could be obtained without undue delay at an establishment having a contractual arrangement with the national insurance fund.

[22–48] The Court of Justice was called upon to clarify its approach in *Geraets-Smits and Peerbooms* in the case of *Watts*, involving a UK national awaiting a hip-replacement from the National Health Service (NHS).[67] Originally diagnosed as having a "routine" condition, an initial waiting time of one year was, three months later, reduced to three to four months when her symptoms were classified as being in more urgent need of treatment. Not wishing to wait, Ms Watts paid directly for the operation in France and sought reimbursement of the cost. Unlike the Dutch insurance scheme, the NHS provided free treatment but had no scheme to reimburse costs incurred through recourse to private hospitals, whether they be in the UK or elsewhere. The Court was asked whether, given the particular nature of the NHS, Art 56 TFEU entitled a UK resident to obtain treatment in another Member State at the expense of the NHS. Applying its earlier case law, the Court confirmed that, without having to decide whether the provision of medical care by the NHS was itself a service, Art 56 applies whenever a "person whose state of health necessitates hospital treatment goes to another Member State and there receives the treatment in question for consideration".[68] As in *Geraets-Smits and Peerbooms*, while a prior authorisation requirement could be justified, it was necessary that it included certain substantial and procedural features:

it should be noted … that the regulations on the NHS do not set out the criteria for the grant or refusal of the prior authorisation necessary for reimbursement of the cost of hospital treatment provided in another Member State, and therefore do not circumscribe the exercise of the national competent authorities' discretionary power in that context.

---

66 *ibid*, 5537.

67 Case C-372/04 *Watts* [2006] ECR I-4325. See Mel Cousins, "Patient Mobility and National Health Systems" (2007) 34 *Legal Issues of Economic Integration* 183; Anthony Dawes, "Bonjour Herr Doctor: National Healthcare Systems, the Internal Market and Cross-Border Medical Care within the EU" (2006) 33 *Legal Aspects of Economic Integration* 167.

68 *ibid*, 4409.

> The lack of a legal framework in that regard also makes it difficult to exercise judicial review of decisions refusing to grant authorisation.
>
> … a refusal to grant prior authorisation cannot be based merely on the existence of waiting lists enabling the supply of hospital care to be planned and managed on the basis of predetermined general clinical priorities, without carrying out in the individual case in question an objective medical assessment of the patient's medical condition, the history and probable course of his illness, the degree of pain he is in and/or the nature of his disability at the time when the request for authorisation was made or renewed.
>
> It follows that, where the delay arising from such waiting lists appears to exceed in the individual case concerned an acceptable period having regard to an objective medical assessment of all the circumstances of the situation and the clinical needs of the person concerned, the competent institution may not refuse the authorisation sought on the grounds of the existence of those waiting lists, an alleged distortion of the normal order of priorities linked to the relative urgency of the cases to be treated, the fact that the hospital treatment provided under the national system in question is free of charge, the duty to make available specific funds to reimburse the cost of treatment provided in another Member State and/or a comparison between the cost of that treatment and that of equivalent treatment in the competent Member State.[69]

[22–49] As in *Geraets-Smits and Peerbooms*, eight Member States, including Ireland, intervened in *Watts* illustrating the sensitive nature of these cases. This sensitivity arose in large part due to the manner in which the Court of Justice, in effect, used the freedom to provide services in order to extend the Union's competence into areas of Member State competence – in particular social security and the provision of health services – by emphasising that, in exercising their national competences in these areas, the Member States must do so in a manner compatible with EU law, and with the right to receive services in particular. This can be seen, too, in *De Coster* and *Mobistar*, discussed above, involving the Member State competence of direct taxation imposed, respectively, on satellite dishes and telecommunication pylons.

[22–50] Gareth Davies has argued that this line of case law has resulted in the paradox that, even if a Member State chooses to organise a sector in an entirely non-economic way, so that its institutions do not offer services within the meaning of the TFEU, "it does not thereby escape the effects of Art 56, since if some actor in another Member State does offer such services for sale this creates an obligation on the state to facilitate defection of clients from the public system to the foreign private one".[70] The result, he suggests, is that:

> states exert considerable policy pressure on each other. If an Austrian hospital or university offers services to the nationals of other Member States for payment – even if most of its services are not offered in this way – then it will be systems in other Member States who will pay the price for this, being compelled to engage with the market despite their own conscious policy decision not to do so. For this reason, the suggestion that Article 56 only "applies" to economic services is rather misleading. It only grants rights to those buying or selling economic services, but it applies to all states and systems who may stand in their way, for their market avoidance is likely to be a "restriction" on movement, and such restrictions, not the services, are the true subject of application of Article 56.[71]

---

69 *ibid*, 4415–4416.

70 Gareth Davies, "The Law of the Free Movement of Services" in Anthony Arnull and Damian Chalmers (eds), *The Oxford Handbook of European Law* (Oxford University Press, 2015) 562.

71 *ibid*, 570.

[22–51] Stephen Weatherill has taken a somewhat less critical view, commenting that:

> By recognising the relevance of the health care system's financial stability in judging the permissibility of prior authorisation requirements, the Court has not thrown the provision of medical care on to the mercy of the market at the expense of State involvement. However, it has adjusted the "balance of power" between the patient's freedom to receive services and the State's competence to define the terms of the provisions of health care. … The Court's case law nudges our assumptions about the discharge of a State's responsibility to its citizens in an era of transnational economic growth.[72]

[22–52] The jurisprudence of the Court of Justice led directly to the adoption of Directive 2011/24/EU on the application of patients' rights in cross-border healthcare, which has been given effect in Irish law by the European Union (Application of Patients' Rights in Cross-Border Healthcare) Regulations 2014 and amending Regulations 2015.[73] According to the recitals, the Directive is intended to achieve a more general and effective application of principles developed by the Court on a case-by-case basis. The Directive applies to all forms of healthcare, regardless of whether it is public or private, but excludes certain treatment such as public vaccination programmes, long-term care and organ transplantation.

[22–53] Negotiation of the Directive involved competing arguments between the European Parliament, wishing for prior authorisation by the home state to be an exceptional requirement, and the Member States, who wished for the inclusion of prior authorisation as the default rule. The compromise reached provides that *non-hospital care* may be delivered in another Member State without prior authorisation, whereas a home Member State may operate a requirement of prior authorisation in respect of healthcare which is made subject to "planning requirements relating to the object of ensuring sufficient and permanent access to a balanced range of high-quality treatment in the Member State concerned or to the wish to control costs and avoid, as far as possible, any waste of financial, technical and human resources" and either involves overnight hospital accommodation for at least one night or requires the use of highly specialised and cost-intensive medical infrastructure or medical equipment.[74]

[22–54] Reflecting the case law, the system of prior authorisation, including the criteria and the application of those criteria, and individual decisions of refusal to grant prior authorisation, is to be restricted to what is necessary and proportionate to the objective to be achieved, and may not constitute a means of arbitrary discrimination or an unjustified obstacle to the free movement of patients. Secondly, authorisation may not be refused when the treatment cannot be provided by the home Member State within a time limit which is medically justifiable, based on an objective medical assessment of the patient's medical condition, the history and probable course of the patient's illness, the degree of the patient's pain and/or the nature of the patient's disability at the time when the request for authorisation was made or renewed. Thirdly, the home Member

---

72 Stephen Weatherill, *Cases and Materials on EU Law* (10th ed, Oxford University Press, 2012) 407.

73 Directive 2011/24/EU of the European Parliament and of the Council of 9 March 2011 on the application of patients' rights in cross-border healthcare [2011] OJ L88/45 and Commission Implementing Directive 2012/52/EU of 20 December 2012 [2012] OJ L356/68 given effect to by SI No 203 of 2014 and SI No 65 of 2015. See Stephane de la Rosa, "The Directive on Cross-Border Healthcare or the Art of Codifying Complex Case Law" (2012) 49 *Common Market Law Review* 15.

74 Art 8.

State is to make publicly available details on which healthcare is subject to prior authorisation, as well as all relevant information on the system of prior authorisation. Individual decisions are to be properly reasoned and subject, on a case-by-case basis, to review and to being challengeable in judicial proceedings, which include provision for interim measures. Statistics for 2017 indicate that, under a prior authorisation regime, Ireland had the highest spend of €3.5m, with 607 patients from Ireland receiving treatment in the UK (and 206 patients from the UK receiving treatment in Ireland). For treatment without prior authorisation, France was by far the largest user, representing 63 per cent of all patient mobility, with €12m reimbursed.[75] That said, take-up of the Directive is regarded as low, without an average of 200,000 claims each year and expenditure incurred under the Directive estimated at 0.004 per cent of the EU-wide annual healthcare budget. According to a 2015 Eurobarometer report, only 20 per cent of citizens were aware of their rights regarding cross-border healthcare.[76]

F. The Services Directive

[22–55] The negotiation of the Services Directive[77] was a protracted and contentious affair, sparking protests in European cities and identified as contributing to the defeat of France's referendum on the Constitutional Treaty in 2005.[78] As initially proposed by the Commission, and developed in a draft known as the "Bolkestein" draft (referred to by some critics as the "Frankenstein" draft), the Directive would have enshrined a country of origin principle, whereby it would be for the home Member State of the service provider to regulate the service, with the host Member State having to accept this level of regulation.[79] Although such a principle had been included in earlier sectoral directives, such as the Television without Frontiers Directive[80] and the e-Commerce Directive,[81] to apply it in a general manner to all services was a highly ambitious goal. In addition to concerns as to how a home country would effectively enforce its regulations

---

[75] Member State Data on Cross-Border Patient Healthcare following Directive 2011/24/EU, Year 2017, 2019; Report from the Commission to the European Parliament and the Council on the operation of Directive 2011/24/EU on the application of patient's rights in cross-border healthcare, COM(2018) 651 final, 21 September 2018.

[76] European Court of Auditors, Special Report No 07/2019, "EU actions for cross-border healthcare: significant ambitions but improved management required", 2019, 7.

[77] Directive 2006/123/EC of the European Parliament and of the Council of 12 December 2006 on services in the internal market [2006] OJ L376/36. See Michele Chang, Dominik Hanf and Jacques Pelkmans, "The Services Directive: Trojan Horse or White Knight?" (2010) 32 *Journal of European Integration* 97; Vassilis Hatzopoulos, "Assessing the Services Directive (2006/123/EC)" (2008) 10 *Cambridge Yearbook of European Legal Studies* 215. For a more recent account in light of emerging case law see Jukka Snell, "Independence Day for the Services Directive: *Visser*" (2019) 56 *Common Market Law Review* 1119.

[78] Joanna Flower, "Negotiating European Legislation: The Services Directive" (2007) 9 *Cambridge Yearbook of European Legal Studies* 217.

[79] See Patrick B Griffin, "Competing Social Models and the Single Market in Services: Has Frankenstein Done for his Maker?" (2006) 13 *Irish Journal of European Law* 13.

[80] Council Directive 89/552/EEC of 3 October 1989 on the coordination of certain provisions laid down by law, regulation or administrative action in Member States concerning the pursuit of television broadcasting activities [1989] OJ L298/23, which is now replaced by the Audiovisual Media Services Directive, Directive 2010/13/EU of the European Parliament and of the Council of 10 March 2010 on the coordination of certain provisions laid down by law, regulation or administrative action in Member States concerning the provision of audiovisual media services [2010] OJ L95/1.

[81] Directive 2000/31/EC of the European Parliament and of the Council of 8 June 2000 on certain

on services being provided in other Member States, there were significant fears that such an approach would lead to a regulatory race to the bottom. In other words, without the Services Directive harmonising a minimum level of common standards, there would be competition amongst the Member States to lower their regulatory standards so as to become the most advantageous for service providers choosing on where to establish their business. Opposition came from the trade union movement, some Member States and, most crucially, the European Parliament, ultimately leading to a much altered "McCreevy" draft, named after the then Commissioner for the Internal Market and Services, Charlie McCreevy. This draft would eventually form the basis of the Services Directive as adopted. The Directive is transposed into Irish law by the European Union (Provision of Services) Regulations 2010.[82]

[22–56] The most significant changes in the McCreevy draft were, first, a narrowing of the scope of the Directive through the removal of eight additional sectors. Article 2 now provides that the Directive shall not apply to: non-economic services of general interest; financial services such as banking, credit, insurance, pensions and investment funds; electronic communications services and networks; transport; temporary work agencies; healthcare services, whether public or private; audiovisual services; gambling; activities connected with the exercise of official authority; social services relating to social housing, childcare and support for those in need provided by the state, by providers mandated by the state or charities; private security services and notaries and bailiffs officially appointed by act of government. In addition, the Directive is "residual" in that Art 3(1) provides that if any of its provisions conflict with a provision of another EU act governing specific aspects of a service activity, or a specific service sector or profession, the provisions of that EU act shall prevail.

[22–57] Secondly, the McCreevy draft saw the replacement, in Art 16, of the country of origin principle by a lesser obligation on the host Member State to ensure "free access to and free exercise of a service activity within its territory" and not to subject such an activity to any requirements which do not respect the three principles of non-discrimination, necessity and proportionality. Of significance here is that "necessity" is defined as meaning that the requirement must be justified by reasons of public policy, public security, public health or the protection of the environment. In other words, a restriction on services to which the Directive applies must be justified by reference to either the three grounds provided for in Art 62 TFEU or the additional ground of protecting the environment. In this regard, Art 16 of the Directive might be contrasted with the much broader and open-ended concept of "overriding reasons relating to the public interest" used in connection with the Directive's rules on the ability of a Member State to impose an authorisation scheme on the establishment, within its territory, of a service provider.[83]

[22–58] The list of four grounds in Art 16 raises an interesting conundrum as to whether the Directive intended (and, indeed, can) abolish other mandatory grounds for justifying non-discriminatory restrictions. Robert Schütze, for instance, suggests that by omitting the unwritten imperative requirements developed by the Court of Justice, other than protection of the environment, "there are strong arguments that the Union

legal aspects of information society services, in particular electronic commerce, in the Internal Market [2000] OJ L178/1.

[82] SI No 533 of 2010.

[83] See ch 21, paras [21–82] to [21–84].

legislator may have abolished them for service provisions falling within Article 16 of the Directive".[84] Similarly, Gareth Davies observes that the "specific mention of one mandatory requirement, the environment, could be argued to emphasise the absence and by implication the exclusion of the others".[85] On the other hand, Davies notes that it is not certain that this is the correct reading of Art 16 given that

> The Treaty itself only allows derogations on public policy, security, and health grounds, but the Court was able to find that other legitimate reasons nevertheless could justify measures, this being somehow implicit. It is hard to see what textual reason prevents it doing precisely the same again. It is therefore quite possible that Article 16 will not be understood to abolish mandatory requirements but simply to be an enactment of the case law as it stands.[86]

[22–59] In addition, Catherine Barnard has made the following constitutional point:

> [C]an the Directive, a piece of secondary legislation, narrow the scope of the (primary) Treaty as interpreted by the Court? An argument in favour is that since the Directive is intended to further integration, and because the broad public interest requirements create barriers to free movement, the Court may very well uphold the narrow justification and not allow States to invoke the full range of public interest justifications. An argument against is that it confuses the hierarchy of norms of [EU] law. On the other hand, it is well known that States cannot invoke justifications or derogations where a [EU] harmonisation measure exists. However, … it is hard to consider the Services Directive, read as a whole, to be a harmonisation measure, although it could be argued that harmonisation has occurred in respect of Articles 16(1) and (3).[87]

[22–60] The Court addressed this issue, albeit in a somewhat vague manner, in *Commission v Portugal*, where an infringement action was taken in respect of Portuguese restrictions on the construction industry. The Court characterised Art 16(1) of the Services Directive as obliging Member States to ensure "access to and exercise of a service activity within their territory by making that access or exercise subject only to non-discriminatory and objectively justified requirements" which, the Court said, stemmed directly from Art 56 TFEU. In comments that may be interpreted as suggesting that Art 16(1) has not abolished the open class of mandatory requirements, the judgment continues to note:

> As to whether there is any objective justification for overriding reasons in the public interest for the restriction of the freedom to provide services that arises from the national scheme at issue, which applies without distinction to any construction undertaking operating within Portuguese territory, it must be observed, first of all, that the reasons put forward by the Portuguese Republic in that regard, namely the requirement to ensure the soundness and safety of buildings and to protect the environment, the architectural heritage as well as consumers and users of buildings, indeed constitute such reasons and it is not necessary to determine for the purposes of the present case whether some of those reasons are, as the Portuguese Republic maintains, a matter of public policy.[88]

---

84 Robert Schütze, *European Union Law* (Cambridge University Press, 2015) 645.

85 Gareth Davies, "The Law on the Free Movement of Services" in Anthony Arnull and Damian Chalmers (eds), *The Oxford Handbook of European Law* (Oxford University Press, 2015) 562, 583.

86 *ibid.*

87 Catherine Barnard, "Unravelling the Services Directive" (2008) 45 *Common Market Law Review* 323, 367.

88 Case C-458/08 *Commission v Portugal* [2010] ECR I-11599, para 89.

[22–61] Possibly by way of partly compensating for the removal of the country of origin principle, the McCreevy draft added, in Art 39(5), a reporting requirement whereby all Member States were to present a report to the Commission by December 2009 on national requirements whose application could be justified, giving reasons. Thereafter, states are to inform the Commission of any changes to the requirements, or any new requirements which are then transmitted to other Member States. Unlike the reporting requirements relating to establishment by service providers, the Commission is not given any decision-making power in respect of new requirements and cannot prevent their adoption by Member States. It has been noted, however, that from the date of implementation of the Services Directive at the end of 2009 to the end of 2015, the Commission received only 1,639 notifications in total.[89] This is compared with an average of around 700 notifications annually in respect of trade in goods. Ireland was among five Member States identified as not having made any notification during that period. As a result of perceived shortcomings, in 2017 the Commission brought forward a proposal to amend the Services Directive and the Internal Market Information System in order to introduce a number of reforms, including by allowing the Commission or other Member States to intervene before a national law is adopted.[90]

[22–62] Other features of the Services Directive include a chapter on "Administrative Simplification" which requires Member States to simplify their administrative procedures, including by permitting formalities to be "easily completed, at a distance and by electronic means", and establishing a single point of contact through which certain information is to be made available. In the case of Ireland, this is made available at the suitably named "www.pointofsinglecontact.ie" website maintained by the Single Market Unit of the Department of Business, Enterprise and Innovation. The Directive also has provisions concerning the rights of recipients of services – enshrining principles of non-discrimination and requiring Member States to make certain information and assistance available – and a chapter on the quality of services, requiring Member States to oblige service providers to make information available, including in relation to the settlement of disputes and, in certain instances, to have professional liability insurance and to provide guarantees.

[22–63] In 2018, a report commissioned by Ireland, the Czech Republic, Finland and Denmark, examined ways in which the Single Market in services could be improved.[91] The report found that, although the Single Market has on average reduced trade costs for manufacturing by 9–20 per cent, for services the reduction has only been around 7 per cent. This, it is said, partly explains why intra-EU trade in services only amounts to a third of intra-EU trade in goods.[92] The report recommends that a full implementation and enforcement of the Services Directive alone will increase intra-EU trade and enhance productivity in the services covered. Among the ways to achieve this, the report

89 European Parliament Briefing, "Reform of Services Notification Procedure", 29 August 2017.

90 Proposal for a directive of the European Parliament and of the Council on the enforcement of Directive 2006/123/EC on services in the internal market, laying down a notification procedure for authorisation schemes and requirements related to services, and amending Directive 2006/123/EC and Regulation (EU) No 1024/2012 on administrative cooperation through the Internal Market Information System COM(2016) 821, 10 January 2017.

91 Eva Rytter Sunesen and Martin Hvidt Thelle, "Making EU Trade in Services Work for All" (Copenhagen Economics, 2018).

92 *ibid*, 18.

suggests revising the Single Market Scoreboard so as to increase the focus placed on services. According to the report:

> the existing toolbox does not provide EU policy makers with an overview of remaining levels of restrictiveness facing services providers or consumers in the EU economy. To measure progress in the Single Market from a business and consumer perspective, an updated Single Market Scoreboard would add this element to the existing tool. The ambition should be to develop a "Single Market Scoreboard 2.0" of the Union's and individual Member States' performances in reducing service restrictiveness and assess whether low performance is due to an adequacy gap, implementation gap or enforcement gap. On this basis, the European Commission could:
>
> – Continue the current monitoring of the elements in the current Single Market Scoreboard;
> – Develop a Single Market Scoreboard 2.0 and use it proactively;
> – Identify best practice amongst the Member States.
>
> To ensure continued focus and improvements, the Commission should urge Member States to make commitments to improve their performance taking account of their existing ranking as to openness to intra-EU services trade.
>
> Based on the scoreboard of services trade openness, it should be clearly stated which Member States are the Single Market Leaders. All Member States should be ranked in groups in a similar manner to the European Innovation Scoreboard which groups all Member States into categories according to level of performance. On this basis, Member States could be obliged to:
>
> – Study the five least restrictive Member States to identify best practices;
> – Set targets to improve, and those below the top category of Leaders should aim to move upwards to the next group.[93]

G. Services of a General Economic Interest

[22–64] A further sensitive aspect of services concerns "services of a general economic interest", which are the subject of Art 14 TFEU, Protocol No 26 on Services of General Interest and Art 36 of the Charter of Fundamental Rights.[94] Although none of these provisions define the actual term, it is understood in practice to refer to services of an economic nature which the Member States or the Union subject to specific public service obligations by virtue of a general interest criterion, such as services "provided by the big network industries such as transport, postal services, energy and communications".[95] According to a Commission Communication of 2001:

> Services of general economic interest are different from ordinary services in that public authorities consider that they need to be provided even where the market may not have

[93] *ibid*, 63–64.

[94] See Leigh Hancher and Wolf Sauter, "Public Services and EU Law" in Catherine Barnard and Steve Peers (eds), *European Union Law* (Oxford University Press, 2017) 543; Leigh Hancher and Pierre Larouche, "The Coming of Age of Regulation of Network Industries and Services of General Economic Interest" in Paul Craig and Gráinne de Búrca (eds), *The Evolution of EU Law* (2nd ed, Oxford University Press, 2011) 743; Wolf Sauter, *Public Services in EU Law* (Cambridge University Press, 2015); Caroline Wehlander, *Services of General Economic Interest as a Constitutional Concept of EU Law* (Springer, 2012); Christopher H Bovis, "Financing Services of General Interest in the EU" (2005) 11 *European Law Journal* 79.

[95] White Paper on Services of General Interest, COM(2004) 374 final, 12 May 2004, 22. See Case C-171/17 *Commission v Hungary* EU:C:2018:881, 7 November 2018, paras 49–60.

sufficient incentives to do so. This is not to deny that in many cases the market will be the best mechanism for providing such services. Many basic requirements, such as food, clothing, shelter, are provided exclusively or overwhelmingly by the market. However, if the public authorities consider that certain services are in the general interest and market forces may not result in a satisfactory provision, they can lay down a number of specific service provisions to meet these needs in the form of service of general interest obligations. The fulfilment of these obligations may trigger, albeit not necessarily, the granting of special or exclusive rights, or the provision of specific funding mechanisms. The definition of a specific mission of general interest and the attendant service required to fulfil that mission need not imply any specific method of service provision. The classical case is the universal service obligation, i.e. the obligation to provide a certain service throughout the territory at affordable tariffs and on similar quality conditions, irrespective of the profitability of individual operations.

... Member States' freedom to define [services of general economic interest] means that Member States are primarily responsible for defining what they regard as [such] services ... on the basis of the specific features of the activities. This definition can only be subject to control for manifest error. They may grant special or exclusive rights that are necessary to the undertakings entrusted with their operation, regulate their activities and, where appropriate, fund them. In areas that are not specifically covered by [EU] regulation Member States enjoy a wide margin for shaping their policies, which can only be subject to control for manifest error. Whether a service is to be regarded as a service of general interest and how it should be operated are issues that are first and foremost decided locally. The role of the Commission is to ensure that the means employed are compatible with [EU] law.[96]

[22–65] In drawing together the results from a consultation process on such services, a 2004 White Paper concluded that in addition to a strong confirmation of the "importance of services of general interest as one of the pillars of the European model of society", there had been:

a broad consensus on the need to ensure the provision of high-quality and affordable services of general interest to all citizens and enterprises in the European Union. It has also confirmed the existence of a common concept of services of general interest in the Union. This concept reflects Community values and goals and is based on a set of common elements, including: universal service, continuity, quality of service, affordability, as well as user and consumer protection.

In the Union, services of general interest remain essential for ensuring social and territorial cohesion and for the competitiveness of the European economy. Citizens and businesses rightly expect to have access to affordable high-quality services of general interest throughout the European Union. For the citizens of the Union, this access is an essential component of European citizenship and necessary in order to allow them to fully enjoy their fundamental rights. For enterprises, the availability of high-quality services of general interest is an indispensable prerequisite for a competitive business environment.[97]

[22–66] Article 14 TFEU, which is worded in very general terms, recalls the "place occupied by services of general economic interest in the shared values of the Union as well as their role in promoting social and territorial cohesion". Given this importance, the Union and the Member States commit to "take care that such services operate on

[96] Communication from the Commission, "Services of General Interest in Europe" [2001] OJ C17/4, paras 14, 22.

[97] *ibid*, 4.

the basis of principles and conditions, particularly economic and financial conditions, which enable them to fulfil their missions". Protocol No 26 supplements Art 14 by providing an agreed interpretation of the reference within that Article to "shared values", as including: (i) the essential role and the wide discretion of national, regional and local authorities in providing, commissioning and organising services of general economic interest as closely as possible to the needs of the users; (ii) the diversity between various services of general economic interest and the differences in the needs and preferences of users that may result from different geographical, social or cultural situations; and (iii) a high level of quality, safety and affordability, equal treatment and the promotion of universal access and of user rights. The Protocol also confirms that the Treaties do not affect in any way the competence of Member States to organise non-economic services of general interest. Finally, Art 36 of the Charter largely mirrors Art 14 TFEU in expressing the Union's recognition of, and respect for, access to services of general economic interest as provided for in national laws and practices, in order to promote the social and territorial cohesion of the Union.

[22–67] The concept of services of a general interest is also taken into account in EU competition law and rules governing state aid. For example, Art 106(2) TFEU provides that Treaty rules on competition shall apply to undertakings entrusted with the operation of services of general economic interest, but only "in so far as the application of such rules does not obstruct the performance, in law or in fact, of the particular tasks assigned to them". This special treatment for certain undertakings was the subject of *BUPA v Commission.*[98] There, a challenge was brought by BUPA against a decision of the Commission, taken pursuant to Art 106(2) TFEU, which had accepted the application of a risk equalisation scheme to private medical insurers in Ireland. Under the scheme, a charge was to be paid to the Health Insurance Authority by insurers whose risk profile was healthier than the average market risk profile, whilst the Authority would make a corresponding payment to insurers whose risk profile was less healthy than the average market risk profile. BUPA claimed that the scheme was advantageous to its competitor, VHI. Ireland intervened in the case in order to support the Commission's defence of its decision, agreeing with the following lines of argument:

> the definition of SGEIs [services of a general economic interest] falls primarily within the competence and discretion of the Member States and that the control which the [EU] institutions are authorised to carry out in that respect is limited to control of a manifest error of assessment, which is not present in this case. The defendant and Ireland submit that PMI [private medical insurance] is an important instrument of the social and health policy pursued by Ireland, a matter which … is essentially reserved for the competence of the Member States, and an important supplement to the public health insurance system, although it does not replace that system. In this case, contrary to the applicants' allegations, the PMI services as such, in conjunction with the PMI obligations, constitute the relevant SGEIs to which the contested decision refers. In particular, the PMI obligations, including open enrolment and community rating, ensure that the PMI services are available to all. In that regard, contrary to the applicants' opinion, it is not necessary that the PMI services be universal and compulsory in the strict sense, that they be free of charge or economically

---

[98] Case T-289/03 *BUPA v Commission* [2008] ECR II-81. See Malcolm Ross, "A Healthy Approach to Services of General Economic Interest? The *BUPA* Judgment of the Court of First Instance" (2009) 34 *European Law Review* 127; Wolf Sauter, "Case T-289/03, *BUPA v Commission*" (2009) 46 *Common Market Law Review* 269; Sybe A De Vries, "BUPA: A Healthy Case, in the Light of a Changing Constitutional Setting in Europe?" in JW van de Gronden et al (eds), *Legal Issues of Services of General Interest* (Springer, 2011) 295.

> accessible to the whole of the Irish population and that they constitute a substitute for the public social security system. Furthermore, in the opinion of the Kingdom of the Netherlands, in light of the dynamic concept of SGEIs, it is sufficient that the State imposes certain requirements, such as PMI obligations, on all insurers, compliance with those requirements being subject to a system of authorisation and control, in order for them to be able to be characterised as SGEIs. Accordingly, the grant of a special or exclusive right to an undertaking is not necessary.[99]

[22–68] The General Court accepted that, in areas falling within their own competence, Member States have a wide discretion to define what they regard as an SGEI and that such definitions could be questioned by the Commission "only in the event of manifest error", finding support for this conclusion in the fact that EU law provided no precise and complete definition of an SGEI, nor was the Commission attributed with a competence to decide on such matters, as well as in Art 14 TFEU. As healthcare fell almost exclusively within Ireland's competence, it primarily had the competence to determine SGEI obligations in this field. Nevertheless, in order to justify its decision a Member State was required to demonstrate: (i) the presence of an act of the public authority entrusting the operators in question with an SGEI mission; (ii) the universal and compulsory nature of that mission; and (iii) the reasons why it considers that the service in question, because of its specific nature, deserves to be characterised as an SGEI and to be distinguished from other economic activities. The General Court concluded:

> the combination of the obligations of open enrolment, community rating, lifetime cover and minimum benefits is apt to guarantee that the Irish population has wide and simple access to PMI services, which entitles those services to be characterised as universal within the meaning of [EU] law. The applicants' argument that, notwithstanding the mutualisation of premiums resulting from the community rating, the PMI services are not universal because they are not available to all strata of the Irish population, cannot be accepted. First, … the criterion of universality does not require that the entire population should have or be capable of having recourse to it in practice. Second, the fact that approximately 50% of the Irish population has subscribed to PMI cover indicates that, in any event, the PMI services respond to a very significant demand on the Irish PMI market and that they make a substantial contribution to the proper functioning of the social security system, in the broad sense, in Ireland.
>
> … [T]he applicants' very general argument concerning the optional, complementary and "luxury" nature of the PMI services cannot succeed. … [T]hey have not submitted a detailed challenge to the argument put forward by the defendant and by Ireland that Irish PMI constitutes, alongside the public health insurance system, the second pillar of the Irish health system, the existence of which fulfils a mandatory objective of social cohesion and solidarity between the generations pursued by Ireland's health policy. According to the explanations provided by Ireland, PMI helps to ensure the effectiveness and profitability of the public health insurance scheme by reducing pressure on the costs which it would otherwise bear, particularly as regards care provided in public hospitals. Within the framework of the restricted control that the [EU] institutions are authorised to exercise in that regard, those considerations cannot be called in question either by the Commission or by the Court. Accordingly, it must be accepted that the PMI services are used by Ireland, in the general interest, as an instrument indispensable to the smooth administration of the national health system and they must be recognised, owing to the PMI obligations, as being in the nature of an SGEI.

---

99 Case T-289/03 *BUPA v Commission* [2008] ECR II-81, para 164.

[22–69] In separate Irish proceedings, the introduction of the risk equalisation scheme was held by the Supreme Court to have been based on an erroneous interpretation of the Health Insurance Act 1994, and so was *ultra vires* the powers of the Minister for Health and therefore quashed.[100]

Overview of Case Law

Definition of a Service	*Luisi and Carbone* *Cowan v Le Trésor Public* *Alpine Investments*
Difference from Establishment	*Gebhard* *Schnitzer*
Direct Effect	*Van Binsbergen* *Walrave and Koch*
Sensitive Nature of Services	*De Coster* *Josemans* *R v Human Fertilisation and Embryology Authority ex p Blood* *SPUC v Grogan*
Non-Discriminatory Restrictions	*De Coster* *Alpine Investments* *Commission v Germany (Insurance Services)* *Säger* *Commission v Italy (Obligation to Contract)* *Mobistar*
Advertising	*Gourmet International* *Bacardi* *Vanderborght*
Grounds for Justifying a Restriction	*Corporación Dermoestética* *De Coster* *Josemans* *Omega* *Commission v Ireland (Vehicle Registration Tax)*
Publicly Funded Services *(i) Education*	 *Belgium v Humbel* *Schwarz*
(ii) Medical Services	*Kohll* *Geraets-Smits and Peerbooms* *Watts*
Services of a General Economic Interest	*BUPA v Commission*

[100] *BUPA Ireland Ltd v Health Insurance Authority* [2012] 3 IR 442.

PART SIX

CHAPTER 23

FREE MOVEMENT OF WORKERS

A. INTRODUCTION

[23–01] Like many areas of EU law, the law in relation to the free movement of workers is best understood by having some knowledge of its historical development, both as regards changes to the Treaties and the interpretation of their provisions, and the introduction of secondary legislation. Whereas the terms of the relevant Treaty provisions have remained largely consistent since 1957 – now found in Arts 45–48 TFEU – their content has undergone extensive elaboration and expansion through the case law of the Court of Justice. Indeed, the Court has declared that the rights set out in Art 45 must be interpreted in a "non-exhaustive way".[1] This, in turn, has led to codifying regulations, the most recent version of which is the highly significant Regulation 492/2011 on the Free Movement of Workers.[2] As a result of this process, it is not always clear whether a particular rule within a regulation or a directive is merely a secondary law measure, susceptible to being amended by subsequent secondary law, or whether it encapsulates an interpretation of a primary law rule based on the TFEU, such that its alteration by secondary law may be found to be contrary to a Treaty guarantee.

1 Case C-292/89 *R v Immigration Appeal Tribunal, ex parte Antonissen* [1991] ECR I-745, 777.

2 Council Regulation (EEC) No 492/2011 of 5 April 2011 on freedom of movement for workers within the Union [2011] OJ L141/1.

[23–02] The regime governing the free movement of workers operates in parallel to the Citizens Directive – Directive 2004/38 – which sets out common rules on the free movement rights of Union citizens that apply, not only to workers, but to all Union citizens "who move to or reside in a Member State other than that of which they are a national, and to their family members … who accompany or join them".[3] In addition to workers, such persons may, for example, be students, self-employed persons or persons of independent means. As will be seen in the next chapter, there is a degree of overlap between the provisions of the Free Movement of Workers Regulation and those of the Citizens Directive, such as the right to enjoy equal treatment with the nationals of the host Member State to which one has moved.

[23–03] While, in some respects, the rules governing the free movement of workers might be viewed as a detailed sub-set of the more general rules set out in the Citizens Directive, chronologically, the rules on the movement of workers date back to the Treaty of Rome of 1957 and form part of the four "Fundamental Freedoms" that provided the cornerstone of the EEC. It is for this reason that they shall be examined first, followed by a look at the Citizens Directive in the next chapter. Nevertheless, the two areas are deeply interrelated. That is not the end of the story, however. Since the entry into force of the Maastricht Treaty on 1 November 1993, the Treaties have conferred the status of "Union citizen" upon the nationals of the Member States. According to Art 21 TFEU:

> 1. Every citizen of the Union shall have the right to move and reside freely within the territory of the Member States, subject to the limitations and conditions laid down in the Treaties and by the measures adopted to give them effect.
>
> 2. If action by the Union should prove necessary to attain this objective and the Treaties have not provided the necessary powers, the European Parliament and the Council, acting in accordance with the ordinary legislative procedure, may adopt provisions with a view to facilitating the exercise of the rights referred to in paragraph 1.

[23–04] In Chapter 25 it will be seen that the development of Union citizenship has greatly impacted the law on the free movement of persons, extending the scope of EU law to situations that would have fallen outside the application of the more longstanding rules on the free movement of workers.

[23–05] The right of workers to move freely within the EU in order to take up employment has a clear link with the prohibition on discrimination on the grounds of nationality set out in Art 18 TFEU. Direct discrimination against non-national workers is prohibited by Art 45 TFEU. So too is *indirect* discrimination resulting from measures that, in practice, are liable to make it easier for nationals of the host Member State to meet relevant requirements, as compared with migrant EU workers. Furthermore, even non-discriminatory measures (ie measures that are neither directly or indirectly discriminatory) may be caught by Art 45 if they constitute an obstacle that affects the ability of workers to access the labour market by precluding or deterring a national from leaving his or her country of origin in order to take up or seek employment in another Member State. Although they are caught by Art 45, measures that pose an obstacle to the free movement of workers may be permitted provided that the measure

[3] Directive 2004/38/EC of the European Parliament of the Council of 29 April 2004 on the rights of citizens of the Union and their family members to move and reside freely within the territory of the Member States [2004] OJ L158/77 (the "Citizens Directive"), Art 3.

is not discriminatory and can be shown to be: (i) objectively justified by an imperative requirement in the general interest; (ii) suitable for the attainment of the objective it pursues; and (iii) proportionate, in the sense that it does not go beyond what is necessary in order to achieve the objective. In contrast, direct discrimination may only be justified by one of the three grounds of limitation provided for in Art 45, namely public policy, public security or public health.

(i) Treaty Law – Article 45 TFEU

[23–06] The 1951 Treaty of Paris establishing the European Coal and Steel Community included a chapter on the free movement of workers employed in the coal and steel industries, as part of which the Member States undertook to renounce, subject to the limitations imposed by the fundamental needs of health and public order, "any restriction based on nationality against the employment in the coal and steel industries of workers of proven qualifications for such industries who possess the nationality of one of the Member States".[4] In addition, the Member States were to: (i) prohibit any discrimination in remuneration and working conditions between national workers and immigrant workers, without prejudice to special measures concerning frontier workers; and (ii) work out among themselves any arrangements necessary so that social security measures did not stand in the way of the movement of labour.[5]

[23–07] The Euratom Treaty of 1957 similarly provided that Member States were to abolish all restrictions based on nationality which had been placed upon access by nationals of any of the Member States to specialised employment in the nuclear field, subject to such limitations as may be imposed by the basic requirements of public order, public safety and public health.[6] A Directive was adopted in 1962 to give effect to this obligation which made clear that, in all other respects, the generally applicable EU rules on the free movement of workers are to apply to those employed in the nuclear field.[7]

[23–08] Under the Treaty of Rome establishing the EEC, a right to reside and to be treated equally in another Member State was extended to all those pursuing an economic activity – not just workers, but also self-employed persons and those availing of a service – reflecting the broad, yet nonetheless economic, orientation of the Treaty as a whole. It remains the case that the "free movement of persons section is firmly anchored in the economic part of the [TFEU], concerned with a basic definition of the internal market outlined in Article 26 TFEU, and not within the social policy section much further on in the treaty".[8] Nevertheless, the social dimension of free movement might be said to receive some acknowledgment within Art 3(2) TEU, which provides that the Union shall offer its citizens an area of freedom, security and justice without internal frontiers where the free movement of persons is ensured. Moreover, as Stephen Weatherill observes, since the right of free movement concerns both labour mobility and the rights of individuals, it has implications beyond the economics of market integration

---

[4] Art 69(1).

[5] Art 69(4).

[6] Art 96.

[7] Euratom Council Directive on freedom to take skilled employment in the field of nuclear energy [1962] OJ P 057 1650.

[8] Nigel Foster, *Foster on EU Law* (5th ed, Oxford University Press, 2015) 300.

and "identifies people as the beneficiaries of the Treaty rules in a more direct sense than any other area of the law of the internal market".[9]

[23–09] Located within Title IV (Free Movement of Persons, Services and Capital) of Part III of the TFEU (Policies and Internal Actions), Art 45(1) provides that, with the exception of employment in the public service, the "freedom of movement for workers shall be secured within the Union". According to Art 45(2), this shall entail the abolition of any discrimination based on nationality, remuneration and other conditions of work and employment. This builds upon Art 18 TFEU, which provides that any discrimination on grounds of nationality shall be prohibited. More specifically, Art 45(3) details that, subject to limitations justified on grounds of public policy, public security or public health, the right of a worker to move entails the right to:

(i) accept offers of employment actually made;
(ii) move freely within the territory of Member States for this purpose;
(iii) stay in a Member State for the purpose of employment in accordance with the provisions governing the employment of nationals of that state laid down by law, regulation or administrative action; and
(iv) remain in the territory of a Member State after having been employed in that state, subject to conditions embodied in implementing regulations drawn up by the Commission.

[23–10] As regards providing a legislative competence in the area, Art 46 TFEU establishes that, acting in accordance with the ordinary legislative procedure and after consulting the Economic and Social Committee, the Parliament and the Council shall issue directives or make regulations setting out the measures required to bring about freedom of movement for workers provided for in Art 45, including certain particular matters highlighted in Art 46. In addition, Art 48 TFEU provides that, acting in accordance with the ordinary legislative procedure, the Parliament and the Council shall adopt such measures in the field of social security as are necessary to provide for the free movement of workers, including making arrangements to ensure the aggregation, for the purpose of acquiring and retaining the right to benefit and of calculating the amount of benefit, of all periods taken into account under the laws of the different countries. Regulation 883/2004 on the coordination of social security systems, as supplemented by Regulation 987/09 on procedural aspects of coordination, are the principal measures governing this aspect of free movement.[10] From an institutional perspective, Art 48 is noteworthy for the inclusion, since the Lisbon Treaty, of an "emergency break" provision, in accordance with which:

> Where a member of the Council declares that a draft legislative act [in the field of social security] ... would affect important aspects of its social security system, including its

[9] Stephen Weatherill, *Cases and Materials on EU Law* (10th ed, Oxford University Press, 2012) 359.

[10] [2004] OJ L166/1 and [2009] OJ L284/1. The right to equal treatment can affect social security agreements entered into by a Member State and a third country. For instance, according to the judgment of the Court of Justice in Case C-55/00 *Gottardo* [2002] ECR I-413, the advantages enjoyed by a Member State's own nationals under a bilateral social security agreement with a third country – in that case concerning the aggregation of periods of insurance for calculating an entitlement to an old-age pension – must also be granted to workers who are nationals of other Member States. There, the Court was not convinced that there was any objective justification that would allow Italy to deprive a French national, who had worked for a time in Switzerland before moving to Italy, of the benefits of a bilateral agreement between Italy and Switzerland on social security. See also Case C-801/18 *EU* (ongoing) [2019] OJ C82/14.

> scope, cost or financial structure, or would affect the financial balance of that system, it may request that the matter be referred to the European Council. In that case, the ordinary legislative procedure shall be suspended. After discussion, the European Council shall, within four months of this suspension, either: (a) refer the draft back to the Council, which shall terminate the suspension of the ordinary legislative procedure, or, (b) take no action or request the Commission to submit a new proposal; in that case, the act originally proposed shall be deemed not to have been adopted.

[23–11] It ought not to be forgotten that the right to free movement is extended to the citizens of Norway, Iceland and Liechtenstein (and for EU citizens, applies to those countries) by virtue of Art 28 of the European Economic Area Agreement (EEA Agreement), which closely mirrors Art 45 TFEU. Article 28(5) of the EEA Agreement provides that "Annex V contains specific provisions on the free movement of persons", and the Annex, which is regularly updated, lists six EU acts which are to apply to Norway, Iceland and Liechtenstein subject to certain adaptations set out therein.[11] Since 2002, certain free movement rights are also afforded to Swiss nationals, under an Agreement on Free Movement between the EU and its Member States and Switzerland. The Agreement also provides for the coordination of social security systems under the principle of equal treatment, as well as the mutual recognition of professional qualifications. Following a referendum in February 2014, however, a new article of the Swiss Federal Constitution set two assignments that were to be completed by February 2017: the introduction of a new autonomous immigration system and the amendment of Switzerland's existing international agreements to the extent that they were contrary to this new immigration system. Rather than pursuing an amendment to its agreement with the EU on the free movement of persons, Switzerland has sought to introduce legislation that will allow, in certain circumstances, for a degree of preference to be given to Swiss job-seekers. In February 2017 the Council issued conclusions on the EU's relations with Switzerland in which it noted:

> the free movement of persons is a fundamental pillar of EU policy and … the internal market and its four freedoms are indivisible. The Council paid close attention to the legislative process in Switzerland which took place following the result of the popular initiative "Against Mass Immigration" of 9 February 2014. The resultant text adopted on 16 December 2016 by the Swiss Federal Assembly can be implemented in a manner compatible with the rights of EU citizens under the Free Movement of Persons Agreement (FMPA) if the necessary implementing ordinance clarifies outstanding open issues, such as the right to information as regards vacancies, and the procedure for the adoption of further measures, in particular with a view to guaranteeing respect for frontier workers' rights.[12]

[23–12] In Council conclusions of February 2019, Switzerland was commended for

---

[11] The six measures listed in Annex V are: (i) Directive 2004/38/EC on the free movement of citizens; (ii) Regulation 492/2011 on the free movement of workers; (iii) Commission Implementing Decision 2012/733/EU of 26 November 2012 implementing Regulation 492/2011 as regards the clearance of vacancies and applications for employment and the re-establishment of EURES; (iv) Commission Regulation (EC) No 635/2006 of 25 April 2006 repealing Regulation (EEC) No 1251/70 on the right of workers to remain in the territory of a Member State after having been employed in that State; (v) Council Directive 77/486/EEC of 25 July 1977 on the education of the children of migrant workers; and (vi) Directive 2014/54/EU of the European Parliament and of the Council of 16 April 2014 on measures facilitating the exercise of rights conferred on workers in the context of freedom of movement for workers.

[12] Council conclusions on EU relations with the Swiss Confederation, 28 February 2017, Press Release 93/17.

its "committed efforts" to implement the result of the 2014 referendum in a manner compatible with the rights of EU citizens under the Free Movement of Persons Agreement.[13] The Council welcomed Switzerland's confirmation that, following the adoption of a Swiss implementing measure, EU and EEA jobseekers will be able to register with regional employment centres.

[23–13] Turkish nationals also enjoy certain free movement rights pursuant to the EU–Turkey Association Agreement and the Additional Protocol thereto. Title II of the Additional Protocol deals with the movement of persons and services, with Art 36 setting out a timetable within which the full free movement of workers is to be achieved. This timetable has, however, slipped, such that the rights of Turkish nationals mainly relate to those who are already legally employed within a Member State, as opposed to a right to enter the Union, which remains within the control of each Member State.[14] Detailed rules on free movement are left to be made by the Council of Association established under the Agreement. Two such decisions relating to the movement of workers, and a third on social security coordination, are of particular importance.[15] The Court of Justice has held that the provisions of these decisions are capable of having direct effect, reasoning that "since they are directly concerned with the Agreement to which they give effect, the decisions of the Council of Association, in the same way as the Agreement itself, form an integral part, as from their entry into force, of the Community legal system".[16]

[23–14] Finally, since the enlargement of 1 May 2004, which increased the EU's population by 75 million, each treaty of accession has provided for transitional arrangements imposing limits on the right of free movement of workers from new Member States. In respect of eight of the 10 states that joined in 2004 (Cyprus and Malta being the exception), existing Member States were entitled to impose restrictions for a two-year period, after which the Commission was required to prepare a report on the functioning of the transitional arrangements for consideration by the Council.[17] Member States were required to inform the Commission of their future intention, with a requirement for free movement to be in place by three years later, on 1 May 2009, unless the Commission authorised a continuation of the transitional measures for a further two years on the basis that the Member State was experiencing serious disturbances within its labour market (a transitional arrangement known as 2+3+2). In addition, as long as one of the existing Member States retained transitional measures in relation to one new Member State, the new Member States were entitled to have recourse to a safeguard clause as between themselves if there were serious disturbances, or the threat thereof, on the labour market due to workers from another new Member State. A "safeguard clause" also provided that, if an existing Member State had stopped applying transitional measures, it could ask to be authorised to re-impose restrictions if it experienced serious problems in its labour market, or a threat thereof. In such a

[13] Council conclusions on EU relations with the Swiss Confederation, 19 February 2019, [2019] OJ C147/2.

[14] See Narin Tezcan/Idriz, "Free Movement of Persons between Turkey and the EU: To Move or Not to Move? The Response of the Judiciary" (2009) 46 *Common Market Law Review* 1621.

[15] Decision 2/76 of 20 December 1976, Decision 1/80 of 19 December 1980 on the Development of the Association, and Decision 3/80 of 19 September 1980 of the EC-Turkey Association Council.

[16] Case C-192/89 *Sevince* [1990] ECR I-3461, 3503.

[17] Communication from the Commission to the Council, the European Parliament, the European Economic and Social Committee and the Committee of the Regions – Report on the Functioning of the Transitional Arrangements set out in the 2003 Accession Treaty (period 1 May 2004–30 April 2006), COM/2006/0048, 8 February 2006.

situation, it would be for the Commission to decide what restrictions could be imposed, and for how long, with any Member State entitled to ask the Council to annul or amend the Commission's decisions acting on the basis of a qualified majority. Only Ireland, the UK and Sweden chose not to apply any transitional arrangements as and from 1 May 2004.[18] Germany and Austria received the final two-year authorisation, with the transitional measures in respect to the 2004 enlargement coming to an end on 1 May 2011. The safeguard clause was never invoked.

[23–15] The same 2+3+2 formula was used in respect of the accession of Bulgaria and Romania on 1 January 2007. On this occasion, Ireland availed of transitional measures so as to require their nationals to continue to obtain an employment permit, as was the case prior to accession. These measures were extended for the additional three-year period, up to the end of 2011, and in December 2011 Ireland obtained permission to continue to apply them for the final two years, up to 1 January 2014. In July 2012, however, the Government decided to end the restrictions with retrospective effect from 1 January 2012. In the case of Croatia, which acceded on 1 July 2013, the same seven-year formula has been employed although Ireland chose not to apply any transitional measures (with only Malta, the Netherlands, Austria, Slovenia and the UK doing so).

(ii) Secondary Legislation – Reg 492/2011

[23–16] The principal legal acts governing the free movement of workers are the Citizens Directive, Directive 2004/38,[19] and the Free Movement of Workers Regulation, Regulation 492/2011.[20] A good familiarity with the content of both of these measures is essential to any proper understanding of the law in relation to free movement of workers. It is worth recalling, however, that earlier legislation had first clarified, and then expanded, the right of workers as originally conceived by the EEC Treaty. First, a 1964 directive set out the circumstances in which a Member State could derogate from the right of free movement.[21] Then, in 1968, a directive required the abolition of administrative restrictions on free movement, while a regulation set out the substantive rights of workers to equal treatment.[22] The content of the two directives is now reflected in the Citizens Directive, while that of the regulation is reflected in the Free Movement

---

18 The UK did, however: (i) impose a requirement that, within 30 days of starting work, workers register with a Workers Registration Scheme; and (ii) deprive workers of their right to have their family members join them during their first year of legal residence in the UK. These restrictions applied until 1 May 2011. See Case C-618/16 *Prefata v Secretary of State for Work and Pensions* EU:C:2018:719, 13 September 2018.

19 Directive 2004/38 of the European Parliament and of the Council of 29 April 2004 on the right of citizens of the Union and their family members to move and reside freely within the territory of the Member States [2004] OJ L158/77.

20 Council Regulation (EEC) No 492/2011 of 5 April 2011 on freedom of movement for workers within the Union [2011] OJ L141/1.

21 Council Directive 64/221/EEC of 25 February 1964 on the co-ordination of special measures concerning the movement and residence of foreign nationals which are justified on grounds of public policy, public security or public health [1964] OJ 56/850.

22 Council Directive 68/360/EEC of 15 October 1968 on the abolition of restrictions on movement and residence within the Community for workers of Member States and their families [1968] OJ L257/13; Regulation (EEC) No 1612/68 of the Council of 15 October 1968 on freedom of movement for workers within the Community [1968] OJ L257/2.

of Workers Regulation. A further regulation in 1970 provided for the right to reside after retiring in another Member State.[23]

[23–17] The adoption of the Single European Act in 1986, which sought to progressively establish an internal market by 1992, "provided the impetus towards the adoption of directives providing for the right of residence for the economically non-active".[24] In 1990, a package of three directives was adopted which respectively conferred a right of residence on (i) those generally with the independent financial means to support themselves[25]; (ii) workers or self-employed persons who had retired[26]; and (iii) students[27]; provided that in each case the individual had comprehensive medical insurance and sufficient resources so as not to become a burden on the host state's social security system.

[23–18] In 2004, the Citizens Directive simplified and consolidated this fragmented area of law by encapsulating the jurisprudence of the Court of Justice and by repealing nine earlier directives. As will be seen in the following chapter, the Directive sets out the rights of entry and residence enjoyed by a range of persons, not just workers, including the self-employed, providers and recipients of services, retired persons, job-seekers and tourists. Thereafter, Chapter 25 will explore the extent to which the development of the concept of Union citizenship since its introduction in the Maastricht Treaty has significantly blurred the traditional distinction between economic actors (be they a worker, self-employed or engaging in a service) and other persons in the context of the exercise of the right to free movement. The remainder of this chapter will examine the way in which the right of workers to move throughout the EU is guaranteed by Art 45 TFEU and regulated by the Free Movement of Workers Regulation, Regulation 492/2011, which codified and updated the rules specific to workers, replacing Regulation 1612/68.

B. Vertical and Horizontal Direct Effect

[23–19] In *Van Duyn v Home Office* it was confirmed that the right of free movement enshrined in Art 45 TFEU has vertical direct effect, "conferring on individuals rights which are enforceable by them and which the national courts must protect".[28]

[23–20] As regards whether the right enjoys horizontal direct effect, in *Bosman*, concerning football player transfer rules, the Court of Justice applied the reasoning it had previously developed in *Walrave and Koch*, a case regarding the freedom to provide services. In that earlier judgment, which concerned the rules of the International

[23] Regulation (EEC) No 1251/70 of the Commission of 29 June 1970 on the right of workers to remain in the territory of a Member State after having been employed in that State [1970] OJ L142/24.

[24] Steve Peers and Nicola Rogers, "Union Citizenship" in Nicola Rogers, Rick Scannell and John Walsh, *Free Movement of Persons in the Enlarged European Union* (2nd ed, Sweet and Maxwell, 2012) 53.

[25] Council Directive 90/364/EEC of 28 June 1990 on the right of residence [1990] OJ L180/26.

[26] Council Directive 90/365/EEC of 28 June 1990 on the right of residence for employees and self-employed persons who have ceased their occupational activity [1990] OJ L180/28.

[27] Council Directive 90/366/EEC of 28 June 1990 on the right of residence for students [1990] OJ L180/30.

[28] Case 41/74 *Van Duyn v Home Office* [1974] ECR 1337, 1347.

Cycling Union as a non-governmental body, the Court had reasoned that since, in addition to national laws and regulations, working conditions are "sometimes governed by agreements and other acts concluded or adopted by private parties", to limit the application of the right to acts of public authorities (ie vertical direct effect) would risk creating an inequality.[29] Accordingly, it was held that the right of free movement could also be invoked against rules of any nature "aimed at regulating in a collective manner gainful employment".[30] In following this approach in *Bosman*, the Court declared that the right of free movement applies to rules laid down by sporting associations such as FIFA and UEFA which determine the terms on which professional sportspersons can engage in gainful employment.[31] Similarly, in *Olympique Lyonnais*, the French Football Player Charter was held to constitute a collective agreement which fell within the scope of Art 45 TFEU, as did a collective agreement with a private employer in *Erny v Daimler*.[32]

[23–21] The precise extent to which Art 45 is capable of having horizontal direct effect in respect of measures taken by an individual employer, rather than some collective regulation of employment as was the case in *Bosman* and *Olympique Lyonnais*, is, however, not entirely clear. The case of *Angonese* is often cited as an instance of when the Court of Justice did afford such a degree of horizontal direct effect.[33] As found by the referring Italian court as a matter of fact, Mr Angonese was bilingual in Italian and German and, when applying for a job with a private bank, had produced certificates to that effect. The bank, however, which was located in the Italian province of Bolzano, insisted that applicants for the position produce a certificate of bilingualism from the Bolzano public authorities on the basis of a particular examination held there.

[23–22] In considering whether the bank's requirement for a particular certificate of language ability was contrary to the right of free movement, the Court began by noting that the principle of non-discrimination in Art 45 is drafted in general terms and is not specifically addressed to the Member States. The Court then recalled its earlier judgments in *Walrave and Koch* and *Bosman*, as well as *Defrenne v Sabena*, in which it held that the principle that men and women were to receive equal pay for like work applied to all agreements intended to regulate paid labour collectively, *as well as to contracts between individuals*, notwithstanding the fact that the relevant Treaty article was addressed to the Member States. In *Angonese*, these considerations were held to apply with even greater force to Art 45, "which lays down a fundamental freedom and which constitutes a specific application of the general prohibition of discrimination".[34] Like the principle of equal pay for men and women, Art 45 was "designed to ensure that there is no discrimination in the labour market. Consequently, the prohibition of discrimination on grounds of nationality laid down in Article [45] must be regarded as applying to private persons as well".[35] The Court went on to hold that where a private employer makes admission to a recruitment competition subject to a requirement to

---

29 Case 36/74 *Walrave and Koch v Association Union Cycliste Internationale* [1974] ECR 1405, 1418–1419.

30 *ibid* 1418.

31 Case C-415/93 *Union Royale Belge des Sociétés de Football Association v Bosman* [1995] ECR I-4921, 5067.

32 Case C-325/08 *Olympique Lyonnais v Bernard* [2010] ECR I-2177; Case C-172/11 *Erny v Daimler* EU:C:2012:399, 28 June 2012.

33 Case C-281/98 *Angonese* [2000] ECR I-4149.

34 *ibid*, 4173.

35 *ibid.*

provide evidence of language ability exclusively by means of one particular certificate that is issued in only one province of a Member State, that requirement constitutes discrimination on the ground of nationality contrary to Art 45.[36]

[23–23] An example of the approach in *Angonese* being followed is found in the 2008 judgment in *Raccanelli v Max-Planck-Gesellschaft*.[37] There, an Italian PhD student in Germany alleged that he had suffered discrimination on the ground of nationality since, unlike German students, he had not been offered the opportunity of choosing between a grant contract and a contract of employment with respect to his research. An issue to be determined was whether Art 45 could be invoked as against a private law association, MPG, responsible for managing a number of Max Planck Institutes. The question referred was described as asking, in essence, whether, notwithstanding its establishment as a private law association, MPG was bound by the principle of non-discrimination as if it had the status of a public-law body. Applying the reasoning from *Angonese*, the Court of Justice held that MPG was required to adhere to the principle of non-discrimination. It was recalled that Art 45 lays down a fundamental freedom which constitutes a specific application of the general prohibition of discrimination contained in Art 18 TFEU, and that the prohibition of discrimination applies equally to all agreements intended to regulate paid labour collectively, as well as to contracts between individuals. As a result, the prohibition of discrimination based on nationality laid down by Art 45 must be held to apply equally to private-law associations such as MPG. It was for the referring court to establish whether, in the particular circumstances, there had been inequality in the treatment of domestic and foreign doctoral students.

[23–24] Notwithstanding the decisions in *Angonese* and *Raccanelli*, Robert Schütze describes the application of Art 45 to actions of individual employers outside the context of collective agreements as "controversial".[38] Derrick Wyatt and Alan Dashwood emphasise the manner in which, in cases against individual private employers, the Court was at pains to limit the application of Art 45 to discrimination claims on the ground of nationality; in their view, to extend the horizontal direct effect of Art 45 to non-discriminatory actions would be "a step too far in that it would risk unduly limiting the freedom of private parties".[39]

C. Scope of Application of the Right

(i) Wholly Internal Situations

[23–25] Before considering, in the following section, the definition of a "worker", it is first necessary to clarify the scope of application of the right of free movement. As might be expected, the right of free movement requires a cross-border element and so does not apply in wholly internal situations. Two illustrations of this are *Saunders* and *Kremzow*, both relating to criminal prosecutions. Ms Saunders was a UK national from Northern Ireland who had pleaded guilty to a charge of theft before a Bristol court and provided an undertaking to return to Northern Ireland and not to re-enter England and

---

36 *ibid*, 4175.

37 Case 94/07 *Raccanelli v Max-Planck-Gesellschaft* [2008] ECR I-5939.

38 Robert Schütze, *European Union Law* (Cambridge University Press, 2015) 577.

39 Alan Dashwood, Michael Dougan, Barry Rodger, Eleanor Spaventa and Derrick Wyatt, *Wyatt and Dashwood's European Union Law* (6th ed, Hart, 2011) 502.

Wales for a period of three years.[40] The undertaking was broken and, when it came to sentencing, the Court made a preliminary reference asking whether the order it had made was compatible with the right of free movement. The Court of Justice responded by confirming that free movement rights cannot be "applied to situations which are wholly internal to a Member State, in other words, where there is no factor connecting them to any of the situations envisaged by [EU] law".[41]

[23–26] Mr Kremzow was an Austrian national who was convicted of murder and sentenced to imprisonment in Austria. Following a finding by the European Court of Human Rights that the conduct of his trial had infringed upon his Convention rights, he brought separate proceedings seeking damages against Austria on the basis that his imprisonment had breached his EU Treaty right of free movement.[42] The Court of Justice held that the criminal law pursuant to which Mr Kremzow had been convicted was not designed to secure compliance with EU rules and so related to a situation that did not fall within the scope of application of EU law.[43]

[23–27] A final example is that of *Moser*, which concerned a German student training to be a teacher.[44] Having completed the first part of a two-stage qualification process, Mr Moser was denied entry to the second stage due to his membership of the Communist Party. The national court considered that the refusal to allow him to proceed could hinder his prospects of obtaining employment as a teacher in another Member State, and referred a question to the Court of Justice asking whether the right to free movement was engaged. Mr Moser had, however, never resided outside of Germany. It was held that a "purely hypothetical prospect of employment in another member state" did not establish a sufficient connection with EU law to justify the application of Art 45 and that, as a result, the situation was wholly internal.[45]

(ii) Reverse Discrimination

[23–28] The concept of a "wholly internal situation", within which the right of free movement does not apply, has a certain logical coherence when considered from the perspective of EU law. From the perspective of the individual affected, however, this may be less clear. For example, workers who exercise a right of free movement enjoy an entitlement under the Citizens Directive to have certain family members from outside the EU join them in the host Member State. This entitlement may go beyond what is provided for in national law with respect to the right of family unification enjoyed by that Member State's own citizens who have not exercised their free movement rights. In *Morson and Jhanjan*, it was held that two Dutch nationals could not rely on this entitlement so as to allow their Surinamese parents join them, as they had remained within the Netherlands and EU law was not, therefore, engaged.[46] The individuals had sought to rely on (now) Art 18 TFEU's prohibition of discrimination on the grounds of nationality but were unsuccessful.

---

[40] Case 175/78 *R v Saunders* [1979] ECR 1129.

[41] *ibid*, 1135.

[42] Case C-299/95 *Kremzow v Austria* [1997] ECR I-2629.

[43] *ibid*, 2646.

[44] Case 180/83 *Moser* [1984] ECR 2539.

[45] *ibid*, 2547.

[46] Cases 35 and 36/82 *Morson and Jhanjan v Netherlands* [1982] ECR 3723.

[23–29] This situation, whereby EU nationals exercising the right of free movement enjoy greater rights than a citizen of an EU Member State who has remained within his or her own country, is known as "reverse discrimination".[47] A similar situation arose in *Uecker and Jacquet*, where German workers in Germany sought to have their Norwegian and Russian wives join them.[48] The Court maintained its view that reverse discrimination was not incompatible with fundamental principles of EU law, holding that "[a]ny discrimination which nationals of a Member State may suffer under the law of that state fall within the scope of that law and must therefore be dealt with within the framework of the internal legal system of that state."[49] In other words, if a Member State wished to avoid a situation whereby the application of EU law resulted in its own citizens, who remained within the state, enjoying lesser rights, it was free to amend its internal law so as to extend the benefits afforded by EU law to such internal situations.

(iii) Exceptions to a Wholly Internal Situation – Frontier Workers and Returnees

[23–30] There are two common situations that, while at first they may appear wholly internal, are in fact regarded as sufficient to engage Art 45 TFEU. The first is that of "frontier workers", where a worker has a cross-border commute having either maintained a residence in one Member State but taken up employment in another,[50] or continued in an existing job but moved to another Member State.[51]

[23–31] The second situation is that of "returnees", where a person has spent time working in another Member State but then returns to his or her home Member State. The issue of returnees has arisen in a number of cases involving the recognition, in the state to which the individual has returned, of a professional qualification obtained in another Member State.[52] It has also given rise to case law concerning the rights of family members, such as the well-known case of *Surinder Singh*.[53] Mr Singh, an Indian national, had married a UK national and moved with her to Germany, where they both worked. After a number of years, they returned to the UK, where Mr Singh's wife sought to establish a business. An issue arose as to whether or not, in returning to the UK, Mr Singh's wife could be said to be engaging EU law. The UK argued that an EU national, such as Mrs Singh, who returned to establish herself in her country of origin, was not in a situation comparable to that of nationals of other Member States, because she entered and remained in that country not by virtue of EU law, but of national law. The Court of Justice adopted a purposive approach to the right of free movement to uphold the application of EU law in such circumstances, reasoning as follows:

> A national of a Member State might be deterred from leaving his country of origin in order to pursue an activity as an employed or self-employed person as envisaged by the Treaty

---

[47] See Alina Tryfonidou, "Reverse Discrimination in Purely Internal Situations: An Incongruity in a Citizen's Europe" (2008) 35 *Legal Issues of Economic Integration* 43; Camille Dautricourt and Sébastien Thomas, "Reverse Discrimination and the Free Movement of Persons under Community Law: All for Ulysses, Nothing for Penelope?" (2009) 34 *European Law Review* 433.

[48] Joined Cases C-64/96 and C-65/96 *Uecker and Jacquet* [1997] ECR I-3171.

[49] *ibid*, 3190.

[50] See, for example, Case C-419/92 *Scholz* [1994] ECR I-505; Case C-385/00 *De Groot* [2002] ECR I-11819; Case C-213/05 *Gevin* [2007] ECR I-6347.

[51] See, for example, Case C-212/05 *Hartmann* [2007] ECR I-6303; Case C-287/05 *Hendrix* [2007] ECR I-6909.

[52] See, for example, Case C-19/92 *Kraus* [1993] ECR I-1663.

[53] Case C-370/90 *Surinder Singh* [1992] ECR I-4265.

in the territory of another Member State if, on returning to the Member State of which he is a national in order to pursue an activity there as an employed or self-employed person, the conditions of his entry and residence were not at least equivalent to those which he would enjoy under the Treaty or secondary law in the territory of another Member State.

He would in particular be deterred from so doing if his spouse and children were not also permitted to enter and reside in the territory of his Member State of origin under conditions at least equivalent to those granted them by [EU] law in the territory of another Member State.

It follows that a national of a Member State who has gone to another Member State in order to work there as an employed person pursuant to Article [45] of the Treaty and returns to establish himself in order to pursue an activity as a self-employed person in the territory of the Member State of which he is a national has the right, under Article [49] of the Treaty, to be accompanied in the territory of the latter State by his spouse, a national of a non-member country, …

Admittedly, as the United Kingdom submits, a national of a Member State enters and resides in the territory of that State by virtue of the rights attendant upon his nationality and not by virtue of those conferred on him by [EU] law. …

However, this case is concerned not with a right under national law but with the rights of movement and establishment granted to a [EU] national by Articles [45] and [49] of the Treaty. These rights cannot be fully effective if such a person may be deterred from exercising them by obstacles raised in his or her country of origin to the entry and residence of his or her spouse. Accordingly, when a [EU] national who has availed himself or herself of those rights returns to his or her country of origin, his or her spouse must enjoy at least the same rights of entry and residence as would be granted to him or her under [EU] law if his or her spouse chose to enter and reside in another Member State. Nevertheless, Articles [45] and [49] of the Treaty do not prevent Member States from applying to foreign spouses of their own nationals rules on entry and residence more favourable than those provided for by [EU] law.[54]

[23–32] This reasoning was tested further in *Akrich*, which concerned a Moroccan national who, following an initial deportation from the UK, returned unlawfully and subsequently married a British national.[55] Mr Akrich was then detained at the beginning of 1997. In June 1997 his spouse moved to Dublin where she found work and, in August 1997, he was deported to Dublin in accordance with his wishes. In 1998 he applied for entry clearance to the UK, in the course of an interview for which his spouse confirmed that they intended to return "because we heard about EU rights, staying six months and then going back to the UK", having been given that information from "solicitors and others in [the] same situation".[56] In replying to a preliminary reference, the Court of Justice made clear that the "motives which may have prompted a worker of a Member State to seek employment in another Member State are of no account as regards his right to enter and reside in the territory of the latter state provided that he there pursues or wishes to pursue an effective and genuine activity".[57] Thus, the fact that Mr Akrich did not have a right of lawful of residence in the UK, the state of nationality of his EU-worker spouse, was not a basis for claiming she was seeking to

---

[54] *ibid*, 4293–4295.
[55] Case C-109/01 *Akrich* [2003] ECR I-9607.
[56] *ibid*, 9681–9682.
[57] *ibid*, 9687.

abuse the right of free movement, absent some further element such as the existence of a marriage of convenience.

[23–33] The right of returnees set out in *Surinder Singh* and *Akrich* was extended one step further in *Eind*. There, a Dutch national went to the UK in 2000 and found employment, on foot of which he successfully applied to have his daughter join him from Surinam.[58] In 2001, Mr Eind returned to the Netherlands with his daughter, where he received social assistance and did not seek employment due to an illness. He had, however, had an interview with an Employment Office and was awaiting a second interview. Before the Court of Justice, the Netherlands argued that an EU national was unlikely to be deterred from moving by the prospect of not being able, on returning to his Member State of origin, to continue a family life which may have been established in the host Member State. More specifically, Mr Eind could not have been deterred from moving to the UK by the fact that it would be impossible for his daughter to reside with him once he returned, given that, at the time of the initial move, his daughter did not have a right to reside in the Netherlands. The Court firmly rejected this argument, reasoning that:

> [a] national of a Member State could be deterred from leaving that Member State in order to pursue gainful employment in the territory of another Member State if he does not have the certainty of being able to return to his Member State of origin, irrespective of whether he is going to engage in economic activity in the latter State.
>
> That deterrent effect would also derive simply from the prospect, for that same national, of not being able, on returning to his Member State of origin, to continue living together with close relatives, a way of life which may have come into being in the host Member State as a result of marriage or family reunification.
>
> Barriers to family reunification are therefore liable to undermine the right to free movement which the nationals of the Member States have under [EU] law, as the right of a [EU] worker to return to the Member State of which he is a national cannot be considered to be a purely internal matter.[59]

[23–34] The Court concluded, therefore, that even though Mr Eind was not economically active, his daughter was to have the right to join him in residing in the Netherlands as, otherwise, he may have been deterred from moving to another EU Member State in the first place.

(iv) Posted Workers

[23–35] In order for a company located in one Member State to be able to provide services in another Member State, there is a likelihood that it may have to transfer some of its employees to that second Member State for a period of time. Such employees are known as "posted workers". It is estimated that, each year, over a million workers are posted by their employers to another EU Member State in order to provide services (indeed, in 2014, the figure was estimated to be as high as 1.9 million workers), representing 0.7 per cent of total EU employment. The posting of workers is particularly prevalent in the construction and business services sectors.

---

[58] Case C-291/05 *Eind* [2007] ECR I-10719.

[59] *ibid*, 10774–10775.

[23–36] The concept of a posted worker is very much associated with the guarantee, under Art 56 TFEU, of the freedom to provide services, and the more accepted view is that such workers do not fall within the scope of Art 45 TFEU since, as the Court of Justice has described, "[w]orkers employed by an undertaking established in one Member State who are temporarily sent to another Member State to provide services do not in any way seek access to the labour market in that second state, if they return to their country of origin or residence after completion of their work."[60] Nevertheless, given the impact that the law on this topic has on individual workers themselves, it is considered appropriate to refer to it here. It ought to be remembered, however, that the overarching right to provide services under Art 56 is a right of the employer, rather than that of the employee.

[23–37] In the 1989 case of *Rush Portuguesa*, the Court of Justice established the principle that a company based in one Member State is entitled to transfer, without being subject to restrictions, its workforce (including third-country nationals) to another Member State for the duration of a project to be carried out there.[61] A few years later the Court further clarified, in *Vander Elst*, that in order for the principle to apply, the employee need not be an EU national, but must have been lawfully and "habitually employed" by the company prior to be being posted.[62] There, a Belgian employer sent employees to France to carry out demolition work, some of whom were Moroccan nationals who were legally resident and permitted to work in Belgium. The Court held that a French requirement that the Moroccan employees obtain work permits went beyond the restrictions that were permitted to be imposed on the freedom to provide services and would amount to a duplication of the procedure already undergone in Belgium.

[23–38] The right established in *Rush Portuguesa* and *Vander Elst* to post workers on a temporary basis could potentially have given rise to a situation in which companies established in Member States with the lowest labour costs could avail of a competitive advantage by using their employees to provide services in other Member States at reduced rates of pay – a phenomenon referred to as "social dumping". Accordingly, the Court entered a critically important caveat to the right to post workers. Provided that it could be justified as being necessary and proportionate to ensure the overriding interest of the protection of workers, Member States were entitled to apply their legislation, including minimum wage laws or collective agreements, to any person temporarily employed within the state, regardless of whether their employer was established in another Member State.[63] This "gave the green light" to the enactment of the Posted Workers Directive in 1996, which has been said to codify a "general presumption that the imposition of the host state's labour laws would generally be justified".[64] The Directive

[60] Case C-43/93 *Vander Elst* [1994] ECR I-3803, 3825. In Joined Cases C-49/98 et al *Finalarte* [2001] ECR I-7884, 7897, the Court followed this passage from *Vander Elst* and concluded, "It follows that Article [45] of the Treaty does not apply in the circumstances of the main proceedings."

[61] Case C-113/89 *Rush Portuguesa* [1990] ECR I-1417.

[62] Case C-43/93 *Vander Elst* [1994] ECR I-3803. See, for example, Case C-18/17 *Denieli* EU:C:2018:904, 14 November 2018.

[63] Case C-165/98, *Mazzoleni* [2001] ECR I-2189, 2222.

[64] Directive 96/71/EC of the European Parliament and of the Council of 16 December 1996 concerning the posting of workers in the framework of the provision of services [1997] OJ L18/1. Catherine Barnard, *The Substantive Law of the EU* (2nd ed, Oxford University Press, 2007) 370; Robert Schütze, *European Union Law* (Cambridge University Press, 2015) 647. See also Directive 2014/67/EU of the European Parliament and of the Council of 15 May 2014 on the enforcement of Directive

provides that, regardless of where an employer is established, posted workers should benefit from the laws, or collective agreements, of the host state governing matters such as minimum rates of pay and holiday pay, maximum work periods, minimum rest periods and health and safety rules.

[23–39] Following lengthy negotiations, an amending Directive on Posted Workers was adopted in 2018, which is to be transposed by Member States by July 2020.[65] The amendment sought to reconcile the interests of Member States with lower wage costs, and those with higher wages, by ensuring fair wages and a level playing field between posting companies and local companies in the host country, whilst at the same maintaining the principle of free movement of services. The Directive provides for the same rules on remuneration as local workers of the host Member State to apply from day one of a posting, introduces clearer rules on allowances and enhances cooperation on fraud and abuse in the context of posting. A new category of long-term posting is introduced, whereby it will be possible for a worker to be posted long-term after 12 months, first with a six-month extension. After this period the posted worker will be subject to nearly all aspects of the labour law of the host country. In addition, the Directive requires temporary work agencies to guarantee to posted workers the same terms and conditions which apply to temporary workers hired in the Member State where the work is carried out. Reflecting, once again, the sensitive nature of regulating posted workers, Poland has brought an annulment action against the new Directive, claiming that it infringes the freedom to provide services as guaranteed by Art 56 TFEU.[66]

[23–40] Finally, it might be noted that the right of free movement under Art 45 TFEU will also apply to a worker from one Member State employed by an international organisation in another Member State, as has been held to be the case in respect of the Commission, Council, Court of Justice, Eurocontrol, European Space Agency, European Patent Office and NATO.[67] Where a worker from one Member State is employed in another Member State, the fact that he or she is temporarily required to work outside of the EU does not prevent reliance on Art 45, provided that the employment relationship retains a sufficiently close link with an EU state.[68]

(v) Employers as Beneficiaries of Article 45

[23–41] It is worth highlighting that, as well as being relied upon by workers, the right

96/71/EC concerning the posting of workers in the framework of the provision of services [2014] OJ L159/11.

65 Directive (EU) 2018/957 of the European Parliament and of the Council of 28 June 2018 amending Directive 96/71/EC concerning the posting of workers in the framework of the provision of services [2018] OJ L173/16. See Piet Van Nuffel and Sofia Afanasjeva, "The Posting of Workers Directive Revised: Enhancing the Protection of Workers in the Cross-Border Provision of Services" (2018) 3 *European Papers* 1401; Rebecca Zahn, "Revision of the Posted Workers Directive: A Europeanisation Perspective" (2017) 19 *Cambridge Yearbook of European Legal Studies* 187.

66 Case C-626/18 *Poland v European Parliament and Council* (ongoing) [2019] OJ C4/12.

67 Case C-411/98 *Ferlini* [2000] ECR I-8081; Case C-137/04 *Rockler* [2006] ECR I-1441 (Commission); Case C-293/03 *My* [2004] ECR I-12013 (Council); Case C-185/04 *Öberg* [2006] ECR I-1453 (Court of Justice); Case C-310/91 *Schmid* [1993] ECR I-3011 (Eurocontrol); Case 389/87 *Echternach* [1989] ECR 723 (European Space Agency); Case C-233/12 *Gardella v INPS* EU:C:2013:449, 4 July 2012 (European Patent Office) and Case C-392/05 *Alevizos* [2007] ECR I-3505 (NATO).

68 Case 237/83 *Sarl Prodest* [1984] ECR 3153, 3162.

of free movement can also be invoked by an employer who, for instance, is faced with a national measure restricting its freedom to hire a worker from another Member State. In *Clean Car Autoservice*, for example, a law requiring the manager of certain trades to be resident within Austria was held to be contrary to the right of free movement as a form of indirect discrimination that was incapable of being justified on the grounds of public policy.[69] Similarly, a Luxembourg law that provided a financial incentive to companies to recruit older workers who were resident in Luxembourg was held to restrict the freedom of companies to employ workers from other Member States.[70]

D. Definition of a "Worker"

[23–42] Since the term "worker" is not defined in Art 45 TFEU, it was left to the Court of Justice to clarify its meaning. The right of free movement is one of the four fundamental freedoms guaranteed by the Treaty. It is unsurprising, therefore, that in order to ensure its effectiveness, the Court interpreted the term in a broad and purposive manner. The Court also made clear that the definition of a worker for the purpose of Art 45 is necessarily a matter of EU law, rather than of national law, so as to maintain a consistent approach throughout the Member States. A series of cases brought in the 1980s – *Levin, Kempf, Raulin, Lawrie-Blum, Steymann* and *Bettray* – clarified the nature of a worker in EU law and provided the framework definition that continues to be used today. As described in *Lawrie-Blum*, the essence of the definition is that, for a certain period of time, a person performs services for and under the direction of another person, in return for which he or she receives remuneration.[71]

[23–43] In *Levin*, the dimension of the work at issue was the level of income it generated. Although Ms Levin, a UK national, worked part-time as a chamber maid, the Dutch authorities argued that she ought not to be classified as a worker because this position did not generate sufficient income to support her and was less than the Dutch minimum legal wage at the time. The Netherlands argued that Art 45 could only be relied upon by persons who "receive a wage at least commensurate with the means of subsistence considered as necessary by the legislation of the Member State in which they work, or who work at least for the number of hours considered as usual in respect of fulltime employment in the sector in question".[72]

[23–44] In replying to a preliminary reference, the Court of Justice had regard to the overall objectives of the Treaty in this area, which included the abolition of obstacles to the free movement of persons so as to promote throughout the EU a "harmonious development of economic activities and a raising of the standard of living".[73] Bearing this in mind, the Court found that:

> since part-time employment, although it may provide an income lower than what is considered to be the minimum required for subsistence, constitutes for a large number of persons an effective means of improving their living conditions, the effectiveness of [EU] law would be impaired and the achievement of the objectives of the Treaty would be

[69] Case C-350/96 *Clean Car Autoservice v Landeshauptmann von Wien* [1988] ECR I-2521.
[70] Case C-379/11 *Caves Krier Frères* EU:C:2012:798, 13 December 2012.
[71] Case 66/85 *Lawrie-Blum* [1986] ECR 2121, 2144.
[72] Case 53/81 *Levin* [1982] ECR 1035, 1048.
[73] *ibid*, 1050.

> jeopardised if the enjoyment of rights conferred by the principle of freedom of movement of workers were reserved solely to persons engaged in full-time employment and earning, as a result, a wage at least equivalent to the guaranteed minimum wage in the sector under consideration.[74]

[23–45] Although accepting that part-time workers may, in principle, fall within the scope of Art 45, in an important and oft-repeated passage the Court emphasised that the rules on free movement "cover only the pursuit of effective and genuine activities, to the exclusion of activities on such a small scale as to be regarded as purely marginal and ancillary", and are intended to guarantee "only the free movement of persons who pursue or are desirous of pursuing a genuine economic activity".[75]

[23–46] A more recent example of this flexible approach towards remuneration is to be found in *Genc*, which concerned the definition of a worker under the EU–Turkey Association Agreement.[76] Ms Genc earned €175 for five-and-a-half hours work each week, which amounted to only a quarter of the sum deemed by German law to be necessary for subsistence. Whilst accepting that very limited hours may be an indication that the activity is marginal and ancillary, the Court of Justice nevertheless emphasised that the "possibility cannot be ruled out that, following an overall assessment of the employment relationship in question, that activity may be considered by the national authorities to be real and genuine", such as to constitute employment as a worker.[77] Other factors to be taken into account as capable of indicating that the economic activity was real and genuine included that Ms Genc had worked for the same undertaking for four years, her contract of employment was subject to a collective agreement, and that she was entitled to 28 days of paid leave and to continued payment in the event of illness.

[23–47] A second issue in *Levin* was whether or not the intention of an individual in moving to another Member State was determinative of whether they could seek to rely on Art 45. The third paragraph of Art 45 provides that the right of free movement shall entail the right to accept offers of employment *actually made* and to move freely within the territory of Member States *for this purpose*. The Netherlands pointed to this wording in arguing that the right under Art 45 applied primarily to a "migrant worker intending to settle in another Member State in response to an actual offer of employment".[78] The suggestion was being made that Ms Levin's primary motive was simply to live in the Netherlands, and that the part-time job was merely a means by which to obtain a right to reside there as an EU worker. The Court rejected this argument, holding that the particular wording used in Art 45 merely gave

> expression to the requirement, which is inherent in the very principle of freedom of movement for workers, that the advantages which [EU] law confers in the name of that freedom may be relied upon only by persons who actually pursue or seriously wish to pursue activities as employed persons. They do not, however, mean that the enjoyment of this freedom may be made to depend upon the aims pursued by a national of a Member State in applying for entry upon and residence in the territory of another Member State, provided that he there pursues or wishes to pursue … an effective and genuine activity as an employed person.

---

74 *ibid.*
75 *ibid.*
76 Case C-14/09 *Genc* [2010] ECR I-931.
77 *ibid*, para 26.
78 Case 53/81 *Levin* [1982] ECR 1035, 1040.

> Once this condition is satisfied, the motives which may have prompted the worker to seek employment in the Member State concerned are of no account and must not be taken into consideration.[79]

[23–48] An example of this disregard for motivation is found in the Court's approach in *Ninni-Orasche*, which concerned a fixed-term contract as a waitress for a two-and-a-half-month period.[80] Ms Ninni-Orasche sought to rely on her status as a worker in order to call in aid the prohibition on discrimination on the grounds of nationality in relation to university finance. The Court held that, in assessing whether the economic activity was effective and genuine, regard ought not to be had to the duration of the employment as compared to the total duration of the individual's stay within the host Member State, which in this case was two-and-a-half years. Nor ought weight to be given to the fact that, shortly after the end of her employment, Ms Ninni-Orasche obtained a diploma entitling her to enrol in university. Indeed, the question of whether she had "sought abusively to create a situation enabling her to claim the status of a worker ... with the aim of acquiring advantages linked to that status" had no bearing on the question of whether or not she met the definition of a worker.[81] This taking advantage of the possibilities created by the right of free movement, and the Court's sanctioning thereof, has variously been termed the "instrumental" exercise of free movement or "legitimate circumvention".[82]

[23–49] The case of *Kempf* involved a music teacher who provided 12 hours of piano lessons a week and whose income was supplemented by a Dutch welfare benefit.[83] A question was referred to the Court asking whether, where a national of another Member State pursues an activity which may in itself be regarded as effective and genuine work within the meaning of *Levin*, did the fact that he claimed financial assistance payable out of public funds in order to supplement his income exclude him from being regarded as a worker. Whereas, in *Levin*, the worker's income had been supplemented by her own resources, including the income of a family member, in *Kempf* the Netherlands argued that work providing an income below the minimum means of subsistence as defined by the host Member State could not be regarded as effective and genuine work if the person was claiming social assistance drawn from public funds. Building upon its reasoning in *Levin*, the Court rejected this argument, holding that a person in effective and genuine part-time employment cannot be excluded from the definition of a worker

> merely because the remuneration he derives from it is below the level of the minimum means of subsistence and he seeks to supplement it by other lawful means of subsistence. In that regard it is irrelevant whether those supplementary means of subsistence are derived from property or from the employment of a member of his family, as was the case in *Levin*, or whether, as in this instance, they are obtained from financial assistance drawn from the public funds of the Member State in which he resides, provided that the effective and genuine nature of his work is established.[84]

[23–50] The issue of "on-call" or "zero-hours" contracts was considered in *Raulin*,

---

79 *ibid*, 1051–1052.

80 Case C-413/01 *Ninni-Orasche* [2003] ECR I-13187.

81 *ibid*, 13230.

82 Niamh Nic Shuibhne, *The Coherence of EU Free Movement Law* (Oxford University Press, 2013) 91.

83 Case 139/85 *Kempf* [1986] ECR 1741.

84 *ibid*, 1750–1751.

which involved an eight-month contract to provide waitress services, during the course of which Ms Raulin had worked for just 16 hours, all of which fell within a 16-day period.[85] Under Dutch law, there was no guarantee as to the hours to be worked, nor was there any obligation on the employee to take up a request to work. The Court held that, whilst the very nature of a zero-hours contract did not preclude the existence of an employment relationship,

> [t]he national court may, however, when assessing the effective and genuine nature of the activity in question, take account of the irregular nature and limited duration of the services actually performed under a contract for occasional employment. The fact that the person concerned worked only a very limited number of hours in a labour relationship may be an indication that the activities exercised are purely marginal and ancillary. The national court may also take account, if appropriate, of the fact that the person must remain available to work if called upon to do so by the employer.[86]

[23–51] In *Lawrie-Blum*, a reference sought the Court's view as to whether a trainee teacher ought to be regarded as a worker in circumstances where, in the second of a two-year teacher training course, she was required to work as a teacher for up to 11 hours a week, initially under the direct supervision of an instructor and later, during the last six months, on her own, and for which she was paid.[87] The Court defined the essential feature of an employment relationship as being that "for a certain period of time a person performs services for and under the direction of another person in return for which he receives remuneration".[88] In finding that these criteria were fulfilled, the Court noted that:

(i) during the entire period of preparatory service the trainee teacher was under the direction and supervision of the school to which she was assigned;
(ii) the school determined the services to be performed and her working hours;
(iii) she was required to carry out the school's instructions and observe its rules;
(iv) during a substantial part of the preparatory service she was required to give lessons to the school's pupils and so provided a service of some economic value to the school; and
(v) the money she received could be regarded as remuneration for the services provided and for the duties involved in completing the period of preparatory service.

[23–52] In addition, the Court reiterated the point established in *Levin* that, provided the work was genuine and effective, the fact that Ms Lawrie-Blum gave lessons for only a few hours a week and was paid remuneration below the starting salary of a qualified teacher did not prevent her from being regarded as a worker. Furthermore, the fact that, like an apprenticeship, teachers' preparatory service could be regarded as practical preparation for an occupation was not a bar to the application of Art 45 if the service was performed under the conditions of an activity as an employed person. This was confirmed in *URSSAF*, in which an Irish student undertaking a vocational course at a technical college in Ireland worked, for a time, in a French hotel as part of her training.[89] It was held that, once the activity was effective and genuine and fulfilled the essential characteristics of employment, it did not matter that her services in the hotel were provided under a traineeship contract. Indeed, in *Raccanelli* it was

---

85 Case C-357/89 *Raulin* [1992] ECR I-1027.
86 *ibid*, 1060.
87 Case 66/85 *Lawrie-Blum* [1986] ECR 2121.
88 *ibid*, 2144.
89 Case C-27/91 *URSSAF* [1991] ECR I-5531.

held that a researcher preparing a doctoral thesis on the basis of a grant contract could be regarded as a worker provided that the research activities were performed for a certain period of time under the direction of the relevant institute, in return for which he received remuneration.[90]

[23–53] A more unusual working relationship and form of remuneration was at issue in *Steymann*, which involved a member of the Bhagwan religious community.[91] The community provided for Mr Steymann's material needs, including pocket money, and in return he contributed to the life of the community by performing plumbing works, household tasks and fundraising activities on the community's premises. It was accepted by the Court of Justice that one could not rule out the possibility that an effective economic activity was being undertaken, and that the services provided by the community to its members could be regarded as being an "indirect quid pro quo for their work".[92]

[23–54] Forms of rehabilitative employment have been considered in *Bettray* and, more recently, *Trojani*. In *Bettray*, an individual with a drug-addiction worked in a rehabilitative employment scheme that aimed to maintain, restore or improve working capacity.[93] The Court found that the essential features of an employment relationship were present, in that Mr Bettray performed services for remuneration under the direction of another person. In contrast to *Levin*, however, where the motivation for performing the activity was held not to be relevant, here the Court proceeded to look behind the position itself, noting that persons engaged on the scheme were not selected on the basis of their capacity to perform a certain activity, but rather the activities were chosen in light of the capabilities of the persons performing them.[94] In addition, the undertakings for which the work was carried out had been created by local authorities solely for this purpose. The Court concluded that the work could not be regarded as an effective and genuine economic activity if it was merely a means of rehabilitation or reintegration.

[23–55] In *Trojani*, the Court distinguished its judgment in *Bettray* on the basis that the scheme in that earlier case had been designed for persons who, due to their circumstances, were for a time unable to work under normal conditions.[95] Mr Trojani lived in a Salvation Army hostel where he carried out chores for 30 hours a week as part of a rehabilitation project, for which he was paid €25 and provided with food and accommodation. As in *Bettray*, the constituent elements of an employment relationship were present in that Mr Trojani carried out paid work at the direction of another person. It was for the national court to determine whether the paid activity was real and genuine and, introducing a new dimension to the case law, "whether the services actually performed … are capable of being regarded as forming part of the normal labour market".[96] Both this addition of a "normal labour market" criterion and the decision in *Bettray* have been criticised for "ab-normalising" the work of persons in rehabilitative employment by imposing "a test against which non-normal work

---

90 Case C-94/07 *Raccanelli v Max-Planck-Gesellschaft* [2008] ECR I-5939.

91 Case 196/87 *Steymann* [1988] ECR 6159.

92 *ibid*, 6173.

93 Case 344/87 *Bettray* [1989] ECR 1621.

94 *ibid*, 1646.

95 Case C-456/02 *Trojani* [2004] ECR I-7573.

96 *ibid*, 7606.

is not valued, exacerbating the danger of disability discrimination".[97] In particular, Charlotte O'Brien points out that "[r]ather than allowing notions of genuine work to be altered *to accommodate* adapted work, it actually uses such adaptations as an indicator *to rule out* that work", in a manner that is "difficult to reconcile with notions of reasonable adjustments and positive discrimination".[98]

(i) Job-Seekers

[23–56] It was noted above that the Court of Justice has adopted a broad and purposive approach to interpreting what constitutes a worker within the meaning of EU law. This expansive attitude is also clearly seen in the Court's treatment of job-seekers. In guaranteeing the free movement of workers, Art 45 TFEU makes no reference to job-seekers. Indeed, in providing for a right to accept offers of employment *actually made* and to move *for this purpose*, a literal reading may have led to the conclusion that a person seeking a job did not come within the scope of the right. This was the argument made by the UK in *Antonissen* and rejected by the Court on the basis that it would "jeopardise the actual chances that a national of a Member State who is seeking employment will find it in another Member State, and would, as a result, make that provision ineffective".[99] Rather, it was necessary to interpret Art 45 as enumerating, "in a non-exhaustive way", certain rights benefiting EU nationals in the context of the free movement of workers, which included the right to move freely within the territory of the other Member States and to stay there for the purposes of seeking employment.

[23–57] As regards the length of time for which an EU national might be permitted to remain as a job-seeker, the Commission and the UK argued that, by analogy with an existing EU regulation on social security schemes, a Member State was entitled to limit the period within which to seek employment to three months. The Court, however, was unwilling to impose a strict time period, preferring instead to take a more open-ended approach:

> In the absence of a [EU] provision prescribing the period during which [EU] nationals seeking employment in a Member State may stay there, a period of six months, such as that laid down in the national legislation at issue in the main proceedings, does not appear in principle to be insufficient to enable the persons concerned to apprise themselves, in the host Member State, of offers of employment corresponding to their occupational qualifications and to take, where appropriate, the necessary steps in order to be engaged and, therefore, does not jeopardize the effectiveness of the principle of free movement. However, if after the expiry of that period the person concerned provides evidence that he is continuing to seek employment and that he has genuine chances of being engaged, he cannot be required to leave the territory of the host Member State.[100]

[23–58] This is now reflected in Art 14(4)(b) of the Citizens Directive. It provides that, for so long as they can provide evidence that they are continuing to seek employment and that they have a genuine chance of being engaged, no expulsion measure can be

---

97 Charlotte O'Brien, "Social Blind Spots and Monocular Policy Making: The ECJ's Migrant Worker Model" (2009) 46 *Common Market Law Review* 1107, 1129.

98 *ibid.*

99 Case C-292/89 *R v Immigration Appeals Tribunal, ex p. Antonissen* [1991] ECR I-745, 777. See Oxana Golynker, "Jobseekers' Rights in the European Union" (2005) 30 *European Law Review* 111.

100 *ibid*, 779.

adopted against an EU citizen (or their family members) who entered the territory of a Member State in order to seek employment.

[23–59] It is important to bear in mind, however, that the Court of Justice has made clear that the status of a job-seeker is not entirely the same as that of a worker in employment. So, for example, whereas Art 24(1) of the Citizens Directive provides for a general right of equal treatment, Art 24(2) provides, by way of derogation, that a host Member State shall not be obliged to confer an entitlement to social assistance during the first three months of a person's residence, or during the period in which a person is seeking employment pursuant to Art 14(4)(b). Two caveats apply to this: first, as will be considered further in Chapter 25, the development of EU citizenship has lessened the significance of the distinction between economically active and non-economically active migrants. In more recent years, however, the Court has tended to place renewed emphasis on the liberty afforded to host Member States by Art 24(2) of the Citizens Directive. Secondly, workers who become involuntarily unemployed, including fixed-term contract workers upon the expiry of their contract, and thereafter seek employment, retain their status as workers. As is now provided for in Art 7(3) of the Citizens Directive:

> … a Union citizen who is no longer a worker or self-employed person shall retain the status of worker or self-employed person in the following circumstances:
> (a) he/she is temporarily unable to work as the result of an illness or accident;
> (b) he/she is in duly recorded involuntary unemployment after having been employed for more than one year and has registered as a job-seeker with the relevant employment office;
> (c) he/she is in duly recorded involuntary unemployment after completing a fixed-term employment contract of less than a year or after having become involuntarily unemployed during the first twelve months and has registered as a job-seeker with the relevant employment office. In this case, the status of worker shall be retained for no less than six months;
> (d) he/she embarks on vocational training. Unless he/she is involuntarily unemployed, the retention of the status of worker shall require the training to be related to the previous employment.

[23–60] Echoing its approach to the rights enumerated in Art 45(3) TFEU, in *Saint Prix,* a case involving a worker who temporarily withdrew from the labour market due to her pregnancy, the Court of Justice made clear that Art 7(3) of the Citizens Directive was not to be interpreted as providing an exhaustive list of the circumstances in which a worker may retain that status.[101] In this regard, the Court noted that an EU citizen "would be deterred from exercising her right to freedom of movement if, in the event that she was pregnant in the host State and gave up work as a result, if only for a short period, she risked losing her status as a worker in that State".[102] As a result, it was necessary to interpret Art 45 TFEU as meaning that "a woman who gives up work, or seeking work, because of the physical constraints of the late stages of pregnancy and the aftermath of childbirth retains the status of 'worker', within the meaning of that

[101] Case C-507/12 *Saint Prix v Secretary of State for Work and Pensions*, ECLI:EU:C:2014:2007, 19 June 2014. See also Case C-544/18 *HM Revenue and Customs v HD* (ongoing) [2018] OJ C436/20, concerning whether a self-employed person retains that status while ceasing her activity during pregnancy.

[102] *ibid*, para 44.

article, provided she returns to work or finds another job within a reasonable period after the birth of her child".[103]

[23–61] Finally, whilst the Citizens Directive imposes a restriction on the entitlement to social assistance, Art 5 of the Free Movement of Workers Regulation provides that an EU national who seeks employment in the territory of another Member State shall receive the same assistance there as that afforded by the employment offices in that state to their own nationals seeking employment.

(ii) The Public Service Exception

[23–62] In a somewhat bald fashion, Art 45(4) TFEU states that the provisions of Art 45 shall not apply to employment in the public service. As a corollary to the broad definition of a worker, this exception to free movement has been interpreted very narrowly, both as regards what constitutes the "public service", but also as to its scope of application. Crucially, it has been held that the exception applies only to *access* to employment, such that it cannot be relied upon in defence of discriminatory treatment once employment has been granted. The rationale for this is, essentially, that the "very fact that [a worker] has been admitted shows indeed that those interests which justify the exceptions … are not at issue".[104]

[23–63] As with the definition of a worker, what constitutes employment in the public service is a matter of EU law, rather than being left to Member States to decide for themselves. The seminal case on this exception remains the 1980 judgment in *Commission v Belgium*, where the Court of Justice had to assess a requirement that, for all positions with local authorities and public undertakings, including jobs such as nurses, electricians, railway workers and gardeners, Belgian nationality was required.[105] A central issue in the case was whether the definition of public service employment ought to be based on an institutional or formal approach, whereby the status of the employment and the employing body would be decisive, or whether it ought instead to depend on a functional approach, focusing on the nature of the tasks actually performed. The Court openly identified what it considered to be the problem:

> in the various Member States authorities acting under powers conferred by public law have assumed responsibilities of an economic and social nature or are involved in activities which are not identifiable with the functions which are typical of the public service yet which by their nature still come under the sphere of application of the Treaty. In these circumstances the effect of extending the exception contained in Article [45(4)] to posts which, whilst coming under the States or other organisations governed by public law, still do not involve any association with tasks belonging to the public service properly so called, would be to remove a considerable number of posts from the ambit of the principles set out in the Treaty and to create inequalities between Member States according to the different ways in which the State and certain sectors of economic life are organized.[106]

[23–64] In order to minimise the number of posts falling within the ambit of the exception, the Court set a high threshold for a post to be regarded as public service

[103] *ibid*, para 47.
[104] Case 152/73 *Sotgiu v Deutsche Bundespost* [1974] ECR 153, 162.
[105] Case 149/79 *Commission v Belgium* [1980] ECR 3881.
[106] *ibid*, 3900–3901.

employment, namely that it involves both (i) direct or indirect participation in the exercise of the powers conferred by public law and (ii) duties designed to safeguard the general interests of the state or of other public institutions. The Court's rationale was that posts meeting these two requirements "presume on the part of those occupying them the existence of a special relationship of allegiance to the state and reciprocity of rights and duties which form the foundation of the bond of nationality".[107]

[23–65] A further narrowing occurred in the *Spanish Merchant Shipping* case, where Spanish law reserved the post of a ship's master to its own nationals.[108] Spain sought to defend the exception by pointing to the fact that, in certain emergency situations, a ship's master had a number of public order powers relating to the maintenance of safety and the exercise of police powers, particularly in the case of a danger on board. The master also had authority in respect of notarial matters and the registration of births, marriages and deaths. The mere conferral of such powers was not sufficient to justify an exception under Art 45(4), however, unless the powers were actually exercised on a regular basis and did not represent a very minor part of the person's activities. As the Court explained, the scope of the derogation "must be limited to what is strictly necessary for safeguarding the general interests of the Member State concerned, which cannot be imperilled if rights under powers conferred by public law are exercised only sporadically, even exceptionally, by nationals of other Member States".[109] In practice, it was only very occasionally that the master of a Spanish registered merchant ship would be required to exercise the duty of representing Spain as the vessel's flag state.

[23–66] Doctors, nurses, school teachers, university teaching assistants and trainee lawyers working in the public sector have all been held not to fall within the public service exception. In order to encourage Member States to open up access to such positions, in 1988 the Commission issued a Communication, *Freedom of Movement of Workers and Access to Employment in the Public Service of the Member States*, in which it set out that posts in bodies responsible for administering commercial services – such as public transport, supply of electricity and gas, airlines and shipping lines, post and telecommunications – and in radio and television companies, public health-care services, state education and research for non-military purposes conducted in public establishments, should be made available to EU workers.[110] It would, in the Commission's view, be rare that a position would fall within Art 45(4), with the examples provided including the police and armed forces, the judiciary, tax authorities and the diplomatic service.

[23–67] The Commission Communication was considered by the High Court of Northern Ireland in the interesting case of *Re Katherine Colgan*, which concerned three Irish nationals living in Belfast who applied for the position of management trainee in the Northern Irish civil service but were unsuccessful due to their nationality.[111] Having reviewed the case law of the Court of Justice, the High Court was satisfied that, in principle, the post came within the public service exception in Art 45(4), such that it could be relied upon by the UK. A difficulty, however, was that Irish nationals

---

107 *ibid*, 3900.

108 Case C-405/01 *Colegio de Oficiales de la Marina Mercante Española (Spanish Merchant Shipping)* [2003] ECR I-10391. See also Case C-47/02 *Anker* [2003] ECR I-10447.

109 *ibid*, 10440.

110 [1988] OJ C72/2.

111 *Re Katherine Colgan* [1997] 1 CMLR 53.

were considered eligible for the same position within the civil service in Great Britain. Furthermore, Commonwealth citizens were also deemed eligible for such positions and, indeed, an Irish national could be considered eligible in the event of an inadequate number of Commonwealth recruits. In seeking to justify the measure, it was argued that there may be discrepancies between states arising from their different and separate historical development, such that once a post fell within Art 45(4) it was for the individual Member State to decide the rules for determining who could apply for such posts. The High Court rejected this, and found that the only permissible justification for relying on the public service exception – namely, the need to protect the interests of the state by excluding non-nationals – was "negatived" by the admission of Commonwealth and Irish citizens to the post in Great Britain, and by the admission of Commonwealth citizens and in certain limited circumstances, Irish nationals, to the post in Northern Ireland.[112]

E. The Right to Equal Treatment

[23–68] The right of workers to enjoy equal treatment and not to be discriminated against is found in a number of provisions. First, Art 45(2) TFEU provides that the right of free movement shall entail the abolition of any discrimination based on nationality as regards employment, remuneration and other conditions of work. Under Art 45(3), subject to limitations justified on grounds of public policy, public security or public health, it shall also entail the right to accept offers of employment actually made and to move freely for this purpose. More generally, Art 18 TFEU provides that, within the scope of application of the Treaties, any discrimination on grounds of nationality shall be prohibited. The Citizens Directive similarly provides in Art 24(1) that all EU citizens residing in a host Member State on the basis of the Directive shall enjoy equal treatment with the nationals of that Member State within the scope of the Treaties.

[23–69] In encapsulating the jurisprudence of the Court of Justice, and codifying and replacing its 1968 predecessor, the Free Movement of Workers Regulation (Regulation 492/2011) sets out the content of the right to equal treatment in considerable detail. It has been said that this secondary legislation "protects and facilitates the exercise of the primary rights conferred by the Treaty, rather than creating rights in itself", albeit that its "degree of detail and specificity goes beyond what is expressed in the Treaty".[113] The Regulation's sixth recital describes how, "in order that it may be exercised, by objective standards, in freedom and dignity", the right of free movement requires that "equality of treatment be ensured in fact and in law in respect of all matters relating to the actual pursuit of activities as employed persons and to eligibility for housing, and also that obstacles to the mobility of workers be eliminated, in particular as regards the conditions for the integration of the worker's family into the host country". To this end, the Regulation guarantees a number of specific rights, including:

- the right to take up available employment in the territory of another Member State with the same priority as nationals of that State (Art 1(2));
- the right to exchange applications for and offers of employment, and conclude and perform contracts of employment, in accordance with the provisions laid down by law, without any discrimination resulting therefrom (Art 2);

[112] *ibid*, 76.
[113] Paul Craig and Gráinne de Búrca, *EU Law* (6th ed, Oxford University Press, 2015) 777.

- the right to receive the same assistance as that afforded by the employment offices of a host Member State to its own nationals who are seeking employment (Art 5);
- other than conditions relating to language ability required by reason of the nature of the post to be filled, provisions laid down by law (or administrative action or practices of a Member State) shall not apply where they limit applications for and offers of employment, or the right of foreign nationals to take up and pursue employment, or subject these to conditions not applicable in respect of their own nationals, including provisions or practices which:
  (i) prescribe a special recruitment procedure for foreign nationals;
  (ii) limit or restrict the advertising of vacancies or subject it to conditions other than those applicable in respect of employers pursuing their activities in the territory of that Member State;
  (iii) subject eligibility for employment to conditions of registration with employment offices or impede recruitment of individual workers, where persons who do not reside in the territory of that state are concerned (Art 3(1)(a) and Art 3(2));
- provisions laid down by law (or administrative action or practices of a Member State) shall not apply where, though applicable irrespective of nationality, their exclusive or principal aim or effect is to keep nationals of other Member States away from the employment offered (Art 3(1)(b));
- provisions laid down by law (or regulation or administrative action of a Member State) shall not apply if they restrict by number or percentage the employment of foreign nationals in any undertaking, branch of activity or region, or at a national level (Art 4);
- the engagement and recruitment of an EU worker shall not depend on medical, vocational or other criteria which are discriminatory on grounds of nationality by comparison with those applied to nationals of the host Member State who wish to pursue the same activity (Art 6);
- the right not to be treated differently from national workers by reason of nationality in respect of any conditions of employment and work, in particular as regards remuneration, dismissal, reinstatement or re-employment (Art 7(1));
- the right to enjoy the same social and tax advantages as national workers (Art 7(2));
- by virtue of the same right and under the same conditions as national workers, the right to access training in vocational schools and retraining centres (Art 7(3));
- any clause of a collective or individual agreement or of any other collective regulation concerning eligibility for employment, remuneration and other conditions of work or dismissal shall be null and void in so far as it lays down or authorises discriminatory conditions in respect of EU workers (Art 7(4));
- equality of treatment as regards membership of trade unions and the exercise of rights attaching thereto, including the right to vote and to be eligible for the administration or management posts of a trade union (Art 8(1));
- all the rights and benefits accorded to national workers in matters of housing, including ownership of required housing (Art 9(1));
- if residing in the host Member State, the child of an EU worker has the right to be admitted to general educational, apprenticeship and vocational training courses under the same conditions as the nationals of that state (Art 10).

[23–70] Discrimination prohibited by Art 45 can take both the form of *direct* discrimination, where the difference in treatment is based upon nationality, or *indirect* discrimination, where, in its application, an apparently neutral or indistinctly applicable rule affects workers from other Member States more than it does workers from the host state. Whereas direct discrimination may only be justified on one of the grounds listed in Art 45 – public policy, public security, public health, or employment in the public service – indirect discrimination can be justified by a broader range of objective reasons based on the public interest, provided that the measure is necessary to achieve the stated aim, is proportionate and the stated aim is compatible with EU law. In addition to measures that discriminate, either directly or indirectly, on the grounds of nationality, the Court has established that even a non-discriminatory measure can be caught by Art 45 if it constitutes an excessive obstacle to free movement by precluding or deterring a national from leaving his or her country of origin in order to work in another Member State. Each of these three types of measure will be considered in turn.

(i) Direct Discrimination

[23–71] Given the extent to which they evidently contradict Art 45, instances of direct discrimination are rare. In *Commission v France*, a law that required a certain percentage of the crew of French registered vessels to be French was held to contravene the right to free movement. The Court of Justice was unwilling to accept France's argument that, in practice, the law was not applied to EU nationals following an official instruction to this effect, as this appeared to be a matter of grace, rather than of law.[114] The case of *Marsman* involved a Dutch metal worker who continued to live in the Netherlands, but who worked in Germany. Following a serious accident at work, he was let go. A German law provided that, in such circumstances, it was necessary to obtain the prior permission of a welfare office before employment could be terminated. With respect to foreign workers, however, this protection only applied if they resided within Germany. As the relevant law failed to give the nationals of other Member States employed in Germany all the advantages which it granted to German workers, it fell foul of the prohibition on discrimination.[115]

(ii) Indirect Discrimination

[23–72] Indirectly discriminatory measures do not, on their face, discriminate on the grounds of nationality, but may operate in practice to have such an effect. This may be because, although neutral in its wording, the measure essentially relates to migrant workers, in that such persons represent the majority of those affected by the measure. Alternatively, the measure may impose a requirement that is more easily satisfied by national workers as compared with workers from other EU Member States. So, for example, if a requirement for some particular position or benefit is that a worker must reside in the host Member State, this is much more likely to be met by that state's own nationals as compared with foreign workers.

[23–73] An indirectly discriminatory measure was at issue in *O'Flynn v Adjudication Officer*.[116] Mr O'Flynn was a retired Irish migrant worker living in the UK. Following the death of his son and his burial in Ireland, Mr O'Flynn sought to claim a funeral allowance benefit but was refused on the ground that the benefit only applied to funerals within the UK. In defending the limitation, the UK argued that the measure was non-discriminatory, in that it applied to both UK and foreign workers in respect of a funeral outside of the UK. The Court of Justice confirmed that:

> unless objectively justified and proportionate to its aim, a provision of national law must be regarded as indirectly discriminatory if it is intrinsically liable to affect migrant workers more than national workers and if there is a consequent risk that it will place the former

[114] Case 167/73 *Commission v France* [1974] ECR 359.
[115] Case 44/72 *Marsman* [1972] ECR 1243, 1248.
[116] Case C-237/94 *O'Flynn v Adjudication Officer* [1996] ECR I-2617.

at a particular disadvantage. It is not necessary in this respect to find that the provision in question does in practice affect a substantially higher proportion of migrant workers. It is sufficient that it is liable to have such an effect.[117]

[23–74] As to whether or not the measure in this case was liable to have such an effect, the Court considered that:

it is above all the migrant worker who may, on the death of a member of the family, have to arrange for burial in another Member State, in view of the links which the members of such a family generally maintain with their State of origin. To make payment of any expenses incurred by a migrant worker in his capacity as responsible member subject to the condition that burial or cremation take place within the United Kingdom therefore constitutes indirect discrimination, unless it be objectively justified and proportionate to the aim pursued.[118]

[23–75] With regard to possible justifications for the limitation, the Court noted that there was nothing to prevent the UK from limiting the allowance to a lump sum or reasonable amount fixed by reference to the normal cost of a burial or cremation within the UK.

[23–76] The cases of *Scholz* and *Köbler v Austria* involved similar residence requirements. In *Scholz*, when recruiting for canteen staff at a university in Sardinia, an advertisement stated that previous experience in the public sector would be taken into account.[119] The university, however, only had regard to experience gained in Italy, and took no account of Ms Scholz's previous position with the German post office. In a short judgment the Court quickly concluded that the refusal to take into consideration employment in the public service of another Member State constituted unjustified indirect discrimination. At issue in *Köbler* was the payment of a salary increment to professors who had completed 15 years' service in Austrian universities.[120] The Court reasoned that the failure to have regard to service accrued in another Member State was likely to impede free movement in two respects. First, it operated to the detriment of migrant workers who had worked as professors in other Member States. Secondly, it was likely to deter Austrian professors from spending part of their career abroad, as no account could be taken of that period upon their return to Austria. The measure was sought to be justified on the basis that it was a bonus aimed at rewarding the loyalty of professors of Austrian universities to their sole employer, namely the state of Austria. The Court rejected this public interest justification, finding that:

Although it cannot be excluded that an objective of rewarding workers' loyalty to their employers in the context of policy concerning research or university education constitutes a pressing public-interest reason, given the particular characteristics of the measure at issue …, the obstacle which it entails clearly cannot be justified in the light of such an objective.

First, although all the professors of Austrian public universities are the employees of a single employer, namely the Austrian State, they are assigned to different universities. However, on the employment market for university professors, the various Austrian universities are in competition not only with the universities of other Member States and those of non-Member States but also amongst themselves. As to that second kind of

---

[117] *ibid*, 2638–2639.

[118] *ibid*, 2639.

[119] Case C-419/92 *Scholz v Opera Universitaria di Cagliari* [1994] ECR I-505.

[120] Case C-224/01 *Köbler v Austria* [2003] ECR I-10239.

> competition the measure at issue in the main proceedings does nothing to promote the loyalty of a professor to the Austrian university where he performs his duties.
>
> Second, although the special length-of-service increment seeks to reward workers' loyalty to their employer, it also has the effect of rewarding the professors of Austrian universities who continue to exercise their profession on Austrian territory. The benefit in question is therefore likely to have consequences in regard to the choice made by those professors between a post in an Austrian university and a post in the university of another Member State.
>
> Accordingly, the special length-of-service increment … does not solely have the effect of rewarding the employee's loyalty to his employer. It also leads to a partitioning of the market for the employment of university professors in Austria and runs counter to the very principle of freedom of movement for workers.[121]

[23–77] It is interesting to compare *Köbler* with another Austrian case concerning benefits that accrue after a certain period of time. *Eurothermen* involved a rule whereby a worker who completed 25 years of service with the same employer was entitled to an additional week of annual leave.[122] For workers who had served with other employers (whether in Austria or elsewhere), only a maximum of five years' service would be taken into account in calculating the 25 year period. So, for example, a worker who had worked 18 years with his current employer, and 10 years with a previous employer, would not qualify, as only 5 of those years would be added to the 18 years spent with the current employer. It was argued that this amounted to indirect discrimination, in that workers from other Member States generally start their career in their country of origin and take up employment in Austria later in their career. The Court of Justice rejected this argument, finding that the law did not provide a greater benefit to Austrians over other workers and so was not indirectly discriminatory. Furthermore, the Court did not accept that the measure would pose an obstacle to the exercise of free movement, by deterring Austrians from leaving their current employer in order to work in another Member State, as they might fail to qualify for the 25 year period were they to return. Such an argument was, in the Court's view, "based on a set of circumstances which are too uncertain and indirect" for the law to be regarded as being liable to hinder the free movement of workers.[123]

[23–78] Residence within a Member State was also a requirement in *Zurstrassen*, where it was a precondition for spouses to be able to make a joint assessment for tax purposes.[124] Mr Zurstrassen and his wife were both Belgian, although he lived and worked in Luxembourg while his wife resided in Belgium. Although he was the sole income-earner, the Luxembourg authorities were unwilling to take account of his wife for tax purposes as she did not reside within the state. In agreeing that such a requirement was likely to render joint assessment more accessible to Luxembourg's own nationals as compared with other EU workers, the Court found it to be incompatible with Art 45. Given that, under certain other conditions, Luxembourg did permit non-residents to be included within a joint assessment, the Court was unwilling to entertain an attempt

---

121 *ibid*, 10319–10320.

122 Case C-437/17 *Eurothermen* EU:C:2019:205, 13 March 2019.

123 *ibid*, para 40.

124 Case C-87/99 *Zurstrassen* [2000] ECR I-3337. See also Case C-174/18 *Jacob v Belgium* EU:C:2019:205, 14 March 2019.

to justify the measure on the grounds of practical necessity in the administration of the tax system.

[23–79] A final example of a residence requirement is *Clean Car Autoservice*, involving a challenge to an Austrian law that required companies to appoint a manager resident in Austria.[125] This was sought to be justified on the basis of an imperative requirement that it was necessary to ensure that managers could act effectively and could be served with notice of any fines which may be imposed, allowing their enforcement. The Court was unwilling to accept this argument, concluding that the residence requirement was either an inappropriate means of ensuring that the aim pursued was achieved, or went beyond what was necessary for that purpose:

> In the first place, the fact that the manager resides in the Member State in which the undertaking is established and exercises its trade does not itself necessarily ensure that he will be in a position to act effectively as manager in the business. A manager residing in the State but at a considerable distance from the place at which the undertaking exercises its trade should normally find it more difficult to act effectively in the business than a person whose place of residence, even if in another Member State, is at no great distance from that at which the undertaking exercises its trade.
>
> Secondly, other less restrictive measures, such as serving notice of fines at the registered office of the undertaking employing the manager and ensuring that they will be paid by requiring a guarantee to be provided beforehand, would make it possible to ensure that the manager can be served with notice of any such fines imposed upon him and that they can be enforced against him.
>
> Finally, it must be added, even such measures as those just indicated are not justified by the aims in question if the service of notice of fines imposed on a manager resident in another Member State and their enforcement against him are guaranteed by an international convention concluded between the Member State in which the undertaking exercises its trade and that in which the manager resides.[126]

[23–80] An example of indirect discrimination based other than on residence is found in *Allué and Coonan*.[127] There, an Italian law limited foreign-language teaching assistants working in Italian universities, irrespective of nationality, to being granted yearly contracts for a maximum of six years in total. As Italy had provided statistics that only 25 per cent of foreign-language assistants were Italian, the Court of Justice was quick to hold that the measure essentially concerned migrant workers. Italy sought to justify the restriction on the basis that it was the only means of ensuring that universities had foreign-language assistants with an up-to-date knowledge and experience of the mother tongue which they taught. Given the increase in cultural exchanges and improved communications, the Court regarded the risk of losing contact with a mother tongue as slight. Moreover, in terms of proportionality, it remained open to universities to simply monitor the language ability of their assistants. Furthermore, the claimed justification for the measure was undermined by the fact that the law in question did not prevent a university from employing a language assistant who had already worked for six years in a different Italian university.

[125] Case C-350/96 *Clean Car Autoservice* [1998] ECR I-2521.
[126] *ibid*, 2548.
[127] Case 33/88 *Allué and Coonan* [1989] ECR 1591, 1610–1611.

[23–81] It should, however, be noted that language requirements receive special treatment in Art 3(1) of the Free Movement of Workers Regulation, which expressly permits the use of "conditions relating to language ability required by reason of the nature of the post to be filled". This was considered in *Groener v Minister for Education*, which involved a Dutch national who applied for a teaching position at the College of Marketing and Design in Dublin. Although the classes were to be conducted in English, and an ability in Irish was not necessary to perform the teaching duties involved, Ms Groener was denied the job as a result of failing an Irish language test. The Court of Justice had regard to a consistent policy as regards Irish as Ireland's first official language and held that, provided the level of knowledge required was not disproportionate and there was no requirement that that knowledge had been acquired in Ireland, the measure was permissible. In the assessment of the Court:

> [T]he policy followed by Irish governments for many years has been designed not only to maintain but also to promote the use of Irish as a means of expressing national identity and culture. It is for that reason that Irish courses are compulsory for children receiving primary education and optional for those receiving secondary education. The obligation imposed on lecturers in public vocational education schools to have a certain knowledge of the Irish language is one of the measures adopted by the Irish Government in furtherance of that policy.
>
> The EEC Treaty does not prohibit the adoption of a policy for the protection and promotion of a language of a Member State which is both the national language and the first official language. However, the implementation of such a policy must not encroach upon a fundamental freedom such as that of the free movement of workers. Therefore, the requirements deriving from measures intended to implement such a policy must not in any circumstances be disproportionate in relation to the aim pursued and the manner in which they are applied must not bring about discrimination against nationals of other Member States.
>
> The importance of education for the implementation of such a policy must be recognised. Teachers have an essential role to play, not only through the teaching which they provide but also by their participation in the daily life of the school and the privileged relationship which they have with their pupils. In those circumstances, it is not unreasonable to require them to have some knowledge of the first national language.
>
> It follows that the requirement imposed on teachers to have an adequate knowledge of such a language must, provided that the level of knowledge required is not disproportionate in relation to the objective pursued, be regarded as a condition corresponding to the knowledge required by reason of the nature of the post to be filled within the meaning of … Article 3(1) of [the Free Movement of Workers] Regulation.[128]

(iii) Non-Discriminatory Measures

[23–82] Of the three types of measure that may be caught by Art 45 TFEU, those of a non-discriminatory nature are the most difficult to assess from the point of view of judging their legality. This is because there are no clearly defined criteria by which to consider whether a measure constitutes an obstacle to the free movement of workers or whether, in contrast, the measure is "too uncertain and indirect" to be regarded as being liable to hinder such free movement.[129]

---

[128] Case 379/87 *Groener v Minister for Education* [1989] ECR 3967, 3993–3994.
[129] Case C-190/98 *Graf* [2002] ECR I-493, 523.

[23–83] It was not until the 1995 judgment in *Bosman* that it was clarified that non-discriminatory measures could indeed be prohibited by Art 45.[130] The case involved two separate rules applicable to a Belgian professional football player wishing to change to a team in France. The first was a discriminatory "nationality clause" that imposed what was known as a "3+2" requirement whereby each team could field only three non-national players, plus two further non-national players provided that they had played in the host state for a certain uninterrupted period of time. The second was a non-discriminatory rule that required the payment of a significant transfer fee to the selling club where the player's existing contract had expired. Mr Bosman's own club, Liège, did not wish to renew his contract. Nevertheless, it was unwilling to release him (and his registration card that entitled him to play) without first receiving a transfer fee, leaving him unable to work as a footballer.

[23–84] A difficulty faced by Mr Bosman in his challenge to the transfer fee rule was that it applied not only to transfers between different states or national football associations, but also to transfers between clubs within a single state or association, thereby applying in a non-discriminatory fashion. In seeking to defend the measure, it was argued that the Court of Justice ought to follow the approach it had adopted with respect to the free movement of goods in its important 1993 judgment in *Keck and Mithouard.* There, it was held that non-discriminatory rules governing selling arrangements were not captured by the Treaty rules on free movement.[131] The Court considered that the transfer fee rule could not be regarded as comparable to the selling arrangements at issue in *Keck* since they "directly affect players' access to the employment market in other Member States and are thus capable of impeding freedom of movement for workers".[132] The manner in which the rule affected access to the market was expressed in general terms, namely by "preventing or deterring [players] from leaving the clubs to which they belong even after the expiry of their contracts of employment with those clubs".[133]

[23–85] In considering whether the restriction, once caught, could be justified, the Court was willing to regard as legitimate the twin aims of maintaining financial and competitive balance between football clubs and supporting young talent. Nevertheless, the requirement of a transfer fee was held not to be an effective means of attaining the first objective, whilst it was considered a disproportionate means of pursuing the second.

[23–86] Writing not long after the judgment, Síofra O'Leary suggested that, although clearly not a statement of principle along the lines of *Cassis de Dijon*, *Bosman* nevertheless provided "unmistakable evidence of movement, as regards Article [45], towards a *Cassis de Dijon* style rule of reason with respect to indistinctly applicable

---

[130] Case C-415/93 *Bosman* [1995] ECR I-4921. See Ester Johnson and David O'Keeffe, "From Discrimination to Obstacles to Free Movement" (1994) 31 *Common Market Law Review* 1313; Luigi Daniele, "Non-Discriminatory Restrictions to the Free Movement of Persons" (1997) 22 *European Law Review* 191; and Cathryn Costello, "Market Access All Areas – The Treatment of Non-Discriminatory Barriers to the Free Movement of Workers" (2000) 27 *Legal Issues of European Integration* 267.

[131] Joined Cases C-267/91 and C-268/91 *Keck and Mithouard* [1993] ECR I-6097. See ch 19, paras [19–66] to [19–72].

[132] Case C-415/93 *Bosman* [1995] ECR I-4921, 5070.

[133] *ibid*, 5069.

measures".[134] As is not infrequently the case, the opinion of the Advocate General provides greater elaboration than the Court's judgment on the question of whether or not Art 45 should capture non-discriminatory measures. Advocate General Lenz concluded that it should, following a close examination of: (i) the precise wording of Art 45; (ii) the systematic context of the right of free movement; and (iii) the nature of free movement as a fundamental right. With respect to the systematic context, particular regard was had to the interpretations previously adopted with respect to the free movement of goods and of services, which led him to the conclusion that:

> The fundamental freedoms of the common market are not only based on a common foundation. They also in my opinion form a unity, and the same criteria should be applied as far as possible in dealing with them. For example, there is no sensible reason discernible why free movement of goods ought to be better protected than free movement of persons, since both are of fundamental importance for the internal market.
>
> … in examining the compatibility of national provisions with the provisions of [EU] law on the fundamental freedoms, it is not so important which specific fundamental freedom a particular factual situation is to be measured against. What should be decisive is rather whether the provisions in question hinder trans-frontier economic activity and – if that is the case – whether those restrictions are justified.[135]

[23–87] With regard to the arguments based upon *Keck*, Advocate General Lenz sought to address those concerns by drawing a distinction between measures that restricted access to a market, on the one hand, and measures that merely affected the exercise of an occupation, on the other. Thus, he posited that it was not necessary that *all* non-discriminatory measures "which actually or potentially restrict freedom of movement must necessarily be subjected to the same strict conditions for justification"; rather, "if one wished to adduce the case-law on [the free movement of goods] by analogy in this respect, one might consider drawing a distinction between measures which regulate *access* to occupational activity and measures which are directed more to the *exercise* of that activity".[136] His opinion then proceeded to apply this reasoning to the transfer rules at issue as follows:

> The transfer rules directly restrict *access* to the employment market in other Member States. Therein they differ very significantly from other rules applicable without distinction which affect the exercise of an occupation. One example may suffice to make the difference clear. The question has just been raised again whether a professional league should for instance have 16, 18 or more clubs. It is perfectly plain that the number of clubs available affects a player's chances of finding employment with a club. The smaller the number of clubs, the more difficult it is likely to be as a rule to find employment. Nevertheless, provisions of *that* nature do not appear to me to raise doubts with respect to Article [45]. They do not concern the possibility of access for foreign players as such, but the exercise of the occupation. The situation with respect to the rules on transfers is quite different: under the applicable rules a player can transfer abroad only if the new club (or the player himself) is in a position to pay the transfer fee demanded. If that is not the case, the player cannot move abroad. That is a direct restriction on access to the employment market.[137]

---

[134] Síofra O'Leary, "The Free Movement of Persons and Services" in Paul Craig and Gráinne de Búrca (eds), *The Evolution of EU Law* (Oxford University Press, 1999) 403.

[135] Case C-415/93 *Bosman* [1995] ECR I-4921, 5006.

[136] *ibid*, 5009.

[137] *ibid*, 5011.

[23–88] It is worth considering the similar case of *Olympique Lyonnais* for the insight it provides as to the Court's methodology in assessing arguments seeking to justify a non-discriminatory measure, and the requirement of proportionality in particular.[138] There, a youth player had spent his early career playing for the French team, Olympique Lyonnais. At the end of his period as a youth player he declined to sign a professional contract with the club and instead signed for the English team, Newcastle United. Under a charter governing French professional football, in such circumstances the former club was entitled to sue the player for damages. It was argued that the measure was justified by the need to encourage the recruitment and training of young players and that its only objective was to permit the club to recover the training costs it had incurred. A difficulty with this argument, however, was that the damages the club could claim were calculated in relation to the loss suffered by it, rather than in relation to the costs it incurred. So, while the clause was held to be caught by Art 45, it could potentially have been justified on the basis of providing a scheme for compensating teams for having recruited and trained a youth player, provided that the scheme was suitable to ensure the attainment of that objective and did not go beyond what was necessary to achieve it. Since the damages were calculated in a way which was unrelated to the actual costs of the training, the measure went beyond what was necessary to attain the objective and so was found to be disproportionate.

[23–89] The Court applied the same reasoning to a non-discriminatory measure in *Terhoeve*.[139] This involved a Dutch national who went to work in the UK from January to November, and then returned to the Netherlands. Under Dutch law, Mr Terhoeve was required to pay a higher social security contribution for that year than would have been the case had he remained within the Netherlands, in return for which he received no additional benefits. The Court reaffirmed its view that, since EU nationals have a Treaty right to leave their state of origin to reside in another Member State in order to pursue an economic activity, provisions which preclude or deter a person from doing so constitute an obstacle to that freedom even if they apply without regard to the nationality of the workers concerned. Such a deterrence could arise from the fact that an EU migrant worker was "required to pay greater social contributions than if he continued to reside in the same Member State throughout the year, without thereby being entitled to additional social benefits such as to compensate for that increase".[140] By posing such an obstacle the measure was held to be caught by Art 45, and thereby in need of justification, and so it was unnecessary, in the Court's view, to consider the further question of whether the measure constituted indirect discrimination on the grounds of nationality. The arguments put forward by the Netherlands in an effort to justify the measure (eg simplifying the tax code or technical difficulties with alternative methods of enforcement) failed to meet with the Court's approval.

[23–90] More recently, a similar issue arose in a successful infringement action brought by the Commission against Cyprus concerning its failure to repeal a national law which provided that civil servants under the age of 45, who left their position in order to carry out work in the private or public sector within Cyprus, were entitled to maintain their future pension rights, whereas the same civil servants leaving in order to take up a position in another EU Member State had no such entitlement and received

---

[138] Case C-325/08 *Olympique Lyonnais* [2010] ECR I-2177.

[139] Case C-18/95 *Terhoeve* [1999] ECR I-345.

[140] *ibid*, 389.

only a lump sum payment.[141] The measure was held to hinder, or make less attractive, the exercise of free movement rights by Cypriot civil servants under the age of 45, thereby directly affecting the access of such workers to the employment market in other EU states, and so constituted an obstacle to free movement that was caught by Art 45. As regards a possible justification, the Court held that Cyprus fell short in that it "merely allude[d] to a risk of imbalances in the social security system and maintain[ed] that the legislation at issue meets the requirements of proportionality".[142] The Court recalled its well-established approach to economic justifications before proceeding to find fault with the lack of evidence adduced:

> [W]hile reasons of a purely economic nature cannot constitute overriding reasons in the public interest justifying a restriction of a fundamental freedom guaranteed by the Treaty, national legislation may, however, constitute a justified restriction on a fundamental freedom when it is dictated by reasons of an economic nature in the pursuit of an objective in the public interest. Therefore, it is conceivable that the risk of seriously undermining the financial balance of the social security system may constitute an overriding reason in the public interest capable of justifying the undermining of the provisions of the Treaty concerning the right of freedom of movement for workers.
>
> However, according to the settled case-law of the Court, it is for the competent national authorities, where they adopt a measure derogating from a principle enshrined by European Union law, to show in each individual case that that measure is appropriate for securing the attainment of the objective relied upon and does not go beyond what is necessary to attain it. The reasons invoked by a Member State by way of justification must thus be accompanied by an analysis of the appropriateness and proportionality of the measure adopted by that State and by specific evidence substantiating its arguments. Such an objective, detailed analysis, supported by figures, must be capable of demonstrating, with solid and consistent data, that there are genuine risks to the balance of the social security system.
>
> It must be noted that in the present case such evidence is lacking.[143]

[23–91] A variant of the scenario in *Commission v Cyprus* was at issue in *Casteels v British Airways*, where a collective agreement between British Airways and a German trade union provided for retention of pension entitlements where an employee transferred between divisions of the airline within Germany, but not where the employee transferred to a division within another Member State.[144] The dissuasive effect of the clause on workers moving from one Member State to another, while remaining with the same employer, was regarded as sufficient to bring it within the scope of Art 45.

[23–92] Two further examples of non-discriminatory measures are *Kranemann* and *Commission v Denmark (Company Cars)*. Mr Kranemann was a temporary civil servant in Germany who, as part of his legal traineeship, was sent to spend some time in a London law firm.[145] Whereas workers in his position were entitled to reimbursement of travel costs incurred within Germany, the entitlement did not extend to additional travel costs incurred in travelling to another Member State. The Court regarded the restriction as creating

---

141 Case C-515/14 *Commission v Cyprus* EU:C:2016:30, 21 January 2016.
142 *ibid*, paras 53–55.
143 *ibid*, paras 54–55.
144 Case C-379/09 *Casteels v British Airways* [2011] ECR I-1379.
145 Case C-109/04 *Kranemann* [2005] ECR I-2421.

> a financial obstacle which may deter trainee lawyers, particularly those with limited financial resources, from taking up a traineeship in another Member State, regardless of whether the decision to undergo such practical training is motivated generally … by reasons relating to the trainee's specialisation or by personal reasons, such as the wish to gain experience of another legal culture.[146]

[23–93] An attempt to justify the measure on the basis of budgetary considerations suffered from the critical flaw that a journey to another Member State could in fact cost less than a journey to a location within Germany.

[23–94] The *Company Cars* case concerned a Danish law which operated to prohibit the use in Denmark of company cars that were only registered in another Member State, affecting Danish frontier workers in particular.[147] The Court satisfied itself that the measure fell within the scope of Art 45 by noting that, whereas it had previously held that to be capable of constituting an obstacle, a measure must affect the ability of workers to access the labour market, the "manner in which an activity is *pursued* is liable also to affect access to that activity. Consequently, legislation which relates to the conditions in which an economic activity is pursued may constitute an obstacle to freedom of movement within the meaning of that case-law".[148]

[23–95] Clearly, the breadth of the test applied in *Company Cars*, potentially capturing all rules governing the manner in which an employment activity is pursued, is extremely broad. It is unsurprising, therefore, that the Court has applied some limit to the test by holding that measures will not be caught by Art 45 if their restrictive effects are too indirect or uncertain. So, in *Graf*, a worker failed in his attempt to argue that an Austrian provision which required a payment to be made to workers upon the involuntary termination of their employment, but not when they voluntarily choose to leave their positions, fell within the scope of Art 45 due to the fact that it deterred cross-border movement.[149] The measure was held not to be such as to preclude or deter the worker from ending his contract of employment in order to take a job with another employer, because the entitlement to compensation was not dependent on the worker's choosing whether or not to stay with his current employer "but on a future and hypothetical event, namely the subsequent termination of his contract without such termination being at his own initiative or attributable to him. Such an event is too uncertain and indirect a possibility for legislation to be capable of being regarded as liable to hinder freedom of movement for workers".[150]

[23–96] In seeking to provide a framework within which to conceptualise the treatment of non-discriminatory measures, Damian Chalmers, Gareth Davies and Giorgio Monti suggest drawing a distinction between two types of measure that can both be caught by Art 45: on the one hand, measures which prevent access to the market, as was suggested as a key rationale by Advocate General Lenz in *Bosman*; on the other, measures which have the lesser effect of deterring workers from taking up positions abroad. Whereas "their extreme restrictive effects" lead the first category to fall within Art 45, the second category comprises measures such as those in *Graf*

---

146 *ibid*, 2442.
147 Case C-464/02 *Commission v Denmark (Company Cars)* [2005] ECR I-7929.
148 *ibid*, 7960. Emphasis added.
149 Case C-190/98 *Graf* [2000] ECR I-493.
150 *ibid*, 523.

and *Kranemann*, the effect of which is not to prevent access to the market, but merely to deter an individual from taking up activities in another Member State because of the economic costs such activity would entail. With regard to this second category of measures that have a deterrent effect, they argue that while *Graf* creates a *de minimis* rule, "*Kranemann* suggests that this will not be applied, or will be less rigorously applied, where the measure specifically targets movement between Member States".[151]

F. Other Rights and Social Advantages

[23–97] While many of the provisions of the Free Movement of Workers Regulation are concerned with guaranteeing equal treatment for workers in, or in connection with, their employment, the Regulation also extends the principle of equal treatment to: (i) social and tax advantages; (ii) training in vocational schools; (iii) housing; and (iv) admission to education for the children of workers.

(i) Social and Tax Advantages – Article 7(2)

[23–98] In simply guaranteeing that a worker "shall enjoy the same social and tax advantages as national workers", Art 7(2) of the Free Movement of Workers Regulation is a deceptively innocuous provision that has proven the source of a number of ancillary rights for EU workers and their families. Motivated by the desire to remove obstacles to the free movement of workers and to assist workers and their families integrate into the society of their host Member State, the Court of Justice has adopted a very expansive interpretation of Art 7(2), whereby the guarantee of equal treatment applies not only to social and tax advantages due to a worker arising from his or her particular position, but also to

> all those advantages which, whether or not they are linked to a contract of employment, are generally granted to national workers, primarily because of their objective status as workers or by virtue of the mere fact of their residence on the national territory and the extension of which to workers who are nationals of other Member States therefore seems suitable to facilitate their mobility.[152]

[23–99] In order to fall within Art 7(2), however, the social advantage must be of some direct or indirect benefit to the worker him or herself, and not just to a family member, although this is interpreted in a flexible way. Indeed, it is not necessary that the worker is the person claiming the social advantage, so long as it benefits him or her – as seen in *Hartmann* where the Court explained that:

> A benefit such as German child-raising allowance, which enables one of the parents to devote himself or herself to the raising of a young child, by meeting family expenses, benefits the family as a whole, whichever parent it is who claims the allowance. The grant of such an allowance to a worker's spouse is capable of reducing that worker's obligation to contribute to family expenses.[153]

---

[151] Damian Chalmers, Gareth Davies and Giorgio Monti (eds), *European Union Law* (3rd ed, Cambridge University Press, 2014) 864. See Max Jansson and Harri Kalimo, "*De Minimis* Meets 'Market Access': Transformations in the Substance – and Syntax – of EU Free Movement Law?" (2014) 51 *Common Market Law Review* 523.

[152] Case 207/78 *Ministère Public v Even* [1979] ECR 2019, 2034.

[153] Case C-212/05 *Hartmann* [2007] ECR I-6303, 6342.

[23–100] There, Mrs Hartmann, who lived in Austria with her children, was denied German children's allowance notwithstanding that her husband was a worker in Germany. The German requirement that the non-working spouse be resident in Germany was held to amount in indirect discrimination contrary to Art 7(2) of the Regulation.

[23–101] In *Cristini v SNCF* the Court expressly stated that Art 7(2) "cannot be interpreted restrictively" and that, "in view of the equality of treatment which the provision seeks to achieve, the substantive area of application must be delineated so as to include all social and tax advantages, whether or not attached to the contract of employment".[154] There, a widow of a migrant worker had been refused a discount card for her and her children to travel on the French railway. The Court concluded that, if the widow and her children would have been entitled to the card upon an application having been made by the worker prior to his death, it would be "contrary to the purpose and spirit of the [EU] rules on freedom of movement for workers to deprive the survivors of such a benefit following the death of the worker whilst granting the same benefit to the survivors of a national".[155]

[23–102] The Court of Justice has held that the following amount to a social advantage within the meaning of Art 7(2) of the Regulation and should, therefore, be made available to workers from other EU Member States:

- children's allowance[156];
- a disability allowance paid to nationals in respect of adult children with a disability[157];
- finance to support study granted to the child of a worker whom the worker is supporting[158] (regardless of whether the child resides in the state of employment)[159];
- a discretionary, interest-free childbirth loan, granted to nationals by a bank incorporated under public law[160];
- benefits made available to larger families on the birth of a third child[161];
- funeral payment allowance.[162]

[23–103] An important case demonstrating the significance of Art 7(2) is that of *Lair*, concerning a French national who had worked intermittently in Germany for a number of years before attending university there.[163] Upon applying for a student maintenance grant, Ms Lair was refused on the basis that she had not worked in Germany for a total period of five years prior to enrolment, a condition that did not apply to German students. The Court was satisfied that an EU migrant worker was "entitled in the same way as national workers to all the advantages available to such workers for improving their professional qualifications and promoting their social advancement", and that the maintenance grant constituted such an advantage.[164] Secondly, the Court confirmed that

---

[154] Case 32/75 *Cristini v SNCF* [1975] ECR 1085, 1094.
[155] *ibid*, 1095.
[156] Case 85/96 *Martinez Sala* [1998] ECR I-2691.
[157] Case 63/76 *Inzirillo* [1976] ECR 2057.
[158] Case C-3/90 *Bernini* [1992] ECR I-1071.
[159] Case C-337/97 *Meeusen* [1999] ECR I-3289.
[160] Case 65/81 *Reina* [1982] ECR 33.
[161] Case C-185/96 *Commission v Greece* [1998] ECR I-6601.
[162] Case C-237/94 *O'Flynn v Adjudication Officer* [1996] ECR I-2617.
[163] Case 39/86 *Lair* [1988] ECR 3161.
[164] *ibid*, 3197.

migrant EU workers are guaranteed certain rights that are sufficiently linked to their status as a worker, even when they are no longer employed:

> In the field of grants for university education, such a link between the status of worker and a grant awarded for maintenance and training with a view to the pursuit of university studies does, however, presuppose some continuity between the previous occupational activity and the course of study; there must be a relationship between the purpose of the studies and the previous occupational activity. Such continuity may not, however, be required where a migrant has involuntarily become unemployed and is obliged by conditions on the job market to undertake occupational retraining in another field of activity.
>
> Such a conception of freedom of movement for migrant workers corresponds, moreover, to current developments in careers. Continuous careers are less common than was formerly the case. Occupational activities are therefore occasionally interrupted by periods of training or retraining.[165]

[23–104] As a result, provided that there was a sufficient link between the previous employment and the course of studies being undertaken, Ms Lair was a worker entitled to avail of the Art 7(2) social advantage of a maintenance grant on an equal basis as German workers, and Germany was unable to impose a five-year employment requirement on EU workers in order to access such grants.

[23–105] Mirroring its approach to the right to equal treatment under Art 45 TFEU, the Court of Justice has confirmed that Art 7(2) of the Regulation prohibits not only direct discrimination on grounds of nationality, such as in *Lair*, but also indirect forms of discrimination which, through the application of other criteria of differentiation, lead to the same result as a matter of fact. So, for example, in *Commission v The Netherlands*, the Commission brought an action in respect of a requirement imposed by the Netherlands on funding for university studies abroad that the student must have been resident in the Netherlands for at least three of the previous six years.[166] Funding was available to both Dutch and EU nationals and the residence requirement applied to both. Naturally, however, the residence requirement would be more readily met by Dutch students. The Court held that such indirect discrimination was impermissible unless it could be objectively justified. The Netherlands sought to justify the residence requirement on two objective bases: namely, in order to avoid an unreasonable financial burden that could have consequences for scheme's very existence and, secondly, to encourage student mobility by targeting the funding towards those students who would otherwise be the least likely to study abroad.

[23–106] Regarding the financial burden argument, the Court reaffirmed its position that although budgetary considerations may underlie a Member State's choice of social policy and influence the nature or scope of the social protection measures which it wishes to adopt, they do not in themselves constitute an aim pursued by that policy and cannot therefore justify discrimination. To accept otherwise would imply that the

---

[165] *ibid*, 3200.

[166] Case C-542/09 *Commission v The Netherlands* EU:C:2012:346, 14 June 2012. See Floris De Witte, "Who Funds the Mobile Student? Shedding Some Light on the Normative Assumptions Underlying EU Free Movement Law: *Commission v Netherlands*" (2013) 50 *Common Market Law Review* 203. See also Case C-20/12 *Giersch* EU:C:2013:411, 20 June 2013; Case C-238/15 *Bragança Linares Verruga* EU:C:2016:949, 14 December 2016; Case C-410/18 *Aubriet* EU:C:2019:582, 10 July 2019.

"application and the scope of a rule of EU law as fundamental as non-discrimination on grounds of nationality might vary in time and place according to the state of the public finances of Member States".[167]

[23–107] The Netherlands suggested that the Court should follow its earlier case law in relation to students and non-economic migrants, where it had accepted that the granting of social assistance could be made dependent upon a required degree of integration within the host state, such as through a three-year residence requirement.[168] However, as the right in this case was that of workers under Art 7(2) of the Regulation, the Court firmly rejected the notion that a degree of integration could be required. Rather, the fact that migrant workers have "participated in the employment market of a Member State establishes, in principle, a sufficient link of integration with the society of that Member State, allowing them to benefit from the principle of equal treatment, as compared with national workers, as regards social advantages".[169] Amongst other things, this link of integration arose from the fact that, "through the taxes which he pays in the host Member State by virtue of his employment, the migrant worker also contributes to the financing of the social policies of that State and should profit from them under the same conditions as national workers".[170]

[23–108] Turning to the second justification, the Court accepted that a residence requirement was appropriate for attaining the legitimate objective of encouraging student mobility by targeting those students who would otherwise be least likely to move. It did not accept, however, that the Netherlands had demonstrated that the "three years out of six" requirement was proportionate, as it had failed to provide evidence substantiating the conclusion that the requirement did not go beyond what was necessary to achieve the objective. Whilst the "standard of proof cannot be so high as to require the Member State to prove, positively, that no other conceivable measure could enable the objective pursued to be attained under the same conditions", it was not sufficient for the Netherlands "simply to refer to two alternative measures which, in its opinion, are even more discriminatory" than the impugned requirement.[171] Rather, it would have been necessary for the Netherlands to

> at least to show why it opted for the "three out of six years" rule, to the exclusion of all other representative elements. It should be pointed out in that regard that the rule is too exclusive. By requiring specific periods of residence in the territory of the Member State concerned, the "three out of six years" rule prioritises an element which is not necessarily the sole element representative of the actual degree of attachment between the party concerned and that Member State.[172]

(ii) Training in Vocational Schools – Article 7(3)

[23–109] Article 7(3) of the Regulation provides that EU workers shall "by virtue of the same right and under the same conditions as national workers, have access to training in vocational schools and retraining centres". As seen above, in *Lair*, the concept of

[167] *ibid*, para 58.
[168] See ch 25, paras [25–49] to [25–50] and [25–53] to [25–54].
[169] Case C-542/09 *Commission v The Netherlands* EU:C:2012:346, 14 June 2012, para 65.
[170] *ibid*, para 66.
[171] *ibid*, para 84–85.
[172] *ibid*, para 86.

social advantages in Art 7(2) was held to apply to university maintenance grants. In that case the Court adopted a narrow interpretation of Art 7(3), in holding that the concept of a vocational school referred "exclusively to institutions which provide only instruction either alternating with or closely linked to an occupational activity, particularly during apprenticeship".[173] Accordingly, the fact that some vocational training is provided is not sufficient for an educational institution to be regarded as a vocational school.

(iii) Housing – Article 9

[23–110] In accordance with Art 9 of the Regulation, EU workers shall "enjoy all the rights and benefits accorded to national workers in matters of housing, including ownership of the housing he needs".

(iv) Education for Workers' Children – Article 10

[23–111] Article 10 of the Regulation provides that the children of a national of a Member State who is or has been employed in the territory of another Member State shall be admitted to that state's general educational, apprenticeship and vocational training courses under the same conditions as the nationals of that state, if such children are residing in its territory. The provision has been interpreted broadly so as to include not only admission criteria but any general measures intended to facilitate educational attendance, such as maintenance grants or student loans.[174] In addition, the concept of "children" for the purposes of Art 10 is noticeably generous, extending to adult children over the age of 21, even where no longer dependent on a parent worker, so long as the child had lived with a parent in the host Member State whilst he or she worked there.[175]

[23–112] Whereas Art 7(3) refers to "vocational schools", which was interpreted narrowly in *Lair*, Art 10 refers much more generally to "educational, apprenticeship and vocational training courses". Vocational training has been given a relatively broad interpretation that includes "any form of education which prepares for a qualification for a particular profession, trade or employment or which provides the necessary skills for such a profession, trade or employment", whatever the age and level of the student.[176] University education will also be considered as vocational training if it provides a required qualification for a particular profession, trade or employment, or the specific training and skills needed for such a position, "even if no legislative or administrative provisions make the acquisition of that knowledge a prerequisite for that purpose".[177] The Court of Justice has observed that, with the exception of certain courses which, "because of their particular nature, are intended for persons wishing to improve their general knowledge rather than prepare themselves for an occupation", university studies will generally fulfil these criteria and so be regarded as vocational training within the meaning of Art 10 of the Regulation.[178]

[23–113] Two final points regarding access to education are worth noting. First, in the 1985 case of *Gravier v City of Liège*, a French student wishing to enrol in a university

---

173 Case 39/86 *Lair* [1988] ECR 3161, 3197.
174 Case 9/74 *Casagrande* [1974] ECR 773.
175 Case C-7/94 *Gaal* [1996] ECR I-1031.
176 Case 293/83 *Gravier v City of Liège* [1985] ECR 593, 614.
177 Case 24/86 *Blaizot* [1988] ECR 379, 404.
178 *ibid.*

course in Belgium sought to argue that the application of a registration fee to other EU nationals, but not to Belgians, was contrary to the Treaty prohibition on discrimination on the grounds of nationality (now found in Art 18 TFEU).[179] Although Ms Gravier was not herself a worker, or the child of an EU worker in Belgium, she claimed to come within the scope of the Treaty by virtue of her accessing of services, in the form of a university course, in another Member State. The Court laid emphasis on the fact that the Treaty provided for a common vocational training policy (now found in Art 166 TFEU), which had led to certain secondary measures. The Court was satisfied that, on the basis of these developments, a common vocational training policy was gradually being established and that it constituted an "indispensable element of the activities of the Community, whose objectives include inter alia the free movement of persons, the mobility of labour and the improvement of the living standards of workers".[180] Moreover,

> [a]ccess to vocational training is in particular likely to promote free movement of persons throughout the Community, by enabling them to obtain a qualification in the Member State where they intend to work and by enabling them to complete their training and develop their particular talents in the Member State whose vocational training programmes include the special subject desired.[181]

[23–114] As a result, the Court was willing to conclude that the conditions of access to vocational training fell within the scope of the Treaty, such that to impose a registration fee on EU nationals, but not on one's own nationals, constituted impermissible discrimination on the grounds of nationality.

[23–115] Secondly, it will be noted that Art 10 of the Regulation refers to children of an EU national "who is *or has been* employed in the territory of another Member State". Accordingly, the fact that the parent worker has ceased working, has died, or no longer resides in the host Member State does not necessarily mean that a child cannot continue to rely on Art 10.[182] Moreover, in *Baumbast* it was held that the right of children, derived from Art 10, to reside in a Member State in order to continue their education gave rise to a further right, vested in the children's primary carer, to reside with them, even if that person was not an EU citizen.[183] Mr Baumbast, who was German, lived and worked in the UK with his Colombian wife and two daughters, one of whom had Colombian nationality and the other had dual Colombian-German nationality. The daughters continued to attend school and live in the UK with their mother, even though their father was required to move outside of the EU in order to seek employment. In challenging a refusal by the UK authorities to grant them indefinite leave to remain, it was argued that the daughters had a continuing right to reside derived from Art 10 of the Free Movement of Workers Regulation, notwithstanding that their EU-worker parent no longer resided in the UK and that Mr and Mrs Baumbast had divorced.

[23–116] The Court observed that the aim of the Regulation was to ensure that the movement of workers be "guaranteed in compliance with the principles of liberty and dignity" through providing the "best possible conditions for the integration of the [EU]

---

[179] Case 293/83 *Gravier v City of Liège* [1985] ECR 593.
[180] *ibid*, 613.
[181] *ibid.*
[182] See Case 76/72 *Michel S* [1973] ECR 457; Joined Cases 389 and 390/87 *Echternach and Moritz* [1989] ECR 723.
[183] Case C-413/99 *Baumbast and R v Secretary of State for the Home Department* [2002] ECR I-7091.

worker's family in the society of the host Member State".[184] In order for such integration to come about, the child of an EU worker must have the possibility of going to school and pursuing further education in the host Member State in order to be able to complete that education successfully. To prevent the child of a Union citizen from continuing his or her education by refusing permission to remain in the state might dissuade that Union citizen from exercising the right of free movement in the first place, and would therefore create an obstacle to the effective exercise of that freedom.[185] Since the right under Art 10 of the Regulation was conferred on the children of an EU worker, the nationality of the child (and any lack of EU citizenship) was irrelevant.

[23–117] Moving on to consider the right of the children's mother to remain in the UK, the Court noted that if she was refused a right to remain in the UK during the period of their education, that might deprive the children of a right which was granted to them by EU law. In addition, it was necessary to interpret the Free Movement of Workers Regulation in light of the obligation to respect family life laid down in Art 8 of the European Convention on Human Rights, which was one of the fundamental rights recognised by EU law. Consequently, in order not to infringe the entitlement of the children to continue their education, it was necessary that their mother also be permitted to reside with them in the UK until their education was completed.

[23–118] As the judgment in *Baumbast* predated the introduction of the Citizens Directive, a question arose as to whether the requirements of that Directive regarding the right of residence were to apply in the case of a non-EU national who sought to remain in the EU on the basis that he or she was a child's primary caregiver. In *London Borough of Harrow v Ibrahim*, a scenario similar to that in *Baumbast* differed to the extent that: (i) the mother of school-going children was not self-sufficient but was dependent on social assistance and (ii) the Citizens Directive had been introduced, which included a requirement that a family member have sufficient resources so as not to become a burden on the social assistance system of the host state.[186] Ireland intervened in the case in support of the UK's argument that, since its entry into force, the Citizens Directive constituted the sole basis for the conditions governing the exercise of the right of residence, such that a right of residence could no longer be derived from Art 10 of the Free Movement of Workers Regulation.

[23–119] Sitting as a Grand Chamber, the Court of Justice found that there was nothing to suggest, either in its terms or the *travaux preparatoires*, that in adopting the Citizens Directive it was intended to alter the scope of Art 10 of the Regulation "so as to limit its normative content from then on to a mere right of access to education".[187] On the contrary, the Directive was designed to be consistent with the judgment in *Baumbast*. Accordingly, the children of a Union citizen who had worked in the host

---

184 *ibid*, 7156.

185 *ibid*, 7157.

186 Case C-310/08 *London Borough of Harrow v Ibrahim* [2010] ECR I-1065. See Charlotte O'Brien, "Case C-310/08, *London Borough of Harrow v Nimco Hassan Ibrahim and Secretary of State for the Home Department*, Judgment of the Court of Justice (Grand Chamber) of 23 February 2010, Case C-480/08, *Maria Teixeira v London Borough of Lambeth and Secretary of State for the Home Department*, Judgment of the Court of Justice (Grand Chamber) of 23 February 2010" (2011) 48 *Common Market Law Review* 203; Peter Starup and Matthew J Elsmore, "Taking a Logical or Giant Step Forward? Comment on *Ibrahim* and *Teixeira*" (2010) 35 *European Law Review* 571.

187 *ibid*, para 45.

Member State but subsequently left, and the parent who was their primary carer, could claim an independent right of residence on the sole basis of Art 10 of the Regulation, without being required to satisfy the conditions laid down in the Citizens Directive.

[23–120] Two further clarifications were made in *Teixeira v London Borough of Lambeth,* which was delivered by the Grand Chamber on the same day as *Ibrahim.*[188] First, in order for a child, and his or her primary carer, to have a right of residence under Art 10 of the Regulation, it is not necessary that one of the child's parents worked as a migrant worker in the host Member State on the precise date on which the child started in education. Rather, it is enough that that child became installed in the host Member State when one of the parents was exercising a right of residence there as a migrant worker. Secondly, the right of residence of the primary carer ends when the child reaches the age of majority, unless the child continues to need the presence and care of that parent in order to be able to complete his or her education.

Overview of Case Law

Art 45 – Vertical Direct Effect	*Van Duyn v Home Office*	
Art 45 – Horizontal Direct Effect	*Bosman* *Olympique Lyonnais* *Erny v Daimler*	*Angonese* *Raccanelli v Max Planck*
Wholly Internal Situations	*Saunders* *Moser*	*Kremzow*
Reverse Discrimination	*Morson and Jhanjan* *Uecker and Jacquet* *Surinder Singh*	*Akrich* *Eind*
Posted Workers	*Rush Portuguesa*	*Vander Elst*
Art 45 – Employers as Beneficiaries	*Clean Car Autoservice*	
Definition of a "Worker"	*Levin* *Genc* *Ninni-Orasche* *Kempf* *Raulin* *Lawrie-Blum*	*URSSAF* *Raccanelli v Max Planck* *Steymann* *Trojani* *Bettray*
Job-Seekers	*Antonissen*	*Saint Prix*
Public Services Exception	*Commission v Belgium* *Spanish Merchant Shipping*	*Re Katherine Colgan*
Direct Discrimination	*Commission v France*	*Marsman*
Indirect Discrimination	*O'Flynn v Adjudication Officer* *Scholz* *Köbler v Austria* *Groener v Minister for Education*	*Clean Car Autoservice* *Allué and Coonan* *Zurstrassen*
Non-Discriminatory Measures	*Bosman Casteels v British* *Airways* *Olympique Lyonnais* *Terhoeve Company Cars* *Commission v Cyprus*	*Kranemann* *Graf*

[188] Case C-480/08 *Teixeira v London Borough of Lambeth* [2010] ECR I-1107.

Social and Tax Advantages	*Hartmann* *Cristini v SNCF*	*Lair* *Commission v Netherlands*
Children's Education	*Gravier v City of Liège* *Baumbast*	*Ibrahim* *Teixeira*

CHAPTER 24

FREE MOVEMENT UNDER THE CITIZENS DIRECTIVE

A. INTRODUCTION

[24–01] Figures compiled by Eurostat indicate that, as of 1 January 2014, of an overall population of 507 million, 17.9 million EU citizens resided in a Member State other than the one in which they were born. In contrast, there were 33.5 million people living in the EU that had been born outside of the Union. According to a 2015 Eurobarometer survey, among those most convinced of the benefits of free movement are the Irish, at 78 per cent, with only four countries having a more positive perception.[1] These figures serve to emphasise the point made by Elspeth Guild, Steve Peers and Jonathan Tomkin that, by establishing a right for EU citizens, and their third-country national (TCN) family members, to move and reside anywhere in the EU, the "relationship of EU citizens and their families to the migration authorities of the Member States has changed fundamentally".[2]

[24–02] As has been seen in earlier chapters, the right of free movement is specifically provided for in the TFEU in respect of workers, those exercising the right of establishment, as well as persons providing or receiving services. Since 1 November 1993, however, free movement has also been guaranteed as an attribute of Union citizenship. As set out in both Art 21 TFEU and Art 45 of the Charter of Fundamental Rights, every citizen of the Union has the right to move and reside freely within the territory of the Member States subject to the limitations and conditions laid down in the Treaties and by the measures adopted to give it effect. The Citizens Directive (Directive 2004/38 – also referred to alternatively as the "Citizens' Rights", the "Citizenship" or the "Free Movement" Directive) was adopted in 2004 in light of the evolving development

---

1 Flash Eurobarometer 430, *European Union Citizenship* (2016) 40, available at <http://ec. europa. eu/commfrontoffice/publicopinion/index.cfm/General/index>.

2 Elspeth Guild, Steve Peers and Jonathan Tomkin, *The EU Citizenship Directive* (Oxford University Press, 2014) 10.

of Union citizenship as the "fundamental status of nationals of the Member States when they exercise their right of free movement and residence".[3] By way of response, it was considered appropriate to codify and review existing EU law contained in a number of secondary legal acts that dealt separately with workers, self-employed persons, as well as students and other inactive persons, "in order to simplify and strengthen the right of free movement and residence of all Union citizens".[4] The Directive is comprised of seven chapters, made up of 42 articles as follows:

Chapter I	**General Provisions**
Art 1	Subject
Art 2	Definitions
Art 3	Beneficiaries
Chapter II	**Right of Exit and Entry**
Art 4	Right of exit
Art 5	Right of entry
Chapter III	**Right of Residence**
Art 6	Right of residence for up to 3 months
Art 7	Right of residence for more than 3 months
Art 8	Administrative formalities for EU citizens
Art 9	Administrative formalities for third-country national (TCN) family members
Art 10	Issue of residence card
Art 11	Validity of residence card
Art 12	Retention of right of residence by family members in event of death or departure of EU citizen
Art 13	Retention of right of residence by family members in event of divorce, annulment of marriage or termination of registered partnership
Art 14	Retention of right of residence
Art 15	Procedural safeguards
Chapter IV	**Right of Permanent Residence**
Art 16	General rule for EU citizens and their family members
Art 17	Exemptions for persons no longer working in the host member state and their family members
Art 18	Acquisition of right of permanent residence by certain TCN family members
Art 19	Document certifying permanent residence for EU citizens
Art 20	Permanent residence card for TCN family members
Art 21	Continuity of residence
Chapter V	**Provisions common to right of residence and right of permanent residence**
Art 22	Territorial scope
Art 23	Related rights
Art 24	Equal treatment
Art 25	General provisions concerning residence documents
Art 26	Checks
Chapter VI	**Restrictions on grounds of public policy, public security or public health**
Art 27	General principles
Art 28	Protection against expulsion

[3] Directive 2004/38/EC of the European Parliament and of the Council of 29 April 2004 on the right of citizens of the Union and their family members to move and reside freely within the territory of the Member States [2004] OJ L158/77, recital 3, adapting well-known language from the judgment in Case C-184/99 *Grzelczyk* [2001] ECR I-6193, 6242.

[4] *ibid.*

Art 29	Public health
Art 30	Notification of decisions
Art 31	Procedural safeguards
Art 32	Duration of exclusion orders
Art 33	Expulsion as a penalty or legal consequence
Chapter VII	**Final Provisions**
Art 34	Publicity
Art 35	Abuse of rights
Art 36	Sanctions
Art 37	More favourable national provisions
Art 38	Repeals
Art 39	Report
Art 40	Transposition
Art 41	Entry into force
Art 42	Addressees

[24–03] The Citizens Directive is transposed into Irish law by the European Communities (Free Movement of Persons) Regulations 2015,[5] which came into operation on 1 February 2016 and contains 30 regulations as follows:

Reg 1	Citation and commencement
Reg 2	Interpretation
Reg 3	Application
Reg 4	Permission for EU citizens and qualifying family members to enter State
Reg 5	Permission for permitted family member to enter State
Reg 6	Residence in the State
Reg 7	Residence card for TCN family member
Reg 8	Validity of residence card
Reg 9	Retention of right of residence by family member in event of death or departure from State of EU citizen
Reg 10	Retention of right of residence by family members in event of divorce, annulment of marriage, annulment or dissolution of civil partnership
Reg 11	Retention of rights of residence
Reg 12	Entitlement to permanent residence in the State
Reg 13	Entitlement to permanent residence in the State of EU citizen no longer working in the State
Reg 14	Issue of permanent residence certificate to EU citizens
Reg 15	Issue of permanent residence card to TCN family member
Reg 16	Production of evidence
Reg 17	Entitlements and matters of equal treatment
Reg 18	Restrictions on right of movement and residence on grounds of public policy and public security
Reg 19	Restrictions on right of movement and residence on grounds of public health
Reg 20	Removal orders – general
Reg 21	Removal orders – procedural requirements
Reg 22	Arrest and detention for purposes of removal from the State
Reg 23	Exclusion orders
Reg 24	Notices
Reg 25	Review of decisions

5 SI No 548 of 2015. See Patricia Brazil, "The Citizens Directive in Irish law – A Cautionary Tale" (2016) 19 *Irish Journal of European Law* 11; Christina Götzelmann, "The Implementation and Administration of Family Reunification Rights in Ireland" (2016) 55 *Irish Jurist* 75; John Stanley, *Immigration and Citizenship Law* (Round Hall, 2017) chs 19–26.

Reg 26	Cooperation with Member State authorities
Reg 27	Cessation of entitlements
Reg 28	Marriages of convenience
Reg 29	Civil partnerships of convenience
Reg 30	Offences

B. Scope of Application of the Citizens Directive

[24–04] Before considering the specific rights provided for in the Citizens Directive, it is worth first considering the personal scope of application of such rights. Article 2 of the Directive sets out a number of definitions, including in Art 2(2) the definition of a "family member" of a Union citizen. Article 3(1) then details the beneficiaries of the Directive and provides that it shall apply to Union citizens who move to or reside in a Member State other than that of which they are a national,[6] and to their family members as defined in Art 2(2) who accompany or join them. It can be seen, therefore, that a degree of cross-border movement is required in order for the Directive to be engaged. In addition, Art 3(2) requires Member States, in accordance with their national law, to facilitate entry and residence for: (a) any other family members, irrespective of their nationality, not falling under the particular definition of a family member in Art 2(2) who, in the country from which they have come, are dependants or members of the household of the Union citizen having the primary right of residence, or where serious health grounds strictly require the personal care of the family member by the Union citizen; and (b) the partner with whom the Union citizen has a durable relationship, duly attested.

[24–05] For the purposes of the Citizens Directive, the family members of a Union citizen are defined in Art 2(2) as comprising:

(a) a spouse;
(b) a registered partner with whom the citizen has contracted a registered partnership, on the basis of the legislation of a Member State, if the legislation of the host Member

---

6 The application of the Citizens Directive to dual nationals was addressed in Case C-165/16 *Lounes v Secretary of State for the Home Department* EU:C:2017:862, 14 November 2017. See Vincent Réveillère, "Family Rights for Naturalized EU Citizens: *Lounes*" (2018) 55 *Common Market Law Review* 1855. There, Ms Ormazabal moved from Spain to the UK to live and work. It was accepted that, as a Spanish national in the UK, she was a beneficiary of the Citizens Directive. She subsequently became a dual British-Spanish national. The Court, sitting as a Grand Chamber, noted that: "since, under a principle of international law, a Member State cannot refuse its own nationals the right to enter its territory and remain there and since those nationals thus enjoy an unconditional right of residence there, Directive 2004/38 is not intended to govern the residence of a Union citizen in the Member State of which he is a national" (para 37). It was held that Ms Ormazabal's acquisition of British citizenship gave rise to a change in the legal rules applicable to her, under both UK law and the Directive. Since then, she had been living in one of the Member States of which she was a national and consequently enjoyed an unconditional right of residence there. Upon acquiring British citizenship, she ceased to fall within the definition of a "beneficiary" within the meaning of Art 3(1) of the Directive, and the Directive no longer governed her residence in the UK, as that residence was inherently unconditional. Accordingly, the Directive stopped applying to her situation upon her becoming a British citizen. Nevertheless, the Court went on to hold that, by virtue of her Union citizenship, Ms Ormazabal was entitled to have the rules set out in the Directive (in this case, relating to family reunification) applied to her by way of analogy. See ch 25, paras [25–75] to [25–76].

State treats registered partnerships as equivalent to marriage and in accordance with the conditions laid down in the relevant legislation of the host Member State;

(c) direct descendants (ie children, grandchildren) who are under 21 or are dependants, of either the citizen or his or her spouse or registered partner;

(d) direct relatives in the ascending line (ie parents, grandparents) of either the citizen or his or her spouse or registered partner.

[24–06] Four aspects of Arts 2 and 3 require further attention. First, certain aspects of the term "spouse" and the relationships that that can encompass. Secondly, the nature of the "dependency" required in respect of direct descendants who are over the age of 21. Thirdly, it will be seen that the concept in Art 3(1) of a family member who wishes to "accompany or join" a Union citizen in a host Member State – and in particular whether that implies that the family member must have previously resided lawfully within an EU Member State – is one area where the Court of Justice has taken the unusual step of departing from its earlier case law. Finally, the parameters of the obligation on a Member State to facilitate the residence of other dependant family members, members of the household, or a partner in a "durable relationship, duly attested" requires further consideration.

(i) Spouses

[24–07] The recent case of *Coman* has clarified that a same-sex spouse, lawfully married in a Member State in accordance with the law of that state, is to be regarded in a host Member State as a spouse within the meaning of Art 2(2) for the purposes of the Directive.[7] This is the case even where same-sex marriage is not otherwise provided for or recognised in the law of the host Member State. Where a spousal relationship experiences difficulty, the fact that a married couple subsequently separate, live apart and even intend to divorce does not alter their status as spouses until a divorce has been finalised.[8] The Directive provides in Art 35 that Member States may adopt necessary and proportionate measures to guard against the abuse of rights or fraud, such as marriages of convenience, including the termination of rights conferred. In a detailed guidance note on the Directive, the Commission follows the recitals in defining a marriage of convenience as a marriage entered into for the sole purpose of enjoying the right of free movement and residence under the Directive that someone would not otherwise have.[9] A marriage cannot be considered as a marriage of convenience simply because it brings an immigration advantage, or indeed any other advantage, and the quality of the relationship is immaterial. The guidance note lists indicative criteria both for and against the presence of a marriage of convenience that might be used as "possible triggers for investigation, without any automatic inferences from results or subsequent investigations. Member States may not rely on one sole attribute; due attention has to be given to all the circumstances of the individual case".[10]

[24–08] By an amendment to s 58 of the Civil Registration Act 2004, s 18 of the Civil

---

[7] Case C-673/16 *Coman* EU:C:2018:385, 5 June 2018. In *Coman*, the Citizens Directive did not apply as the EU citizen was a Romanian national, returning to Romania. As a result, the Court applied Art 21 TFEU by analogy with the Directive. See ch 25, para [25–78].

[8] Case 267/83 *Diatta* [1985] ECR 567.

[9] COM (2009) 313, Communication from the Commission to the European Parliament and the Council on guidance for better transposition and application of Directive 2004/38/EC, 2 July 2009, 15.

[10] *ibid*, 16–17.

Registration (Amendment) Act 2014 provides new powers for registrars with respect to marriages of convenience. The Act adopts the definition used by the Commission, as well as employing an indicative list of ten criteria. A similar approach is taken, in the immigration context, by regulation 28 of the European Communities (Free Movement of Persons) Regulations 2015.[11] There it is provided that, in making a determination of any matter relevant to the Regulations, the Minister for Justice and Equality may disregard a particular marriage as a factor bearing on that determination where the Minister deems or determines that marriage to be a marriage of convenience. Where the Minister has reasonable grounds for considering that the marriage is a marriage of convenience, he or she may send a notice to the parties to the marriage requiring the persons concerned to provide, within a specified time, such information as is reasonably necessary to satisfy the Minister that the marriage is not a marriage of convenience.

(ii) Dependency

[24–09] The Court of Justice has been called upon to clarify the meaning of dependency in a number of cases, and has confirmed that dependency ought to be assessed as a factual situation. In other words, regardless of the reasons why support is given or whether the family member could, as an alternative, take up employment as a means of supporting himself or herself, is that person, as a matter of fact, dependent on support received from the Union citizen?

[24–10] An example of this is the case of *Reyes*, which concerned a citizen of the Philippines who sought to join her mother in Sweden on the basis of being a dependent daughter.[12] As Ms Reyes' mother had moved to Europe while she was young, she had been raised by her grandmother, with her mother sending money on a monthly basis. In the Philippines, Ms Reyes qualified as a nursing assistant, as part of the training for which she completed some work experience. She did not, however, take up employment, but assisted in looking after her sister's children. Nor did she apply for any social security allowances. Sweden argued that Ms Reyes had failed to prove dependency on her mother in that she: (i) had failed to show that the money which was transferred by her mother had been used to supply basic needs in the form of board and lodging and access to healthcare in the Philippines; (ii) had failed to show how the Philippines social insurance and security system could cover a citizen in her situation; (iii) in contrast, she had shown that she held qualifications and had carried out work experience; and (iv) she had shown that she had, in fact, been economically dependent on her grandmother throughout her childhood and adolescence.

[24–11] The Court was unwilling to accept these arguments, holding that Sweden could not make the concept of dependency conditional on a requirement that Ms Reyes had tried unsuccessfully to obtain employment or to obtain subsistence support in the Philippines. Furthermore, the fact that, due to personal circumstances such as age, education and health, a family member is deemed to be well placed to obtain employment and, indeed, intends to start work in the Member State, did not affect the interpretation of the dependency requirement. In so finding, the Court reasoned as follows:

---

11 SI No 548 of 2015. See John Stanley, *Immigration and Citizenship Law* (Round Hall, 2017) 823–827.

12 Case C-423/12 *Reyes* ECLI:EU:C:2014:16, 16 January 2014.

[D]ependent status is the result of a factual situation characterised by the fact that material support for that family member is provided by the Union citizen who has exercised his right of free movement or by his spouse.

In order to determine the existence of such dependence, the host Member State must assess whether, having regard to his financial and social conditions, the direct descendant, who is 21 years old or older, of a Union citizen, is not in a position to support himself. The need for material support must exist in the State of origin of that descendant or the State whence he came at the time when he applies to join that citizen.

However, there is no need to determine the reasons for that dependence or therefore for the recourse to that support. That interpretation is dictated in particular by the principle according to which the provisions, such as Directive 2004/38, establishing the free movement of Union citizens, which constitute one of the foundations of the European Union, must be construed broadly.

The fact that … a Union citizen regularly, for a significant period, pays a sum of money to that descendant, necessary in order for him to support himself in the State of origin, is such as to show that the descendant is in a real situation of dependence vis-à-vis that citizen.

In those circumstances, that descendant cannot be required, in addition, to establish that he has tried without success to find work or obtain subsistence support from the authorities of his country of origin and/or otherwise tried to support himself.

The requirement for such additional evidence, which is not easy to provide in practice, … is likely to make it excessively difficult for that descendant to obtain the right of residence in the host Member State, while the facts … already show that a real dependence exists. Accordingly, that requirement is likely to deprive Articles 2(2)(c) and 7 of Directive 2004/38 of their proper effect.

Furthermore, it is not excluded that that requirement obliges that descendant to take more complicated steps, such as trying to obtain various certificates stating that he has not found any work or obtained any social allowance, than that of obtaining a document of the competent authority of the State of origin or the State from which the applicant came attesting to the existence of a situation of dependence. The Court has already held that such a document cannot constitute a condition for the issue of a residence permit.

…. it must be noted that the situation of dependence must exist, in the country from which the family member concerned comes, at the time when he applies to join the Union citizen on whom he is dependent.

It follows that … any prospects of obtaining work in the host Member State which would enable, if necessary, a direct descendant, who is 21 years old or older, of a Union citizen no longer to be dependent on that citizen once he has the right of residence are not such as to affect the interpretation of the condition of being a "dependant" referred to in Article 2(2)(c) of Directive 2004/38.

Furthermore, … the opposite solution would, in practice, prohibit that descendant from looking for employment in the host Member State and would accordingly infringe Article 23 of that directive, which expressly authorises such a descendant, if he has the right of residence, to take up employment or self-employment.[13]

[13] *ibid*, paras 20–32.

(iii) "Accompany or Join" – Whether Prior Lawful Residence is Required

[24–12] An element of Art 3(1) requiring elaboration is the qualifier that family members, within the meaning of the definition, must either "accompany or join" the Union citizen. It is clearly the case that if an EU citizen, intending to move from one Member State to another, is unable to be joined by a TCN family member with whom they live in the first Member State, that will serve as a significant obstacle to, or have a dissuasive effect on, the exercise of the right of free movement. Can the same be said, however, as regards a family member who did not reside within the EU when the move takes place, or who does not have a right to reside in the Member State from which the Union citizen intends to move?

[24–13] In discussing the concept of "reverse discrimination" in the previous chapter, it was seen that the principle in *Surinder Singh* is of particular benefit to TCN family members in what might otherwise be regarded as an internal situation.[14] This arises, for example, where a Union citizen moves to another Member State where he or she subsequently marries a TCN. The *Surinder Singh* principle dictates that, in the event of the Union citizen returning to their own state of nationality, he or she is to be regarded as exercising an EU law right of free movement, such that their spouse is entitled to rely on the right of family unification in order to join or accompany them. It has been confirmed, in the recent case of *Banger*, that the principle applies not only to the TCN family members as defined in Art 2(2) of the Citizens Directive, but also to other beneficiaries as provided for in Art 3(2) of the Directive, such as a partner with whom the Union citizen has a durable relationship, duly attested.[15]

[24–14] In the 2003 case of *Akrich* – concerning the Free Movement of Workers Regulation – Mr Akrich was a Moroccan national who had been deported from the UK and subsequently returned unlawfully and married a British national. The couple had expressly made known that their brief stay in Ireland was for the purpose of relying on the *Surinder Singh* principle in order to obtain a right to reside in the UK.[16] The Court of Justice once again confirmed that the intentions of the Union citizen in moving were not relevant. The Court did, however, impose a critically important limitation on the rights of family members, holding that in order to rely on (what is now) Art 3 of the Citizens Directive, it was necessary that the TCN must have already been lawfully resident in a Member State when he or she moves to another Member State to which the Union citizen is migrating or has migrated.[17] This is known as a "prior lawful residence" requirement, and the Court explained the rationale behind it as follows:

> [W]here a citizen of the Union, established in a Member State and married to a national of a non-Member State without the right to remain in that Member State, moves to another Member State in order to work there as an employed person, the fact that that person's spouse has no right … to install himself with that person in the other Member State cannot constitute less favourable treatment than that which they enjoyed before the citizen made use of the opportunities afforded by the Treaty as regards movement of persons. Accordingly, the absence of such a right is not such as to deter the citizen of the Union from exercising the rights in regard to freedom of movement conferred by Article [45 TFEU].[18]

---

[14] Case C-370/90 *Surinder Singh* [1992] ECR I-4265.
[15] Case C-89/17 *Secretary of State for the Home Department v Banger* EU:C:2018:570, 12 July 2018.
[16] Case C-109/01 *Akrich* [2003] ECR I-9607.
[17] *ibid*, 9686.
[18] *ibid*, 9687.

[24–15] In his opinion, Advocate General Geelhoed drew a distinction between two areas of competence that had an important influence on his overall approach to the case – Member State competence concerning immigration from a third country and EU competence regarding the free movement of persons within the EU. The Advocate General observed that, from the point of view of the free movement of persons, it was logical for the spouse of an EU citizen to be exempt from national competence in immigration matters. Nevertheless,

> this logic applies primarily to non-Member country spouses who have already been admitted to the territory of a Member State and are thus legally within the territory of the European Union. It is less self-evident also to grant a right of residence under [EU] law to spouses from non-Member States who have not yet been so admitted or who, as in the case of Mr Akrich, are within the territory of the European Union without leave to remain. The spouse's right to remain is quite a different matter from admission to the territory of the European Union. That is well illustrated by the present case in which entry to the European Union was earlier refused by [the UK] on the basis of a competence pertaining to that Member State.
>
> Thus, in the present case [EU] law is being invoked in a matter essentially involving national competence in the area of immigration. For the nub of this case is not that a [Union] worker, exercising a freedom conferred on her by the [TFEU], wishes to be accompanied by her spouse but that a national of a non-Member State wishes to secure entry to a Member State, in this case the United Kingdom, on the basis of rights conferred on him by [EU] law as the spouse of an [EU] national.[19]

[24–16] The judgment in *Akrich* came before the introduction of the Citizens Directive in 2004, which Member States were required to transpose into national law by April 2006. In the Regulations introduced to give effect to the Directive, Ireland was among eleven Member States to include a prior lawful residence requirement.[20] The case of *Eind*, however, in which the Court gave judgment in 2007, soon cast doubt on the division of competence rationale that had underscored the approach in *Akrich.*

[24–17] Mr Eind was a Dutch national who went to the UK and found employment, on foot of which he successfully applied to have his daughter join him from Surinam. The following year, he returned to the Netherlands with his daughter. Before the Court of Justice, the Netherlands argued that Mr Eind could not have been deterred from moving to the UK by the fact that it would be impossible for his daughter to reside with him once he returned, given that at the time of the initial move his daughter did not have any right to reside in the Netherlands. The Court firmly rejected this argument, reasoning that the right of an EU worker, such as Mr Eind, to return to the Member State of which he is a national cannot be considered to be a purely internal matter, since free movement could be deterred "simply from the prospect … of not being able, on returning to his Member State of origin, to continue living together with close relatives, a way of life which may have come into being in the host Member State as a result of marriage or family reunification".[21] Thus, EU law had a role to play in determining whether a TCN, Mr Eind's Surinamese daughter, had a right to reside in the Netherlands, following on

---

19 *ibid*, 9611–9612.

20 European Communities (Free Movement of Persons) (No 2) Regulations 2006 (SI No 656 of 2006). See Cathryn Costello, "Metock: Free Movement and 'Normal Family Life' in the Union" (2009) 46 *Common Market Law Review* 587, 595.

21 Case C-291/05 *Eind* [2007] ECR I-10719, 10775.

from the fact that her right to reside in the UK was to be understood as having derived not from the UK's grant of a residence permit to her, but rather from EU law. Similarly, in returning to the Netherlands as an EU worker, Mr Eind's situation fell within the scope of EU law, giving his daughter a right to reside there with him.

[24–18] Cathryn Costello points out that it emerges clearly from *Eind* that prior lawful residence in the EU citizen's state of nationality, in this case the Netherlands, is not a requirement that that state may impose. Furthermore, the language and tone of the Court's reasoning "suggest that a general lawful residence pre-condition would also be inappropriate. This conclusion is supported by the fact that the ECJ did not examine the quality of [Ms Eind's] prior residence in the UK, but rather insisted that she derived a right of residence in the Netherlands from [EU] law".[22]

[24–19] Doubt as to the lawfulness of the prior lawful residence requirement imposed by the Irish implementing regulations led to the High Court making a preliminary reference in *Metock*, a case involving four TCNs who, whilst living in Ireland as (ultimately unsuccessful) asylum applicants, met and married Union citizens also residing here.[23] The reason for the refusal by the Minister for Justice to issue a residence permit was that the applicants had not submitted evidence showing lawful residence in another EU Member State prior to arrival in Ireland, as required by the regulations.

[24–20] Basing its interpretation of the Citizens Directive on the approach in *Akrich*, Ireland argued before the Court of Justice that the division of competences between the Union and the Member States was such that the Member States had competence in respect of the admission into their territory of TCNs coming from outside the EU, while the Union had competence to regulate the movement of EU citizens and their family member within the EU. It contested that "in a context typified by strong pressure of migration" it was necessary to control immigration at the external borders of the EU, which presupposed an individual examination of all the circumstances surrounding a first entry into EU territory.[24] Supported by 10 intervening Member States, Ireland argued that to interpret the Directive as prohibiting host Member States from requiring prior lawful residence within the EU would undermine their ability to control immigration at their external frontiers, with "serious consequences for the Member States by bringing about a great increase in the number of persons able to benefit from a right of residence in the [Union]".[25]

[24–21] The Court began its analysis by noting that there was no express provision of the Citizens Directive that required prior lawful residence within the EU. Nor did the Directive's definition of a family member distinguish according to whether or not the individual had already resided lawfully in another Member State. Whilst acknowledging that its judgment in *Akrich* had required prior lawful residence in the context of the Free Movement of Workers Regulation, the Court made the unusual step of declaring that "that conclusion must be reconsidered".[26] The Court then turned to the question of

---

[22] Cathryn Costello, "Metock: Free Movement and 'Normal Family Life' in the Union" (2009) 46 *Common Market Law Review* 587, 594.

[23] *Metock v Minster for Justice, Equality and Law Reform* [2008] IEHC 77, Finlay Geoghegan J, 14 March 2008.

[24] Case C-127/08 *Metock* [2008] ECR I-6241, para 71.

[25] *ibid*, para 72.

[26] *ibid*, para 58.

competence and rejected the argument put forward by several Member States, including Ireland, as follows:

> [I]f Union citizens were not allowed to lead a normal family life in the host Member State, the exercise of the freedoms they are guaranteed by the Treaty would be seriously obstructed.
>
> Consequently, within the competence conferred on it by ... the Treaty, the [Union] legislature can regulate the conditions of entry and residence of the family members of a Union citizen in the territory of the Member States, where the fact that it is impossible for the Union citizen to be accompanied or joined by his family in the host Member State would be such as to interfere with his freedom of movement by discouraging him from exercising his rights of entry into and residence in that Member State.
>
> The refusal of the host Member State to grant rights of entry and residence to the family members of a Union citizen is such as to discourage that citizen from moving to or residing in that Member State, even if his family members are not already lawfully resident in the territory of another Member State.
>
> It follows that the [Union] legislature has competence to regulate, as it did by Directive 2004/38, the entry and residence of nationals of non-member countries who are family members of a Union citizen in the Member State in which that citizen has exercised his right of freedom of movement, including where the family members were not already lawfully resident in another Member State.
>
> ... Indeed, to allow the Member States exclusive competence to grant or refuse entry into and residence in their territory to nationals of non-member countries who are family members of Union citizens and have not already resided lawfully in another Member State would have the effect that the freedom of movement of Union citizens in a Member State whose nationality they do not possess would vary from one Member State to another, according to the provisions of national law concerning immigration, with some Member States permitting entry and residence of family members of a Union citizen and other Member States refusing them.
>
> That would not be compatible with the objective ... of an internal market characterised by the abolition, as between Member States, of obstacles to the free movement of persons. Establishing an internal market implies that the conditions of entry and residence of a Union citizen in a Member State whose nationality he does not possess are the same in all the Member States. Freedom of movement for Union citizens must therefore be interpreted as the right to leave any Member State, in particular the Member State whose nationality the Union citizen possesses, in order to become established under the same conditions in any Member State other than the Member State whose nationality the Union citizen possesses.[27]

[24–22] In analysing the passage above, Cathryn Costello has highlighted the manner in which the Court of Justice roughly equated a "serious obstruction" to the exercise of the right of free movement with a "discouragement" to movement, thereby endorsing a broad notion of barriers to free movement. Given that this was then used by the Court to identify EU competence with respect to the first entry into the EU of TCNs, Costello argues that this "potentially subjects a broad range of national measures not only to its judicial review, but also to legislative harmonisation".[28] The judgment, she suggests,

[27] *ibid*, paras 62–68.

[28] Cathryn Costello, "Metock: Free Movement and 'Normal Family Life' in the Union" (2009) 46 *Common Market Law Review* 587, 602.

Turns on the ECJ's characterisation of host States' failure to accommodate the TCN family members of migrant EU citizens as discouraging free movement, as a non-discriminatory barrier to free movement. In this respect, *Metock* confirms the trend in the case law, confirming that non-discriminatory barriers to the movement of EU citizens *per se* also requires justification, as is the case with the free movement of worker and service providers.[29]

[24–23] It is fair to say that the judgment in *Metock* was unpopular with a number of Member States. It led to political discussions within the Justice and Home Affairs Council, the conclusions to which made express reference to the case and noted the concern that the Citizens Directive "should be fully and correctly implemented in order to improve the prevention and combating of misuses and abuses, while adhering to the principle of proportionality".[30] While the Commission resisted calls by some for the Citizens Directive to be amended, it did respond to the Council's request to issue guidance on "better transposition and application of the Directive". In Ireland, the implementing regulations were amended in order to give effect to the judgment.[31] Academic commentary, however, was more welcoming, as seen in the following assessment by Samantha Currie:

> [W]hen the judgment is considered in light of the case law pre-dating *Akrich* on TCN family members, and subsequent developments which have placed an increasing emphasis on the protection of family life as a fundamental right, *Metock* is not unreasonable. If anything, *Akrich* can be classified as an erroneous judgment due to its apparent contradiction of the case law before it. *Metock* also represents recognition of the reality of family life in the context of mobility and accepts that family relationships which arise in the aftermath of migration are worthy of some protection. In essence, the ruling enshrines a more equitable approach to TCN family members of the Union in circumstances of genuine family union.[32]

[24–24] Two further points are worth noting. First, by applying to a situation such as that in *Metock*, where a TCN and Union citizen first meet in Ireland and establish their relationship here, the judgment not only facilitates family reunification, but also family formation, "two modes of family migration that Member States often seek to differentiate".[33] Secondly, by enhancing the rights of Union citizens, the judgment potentially has the effect of exacerbating the concept of reverse discrimination, whereby Union citizens residing in a Member State other than their own may enjoy greater rights, derived from EU law, than nationals of that state residing there. Following the principle in *Surinder Singh*, returnees – EU citizens who have exercised a right to free movement and then return to their Member State of nationality – may also enjoy greater rights to family reunification/formation than their compatriots who have never resided elsewhere.

---

29 *ibid*, 604.

30 Justice and Home Affairs Council Conclusions, 27–28 November 2008, 28.

31 European Communities (Free Movement of Persons) (Amendment) Regulations 2008 (SI No 310 of 2008). See Clíodhna Murphy, "Immigration and Family Life: Reunification in Irish law" (2011) 34 *Dublin University Law Journal* 221; John Stanley, *Immigration and Citizenship Law* (Round Hall, 2017) 690–691.

32 Samantha Currie, "Accelerated Justice or a Step too Far? Residence Rights for Non-Family Members and the Court's Ruling in Metock" (2009) 34 *European Law Review* 310, 325.

33 Cathryn Costello, "Metock: Free Movement and 'Normal Family Life' in the Union" (2009) 46 *Common Market Law Review* 587, 601.

(iv) Other Beneficiaries

[24–25] In addition to the rights of family members as defined in Art 2 of the Directive, Art 3(2) provides that a host Member State shall, in accordance with its national legislation, facilitate entry and residence for: (a) any other family member, irrespective of nationality, not falling within the definition in Art 2, who in the country from which they have come, are dependants or members of the household of the Union citizen having the primary right of residence, or where serious health grounds strictly require the personal care of the family member by the Union citizen; and (b) the partner with whom the Union citizen has a durable relationship, duly attested. In respect of these two categories of person, the host Member State is required by Art 3(2) to "undertake an extensive examination of the personal circumstances and shall justify any denial of entry or residence to these people".

[24–26] It can be seen, therefore, that while the admission of family members falling within the definition in Art 2 is mandatory, the host Member State has some degree of discretion in deciding whether or not to admit family members falling within the two categories in Art 3(2). The relevant Irish regulations distinguish between family members under Art 2 and Art 3(2) by referring to them as "qualifying" family members and "permitted" family members respectively.[34] As expressed in the Directive, a permitted family member does not have a right of entry and residence, but rather they have a right to have their entry and residence "facilitated" by the host Member State. What this somewhat vague obligation entails was first clarified in the 2012 judgment of *Rahman.*[35]

[24–27] Mr Rahman moved from Bangladesh to the UK, where he married an Irish woman. Subsequently, Mr Rahman's brother, half-brother and nephew applied for permission to move to the UK as dependants of Mr and Mrs Rahman, within the meaning of Art 3(2)(a) of the Directive. A lack of clarity as to the nature of the host state's discretion led to a number of questions being referred to the Court of Justice, in response to which the Court explained that Art 3(2)

> imposes an obligation on the Member States to confer a certain advantage, compared with applications for entry and residence of other nationals of third States, on applications submitted by persons who have a relationship of particular dependence with a Union citizen.
>
> In order to meet that obligation, the Member States must … make it possible for persons envisaged in the first subparagraph of Article 3(2) to obtain a decision on their application that is founded on an extensive examination of their personal circumstances and, in the event of refusal, is justified by reasons.
>
> As is clear from recital 6 in the preamble to Directive 2004/38, it is incumbent upon the competent authority, when undertaking that examination of the applicant's personal circumstances, to take account of the various factors that may be relevant in the particular case, such as the extent of economic or physical dependence and the degree of relationship between the family member and the Union citizen whom he wishes to accompany or join.
>
> In the light both of the absence of more specific rules in Directive 2004/38 and of the use

[34] See John Stanley, *Immigration and Citizenship Law* (Round Hall, 2017) 692–694.

[35] Case C-83/11 *Secretary of State for the Home Department v Rahman* EU:C:2012:519, 5 September 2012.

of the words "in accordance with its national legislation" in Article 3(2) of the directive, each Member State has a wide discretion as regards the selection of the factors to be taken into account. None the less, the host Member State must ensure that its legislation contains criteria which are consistent with the normal meaning of the term "facilitate" and of the words relating to dependence used in Article 3(2), and which do not deprive that provision of its effectiveness.

Finally, even though … the wording used in Article 3(2) of Directive 2004/38 is not sufficiently precise to enable an applicant for entry or residence to rely directly on that provision in order to invoke criteria which should in his view be applied when assessing his application, the fact remains that such an applicant is entitled to a judicial review of whether the national legislation and its application have remained within the limits of the discretion set by that directive.

In the light of the foregoing, the answer to the first and the second question referred is that, on a proper construction of Article 3(2) of Directive 2004/38:

– the Member States are not required to grant every application for entry or residence submitted by family members of a Union citizen who do not fall under the definition in Article 2(2) of that directive, even if they show, in accordance with Article 10(2) thereof, that they are dependants of that citizen;
– it is, however, incumbent upon the Member States to ensure that their legislation contains criteria which enable those persons to obtain a decision on their application for entry and residence that is founded on an extensive examination of their personal circumstances and, in the event of refusal, is justified by reasons;
– the Member States have a wide discretion when selecting those criteria, but the criteria must be consistent with the normal meaning of the term "facilitate" and of the words relating to dependence used in Article 3(2) and must not deprive that provision of its effectiveness; and
– every applicant is entitled to a judicial review of whether the national legislation and its application satisfy those conditions.[36]

[24–28] As regards the criteria that may be imposed, the Court elaborated that in order in to satisfy themselves that the situation of dependence is genuine and stable, and has not been brought about with the sole objective of obtaining entry and residence, Member States may lay down in their legislation particular requirements as to the nature and duration of dependence. Any such requirements, however, must be consistent with the normal meaning of the words relating to the dependence referred to in Art 3(2)(a), and not be such as to deprive that provision of its effectiveness. In prescribing the procedure for such applications, Regulation 5 of the European Communities (Free Movement of Persons) Regulations 2015 sets out six criteria to be taken into account by the Minister for Justice and Equality in making his or her determination.[37]

---

36 *ibid*, paras 21–26.

37 The criteria set out in Reg 5(5) are as follows: "(a) where the applicant is a dependant of the Union citizen concerned, the extent and nature of the dependency and, in the case of financial dependency, the extent and duration of the financial support provided by the Union citizen to the applicant prior to the applicant's coming to the State, having regard, amongst other relevant matters, to living costs in the country from which the applicant has come, whether the financial dependency can be satisfied by remittances to the applicant in the country from which the applicant has come and other financial resources available to him or her; (b) where the applicant is a member of the household of the Union citizen concerned, the duration of the period during which he or she has been living within the household of the Union citizen; (c) where, on the basis of serious health grounds, the applicant strictly requires the personal care of him or her by the Union citizen concerned, the nature of the serious health grounds and the duration of the period in which they have existed; (d) where the applicant is in a durable relationship with the Union citizen concerned, the nature and duration

[24–29] The Court of Justice further clarified that, with respect to dependants, the situation of dependency must exist in the country from which the family member concerned comes, at the very least at the time when he or she applies to join the Union citizen on whom he or she is dependent. It was not necessary, however, that the dependent family member and the Union citizen both lived in that country during the period of dependency, nor that the country be the same country in which the Union citizen resided before moving to the host Member State.

[24–30] In light of the judgment in *Rahman*, Art 3(2) has been described as entailing both substantive and procedural obligations. Substantively, Member States "must ensure a margin of preference for the extended family members of EU citizens" as compared to other TCNs, as well as ensuring that national rules are consistent with the correct interpretation of the two categories of person in Art 3(2) of the Directive.[38] Procedurally, Member States must make a reasoned decision on any application which, according to the Commission guidance, ought to be provided in writing, as well as entitling the applicant to judicially review the exercise of the discretion.[39]

C. Rights under the Citizens Directive

[24–31] The substantive rights provisions of the Citizens Directive are contained in Chapters II–V, which deal respectively with: the right to enter and exit a Member State (Chapter II); the right to reside in a Member State other than one's own for an initial period of three months and, following that, for longer periods (Chapter III); a right of permanent residence in a Member State other than one's own (Chapter IV) and certain provisions common to both the right of residence and the right of permanent residence, most importantly the right to equal treatment and the right of family members to work (Chapter V). These rights will be briefly considered in this section, while the following section will examine the permissible restrictions that may be imposed on the grounds of public health, policy or security, as provided for in Chapter VI of the Directive. An important preliminary point to remember is that, as the Court of Justice has stated, since the purpose of the Directive is to strengthen the rights of citizens, its provisions cannot be interpreted in a manner that would result in a reduction in such rights as compared with the position under earlier secondary measures which the Directive amended or repealed.[40]

(i) Right to Enter and Exit

[24–32] Article 4 of the Directive provides that, without prejudice to the provisions on

---

of the relationship; (e) whether the relationship described in subparagraph (a), (b), (c) or (d), as the case may be, was brought about with the objective of obtaining permission to remain in the State or a Member State; (f) the capacity of the Union citizen concerned to continue to support the applicant in the State in the event that the applicant is to be treated as a permitted family member under these Regulations."

38 Elspeth Guild, Steve Peers and Jonathan Tomkin, *The EU Citizenship Directive* (Oxford University Press, 2014) 74.

39 See Reg 5(6)(b) of the European Communities (Free Movement of Persons) Regulations 2015 (SI No 548 of 2015).

40 Case C-127/08 *Metock* [2008] ECR I-6241, paras 59 and 82; Case C-162/09 *Lassal* [2010] ECR I-9217, para 30.

travel documents applicable to national border controls, all Union citizens with a valid identity card or passport, and their TCN family members who hold a valid passport, shall have the right to leave the territory of one Member State to travel to another. For such persons, no exit visa or equivalent formality may be imposed. In mirroring terms, Article 5 provides for the right of entry into a Member State by a Union citizen and their TCN family members, however here the prohibition on the imposition of entry visas or equivalent formalities applies only to Union citizens. In contrast, TCN family members shall only be required to have an entry visa in accordance with Regulation No 539/2001 or, where appropriate, with national law.[41] Member States are required to grant such persons every facility to obtain the necessary visas, which are to be issued free of charge as soon as possible and on the basis of an accelerated procedure.

[24–33] As Ireland does not participate in Regulation No 539/2001, national law applies in determining the need for entry visas by TCN family members. According to Regulation 4(3) of the European Communities (Free Movement of Persons) Regulations, a TCN family member who is not visa-exempt shall be in possession of a valid Irish visa as a condition of being granted permission to enter the State. The Minister for Justice and Equality shall grant the person every facility to obtain an Irish visa and, on the basis of an accelerated process, consider an application for an Irish visa as soon as possible.[42] In considering what is to be regarded as an "accelerated process" for visa applications, in *Mahmood v Minister for Justice and Equality* the High Court observed that the framers of Art 5 of the Directive "had in mind a considerably shorter time span than six months for the issuing of visas to qualifying family members of EU citizens who have or intend to exercise their free movement rights, given the urgency which informs the language used in the provision".[43] On appeal, the Court of Appeal expressed concern lest the delays in the cases before it

> go beyond that which is contemplated by Article 5(2) of the 2004 Directive. While recognising the concerns of the Minister in relation to matters such as fraud, abuse of rights and marriages of convenience, one might think that if the 2004 Directive permitted a Member State to delay processing a visa application for a period of a year or more this would have been expressly stated, whether in Article 35 or elsewhere.[44]

[24–34] Accordingly, the Court of Appeal requested a preliminary ruling from the Court of Justice as to whether a Member State is in breach of its obligation to issue a visa as quickly as possible to the family member of a Union citizen exercising free movement rights where the delays in processing such an application exceed 12 months or more. In addition, the reference asked whether delays in deciding on an application are justifiable, and so not in breach of Art 5, where they arise from: (i) the necessity to ensure by way of background checks that the application is not fraudulent or an abuse of rights, including that the marriage does not amount to a marriage of convenience; (ii) the necessity to conduct extensive background and security checks on persons coming

[41] Council Reg (EC) No 539/2001 of 15 March 2001 listing the third countries whose nationals must be in possession of visas when crossing the external borders and those whose nationals are exempt from that requirement [2001] OJ L81/1.

[42] Reg 4(3)(b) of the European Communities (Free Movement of Persons) Regulations 2015 (SI No 548 of 2015).

[43] *Mahmood v Minister for Justice and Equality* [2016] IEHC 600, unreported, High Court, Faherty J, 14 October 2016, para 137.

[44] *Mahmood v Minister for Justice and Equality* [2018] IECA 3, unreported, Court of Appeal, 26 January 2018, para 59.

from certain third countries because of specific concerns relating to security in respect of travellers coming from those third countries; or (iii) arising from a sudden and anticipated surge in applications coming from certain third countries which are thought to present real security concerns.[45] As visas were in fact refused in each of the cases at issue, the Court of Justice declined to provide a preliminary ruling, considering that the reference had become devoid of purpose. This was notwithstanding the fact that the Court of Appeal had expressed a wish to maintain its request for a ruling, "since such an answer would have implications for thousands of cases currently being processed".[46]

[24–35] Regulation 4(5) provides that where a Union citizen or TCN family member does not have a valid identity card or passport or, if needed, an Irish visa, before refusing permission to enter the State an immigration officer is required to give the person every reasonable opportunity to obtain the necessary documents, present the necessary documents to the immigration officer within a reasonable period and/or corroborate or prove by other means that he or she is entitled to enter the State. Ireland's compliance with its obligations under Art 5 of the Directive was the subject of High Court proceedings in *Raducan v Minister for Justice and Equality*. There, Hogan J found that the TCN spouse of a Union citizen had not been afforded every reasonable opportunity to obtain the necessary documents or to corroborate her status by other means.[47] Moreover, given that there was no facility for a TCN spouse to apply for a visa at the airport it could not be said that such persons were afforded "every facility to obtain the necessary visas", or that such visas were issued "as soon as possible and on the basis of an accelerated procedure", as required by the Directive. Hogan J went on to hold that Mrs Raducan's detention for three days pending her removal constituted a violation of her constitutional rights, for which she was awarded €2,500 for each day that she was detained.

[24–36] In *McCarthy*, the Court of Justice rejected an attempt by the UK to rely on Art 35 of the Citizens Directive – which permits Member States to adopt measures necessary in the case of abuse of rights such as fraud – and Protocol No 20 to the TEU and TFEU on the application of certain aspects of Art 26 TFEU to the UK and Ireland, in order to justify the imposition of a visa requirement on TCN family members resident in another EU Member State and in possession of a valid residence card issued by that Member State.[48] Arising from the fact that it remains outside of the Schengen Area, Art 1 of Protocol No 20 provides that the UK is entitled to exercise at its frontiers with other Member States such controls on persons seeking to enter the UK as it may consider necessary for the purpose: (a) of verifying the right to enter the UK of EU citizens and of their dependants exercising rights conferred by EU law and (b) of determining whether or not to grant other persons permission to enter the UK. So long as the Common Travel Area between the UK and Ireland is maintained, Ireland is entitled to exercise the same measures.[49]

---

[45] Case C-169/18 *Mahmood v Minister for Justice and Equality* EU:C:2019:5, 10 January 2019.

[46] *ibid*, para 20.

[47] [2012] 1 ILRM 419.

[48] Case C-202/13 *McCarthy v Secretary of State for the Home Department* ECLI:EU:C:2014:2450, 18 December 2014.

[49] See Gavin Barrett and Graham Butler, "Europe's 'Other' Open-Border Zone: the Common Travel Area under the Shadow of Brexit" (2018) 20 *Cambridge Yearbook of European Legal Studies* 252; Bernard Ryan, "The Common Travel Area between Britain and Ireland" (2001) 64 *Modern Law Review* 855.

[24–37] Mr McCarthy was a UK citizen who resided in Spain with his Colombian wife. Although Mr McCarthy's wife possessed a Spanish residence card issued on a five-year basis, in order to travel to the UK (where Mr McCarthy maintained a home and regularly received medical treatment), the UK required that she obtain an entry permit, valid for six months, from the British embassy in Madrid. The UK argued that such a measure was required due to a systemic risk of abuse of free movement rights or fraud. With regard to Art 35 of the Directive, the Court of Justice held that it was not open to a Member State to refuse entry to a TCN family member, in possession of a valid residence card from another Member State, in the absence of an individual examination of the particular case having been carried out by the competent national authorities. The UK was, therefore, required to recognise her residence card for the purposes of entry without a visa, unless doubt was cast on the authenticity of the card and the correctness of the data appearing on it by concrete evidence that related to her individually and justified the conclusion that there was an abuse of rights or fraud.

[24–38] As to the proper interpretation of Protocol No 20, the Court took the view that, while the Protocol authorises the UK to verify whether a person seeking entry in fact fulfils the conditions for entry, including those provided for by EU law, it does not permit it to determine the conditions for entry of persons who have a right of entry under EU law and, in particular, to impose upon them extra conditions for entry or conditions other than those provided for by EU law.

(ii) Right to Reside

[24–39] The right to reside in another Member State is broken down into three time periods: (i) an initial period of up to three months; (ii) between three months and five years; and (iii) a right of permanent residence following a continuous period of five years residing legally in the host state. So, Art 6 of the Directive provides that Union citizens shall have the right to reside in a Member State for up to three months without any conditions or formalities other than the requirement to hold a valid passport or identity card. This right is, however, subject to Art 14, which adds that EU citizens shall enjoy the right "as long as they do not become an unreasonable burden on the social assistance system of the host Member State".

[24–40] Article 7 deals with residence for more than three months and affords this right to the following categories of migrant and their family members:

(i) workers or self-employed persons;

(ii) those who have sufficient resources for themselves and their family members not to become a burden on the social assistance system of the host Member State and have comprehensive sickness cover in the host Member State;

(iii) those who are enrolled in a private or public establishment, accredited or financed by the host Member State on the basis of legislation or administrative practice, for the principal purpose of following a course of study, including vocational training and who (a) assure the relevant national authority that they have sufficient resources for themselves and their family members not to become a burden on the social assistance system and (b) have comprehensive sickness cover in the host member state.

[24–41] Furthermore, workers or self-employed persons can retain this status where they are:

(i) temporarily unable to work due to illness or an accident;
(ii) in duly recorded involuntary unemployment after having been employed for more than one year and having registered as a job-seeker with an employment office;
(iii) embarking on vocational training, although in the case of voluntary unemployment the training must be related to previous employment;
(iv) in addition, a person who is involuntarily made unemployed after working for less than a year (including where a fixed-term contract was for less than a year) and registers with an employment office may retain the status of a worker for no less than six months. The Irish Regulations confine the retention of the right to a six-month period only, unless the person enters employment within that time.[50]

[24–42] The Citizens Directive prescribes the circumstances in which a family member may retain the right to reside in the event of the death or departure of a Union citizen (Art 12) or divorce/annulment of marriage/termination of a registered partnership (Art 13). Whilst the right to reside of Union citizen family members will generally continue, in respect to TCN family members the retention of the right to reside does not arise in the case of the departure of the Union citizen, and in the case of death or divorce it is subject to certain conditions.[51] Irrespective of nationality, however, the death or departure of a Union citizen does not entail the loss of a right of residence for any child of that citizen, or for the parent with custody of the child, for so long as the child is enrolled in an educational establishment in the host Member State pending the completion of his or her studies.[52]

[24–43] Under Art 8 of the Directive, it is open to Member States to require a person wishing to reside for longer than three months to register with the relevant authorities. Failure to do so, however, cannot result in expulsion or imprisonment, but may only be subject to "proportionate and non-discriminatory sanctions".[53] While most Member States apply such a registration requirement, Ireland does not, with the result that an "application for a residence card for a family member, or an application for a permanent residence for the EU citizen, may be the first occasion on which the presence of an EU citizen in the State comes to the attention of the Irish immigration authorities".[54] Where the person is a worker, self-employed person or student, Member States are permitted to require proof of this status. Where sufficient resources so as not to become a burden on the social assistance system are required to be shown, Member States are not permitted

---

50 Reg 6(3)(d) of the European Communities (Free Movement of Persons) Regulations 2015 (SI No 548 of 2015).

51 In the case of the death of a Union citizen spouse, a TCN family member has a right to remain provided they have been residing in the host Member State as a family member for at least one year prior to the death. In the case of divorce, etc, in order for a TCN to retain the right to reside one of four conditions set out in Art 13(2) must be met: (a) prior to the initiation of the divorce, the marriage has lasted for at least three years, including one year in the host Member State; (b) by agreement or by court order, the TCN spouse has custody of a child of the Union citizen; (c) particularly difficult circumstances exist, such as domestic violence; or (d) by agreement or court order, the TCN is to have access to a minor child in the host Member State. In a preliminary reference from Ireland, Case C-218/14 *Singh v Minister for Justice and Equality*, the Court of Justice held that a TCN could not retain a right of residence in Ireland on the basis of Art 13(2)(a) where the commencement of the divorce proceedings was preceded by the departure from Ireland of the Union citizen spouse in order to return to Latvia, her state of nationality, even though the spouses had been married for more than three years, including one year in Ireland (EU:C:2015:476, 16 July 2015).

52 See ch 23, paras [23–117] to [23–120].

53 Case 48/75 *Royer* [1976] ECR 497.

54 John Stanley, *Immigration and Citizenship Law* (Round Hall, 2017) 728.

to lay down a fixed amount which they regard as comprising sufficient resources, but rather must take into account the personal situation of the individual concerned. The amount required to be at the disposal of any individual must not be higher than the threshold below which nationals of the host state become eligible for social assistance.

(iii) Right to Permanent Residence

[24–44] The Citizens Directive provides for two grounds on which a person may be entitled to reside permanently in a host Member State. The first, and more common, is found in Art 16, which provides that a Union citizen, and his or her family members, who has legally resided in the host state for a continuous period of five years shall have the right of permanent residence there. Continuity of residence is not affected by temporary absences which, in total, do not exceed six months a year, or by one absence of 12 consecutive months for an important reason such as pregnancy, serious illness, study or vocational training or a posting to another country. Once acquired, the right to permanent residence may only be lost through an absence of more than two consecutive years.

[24–45] In *Lassal*, the Court of Justice established that residence accrued prior to the date for transposition of the Citizens Directive, 30 April 2006, counted towards the five-year period required by Art 16.[55] In *Dias* it was further held that time accrued prior to the migrant's state of nationality acceding to the EU could also be taken into account (in that case, Polish migrants living in Germany prior to Poland's accession in 2004).[56] The question of interpretation at issue in *Lassal* was the subject of proceedings in *Ogieriakhi v Minister for Justice and Equality*. There, the High Court held that the State's incorrect interpretation of Art 16, in excluding residence in Ireland by Mr Ogieriakhi's spouse prior to 30 April 2006, was a serious breach of EU law such as to give rise to *Francovich* damages.[57] As Mr Ogieriakhi was let go from his employment with An Post as a result of the residence decision, the High Court awarded damages for the loss he incurred. On appeal, however, the Court of Appeal held that the State's "inadvertent error" in transposing the Directive was not such as to give rise to a *Francovich* claim.[58] The Supreme Court upheld this decision, although it adopted somewhat different reasoning.[59]

[24–46] Article 17 provides for three scenarios whereby a right to permanent residence may arise before a five-year period of residence is reached. First, a person who has resided continuously for more than three years and has worked for at least the preceding 12 months, may reside permanently upon reaching pensionable age (in the case of Ireland, as defined in the Social Welfare Acts) or upon taking early retirement. Secondly, a person who has resided continuously for more than two years may reside permanently in the event that he or she ceases to be employed, or self-employed, as a result of a permanent incapacity. If the incapacity is due to an accident at work or occupational illness entitling him or her to a pension or other benefit payable in whole

55 Case C-162/09 *Lassal* [2010] ECR I-9217.

56 Case C-325/09 *Dias* [2011] ECR I-6387.

57 [2015] 1 ILRM 344. See also Case C-244/13 *Ogieriakhi v Minister for Justice and Equality* EU:C:2014:2068, 10 July 2014.

58 [2016] 1 ILRM 504.

59 *Ogieriakhi v Minister for Justice and Equality* [2017] 2 ILRM 340. See ch 14, paras [14–67] to [14–69].

or part by the state, no continuous residence requirement is imposed. Thirdly, after three years of continuous residence and employment in the host Member State, if a person becomes a frontier worker or self-employed person in another Member State, but retains a residence in the first Member State to which they return each day, or at least once a week, a right of permanent residence accrues (the Irish Regulations refer merely to returning at least once a week).[60]

(iv) Right to Equal Treatment

[24–47] In addition to providing for the right to reside itself, through the seemingly innocuous Art 24 the Citizens Directive also confers the critically important right to equal treatment on EU citizens residing on the basis of the Directive in another Member State, as well as on their TCN family members who have a right of residence. A number of caveats apply, however. First, the right to equal treatment is stated to be confined to matters "within the scope of the Treaty". Secondly, the right is made "[s]ubject to such specific provisions as are expressly provided for in the Treaty and secondary law", with the result that the right to equal treatment can be qualified on the grounds of public policy, public security or public health, by the public-sector employment exemption, or by criteria found in secondary law such as the requirement to have sufficient resources not to become a burden on the social assistance system of the host state and to have medial insurance. Thirdly, Art 24 provides that a host Member State is not obliged to confer an entitlement to social assistance during the first three months of residence or, in respect of job-seekers, throughout the period in which a job-seeker can provide evidence that he or she is seeking employment and has a genuine chance of being engaged. Fourthly, before a person acquires a right to permanent residence, a host Member State is not obliged to grant him or her maintenance aid for studies, including vocational training, consisting in student grants or student loans unless the person is a worker, self-employed, has retained such status, or is a family member of such a person.

[24–48] It can be seen that the right to equal treatment guaranteed by Art 24 of the Directive overlaps to a significant extent with both the right of equal treatment of workers, provided for in the Free Movement of Workers Regulation, as well as the Treaty guarantee of non-discrimination on the grounds of nationality in Article 18 TFEU. The right to equal treatment is also closely related to Union citizenship more generally, as conferred by Art 20 TFEU. As will be seen in the following chapter, the exceptions to the right to equal treatment contained in Art 24 as regards access to social assistance and maintenance aids sit uneasily with a fully comprehensive concept of Union citizenship. While arguments have been made that this provision of the Citizens Directive ought to be interpreted in light of the fundamental status of Union citizenship, in more recent cases the Court of Justice has emphasised that Art 21 TFEU explicitly subjects the rights of Union citizens to move and reside freely within the territory of the Member States "to the limitations and conditions laid down in the Treaties and *by the measures adopted to give them effect*". This includes, therefore, the various limitations set out in the Citizens Directive, including Art 24.

[60] Reg 13(3) of the European Communities (Free Movement of Persons) Regulations 2015 (SI No 548 of 2015).

D. Grounds for Exclusion

[24–49] Article 45(3) TFEU allows for limitations to be placed on the free movement of workers on the grounds of public policy, public security or public health. Articles 52 and 62 provide for the same grounds in respect of the freedom of establishment and the provision of, or access to, services. Whereas indirect discrimination and non-discriminatory measures that impede or discourage free movement may be justified, not only by these three grounds, but also by other objective reasons or "overriding requirements of the public interest", *direct* discrimination can only be defended by reference to the three grounds alone. The grounds apply to all measures of exclusion regardless of the particular form it takes, eg refusal of entry or prevention of exit, the issue or renewal of a residence card, or expulsion.[61] The focus here is on restrictions on the right to move and reside as provided for in the Citizens Directive, and efforts to justify such restrictions on the ground of public policy, public security or public health.

[24–50] A 1964 Directive provided guidance as to how such limitations could be applied in response to conduct by individuals, as did a Commission Communication on the matter issued in 1999.[62] More comprehensive treatment of this issue is now set out in Chapter VI of the Citizens Directive (Arts 27–33), which are implemented in Regulations 18 and 19 of the Irish regulations. These articles codify much of the case law that had developed in interpreting the 1964 Directive. Account has also clearly been taken of the approach of the European Court of Human Rights in cases such as *Boultif v Switzerland*[63] and *Uner v The Netherlands*,[64] as reflected in recitals 23–27 of the Citizens Directive:

> Expulsion of Union citizens and their family members on grounds of public policy or public security is a measure that can seriously harm persons who, having availed themselves of the rights and freedoms conferred on them by the Treaty, have become genuinely integrated into the host Member State. The scope for such measures should therefore be limited in accordance with the principle of proportionality to take account of the degree of integration of the persons concerned, the length of their residence in the host Member State, their age, state of health, family and economic situation and the links with their country of origin.
>
> Accordingly, the greater the degree of integration of Union citizens and their family members in the host Member State, the greater the degree of protection against expulsion should be. Only in exceptional circumstances, where there are imperative grounds of public security, should an expulsion measure be taken against Union citizens who have resided for many years in the territory of the host Member State, in particular when they were born and have resided there throughout their life. In addition, such exceptional circumstances should also apply to an expulsion measure taken against minors, in order to protect their links with their family, in accordance with the United Nations Convention on the Rights of the Child, of 20 November 1989.

---

61 Elspeth Guild, Steve Peers and Jonathan Tomkin, *The EU Citizenship Directive* (Oxford University Press, 2014) 246.

62 Council Directive 64/221/EEC of 25 February 1964 on the coordination of special measures concerning the movement and residence of foreign nationals, which are justified on grounds of public policy, public security or public health, *Official Journal* 1963–1964, Special Edition Series I, 117; Commission Communication to the Council and the European Parliament on the Special Measures concerning the movement and residence of citizens of the Union which are justified on the grounds of public policy, public security, or public health: COM (99) 372.

63 [2001] ECHR 497; (2000) 22 EHRR 50.

64 [2006] ECHR 873; (2007) 45 EHRR 14.

Procedural safeguards should also be specified in detail in order to ensure a high level of protection of the rights of Union citizens and their family members in the event of their being denied leave to enter or reside in another Member State, as well as to uphold the principle that any action taken by the authorities must be properly justified.

In all events, judicial redress procedures should be available to Union citizens and their family members who have been refused leave to enter or reside in another Member State.

In line with the case-law of the Court of Justice prohibiting Member States from issuing orders excluding for life persons covered by this Directive from their territory, the right of Union citizens and their family members who have been excluded from the territory of a Member State to submit a fresh application after a reasonable period, and in any event after a three year period from enforcement of the final exclusion order, should be confirmed.

[24–51] Article 27 of the Citizens Directive allows Member States to restrict the freedom of movement and residence of Union citizens and their family members on grounds of public policy, public security or public health, provided that these grounds are not invoked to serve economic ends. There is a difference in treatment as between the grounds of public policy and public security, which are dealt with in Arts 27 and 28, and the ground of public health, which is dealt with in Art 29. Whereas an express proportionality requirement is built in to Art 27, proportionality is not referred to in Art 29, which instead provides a very limited basis on which public health may be invoked as a ground for expulsion:

(1) The only diseases justifying measures restricting freedom of movement shall be the diseases with epidemic potential as defined by the relevant instruments of the World Health Organisation and other infectious diseases or contagious parasitic diseases if they are the subject of protection provisions applying to nationals of the host Member State.

(2) Diseases occurring after a three-month period from the date of arrival shall not constitute grounds for expulsion from the territory.

(3) Where there are serious indications that it is necessary, Member States may, within three months of the date of arrival, require persons entitled to the right of residence to undergo, free of charge, a medical examination to certify that they are not suffering from any of the conditions referred to in paragraph 1. Such medical examinations may not be required as a matter of routine.

[24–52] It can be seen from Art 29 that the public health ground may only be used to restrict an EU citizen's initial entry into a Member State, or within the three-month residence period following entry. Thereafter, the public health ground cannot be invoked as a ground for exclusion.

[24–53] Reflecting the case law of the Court of Justice, Art 27 of the Citizens Directive establishes the following five principles which are to be applied by a Member State whenever it is considering applying the grounds of public policy or public security in order to restrict the right of free movement:

(i) measures taken on grounds of public policy or public security shall comply with the principle of proportionality;
(ii) such measures shall be based exclusively on the personal conduct of the individual concerned;
(iii) previous criminal convictions shall not in themselves constitute grounds for taking such measures;

(iv) the personal conduct of the individual concerned must represent a genuine, present and sufficiently serious threat affecting one of the fundamental interests of society; and
(v) justifications that are isolated from the particulars of the case or that rely on considerations of general prevention shall not be accepted.

[24–54] In addition, Art 28 requires that, before making a decision to expel a person, a host Member State must take into account considerations such as his or her: (i) length of time residing in the territory; (ii) age; (iii) state of health; (iv) family and economic situation; (v) social and cultural integration into the host Member State; and (vi) the extent of links with the country of origin.

[24–55] In contrast to the three-month period in which public health may be invoked as a ground for exclusion, the grounds of public security and public policy may be invoked for a much longer period, but according to a tapered approach that in some ways mirrors the staggered accrual of residence rights. Should it consider it essential, and not as a matter of routine, when a host Member State is issuing a registration certificate or, in the absence of a registration system, within the first three months from arrival, or when issuing a residence card, it may request another Member State to provide information on any police record a person may have, with a reply to be issued within two months. Once a person has become entitled to permanent residence – usually after five years continuous residence – Art 28 permits public order or public safety to be relied upon only if there are "serious" grounds for doing so. In respect of Union citizens (but not TCN family members) that have resided in a host Member State for the previous 10 years, "imperative grounds of public security" are necessary in order to justify their expulsion. Finally, unless it happens to be in the child's best interests, an expulsion decision may not be taken against a Union citizen minor unless there are imperative grounds of public security for doing so.

[24–56] The proper interpretation of "serious grounds" and "imperative ground of public security" was considered by the Court of Justice in *Tsakouridis*.[65] There, German authorities had considered a conviction for dealing in drugs as part of an organised gang, together with a number of other convictions, to be an imperative ground of public security. As regards the definition of "public security", the Court outlined that this covers both internal and external security and can include a "threat to the functioning of the institutions and essential public services and the survival of the population, as well as the risk of a serious disturbance to foreign relations or to peaceful coexistence of nations, or a risk to military interests".[66] The Court took the view that the fight against crime in connection with dealing in drugs as part of an organised gang could, in principle, fall within the meaning of "public security", given that: (i) "drug addiction represents a serious evil for the individual and is fraught with social and economic danger to mankind"; (ii) "[d]ealing in narcotics as part of an organised group is a diffuse form of crime with impressive economic and operational resources and frequently with transnational connections"; and (iii) "trafficking in narcotics as part of an organised group could reach a level of intensity that might directly threaten the calm and physical security of the population as a whole or a large part of it".[67]

[65] Case C-145/09 *Tsakouridis* [2010] ECR I-11979.
[66] *ibid*, para 44.
[67] *ibid*, paras 46–47.

[24–57] The Court confirmed that the concept of "imperative grounds of public security" was considerably stricter than "serious grounds" within the meaning of Art 28(2), and was intended to be confined to "exceptional circumstances" which presupposed "not only the existence of a threat to public security, but also that such threat is of a particularly high degree of seriousness".[68]

[24–58] In terms of categorising the severity of conduct that is considered to be contrary to public policy or public security, in one of the earliest cases in this area, *Van Duyn v Home Office*, the Court of Justice did not consider it fatal to the UK's argument that its own citizens were not prohibited from engaging in the same conduct as that which had led to Ms Van Duyn being excluded from the UK.[69] Ms Van Duyn had wished to take up employment in the UK with the Church of Scientology, of which the UK disapproved but did not prohibit by law. The Court concluded that where a Member State had taken administrative measures to counteract what it considered to be a socially harmful activity, it was not required, in order to be able to rely on the public policy ground, to make such activity unlawful if it did not consider this to be appropriate in the circumstances. The Court sought to strike a balance, noting on the one hand that the public policy exception must be interpreted strictly, while at the same time recognising that the "particular circumstances justifying recourse to the concept of public policy may vary from one country to another and from one period to another, and it is therefore necessary in this matter to allow the competent national authorities an area of discretion within the limits imposed by the Treaty".[70]

[24–59] In two cases following very shortly after *Van Duyn*, however, the Court took a less generous approach to reliance on public policy grounds. First, in the 1977 case of *Bouchereau*, the Court had to consider a proposed decision by the UK authorities to deport a French national upon his second conviction for the unlawful possession of drugs.[71] In addition to finding that a previous criminal conviction could only be taken into account "in so far as the circumstances which gave rise to that conviction are evidence of personal conduct constituting a *present* threat to the requirements of public policy", the Court also observed that recourse by a state to the public policy ground "presupposes, in any event, the existence, in addition to the perturbation of the social order which any infringement of the law involves, of a genuine and sufficiently serious threat to the requirements of public policy affecting one of the fundamental interests of society".[72] Secondly, in 1982 in *Adoui and Cornuaille*, the Court was faced with a decision to require two French nationals to leave Belgium as they had "worked in a bar which was suspect from the point of view of morals and in which waitresses displayed themselves in the window and were able to be alone with their clients".[73] In a preliminary reference, the Court was asked whether it was conceivable that personal conduct said to constitute a genuine and sufficiently serious threat affecting one of the fundamental interests of society could, nevertheless, not be criminally punishable in the Member State wishing to rely on that conduct in order to expel an individual. It was also asked whether such a scenario was consistent with the prohibition of discrimination on the grounds of nationality. Differing from its approach in *Van Duyn*, the Court held that:

[68] *ibid*, para 41.
[69] Case 41/74 *Van Duyn v Home Office* [1974] ECR 1337.
[70] *ibid*, 1350.
[71] Case 30/77 *Bouchereau* [1977] ECR 1999.
[72] *ibid*, 2012, 2014. Emphasis added.
[73] Joined Cases 115/81 and 116/81 *Adoui and Cornuaille* [1982] ECR 1665, 1708.

> Although [EU] law does not impose upon the Member States a uniform scale of values as regards the assessment of conduct which may be considered as contrary to public policy, it should nevertheless be stated that conduct may not be considered as being of a sufficiently serious nature to justify restrictions on the admission to or residence within the territory of a Member State of a national of another Member State in a case where the former Member State does not adopt, with respect to the same conduct on the part of its own nationals repressive measures or other genuine and effective measures intended to combat such conduct.[74]

[24–60] A more recent case which can be seen to have influenced the Citizens Directive is that of *Orfanopoulos*.[75] Mr Orfanopoulos was a Greek national who moved to Germany in 1972, aged 13, in order to join his parents, and who later married a German with whom he had three children. He developed a drug addiction and had nine convictions in relation to drug possession and acts of violence. On the two occasions on which he attended specialised drug-treatment centres he was discharged for disciplinary reasons. An exclusion order was made against him on the basis of the number and seriousness of the offences committed and of the real risk of him offending in future, by reason of his dependency on drugs and alcohol. While the Court of Justice accepted that a Member State may consider illegal drug use as constituting a danger for society such as to justify special measures against foreign nationals, it was necessary to interpret the public policy exception restrictively. As a result, the existence of a previous criminal conviction could justify an expulsion order only in so far as the circumstances which gave rise to that conviction evidenced personal conduct constituting a present threat to the requirements of public policy. Accordingly, the Court concluded that EU law

> precludes the deportation of a national of a Member State based on reasons of a general preventive nature, that is one which has been ordered for the purpose of deterring other aliens in particular where such measure automatically follows a criminal conviction, without any account being taken of the personal conduct of the offender or of the danger which that person represents for the requirements of public policy.[76]

[24–61] In order to assess the personal circumstances of the individual, Member States were first required to examine, on a case-by-case basis, whether his or her conduct constituted a *present threat* to the requirements of public policy. If necessary, Member States were then required, in compliance with the general principles of EU law, to assess where the fair balance lay between the legitimate interests in issue. Such an assessment must take into account: (i) the particular legal position of persons subject to EU law; (ii) the fundamental nature of the principle of free movement; and (iii) the fundamental rights whose observance the Court ensures, having regard to the fact that it is only if a national measure takes account of such rights that reasons of public interest may be invoked to justify a measure which is likely to obstruct the exercise of freedom of movement. In addition, the Court went on to note that:

> the importance of ensuring the protection of the family life of [EU] nationals in order to eliminate obstacles to the exercise of the fundamental freedoms guaranteed by the Treaty has been recognised under [EU] law. It is clear that the removal of a person from the country where close members of his family are living may amount to an infringement

---

[74] *ibid.*

[75] Joined Cases C-482/01 and C-493/01 *Orfanopoulos* [2004] ECR I-5257. See also Joined Cases C-331/16 and C-366/16 *K* EU:C:2018:296, 2 May 2018 and Joined Cases C-381/18 and C-382/18 *GS* EU:C:2019:608, 11 July 2019 (Opinion of Advocate General Pitruzzella) (ongoing).

[76] *ibid*, 5317–5318.

of the right to respect for family life as guaranteed by Article 8 of the ECHR, which is among the fundamental rights, which, according to the Court's settled case-law, are protected in [EU] law.

Finally, the necessity of observing the principle of proportionality must be emphasised. To assess whether the interference envisaged is proportionate to the legitimate aim pursued, in this instance the protection of public policy, account must be taken, particularly, of the nature and seriousness of the offences committed by the person concerned, the length of his residence in the host Member State, the period which has elapsed since the commission of the offence, the family circumstances of the person concerned and the seriousness of the difficulties which the spouse and any of their children risk facing in the country of origin of the person concerned.[77]

[24–62] Similar reasoning can be seen in the Court's approach in cases decided since the introduction of the Citizens Directive. For example, in *Tsakouridis*, referred to above, a Greek national who was born and spent, effectively, all of his life in Germany, was ordered to be expelled following a conviction for drug dealing as part of an organised gang.[78] The Court of Justice reaffirmed much of its existing practice: a criminal sentence cannot automatically lead to an expulsion, but rather must be taken into account with all other relevant factors; there must be an individual examination of the facts of the specific case; account must be taken of fundamental rights, including the rights of privacy and family life as guaranteed by the Charter and the European Convention on Human Rights, and the expulsion must be proportionate in that it is necessary for the protection of the interests it aims to secure and that objective cannot be attained by less restrictive means. In addition to the list of factors identified in *Orfanopoulos*, the Court referred to the "solidity of the social, cultural and family ties with the host Member State" and observed that, in the case of an EU citizen who has lawfully spent most or even all of his childhood and youth in the host Member State, "very good reasons would have to be put forward to justify the expulsion measure".[79]

[24–63] An example of reliance by Ireland on the grounds of public policy and security is *Kovalenko v Minister for Justice and Equality*.[80] There, a Union citizen sought to judicially review the Minister's decision to order his exclusion for 10 years following his conviction for two rape offences, arising out of a single incident, for which he was given two concurrent terms of seven years. In deciding whether the conviction could give rise to an invocation of the public policy or public security grounds, McDermott J observed that the legislature's treatment of sexual offences, including the imposition of severe penalties, indicated that not only was such conduct to be condemned and punished, but that "it is a matter of public policy that women and girls be protected from such vicious assaults".[81] Having considered the approach of the Court of Justice in cases such as *Bouchereau*, *Orfanopoulos* and *Tsakouridis*, it was held that the Minister was entitled to regard the conduct which resulted in the conviction as, of itself, constituting a threat to the requirements of public policy, albeit that it was only

77 *ibid*, 5327.

78 Case C-145/09 *Tsakouridis* [2010] ECR I-11979.

79 *ibid*, para 53.

80 [2014] IEHC 624, McDermott J, 12 December 2014. See also *Balc v Minister for Justice and Equality* [2018] IECA 76, Peart J, 7 March 2018; *DS v Minister for Justice and Equality* [2015] IEHC 643, McDermott J, 20 October 2015; *PR v Minister for Justice and Equality* [2015] IEHC 201, McDermott J, 24 March 2015.

81 *ibid*, para 47.

one factor to be considered. Although the applicant sought to highlight his ongoing rehabilitation, the resumption of his family life upon release from prison, and the fact that he had not reoffended, the High Court found that the Minister had been entitled to reach the decision made, including by having regard to the lack of any statement of remorse by the applicant.

[24–64] The High Court has also held that repeat offending may give rise to grounds for expulsion, even if some of the offences taken in isolation would not constitute a serious threat to public security. In *Lukasz v Minister for Justice and Equality*, the High Court upheld an expulsion order made against a Union citizen with a right of permanent residence in Ireland.[82] The decision to expel had been taken on the basis that the individual's continued pattern of criminal behaviour – comprising convictions for 40 offences while resident in Ireland, including assault, theft, damage to property, road traffic offences and possession of drugs for sale or supply – indicated a "proclivity to offend".[83] In so deciding, Faherty J reasoned as follows:

> It is certainly the case from established ECJ jurisprudence that, subject to the strictures set out therein, a recidivist tendency can constitute the basis for a Removal Order on serious grounds of public policy. Counsel for the applicant however cites the decision of the ECJ in [*Orfanopoulous*] where the ECJ considered, inter alia, whether individuals who had served a number of custodial sentences for drugs offences and showed a capacity for recidivism could be subjected to an exclusion order. The Court held that derogations from the principle of free movement had to be interpreted particularly restrictively where the subject of a Removal Order was a Union citizen, again emphasising that measures of public policy "must be based exclusively on the personal conduct of the individual concerned". The applicant contends that, based on the approach of the ECJ in that case, the first named respondent was required to identify specifically why each of the applicant's relevant convictions engenders a public policy concern.
>
> … However, I agree with counsel for the respondents that the ECJ's pronouncements in *Orfanopoulous* … have to be seen in the context that the particular provisions of German law which the Court was considering in that case allowed for an alien to be expelled if he had been sentenced to a term of two years or more imprisonment for drugs offences or for a breach of the peace and the sentence had not been suspended. I also agree that that case is not authority for the proposition that the [Minister for Justice] was required to set out why each of the applicant's individual convictions engenders a public policy concern. As set out by the ECJ …, recidivism may justify the making of an expulsion order. This is subject to the proviso that the behaviour of the individual against whom the Removal Order [is made] must constitute a genuine and sufficiently serious threat to a fundamental interest of society.
>
> … I do not hold with the contention that the applicant's offences (even when viewed cumulatively) could not constitute a serious threat to the requirements of public policy, given that the ECJ has recognised that the cumulative effect of the applicant's offences may entitle the [Minister] to view the applicant's recidivism as a threat to public policy. A Member State is entitled to consider that it is in its fundamental public policy interest to take effective measures to remove a present and genuine threat to the social order that recidivist criminal behaviour presents.[84]

[24–65] A rare example of the Irish courts considering public policy as a ground,

[82] [2017] IEHC 619, Faherty J, 21 July 2017.
[83] *ibid*, para 81.
[84] *ibid*, paras 82–85.

outside of the context of criminal behaviour, is *Kweder v Minister for Justice*.[85] There, the maintenance of the Common Travel Area between Ireland and the UK was considered to be a fundamentally important public policy, which could be affected by the cumulative impact of individual instances of Ireland being used as a means of illegal entry to the UK. There, a British citizen had moved to Ireland and sought a visa for her third-country spouse to join her. Her spouse had previously been deported from the UK for breaching the terms of his visa. In a judicial review of the Minister's refusal to grant an Irish visa, the High Court accepted that the maintenance of the Common Travel Area was a legitimate public policy ground on which to base such a decision. On the other hand, given that the entitlement to reside with one's spouse working in a Member State was clearly a fundamental right under EU law, a public policy defeating it could not lightly be invoked. According to Geoghegan J:

> To justify a refusal of entry in a case such as the applicant's it is not sufficient for the Minister or the Department of Justice merely to harbour a suspicion that the real purpose of the application was to achieve an illegal entry into the United Kingdom. In my view, the Minister, via her officers in the Department, must reasonably form the view on evidence before her, that as a matter of probability the application for the visa is not a bona fide application to reside in Ireland with a lawful spouse but in reality a device in order to obtain entry into the United Kingdom contrary to the Deportation Order.[86]

[24–66] As the High Court was not satisfied that such an approach had been followed in this particular instance, the Minister's decision to refuse the visa was quashed.

[24–67] Once again reflecting the jurisprudence of the Court of Justice, Art 33 of the Citizens Directive prohibits the use of an expulsion order as a penalty or legal consequence of a custodial penalty unless it otherwise conforms to the requirements in the Directive. In addition, if a Member State has not enforced an expulsion order within two years of issuing it, it is obliged to confirm that the individual remains a current and genuine threat to public security and assess whether there has been any material change in circumstances since the order was made. The Directive further provides in Art 32 that a person excluded on the grounds of public policy or public security can apply to be permitted to re-enter "after a reasonable period, depending on the circumstances, and in any event after three years" from the enforcement of an exclusion order. Such an application must put forward arguments to establish a material change in the circumstances that had justified the making of the exclusion order in the first place.

[24–68] Finally, Arts 30 and 31 of the Directive guarantee certain procedural safeguards in respect of any decision to expel. First, an affected individual is to be given written notification of the decision in a manner that enables him or her to understand its content and implications, as well as specifying the court or body with whom to lodge an appeal and the time within which it must be lodged. Unless contrary to the interests of state security, he or she is also to be told, "fully and precisely", of the ground on which the decision is based. Except in "duly substantiated cases of urgency", he or she must be given no less than one month from the date of notification in which to leave the country.

---

85 [1996] 1 IR 381.

86 *ibid*, 387. See Bernard Ryan, "The Common Travel Area between Britain and Ireland" (2001) 64 *Modern Law Review* 855.

[24–69] Secondly, the individual is to have access to judicial and, where appropriate, administrative redress procedures to appeal against or seek to review any such decision. The procedures must provide for an examination of the legality of the decision, including its proportionality, as well as of the facts on which the proposed measure is based. This issue was considered by the High Court in *Kovalenko v Minister for Justice and Equality* where it was successfully argued that the failure to give the applicant prior notice that material concerning his commission of offences against prison discipline were to be considered by the Minister in deciding whether or not to order expulsion amounted to a breach of his fair procedures.[87] The High Court also considered the partial involvement of the same civil servant in both the initial decision, and the review thereof, to be contrary to fair procedures and to the spirit of the implementing Regulations governing the review. As a result of these failings, the order was quashed.

Overview of Case Law

Spouses	*Coman*
Dependency	*Reyes*
Prior Lawful Residence	*Akrich* *Eind* *Metock*
Other Beneficiaries/"Permitted" Family Members	*Rahman* *Banger*
Right to Enter	*Mahmood v Minister for Justice and Equality* *Raducan v Minister for Justice and Equality* *McCarthy*
Right to Permanent Residence	*Lassal* *Dias* *Ogieriakhi v Minister for Justice and Equality*
Grounds for Exclusion	*Van Duyn v Home Office* *Bouchereau* *Adoui and Cornuaille* *Orfanopoulos* *Tsakouridis* *Kovalenko v Minister for Justice and Equality* *Lukasz v Minister for Justice and Equality* *Kweder v Minister for Justice*

87 [2014] IEHC 624, unreported, High Court, McDermott J, 12 December 2014.

CHAPTER 25

UNION CITIZENSHIP

A. INTRODUCTION

[25–01] In its traditional sense, citizenship is concerned with the rights conferred by a state on its nationals and the corresponding duties owed by nationals to their state. In this way, citizenship is about identity and demarcation, identifying those included within a state's embrace and those who, by definition, are excluded from it and so form the "other" in opposition to which a particular citizenship is defined. In this sense, as traditionally conceived, citizenship is closed and is concerned with bounded communities. Drawing on the work of political theorist David Held, Catherine Barnard suggests viewing citizenship as made up of three component elements: (i) membership; (ii) participation; and (iii) rights and duties.[1]

[25–02] Given the unique nature of the EU as a transnational political project, it is to be expected that its concept of citizenship will differ significantly from that applied to nation states. Indeed, for most of its history, from 1957 until the entry into force of the Maastricht Treaty on 1 November 1993, EU law did not provide for citizenship at all. Whatever rights the nationals of EU Member States derived from EU law were largely related to their exercise of free movement as economic actors, combined with the prohibition of discrimination on the grounds of nationality as now found in Art 18 TFEU. Consequently, the exercise of the right to free movement has a dominant place in the concept of Union citizenship quite unlike the citizenship of a single state, and in many respects remains its cornerstone. This is illustrated by the fact that, as seen in the previous chapter, what is known, in shorthand, as the "Citizens Directive" – Directive 2004/38 – is in substance concerned exclusively with the right to exit, enter and reside in Member States, as its full title indicates.[2] Adopted in 2004, the Citizens Directive sought

---

1 Catherine Barnard, *The Substantive Law of the EU* (4th ed, Oxford University Press, 2013) 433.

2 Directive 2004/38/EC of the European Parliament and of the Council of 29 April 2004 on the right of citizens of the Union and their family members to move and reside freely within the territory of the Member States [2004] OJ L158/77 (the "Citizens Directive").

to codify, streamline and strengthen the complex body of EU law that had developed governing the right of EU citizens to move and reside in a Member State other than their own. This included bringing together within one directive a number of sectoral measures that had separately dealt with categories of migrants such as workers, self-employed persons, students or persons who were retired or otherwise self-sufficient. As seen in Chapter 23, however, the Citizens Directive does continue to be supplemented by a separate Regulation on the Free Movement of Workers – Regulation 492/2011.[3]

[25–03] The complexity of the law in this area derives, in part, from the fact that Union citizenship evolved in a gradual manner ever since its introduction by the Maastricht Treaty in 1993. Then, in 2004, certain aspects of this evolution, together with elements of the case law of the Court of Justice on the free movement of persons, were codified into a detailed set of rules in the form of the Citizens Directive. Since 2004, however, the nature of Union citizenship has continued to evolve significantly, sometimes in interaction with the Citizens Directive and sometimes independently of it with reference to the Treaty guarantees themselves.[4] Direct reliance on Union citizenship as conferred by the Treaties can arise particularly in connection with situations that are purely internal to one Member State, or where a Union citizen seeks to rely on EU law against their own Member State of nationality having returned there from another Member State. It can also arise where a Union citizen seeks to rely on the principle of equal treatment when residing in a Member State of which they are not a national, but where their right of residence derives from the domestic law of that Member State (eg through the granting of a residence permit) rather than through EU law itself.[5] In addition, the Lisbon Treaty's entry into force on 1 December 2009 brought about many changes in the area of citizenship, particularly regarding the elements of membership and participation. Indeed, it has been observed that, due to its "intersections with questions of a constitutional nature about sovereignty, rights and the boundaries between EU and state competences", the development of Union citizenship "represents, in several respects, a microcosm of the development of EU law more generally".[6]

[25–04] As a way of introducing this intricate field of law, this chapter will begin by setting out the current Treaty articles relating to citizenship, so that the overarching framework can be understood. We will then return to the origins of Union citizenship. Borrowing from Alina Tryfonidou's categorisation, we will trace its development through the four stages of infancy (1993–1997), growth (1998–2005), adolescence

---

3 Council Regulation (EEC) No 492/2011 of 5 April 2011 on freedom of movement for workers within the Union [2011] OJ L141/1.

4 See Daniel Thym (ed), *Questioning EU Citizenship* (Hart, 2017); Elspeth Guild, Cristina Gortázar Rotaeche and Dora Kostakopoulou (eds), *The Reconceptualization of European Union Citizenship* (Martinus Nijhoff, 2014); Dimitry Kochenov, "The Essence of EU Citizenship from the Last Ten Years of Academic Debate: Beyond the Cherry Blossoms and the Moon?" (2013) 62 *International and Comparative Law Quarterly* 97; Michael Dougan, Niamh Nic Shuibhne and Eleanor Spaventa (eds), *Empowerment and Disempowerment of the European Citizen* (Hart, 2012); Jo Shaw, "Citizenship: Contrasting Dynamics at the Interface of Integration and Constitutionalism" in Paul Craig and Gráinne de Búrca (eds), *The Evolution of EU Law* (2nd ed, Oxford University Press, 2011) 575; Dora Kostakopoulou, "European Union Citizenship: Writing the Future" (2007) 13 *European Law Journal* 623.

5 Niamh Nic Shuibhne, "The Developing Legal Dimensions of Union Citizenship" in Anthony Arnull and Damian Chalmers (eds), *The Oxford Handbook of European Union Law* (Oxford University Press, 2015) 477, 498.

6 *ibid*, 478.

(2006–2009) and coming of age (from 2010 onwards).[7] As mentioned above, aspects of these developments interact with the application of the Free Movement of Workers Regulation and the Citizens Directive. Unavoidably, therefore, a full understanding of this chapter will benefit from having read the previous two chapters – which consider in greater detail the rules codified in the Regulation and the Directive respectively – and vice versa. This chapter will then conclude by exploring the membership and participation elements of Union citizenship in the form of consular protection, voting rights, the right to petition the European Parliament, complain to the Ombudsman or correspond in an official Treaty language, and the Citizens' Initiative.

[25–05] Since the entry into force of the Lisbon Treaty, provisions on citizenship are now found in Arts 9–11 TEU, Arts 20–25 TFEU and Title V of the Charter of Fundamental Rights. Beginning with the Charter, Title V on Citizens' Rights contains the following provisions, most of which echo similar guarantees found in the TEU and TFEU:

> Art 39 – Right to vote and to stand as a candidate at elections to the European Parliament
> Art 40 – Right to vote and to stand as a candidate at municipal elections
> Art 41 – Right to good administration
> Art 42 – Right of access to documents
> Art 43 – European Ombudsman
> Art 44 – Right to petition the European Parliament
> Art 45 – Freedom of movement and of residence
> Art 46 – Diplomatic and consular protection

[25–06] Other provisions of the Charter that may be relevant to the exercise of Union citizenship include Art 1 on human dignity, Art 7 on respect for private and family life, Arts 15 and 16 on the right to work and to start a business, Art 21(2) on non-discrimination on the grounds of nationality and Art 34 on access to social security and social assistance.[8]

[25–07] Article 9 TEU brings together the principle of equality and Union citizenship, providing that in all its activities, the Union "shall observe the principle of the equality of its citizens, who shall receive equal attention from its institutions, bodies, offices and agencies. Every national of a Member State shall be a citizen of the Union. Citizenship of the Union shall be additional to national citizenship and shall not replace it." This is mirrored in Art 20(1) TFEU, which reads: "Citizenship of the Union is hereby established. Every person holding the nationality of a Member State shall be a citizen of the Union. Citizenship of the Union shall be additional to and not replace national citizenship." Articles 10 and 11 TEU then proceed to describe the nature of the Union as being founded on representative democracy, and the role of the citizen therein. These articles, therefore, deal with the membership and participation elements of citizenship, reading as follows:

> Article 10
> 1. The functioning of the Union shall be founded on representative democracy.

[7] Alina Tryfonidou, *The Impact of Union Citizenship on the EU's Market Freedoms* (Hart, 2016) 27–57.

[8] See Niamh Nic Shuibhne, "Integrating Union Citizenship and the Charter of Fundamental Rights" in Daniel Thym (ed), *Questioning EU Citizenship* (Hart, 2017) 209.

2. Citizens are directly represented at Union level in the European Parliament.

Member States are represented in the European Council by their Heads of State or Government and in the Council by their governments, themselves democratically accountable either to their national Parliaments, or to their citizens.

3. Every citizen shall have the right to participate in the democratic life of the Union. Decisions shall be taken as openly and as closely as possible to the citizen.

4. Political parties at European level contribute to forming European political awareness and to expressing the will of citizens of the Union.

Article 11
1. The institutions shall, by appropriate means, give citizens and representative associations the opportunity to make known and publicly exchange their views in all areas of Union action.

2. The institutions shall maintain an open, transparent and regular dialogue with representative associations and civil society.

3. The Commission shall carry out broad consultations with parties concerned in order to ensure that the Union's actions are coherent and transparent.

4. Not less than one million citizens who are nationals of a significant number of Member States may take the initiative of inviting the Commission, within the framework of its powers, to submit any appropriate proposal on matters where citizens consider that a legal act of the Union is required for the purpose of implementing the Treaties. ...

[25–08] These membership and participation components are further expanded upon in Part Two of the TFEU (Arts 18–25), which is now titled "Non-discrimination and Citizenship of the Union" – a change that has been described as codifying "an established conceptual link between citizenship and the principle of equality".[9] Within Part Two, Art 22 guarantees the right to vote and stand as a candidate in municipal and European Parliament elections, Art 23 provides for right to consular protection, Art 24 details the Citizens' Initiative, the right of petition and the entitlement to correspond with the institutions in any of the official languages, and Art 25 requires the Commission to report on the application of these provisions every three years.[10]

[25–09] Article 18 TFEU is of critical importance and sets out the core principle of non-discrimination. It provides that, within the scope of application of the Treaties, any discrimination on grounds of nationality shall be prohibited. As will be seen throughout this chapter, Union citizenship often operates in conjunction with the right to equal treatment based on Art 18 TFEU. Other forms of discrimination are dealt with in Art 19, which provides a legal base for the adoption of measures to combat discrimination based on sex, racial or ethnic origin, religion or belief, disability, age or sexual orientation.

[25–10] The rights and duties of Union citizenship are then described in Art 20. According to Art 20(2), "citizens of the Union shall enjoy the rights and be subject to the

---

9 Niamh Nic Shuibhne, *The Coherence of EU Free Movement Law: Constitutional Responsibility and the Court of Justice* (Oxford University Press, 2013) 144, cited in Alina Tryfonidou, *The Impact of Union Citizenship on the EU's Market Freedoms* (Hart, 2016) 25.

10 See European Commission, "Strengthening Citizens' Rights in a Union of Democratic Change EU – Citizenship Report 2017", COM/2017/030 final, 24 January 2017.

duties provided for in the Treaties", which include: the right to move and reside freely within the territory of the Member States; the right to vote and to stand as candidates in elections to the European Parliament and in municipal elections in their Member State of residence, under the same conditions as nationals of that state; the right to consular protection, and the right to petition the European Parliament, to apply to the European Ombudsman, and to address the institutions of the Union in any of the Treaty languages and to obtain a reply in the same language. Article 21 TFEU further elaborates on the right to reside by affirming that:

> Every citizen of the Union shall have the right to move and reside freely within the territory of the Member States, subject to the limitations and conditions laid down in the Treaties and by the measures adopted to give them effect.

[25–11] In the context of Union citizenship, the component of "rights and duties" is primarily concerned with this right of citizens to move and reside freely in another Member State. As expanded upon in the Citizens Directive, this includes the right of Union citizens to be accompanied in a host Member State, on the same basis, by their core "family members" of any nationality, namely their spouse or registered partner, their children or grandchildren who are under the age of 21 or dependent (or those of their spouse or partner), and their parents or grandparents who are dependent (or those of their spouse or partner).[11] Migrant students are treated slightly differently, in that there is no automatic entitlement to be accompanied by one's dependent parents or grandparents.[12]

[25–12] The citizenship right of free movement and residence now found in Arts 20 and 21 TFEU is often described as an "autonomous" right, in the sense that it is not dependent on an individual being a worker, a self-employed person or a provider or recipient of a service, but rather rests upon his or her status as a Union citizen. Whilst there had previously been a directive that provided a right of residence to non-economically active citizens who had both adequate resources not to become a burden on social assistance schemes and comprehensive health insurance, Arts 20 and 21 elevated this right to Treaty status.[13] Indeed, as was first held in the 2002 case of *Baumbast*, the right of free movement is now "conferred directly on every citizen of the Union by a clear and precise provision" of the TFEU, and so is directly effective.[14] Nevertheless, as was seen in the previous chapter, extensive limitations and conditions on the right to move and reside within another Member State are largely codified in the Citizens Directive. These limitations are far-reaching, particularly for citizens who are not economically active or otherwise self-sufficient, such that it would be wrong to view Art 21 TFEU as guaranteeing a straightforward right to reside indefinitely wherever one may choose throughout the EU. In this regard, it has been observed that the requirement in the Citizens Directive for economic activity or self-sufficiency does "mark a point of tension with the rule in free movement law more generally that states cannot be excused of their obligations under the Treaty on purely economic grounds".[15]

---

[11] Art 2(2) of the Citizens Directive 2004/38.

[12] Art 3(4) of the Citizens Directive 2004/38.

[13] Council Directive 90/364/EEC of 28 June 1990 on the right of residence [1990] OJ L180/26.

[14] Case C-413/99 *Baumbast v Secretary of State for the Home Department* [2002] ECR I-7091, 7166.

[15] Niamh Nic Shuibhne, "The Developing Legal Dimensions of Union Citizenship" in Anthony Arnull and Damian Chalmers (eds), *The Oxford Handbook of European Union Law* (Oxford University Press, 2015) 477, 481.

[25–13] The first thing to notice about the citizenship provisions in the TEU, TFEU and the Charter of Fundamental Rights is the manner in which the right to free movement is intertwined with articles dealing with membership and participatory rights, emphasising the exalted status given to that right. Secondly, as regards membership, it will be seen that Union citizenship is additional to national citizenship, and shall not replace it. Accordingly, it is for each Member State to determine who is a national citizen but, once having done so, that person is automatically a Union citizen as well.[16] A person of dual-nationality, one of which is that of an EU Member State, is entitled to have their Union citizenship recognised.[17]

[25–14] One aspect where EU law does have a bearing on the attribution of national citizenship is where the revocation of citizenship would result in a person losing their Union citizenship, as was the case in *Rottmann*.[18] Mr Rottmann was an Austrian who obtained German citizenship by naturalisation, as a result of which Austrian law prescribed that he lost his Austrian citizenship. When it subsequently transpired that he had failed to disclose that he was subject to serious criminal proceedings in Austria, Germany sought to revoke his citizenship. The Court of Justice held that, by reason of the nature and the consequences of any German decision which had the effect of causing Mr Rottmann to lose his Union citizenship, the matter fell within the ambit of EU law. Since Germany was required to exercise its powers in the sphere of nationality having due regard to EU legal principles, it followed that any decision taken by Germany to revoke his citizenship was amenable to judicial review carried out in the light of such principles. A review would have to consider whether the revocation was proportionate in light of the state's legitimate interest in protecting the special relationship of solidarity amongst its citizens, as weighed against

> the consequences that the decision entails for the person concerned and, if relevant, for the members of his family with regard to the loss of the rights enjoyed by every citizen of the Union. In this respect it is necessary to establish, in particular, whether that loss is justified in relation to the gravity of the offence committed by that person, to the lapse of time between the naturalisation decision and the withdrawal decision and to whether it is possible for that person to recover his original nationality.[19]

[25–15] The concept of "additional" citizenship clearly distinguishes Union citizenship from more traditional notions of bounded communities and has fed into new ways of thinking about citizenship and belonging, as exemplified by works of German philosopher Jürgen Habermas, such as "Citizenship and National Identity: Some Reflections on the Future of Europe" and *The Postnational Constellation*.[20] In

---

16 Case C-192/99 *Kaur* [2001] ECR I-1237.

17 Case C-369/90 *Micheletti* [1992] ECR I-4239; Case C-138/02 *Collins v Secretary of State for Work and Pensions* [2003] ECR I-2703.

18 Case C-135/08 *Rottmann* [2010] ECR I-449. See also Case C-221/17 *Tjebbes* EU:C:2018:572, 12 March 2019; HU Jessurun d'Oliveira, "Decision of 2 March 2010, Case C-135/08, *Janko Rottman v Freistaat Bayern* – Case Note I – Decoupling Nationality and Union Citizenship?" (2011) 7 *European Constitutional Law Review* 138; Gerard-René De Groot and Anja Seling, "Case Note II – The Consequences of the *Rottman* Judgment on Member State Autonomy: The European Court of Justice's Avant-Gardism in Nationality Matters" (2011) 7 *European Constitutional Law Review* 150.

19 *ibid*, paras 48, 51, 56. See *AP v Minister for Justice and Equality* [2019] IESC 47, 31 May 2019, Clarke CJ, paras 6.1–6.9.

20 Jürgen Habermas, "Citizenship and National Identity: Some Reflections on the Future of Europe" (1992) 12 *Praxis International* 10; and Jürgen Habermas, *The Postnational Constellation* (MIT

this novel form, the membership component of citizenship tends to be weaker than as compared to the closed nationhood of states, with a greater emphasis placed on facilitating participation in democratic processes in order to develop a European-wide civic solidarity. Consider, for example, the remarks by the Court of Justice in *Rottmann* to the effect that, notwithstanding Union citizenship, it remained "legitimate for a Member State to wish to protect the special relationship of solidarity and good faith between it and its nationals and also the reciprocity of rights and duties, which form the bedrock of nationality".[21] That said, awareness of Union citizenship is more extensive than perhaps might be expected, with a 2015 Eurobarometer survey finding 87 per cent of respondents to be familiar with the term "citizen of the European Union" (88 per cent in Ireland), with 42 per cent feeling informed as to their rights as a citizen (52 per cent in Ireland).[22] Indeed, according to a 2018 survey, the Irish are second only to Luxembourgers in seeing themselves as citizens of the Union, with 85 per cent doing so, and 46 per cent having a definite feeling of Union citizenship.[23]

[25–16] As Catherine Barnard has observed, the EU has been proactive in seeking to foster a sense of belonging through initiatives such as the EU flag, anthem ("Ode to Joy" from Beethoven's Ninth Symphony), motto ("United in diversity"), day (9 May, being the anniversary of the Schuman Declaration), burgundy passport,[24] pink driving licence,[25] town-twinning, and Erasmus/Socrates student mobility programmes.[26] It might be noted that Ireland is not among the 16 Member States to have declared, in Declaration No 52 to the TEU and TFEU, that for them, the EU symbols of the flag, anthem, motto, Europe Day and euro currency will "continue as symbols to express the sense of community of the people in the European Union and their allegiance to it".[27]

[25–17] As against this, it remains the case that EU migrants do not have an entitlement to vote or stand as a candidate in the all-important national elections held within Member States (as compared with municipal and European Parliament elections). Even regarding the right to vote in municipal elections, in setting out arrangements for the exercise of this right, a Council Directive permits a Member State to invoke certain derogations so as to limit the franchise to those who have resided within the state for a minimum period where, within the state, the proportion of EU citizens of voting age residing there, but who are not nationals of it, exceeds 20 per cent of the total number

---

Press, 2001). See also Jürgen Habermas, *The Crisis of the European Union. A Response* (Polity Press, 2012); Oliver Garner, "The Existential Crisis of Citizenship of the European Union: The Argument for an Autonomous Status" (2018) 20 *Cambridge Yearbook of European Legal Studies* 1; Dimitry Kochenov, "EU Citizenship: Some Systemic Constitutional Implications" (2018) 3 *European Papers* 1061.

21 *ibid*, para 51. See also Case C-22/18 *TopFit* EU:C:2019:497, 13 June 2019, para 50, where it was held that it was "legitimate to limit the award of the title of national champion in a particular sporting discipline to a national of the relevant of Member State … However, it is vital that the restrictions resulting from the pursuit of that objective should observe the principle of proportionality."

22 Flash Eurobarometer 430, *European Union Citizenship, Ireland Factsheet* (2016), available at <http://ec. europa.eu/commfrontoffice/publicopinion/index.cfm/General/index>.

23 Standard Eurobarometer 89, European Citizenship, 2018, 30–31.

24 Resolution of the Representatives of the Governments of the Member States of the European Communities, meeting within the Council of 23 June 1981 [1981] OJ C241/1.

25 Directive 2006/126/EC of the European Parliament and of the Council of 20 December 2006 on driving licences [2006] OJ L403/18.

26 Catherine Barnard, *The Substantive Law of the EU* (4th ed, Oxford University Press, 2013) 478.

27 The 16 Member States being Belgium, Bulgaria, Germany, Greece, Spain, Italy, Cyprus, Lithuania, Luxemburg, Hungary, Malta, Austria, Portugal, Romania, Slovenia and Slovakia.

of EU citizens residing there who are of voting age.[28] Although Luxembourg is the only Member State to have invoked the derogation, its mere presence is revealing of a certain tension. With respect to European Parliament elections, whilst Art 10 TEU refers to citizens being directly represented in the Parliament, a curious feature arising from the nature of EU citizenship is that a Member State is permitted to grant the right to vote and stand in these elections to "certain persons who have a close link with it without however being nationals of that State or another Member State".[29] Furthermore, Arts 45 and 51 of the TFEU allow for exceptions to the right of free movement as regards employment in the public service and the provision of services that are connected "even occasionally, with the exercise of official authority". These exceptions have been said to "reveal starkly the limits of Union citizenship. There is an inner core of national membership to which the migrant is not admitted. Fundamentally, she cannot be trusted, because she is foreign."[30]

[25–18] This somewhat incomplete form of membership can be seen to lie behind Art 25 TFEU, which provides that the Commission shall report every three years on the application of the citizenship provisions, on the basis of which the Council, acting unanimously in accordance with a special legislative procedure and after obtaining the consent of the European Parliament, may adopt provisions to strengthen or add to the rights listed in Art 20(2). In addition to the use of the special legislative procedure, the potential sensitivity of such proposals for Member States is reflected in the fact that any such provisions are only to enter into force "after their approval by the Member States in accordance with their respective constitutional requirements". It has been suggested that, following the guiding concept in Art 1 TEU of the EU developing as an ever-closer union among the peoples of Europe, Art 25 TFEU "serves a dynamic evolution and expansion" of Union citizenship.[31]

B. The Development of Citizenship

[25–19] Union citizenship is unusual in that, whilst Art 20(1) TFEU provides that citizens of the Union shall enjoy the rights and be subject to the duties provided for in the Treaties, as Catherine Barnard points out, "one of the conundrums of EU citizenship is that rights intended to foster a commitment *to the Union* are actually being exercised against the Member States", the right to free movement being the most obvious example.[32] In reality, Union citizens also continue to owe most of their duties to their state of nationality, and the duty to pay taxes most particularly.[33] Despite Union citizenship, therefore, there continues to remain a strong bond between a Member State and its citizenry as regards taxation, public expenditure and social welfare entitlements, which inevitably influences the extent to which Union citizens can be said to truly enjoy

---

[28] Council Directive 94/80/EC of 19 December 1994 laying down detailed arrangements for the exercise of the right to vote and to stand as a candidate in municipal elections by citizens of the Union residing in a Member State of which they are not nationals [1994] OJ L368/38.

[29] Case C-145/04 *Spain v United Kingdom* [2006] ECR I-7917, 7987.

[30] Damian Chalmers, Gareth Davies and Giorgio Monti, *European Union Law* (3rd ed, Cambridge University Press, 2014) 515.

[31] Rudolf Geiger, Daniel Erasmus-Khan and Markus Kotzur, *European Union Treaties* (Hart, 2015) 264.

[32] Catherine Barnard, *The Substantive Law of the EU* (4th ed, Oxford University Press, 2013) 436. Emphasis added.

[33] See Dimitry Kochenov, "EU Citizenship without Duties" (2014) 20 *European Law Journal* 482.

a right to reside freely within the territory of the Member States, as provided for in Art 21(1) TFEU. In practice, other than for an initial three-month period, the right of a Union citizen to reside in a Member State other than their state of nationality continues to largely depend upon either economic activity or economic self-sufficiency. It has been said, therefore, that the "exclusion of the disadvantaged from migration rights inspires the criticism that Union citizenship is still a quasi-economic policy as opposed to a proper constitutional citizenship embodying solidarity, equality and universality".[34]

[25–20] The notion of "solidarity" referred to here is of particular importance in the evolution of EU citizenship, where it has found itself at the centre of a tug-of-war between competing notions of loyalty and permitted differences in treatment. A key question has been, given the right to free movement and the right to equal treatment to which it gives rise, can certain differences in treatment be justified on the grounds of the special bonds of solidarity that are owed among citizens (and, perhaps, also residents) of a particular Member State, as compared with EU nationals present in the state by virtue of exercising the right of free movement. In essence, what one is talking about here are two competing versions of solidarity: solidarity amongst the nationals of a Member State versus EU-wide solidarity. This tension arose even before the introduction of citizenship via the Maastricht Treaty.

[25–21] In Chapter 23, when considering the right of children of workers to access education under the Free Movement of Workers Regulation, reference was made to the 1985 case of *Gravier v City of Liège*.[35] There, a French student wishing to enrol in a university course in Belgium sought to argue that the application of a registration fee to EU nationals, but not to Belgians, was contrary to the Treaty prohibition on discrimination on the grounds of nationality. As she was not a migrant worker, or the child of a migrant worker, Ms Gravier claimed to come within the scope of the Treaty by virtue of her accessing of services, in the form of a university course, in another Member State.

[25–22] In seeking to defend the registration fee, Belgium argued that it was due to an imbalance between the number of foreign students studying in Belgium and the number of Belgian students going abroad, which was having serious consequences for the national education budget. As a result, it was necessary to ask students from other Member States, and who normally did not pay taxes in Belgium, to make a proportional contribution to the cost of their education. It was argued that, "far from being discriminatory, such a contribution puts foreign students on the same footing as Belgian nationals".[36] Intervening in the case, Denmark and the UK argued that the Treaty prohibition on discrimination on the grounds of nationality was not intended to prevent a Member State from treating its own nationals more favourably as regards access to education, grants and the contribution by students to the cost of education, in respect of which each state "has special responsibilities toward its own nationals".[37]

[25–23] The Court of Justice rejected both of these arguments – which were essentially based on a conception of national solidarity that overrode principles of

---

34 Damian Chalmers, Gareth Davies and Giorgio Monti (eds), *European Union Law* (3rd ed, Cambridge University Press, 2014) 467.

35 Case 293/83 *Gravier v City of Liège* [1985] ECR 593, 613.

36 *ibid*, 610.

37 *ibid*, 611.

equal treatment and non-discrimination for EU nationals exercising the right of free movement – by laying emphasis on the fact that, as provided for in the Treaty, a common vocational training policy was gradually being established. The "conditions of access to vocational training" were held to fall within the scope of the Treaty, such that to impose a registration fee on EU nationals, but not on one's own nationals, constituted impermissible discrimination on the grounds of nationality. The judgment has been said to have suggested "as early as the 1980s, a reduction of Member State sovereignty in the social welfare field, as well as increased tension between migration in the EC and the protected sphere of national citizenship".[38] The Court subsequently lessened the financial implications of its judgment by ruling that "conditions of access to vocational training" related only to matters such as registration fees and tuition fees, and did not extend to maintenance grants and scholarships *etc*.

[25–24] The 1989 case of *Cowan v Le Trésor public* has been described as a "precursor of EU citizenship if ever there was one".[39] Mr Cowan had been in France, exercising the right of free movement in relation to services as a tourist, when, upon leaving a metro station, he was violently assaulted. As his assailants were never identified, Mr Cowan applied to a French compensation scheme for victims of violence. He argued that the refusal of his application on the grounds that it did not fulfil the scheme's requirement that he be either a French national or resident in France was contrary to the Treaty prohibition on discrimination on the grounds of nationality. Echoing the arguments of Denmark and the UK in *Gravier*, France argued that the right to apply to the compensation scheme was a "manifestation of the principle of national solidarity" and that it presupposed a "closer bond with the State than that of a recipient of services, and for that reason it may be restricted to persons who are either nationals of that State or foreign nationals resident on the territory of that State".[40] Without engaging with the argument made by France, the judgment of the Court of Justice rejected this proposition. According to the Court, when EU law guarantees the right of individuals to go to another Member State,

> the protection of that person from harm in the Member State in question, on the same basis as that of nationals and persons residing there, is a corollary of that freedom of movement. It follows that the prohibition of discrimination is applicable to recipients of services within the meaning of the Treaty as regards protection against the risk of assault and the right to obtain financial compensation provided for by national law when that risk materialises. The fact that the compensation at issue is financed by the Public Treasury cannot alter the rules regarding the protection of the rights guaranteed by the Treaty.[41]

[25–25] The argument has been made that the most obvious characteristic of Union citizenship is not its "postnational" nature, but rather its "transnational" one. This reflects the reality that Union citizenship is predominantly engaged as a result of the exercise of free movement across national boundaries within the EU. If this cross-border movement is understood as the horizontal dimension of citizenship, its vertical dimension would represent the direct relationship between a citizen and the Union as such. As Jo Shaw has observed, "[b]ecause of the weakness of the vertical bonds, the

---

[38] Síofra O'Leary, "Solidarity and Citizenship Rights in the Charter of Fundamental Rights of the European Union", in Gráinne de Búrca (ed), *EU Law and the Welfare State* (Oxford University Press, 2005) 59.

[39] *ibid*, 58.

[40] Case 186/87 *Cowan v Le Trésor Public* [1989] ECR 195, 221.

[41] *ibid.*

'static' European citizen, in contrast to the mobile transnational one, does not seem to derive many benefits from the institution of citizenship as a fundamental building block of the European Union."[42] The ongoing development of Union citizenship has, in many respects, concerned the extent to which it is capable of moving beyond its transnational origins that are epitomised by the label "EU *market* citizenship".[43] As will be seen, however, the jurisprudence in relation to Union citizenship is highly atomistic, with distinctive individual judgments often occurring in isolation, without any clear linear trend emerging. There have been moments of judicial activism followed by periods of retrenchment, or indeed times when the Court of Justice has adopted a maximalist approach to certain aspects of citizenship, but a more moderate approach to others. While the chronological account that follows is one way of providing a framework in which to consider this case law, it is also possible to analyse the jurisprudence from various thematic perspectives.

(i) Infancy: 1993–1997

[25–26] In the infancy phase identified by Alina Tryfonidou, between its introduction in 1993 and 1997, the case law of the Court of Justice is marked by restraint or minimalism, and by having recourse to the market freedoms as a means of avoiding having to grapple with the incipient meaning behind the new concept of Union citizenship.[44] It was during this early period that the Court was first confronted with the argument that "reverse discrimination" – whereby Union citizens who have moved to another Member State may enjoy greater legal rights there than the nationals of the host Member State under its domestic law – was contrary to the notion of Union citizenship. As seen in Chapter 23, in *Uecker and Jacquet*, two German workers who had remained living in Germany were unsuccessful in seeking to rely on the Free Movement of Workers Regulation in order to claim a right of residence for their Norwegian and Russian wives.[45] According to the Court of Justice, any lesser treatment or "reverse discrimination" which nationals of a host Member State may suffer under the law of that state, as compared with other EU nationals who have moved there, falls within the scope of that law and must therefore be dealt with within the framework of the internal legal system of that state. In other words, if it were to choose to do so, Germany was free to amend its domestic law so as to afford the same family reunification rights available under EU law to its own nationals. With regard to the newly introduced concept of Union citizenship, the Court simply noted that it was not intended to extend the material (*ratione materiae*) or subject-matter scope of the Treaties to internal situations which have no link with EU law.[46]

---

42 Jo Shaw, "Citizenship: Contrasting Dynamics at the Interface of Integration and Constitutionalism" in Paul Craig and Gráinne de Búrca (eds), *The Evolution of EU Law* (2nd ed, Oxford University Press, 2011) 575, 587.

43 See Niamh Nic Shuibhne, "The Resilience of EU Market Citizenship" (2010) 47 *Common Market Law Review* 1597; Ferdinand Wollenschläger, "A New Fundamental Freedom beyond Market Integration: Union Citizenship and Its Dynamics for Shifting the Economic Paradigm of European Integration" (2011) 17 *European Law Journal* 34.

44 See Dimitry Kochenov and Richard Plender, "EU Citizenship: From Incipient Form to Incipient Substance? The Discovery of the Treaty Text" (2012) 37 *European Law Review* 369; David O'Keeffe and Margot Horspool, "European Citizenship and the Free Movement of Persons" (1996) 31 *The Irish Jurist* 145.

45 Cases C-64 and 65/96 *Uecker and Jacquet* [1997] ECR I-3171.

46 *ibid*, 3190.

(ii) Growth: 1998–2005

[25–27] The right to non-discrimination as guaranteed by Art 18 TFEU is expressly limited to matters "within the scope of application of the Treaties". The question of the material and personal scope of EU law, and how both of these elements were required to be fulfilled in order to avail of citizenship rights, featured significantly in the growth phase, running from 1998 to 2005. It was in this phase that it first became clear the Union citizenship was capable of having independent effects, separate from the market freedoms. In this way, the growth phase saw the Court of Justice adopt a more maximalist approach and the "placing of the first building blocks of a vertical relationship between the EU and the Union citizen".[47]

[25–28] While the facts of *Martínez Sala* are complex, it continues to be identified as the very first judgment in which the Court of Justice relied on Union citizenship alone in order to bring a situation within the personal scope of EU law.[48] There, Ms Martínez Sala sought to rely on either the Free Movement of Workers Regulation, or a Regulation on the application of social security schemes to employed persons moving within the EU, in order to claim an entitlement to child benefit in Germany on the same basis as German nationals. Ms Martínez Sala had moved from Spain to Germany as a young teenager and later worked there up until 1986, and then again for a number of weeks in 1989. She was granted a series of residence permits by the German authorities, although it was during a gap in these permits that she applied for child benefit for a newly born child. Her application was refused on the grounds that, as a non-national, she was required by German law to hold a valid, particular form of residence permit in order to claim the benefit. The referring court noted that delay in granting residence permits for purely technical administrative reasons could materially affect the substance of the rights enjoyed by Union citizens.

[25–29] On a preliminary reference, the Court of Justice was satisfied that the child benefit at issue was an applicable family benefit within the meaning of the Social Security Regulation, and was a social advantage within the meaning of the Free Movement of Workers Regulation. As a result, the German child benefit fell within the material scope (or scope *ratione materiae*) of EU law. The Court considered that it had not been provided with sufficient information to determine if Ms Martínez Sala remained a "worker" within the meaning of the Free Movement of Workers Regulation, such as by being a job-seeker since ending her employment. The definition of a "worker" within the Social Security Regulation was different, however, and applied to employees who are, *or have been*, subject to legislation in one or more Member States. Again, the Court considered that it had insufficient information to determine whether she met the definition of a worker for either Regulation.

[25–30] In reply to a further question referred by the German court, the Court of Justice ruled that to require a Union citizen to produce a residence permit in order to be entitled to child benefit, when its own nationals were not required to produce any document of that kind, amounted to unequal treatment. In the sphere of application of the Treaty, and absent any justification, the unequal treatment constituted discrimination contrary to (what is now) Art 18 TFEU. In arguing against such a finding, Germany

---

47 Alina Tryfonidou, *The Impact of Union Citizenship on the EU's Market Freedoms* (Hart, 2016) 42.

48 Case C-85/96 *Martínez Sala* [1998] ECR I-269.

argued that the facts of the case were outside both the personal and the material scope of the Treaty.

[25–31] As per its answers to the earlier questions, the Court repeated that the child benefit was within the material scope of EU law. Regarding personal scope, the Commission argued that even if the national court were to find that Ms Martínez Sala was not a worker, since the entry into force of the Maastricht Treaty she was a Union citizen and, as such, had a right to reside within the EU. Given that she was in possession of a residence permit, the Court deemed it unnecessary to consider whether citizenship, by itself, could be relied upon to obtain a new right to reside. Nonetheless, it went on to find that, as a national of a Member State lawfully residing in the territory of another Member State, she came within the personal scope (or scope *ratione personae*) of the Treaty provisions on citizenship. According to the Court, (what is now) Art 20 TFEU attaches to the status of Union citizen the rights and duties laid down by the Treaty, including the right not to suffer discrimination on grounds of nationality within the scope of application *ratione materiae* of the Treaty. It followed that a Union citizen

> such as the appellant ..., lawfully resident in the territory of the host Member State, can rely on [Art 18 TFEU] in all situations which fall within the scope *ratione materiae* of [EU] law, including the situation where that Member State delays or refuses to grant to that claimant a benefit that is provided to all persons lawfully resident in the territory of that State on the ground that the claimant is not in possession of a document which nationals of that same State are not required to have and the issue of which may be delayed or refused by the authorities of that State.[49]

[25–32] As Alina Tryfonidou has described, the importance of the *Martínez Sala* judgment lies in the fact that it signified, for the first time, that

> in order for the principle of non-discrimination on the grounds of nationality to apply, it was no longer necessary to establish a link between the contested differential treatment and an impediment to the exercise of free movement between Member States: the German refusal to extend to Ms Martínez Sala the child-raising allowance under the same conditions as was granted German nationals, would not appear to be capable of causing her to leave Germany; or, if it is asked whether she would in the first place be deterred from moving to Germany if she knew that she would be refused the benefit under the circumstances, again the answer would be in the negative. ... Hence, this case demonstrated that in a Citizens' Europe, the principle of equality is important as such, and not merely as an instrument for the achievement of the EU's aims. The Court endorsed this reasoning, by explicitly detaching the material from the personal scope of EU law. Hence, on the facts, a Union citizen who was lawfully resident in the territory of another Member State and, by virtue of that, fell within the personal scope of EU law via (what is now) Article 20 TFEU could rely on the prohibition of discrimination on the ground of nationality to claim a social assistance benefit that was traditionally granted only to "workers".[50]

[25–33] Three years later, in its 2001 judgment in *Grzelczyk*, the Court of Justice famously declared that Union citizenship was "destined to be the fundamental status of nationals of the Member States, enabling those who find themselves in the same situation to enjoy the same treatment in law irrespective of their nationality, subject

[49] *ibid*, 2726.

[50] Alina Tryfonidou, *The Impact of Union Citizenship on the EU's Market Freedoms* (Hart, 2016) 31–32.

to such exceptions as are expressly provided for".[51] This quotation is frequently cited by the Court and, in more recent instances, has been adjusted to state more concretely that Union citizenship is *intended* to be the fundamental status of nationals of the Member States.[52]

[25–34] Rudy Grzelczyk was a French student in Belgium who had previously worked while studying. Given the extra demands of his final year, he stopped working and applied for a minimum income guarantee (the "minimex") from the Belgian authorities. For the purpose of EU law, the minimex was not regarded as student finance but rather as a social advantage. In responding to a request for a preliminary reference, on the basis of the information provided by the national court, the Court of Justice proceeded on the assumption that Mr Grzelczyk was not a worker. Belgium argued that, notwithstanding the introduction of Union citizenship, EU law did not confer an entitlement to the minimex on all Union citizens. Rather, the entitlements of citizenship were subject to limitations, such as the requirement for non-workers to demonstrate sufficient resources and social security cover. According to Belgium, Union citizenship did not mean that Union citizens obtained rights that were new or more extensive than those already deriving from the Treaties and secondary legislation. In its view, Union citizenship "has no autonomous content, but is merely linked to the other provisions of the Treaty".[53]

[25–35] The Court of Justice recalled that, within the sphere of application of the Treaties, discrimination on the grounds of nationality was prohibited. In order to determine the sphere of application of (now) Art 18 TFEU, it needed to be read in conjunction with the Treaty provisions concerning Union citizenship. From its ruling in *Martínez Sala* the Court recalled that a Union citizen, lawfully resident in the territory of a host Member State, can rely on Art 18 TFEU in all situations which fall within the scope *ratione materiae* of EU law. The relevant directive at the time governing the free movement of students made the right to reside conditional on demonstrating (by way of a declaration or otherwise) sufficient resources to avoid becoming a burden on the social assistance system of the host Member State and comprehensive health insurance. The directive also envisaged that beneficiaries of the right of residence must not become an "unreasonable" burden on the public finances of the host Member State. In the view of the Court of Justice, therefore, the directive "accepts a certain degree of financial solidarity between nationals of a host Member State and nationals of other Member States, particularly if the difficulties which a beneficiary of the right of residence encounters are temporary".[54] In this regard, the Court noted that since a student's financial position may change with the passage of time for reasons beyond his or her control, the truthfulness of a student's declaration of means was to be assessed only as of the time at which it was made. On the combined basis of the Treaty provisions on citizenship and non-discrimination, therefore, the Court held that the entitlement to a minimex could not be made conditional on being a "worker", within the meaning of EU law, where no such condition applied to Belgian nationals.

[25–36] This was reaffirmed in the case of *Trojani*, which concerned a French national living in a Salvation Army hostel in Belgium who possessed a residence permit allowing

---

[51] Case C-184/99 *Grzelczyk* [2001] ECR I-6193, 6242.

[52] Case C-135/08 *Rottmann* [2010] ECR I-1449, para 43; Case C-679/16 *A* EU:C:2018:601, 25 July 2018, para 56.

[53] *ibid*, 6240.

[54] *ibid*, 6245.

him to remain in Belgium for a period of time.[55] It was confirmed that, as a Union citizen, Mr Trojani was entitled to rely directly on the right to reside in (now) Art 20 TFEU, albeit that that was subject to limitations and conditions. While he did not have sufficient resources that would have permitted him to remain, he was nevertheless in possession of a Belgian residence permit. While this persisted, Mr Trojani was entitled to rely on Art 18 TFEU to claim an entitlement to the minimex on the same basis as Belgian nationals.

[25–37] One year after *Grzelczyk*, the Court delivered another expansive judgment in *Baumbast*, a case already encountered in Chapter 23.[56] Mr Baumbast, who was German, lived and worked in the UK as an employee and later as owner of his own company. When his company was no longer viable he took up employment with a German company that involved him travelling abroad to work. He owned a home in the UK, had a family there, and had health insurance in Germany, to where he and his family travelled for any medical needs. The UK refused a renewal of his residence permit (and that of his family members) on the basis that, as a person of independent means, he did not have comprehensive health insurance in the UK, which would include emergency treatment. A preliminary reference inquired as to whether, by virtue of being a Union citizen, Mr Baumbast had a right to reside in the UK even though he no longer had the status of a migrant worker.

[25–38] The UK argued that a right of residence could not be derived directly from (what is now) Art 21 TFEU since the limitations and conditions referred to in the article showed that it was not intended to be a free-standing provision. The Commission, too, considered that the right to move and reside under Art 21 was conditioned by the pre-existing primary and secondary rules, which defined the categories of persons eligible for it by reference to either an economic activity or to having sufficient resources. As Mr Baumbast had no other foundation in EU law for his right to reside in the UK, the Commission considered that Art 21 could not be of any use to him.

[25–39] In addressing this question, the Court first rejected the position of the UK and the Commission and held that, as a result of the introduction of Union citizenship, non-economic migrants could rely directly on the right of citizens to move and reside freely as enshrined in (now) Art 21 TFEU. In its assessment:

> Although, before the Treaty on European Union entered into force, the Court had held that that right of residence, conferred directly by the [TFEU], was subject to the condition that the person concerned was carrying on an economic activity within the meaning of … the [TFEU], it is none the less the case that, since then, Union citizenship has been introduced into the [TFEU] and Article [21 TFEU] has conferred a right, for every citizen, to move and reside freely within the territory of the Member States.
>
> … Moreover, the Treaty on European Union does not require that citizens of the Union pursue a professional or trade activity, whether as an employed or self-employed person, in order to enjoy the rights provided … on citizenship of the Union. Furthermore, there is nothing in the text of [the Treaties] to permit the conclusion that citizens of the Union who have established themselves in another Member State in order to carry on an activity as an employed person there are deprived, where that activity comes to an end, of the rights which are conferred on them by the [Treaties] by virtue of that citizenship.

---

[55] Case C-456/02 *Trojani* [2004] ECR I-7573.

[56] Case C-413/99 *Baumbast v Secretary of State for the Home Department* [2002] ECR I-7091.

> As regards, in particular, the right to reside within the territory of the Member States under Article [21 TFEU], that right is conferred directly on every citizen of the Union by a clear and precise provision of the [Treaty]. Purely as a national of a Member State, and consequently a citizen of the Union, Mr Baumbast therefore has the right to rely on Article [21 TFEU].[57]

[25–40] Having held that Art 21 TFEU could be relied upon directly, the question arose as to what effect this change in primary EU law would have for Mr Baumbast and his family, and for the manner in which the UK authorities were to consider their application for residence permissions. While the Court accepted that the right of Union citizens to reside within another Member State was subject to the limitations and conditions laid down by the TFEU and by the measures adopted to give it effect, crucially the application of these limitations and conditions was, first, subject to judicial review and, secondly, could not prevent Art 21 from conferring on individuals rights which are enforceable by them and which the national courts must protect. According to the Court's reasoning:

> the limitations and conditions which are referred to in Article [21 TFEU] and laid down by [now, the Citizens Directive] are based on the idea that the exercise of the right of residence of citizens of the Union can be subordinated to the legitimate interests of the Member States. In that regard, according to the [tenth] recital in the preamble to [the Citizens Directive] beneficiaries of the right of residence must not become an "unreasonable" burden on the public finances of the host Member State.
>
> However, those limitations and conditions must be applied in compliance with the limits imposed by [EU] law and in accordance with the general principles of that law, in particular the principle of proportionality. That means that national measures adopted on that subject must be necessary and appropriate to attain the objective pursued.[58]

[25–41] Applying a proportionality assessment to the facts in Mr Baumbast's case, the Court observed that: he had sufficient resources; he had worked in the UK for a number of years initially as an employee and then as a self-employed person; his family had resided with him in the UK and remained there while he travelled abroad to work; neither he nor his family had become a burden on the UK public finances and both he and his family had comprehensive health insurance in Germany. To refuse a right of residence merely on the ground that the German health insurance did not cover emergency treatment in the UK would, in the Court's view, amount to a disproportionate interference with the exercise of the right of Union citizens to reside throughout the EU.

[25–42] The significance of these 2001 and 2002 judgments during citizenship's growth phase has been explained by Catherine Barnard as follows:

> Extending the *Baumbast* reasoning to the facts of *Grzelczyk,* Grzelczyk had completed three out of four years of his degree. It would be disproportionate to interfere with his free movement rights by denying him access to the minimex. Conversely, extending the *Grzelczyk* reasoning to *Baumbast,* Baumbast was sufficiently integrated into UK society that there was a sufficient degree of solidarity between UK taxpayers and sick Germans and their families that Mr Baumbast and his family should be entitled to emergency medical treatment in the UK.

---

57 *ibid,* 7165–7166.
58 *ibid,* 7167–7168.

> The striking feature of these two cases is that the Court used EU citizenship law to establish the right to equal treatment. It also used EU citizenship rules to impose limits on the limits to equal treatment. It was enough for students and persons of independent means to have *sufficient* medical insurance and resources, not comprehensive resources. The cases also established that the concept of EU citizenship was a dynamic tool which could be used to achieve quite radical surgery on the secondary legislation.[59]

[25–43] A few months before its ruling in *Baumbast*, the Court of Justice had responded to another preliminary reference from the UK in *Carpenter*.[60] Although the Court's judgment is not framed in terms of Union citizenship per se, it is worth noting as being emblematic of the Court's maximalist approach during this period. As Stephen Weatherill has commented, it is striking how easy the Court found it to establish a connection between the threatened deportation of Mrs Carpenter – a Philippines national who had moved to the UK and later married a British man whose business extended to providing services in other EU Member States – and a perceived impediment to trade. The judgment, he suggests,

> represents a powerful assertion by the Court that once a matter is shown to fall within the scope of application of the EU's rules on the free movement of persons, the range of legal sources that become relevant in influencing the legal protection afforded by what is nominally "trade law" is broad indeed.[61]

[25–44] Mrs Carpenter originally obtained a six-month visa to live in the UK. She remained in the UK, however, without obtaining a further permission and two years later married a British national. In seeking to challenge an order for her deportation, it was argued that since a significant portion of her husband's business – selling advertising in scientific journals – was carried out in other EU Member States, and involved him travelling within the EU, her deportation would interfere with his right under (now) Art 56 TFEU to provide services. Mrs Carpenter looked after her husband's children and, in this way, it was also claimed that she assisted in his ability to carry out his business. The Court of Justice considered it noteworthy that, as exemplified by the Free Movement of Workers Regulation, the Union legislature had "recognise[d] the importance of ensuring the protection of the family life of nationals of the Member States in order to eliminate obstacles to the exercise of the fundamental freedoms guaranteed by the Treaty".[62] The Court went on to reason as follows:

> It is clear that the separation of Mr and Mrs Carpenter would be detrimental to their family life and, therefore, to the conditions under which Mr Carpenter exercises a fundamental freedom. That freedom could not be fully effective if Mr Carpenter were to be deterred from exercising it by obstacles raised in his country of origin to the entry and residence of his spouse.
>
> A Member State may invoke reasons of public interest to justify a national measure which is likely to obstruct the exercise of the freedom to provide services only if that measure is compatible with the fundamental rights whose observance the Court ensures.

---

[59] Catherine Barnard, "Free Movement of Natural Persons and Citizenship of the Union" in Catherine Barnard and Steve Peers (eds), *European Union Law* (2nd ed, Oxford University Press, 2017) 367, 394.

[60] Case C-60/00 *Carpenter v Secretary of State for the Home Department* [2002] ECR I-6279.

[61] Stephen Weatherill, *Cases and Materials on EU Law* (10th ed, Oxford University Press, 2012) 413.

[62] *ibid*, 6320.

> The decision to deport Mrs Carpenter constitutes an interference with the exercise by Mr Carpenter of his right to respect for his family life within the meaning of Article 8 of the [European] Convention for the Protection of Human Rights and Fundamental Freedoms … which is among the fundamental rights which, according to the Court's settled case-law … are protected in [EU] law.
>
> … A decision to deport Mrs Carpenter, taken in circumstances such as those in the main proceedings, does not strike a fair balance between the competing interests, that is, on the one hand, the right of Mr Carpenter to respect for his family life, and, on the other hand, the maintenance of public order and public safety.[63]

[25–45] A further instance of the Court adopting a broad approach in assessing the scope of EU law is *Garcia Avello*, which concerned an application by dual Spanish-Belgian national children to have their surname registered in Belgium so as to include their mother's surname, as per the Spanish practice.[64] The children were born in Belgium to a Belgian mother and a father who had moved from Spain. When a refusal to allow the registration led to a preliminary reference, Belgium argued that the matter did not come within the scope of EU law and that the situation was purely an internal one. The Court first observed that, as a result of the status of Union citizenship, EU nationals who find themselves in the same situation are entitled to enjoy, within the material scope of the Treaties, the same treatment in law irrespective of their nationality. Situations falling within the material scope of EU law included those involving the exercise of the freedom to move and reside in another Member State. In finding that the children were entitled to rely on Art 18 TFEU, the Court explained:

> Although, as [EU] law stands at present, the rules governing a person's surname are matters coming within the competence of the Member States, the latter must none the less, when exercising that competence, comply with [EU] law, in particular the Treaty provisions on the freedom of every citizen of the Union to move and reside in the territory of the Member States.
>
> Citizenship of the Union … is not, however, intended to extend the scope *ratione materiae* of the Treaty also to internal situations which have no link with [EU] law.
>
> Such a link with [EU] law does, however, exist in regard to persons in a situation such as that of the children of Mr Garcia Avello, who are nationals of one Member State lawfully resident in the territory of another Member State.
>
> That conclusion cannot be invalidated by the fact that the children involved in the main proceedings also have the nationality of the Member State in which they have been resident since their birth … It is not permissible for a Member State to restrict the effects of the grant of the nationality of another Member State by imposing an additional condition for recognition of that nationality with a view to the exercise of the fundamental freedoms provided for in the Treaty.[65]

[25–46] Although not expressly repeated by the Court, the reasoning of Advocate General Jacobs is instructive. While, technically, the Belgian proceedings had been begun by the father as his children's legal representative, the Advocate General considered the matter to affect both generations. In his view,

---

63 *ibid*, 6320–6321.

64 Case C-148/02 *Garcia Avello* [2003] ECR I-11613. See also Case C-541/15 *Florian Freitag* EU:C:2017:432, 8 June 2017.

65 *ibid*, 11645–11646.

> [t]he refusal to allow Mr Garcia Avello's surname to be passed on in accordance with its method of formation is a consequence of his exercise of the right of freedom of movement since, had he not exercised that right, the situation in which the refusal was made would not have arisen. The existence of an administrative practice leading systematically to such a refusal is thus likely to render the exercise of that right less attractive.[66]

[25–47] As Jo Shaw has observed, cases such as *Garcia Avello* have seen the Court of Justice make determinations on matters of national law that "fall beyond the scope of EU law in ordinary circumstances, but which are caught by the principle that the Member States must exercise *their* competences in compatibility with their duties under EU law".[67] When this is then combined with the Court's willingness to "impose a low threshold for triggering the applicability of EU law, by requiring the Member States to take care not to place obstacles in the way of exercising free movement rights, this generates a huge potential for the Court to intrude substantially into areas which are matters for national law".[68] An example of this can be seen in *Collins v Secretary of State for Work and Pensions*, although here the Court of Justice did acknowledge the legitimate interests of the Member States and afforded them some leeway in how to apply the principle of equal treatment to eligibility for job-seekers allowance, with a view to curbing so-called "benefit tourism".[69] Mr Collins was a dual US and Irish national who had lived mainly in the United States. He had spent a number of months in the 1980s in the UK working in pubs and bars. In the late 1990s he returned to the UK to seek employment in the social services sector. A refusal to grant him job-seekers allowance on the basis that he had not been habitually resident in the UK led to a preliminary reference which asked, *inter alia*, whether, assuming Mr Collins was not a "worker" for the purposes of EU secondary legislation, did any provision or principle of EU law require the payment of job-seekers allowance.

[25–48] After recalling its judgments in *Grzelczyk* and *Garcia Avello*, the Court declared that, in view of the establishment of Union citizenship and its earlier case law on the interpretation of the right to equal treatment, it was no longer possible to exclude from the scope of (now) Art 45(2) TFEU a "benefit of a financial nature intended to facilitate access to employment in the labour market of a Member State. The interpretation of the scope of the principle of equal treatment in relation to access to employment must reflect this development".[70] Since the requirement of habitual residence was more easily met by the UK's own nationals, the rules "place at a disadvantage Member State nationals who have exercised their right of movement in order to seek employment in the territory of another Member State".[71] As a result, such a requirement could only be justified if it was based on objective considerations that were independent of the nationality of the persons concerned and proportionate to the legitimate aim of the national provisions. In this regard, the Court accepted that it was

---

66 *ibid*, 11631.

67 Jo Shaw, "Citizenship: Contrasting Dynamics at the Interface of Integration and Constitutionalism" in Paul Craig and Gráinne de Búrca (eds), *The Evolution of EU Law* (2nd ed, Oxford University Press, 2011) 575, 589–590.

68 *ibid.*

69 Case C-138/02 *Collins v Secretary of State for Work and Pensions* [2004] ECR I-2703. See also Case C-224/02 *Pusa* [2004] ECR I-5763.

70 *ibid*, 2753. Article 45(2) reads: "Such freedom of movement [of workers] shall entail the abolition of any discrimination based on nationality between workers of the Member States as regards employment, remuneration and other conditions of work and employment".

71 *ibid*, 2754.

legitimate for a Member State to seek to ensure that there was a "genuine link" between an applicant for job-seekers allowance and the employment market of that state. The existence of such a link could be determined by establishing that the applicant had, for a reasonable period, genuinely sought work in the Member State. However, in order to be proportionate, a residence requirement could not go beyond what was necessary to achieve the objective of satisfying oneself that the applicant was genuinely seeking work in the UK.

[25–49] A similar issue arose in *Bidar*, where a French student living in the UK for a number of years attending secondary school sought access to a government student loan facility upon commencing university.[72] Mr Bidar was refused on the basis that he was not "settled" in the UK, within the meaning of national immigration law – a status that was not open to students from other EU Member States. Eligibility for the loan facility also required that an applicant had been residing in the UK for the previous three years. The UK argued that student loans fell outside the scope of (now) Art 18 TFEU. Indeed, earlier case law of the Court of Justice supported this. Nevertheless, the Court of Justice noted that its earlier judgments had predated the introduction of Union citizenship, as well as new Treaty provisions on education and student mobility. As a result, the Court concluded that where a Union citizen lawfully resided in another Member State as a student, access to student loans did come within the scope of EU law and the guarantee of equal treatment in Art 18 TFEU.

[25–50] In seeking to defend the residence requirement, the UK argued that it was legitimate to ensure that: (i) the contribution made by parents or students through taxation was, or would be, sufficient to justify the subsidised loan and (ii) there was a genuine link between the student and the UK employment market. In order that a student loan scheme did not become an unreasonable burden, the Court accepted that it was legitimate for a Member State to restrict such a scheme to "students who have demonstrated a certain degree of integration into the society of that state".[73] In the view of the Court, it was not permissible to require a student to establish a link with the national employment market. It was, however, reasonable to require a certain period of residence within the host Member State in order to establish a degree of integration. As the "settled status" requirement precluded EU nationals from being eligible for student loans, that requirement was contrary to Art 18 TFEU and so was impermissible.

[25–51] The judgments in *Collins* and *Bidar* have been said to have explicitly mandated "mainstreaming the demands of EU citizenship" in the interpretation of the personal market freedoms, whereby a "kind of spill-over effect" allows Union citizenship to permeate the interpretation of free movement rights.[74] A final judgment from this growth period is that of *Chen*, where a Chinese national moved to Northern Ireland in order to ensure that her daughter would be conferred with Irish citizenship as a result of being born on the island of Ireland (as was then the position under Irish

---

72 Case C-209/03 *Bidar* [2005] ECR I-2119. See Catherine Barnard, "Case C-209/03 *R (on the application of Danny Bidar) v London Borough of Ealing*" (2005) 42 *Common Market Law Review* 1465.

73 *ibid*, 2170.

74 Alina Tryfonidou, *The Impact of Union Citizenship on the EU's Market Freedoms* (Hart, 2016) 81–82, quoting in part Christiaan Timmermans, "*Martinez Sala* and *Baumbast* revisited" in Miguel Poiares Maduro and Loic Azoulai (eds), *The Past and Future of EU Law: The Classics of EU Law Revisited on the 50th Anniversary of the Rome Treaty* (Hart, 2010) 353.

law).[75] Mrs Chen then moved with her daughter to Wales. As both of the child's parents were Chinese, and had not previously been residing in the UK, the child did not acquire British nationality. Mr and Mrs Chen were self-sufficient and had health insurance, but were refused a residence permit by the UK authorities.

[25–52] In a preliminary reference, the Court of Justice was asked, *inter alia*, whether Art 21 TFEU conferred a right of residence on baby Chen, as a Union citizen who was availing of childcare services in another Member State and, if so, whether that right of residence extended to conferring her mother with a similar entitlement. Both the UK and Ireland argued that as baby Chen had only ever lived in the UK, she was not in a position to invoke Art 21 TFEU. This was rejected by the Court which, recalling its ruling in *Baumbast*, affirmed that, subject to the limitations and conditions imposed by the TFEU and the measures adopted to give it effect, the right to reside "is granted directly to every citizen of the Union by a clear and precise provision of the Treaty. Purely as a national of a Member State, and therefore as a citizen of the Union", baby Chen was entitled to rely on Article 21 TFEU.[76] Given that she had health insurance and her parents had sufficient resources to prevent her becoming a burden on the UK, there was no legitimate or proportionate justification to restrict baby Chen's right to reside, nor was the fact that the birth had deliberately taken place in Northern Ireland a relevant consideration. Furthermore, a refusal to allow baby Chen's parent and carer to reside in the UK

> would deprive the child's right of residence of any useful effect. It is clear that enjoyment by a young child of a right of residence necessarily implies that the child is entitled to be accompanied by the person who is his or her primary carer and accordingly that the carer must be in a position to reside with the child in the host Member State for the duration of such residence.
>
> For that reason alone, where … Article [21 TFEU] and [the Citizens Directive] grant a right to reside for an indefinite period in the host Member State to a young minor who is a national of another Member State, those same provisions allow a parent who is that minor's primary carer to reside with the child in the host Member State.[77]

(iii) Adolescence: 2006–2009

[25–53] The "adolescent" period of Union citizenship is defined by Tryfonidou as the years when it marked its 13th to 16th anniversaries, from 2006 to 2009, a relatively uneventful phase characterised by confusion, mixed signals and some backwards steps, indicating a desire by the Court of Justice to impose certain limits on the principles established during the growth phase.[78] Perhaps most representative of this phase is the case of *Förster*, which dealt with similar issues to those in *Bidar*.[79]

[25–54] Ms Förster was a German student in the Netherlands who was refused

---

[75] Case C-200/02 *Zhu and Chen v Secretary of State for the Home Department* [2004] ECR I-9925. See Bernhard Hofstötter, "A Cascade of Rights, or Who Shall Care for Little Catherine? Some Reflections on the *Chen* Case" (2005) 30 *European Law Review* 548.

[76] *ibid*, 9965.

[77] *ibid*, 9969.

[78] Alina Tryfonidou, *The Impact of Union Citizenship on the EU's Market Freedoms* (Hart, 2016) 43.

[79] Case C-158/07 *Förster* [2008] ECR I-8507.

a maintenance grant as she did not fulfil the requirement of being resident in the Netherlands for the previous five years – a condition that did not apply to Dutch nationals. Following *Bidar*, the Court of Justice confirmed that: (i) as a Union citizen lawfully residing in another Member State, the principle of equal treatment did apply, pursuant to (now) Art 18 TFEU; (ii) in the application of their social assistance systems, Member States were required to show a degree of financial solidarity with nationals of other Member States; (iii) it was permissible for Member States to ensure that access to maintenance grants to students from other Member States did not impose an unreasonable burden which would affect the overall level of assistance that could be granted, and (iv) it was legitimate for a Member State to restrict access to maintenance grants to those students who had demonstrated a certain degree of integration into its society, which may be established by a finding that the student had resided there for a certain length of time. According to the Court, the requirement for five years residence was proportionate in that it "does not go beyond what is necessary to attain the objective of ensuring that students from other Member States are to a certain degree integrated into the society of the host Member State".[80] It has been suggested that the judgment was a step backwards from *Bidar* in that, whereas there the Court indicated that a student may be able to demonstrate sufficient integration by other means, in *Förster* it was established that it is permissible for a Member State to impose a blanket requirement of five years continuous residence, regardless of what other links one might have.[81]

(iv) Coming of Age: 2010 Onwards

[25–55] The current phase of the Court's case law contains two distinct strands of a contrasting nature. The first strand is marked by conservativism and a concern to restrain the entitlement of non-economically active migrants to social assistance. As will be seen, in a series of judgments the Court has adopted a quite different approach to that taken in cases such as *Bidar* and *Trojani*. Rather than emphasising the right of an individual to equal treatment by virtue of the directly effective primary right deriving from Union citizenship, the Court determined these cases by applying the rules and limitations set down in the Citizens Directive (Directive 2004/38), and Art 24 of the Directive in particular. In stark contrast, the second strand has been described as the "jewel in the crown" of this phase of Union citizenship. In landmark cases such as *Rottmann* and *Ruiz Zambrano*, the Court has made clear that Art 20 TFEU will prohibit a national measure that deprives a Union citizen of the genuine enjoyment of the substance of the rights conferred by virtue of such citizenship, regardless of whether or not there had been any cross-border element. The judgment in *Ruiz Zambrano*, in particular, opened up a new phase in the development of Union citizenship.

[25–56] Considering, first, the question of social assistance, the Court's conservative turn in this area can be seen by contrasting its decision in *Brey* with its later decisions in *Dano* and *Alimanovic*. Under Art 7 of the Citizens Directive, one of the bases on which there is a right to reside for longer than three months is if a Union citizen has sufficient resources for themselves and their family members not to become a burden on the social assistance system of the host Member State during their period of residence

---

[80] *ibid*, para 58.

[81] Alina Tryfonidou, *The Impact of Union Citizenship on the EU's Market Freedoms* (Hart, 2016) 45. See Síofra O'Leary, "Equal Treatment and EU Citizens: A New Chapter on Cross-Border Educational Mobility and Access to Student Financial Assistance" (2009) 34 *European Law Review* 612.

and has comprehensive sickness insurance cover in the host Member State. By way of a derogation from the principle of equal treatment in Art 24(1) of the Citizens Directive, in accordance with Art 24(2) it is left to the host Member State to decide whether it will grant social assistance during the first three months of residence, or for a longer period in the case of job-seekers, to Union citizens other than those who are workers or self-employed persons or who retain that status or their family members.

[25–57] In the case of *Brey*, a German couple moved to Austria where they were in receipt of a pension and welfare benefits.[82] When they applied for an additional supplementary benefit it was automatically refused on the basis that they did not have sufficient resources. This was because Austrian law expressly made the granting of the supplementary benefit conditional upon the applicant meeting the requirements for obtaining a right of residence. The question for the Court of Justice, therefore, was whether the Citizens Directive should be interpreted as precluding national legislation which did not allow the grant of a benefit to a national of another Member State who was not economically active on the following ground: despite having been issued with a certificate of residence, the individual did not meet the necessary requirements for obtaining a legal right to reside on the territory of the host Member State for a period of longer than three months, since such a right of residence is conditional upon that national having sufficient resources so as not to need to apply for the benefit. As only persons who met the conditions to be entitled to a right to reside could claim the Austrian supplementary benefit, that benefit could not be awarded to a person who otherwise had insufficient resources to claim a right to reside.

[25–58] The Court accepted that the fact that a national of another Member State who was not economically active may be eligible, in light of his low pension, to receive a supplementary benefit could be an indication that he does not have sufficient resources to avoid becoming an unreasonable burden on the social assistance system of the host Member State for the purposes of Art 7 of the Citizens Directive. Crucially, however,

> the competent national authorities cannot draw such conclusions without first carrying out an overall assessment of the specific burden which granting that benefit would place on the national social assistance system as a whole, by reference to the *personal circumstances* characterising the individual situation of the person concerned.
>
> ... it should be borne in mind that, since the right to freedom of movement is – as a fundamental principle of EU law – the general rule, the conditions laid down in Article [7 of the Citizens Directive] must be construed narrowly and in compliance with the limits imposed by EU law and the principle of proportionality.
>
> ... the mere fact that a national of a Member State receives social assistance is not sufficient to show that he constitutes an unreasonable burden on the social assistance system of the host Member State.
>
> As regards the legislation at issue ..., it is clear from the explanation provided by the Austrian Government at the hearing that, although the amount of the compensatory supplement depends on the financial situation of the person concerned as measured against the reference amount fixed for granting that supplement, the mere fact that a national of another Member State who is not economically active has applied for that benefit is sufficient to preclude that national from receiving it, regardless of the duration of residence, the amount of the benefit and the period for which it is available, that is to

[82] Case C-140/12 *Brey* EU:C:2013:565, 19 September 2013.

> say, regardless of the burden which that benefit places on the host Member State's social assistance system as a whole.
>
> Such a mechanism, whereby nationals of other Member States who are not economically active are automatically barred by the host Member State from receiving a particular social security benefit, even for the period following the first three months of residence referred to in Article 24(2) of Directive 2004/38, does not enable the competent authorities of the host Member State, where the resources of the person concerned fall short of the reference amount for the grant of that benefit, to carry out – in accordance with the requirements under, inter alia, Articles 7(1)(b) and 8(4) of that directive and the principle of proportionality – an overall assessment of the specific burden which granting that benefit would place on the social assistance system as a whole by reference to the personal circumstances characterising the individual situation of the person concerned.
>
> In particular, in a case such as that before the referring court, it is important that the competent authorities of the host Member State are able, when examining the application of a Union citizen who is not economically active and is in Mr Brey's position, to take into account, inter alia, the following: the amount and the regularity of the income which he receives; the fact that those factors have led those authorities to issue him with a certificate of residence; and the period during which the benefit applied for is likely to be granted to him. In addition, in order to ascertain more precisely the extent of the burden which that grant would place on the national social assistance system, it may be relevant … to determine the proportion of the beneficiaries of that benefit who are Union citizens in receipt of a retirement pension in another Member State.
>
> In the present case, it is for the referring court, which alone has jurisdiction to assess the facts, to decide, in light of those elements in particular, whether granting a benefit such as the compensatory supplement to a person in Mr Brey's situation is likely to place an unreasonable burden on the national social assistance system.[83]

[25–59] One year later, however, the Court adopted a noticeably different approach and tone in *Dano*, which concerned a Romanian national living in Germany for more than three months, but less than five years, who had been refused access to a form of social assistance on the basis that she was not economically active.[84] Ms Dano had not worked in Germany, nor had she looked for work. The Court of Justice was asked whether Arts 18 and 20 TFEU, together with Art 24 of the Citizens Directive, must be interpreted as precluding legislation under which nationals of other Member States who are not economically active are excluded from receiving a social assistance benefit that is granted to nationals of the host Member State who are in the same situation. While the Court confirmed the "fundamental nature" of Union citizenship and the right to equal treatment to which it gives rise, it then noted that the "principle of non-discrimination, laid down generally in Article 18 TFEU, is given more specific expression in Article 24 of Directive 2004/38 in relation to Union citizens who, like the applicants in the

---

83 *ibid*, paras 75–79. Emphasis added.

84 Case C-333/13 *Dano* EU:C:2014:2358, 11 November 2014. See Daniel Carter and Moritz Jesse, "The '*Dano* Evolution': Assessing Legal Integration and Access to Social Benefits for EU Citizens" (2018) 3 *European Papers* 1179; Adrienne Yong, "Driving a Wedge between Friends? The Court of Justice of the EU and its Citizens in the Case of Welfare Benefits" (2016) 6 *European Human Rights Law Review* 664; Herwig Verschueren, "Preventing 'Benefit Tourism' in the EU: A Narrow or Broad Interpretation of the Possibilities Offered by the ECJ in *Dano*?" (2015) 52 *Common Market Law Review* 363; Daniel Thym, "When Union Citizens Turn into Illegal Migrants: The *Dano* Case" (2015) 40 *European Law Review* 249; Niamh Nic Shuibhne, "Limits Rising, Duties Ascending: The Changing Legal Shape of Union Citizenship" (2015) 52 *Common Market Law Review* 889.

main proceedings, exercise their right to move and reside within the territory of the Member States".[85]

[25–60] Since Art 24 of the Citizens Directive provides that all Union citizens residing *on the basis of the Directive* in the territory of the host Member State are to enjoy equal treatment with the nationals of that Member State within the scope of the Treaty, it followed that, so far as concerns access to social benefits, a Union citizen can claim equal treatment with nationals of the host Member State only if his or her residence complies with the conditions of the Directive.[86] For periods of residence longer than three months, the right of residence was retained only if the conditions prescribed by Art 7 of the Directive were fulfilled. Significantly, the Court observed that, from the recitals, it was apparent that "those conditions are intended, inter alia, to prevent such persons from becoming an unreasonable burden on the social assistance system of the host Member State".[87] Indeed, in the Court's view:

> To accept that persons who do not have a right of residence under Directive 2004/38 may claim entitlement to social benefits under the same conditions as those applicable to nationals of the host Member State would run counter to an objective of the directive, set out in recital 10 in its preamble, namely preventing Union citizens who are nationals of other Member States from becoming an unreasonable burden on the social assistance system of the host Member State.[88]

[25–61] Accordingly, in order to determine whether, as an economically inactive Union citizen residing in Germany for more than three months but less than five years, Ms Dano could claim equal treatment with German nationals to social benefits, it had to be examined whether her residence complied with the conditions in Art 7 of the Citizens Directive, including the requirement that economically inactive citizens must have sufficient resources for themselves and their family members. In the view of the Court, this requirement "seeks to prevent economically inactive Union citizens from using the host Member State's welfare system to fund their means of subsistence".[89] The Court went on to reason that:

> any unequal treatment between Union citizens who have made use of their freedom of movement and residence and nationals of the host Member State with regard to the grant of social benefits is an inevitable consequence of Directive 2004/38. Such potential unequal treatment is founded on the link established by the Union legislature in Article 7 of the directive between the requirement to have sufficient resources as a condition for residence and the concern not to create a burden on the social assistance systems of the Member States.
>
> A Member State must therefore have the possibility, pursuant to Article 7 of Directive 2004/38, of refusing to grant social benefits to economically inactive Union citizens who exercise their right to freedom of movement solely in order to obtain another Member State's social assistance although they do not have sufficient resources to claim a right of residence.
>
> To deny the Member State concerned that possibility would … have the consequence that

[85] *ibid*, para 61.
[86] *ibid*, para 69.
[87] *ibid*, para 71.
[88] *ibid*, para 74.
[89] *ibid*, para 76.

persons who, upon arriving in the territory of another Member State, do not have sufficient resources to provide for themselves would have them automatically, through the grant of a special non-contributory cash benefit which is intended to cover the beneficiary's subsistence costs.

Therefore, the financial situation of each person concerned should be examined specifically, without taking account of the social benefits claimed, in order to determine whether he meets the condition of having sufficient resources to qualify for a right of residence under Article 7(1)(b) of Directive 2004/38.

In the main proceedings, according to the findings of the referring court the applicants do not have sufficient resources and thus cannot claim a right of residence in the host Member State under Directive 2004/38. Therefore … they cannot invoke the principle of non-discrimination in Article 24(1) of the directive.[90]

[25–62] Finally, the Court of Justice did not regard the Charter of Fundamental Rights as being applicable in that the conditions governing access to the social assistance at issue were not prescribed by EU law. Rather, it was the Member States who had the competence to determine the extent and the conditions for the grant of such benefits, and in doing so they were not implementing EU law. The following year, in *Alimanovic*, the Court repeated this approach.[91] The Alimanovic family were Swedish nationals with a right of permanent residence in Germany. Ms Alimanovic was denied an entitlement to social assistance on the basis that, although she had worked for a number of months, she subsequently became a job-seeker. The Court of Justice was asked whether Arts 18 and 45 TFEU, together with Art 24 of the Citizens Directive, permitted Germany to refuse access to social assistance in circumstances where such assistance was available to German job-seekers in the same position.

[25–63] As per its decision in *Dano*, the Court confirmed that in order to determine whether social assistance may be refused on the basis of the derogation laid down in Art 24(2) of Citizens Directive, it is first necessary to determine whether the principle of equal treatment referred to in Art 24(1) is applicable and, accordingly, whether the Union citizen concerned is lawfully resident on the territory of the host Member State. As Ms Alimanovic had been unemployed for more than six months, she had lost her status as a worker. If Ms Alimanovic was regarded as a job-seeker, Art 24(2) expressly provided that a Member State may refuse to grant any social assistance to a Union citizen whose right of residence is based solely on being a job-seeker. In this context, the Court explicitly declared that, although in *Brey* it had held that the Citizens Directive requires a Member State to take account of the individual situation of the person concerned before it finds that his or her residence is placing an unreasonable burden on its social assistance system, "no such individual assessment is necessary in circumstances such as those at issue" in *Alimanovic.*[92] Rather, by "establishing a gradual system as regards the retention of the status of 'worker' which seeks to safeguard the right of residence and access to social assistance, [the Citizens Directive] itself takes into

[90] *ibid*, paras 77–81.

[91] Case C-67/14 *Alimanovic* EU:C:2015:597, 15 September 2015. See Anastasia Iliopoulou-Penot, "Deconstructing the Former Edifice of Union Citizenship? The *Alimanovic* Judgment" (2016) 53 *Common Market Law Review* 1007; Niamh Nic Shuibhne, "'What I Tell You Three Times is True': Lawful Residence and Equal Treatment after *Dano*" (2016) 23 *Maastricht Journal of European and Comparative Law* 908; Anita Heindlmaier and Michael Blauberger, "Enter at Your Own Risk: Free Movement of EU Citizens in Practice" (2017) 40 *West European Politics* 1198.

[92] *ibid*, para 59.

consideration various factors characterising the individual situation of each applicant for social assistance and, in particular, the duration of the exercise of any economic activity".[93] According to the Court:

> By enabling those concerned to know, without any ambiguity, what their rights and obligations are, the criterion referred to [in German law and in Art 7 of the Citizens Directive], namely a period of six months after the cessation of employment during which the right to social assistance is retained, is consequently such as to guarantee a significant level of legal certainty and transparency in the context of the award of social assistance by way of basic provision, while complying with the principle of proportionality.
>
> Moreover, as regards the individual assessment for the purposes of making an overall appraisal of the burden which the grant of a specific benefit would place on the national system of social assistance ... as a whole, it must be observed that the assistance awarded to a single applicant can scarcely be described as an "unreasonable burden" for a Member State, within the meaning of [the Citizens Directive]. However, while an individual claim might not place the Member State concerned under an unreasonable burden, the accumulation of all the individual claims which would be submitted to it would be bound to do so.[94]

[25–64] In *García-Neto*, the Court confirmed that an individual assessment is also not necessary in considering an application for social assistance from a person who is not a worker or a former worker, but who is relying on the right to reside for up to three months under the Citizens Directive.[95] In its view, the derogation from the principle of equal treatment in Art 24(2) was consistent with the objective of maintaining the financial equilibrium of the social assistance systems of the Member States. The Court reasoned that

> [s]ince the Member States cannot require Union citizens to have sufficient means of subsistence and personal medical cover for a period of residence of a maximum of three months in their respective territories, it is legitimate not to require those Member States to be responsible for those citizens during that period.[96]

[25–65] Just one week before the UK's referendum on EU membership in June 2016 – in which the free movement of persons and alleged "benefit tourism" were prominent issues – the Court of Justice confirmed its approach in *Dano* and *Alimanovic* in *Commission v UK*.[97] There, the Commission had brought infringement proceedings in respect of legislation that made the grant of child benefit conditional on confirming a right of lawful residence in the UK. The Commission also claimed that a residence requirement amounted to indirect discrimination, in that it was more easily satisfied by UK nationals. The Court reiterated that there was nothing to prevent, in principle, the grant of social benefits to Union citizens who are not economically active being made subject to the requirement that those citizens fulfil the conditions for possessing a right to reside lawfully in the host Member State. On the basis of the information provided by the UK, the Court was satisfied that claimants were required to provide, on the claim form, a set of data which revealed whether or not they had a right to reside in the UK. Following checks by the UK authorities, it was only in the event of doubt

---

93 *ibid*, para 60.
94 *ibid*, paras 61–62.
95 Case C-299/14 *García-Nieto* EU:C:2016:114, 25 February 2016.
96 *ibid*, para 45.
97 Case C-308/14 *Commission v United Kingdom* EU:C:2016:436, 14 June 2016.

that claimants would be required to prove that they in fact enjoyed a right to reside as declared by them in the claim form. As a result, the legislation did not breach the Citizens Directive's prohibition on systematic checks. The Court was satisfied that the UK's requirements were proportionate for the purpose of securing the objective of protecting public finances.

[25–66] For some, the *Dano, Alimanovic, García-Nieto* line of case law represents a "swift dismantling" of the Court's earlier jurisprudence that had given meaning to the fundamental status of Union citizenship.[98] By way of example, Dion Kramer has argued that:

> The "heydays" of Union citizenship were probably situated around the turn of the century, when the Court employed the primary right of equal treatment attached to Union citizenship to extend social welfare entitlements to mobile Union citizens regardless of their economic status, thereby including the "economically inactive", "simply" on the basis of their being citizens of the Union. As this bold move was neither anticipated nor considered politically and historically neutral, it was no surprise that it provoked a lively debate on Union social citizenship. Since the start of this debate, discourses on Union citizens' "earning and deserving" have featured prominently and have re-emerged in the context of debates on "welfare tourism" and the British referendum. An early critic, for example, submitted that by offering "radical equality" to those Union citizens who have not earned social welfare benefits on account of participation in the collective work process of a given society, the Court undermines the systems of reciprocity underpinning national welfare states. … With respect to its more recent case law, however, the Court is facing equal criticism from the opposite direction: by sacrificing the "fundamental status" so dear to the Court in its earlier case law, it now presents a picture of the economically inactive migrant who is only one step above the "alien" whose rights have to be "*earned* through wealth, health and good behaviour".[99]

[25–67] In parallel to this conservative turn, the "coming of age" phase has also witnessed a series of ground-breaking judgments that have added a new and important dimension to Union citizenship. These began with *Rottmann* which, as we have already seen, concerned Germany's proposed revocation of Mr Rottmann's citizenship, which would result in him also losing Union citizenship.[100] The Court of Justice held that, by reason of the nature and the consequences of any such decision, the matter fell within the scope of EU law and Germany was required to exercise its powers in the sphere of nationality having due regard to EU law. As a consequence, any decision to revoke his citizenship was amenable to judicial review carried out in the light of EU law. Such a review would have to consider whether the revocation was proportionate in light of Germany's legitimate interest in protecting the special relationship of solidarity amongst

---

98 Charlotte O'Brien, "The ECJ Sacrifices EU Citizenship in Vain: *Commission v United Kingdom*" (2017) 54 *Common Market Law Review* 209, 210.

99 Dion Kramer, "Earning Social Citizenship in the European Union: Free Movement and Access to Social Assistance Benefits Reconstructed" (2016) 18 *Cambridge Yearbook of European Legal Studies* 270, 271–272.

100 Case C-135/08 *Rottmann* [2010] ECR I-449. See HU Jessurun d'Oliveira, "Decision of 2 March 2010, Case C-135/08, *Janko Rottman v Freistaat Bayern* – Case Note I – Decoupling Nationality and Union Citizenship?" (2011) 7 *European Constitutional Law Review* 138; Gerard-René De Groot and Anja Seling, "Case Note II – The Consequences of the *Rottman* Judgment on Member State Autonomy – The European Court of Justice's Avant-Gardism in Nationality Matters" (2011) 7 *European Constitutional Law Review* 150. See *AP v Minister for Justice and Equality* [2019] IESC 47, 31 May 2019, Clarke CJ, paras 6.1–6.9.

its citizens, as weighed against the consequences for Mr Rottmann with regard to the loss of the rights enjoyed as a Union citizen.

[25–68] More recently, in *Tjebbes*, a Grand Chamber of the Court has reaffirmed that a Member State's laws on the loss of nationality, where this entails a loss of Union citizenship, must be consistent with principle of proportionality.[101] In order to remain proportionate, it is necessary to permit an individual examination of the consequences of that loss of citizenship for the persons affected from the point of view of EU law. There, Dutch law provided for the automatic loss of Dutch citizenship by any national who had another nationality and who resided outside the Netherlands and the EU for an uninterrupted period of 10 years. Citizenship would not be lost, however, if during that time the person applied for a Dutch passport or identity card, or sought a declaration of citizenship. The Minister for Foreign Affairs decided not to examine Ms Tjebbes' application for a passport on this basis that her citizenship had been lost due to her residence outside the Netherlands. As her other nationality was Canadian, the operation of Dutch law deprived her of her Union citizenship. According to the Grand Chamber, while such a national measure was permissible in principle, it must allow for the possibility of

> an individual assessment of the situation of the person concerned and that of his or her family in order to determine whether the consequences of losing the nationality of the Member State concerned, when it entails the loss of his or her citizenship of the Union, might, with regard to the objective pursued by the national legislature, disproportionately affect the normal development of his or her family and professional life from the point of view of EU law. Those consequences cannot be hypothetical or merely a possibility.
>
> As part of that examination of proportionality, it is, in particular, for the competent national authorities and, where appropriate, for the national courts to ensure that the loss of nationality is consistent with the fundamental rights guaranteed by the Charter, the observance of which the Court ensures, and specifically the right to respect for family life as stated in Article 7 of the Charter, that article requiring to be read in conjunction with the obligation to take into consideration the best interests of the child, recognised in Article 24(2) of the Charter.
>
> As regards the circumstances of the individual situation of the person concerned, which are likely to be relevant in the assessment that the competent national authorities and national courts are to carry out in the present case, it must be mentioned, in particular, that following the loss, by operation of law, of Netherlands nationality and of citizenship of the Union the person concerned would be exposed to limitations when exercising his or her right to move and reside freely within the territory of the Member States, including, depending on the circumstances, particular difficulties in continuing to travel to the Netherlands or to another Member State in order to retain genuine and regular links with members of his or her family, to pursue his or her professional activity or to undertake the necessary steps to pursue that activity. Also relevant … [is] the serious risk, to which the person concerned would be exposed, that his or her safety or freedom to come and go would substantially deteriorate because of the impossibility for that person to enjoy consular protection under Article 20(2)(c) TFEU in the territory of the third country in which that person resides.[102]

[25–69] One year after the decision in *Rottmann*, in 2011, a Grand Chamber of the Court delivered a landmark judgment in *Ruiz Zambrano*, which was quickly followed

[101] Case C-221/17 *Tjebbes* EU:C:2019:189, 12 March 2019.

[102] *ibid*, paras 44–46.

by clarifying judgments in *McCarthy* and *Dereci*. The Ruiz Zambranos were Colombian nationals who had unsuccessfully sought asylum in Belgium.[103] As a result of the principle of non-refoulement, however, they could not be deported to Colombia. While living in Belgium they had two children, both of whom were granted Belgian citizenship by operation of national law. Subsequently, Mr and Mrs Ruiz Zambrano applied for a right of residence but were refused, nor were they allowed a right to work or access to unemployment benefit. A preliminary reference required the Court of Justice to consider whether the Treaty and Charter provisions on Union citizenship conferred on a third-country national parent of a Union citizen dependent child, a right of residence in the Member State of which the child is a national and resides. If so, did those provisions also exempt such a parent from having to obtain a work permit in that Member State?

[25–70] The Commission and eight Member States (including Ireland) submitted observations to the Court, all of which argued that as the children had been born in Belgium, had Belgian nationality, and had never left, the situation was wholly internal and so the provisions of EU law invoked by the applicant did not apply. The Court accepted that as the Citizens Directive applies to Union citizens "who move to or reside in a Member State other than that of which they are a national, and to their family members", it was not applicable. On the other hand, the Court confirmed that, as established in *Rottmann*,

> Article 20 TFEU precludes national measures which have the effect of depriving citizens of the Union of the genuine enjoyment of the substance of the rights conferred by virtue of their status as citizens of the Union.
>
> A refusal to grant a right of residence to a third country national with dependent minor children in the Member State where those children are nationals and reside, and also a refusal to grant such a person a work permit, has such an effect.
>
> It must be assumed that such a refusal would lead to a situation where those children, citizens of the Union, would have to leave the territory of the Union in order to accompany their parents. Similarly, if a work permit were not granted to such a person, he would risk not having sufficient resources to provide for himself and his family, which would also result in the children, citizens of the Union, having to leave the territory of the Union. In those circumstances, those citizens of the Union would, in fact, be unable to exercise the substance of the rights conferred on them by virtue of their status as citizens of the Union.
>
> Accordingly, ... Article 20 TFEU is to be interpreted as meaning that it precludes a Member State from refusing a third country national upon whom his minor children, who are European Union citizens, are dependent, a right of residence in the Member State of

[103] Case 34/09 *Ruiz Zambrano* [2011] ECR I-1177. See Urska Sadl, "*Ruiz Zambrano* as an Illustration of How the Court of Justice of the European Union Constructs its Legal Arguments" (2013) 9 *European Constitutional Law Review* 205; Iyiola Solanke, "Using the Citizen to Bring the Refugee In: *Gerardo Ruiz Zambrano v Office national de l'emploi (ONEM)*" (2012) 75 *Modern Law Review* 101; Kay Hailbronner and Daniel Thym, "Case C-34/09, *Gerardo Ruiz Zambrano v Office national de l'emploi (ONEM)*, Judgment of the Court of Justice (Grand Chamber) of 8 March 2011" (2011) 48 *Common Market Law Review* 1253; Robin Morris, "*Gerardo Ruiz Zambrano v Office national de l'emploi (ONEM)*: European Citizenship and the Right to Move Freely: Internal Situations, Reverse Discrimination and Fundamental Rights" (2011) 18 *Maastricht Journal of European and Comparative Law* 179; Janet T Nowak, "Case Note – Case C-34/09, *Gerardo Ruiz Zambrano v Office national de l'emploi (ONEM)* and Case C-434/09, *Shirley McCarthy v Secretary of State for the Home Department*" (2011) 17 *Colombia Journal of European Law* 673; Alicia Hinarejos, "Extending Citizenship and the Scope of EU Law" (2011) 70 *Cambridge Law Journal* 309.

> residence and nationality of those children, and from refusing to grant a work permit to that third country national, in so far as such decisions deprive those children of the genuine enjoyment of the substance of the rights attaching to the status of European Union citizen.[104]

[25–71] The paragraphs quoted above are the extent of the reasoning provided by Court, and so it is unsurprising that the judgment has been described as "terse" and "elliptical".[105] In Ireland, a *Policy Document on Non-EEA Family Reunification* sought to provide some guidance, and an administrative scheme was introduced for seeking permission to remain in the State on the basis of the principles outlined by the Court of Justice.[106] A number of clarifying judgments quickly followed, beginning with *McCarthy*, a case in which a dual Irish and British national, who was born and lived all her life in the UK, sought to rely on her Irish nationality in order to avail of EU law rights to family reunification so as to allow her Jamaican husband remain in the UK.[107] In contrast to *Ruiz Zambrano*, the failure to provide her husband with a residence permit was not regarded by the Court of Justice as depriving Mrs McCarthy of the genuine enjoyment of the substance of the rights associated with her status as a Union citizen, or of impeding her right to move and reside freely within the territory of the Member States. Whereas this may have been interpreted as limiting *Ruiz Zambrano* to cases involving minors, it has been suggested that the next ruling, in *Dereci*, lends no support to that view and, instead, "whether the EU citizen would have to leave 'territory of the Union' is open for assessment in all situations".[108]

[25–72] Mr Dereci was a Turkish national who moved to Austria without having a lawful right of residence.[109] He married an Austrian and had children, all of whom were Austrian citizens. When his application for a residence permit was rejected, he was made the subject of an expulsion order. Unlike in *Ruiz Zambrano*, the children were not dependent on their father for their subsistence, in the sense that if Mr Dereci was

---

104 *ibid*, paras 42–45.

105 Cathryn Costello, "Child Citizens and De Facto Deportation: Tender Years, Fragile Ties and Security of Residence" in Kieran Bradley, Noel Travers and Anthony Whelan (eds), *Of Courts and Constitutions: Liber Amicorum in Honour of Nial Fennelly* (Hart, 2014) 411, 422.

106 Department of Justice and Equality, "Policy Document on Non-EEA Family Reunification" (December 2013, updated December 2016) available at <http://www.inis.gov.ie/en/INIS/Pages/immigration-policy-family-reunification>. For a detailed discussion of the application of *Ruiz Zambrano* by the Irish courts see John Stanley, *Immigration and Citizenship Law* (Round Hall, 2017) 837–852, 235–237.

107 Case C-434/09 *McCarthy* [2011] ECR I-3375. See Janet T Nowak, "Case Note – Case C-34/09, *Gerardo Ruiz Zambrano v Office national de l'emploi (ONEM)* and Case C-434/09, *Shirley McCarthy v Secretary of State for the Home Department*" (2011) 17 *Colombia Journal of European Law* 673.

108 Cathryn Costello, "Child Citizens and De Facto Deportation: Tender Years, Fragile Ties and Security of Residence" in Kieran Bradley, Noel Travers and Anthony Whelan (eds), *Of Courts and Constitutions: Liber Amicorum in Honour of Nial Fennelly* (Hart, 2014) 411, 423. See Niamh Nic Shuibhne, "(Some of) The Kids Are All Right: Comment on *McCarthy* and *Dereci*" (2012) 49 *Common Market Law Review* 349; Stanislas Adam and Peter Van Elsuwege, "Citizenship Rights and the Federal Balance between the European Union and its Member States: Comment on *Dereci*" (2012) 39 *European Law Review* 176.

109 Case C-256/11 *Dereci* [2011] ECR I-11315. See also Case C-40/11 *Iida* EU:C:2012:691, 8 November 2012; Case C-357/11 *O and S* EU:C:2012:776, 6 December 2012; Case C-87/12 *Ymeraga* EU:C:2013:291, 8 May 2013; Case C-86/12 *Alokpa* EU:C:2013:645, 10 October 2013; Case C-115/15 *NA* EU:C:2016:487, 30 June 2016; Case C-304/14 *CS* EU:C:2016:674, 13 September 2016; and Case C-165/14 *Rendón Marín* EU:C:2016:675, 13 September 2016.

required to leave Austria, they could continue to live there with their mother. According to the Court of Justice:

> the criterion relating to the denial of the genuine enjoyment of the substance of the rights conferred by virtue of European Union citizen status refers to situations in which the Union citizen has, in fact, to leave not only the territory of the Member State of which he is a national but also the territory of the Union as a whole.
>
> … Consequently, the mere fact that it might appear desirable to a national of a Member State, for economic reasons or in order to keep his family together in the territory of the Union, for the members of his family who do not have the nationality of a Member State to be able to reside with him in the territory of the Union, is not sufficient in itself to support the view that the Union citizen will be forced to leave Union territory if such a right is not granted.
>
> … if the referring court considers, in the light of the circumstances of the disputes in the main proceedings, that the situation of the applicants … is covered by European Union law, it must examine whether the refusal of their right of residence undermines the right to respect for private and family life provided for in Article 7 of the Charter.[110]

[25–73] The nature of the dependency required was further elaborated by the Court in the more recent case of *Chavez-Vilchez*.[111] Ms Chavez-Vilchez was a Venezuelan national who, while on a tourist visa in the Netherlands, entered into a relationship with a Dutch national, with whom she had a child. Ms Chavez-Vilchez and her child were subsequently compelled to leave the family home and enter an emergency refuge. She remained responsible for the care of the child and the father did not contribute to the child's support or upbringing. The Netherlands argued that the mere fact that a third-country national parent undertakes the day-to-day care of the child and is the person on whom that child is in fact dependent, legally, financially or emotionally, even in part, did not permit the automatic conclusion that a child who is a Union citizen would be compelled to leave the Union if a right of residence were refused to that third-country national. According to the Netherlands, the presence in the Member State of which the child is a national or in the Union as a whole of a Union citizen parent who is capable of caring for the child is a significant factor in any assessment of dependency.

[25–74] The Court of Justice clarified that, for the purposes of determining whether a refusal to grant a right of residence to a third-country national parent means that a Union citizen child is deprived of the genuine enjoyment of the substance of his or her citizenship rights, relevant factors include the question of who has custody of the child and whether the child is legally, financially or emotionally dependent on the third-country national parent.[112] In this regard,

> it is the relationship of dependency between the Union citizen who is a minor and the third country national who is refused a right of residence that is liable to jeopardise the effectiveness of Union citizenship, since it is that dependency that would lead to the Union

[110] *ibid*, paras 66, 68 and 72.

[111] Case C-133/15 *Chavez-Vilchez* EU:C:2017:354, 10 May 2017. See Fulvia Staiano, "Derivative Residence Rights for Parents of Union Citizen Children under Article 20 TFEU: *Chavez-Vilchez*" (2018) 55 *Common Market Law Review* 225; Hanneke Van Eijken and Pauline Phoa, "The Scope of Article 20 TFEU Clarified in *Chavez-Vilchez*: Are the Fundamental Rights of Minor EU Citizens Coming of Age?" (2018) 43 *European Law Review* 949.

[112] *ibid*, para 68.

> citizen being obliged, in practice, to leave not only the territory of the Member State of which he is a national but also that of the European Union as a whole, as a consequence of such a refusal.
>
> … it is important to determine … which parent is the primary carer of the child and whether there is in fact a relationship of dependency between the child and the third-country national parent. As part of that assessment, the competent authorities must take account of the right to respect for family life, as stated in Article 7 of the Charter of Fundamental Rights of the European Union, that article requiring to be read in conjunction with the obligation to take into consideration the best interests of the child, recognised in Article 24(2) of that Charter.
>
> For the purposes of such an assessment, the fact that the other parent, a Union citizen, is actually able and willing to assume sole responsibility for the primary day-to-day care of the child is a relevant factor, but it is not in itself a sufficient ground for a conclusion that there is not, between the third-country national parent and the child, such a relationship of dependency that the child would be compelled to leave the territory of the European Union if a right of residence were refused to that third-country national. In reaching such a conclusion, account must be taken, in the best interests of the child concerned, of all the specific circumstances, including the age of the child, the child's physical and emotional development, the extent of his emotional ties both to the Union citizen parent and to the third-country national parent, and the risks which separation from the latter might entail for that child's equilibrium.[113]

[25–75] The "coming of age" period has continued to see the Court of Justice place emphasis on the fundamental status of Union citizenship and the right of Union citizens to move freely throughout the Union. In the three significant cases of *Lounes, Coman* and *Banger*, the Court can be seen to take an expansive approach to citizenship rights under Art 21 TFEU, in circumstances where the Citizenship Directive did not apply as the Union citizen was living in a Member State of which they had nationality. It is also noteworthy that in each of these preliminary references, the Court chose to expand on the request for a ruling, going beyond questions referred concerning the application of the Citizens Directive to look more broadly at the implications of Union citizenship for the cases at hand.

[25–76] In *Lounes*, the UK argued that a dual Spanish–UK national, Ms Ormazabal, who had exercised her right of free movement to move from Spain to the UK and subsequently acquired British citizenship, could not rely on her EU law right to family reunification in respect of her Algerian husband, as she was now a British citizen.[114] The Court rejected the argument that the situation could be equated to one that was wholly internal, given that Ms Ormazabal had in fact moved from one Member State to another. As a result, she could not be denied her rights under Art 21 TFEU merely because she had acquired British nationality, in addition to her Spanish citizenship, as this would undermine the effectiveness of Art 21. To deny her the right of family reunification would amount to treating her the same as a British citizen who had never left the UK, disregarding the fact that she had exercised her freedom of movement and had retained her Spanish nationality. In addition,

[113] *ibid*, paras 69–71.

[114] Case C-165/16 *Lounes v Secretary of State for the Home Department* EU:C:2017:862, 14 November 2017. See Vincent Réveillère, "Family Rights for Naturalized EU Citizens: *Lounes*" (2018) 55 *Common Market Law Review* 1855; David AJG de Groot, "Free Movement of Dual EU Citizens" (2018) 3 *European Papers* 1075.

> the rights conferred on a Union citizen by Article 21(1) TFEU, including the derived rights enjoyed by his family members, are intended, amongst other things, to promote the gradual integration of the Union citizen concerned in the society of the host Member State.
>
> Union citizens, such as Ms Ormazabal, who, after moving, in the exercise of their freedom of movement, to the host Member State and residing there for a number of years pursuant to and in accordance with Article 7(1) or Article 16(1) of Directive 2004/38, acquire the nationality of that Member State, intend to become permanently integrated in that State.
>
> … it would be contrary to the underlying logic of gradual integration that informs Article 21(1) TFEU to hold that such citizens, who have acquired rights under that provision as a result of having exercised their freedom of movement, must forego those rights – in particular the right to family life in the host Member State – because they have sought, by becoming naturalised in that Member State, to become more deeply integrated in the society of that State.
>
> It would also follow that Union citizens who have exercised their freedom of movement and acquired the nationality of the host Member State in addition to their nationality of origin would, so far as their family life is concerned, be treated less favourably than Union citizens who have also exercised that freedom but who hold only their nationality of origin. The rights conferred on Union citizens in the host Member State, particularly the right to a family life with a third-country national, would thus be reduced in line with their increasing degree of integration in the society of that Member State and according to the number of nationalities that they hold.[115]

[25–77] As a result, even though the Citizens Directive did not apply to her situation as she was not residing in a Member State of which she was not a national, Art 21 TFEU nevertheless required that it be applied to her situation by analogy so as to ensure that her citizenship right of free movement was effective and to uphold Art 21's "underling logic of gradual integration".[116]

[25–78] A number of months later, in *Coman*, the Court ruled that Art 21 TFEU required a Member State in which same-sex marriage is not provided for to nonetheless recognise, for the purposes of family reunification, a same-sex spouse of a Union citizen where their marriage was concluded in a Member State in accordance with the law of the state.[117] Mr Coman was a Romanian national who had lived in Belgium and, while there, married an American man. When he sought to return to Romania he was informed that his husband would not be granted a right of residence on family reunion grounds as same-sex marriage was not recognised in its national law. As explained by the Court of Justice, notwithstanding that the Citizens Directive did not apply to Mr Coman when residing in Romania, Art 21 TFEU conferred on him a right to lead a normal family life both in the host Member State to which he had moved, and in his Member State of nationality to which he returns. Whilst Member States retained the competence to decide whether or not to allow for same-sex marriage, in doing so they must comply with EU law. In the view of the Court, to allow Member States to grant

[115] *ibid*, paras 56–59.

[116] The importance of integration within the host Member State has been emphasised by the Court again in *TopFit* EU:C:2019:497, 13 June 2019, paras 26–48, which concerned national athletics competitions in Germany that were not open to an Italian national who had lived in Germany for 15 years. Such rules were held to constitute a restriction on the free movement of EU citizens within the meaning of Art 21 TFEU and so needed to be justified by objective considerations that were proportionate to the legitimate objective pursued.

[117] Case C-673/16 *Coman* EU:C:2018:385, 5 June 2018.

or refuse a spouse the right of residence on the basis of national law would have the effect that the freedom of movement of Union citizens would vary from one Member State to another. Moreover, it could have the effect that a Union citizen could be denied the possibility of returning to his or her Member State of nationality together with his or her spouse. The Court rejected the suggestion that public policy grounds, based on the national identity of the Member States, could justify such a restriction on the right to free movement, noting that the obligation to recognise the marriage was confined to enabling the persons to exercise their EU law rights and did not require national law to recognise the institution of marriage between same-sex couples. Furthermore, Art 7 of the Charter of Fundamental Rights guaranteed the right to respect for private and family life and was to have the same meaning and scope as the equivalent right within the European Convention on Human Rights. As interpreted by the European Court of Human Rights, the right to private and family life equally applied to same-sex relationships.

[25–79] The following month, the Court delivered a judgment that followed similar reasoning in *Banger*.[118] There, Ms Banger, a South African national, had lived with her British partner in South Africa and later in the Netherlands. In the Netherlands, Ms Banger was given a residence card on the basis that she was an extended family member of her Union citizen partner. When they subsequently moved to the UK, she sought a residence card on the basis of the *Surinder Singh* principle, in the sense that her partner was an EU citizen who had exercised his right of free movement in the Netherlands and was now returning to his Member State of nationality. The UK refused her application on the basis that the *Surinder Singh* principle was confined to spouses, and did not extend to unmarried partners. As in *Lounes* and *Coman*, because Ms Banger's partner was now residing in a Member State of which he was a national, the Citizen's Directive did not apply. Nevertheless, once again it was possible that a third-country national could derive a right of residence on the basis of Art 21 TFEU. It was held that, in principle, such a derived right of residence ought to be granted on conditions that were no stricter than those set down in the Directive. This meant that Art 21 TFEU was to be interpreted as requiring the UK to facilitate the provision of a residence authorisation to Ms Banger as a third-country national with whom a Union citizen – returning to his home Member State after exercising his right of free movement in another Member State – was in a durable relationship that was duly attested.[119]

[25–80] Delivered around the same time, the case of *A* concerned a Finnish national with severe disabilities who applied for a personal assistance allowance to pay for the carrying out of household chores such as shopping and laundry.[120] His application was denied on the basis that, although he was maintaining his habitual residence in Finland, he intended to spend three to four days each week in Estonia, where he was to undertake higher education studies. In a preliminary reference, having confirmed that the allowance did not come within the scope of Regulation 883/2004 on the coordination of social security systems, the Court had to consider whether the denial of the allowance was contrary to Mr A's Union citizenship rights. In finding that the refusal was a restriction on his citizenship right of free movement, the Court observed that:

> the opportunities offered by the Treaty in relation to freedom of movement for citizens

[118] Case C-89/17 *Secretary of State for the Home Department v Banger* EU:C:2018:570, 12 July 2018.
[119] *ibid*, para 35.
[120] Case C-679/16 *A* EU:C:2018:601, 25 July 2018.

> of the Union cannot be fully effective if a national of a Member State can be dissuaded from using them by obstacles resulting from his stay in another Member State, because of legislation of his State of origin which penalises the mere fact that he has used those opportunities.
>
> That consideration is particularly important in the field of education, in view of the aims pursued by Article 6(e) TFEU and the second indent of Article 165(2) TFEU, namely, amongst other things, encouraging mobility of students and teachers.
>
> The [relevant] case-law … is applicable even though the personal assistance at issue … is not granted exclusively for the pursuit of studies, but for the social and economic integration of persons who are severely disabled in order to enable them to make their own choices, including as to whether to follow a course of study.[121]

[25–81] One final area where Union citizenship has had an increasing impact during the "coming of age" phase has been in relation to extradition. In *Petruhhin*, an Estonian living in Latvia was arrested on foot of a Russian request for his extradition.[122] Whereas an extradition treaty between Latvia and Russia precluded the extradition of Latvian nationals, there was no such bar on extraditing other Union citizens. The Court of Justice accepted that this difference in treatment engaged Arts 18 and 21 TFEU and was liable to affect the freedom of nationals of other EU Member States to move within the Union. As a restriction on the right of free movement, it was necessary for Latvia to justify the measure as being a proportionate means of pursing a legitimate public interest, such as preventing impunity for criminal offences. In this regard, the Court determined that it was necessary to ascertain whether there was an alternative measure less prejudicial to Art 21 TFEU would which be equally effective in achieving that objective.[123] According to the Court, in the absence of any EU-wide extradition agreement with Russia, it was necessary to give priority to an exchange of information with Estonia in order to allow the Estonian authorities the opportunity to issue a European Arrest Warrant for the individual, should its national law grant it jurisdiction to prosecute.

[25–82] This issue arose again in *Pisciotti*, where an Italian was arrested on foot of a US extradition request when making a stopover at Frankfurt airport.[124] Unlike *Petruhhin*, however, Mr Pisciotti was extradited pursuant to an EU–US extradition agreement rather than a bilateral agreement between Germany and the United States. In accordance with that agreement, Member States were permitted to refuse the extradition of their own nationals if a bilateral agreement with the US so provided, as was the case with respect to Germany. The Court followed its decision in *Petruhhin* and held that the same principle applied, even in the context of applying an EU extradition agreement with a third country. Whilst Member States were permitted to differentiate in the treatment of their own citizens, before acceding to an extradition request for a Union citizen it was necessary to first put that person's national authorities in a position to seek his or her surrender by issuing a European Arrest Warrant.

---

121 *ibid*, paras 61–63.

122 Case C-182/15 *Petruhhin* EU:C:2016:630, 6 September 2016. See Martin Böse, "Mutual Recognition, Extradition to Third Countries and Union Citizenship: *Petruhhin*" (2017) 54 *Common Market Law Review* 1781; Miguel João Costa, "The Emerging EU Extradition Law: *Petruhhin* and Beyond" (2017) 8 *New Journal of European Criminal Law* 192.

123 *ibid*, para 41.

124 Case C-191/16 *Pisciotti* EU:C:2018:222, 10 April 2018. See Stephen Coutts, "From Union citizens to national subjects: *Pisciotti*" (2019) 56 *Common Market Law Review* 521.

Overview of Case Law

Pre-Maastricht Treaty	*Gravier v City of Liège* *Cowan v Le Trésor public*	1985 1989
Infancy: 1993–1997	*Uecker and Jacquet*	1997
Growth: 1998–2005	*Martinez Sala* *Grzelczyk* *Baumbast* *Carpenter* *Garcia Avello* *Collins* *Trojani* *Chen* *Bidar*	1998 2001 2002 2002 2003 2004 2004 2004 2005
Adolescence: 2006–2009	*Förster*	2008
Coming of Age: 2010 Onwards *(i) Limiting Social Assistance*	 *Brey* *Dano Case* *Alimanovic* *García-Nieto* *Commission v UK*	 2013 2014 2015 2016 2016
(ii) "Genuine Enjoyment" Test	*Rottmann* *Tjebbes* *Ruiz Zambrano* *McCarthy* *Dereci* *Chavez-Vilchez*	2010 2019 2011 2011 2011 2017
Citizens Directive not applicable as person living within Member State of which they are a national	*Lounes* *Coman* *Banger* *A*	2017 2018 2018 2018
Extradition	*Petruhhin* *Pisciotti*	2016 2018

C. Membership and Participation

(i) Right to Consular Protection

[25–83] One aspect of the membership component of Union citizenship is the right to receive consular protection, as provided for in Arts 20(2)(c) and 23 TFEU and Art 46 of the Charter of Fundamental Rights. Consular protection is further elaborated upon in Council Directive 2015/637, the recitals to which note that it is an "expression of European solidarity" that provides an "external dimension to the concept of citizenship of the Union and strengthens the identity of the Union in third countries".[125]

[125] Council Directive (EU) 2015/637 of 20 April 2015 on the coordination and cooperation measures to facilitate consular protection for unrepresented citizens of the Union in third countries and repealing Decision 95/553/EC, [2015] OJ L106/1, recital (3). See Madalina Moraru, "An Analysis of the Consular Protection Directive: Are EU Citizens now Better Protected in the World?" (2019) 56 *Common Market Law Review* 417; Jan Wouters, Sanderijn Duquet and Katrien Meuwissen, "Caring for Citizens Abroad: The European Union and Consular Tasks" (2014) 19 *European Foreign Affairs*

The Directive has been transposed into Irish law by the European Union (Consular Protection) Regulations 2018.[126]

[25–84] Any Union citizen in a third country in which his or her own state is not represented is entitled to receive consular protection from the embassy or consulate of another EU Member State on the same conditions as that state applies to their own nationals. Accordingly, the Directive does not affect the competence of Member States to determine the scope of the protection to be provided to their own nationals, but once certain protection is provided it must be made available, on an equal basis, to any unrepresented Union citizen who wishes to avail of it. According to the implementing regulations, an Irish embassy or consulate (not including an honorary consulate) shall provide consular protection to unrepresented Union citizens who seek such protection on the same conditions as to Irish citizens.[127]

[25–85] A Member State is considered not to be represented in a third country if it has no embassy or consulate established there on a permanent basis, or if it has no embassy, consulate or honorary consul there which is effectively in a position to provide consular assistance in a given case. The recitals to the Directive indicate that a broad meaning is to be given to the notion of not being "effectively in a position" to provide assistance, stating that:

> a citizen who seeks consular protection or assistance from the embassy or consulate of another Member State should not be redirected to the embassy, consulate or honorary consul of his or her own Member State of nationality when it is not possible, due to local circumstances or lack of resources, for the citizen safely to reach or be reached by those latter instances in a way allowing him or her to receive consular protection. The notion of absence of representation should be interpreted with a view to ensuring the effectiveness of the right of unrepresented citizens to be protected by another Member State's embassy or consulate in a non-discriminatory way, taking into account the circumstances of each particular case.[128]

[25–86] The types of protection envisaged include assistance in situations of arrest or detention, being a victim of crime, a serious accident, serious illness or death and relief and repatriation in case of an emergency. It also includes the need for emergency travel documents as provided for in an earlier Decision from 1996, provision for which is made in s 28 of the Passport Act 2008.[129] The Directive calls for the diplomatic and consular authorities of Member States to closely cooperate and coordinate with one another, and with the EU's own delegations in third countries and the External Action Service,

Review 563; Alessandro Ianniello Saliceti, "The Protection of EU Citizens Abroad: Accountability, Rule of Law, Role of Consular and Diplomatic Services" (2011) 17 *European Public Law* 91. On the interaction between this EU law right and public international law, see Annemarieke Vermeer-Kunzli, "Where the Law Becomes Irrelevant: Consular Assistance in the European Union" (2011) 60 *International and Comparative Law Quarterly* 965.

126 SI No 123 of 2018.

127 *ibid*, Reg 3.

128 Recital (8).

129 Decision 96/409/CFSP of the Representatives of the Governments of the Member States, meeting within the Council of 25 June 1996 on the establishment of an emergency travel document [1996] OJ L168/4. Council Directive (EU) 2019/997 of 18 June 2019 establishing an EU Emergency Travel Document and repealing Decision 96/409/CFSP [2019] OJ L163/1 repeals the earlier Decision but only with effect from 36 months after the adoption of additional technical specifications referred to in Art 9 of the Directive.

to ensure protection of unrepresented citizens. There are also financial procedures for the reimbursement of costs incurred by the assisting Member State from the state of nationality, in order to allow for adequate burden sharing.

(ii) Right to Vote

[25–87] As noted above, newly evolving conceptions of shared and multiple citizenship tend to stress the importance of participatory actions and engagement with democratic processes over more traditional forms of passive membership in clearly defined, closed communities.[130] This can be seen in Arts 39 to 44 of the Charter of Fundamental Rights, in particular, which refer to the right: (i) to vote and stand as a candidate in municipal and European Parliament elections; (ii) to good administration; (iii) to be heard and to be given reasons for a decision; (iv) to have access to one's file; (v) to have made good any damage caused by an EU institution; (vi) to write to, and receive a reply from, an EU institution in any of the Treaty languages; (vii) to access documents of the Parliament, Council and Commission; (viii) to refer instances of maladministration to the Ombudsman; and (ix) to petition the European Parliament. In addition, as introduced by the Lisbon Treaty, Art 11(4) TEU provides for a mass petition to the Commission, known as the "Citizens' Initiative".

[25–88] Rules governing elections to the European Parliament are set out in an Act of 1976, as amended by Council Decisions in 2002 and 2018.[131] Directives have also been adopted setting out more detailed rules for voting in municipal[132] and European Parliament[133] elections by Union citizens residing in a Member State of which they are not a national. The European Parliament Elections Acts 1992 to 2019 provide the arrangements for European Parliament elections in Ireland, including voting by Union citizens.[134] In order to be registered as a European elector a Union citizen, other than a British citizen, must complete an "EP1" form and make a statutory declaration confirming that he or she is a Union citizen ordinarily resident in Ireland and that they "intend to exercise the right to vote at a European election in Ireland only".[135] In order to avoid double voting, which is a criminal offence, the statutory declarations are made available to the Member States of nationality. Irish turnout in European Parliament elections tends to be above the EU average, with turnouts of 59 and 52 per cent in 2009

---

[130] See Jo Shaw, *The Transformation of Citizenship in the European Union: Electoral Rights and the Restructuring of Political Space* (Cambridge University Press, 2015).

[131] The Act concerning the election of the members of the European Parliament by direct universal suffrage (which is known as the "Electoral Act") is annexed to Decision 76/787/ECSC, EEC, Euratom of the representatives of the Member States meeting in the Council relating to the Act concerning the election of the representatives of the Assembly by direct universal suffrage [1976] OJ L278/1; Council Decision 2002/772/EC, Euratom of 25 June and 23 September 2002 [2002] OJ L283/1; Council Decision (EU, Euratom) 2018/994 of 13 July 2018 [2018] OJ L178/1.

[132] Council Directive 94/80/EC of 19 December 1994 laying down detailed arrangements for the exercise of the right to vote and to stand as a candidate in municipal elections by citizens of the Union residing in a Member State of which they are not nationals [1994] OJ L368/38.

[133] Council Directive 2013/1/EU of 20 December 2012 [2013] OJ L26/27 and Council Directive 93/109/EC of 6 December 1993 [1993] OJ L329/34 laying down detailed arrangements for the exercise of the right to vote and stand as a candidate in elections to the European Parliament for citizens of the Union residing in a Member State of which they are not nationals.

[134] The European Parliament Elections Acts 1997, 2004, 2014 and 2019 and relevant sections of the Electoral Acts, in particular the Electoral Act 1992 (known collectively as the European Parliament Elections Act 1992 to 2019).

[135] s 6 of the European Parliament Elections Act 1997.

and 2014, compared to an EU-wide turnout of 43 per cent in both years. The 2019 elections bucked this trend. Whereas turnout across the EU reached a twenty year high of 51 per cent, in Ireland it fell below the EU average to 50 per cent.

[25–89] Although the Court of Justice has confirmed that Member States are entitled to make the right to vote and stand in European Parliament elections subject to a residency requirement, it has shown a willingness to review such restrictions from an EU law perspective. In *Eman and Sevinger*, the Court held that it was contrary to the principle of equal treatment for the Netherlands to allow its nationals resident in a third country to vote and stand in European Parliament elections, but not to allow its nationals resident in Dutch Antilles or Aruba to do so.[136] The principle of equal treatment precluded the imposition of any criteria which resulted in nationals who were in comparable situations from being treated differently, unless that difference in treatment was objectively justified, which the Netherlands had failed to demonstrate.

[25–90] The EU is a polity whose own elections, in the form of elections to the European Parliament, "tend to be fought on the basis of national political platforms by national political parties fielding national candidates, despite the existence of electoral rights for EU citizens under Articles 22(2)(b) and 23 TFEU. In practice, most of the legal regulations governing the European Parliament elections are national, not European in character".[137] In 2017, President Macron of France proposed that some of the 73 seats that would be freed up as a result of the UK's withdrawal from the EU should be used to create transnational lists of Union-wide constituencies. It was argued that this would contribute to strengthening European democracy by creating debates on European challenges and not strictly national ones during European Parliament elections. Whilst the Commission had expressed sympathy for the proposal, it was ultimately rejected by the European Parliament itself and did not form part of the 2018 amendment to the Electoral Act of 1976.[138] One amendment that was introduced in 2018, however, was to allow for the possibility of the name of a relevant European political party or group to be included on ballot papers, a reform that should contribute to increasing the level of awareness of European-wide parties or groupings to which Irish political parties or independent candidates affiliate.[139]

(iii) Petition the European Parliament

[25–91] Although the rights to petition the European Parliament and refer a complaint to the Ombudsman already existed and so were not first created by the Lisbon Treaty, that Treaty did elevate their status in Arts 20 and 24 TFEU, as part of the strengthening of the provisions on Union citizenship. They are also found in Arts 43 and 44 of the

[136] Case C-300/04 *Eman and Sevinger* [2006] ECR I-8055. In seeking to justify the exclusion, it was perhaps a weakness that, whereas Dutch nationals of Antilles or Aruba were unable to vote while living there, if they moved to another third country, say neighbouring Venezuela, they were entitled to vote on the same basis as a Dutch national from the Netherlands who had moved to Venezuela. See Leonard Besselink, "Case Notes on *Gibraltar, Aruba* and *Sevinger and Eman v The Netherlands*" (2008) 45 *Common Market Law Review* 787.

[137] Jo Shaw, "Citizenship: Contrasting Dynamics at the Interface of Integration and Constitutionalism" in Paul Craig and Gráinne de Búrca (eds), *The Evolution of EU Law* (2nd ed, Oxford University Press, 2011) 575, 577.

[138] European Commission Press Release, "A Europe that Delivers: Commission Presents Ideas for a More Efficient European Union", 14 February 2018.

[139] European Parliament Elections (Amendment) Act 2019, s 6.

Charter of Fundamental Rights. With respect to submitting a petition, Art 227 TFEU further provides that:

> Any citizen of the Union, and any natural or legal person residing or having its registered office in a Member State, shall have the right to address, individually or in association with other citizens or persons, a petition to the European Parliament on a matter which comes within the Union's fields of activity and which affects him, her or it directly.

[25–92] The right to petition the Parliament has been described by the Court of Justice as a fundamental right and an "instrument of citizen participation in the democratic life of the European Union. It is one of the means of ensuring direct dialogue between citizens of the European Union and their representatives".[140] In 2016, 1,569 petitions were received, of which 1,110 were deemed admissible, dealing with issues in the areas of the Internal Market (10 per cent), justice (7 per cent), fundamental rights (7 per cent), and property, health and social affairs (4 per cent each).[141] Sixteen petitions were from Irish citizens or otherwise had a connection to Ireland. The main reasons why a petition is deemed inadmissible is that the matter does not relate to an EU competence and so does not come within the Union's field of activity, or there is confusion as between the means of redress provided by the EU and the Council of Europe. A "Petitions' Portal" website allows for the submission of a new petition, or expression of support for an existing petition, online, and 68 per cent of submissions in 2016 were made electronically via the web portal.[142]

[25–93] In accordance with Rules 215–217 of the Parliament's Rules of Procedure, together with Part XX of Annex VI, petitions are examined by the Parliament's Committee on Petitions, which takes a decision on their admissibility and is responsible for dealing with them in conjunction with the Commission, which is usually asked to provide information or to give its opinion on the issues raised. The Committee may also pose questions to the Ombudsman and/or consult with other parliamentary committees, hold hearings or send members on fact-finding visits. The outcome will vary depending on the nature of the issue raised and, in particular, whether it is a specific claim relating to an individual, in which case the Committee may contact the relevant national authorities or intervene through the relevant permanent representation. If the petition relates to a matter of more general interest, the outcome may take the form of political action by the Parliament or Commission, or in the case of a breach of EU law, may lead to infringement proceedings being considered by the Commission.

[25–94] The Court of Justice has confirmed that a decision by the Parliament to deem a petition inadmissible for failing to meet the conditions laid down in Art 227 TFEU must be amenable to judicial review, since it is liable to affect the right of petition of the person concerned, and must be accompanied by a sufficient statement of reasons to allow the petitioner to know which of the conditions was not met. Once having decided that a petition is admissible, however, the Parliament has a broad discretion, of a political nature, as regards how that petition should be dealt with, which is not amenable to review.[143]

---

140 Case C-261/13P *Schönberger v Parliament* EU:C:2014:2423, para 17.

141 European Parliament Report under Rule 216(7) on the deliberations of the Committee on Petitions during the year 2016, 30 November 2017, 15, 17.

142 *ibid*, 14. The portal is available at <https://petiport.secure.europarl.europa.eu/petitions/en/main>.

143 Case C-261/13P *Schönberger v Parliament* EU:C:2014:2423, paras 22–24.

(iv) Complain to the Ombudsman

[25–95] In addition to Arts 20 and 24 TFEU, the role of the Ombudsman is the subject of Art 228 TFEU, which provides that:

> A European Ombudsman elected by the European Parliament shall be empowered to receive complaints from any citizen of the Union or any natural or legal person residing or having its registered office in a Member State concerning instances of maladministration in the activities of the Union institutions, bodies, offices or agencies, with the exception of the Court of Justice and acting in its judicial role. He or she shall examine such complaints and report on them. In accordance with his duties, the Ombudsman shall conduct inquiries for which he finds grounds, either on his own initiative or on the basis of complaints submitted to him direct or through a Member of the European Parliament, except where the alleged facts are or have been the subject of legal proceedings. Where the Ombudsman establishes an instance of maladministration, he shall refer the matter to the institution concerned, which shall have a period of three months in which to inform him of its views. The Ombudsman shall then forward a report to the European Parliament and the institution, body, office, or agency concerned. The person lodging the complaint shall be informed of the outcome of such inquiries. The Ombudsman shall submit an annual report to the European Parliament on the outcome of his inquiries.[144]

[25–96] The Ombudsman's powers include the right to inspect EU documents, call officials to testify, and to open strategic inquiries on her own initiative. The Ombudsman plays an important role with respect to requests for access to EU documents and the current office holder, Emily O'Reilly (who previously held the equivalent position in Ireland), has placed an emphasis on ensuring transparency, which tends to account for between 20 and 30 per cent of complaints. For instance, an own-initiative inquiry was established concerning transparency and public participation in relation to the Transatlantic Trade and Investment Partnership negotiations with the United States, prompting the Council and the Commission to permit greater detail to be made known, while a complaint was upheld concerning the refusal of the European Central Bank to release a three-year old letter issued from its former President to the Irish Finance Minister at the height of the financial crisis, leading to the release of the letter. A strategic initiative between the Ombudsman and the Council on the transparency of the negotiations on the UK withdrawal from the EU was closed in 2019, reaching the conclusion that the EU had "had overall pursued a proactive approach anticipating citizens' and businesses' legitimate need for information" and that the "level of transparency achieved by the EU thus far has been very high when compared to for example international negotiations that the EU has conducted in the past".[145] In 2018, the Ombudsman introduced a new fast-track procedure for dealing with complaints relating to access to documents, which sets out a two-month timeframe within which a complaint should be addressed. Out of a total of 2,216 complaints made to the Ombudsman in 2017, and 433 investigations opened, 60 came from Ireland, 19 of which led to the opening of investigations.[146]

---

[144] See Nikos Vogiatzis, *The European Ombudsman and Good Administration in the European Union* (Palgrave Macmillan, 2018).

[145] European Ombudsman, "Closing Note on the Strategic Initiative with the Council of the EU concerning public information on the UK's withdrawal from the EU" (SI/3/2017/KR), 6 May 2019.

[146] European Ombudsman, *Annual Report 2017*, 15 May 2018, 36.

(v) Correspond in an Official Treaty Language

[25–97] The right of a citizen to correspond with an EU institution in any one of the official Treaty languages mentioned in Art 55(1) TEU had already been provided for in a 1958 Council Regulation,[147] but was raised to primary law status by the Treaty of Amsterdam. It is now confirmed in Art 24 TFEU and Art 41(4) of the Charter. Although correspondence with the institutions could be conducted in Irish from the entry into force of the Treaty of Amsterdam on 1 May 1999, Irish did not become an official *working* language of the EU until 1 January 2007, the date upon which Council Regulation (EC) No 920/2005 entered into force, bringing to an end a derogation from the 1958 Council Regulation whereby Irish, although an official Treaty language, was not a working language pursuant to the Regulation.[148] Even then, however, a limited form of derogation was retained, with the recitals to Regulation No 920/2005 noting:

> It is however appropriate to decide that, for practical reasons and on a transitional basis, the institutions of the European Union are not to be bound by the obligation to draft and translate all acts, including judgments of the Court of Justice, in the Irish language. It is also appropriate to provide that such a derogation be partial, to exclude from its scope Regulations adopted jointly by the European Parliament and the Council and to empower the Council to determine unanimously, within a period of four years after the date of application of this Regulation and at five-yearly intervals thereafter, whether to put an end to that derogation.[149]

[25–98] The derogation was extended once again in 2010, until 31 December 2016, and again by Council Regulation 2015/2264, until 31 December 2021.[150] On this occasion, however, the Regulation committed to a gradual reduction in the scope of the derogation with a view to not renewing it further at the end of the five-year period, as well as an urging of the institutions to "continue their proactive approach to increasing the availability of information in Irish on the activities of the Union". The Irish authorities are to meet regularly with the Commission to monitor the recruitment of a sufficient number of Irish-language personnel by the institutions in order to successfully handle a gradual reduction of the derogation, by extending the obligation to translate as follows:

No later than 1 January 2017	Directives adopted by the Parliament and the Council
No later than 1 January 2018	Decisions adopted by the Parliament and the Council
No later than 1 January 2020	(i) Directives adopted by the Council addressed to all Member States; (ii) Regulations adopted by the Council; and (iii) Decisions adopted by the Council which do not specify to whom they are addressed.
No later than 1 January 2021	(i) Regulations adopted by the Commission; (ii) Directives adopted by the Commission which are addressed to all Member States; and (iii) Decisions adopted by the Commission which do not specify to whom they are addressed.

---

[147] EEC Council Regulation No 1 of 15 April 1958 determining the languages to be used by the European Economic Community [1958] OJ 17/385. See Sean Ó Riain, *The EU and the Irish Language: Identity and Linguistic Diversity* (Clódhanna Teo, 2001).

[148] Council Regulation (EC) No 920/2005 of 13 June 2005 amending Regulation No 1 of 15 April 1958 [2005] OJ L156/3.

[149] *ibid*, recital 4.

[150] Council Regulation (EU) No 1257/2010 of 20 December 2010 [2010] OJ L343/5 and Council Regulation (EU) No 2015/2264 of 3 December 2015 [2015] OJ L322/1.

[25–99] No later than October 2019, the Commission is to report to the Council on the progress made towards achieving these goals, on foot of which the Council may decide by unanimity, in accordance with Art 342 TFEU, to revise the target dates set out above.[151] No later than June 2021, the Commission is to again report to the Council, this time setting out whether the institutions have sufficient capacity to remove the derogation from the 1958 Regulation entirely, as is planned.

(vi) Citizens' Initiative

[25–100] Introduced by the Lisbon Treaty, the Citizens' Initiative is provided for in Art 11 TEU, with Art 24 TFEU laying down the legislative procedure for the specification of its precise modalities.[152] These rules are set out in Regulation No 211/2011 and three additional implementing acts,[153] which have been given further effect in Irish law.[154] Although Art 11 TEU merely refers to a requirement for one million signatories to be obtained, the Regulation adds a number of complex requirements, including that the signatories must come from at least a quarter of the Member States – ie from at least seven states – in each of which there must be a minimum number of signatories corresponding to that state's number of members of the European Parliament multiplied by 750. In response to perceived technical and logistical difficulties in the implementation of the Citizens' Initiative, in 2017 a consultation process was launched which resulted in a Commission proposal for a new regulation that would make the initiative more accessible and easier to use for organisers and supporters. From 1 January 2020, Regulation 211/2011 will be repealed and replaced by Regulation 2019/788.[155]

[25–101] An initiative begins life by being launched by a citizens' committee, which is then registered by the Commission provided that the conditions for admissibility are met, in particular the fact that the initiative does not manifestly fall outside the Commission's powers. The decision as to whether to register an initiative is now taken by the College of Commissioners, which is said to demonstrate the importance given by the Commission to the Citizens' Initiative and to the priority of listening to citizens and their concerns.[156] The refusal to register a proposed initiative has led to a number of legal challenges.[157] Once an initiative is registered, the collection of the required

[151] According to Art 342 TFEU: "The rules governing the languages of the institutions of the Union shall, without prejudice to the provisions contained in the Statute of the Court of Justice of the European Union, be determined by the Council, acting unanimously."

[152] See Fernando Mendez and Mario Mendez, "The Promise and Perils of Direct Democracy for the European Union" (2017) 19 *Cambridge Yearbook of European Legal Studies* 48; Nikos Vogiatzis, "Is the European Citizens' Initiative a Serious Threat for the Community Method" (2013) 6 *European Journal of Legislative Studies* 91; Michael Dougan, "What Are We to Make of the Citizens' Initiative?" (2011) 48 *Common Market Law Review* 1807; Editorial, "Direct Democracy and the European Union … Is that a Threat or a Promise?" (2008) 45 *Common Market Law Review* 929.

[153] Regulation (EU) No 211/2011 of the European Parliament and of the Council of 16 February 2011 on the citizen's initiative [2011] OJ L65/1; Commission Delegated Regulation 887/2013 [2013] OJ L247/11; Commission Implementing Regulation 1179/2011 [2011] OJ L301/13; Commission Delegated Regulation 2019/714 [2019] OJ L123/30.

[154] European Union (Citizens' Initiative) Regulations 2012 (SI No 79 of 2012) and European Union (Citizens' Initiative) (Amendment) Regulations 2014 (SI No 94 of 2014).

[155] Regulation (EU) 2019/788 of the European Parliament and of the Council of 17 April 2019 on the European citizens' initiative [2019] OJ L130/55.

[156] European Commission, *Report on the Application of Regulation (EU) No 211/2011 on the Citizens' Initiative*, COM(2018) 157 final, 28 March 2018, 5.

[157] See Case C-420/16 P *Izsák v Commission* EU:C:2019:177, 7 March 2019; Case C-589/15

statements of support can begin. If the verification of statements of support by Member States' competent authorities (in Ireland, the Department of Housing, Planning and Local Government) confirms that the minimum number of signatories has been reached, organisers submit their initiative to the Commission, which has three months to reply.

[25–102] Since its introduction up to March 2018, 48 initiatives had been registered, amassing a total of around nine million signatures, while 22 requests for registration were refused.[158] Of these, four initiatives successfully reached the required number of signatories. The first concerned the right to water, and called upon the Commission to "propose legislation implementing the human right to water and sanitation as recognised by the United Nations, and promoting the provision of water and sanitation as essential public services for all". The second sought to "establish a ban and end the financing of activities which presuppose the destruction of human embryos, in particular in the areas of research, development aid and public health", while the third sought to end the use of live animals in scientific experimentation and the fourth urged a ban on glyphosate and the protection of people and the environment from toxic pesticides.[159] Taken together, Irish support for these petitions totalled just under 24,000 statements of support, the seventh lowest amongst the Member States.

[25–103] In the three months following the submission of a successful initiative, the Commission will meet with the organisers so as to allow them the opportunity to explain in detail the issues raised. The organisers also have the opportunity to present their initiative at a public hearing in the European Parliament. The Commission will then adopt a formal response, in the form of a communication adopted by the College of Commissioners, spelling out what action, if any, it will propose in response to the initiative, and the reasons for doing so.[160] In certain cases, the Commission may only present its preliminary opinion and decide to carry out further studies before making its final decision. Crucially, there is no obligation on the Commission to propose legislation as a result of an initiative if it does not consider that this is appropriate.

Anagnostakis v Commission ECLI:EU:C:2017:663, 12 September 2017; Case T–754/14 *Efler v Commission* EU:T:2017:323, 10 May 2017; Case T–646/13 *Minority SafePack – One Million Signatures for Diversity in Europe v Commission* EU:T:2017:59, 3 February 2017; Case T–44/14 *Costantini v Commission* EU:T:2016:223, 19 April 2016; Anastasia Karatzia, "The European Citizens' Initiative and Greek debt relief: *Anagnostakis*" (2019) 56 *Common Market Law Review* 1069; Anastasia Karatzia, "Revisiting the Registration of European Citizens' Initiatives: The Evolution of the Legal Admissibility Test" (2018) 20 *Cambridge Yearbook of European Legal Studies* 147; Natassa Athanasiadou, "The European Citizens' Initiative in Times of Brexit" (2018) 3 *European Papers* 1379.

[158] European Commission, *Report on the Application of Regulation (EU) No 211/2011 on the Citizens' Initiative*, COM(2018) 157 final, 28 March 2018, 3.

[159] See <http://ec.europa.eu/citizens-initiative/public/initiatives/successful>.

[160] See Commission Communication on the European Citizens' Initiative "Ban Glyphosate and Protect People and the Environment from Toxic Pesticides", C(2017) 8414 final, 12 December 2017; Commission Communication on the European Citizens' Initiative "Stop Vivisection", C(2015) 3773 final, 3 June 2015; Commission Communication on the European Citizens' Initiative "One of Us", COM(2014) 355 final, 28 May 2014; Commission Communication on the European Citizens' Initiative "Water and Sanitation Are a Human Right! Water Is a Public Good, Not a Commodity!", COM(2014) 177 final, 19 March 2014.

PART SEVEN

CHAPTER 26

FREE MOVEMENT OF CAPITAL

A. INTRODUCTION

[26–01] The movement of capital can be understood as the movement across borders of resources that are "used for, or capable of, investment intended to generate revenue".[1] Such resources can include cash, shares, bonds and other debt instruments, and even goods when they take the form of charitable gifts. Within the EU, the freedom to move capital is intended to allow individuals or legal entities to operate on a cross-border basis in order to carry out a range of activities such as transporting cash, opening and closing bank accounts, making bank deposits and withdrawals or taking out loans, registering mortgages, buying and selling shares and receiving dividends, or even giving and receiving gifts.[2]

[26–02] The free movement of capital is one of the four fundamental freedoms. As originally provided for in the Treaty of Rome, however, it was treated much less ambitiously than the free movement of goods, workers and services. At the time, Member States tended to seek to control the movement of capital into and out of their jurisdiction, such as through restrictions on the exchange of currency. This was because large movements of capital have the potential to influence both exchange rates and interest rates. A significant outflow of capital can lead to higher interest rates and a currency devaluation, with a significant inflow having the opposite effect. As a result, "capital movements will either require the exchange rate to adjust to in- and outflows, or interest rates will have to be used to defend the exchange rate".[3] Large inflows of capital can also be a factor leading to the ready availability of credit. This might cause an increase in consumer spending, which in turn can fuel inflation and result in a growth in imports, affecting a country's balance of payments.

[26–03] Prior to the creation of the euro and the European Central Bank, the ability to alter interest rates or devalue a currency were important monetary policy tools available

[1] Leo Flynn, "Free Movement of Capital" in Catherine Barnard and Steve Peers (eds), *European Union Law* (2nd ed, Oxford University Press, 2017) 447, 452.
[2] *ibid*, 451.
[3] Jukka Snell, "Free Movement of Capital: Evolution as a Non-Linear Process" in Paul Craig and Gráinne de Búrca (eds), *The Evolution of EU Law* (2nd ed, Oxford University Press, 2011) 547, 550.

to Member States in protecting their own economies. While inward investment will usually be welcomed, Member States wished to retain a degree of control over inward and outward capital flows for these purposes. Naturally, therefore, the free movement of capital has remained very closely intertwined with the development of the EU's economic and monetary union, which is the subject of Chapter 27.

[26–04] The Treaty of Rome's guarantee of the free movement of capital reflected this concern by providing, in general and somewhat aspirational terms, that "to the extent necessary to ensure the proper functioning of the common market, Member States shall progressively abolish between themselves all restrictions on the movement of capital belonging to persons resident in Member States and any discrimination based on the nationality or place of residence of the parties or on the place where such capital is invested". This difference in treatment led the Court of Justice in *Casati* to conclude that, unlike the other fundamental freedoms, the Treaty guarantee of the free movement of capital was not capable of having direct effect. As explained by the Court:

> Freedom to move certain types of capital is, in practice, a pre-condition for the effective exercise of other freedoms guaranteed by the Treaty, in particular the right of establishment. However, capital movements are also closely connected with the economic and monetary policy of the Member States. At present, it cannot be denied that complete freedom of movement of capital may undermine the economic policy of one of the Member States or create an imbalance in its balance of payments, thereby impairing the proper functioning of the Common Market. For those reasons [the Article on free movement of capital] differs from the provisions on the free movement of goods, persons and services in the sense that there is an obligation to liberalise capital movements "only to the extent necessary to ensure the proper functioning of the Common Market". The scope of that restriction … varies in time and depends on an assessment of the requirements of the Common Market and on an appraisal of both the advantages and risks which liberalisation might entail for the latter, having regard to the stage it has reached and, in particular, to the level of integration attained in matters in respect of which capital movements are particularly significant.[4]

[26–05] In a separate provision of the Treaty of Rome, the Member States undertook to authorise, in the currency of the Member State in which a creditor resides, any *payments* connected with the movement of goods, services and capital. Whereas the provision on the free movement of capital dealt mainly with financial operations concerning investment of funds and was not capable of direct effect, the provision on payments dealt with payment in a foreign currency for the provision of goods or services and was held to be directly effective.[5] Since the ability to transfer payments was not to be interfered with, the Court of Justice confirmed that the physical transfer of bank notes could not be classified as a movement of capital where the transfer corresponded to an obligation to pay arising from a transaction involving the movement of goods or services.[6]

[26–06] In 1990, an important directive – Directive 88/361 or the "Third Capital Directive" – entered into force and further implemented the Treaty's provision on the

---

4 Case 203/80 *Casati* [1981] ECR 2595, 2614. See John A Usher, "The Evolution of the Free Movement of Capital" (2007) 31 *Fordham Journal of International Law* 1533; Leo Flynn, "Coming of Age: The Free Movement of Capital Case Law 1993–2002" (2002) 39 *Common Market Law Review* 773.

5 Joined Cases 286/82 and 26/83 *Luisi and Carbone* [1984] ECR 377.

6 *ibid*, 404. See Reg (EC) No 1889/2005 of the European Parliament and of the Council of 26 October 2005 on controls of cash entering or leaving the Community [2005] OJ L309/9.

free movement of capital.[7] It provided that, to facilitate its application, movements of capital were to be classified in accordance with a nomenclature (and explanatory notes) set out in an annex as follows:

Direct Investments
Investments in Real Estate
Operations in Securities
Operations in Collective Investment Undertakings
Operations in Securities and Other Instruments Normally Dealt with on the Money Market
Operations in Current and Deposit Accounts with Financial Institutions
Credits Related to Commercial Transactions or the Provision of Services
Financial Loans and Credits
Sureties, Other Guarantees and Rights of Pledge
Transfers Performance or Insurance Contracts
Personal Capital Movements (Inheritances, Dowries)
Physical Import and Export of Financial Assets

[26–07] In defining what constitutes a movement of capital, the Court of Justice has made frequent use of the non-exhaustive list set out in the Third Capital Directive, for which purpose it has been said to retain an "indicative value".[8] Rather than following the approach taken in respect of goods, workers or services, whereby it might have developed a broad, abstract definition of the movement of capital, the Court has further elaborated on the meaning of each of the various terms set out in the annex. For example, the Court has clarified that direct investment involves "participation in an undertaking through the holding of shares which confers the possibility of participating effectively in its management and control", as compared with portfolio investment which entails the "acquisition of shares on the capital market solely with the intention of making a financial investment without any intention to influence the management and control of the undertaking".[9] While it got off to a slow start, over the past 15 years, in particular, a sudden growth in litigation regarding the free movement of capital has seen the Court's case law on the topic shifting "from the shadows to the foreground of market integration".[10]

[26–08] As direct investment involves participation in an undertaking, rules concerning the movement of capital will often have a bearing on related fields such as the right of establishment, cross-border acquisitions and rules of company law

[7] Council Directive 88/361/EEC of 24 June 1988 for the implementation of Article 67 of the Treaty [1988] OJ L178/5.

[8] Case C-510/08 *Mattner* [2010] ECR I-3553, para 19.

[9] Case C-182/08 *Glaxo Wellcome* [2009] ECR I-8591, para 40. See also Case C-452/04 *Fidium Finanz* [2006] ECR I-9521; Case C-98/01 *Commission v UK* [2003] ECR I-4641; Case C-279/00 *Commission v Italy* [2002] ECR I-1425; Case C-222/97 *Trummer and Mayer* [1999] ECR I-1661. The distinction between direct investment and non-direct investment, such as portfolio investment, has been replicated at the external level, with the Court of Justice clarifying the scope of "foreign direct investment" as part of the Common Commercial Policy in *Opinion 2/15* EU:C:2017:376, 16 May 2017. See Rumiana Yotova, "Opinion 2/15 of the CJEU: Delineating the Scope of the New EU Competence in Foreign Direct Investment" (2018) 17 *Cambridge Law Journal* 29; Marise Cremona, "Shaping EU Trade Policy Post-Lisbon: Opinion 2/15 of 16 May 2017" (2018) 14 *European Constitutional Law Review* 231.

[10] Thomas Horsley, "Death, Taxes, and (Targeted) Judicial Dynamism. The Free Movement of Capital in EU Law" in Anthony Arnull and Damian Chalmers (eds), *The Oxford Handbook of European Union Law* (Oxford University Press, 2015) 784, 788.

governing ownership and shareholding.[11] For instance, certain national restrictions may impair both the free movement of capital and the right of establishment, such as a limit placed by a host state on the amount of voting shares that investors from other Member States may acquire in domestic companies. In very general terms, the approach of the Court of Justice in deciding whether the freedom of establishment or the free movement of capital governs a dispute is to examine the extent to which the investment or shareholding at issue gives the investor a "definite influence" over the company's decisions. The greater the level of direct influence, the more likely it is that the rules on establishment will apply rather than those on the free movement of capital.[12] While Art 65(2) TFEU acknowledges that a degree of overlap between the two freedoms can apply, the situation is different in cases involving third-country nationals or entities. Since only the free movement of capital extends to third countries, the determination of which freedom applies will be of much greater significance in such cases.

[26–09] The free movement of capital is also closely related to the freedom to provide services, and financial services in particular.[13] This is reflected in the TFEU, which provides that the liberalisation of banking and insurance sectors connected with movements of capital shall be effected in step with the liberalisation of movement of capital.[14] Finally, by limiting the ability of Member States to restrict flows of capital, EU law may deprive Member States of their autonomy to tax income received from investments abroad differently from income received from domestic investments. Consequently, much of the Court's case law on the free movement of capital concerns the tax laws of Member States and whether the TFEU has been infringed by any preferential treatment being afforded to domestic investments over investments made in other Member States. Indeed, between 2008 and 2013, out of 57 judgments on intra-EU capital movements, 46 concerned disputes involving taxation.[15]

[26–10] The free movement of capital is the only one of the four freedoms to have undergone any substantive amendment. This occurred with the entry into force of the Maastricht Treaty in 1993, which introduced into the Treaties the core elements of Third Capital Directive and merged the separate provisions on capital and payments. The free movement of capital and of payments is now provided for in Arts 63–66 TFEU, which make up Chapter 4 of Title IV of Part Three of the TFEU (the Title dealing with the free movement of persons, services and capital).

[26–11] Article 63 enshrines the general prohibition of restrictions on the movement of capital and payments. Uniquely amongst the four freedoms, this prohibition is not confined to movements as between EU Member States but extends to movements to and from third countries. Reflecting the unique and expansive nature of this extension, Art

---

11 See Wolf-Georg Ringe, "Company Law and Free Movement of Capital" (2010) 69 *Cambridge Law Journal* 378.

12 See Case C-31/11 *Scheunemann* EU:C:2012:481, 19 July 2012; Case C-531/06 *Commission v Italy* [2009] ECR I-4103; Case C-231/05 *Oy AA* [2007] ECR I-6373; Case C-196/04 *Cadbury Schweppes* [2006] ECR I-7995; Case C-436/00 *X and Y* [2002] ECR I-10829; Case C-251/98 *Baars* [2000] ECR I-2787.

13 See Case C-452/04 *Fidium Finanz* [2006] ECR I-9521.

14 Article 58(2) TFEU.

15 Thomas Horsley, "Death, Taxes, and (Targeted) Judicial Dynamism: The Free Movement of Capital in EU Law" in Anthony Arnull and Damian Chalmers (eds), *The Oxford Handbook of European Union Law* (Oxford University Press, 2015) 784, 789.

64 places a number of limitations on the general prohibition as it applies to movements to and from third countries, while Art 66 allows for the adoption of six-month safeguard measures where movements of capital to or from third countries cause, or threaten to cause, serious difficulties for the operation of economic and monetary union.

[26–12] By way of derogation from Art 63, Art 65 allows certain Member State measures that either: (i) are justified on grounds of public policy or public security; (ii) include different treatment in tax law based on the taxpayer's place of residence or the place where their capital is invested; (iii) are aimed at preventing infringements of national law, particularly in the field of taxation and the prudential supervision of financial institutions; or (iv) prescribe procedures for the declaration of capital movements for purposes of administrative or statistical information. However, any such measures must not constitute a means of arbitrary discrimination or a disguised restriction on the free movement of capital.

[26–13] A separate provision related to the movement of capital and payments is found in Title V of the TFEU dealing with the Area of Freedom, Security and Justice. Article 75 provides that, where necessary to achieve justice and security objectives concerning the prevention and combatting of terrorism and related activities, the Parliament and Council shall define a framework for administrative measures with regard to capital movements and payments, such as the freezing of funds, financial assets or economic gains belonging to, or owned or held by, natural or legal persons, groups or non-state entities. Unlike Art 215 TFEU, which allows for the imposition of restrictive measures (ie sanctions) in the context of the Union's foreign policy and has been widely used, Art 75 has not been used to date. Declaration No 25 to the TEU and TFEU on Arts 75 and 215 recalls that respect for fundamental rights and freedoms implies, in particular, that proper attention is given to the protection and observance of the due process rights of the individuals or entities concerned. For this purpose and in order to guarantee a thorough judicial review of decisions subjecting an individual or entity to restrictive measures, such decisions must be based on clear and distinct criteria. Through Protocol No 21 to the TEU and TFEU, Ireland has the right to choose whether or not to opt-in to any measure adopted under Title V TFEU. As an exception to this, however, the Protocol provides that, with respect to Ireland, any measure adopted pursuant to Art 75 shall apply automatically.

B. No Restrictions on the Movement of Capital – Article 63 TFEU

[26–14] Article 63 TFEU prohibits "all restrictions" on the movement of capital or payments between Member States. Uniquely among the four freedoms, this prohibition is also extended to movements as between Member States and third countries. This extension to third countries is limited, however, by that fact that Art 64 allows any restrictions that were in place on 31 December 1993 to remain in force.[16] Secondly, the Council is merely required to adopt measures in order to endeavour to "achieve the objective of free movement of capital between Member States and third countries to the greatest extent possible". Thirdly, Art 65(4) provides that, in the absence of measures by the Council to restrict the movement of capital to and from third countries,

[16] See Case C-135/17 *X GmbH v Finanzamt Stuttgart* EU:C:2019:136, 26 February 2019.

the Commission or, in the absence of a Commission decision within three months, a unanimous Council, may adopt a decision stating that restrictive tax measures adopted by a Member State concerning a third country are compatible with the Treaties as being justified by a Union objective and the proper functioning of the Internal Market. The unusual nature of this provision has been described by Jukka Snell, for whom Art 65(4) is remarkable in that:

> it places the Member States in the Council in the position to rule on the legality of national measures, something that is normally reserved for the Court. … The criteria employed – justification by one of the objectives of the EU and compatibility with functioning of the internal market – are extremely wide, and do not in practice curtail the discretion of the Council much … [and] the wide discretion granted to the Council will make judicial review of its decisions difficult. From a wider perspective, the inclusion of the Article in the Lisbon Treaty clearly demonstrates a distrust of the Court on the part of the Member States when it comes to deciding on tax matters and their willingness to curtail the free movement of capital to and from third countries. The Court, for its own part, seems to have received the message sent by the Member States, and has chosen to tread lightly in the third country context.[17]

[26–15] While the Court of Justice has linked the extension of the prohibition to third states with the aim of maintaining financial centres of a global nature within the Member States, Snell suggests that it may also be seen as supporting the promotion of the euro as a global currency, on the basis that "overseas investments in euros are facilitated by a legal regime that guarantees the free repatriation of those investments without capital export controls".[18] Finally, in relation to third countries, it is worth noting that since the entry into force of the European Economic Area Agreement in 1995, it appears that the EEA countries of Iceland, Liechtenstein and Norway are not to be regarded as third countries for the purpose of Arts 63–66 TFEU, such that the limitations that may be placed on the free movement of capital do not apply to them.[19]

[26–16] Like the free movement of goods, workers and services, Art 63 has been held to be capable of having vertical direct effect – even with respect to movements of capital to and from third states – although the extent to which it can have horizontal direct effect remains unclear.[20]

[26–17] Article 63 prohibits "all restrictions" on the movement of capital, which includes both restrictions on imports and exports of capital. As with Art 34 TFEU on the free movement of goods, Art 63 covers administrative obstacles and not just legislative or regulatory acts. Similarly, like Art 34, Art 63 not only prohibits *discriminatory* measures that restrict the movement of capital (both direct and indirect) but has also been held to prohibit certain *non-discriminatory* measures that are likely to deter foreign

---

17 Jukka Snell, "Free Movement of Capital: Evolution as a Non-Linear Process" in Paul Craig and Gráinne de Búrca (eds), *The Evolution of EU Law* (2nd ed, Oxford University Press, 2011) 547, 553–554.

18 *ibid*, 564. See Commission Communication, "Towards a Stronger International Role of the Euro" COM(2018) 796 final, 5 December 2018.

19 Case C-110/17 *Commission v Belgium* EU:C:2018:250, 12 April 2018, paras 63–65; Case C-98/16 *Commission v Greece* EU:C:2017:346, 4 May 2017, paras 49–51; Case C-250/08 *Commission v Belgium* EU:C:2011:793, 1 December 2011, para 83; Case C-452/01 *Ospelt* [2003] ECR I-9743.

20 Joined Cases C-163/94, C-165/94 and C-250/94 *Sanz de Lera* [1995] ECR I-4830; Case C-101/05 *Skatteverket v A* [2007] ECR I-11531; Case C-112/05 *Commission v Germany (Volkswagen)* [2007] ECR I-8995.

investors from making investments, or borrowers from seeking loans in other Member States, and so affect access to the market. Just as the concept of "capital" has evaded a core definition of general application, so too has the notion of restrictions on the movement of capital. As one writer has described, while the reference to restrictions in Art 63 clearly goes beyond non-discrimination on the grounds of nationality and envisages a regulatory regime that facilitates the free flow of capital,

> this general thrust of the provision creates an inherent tension that is not, at least not to the same extent, present in the other market freedoms. As opposed to the free movement of goods, services or persons, movement of capital generally presupposes the existence of a regulatory framework. While the other freedoms … refer to objects or persons that exist notwithstanding any legal qualification of their characteristics or relations, the term "capital movements" concerns activities that have a necessary legal dimension, such as direct investment by means of the acquisition of undertakings, transactions in securities, or the granting of loans. As one commentator put it in a different context, many rules that may constitute obstacles to the free movement of capital are essential to "structure" or establish the market and thus make capital movements possible in the first place. We are, therefore, confronted with the potentially difficult task of identifying those rules that do not merely establish the market, but restrict market movements.[21]

[26–18] The unique and complex nature of restrictions on the free movement of capital is particularly evident in the context of the treatment of national tax laws and non-discriminatory restrictions that are alleged to restrict or dissuade the movement of capital. Before considering these, we will first consider the category of discriminatory measures. This category includes both direct discrimination – which is only capable of being justified by one of the express grounds for derogation listed in Art 65 – and indirect discrimination, which may also be justified on the basis of an overriding public interest, provided that it is suitable to achieve that objective and is proportionate in that it does not go beyond what is necessary to achieve it.

(i) Discriminatory Restrictions

[26–19] An example of a directly discriminatory measure is seen in *Albore*.[22] There, a German purchaser of property in Italy was informed that only Italian nationals were permitted to buy in the particular area, which had been designated to be of military importance. In the absence of any specific risk having been identified by Italy, the Court of Justice considered the measure to be a restriction on the free movement of capital that was prohibited by Art 63.

[26–20] One common directly discriminatory restriction that will prima facie be caught by Art 63 is a requirement that any transaction conducted by a foreign national must receive a prior authorisation. As was stated in the *Church of Scientology* case, to be justified such a restriction must be necessary in order to enable the national authorities to carry out checks designed to prevent infringements of their laws, or for the protection of public policy or public security.[23] There, a French law provided that, subject to certain exceptions, all foreign direct investments made in France were subject to prior authorisation by the relevant minister. An authorisation was to be deemed to

---

[21] Carsten Gerner-Beuerle, "Shareholders between the Market and the State: The *VW* Law and Other Interventions in the Market Economy" (2012) 49 *Common Market Law Review* 97, 136–138.

[22] Case C-423/98 *Albore* [2000] ECR I-5965.

[23] Case C-54/99 *Church of Scientology* [2000] ECR I-1335.

have been obtained one month after receipt of the investment declaration unless the minister had declared the transaction to be deferred. Emphasising the general nature of the authorisation requirement, and the absence of any specified risk, the Court found the restriction to be contrary to Art 63, reasoning as follows:

> In the case of direct foreign investments, the difficulty in identifying and blocking capital once it has entered a Member State may make it necessary to prevent, at the outset, transactions which would adversely affect public policy or public security. It follows that, in the case of direct foreign investments which constitute a genuine and sufficiently serious threat to public policy and public security, a system of prior declaration may prove to be inadequate to counter such a threat.
>
> In the present case, however, the essence of the system in question is that prior authorisation is required for every direct foreign investment which is "such as to represent a threat to public policy [and] public security", without any more detailed definition. Thus, the investors concerned are given no indication whatever as to the specific circumstances in which prior authorisation is required.
>
> Such lack of precision does not enable individuals to be apprised of the extent of their rights and obligations deriving from Article [63 TFEU]. That being so, the system established is contrary to the principle of legal certainty[24]

[26–21] The essence of an indirectly discriminatory restriction is that, although not expressly applying criteria based on nationality, in practice the criteria established by the restriction are more likely to be met by nationals of the host state as compared with nationals of any other Member State. It might take the form of, say, a national rule that precludes the registration of a mortgage in a currency other than that of the Member State of registration.[25] For example, in *Segro*, a company owned by German nationals was deprived by a Hungarian law of its legal right to use land owned by others (the right of "usufruct") due to the fact that it did not have a close family tie with the owner of the land. As this requirement was much more likely to be met by Hungarian nationals than others, it was held to amount to indirect discrimination that was caught by Art 63 and was therefore in need of justification from the Member State.[26]

(ii) Taxation

[26–22] The typical understanding of indirect discrimination requires some adjustment in the context of direct taxation. Although direct taxation remains within the competence of the Member States, that competence must be exercised in a manner that is consistent with EU law. As the Court of Justice explained in *Schumacker*, in principle, favourable tax treatment based on residence in the taxing state is likely to benefit a Member State's own nationals over others, and so would prima facie amount to indirect discrimination.[27] As against this, however, tax law has traditionally drawn distinctions based on residence which, in this context, have long been regarded as legitimate. The Court has accepted that this is a long-standing characteristic of how Member States apply direct taxation. From a discrimination perspective, the Court

---

24 *ibid*, 1362–1363.

25 Case C-222/97 *Trummer and Meyer* [1999] ECR I-9409.

26 Joined Cases C-52/16 and C-113/16 *Segro* EU:C:2018:157, 6 March 2018. See also Case C-235/17 *Commission v Hungary* EU:C:2019:432, 21 May 2019.

27 Case C-279/93 *Schumacker* [1995] ECR I-225.

has rationalised this acceptance by describing different places of residence as being – for tax purposes – non-comparable situations, such as not to require equal treatment. According to the Court:

> national rules … under which a distinction is drawn on the basis of residence in that non-residents are denied certain benefits which are, conversely, granted to persons residing within national territory, are liable to operate mainly to the detriment of nationals of other Member States. Non-residents are in the majority of cases foreigners.
>
> In those circumstances, tax benefits granted only to residents of a Member State may constitute indirect discrimination by reason of nationality.
>
> It is also settled law that discrimination can arise only through the application of different rules to comparable situations or the application of the same rule to different situations. In relation to direct taxes, the situations of residents and of non-residents are not, *as a rule*, comparable.
>
> Income received in the territory of a Member State by a non-resident is in most cases only a part of his total income, which is concentrated at his place of residence. Moreover, a non-resident's personal ability to pay tax, determined by reference to his aggregate income and his personal and family circumstances, is more easy to assess at the place where his personal and financial interests are centred. In general, that is the place where he has his usual abode. Accordingly, international tax law … recognises that in principle the overall taxation of taxpayers, taking account of their personal and family circumstances, is a matter for the State of residence.
>
> The situation of a resident is different in so far as the major part of his income is normally concentrated in the State of residence. Moreover, that State generally has available all the information needed to assess the taxpayer's overall ability to pay, taking account of his personal and family circumstances.
>
> Consequently, the fact that a Member State does not grant to a non-resident certain tax benefits which it grants to a resident is not, *as a rule*, discriminatory since those two categories of taxpayer are not in a comparable situation.
>
> Accordingly, … the Treaty does not *in principle* preclude the application of rules of a Member State under which a non-resident working as an employed person in that Member State is taxed more heavily on his income than a resident in the same employment.
>
> The position is different, however, … where the non-resident receives no significant income in the State of his residence and obtains the major part of his taxable income from an activity performed in the State of employment, with the result that the State of his residence is not in a position to grant him the benefits resulting from the taking into account of his personal and family circumstances.
>
> There is no *objective difference* between the situations of such a non-resident and a resident engaged in comparable employment, such as to justify different treatment as regards the taking into account for taxation purposes of the taxpayer's personal and family circumstances.
>
> In the case of a non-resident who receives the major part of his income and almost all his family income in a Member State other than that of his residence, discrimination arises from the fact that his personal and family circumstances are taken into account neither in the State of residence nor in the State of employment.[28]

---

[28] *ibid*, 259–260. Emphasis added.

[26–23] From the judgment in *Schumacker*, therefore, it can be seen that the default position was that residence in the taxing state and residence elsewhere were not considered to be comparable situations, such that it did not amount to indirect discrimination to treat them differently. This default position would not apply, however, if the particular circumstances were such that, as a matter of fact, there was no objective difference in the two situations, such that they were comparable after all. In order to be permissible in such a scenario, any indirect discrimination would need to be capable of justification by the taxing state on the basis of either an express derogation in Art 65 TFEU or an overriding public interest.

[26–24] As part of the changes brought about by the Maastricht Treaty, what is now Art 65(1)(a) TFEU was first introduced into the Treaty provisions on the movement of capital to address the question of tax treatment based upon place of residence or of investment. Article 65(1)(a) provides that the prohibition on restrictions on the movement of capital in Art 63 shall be without prejudice to the right of Member States to apply the relevant provisions of their tax law which distinguish between taxpayers who are not in the same situation with regard to either their place of residence or the place where their capital is invested. This is subject to the proviso in Art 65(3) that any such measures must not constitute a means of arbitrary discrimination or a disguised restriction on the free movement of capital. In addition, a declaration to the Maastricht Treaty affirmed that, in relation to capital movements between Member States, Art 65(1)(a) would be confined to provisions of tax law that were in force at the end of 1993, and so could not be used to introduce new tax provisions.[29]

[26–25] According to some commentators, if the insertion of Art 65(1)(a) had been intended to provide an additional level of protection for Member States in relation to their tax treatment of capital movements between Member States, "it clearly failed in its objective".[30] This is because the Court of Justice has interpreted Art 65(1)(a) very strictly. In *Verkooijen*, Dutch tax law allowed for a certain exemption in respect of share dividends received from companies established in the Netherlands, without providing for a similar exemption in respect of dividends from companies established elsewhere. The Court of Justice described the exemption as fulfilling a twofold objective. First, it was intended to increase the level of equity capital that could be raised by companies and to stimulate the interest of private individuals in investing in Dutch-based shares. Secondly, it was intended to provide some compensation for the double taxation that would otherwise result from the levying of corporation tax on company profits followed by income tax on the income of private shareholders derived from dividends distributed by those companies.[31] Bearing this in mind, the Court was satisfied that the preferential treatment did amount to a restriction on the movement of capital since it: (i) had the effect of dissuading nationals of a Member State residing in the Netherlands from investing their capital in companies which had their seat in another Member State; (ii) was intended specifically to promote investments by individuals in companies established in the Netherlands in order to increase their equity capital; and (iii) constituted an obstacle to the raising of capital in the Netherlands since the dividends which non-Dutch

[29] Declaration on Article 73d of the Treaty Establishing the European Community.

[30] Thomas Horsley, "Death, Taxes, and (Targeted) Judicial Dynamism: The Free Movement of Capital in EU Law" in Anthony Arnull and Damian Chalmers (eds), *The Oxford Handbook of European Union Law* (Oxford University Press, 2015) 784, 792.

[31] Case C-35/98 *Verkooijen* [2000] ECR I-4071, 4119.

companies paid to Dutch residents received less favourable tax treatment, making their shares less attractive to investors residing in the Netherlands.[32]

[26–26] Although the facts in *Verkooijen* had arisen before the entry into force of the Maastricht Treaty, the Dutch Government sought to place reliance on (what is now) Art 65(1)(a) TFEU. The Court dealt with the case on the basis of the Treaty provisions in force at the time that the dispute arose. Nevertheless, in commenting on the newly introduced provision, the Court made clear that it did not regard Art 65(1)(a) as having made any significant change to the approach it had set out in *Schumacker.* It recalled that, according to its earlier case law, distinctions based on residence could be compatible with EU law provided that they applied to situations which were not objectively comparable or could be justified by overriding reasons in the general interest, in particular in relation to the cohesion of the tax system. The Court also observed that, even under the new provision, any distinctions based on residence were not permitted to constitute a means of arbitrary discrimination or a disguised restriction on the free movement of capital.[33]

[26–27] While these statements were of an *obiter* nature in *Verkooijen*, they pointed towards a direction of travel that was taken up by the Court a few years later in *Manninen.*[34] Here, Finnish tax law provided for similar preferred treatment for dividends paid by Finnish companies, as opposed to companies based elsewhere. The Court followed its earlier reasoning to find that, as the provision had the effect of deterring taxable persons in Finland from investing their capital in companies established in another Member State, it constituted a restriction on the free movement of capital within the meaning of Art 63. Next, the Court considered whether the restriction was capable of justification. According to Finland, Art 65(1)(a) clearly showed that Member States were entitled to reserve the benefit of a tax credit for dividends paid by companies established in their territory. Recalling that the measures envisaged by Art 65(1)(a) must not constitute a means of arbitrary discrimination or a disguised restriction on the movement of capital, the Court confirmed that, as a derogation from one of the fundamental freedoms, Art 65(1)(a) must be interpreted strictly and cannot be interpreted as meaning that any tax law making a distinction between taxpayers by reference to the place where they invest their capital is *automatically* compatible with the Treaty.[35] In order to be capable of justification, the difference in treatment of Finnish-based dividends and other dividends must either (i) concern situations which are not objectively comparable or (ii) be justified by overriding reasons in the general interest, such as the need to safeguard the coherence of the tax system or effective fiscal supervision, with the difference in treatment not going beyond what is necessary in order to attain that objective.

[26–28] Other examples of tax treatment being found to amount to a restriction on the movement of capital include infringement proceedings brought against Portugal in respect of a tax amnesty it had introduced for undeclared assets. While a 5 per cent

---

32 *ibid*, 4127.

33 *ibid*, 4129.

34 Case C-319/02 *Manninen* [2004] ECR I-7477. See also Case C-685/16 *EV* EU:C:2018:743, 20 September 2018; Case C-184/14 *Patrício Teixeira* EU:C:2018:694, 6 September 2018; Case C-110/17 *Commission v Belgium* EU:C:2018:250, 12 April 2018; Case C-98/16 *Commission v Greece* EU:C:2017:346, 4 May 2017; Case C-479/14 *Hünnebeck* EU:C:2016:412, 8 June 2016.

35 *ibid*, 7507. Emphasis added.

tax applied to all previously undeclared assets that were disclosed, a lower rate of 2.5 per cent applied to Portuguese state securities, or to the proceeds of any assets that were held abroad but were returned to Portugal and invested in state securities.[36] Such a difference in treatment was likely to deter Portuguese taxpayers from investing in public debt securities issued by other Member States and so was a restriction caught by Art 63.

[26–29] In *Persche*, a German national made a gift of bed linen, zimmer frames and toys to a Portuguese retirement and children's home.[37] Although the home had charitable status in Portugal, German law only permitted a tax deduction for charitable donations made to bodies established in Germany. The Court of Justice first confirmed that, where a taxpayer claims a tax deduction for gifts made to bodies established and recognised as charitable in another Member State, such gifts come within the scope of the free movement of capital, even if they are gifts-in-kind in the form of everyday consumer goods. The Court then held that the difference in tax treatment did amount to a restriction, since the possibility of obtaining a tax deduction can have a significant influence on the decision of a donor to make a donation, or where to make it. The inability to avail of a tax deduction in respect of gifts to charities in other Member States was likely to affect the willingness of German taxpayers to make such gifts.

(iii) Non-Discriminatory Restrictions

[26–30] Displaying a certain symmetry with its approach to defining measures equivalent to quantitative restrictions on the free movement of goods, the Court of Justice has made clear that even where a regulatory measure does not entail any direct or indirect discrimination it may, nonetheless, be deemed to be a restriction on the free movement of capital within the meaning of Art 63. A striking example of this is the judgment in *Sandoz*, dating from 1999, although this perhaps represents a highwater mark in terms of the strictness of the Court's approach to such measures.[38] There, Austrian law imposed a stamp duty on all loans, regardless of where they were taken out. A loan was taken out from a Belgian company which, under Belgian law, was entitled to provide tax free loans. According to the Court, the law was caught by Art 63 (and so was required to be justified) since it deprived Austrian residents of the "possibility of benefiting from the absence of taxation which may be associated with loans obtained outside the national territory. Accordingly, such a measure is likely to deter such residents from obtaining loans from persons established in other Member States."[39] As will be seen below, the measure was ultimately found to be capable of being justified by Austria in order to prevent the infringement of national tax law. The fact that it was deemed to be a restriction, however, meant that the onus was transferred onto Austria to demonstrate why it was both necessary and proportionate.

[26–31] It has been observed that this expansive approach has considerable implications for Member State autonomy. By moving beyond a purely discrimination model of Art 63, the Court of Justice "enables litigants (including the Commission

---

36 Case C-20/09 *Commission v Portugal* [2011] ECR I-2637.

37 Case C-318/07 *Persche* [2009] ECR I-359.

38 Case C-439/97 *Sandoz* [1999] ECR I-7041. See Karen Banks, "The Application of the Fundamental Freedoms to Member State Tax Measures: Guarding Against Protectionism or Second-Guessing National Policy Choices?" (2008) 33 *European Law Review* 482.

39 *ibid*, 7074–7075.

under Art 258 TFEU) to scrutinise the existence of Member State regulation *per se*".[40] This intrusive approach in the regulatory sphere may result in Member States being called upon to justify measures "that merely 'dissuade', 'deter' or 'render less attractive' intra-EU capital movements".[41] In *Burtscher*, for instance, an Austrian law required that, before a purchase of land could be entered onto the land register, a declaration had to be filed with the relevant local authority stating whether the property had been bought for holiday purposes.[42] The failure to do so within two years rendered the contract for sale invalid. In a preliminary ruling concerning this sanction for failing to file the necessary declaration, the Court found it to be a restriction on the movement of capital that was disproportionate and so contrary to Art 63. Given the particular facts of the case, the judgment in *Burtscher* may be seen as understandable. Nevertheless, Jukka Snell has argued that the willingness of the Court to view the declaration system as, "by its very purpose", having the effect of restricting the free movement of capital, is an example of the Court casting the net of the free movement of capital very wide. This, in turn, enables the Court

> to consider the proportionality of many non-discriminatory registration formalities and the penalties attached to non-compliance. As such registration requirements are very common and often long-standing, and as consequences of variable severity attach to non-compliance, this represents a significant extension of the Court's reach. In sum: in the context of national regulatory measures, the concept of restriction is a very wide one and does not require any disparate effect to the detriment of cross-border capital movements.[43]

[26–32] More recently, a series of so-called "golden share" cases have come to be regarded as emblematic of the Court's approach to non-discriminatory restrictions. These cases have tended to arise out of the privatisation of state-owned companies where governments sought to retain special powers for themselves through carefully crafted share rules. In the *British Airport Authority* case, for example, UK legislation privatised its airports and allowed the Secretary of State for Transport to approve the Articles of Association of the newly established British Airport Authority company.[44] The Articles of Association created a special share that was held by the Secretary of State and allowed the Secretary to veto the sale of certain airports or the winding-up of the Authority. In addition, the Articles limited the maximum shareholding to 15 per cent of the equity. In infringement proceedings, the Court rejected the UK's argument that, as a non-discriminatory measure, the restrictions within the Articles of Association were not caught by Art 63, or indeed that the Court ought to follow by analogy its judgment in *Keck and Mithouard* concerning the free movement of goods. As explained by the Court:

> The United Kingdom Government argues that the rules in question apply without

---

[40] Thomas Horsley, "Death, Taxes, and (Targeted) Judicial Dynamism: The Free Movement of Capital in EU Law" in Anthony Arnull and Damian Chalmers (eds), *The Oxford Handbook of European Union Law* (Oxford University Press, 2015) 784, 794.

[41] *ibid.*

[42] Case C-213/04 *Burtscher* [2005] ECR I-10309.

[43] Jukka Snell, "Free Movement of Capital: Evolution as a Non-Linear Process" in Paul Craig and Gráinne de Búrca (eds), *The Evolution of EU Law* (2nd ed, Oxford University Press, 2011) 547, 557.

[44] Case C-98/01 *Commission v United Kingdom* [2003] ECR I-4641. See also Case C-112/05 *Commission v Germany (Volkswagen)* [2007] ECR I-8995; Case C-367/98 *Commission v Portugal* [2002] ECR I-4731; Case C-483/99 *Commission v France* [2002] ECR I-4781; Erika Szyszczak, "Golden Shares and Market Governance" (2002) 29 *Legal Issues of Economic Integration* 255.

distinction on grounds of nationality. There is thus no discrimination as regards nationals of other Member States. Consequently, those rules do not amount to a restriction on the free movement of capital.

That argument cannot be accepted. It is clear … that the prohibition laid down in Article [63 TFEU] goes beyond the mere elimination of unequal treatment, on grounds of nationality, as between operators on the financial markets.

Rules which limit the acquisition of shareholdings in the way that … BAA's Articles of Association does, or which restrict in some other way the scope for participating effectively in the management of a company or in its control, as is the case of the system of prior approval provided for in … the Articles, constitute a restriction on the free movement of capital.

In particular, the United Kingdom Government's argument that the measures at issue do not restrict access to the market within the meaning of *Keck and Mithouard* cannot be accepted. The measures at issue are not comparable to the rules concerning selling arrangements which were found in that judgment not to fall within the scope of Article [34 TFEU].

According to that judgment, the application to products from other Member States of national provisions restricting or prohibiting, within the Member State of importation, certain selling arrangements is not such as to hinder trade between Member States so long as, first, those provisions apply to all relevant traders operating within the national territory and, second, they affect in the same manner, in law and in fact, the marketing of domestic products and of those from other Member States. The reason is that the application of such provisions is not such as to prevent access by the latter products to the market of the Member State of importation or to impede such access more than it impedes access by domestic products.

In this instance, although the relevant restrictions on investment operations apply without distinction to both residents and non-residents, it must none the less be held that they affect the position of a person acquiring a shareholding as such and are thus liable to deter investors from other Member States from making such investments and, consequently, affect access to the market.[45]

[26–33] The Court also rejected an argument that the Articles of Association were a private law matter, for which the UK could not be held responsible by virtue of the fact that the direct effect of Art 63 was *vertical* only in nature. In the view of the Court:

The restrictions at issue do not arise as the result of the normal operation of company law. BAA's Articles of Association were to be approved by the Secretary of State pursuant to the Airports Act 1986 and that was what actually occurred. In those circumstances, the Member State acted in this instance in its capacity as a public authority.

Consequently, the rules at issue constitute a restriction on the movement of capital for the purposes of Article [63 TFEU]. …

It must therefore be held that, by maintaining in force the provisions limiting the possibility of acquiring voting shares in BAA as well as the procedure requiring consent to the disposal of the company's assets, to control of its subsidiaries and to winding-up, the United Kingdom has failed to fulfil its obligations under Article [63 TFEU].[46]

---

45 *ibid*, 4662–4663.
46 *ibid*, 4663–4664.

C. Permissible Derogations – Article 65 TFEU

[26–34] The law in relation to permissible derogations from Art 63 is broadly similar in outline to that governing derogations from Art 34 TFEU, guaranteeing the free movement of goods. In both cases, a court is first required to determine whether a particular national measure is "caught" by the general prohibition. If the measure is caught, it will then require justification by the Member State in order not to be found to be in breach of the prohibition. As with the free movement of goods, Art 65(1) TFEU prescribes an exhaustive list of grounds that may be used to justify a directly discriminatory measure, provided that any such measure does not constitute a means of arbitrary discrimination or a disguised restriction on the free movement of capital or payments. It provides that Art 63 is to be without prejudice to the right of Member States:

> (a) to apply the relevant provisions of their tax law which distinguish between taxpayers who are not in the same situation with regard to their place of residence or with regard to the place where their capital is invested;
> (b) to take all requisite measures to prevent infringements of national law and regulations, in particular in the field of taxation and the prudential supervision of financial institutions, or to lay down procedures for the declaration of capital movements for purposes of administrative or statistical information, or to take measures which are justified on grounds of public policy or public security.

[26–35] The Court of Justice has confirmed that the fields set out in Art 65(1)(b) are non-exhaustive, and so might include measures aimed at preventing serious illegal activities, such as drug trafficking, money laundering or terrorism.[47] The prudential supervision of financial institutions entails matters such as regulating the liquidity of banks by enforcing a minimum loan-to-deposit ratio.

[26–36] In a further parallel with the free movement of goods, in addition to the exhaustive grounds listed in Art 65(1), measures that are either indirectly discriminatory or non-discriminatory are capable of being justified pursuant to a "rule of reason" approach. More specifically, a measure that is applicable to all persons and undertakings pursuing an activity in the host Member State may be justified by an *overriding requirement of general interest*, provided that it accords with the principle of proportionality by being suitable for achieving the objective pursued and not going beyond what is necessary to achieve it. While the category of overriding requirements of general interest is open-ended, it may not include the general interest in safeguarding a Member State's financial or purely economic interests, such as maintaining sources of tax revenue. Matters such as the continuity of public services, preserving agricultural communities, town planning, public-housing policy, protection of minority shareholders, protection of workers, fiscal supervision and maintaining energy supplies have been acknowledged by the Court to be overriding public interests.

[26–37] Taking the cases referred to above as illustration, in *Albore* Italy sought to justify the restriction on foreign nationals buying property in a designated military area on the basis of public security. Given the absence of any specific, identifiable risk, the Court of Justice was unimpressed, remarking that

> a mere reference to the requirements of defence of the national territory … cannot suffice to justify discrimination on grounds of nationality against nationals of other Member

[47] Joined Cases C-358/93 and C-416/93 *Bordessa* [1995] ECR I-361, 385.

> States regarding access to immovable property on all or part of the national territory of the first State.
>
> The position would be different only if it were demonstrated, for each area to which the restriction applies, that non-discriminatory treatment of the nationals of all the Member States would expose the military interests of the Member State concerned to real, specific and serious risks which could not be countered by less restrictive procedures.[48]

[26–38] As we have seen, the result in the *Church of Scientology* case was essentially to the same effect. Whereas, in principle, a Member State might justify a prior authorisation requirement in respect of foreign direct investments which constitute a "genuine and sufficiently serious threat to public policy and public security", the requirement was being applied by France in a sweeping manner that failed to identify the particular security or policy concern at stake. The Court recalled that, as derogations from the fundamental principle of free movement of capital, the requirements of public policy and public security must be interpreted strictly, so that their scope cannot be determined unilaterally by each Member State without any control by the Union institutions.[49] Moreover, the derogations must not be misapplied so as to serve purely economic ends. A public security justification was, however, successful in a "golden share" case, where Belgium was held to be entitled to oppose certain management decisions within an energy distribution firm that were contrary to Belgian energy policy.[50] In contrast, an attempt to use a similar clause by France was held not to be justified on the basis that it was less specific than the Belgian law and went beyond what was necessary to achieve the goal.[51]

[26–39] In *Segro*, Hungary sought to justify its restriction on the right to use agricultural land to those with a close family tie to the owner of the land by reference to the objective of preventing land being acquired for speculative purposes. The Court considered that the restriction was unrelated to this objective and was disproportionate, given that a person with a close family tie could just as easily be acquiring the land for speculative reasons, while a person without a family tie may wish to farm the land and have no interest in speculation.[52] Similarly, in *Burtscher*, the Court accepted that Austrian restrictions on the establishment of second homes in a particular area in order to maintain a permanent population and economic activity independent of the tourist sector may be regarded as contributing to objectives in the public interest, as could the need to ensure that planning rules were applied in compliance with the requirement of legal certainty of transactions.[53] As regards the proportionality of the penalty of invalidating the transaction if a declaration was not filed within the two-year period, Austria claimed that, by dint of its automatic nature, this served to ensure that the relevant authorities were properly informed and were in a position to take action within a reasonable period. It was claimed that an administrative penalty would not, necessarily, be less severe, in that it would be imposed after a much shorter time and would be less effective. The Court, however, remained unconvinced that measures with less wide-ranging effects,

---

48 Case C-423/98 *Albore* [2000] ECR I-5965, 6003.

49 Case C-54/99 *Church of Scientology* [2000] ECR I-1335, 1361.

50 Case C-383/98 *Commission v Belgium* [2002] ECR I-4809.

51 Case C-483/98 *Commission v France* [2002] ECR I-4781.

52 Joined Cases C-52/16 and C-113/16 *Segro* EU:C:2018:157, 6 March 2018. See also Case C-235/17 *Commission v Hungary* EU:C:2019:432, 21 May 2019.

53 Case C-213/04 *Burtscher* [2005] ECR I-10309, 10342–10343.

such as fines, could not be effective in penalising the late submission of a declaration. In contrast, the penalty of invalidity was

> imposed automatically, following the mere passing of the time-limit for submitting the requisite declaration, irrespective of the reasons for its being late. …
>
> Secondly, for no reason deriving from infringement of the applicable substantive rules, such a penalty radically calls into question an agreement expressing the intentions of the parties and cannot therefore reflect the requirements of legal certainty, which are particularly important in relation to property acquisitions. The fact that that time-limit is … "calculated generously" is not therefore sufficient for that penalty to be regarded as proportionate to the objectives envisaged.[54]

[26–40] In response to the Commission's infringement proceedings concerning the UK's "golden share" in the British Airport Authority, the UK contested that the arrangements amounted to a restriction on the movement of capital, but declined to seek to rely on any of the grounds for derogation. In another golden share case, Germany sought to defend a law according to which fundamental company decisions by Volkswagen required support by more than four-fifths of the share capital, and no single shareholder could exercise voting rights beyond one-fifth of the share capital.[55] As it happened, only one shareholder – the State of Lower Saxony – held one-fifth of the share capital, granting it a blocking minority that was likely to deter investors from other Member States.

[26–41] According to Germany, the law was justified in order to protect the interests of workers and of minority shareholders, as well as due to the fact that the activities of a company as large as Volkswagen could have an impact on the general interest. While the Court of Justice accepted that these were public interest concerns, Germany had been unable to explain, "beyond setting out general considerations as to the need for protection against a large shareholder which might by itself dominate the company, why, in order to meet the objective of protecting Volkswagen's workers, it is appropriate and necessary for the Federal and State authorities to maintain a strengthened and irremovable position in the capital of that company".[56] Nor had it shown why, in order to protect the general interests of minority shareholders, it was appropriate or necessary to maintain such a position for the benefit of the Federal and State authorities.

[26–42] Turning lastly to the tax-related cases, in *Sandoz*, Austria was successful in claiming that its imposition of stamp duty on all loans, including those taken out abroad, was in order to ensure the coherence of its indirect tax system and the need to observe the principle that residents should be treated equally for tax purposes.[57] The Court accepted that the measure was aimed at preventing taxable persons from evading the requirements of domestic tax legislation through the exercise of freedom of movement of capital. As such, the measure was justified on the basis of Art 65(1)(b), which allows Member States to take measures in order to prevent infringements of national law, particularly in the field of taxation and the prudential supervision of financial institutions.

---

[54] *ibid*, 10346.

[55] Case C-112/05 *Commission v Germany (Volkswagen)* [2007] ECR I-8995.

[56] *ibid*, 9042.

[57] Case C-439/97 *Sandoz* [1999] ECR I-7041

[26–43] In *Manninen*, Finland argued that the preferential treatment of dividends paid out by Finnish companies was necessary in order to maintain the cohesion of the national tax system, bearing in mind that there was a direct link between the taxation of the company's profits and the tax credit granted to the shareholder receiving the dividends.[58] While acknowledging that the need to preserve the cohesion of a tax system might justify a restriction on the free movement of capital, the Court noted that for such a justification to succeed, a direct link had to be established between the tax advantage concerned and the offsetting of that advantage by a particular tax levy. The aim of the relevant provision of the tax law was to prevent double taxation of company profits distributed to shareholders. Having regard to this objective, the Court observed that

> the cohesion of that tax system is assured as long as the correlation between the tax advantage granted in favour of the shareholder and the tax due by way of corporation tax is maintained. Therefore, … the granting to a shareholder who is fully taxable in Finland and who holds shares in a company established in Sweden of a tax credit calculated by reference to the corporation tax owed by that company in Sweden would not threaten the cohesion of the Finnish tax system and would constitute a measure less restrictive of the free movement of capital than that laid down by the Finnish tax legislation.
>
> … Whilst, for the Republic of Finland, granting a tax credit in relation to corporation tax due in another Member State would entail a reduction in its tax receipts in relation to dividends paid by companies in other Member States, it has been consistently held in the case-law that reduction in tax revenue cannot be regarded as an overriding reason in the public interest which may be relied on to justify a measure which is in principle contrary to a fundamental freedom.
>
> … the calculation of a tax credit granted to a shareholder fully taxable in Finland, who has received dividends from a company established in Sweden, must take account of the tax actually paid by the company established in that other Member State, as such tax arises from the general rules on calculating the basis of assessment and from the rate of corporation tax in that latter Member State. Possible difficulties in determining the tax actually paid cannot … justify an obstacle to the free movement of capital such as that which arises from the legislation at issue …[59]

[26–44] Similar issues of practicality arose in *Persche*.[60] There, Germany sought to defend confining a tax deduction for charitable donations to gifts made to German-based charities on the ground of fiscal supervision, in the sense of having to ensure that the alleged charitable donation was genuinely made – an argument supported by a number of Member States, including Ireland. While accepting the public interest involved, the Court was not persuaded of the necessity or proportionality of the measure. In particular, the Court noted that nothing would prevent the tax authorities from requiring the taxpayer to provide such proof as they may consider necessary in order to determine whether the conditions for deducting expenses had been met. In the Court's assessment

> the possibility cannot be excluded *a priori* that the taxpayer is able to provide relevant documentary evidence enabling the tax authorities of the Member State of taxation to ascertain, clearly and precisely, the nature and genuineness of the expenditure incurred in other Member States.
>
> … before granting a tax exemption to a body established and recognised as having

---

58 Case C-319/02 *Manninen* [2004] ECR I-7477.

59 *ibid*, 7512–7514.

60 Case C-318/07 *Persche* [2009] ECR I-359.

> charitable status in another Member State, a Member State is authorised to apply measures enabling it to ascertain in a clear and precise manner whether the body meets the conditions imposed by national law in order to be entitled to the exemption and to monitor its effective management, for example, by requiring the submission of annual accounts and an activity report. Any administrative disadvantages arising from the fact that such bodies may be established in another Member State are not sufficient to justify a refusal on the part of the authorities of the State concerned to grant such bodies the same tax exemptions as are granted to national bodies of the same kind.
>
> The same applies in the case of the taxpayer who claims a tax deduction in a Member State for a gift to a body established and recognised as charitable in another Member State, even if … the taxpayer from whom the tax authorities have to obtain the necessary information is not the body which received the gift but, indeed, the actual donor.
>
> Whilst it is true that, in contrast to such a recipient body, the donor does not himself have all the information necessary for the tax authorities to verify whether that body satisfies the conditions required by the national legislation for the grant of tax advantages, … it is usually possible, for a donor, to obtain from that body documents confirming the amount and nature of the gift made, identifying the objectives pursued by the body and certifying the propriety of the management of the gifts which were made to it during previous years.[61]

[26–45] The Court also observed that the argument could not be made that, for the purposes of Art 65, there was a justifiable public policy or overriding public interest in encouraging charitable donations *within* Germany that would serve to free up government expenditure – that might otherwise have been spent on these services – for other causes. Settled case law had determined that the need to prevent the reduction of tax revenues was neither among the objectives stated in Art 65, nor an overriding reason in the public interest capable of justifying a restriction on one of the four freedoms. This also applied in the infringement proceedings against Portugal for applying a lower rate of tax to undeclared assets in Portuguese state securities, or assets that were repatriated into such securities, as compared with all other undeclared assets. Whilst the aim of combatting tax evasion and tax avoidance could justify proportionate restrictions on the free movement of capital that were appropriate to achieve that objective and did not go beyond what was necessary to attain it, this could not be said of the measures in question. As Advocate General Mengozzi reasoned:

> the Portuguese Government has neither explained nor *a fortiori* demonstrated why it is indispensable for there to be a difference in rates as between public debt securities issued by the Portuguese State and those issued by other Member States in order to achieve *the general-interest objectives that it seeks to pursue.* The other rules … applicable to taxable persons wishing to regularise their tax situations applied regardless of the place where the capital was invested. In fact, the explanation that the rate difference is justified, in essence, as a compensatory indemnity that is higher on regularised investments in public debt securities issued by other Member States comes down, in my view, to an attempt to justify a measure restricting the free movement of capital by pursuit of an objective that is plainly financial in nature, that is to say offsetting the Member State's lost tax revenue. However, in accordance with the Court's caselaw, a ground of a financial nature certainly cannot justify a measure contrary to Article [63 TFEU]. If the taxable persons concerned were all invited to regularise their situations in respect of taxes unpaid in Portugal, I do not at all see why in the event of tax evasion, only those who invested in public debt securities issued by the Portuguese State ought to enjoy the benefit of preferential treatment.[62]

---

[61] *ibid*, paras 52–57.

[62] Case C-20/09 *Commission v Portugal* EU:C:2010:350, 17 June 2010, para 89.

[26–46] There is one final point worth noting regarding the derogation in relation to tax treatment that is found in Art 65(1)(a). The assessment of whether taxpayers residing abroad (or capital invested abroad) are in a *comparable situation* to taxpayers residing in the host state (or capital invested there), does not take place at the initial stage of deciding whether a particular measure is a restriction caught by Art 63. Rather, reflecting that Art 65(1)(a) is a derogation from the general rule, a measure will first be determined to be a restriction before considering the question of whether the situations are, in fact, not objectively comparable, such that the difference in treatment is justifiable. The onus will, therefore, have shifted onto the Member State to show that this is the case. In *Persche*, for instance, Germany sought to argue that the situation of donating to foreign charities was not comparable to donating to German charities given that Member States may apply different concepts of benevolence as well as different requirements for recognition of acts of benevolence. Furthermore, it was said that if a Member State provides a tax deduction for donations to charities established within its territory, that is because such bodies absolve the Member State of certain charitable tasks which it would otherwise have to fulfil itself using tax revenues. As we have seen above, the Court rejected the second argument on the grounds that the need to prevent the reduction of tax revenues is not an overriding reason in the public interest. More generally, the Court concluded:

> where a body recognised as having charitable status in one Member State satisfies the requirements imposed for that purpose by the law of another Member State and where its object is to promote the very same interests of the general public, so that it would be likely to be recognised as having charitable status in the latter Member State, which it is a matter for the national authorities of that same Member State, including its courts, to determine, the authorities of that Member State cannot deny that body the right to equal treatment solely on the ground that it is not established in that Member State.
>
> … a body which is established in one Member State but satisfies the requirements imposed for that purpose by another Member State for the grant of tax advantages, is, in respect of the grant by the latter Member State of tax advantages intended to encourage the charitable activities concerned, in a situation comparable to that of bodies recognised as having charitable purposes which are established in the latter Member State.[63]

[63] Case C-318/07 *Persche* [2009] ECR I-359, paras 49–50.

CHAPTER 27

ECONOMIC AND MONETARY UNION

A. INTRODUCTION

[27–01] This book began by noting the optimistic spirit that pervaded the opening of the Bretton Woods Conference in 1944. In seeking to avoid mistakes made following the end of the First World War, the Conference reflected on economic factors that had contributed to the outbreak of a second world war just 20 years later. Not only had the Great Depression of the 1930s paved the way for a rise in populist political movements, it also led to a breakdown in the international financial system. Attempting to improve their situations, some struggling states engaged in competitive devaluation, deliberately lowering the value of their currency in order to make their exports more competitive and imports more expensive. In this unstable environment of free-floating currencies, the inter-War period also saw a large increase in the international flow of speculative financial capital.

[27–02] A key innovation of the Bretton Woods System, therefore, was to introduce an international monetary system of fixed exchange rates as a means of maintaining global stability and reducing a significant barrier to cross-border trade. States were required to maintain their national currency's exchange rate within a 1 per cent band of a "pegged" reserve currency (the US dollar, which in turn maintained a link with gold) by buying or selling foreign money on the foreign exchange markets as needs be. This was to be supported by controls on capital movements that were aimed at reducing speculative financial flows and redirecting capital into more tangible foreign direct investment, such as investing in factories or infrastructure. In 1971, however, the "Nixon Shock" occurred when – in the midst of its economic woes during the Vietnam War – the US ended the direct convertibility of the dollar into gold. Addressing the nation, President Nixon sought to "lay to rest the bugaboo of what is called devaluation. If you want to buy a foreign car or take a trip abroad, market conditions may cause your dollar to buy slightly less. But if you are among the overwhelming majority of Americans who buy American-made products in America, your dollar will be worth just as much tomorrow as it is today." Two years later, in 1973, the dollar was devalued by 10 per cent, leading to the breakdown of the Bretton Woods monetary system, to be replaced by a series of free-floating currencies.

[27–03] It is against this background that consideration was first being given to the development of a distinct European policy on economic and monetary matters. The origins of this can dated to 1970, when the Werner Report presented to the EEC Member States a fully fledged blueprint for achieving an economic and monetary union by the end of the decade. This would include irrevocably fixed exchange rates, a pooling of monetary reserves, a single institution to control monetary policy and the complete liberalisation of capital movements within the EEC. According to the report, such a union "will make it possible to realise an area within which goods and services, people and capital will circulate freely and without competitive distortions, without thereby giving rise to structural or regional disequilibrium".[1] While the recommendations of the Werner Report would not come to pass within the timeframe envisaged, they do demonstrate the longevity of economic policy ideas that continue to be debated today. An early attempt was made, however, at maintaining a close degree of parity in exchange rates, through what became known as "the snake", first established in 1972. This was replaced in 1979 by the establishment of the European Monetary System, with its own Exchange Rate Mechanism, through a resolution of the European Council. The Exchange Rate Mechanism (ERM) pegged national currencies against a notional unit of account – the European Currency Unit or ECU – around which they were permitted to fluctuate within a margin of plus or minus 2.5 per cent, with the central banks of each Member State being required to intervene to rectify any fluctuation that went beyond this.[2]

[27–04] When it came to the first major Treaty amendment in 1986, the Single European Act recalled in a recital that, in 1972, the heads of state and government had approved the objective of the progressive realisation of economic and monetary union. Nevertheless, the Act's corresponding amendment to the Treaty of Rome was modest. While a new chapter was inserted, entitled "Co-operation in Economic and Monetary Policy (Economic and Monetary Union)", it comprised just a single short article. Member States undertook to cooperate in order to ensure the convergence of economic and monetary policies necessary for the further development of the Community, taking account of the experience acquired within the framework of the European Monetary System.

[27–05] From the previous chapter it will be recalled that there is a very close link between monetary policy, as pursued through the fixing of exchange rates and interest rates, and the movement of capital. For example, in the 1960s, France and Italy were particularly concerned about high levels of unemployment. Such was the extent of this problem that it outweighed countervailing concerns that they may have had regarding

---

1 Report to the Council and the Commission on the Realisation by stages of economic and monetary union in the Community, 8 October 1970, 9 [1970] OJ C136/1.

2 See Jean-Victor Louis and Etienne de Lhoneux, "The Development of the Use of the ECU: Legal Aspects" (1991) 28 *Common Market Law Review* 335.

rising inflation.[3] In contrast, since, historically, Germany had experienced great difficulty with rapid inflation, it had come to prioritise keeping it strictly under control. At this time, Germany enjoyed strong economic growth and so employment levels were low. As a result, whereas German monetary policy favoured an interest rate of over 4 per cent, the interest rate in France and Italy was around 2 per cent. The consequence of this for any proposed system of fixed exchange rates or single currency has been described as follows:

> If interest rates differ between two countries with fixed currency values, investors will take their money from the low interest rate to the high interest rate country. In the 1960s they would have pulled money out of France and Italy and put it in Germany, and they would have kept doing so until interest rates in France and Italy went up to German levels. It was this problem that led ... the ... architects of Bretton Woods to want controls on short-term international investments. They did not want to restrict the ability of companies to invest in other markets ... However, they did want to make it difficult or impossible for investors to speculate on interest rate differences among countries with flows of what was branded "hot money".
>
> For national governments to pursue their own monetary policies, with fixed exchange rates, they had to make it hard to send *short-term investments* from one country to another. So the Bretton Woods system pre-supposed capital controls, taxes or prohibitions on moving money across borders for "speculative" purposes. The Europeans had a solid array of such measures, relaxed but not removed after the 1950s.[4]

[27–06] It has been said that the following "unholy trinity" are, in principle, incompatible, such that eventually one of these three things will have to give way: (i) fixed exchange rates among a number of national currencies; (ii) full free movement of capital between those countries; and (iii) independent monetary policies in the countries concerned.[5] With the adoption of the Exchange Rate Mechanism in 1979, the EEC Member States were seeking to maintain close parity among their national currencies. Yet, so long as Member States were able to exercise a degree of control over capital movements, they still retained an ability to pursue an independent monetary policy through the fixing of interest rates. As was seen in the previous chapter, although the Treaty of Rome did include the free movement of capital as one of the four fundamental freedoms, unlike goods, workers and services, this was treated less ambitiously, lacked direct effect and was to be achieved progressively. The adoption of the Third Capital Directive in 1988 – with its entry into force scheduled for 1 July 1990 – therefore clearly presented a very significant dilemma.[6] By substantially liberalising capital movements, the Directive would radically reduce the remaining ability of Member States to pursue their own monetary policies. It is unsurprising then that attention turned, once again, to the notion of a comprehensive economic and monetary union, with Commission President Jacques Delors tasked with picking up from where the Werner Report had left off.

---

3 This comparison is taken from Jeffry A Frieden, *Global Capitalism* (Norton, 2007) 291.

4 *ibid*, 291–292.

5 John Grahl and Paul Teague, *1992 – The Big Market* (Lawrence & Wishart, 1990) 129, cited in Francis Snyder, "EMU – Integration and Differentiation: Metaphor for European Union" in Paul Craig and Gráinne de Búrca (eds), *The Evolution of EU Law* (2nd ed, Oxford University Press, 2011) 686, 692.

6 Council Directive 88/361/EEC of 24 June 1988 for the implementation of Art 67 of the Treaty [1988] OJ L178/5.

(i) Delors Report

[27–07] The Delors Report emphasised that, as the Single Market moved towards completion, the economies of the Member States became more and more interdependent, thereby reducing the room for independent policy manoeuvre. In particular, the full free movement of capital and integration of financial markets would cause any incompatible national policies to result in exchange-rate tensions and place considerable strain on monetary policy. The Report described the mutual dependency of an economic and a monetary union (EMU) as follows: whereas a coherent set of *economic* policies at the Community and national levels was necessary to maintain permanently fixed exchange rates between national currencies, a common *monetary* policy in support of a single currency area was equally necessary for the Community to develop into an economic union.

[27–08] The proposed economic union would combine the Single Market with three additional elements: (i) competition policy and other measures aimed at strengthening market mechanisms; (ii) common policies aimed at structural change and regional development; and, most significantly, (iii) macroeconomic policy coordination, including binding rules for budgetary policies. Because uncoordinated and divergent national budgetary policies would undermine monetary stability and generate imbalances, macroeconomic coordination would require binding rules governing both the size and the financing of national budget deficits. For example, if one Member State borrowed excessively, this could lead to a high rate of inflation within that state. In response, the centrally set interest rate might have to be raised, making it more expensive for other Member States to borrow, even though they might have been exercising strict budgetary discipline. Given this shared fate, coordination within an economic union would ensure that Member States remained team-players, pursuing policy choices that were consistent with the economic well-being of the Community as a whole.

[27–09] Regarding monetary union, the Delors Report repeated the conclusions of the Werner Report that the necessary conditions for such a union included the irrevocable locking of exchange rates, the complete liberalisation of capital movements and the full integration of banking and other financial markets. While a single currency, as such, was not strictly necessary, for economic, psychological and political reasons it could be seen as a natural further development of monetary union. A single currency would "clearly demonstrate the irreversibility of the move to monetary union, considerably facilitate the monetary management of the Community and avoid the transaction costs of converting currencies".[7] A further recommendation was the creation of a new monetary institution, which would be needed due to the fact that

> a single monetary policy cannot result from independent decisions and actions by different central banks. Moreover, day-to-day monetary policy operations cannot respond quickly to changing market conditions unless they are decided centrally. Considering the political structure of the Community and the advantages of making existing central banks part of a new system, the domestic and international monetary policy-making of the Community should be organised in a federal form, in what might be called a *European System of Central Banks.*[8]

---

[7] Committee for the Study of Economic and Monetary Union, *Report on Economic and Monetary Union in the European Community*, 1989, para 23.

[8] *ibid*, para 32.

[27–10] Given the ambition of what was being proposed, it is unsurprising that the Delors Report prompted intense political debate. The UK, in particular, was fearful of the loss of national sovereignty that EMU would entail. According to Prime Minister Thatcher, the Exchange Rate Mechanism was already "tearing the heart out of parliamentary sovereignty", while handing over monetary policy to a European institution would reduce "national finance ministers to the status of innocent bystanders at the scene of an accident".[9] For other Member States, however, the centralising of monetary policy would in fact *increase* their opportunities to exercise influence, given that in practice the ERM saw their currencies pegged to the ECU, which was dominated by the German mark and so heavily influenced by the economic and monetary policy followed by Germany. As one writer has described:

> Most ERM participants had already lost control over national monetary policy. By the late 1980s their currencies were pegged to the mark, the system's unofficial anchor. The Bundesbank formulated monetary policy in the EMS, and Member States reaped the political and economic rewards of low inflation and stable exchange rates. In effect, Germany's partners in the EMS gave up using interest rates and nominal exchange rates as instruments of national policy. …
>
> As far as monetary policy was concerned, most ERM participants stood to regain sovereignty rather than lose it. By joining a federal monetary system, they would wrest some power back from the Bundesbank. … By the same token, Germany should have been the least happy about monetary union. Indeed, the Bundesbank had serious concerns about surrendering its virtual monopoly of decision making, at least until it could be sure than an alternative arrangement offered as good a prospect of price stability as did the existing mechanism. But the German government, which in any event supported monetary union for political reasons, could hardly argue in favour of maintaining a monopoly over monetary policy in the EC.[10]

[27–11] In endorsing the Delors Report, the European Council adopted a three-phase approach to achieving EMU. Stage I ran from the entry into force of the Third Capital Directive on 1 July 1990 to 1 January 1994 and was to see closer monetary and macro-economic cooperation between Member States and their central banks and the full free movement of capital. During this period, the German mark steadily increased in value, placing pressure on other currencies, including sterling. This pressure was exacerbated by the loosening of capital controls, which made it easier than ever to speculate on currency fluctuations. Just three days before France voted in a referendum on the Maastricht Treaty, on "Black Wednesday", 16 September 1992, the UK was forced to withdraw from the ERM, having first raised interest rates as high as 15 per cent in a vain attempt to remain above the minimum permitted floor. In order to stay within the ERM other Members States were required to devalue their currency, including the Irish punt which was devalued by 10 per cent on 30 January 1993. Following rejection in the first of two Danish referendums, which led to a protocol permitting Denmark to opt-out of joining the single currency, the Maastricht Treaty finally entered into force on 1 November 1993.

---

9 Desmond Dinan, *Ever Closer Union* (2nd ed, Palgrave, 1999) 459.

10 *ibid*, 458.

B. Maastricht Treaty Architecture

[27–12] Whereas the Delors Report had stopped short of calling for the introduction of a single currency (as opposed to fixed exchanges rates), the Maastricht Treaty took the extra step of identifying a single currency as the EMU's ultimate goal, to be achieved at the end of Stage III.[11] Stage II was to begin on 1 January 1994 and, in addition to further economic convergence and coordination of monetary policies, would see the establishment of the European Monetary Institute – as the forerunner to the European Central Bank (ECB) – and a ban on the granting of credit to Member States by either the ECB or any national central bank. This stage was also to see a progressive narrowing of the margins of fluctuation in exchange rates. To this end, the Maastricht Treaty conferred on the Community the competence to establish an Economic and Monetary Union in which, together with the Member States, it would conduct a single monetary policy and exchange rate policy with the express objective of maintaining price stability.

[27–13] The Werner Report had originally envisaged that, in support of fixed exchange rates, the EMU would require the transfer of competence to the Community to make principal decisions on economic policy as a whole. In contrast, the Delors Report recommended an approach that differentiated as between monetary and economic integration. This differentiated approach is most readily apparent in comparing the Union's current competence in these fields under the TFEU. Whereas monetary policy for the Member States whose currency is the euro is an *exclusive* EU competence under Art 3 TFEU, the Union has only a *coordinating* competence in respect of the Member States' economic, employment and social policies, as reflected in Art 5 TFEU. Included among the overall aims of the Union in Art 3 TEU is the sustainable development of Europe based on economic growth and price stability, a highly competitive social market economy, aiming at full employment and social progress, and a high level of protection of the environment. This is expanded upon in Art 119 TFEU which provides that, for the purposes set out in Art 3 TEU, the activities of the Member States and the Union shall include the adoption of an economic policy conducted in accordance with the principle of an open market economy and free competition, and which is based on: (i) the Internal Market; (ii) the definition of common objectives; and (iii) the close coordination of Member States' own economic policies. These activities are to be conducted in compliance with the principles of stable prices, sound public finances and monetary conditions, and a sustainable balance of payments.

[27–14] The following institutional architecture is set out in the TFEU and in related protocols and regulations. The general schema, however, derives from the approach originally taken in the Maastricht Treaty, and includes as central elements the (i) Multilateral Surveillance Procedure; (ii) Excessive Deficit Procedure; (iii) Stability and Growth Pact; (iv) prohibition on monetary financing; and (v) no bail-out clause.

[27–15] In accordance with Art 121 TFEU, Member States are to regard their economic policies as a matter of common concern, to be coordinated within the

[11] See Jörn Pipkorn, "Legal Arrangements in the Treaty of Maastricht for the Effectiveness of the Economic and Monetary Union" (1994) 31 *Common Market Law Review* 263; Maurice O'Connell, "The Maastricht Treaty and Aspects of Monetary Union" (1995) 1 *Irish Journal of European Law* 5; Pieter Ver Loren Van Themaat, "Some Preliminary Observations on the Intergovernmental Conferences: The Relations between the Concepts of a Common Market, a Monetary Union, an Economic Union, a Political Union and Sovereignty" (1991) 28 *Common Market Law Review* 291.

Council. On a recommendation from the Commission, the Council is mandated to formulate draft *Broad Guidelines of Economic Policies* of the Member States to be considered by the European Council. On foot of European Council conclusions, the Council then adopts the Guidelines in the form of a recommendation, of which the European Parliament is informed.[12] On the basis of reports by the Commission, the Council monitors economic developments within the Member States on an ongoing basis, including the consistency of their economic policies with the Broad Guidelines. This is termed the *Multilateral Surveillance Procedure*. If a Member State's economic policies are found to be inconsistent with the Broad Guidelines, or risk jeopardising the proper functioning of the EMU, the Council can address specific recommendations to the Member State concerned and can decide to make these recommendations public.

[27–16] Member States have also committed to avoiding excessive government deficits and debts, with Art 126 TFEU providing an *Excessive Deficit Procedure* to monitor and ultimately enforce adherence to agreed criteria. As defined in Protocol No 12 to the Treaties, an excessive government *deficit* in any given year is where it rises above 3 per cent of GDP. An excessive government *debt* is one where the total debt is greater than 60 per cent of GDP. If a Member State breaches either of these criteria, the Commission is to prepare a report. While the two criteria are clearly central to this process, they are not by themselves determinative. In preparing its report, the Commission is required to take into account whether the government deficit exceeds government investment expenditure and all other relevant factors, including the medium-term economic expenditure and budgetary position of the Member State. If the Commission considers there to be an excessive deficit, it addresses an opinion to the Member State and informs the Council. If the Council does decide that an excessive deficit exists, it shall adopt recommendations addressed to the Member State with a view to bringing the situation to an end within a given period.

[27–17] With regard to Member States of the Euro Area, if such recommendations are not taken up, the Council may require the Member State to take specified measures within a set period of time.[13] If a Member State fails to comply, by way of a sanction the Council may: (i) require the Member State to publish additional information before issuing bonds or securities; (ii) invite the European Investment Bank to reconsider its lending policy towards the Member State; (iii) require the Member State to make a non-interest-bearing deposit with the Union until the excessive deficit has been corrected; and/or (iv) impose a fine. This process takes the place of any infringement proceedings possibly being brought by the Commission or a Member State, since Art 126 expressly excludes the right to bring such actions within the framework of the Excessive Deficit Procedure. To date, sanctions have yet to be imposed on any Member State. A finding of an excessive deficit was made against Ireland in 2009, which was eventually abrogated in 2016.[14]

[12] See Council Recommendation 2010/410/EU of 13 July 2010 on Broad Guidelines for the Economic Policies of the Member States and the Union [2010] OJ L191/28.

[13] For Member States with a derogation from the adoption of the euro, Art 139(2)(b) TFEU excludes the application of the coercive means of remedying excessive deficits set out in Art 126(9) and (11).

[14] Council Decision of 27 April 2009 on the existence of an excessive deficit in Ireland (2009/416/EC) [2009] OJ L135/23; Council Decision (EU) 2016/1000 of 17 June 2016 abrogating Decision 2009/416/EC on the existence of an excessive deficit in Ireland [2016] OJ L164/12.

[27–18] Both the preventative Multilateral Surveillance Procedure and the corrective Excessive Deficit Procedure were strengthened in 1997 by twin regulations that implemented an important European Council resolution known as the *Stability and Growth Pact*.[15] As part of the Pact, Member States agreed to submit an annual *Stability Programme* or, for non-Euro Area states, a *Convergence Programme*, to the Council and Commission, which would take account of the Council's Broad Guidelines of Economic Policies. The Stability Programme would set out the Member State's: (i) medium-term objectives for achieving a budgetary position of close to balance, or in surplus; (ii) the budgetary and other economic policy measures being taken to achieve the objectives; and (iii) the main assumptions about expected economic developments and important economic variables.

[27–19] In the early 2000s it became apparent that the Council's role in the Excessive Deficit Procedure meant that, in practice, it was likely to prove ineffective, particularly in the face of a breach by a larger Member State. When the Council declined to pursue Commission recommendations in respect of deficits in France and Germany, the Commission sought to have this annulled by the Court of Justice. While the Court of Justice, sitting as a Full Court, found fault with the Council's attempt to develop an ad hoc procedure of its own design – whereby Council conclusions placed the Excessive Deficit Procedure into abeyance pending further action by the states concerned – it ruled that a failure by the Council to adopt the Commission's recommendation was not, of itself, a decision that was capable of being subject to an annulment action.[16] In order not to have the credibility of the Stability and Growth Pact undermined by such responses within the Council, in 2005 the Pact was reformed in order to increase the degree of discretion afforded to the institutions, thereby bringing the Pact into line with the Council's more flexible approach.[17]

[27–20] Finally, the TFEU contains two important prohibitions intended to prevent Member States or the Union from interfering with a monetary policy aimed at controlling inflation, or from avoiding the higher interest rates that should apply to borrowing under normal economic conditions, both of which could lead to financial ill-discipline on the part of Member States. First, Art 123 TFEU prohibits either the Union or the Member States (in the form of central governments, regional, local or other public authorities, other bodies governed by public law or public undertakings) from availing of any

---

[15] Council Regulation 1466/97 on the Strengthening of the Surveillance of Budgetary Positions and the Surveillance and Coordination of Economic Policies [1997] OJ L209/1; Council Regulation 1467/97 on Speeding Up and Clarifying the Implementation of the Excessive Deficit Procedure [1997] OJ L209/6. See Hugo Hahn, "The Stability Pact for European Monetary Union: Compliance with Deficit Limit as a Constant Legal Duty" (1998) 35 *Common Market Law Review* 77; European Court of Auditors, Special Report No 18, "Is the Main Objective of the Preventative Arm of the Stability and Growth Pact Delivered?" (2018).

[16] Case C-27/04 *Commission v Council* [2004] ECR I-6649. See Imelda Maher, "Economic Policy Coordination and the European Court: Excessive Deficits and ECOFIN Discretion" (2004) 29 *European Law Review* 831; Fabian Amtenbrink and Jakob De Haan, "Economic Governance in the European Union – Fiscal Policy Discipline versus Flexibility" (2003) 40 *Common Market Law Review* 1075.

[17] Council Regulation (EC) No 1055/2005 of 27 June 2005 [2005] OJ L174/1, and Council Regulation (EC) No 1056/2005 of 27 June 2005 [2005] OJ L174/5. See Patrick Leblond, "The Political Stability and Growth Pact is Dead: Long Live the Economic Stability and Growth Pact" (2006) 44 *Journal of Common Market Studies* 969; Francis Snyder, "EMU – Integration and Differentiation: Metaphor for European Union" in Paul Craig and Gráinne de Búrca (eds), *The Evolution of EU Law* (2nd ed, Oxford University Press, 2011) 687, 705–709.

overdraft facility or any other type of credit facility from the ECB or the central bank of a Member State. This is known as the "prohibition on monetary financing". Secondly, Art 125 TFEU comprises a "no bail-out clause", providing that the Union shall not be liable for or assume the commitments of a Member State, nor shall any Member State be liable for or assume the commitments of another.

[27–21] Both of these provisions were originally introduced in the Maastricht Treaty with a view to requiring the maintenance of each Member State's fiscal independence. As described by the Court of Justice in *Pringle*, the aim of Art 125 is to protect the financial stability of the monetary union by requiring Member States to follow a sound budgetary policy by keeping them "subject to the logic of the market when they enter into debt, since that ought to prompt them to maintain budgetary discipline".[18] For some Member States, such as Germany, the no bail-out clause was also a means of guaranteeing that the EMU was not turned into a transfer union, whereby financial resources would be moved from prudently managed Member States to those less fiscally responsible. It has been said that the "authors of the Maastricht Treaty were convinced that Art 125 TFEU would prevent Member States from defaulting by a mechanism of self-discipline but they did not develop a concept for a failure of this mechanism", thus necessitating a rereading when the sovereign debt crisis emerged in 2008.[19]

[27–22] Reflecting the differentiated nature of EMU, Paul Craig and Gráinne de Búrca have described the architecture established by the Maastricht Treaty as having been predicated on a dichotomy between monetary and economic union, which remained largely unchanged in the Lisbon Treaty.[20] While it was integral to the Maastricht settlement that monetary policy was to be Europeanised – reinforced by mandatory Treaty provisions precluding instructions or interference from any outside party, whether a Member State or another EU institution – the treatment of economic policy was markedly different and rested on two related assumptions: the need to preserve both *national authority* and, as a result, *national liability*. As Craig and de Búrca explain:

> [National authority] was reflected in the fact that Member States retained fiscal authority for national budgets, subject to oversight and coordination from the EU designed to persuade Member States, with the ultimate possibility of sanctions, to balance their budgets and not run excessive deficits.
>
> The ... preservation of national liability was the consequence of [the preservation of national authority]. It finds its most powerful expression in the no bail-out provision ... The message was that national governments retained authority over national economic policy, subject to the Treaty rules designed to persuade them to balance their budgets, the corollary being that if they did not do so then the liabilities remained their own ...
>
> The Member States recognised the proximate connection between economic and monetary policy ... They were however mindful of the policy decisions made in and through national budgets, including those of a redistributive nature, and were unwilling to accord the EU too much control over such determinations ...[21]

[18] Case C-370/12 *Pringle v Government of Ireland* EU:C:2012:756, 27 November 2012, para 135.

[19] Clemens Richter in Rudolf Geiger, Daniel-Erasmus Khan and Markus Kotzur (eds), *European Union Treaties* (Beck, 2015) 592.

[20] Paul Craig and Gráinne de Búrca, *EU Law* (6th ed, Oxford University Press, 2015) 727.

[21] *ibid*, 728.

[27–23] In broad terms, the differentiated form of integration that makes up EMU, as first established in the Maastricht Treaty, can be represented as follows:

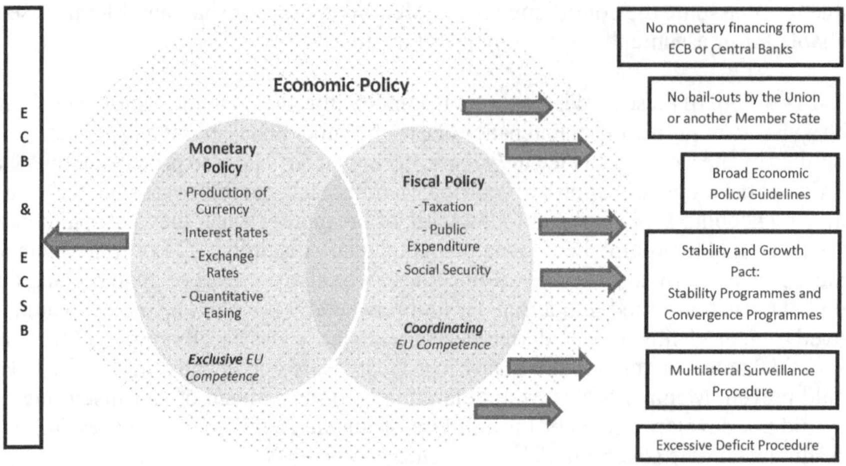

(i) Creating the Euro

[27–24] Before the third and final stage of EMU began on 1 January 1999, on 1 June 1998 the European Monetary Institute was replaced by the European Central Bank (ECB). The ECB, together with the central banks of the Member States, would form the European System of Central Banks and was charged with conducting the Union's monetary policy. This had been preceded in May 1998 by a decision of the heads of state and government as to which Member States had fulfilled the convergence criteria necessary in order to be permitted to adopt the euro. On 31 December 1998, the exchange rates of 11 participating states, including Ireland, were fixed and the following day the euro became their currency, albeit in "virtual" form. Preparations for the introduction of banknotes and coins began, with their circulation commencing three years later on 1 January 2002.[22] Today, the euro is used in 19 Member States, with two Member States – the UK and Denmark – having protocols exempting them from any obligation to adopt the single currency. The remaining seven Member States – Bulgaria, Croatia, Czech Republic, Hungary, Poland, Romania and Sweden – are known as "countries with a derogation" and are committed to adopting the euro whenever they fulfil the convergence criteria set out in Art 140 TFEU and Protocol No 13 to the TEU and TFEU, namely:

(i) to have participated in the Exchange Rate Mechanism (ERM II), which allows fluctuation of plus or minus 15 per cent from a central rate that has been agreed between the euro and the country's currency, for at least two years without devaluing against the euro.[23] Notwithstanding its opt-out, Denmark is in ERM II and is currently the only participating state. For example, Sweden, which rejected joining the euro in a 2003 referendum, is not in ERM II;

---

[22] See John Kelly, "The Irish Pound: From Origins to EMU" (2003) Central Bank of Ireland, *Spring Quarterly Review* 89.

[23] Agreement of 16 March 2006 between the European Central Bank and the national central banks of the Member States outside the euro area laying down the operating procedures for an exchange-rate mechanism in stage three of Economic and Monetary Union, [2006] OJ C73/21.

(ii) to have a sustainable government financial position that has avoided an excessive government deficit (ie the annual deficit must not exceed 3 per cent of GDP while the total deficit must not exceed 60 per cent of GDP);
(iii) to have achieved a high degree of price stability, indicated by the fact that the annual rate of inflation is not more than 1.5 percentage points above the three best performing Member States; and
(iv) to have long-term interest rates that are not more than 2 percentage points above the three best performing Member States in terms of price stability.

[27–25] While, in theory, all Member States with a derogation other than Denmark and the UK have a legal obligation to join the euro, in practice this is a difficult obligation to enforce given the need to fulfil the convergence criteria. A specific chapter of the TFEU, Chapter 5 of Title VIII of Part Three, is dedicated to such states, dealing with issues such as: identifying the provisions of the TFEU that do not apply to them[24]; voting procedures in the Council on matters concerning the Euro Area or Euro Area states[25]; the requirement for a convergence report every two years detailing the progress made in fulfilling their obligation to achieve EMU[26]; the role of the ECB with regard to states with a derogation,[27] and a requirement on such states to treat their exchange rate policy as a matter of common interest.[28] A further degree of differentiation arose through the establishment of the Euro Group in 1998, which is now formally recognised in Art 137 TFEU and in Protocol No 14. The short protocol comprises just two articles and provides that the ministers of Euro Area states shall meet informally, when necessary, to discuss questions related to the specific responsibilities they share with regard to the euro. Since 2005, the members of the Euro Group have elected a president, which the Protocol provides shall be for a two-and-a-half year term. The Commission takes part in Euro Group meetings, while the ECB may be invited to do so.[29]

C. European Central Bank

[27–26] Economic and monetary policy now forms Title VIII of Part Three of the TFEU. In addition to Art 119, setting out general principles, Title VIII comprises five chapters as follows: Economic Policy (Arts 120–126); Monetary Policy (Arts 127–133); Institutional Provisions (Arts 134–135); Provisions Specific to Member States whose currency is the euro (Arts 136–138) and Transitional Provisions relating to Member States with a derogation (Arts 139–144). As we have already seen, in setting out the general principles regarding coordination on economic policies, Chapter 1 includes the prohibition on monetary financing (Art 123), no bail-out clause (Art 125), Multilateral Surveillance Procedure (Art 121) and Excessive Deficit Procedure (Art 126). In this section we shall focus on the role of the European System of Central Banks (ESCB)

---

[24] Art 139(2) TFEU.

[25] Art 139(4)

[26] Art 140 TFEU.

[27] Art 141 TFEU.

[28] Art 142 TFEU.

[29] For a discussion of the legal status of the Euro Group see the opinion of Advocate General Wathelet in Joined Cases C-105/15 P to C-109/15 P *Mallis v Commission* EU:C:2016:294, 21 April 2016, paras 54–67; Case T–786/14 *Bourdouvali* EU:T:2018:487, 13 July 2018, paras 102–111. For a critical assessment of the Euro Group from the perspectives of transparency and accountability, see Benjamin Braun and Marina Hübner, *Vanishing Act: The Eurogroup's Accountability* (Transparency International EU, 2019).

and the European Central Bank. Since the entry into force of the Lisbon Treaty, the ECB is now one of the Union's seven institutions, further provision for which is made in Arts 282–284 TFEU and in the Statute of the ECSB and ECB that forms Protocol No 4 to the Treaties.

[27–27] Article 282 TFEU provides that the European System of Central Banks shall comprise the European Central Bank and national central banks. However, the ECB and the national central banks of the Member States whose currency is the euro constitute the Eurosystem, which shall conduct the EU's monetary policy. The ESCB is governed by the decision-making bodies of the ECB – its Governing Council and Executive Board – and has as its primary objective the maintenance of price stability with the supplemental aim of supporting the Union's general economic policies.[30] Here, price stability is defined by the ECB as a year-on-year increase in the Harmonised Index of Consumer Prices of below 2 per cent. The basic tasks to be carried out through the ESCB are identified in Art 127 TFEU as being to: (i) define and implement the Union's monetary policy; (ii) conduct foreign-exchange operations; (iii) hold and manage the official foreign reserves of the Member States; and (iv) promote the smooth operation of payment systems. The ESCB is also to contribute to the smooth conduct of policies pursued by competent authorities relating to the prudential supervision of credit institutions and the stability of the financial system. As Damian Chalmers observes, although monetary policy is to be defined and implemented through the ESCB, the ECB has a *primus inter pares* position within the ESCB, with "a monopoly control over the central tool of monetary policy, the authorisation of the issue of euros, and, thereby, the setting of short-term interest rates".[31]

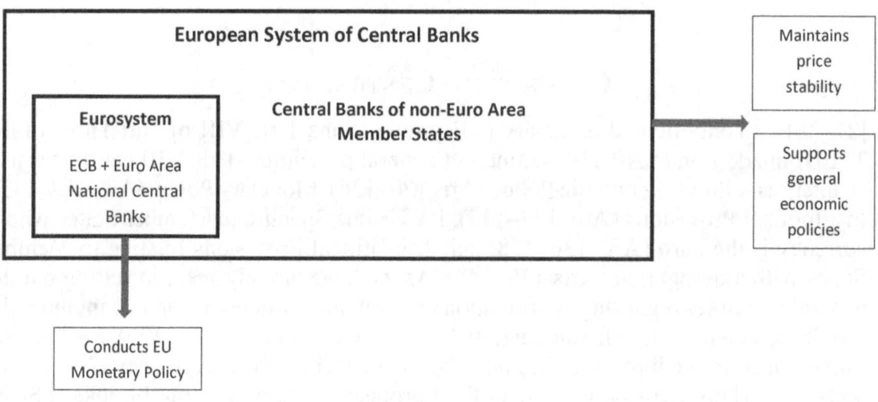

[27–28] Uniquely amongst the EU institutions, the ECB is said to enjoy institutional isolationism, with Art 130 TFEU providing that, in exercising the tasks conferred upon them by the Treaties, neither the ECB, nor the national central banks, nor any member of their decision-making bodies, shall take or seek instructions from a Union institution, Member State government or any other body. As a corollary, the Union institutions

[30] See Bernd Krauskopf and Christine Steven, "The Institutional Framework of the European System of Central Banks: Legal Issues in the Practice of the First Ten Years of its Existence" (2009) *46 Common Market Law Review* 1143.

[31] Damian Chalmers, Gareth Davies and Giorgio Monti, *European Union Law* (3rd ed, Cambridge University Press, 2014) 731.

and the Member States undertake not to seek to influence the members of the ECB's decision-making bodies. Since the Governing Council of the ECB is comprised of the governors of the central banks of Euro Area Member States, this also serves to ensure the independence of such officials within their own Member State. For example, the ECB recently obtained a ruling from the Court of Justice that Latvia's suspension of its central bank governor, thereby preventing him from serving on the ECB's Governing Council, was in breach of the Statute of the ECSB and ECB.[32] This was the first such case heard by the Court on the basis of a specific jurisdiction conferred on it by Art 14 of the Statute. Unlike the jurisdiction of the Court under the TEU and TFEU, uniquely the Court's jurisdiction under this provision of the Statute was held to empower it to *annul* a national decision to relieve a central bank governor of his or her duties. According to the Court:

> It is true that, inasmuch as it expressly entrusts the Court with power to review the lawfulness of an act of national law in light of "[the] Treaties or of any rule of law relating to their application", the second subparagraph of Article 14.2 of the Statute of the ESCB and of the ECB derogates from the general distribution of powers between the national courts and the courts of the European Union as provided for by the Treaties and in particular by Article 263 TFEU, as an action under that article may concern only acts of EU law. However, that derogation can be explained by the particular institutional context of the ESCB within which it operates. The ESCB represents a novel legal construct in EU law which brings together national institutions, namely the national central banks, and an EU institution, namely the ECB, and causes them to cooperate closely with each other, and within which a different structure and a less marked distinction between the EU legal order and national legal orders prevails.
>
> Article 14.2 of the Statute of the ESCB and of the ECB reflects the logic of this highly integrated system which the authors of the Treaties envisaged for the ESCB and, in particular, of the dual professional role of the governor of a national central bank, who is certainly a national authority but who acts within the framework of the ESCB and sits, where he is the governor of a national central bank of a Member State whose currency is the euro, on the main decision-making body of the ECB. It is because of this hybrid status and … in order to guarantee the functional independence of the governors of the national central banks within the ESCB that, by way of exception, a decision taken by a national authority relieving one of those governors from office may be referred to the Court.
>
> Article 14.2 of the Statute [of the ESCB and of the ECB] thus adds a legal remedy to the system of legal remedies laid down by the Treaties which is very specific, as is apparent from the very small number of persons to whom it is available, the unique subject matter of the decisions against which it may be used and the exceptional circumstances in which it may be exercised.
>
> In the third place, the nature of the action provided for in Article 14.2 of the Statute [of the ESCB and of the ECB] is also made clear by the objective in view of which it was introduced. … [T]hat action is one of the main guarantees that the governors, although appointed by and, as the case may be, dismissed by the Member States, are to carry out independently the tasks that are conferred on them by the Treaties and are not, pursuant to Article 130 TFEU and Article 7 of the Statute of the ESCB and of the ECB, to take any instructions from national authorities. It thus represents an essential component of the institutional balance necessary for close cooperation between the national central banks and the ECB within the ESCB.[33]

---

[32] Case C-238/18 *European Central Bank v Latvia* EU:C:2019: 139, 26 February 2019 with limited interim measures granted on 20 July 2018, EU:C:2018:581.

[33] *ibid*, paras 69–72.

[27–29] The aim of guaranteeing the ECB's independence is to ensure that the policy objective of maintaining price stability is not diluted by short-term government interests. The potential downside of insulating the Bank from any outside direction is that it operates free from typical democratic controls.[34] From this perspective, it has been suggested that the "failure of EMU's architects to embed the ECB in a 'wider European polity' … leaves the euro's legitimacy dangerously dependent on its perceived economic benefits and hence on short-term economic fluctuations".[35]

[27–30] The Bank's decision-making bodies are its Governing Council and Executive Board. The Executive Board is made up of a President, Vice-President and four other members who are appointed by the European Council from among persons of recognised standing and professional experience in monetary or banking matters.[36] In 2019, the governor of the Central Bank of Ireland, Philip Lane, became the first Irish person to be appointed as a member of the Executive Board, upon which he was required to leave his post in the Central Bank. The Governing Council comprises the Executive Board and the governors of the central banks of the Member States whose currency is the euro. The Executive Board is responsible for day-to-day business and for implementing monetary policy in accordance with the guidelines and decisions of the Governing Council, including by giving necessary instructions to national central banks. The Executive Board prepares the meetings of the Governing Council, which are chaired by the President of the Executive Board. Through its decisions, the Governing Council is to formulate the EU's monetary policy including matters such as key interest rates and the supply of reserves in the ESCB.

[27–31] The tasks and powers of the ECB are further elaborated upon in its Statute. In order to achieve the objectives of the ESCB, the ECB and national central banks may operate in the financial markets by buying and selling outright claims and marketable instruments and may conduct credit operations with credit institutions and other market participants.[37] The ECB may require credit institutions established in Member States to hold minimum reserves on accounts with the ECB and national central banks in pursuance of monetary objectives.[38] The ECB and national central banks may provide facilities, and the ECB may make regulations, to ensure efficient clearing and payment systems within the Union and with other countries.[39] In accordance with any regulations adopted unanimously by the Council using the special legislative procedure, the ECB may perform tasks aimed at the prudential supervision of credit and other financial

---

34 See Leo Hoffmann-Axthelm, *Two Sides of the Same Coin? Independence and Accountability of the European Central Bank* (Transparency International EU, 2017); Fabian Amtenbrink and Kees Van Duin, "The European Central Bank before the European Parliament: Theory and Practice after 10 Years of Monetary Dialogue" (2009) 34 *European Law Review* 561; Lorenzo Bini Smaghi, "Central Bank Independence in the EU: From Theory to Practice" (2008) 14 *European Law Review* 446; Roger J Goebel, "Court of Justice Oversight over the European Central Bank: Delimiting the ECB's Constitutional Autonomy and Independence in the *OLAF* Judgment" (2005) 29 *Fordham International Law Journal* 610.

35 Dermot Hodson, "Managing the Euro: The European Central Bank" in John Peterson and Michael Shackleton (eds), *The Institutions of the European Union* (3rd ed, Oxford University Press, 2012) 214.

36 Art 283(2) TFEU.

37 Art 18, Statute of the ESCB and ECB.

38 Art 19, Statute of the ESCB and ECB.

39 Art 22, Statute of the ESCB and ECB.

institutions.[40] To the extent necessary to implement its tasks, the ECB is empowered to make regulations and recommendations, take decisions and deliver opinions.[41] As provided for by the Council, the ECB may impose fines or periodic penalty payments on undertakings for failure to comply with obligations under its regulations and decisions.[42]

D. Responding to Financial Crisis

[27–32] In September 2008, the fourth largest investment bank in the United States – Lehman Brothers – collapsed, becoming a totemic victim of the US subprime mortgage crisis. This triggered the beginning of a crisis in the global financial system itself, causing a credit crunch that ended the ready availability of loans such as mortgages. In Ireland, this led to a general economic crash and a rapid fall in house prices. Benefitting from lower interest rates within the Euro Area, as set by the ECB, in the years leading up to 2008 Irish banks had relied excessively upon wholesale borrowing on the international markets to support a very rapid expansion of their balance sheets in order to finance the property boom. The fall in the property market therefore seriously undermined the funding base of Irish banks, leading to deposits being withdrawn from the system. In parallel, as the property boom had increased the proportion of total tax revenue derived from property-based taxes such as stamp duty, its collapse depleted an important source of government revenue and caused the banking problem to precipitate a fiscal problem.[43] As has been described, the property boom in Ireland, the "counterpoint of which was an increase in private debt, temporarily masked an underlying fiscal weakness because tax receipts depended heavily on debt-fuelled consumption and property-related transactions. As windfall revenues were typically used to fund expenditure programmes, large and irreversible deficits appeared when these, essentially temporary, sources of revenue dried up."[44]

[27–33] According to the critical assessment of one economist, when money rushed into Ireland following the introduction of the euro, and especially in the years preceding 2008, "lenders somehow thought that the elimination of exchange-rate risk meant the elimination of *all* risk", which was reflected in the low interest rates that Ireland had to pay to borrow.[45] Joseph Stiglitz has gone on to describe how:

> In the absence of the eurozone, a country flooded with speculative money could have raised interest rates to dampen the real estate bubble. But being part of the euro made this

---

[40] Art 25, Statute of the ESCB and ECB.

[41] Art 132(1) TFEU; Art 34.1, Statute of the ESCB and ECB.

[42] Art 132(2) TFEU; Art 34.3, Statute of the ESCB and ECB. See Regulation (EC) No 2532/98 of 23 November 1998 concerning the powers of the European Central Bank to impose sanctions [1998] OJ L318/4.

[43] Alan Dukes, "The Euro Crisis: An Agenda for Reform" (Institute of International and European Affairs, 2011) 2. For a detailed account of the responses to the debt crisis in Ireland see Stephen Coutts, "Ireland and the European Union" (2011) 6 *Irish Yearbook of International Law* 127; Stephen Coutts, "Ireland and the European Union 2012" (2012) 7 *Irish Yearbook of International Law* 185; Roderic O'Gorman, "Ireland and the European Union 2013" (2013) 8 *Irish Yearbook of International Law* 121; Patrick Honohan, *Currency, Credit and Crisis: Central Banking in Ireland and Europe* (Cambridge University Press, 2019); Patrick Honohan, "Resolving the Irish Banking Crisis" (2009) 40 *Economic and Social Review* 207.

[44] Pat McArdle, "The Euro Crisis: Economic Governance and Budgetary Surveillance" (Institute of International and European Affairs, 2011) 7.

[45] Joseph Stiglitz, *The Euro* (Penguin, 2016) 114. Emphasis added.

> impossible. Countries like Spain and Ireland facing a real estate bubble could and should have imposed capital gains taxes or imposed restrictions in lending by local banks. But the market fundamentalist ideology dominant in the euro-zone ruled these measures out.
>
> The government could, alternatively, have cut back on its spending … But the governments of Spain and Ireland were flush with tax revenues generated by the boom, and they felt no need to do so. Both countries were in surplus. Managing inflation was the job of the ECB, not their job. Their job was to stick within the budget constraints demanded by the Maastricht Treaty and spend money well; and they were doing that. According to the convergence criteria – and the ideology of the time – everything was fine.[46]

[27–34] The financial crisis in the Irish banks soon led to a sovereign debt crisis. With the aim of ensuring the stability of the Irish financial system, on 30 September 2008 the Government guaranteed the deposits and borrowings of banks incorporated in Ireland. This was done so as to enable Irish banks to access liquidity, in the form of cash, in order to conduct their business. When depositors and bondholders cashed in on this guarantee, Ireland's credit rating started to fall and the yield on Irish government debt rose rapidly. Having had a surplus in 2007, by 2010 the budget deficit had rocketed to 32 per cent of GDP. By the autumn of 2010,

> the loss of investor confidence in Ireland triggered a vicious cycle. Deposit outflows from the banking sector accelerated and the cost of government borrowing reached unsustainable highs. As financing costs increased and renewed banking losses were revealed, investors were increasingly concerned about the capacity of the government to deal with the dual challenge of a large fiscal deficit and the state's commitment to finance the growing cost of supporting a severely damaged banking sector. The credibility and thus the effectiveness of the government guarantees in the banking sector faded. More outflows and increasing borrowing costs further damaged confidence.[47]

[27–35] Unable to afford borrowing at market prices, in November 2010 the Government entered into a "bail-out" agreement with the International Monetary Fund (IMF), the European Commission and the ECB (the "Troika") titled the European Adjustment Programme for Ireland.[48] As part of this, Ireland would receive €22.5 billion from each of the IMF, the European Financial Stabilisation Mechanism (EFSM) and the European Financial Stability Facility (EFSF), with the EFSF contribution made up in part by bilateral loans from the non-Euro Area states of the UK (€3.8bn), Sweden

---

46 *ibid*, 114–115.

47 *The Economic Adjustment Programme for Ireland*, European Commission, European Economy Occasional Papers No 76, 2011, 5.

48 The agreement took the form of three Memorandums of Understanding signed on 16 December 2010: Memorandum of Economic and Financial Policies; Memorandum of Understanding on Specific Economic Policy Conditionality and Technical Memorandum of Understanding, which set out the Loan Facility Agreement itself. The texts of the Memorandums are annexed in *The Economic Adjustment Programme for Ireland*, European Commission, European Economy Occasional Papers No 76, 2011. See Council Implementing Decision of 7 December 2010 on granting financial assistance to Ireland (2011/77/EU) [2011] OJ L54/34, as amended by Council Implementing Decisions of: 30 May 2011 (2011/326/EU) [2011] OJ L147/17; 2 September 2011 (2011/542/EU) [2011] OJ L240/11; 11 October 2011 (2011/682/EU) [2011] OJ L269/31; 30 November 2011 (2011/827/EU) [2011] OJ L329/7; 22 June 2012 (2012/375/EU) [2012] OJ L182/37; 22 January 2013 (2013/48/EU) [2013] OJ L21/30; 21 June 2013 (2013/313/EU) [2013] OJ L173/40; 9 July 2013 (2013/372/EU) [2013] OJ L191/9; 22 October 2013 (2013/525/EU) [2013] OJ L282/71. See also Council Implementing Decision of 9 July 2013 approving the update of the macroeconomic adjustment programme in Ireland (2013/373/EU) [2013] OJ L191/10.

(€0.6bn) and Denmark (€0.4bn). As the name suggests, the Adjustment Programme involved loans being made available to Ireland with a range of conditions attached. As part of the required fiscal reforms, a fiscal consolidation of €15 billion was to be achieved by 2014, through a €7 billion reduction in capital expenditure, €3 billion reduction in current expenditure and an increase in revenue of €5 billion. Other conditions included matters such as a reduction in the national minimum wage; a reorganisation of the banking sector; an increase in the age of entitlement to the state pension; and the introduction of legislative changes to remove restrictions to trade and competition in "sheltered sectors" including the legal profession, medical services and the pharmacy profession. As has been observed, while the Adjustment Programme did not directly require the enactment of implementing legislation,

> the detailed terms have had profound implications in terms of policy and many associated legislative commitments linked to the payment of the staged payments … of the funding envisaged in the agreement. These include: the enactment of a Fiscal Responsibility Act, including the creation of a Fiscal Council and, in effect, a legally binding requirement to aim for a balanced budget; the enactment of Central Bank Acts aimed at further regulating the financial services sector; the rationalisation of the financial services sectors, including provision for the liquidation of banks; fundamental reform of the law on personal insolvency; and reform of certain professions, including the dental and legal professions.[49]

[27–36] While Ireland exited the Adjustment Programme in December 2013, it does remain subject to post-programme surveillance until at least 75 per cent of the financial assistance received has been repaid, which is scheduled to be no earlier than 2031. The surveillance is intended to measure Ireland's capacity to repay its outstanding loans to the EFSF and EFSM. The Commission and the ECB undertake the surveillance by regular missions to Ireland to assess the economic, fiscal and financial situation, which are the subject of six-monthly reports which identify any corrective measures that are deemed necessary.[50]

(i) Initial Ad Hoc Responses

[27–37] Since Art 123 TFEU prohibits monetary financing or the provision of credit by the ECB or national central banks in favour of the Union or a Member State, and Art 125 TFEU prohibits the ECB or Member States from bailing out a Member State, how was the EU to respond to the sovereign debt crisis being experienced in Greece, Spain, Portugal and Ireland? Initially, reliance was placed on Art 122(2) TFEU. It provides that where a Member State is in difficulties or is seriously threatened with severe difficulties caused by natural disasters or exceptional occurrences beyond its control, the Council may grant Union financial assistance to the Member State concerned.[51] This was the legal basis on which the European Financial Stabilisation Mechanism (EFSM) was established by a regulation in May 2010.[52] Contributed to by all Member States, the EFSM was a fund of €60 billion from which, in order to preserve the financial stability of the Union, loans could be made available to a state

---

49 Raymond Byrne and William Binchy, *Annual Review of Irish Law 2010* (Round Hall 2011), 56.

50 For example, see *Post-Programme Surveillance Report: Ireland, Autumn 2018*, European Commission, Institutional Paper 98, 7 February 2019.

51 See Council Regulation (EU) 2016/369 of 15 March 2016 on the provision of emergency support within the Union [2016] OJ L70/1.

52 Council Regulation (EU) No 407/2010 of 11 May 2010 establishing a European financial stabilisation mechanism [2010] OJ L118/1.

experiencing, or seriously threatened with, a severe economic or financial disturbance caused by exceptional occurrences beyond its control.

[27–38] Around the same time, the European Financial Stability Facility (EFSF) was created through the combination of a framework agreement between the Euro Area states and the establishment of the Facility as a private law company incorporated in Luxembourg.[53] The Facility comprised a fund of €440 billion that, through the issue of bonds or other debt instruments on the market, could raise funds needed to provide loans to Euro Area countries in financial difficulty. The Facility made loans available to Ireland, Greece and Portugal.[54] Whilst it has ceased to provide any new loans, it will continue to operate in carrying out tasks related to loans and EFSF bonds until they are repaid in full.

[27–39] In addition to the establishment of the EFSM and EFSF, the ECB also responded to the debt crisis by adopting what it termed "non-standard monetary policy measures". Because sovereign bonds played a crucial role in benchmarking private sector lending rates and formed an important part of banks' balance sheets and liquidity operations, the ECB considered that the debt crisis was impairing its ability to transmit its monetary policy – through decisions on interest rates – to the real economy. Accordingly, in May 2010, the ECB decided to launch a Securities Markets Programme whereby it would purchase sovereign bonds of Euro Area Member States on the secondary markets.[55] In September 2012, this Programme was replaced by an Outright Monetary Transactions (OMT) Programme. Unlike the Securities Market Programme, the scope of the OMT Programme was unlimited, linked to the widely reported remarks of the ECB President that the Bank would do "whatever it takes" to save the euro. In further contrast to the earlier Programme, to benefit from the OMT Programme a Member State would first have to have agreed to an adjustment programme, or some other form of conditionality, as part of a loan from the European Financial Stability Facility, or its successor, the European Stability Mechanism (ESM). The ECB would consider OMTs to the extent that they were warranted from a monetary policy perspective and as long as EFSF/ESM programme conditionality was being fully respected, terminating them once their objectives were achieved or whenever there was non-compliance with the EFSF/ESM programme conditionality.

[27–40] Each of these measures – the EFSF, the EFSM, the Securities Markets Programme and, later, the OMT Programme – were all shadowed by an overriding concern as to their legality given the TFEU's clear prohibitions against monetary financing and bail-outs and the very narrow exception permitted by Art 122 in respect of "natural disasters or exceptional occurrences" beyond a state's control.[56] As we have seen

---

[53] EFSF Framework Agreement between Belgium, Germany, Ireland, Spain, France, Italy, Cyprus, Luxembourg, Malta, the Netherlands, Austria, Portugal, Slovenia, Slovakia, Finland, Greece and the European Financial Stability Facility, 7 June 2010. The text of the Framework Agreement is scheduled to the European Financial Stability Funding Act 2010, as amended by the European Financial Stability Facility and Euro Area Loan Facility (Amendment) Act 2011. See Ledina Gocaj and Sophie Meunier, "Time Will Tell: The EFSF, the ESM, and the Euro Crisis" (2013) 35 *Journal of European Integration* 239.

[54] See "Testing the EFSF: the case of Ireland" in *Safeguarding the Euro in Times of Crisis: the inside story of the ESM* (European Stability Mechanism, 2019) 91.

[55] Decision of the European Central Bank of 14 May 2010 establishing a Securities Markets Programme (ECB/2010/5) (2010/281/EU) [2010] OJ L124/8.

[56] See Jean-Victor Louis, "The No-Bailout Clause and Rescue Packages" (2010) 47 *Common Market*

in Chapter 13, the OMT Programme would prompt the German Constitutional Court to make its first ever reference to the Court of Justice, with that Court upholding the lawfulness of the Programme provided that its operation abided by certain conditions.[57] These concerns contributed to the making of the "Deauville Declaration" in October 2010 by the leaders of France and Germany. Just ten months after the entry into force of the Lisbon Treaty, both countries called for an amendment to the Treaties in order to establish a permanent framework to ensure orderly crisis management in the future and allow all Member States to adopt coordinated measures to safeguard the financial stability of the Euro Area. Secondly, it was proposed that the Treaties should be amended so as to allow for the suspension of voting rights in the Council in the event of a Member State's serious violation of basic principles of EMU.

[27–41] Rather than lead to substantive Treaty change, the Deauville Declaration marked the start of an intense period of EMU reform that would see the conclusion of two international agreements outside of the EU framework – the Treaty Establishing the European Stability Mechanism (the "ESM Treaty") and the Treaty on Stability, Coordination and Governance in the Economic and Monetary Union (also known as the "Fiscal Treaty") – and a much strengthened Stability and Growth Pact bolstered by the so-called "Six Pack" and "Two Pack". In order to provide a Treaty legal base for the conclusion of the ESM Treaty, a new paragraph (3) was inserted into Art 136 TFEU pursuant to the simplified revision procedure, as follows: "The Member States whose currency is the euro may establish a stability mechanism to be activated if indispensable to safeguard the stability of the euro area as a whole. The granting of any required financial assistance under the mechanism will be made subject to strict conditionality."[58] To date, this is the only amendment to the TEU or TFEU to have resulted from the debt crisis. It also remains the only occasion on which the simplified revision procedure has been used to amend the Treaties.[59]

Law Review 971; Matthias Ruffert, "The European Debt Crisis and European Union Law" (2011) 48 *Common Market Law Review* 1777; Rainer Palmstorfer, "To Bail Out or Not to Bail Out? The Current Framework of Financial Assistance for Euro Area Member States Measured Against the Requirements of EU Primary Law" (2012) 37 *European Law Review* 771; Alicia Hinarejos, "The Euro Area Crises and Constitutional Limits to Fiscal Integration" (2012) 14 *Cambridge Yearbook of European Legal Studies* 243; Thomas Beukers, "The New ECB and its Relationship with the Eurozone Member States: Between Central Bank Independence and Central Bank Intervention" (2013) 50 *Common Market Law Review* 1579.

57 Case C-62/14 *Gauweiler v Deutscher Bundestag* EU:C:2015:400, 16 June 2015. See Takis Tridimas and Napoleon Xanthoulis, "A Legal Analysis of the *Gauweiler* Case: Between Monetary Policy and Constitutional Conflict" (2016) 23 *Maastricht Journal of European and Comparative Law* 17; Vestert Borger, "Outright Monetary Transactions and the Stability Mandate of the ECB: *Gauweiler*" (2016) 53 *Common Market Law Review* 139; Paul Craig and Menelaos Markakis, "*Gauweiler* and the Legality of Outright Monetary Transactions" (2016) 41 *European Law Review* 4; Dariusz Adamski, "Economic Constitution of the Euro Area after the *Gauweiler* Preliminary Ruling" (2015) 52 *Common Market Law Review* 1451.

58 European Council Decision of 25 March 2011 amending Art 136 of the Treaty on the Functioning of the European Union with regard to a stability mechanism for Member States whose currency is the euro (2011/199/EU) [2011] OJ L91/1; Irish Treaty Series No 14 (Treaty Action) of 2014. The European Communities (Amendment) Act 2012 amended the definition of "treaties governing the European Union" in s 1 of the European Communities Act 1972 so as to include the European Council Decision of 25 March 2011.

59 The nature of Ireland's freedom to choose whether or not to proceed with approving the European Council Decision in accordance with its constitutional requirements was the subject of litigation in *Doherty v Referendum Commission* [2012] 2 IR 594. In the context of the referendum campaign on the Treaty on Stability, Coordination and Governance in the EMU, the Chairman of the

(ii) European Stability Mechanism

[27–42] Even before the European Council Decision to amend Art 136 TFEU had been brought into force through ratification by all Member States, the Euro Area Member States had proceeded to sign the Treaty Establishing the European Stability Mechanism, replacing the EFSM and the EFSF with a new permanent mechanism capable of lending up to €500 billion.[60] Based in Luxembourg, the Mechanism is an international organisation with its own legal personality.[61] The ESM is provided for in Irish law through the European Stability Mechanism Act 2010, as amended by the European Stability Mechanism (Amendment) Act 2014. According to Art 3 of the Treaty, the purpose of the ESM is to:

> mobilise funding and provide stability support under strict conditionality, appropriate to the financial assistance instrument chosen, to the benefit of ESM Members which are experiencing, or are threatened by, severe financing problems, if indispensable to safeguard the financial stability of the euro area as a whole and of its Member States. For this purpose, the ESM shall be entitled to raise funds by issuing financial instruments or by entering into financial or other agreements or arrangements with ESM Members, financial institutions or other third parties.

[27–43] The ways in which financial assistance can be provided to a Member State include loans,[62] a market support facility whereby the ESM will purchase a state's sovereign bonds on the primary or secondary markets,[63] or through financial assistance for the re-capitalisation of a state's financial institutions.[64] If the ESM Governing Board decides to grant stability support, the Board entrusts the European Commission – in liaison with the ECB and, wherever possible, together with the IMF – with the task of negotiating a memorandum of understanding detailing the conditionality attached to the financial assistance. The content of the memorandum is to (i) reflect the severity of the weaknesses to be addressed and the financial assistance instrument chosen and (ii) be fully consistent with the measures of economic policy coordination provided for in the TFEU, including any act of EU law and any opinion, recommendation or decision addressed to the state concerned.[65] Following approval by the ESM Board of Governors, the memorandum is signed on behalf of the ESM by the Commission and it is the Commission – in liaison with the ECB and, wherever possible, together with the IMF – that is entrusted with monitoring compliance with the conditionality.

Referendum Commission indicated that, after agreeing to the adoption of the Decision within the European Council, Ireland could not oppose the Decision's entry into force. The High Court (Hogan J) confined itself to finding that the statement of the Referendum Commission was not clearly wrong, nor could it be said that it was likely to affect the outcome of the referendum, and so the Court declined the reliefs sought. As there was room for legitimate debate as to the merits of the competing interpretations put forward, any definitive choice from amongst them would require a preliminary ruling from the Court of Justice.

60 Irish Treaty Series No 14 of 2013. An earlier version of the Treaty was signed on 11 July 2011 but was subsequently deemed to be inadequate in certain respects and so a revised version was signed on 2 February 2011, which was ratified by Ireland on 1 August 2012 and entered into force on 27 September 2012. See *Safeguarding the Euro in Times of Crisis: the inside story of the ESM* (European Stability Mechanism, 2019).

61 Arts 31 and 32, ESM Treaty.

62 Art 16, ESM Treaty.

63 Arts 17 and 18, ESM Treaty.

64 Art 15, ESM Treaty.

65 Art 13, ESM Treaty.

[27–44] Each ESM member contributes to the Mechanism's total authorised capital stock of €700 billion in accordance with a contribution key based on their respective share of the EU total population and GDP.[66] So, for example, whereas Germany's contribution key is 27 per cent, with a subscribed capital of €190 billion, Ireland's contribution key is 1.6 per cent, with a subscribed capital of just over €11 billion. Subject to approval by the Board of Governors, the ESM Treaty is open for accession for new members of the Euro Area and, since its establishment, has been acceded to by Latvia and Lithuania. As the accession of new members is factored into the total capital stock it slightly reduces the founding members' contribution keys. Each ESM member appoints a member to the Board of Governors which, subject to one exception, makes decisions on the granting of assistance by unanimity. Where, however, both the Commission and the ECB conclude that a failure to urgently grant assistance would threaten the economic and financial sustainability of the Euro Area, a decision requires only 85 per cent of the votes cast.[67] Since the voting rights of members are equal to the percentage allocation of authorised capital stock, only Germany (27 per cent), France (20 per cent) and Italy (18 per cent) have a veto in such circumstances. Any dispute arising between the ESM and a Member State, or between Member States, is to be determined by the Board of Governors. If an ESM member contests the decision of the Board, the dispute is submitted to the Court of Justice whose judgment shall be binding on the parties in the procedure. The parties shall take the necessary measures to comply with the judgment within a period prescribed by the Court.[68] As will be seen below, this model of adopting an intergovernmental agreement outside of the formal EU legal framework, whilst making use of its institutions, was followed a month later in the Treaty on Stability, Coordination and Governance in the EMU. While this can seem like a pragmatic solution in the context of the need to address the sovereign debt crisis, it does raise principled concerns as regards differentiated forms of EU law and whether this vehicle allows selective "cherry-picking" to take place whereby inconvenient aspects of the EU architecture, such as democratic controls or transparency, can be circumvented.[69]

---

[66] Art 8, ESM Treaty.

[67] Art 4(4) ESM Treaty.

[68] Art 37, ESM Treaty.

[69] See Imelda Maher, "Economic Governance: Hybridity, Accountability and Control" (2007) 13 *Columbia Journal of European Law* 679; Alberto de Gregorio Merino, "Legal Developments in the Economic and Monetary Union during the Debt Crisis: The Mechanisms of Financial Assistance" (2012) 49 *Common Market Law Review* 1613; Steve Peers, "Towards a New Form of EU Law?: The Use of EU Institutions Outside the EU Legal Framework" (2013) 9 *European Constitutional Law Review* 37; Edoardo Chiti and Pedro Gustavo Teixeira, "The Constitutional Implications of the European Responses to the Financial and Public Debt Crisis" (2013) 50 *Common Market Law Review* 683; Mark Dawson and Floris de Witte, "Constitutional Balance in the EU after the Euro-Crisis" (2013) 76 *Modern Law Review* 817; Paul Craig, "*Pringle* and Use of EU Institutions outside the EU Legal Framework: Foundations, Procedure and Substance" (2013) 9 *European Constitutional Law Review* 263; Jonathan Tomkin, "Contradiction, Circumvention and Conceptual Gymnastics: The Impact of the Adoption of the ESM Treaty on the State of European Democracy" (2013) 14 *German Law Journal* 169; Claire Kilpatrick, "On the Rule of Law and Economic Emergency: The Degradation of Basic Legal Values in Europe's Bailouts" (2015) 35 *Oxford Journal of Legal Studies* 1; René Repasi, "Court of Justice Judicial Protection against Austerity Measures in the Euro Area: *Ledra* and *Mallis*" (2017) 54 *Common Market Law Review* 1123; Anastasia Karatzia and Menelaos Markakis, "What Role for the Commission and the ECB in the European Stability Mechanism?" (2017) 6 *Cambridge International Law Journal* 232; Paul Dermine, "The End of Impunity? The Legal Duties of 'Borrowed' EU Institutions under the European Stability Mechanism Framework" (2017) 13 *European Constitutional Law Review* 369; Menelaos Markakis and Paul Dermine, "Bailouts, the Legal Status of Memoranda of Understanding, and the Scope of Application

[27–45] In July 2012, after Ireland had signed the ESM Treaty but before it had ratified it, Thomas Pringle TD brought an action in the High Court claiming that Ireland's ratification of the Treaty would require prior approval in a referendum. Secondly, it was claimed that the European Council Decision to amend Art 136 TFEU using the simplified revision procedure was contrary to EU law or, alternatively, that it was not open to Euro Area Member States to ratify the ESM Treaty prior to the entry into force of the European Council Decision providing the necessary TFEU legal base. On appeal, on 31 July 2012 the Supreme Court rejected the constitutional law claims and decided to refer the two questions of EU law to the Court of Justice.[70] The Supreme Court declined to grant an injunction restraining the State from ratifying the Treaty and Ireland proceeded to do so the following day.

[27–46] The *Pringle* case offered the Court of Justice its first opportunity to address the legal aspects of the Union's approach to the debt crisis.[71] Its exceptional nature was reflected in the Court's exceedingly rare decision to sit as a "Full Court", comprising the judges of all Member States. The reference required the Court to consider two principal questions. First, was the use of the simplified revision procedure a correct application of Art 48(6) TEU? In other words, did the insertion of Art 136(3) TFEU solely concern Part Three TFEU and did it refrain from increasing the competences of the Union? Secondly, was it compatible with the TEU and TFEU for a Euro Area Member State to ratify an international agreement such as the ESM Treaty, particularly given the prohibitions on monetary financing and bail-outs in Arts 123 and 125 TFEU?

[27–47] An assessment as to whether proper use had been made of the simplified revision procedure essentially revolved around whether allowing the Euro Area Member States to establish a stability mechanism, to be used if indispensable to safeguard the stability of the Euro Area as a whole, in which case financial assistance would be granted subject to strict conditionality, concerned the Union's exclusive competence with respect to monetary policy (found in Part One TFEU), or the Union's coordinating competence with respect to economic policy. According to the Court, the objective of the stability mechanism – to safeguard the stability of the Euro Area as a whole – was:

> clearly distinct from the objective of maintaining price stability, which is the primary objective of the Union's monetary policy. Even though the stability of the euro area may have repercussions on the stability of the currency used within that area, an economic policy measure cannot be treated as equivalent to a monetary policy measure for the sole reason that it may have indirect effects on the stability of the euro.
>
> ... The grant of financial assistance to a Member State ... clearly does not fall within monetary policy...
>
> ... In the light of the objectives to be attained by the stability mechanism ..., the instruments provided in order to achieve those objectives and the close link between that mechanism, the provisions of the [TFEU] relating to economic policy and the regulatory framework

of the EU Charter: *Florescu*" (2018) 55 *Common Market Law Review* 643; Paul Gallagher, "The Financial Crisis, the Banking Union and the Rule of Law" in Kieran Bradley, Noel Travers and Anthony Whelan (eds), *Of Courts and Constitutions: Liber Amicorum in Honour of Nial Fennelly* (Hart, 2014) 127.

70 *Pringle v Government of Ireland* [2013] 3 IR 1. See ch 2, paras [2–24] to [2–28].

71 Case C-370/12 *Pringle v Government of Ireland* EU:C:2012:756, 27 November 2012.

> for strengthened economic governance of the Union, it must be concluded that the establishment of the mechanism falls within the area of economic policy.[72]

[27–48] The Court was also satisfied that the amendment to Art 136 TFEU did not confer any new competence on the Union and did not create a legal basis for the Union to be able to undertake any action which was not possible before the entry into force of the amendment. In itself, the decision of the European Council provided only for the establishment of a stability mechanism by the Member States and was silent on any possible role for the Union's institutions. The fact that the ESM Treaty did in fact make use of the Union's institutions – giving specific roles to the Commission and the ECB – was not capable of affecting the validity of the European Council's decision.[73] Accordingly, the Court upheld the use of the simplified revision procedure to amend Art 136 TFEU. Later in the judgment the Court confirmed that, in areas which do not fall under the Union's exclusive competence, Member States are entitled to entrust tasks to the institutions outside of the Union framework, provided that they do not alter the essential character of their powers. It found that the duties conferred on the Commission and the ECB: (i) did not entail any power to make decisions of their own; (ii) solely committed the ESM; and (iii) supported the general interests and economic policies of the Union.[74]

[27–49] Secondly, the Court assessed whether any provision of the TEU or TFEU rendered it impermissible for the Euro Area Member States to become a party to the ESM Treaty. First, it was argued by Mr Pringle that the ESM Treaty encroached upon the Union's exclusive competence over monetary policy, since the granting of financial assistance on the scale envisaged by the ESM Treaty would increase the amount of euro currency in circulation, having a direct impact on inflation and price stability. It was claimed that as the ECB had the exclusive power to regulate money supply in the Euro Area, the Treaties did not permit a second entity to carry out such tasks in parallel to the ECB and outside of the EU legal framework. Mirroring its finding with regard to the European Council decision, the Court did not regard the activities of the ESM as falling within the Union's monetary policy. In the view of the Court:

> it is not the purpose of the ESM to maintain price stability, but rather to meet the financing requirements of ESM Members, namely Member States whose currency is the euro, who are experiencing or are threatened by severe financing problems, if indispensable to safeguard the financial stability of the euro area as a whole and of its Member States. To that end, the ESM is not entitled either to set the key interest rates for the euro area or to issue euro currency, while the financial assistance which the ESM grants must be entirely funded – the provisions of Article 123(1) TFEU being respected – from paid-in capital or by the issue of financial instruments, as provided for in Article 3 of the ESM Treaty.
>
> … any effect of the activities of the ESM on price stability is not such as to call into question that finding. Even if the activities of the ESM might influence the rate of inflation, such an influence would constitute only the indirect consequence of the economic policy measures adopted.[75]

[27–50] Secondly, it was argued by Mr Pringle that the ESM Treaty encroached upon

---

[72] *ibid*, paras 56–60.
[73] *ibid*, paras 73–74.
[74] *ibid*, paras 155–169.
[75] *ibid*, paras 96–97.

EU rules and competences governing the coordination of economic policy amongst the Member States, including the ability of the Council to issue recommendations to a state with an excessive deficit. This too was rejected by the Court, which reasoned as follows:

> the Member States have the power to conclude between themselves an agreement for the establishment of a stability mechanism such as the ESM Treaty provided that the commitments undertaken by the Member States who are parties to such an agreement are consistent with European Union law.
>
> … the ESM is not concerned with the coordination of the economic policies of the Member States, but rather constitutes a financing mechanism. … the purpose of the ESM is to mobilise funding and to provide financial stability support to ESM Members who are experiencing, or are threatened by, severe financing problems.
>
> While it is true that … the financial assistance provided to a Member State that is an ESM Member is subject to strict conditionality, appropriate to the financial assistance instrument chosen, which can take the form of a macro-economic adjustment programme, the conditionality prescribed nonetheless does not constitute an instrument for the coordination of the economic policies of the Member States, but is intended to ensure that the activities of the ESM are compatible with, inter alia, Article 125 TFEU and the coordinating measures adopted by the Union.
>
> The … ESM Treaty expressly provides that the conditions attached to any stability support are to be "fully consistent with the measures of economic policy coordination provided for in the [TFEU]". Further, … the Commission is to check, before signing the MoU defining the conditionality attached to stability support, that the conditions imposed are fully consistent with the measures of economic policy coordination.
>
> Lastly, nor does the ESM Treaty affect the competence of the Council of the European Union to issue recommendations … to a Member State in which an excessive deficit exists. First, the ESM is not called upon to issue such recommendations. Secondly, … the ESM Treaty provide[s] that the conditions imposed on ESM Members who receive financial assistance must be consistent with any recommendation which the Council might issue …[76]

[27–51] Following these broad-natured assessments, the Court was called upon to consider the ESM Treaty's compatibility with Art 122 TFEU (Union assistance in the case of a natural disaster or exceptional circumstance), Art 123 TFEU (prohibition on monetary financing) and Art 125 TFEU (no bail-out clause).

[27–52] Regarding Art 122 TFEU, the Irish Supreme Court had asked whether that provision exhaustively defined the exceptional circumstances in which it is possible to grant financial assistance to a Member State, and whether the ability to do so was confined exclusively to the Union's institutions. In response, the Court of Justice gave Art 122 a narrow interpretation, observing that it was solely concerned with the granting of financial assistance by the Union and not that granted by a Member State. The exercise by the Union of the competence conferred on it by Art 122 was not affected by the establishment of the ESM, nor did anything in Art 122 indicate that the Union had exclusive competence to grant financial assistance to a Member State.

[27–53] Similarly, with regard to the ban on monetary financing in Art 123 TFEU, the Court construed the provision narrowly, finding that Art 123 "is addressed specifically

[76] *ibid*, paras 109–113.

to the ECB and the central banks of the Member States. The grant of financial assistance by one Member State or by a group of Member States to another Member State is therefore not covered by that prohibition."[77]

[27–54] Finally, the Court adopted the same narrow and teleological approach to the no bail-out clause found in Art 125 TFEU, which provides that neither the Union nor a Member State are to be liable for or assume the commitments of another Member State. It began by noting that this wording does not prohibit either the Union or a Member State from granting any form of financial assistance whatever to another Member State. The Court then buttressed this by observing, first, that if a fully comprehensive prohibition had been intended, Art 122 would have had to state that it derogated from the total prohibition in Art 125. Secondly, in prohibiting monetary financing, Art 123 employs stricter wording than Art 125, suggesting that the no bail-out clause is not intended to prohibit any financial assistance whatsoever.

[27–55] Having established that Art 125 leaves the door open to certain types of financial assistance, the Court sought to determine the overall objective pursued by the Article, which in turn would determine the circumstances in which financial assistance would be permitted. According to the Court:

> It is apparent from the preparatory work relating to the Treaty of Maastricht that the aim of Article 125 TFEU is to ensure that the Member States follow a sound budgetary policy. The prohibition laid down in Article 125 TFEU ensures that the Member States remain subject to the logic of the market when they enter into debt, since that ought to prompt them to maintain budgetary discipline. Compliance with such discipline contributes at Union level to the attainment of a higher objective, namely maintaining the financial stability of the monetary union.
>
> Given that that is the objective pursued by Article 125 TFEU, it must be held that that provision prohibits the Union and the Member States from granting financial assistance as a result of which the incentive of the recipient Member State to conduct a sound budgetary policy is diminished. ... the activation of financial assistance by means of a stability mechanism such as the ESM is not compatible with Article 125 TFEU unless it is indispensable for the safeguarding of the financial stability of the euro area as a whole and subject to strict conditions.
>
> However, Article 125 TFEU does not prohibit the granting of financial assistance by one or more Member States to a Member State which remains responsible for its commitments to its creditors provided that the conditions attached to such assistance are such as to prompt that Member State to implement a sound budgetary policy.
>
> As regards the ESM Treaty, it is clear, first, that the instruments for stability support of which the ESM may make use ... demonstrate that the ESM will not act as guarantor of the debts of the recipient Member State. The latter will remain responsible to its creditors for its financial commitments.
>
> ... Secondly, the ESM Treaty does not provide that stability support will be granted as soon as a Member State whose currency is the euro is experiencing difficulties in obtaining financing on the market. ... stability support may be granted to ESM Members which are experiencing or are threatened by severe financing problems only when such support is indispensable to safeguard the financial stability of the euro area as a whole and of its

[77] *ibid*, para 125.

> Member States and the grant of that support is subject to strict conditionality appropriate to the financial assistance instrument chosen.
>
> … the purpose of the strict conditionality to which all stability support provided by the ESM is subject is to ensure that the ESM and the recipient Member States comply with measures adopted by the Union in particular in the area of the coordination of Member States' economic policies, those measures being designed, inter alia, to ensure that the Member States pursue a sound budgetary policy.[78]

[27–56] The novel nature of the Court's reasoning has prompted much analysis.[79] Bruno de Witte and Thomas Beukers deliver a positive assessment overall, pointing out the several methods of interpretation employed in interpreting Art 125:

> A textual or literal interpretation leads to the conclusion that Article 125 TFEU is not intended to prohibit *any* form of financial assistance to another Member State. A contextual or systematic interpretation finds support for this reading in the wording of Article 122 TFEU (which is not formulated as an exception) and 123 TFEU (which applies stricter language). From a historical interpretation it follows that the prohibition of Article 125 TFEU was included in the Maastricht Treaty to ensure that Member States follow a sound budgetary policy. The teleological interpretation of Article 125 TFEU (sound budgetary policy) is complemented by an *ultima ratio* interpretation, namely that compliance with budgetary discipline contributes to the higher objective of maintaining the financial stability of the monetary union. The reference to the preparatory works of the Maastricht Treaty, and especially the *ultima ratio* interpretation are exceptional, but methodologically all this can be very well defended.[80]

[27–57] De Witte and Beukers do go on to highlight, however, that in crafting an elegant solution to concerns about the no bail-out clause, the Court of Justice developed two requirements of its own that have to be met in order for financial assistance to be compatible with Art 125. First, the assistance must be indispensable for safeguarding the financial stability of the Euro Area as a whole. Secondly, the assistance must be subject to strict conditionality aimed at ensuring sound budgetary policy on the part of the recipient. Expressing a degree of scepticism, Damian Chalmers notes that while

---

78 *ibid*, paras 135–143.

79 See Gunnar Beck, "The Court of Justice, Legal Reasoning, and the *Pringle* Case-Law as the Continuation of Politics by Other Means" (2014) 39 *European Law Review* 234; Paul Craig, "*Pringle* and the Nature of Legal Reasoning" (2014) 21 *Maastricht Journal of European and Comparative Law* 205; Etienne de Lhoneux and Christos A Vassilopoulos, *The European Stability Mechanism before the Court of Justice of the European Union: Comments on the Pringle Case* (Springer, 2014); Bruno de Witte and Thomas Beukers, "The Court of Justice Approves the Creation of the European Stability Mechanism: *Pringle*" (2013) 50 *Common Market Law Review* 805; Alicia Hinarejos, "The Court of Justice of the EU and the Legality of the European Stability Mechanism" (2013) 72 *Cambridge Law Journal* 237; Paul Craig, "*Pringle*: Legal Reasoning, Text, Purpose and Teleology" (2013) 20 *Maastricht Journal of European and Comparative Law* 3; Paul Craig, "*Pringle* and Use of EU Institutions outside the EU Legal Framework: Foundations, Procedure and Substance" (2013) 9 *European Constitutional Law Review* 263; Stanislas Adam and Francisco Javier Mena Parras, "The European Stability Mechanism through the Legal Meanderings of the Union's Constitutionalism: Comment on *Pringle*" (2013) 38 *European Law Review* 848; Chris Koedooder, "The *Pringle* Judgment: Economic and/or Monetary Union?" (2013) 37 *Fordham International Law Journal* 111; Gunnar Beck, "The Legal Reasoning of the Court of Justice and the Euro Crisis – The Flexibility of the Court's Cumulative Approach and the *Pringle* Case" (2013) 20 *Maastricht Journal of European and Comparative Law* 635.

80 Bruno de Witte and Thomas Beukers, "The Court of Justice Approves the Creation of the European Stability Mechanism: *Pringle*" (2013) 50 *Common Market Law Review* 805, 838.

the Court's use of a substantive argument in order to qualify what constitutes permitted assistance under Art 125 may be persuasive in policy terms, particularly in the midst of the debt crisis, nevertheless:

> the Court of Justice is not acting as a policy actor in which it decides when it is economically appropriate for states to support other states. This engagement with policy stands out in the judgment with the interpretive reasoning being very thin. The consequence, of course, is that EU law becomes *relativised*. Its meaning is given a flexibility and indeterminacy which allows it to be tailored to the circumstances.[81]

[27–58] For many, the judgment's pragmatic approach is unsurprising given the heightened circumstances in which it was delivered. As Alicia Hinarejos has remarked, the "EMU provisions in the Treaties were designed to prevent a crisis, but not to manage one; as such, they needed to be interpreted in a purposive and dynamic manner to ensure that the EU's legal framework does not become obsolete and that the Eurozone is capable of dealing effectively with this crisis of confidence."[82]

(iii) The European Semester and the Six Pack

[27–59] In parallel to the development of the ESM as a means of providing indispensable financial assistance, the Union sought to significantly strengthen the Stability and Growth Pact through a package of five regulations and a directive adopted in 2011 known as the Six Pack. Alongside amendments to the two original 1997 regulations,[83] these comprised three new regulations dealing with the Prevention and Correction of Macro-Economic Imbalances,[84] Enforcement Measures to Correct Excessive Macro-Economic Imbalances in the Euro Area[85] and Effective Enforcement of Budgetary Surveillance in the Euro Area,[86] and a directive on Requirements for Budgetary Frameworks of the Member States.[87] The Six Pack was further supplemented by two additional regulations adopted in 2013, known as the Two Pack, which provide for greater surveillance of national budgets of states in receipt of financial assistance and for all other Euro Area states respectively.[88]

---

81 Damian Chalmers, Gareth Davies and Giorgio Monti, *European Union Law* (3rd ed, Cambridge University Press, 2014) 723. Emphasis added.

82 Alicia Hinarejos, "Economic and Monetary Union" in Catherine Barnard and Steve Peers (eds), *European Union Law* (2nd ed, Oxford University Press, 2017) 513, 586.

83 Regulation 1175/2011 amending Regulation 1466/97 on the Strengthening of the Surveillance of Budgetary Positions and the Surveillance and Coordination of Economic Policies [2011] OJ L306/12; Regulation 1177/2011 amending Regulation 1467/97 on Speeding Up and Clarifying the Implementation of the Excessive Deficit Procedure [2011] OJ L306/33.

84 Regulation 1176/2011 of the European Parliament and of the Council of 16 November 2011 on the prevention and correction of macroeconomic imbalances [2011] OJ L306/25.

85 Regulation 1174/2011 of the European Parliament and of the Council of 16 November 2011 on enforcement measures to correct excessive macroeconomic imbalances in the euro area [2011] OJ L306/8.

86 Regulation 1173/2011 of the European Parliament and of the Council of 16 November 2011 on the effective enforcement of budgetary surveillance in the euro area [2011] OJ L306/1.

87 Directive 2011/85/EU of 8 November 2011 on requirements for budgetary frameworks of the Member States [2011] OJ L306/41. See European Union (Requirements for Budgetary Frameworks of Member States) Regulations 2013 (SI No 508 of 2013).

88 Regulation 472/2013 on the Strengthening of Economic and Budgetary Surveillance of Member States in the Euro Area experiencing or threatened with serious difficulties with respect to their Financial Stability [2013] OJ L140/1; Regulation 473/2013 on Common Provisions for Monitoring

[27–60] A key element of the reforms introduced by the Six Pack was the formal establishment of what is known as the European Semester, which is an annual cycle of economic coordination and surveillance. The European Semester for Economic Policy Cooperation had in fact been announced by the Commission in 2010, became operational in 2011 and later that year was incorporated in legal form within one of the Six Pack regulations that amended the original Stability and Growth Pact.[89] The European Semester has two main phases: the European Phase, which runs from November to February, and the National Phase, which runs from February to June.

[27–61] The Six Pack introduced certain common budgetary rules and timeframes, requiring Member States to produce their Stability Programme, fiscal plan and medium-term budgetary frameworks (of at least three years' duration) by the end of April, with a draft budget to be submitted to the Commission and the Euro Group no later than 15 October. By the end of November, the Commission presents an assessment of the draft budget to the Euro Group, which discusses it. The budget is then required to be adopted by the Member State before the end of the year. In the case of serious non-compliance, the Commission may request the submission of a revised budget. Each Member State is to develop its own fiscal rules which will allow for multi-annual compliance with its budgetary obligations, to be monitored by an independent fiscal council. Under the Fiscal Responsibility Act 2012, the Irish Fiscal Advisory Council is tasked with assessing official forecasts and, in relation to each budget and Stability Programme, whether the fiscal stance is conducive to prudent economic and budgetary management, including by reference to the provisions of the Stability and Growth Pact.[90]

[27–62] In November of each year the Commission will also publish what is termed the *Annual Growth Survey*,[91] setting out high-level economic guidelines and priorities for the following year, together with *Euro Area Recommendations*, addressing issues critical to the functioning of the Euro Area and suggesting concrete measures national governments can implement. November also sees the launch of the *Macroeconomic Imbalance Procedure* (MIP), through the Commission's publication of the *Alert Report Mechanism* (ARM) and the *MIP Scoreboard*.[92] In light of lessons learned from the financial crisis of 2008, the Macroeconomic Imbalance Procedure is intended to broaden out budgetary surveillance in order to detect emerging trends that are likely to lead to macroeconomic imbalances. The MIP Scoreboard assesses a range of indicators including the long-term, youth and overall unemployment rates, labour costs, house price index, private sector debt, international investment, current account balance and global export market share. The MIP Scoreboard is used to screen out those Member States that may be affected by economic imbalance and for which the Commission should undertake further In-Depth Reviews.

---

and Assessing draft budgetary plans and Ensuring the Correction of Excessive Deficit of the Member States in the Euro Area [2013] OJ L140/11.

[89] Regulation 1175/2011 amending Regulation 1466/97 on the Strengthening of the Surveillance of Budgetary Positions and the Surveillance and Coordination of Economic Policies [2011] OJ L306/12. See Kenneth Armstrong, "The New Governance of EU Fiscal Discipline" (2013) 38 *European Law Review* 601.

[90] s 8(4) of the Fiscal Responsibility Act 2012, as amended by the Ministers and Secretaries (Amendment) Act 2013.

[91] See, for example, *Annual Growth Survey 2019*, Commission Communication COM(2018) 770 final, 21 November 2018.

[92] See, for example, *Alert Mechanism Report 2019*, Report from the Commission COM(2018) 758 final, 21 November 2018.

[27–63] In February, *Country Reports* are published as staff working documents of the Commission, detailing the overall economic outlook with particular attention given to imbalances, risks and adjustments. The Country Report reviews progress made on the previous year's Country Specific Recommendations and MIP Scoreboard.[93] If an In-Depth Review had been deemed necessary, it will be set out in the Country Report. For example, Ireland's Country Report for 2019 included an In-Depth Review on foot of the findings of the Alert Mechanism Report published in November 2018.[94]

[27–64] If an In-Depth Review finds that imbalances do exist that require action, these can be the subject of Country Specific Recommendations or specific monitoring of the country concerned. In the more extreme scenario of where an imbalance is found to be excessive, the Council may adopt a recommendation from the Commission establishing an excessive imbalance and prescribing corrective action within a set timeframe.[95] This is known as the *Excessive Imbalance Procedure*. The Commission will monitor the implementation of the corrective action. If a Member State is found to be at fault, the Council may adopt a decision to that effect which, ultimately, may lead to the Member State being sanctioned.[96]

[27–65] The European Council in March sees the consideration of the Annual Growth Survey, in light of which the European Council will adopt economic priorities for the coming year. This is followed in April by the submission by the Member States of their *National Reform Programmes* and their *Stability Programmes* (or *Convergence Programmes* for non-Euro Area Member States). The National Reform Programme provides an overview of planned structural reforms, including action being taken on foot of the previous year's Country Specific Recommendations. Ireland's National Reform Programme is prepared by the Department of the Taoiseach and a draft version is presented to the Joint Oireachtas Committee on EU Affairs before its submission. The Stability Programme is concerned with demonstrating a Member State's compliance with fiscal rules and sets out the state's Medium Term Budgetary Objective for the following three years. Ireland's Stability Programme is prepared by the Department of Finance and a draft version is presented to the Oireachtas Joint Committee on Finance before its submission.

[27–66] On the basis of the Country Reports and any In-Depth Reviews, in May the Commission will propose Country Specific Recommendations, which are then discussed by the Council and eventually endorsed by the European Council in June.

---

93 See Tim Costello, "Six Years On: Assessment the Impact of Country Specific Recommendations" (Institute of International and European Affairs, 2017).

94 Commission Staff Working Document, *Country Report Ireland 2019 Including an In-Depth Review on the Prevention and Correction of Macroeconomic Imbalances*, SWD(2019) 1006 final, 27 February 2019.

95 Regulation 1176/2011, Art 7(2).

96 *ibid*, Art 10(4).

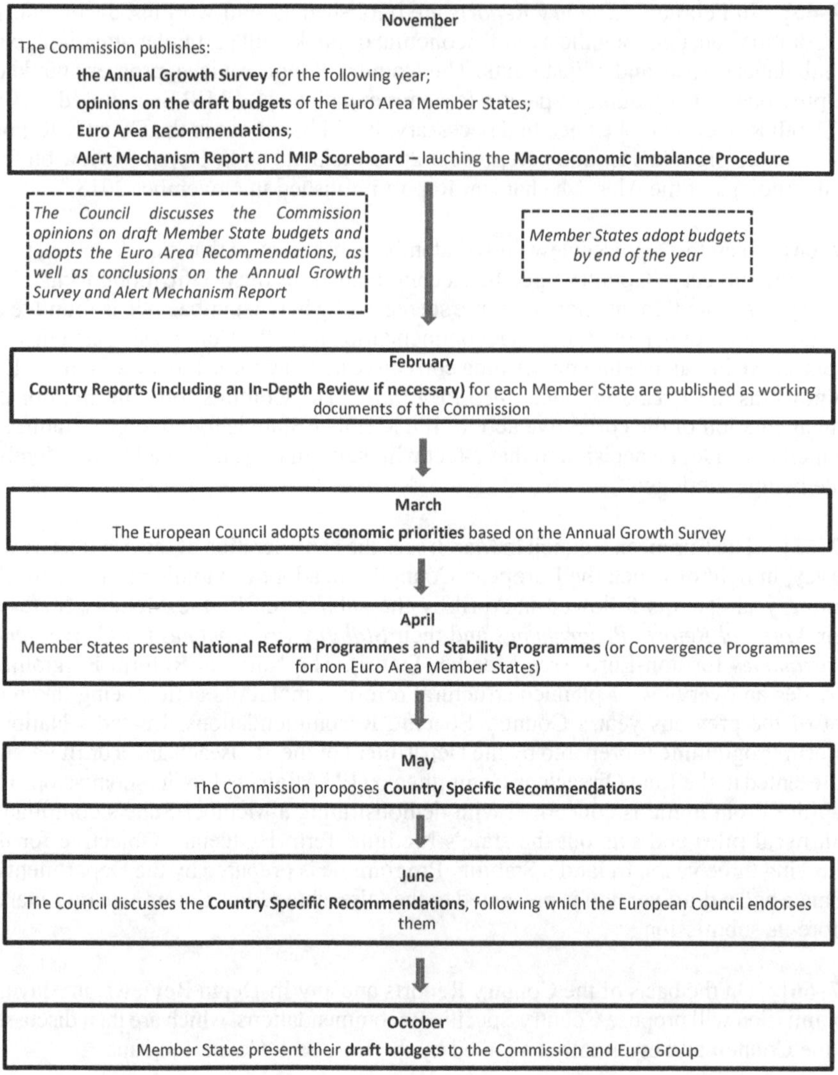

(iv) Treaty on Stability, Coordination and Governance in the EMU

[27–67] It will be recalled that in the Deauville Declaration of 2010, the leaders of France and Germany called for the EU Treaties to be amended so as to provide a permanent framework to ensure the financial stability of the Euro Area – which came to pass in the separate ESM Treaty – and to allow for the suspension of a Member State's voting rights in the case of a serious violation of basic principles of the EMU. This second proposal was developed in suggestions to incorporate elements of the Stability and Growth Pact into the Treaties. This became known as the "Fiscal Compact". However, when the UK made clear that it was unwilling to become a party to this agreement, it was decided to proceed with the Compact as an intergovernmental agreement outside of the EU framework, albeit placing some reliance on the EU institutions.

[27–68] Possibly with a view to avoiding the need for a referendum, Ireland had tended to favour using existing mechanisms to ensure compliance with fiscal rules, rather than amending the primary EU Treaties. For others, however, it was desirable to strengthen the Stability and Growth Pact by requiring the Member States to give the fiscal rules constitutional status within their own legal systems. The desire to avoid referendums led to this requirement taking an optional form, whereby parties to the agreement are obliged to introduce an "automatic correction mechanism" that takes the form of "provisions of binding force and permanent character, *preferably constitutional*, or otherwise guaranteed to be fully respected and adhered to throughout the budgetary process".[97]

[27–69] The agreement that finally emerged is titled the Treaty on Stability, Coordination and Governance in the Economic and Monetary Union.[98] Confusingly, Title III of the Treaty is termed the "Fiscal Compact", and the Treaty is often referred to by this name or by "Stability Treaty" or "Fiscal Stability Treaty". Article 2 addresses the Treaty's relationship with the EU framework by providing that it shall be applied and interpreted in conformity with the EU Treaties and EU law, including procedural law whenever the adoption of secondary legislation is required. Moreover, the Treaty is to apply insofar as it is compatible with the EU Treaties and EU law, and shall not encroach upon the competence of the Union to act in the area of the economic union.[99] The Treaty includes a commitment that, within five years of its entry into force on 1 January 2013, the necessary steps would be taken with the aim of incorporating the substance of the Treaty into the EU legal framework.[100] This has yet to be achieved. The Treaty is also linked to the ESM Treaty to the extent that one of its recitals establishes that, as of 1 March 2013, the granting of financial assistance under new ESM programmes will be conditional on the ratification of the Treaty on Stability, Coordination and Governance.

[27–70] As part of the Fiscal Compact in Title III of the Treaty, the parties agree to maintain an annual budget that is either balanced or in surplus. This is deemed to be respected if the government's "annual structural balance" (ie the cyclically adjusted budget) is at its country-specific medium-term objective, as defined by the Stability and Growth Pact.[101] The parties commit to ensuring "rapid convergence towards their respective medium-term objective", the timeframe for which is proposed by the Commission. This may only be deviated from in the event of "exceptional circumstances" which are defined as periods of severe economic downturn or an unusual event outside the control of a state which has a major impact on the government's financial position.[102] Crucially, in the event of significant observed deviations from the medium-term objective or the adjustment path towards it, a correction mechanism is to be triggered automatically which shall require the taking of measures to address the deviations over a defined period of time.

---

97 Art 3(2), Treaty on Stability, Coordination and Governance in the EMU.

98 Irish Treaty Series No 21 of 2013. See Paul Craig, "The Stability, Coordination and Governance Treaty: Principle, Politics and Pragmatism" (2012) 37 *European Law Review* 235; Federico Fabbrini, "The Fiscal Compact, the 'Golden Rule' and the Paradox of European Federalism" (2013) 36 *Boston College International and Comparative Law Review* 1; Steve Peers, "The Stability Treaty: Permanent Austerity or Gesture Politics?" (2012) 8 *European Constitutional Law Review* 404.

99 Art 2, Treaty on Stability, Coordination and Governance in the EMU.

100 Art 16, Treaty on Stability, Coordination and Governance in the EMU.

101 Art 3, Treaty on Stability, Coordination and Governance in the EMU.

102 Art 3(3)(b), Treaty on Stability, Coordination and Governance in the EMU.

[27–71] It is these rules that the parties are obliged to incorporate into national law "through provisions of binding force and permanent character, preferably constitutional, or otherwise guaranteed to be fully respected and adhered to throughout the national budgetary processes". While Ireland was the only country to hold a referendum on the Treaty's ratification, it did not choose to enshrine the fiscal rules within the Constitution. Rather, following a 60 per cent vote in favour, the Constitution was amended so that Art 29.4.10° now provides that, in addition to permitting the State to ratify the Treaty on Stability, Coordination and Governance in the EMU, no provision of the Constitution invalidates laws enacted, acts done or measures adopted by the State that are necessitated by its obligations under the Treaty, or prevents laws enacted, acts done or measures adopted by bodies competent under the Treaty from having the force of law in the State.[103]

[27–72] The Fiscal Responsibility Act 2012, as amended by the Ministers and Secretaries (Amendment) Act 2013, enshrines in law a budgetary rule, a deficit rule, a medium-term budgetary objective and a correction mechanism. Section 2 of the Act imposes an express duty on the Government to ensure that the budgetary rule and deficit rule which derive from the Treaty are complied with. In addition, the 2013 Act amended the Ministers and Secretaries (Amendment) Act 2011 so as to provide, *inter alia*, that each financial year the Government shall make a decision approving an upper limit on the amount of Government expenditure for each of the following three years, and that this ceiling shall not be exceeded.[104]

[27–73] If either the Commission or another contracting party considers that a state has failed to comply with its obligation to incorporate the Treaty obligations in national law, it may bring the matter before the Court of Justice. If a second set of proceedings are brought on foot of a failure to implement the Court's judgment, and the Court upholds such a finding, it may impose a lump sum or a penalty payment appropriate in the circumstances that shall not exceed 0.1 per cent of the state's GDP.[105]

[27–74] As well as the budgetary rules set out in Art 3 of the Treaty, where a contracting party has an excessive deficit within the meaning of Protocol No 12, in that its debt is greater than 60 per cent of GDP, it is obliged under the Treaty to reduce the debt to GDP ratio by one-twentieth each year.[106] Countries subject to the Excessive Deficit Procedure are required to put in place a budgetary and economic partnership programme including a detailed description of the structural reforms which must be implemented to ensure an effective and durable correction of its excessive deficit.[107] While avoiding an amendment of the TFEU to change the voting procedure under Art 126, the Treaty nevertheless commits the contracting parties to applying a form of "reverse qualified majority" whenever the Commission recommends a finding of an excessive deficit. The parties "commit to support" the recommendation submitted by the Commission, unless it is apparent that it is opposed by a qualified majority of them.[108]

---

[103] See Gavin Barrett, "The Evolving Door to Europe: Reflections on an Eventful Forty Years for Article 29.4 of the Irish Constitution" (2012) 48 *Irish Jurist* 132, 167–171.

[104] s 17(2) of the Ministers and Secretaries (Amendment) Act 2011, as inserted by s 1 of the Ministers and Secretaries (Amendment) Act 2013.

[105] Art 8, Treaty on Stability, Coordination and Governance in the EMU.

[106] Art 4, Treaty on Stability, Coordination and Governance in the EMU.

[107] Art 5, Treaty on Stability, Coordination and Governance in the EMU.

[108] Art 7, Treaty on Stability, Coordination and Governance in the EMU.

[27–75] Finally, the Treaty on Stability, Coordination and Governance supplements the Euro Group – which was given formal recognition in the Lisbon Treaty – by institutionalising the Euro Summit meetings of heads of state or government of Euro Area contracting parties and the President of the Commission, with the President of the ECB as invited. The Euro Group is charged with preparing and following-up on Euro Summit meetings, and the President of the Euro Group may be invited to attend for that purpose.[109]

E. Banking Union

[27–76] In the midst of the financial crisis, it was readily apparent that responsibility for much of the difficulty lay at the door of commercial banks. As has been described, the first phase was triggered by the US sub-prime mortgage crisis, which then "extended into Europe because some EU banks had purchased derivatives linked to US mortgages that became worthless. Virtually overnight, the interbank market dried up, switching the focus to banks like Northern Rock in the UK and to the Irish banks, which had borrowed to excess and/or had funding models that were no longer sustainable."[110] While only a very small portion was ever activated, guarantees of over €800 billion were required to keep the Euro Area financial sector afloat.[111] By the time of its June 2009 summit, the European Council agreed a detailed set of conclusions calling for rapid reforms aimed at the strengthened supervision and regulation of financial institutions:

> The financial crisis has clearly demonstrated the need to improve the regulation and supervision of financial institutions, both in Europe and globally. Addressing the failures exposed by the present crisis will contribute to preventing future ones. It will also help restore confidence in the financial system, in particular by enhancing the protection of depositors and consumers, and will thus facilitate the recovery of the European economy.
>
> Significant progress has already been achieved on improving the EU's regulatory framework, in particular with the agreement reached on the Capital Requirements Directive, the Credit Rating Agencies Regulation and the Solvency II Directive. The European Council calls for further progress to be made in the regulation of financial markets, notably on the regulation of alternative investment funds, the role and responsibilities of depositaries and on the transparency and stability of derivatives markets.
>
> … The European Council supports the creation of a European Systemic Risk Board which will monitor and assess potential threats to financial stability and, where necessary, issue risk warnings and recommendations for action and monitor their implementation. The members of the General Council of the ECB will elect the chair of the European Systemic Risk Board.
>
> The European Council also recommends that a European System of Financial Supervisors, comprising three new European Supervisory Authorities, be established aimed at upgrading the quality and consistency of national supervision, strengthening oversight of cross-border groups through the setting up of supervisory colleges and establishing a European single rule book applicable to all financial institutions in the Single Market. Recognising the potential or contingent liabilities that may be involved for Member States, the European Council stresses that decisions taken by the European Supervisory Authorities should

[109] Art 12, Treaty on Stability, Coordination and Governance in the EMU.

[110] Pat McArdle, *Banking Union: Progress and Prospects* (Institute of International and European Affairs, 2015) 20–21.

[111] *ibid*, 21.

> not impinge in any way on the fiscal responsibilities of Member States. … the European Council agrees that the European System of Financial Supervisors should have binding and proportionate decision-making powers in respect of whether supervisors are meeting their requirements under a single rule book and relevant Community law and in the case of disagreement between the home and host state supervisors, including within colleges of supervisors.[112]

[27–77] Before the end of the following year the European System of Financial Supervision was established through the creation of three European Supervisory Authorities: the European Banking Authority,[113] the European Insurance and Occupational Pensions Authority,[114] and the European Securities and Markets Authority.[115] At the same time, the European Systemic Risk Board was set up with the task of providing macro-prudential oversight of the EU financial system in order to prevent and mitigate systemic risk.[116] The Board monitors and assesses systemic risks and issues warnings and recommendations, covering a remit that includes banks, insurers, asset managers, financial market infrastructures (such as payment systems and securities settlement facilities) and other financial institutions and markets.

[27–78] Having established the European System of Financial Supervisors and the foundations of a Single Rulebook, by 2012 thinking had progressed further and coalesced around the idea of creating a Banking Union. The aim of a Banking Union would be to "place the banking sector on a more sound footing and restore confidence in the Euro as part of a longer term vision for economic and fiscal integration. Shifting the supervision of banks to the European level is a key part of this process, which must subsequently be combined with other steps such as a common system for deposit protection, and integrated bank crisis management."[117] These three elements form the key components of the Banking Union: (i) effective supervision of prudential rules by the Single Supervisory Mechanism; (ii) a fund contributed to by banks that would protect taxpayers from bearing the cost of overseeing the winding-down of non-viable financial institutions, provided by the Single Resolution Mechanism; and (iii) a yet-to-be-established European Deposit Insurance Scheme that would supplement at the EU level national deposit guarantee schemes.

---

112 Presidency Conclusions, European Council, 18–19 June 2009, 11225/2/09, paras 17–20.

113 Regulation 1093/2010 establishing a European Supervisory Authority (European Banking Authority) [2010] OJ L331/12.

114 Regulation 1094/2010 establishing a European Supervisory Authority (European Insurance and Occupational Pensions Authority) [2010] OJ L331/48.

115 Regulation 1095/2010 establishing a European Supervisory Authority (European Securities and Markets Authority) [2010] OJ L331/84.

116 Regulation 1092/2010 on European Union Macro-Prudential Oversight of the Financial System and establishing a European Systemic Risk Board [2010] OJ L331/1.

117 Commission Communication, *A Roadmap towards a Banking Union*, COM/2012/0510 final, 12 September 2012, 3. See also *Towards a Genuine Economic Union*, Report by the President of the European Council, EUCO 120/12, 26 June 2012; Gavin Barrett, "The European Banking Union and the Economic Monetary Union – A re-telling of *Cinderella* with an uncertain happy ever after?" in Gianni Lo Schiavo (ed), *The European Banking Union and the Role of Law* (Edward Elgar, 2019) 10.

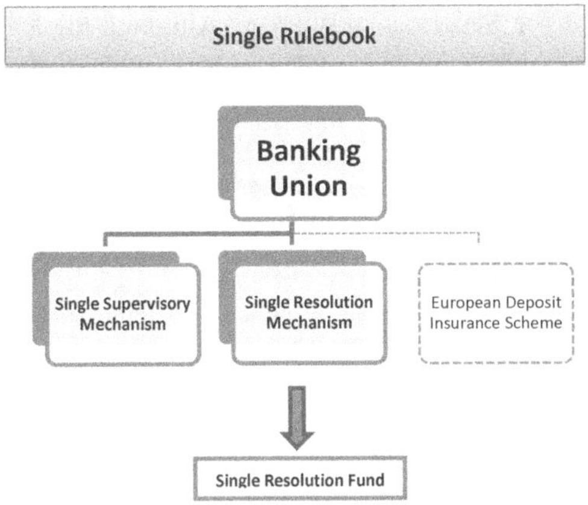

(i) Single Supervisory Mechanism

[27–79] The Single Supervisory Mechanism (SSM) was established by regulation in 2013 by conferring additional powers on the ECB.[118] Institutionally, the SSM takes the form of a Supervisory Board that is delegated certain functions by the Governing Council of the ECB. In order to maintain the independence of the SSM and the ECB a "non-objection" procedure is operated whereby decisions of the Supervisory Board are deemed adopted unless the Governing Council objects within 10 days. In the case of a fundamental disagreement, mediation must be convened to resolve the dispute.

[27–80] The SSM is responsible for the prudential supervision of all banks in the Euro Area or other Member States that choose to participate in the SSM. For the vast majority of almost 5,000 banks, direct supervision continues to be carried out by the national competent authorities, overseen by the SSM which can choose to exercise direct control if this is deemed necessary. Otherwise, it is only banks that meet the criteria of being "significant institutions" – of which there are around 120 – that are under the direct supervision of the SSM. These criteria include: banks with assets of over €30 billion; the three most significant banks in each participating state; banks deemed by a national competent authority to be of significant importance to the domestic economy; banks deemed by the ECB to have systematically significant cross-border activities, and banks that have previously received financial assistance from the ESM or EFSF.

[27–81] A complication in reaching agreement on the SSM was the dissatisfaction of the European Parliament with the degree of democratic accountability that would pertain in relation to it. Eventually, a far-reaching inter-institutional agreement was adopted

[118] Regulation 1024/2013 conferring specific tasks on the European Central Bank concerning policies relating to the prudential supervision of credit institutions [2013] OJ L287/63; Regulation (EU) No 1022/2013 amending Regulation (EU) No 1093/2010 establishing a European Supervisory Authority (European Banking Authority) as regards the conferral of specific tasks on the European Central Bank pursuant to Council Regulation (EU) No 1024/2013 [2013] OJ L287/5. See also the European Union (Single Supervisory Mechanism) Regulations 2014 (SI No 495/2014). See Report from the Commission on the Single Supervisory Mechanism, COM(2017) 591 final, 11 October 2017.

by the Parliament and the ECB whereby the ECB must answer questions and report regularly to the Parliament on its supervisory activities, and provide a comprehensive record of meetings of the Supervisory Board.[119] Although the SSM is still a young institution, Pat McArdle has reached the positive assessment that:

> Though the idiosyncratic governance design was an exercise in creativity under legal constraint, and the incomplete denationalisation of its governance and operational structure is less than ideal, these shortcomings should not be overstated: the successful first year of the SSM's existence has shown that a complex organisational structure does not necessarily imply that the mechanism is fatally flawed. On the contrary, the SSM and the common supervisory culture it will impose on the European banking sector, which will over time become stricter than those applied by national supervisors, will eventually prove an effective instrument and should be inherently superior to the fragmented model of the past.[120]

(ii) Single Resolution Mechanism and Fund

[27–82] The second element of the Banking Union is the Single Resolution Mechanism (SRM), which was established by regulation in 2014.[121] A "resolution" occurs when a competent authority determines that a failing bank cannot go through normal insolvency proceedings without harming public interest and causing financial instability. Resolution tools are used to manage the bank's failure in an orderly manner through a restructuring that ensures the continuity of its critical functions, preservation of financial stability and the restoration to viability of all or part of its business. Any remaining part of the bank that cannot be made viable again goes through normal insolvency proceedings. A harmonised means of resolving failing banks was regarded as a necessary accompaniment to a Single Supervisory Mechanism and would further contribute to breaking the link between banks and states that had led to the sovereign debt crisis, as well as assisting in the deepening of the internal market in financial services.

[27–83] The SRM Regulation built upon the Bank Recovery and Resolution Directive that had been adopted a few months earlier and introduced harmonised technical standards for dealing with failing banks.[122] Under the Directive, banks are required to prepare recovery plans to overcome financial distress, while Member States must establish a national resolution fund to which all financial institutions must contribute in accordance with their size and risk profile. A "bail-in" mechanism is provided for

---

[119] Interinstitutional Agreement between the European Parliament and the European Central Bank on the Practical Modalities of the Exercise of Democratic Accountability and Oversight over the Exercise of the tasks conferred on the ECB within the framework of the Single Supervisory Mechanism (2013/694/EU) [2013] OJ L320/1.

[120] Pat McArdle, *Banking Union: Progress and Prospects* (Institute of International and European Affairs, 2015) 64–65.

[121] Regulation (EU) No 806/2014 establishing uniform rules and a uniform procedure for the resolution of credit institutions and certain investment firms in the framework of a Single Resolution Mechanism and a Single Resolution Fund and amending Regulation (EU) No 1093/2010 [2014] OJ L225/1. See also the European Union (Single Resolution Mechanism) Regulations 2015 (SI No 568/2015).

[122] Directive 2014/59/EU of the European Parliament and of the Council of 15 May 2014 establishing a framework for the recovery and resolution of credit institutions and investment firms [2014] OJ L173/190. See also the European Union (Bank Recovery and Resolution) Regulations 2015 (SI No 289 of 2015), as amended by SI No 516 of 2015, SI No 522 of 2015, SI No 568 of 2015 and SI No 202 of 2016.

whereby a bank's shareholders and creditors must pay their share of the costs. If this is insufficient, the national resolution fund can provide the resources needed to continue operating while the bank is restructured.

[27–84] The Single Resolution Mechanism is made up of the Single Resolution Board – which is an EU agency – and the national resolution authorities of Euro Area members and other states participating in the SRM. Its purpose is to act as a centralised decision-making body that can coordinate and assist the national resolution authorities. Once the Single Resolution Board is informed that a bank is failing or likely to fail, it aims to adopt a resolution scheme within 32 hours if this is deemed to be in the public interest (otherwise the bank will be wound-up). The resolution scheme places the bank under resolution, identifies the appropriate resolution tools and determines whether the Single Resolution Fund can be used to assist, and if so the amount to be provided. The resolution scheme must be endorsed by the Commission.

[27–85] By the end of 2023, the Single Resolution Fund, established by the SRM Regulation, is to comprise 1 per cent of the amount of covered deposits of all credit institutions within the Banking Union. The idea is that the Single Resolution Fund will replace the national funds established under the Banking Recovery and Resolution Directive. The merging of funds in this way is known as mutualisation. Mutualisation is a particularly sensitive aspect of the Fund and raised constitutional concerns in Germany. As a result, an intergovernmental agreement was concluded dealing with the mutualisation of contributions and certain aspects of how the Fund can be used.[123] During a transition period that runs from 2016 to 2023, national contributions will, at first, be compartmentalised within the Fund, and thereafter progressively mutualised so that the compartments will cease to exist. Although outside the EU law framework, the Agreement does use the Court of Justice in the event of a dispute and requires the Single Resolution Board to make regular reports to the European Parliament and to the Council on its implementation and on the Fund's impact on financial stability and the Internal Market. In addition, the contracting parties have agreed that, no more than 10 years after its entry into force (ie by 1 January 2026), necessary steps shall be taken with the aim of incorporating the substance of the Agreement into the Union's legal framework.[124]

[27–86] The purpose of the Single Resolution Fund is to make loans to a bank under resolution, or to buy its assets, as part of the resolution tools being employed. It is not the purpose of the Fund to recapitalise the bank, or to absorb its losses. In order to more fully break the link between sovereign debt and the banking sector, it is considered that to prepare for the possibility of a future financial crisis it is necessary to put in place a further "backstop" that would make additional funding available should the Single Resolution Fund prove inadequate. This, together with the establishment of a European Deposit Insurance Scheme, forms part of an ongoing debate on the Future of Europe, and on the completion of EMU more particularly. Although a recast directive on Deposit Guarantee Schemes was introduced in 2014, harmonising protection for deposits of up to €100,000, the European Deposit Insurance Scheme was envisaged as the third pillar of the Banking Union but has yet to be established.[125] Compared with national

[123] Agreement on the Transfer and Mutualisation of Contributions to the Single Resolution Fund, Irish Treaty Series No 1 of 2016.

[124] *ibid*, Art 16(2).

[125] Directive 2014/49/EU of the European Parliament and of the Council of 16 April 2014 on deposit

schemes, a European Deposit Insurance Scheme is seen as being more resilient to any future large-scale crises and likely to be more fiscally neutral over time, since risks would be spread more widely and private contributions would be raised over a much larger pool of financial institutions.[126]

F. Completing the EMU

[27–87] In March 2017, the leaders of the Member States gathered in Rome to celebrate the 60th anniversary of the Treaty of Rome. Notwithstanding the decision of the UK to leave the European Union – the letter formally triggering the withdrawal process would be delivered just four days later – the focus was very much on the Union's future and the vision that should guide the way towards 2025. Naturally, having spent much of the last decade responding to the financial crisis, a key area of debate revolved around the further deepening of the Economic and Monetary Union. Already, in 2015, the Commission President, in cooperation with the Presidents of the Euro Summit (ie the Presidents of the European Council, the Euro Group, the ECB and the European Parliament), had published the Five Presidents' Report on completing the EMU. At the heart of the debate on the future of the EMU lies a difference of views as regards whether the primary deficiency lies in a lack of solidarity or mutualised risk amongst the Member States, or whether what is needed most is in fact greater responsibility and discipline within each Member State. As the Five Presidents' Report observes:

> The euro is more than just a currency. It is a political and economic project. All members of our Monetary Union have given up their previous national currencies once and for all and permanently share monetary sovereignty with the euro area countries. In return, countries gain the benefits of using a credible and stable currency within a large, competitive and powerful single market. This common destiny requires *solidarity* in times of crisis and *respect for commonly agreed rules* for all members.[127]

[27–88] Among the recommendations made in the Report were:

- the establishment of a European Deposit Insurance Scheme;
- the creation of a backstop to the Single Resolution Fund;
- strengthening the Single Rulebook governing financial institutions, as well as the macro-prudential institutions, building on the roles of the ECB and the European Systemic Risk Board;
- launching a Capital Markets Union[128] where investors can invest without hindrance across borders and businesses can raise funds from a diverse range of sources, irrespective of their location;
- the further stabilisation of the Fiscal Union through the development, within the

guarantee schemes [2014] OJ L173/149. See the Financial Services (Deposit Guarantee) Act 2009, as amended by the Finance (Miscellaneous Provisions Act) 2015, and the European Union (Deposit Guarantee Schemes) Regs 2015 (SI No 516 of 2015).

126 See Proposal for a Regulation of the European Parliament and of the Council amending Regulation (EU) 806/2014 in order to establish a European Deposit Insurance Scheme, COM/2015/0586 final, 2015/0270(COD), 24 November 2015. See also Daniel Gros and Dirk Schoenmaker, "European Deposit Insurance and Resolution in the Banking Union" (2014) 52 *Journal of Common Market Studies* 529.

127 European Commission, *Completing Europe's Economic and Monetary Union* (The Five Presidents' Report), 22 June 2015, 4.

128 See Commission Communication, *Capital Markets Union – Accelerating Reform*, COM/2016/0601 final, 14 September 2016.

Union framework, of a common macro-economic stabilisation function for the Euro Area that would not be a crisis management instrument but rather would improve the overall resilience of the EMU and Euro Area states;

- a strengthening of the European Semester, including the Macro-economic Imbalance Procedure and the Country Specific Recommendations;
- integrating the various intergovernmental agreements into the EU legal framework;
- an increased role for the European Parliament, as well as national parliaments in order to improve democratic accountability and legitimacy within the EMU;
- a more unified means of providing the EMU with external representation;
- further consideration to be given to the idea of a Euro Area Treasury.

[27–89] In 2017, the Commission made further contributions to this debate by publishing a Reflection Paper on deepening EMU, followed by a Roadmap setting out further steps towards completing EMU.[129] Among the proposals set out in the Roadmap were the transforming of the European Stability Mechanism into a European Monetary Fund within the EU legal framework.[130] The European Monetary Fund would continue to provide financial support to Member States in need and to raise funds by issuing capital market instruments and engage in money-market transactions. In addition, however, it would provide a common backstop to the Single Resolution Fund. Secondly, the Roadmap recommended that the Treaty on Stability, Coordination and Governance in the EMU be incorporated into the EU legal framework by way of a directive.[131] Thirdly, it was suggested that a position of European Minister of Economy and Finance be created as a means of "strengthening the coherence, efficiency, transparency and democratic accountability of EU economic governance", as well as providing for a more unified external representation of the Euro Area.[132] As well as calling for completion of the Banking Union through the establishment of a European Deposit Insurance Scheme, and further work on a Capital Markets Union, the Roadmap expressed support for the idea of European Sovereign Bond-backed Securities and recommended further work on a stabilisation function that could take the form of a European Investment Protection Scheme, a European Unemployment Reinsurance Scheme or a rainy day fund that would accumulate funds on a regular basis for disbursement in order to cushion a large shock. At its height, and as a longer-term goal, stabilisation could be provided by a form of Euro Area budget, as was subsequently envisaged by President Macron of France in a speech to the Sorbonne University in September 2017:

> We need convergence and stability through national reforms, but also by coordinating our economic policies and a common budget. If we want to reduce our differences and develop our common goods – … security, protection in the context of migration, digital transition, ecological transition, a genuine development and partnership policy – these

---

[129] Reflection Paper on the Deepening of the Economic and Monetary Union, European Commission, COM(2017) 291, 31 May 2017; Commission Communication, *Further Steps Towards Completing Europe's Economic and Monetary Union: A Roadmap* COM(2017) 821 final, 6 December 2017. See Editorial, "Tinkering with Economic and Monetary Union" (2018) 55 *Common Market Law Review* 709; Luca Lionello, "Establishing a Budgetary Capacity in the Eurozone: Recent Proposals and Legal Challenges" (2017) 24 *Maastricht Journal of European and Comparative Law* 822.

[130] Proposal for a Council Regulation on the establishment of the European Monetary Fund, COM(2017) 827 final, 6 December 2017.

[131] Proposal for a Council Directive laying down provisions for strengthening fiscal responsibility and the medium-term budgetary orientation in the Member States, COM(2017) 824 final, 6 December 2017.

[132] Reflection Paper on the Deepening of the Economic and Monetary Union, European Commission, COM(2017) 291, 31 May 2017, 10.

common goods, foremost among which is our currency, must be financed. And we therefore need more investment, we need the means to provide stability in the face of economic shocks, as no state can tackle an economic crisis alone when it no longer controls its monetary policy. So for all these reasons, yes we need a stronger budget within Europe, at the heart of the eurozone.

This budget's resources must reflect its ambition. European taxes in the digital or environmental fields could thus form a genuine European resource to fund common expenditure. And beyond that, we must discuss partly allocating at least one tax to this budget, such as corporation tax once it has been harmonised.

The *solidarity* required for a budget must be combined with increased *responsibility*, which starts by observing the rules we have set ourselves and implementing essential reforms.

A budget must be placed under the strong political guidance of a common minister and be subject to strict parliamentary control at European level. Only the eurozone with a strong and international currency can provide Europe with the framework of a major economic power.[133]

[27–90] This competing emphasis as between solidarity and responsibility still largely characterises the ongoing debate on the future of the EMU. It has been suggested that while President Macron and Chancellor Merkel of Germany may agree on the establishment of a European Monetary Fund, they disagree on what its purpose should be. While Chancellor Merkel seems attracted to the idea that it be used to strictly enforce the fiscal rules, President Macron appears to favour using it as a Euro Area stabilisation mechanism.[134]

[27–91] In 2017, the President of the European Council initiated the Leaders' Agenda, a series of consultations and discussions amongst the members of the European Council. As part of this Leaders' Agenda process, at the Euro Summit in March 2018 the theme for discussion was the future of the EMU, with a short preparatory document framing the topic as follows:

Fiscal capacity. Should a fiscal capacity for the euro area be set up? What would be its main purposes (eg macroeconomic stabilisation, support to investment and employment, promotion of structural reforms)? Should it be part and parcel of the EU budget or an instrument outside the EU budget?

Promotion of good policy-making. Should more be done at the European level to promote competitiveness- and growth-enhancing structural reforms, reduce imbalances and ensure sustained convergence? Should more be done to ensure fiscal responsibility? Which instruments should be used to this effect? [135]

[27–92] While there were no written conclusions from the discussion, it was agreed that the most urgent political priorities were strengthening of the Banking Union and reform of the European Stability Mechanism. Prior to the discussion, the finance ministers of Ireland and seven other Member States (a grouping that has become known as the new "Hanseatic League") published a paper setting out their shared views and

---

[133] "Initiative for Europe", Speech by President Emmanuel Macron at Sorbonne University, 26 September 2017. Emphasis added.

[134] André Sapir and Dirk Schoenmaker, "The Time is Right for a European Monetary Fund", Breugel Policy Brief, Issue 4, October 2017.

[135] Leaders' Agenda Note on Economic and Monetary Union, March 2018.

values on the creation of a stronger EMU.[136] These included that a stronger EMU requires, first of all, full compliance with existing fiscal rules. After this, as opposed to more "far-reaching proposals", priority should be given to those areas with the greatest convergence of views amongst Member States such as completion of the Banking Union and the transformation of the European Stability Mechanism into a European Monetary Fund. Further deepening of the EMU should stress real value-added, not far-reaching, transfer of competence to the European level. While the European Stability Mechanism should be strengthened and possibly developed into a European Monetary Fund, the current voting rules should be preserved and decision-making remain firmly in the hands of the Member States. It was also agreed that discussions should continue on a common backstop for the Single Resolution Fund and a European Deposit Insurance Scheme, and that progress should be made with the development of a Capital Markets Union in order to foster cross-border private risk-sharing. On 1 November 2018, the eight "Hansa" states, joined by the Czech Republic and Slovakia, again came together to set out their shared views on reform of the ESM.

[27–93] In their Meseberg Declaration of June 2018, France and Germany sought to reconcile their views and set out a common vision for a Roadmap on strengthening the Euro Area.[137] This would include: (i) amending the ESM Treaty so as to include a common backstop instrument; (ii) incorporating the ESM into the EU legal order; (iii) making the ESM the backstop to the Single Resolution Fund by 2024 at the latest; (iv) beginning negotiations on the European Deposit Insurance Scheme; (v) establishing a Eurozone budget by 2021 to promote competitiveness, convergence and stabilisation in the Euro Area; and (vi) examining the issue of a European Unemployment Stabilisation Fund for the case of severe economic crises, without transfers. At the Euro Summit held later that month, it was agreed that the ESM would be reformed to provide a common backstop to the SRF and that a Roadmap be prepared on the development of the European Deposit Insurance Scheme.[138] The Euro Group was tasked with preparing a report to the Leaders on deepening the EMU, which was endorsed at the next Euro Summit meeting in December 2018, together with a term sheet on reform of the ESM.[139] In setting out a Roadmap of further measures to be taken forward in the short term, the Euro Summit

- endorsed the terms of reference of a common backstop to the Single Resolution Fund, which set out how the backstop will be operationalised in the form of the ESM providing a revolving credit line to the SRF;
- asked the Euro Group to prepare the necessary amendments to the ESM Treaty (including the common backstop to the SRF) by June 2019;
- called for work to advance on the Banking Union the Capital Markets Union;
- mandated the Euro Group to work on the design, means of implementation and timing of a Budgetary Instrument for Convergence and Competitiveness for the Euro Area (and ERM II Member States on a voluntary basis). The features of the instrument are to be agreed in June 2019. The instrument will be part of the EU budget, coherent with other EU policies, and subject to criteria and strategic guidance from the Euro Area Member States; and

136 "Finance Ministers from Denmark, Estonia, Finland, Ireland, Latvia, Lithuania, the Netherlands and Sweden Outline their Shared Views and Values in the Discussion on the Architecture of the EMU", 6 March 2018.

137 Meseberg Declaration, "Renewing Europe's Promises of Security and Prosperity", 19 June 2018.

138 Euro Summit Meeting Statement, EURO 502/18, 29 June 2018.

139 Euro Summit Meeting Statement, EURO 503/18, 14 December 2018.

– encouraged work to be taken forward on a stronger international role for the euro.

[27–94] At the Euro Summit in June 2019, the work of the Euro Group was endorsed on the three elements of: (i) revising the ESM Treaty, including so as to provide for a common backstop for bank resolution; (ii) further strengthening the Banking Union, including through a European Deposit Insurance System and (iii) developing a Budgetary Instrument for Convergence and Competitiveness (BICC).[140] Since December 2018, broad agreement had been reached on the text of a revised ESM Treaty, such that the aim is to achieve agreement on the final package by December 2019. Secondly, progress had been made on identifying the principles that should guide the further strengthening of the Banking Union. Technical work would continue on a roadmap for beginning political negotiations on a European Deposit Insurance System, reporting back to the Euro Summit in December 2019. Thirdly, the main features of the Budgetary Instrument for Convergence and Competitiveness had been agreed. As a rule, the Instrument should support both structural reforms and public investment through a coherent package reflecting the key objective to increase the degree of convergence and competitiveness within the Euro Area. The Euro Summit and the Euro Group will give strategic guidance on the key reform and investment priorities for the convergence and competitiveness of the Euro Area, and will review these priorities annually. Grants will be issued on the basis of detailed reform and investment proposals put forward by a Member State. The Instrument will be part of the EU budget, with its size being determined in the context of the Multiannual Financial Framework. Continued discussion was needed, however, on two different options for the financing of the Instrument: general own resources with or without additional national contributions.

Timeline

1944	Bretton Woods Agreement establishes a new international monetary system with currencies pegged to a reserved currency (the US dollar, which in turn maintained a link and convertibility with gold)
1970	The Werner Report proposes that the EEC Member States establish an economic and monetary union by 1980
August 1971	The "Nixon Shock" announces the end of the direct convertibility of the dollar into gold
March 1972	Establishment of the European currency "snake"
February 1973	A 10 per cent devaluation of the dollar is announced, leading to the end of the Bretton Woods monetary system, to be replaced by free-floating currencies
1979	Economic Monetary System and Exchange Rate Mechanism (ERM-I) established pursuant to a Resolution of the European Council
February 1986	Economic Monetary System is given recognition in the Single European Act, which also recalls the 1972 commitment of aiming towards EMU
26–27 June 1989	Adoption of the Delors Report on EMU by the European Council
1 July 1990	First Stage of Economic and Monetary Union begins (coinciding with the date on which free movement of capital, under the Third Capital Directive, was to be achieved)

[140] Euro Summit Meeting Statement, EURO 502/19, 21 June 2019.

7 February 1992	Signing of the Treaty on European Union (the Maastricht Treaty)
16 September 1992	"Black Wednesday", on which the UK withdraws sterling from ERM–I as it is unable to remain within the agreed fluctuation bands
30 January 1993	Ireland devalues the punt by 10 per cent in order to remain with ERM–I
1 November 1993	Entry into force of the Maastricht Treaty
1 January 1994	Second Stage of Economic and Monetary Union begins and European Monetary Institute (forebear of European Central Bank) established
7 July 1997	Adoption of regulations comprising the Stability and Growth Pact
1 June 1998	Creation of the European System of Central Banks (ESCB), as part of which the European Central Bank (ECB) replaces the European Monetary Institute
1 January 1999	Third Stage of Economic and Monetary Union begins. The exchange rate as between national currencies and the European Currency Unit (ECU) become fixed and the ECU becomes a currency in its own right. ECSB and ECB begin to operate fully
1 January 2002	Euro notes and coins put into circulation, with national currencies withdrawn by 28 February 2002
September 2008	Collapse of Lehman Brothers leads to a financial crisis, credit crunch and drop in Irish property prices
30 September 2008	Irish Government guarantees all deposits and borrowings of Irish banks
27 April 2009	The Council decides that Ireland has an excessive deficit
1 December 2009	Entry into force of the Lisbon Treaty
9 May 2010	Agreement to establish the European Financial Stability Facility (EFSF), which is the subject of a Framework Agreement between the Euro Area Member States and the Facility on 7 June 2010
11 May 2010	Adoption of Regulation establishing the European Financial Stability Mechanism (EFSM)
14 May 2010	ECB decides to commence a Securities Markets Programme to purchase sovereign bonds of Euro Area Member States on the secondary markets
September 2010	Establishment of the annual European Semester for Economic Policy Coordination
18 October 2010	Germany and France jointly call for an amendment to the TFEU to establish a permanent crisis framework for safeguarding the financial stability of the Euro Area (the Deauville Declaration)
24 November 2010	Adoption of regulations establishing the European Banking Authority, the European Insurance and Occupational Pensions Authority, the European Securities and Markets Authority and the European Systemic Risk Board
29 November 2010	Ireland is granted a "bail-out" of €67.5 billion from the IMF (€22.5), European Financial Stability Mechanism (€22.5) and the European Financial Stability Facility (€22.5 including bilateral loans from the UK, Sweden and Denmark)
25 March 2011	European Council adopts a decision to amend Art 136 TFEU by the simplified revision procedure to provide a legal base for the ESM Treaty

November 2011	Adoption of the Six Pack of five regulations and a directive
2 February 2012	Signing of the Treaty Establishing a European Stability Mechanism (ESM Treaty)
2 March 2012	Signing of the Treaty on Stability, Coordination and Governance in the Economic and Monetary Union
31 May 2012	A referendum approves Ireland's ratification of the Treaty on Stability, Coordination and Governance in the Economic and Monetary Union by 60 per cent to 40 per cent
26 July 2012	Ireland returns to the financial markets for the first time since 2010
31 July 2012	Supreme Court delivers its ruling in *Pringle v Government of Ireland*
1 August 2012	Ireland ratifies the Treaty Establishing the European Stability Mechanism (ESM Treaty)
6 September 2012	ECB replaces its Securities Markets Programme with an Outright Monetary Transactions (OMT) Programme
12 September 2012	German Federal Constitutional Court permits Germany's ratification of the ESM Treaty and the Treaty on Stability, Coordination and Governance in the Economic and Monetary Union, subject to certain conditions
27 September 2012	Entry into force of the Treaty Establishing the European Stability Mechanism (ESM Treaty)
27 November 2012	Judgment of the Court of Justice in *Pringle v Government of Ireland*
1 January 2013	Entry into force of the Treaty on Stability, Coordination and Governance in the Economic and Monetary Union
1 May 2013	Entry into force of the European Council Decision to amend Art 136 TFEU
13 May 2013	Adoption of the Two Pack Regulations, further strengthening the Stability and Growth Pact for Euro Area Member States
15 October 2013	Adoption of regulations establishing the Single Supervisory Mechanism
15 December 2013	Ireland exits its "bail-out" programme
21 May 2014	Signing of the Agreement on the Transfer and Mutualisation of Contributions to the Single Resolution Fund
16 April 2014	Adoption of directive on Deposit Guarantee Schemes
15 July 2014	Adoption of the regulation establishing the Single Resolution Mechanism
16 June 2015	Judgment of the Court of Justice in *Gauweiler* upholding the lawfulness of the ECB's Outright Monetary Transaction (OMT) programme
22 June 2015	Publication of the Five Presidents' Report on *Completing Europe's Economic and Monetary Union*
1 January 2016	The Single Resolution Fund becomes operational with the entry into force of the Agreement on the Transfer and Mutualisation of Contributions to the Single Resolution Fund
17 June 2016	The Council abrogates its 2009 decision finding an excessive deficit in Ireland
1 March 2017	Publication of the Commission's White Paper on the *Future of Europe*

31 May 2017	Publication of the Commission's Reflection Paper on *Deepening of the EMU*
26 September 2017	French President proposes a Euro Area budget and finance minister, funded in part through European taxes
6 December 2017	Publication of the Commission's *Roadmap Towards Completing the EMU*
6 March 2018	Finance Ministers of Ireland, Denmark, Estonia, Finland, Latvia, Lithuania, the Netherlands and Sweden set out their shared views and values to create a stronger EMU
23 March 2018	Leaders' Agenda discussion at the Euro Summit on the future of the EMU
19 June 2018	Meseberg Declaration by France and Germany sets out Roadmap for strengthening the Euro Area
29 June 2018	Euro Summit agrees to reform European Stability Mechanism so as to make it a common backstop to the Single Resolution Fund
1 November 2018	Finance Ministers of Ireland, Denmark, Estonia, Finland, Latvia, Lithuania, the Netherlands, Sweden, Czech Republic and Slovakia set out their shared views on ESM reform
14 December 2018	Euro Summit endorses the Euro Group report to Leaders on Deepening EMU
21 June 2019	Euro Summit endorses the work of the Euro Group on: (i) revising the ESM Treaty, including so as to provide for a common backstop for bank resolution; (ii) further strengthening the Banking Union, including through a European Deposit Insurance System and (iii) developing a Budgetary Instrument for Convergence and Competitiveness.

INDEX